# THE OXFORD COMPANION TO
# CLASSICAL LITERATURE

# THE OXFORD COMPANION TO
# CLASSICAL LITERATURE

THIRD EDITION

EDITED BY

M. C. HOWATSON

**OXFORD**
UNIVERSITY PRESS

# OXFORD
UNIVERSITY PRESS

Great Clarendon Street, Oxford OX2 6DP

Oxford University Press is a department of the University of Oxford.
It furthers the University's objective of excellence in research, scholarship,
and education by publishing worldwide in

Oxford New York

Auckland Cape Town Dar es Salaam Hong Kong Karachi
Kuala Lumpur Madrid Melbourne Mexico City Nairobi
New Delhi Shanghai Taipei Toronto

With offices in

Argentina Austria Brazil Chile Czech Republic France Greece
Guatemala Hungary Italy Japan Poland Portugal Singapore
South Korea Switzerland Thailand Turkey Ukraine Vietnam

Oxford is a registered trade mark of Oxford University Press
in the UK and in certain other countries

Published in the United States
by Oxford University Press Inc., New York

British Library Cataloguing in Publication Data
Data available

Library of Congress Cataloging in Publication Data
Data available

Typeset by SPI Publisher Services, Pondicherry, India
Printed in Great Britain
on acid-free paper by
Clays Ltd, St Ives plc

ISBN 978-0-19-954854-5

1 3 5 7 9 10 8 6 4 2

# PREFACE

This new, third, edition of the *Oxford Companion to Classical Literature* is a revised version of the second edition, published in 1989. It has been a privilege to be allowed to attempt a second revision of Sir Paul Harvey's original *Companion* of 1937.

Harvey's main intention was that his book should be a companion for the general reader, and this remains the ideal. But what does the general reader want nowadays with a companion to classical literature? Harvey's reader was likely to have acquired some knowledge of the classical world in the course of learning Latin and Greek, whereas today's general readers are almost entirely ignorant of these languages. Yet today's readers are far more knowledgeable in other ways; they are widely travelled and more sophisticated. My aim is therefore not only to give some account of the literatures of Greece and Rome, which are after all their most precious legacy to the modern world, but also to set them against the concerns and constraints of their societies and institutions; As well as giving answers to 'who?', 'what?', and 'when?' the *Companion* sometimes tries to answer the question 'why?', and to be a guide for those who wish to find out more.

All the entries taken over from the 1989 edition have been scrutinized and most have been revised. There are around 200 new entries, many of which reflect the way we view our own societies and the subjects which engage our interest at the present day: they deal with, for example, freedom, death, art, love and sexuality, science, and technology. Harvey set store by his synopses of what he considered the most significant works of classical literature, and these survive very much as he wrote them. In this edition they have been supplemented by other summaries, including the ancient novels and the scientific treatises of Aristotle. On the other hand, since Harvey's day interest in some topics and authors has diminished almost to vanishing point. This is the case with political oratory and with the history of administration and of constitutions. Law does not fare much better. The previous entries on Demosthenes, Isocrates, and the Roman orator Cicero have accordingly been shortened, although it may be regretted that the modern attitudes towards political oratory, of boredom and suspicion, deform our understanding of an important part of the classical experience, in particular of the politics of Athens in the time of Demosthenes and Isocrates, and the education that prepared the Greek adult male to take part in it. A few longer entries on the historical or political background have also been abridged and some minor entries omitted for this edition. But no topic in classics can nowadays be regarded a priori as totally lacking in interest: many topics once considered marginal are now rightly seen to be well worth studying in the classical context: concepts of character, friendship, and good government (*eunomia*); anti-Semitism; the rise of Christianity; the attitudes of Athens and Rome to problematic citizens like Socrates and Catiline, and to children; there are entries which allude to all of these. A new development is the inclusion of additional entries in the online edition (Oxford Reference Online: http://www.oxfordreference.com/), for some of which there is no space in the printed *Companion*; others have been judged to be slightly outside its range, either because they are not specifically literary, such as *army*, or because they have been written with classical specialists in mind, such as *metre*.

The *Companion* is still a book for browsing. Extensive, but it is hoped not intrusive, cross-referencing will lead the reader into further byways. An asterisk before a word draws the reader's attention to its existence as a separate entry only where more information may be found of direct relevance to the subject. The period covered begins about 2000 BC with the migrations into the Balkan peninsula of an Indo-European people whose languages subsequently evolved into a tongue recognizably Greek. The stopping-point is less easily identifiable. In the main my aim has been to cover as fully as possible the period up to AD 180, the date of the accession of the Roman emperor Commodus, the last of the Antonine emperors whose reigns the English historian Edward Gibbon judged to be most happy and prosperous for the human race. Entries after that date are fewer than in the previous edition and mostly relate to the survival of classical literature.

The book requires no knowledge of Greek or Latin. All Greek is transliterated ($v$ = y, $\chi$ = ch, $ov$ = u). In the printing of the headwords some guidance is given to their commonest pronunciation in English, but there are no hard-and-fast rules. Proper nouns are generally spelt in the Latinized form in which they have become familiar in English, but where these are headwords their transliterated Greek form is also given. Roman names appear in the form in which they are most familiar, either under the *nomen* (second name, or middle name of three), e.g. Gaius *Marius*, Quintus *Fabius* Maximus, or, where the subject is best known by his *cognomen* or third name, under that headword, e.g. Marcus Tullius *Cicero*, Lucius Aemilius *Paullus*.

A chronological table and set of maps, revised and improved for this edition and provided with a gazetteer, are included. The chronological table records the major literary and historical events from 2000 BC to AD 529. The maps are intended to show those places mentioned in the text, irrespective of size and importance. Places east of Iran are not shown, since they are relevant only to the journeys of Alexander the Great. Geographical names are mostly given in Latinized form (except for those which are very commonly used in English even in a classical context, e.g. Athens, Adriatic Sea). Modern equivalents, where they are judged to be helpful or interesting, have been added. Where several variants of a place-name are recognized, only the most commonly used is given.

This *Companion* maintains the policy of the original in not being a dictionary of classical mythology. To make it so would have increased its bulk and changed its focus out of all proportion. Only those names and stories which occur most often in literature are included.

I am very grateful to those readers who took the trouble to point out mistakes and other failings in the last edition, or to offer opinions and advice; for the most part these suggestions have been incorporated in the new edition. I have consulted and pestered many friends and colleagues, for whose advice and patience I offer warmest thanks. In particular I should like to acknowledge the generous help of Professor Hilary Mackie of Rice University, Dr Clare Sharp of St Paul's Girls' School, and the librarians of St Anne's College. The support of Pam Coote, the doyenne of the Reference Division at OUP, the Production Editor Clare Jenkins, and the other editors through whose hands I passed—Vicki Donald, Rebecca Lane, and Joanna Harris—has been a constant reassurance, and I am much indebted to them all. I should like to thank the copy-editor Jeff New for his prompt and invaluable help and advice, and for saving me from many embarrassing mistakes; I am also very grateful to Penny Trumble for meticulous proof-reading. Errors that remain must be attributed, alas, solely to me. Through all stages of composition this book has benefited immeasurably from the critical acumen of Alastair Howatson, to whom I am deeply indebted.

M. C. H.

# CONTENTS

# A

**Abdera** Greek city on the coast of Thrace, founded in the seventh century BC and refounded in the sixth by Ionians from Teos in Asia Minor, among them the Greek lyric poet *Anacreon. It was the birthplace of the sophist *Protagoras and the philosopher *Democritus, but was nevertheless proverbial for the stupidity of its inhabitants.

**Abȳ'dos** Milesian colony on the eastern, Asiatic, side of the Hellespont, at its narrowest point. Here *Xerxes crossed to Europe in 480 BC during the *Persian Wars, and here, in Greek myth, lived *Leander.

**Acadē'mica** ('Concerning Academic philosophy') Dialogue by *Cicero (1) of 45 BC discussing the philosophical views of the Greek New *Academy, particularly the Sceptic view of *Carneades. While Cicero's friend Atticus was having copies of the original two books produced for the public at large, Cicero remodelled it into four books. Both editions went into circulation; of the first edition we possess the second book, *Lucullus*; of the second edition we possess part of the first book, known as *Academica posteriora* ('Concerning Academic philosophy Part 2'). In the latter, *Varro expounds the evolution of the doctrines of the Academy, from early dogmatism to the Scepticism of Arcesilaus and Carneades. In *Lucullus* that interlocutor attacks the position of the Sceptics. Cicero defends the Sceptic view and approves Carneades' stance of accepting what seems most probably true.

**Acadē'mus** *See* ACADEMY.

**Academy (Akadēmia, Akadēmeia)** Originally a shrine to a *hero, Akademos, and a public gymnasium just north of Athens near the hill of Colonus (*see also* DIOSCURI). It gave its name to the school Plato established there in the early fourth century BC, which survived in some form until AD 529 when the Christian emperor Justinian's campaign against paganism led to the closure of the philosophy schools in Athens. Plato was buried nearby. The Roman general Sulla cut down the trees during his siege of Athens in 87–86 BC, but they must have grown again, for Horace, who studied at Athens, refers in his *Epistles* to the 'woods of Academus'. Recent finds on the site included schoolboys' slates, some with writing on them.

The *Old (Early) Academy* describes the period when the school was headed by Plato (d. 347 BC) and his conservative successors Speusippus, Xenocrates, Polemon, and Crates, down to c.265 BC. The *Middle Academy* is the term sometimes used for the period initiated by Arcesilaus of Pitane (c.315–242 BC) who interpreted true Platonism as Scepticism (*see* SCEPTICS), an approach which the school kept with variations until the time of Antiochus of Ascalon (below) in the first century BC. Arcesilaus followed that aspect of Plato which was derived from Socrates' negative style of argument, in which no positive conclusion is reached (*see* ELENCHUS). The *New Academy*, sometimes taken to include Arcesilaus, is often described as having started in the mid-second century BC under Carneades (d. 129) who extended Scepticism into new areas.

The destruction of the Academy with its library during the sack of Athens by Sulla in 86 BC broke the direct link with Plato. At this time the head of the Academy was Philon of Larissa. The philosopher Antiochus of Ascalon (d. 68 BC) left the Academy because of Philon's Scepticism, which he thought an aberration, and founded his own school on Stoic and *Peripatetic lines, calling it in consequence the Old Academy. Antiochus aimed to return to what he thought was genuine Platonism by maintaining that there was essential agreement between the doctrines of the Old Academy, the Aristotelians (Peripatetics), and the Stoics. Although not original he exerted great influence; his lecture audience included Cicero, who found his eclecticism appealing and who later proclaimed himself an Academic (*see* ACA-DEMICA). The school of Antiochus appears not to have survived for long after his death. Philon seems to have been the last head of the original Academy in the direct succession from Plato. After him the Academy disintegrated as an institution, although the term Academic to describe a Platonist philosophy survived. For the development of Platonism after Antiochus *see* MIDDLE PLATONISM.

Little is known of the Academy itself in the following centuries until it appears in the fifth century AD as a centre of Neoplatonism, particularly under the leadership of *Proclus, who powerfully influenced the form in which the Greek philosophical inheritance was passed on to Renaissance Europe.

**Aca'stus** Son of *Pelias and Anaxibia, and brother of Alcestis. He sailed with the *Argonauts against his father's wishes. *See also* PELEUS.

**acatalectic** A metrical term; *see* CATALECTIC.

**accents, Greek** The diacritic marks ´ (acute), ^ (circumflex) and ` (grave) placed over vowels to indicate the pitch of the predominant syllable in a Greek word. Spoken Greek in antiquity indicated the predominant syllable by the pitch of the voice, as in modern Japanese, not by stress as in modern Greek and English. The invention of written accents, attributed to the Alexandrian scholar *Aristophanes of Byzantium (*c.*257–180 BC), was intended to make it easier for readers of Homer and the other early poets to recognize and pronounce words which had become unfamiliar by his time. This was a period when written texts did not leave spaces between words (*see* BOOKS, GREEK AND ROMAN 2) and the use of accents made rare words more readily identifiable. The acute accent indicates a high pitch, and a circumflex, used only on long vowels and diphthongs, a high-descending-to-lower pitch. The pitch did not jump from one note to another, as in singing; rather there was a gradual rise or fall. Only the predominant syllable of a word carries an accent. In the case of a word with an acute accent on the final syllable, if the word is followed by another word in the same sentence the acute is generally replaced by a grave. This is the only circumstance in which the grave accent is used, and it seems to indicate that the syllable in question is to be pronounced at a higher pitch than the preceding unaccented syllable but lower than if the acute accent had been retained. By the end of the fourth century AD the pitch accent seems to have been entirely replaced by a stress accent. In the case of ancient Greek words which survived into modern Greek, the present-day stress accent is generally on the same syllable as the ancient pitch accent.

The merit of retaining accents in modern times is debatable. A nineteenth-century authority on the positioning of accents (Chandler) drew attention to the absurdity of those who 'persist in ornamenting their Greek with three small scratches'.

**accidence** That aspect of grammar which is concerned with inflections, i.e. the various modifications which might be applied to any individual word. In Greek and Latin this includes the declension of nouns, adjectives, and pronouns, and the conjugation of verbs.

**A'ccius, Lucius** (170–*c.*86 BC) Latin poet and literary scholar, from Picenum in Umbria. He was a younger contemporary of the tragedian *Pacuvius and the last great Roman writer of tragedy. The titles of some 45 of his tragedies are known, the subjects drawn from Greek myth and especially from the Trojan War and the family of Atreus. Roman subjects were treated in two plays, *Brutus* (about the overthrow of the last Roman king, the tyrannical Tarquinius Superbus) and *Decius* (about the self-sacrifice of the general *Decius Mus at the battle of Sentinum in 295 BC; *see* FABIUS (1)). No play survives intact but there are numerous fragments of the tragedies, many preserved because Cicero quoted them in his rhetorical and philosophical works. Cicero, who heard Accius speak in his old age, admired his lofty and vigorous style, and Ovid called him 'impassioned'. His tragedy *Atreus* contained the phrase *oderint dum metuant* ('let them hate, so long as they fear'), frequently quoted, says Suetonius, by the emperor Caligula.

Among various scholarly works Accius wrote a long hexameter poem *Annales* ('Annals') in which he demonstrated the Greek origins for Roman religious festivals, and *Didascalia*, a history in at least nine books of the Attic (Greek) and Roman theatre (*see* DIDASCALIA; the term came to mean 'stage records'). Its apparent mixture of prose and verse indicates that in form it was a forerunner of the so-called Menippean satire, as written by the polymath Varro. Accius' attempts to reform Latin spelling so as to conform with pronunciation met with no success, but Varro seems to have dedicated to him one of his own works written on similar lines.

**Achae'a, Achae'ans** Geographical terms referring to Greece which changed their meaning over time. (*See also* AHHIYAWA.)

**1.** In Homer's epics the term 'Achaeans' is applied collectively to all the peoples of Greece and all those fighting on the Greek side under Agamemnon. (Occasionally the terms 'Argives' or 'Danaans' are used in this sense also. 'Hellenes', the word for 'Greeks' in historical times, is a local name in Homer, applied only to the people of a part of central Greece.) Achaeans all speak one language and have the same norms of behaviour, and their unity is taken for granted. Nevertheless they are divided into small, politically independent states, many of which were still in existence in historical times.

**2.** In historical times, Achaea meant a region in the north Peloponnese on the Gulf of Corinth. In the eighth century BC Achaea founded an important group of Greek colonies at the southern tip of Italy including Sybaris (720 BC) and Croton (708 BC). Otherwise Achaea plays little part in classical Greek history, being neutral in the Persian Wars and not conspicuous in the Peloponnesian War. For the third and second centuries BC see ACHAEAN CONFEDERACY.

**Achaean confederacy, Achaean league** A federal organization which in the third and second centuries BC was the chief power in Greece. A revival in 280 BC of an older confederacy, it consisted of the twelve Achaean cities united in the cult of Zeus. Soon after 283 BC the confederacy admitted non-Achaean members on terms of equality, which was a step towards the growth of *federal states, something which had scarcely been attempted before. In the second century BC under military threat it came to support Rome against Macedon, while at the same time expanding to admit the whole Peloponnese including Sparta (*see* PHILOPOEMEN). Tension with Rome in 167 BC led to the deportation and detention in Italy of a thousand leading Achaeans, including the historian *Polybius,

for political investigation. They were released in 150, but continuing tension led to the Achaean War with Rome (146–145). The war ended with the complete destruction of the city of Corinth in 146, the virtual dismemberment of the confederacy, and the end of Achaean political independence.

**Achaemenids** Members of one of the three clans of the Pasargadae tribe to which Herodotus believed the Persian kings belonged. They were centred on an area north-east of Persepolis. The name derives from a legendary hero Achaemenes (Persian: Hexāmanish), the probably fictional ancestor perhaps created by Darius I to give authority to his claim to the throne and to his membership of the same clan as Cyrus I, the Great, and Cambyses. Alexander the Great put an end to the dynasty when he defeated Darius III (d. 330 BC).

**Acharnae** The largest Attic deme or district, lying north-west of Athens near the foot of Mount Parnes, whose inhabitants, charcoal-burners (according to Aristophanes) and small farmers, were famously brave. 'Acharnae, famous for heroes', says Pindar in an ode to an Acharnian.

*Acha'rnians* (*Acharnēs*) The earliest surviving complete Attic Greek comedy. Written by *Aristophanes, it achieved first prize at the *Lenaea in 425 BC. It was produced under the name of Callistratus, perhaps because the author considered himself too young to produce it himself.

For six years of the *Peloponnesian War the Acharnians, with everyone else from the Attic countryside, had sacrificed their farms and crowded into Athens where there had been plague and food shortage. The Acharnians, who make up the chorus of the play, had seen their land repeatedly laid waste. The play opens with Dikaiopolis, an Athenian with a farm in the countryside, sitting and waiting for the meeting of the assembly, sighing for the good times of peace. Amphitheos ('Demigod') appears, sent by the gods to arrange peace with Sparta, but unfortunately lacking the necessary travelling-money. This Dikaiopolis provides, but the treaty with Sparta is to be a private one for himself alone. Amphitheos presently brings the treaty, narrowly escaping from the chorus of bellicose and infuriated Acharnians. Dikaiopolis is now able to celebrate the festival of the Rural *Dionysia with a procession consisting of his daughter and servants, and this leads to a dispute between Dikaiopolis and the chorus on the question of peace or war, in which *Lamachus, portrayed as a typical general, takes part. Dikaiopolis is allowed to make a speech before being executed as a traitor; and to render this more pathetic borrows from the tragedian Euripides some of the stage properties which make the latter's tragedies so moving. As a result the chorus are won over to the pro-peace view of Dikaiopolis. After the *parabasis* (*see* COMEDY [Greek 3]), in which the poet defends himself against charges that he insulted the city in the previous year's play, *Babylonians*, there is a succession of satirical scenes illustrating the benefits of peace. A Megarian comes to Dikaiopolis to buy food (Athens had been trying to starve out Megara by a blockade), offering in exchange his little daughters disguised as pigs in sacks. A Boeotian brings eels and other good things, and wants in return local produce of Attica; he is given an informer tied up in a sack (*see* SYCO-PHANT). A farmer wants peace-salve for his eyes, which he has cried out over the loss of his oxen; and so on. Finally Lamachus has to march off through the snow against the Boeotians, and returns wounded by a vine-stake on which he has impaled himself, while Dikaiopolis celebrates the Anthesteria with the priest of Dionysus.

This play is sometimes interpreted as a serious plea for peace on the part of the poet.

**Achā'tēs** In Virgil's *Aeneid*, the friend and lieutenant of Aeneas, frequently referred to as *fidus Achates*, 'faithful Achates'. He is in the epic tradition of faithful friends, comparable with Patroclus, friend to Achilles, and with Peirithous, friend to Theseus. *See* FRIENDSHIP.

**A'cheron** In Greek myth, one of the rivers of the Underworld (*see* HADES). The name was also that of an actual river in southern Epirus, which, issuing from a deep and gloomy gorge, passed through the lake Acherusia and after receiving the waters of the tributary Cocytus fell into the Thesprotian Gulf. In Hellenistic and Latin poetry the name denoted the Underworld itself.

**Achillē'id** (*Achillēis*) Latin epic poem in hexameters by the Roman poet *Statius on the story of *Achilles, of which only the first book and part of the second exist, the work having been cut short by the poet's death.

The poem describes how Thetis, anxious that her son Achilles shall not take part in the Trojan War (from which she knows he will not return), removes him from the care of the Centaur *Chiron to the island of Scyros. It relates his adventures there in the disguise of a girl, his discovery by Ulysses, and departure for Troy.

**Achi'llēs** (Akhilleus) In Greek myth, the greatest of the Greek heroes in the Trojan War and the central character of Homer's *Iliad*. The plot of the *Iliad* turns on his excessive and destructive anger. Achilles was the only son of the mortal Peleus, king of Phthia in south Thessaly, and of the sea-nymph Thetis, daughter of Nereus (*see* PARIS, JUDGEMENT OF). He came to Troy with fifty ships and many followers, the Myrmidons (for this name *see* AEACUS). As a fighter and a hero he is unquestionably supreme, repeatedly called 'the best of the Achaeans'. But he knows that if he pursues personal glory, as befits a hero, he will die young; his death at Troy was foretold. When Agamemnon takes his concubine, Achilles' anger seems natural both to the gods and to the Achaeans but his continuing refusal to fight after Agamemnon has offered generous compensation and when his own side are suffering heavy losses is felt to be excessive. After his friend Patroclus is killed he is moved by grief to be reconciled with Agamemnon and return to battle. He takes heroic but terrible revenge on the Trojans and on the body of their hero Hector whom he kills. All this may be thought of as typical behaviour of a hero, but Achilles himself when he has rejected Agamemnon's offer of compensation questions the heroic code, so-called, and a life devoted to the pursuit of honour, saying that he would prefer a life lived quietly. After maltreating Hector's body by dragging it behind his chariot, he is moved by a sense of common humanity as well as by the will of the gods to allow Hector's father Priam to pay ransom for it. Yet a lurking anger still remains.

The poets of the *Epic Cycle and later writers add to the story of Achilles. It was said that in infancy he was dipped in the river Styx by his mother Thetis (or anointed with *ambrosia by day and held in the fire at night) to make him invulnerable. She was interrupted by Peleus, and in anger abandoned her husband and the child, who remained vulnerable in the heel by which she had held him. It was in his heel that Achilles, according to epic tradition, received his death wound from an arrow shot by Paris. He had his education from the Centaur *Chiron. When the Greek contingents were gathering for Troy, Thetis, seeking to save him from his fated death, hid him on the island of Scyros at the court of King Lycomedes dressed as a girl and called, according to one source, Pyrrha. (Suetonius says that the emperor Tiberius liked to puzzle the scholars at his court with questions such as, 'What was the name of Achilles when he hid himself among the girls?') The king's daughter Deidameia bore him a son *Neoptolemus (sometimes called Pyrrhus). When the seer Calchas told the Greeks that Troy could not be captured without Achilles, Odysseus sought him out, after which he went willingly to Troy, by way of, first, Mysia, where he wounded *Telephus, secondly Aulis, where the events concerning *Iphigeneia took place, and thirdly Tenedos, where he slew Tenes, king of the island and son of Apollo.

Aeschylus in a lost play made Achilles and Patroclus lovers. There are also various stories of Achilles' exploits at Troy which are not related in the *Iliad*, notably the killing of *Cycnus (2) and *Troilus, stories popular with vase-painters.

**Achi'llēs Ta'tius** (from Alexandria, fl. AD 150; nothing certain is known of him) Author of the Greek novel *Leucippe and Cleitophon*.

**Ācis** *See* GALATEA.

**Aco'ntius** In myth, a young man from the Greek island of Ceos. He was in love with an Athenian girl Cydippe, and threw her an apple on which he had written: 'I swear to Artemis to marry none but Acontius.' She read this aloud, the usual way of reading in the ancient world, and so being under oath she fell ill whenever her parents tried to marry her elsewhere. In this way Acontius won her.

**A'cragas** (Lat. Agrigentum, modern Agrigento) One of the richest and most famous of the Greek cities in Sicily, founded c.580 BC on the central south coast by a colony from nearby Gela, itself founded by Cretans and Rhodians. It first came to power under the tyrant *Phalaris and continued to prosper under the tyrant *Theron. After Theron's death in 472 his son Thrasydaeus was overthrown and a democracy established in which the philosopher *Empedocles took part. The democracy continued until Acragas was sacked by the Carthaginians

in 406. It revived to some extent in the time of Timoleon (d. c.334 BC; *see* SYRACUSE) but suffered badly in the First Punic War. After the Roman capture of Syracuse in 211 BC all Sicily became a Roman province. In the time of the Roman governor *Verres and the late republic Acragas was again wealthy, and with the rest of Sicily received Latin rights under Augustus.

**Acri'sius** In Greek myth, son of Abas, king of Argos, and father of *Danae. His brother was *Proetus.

**acro'polis** ('upper city', 'citadel') The central stronghold of a Greek city, usually standing on higher ground. It was often referred to simply as *polis*, the rest of the city being called *asty*.

**Acropolis of Athens** The central stronghold of the city and the main sanctuary of Athena, the patron-goddess. It was built on a rocky plateau about 50m (165 ft.) high, the flat summit measuring about 300m east to west and 150m north to south, and inaccessible except by a steep slope on the west. In the thirteenth century BC it was enclosed by a massive wall containing traces of Mycenaean terracing (*see* ATHENS 1). All previous fortifications, buildings, and statues were destroyed in the Persian occupation of 480–479 BC (*see* PERSIAN WARS). In the 450s, in celebration of the final defeat of the Persians, a statue of Athena Promachos by *Pheidias was erected. It stood 10m (33 ft.) high and the helmet and spear-tip were visible to sailors at Sunium. Pheidias was directed by *Pericles to superintend the latter's general scheme for the rebuilding of the Acropolis. First came the *Parthenon, then the *Propylaea, Temple of Athena Nike, and Erectheum, as well as many lesser sanctuaries such as that of *Artemis Brauronia. There were also large numbers of marble slabs and columns, with inscriptions of decrees, memorials, casualty lists, treaties and alliances, public accounts, inventories, etc. Many of these inscriptions, more or less mutilated, have survived. The Romans added after 27 BC a small round temple dedicated to Rome and Augustus.

**acta** [Lat., 'the things that have been done']
**1.** *acta diurna* ('events of the day'), at Rome, a gazette of social and political news published daily from at least 59 BC and read both in the city and in the provinces.
**2.** *acta senatūs* ('proceedings of the senate'), first published in 59 BC. Under the Roman

empire, the official record of proceedings in the senate. Augustus forbade their circulation beyond senators.

**3.** An emperor's enactments which magistrates and succeeding emperors swore to observe, unless they had been explicitly rescinded immediately after an emperor's death. Magistrates first took the oath in 45 BC when they swore to observe the *acta* of Julius Caesar.

**Actae'on** In Greek myth, son of *Aristaeus and Autonoe, daughter of *Cadmus. For some offence, either because he boasted that he was a better hunter than Artemis or because he came upon her bathing, the goddess changed him into a stag, and he was torn to pieces by his own hounds.

**Actium** A promontory on the west coast of Greece in the extreme north-west of Acarnania at the entrance to the Ambracian Gulf. It gave its name to the naval battle fought just outside the Gulf between Mark Antony and Octavian on 2 September 31 BC (*see* ROME 4). Antony's defeat signalled the end of the Roman republic and the establishment of the empire.

In western Greece, which had become the arena of war, during the months leading up to the battle Antony had gradually been losing the support of powerful friends, ostensibly because of Cleopatra's presence in his camp, and losing also his numerical superiority. For several months the opposing armies and fleets confronted each other, until Antony decided to break out of a virtual blockade. Much mystery surrounds the campaign, and no source is clear about what exactly happened. Plutarch represents Cleopatra's contingent of sixty ships as deserting southwards at the height of the battle, followed by Antony. His cause was lost, and in the following months his supporters went over to Octavian. According to Virgil, in book 8 of the *Aeneid*, the defeated fleet, sheltered by the Nile-God, was depicted on the shield of Aeneas. Alexandria surrendered and Antony committed suicide in the following year, 30 BC.

**actors** *See* COMEDY [Greek 3 and 6, and Roman]; THEATRE; TRAGEDY 1 and 2; DIONYSUS, ARTISTS OF.

**Adelphoe, Adelphi** ('The brothers'; the ending -oe represents the Greek spelling, the ending -i the Latin) Roman comedy by *Terence, based on a Greek original by Menander with a scene added from a play of Diphilus ('Comrades in death'); *see* COMEDY [Greek 6]. It was first performed at the funeral games of Aemilius *Paullus in 160 BC.

Aeschinus and Ctesipho are the two sons of Demea. Ctesipho is brought up by his father in the country, but Aeschinus is entrusted to his uncle Micio and brought up in the town. The theme of the comedy is the contest between two methods of education. Demea makes himself hated and distrusted by his harshness and frugality; Micio makes himself loved and trusted by his indulgence and open-handedness. Aeschinus loves and wishes to marry an Athenian girl Pamphila, living in a poor way, who is about to have his child. Ctesipho, whom his father believes a model of virtue, has fallen in love with a music-girl. Aeschinus, to help his brother, carries off this girl from her pimp and brings her to Micio's house. He is therefore suspected of carrying on an affair with her just when his own girlfriend needs his support. The truth becomes known; Aeschinus is forgiven by Micio and his marriage arranged. Demea is mortified at the revelation of Ctesipho's behaviour. Finding that his boasted method of education has earned him only hatred, he suddenly changes his attitude and makes a display of geniality. He allows Ctesipho to marry his music-girl, and forces his old bachelor brother Micio into a reluctant marriage with the bride's mother and into endowing one of her relatives with a farm at Micio's expense, and obliging him to free his slave and give him a good start in life—showing his sons that indulgence and extravagance can be overdone. As in *Heauton timorumenos* the plot focuses on the question of openness between fathers and sons.

**ad Here'nnium, Rheto'rica** *See* RHETORICA AD HERENNIUM.

**Admē'tus** In Greek myth, son of Pheres and king of Pherae in Thessaly. When Zeus killed *Asclepius for restoring Hippolytus to life at the entreaty of Artemis, Apollo, the father of Asclepius, killed in vengeance the *Cyclopes who had forged Zeus' thunderbolt. To expiate this crime Zeus made him for a year the servant of Admetus, who treated him kindly. Apollo in gratitude helped him to win *Alcestis as his bride. At the bridal feast it was revealed that Admetus was fated to die imminently, but Apollo again intervened and persuaded the

Fates to grant Admetus longer life, provided that he could persuade someone else to die for him. According to Euripides' treatment of the story, Admetus' father and mother refused, but his wife Alcestis consented, and accordingly died. Just after this, Heracles visited the palace of Admetus who, in obedience to the laws of hospitality, concealed his wife's death and welcomed the hero. Heracles discovered the truth, went out to intercept Death, set upon him, and took Alcestis from him. He then restored her to her husband. *See also* ALCESTIS.

**Adoniazū'sae** The title of Idyll 15 of *Theocritus.

**Adō'nis** In Greek myth, a beautiful youth, son of *Cinyras, king of Cyprus, by his daughter Zmyrna or Myrrha. Their union was brought about by Aphrodite in revenge for Zmyrna's refusal to honour the goddess. When her father discovered the truth and was about to kill her the gods turned her into a myrrh tree. Adonis was born from this tree. He was very beautiful from birth, and Aphrodite fell in love with him. One story says that she placed him in a chest and gave him to Persephone to take care of. When she refused to give him back Zeus decreed that for part of the year he should stay with her in the Underworld and for the remaining part with Aphrodite. Another story relates that Adonis, having been brought up by nymphs, was out hunting when Aphrodite met him and fell in love with him. He was killed by a wild boar, and from his blood sprang the rose, or from Aphrodite's tears the anemone.

Many explanations of this strange myth have been suggested. The name could be oriental in origin, from the Semitic *Adon*, 'Lord'. In fifth-century Athens the festival of Adonis was marked by women mourning and lamenting his death, and by the setting on the housetops of the 'Gardens of Adonis', seedlings in shallow soil which withered as soon as they sprang up. *See also* THEOCRITUS (Idyll 15).

**Adra'stus** Mythical king of Argos at the time of the conflict of Polyneices and Eteocles for the kingdom of Thebes (*see* OEDIPUS). He was the son of Talaus and Lysimache. After a quarrel with another branch of the royal family he fled to Sicyon, where the king made him his heir. He became king of Sicyon, but then made his peace at Argos and returned there, giving his sister Eriphyle in marriage to Amphiaraus. To his court came the exiles *Tydeus

and Polyneices. The latter married his daughter Argeia, the former her sister Deipyle. Adrastus undertook to restore them to their kingdoms and began by leading an army, the *'Seven against Thebes', to set Polyneices on the throne of Thebes. When the expedition was defeated, Adrastus escaped on his divine horse Arion, the offspring of Poseidon and Demeter. In his old age he successfully led the sons of the Seven, the *Epigoni, against Thebes, but died on his way home from grief at the loss of his son, Aegialeus, who alone had fallen in the attack. His grandson Diomedes, the Homeric hero, became king.

**adultery** In Greece, sexual relations between the wife, widowed mother, unmarried daughter, sister, or niece of a citizen and a man who was not her husband. At Athens the law allowed a plea of justifiable homicide in the case of a man who killed another man whom he could prove he had caught in the sexual act with his wife or close female relation. The adulterer could also be held for ransom. Adulterous wives had to be divorced and were not allowed to take part in public sacrifices. At Sparta the tradition was that there was no penalty for adultery.

In the Roman republic, before the law of *Augustus on the repression of adultery (passed shortly after 18 BC), it is probable that it was left to the family rather than the law to deal with cases of adultery, though magistrates occasionally proceeded against adulterers and adulteresses. Roman tradition, as well as the Augustan law, allowed (within strict limits) the *paterfamilias to kill an adulterous wife or daughter caught in the sexual act. (Acts of sexual violence against the adulterous male, as literature attests, were also permitted.) The Augustan law made adultery with a respectable free woman a crime, the normal punishment being banishment of one or both parties to different islands and some confiscation of property. Adulterous wives had to be divorced, and marriage to a convicted adulteress was forbidden to free-born citizens.

**advocacy** The profession of those who plead causes in a court of law. For advocacy at Athens *see* LOGOGRAPHERS.

In Rome advocates like Cicero appear in the late republic. They did not necessarily have specialized knowledge of the law; their skill lay in rhetoric and their ability to plead their client's cause. Advocates were supposed not to accept rewards from their clients, but ways were clearly found to get around this condition. *See* LAW, ROMAN.

**Ae'a** In the story of the *Argonauts, the realm of *Aeētes, later identified with Colchis.

**Ae'acus** In Greek myth, son of Zeus and the nymph Aegina. He married Endeis and became the father of *Telamon (father of the Greater Ajax) and of *Peleus (father of Achilles). He was a man of great piety: his prayers once ended a drought in Greece. On another occasion when the inhabitants of his island, Aegina, were destroyed by a plague, Zeus, to reward him, re-peopled it by creating human beings out of ants (*myrmekes*); they were therefore called Myrmidons, the name by which the subjects of Peleus and Achilles are known in Homer. After his death he became, with *Minos and *Rhadamanthys, a judge of the dead in the Underworld, imposing punishments for misdeeds in life.

**Aeae'a (Aiaiē)** In Homer's *Odyssey*, the island of *Circe, situated in the stream of Ocean (*see* OCEANUS).

**aediles** At Rome, magistrates, at first two in number, elected annually as subordinate officers to the *tribunes of the plebs whose inviolability they shared. Their name derived from the *aedes* or temple of Ceres on the Aventine hill, their original function being to superintend that cult, which was particularly important to the plebs. In 367 BC their number was increased to four by the addition of two *'curule' aediles elected from the patricians and the office became a magistracy of the whole people. The office was not essential in the *cursus honorum* but was the lowliest office to permit its holder to enter the senate. Aediles were protectors of the plebs and responsible for the care of the city and what went on in it, including the water supply, the corn supply, and the market. They also administered the public games, and in the heated politics of the late republic they tended to spend more of their own money on the games to gain favour with the people. Augustus transferred care of the games to the praetors.

**Ăē'don** In Greek myth, daughter of Pandareōs and wife of Zethus. Envying Amphion's wife *Niobe for her many children, she plotted to kill them. By mistake she slew her own child,

Itylus (or Itys), and mourned for him so bitterly that the gods changed her into a nightingale, *aēdon*. (Compare the story of Procne: *see* PHILOMELA.)

**Ae'dui (Haedui)** A highly developed Gallic people who in Roman times occupied most of modern Burgundy. They became allies of Rome *c.*121 BC, and gave support to Julius Caesar during most of the Gallic Wars, joining Vercingetorix (of the Arverni) somewhat reluctantly in his revolt of 52 BC. Their chief settlement was originally the hill fort of Bibracte (Mont-Beuvray) but *c.*12 BC it was abandoned for Augustodunum (Autun), a city covering an unusually large area in the plain of the Arroux. Under the emperor Claudius the Aedui were the first Gallic tribe to have members in the senate at Rome.

**Aeē'tēs** In Greek myth, king of Colchis; he was the son of *Helios, brother of *Circe, and father of *Medea. *See* ATHAMAS and ARGONAUTS.

**Aegae** (modern Vergina) In north-east Greece overlooking the coastal plain of Macedonia, the site of the Macedonian royal tombs. Some of these have been and continue to be excavated. Those of the fourth century BC have roused great interest because of the possibility that they were the tombs of well-known rulers including Philip II. They are also outstanding for the artistic merit of the contents—frescos, fine weaponry, and offerings in ivory and precious metals.

**Aega'tēs I'nsulae** Islands off Lilybaeum (Marsala), the westernmost point of Sicily. Here a naval battle was fought in 241 BC in which C. Lutatius Catulus, the Roman admiral, defeated the Carthaginian fleet, so ending the First *Punic War.

**Aegeus** *See* THESEUS.

**Aegi'aleus** Son of *Adrastus and the only one of the *Epigoni to be killed in the expedition against Thebes.

**Aegi'mius** The king of Doris in central Greece who sought Heracles' help in expelling the *Lapiths from his land. Heracles asked as his reward the right of his descendants to claim asylum in Doris. Later the *Heracleidae (from whom the Dorian kings claimed descent) were believed to have settled there, and thus were 'Dorians'. Aegimius' sons Dymas and Pamphylus together with Heracles' son Hyllus gave their names to the three Dorian tribes. *See* DORUS.

**Aegī'na 1.** Nymph, daughter of the river-god Asopus. She was carried to the island of that name (2) by Zeus, to whom she bore *Aeacus.
**2.** Island of some 90 sq. km (35 sq. miles) in the Saronic Gulf, about 20km (13 miles) south-west of Athens, the realm of the mythical *Aeacus. At some early period it was settled by Greeks from Epidaurus and so was Dorian. Relatively poor in terms of land it grew rich on trade. At some time, probably in the early seventh century BC, it was ruled by the tyrant *Pheidon of Argos, and in the sixth century was one of the earliest cities to mint coins (*see* MONEY AND COINS), a great facilitator of trade. In that century it built up a navy which by 500 BC had no rival in Greece. At roughly the same time began the long feud with neighbouring Athens, whose navy was developed partly to combat the Aeginetans. The Aeginetan navy fought well on the Greek side in the Persian Wars, but hostility to Athens continued. In 458/7 Aegina was decisively defeated by Athens and compelled to join the *Delian League despite being Dorian rather than Ionian, paying a heavy annual tribute of 30 talents (*see* PELOPONNESIAN WAR, FIRST). In 431, at the outbreak of the Peloponnesian War, the Athenians evicted the Aeginetans from the island on the pretext that they had helped foment the war, and installed Athenian *cleruchs in their place. The exiles were restored by Lysander in 405, after which Aegina played a minor role in history. Some of Pindar's greatest odes were written for the Aeginetans.

**aegis** The attribute of the Greek gods Zeus and Athena, also used by Apollo. It is difficult to find out how the Greeks imagined it. ('Ageless and deathless', and 'with a hundred gold tassels', is how Homer describes it.) The name possibly suggests a goat-skin, and *Eratosthenes says that Zeus used the skin of the goat *Amaltheia to defeat the Titans. In art Athena wears it like a skin thrown over the shoulders. It is also depicted as a shield with a shaggy fringe and the *Gorgon's head in the centre. It symbolized power, and when brandished it struck terror into the enemy. In Hellenistic times and after it became part of the iconography of rulers.

**Aegi'sthus** *See* PELOPS.

**Aegospo'tami (Aigospotamoi)** ('goat's rivers') Small river in the Thracian Chersonese, with at one time a town of the same name on it. Off the mouth of the river Athens suffered her final naval defeat of the *Peloponnesian War in 405 BC. For the famous fall of a meteorite there *see* ANAXAGORAS.

**Aegy'ptus 1.** *See* DANAUS. **2.** *See* EGYPT.

**Ae'lian (Claudius Aeliānus)** (AD *c.*170–*c.*235) A rhetorician and writer in Greek, born in Praeneste near Rome. His two surviving works, *De animalium natura* ('On the nature of animals', in seventeen books) and the *Varia historia* ('Miscellany', in fourteen books), have the expressed purpose of demonstrating the workings of divine providence in the animal kingdom and in human life, and are full of extraordinary anecdotes collected from earlier writers. The self-conscious simplicity of the Greek was much admired, and later moralists drew heavily on the work.

**Aemi'lius Paullus, Lucius** *See* PAULLUS.

**Aenē'as** In Greek and Roman myth and literature, one of the Trojan leaders in the Trojan War, son of *Anchises and the goddess Aphrodite (at Rome, Venus), and the subject of Virgil's Latin epic, the *Aeneid*. In the account of the Trojan War given in Homer's *Iliad* he is a notable hero, although descended from the younger branch of the Trojan royal house (Priam, king of Troy, was of the older branch). The Greek god Poseidon prophesies that he and his descendants will rule over the Trojans, a prophecy echoed by Aphrodite in the Homeric Hymn to Aphrodite. By tradition, then, Aeneas survives the war. In *Iliad* 20 he duels with Achilles but is snatched from danger by Poseidon. Hence there developed, after Homer, in the lost poem of the *Epic Cycle *Iliupersis*, the legend of his flight from ruined Troy with his father, son Ascanius, and the *penates* (indicative of his pious and dutiful nature), and of his subsequent wanderings. The story that his voyages took him to Italy may possibly have existed in the sixth or fifth centuries BC (*see* TABULAE ILIACAE). It was certainly known to the Greek historian *Timaeus, who in the third century BC speaks of Lavinium as Aeneas' first foundation in Italy. The story of Rome's Trojan origin had taken full shape in the fourth century BC when it was synthesized with the chronologically difficult legend of the city's foundation by *Romulus (a descendant of Aeneas through his mother). Rome soon developed the legend of Aeneas as founder of the Romans, national pride leading her to connect her own history with that of the Greek world, and by the third century BC the story later known to Virgil was well established and familiar.

When *Pyrrhus, king of Epirus, launched his attack against Rome in 281 BC he saw himself as the descendant of Achilles making war on a colony of Troy. Probably both *Fabius (3), the first Roman historian, and the Roman poet *Ennius filled the gap between the supposed dates of the fall of Troy (1184) and Romulus' foundation of Rome (753)—both dates have variants—with the story of a sojourn by Aeneas' descendants at Alba Longa. From the second century BC the Julian gens ('clan'; see JULIA, GENS), and Julius Caesar above all, exploited their descent from Aeneas and Venus for political aggrandizement. Virgil seems deliberately to create a typological link between Aeneas and the emperor Augustus.

Virgil's Aeneas retains his epic characterization as a heroic warrior, but at the fall of Troy he does not seek personal glory; instead he leaves the fight to carry his father on his shoulders out of Troy—a famous image in ancient art from the late sixth century BC and a sign of his *pietas* ('sense of duty'). He rejects personal happiness with Dido in Carthage and subordinates his own interest to that of a higher authority, as a Roman should. Yet despite his self-control he can sometimes yield to human weakness and passion.

**Aene'as Ta'cticus** ('the tactician') Probably Aeneas of Stymphalus, an Arcadian general of the early fourth century BC, named 'Tacticus' for his military treatises, one of which has survived, *Poliorcetica* ('On the defence of fortified positions'). It is also interesting for revealing social and political conditions in early fourth-century cities under threat of attack from inside as well as from foreigners, and for being a work outside the Attic literary tradition of its time.

**Aeneid (Aeneis)** Latin epic poem in twelve books of hexameters by *Virgil. It was composed during the last ten years of the poet's life, 29–19 BC, after the battle of *Actium (31 BC) had finally established the imperial-style rule of Octavian (later the emperor Augustus) at

Rome. In the introduction to his earlier *Georgics* book 3 Virgil appears to be promising to write of Octavian's 'fiery battles' and so immortalize his name in an epic, something which Propertius and Horace declined to do. In the event the *Aeneid* was a work immeasurably greater in scope and subtlety than the traditional Roman panegyric *epic by being set in the past and prefiguring the present; to write of recent wars would be tactless and might be dangerous; history was safer and admitted greater freedom. Before long the image Augustus wished to promote of himself would be that of the bringer of peace and the restorer of the *Golden age.

For his subject Virgil goes back to the legends about the arrival in Italy of the Trojan hero *Aeneas, his son Ascanius (also known as Iulus, the ancestor of the gens *Julia) and the weary remnants of his followers after the fall of Troy (traditionally 1184 BC; see ERATOSTHENES), and concludes his poem when the settlement that will lead eventually to the foundation of Rome is no more than a camp. Thus the poet conceives of his narrative as symbolic, with no more than implications for the rule of Augustus. Even so Augustus eagerly awaited its completion, and in 23 BC had the poet read books 2, 4, and 6 to the imperial family.

The Latin sources for the legends of Rome's early history were multiple, and Virgil may even have made up stories for his own purposes. The influences of many literary genres have been detected in the *Aeneid*, including tragedy (Greek and Roman) and Hellenistic poetry. It is clear that Virgil studied carefully the *Annales* of Ennius, which presented in epic verse the history of Rome from Aeneas to Ennius' own day (d. 169 BC). One very important literary influence was the Greek *Argonautica* of *Apollonius Rhodius (translated into Latin by an older contemporary of Virgil; see VARRO (2)). As in that work each book of the *Aeneid* is a unity. However, the first line of the *Aeneid*, 'Arms and the man I sing', establishes the conception of the poem as Homeric: in books 1-6, warfare as in the *Iliad*, and in books 7-12, a hero's adventurous journeying towards the desired conclusion as in the *Odyssey* (though the final act in the *Aeneid*, the killing of Turnus by Aeneas, seems more like Achilles' slaying of Hector in the *Iliad* than Odysseus' slaughter of the suitors). As in Homer, the narrator, inspired by the Muse, is omniscient, but remote from the events he describes. A striking aspect of Virgil's narrative is the constant foreshadowing of the future heroism and glory of Rome.

The role of the gods, so central in Homeric epic, is an elusive one in Virgil, especially in the case of Juno. Sometimes the gods' influence on human affairs can be seen as metaphor for the psychological states or the decisions of the individuals concerned, but the gods are more than allegorical: they have their own personalities and motivations. This is so with Venus, and especially with Juno, implacable in her long-standing hatred of the Trojans. In the end she has to accept, with some compromise, that the fate of Aeneas must be what it is. Fate itself is mysterious: though it coincides with the will of Jupiter it yet remains a force apart from divine will.

Females play a conspicuous role in the *Aeneid*, not only as goddesses but also as humans. Women, significant individuals and nameless Trojan matrons alike, are the victims of events which they cannot influence and for the most part have no interest in. Their sufferings draw attention to the extent to which the ostensible purpose of the *Aeneid* (praise of Augustus in the ancient view, or the celebration of power, to put it in a modern light) is undercut by consciousness of the pain and loss involved in vastly ambitious enterprises, and there is powerful pathos in the descriptions of so many deaths, especially of the young. There are many such oppositions, or 'contrary voices', in the *Aeneid*. Despite the imposition of order the threat of overwhelming disorder is always present, and success seems close to failure.

Several explicitly philosophical passages pose questions about Virgil's philosophical allegiances or religious beliefs but offer little clue as to answers. Is Aeneas Stoic, discounting the emotions (book 4), or Peripatetic, accepting a right amount of anger (book 12)? The most interesting is Anchises' Platonic account (with some Stoic elements) of the soul and its rebirth in book 6, a passage completely at odds with the rationalism of Lucretius, for example. A purely structural explanation for its inclusion—that the notion of rebirth makes it possible for Aeneas to view a procession of Roman heroes yet to be born—seems hardly sufficient.

The *Aeneid* was edited after Virgil's death by his friends *Varius Rufus and Plotius Tucca. The events are as follows.

*Book 1.* It is seven years since the fall of Troy. Aeneas has been making his way to Latium in Italy with the Trojan fleet and has just left Sicily. The goddess Juno, enemy of Troy and guardian of Carthage (which she knows is fated to be destroyed by a race of Trojan descent), persuades the wind-god Aeolus to send a storm against the fleet. Some of the ships are wrecked, but the sea-god Neptune calms the storm; Aeneas and the remaining ships reach the Libyan coast. The goddess Venus, mother of Aeneas, complains to Jupiter of promises unfulfilled, and Jupiter reveals the future until the time of Augustus Caesar when war will cease. The Trojans enter Carthage and Aeneas is comforted by seeing pictures in a temple of the wars of Troy. The visitors are well received by Dido, queen of the newly founded Carthage; she has fled from Tyre, where her husband Sychaeus has been killed by his brother Pygmalion, the king. Venus distrusts Juno and the Tyrians, and sends her son Cupid, in the appearance of Aeneas' son Ascanius, to make Dido fall in love with Aeneas.

*Book 2.* At Dido's request, Aeneas relates to her court the fall of Troy and the subsequent events: the building of the Trojan Horse and the cunning of Sinon, the death of *Laocoon, the entry of the Wooden Horse and the firing of the city, the desperate but useless resistance by the Trojans, Priam's death, and Aeneas' own flight at the bidding of Venus; he tells how he carried his father Anchises on his shoulders and took his son Ascanius by the hand, how his wife Creusa, who followed, was lost, and his destiny was revealed to him by her ghost. At daybreak he sees that his followers have increased greatly in number, and they begin a retreat to the mountains.

*Book 3.* Aeneas continues his story. At the foot of the mountains they build a fleet and sail north. They land at Thrace, but leave after Aeneas finds there the grave of his murdered kinsman Polydorus, and hears his voice; they sail south to Delos. The god Apollo tells them to seek the land that first bore the Trojan race. This they wrongly think means Crete, from where they are driven by plague. Aeneas now learns in a dream that Italy is meant. On their way there the Trojans land on the island of the *Harpies and attack them. The Harpy Celaeno prophesies that they shall found no city until hunger makes them 'eat their tables' (book 7). At Buthrotum in Epirus they find Helenus the seer (son of Priam) and Andromache. The seer tells Aeneas the route he must follow, visiting the Cumaean Sibyl and founding his city where by a stream he will find a white sow with a litter of thirty young. Going on his way, Aeneas visits the country of the *Cyclopes near Etna in Sicily and sees Polyphemus. The Trojans rescue the abandoned Greek Achaemenides. At Drepanum Anchises dies. From there winds drive the fleet to Libya and the Trojans arrive at Dido's court.

*Book 4.* Dido, though bound by a vow to her dead husband, confesses to her sister Anna her love for Aeneas. Juno and Venus arrange that the union of Dido and Aeneas should be sealed when a hunting expedition is interrupted by a storm and they take shelter in the same cave. Dido refers to their relationship as marriage. The rumour of their love reaches Iarbas, a neighbouring king, who has been rejected by Dido and now in his anger appeals to Jupiter. The god commands that Aeneas should leave Carthage. When Dido realizes that the fleet is preparing to sail, she confronts Aeneas and pleads with him. He replies that he has no choice, and must go to Italy even against his will. Dido's fury does not stop the Trojan preparations, and even a last entreaty from her fails to weaken Aeneas' resolve. She prepares for death, and, having seen the Trojan fleet depart, takes her own life while cursing Aeneas and his descendants.

*Book 5.* Threatening weather warns the Trojans to return to Sicily where they are received by their compatriot Acestes. It is a year since Anchises died in the same place, and the anniversary is celebrated with sacrifices and games. The first event of the latter is a race between four ships. Gyas, captain of *Chimaera*, angrily pushes his helmsman overboard when he loses the lead to Cloanthus in *Scylla*; Sergestus in *Centaur* runs aground; Mnestheus in *Pristis* overtakes Gyas but just fails to catch Cloanthus. There follows a foot-race in which the leader, Nisus, having slipped and fallen, deliberately trips Salius so as to let his friend Euryalus win. In a boxing match between the Trojan Dares and Entellus of Sicily, Aeneas stops the fight when Dares is savagely attacked by the Sicilian. Next comes an archery competition, and finally a display by thirty-six young horsemen led by Ascanius, an event which was later to become a tradition at Rome. Meanwhile Juno incites the Trojan women to express their weariness with the endless voyaging by setting fire to the ships; but only four are

destroyed before a rainstorm quenches the flames in answer to Aeneas' prayer. Nautes advises him to proceed to Italy, leaving some behind to found a new city under Acestes. Anchises appears to Aeneas giving the same advice and also telling him to see him in Elysium. Later the Trojans set sail again. The helmsman Palinurus falls asleep and is lost overboard.

*Book 6.* Aeneas lands in Italy and visits the Cumaean *Sibyl who foretells the trials he will face in Latium and what he must do to enter the Underworld. She also tells him of the death of Misenus, and Aeneas, returning to the fleet, goes to gather wood for his funeral pyre. He sees and picks the *Golden Bough as the Sibyl had instructed, and they both descend through the cave of Avernus to the Underworld. Arriving at the river Styx they see the ghosts of the unburied dead unable to cross; among them is the helmsman Palinurus, who recounts his fate and begs for burial. On seeing the Golden Bough, Charon allows Aeneas and the priestess to cross the Styx; they send *Cerberus to sleep with a drugged cake. Beyond his cave they find various groups of the dead: infants, those unjustly condemned, those who have died of love (among them Dido, not appeased by the excuses Aeneas offers), and those killed in battle. They arrive at the entrance to Tartarus, where the worst sinners suffer torments, but go on until they reach Elysium, where the souls of the virtuous live in bliss. Here Aeneas greets his father Anchises, but tries in vain to embrace him. Aeneas sees ghosts drinking at the river *Lethe, and Anchises explains how they are those who will be reincarnated: over a long period they have been purged of all evil and now drink the waters so as to lose all memory. Anchises points out the souls of men who are destined to be illustrious in Roman history: Romulus, the early kings, the great generals, Augustus himself, and his nephew *Marcellus (to whose brief life Virgil alludes). After this Aeneas and the Sibyl leave the Underworld through the Ivory Gate, by which false visions also are sent to mortals. Aeneas and the Trojans sail north to Caieta.

*Book 7.* Virgil describes this second half of the *Aeneid* as a *maius opus* (7.44), a 'greater work'. The Trojans reach the mouth of the Tiber and land in Latium. They fulfil the prophecy of the Harpy Celaeno (book 3) by eating the bread cakes which they have used as platters during a meal.

Lavinia, the daughter and heir of Latinus, king of Latium, has many suitors, the most favoured being Turnus, king of the Rutulians (who occupied part of Latium); but Latinus has been told by the oracle of Faunus that she must marry not a Latin but a stranger who will arrive. While Aeneas fortifies the camp, his ambassadors, bearing presents, are welcomed by Latinus. He offers Aeneas alliance and his daughter in marriage. Juno sees the Trojans preparing to settle and summons the Fury Allecto. Allecto stirs up passionate fury against the Trojans in Lavinia's mother, Queen Amata, who favours Turnus as a son-in-law, and in Turnus himself. When Ascanius is hunting, Allecto causes him to wound a stag which is kept as a pet, and a fight between Latins and Trojans ensues. Latinus is powerless to stop the preparations for war. There follows a catalogue of the Italian forces gathered under their leaders; among these, apart from Turnus, are an Etruscan king Mezentius, scorner of gods and a hated tyrant, Messapus, Virbius (son of *Hippolytus), and the Volscian warrior-maiden Camilla.

*Book 8.* The god of the river Tiber encourages the anxious Aeneas, telling him to seek alliance with the enemies of the Latins, the Arcadians under Evander, who have founded a city on the Palatine hill (which will in the future be part of Rome). Rowing up the river, Aeneas sees on the bank a white sow with her litter, as prophesied to be the site of his future city (book 3). Evander promises his support, and in explanation of the festival they are celebrating tells the story of Cacus. Vulcan, at the request of Venus, makes armour for Aeneas. Evander, who has shown Aeneas a number of places in his city (which will eventually be famous sites in Rome), urges alliance with the Etruscans who have revolted from their king Mezentius. Evander's son Pallas accompanies the Trojans to the Etruscan camp. Venus brings Aeneas his armour; it includes a shield on which are depicted various events in the future of Rome, down to the battle of Actium (31 BC).

*Book 9.* Aeneas has told the Trojans to keep to their camp in his absence, and they refuse to join battle even when Turnus and his forces surround them. When Turnus tries to set fire to the Trojan ships, Neptune changes them into sea-nymphs, an omen which, to reassure his followers, Turnus interprets as hostile to the Trojans. At night the Trojans Nisus and Euryalus leave the camp in order to summon Aeneas. They kill a number of the enemy in their drunken sleep, but are seen by Latin horsemen and surrounded; both are killed, after Nisus has bravely tried to save his friend. The Rutulians attack the Trojan camp in revenge for their own losses, and Ascanius, in his first feat of battle, kills one who has been shouting taunts. Turnus is cut off inside the camp, and kills many Trojans before plunging into the river to escape.

*Book 10.* On Olympus the gods debate the conflict, and Jupiter declares that the Fates must have their way. Aeneas secures the alliance of Tarchon, a king of the Etruscans, and sets out with him and with Pallas, Evander's son, to return to the Trojans. Turnus attacks them as their ships reach the shore. In the battle which follows Turnus kills Pallas but returns his body to his companions. In order to save Turnus Juno contrives a phantom of Aeneas; Turnus pursues it on board a ship which bears him away to safety. Aeneas wounds Mezentius and reluctantly kills the latter's son Lausus as he tries to protect his father; Mezentius mounts his faithful horse Rhaebus for a last attack on Aeneas before the latter kills both horse and rider.

*Book 11.* Aeneas celebrates the Trojan victory and laments the death of Pallas. The Latins send ambassadors and a truce is arranged. King Latinus and the Italian chiefs debate; Drances proposes that Turnus, being mainly responsible for the war, should settle it by meeting Aeneas in single combat. Turnus, scornful of Drances, accepts the challenge. The Latins now hear that the Trojans and Etruscans are advancing against them; Camilla and her Volscian cavalry confront the attackers. In the battle which follows Tarchon drags Venulus from his horse; Arruns seeks out and kills Camilla, who is avenged by Opis, messenger of the goddess Diana. The Volscians are defeated.

*Book 12.* The Latins are discouraged, and Turnus decides to fight Aeneas alone despite the efforts of Latinus and Amata to dissuade him. Preparations for the duel are made, but the Rutulians, already anxious about the outcome, are stirred up to break the truce by Turnus' sister Juturna; the two armies join battle again. Aeneas is wounded by an arrow, but

Venus heals him and he pursues Turnus; then Aeneas sees that the city of the Latins is unguarded and turns the Trojan army to attack it with fire. Amata, distraught, takes her own life. Turnus seeks out Aeneas and the armies draw back while the two leaders fight. Aeneas wounds Turnus and hesitates over killing him, but in grief and rage at the sight of him wearing the sword and belt taken from Pallas, kills him with his sword.

**Ae'olis** The name given in classical times to the territory in the northern part of the west coast of Asia Minor, from the Troad to the river Hermus, which had been occupied by Aeolian Greeks (for the name *see* AEOLUS (2)). These Greeks, around the end of the second millennium BC, migrated from Boeotia and Thessaly, bringing with them their own dialect, and founded their first settlements in Lesbos (*see* GREECE 2). From there they spread northwards and along the coast. Their chief city was Cyme.

**Ae'olus 1.** Described in Homer's *Odyssey* as the son of Hippotes, a mortal, king of the floating island of Aeolia and friend of the gods, to whom Zeus gave the custodianship of the winds. Later he was thought of as the god of the winds. He received Odysseus hospitably and gave him a leather bag in which he had secured those winds adverse to the latter's voyage. Virgil depicts him as keeping the winds imprisoned in a cave (*Aeneid* 1.50-9). He is sometimes confused with (2) below.

**2.** Son of *Hellen and the legendary ancestor of the Aeolians; he was the father of *Sisyphus, *Athamas, *Salmoneus, *Alcyone, Calyce (mother of *Endymion), *Canace, and other children.

**Āĕ'ropē** Wife of Atreus, seduced by Thyestes (*see* PELOPS).

**aes** (Lat.) Bronze; more loosely, copper or brass. *See* MONEY AND COINS 2.

**Ae'schinēs** (*c.*397–*c.*322 BC) Athenian orator and politician, great rival of *Demosthenes (2). Only three of the speeches attributed to him were judged to be genuine by the Roman critics, and these survive. Demosthenes mocked his upbringing as the son of a poor schoolteacher; if that is true Aeschines displays his education by frequent quotations from poetry. He embarked on a political career as a

supporter of *Eubulus, who controlled Athenian finances. When it was known that under *Philip II Macedonian influence was spreading as far south as Arcadia in the Peloponnese, Aeschines supported Eubulus in the proposal for creating a Common Peace (i.e. a treaty open to all autonomous Greek states) to provide common action against aggressors so that no state under threat would need to seek help from Macedon. Aeschines was sent to Megalopolis to dissuade the Arcadians from having dealings with Philip, but the scheme failed. Athens then realized that she and her allies must make an alliance with Philip, and an embassy under the leadership of *Philocrates, including Aeschines and Demosthenes, was hastily sent to negotiate terms. Peace and alliance between Philip and Athens (and the Second Athenian League) were finally agreed in 346, known as the Peace of Philocrates. But by this time Philip had encroached still further south and finally taken Thermopylae. The Peace of Philocrates was clearly ineffectual and discredited. Aeschines spoke in an attempt to reconcile the Athenians to the facts of the situation, but Demosthenes was now anxious to dissociate himself from the Peace, and became implacably hostile to Aeschines, its supporter, choosing to believe that the latter had been won over by Macedonian bribes.

In 346/5 Demosthenes began a prosecution against him for his part in the peace negotiations, with the support of Timarchus. The latter was a man long active against Philip but notorious for his private life. Aeschines replied with a speech of counter-accusation, *Against Timarchus* (still extant), in which he invoked a law forbidding those of known misconduct from addressing the assembly. He was successful, but the mood of Athens was becoming more hostile to Macedon.

In the sixteen years that followed, the speeches exchanged between Aeschines and Demosthenes provide much of the evidence for the relations between Athens and Macedon in this period. In 343 Demosthenes rose to the attack again in a speech *On the False Embassy*, as if Aeschines had been solely responsible for the discredited Peace, and had supported it because he was bribed. Aeschines replied in a speech of the same title (which also survives) and was narrowly acquitted of wrongdoing. He continued to be influential in the Assembly

and in 340 was sent as one of Athens' representatives to the Amphictyonic Council (*see*
AMPHICTYONY), where he notably failed in judgement by provoking a Sacred War at the very
time when Greek unity was essential to avoid
giving Philip an opportunity to intervene in
Greek affairs.

Philip's subsequent advance south ended
with the defeat of Athens and Thebes at
the battle of *Chaeronea in 338, and Aeschines
was a member of the embassy sent to negotiate
with Philip after the battle. In 336 Demosthenes' friend Ctesiphon proposed that
Demosthenes should be crowned in the theatre at the *Dionysia for his patriotic services to
the city. Aeschines indicted Ctesiphon for the
alleged illegality of the proposal but did not
proceed with the indictment until 330 when
Athens was in almost complete isolation, with
no prospect of liberation from Macedon. In his
speech *Against Ctesiphon* he attacked the
whole career of Demosthenes as injurious to
Athens. Demosthenes replied in his speech *On
the Crown* (*De corona*) with such devastating
effect that Aeschines failed to obtain the necessary fifth of the jury's votes to save himself
from a fine. He retired from Athens to Rhodes,
where he died in about 322. At Rhodes he gave
declamations, and on one occasion delivered
his speech *Against Ctesiphon*. When the islan-
ders expressed amazement that it did not win
he replied, 'You would not wonder if you had
heard Demosthenes'.

Aeschines was not a professional rhetorician. A story tells that when the Rhodians
asked him to teach rhetoric he replied that he
was ignorant of it himself. He seems not to
have written speeches for others, and it is
probable that he received no rhetorical training, but he was thoroughly familiar with all the
conventions. He was famous for his dignified
presence and splendid voice. In ancient as well
as modern times he has suffered from comparison with Demosthenes. The general aim of his
activities was to find a compromise between
Athens and Macedon which would leave
Athens independent and at peace, and inevitably he had to trust Macedon to some extent. It
was not a noble policy, nor was it possible to
give it rhetorical expression. In consequence
he avoided deeper issues of principle, and in
contrast with Demosthenes, who was forever
generalizing and broadening the issues, he
seems lacking in a wider vision.

**Ae'schylus** (525–456 BC) The earliest Greek
tragic poet whose work survives. Born at Eleusis, near Athens, of a noble family, he witnessed in his youth the end of tyranny at
Athens, and in his maturity the growth of democracy. He took part in the Persian Wars, at
the battle of Marathon in 490 (where his brother was killed) and probably at Salamis in 480
(which he describes in the *Persians*). He visited Syracuse at the invitation of the tyrant
Hieron I more than once and died at Gela in
Sicily; an anecdote relates that an eagle
dropped a tortoise on his bald head and killed
him. Soon after his death it was decreed as a
unique honour that anyone who wished to
produce his plays should be 'granted a chorus'
(*see* TRAGEDY 2). His epitaph does not mention
his plays, only that he fought at Marathon. One
of his sons, Euphorion, was also a tragic poet.

Aeschylus wrote some seventy to ninety
plays (including *satyr plays) and won his first
victory in the dramatic competitions of 484. He
won thirteen victories altogether. In his early
days he was the rival of Pratinas, Phrynichus,
and Choerilus of Athens, and in later life
of Sophocles, who defeated him in 468. Seven
plays only have come down to us, six of which
we know to have come from prize-winning
*tetralogies: the *Persians*, produced in 472,
the *Seven against Thebes* (*Septem*) in 467, the
*Oresteia* trilogy, comprising the *Agamemnon*,
the *Choephoroe* ('Libation bearers'), and the
*Eumenides* ('The kindly ones'), in 458, and
the *Suppliants*; this last used commonly to
be regarded as the earliest play because of
certain archaic features, but a papyrus fragment containing a note on its production
shows that it must be later than 467, and 463
is a likely date. The other surviving play, *Prometheus Bound*, if by Aeschylus, has several
features not found elsewhere in the plays. It
may have been composed in Sicily and produced posthumously by Euphorion, perhaps
partially written by him but produced as
Aeschylus' work. There are substantial fragments of the satyr plays 'Netfishers' (*Dic-
tyoulkoi*) and 'Spectators at the Isthmian
games' (*Theoroi* or *Isthmiastai*) surviving on
papyri (*see* PAPYROLOGY), and many titles of
plays are known.

Aeschylus is generally regarded as the real
founder of Greek tragedy. The surviving plays
cover a period of only fourteen years but they
show considerable structural development.

In the *Persians, Seven against Thebes,* and *Suppliants* where there are only two actors, the pace of action is slow. Conversations are still mainly between chorus and actors who enter, speak to the chorus, and exit again, and each episode is followed by a song from the chorus. By the addition of a third actor and the reduction of the part taken by the chorus, innovations ascribed to either Aeschylus or Sophocles, true dialogue and dramatic action became possible. Three actors are used in Aeschylus' later plays.

Also by the date of the *Oresteia,* 458, more stage properties were available to him, such as the *skene* (stage building), *ekkyklema* (a wheeled platform), and *mechane* (machine, Lat. *machina*); *see* THEATRE [Greek]. So, in *Agamemnon,* the watchman keeps watch from the roof of the *skene,* and the murdered bodies of Agamemnon and Cassandra are wheeled on stage from the door of the *skene* by means of the *ekkyklema.*

The visual aspects of the plays are exciting: in the *Persians* alone, the sumptuous costume of Atossa contrasted later with Xerxes' rags, and the chorus of Persian elders calling up the spirit of Darius (as Aristophanes in the *Frogs* noted); the Furies, before they become 'the kindly ones', tracking Orestes like hounds by the scent of blood; and in *Agamemnon,* the purple cloth on which Agamemnon fatally walks as he enters the palace.

Aeschylus' language has a grandeur which could verge on the bathetic (again, according to Aristophanes), though his dialogue sometimes seems stiff. He coins long compound words and is lavish with epithets and bold metaphors. The lyric poetry of the choruses is markedly Homeric in language and owes much to earlier lyric, but simple in metre and free-flowing. It is powerful in suggesting a mood or a theme that may run throughout the play. Thus the choral odes are relevant to the action, often explaining the significance of events that preceded the drama. Choruses in Aeschylus, in comparison with Sophocles and Euripides, have a marked corporate personality—the Danaids, who are the actual Suppliants, determined to reject marriage to the death; the Argive elders in *Agamemnon,* powerless in their old age, pondering the workings of justice with a sense of foreboding.

The principal characters are strongly drawn; even if they seem to lack complexity, they say and do with intensity what their role requires of them. Most memorable is Clytemnestra, depicted as a woman completely out of the ordinary, one capable of ruling, 'a woman with a man's mind' (*androboulon*). Aristophanes comments on one peculiarity: the tendency of Aeschylus to introduce a character early on who remains mute for a large part of the action, as happens in the case of Cassandra in *Agamemnon.*

The plot of an Aeschylean tragedy as we know it is generally of the kind that Aristotle in the *\*Poetics* calls 'simple'; it moves towards its end without 'a surprising turn of events' (Aristotle's *peripeteia*) because the events that precipitated it have occurred long before. The climax is prepared for by a gradual increase of tension. One effect of this form of plot is to suggest the slow but certain workings of a divine justice. It is through suffering that mortals eventually learn the will of Zeus but, in line with traditional Greek thought, it may be in the person of their descendants.

In Athens dramatic festivals were also religious and civic occasions. The end of the *Oresteia,* which shows the healing effect of compromise and reconciliation, suggests the political as well as the religious dimension of Attic drama. It was impossible to separate drama from politics and from the duties and privileges of the citizens of a democratic \*city-state who comprised most of the audience.

**Aescula'pius** The Latin form of the name of the Greek god of healing, \*Asclepius. His cult was brought to Rome from the famous temple at Epidaurus in Argos in 293 BC, after the Romans had consulted the Sibylline books (*see* SIBYL) because of a severe pestilence. The temple, with a sanatorium, stood on the island of the river Tiber, where an important healing-cult developed.

**Aesop (Aisōpos)** The traditional composer of Greek \*fables. The story of his life, which was already known to Herodotus in the fifth century BC, has been overlaid by many fictions. He is said to have been a Phrygian slave living on the island of Samos in the early sixth century BC. *See also* RHODOPE.

**aesthetics** The study of concepts of beauty, or, in particular, the study of the rules and principles of art, including the nature of the arts in general. These categories of thought did not exist as such in the ancient world. However, modern aesthetics often takes as a starting point ideas already found in Greek and Roman literature, particularly in philosophy, literary or art criticism, and *rhetoric. Aesthetic criticism is very often close to moral criticism in the ancient world. In Aristophanes' *Frogs* (405 BC), for example, the literary grandeur of Aeschylus is associated with his 'moral worth'. Deeper questions about the value of art and the relation of art to ethics go back to Plato's original attack on art in the fourth century BC and Aristotle's answers to that attack.

Plato is the first to subject the arts to rigorous philosophical investigation to assess their value. Though he includes painting (to a limited extent) and also music in his investigation, his focus is on poetry, and beyond poetry on the similar art, as it seemed to him, of contemporary rhetoric. The poets, rhetors, and sophists all claim to have knowledge, and aim to produce conviction in the minds of their audience. The poets' claim to knowledge is based on inspiration imparted by the *Muses. Is their claim well founded?

Greeks of Plato's day assumed that in addition to giving pleasure the function of poetry was to teach (as it was the function of painting and sculpture to produce likenesses of the original). Plato is not interested in the arts for their own sake. 'To write well a good poet must know his subject; otherwise he would not write about it', he says in the *Republic*. Inspiration, as claimed by the poets, did not lead to knowledge. As Socrates observes in the *Apology*, poets are often at a loss to explain their own poetry. Plato believes that the only true objects of knowledge are the Forms, ideals of the things of this world. Thus he originated the concept of art as *mimesis*, 'imitation'; he compares it to holding up a mirror to objects. An artist's picture of a bed (in Plato's example) is an 'imitation' of an actual bed, and that actual bed is itself an 'imitation' of the true Form of Bed. 'All poetry, from Homer onwards, imitates images of its subject, whatever that may be, and has no grasp of reality.'

Moreover, art has the power to arouse the emotions, the non-rational part of a person, and so is damaging to rationality and must be subject to censorship. Poets often portrayed gods and heroes behaving in an immoral way, and so failed in their educative function of promoting correct values. Hence the paradox that Plato, the most self-conscious of literary craftsmen, who had an admitted love of poetry, would banish the poets from his ideal state,

and only a small fraction of poetry would be reprieved: 'praises of the gods and eulogies of good men' (*see* REPUBLIC).

Some have thought that when Plato talks of 'love of the beautiful' he may be talking in a positive way about a philosophy of art, but Plato does not seem to give any autonomous value to art. The best he can say for poets is that a true poet is inspired by the divine in a way that is akin to madness. No role is afforded to the arts in the 'long-standing quarrel between poetry and philosophy'. Knowledge of the Form of the Beautiful can only be arrived at, if at all, by philosophy.

The first philosophical work of aesthetic theory is Aristotle's *Poetics*. Like his *Rhetoric* it is a 'study of productive activity', in this case how to write tragedy, but it is also a work of aesthetic theory because it answers the questions, What is poetry? What kind of poetry is tragedy? What are the essential constituents of tragedy? Aristotle is in part replying to Plato's conclusion that poetry should be banned in the (ideal) city-state because of its harmful effects, which are, that it cannot transmit knowledge, that it encourages irrationality, and that it presents sufferings to which we respond, thus making us less able to endure our own. Aristotle justifies poetry and especially tragedy by appealing to its essential seriousness: 'poetry is more philosophical than history' because it deals with the general rather than the particular, and therefore has important ethical and educative effects. However, he does not explicitly say that these follow from poetry's *artistic* effects. The role of art in moral education is still today a matter for argument. For Aristotle the meaning of beauty is relative: it varies with the thing to which beauty is being ascribed. The concept of beauty itself has no role to play in his discussion of poetry.

Followers of *Epicurus naturally rejected the mythical content of poetry since they thought that the religious beliefs underlying the myths were false. However, because their criterion of value was pleasure they could still allow themselves to enjoy artistic performances and, as the Epicurean Latin poet *Lucretius showed, giving pleasure could be combined with Epicurean teaching. *Eratosthenes too (late third century BC), himself a poet as well as an exceptionally versatile scholar, declared that the aim of poetry was to entertain not to instruct. The Epicurean philosopher and poet *Philodemus (first century BC), whose writings are still being deciphered, seems refreshingly modern. His theory of art, which included music, was that art had no moral attributes or logic and did not influence character; its value, decided on grounds of form and beauty, consisted in giving pleasure. However, Stoics, like Strabo, who quoted Eratosthenes' dictum, retained under Plato's influence a moralistic view of poetry; in difficult cases they interpreted it allegorically (*see* ALLEGORY) or simply accepted that it could not be judged as strict truth. Stoic attitudes were very influential in later centuries.

See also ARS POETICA; LONGINUS ON THE SUBLIME; LITERARY CRITICISM; PLOTINUS; ART, ATTITUDES TO.

**aether** [Gk. *aither*, in Greek myth a primordial deity, otherwise 'upper air'] In early Greek thought the sky was imagined as a solid hemispherical bowl covering the round, flat earth. The part nearest earth was the *aēr*, the misty air including the clouds. The shining upper air was the *aither*, the rarified and pure atmosphere in which the Greeks imagined the gods to live and the heavenly bodies to exist. The name is sometimes given to heaven itself (*see* URANUS). The *Presocratic philosophers interpreted *aither* to suit their own individual cosmological theories. *See also* ELEMENT.

*Aethio'pica* (in full, 'Ethiopian story of Theagenes and Charicleia') A Greek *novel by Heliodorus in ten books. The date is uncertain: a date in the fourth century AD has been argued for, but other indications suggest some time in the first half of the third century AD.

The narrative opens in mid-story and earlier events are only gradually revealed in a long and much-interrupted recapitulation by Calasiris. The heroine Charicleia is the daughter of the Ethiopian queen. Born white and therefore exposed by her mother (*see* INFANTICIDE), she is taken by a Greek traveller to Delphi where she is brought up and becomes a priestess. At a festival she and Theagenes, a Thessalian aristocrat, fall in love and aided by Calasiris, a priest sent by Charicleia's mother to find her, leave for Egypt. After a series of adventures they at last reach Meroe in Ethiopia, where Charicleia, on the point of being sacrificed, is recognized by her parents and the lovers are then happily married. Much of the charm of the novel lies in the lively and practical character of Charicleia.

*Ae'thiopis* ('The Ethiopian poem', referring to Memnon's Ethiopian followers) A lost poem of the *Epic Cycle in five books, ascribed to Homer or Arctinus of Miletus. It covered the deaths of *Penthesilea, *Thersites (killed for mocking Achilles in his grief at the death of Penthesilea), *Memnon (king of Ethiopia, hence the title), and Achilles (*see* AJAX (1)). Very few fragments survive.

**Aethra** In Greek myth, daughter of Pittheus, king of Troezen, and mother of *Theseus.

**Aetna 1.** Europe's highest active volcano, in Sicily. Eruptions were attributed in literature to the mythical monster *Typhon or the Giant Enceladus (*see* GIANTS) imprisoned by Zeus beneath the mountain; occasionally it was described as the workshop of *Vulcan. Various notable eruptions are recorded in antiquity, Pindar in his first Pythian ode refers to one in 475 BC, and there were others in 396 BC and 122 BC.

**2.** The city of Catana (Gk. Katane, modern Catania) at the foot of Mount Aetna. This name was given to it by Hieron I, tyrant of Syracuse, when he refounded the city in 475 BC, removing the former Ionian inhabitants and re-peopling it with Dorian mercenaries. In 461 these were expelled and the old name restored. The name Aetna was then transferred with the mercenaries to the nearby city of Inessa.

*Aetna* Latin didactic poem in 645 hexameters of unknown authorship. It attempts to explain the volcanic activity of Mount Aetna. Attributed by its manuscripts and doubtfully by *Donatus (1) to Virgil, it is almost certainly not by him. The authorship and date have been the subject of much speculation with no agreement reached, but the style seems to point to the first century AD. The author rejects mythological explanations and attributes eruptions to wind at high pressure acting on subterranean fires in cavities of the earth (substantially the same explanation as that of Lucretius, *De rerum natura* 6.680). The poem is enlivened by digressions and closes with a story to illustrate justice in natural events: on the occasion of a sudden eruption the inhabitants of Catana hastily fled, each carrying the property he thought most precious; they were overwhelmed, but a certain Amphinomus and his brother, who carried away nothing but their aged father and mother and their household gods, were spared.

**Afrā'nius, Lucius** (active *c.*160–120 BC) Writer of Roman comedies, *fabulae *togatae*, 'dramas in a toga', i.e. about Italian life and characters. Only scanty fragments and forty-two titles survive. Horace says that admirers compared him with the Greek writer of comedy Menander, and Afranius acknowledges his indebtedness to the latter. The popularity of his plays continued under the empire; the emperor Nero staged a realistic and costly performance of *The Fire*, allowing the actors to keep what furniture they could rescue from a house which was actually set on fire.

**Africa** (i.e. *Africa terra*, the land of the Afri) The Latin name for the territory in the north of Africa, and later extended to the whole continent. From *c.*500 BC the Greeks recognized it as a third continent after Europe and Asia. They divided Africa from Asia at first by the Nile and later by the Red Sea, and called the part of it they knew (the pastoral land in the north near Egypt) Libya, after the indigenous people of North Africa. After they had colonized the area, the name Libya usually denoted the colonial area around Cyrene, but sometimes the whole of the North African coastal area, or even the whole continent. Herodotus believed the continent was circumnavigable, and Strabo thought it triangular in shape. The interior remained largely unknown to them, and likewise the coast south of the Canaries in the west, roughly, and Zanzibar in the east.

**Africa, Roman** After finally defeating Carthage in 146 BC (*see* PUNIC WARS), Rome acquired what is now north and central Tunisia as the new and very fertile province of Africa. Most of the land became *ager publicus*, and many Romans and Italians settled there, some on land beyond the provincial boundary. After 46 BC (*see* THAPSUS) Julius Caesar added more territory, and with the planting of new colonies the province stretched along the north coast from Cyrenaica (which remained Greek-speaking) to the Atlantic. The area was heavily urbanized, with a number of towns of Phoenician or Carthaginian origin surviving, such as Lepcis Magna (where the emperor Septimius Severus was born). During the second century AD African senators at Rome (who included the orator Fronto) comprised the largest group from the western provinces. The wealth of Roman Africa was proverbial, derived largely from the chief export, corn, and Africa replaced Sicily as Italy's main supplier. In the third century Christianity spread rapidly in the province: Cyprian, Tertullian, and Augustine were all African by birth. *See also* ASIA; CARTHAGE; EGYPT; and GEOGRAPHY.

**Africanus** *See* SCIPIO (1 and 2).

**after-life** *See* DEATH, ATTITUDES TO; ELYSIUM; HADES; ORPHISM; *REPUBLIC*; SOUL; TARTARUS.

**Agamē′dēs** *See* TROPHONIUS.

**Agamemnon** In Greek myth, king of Mycenae or Argos. He was the son of *Atreus, brother of *Menelaus, and husband of *Clytemnestra. Because of his superiority in wealth and power he was commander-in-chief of the Greek forces in the Trojan War; his contingent of a hundred ships was the largest. He is represented in Homer's *Iliad* as a valiant fighter, a proud and passionate man, but vacillating in purpose and easily discouraged. His quarrel with *Achilles is the mainspring of the poem's action. The *Odyssey* tells how, on his return from Troy, he was feasted in the palace of his wife's lover in Argos, and there murdered by them both, together with his captive *Cassandra. This story is retold by later authors, with minor variants (*see esp.* ORESTEIA). All accounts include a son *Orestes among his children, who avenged his father's murder, usually with the help of his sister *Electra. The *Cypria* is the earliest witness to the story that Agamemnon was required to sacrifice his daughter Iphigeneia to atone for an offence against Artemis, who in anger was keeping the Greek fleet windbound at Aulis. *See* IPHIGENEIA AMONG THE TAURIANS and IPHIGENEIA AT AULIS.

**Agamemnon** 1. Greek tragedy by *Aeschylus; for the plot *see* ORESTEIA.
2. Roman tragedy by Seneca the Younger (*see* SENECA (2) 4). The play shows variation in details from the *Agamemnon* of Aeschylus. There is a chorus of captive Trojan women and one of women from Argos; the ghost of Thyestes is introduced urging Aegisthus to murder Agamemnon, and Aegisthus strengthens a weaker Clytemnestra's resolve. Cassandra is not murdered with Agamemnon but later. Electra is included in the play and contrives the escape of her brother Orestes.

**Agapē′nor** In Greek myth, leader of the Arcadian contingent against Troy in the Trojan War. On the way back he arrived at Cyprus where he founded the city of Paphos.

**Aga'thias** (AD *c.*532–*c.*580) Greek poet and historian in Constantinople, author of a (now lost) epic in nine books, the *Daphniaca*. *See* ANTHOLOGY [Greek].

**Aga'thoclēs** Tyrant of *Syracuse in the late fourth century BC.

**A'gathon** (*c.*445–*c.*400 BC) Athenian tragic poet, perhaps the most important apart from the three great tragedians (*see* TRAGEDY 4) and celebrated for his good looks. Fewer than fifty lines of his work survive. His first victory in the dramatic competitions was gained at the *Lenaea in 416 BC when he was probably just under 30. It is the banquet held at his house to celebrate this victory that forms the setting of Plato's *Symposium*. He appears as a youth in Plato's *Protagoras* (dramatic date *c.*432 BC). Agathon was innovative: he wrote a tragedy on an imaginary subject with imaginary characters rather than taking both from myth; he made the songs of the chorus mere interludes (*embolima*, 'interpolations') without reference to the subject of the play, thus preparing the way for the division of a tragedy into acts; and he also introduced some changes in the character of the music. Aristophanes in the *Thesmophoriazusae* parodies Agathon's lyrics, hinting that they are voluptuous and effeminate and at one point describing them as like the walking of ants, and also mocks his effeminacy. When, towards the end of the Peloponnesian War, Agathon, like Euripides, withdrew to the court of Archelaus of Macedon with his long-term lover Pausanius, Aristophanes in the *Frogs* (84) regrets his abandonment of Athens. He died in Macedon.

**Aga'vē (Agauē)** In Greek myth, the mother of Pentheus (*see* BACCHAE). For the pantomime with this title *see* STATIUS.

**Agdistis** The Phrygian name of *Cybele; *see* also* ATTIS.

**age** For age in the sense of era *see* BRONZE AGE; MYCENAE; CALENDARS.

**age groups** (childhood, adulthood, old age) Homer often stresses the particular closeness that is felt between men of the same age, apart from the usual ties of friendship, and between women too (in the case both of Helen and of Nausicaa). This may have arisen from shared puberty rites. The ancient world was particularly conscious of age groups and the

activities appropriate to childhood and early youth, adulthood, and old age. *See* AGE QUALIFICATION.

**Agē'nōr** In Greek myth, king of Tyre, twin-brother of *Belus, and father of *Cadmus and *Europa.

**age qualification** In Greece and Rome, the minimum and maximum ages for undertaking certain responsibilities. For service in the army these were governed by physical capability. At Athens a man underwent military training between 18 (when he ceased technically to be a boy, *pais*, and came of age and if qualified was enrolled as a citizen; *see* EPHEBOI) and 20, and could then be required to serve until he was 49. From 50 to 60 he was liable only for garrison duty. The upbringing of a Spartan male from 7 to 29, known as *agōge*, was particularly regulated by age. Boys were removed from their mothers at the age of 7 into individual year groups and at 12 entered into an institutionalized pederastic relationship with a young adult. At 20 they joined the army and could marry, although they continued to live in barracks, and they were liable for military service until the age of 60. The Roman boy became a youth, *iuvenis*, and put on the plain white *toga virilis*, the toga of a man, at about 14. From 14 to 17 these *iuvenes* served their 'apprenticeship' (*tirocinium*) to military service, for which the age range was from 17 to 46.

The ancient world believed that mental maturity came with age. At Athens a *strategos* or a member of the *boule* had to be at least 30, as (probably) did a Spartan *ephor*. The Roman *cursus honorum* (the sequence of political offices) prescribed minimum ages for all offices. The minimum age for the highest, the consulship, was 42. In Athens and Rome there were legal minimum ages for marriage; in Athens a man could marry when he came of age at 18 and a woman when she reached puberty, i.e. was 14. In Rome both could marry at puberty though the consent of the father was needed if either was under his control (*see* PATRIA POTESTAS).

**ager pu'blicus** ('public land') Land confiscated during the Roman conquest of Italy, from communities which had put up a strong resistance or subsequently rebelled. (Some land in the provinces could also be so described.) Some of the land was assigned to individuals and much was allocated to colonies, but from earliest times most of it became the subject of dispute between the *plebs* who wished it to be distributed among themselves and the patricians who preferred to maintain public ownership so that they could be *possessores*. The *possessores* were supposed to pay dues to the state in return for occupying the land. After the extensive confiscations of the Second Punic War some *ager publicus* was leased by the censors and brought in a good rent to the state, but large tracts especially in the south were held by *possessores* and mostly used for ranching. The aim of the *Gracchi was to distribute the excess land in smallholdings. An end was put to many disputes by a law of 111 BC which said that all state land was to become the private property of its occupants. The question of *ager publicus* became an issue on several occasions afterwards as victorious generals like Sulla and Julius Caesar wanted land for their veterans. It was not until AD 6 in the time of the emperor Augustus that a pension scheme, *aerarium*, as a means of support other than grants of land, was devised for discharged soldiers. Thereafter public land in Italy consisted only of common pasture or what belonged to municipalities.

**Agesilā'us II** (*c.*445–359 BC) Spartan king of the *Eurypontid line who unexpectedly succeeded his elder brother in 399 BC. Born lame in one leg, he was a man of great efficiency and Spartan virtues. His successful campaigns against the Persians in 396–395 and his victory over the Boeotians and Athenians at Coronea in 394 are related by his friend the Athenian historian Xenophon in his *Hellenica*. Spartan intervention in the affairs of autonomous states, most flagrantly in Thebes (382), which Agesilaus condoned, resulted in an alliance between Thebes and Athens which his invasions of Boeotia in 378 and 377 did not succeed in disrupting. His refusal in 371 to admit *Epaminondas' claim to represent all Boeotia at the peace congress in Sparta precipitated the battle of Leuctra at which Sparta lost the leadership of Greece. The Theban ascendancy which followed, and the consequent liberation of *Messenia from Sparta, were the result of Agesilaus' hostility to Thebes. He organized the defence of Sparta against Epaminondas and in order to increase the revenue of the state he conducted an expedition against Persia in 361, in aid of an Egyptian prince. During this he met his death

(in his middle eighties). His Life was written by *Nepos and by Xenophon (*see* AGESILAUS).

**Agesilā'us** One of the minor works of Xenophon, a biographical essay on his friend the Spartan king (*see* AGESILAUS II). Xenophon relates in some detail the campaign of Agesilaus against the Persian satrap *Tissaphernes in 395 BC and the march back to Greece through Macedonia and Thessaly, and gives a full description of the battle of *Coronea in 394 at which, according to Plutarch, Xenophon fought for his friend and against his fellow-countrymen. The remaining events of Agesilaus' reign are touched on more briefly. Xenophon then passes from his deeds to his virtues, and ends with an encomium on his piety, justice, wisdom, and patriotism.

**A'giads (Agiadai)** The senior royal house at *Sparta, the name derived from king Agis, son of Eurysthenes (*see* HERACLEIDAE). The junior branch was the Eurypontid.

**agnosticism** The view that it is impossible to have knowledge of the existence, or non-existence, of gods. In the ancient world it is not easy to distinguish between agnostic and atheistic views. The Greeks had no word for agnostic and did not make fine distinctions in the matter: those who disbelieved in the gods who were usually worshipped and believed in were liable to be called atheists (*athēoi*). From the sixth century BC onwards philosophers, especially those with views on cosmological matters which seemed to indicate disbelief in the traditional gods, could be called atheists, and similarly the sophists (*see* e.g. ANAXAGORAS and PRODICUS respectively). The most trenchant expression of a strictly agnostic viewpoint in ancient Greece was that of the sophist Protagoras: 'Concerning the gods I have no means of knowing whether they exist or not, or what they are like in form. Many things prevent knowledge: the uncertainty of the subject and the brevity of human life.' *See* ATHEISM.

**agō'gē** [Gk., 'leading', 'guidance', and so 'system of education'] The name given to the public and military upbringing of males at Sparta in particular. *See* AGE QUALIFICATION; EDUCATION 2; SPARTA.

**agōn** (pl. *agonēs*) Greek for 'contest', 'struggle'. The Greeks, being intensely competitive, applied this word and its derivatives to all the rivalries of Greek life—war, public debate, jealous ambition, and also to set-piece arguments or debates in tragedy and comedy. In particular *agon* denoted, at Greece and later at Rome, a public festival in which contenders competed for a prize. These could be musical or dramatic competitions (*see* DIONYSIA), but those creating most excitement were *athletic competitions and *horse- and chariot-races—the games.

**a'gora** [In Greek literally 'assembly', especially of the people, then 'place of assembly', 'market-place'; Lat. *forum*] The commercial, social, and political centre of a Greek city. At Athens the agora was established in the time of Solon in the early sixth century BC, on ground sloping down to the river Eridanus, to the north-west of the Acropolis. It was lined by the principal administrative buildings, many erected at the end of the century under the Peisistratids: bouleuterion, tholos, Metrōon, mint, law-courts, magistrates' offices, stoas, and many sanctuaries. The Panathenaic Way ran through it. The Athenian agora stood for over 800 years, being finally destroyed in the invasions of the Heruli (a Germanic people from the Black Sea area) in AD 267. *See also* PEISISTRATUS; STOA; OLYMPIEUM.

**Agri'cola, Gnaeus Julius** (AD 40–93) From the Roman colony of Forum Julii (Fréjus), Roman general and governor of *Britain (4), known almost entirely from the biography written by his son-in-law the historian Tacitus (*see* AGRICOLA). Agricola did his early military service in Britain as the (senatorial) *tribunus militum* during *Boudicca's rebellion (AD 60–1). He was quaestor of Asia, tribune of the people, praetor, and then in AD 71–3 commander of the Twentieth Legion in Britain. After that he became governor of Aquitania, then consul for part of 77. Later that year he returned to Britain as legate (governor) at an unusually young age. He remained for seven years, the longest-known governorship. In his first year he subdued Anglesey, and in his second advanced to northern England and southern Scotland. This advance was made by stages during 80 and 81, with gains consolidated by fortifications including some on a line between the rivers Forth and Clyde. Agricola finally succeeded in bringing about a pitched battle with the Caledonians in September 83 at Mons Graupius (a much-sought battlefield, but the discovery of a large Roman camp near Inverurie in Aberdeenshire suggests that it may be the mountain now called Bennachie).

Agricola's victory in this battle was final for its generation. After it he ordered the fleet to circumnavigate Britain (a feat remembered by later Roman historians), thus proving that it was an island. In spring 84 he was recalled to Rome and given no further command, because of Domitian's jealousy according to Tacitus. He lived long enough to see Rome abandon the system of forts with which he had blockaded the Highlands and secured the northern frontier. The excavations at Inchtuthil in Perthshire are a notable revelation of an outpost systematically demolished before it had been properly occupied. His civil policy encouraged urbanization and he founded many small quasi-independent 'states' in southern Britain to fill the administrative gap caused by moving the legions north.

**Agri'cola** Biography by *Tacitus of his father-in-law, the Roman governor of Britain (*see* AGRICOLA, GNAEUS JULIUS). Though it is naturally not as informative as one might hope about the geography and ethnography of Britain, the account of continual rain and cloud and the long days and short nights of the north European summer strikes a chord with present-day visitors. Tacitus' laudatory account of his subject emphasizes Agricola's sympathy and justice towards the provincials which enabled him to pacify the country, and the military skills, particularly his good eye for terrain, which helped him to extend Roman occupation some distance into Scotland. *Agricola*, though less epigrammatic in style than Tacitus' other work, includes phrases that have become memorable; for example, from the speech of the Caledonian leader Calgacus before the battle at Mons Graupius: *omne ignotum pro magnifico est* ('what men know nothing about they see as wonderful'), and *ubi solitudinem faciunt, pacem appellant* ('when they create a desolation they call it peace').

*See also* BIOGRAPHY.

**agricultural writers** Writers of treatises on methods of agriculture, a popular literary genre in Greece and Rome. Most of these works have not survived. *See* CATO (1), COLUMELLA, and VARRO. The Greek poet Hesiod, in *Works and Days* (381–617), gives interesting information on the year's agricultural tasks in Greece during the early archaic age. In recent years surveys of rural areas, excavations of farms, and study of ancient seeds and pollen have been greatly extending knowledge of Roman agriculture and sometimes confirming written accounts of agricultural practice which some scholars had doubted.

**Agrige'ntum** *See* ACRAGAS.

**Agri'ppa, Marcus Vipsā'nius** (64–12 BC) Lifelong friend and supporter of the Roman emperor Augustus and by the end of his life nearly his equal in power. After Caesar's murder he accompanied Octavian (as Augustus was then called) to Rome. He was tribune of the people in 43 BC, and as governor of Gaul in 38 he suppressed rebellion. Appointed consul in 37 he won two naval victories in the following year against Sextus Pompeius. His naval operations against Mark Antony were the main cause of Antony's defeat and at *Actium he famously commanded the left wing of the fleet. During Augustus' protracted absences from Italy, Agrippa, with Maecenas, managed affairs. He held second and third consulships in 28 and 27, and in 23 BC Augustus, when very ill, seemed to indicate that Agrippa should succeed him. After absence in the east Agrippa went to Gaul and Spain in 20 and 19, where he put down a revolt. In 13 the power of his *imperium* was apparently made virtually equal to that of Augustus. His second visit to the East is notable for his friendship with Herod (1) the Great and the goodwill he showed towards the Jews. He died in the following year, 12 BC, and was buried in Augustus' own mausoleum.

Agrippa devoted his life and his immense wealth to Rome and the empire, and left most of his property to Augustus at his death. Among his many public works were the building of the *Pantheon and the first great public *baths at Rome, and the renewal of the water-supply and sewage systems (*see* CLOACA MAXIMA). He built the harbour, Portus Julius, on Lake Avernus, and also carried out many works in the provinces; the system of main roads radiating from Lugdunum (Lyons) is his. He wrote an autobiography and a geographical commentary, both now lost. He married first the daughter, known as Attica, of Cicero's friend Titus Pomponius *Atticus; she bore him a daughter Agrippina who was to marry the emperor Tiberius. Secondly he married Augustus' niece Marcella; thirdly, Augustus' daughter Julia, who bore him five children including Gaius and Lucius Caesar who were adopted by Augustus but died young (AD 2 and 4 respectively), and Agrippina ('the Elder'), who married Germanicus.

**Agrippī'na 1. Vipsānia Agrippina** (d. AD 20) Daughter of *Agrippa and Attica, first wife of the Roman emperor Tiberius and mother of his son Nero Claudius Drusus. Augustus forced Tiberius to divorce her and marry his daughter Julia. Agrippina later married C. Asinius Gallus and bore at least five sons.

**2. Vipsania Agrippina** ('the Elder Agrippina', *c.*14 BC–AD 33) Daughter of *Agrippa and wife of *Germanicus to whom she bore nine children. She was present at his deathbed in Syria in AD 19 and brought back his ashes to Rome. There she became a rallying point for those who were opposed to Sejanus. The hostility that she showed to Tiberius, who refused her permission to marry again and to whose agency (though without evidence) she attributed her husband's suspicious death, led to her arrest in 29 and banishment by the senate to the island of Pandateria (Ventotene). There she starved to death in 33. She was the mother of the future emperor Caligula (*see* GAIUS CAESAR) and of Julia Agrippina ('the Younger Agrippina' (3)).

**3. Julia Agrippina** ('the Younger Agrippina', AD 15–59) Daughter of the Elder Agrippina (2) and Germanicus. She married Cn. Domitius *Ahenobarbus, to whom she bore one son, later the emperor *Nero. On suspicion of plotting against her brother the emperor Caligula (*see* GAIUS CAESAR) she was exiled in 39, but was recalled in 49 by Claudius, her uncle, who married her when she was widowed. She persuaded Claudius to adopt Nero as guardian to his own son Britannicus, and when Claudius died in 54 she was generally believed to have poisoned him to make way for Nero. 'Let him kill me, provided that he rules', Tacitus represents her as saying. In the early years of Nero's reign she was almost co-regent with him (though Tacitus suggests that her influence may have been less than it seemed) but eventually lost favour. In 59 Nero had her stabbed at her villa in Baiae after he had failed to drown her by scuttling her ship. 'Strike my womb!' were her famous last words.

**Ahenoba'rbus** ('Bronze-beard') The *cognomen* or nickname (*see* NAMES [Roman]) of a branch of the Roman *gens* ('clan'), the Domitii, many of whom were famous through several centuries of Roman history. Legend relates that the *Dioscuri announced to an early member of the family, Gnaeus Domitius, the victory of Lake Regillus (496 BC). To prove their supernatural powers they stroked his black beard, which immediately turned bronze-coloured, and he took the cognomen Ahenobarbus. One Gnaeus Domitius Ahenobarbus, after fighting against Julius Caesar in 49 BC and being subsequently pardoned by him, was one of the republican leaders after Caesar's murder, and commanded a fleet against the triumvirs. Consul in 32 BC, he soon fled to join Mark Antony. He was hostile to Cleopatra's presence in Antony's camp, and went over to Octavian before the battle of Actium, already suffering from the fever which soon killed him. He figures in Shakespeare's *Antony and Cleopatra*.

Another Gnaeus Domitius, who was consul in AD 32, married Julia Agrippina ('the Younger'; *see* AGRIPPINA (3)) and became the father of Lucius Domitius Ahenobarbus, later the emperor Nero. According to Suetonius the family possessed a streak of vicious cruelty.

**Ahhiyawa, Ahhiya** In the Hittite clay tablets of the fifteenth to thirteenth centuries BC, the name of a foreign country which at one time was ruled by a 'Great King'. Some evidence for the presence of Mycenaeans in western Anatolia has strengthened the idea that this name denotes 'Achaea', i.e. Mycenaean Greece, but the identification poses problems and is controversial.

**Aias** *See* AJAX.

**Aïdēs, Aïdō'neus** Variant forms of *Hades.

**aidōs** [Gk., 'shame'] For Greeks 'shame' may transcend concern for how one appears in the eyes of others and be directed towards how one appears to oneself, a realization of what one is, perhaps contrasted with what one hoped to be. Homer's world has been called a 'shame culture', meaning that shame has ethical force for those living in that heroic world. In some Greek tragedies, notably Sophocles' *Ajax* and *Philoctetes*, and Euripides' *Hippolytus*, this emotion and its complexities are examined. Aristotle, who observes in the *Nicomachean Ethics* that shame is a feeling rather than a disposition of character, states that it is fitting only for youth. *See also* PROTAGORAS.

**Aisa** *See* FATE.

**aisymnetēs** *See* PITTACUS.

**aither** *See* AETHER.

**Ajax 1.** In Greek myth, son of *Telamon, hence 'Telamonian' Ajax or 'the Greater Ajax', to distinguish him from Ajax (2). His father was king of Salamis (in the Saronic Gulf off Attica), and his mother was Eriboea (or Periboea). As leader of the Salaminians he brought twelve ships to the siege of Troy. He is represented by Homer in the *Iliad* as being of great size and of dogged courage, the greatest of the Greek warriors after Achilles and the 'bulwark' of the Achaeans, who repeatedly leads the Greek attack or covers the retreat. His characteristic attribute is the all-enveloping body-shield of sevenfold oxhide. The *Aethiopis* tells how Ajax carried off the dead body of Achilles from the battlefield while Odysseus warded off the Trojans. In the *Odyssey* his suicide is mentioned in a version that has become famous through Sophocles' tragedy *Ajax* and was narrated in the *Little *Iliad*. After Achilles' death there was a dispute between Ajax and Odysseus over who should receive his armour as a mark of personal prowess, and by the votes of the Greek leaders the armour was awarded to Odysseus; Ajax went mad with resentment and killed himself. He was then denied the customary burial rites (in Sophocles' *Ajax* he is finally given honourable burial). In the *Odyssey*, when Odysseus meets Ajax in the Underworld Ajax refuses to speak to him.

**2.** In Greek myth, son of Oileus (or Ileus), 'the Lesser Ajax', the captain of the Locrian contingent on the Greek side at the siege of Troy and the fastest runner, brave but arrogant and hated by the gods, particularly Athena. He was killed by the sea-god Poseidon on the way home from Troy for boasting that he had escaped from shipwreck without divine aid. At the fall of Troy he dragged King Priam's daughter Cassandra by her hair from the altar of Athena, together with the statue (*Palladium) which she was embracing (a story told in the *Iliupersis*). For this impiety the Locrians continued to make atonement (for a thousand years, the Locrians maintained), by sending every year two virgins of noble birth to serve in the temple of Athena at Troy.

**Ajax** Greek tragedy by *Sophocles, of unknown date, perhaps his earliest and written before 441 BC.

Ajax son of Telamon (*see* AJAX (1)), bitterly resentful that Achilles' arms had been awarded to Odysseus, planned a night attack on the Greek leaders but, having been driven mad by the goddess Athena, killed cattle and sheep instead. When the play opens he is still mad and gloating over his supposed captives, but he recovers and is stricken with shame, while his concubine Tecmessa and the chorus of Salaminian sailors try to soothe him. He calls for his son Eurysaces, gives him his shield, and in his grief resolves upon suicide. After an interval Ajax speaks more calmly before going away to purify himself and to bury his sword. The chorus and Tecmessa are reassured, only to learn from his half-brother Teucer that the seer Calchas has declared calamity can be averted only if Ajax, who has angered the gods by his arrogance, is kept within his tent for that day. But it is too late; Ajax is found having fallen upon his sword. Menelaus forbids his burial, as an enemy to the Greeks; Agamemnon confirms the edict but is persuaded by Odysseus to relent, and Ajax is carried to an honourable burial.

**akrasia** *See* NICOMACHEAN ETHICS.

**Alba Longa** Ancient Latin city (*see* LATIUM) built on the northern slope of the *Albanus mons* near modern Castel Gandolfo some 20km (13 miles) south-east of Rome. It was traditionally founded *c.*1152 BC by Aeneas' son Ascanius, who moved his seat of government there from Lavinium. It appears once to have headed a league of Latin cities, but lost its primacy in Latium in about the seventh century BC, being destroyed allegedly by Rome in the reign of Tullus Hostilius. Some Alban families, including the Julii, are said to have migrated to Rome. The city was never rebuilt, though the name survives in modern Albano. *See also* ROMULUS and HORATII AND CURIATII.

**Albion** The ancient (Celtic or pre-Celtic) name for the mainland of Britain, first recorded in the first century AD, when it had been replaced among Romans by 'Britannia' (*see* BRITAIN 1). The Romans connected it with *albus*, 'white', in reference to the cliffs of Dover.

**Alcae'us** Greek lyric poet (b. a little before 620 BC) from Mytilene, chief city of Lesbos. Until comparatively recent times his poetry survived only in quotations made by later authors, but since the decipherment in the

twentieth century of certain Egyptian papyri (*see* PAPYROLOGY) much more of his poetry has come to light, though the tattered fragments have yielded very few complete poems. Many of the poems concern the politics of the time, in which Alcaeus was closely involved. After the overthrow of the ruling family, the Penthilidae, Mytilene was governed by a series of tyrants, Melanchrus (612–609), Myrsilus, and *Pittacus (590–580) as 'dictator', all of whom were generally opposed by Alcaeus' family or party, who wished to restore the old aristocratic rule. There was a closing of ranks when the Lesbians, Alcaeus among them, fought under Pittacus against the Athenians, *c.*606 BC, for the possession of Sigeum, a key stronghold on the Hellespont. Athens held Sigeum and Alcaeus describes himself as abandoning his shield in the retreat, as the poet Archilochus did before him. At some stage when Pittacus was ruling, Alcaeus went away to Egypt and his brother Antimenidas became a mercenary of Nebuchadnezzar, king of Babylon. The tradition, perhaps untrue, is that he was eventually reconciled with Pittacus before the latter laid down the tyranny in 580, and returned home. The date of his death is unknown.

His poetry consists of lyrical songs, mostly monodies (*see* LYRIC POETRY) in two- or four-lined stanzas, in a great variety of metres. Many of these were later adapted to Latin poetry by Horace, who imitated and wrote variations upon Alcaic themes throughout his *Odes*. As well as writing of politics and personalities with passion and gusto, Alcaeus composed love-songs (not always in his own person), now almost totally lost, drinking-songs, and hymns to the gods, all with simple directness, economy, and little imagery. (In two of his political poems he may be writing allegorically, using the image of the ship of state tossed by storm to describe political strife.) His language was the Aeolic vernacular spoken in Lesbos at that time, with a few Homeric forms.

**Alce'stis** In Greek myth, daughter of Pelias and Anaxibia, and wife of *Admetus. Her father would let her marry only a suitor who could yoke a lion and a boar to a chariot and drive it, a condition fulfilled by Admetus with the help of the god Apollo. *See* ALCESTIS.

**Alce'stis** Greek tragedy by *Euripides, produced in 438 BC and our earliest dated play by that author. It was the final drama of a tetralogy which included the famous *Telephus* and which won second prize in the tragedy competition. *Alcestis*, which has a happy ending, is sometimes described by modern critics, perhaps wrongly, as being in place of a *satyr play. The character of the genial, drunken Heracles gives humour to one scene. For the background to the play *see* ADMETUS.

In the prologue Death arrives to carry off Alcestis but Apollo tells him he will not in the end succeed. When the first scene opens Alcestis is dying and makes her farewells to husband, household, and children. She dies, and then Heracles arrives unexpectedly. He is not given the news for reasons of hospitality but finds out from a servant and goes off to rescue Alcestis. Admetus and his father Pheres quarrel over the parents' refusal to die for their son. Heracles returns with a veiled woman who is eventually revealed to be Alcestis, and the play ends with rejoicing.

**Alcibī'adēs** (451–404 BC) As politician and general, the outstanding personality of his generation at Athens and famous also for his good looks. He was the elder son of Cleinias and Deinomache, who was an *Alcmaeonid, and brought up in the household of *Pericles. He married Hipparete, daughter of Hipponicus (son of *Callias) who was reputed to be the richest man in Greece. He was thus connected with rich and powerful families. His career spanned the first Peloponnesian War; his first military service was at the siege of Potidaea (432–430), where Socrates also served, and he was present at the battle of Delium in 424, when the Athenians were routed by the Boeotians. His experience led to his election as *strategos* in 420, probably at the earliest legal age, and at a time when he had already become a leader of the extreme democrats. His ambitious imperialism contributed most to the breakdown of the Peace of Nicias (made in 421) and to the launching in 415 of the disastrous *Sicilian Expedition, of which he was appointed one of the three generals. The mutilation of the *herms just before its departure was believed to be the work of Alcibiades and his associates (*see* ANDOCIDES), and he was also accused of profaning the Eleusinian *mysteries; nevertheless it was decided that he should embark and be tried later. When summoned back to Athens from Sicily for this purpose, he was allowed to make the journey in his own ship, but escaped at Thurii in south Italy.

In his absence Alcibiades was condemned to death and his property confiscated. He made his way to Sparta, where he gave the Spartans the valuable advice that their general Gylippus should be sent to aid the Syracusans, and that *Decelea in Attica should be occupied as a permanent threat to Athens. In 412 he went to Ionia and with a Spartan squadron fomented revolt against Athens, first in Chios and then more widely, but he soon became mistrusted by the Spartans (perhaps an intrigue with the wife of the Spartan king Agis had soured relations). He entered into negotiations with *Tissaphernes, the Persian satrap, who tantalizingly seemed to support neither the Athenian nor the Spartan cause. He was now anxious to return to Athens. After months of delicate diplomacy the Athenian fleet at Samos made him general in the summer of 411 and he won a naval victory over the Spartans at Cyzicus in 410. From then until 406 he directed their war operations with brilliant success. In 407 the restored democracy at Athens recalled him, and cleared him of religious charges, hoping to find in him a capable commander and a means of alliance with the Persians. However, the defeat of a subordinate in the sea-battle at Notium (fought against his orders) in 406 lost him his prestige, and he was not elected *strategos* for 406/5. He retired to the Thracian Chersonese, where the good advice he gave to the Athenian commanders before the battle of Aegospotami in 405 was disregarded and the Athenians suffered total defeat. He was finally assassinated in Phrygia in 404, perhaps through the influence of the *Thirty Tyrants and *Lysander.

The biographical tradition for Alcibiades was exceptionally rich, owing to his immense reputation and his connection with Socrates. The chief surviving authority for his career is his contemporary Thucydides. He figures in Plato's *Symposium* and the perhaps spurious Platonic dialogues that bear his name (*see* AL-CIBIADES), and there are Lives of him by Nepos and Plutarch. He was an outstandingly able politician and military leader, able to adapt to varying circumstances; Plutarch thought his ingratiating ways towards markedly different people showed inconstancy of character. He had great personal magnetism, but his unscrupulous personal ambition, his vanity, and his dissolute life aroused the distrust of the

Athenians at times when his leadership might well have been a decisive factor in the Peloponnesian War. In Aristophanes' *Frogs* (produced in 405), when the tragic poets are required to give a sample of their political advice, it is their opinion of Alcibiades that is sought: Aeschylus thinks it 'wiser not to rear a lion's whelp, but if you do, you must accept its ways'. One of his most spectacular acts was to enter seven chariots for the Olympian games (perhaps those of 416 BC), in which he won first, second, and fourth places. Alcibiades' career is referred to in two speeches of Lysias directed against his son, the younger Alcibiades (b. *c*.416), for whom Isocrates wrote one in support.

***Alcibī'adēs I and II*** Two dialogues attributed to Plato. *Alcibiades I*, a short and relatively trivial dialogue, is thought to be spurious by most scholars, but opinion is still divided about the authenticity of *Alcibiades II*, which has been described as an introduction to Socratic philosophy for beginners and has been dated to about the middle of the fourth century BC, i.e. about the time of Plato's death. It argues that the body is not the real person but only an instrument which the soul uses. It consists of a dialogue between the 19-year-old *Alcibiades and the mature Socrates.

**Alci'damas** (early fourth century BC) Greek *sophist and rhetorician from Elaea in Aeolis, follower of *Gorgias, and opposed to the teaching of *Isocrates. One genuine work of his survives, 'On the sophists', in which he argues in favour of extempore rather than prepared speeches. *See* CERTAMEN HOMERI ET HESIODI.

**Alci'dēs (Alkeidēs)** In Greek myth, a name, meaning 'descendant of Alcaeus', used to designate Heracles, whose mortal father *Amphitryon was the son of Alcaeus, king of Tiryns.

**Alci'nŏus** In Homer's *Odyssey*, king of the Phaeacians in Scheria, husband of Arete and father of *Nausicaa. He received Odysseus on his wanderings and sent him home to Ithaca on a magic ship.

**A'lciphron** (*c*.AD 200) Greek sophist (*see* SECOND SOPHISTIC). He was the author of fictitious letters (of which we have about a hundred) purporting to be by Athenians of various classes of society in the fourth century BC, depicting Athenian life much as it is shown in New Comedy.

**Alcmae'on (Alkmaion)** In Greek myth, son of *Amphiaraus. In accordance with his father's command he became leader of the expedition of the *Epigoni which took Thebes. On his return, in further execution of his father's commands, he avenged him by killing his own mother Eriphyle (in some sources, the matricide came before the expedition). For this murder he was (like Orestes) pursued from place to place by the Furies. At Psophis in Arcadia he received partial purification from Phegeus, whose daughter Arsinoe, or Alphesiboea, he married. To her he gave the necklace of Harmonia (*see* CADMUS (1)). But the crops of the country began to fail, and Alcmaeon set out again to discover a land on which the sun had not shone when he murdered his mother. This he found in an island newly thrown up at the mouth of the river Achelous. Here he married Callirrhoe, a daughter of Achelous, and the land was called Acarnania after their son Acarnan. She in turn begged for the necklace of Harmonia, and Alcmaeon obtained it from Phegeus on a false pretence. But the brothers of Arsinoe waylaid and killed him, afterwards shutting their sister up in a chest because she protested, and selling her as a slave. Acarnan and Amphoteros, the sons of Alcmaeon and Callirrhoe, avenged their father by killing Phegeus and his sons, and the fatal necklace was dedicated to Apollo at Delphi. A later story tells that it was stolen by a Phocian when Phocis was at war with Philip of Macedon, and that it brought ill-luck to the thief.

**Alcmaeonidae (Alkmaiōnidai)** A noble (Eupatrid) Athenian *genos ('clan') prominent in politics. Its origins are obscure, but its name seems to derive from that Alcmaeon who commanded the Athenian forces in the First Sacred War from *c*.595 BC onwards, and who in 592 won his family's and Athens' first victory in the Olympian games in the chariot-race. The first notable member of this family was Alcmaeon's father *Megacles (1) who as archon in perhaps 632 incurred a hereditary pollution (*see* CYLON) which made all his descendants liable to banishment, a sentence that was periodically enforced against them for political reasons. Banished at some time after 632 they were back in Athens under Solon. Alcmaeon's son Megacles (2) married the daughter of Cleisthenes (1), tyrant of Sicyon. They were banished again during the tyranny of *Peisistratus (who was briefly and unsuccessfully married to a daughter of Megacles (2)) but returned once more to Athens before the archonship in 525 of Cleisthenes (2), son of Megacles (2). They were in exile again in the last years of Hippias' tyranny (after 514). The later claim of the family to be 'tyrant-haters' makes it difficult to assess their role in the expulsion of Hippias. Cleisthenes returned to Athens and initiated reforms in 508. In the fifth century the pollution was invoked at intervals by their political enemies. *Pericles, like *Alcibiades an Alcmaeonid on his mother's side, was able to ignore the Spartan appeal to the pollution in 432. It does not appear to have been invoked against Alcibiades.

**Alcman** Greek *lyric poet who lived in Sparta in the second half, perhaps the last quarter, of the seventh century BC. In antiquity it was a matter of dispute whether he was a Laconian or whether he came from Sardis in Lydia. His works contain no direct reference to contemporary history but seem to belong to a period of peace, and are mainly choral lyrics for the festivals. His poems were collected in six books, now all lost except for a few quotations and papyrus fragments. His *partheneia ('maiden-songs'), probably in two books, were especially celebrated but we hear also of hymns and wedding-songs. Most of the surviving fragments defy classification, but one or two are obviously from love-songs. The longest pieces of his poetry and the earliest choral lyric we possess come from fragments of two partheneia. The first shows the features later thought of as typical of choral lyric: a myth, a moral, and some reference to the occasion. The song was performed at dawn in honour of a goddess Aotis. The second partheneion, which is more fragmentary, concerns the actions of one of the performers (it is presumed). Both show humour, personal intimacy, and a lightness of touch that seem unlike the usual perception of Sparta. Alcman's dialect is for the most part the Laconian vernacular with some Homerisms. His simple metres were markedly dactylic, with some iambo-trochaic and aeolic elements. It is not certain whether his lyric was *triadic in structure or composed in stanzas.

**Alcme'ne** (Alkmēnē) *See* AMPHITRYON.

**Alcy'onē** In Greek myth, a daughter of *Aeolus (2) and wife of Ceyx. They were changed into birds, she into the halcyon (kingfisher), Ceyx into the bird of his name (perhaps a tern or gannet), either because he was drowned at sea and her despair was so great that the gods reunited them, or because of their impiety (they called themselves Zeus and Hera). 'Halcyon days' were fourteen days of calm weather around the winter solstice, supposed to be sent by Aeolus when the halcyon bird was brooding.

**Alexander** (Alexandros) **1. Alexander the Great** (Alexander III of Macedon, 356–323 BC, son of *Philip II and Olympias)

**1. Early life.** In his youth, Alexander was taught by Aristotle from 342 BC. He showed his intelligence and power of command at an early age; when only 18 he led the Macedonian cavalry with distinction at the battle of Chaeronea (338) which saw the defeat of Thebes and Athens by Macedon. When his father was murdered in 336 he succeeded, after the elimination of his rivals, to the kingdom of Macedon and the leadership of the Greek city-states (*see* CORINTH). Before his death Philip had been about to lead an army against Persia in punishment for the wrongs inflicted on Greece in the Persian Wars 150 years earlier. Alexander aimed to continue this war, but first he secured his position in Greece and stabilized the northern frontiers by defeating the Danubian tribes of that area. It was while he was at Corinth that he is reputed to have met the *Cynic philosopher Diogenes.

A false rumour of Alexander's death caused several Greek states to revolt (335), but only Thebes openly rebelled. Alexander arrived in Greece from the north with startling rapidity (his most impressive military quality) and stormed the city. The other Greek states were asked to decide Thebes' fate, and voted for its destruction. Only the house once lived in by the poet Pindar was spared.

**2. 334–332 BC.** With his Greek territory secured and left in the control of his general Antipater, Alexander crossed the Hellespont into Asia in 334 to join the remnants of his father's advance army. He had a force of about 43,000 men and a fleet of the Greek allies with about fifty warships. Like the mythical Greek hero *Protesilaus on his way to Troy, Alexander, who modelled his behaviour on the Homeric heroes, was the first ashore. He visited Troy and paid sacrifice at the tombs of various heroes. He soon achieved his desire for a pitched battle with the Persians, and at the river Granicus (334) defeated Darius III and a slightly smaller Persian army. The nucleus of the Greek infantry was the 15,000 strong Macedonian phalanx, divided into regional units. Armed with the six-metre *sarisa* (a pike, nearly twenty feet long) it was virtually irresistible in pitched battle, when the final blow was usually delivered by a cavalry charge from the right flank. As a result of the battle, from which Darius escaped unscathed, Alexander's way into Asia Minor had been opened up. He moved fast and took the cities of Sardis, Ephesus, and Miletus. Halicarnassus fell only after a stubborn siege. Democracies were reestablished in these cities which, though he came as the leader of a league of Greek states, became virtually a part of Alexander's own empire.

Having completed the conquest of western and southern Asia Minor Alexander reached Gordium, the ancient capital of King *Midas' Phrygian empire. Here he 'cut' the *Gordian knot, thus proving, according to local legend, his destiny to rule 'Asia', that is the whole Persian empire. Perhaps the idea of an Alexander of mythical prowess was already being propagated. At Gordium in the spring of 333 Alexander heard that the Persian commander Memnon had been successful in winning back some Greek cities, but it was Alexander's good fortune that the able Memnon died at the siege of Miletus.

Still in pursuit of Darius, Alexander made Cilicia his base. He lured Darius and his large army into the narrow coastal plain south of Issus (near the north-east corner of the Mediterranean) late in 333. Alexander's cavalry charge began the Persian defeat, which turned into a rout when Darius was seen to leave the battle at a crucial juncture. He escaped capture but left behind his wife, mother, and children. Included in the booty was a precious casket in which Alexander decided to store his copy of Homer's *Iliad*. By this victory Alexander won control of the Near East as far east as the Euphrates. Darius offered generous terms for peace which Alexander refused. An anecdote relates that when his general Parmenio said he would accept the terms if he were Alexander, the latter replied, 'So would I were I Parmenio.'

**3. 332–331 BC.** After wintering in Egypt (332–331), where he had been welcomed enthusiastically, Alexander became aware of the commercial and military possibilities of the western side of the Delta as a site for a city. Thus began *Alexandria, 'like a navel at the middle of the civilized world', based, like all the cities founded by Alexander, on an earlier military fort. From Egypt he made a gratuitous journey to the desert oracle of Zeus *Ammon at the oasis of Siwa. He kept secret the questions he asked and the answers he received, but the priest had already hailed him as 'Son of Ammon'. As a descendant of the heroes Heracles and Perseus he now began to represent himself as the son of Zeus.

**4. 331–330 BC.** When Alexander left Egypt in the spring of 331, he made for Persis, the original home province of the Persians. Darius had had over a year in which to mobilize his forces. These awaited Alexander east of the river Tigris at Gaugamela (near Arbela); once more the Persians were routed and Darius fled. After the battle Alexander turned south to *Babylonia, a land of exceptional fertility which had fallen to the Persians 200 years previously and whose city now welcomed him as a deliverer; thence he proceeded to the province and Persian palace of Susa at the end of the *Royal Road. Early in 330 Persepolis, the ritual centre of the Persian empire and symbol of all that was most hateful to the Greeks, fell to Alexander with its treasury. During a wild victory banquet it was burnt to ashes by his hand, perhaps not altogether intentionally: the story is that the Athenian *hetaira* Thaïs incited him to this act, which he later regretted. The enormous treasure found at Persepolis was transported to a central treasury at Hamadan under his trusted general Parmenio. When Darius was found soon after this murdered by Bessus, the satrap of Bactria, thus ending the line of the Achaemenidae, Alexander held himself to be the legitimate ruler of the Persian empire, bound to punish the regicide Bessus and to treat further resistance as rebellion. He marked the end of the war by discharging all the allied troops and Thessalian cavalry. He now assumed, significantly, parts of the Persian royal dress, the striped tunic, girdle, and diadem. His friend Hephaestion approved; others did not. It was now clear that his aim was the conquest of the whole empire.

**5. 330–327 BC.** The pursuit of Bessus took Alexander into outer Iran and lasted from 330 to 327, during which time he subdued vast tracts of the outlying areas of the empire—Hyrcania, Areia, Drangiana, Bactria, and Sogdiana—but his Macedonian soldiers were becoming increasingly reluctant to advance further. Advancing from Drangiana Alexander performed the feat of taking his army across the snows of the Hindu Kush. He descended into Sogdiana, and eventually captured and killed Bessus. In 328 he reached the furthest north-east boundary of the Persian empire, the river Jaxartes (Syr Darya), and here he founded Alexandria Eschate, 'the furthest'. Later that year after a violent quarrel at a banquet he killed his lifelong friend Cleitus with one blow, a rash act of which he bitterly repented, retiring to his tent in the manner of Achilles in Homer's *Iliad*.

By early 327 Alexander had overcome the last resistance in the north-east borders by the spectacular capture of two apparently impregnable mountain fortresses. Among the captives was Roxane (Roxana), the daughter of a Sogdian baron, whom Alexander loved at sight and immediately married, in the customary form of Macedonian marriage. She became the mother of his son, Alexander IV. In the same year another plot was discovered against his life, implicating *Callisthenes, the nephew of Aristotle and the expedition's historian, who was eventually killed. Callisthenes was reputed to have refused Alexander the obeisance, *proskynesis*, traditionally given to the Persian kings. Although *proskynesis* might involve no more than kissing the tips of one's fingers towards a person or god, to the Greeks it meant prostrating oneself on the ground, which they regarded as impious when done before men.

**6. 327–323 BC.** In summer 327 Alexander descended to the plains of India. His motives for doing so will never be certain, but perhaps India appealed as much to his curiosity as to a longing for further conquest. For the Macedonians it was a mythical world full of wonders, the home of the god Dionysus whose cult was strong in Macedonia. None of these wonders made more impact on the West than the *Gymnosophists ('naked philosophers'), whose meetings with Alexander became part of his legend and whose asceticism became an ideal to many. In 326 he reached the river Hydaspes (Jhelum). Here he fought his last great pitched battle to defeat the local king Porus and his formidable elephants. This was the last battle too for *Bucephalas, Alexander's horse since childhood, which was wounded

and died soon after the battle. An enormous fleet was constructed to transport the army—perhaps by now as many as 120,000 men—and its baggage downstream. It was put under the command of Nearchus, while Onesicratus, who wrote an account of the expedition, had charge of Alexander's ship. Army detachments accompanied the boats along each shore. They reached the Indus delta in summer 325, and started on a land march homewards, choosing a route through the waterless waste of Gedrosia (Baluchistan) at the cost of much loss of life. The fleet suffered too but arrived safely

When Alexander reached Susa he found misgovernment and disloyalty among his subordinates, whom he ruthlessly purged. His friend and treasurer Harpalus fled to Greece with a large sum of money (*see* DEMOSTHENES (2) 4). There was unrest in Greece, especially about Alexander's proclamation that exiles should be allowed to return to their cities. At midsummer he arranged marriages between his officers and men and Persian women, and encouraged those soldiers who had Asian mistresses to keep them as official wives. He himself married Stateira, daughter of Darius. Undoubtedly anger and jealousy were felt by some at the equality of status the Orientals now seemed to enjoy, particularly when large numbers of Persians were enrolled into the army, and these feelings found expression in a mutiny at Opis in 324 when Alexander tried to send some veterans home to Macedonia. He executed the ringleaders and retired in anger to his tent, thus frightening his troops into a change of heart. In the autumn his intimate friend Hephaestion died, and Alexander gave himself up to passionate expressions of grief, as, in Homer's *Iliad*, Achilles did for Patroclus. Afterwards he returned to Babylon, where in 323 he fell suddenly ill at a drinking-party, perhaps through fever, perhaps through poison, and after ten days died. He was 32. His body was finally brought to rest in Alexandria, where three centuries later his coffin was seen by the young emperor Augustus. It was probably destroyed in the riots of the late third century AD.

**7. Character and reputation.** Alexander is the greatest general of antiquity. This position he owes partly to the splendidly organized Macedonian army and its technically improved siege weapons, partly to his own versatile and intelligent strategy, but much more to qualities that were uniquely his: an unprecedented speed of movement, resolution in tackling the seemingly impossible, personal involvement in the dangers of battle and the rigours of campaigning, and his heroic style. To these qualities as well as to his generosity Alexander owed his ascendancy over the army. He regarded himself as the ruler of the Persian empire by right of conquest, and his assumption of Persian dress announces this fact, as does his addition of Persian ceremonial and his employment of Persian nobles, even among the Companions (*see* HETAIROI). There is no evidence that he had a policy of mixing Greeks and Persians in pursuit of an ideal. Even in the case of the Susa marriages he may have wished to cut across the family and regional loyalties which had bedevilled Persians and Macedonians alike and to promote able men of either race whose loyalty was to him alone.

The famous profile of Alexander with head and hair thrown back which appears repeatedly on coins was derived from the model by the sculptor Lysippus.

**8. The literature on Alexander.** Most of the history of Alexander depends upon sources written some 300 years after his death. The principal extant authority for the history of his campaigns is the *Anabasis* of *Arrian, who used the writings, now lost, of Alexander's officers Ptolemy (later King Ptolemy I Soter of Egypt) and Aristobulus of Cassandreia, who may both have used the court historian Callisthenes (Aristotle's nephew). All these were sympathetic to Alexander. Arrian may also have consulted Alexander's lost journal (*Ephemerides*), but many scholars doubt the existence of an authentic journal. There is also a tradition, which may be seen in the fragmentary history of Quintus *Curtius, of writers hostile to Alexander, who represented him as a tyrant corrupted by power; most of them are of the *Peripatetic (Aristotelian) School, whose hostility was natural enough after the death of Callisthenes. Plutarch's Life, which is paired with that of Julius Caesar, is compiled from every kind of source, good and bad. The most influential tradition, however, stems from the narrative of an accompanying historian Cleitarchus, written in the third century BC and known to us through the writings of *Diodorus Siculus. Cleitarchus introduced the fabulous, an element that was further developed in the various Eastern versions of Alexander's life. From Latin versions supposedly translated from Callisthenes the legends passed into French poetry of the twelfth and thirteenth centuries, thus giving the twelve-syllabled alexandrine line its name. There are two Old English works of the eleventh century based on the Latin legend, but it is from the French poems that the Alexander legends passed into the Middle English metrical romances such as *King Alisaunder* of the early fourteenth century.

**2. Alexander IV** (323–*c.*310 BC) Posthumous son of Alexander the Great and Roxane. After the death of his father the infant Alexander, together with the new king Philip Arrhidaeus, came into the custody of *Perdiccas. In 317 he was a pawn in the struggle for the throne of Macedon, but when his grandmother Olympias was overthrown he fell into the hands of *Cassander and was killed *c.*310. One of the tombs at Aegae has been tentatively identified as his.

**3. Alexander of Aphrodisias** (fl. *c.*AD 200) The most important of the early commentators on Aristotle. Of his commentaries (in Greek) a few survive, and a fragment of one, on *Categories*, has been found on the *Archimedes palimpsest. His works are widely quoted by later writers.

**4. Alexander of Pherae** Nephew and successor of *Jason, tyrant of Pherae (in Thessaly) 369–358 BC. He was opposed by most of the cities of Thessaly and allied himself with Athens to counteract Theban expansion. When the Theban general *Pelopidas visited him on one of his expeditions, he detained the general as a hostage until the latter was eventually rescued by a second Theban expedition in 367. As the result of a fresh appeal from Thessaly in 364, Pelopidas marched against him and defeated him at Cynoscephalae, but was himself killed. Later, a larger Theban army defeated Alexander and forced him to become the ally of the Thebans. In 362 he felt free to make piratical raids against Athens and raided the Piraeus. He was assassinated in 358 by his wife's brothers.

**5.** Alternative name for *Paris (1).

**Alexandria** City on the north coast of Egypt, near the Canopic or western mouth of the Nile, founded by Alexander the Great in 331 BC on the site of a fort called Rhacotis. It was the first of his many foundations. On a barren coast this area alone had possibilities for a harbour to accommodate a large fleet and for further development. There was a long bay west of the silt-producing mouths of the Nile, protected by the island of Pharos (now joined to the mainland by a bridge of silted-up land), with a ridge of rising ground parallel to the coast between the sea and Lake Mareotis (Maryût) inland. The climate was equable. According to the historian Arrian, Alexander himself established where the main points of the city, the agora and the temples, should be, and drew the line of the city walls with the meal which his soldiers were carrying, a good omen for the city's future prosperity. After Alexander's general Ptolemy had established his authority in Egypt, the seat of government was transferred from the ancient city of Memphis to Alexandria. It was a theoretically autonomous city, *polis*, of the Greek type, modelled on Athens, with *demes, and assembly (*ecclesia*), council (*boule*) and magistrates, and its own coinage and laws. Its citizens came from all over the Greek world, and there were many representatives of other ethnic groups, including a very large community of Jews (a million strong in Alexandria and Egypt, according to Philo), who were not citizens, although they had special privileges. The new city grew rapidly and by 200 BC was the largest in the world (later to be surpassed by Rome), a centre of learning as well as of commerce and industry. In the Roman period, with well over 500,000 inhabitants, it counted as the second city of the empire, after Rome itself. It did not decline in importance to the West until the Arab conquest in the seventh century.

The plan of ancient Alexandria is difficult to reconstruct, partly because of subsidence, which has resulted in much of the ancient city being covered by the coastal waters, and partly because of modern building and reconstruction of the coast. It was laid out on the sandy ridge running east and west between Lake Mareotis and the sea. A broad street ran east and west through the centre of it and was crossed by another running north and south. On the island of Pharos, which Alexander connected with the mainland by a mole over a kilometre long so as to provide a double harbour, a lighthouse, also known as the Pharos, was built to mark the harbour (and perhaps warn of the dangerous entrance),

probably in the reign of Ptolemy II Philadelphus. It seems to have been the first of its kind, and was one of the *Seven Wonders of the ancient world.

In the Ptolemaic period the city was divided into five 'quarters'. Near the eastern sea-harbour lay the area known originally as the 'Palaces' and as Brucheion in the Roman period, in which stood royal palaces and buildings, shrines, pleasure-gardens, and a zoo built by Ptolemy II. It occupied much of the northern and central area of the city, perhaps a square mile (two or more square kilometres) in total, and was clearly the most pleasant part to live in. Here also was the Museum, and perhaps the Library, about whose location the literary sources are silent, and the *Sēma* (or *Sōma*), the tomb of Alexander, whose body was brought to the city by Ptolemy I Soter and encased in a magnificent gold coffin. (This was later removed by Ptolemy X when short of funds, and replaced by alabaster.) To the south-west of this, in the ancient Egyptian quarter (Rhacotis, above), stood the Serapeum (temple of Serapis), built on a largely artificial hill by Ptolemy III Euergetes and greatly extended in Roman times. Here still stands today the column known as 'Pompey's Pillar', dedicated to the emperor Diocletian. The royal residence itself has now disappeared. Above the harbour a large theatre was built. Also in that area were the *emporion* (the general trading centre), warehouses, and the Caesareum, the temple of the emperor Augustus, finally destroyed in AD 912. Of the two obelisks which stood before it, one was given to Britain in 1877 and stands by the Thames in London, where it is known as Cleopatra's Needle, the other in 1879 to New York where it was erected in Central Park. Both had been brought to Alexandria from a temple in the ancient Egyptian city of Heliopolis.

Intermarriage between Greeks and Egyptians began in the second century BC, and the mixed population (with the exception of the Jews and some of the Greeks) gradually blended into a more or less homogeneous whole. Under the Ptolemies the city was nominally a democracy. Under the Romans it was assigned to the emperor. Augustus refused it self-government, but in Egypt only the Alexandrians could become Roman citizens. In AD 200 it was given a senate by the Roman emperor Severus.

*See also* ALEXANDRIAN LIBRARY; MUSEUM; HELLENISTIC AGE; PTOLEMIES.

**Alexandrian** Term used for the culture (especially literary) of Alexandria in the *\*Hellenistic age.

**Alexandrianism, Latin** Term used of the influence of the Alexandrian school of Greek poets of the third and second centuries BC (*see* HELLENISTIC AGE) on Roman poets.

**Alexandrian Library** The famous library perhaps founded by Ptolemy I Soter (reigned 323–283 BC) but greatly augmented by his son Ptolemy II Philadelphus (*see* PTOLEMIES and DEMETRIUS (1)). Such evidence as there is suggests that it was in the 'palace quarter' of Alexandria, perhaps adjacent to the Museum, and was supplemented by a subsidiary building near the Serapeum. At its head was placed a series of distinguished scholars, Zenodotus, Apollonius Rhodius, Eratosthenes, Aristophanes of Byzantium, Aristarchus; the poet Callimachus also worked there (*see* TEXTS, TRANSMISSION OF ANCIENT 1). The library was said to contain nearly 500,000 papyrus rolls, i.e. perhaps 100,000 \*books (*see* 2) if the figure can be trusted. There was keen rivalry between the kings of Alexandria and Pergamum in the enlargement of their respective libraries. It is said that Ptolemy II purchased the library that Aristotle had formed; and that Ptolemy III appropriated the official copies of the texts of Aeschylus, Sophocles, and Euripides (*see* LYCURGUS (3)), forfeiting the large deposit he had paid when borrowing them from Athens. The library became the great centre of literature in the Hellenistic world and the practice of its copyists was probably decisive in the forms of book production (*see also* MUSEUM). Callimachus made catalogues (*pinakēs*) of its contents. According to Plutarch, in 47 BC when Julius Caesar was in Alexandria the main library was burnt. Later legend magnified this episode.

**Alexandrian literature, scholars** *See* ALEXANDRIAN LIBRARY; HELLENISTIC AGE; MUSEUM.

**Ale'xis** (*c*.375–*c*.275 BC) Greek comic poet of Middle and New Comedy, who lived most of his life at Athens. He was a prolific writer. It is difficult to assess from his few remaining fragments the part he played in the transition from the older to the newer forms of comedy, but he seems to have used the kind of plot especially associated with New Comedy, concerning love affairs of an intricate kind, and to have been clever and amusing. His fame continued to Roman times when his plays were adapted by Roman comedians. *See also* COMEDY [Greek 5].

**Alle'cto** *See* FURIES.

**allegory** In literature the presentation or interpretation of a subject in terms of another subject which suggestively resembles it. Allegory had a long history in classical literature. (The Greek word *allēgoria*, 'figurative language' in a wide sense, is post-classical.) Fables (*see* AESOP) are a form of allegory, and one of the earliest, the fable of the hawk and the nightingale, appears in Hesiod's *Works and Days*. As a device of literary interpretation in Greece it flourished in the late fifth century BC, when \*Prodicus composed his famous *Choice of Heracles*. One motive at this time may have been to conserve religious tradition and the ethical teaching of the poets, particularly Homer and Hesiod, with their sometimes strange or even immoral stories of the gods, and so maintain their important role in education, while also taking account of science, including cosmology, and the new learning. Plato distinguished between a factual statement (*logos*) and the story (*mythos*) which overlaid it. This kind of allegorizing was sometimes connected with \*etymology, at that time a pseudo-science which dealt in the 'true' meaning of words and names as revealed by basic sound-elements. (*See also* ANALOGY AND ANOMALY and *CRATYLUS*.) The main proponents of allegory after the Platonists were the Stoic philosophers of the third century BC onwards (*see* CHRYSIPPUS and CLEANTHES), who felt that poetry was, in fact and intention, educative, and so adopted allegory for the illustration and corroboration of their doctrines. From them derive the surviving collections of allegorical interpretations of Homer. In this Hellenistic period and in Greek-speaking areas under the Roman empire allegory could also be a device for integrating non-Greek religions into a widely acceptable philosophical attitude to the gods.

The Romans, following the Greeks, found certain moral meanings implicit in Homer, and Horace took over the allegory of the 'ship of state', a familiar topic in Greek poetry first employed by the early lyric poet Alcaeus, but they did not compose large-scale allegories. Instead they used numerous poetic conceits and personifications (such as calling the sea Neptune—metonomy rather than allegory), often in a way that suggests rather the influence of symbolic painting. A Roman innovation was the allegorical representation of contemporary persons and events, as in Virgil's *Eclogues*, but perhaps this too had been done before by Theocritus (in Idyll 7), and scholars of both poets still dispute the degree of correspondence with real people. The descriptions of weather or the changing seasons in the *Odes* of Horace have suggested a deeper, allegorical meaning to many readers. The profundity and ambiguity of much of the *Aeneid* led interpreters from the fourth century AD onward to find in it an allegory of ideas rather than of facts. Allegory entered Christian literature from Stoic sources. *See also* BARBARIAN; HERACLEITUS (3); PASTORAL POETRY.

**A'llia** A small stream flowing into the Tiber from the east about 18km (11 miles) north of Rome, near which the Romans suffered a notable defeat by Brennus and the Gauls *c.*385 BC (*see* GAUL 1). The disaster was said to have occurred on 18 July, the anniversary of the ambush of the Fabii (*see* FABIA, GENS) by the Veientes in 479 BC, which was kept as an unlucky day.

**alliteration** The literary device in which two or more words in close connection begin with the same letter (*see* ASSONANCE [Latin]). It was not a common device of Greek poetry, but is a feature in Latin Saturnian verse, and was adopted by later Roman poets including Ennius and Virgil, as when Ennius writes:

*fraxinu' frangitur atque abies consternitur alta.*
*pinus proceras pervortunt.*

('The ash tree is shattered and the lofty fir laid low. They overturn the tall pines.')

It is carried to grotesque excess by the same poet in the line:

*o Tite tute Tati tibi tanta tyranne tulisti.*

('O Titus Tatius, such great things you brought upon yourself, you arrogant ruler.')

**A'lmagest** *See* PTOLEMY.

**Alō'adae (Alōï'dae)** *See* OTUS.

**alphabet** The cuneiform and hieroglyphic writing systems of the Babylonians and Egyptians, each with hundreds of signs partly phonetic and partly symbolic, meant that only a small professional class could read and write. An alphabet such as the Greek made reading and writing easier.

**Greek.** The earliest examples of Greek writing to survive are all inscribed on Greek pottery from the second half of the eighth century BC, and examples are found almost simultaneously in all parts of the Greek world. In these examples the writing runs from right to left in odd-numbered lines and from left to right in even-numbered lines, a form known as *\*boustrophēdon*, 'as the ox turns'.

The standard Greek alphabet, still in use today, is as follows:

| Small letters | Capital letters | Greek names | English equivalents |
|---|---|---|---|
| α | A | alpha | a |
| β | B | bēta | b |
| γ | Γ | gamma | g |
| δ | Δ | delta | d |
| ε | E | epsīlon | ĕ |
| ζ | Z | zēta | z (pronounced sd) |
| η | H | ēta | ē |
| θ | Θ | thēta | th |
| ι | I | iōta | i |
| κ | K | kappa | hard c or k |
| λ | Λ | lam(b)da | l |
| μ | M | mū | m |
| ν | N | nū | n |
| ξ | Ξ | xī | x (pronounced ks) |
| o | O | omīcron | ŏ |
| π | Π | pī | p |
| ρ | P | rhō | r (or rh) |
| σ, s† or ϲ | Σ or ϲ | sigma | s |
| τ | T | tau | t |
| υ | Y | upsī'lon | u (usually transliterated y) |
| φ | Φ | phī | ph |
| χ | X | chī | kh (sometimes transliterated ch) |
| ψ | Ψ | psī | ps |
| ω | Ω | ōmega | ō |

† *s* is the form used at the end of a word; ϲ is an alternative to either form.

Small letters came into existence from the late fourth century BC onwards as a result of writing with a pen in ink, which produced rounded forms (e.g. $\epsilon$ instead of $E$) often described as 'cursive'. A distinction between 'capital' (upper-case) and 'small' (lower-case) letters was not clearly made until the ninth century AD. Small letters are used conventionally in what follows.

In early Greece, though various forms of the alphabet from alpha to tau were in use, they were all derived from the north-Semitic Phoenician script. The introduction of the alphabet into Greece in the late ninth or early eighth century BC is perhaps reflected in the myth which tells how *Cadmus, son of Agenor king of Tyre, brought letters to Thebes, the city he had founded. The shapes of the letters, their names and their order are virtually the same in both Greek and Semitic alphabets but they do not necessarily represent the same sounds. The Semitic alphabet has no characters for vowels, and the Greek therefore used for its vowels Semitic characters for consonants not in use in Greece. Thus Semitic consonant characters were used for $\alpha$, $\epsilon$, $o$, and $\iota$. The character for upsilon, $\upsilon$, was taken over from a *cursive Phoenician script and added to the alphabet after tau. $\upsilon$, $\phi$, $\chi$, $\psi$, and $\omega$ are all Greek additions. In Greece local variations lasted for centuries. Some dialects had an extra letter, $F$, between epsilon and zeta, pronounced like English w and called first 'vau' by the Greeks and later digamma. It disappeared in pre-classical times from the Attic–Ionic dialects and does not appear in the standard alphabet given above. The alphabet thus obtained, comprising the first 22 letters of the 24 listed above, was used by the Athenians down to the end of the fifth century BC. The sounds represented have not changed, except that the letter eta ($\eta$) up to that time stood for the aspirate (h). Epsilon ($\epsilon$) was written to represent all forms of the e sound and omicron ($o$) for all forms of the o sound. In 403 BC, in the archonship of Eucleides, Athens adopted the more developed East Ionic (Milesian) alphabet which by $c$.370 BC was accepted by the whole Greek world. It distinguished between short and long o sounds by using $o$ and $\omega$ respectively, and between short and long e by using $\eta$ for the latter, as well as admitting diphthongs in its spelling to express variations of these sounds. All Ionic dialects, however, lacked the aspirate, and when the East Ionic alphabet was adopted the aspirate (for which $\eta$ was no longer available)

was ignored in writing. In some scripts this deficiency was remedied by the sign $\vdash$ (the left half of capital eta). The Alexandrian scholar *Aristophanes of Byzantium subsequently introduced both $\vdash$ and $\dashv$ written above initial vowels to mark the presence or absence of the aspirate (known as 'rough breathing' and 'smooth breathing'). These are written in modern texts as ' and ' respectively.

**Latin.** The Latin alphabet seems to have come from an early form of Etruscan script which was itself derived in the late eighth century BC from the (Euboean) Greek alphabet as used at Cumae (in Campania), a Greek colony from Chalcis in Euboea. Many more Etruscan texts of the seventh century survive than Latin. The early Latin alphabet was the same as its modern English derivative except that it lacked the letters G, J (for which I did duty), U, W (for which V also served), Y, and Z. The character X represented a probably more complicated sound than English x. H represented the aspirate (for its varying significance in Greek see above). Greek gamma was represented by the character C which was at first used for the G sound as well as for the K sound (compare the names Gaius and Gnaeus which when abbreviated were written in archaic fashion C. and Cn.); the character G was introduced in the third century BC. Originally the character K was written instead of C where the following letter was A, but it was later replaced by C and K became redundant (a relic of this old spelling is *Kalendae*, 'the Calends'). The letter Q (from Greek $\varphi$, koppa, found in some Greek alphabets after pi), originally written instead of C before O and U, was later used only before U (like English q). Z was introduced to express the original ds sound in words borrowed from Greek, and was added at the end of the alphabet, its seventh place in the Greek alphabet (after digamma) having been occupied by G. The Latin f sound was most closely represented by the Greek digamma. V (a form of capital upsilon) represented both the vowel and the semivowel U. Y (the usual form of capital upsilon) was added in the late republic to transliterate Greek words containing upsilon, and was pronounced ü.

*See also* BOOKS, GREEK AND ROMAN and EPIGRAPHY.

**Alphesiboe'a** *See* ALCMAEON.

**altars** Sacrificial tables. As almost every religious act in the ancient world was accompanied by sacrifice, altars as sacrificial tables were an indispensable part of the cult of a god or hero (but not of an Underworld deity, to whom offerings were made in pits). Thus altars as a focus for worship existed long before temples, and after temples were built the altar generally stood outside, opposite the main door so that the steam of the sacrifice could waft upwards to the gods. Altars inside were only for incense or bloodless offerings. In Greece the chief type was the *bōmos*, block-like in form, on which the entrails were roasted and the bones and fat cremated (*see* SACRIFICE). In the case of hero-cults in particular the *eschara* ('hearth'), a low altar, was used; it was also used for burnt offerings. Incense and bloodless sacrifices were made only on the small domestic altar or on the hearth, which was a sacred place. Roman altars also varied in size according to purpose. Most altars were dedicated to a particular god, and were places of refuge for suppliants, who then came under the protection of the deity concerned. Cicero says that it was a Greek practice to take solemn oaths at altars.

**Althae'a** In Greek myth, mother of *Meleager.

**Alyattes** (d. 560 BC) Lydian king, succeeded by his son *Croesus.

**Amalthē'a (Amaltheia)** In Greek myth, the goat that suckled the infant *Zeus in Crete; or a nymph (according to one version the daughter of Melissus, king of Crete) who fed Zeus with the milk of a goat. Zeus gave her the horn of the goat; it had the power of producing whatever its possessor wished, and was known (in Latin) as the *cornu copiae*, 'horn of plenty'.

**Amā'ta** In Virgil's *Aeneid*, the wife of *Latinus and mother of *Lavinia.

**Amazons (Amāzonĕs)** Mythical nation of female warriors supposed by the Greeks to have lived in the time of the heroes. Their home is always imagined as being on the bounds of the known world, usually in remote north-east Asia. They figure in the exploits of various Greek heroes down to Alexander the Great, who according to legend met their queen on the borders of India, and are very popular in art from at least the seventh century BC. Their name, supposedly meaning 'breastless', was said to derive from their custom of removing the right breast to facilitate the use of arms in battle. Their occupations are hunting and fighting, always from horseback. They

propagate their kind by associating for a time with men from a neighbouring tribe and rearing only their daughters. They are mentioned in Homer's *Iliad* and appear as allies of the Trojans in Arctinus' *Aethiopis*; their queen Penthesilēa was killed by Achilles. They also play a part in the careers of Heracles (*see* HERACLES, LABOURS OF 9) and *Theseus.

**A'mbiorix** Leader of the Gallic tribe of the Eburōnēs in their revolt against the Romans in 54–53 BC. He successfully evaded capture. *See COMMENTARIES* 1 [books 5 and 6].

**ambitus** ('a going round') In Rome, seeking electoral support through bribery, direct or indirect. The practice continued, although there may have been (ineffective) laws against it, and was used particularly by 'new men' (*see* NOVUS HOMO) who outraged old-established families by spending money and so outbidding the traditional claims of patronage.

**ambrosia and nectar** The mythical food and drink of the gods, associated with divine immortality. A mortal who took them became immortal; shed on a corpse they kept it from decay. Various things connected with the gods are described as ambrosial, sometimes with the connotation of 'sweet-smelling'.

**amicitia** *See* FRIENDSHIP.

**Ammiā'nus Marcellī'nus** (*c.*AD 330–95) The last great Roman historian to write in Latin, although he was a Greek born at Syrian Antioch. His history in 31 books was a continuation of the histories of Tacitus, covering the years AD 96–378, from the death of Domitian to the disastrous defeat of the Romans by the Goths at Adrianople in 378. Books 1–13 have been lost. The remaining books 14–31 deal in considerable detail with the years 353–78, covering events in his own lifetime, many of which he witnessed himself and, it is believed, reported accurately. As a young man he joined the army and served in Gaul under Julian (later emperor), whom he admired but not uncritically. Like Julian he was a pagan, but of a more restrained sort. He took part in Julian's fatal invasion of Persia in 363, and later visited the Black Sea, Egypt, and Greece before settling in Rome in the mid-380s. Here he completed his history. Ammianus' narrative is interesting and enlivened by digressions—on the Egyptian obelisks and their hieroglyphics, earthquakes, lions in Mesopotamia, the artillery of his time.

The work culminates in the Gothic invasions of 376–8 and the battle of Adrianople (9 August 378). The latest dateable events occur in 391, and the history was probably completed soon after. He writes largely without prejudice on the various nations dealt with, on the Christians, and on the emperors themselves.

Ammianus' work was greatly admired by the historian Edward Gibbon. The influence of Tacitus on his style is strong, but more pervasive is that of Cicero, who is constantly alluded to. His reading of the Greek historians is less in evidence.

**Ammon (Amo(u)n)** Greek form of Amun, the great god of Egyptian Thebes (Luxor), identified by the Greeks with Zeus. His *oracle at the oasis of Siwa in the Libyan desert became known to the Greeks probably through the north African Greek colony of Cyrene. Its fame rivalled that of Delphi and Dodona, and it was consulted on a notable occasion in 331 BC by *Alexander the Great. The poet Pindar wrote a hymn to the god, and his cult had arrived at Athens by the fourth century BC. Ammon was usually portrayed in the Greek world with the head of Zeus bearing a ram's curling horns. *See also* ANDROMEDA.

**amoebe'an verse** Literary form found mainly in bucolic poetry (*see* PASTORAL POETRY), for example in Theocritus and Virgil, consisting of couplets or 'stanzas' assigned alternately to two characters, usually in singing matches where the verses of one character are capped by the other.

**Amores** A collection of fifty love poems by the Roman poet *Ovid, written in elegiac couplets. They are among his earliest works. The first edition, in five books, may have been published in the late 20s BC. The second (presumably revised) edition is the one we possess, in three books, published after 11 BC. The poems are or purport to be autobiographical, describing episodes in the poet's love life. His married mistress is called *Corinna, a Greek name which recalls the love-poems of Catullus to his 'Lesbia' (the name suggesting another Greek poet, Sappho from Lesbos). The poet knows the rules of the game of love and the conventions governing its expression in poetry. The result is witty, self-mocking, and sophisticated. There are interesting illustrations of contemporary life—a scene at the circus, or a festival of Juno, for example. Poem 3.9 is a touching lament for the death of the poet Tibullus.

**Amphiarā'us** In Greek myth, an Argive hero and seer, descended from *Melampus. He played an important part in the stories of the Greek *Epic Cycle which relate to two generations earlier than the heroes of the Trojan War. (For the chronology *see* ADRASTUS.) He married Eriphyle, whom Polyneices bribed, with the necklace of Harmonia (*see* CADMUS (1)), to persuade Amphiaraus to take part in the expedition of the Seven against Thebes (*see* OEDIPUS), although the seer knew that none of the Seven except Adrastus would return from it alive. He set out reluctantly, but before starting commanded his children to avenge his death by killing their mother, and by making a second expedition against Thebes (*see* ALCMAEON). He attacked Thebes but was driven off, and as he fled was swallowed up in a cleft in the ground made by Zeus' thunderbolt. Thus originated the famous oracular shrine of Amphiaraus at Oropus (between Attica and Boeotia), where oracles were given by the interpretation of dreams.

**amphi'ctyony (*amphiktyoneia*)** [from *amphictyones*, 'dwellers around'] Religious association or league of Greek communities who lived in the neighbourhood of, and had some responsibility for, the sanctuary of a god. The most important, such as that of Delphi, came to include representatives from much of Greece. The Delphic league administered the temple of Apollo and conducted the Pythian games. Sacred wars were occasionally proclaimed against violators of amphictyonic laws.

**Amphidromia** *See* CHILDBIRTH.

**Amphī'on and Zethus** *See* ANTIOPE.

**Amphi'polis** City founded by a colony of Athenians in 437 BC, of great strategic and commercial importance, particularly in the Peloponnesian War. Situated near the coast on the east bank of the river Strymon, the boundary between Macedonia and Thrace, it commanded the only crossing-place on the southern reaches of that river and thus the route into Greece from the Hellespont. In 424 BC during the Peloponnesian War Amphipolis surrendered to the Spartans; the historian Thucydides was held responsible for the loss and exiled. In an unsuccessful attempt to recapture it in 422 the Athenian and Spartan commanders Cleon and Brasidas were both killed. Amphipolis was to have been restored to Athens by the Peace of Nicias in 421 but it remained practically independent, despite Athenian pressure, until it was annexed by Philip II of Macedon in 357 BC. Under the Romans it was an important station on the Via Egnatia.

**amphitheatre** Roman theatre constructed in a circular or elliptical shape so as to contain the combats of gladiators, wild animals, and even ships and to make them visible to a large number of spectators. The earliest surviving examples are in Campania; the one at Pompeii was built *c*.80 BC and is the earliest stone building of that type to survive. It could accommodate 20,000 spectators, drawn from the surrounding area. Rome's first permanent stone amphitheatre was erected in 29 BC in the Campus Martius at a time when many others were being constructed throughout the empire. Imperial architects rapidly developed very large buildings with ingenious systems for access and circulation. The most famous is the *Colosseum in Rome (AD 80), which could accommodate 50,000 people (at a time when the city's population may have numbered about a million).

**Amphitrī'tē** Nereid (*see* NEREUS), wife of the god *Poseidon.

***Amphi'truo*** Roman comedy by *Plautus (perhaps *c*.195 BC), his only mythological comedy. It may be an adaptation of a Greek Middle Comedy on the subject of the cuckolding of Amphitruo (Gk. *Amphitryon) by the god Jupiter (Gk. Zeus). Jupiter takes on the appearance of Amphitruo after the latter's departure for war, and seduces his virtuous wife Alcmena. Plautus calls the play a *tragico-comoedia* because of the unusual blend of contrasting elements, the morally virtuous but unwittingly unchaste wife, and the burlesque situation of the outraged husband. Foils are provided by the god Mercury and Sosia, the long-suffering but cheerful slave. The theme proved popular with later comic dramatists.

**Amphi'tryon** In Greek myth, son of Alcaeus king of Tiryns, and Astydameia; grandson of *Perseus. His sister Anaxo married her uncle Electryon (brother of Alcaeus), king of Mycenae, and their daughter Alcmene was engaged to be married to Amphitryon. After the death of his sons in a feud Electryon handed over his

kingdom to Amphitryon, but the latter, while helping to recover stolen cattle, accidentally killed Electryon and so had to take refuge with Creon, king of Thebes. Alcmene wished Amphitryon to avenge her brothers before she would marry him, and this he did; but during his absence Zeus fell in love with her and just before Amphitryon's return made love to her in the guise of her husband. Alcmene gave birth to twin sons, Iphicles the child of Amphitryon and *Heracles the child of Zeus. Amphitryon's supposed tomb was at Thebes, where he seems to have been regarded as a hero (*see* HEROES).

**amphora** [Lat.; Gk. *amphoreus*, 'carried on both sides'] Greek and Roman two-handed clay pot with narrow mouth and, usually, a pointed base (though some had flat bases), used in the ancient world for storage and transport. The shape tended to be slim and elongated to make them easier to store on board ship. The original foot turned almost into a spike to facilitate pouring. It could be stood in sand, but decorated amphorae with pointed ends often had a stand. An amphora was intended to be portable by at most two people. In Greece the earliest amphorae contained oil, later wine, supplanting skins as containers. They were also used for pitch and dried fish. The average capacity in classical and Hellenistic Greece was 20–5 litres (about five Imperial gallons). The Romans transported many comestibles in amphorae—olive oil, wine, preserved fish or fruit, fish-sauce. The contents could be indicated by a distinctive appearance, but also by painted signs. For purposes that remain uncertain (and probably varied) amphorae often had a stamp impressed into the wet clay. The stamps are of especial importance when they indicate where the amphorae came from, and also the date of dispatch. Classification of these stamps has greatly contributed to our knowledge of the economic history of Greece and Italy, and has yielded valuable information about dates. Underwater finds of undisturbed cargoes in shipwrecks can be particularly significant.

**Amū'lius** *See* ROMULUS.

***Ana'băsis*** (in full, *Kyrou anabasis*, 'Cyrus' expedition inland', often called in English 'The Persian expedition') Prose narrative in seven books by *Xenophon, describing the expedition of the younger *Cyrus, son of king Darius II of Persia, against his elder brother Artaxerxes II, the then king. Xenophon seems to have first published the work under the pseudonym of Themistogenes of Syracuse, but later he abandoned the pretence and magnified his own role in the expedition.

Cyrus, who was satrap of Lydia, was disappointed that he had not been chosen to succeed his father, as the favourite son. His resentment against his brother was increased, according to Xenophon, when he was arrested by Artaxerxes, soon after the latter's accession, on a false charge of conspiracy. Cyrus prepared to attack Artaxerxes, and recruited an auxiliary force of more than 10,000 Greeks, mostly hoplites. Xenophon accompanied the 'Ten Thousand' at the suggestion of his friend Proxenus, one of the Greek generals, from Sardis to the neighbourhood of Babylon in 401 BC. It was interrupted by the reluctance of some of the troops to proceed when they discovered the true object of the expedition, which had been concealed from them. The majority were persuaded to go on, and fought in the battle of Cunaxa (near Babylon) between Cyrus and Artaxerxes in 401. Cyrus was killed, his Asiatic troops took flight, and his cause was lost.

This disaster dismayed the Greeks, but they resisted the attempts of Artaxerxes to induce them to surrender. Their dismay increased when the satrap *Tissaphernes, who had been conducting the negotiations on the Persian side, lured the Greek generals into his quarters to have them seized and beheaded. At this point Xenophon induced the remaining officers to reorganize the force and arrange a safe retreat. Cheirisophus commanded the van while Xenophon took the more dangerous command at the rear. His advice on the route through Mesopotamia, Armenia, and northern Anatolia, and his courage and resourcefulness enabled the Greek army to reach the Black Sea. Xenophon's account includes a famous description (4.7.20–6) of the scene when the Greek vanguard, climbing Mount Theches, at last saw a glimpse of the sea and cried *thalatta, thalatta!* ('the sea, the sea!'). They now reached comparative safety at Trapezus, a Greek colony on the Black Sea coast; but difficulties had still to be overcome, and there was dissension among the troops before they reached Byzantium. At one stop on their journey a review showed that they then numbered 8,600. After spending a winter in the service of the treacherous Seuthes, a Thracian, Xenophon handed over the survivors to the Spartan Thimbron, for the war against Persia. The work ends with him

at Pergamum near the coast of Asia Minor, reunited with the horse he had had to sell, and amply rewarded with booty.

**Anacha'rsis** According to Herodotus, a Scythian prince of the sixth century BC who travelled widely and acquired a high reputation for wisdom. On his return to Scythia he was put to death for trying to introduce the cult of Magna Mater ('Great Mother'; see CYBELE). It is impossible to say what, if anything, is historical in his story. Later writers made him the guest of Solon at Athens and include him among the *Seven Sages. He was traditionally supposed to have despised all Greeks except the Spartans, and thus arose the picture of him as a 'noble savage' typifying barbarian criticism of Greek customs.

**anachrony** The narration of events taken outside their chronological sequence, usually in a narrator's recapitulation of past happenings. See e.g. *Odyssey* books 9–12, *Aeneid* books 2 and 3, and the Greek novel *Aethiopica*.

**Ana'creon** (b. *c.*570 BC) Greek lyric poet, born in the Ionian city of Teos on the coast of Asia Minor. He probably migrated in 545 BC when the Persians threatened, and joined other Teians in the foundation of Abdera in Thrace. Some time later he moved to the court of Polycrates, tyrant of Samos *c.*533–522, to whom he wrote many poems, though in the extant fragments Polycrates' name is nowhere found. After the murder of Polycrates, Hipparchus, brother of the Athenian tyrant Hippias, brought him to Athens; it is probable that after Hipparchus' murder he went to Thessaly. The place of his death, at an advanced age, is unknown. He wrote in the Ionic Greek dialect perhaps five books of lyric, iambic, and elegiac poetry from which only a few complete poems survive, more often in the quotations of later grammarians and metricians than in fragments of papyrus (*see* PAPYROLOGY). Most of his surviving fragments are from poems composed in simple metres (especially anacreontics and glyconics), which speak of love and the pleasures of the *symposium. His love-poems are tender and delicately sensuous, often characterized by a self-deprecating humour and verbal wit. They are far removed from the mere 'prettiness' of later imitators (*see* ANACREONTEA).

**Anacreontēa** A body of short poems mostly on the subject of wine and love composed at various times between the first and fifth centuries AD. They were modelled, not very accurately, on the style and subject-matter of *Anacreon and often ascribed to him, so much so that his fame in Europe after the Renaissance depended very largely on these imitations. With their literary conceits and prettiness the best of them have charm despite their slightness.

**anacrū'sis** ('upbeat') In metric, an alternative term for *arsis.

**anagnō'risis** ('recognition') See POETICS.

**analogy and anomaly** Two contrasting principles in the approach to language taken by mainly Hellenistic scholars of the second century BC, the words in this context roughly denoting 'regularity' and 'irregularity'. This was a period in which for the first time scholars, groping their way towards a written grammar, were investigating the extent to which linguistic regularity, 'analogy' (i.e. 'how this is like that') could be expressed in rules and paradigms. These principles of approach were partly connected with contemporary philosophical arguments about whether norms of thought and behaviour exist by nature (*physis*) or by human convention or law (*nomos*; see NOMOS–PHYSIS ANTITHESIS). In establishing the text of Homer and in striving to understand the Greek language the Alexandrian scholars, notably *Aristophanes of Byzantium and *Aristarchus, were analogists; the scholars of Pergamum, notably *Crates (1), were anomalists. The latter thought that variations in the endings of Greek words, as in the declension of nouns for example, showed human confusion inflicted upon nature's original true and perfect product. However, only by using the evidence of analogies could language be seen to possess a rational order.

In the Roman world, *Varro (first century BC) in his *De lingua Latina* ('On the Latin language') used analogy to set out his paradigms of Latin nouns and verbs. In this he was followed by later Latin grammarians, who eventually established the case endings of the five declensions as we now know them. Julius Caesar, an outstanding orator among his many other achievements, was an analogist, and wrote a treatise on the subject (which does not survive).

**Analytics** (*Analy'tica prio'ra, Analytica posterio'ra*) Two works on logic by Aristotle dealing with syllogisms; *see* PRIOR and POSTERIOR ANALYTICS.

**Anatolia** ('the East') The late Greek name for that part of Asia which is roughly equivalent to modern Turkey, often used nowadays to denote that part of the world in ancient times.

## anatomy and physiology

1. The Greeks often grouped anatomy and physiology with other subjects with which it seems to us they have little or no connection—structure of the universe, for example. For them there was nothing strange in a doctor being a cosmologist as well (or vice versa). Observations of physiological processes such as breathing or digestion were often combined with fanciful theories which bore no relation to the phenomena being observed. Scenes of wounding described in Homer perpetuated traditional ideas about the internal structure of the body in language scarcely meaningful. Also influential was the assumption that the external symmetry of the body reflected some sort of internal symmetry. The result was that even as late as the fourth century BC empirical knowledge of internal anatomy was still lacking. There was even speculation about the seat of cognition (the Greeks tended to think that the separation of thought and emotion was unnatural): some, including apparently Philolaus, argued for the brain, which Plato accepted, but others, including Aristotle, Epicurus, and the Stoics, for the heart (*see* HEROPHILUS). For the Romans the Latin *cor*, 'heart', also denoted 'mind', 'soul', and 'spirit', the seat of the intelligence and the emotions.

2. The earliest medical writings, attributed to *Hippocrates, writing in the fifth century BC, contain no treatise on anatomy or physiology and no certain evidence for dissection as a method of investigation. The reason for this failure to investigate, according to Galen (below), was that early doctors treated medicine not as a branch of learning but as a craft in which skill was handed down from father to son. There was therefore no need to write anything down or seek to advance knowledge. In any case the Greeks had a strong distaste for dissecting bodies. *Celsus can see the argument for vivisection of criminals (Proem 26) but still condemns it for cruelty and on the grounds that the violated body cannot exhibit the same appearance as the healthy one, and vivisection is ineffective when the victim dies.

In the case of Aristotle there is more evidence that physiological theory was related to experiment. As well as propounding theory, Aristotle gave accounts of the layout of organs and of the vascular system through actually examining animals (see ANIMALS, ARISTOTLE ON). After Aristotle animal dissection became more common. In the third century BC the dissections—including, it seems, human dissection—carried out by Herophilus (in Alexandria) and *Erasistratus (in Ceos), led to rapid advances in anatomical knowledge.

In Hellenistic physiological theory we find anatomy allied to knowledge of mechanics in order to attempt an explanation of the circulation of the blood. Erasistratus in fact produced a single comprehensive physiology. In the first century BC the theory of Asclepiades was that the body is made of corpuscles and ducts, and if the constant motion of the corpuscles is impeded or altered, this could lead to disease. His treatments were benign—massage and baths and the judicious use of wine. Against such theorists were those who trusted rather to experience. An outstanding physician of the first and second centuries AD was *Soranus, who made a substantial contribution to knowledge of the female anatomy (see GYNAECOLOGY). But the greatest anatomist and physiologist of antiquity was the polymath *Galen of Pergamum (second century AD), whose knowledge embraced all aspects of medicine, and philosophy as well. The foundation of much of his anatomical and physiological knowledge was the careful dissection of animals, through which he was able to correct his predecessors. His summary of their work, as well as his own, preserved ancient knowledge of these subjects through the centuries which followed.

**Anaxa'goras** (c.500–c.428 BC, of Clazomenae in Ionia) *Presocratic Greek philosopher, the first philosopher to settle in Athens, indicative, perhaps, of Athens' growing cultural prestige. He became the friend and mentor of Pericles, but according to tradition he was later prosecuted for impiety, perhaps by Pericles' political enemies, and so withdrew to Lampsacus, where he founded a school and was held in high esteem. He appears to have written only one book, *On Nature*, a prose work of which several extensive fragments are preserved by quotation. It seems to have been written c.470 BC, and it is debatable whether or not he was influenced by Parmenides. Anax-

agoras belongs to the Ionian tradition of philosophy (see PHILOSOPHY [Greek] and PROSE, DEVELOPMENT OF [Greek]), and his interests were in cosmology and physics.

His book began, 'All things were together', indicating the fundamental homogeneity of reality. The longest fragment explains how the universe as it exists now, made up of differentiated substances, was created out of the original relatively homogeneous mix by the action of Mind (Gk. *nous*), a separate entity which is present only in some things: 'In everything there is a portion of everything except Mind; and there are some things in which there is Mind as well.'

Mind has the capability of initiating the rotation in which items in the mixture begin to separate and display distinctive characteristics according to the predominating constituent, but it is also capable of ordering and arranging everything else. Plato's Socrates (in *Phaedo*) thought this was a mechanistic explanation, which seemed to him to fail to reveal how Mind directed natural processes. But as for the differentiated substances, 'as things were in the beginning so are they now all together'; 'all things share a portion of everything'. Every distinct substance not only takes its identity from its dominating constituent but at the same time contains infinitesimal particles of every other substance. Thus sperm, for example, contains flesh and hair and everything else, for 'hair cannot come from not-hair, nor flesh from not-flesh', etc. Moreover, 'the small is unlimited', i.e. no division however far it proceeds could reach pure flesh, for example. The ultimate constituents of the universe are the 'seeds' of which there was an infinity 'both in the beginning and now in our world', and these should probably be thought of as potentialities.

Anaxagoras' cosmology seems to be very like that of *Anaximenes. Public opinion was shocked by the former's claim that the sun, far from being divine, is a fiery stone 'larger than the Peloponnese', torn from the earth and made incandescent by its motion, and this may have contributed to his withdrawal from Athens. (His view may have been influenced by the famous fall of a meteorite in the region of Aegospotami in Thrace in 467 BC.) Anaxagoras' work had influence on Athenian thought towards the second half of the fifth century BC.

Like Anaximenes, Anaxagoras believed that the earth was flat and floated on air, but he understood that the heavenly bodies rotated and that the moon received its light from the sun, and he therefore grasped the principle of eclipses. Doctrines such as his, destructive of the traditional and official pantheon, exerted great influence on late fifth-century thinkers but made him generally unpopular. His ideas have been detected in Aeschylus' *Supplices* (*c.*463 BC) and *Eumenides* (458 BC).

**Anaxima'nder (Anaximandros)** (d. *c.*545 BC) Ionian philosopher of Miletus, a so-called *Presocratic, the first Greek known to have written a prose treatise (but *see* PHERECYDES), 'On the nature of things', now lost except for one quotation (a fragment which is the earliest surviving piece of European philosophical prose). It was said that he constructed the first map of the inhabited world and according to some sources the first celestial globe. (A Babylonian clay tablet of perhaps 600 BC, now in the British Museum, gives a stylized picture of the world from a Babylonian perspective.)

Anaximander is the first philosopher we know of who tried to explain rationally the origins of the world and of humankind. He declared that the originative principle of the cosmos was not water (*see* THALES) or any other element but 'the unbounded' or 'the indefinite', which is also 'the divine', being immortal and everlasting. This 'enfolded' and 'controlled' the *cosmos* (how is not clear), or indeed many *cosmoi* (whether successive or coexistent is not clear either). It was the source of all the many elements in the cosmos. The most important forces at work in the cosmos and the agents of physical change were pairs of opposites, chiefly the hot and the cold, the wet and the dry. Anaximander thought that the earth was a shallow cylinder with a diameter three times its depth, 'like the drum of a column', its people living on its upper surface. He was reported by *Eudemus as being the first to give some account of the relative distances of the sun, moon, and stars from the earth, specifying various ratios of size. Of his many interesting ideas about details of our cosmos two are notable. Alone of the Presocratics he explained why the earth remains in the same place without postulating some material support, declaring that there was no reason why what was symmetrically placed in the middle, equidistant from the extremities, should move downwards rather than in any other direction.

The second is his conjecture about the origins of animal and human life. He supposed that the first living creatures were produced by spontaneous generation from the moist world by the heat of the sun, and this became a standard account. Further, he inferred from the helpless condition of humans in infancy that they could not have survived in primitive conditions without protection, and so conjectured that in the beginning they were reared in fish-like creatures from which they burst out when they were able to nourish themselves and reproduce.

**Anaxi'menēs** (fl. *c.*546 BC) Ionian philosopher of Miletus and a so-called *Presocratic, younger contemporary of Anaximander. His prose treatise is lost and our knowledge of it depends on the statements of later writers. For Anaximenes the originative principle of the cosmos was the *element air; when air was rarified as fire or condensed progressively as water, then earth, then stones, these things compounded together could make up the wide diversity of the natural world. Furthermore air was the actual breath of the cosmos and so its ever-living and therefore divine source. Anaximenes thought that the earth was a flat disc supported by air, and in this he was followed by Anaxagoras and Democritus. His theory of condensation and rarefaction as observable means of change from the basic form of matter to the diversity of natural substances was his important contribution to the thought of his time.

**anceps** ('ambivalent') In metre, a syllable that can be scanned either long or short.

**Anchī'sēs** In Greek myth, a Trojan prince, great-grandson of *Tros and a member of the younger branch of the Trojan royal house. The goddess Aphrodite fell in love with him, and the child of their union was *Aeneas. Anchises when drunk boasted of the goddess's favour and was struck blind, or paralysed, by the thunderbolt of Zeus. We are told in the *Aeneid* that he was carried from burning Troy on his son's shoulders, and accompanied him in his wanderings. Virgil places his death at Drepanum in Sicily (*Aeneid* [book 3]).

**ancī'lia** At Rome a shield (*ancīle*) was said to have fallen from heaven during the reign of *Numa (715–673 BC), and an oracle declared that the seat of empire would lie wherever that shield should be. Thereupon Numa caused eleven other shields to be made like it, so that, if a traitor should wish to remove it, the genuine shield could not be distinguished. These shields were of the ancient 'figure of eight' shape, known from Mycenaean art, and were preserved in the temple of Mars (part of the old royal palace in the Forum) in the custody of the *Salii. They were carried round the city yearly in solemn procession in the month of March, the shield being supposed to have fallen on the first day of that month. On a declaration of war, the Roman general moved the shields, with the words 'Awake, Mars!'

**Ancus Ma'rcius** The fourth of the legendary seven *kings of Rome, who traditionally reigned 640–617 BC. He is credited with annexing the Janiculum hill, establishing a settlement at Ostia, and constructing the Sublician bridge (*see* PONS SUBLICIUS). He was characterized as a good king.

**Ancȳrā'num Monumentum** *See* RES GESTAE.

**Ando'cidēs** (*c.*440–*c.*390 BC) One of the earlier Attic orators and member of a distinguished aristocratic Athenian family. In 415, shortly before the *Sicilian Expedition set sail, he was accused of sacrilege in having shared in the mutilation of the *herms around the city. Subsequently he and his associates were accused of having profaned the Eleusinian *mysteries (*see also* ALCIBIADES), and in order to secure his own immunity and, he claimed, to save his father, who had been implicated, confessed to taking part in these affairs. He subsequently repudiated the confession, but at the time his account was accepted by the Athenians. When a decree was passed limiting citizen rights for those confessing to an act of impiety, he retired from Athens and began to trade as a merchant. We possess three of his speeches, the first, *On his Return*, delivered in the *ecclesia*, probably in 410, when he unsuccessfully pleaded for the removal of the limitation on his rights. The second, *On the Mysteries*, was made in 399 when, having been restored to full public rights under the amnesty of 403, he successfully defended himself against a charge of still being subject to the former limitation (the sixth speech in the works of Lysias, *Against Andocides*, is apparently part of the prosecution); it is interesting as an eyewitness account of these events in Athenian history. His third speech, *On the Peace*, is a political discourse urging peace with Sparta in 390, the fourth year of the Corinthian War. The Athenians rejected the peace, and Andocides retired into exile and oblivion. He was not, like the other orators, a trained or professional rhetorician, but a man of ability and shrewdness, who had a natural gift of expression.

**A'ndria** ('Woman of Andros') The first comedy of *Terence, produced in 166 BC, based on a play by Menander with material from the latter's *Perinthia* ('Girl from Perinthos'). An anecdote, perhaps apocryphal, relates that Terence appeared before the elderly comic dramatist Caecilius by order of the *aediles to read his first play to him when Caecilius was at dinner. The latter was so impressed that Terence was invited to share the meal.

Pamphilus, a young Athenian, has seduced Glycerium, supposed to be the sister of a courtesan from Andros, and is devoted to her. His father, Simo, has arranged a match for him with the daughter of his friend Chremes. But Chremes has heard of the relations between Pamphilus and Glycerium and withdraws his consent to the match. Simo conceals this and pretends to go on with preparations for an immediate marriage, hoping by this means to put an end to the affair. Pamphilus, learning from his cunning slave Davus that the intended marriage is a pretence, temporizes and offers no objection. Simo now persuades Chremes to withdraw his objection, so reducing Pamphilus to despair. At this stage Glycerium bears a son to Pamphilus, and Davus arranges to have this made known to Chremes, who now finally breaks off the match. At this point an acquaintance newly arrived from Andros reveals to Chremes that Glycerium as a child was shipwrecked there in circumstances which show that she is in fact his daughter. Chremes and Simo consent to the marriage of Pamphilus and Glycerium, and all ends happily.

The play contains the often-quoted phrases 'hence those tears', *hinc illae lacrimae*, and 'the quarrels of lovers are the renewal of love', *amantium irae amoris integratiost*.

**Androclus and the Lion** *See* GELLIUS, AULUS.

**Andro'machē** In Greek myth, daughter of Ēëtiōn king of Thebe in Cilicia, and wife of *Hector. Her father and seven brothers were killed by Achilles, her mother ransomed for a large sum. Her son Astyanax was put to death by the Greeks after the fall of Troy (*see* *Trojan Women*) and she herself fell to the lot of Neoptolemus to whom she bore three sons, Molossus (eponym of the Molossians), Pielus, and Pergamus (named after the citadel of Troy). The conflict between her and Hermione, the jealous, childless wife of Neoptolemus, is the theme of Euripides' play *\*Andromache*. After Neoptolemus' death she married the Trojan seer Helenus, a son of Priam, and lived in Epirus. When Helenus died she was taken by her son Pergamus to Asia Minor, where he founded the city of Pergamum.

**Andro'machē** Greek tragedy by *\*Euripides, produced *c*.426 BC, in the early part of the Peloponnesian War.

The play deals with that period in the life of *\*Andromache when she was living as the concubine of Neoptolemus in Thessaly. She had borne him a son, Molossus. After ten years Neoptolemus had married Hermione, daughter of Menelaus; she remained childless and suspected that this was the doing of her hated rival Andromache. Helped by Menelaus, Hermione takes advantage of the absence of Neoptolemus on a journey to Delphi to draw Andromache, by the threat to kill Molossus, from the shrine of Thetis where she had taken refuge, in order to kill both mother and son. They are saved by the intervention of the aged Peleus, the grandfather of Neoptolemus. *\*Orestes, who has contrived the murder of Neoptolemus at Delphi and who arrives unexpectedly, carries off Hermione, to whom he had been betrothed before Neoptolemus had claimed her. The death of Neoptolemus is announced. Thetis appears and arranges matters. The odious character which the poet attributes to (the Spartan) Menelaus has been seen as according with the feeling against Sparta which prevailed at this time at Athens.

**Andro'meda (Andromedē)** In Greek myth, daughter of Cepheus king of the Ethiopians and Cassiopeia, his wife. Cassiopeia had boasted that her daughter was more beautiful than the Nereids (sea-nymphs). They complained to the sea-god Poseidon, who sent a sea-monster to ravage the country. The oracle of *\*Ammon said it could be appeased only by the sacrifice of Andromeda, who was accordingly fastened to a rock on the sea-shore. Perseus changed the monster to stone by showing it the *\*Gorgon's head, and married Androm-

eda, after first fighting and turning to stone her uncle Phineus, who had been betrothed to her and who now attacked him. Their children included Alcaeus and Electryon.

**Andronī'cus, Lucius Livius** *See* Livius Andronicus.

**animals, Aristotle on** About one-fifth of *\*Aristotle's writings are concerned with the biological aspects of animals. His reputation as a research scientist rests primarily on these works.

1. *Historia animalium* ('Inquiry into animals'). A work of natural history, in ten books of which the last is spurious. The range of animals covered is very large—some 540 different genera.

*Book 1.* A survey of the very many ways in which the various genera differ from one another. The parts of animals, as compared with the animal we know best, the human, which is described in some detail. Some physical features indicate temperament or characteristic behaviour.

*Book 2.* About individual animals; comparisons of movement, genitals, teeth. Animals discussed include the camel, elephant, Egyptian hippopotamus, ape and monkey, crocodile, and chameleon.

*Book 3.* This book begins with an important survey of previous writers on the blood vessels, a very difficult topic to investigate because blood vessels collapse when blood leaves the body at death. (As a good investigative method Aristotle recommends starving an animal to emaciation then strangling it.) In this area Aristotle is accurate in many ways but often obscure. The book includes descriptions of those constituents of the body which can be called by the same name whether the name refers to the whole or a part—flesh or bone, for example.

*Book 4.* On various genera of bloodless animals—crustaceans, sea urchins, insects, etc. On the senses, including the eyes of moles, and hearing, smell, and taste in fishes. Aristotle writes as one who has himself handled and examined (and sometimes eaten) these creatures. He notes the singularity of the sea urchin, for example, in having its mouth underneath and its anal vent on top because its food 'lies down below'.

*Book 5.* On the breeding habits of a large variety of creatures, including the clothes-moth and the silkworm. Aristotle accurately describes how the filament of the wild silkworm in Cos, now probably extinct, was woven into garments valued for their sheen.

*Book 6.* On the pairing of birds and the mating of some sea-creatures and animals which give birth to their young alive (viviparous). Aristotle is interested in the life-span of animals. His story of the 80-year-old mule at Athens who was allowed by public decree to help itself from any baker's bread-tray is repeated by several later writers.

*Book 7.* On human reproduction.

*Book 8.* Since the life of animals consists of procreation and feeding, Aristotle turns now to diet in animals, and then to their diseases and the effect of climate.

*Book 9.* On the psychology, habits, and intelligence of animals, especially of birds, including the way of life of bees and the loving nature of dolphins.

**2. *De partibus animalium*** ('On the parts of animals'). A work of natural history in four books. Chapter 5 of book 1 contains the eloquent and deservedly famous exhortation to the study of the natural world. His thesis is that it is the contemplation of what is imperishable and eternal that gives us the greatest pleasure, 'just as a half-glimpse of people we love is more delightful than a leisurely view of other things'. Nevertheless, a more certain and complete knowledge is to be gained from studying the world around us. 'For in the matter of studying animals, as *Heracleitus said to visitors who found him warming himself at the stove and hesitated to approach, they should not be afraid to enter because even there gods are present.'

In *De partibus animalium* Aristotle now considers the problems arising from consideration of the parts of animals in more detail than in *Historia animalium* and explains their existence in terms of their purpose. He explains the causes by which each animal has the nature it has, and develops his ideas on classification.

**3. *De motu animalium*** ('On the movement of animals') and ***De incessu animalium*** ('On the progression of animals'). Aristotle's investigations on the origin of movement in animals—how does soul move body?—as well as the means. 'Nature makes nothing without purpose but always regards what is the best possible for each individual.'

**4. *De generatione animalium*** ('On animal reproduction'). A work in five books dealing specifically with those parts of animals concerned in reproduction, and a detailed account of generation in the different classes of animals. Book 5 deals with development after birth and the differences between individuals of the same species in for example hearing, hair, voice, and teeth.

**animals, attitudes to** The philosophers Pythagoras in the sixth century BC and Empedocles in the fifth had both believed in the transmigration of the soul and its reincarnation, possibly in an animal body, and so opposed the harming of animals and the killing of them for food. Pythagoreanism imposed taboos on various other foodstuffs including certain kinds of fish, but the rules of their vegetarianism are not consistent in our sources. Total vegetarianism prevented adherents from taking part in public sacrifice, the main occasion in Greece when meat was eaten, and was therefore associated with an ascetic and Orphic lifestyle (*see* ORPHEUS) which tended to marginalize members of those sects. The Theban general Epaminondas was reputedly a vegetarian as a result of being educated by a Pythagorean.

Aristotle wrote the earliest surviving work on the physical and psychological nature of animals. He interpreted their temperament to some extent in human terms: they were e.g. good- or quick-tempered, intelligent, timid; the snake was 'mean and treacherous', the dog spirited, affectionate, but fawning, the lion noble, courageous, and high-bred (but nevertheless fears fire, 'as Homer says'). But he thought there were radical differences. 'As regards humans and animals, certain psychological qualities in each are identical, and others resemble or are analogous to each other. For example, with regard to intelligence there is something in animals equivalent to understanding. But only humans have reason, and though many animals have memory, only humans can recall the past at will.' Sympathy for another order of creation pervades even the most scientific parts of Aristotle's work: he tells us what to do when our elephant has insomnia, or aches in the shoulder, and treats the gentle and intelligent dolphin appreciatively. (The dolphin was the subject of a famous story in Herodotus: *see* ARION.)

In the case of the elephant it seems that ancient and modern sentiments coincide. At the Roman *venationes* ('huntings', fights between animals or between men and animals organized as a public entertainment), where elephants sometimes made an appearance, the crowd was concerned. Cicero notes in a letter public distress at Pompey's slaughter of them at his show in 55 BC. Dogs were admired for their loyalty. The faithfulness of *Xanthippus' dog recalls that of Odysseus' dog Argus who recognizes his master after twenty years' absence.

Aristotle's successor at the Lyceum in the late fourth century BC, Theophrastus, used an argument for vegetarianism based on the affinity between humans and animals, stating that humans and animals were akin even in reasoning, and that it is unjust to kill non-dangerous animals. Nevertheless, animal pain or distress seems not to have been much considered, even by philosophers, despite the prevalence of pets. The Greek rhetorician and philosopher Plutarch, of the late first century AD, argued that animals possessed both feeling and reasoning. (He also seems to have leaned towards vegetarianism.) At best the Stoics conceded that animals might have a kind of instinctive sagacity, but no individual animal could be credited with a deliberately conscious act, and so no animal behaved virtuously (virtue being controlled by reason, Plato's argument). Since the lower elements in the universe were for the sake of the higher, the Stoics believed, it followed that animals were for the sake of humans, a belief with long-lasting consequences for morality, theology, and psychology

This attitude was countered by a vast body of zoological observations made by Aristotle and his followers (*see* ANIMALS, ARISTOTLE ON), and in the less scientific compilations of 'remarkable stories about animals'. Both strands came together in *Aelian and in the *Natural History* of the Elder *Pliny. Pliny presents the largest collection of material on animals, much of it derived from Aristotle and Theophrastus. Like Aristotle he believes that animals are incapable of reasoning but they can learn and they have their own world and way of functioning for which humans may feel sympathy. The philosopher *Porphyry (third century AD) wrote a treatise 'On abstinence from animal food', in defence of vegetarianism and attacking animal sacrifice.

*See also* ANYTE and SACRIFICE 3.

**Anna** Sister of *Dido. According to the poet Ovid, Anna came to Italy after *Aeneas had established himself there, and was entrusted by him to his wife Lavinia. But Lavinia was jealous of her, and Anna fled to the river Numicius and was taken by the river-god into his care. The story is not in Virgil's *Aeneid*.

**Annā'lēs 1.** Of Ennius, *see* ENNIUS. **2.** Of Tacitus, *see* ANNALS.

**annals (*annales*)** At Rome, 'year by year records'. Records at Rome went back to at least the fourth century BC and possibly earlier. The *annales maximi*, 'the most important records', were kept by the *pontifex maximus* ('chief priest') and inscribed on the *tabulae pontificum* ('the boards of the priests') outside his official residence (*Regia). About 130 BC the pontifex maximus P. Mucius Scaevola put an end to the annual display and authorized the publication of all the past annals. The material amassed filled eighty books. The earliest Roman historians used the annals as a source and perhaps continued the year-by-year arrangement. They may even have called their own work 'annals' (though the first writer known to have used the term as a title was *Ennius). These are the historians, whose works are lost, who are frequently referred to as 'annalists'. *See* HISTORIOGRAPHY [Roman].

**Annals (*Annales*)** (properly *Ab excessu divi Augusti*, 'From the death of the late emperor Augustus'; the title 'Annals' dates from the sixteenth century) Tacitus' history of the reigns of the Julio-Claudian emperors Tiberius, Caligula, Claudius, and Nero, written after his *Histories*. There is evidence that Tacitus was writing it in AD 115, so the last books were perhaps written *c*.120. The surviving portions are books 1–4, a small piece of 5, 6, part of 11, 12–15, and part of 16. The work is notable for its style, concise to the point of obscurity, its sustained dignity and vividness, and its epigrammatic sayings, memorable for their irony or melancholy. The record is in the main gloomy and depressing, and although Tacitus bears occasional witness to the efficient civil administration of the empire, the emphasis is rather on the crimes, the sycophancy, the informing, and the oppression that marked this period at Rome. Tacitus claims to write without partiality and prejudice, to aim at saving worthy actions from oblivion while recording evil deeds for posterity (3. 65), but he has in fact a republican bias. It is generally recognized that the impression he gives of Tiberius is unduly dark, and the life of debauchery imputed to him in his last years at Capri inherently improbable. The most important matters covered in the surviving books are as follows.

### Books 1–6: Tiberius

*Book 1.* (AD 14–15) A rapid review of the reign of Augustus, passing to that of Tiberius. The suppression by Germanicus of the mutiny of the legions in Pannonia and Germany in 14, and his first two campaigns (14–15) against the Germans. Death of *Julia (4). Description of the visit of the Roman army to the scene of the disaster of *Varus, and a hard-fought victory against Arminius.

*Book 2.* (AD 16–19) The third campaign of Germanicus (16) in which he defeats Arminius. Prosecution and death of Libo Drusus. Germanicus' expedition to the East with Cn. Calpurnius Piso (17), with whom he quarrels, and his death, which some suspected to be due to Piso and his wife Plancina. Piso returns to Rome. Death of Arminius.

*Book 3.* (AD 20–2) The return of Agrippina, the widow of Germanicus, to Italy, and the trial (20) and apparent suicide of Piso. Acquittal of Plancina. Death of Vipsania *Agrippina. The growth of luxury and sycophancy at Rome.

*Book 4.* (AD 23–8) The character and career of Sejanus, who, in league with Livia (2), the wife of Drusus (son of Tiberius), has Drusus poisoned (23) and plots against the children of Germanicus. After describing a series of trials brought about by informers, such as that of Cremutius Cordus, accused of having in a history praised Brutus and Cassius, Tacitus apologizes for relating 'dismal misery' in Rome and 'trifling events', but explains that great changes may arise from them. The proposal of Sejanus' marriage to Livia is set aside by Tiberius. An amphitheatre collapses at Fidena with enormous loss of life, and a fire destroys the buildings on Mount Caelius. Death of Augustus' granddaughter Julia, daughter of *Julia (4), who had been banished for adultery. In 26 Tiberius withdraws to Capri.

*Book 5.* (AD 29–31) Death of Tiberius' mother, *Livia, known later as Julia (5) Augusta. The story of the conspiracy and fall of Sejanus in 31, which formed part of this book, is lost.

*Book 6.* (AD 32–7) Tiberius at Capri; his vicious life, anguish, and ferocity. The death of Drusus (son of Germanicus) by starvation in prison, and of Agrippina his mother in 33. The cease-

less bloodshed at Rome, by executions and suicides. The death of Tiberius in 37, and a summary of his life.

The next four books and the beginning of Book 11 covered the period AD 37–47. They included the reign of Gaius Caesar (Caligula) and the first six years of the reign of Claudius.

### Books 11–16: Claudius and Nero

*Book 11.* (AD 47–9) The seventh year of the reign of Claudius (47). The excesses of his wife Messalina. The *Aedui are admitted to the Senate. Messalina goes through a marriage ceremony with Silius. The dismay of the emperor, and the execution in 48 of Silius and Messalina at the urging of the freedman Narcissus.

*Book 12.* (AD 49–54) Claudius marries in 49 his widowed niece Agrippina (3), daughter of his brother Germanicus. Through her influence her son, the future emperor Nero, is adopted by Claudius, preferred to his own son Britannicus, and married to his daughter Octavia. Silanus, who was expecting to marry Octavia, is brought to ruin and death in 49 by Agrippina. Seneca is recalled from exile to be Nero's tutor. The insurrection in Britain and the defeat (50) of Caratacus, king of the Silures, who is brought to Rome and pardoned. Claudius is poisoned by Agrippina, and Nero becomes emperor (54).

*Book 13.* (AD 54–8) Narcissus commits suicide. The promising beginning to the reign of Nero, who is restrained by Seneca and Burrus, the prefect of the praetorians. Cn. Domitius Corbulo is sent to the East to resist Parthian aggression. Agrippina, whose influence is weakened, takes up the cause of Britannicus; Nero has him poisoned (55) and Agrippina removed from the palace. Nero in love with Poppaea Sabina.

*Book 14.* (AD 59–62) The attempt to remove Agrippina by scuttling her ship, followed by her brutal murder (61). Armenia is recovered from the Parthians by the Romans under Corbulo. The great rising of 61 in Britain under Boudicca, and its suppression (London is mentioned as 'much used by merchants and trading vessels'). The death of Burrus in 62 and the retirement of Seneca. Nero marries Poppaea; his virtuous former wife Octavia is banished to Pandataria (Ventotene) and there murdered.

*Book 15.* (AD 62–5) The ignominious defeat of Caesennius Paetus in Armenia, followed by the reduction of the country by a Roman army under Corbulo to a dependency of the empire

(63). The great fire of Rome (64), which affects ten out of the city's fourteen districts, and its rebuilding on an improved plan. (It is rumoured that during the fire the emperor appeared on stage singing of the destruction of Troy.) The persecution of the Christians, to whom Nero attributes the fire. The conspiracy of C. Calpurnius Piso and the ordering of death to Seneca and Lucan in 65.

*Book 16.* (AD 65–6) The extravagances of Nero, who appears in public as a singer; the death of Poppaea (65). The suicide of the Stoic Thrasea and the banishment of his son-in-law Helvidius in 66. In chapter 16 of this book, one of the last surviving, Tacitus laments the melancholy and monotonous record of bloodshed. The part relating to the last two years of Nero's reign is lost.

**Anna Pere'nna** Roman goddess celebrated with much jollity on 15 March (the Ides) at the time of the full moon (reckoned as the first of the Roman New Year when that began on 1 March; *see* CALENDARS). She was probably a year-goddess.

**annona** The Roman corn supply.

**anomaly** *See* ANALOGY AND ANOMALY.

**Antae'us** In Greek myth, a giant, son of Poseidon and Gaia (Earth), who lived in Libya. Heracles wrestled with him while on his way to fetch the golden apples of the Hesperides (*see* HERACLES, LABOURS OF 11). Whenever Antaeus was thrown, he arose stronger than before from contact with his mother Earth. Heracles, perceiving this, lifted him in the air and crushed him to death.

**Antalcidas** *See* KING'S PEACE.

**Antē'nor** One of the elders of Troy during the siege. He was in favour of restoring Helen to the Greeks, since she had been taken by treachery. It was said that the Greeks, recognizing his fairness, spared him and his family when the city was captured. Later legend made him out a traitor to the Trojans, telling the Greeks to steal the *Palladium and build the Wooden Horse. Several stories were told of what happened to him after the Trojan War. One legend known to Livy, which may be as old as Sophocles' lost tragedy *Antenoridae* ('sons of Antenor'), relates that Antenor led the Eneti, who had lost their king at Troy, from Paphlagonia to the head of the Adriatic

Sea, where they settled in Venetia and founded the city of Patavium (Padua).

**A'nthimus** Greek doctor who wrote soon after AD 511, in the form of a letter to Theoderic Strabo king of the Ostrogoths, a short Latin treatise 'On dietetics', *De observatione ciborum*, half medical textbook, half cookery book. The book is of great interest for the picture it gives of the eating and drinking habits of a Germanic people, and for the unclassical nature of the author's language which he had learnt entirely from popular speech (*see* LATIN LANGUAGE).

**anthology** [Gk. *anthologia*, 'flower-gathering'] The name (coined perhaps in the second century AD) for a collection of short poems in elegiac metre (*epigrams).

**Greek.** Though many such collections were made in Greece from the fourth century BC onwards, the first known to be made on artistic principles was the *Garland* (Gk. *Stephanos*) of Meleager *c.*100 BC. This survives in part in the very large collection of (mostly) elegiac poems known as the *Greek Anthology*. Among the contents, which range in time from the seventh century BC to the tenth century AD, is Meleager's Preface, listing all the poets he included, and some blocks of poems by them. Another 'Garland' was compiled by Philip of Thessalonika in the mid-first century AD, and the next notable collection, of contemporary poems, was made in the sixth century AD by the Byzantine poet and scholar Agathias. These three anthologies became the principal sources for an important and comprehensive anthology compiled *c.*AD 900 by the learned Constantine Cephalas, an official of the Imperial Palace at Byzantium, who included most importantly epigrams from inscriptions found in various parts of Greece. All these various collections have perished as such; the surviving *Greek Anthology*, a collection of sixteen books of epigrams, is derived from two Byzantine compilations which were based on Cephalas' work but with many additions. The first and larger is the Palatine Anthology, so-called because the unique tenth-century manuscript which contains it was found in the Count Palatine's Library at Heidelberg. The second is a collection made by the scholarly Byzantine monk Maximus Planudes about 1300, and the only one known until the Palatine manuscript was discovered by the young French scholar

Salmasius (Claude de Saumaise) in 1606 (and not published until the nineteenth century). Those epigrams of Planudes which are not found in the Palatine manuscript are now published as book 16 of the Palatine Anthology.

The *Greek Anthology* contains a wide variety of poems, many of great charm. There are epitaphs (including the famous epitaphs attributed to Simonides), dedications, reflections on life and death and fate, poems on love and sex, on family life, on great poets and artists and their works, and on the beauties of nature. A certain proportion are humorous or satirical, making fun of doctors, rhetoricians, athletes, etc., or of personal peculiarities, such as Nicon's long nose.

The Planudean Anthology was, until 1606 and beyond, *the* Greek Anthology, and after its publication in 1494 exerted a wide influence throughout the Renaissance.

**Latin.** The *Anthologia Latina* is the title given to a collection made in modern times of short Latin poems. The largest block comes from the famous Codex Salmasianus of the eighth or ninth century (named after its former owner Salmasius: see above). The collection contains poems written by African poets during the Vandal occupation (fifth to early sixth century) and a few miscellaneous earlier pieces, including the *Pervigilium Veneris* and three epigrams of the philosopher Seneca.

**anthropomorphism** The attribution of human form and behaviour to gods, animals etc. In Greek *religion, the poems of Hesiod and Homer gave the Greeks a strongly anthropomorphized conception of the Olympian gods, their appearance, behaviour, and society. The gods were represented as possessing human traits and desires but greatly exceeding them in size, beauty, and power. And, of course, they were immortal. The important Roman gods were also regarded as anthropomorphic, but the Romans lacked the large body of myth available to the Greeks which gave the Greek gods their rich characterization.

**Anticle'a (Antikleia)** In Greek myth, the wife of Laertes and mother of *Odysseus.

**antidosis** ('exchange') At Athens, wealthy citizens were taxed by being required to undertake certain public services (*see* LITURGY). A citizen who thought that his wealth assessment was unfairly large might challenge some other, whose wealth he thought greater than his own, either to undertake the service or to make an exchange, *antidosis*, of properties. This might lead to a law-suit, if the other citizen refused, as in the case of *Isocrates.

**Anti'gonē** In the version of the myth of *Oedipus most familiar to us from Greek literature, one of the four children (two daughters and two sons) of Oedipus by his union with his mother Jocasta. Antigone's part in the myth seems to have originated largely in fifth-century Attica. She accompanied the blind Oedipus after his banishment from Thebes, and they eventually arrived at Colonus, near Athens. When Oedipus' sons Polyneices and Eteocles died by each other's hand as they fought for the kingdom of Thebes (*see* SEVEN AGAINST THEBES), Jocasta's brother Creon, now king of Thebes, forbade the burial of Polyneices as being the aggressor. Antigone refused to accept this decree, gave the body a token burial, was discovered, and by Creon's order walled up alive in a tomb although she was betrothed to his son Haemon. She hanged herself and Haemon stabbed himself beside her body. This is the version in Sophocles' *Antigone*. A play by Euripides (now lost) with the same title told a modified version.

**Anti'gonē** Greek tragedy by *Sophocles, possibly written in 441 BC.

Creon, king of Thebes, has forbidden the burial of the body of Polyneices (*see* ANTIGONE); the body has nevertheless been found buried but it has been exposed again. Antigone, Creon's niece, is caught performing fresh funeral rites for her brother, and is brought before the king. She pleads that her act is in accordance with the unwritten but overriding laws of the gods. Creon is unrelenting and condemns her to be imprisoned in a tomb and left to die. Her sister Ismene, who has refused to share in Antigone's actions, now claims a share in her guilt and punishment, but the king regards her as demented. Creon's son Haemon, who is to marry Antigone, pleads with his father in vain; he leaves with a warning that he will die with her. The seer Teiresias reveals to the king that the gods are angry at the exposure of Polyneices' body and the entombment of Antigone. Creon, at last moved, buries the body and goes to the tomb. He finds Haemon clasping the dead body of Antigone, who has hanged herself. Haemon then kills himself in front of his father. Creon returns to his palace, to find that his wife Eurydice, in despair, has taken her own life.

**Anti'gonus, Anti'gonids** The first Antigonus whom we hear about ('Antigonus the One-eyed') was one of the generals of Alexander the Great, the son of a noble Macedonian family, who was satrap of Phrygia at the time of Alexander's death in 323 BC and eventually aspired to rule all the empire. He was defeated and killed at the battle of Ipsus in 301 by Lysimachus, a Macedonian, and *Seleucus. His grandson Antigonus II Gonatas, son of *Demetrius Poliorcetes and king of *Macedon, established the Antigonid dynasty which maintained a partial control over Greece. After Gonatas the most prominent of the Antigonids was his grandson *Philip V (238–179 BC) who, by provoking Rome into the Macedonian Wars, was largely responsible for bringing Greece under Roman domination. After the Macedonian army was practically annihilated by the Romans at the battle of Pydna in 168 BC the Antigonids were dethroned and the Macedonian realm broken up into four federal republics. In 146 BC it became a Roman province.

**Anti'lochus** In Greek myth, son of Nestor, in Homer's *Iliad* a brave fighter for the Greeks in the Trojan War. The *Aethiopis* described how he was killed defending his father against Memnon.

**Anti'machus** (of Colophon, fl. c.400 BC) The first Greek 'scholar-poet' and as such a forerunner of the Hellenistic poets, anticipating them in their learned obscurities. He wrote an epic on Thebes, and in his long elegiac poem *Lyde* was the originator of narrative *elegy, a genre in which he had many imitators. Only scanty fragments of his works survive. The *Lyde* was much admired by some Hellenistic poets, but objected to by Callimachus (*see* his *Answer to the Telchines*) on the grounds of excessive length and obscurity.

**Anti'nŏus 1.** In Homer's *Odyssey*, the most arrogant of the suitors of Odysseus' wife Penelope, and the first of them to be killed by Odysseus.

**2.** Bithynian youth of great beauty, and the beloved of the emperor *Hadrian (for the term 'beloved' *see* LOVE AND SEXUALITY). He was drowned in the Nile in AD 130 and gossip surrounded his death with romantic legends of suicide or ritual sacrifice. He was deified and Hadrian founded the city of Antinoopolis on the Nile and created temples and cults in his memory. Antinous was frequently represented in sculpture, and some of these representations survive.

**A'ntioch (Antiocheia)** The name of several Asian capital cities founded by the *Seleucids.
  **1.** Syrian Antioch, on the river Orontes, founded by Seleucus I about 300 BC and named after his father Antiochus. It became a centre of trade and a city of pleasure; the Greek poet Aratus of Soli lived there for a time at the court of Antiochus I (ruled 281–261 BC). Antiochus III ('the Great'), king of Syria 223–187 BC, adorned it with works of art, a theatre, and a public library of which he appointed the Greek poet Euphorion librarian. Antiochus IV Epiphanes (ruled 175–163 BC), an ardent lover of classical Greek culture, considerably beautified the city. It was annexed by Pompey in 64 BC and became the capital of the province of Syria. Antioch was prominent in Christian life: it was here that Christians were first so called (Acts 11: 26). It was the third city in the East (after Alexandria and Seleuceia on the Tigris) and ranked after Rome and Jerusalem as the third Patriarchal See. After the inauguration of Constantinople in AD 330 Antioch slipped in importance. It was sacked in the Persian invasion of AD 540 and captured by the Arabs in 641, but it survived these events as a city still of some consequence.
  **2.** Pisidian Antioch, a city in Phrygia, north of Pisidia, founded by the Seleucids in the third century BC. It gained in status to become the most important Roman colony in Asia Minor under Augustus; St Paul chose Antioch as his main target when he made his first missionary journey to Asia Minor c.AD 47 (Acts 13: 13–52). Large imperial buildings dominated the centre of the city and a copy of Augustus' *Res Gestae was displayed. Two large fourth-century churches still survive.

**Anti'ochus 1.** The name of several of the *Seleucid kings of Asia; *see* ANTIOCH (1).
  **2.** Of Ascalon; *see* ACADEMY.
  **3.** Of Syracuse, a western Greek historian of the fifth century BC, who overlapped both Herodotus and Thucydides. He wrote *Sicelica*, a history of Sicily in nine books based on oral tradition, and a book on the foundation of Greek cities in south Italy. Very little survives. It is thought that Thucydides used his work as a source.

**Anti'opē** In Greek myth, daughter of Nycteus, king of Boeotia. Her story has come
down to us chiefly through Euripides' tragedy
*Antiope*, now lost. Antiope was seduced by
Zeus and became the mother of the twin
brothers Amphion and Zethus. To avoid her
father's anger she fled to Sicyon. Nycteus in
despair killed himself, but first charged his
brother, Lycus, who was king of Thebes during
the minority of *Laius, to punish Antiope.
Lycus captured Sicyon and imprisoned Antiope; her treatment was made more cruel by the
jealousy of Dirce, the wife of Lycus. At last
Antiope escaped and joined her sons, now
grown to maturity. These avenged her by
tying Dirce to the horns of a bull, so that she
was dragged to death; and they killed or deposed Lycus. Amphion and Zethus now became rulers of Thebes and built its walls. (In
Homer's *Odyssey* they are represented as the
city's first founders.) Amphion was a harper of
such skill that the stones were drawn into their
places by his music. He married *Niobe, and
Zethus (according to some) married the river-
nymph Thebe, whence the name of Thebes.

**Anti'pater (Antipatros) 1.** (*c.*397–319 BC)
One of the most able generals of Philip II of
*Macedon and subsequently of his son Alexan-
der (the Great). During Alexander's absence in
the East he was the governor of Macedonia and
the Greek states. After the death of Alexander
he was faced with a revolt by a league of Greek
states (*see* LAMIAN WAR) but was eventually victorious at Crannon (*see* ATHENS 4); he drove the
Athenian orator Demosthenes to suicide by
demanding his surrender. He remained loyal
to the Macedonian dynasty, and it was his
death in 319 that precipitated the break-up of
Alexander's empire. His son was *Cassander.
    **2.** Of Sidon (fl. *c.*120 BC), Greek writer of
short elegiac poems, some of which are preserved in the *Greek *Anthology*.

**Anti'phanes** Greek poet of Middle Comedy;
*see* COMEDY [Greek 5].

**A'ntiphon** (*c.*480–411 BC) Athenian orator
from a prominent family whose surviving
speeches are the earliest we have. He gained
a great reputation by writing speeches for other
litigants to deliver in their own person—at
Athens litigants were required to plead in person—and thus he was the first to circulate
written speeches. We possess three of his
speeches for murder trials, written between

430 and 411 BC). In *Against the Stepmother* a
young man accuses his stepmother of poisoning his father through a servant (offering very
little evidence). In the *Murder of Herodes* a
man from Mitylene defends himself from the
charge of having murdered Herodes during a
sea-voyage—Herodes went ashore on a stormy
night and never returned. He appeals to evidence and probabilities, and alleges political
and financial motives on the part of the accuser. In *On the Chorus-boy* the defendant,
the chorus-leader (*see* CHOREGIA), who is accused of accidentally killing the boy by giving
him a drug to improve his voice, argues that he
was not present at the time and that the prosecution is politically motivated.

The name Antiphon was common in Attica
and this fact, together with his apparently
many-sided activities, makes it difficult to be
sure that all the writings and activities ascribed
to this name are the work of one and the same
person. Attributed to this same orator but perhaps wrongly are the *Tetralogies*, which seem
to be an earlier work, although their arguments
about causation and probability fit the second
half of the fifth century BC and Antiphon's
reasoning in the speeches above. The *Tetralogies* are rhetorical exercises in which the author
composes two model speeches for the prosecution and two for the defence (the four
making a tetralogy) in three imaginary homicide trials. The speeches illustrate methods of
argument that could be applied to a variety of
actual cases but would be especially helpful to
a defence. In the first case the defendant argues that though circumstantial evidence
points to his being guilty of murder there are
others more likely to have committed the
crime. In the second, concerning a boy accidentally killed by a javelin in the gymnasium,
the defendant argues that the boy not the
thrower was guilty of unintentional homicide
because he brought about his own death by
inadvertence. In the third, a man dies after a
fight and the defendant argues that the man
himself was to blame because he started the
fight.

Antiphon is sometimes identified with Antiphon 'the Sophist', fragments of whose work
*Truth* survive. This is concerned with the
nature of justice and is critical of conventional
morality (*nomos*) from the point of view of self-
interest (*see* NOMOS–PHYSIS ANTITHESIS).

Antiphon was one of the very few men
praised by Thucydides, who was reputedly

his pupil, for his 'virtue' (*arete*), as well as his intelligence and power of expression. According to Thucydides, Antiphon was responsible for the oligarchic revolution which overthrew the democracy at Athens for a few months in 411 (*see* FOUR HUNDRED). When the democracy was restored, Antiphon was tried for treason, found guilty, and put to death. His defence speech (of which a small fragment survives on papyrus) was the finest speech Thucydides knew. Aristotle tells the story that when *Agathon congratulated him on it he replied that he would rather satisfy one man of good taste than any number of common people.

Antiphon stands at the beginning of extant Greek prose. In comparison with his successors in oratory Lysias and Demosthenes his speeches lack charm, variety, and to some extent clarity, but are nevertheless very interesting on their own terms.

**anti-Semitism** Conflict between Jews and the Greeks and Romans, when it arose, was a Roman rather than a Greek problem. The classical Greek world was unaffected by the Diaspora (the dispersal of the Jews) which began with the Assyrian deportation in 722 BC and continued in the early sixth century BC when Nebuchadnezzar took the Jews of Jerusalem into captivity in Babylon. However, during the Hellenistic period, from the fourth century BC onwards, the Jews spread widely in the Hellenized eastern Mediterranean world, the Jewish community at Alexandria in particular becoming the largest and most important of its kind at that time. The causes of subsequent anti-Jewish movements in the ancient world have been much debated, and study has focused on several episodes: first, the overturning, by the Seleucid king Antiochus IV when he ruled Palestine, of the liberal dispensation of Antiochus III for the Jews, and his hellenizing measures such as the installation of a pagan cult in the Temple at Jerusalem in 167 BC; secondly, in cities where Jews sometimes had special and long-standing privileges (notably Alexandria and Syrian Antioch) the occasional stand-offs between the citizens and the metic (non-citizen) Jews; thirdly, the occasions when Jews were expelled from Rome. The question is whether these events were motivated by a prejudice against Jews in particular on the grounds of religion and culture (an antipathy which would be unique in

the ancient world), or whether the conflicts were due to local factors, often connected with the granting or removal of privileges, and with questions of citizenship. There are scholars who believe that anti-Semitism as a phenomenon arose later than Greco-Roman antiquity and is driven by an ideology, in the sense of a body of ideas reflecting group beliefs and interests, which had no equivalent in the ancient world.

**Anti'sthenēs** (*c*.445–*c*.360 BC) At Athens, a devoted follower of Socrates, present at his final conversation. He was depicted with some humour by Plato. Like the sophists he wrote on a wide range of subjects, which included Socratic *dialogues in the manner of Plato (against whom, among others, he wrote a diatribe). All his works except for a few fragments have been lost. He believed, with Socrates, that virtue is sufficient for happiness, and therefore he emphasized, emulated, and even exceeded the austerity of Socrates' lifestyle, but unlike Socrates, who enjoyed the good life too, was hostile to pleasures except those of the simplest and most natural kind. For that reason later *Cynic philosophers regarded him as the real founder of Cynicism (*see* CYNOSARGES). He criticized polytheism in the manner of Xenophanes, maintaining that though in conventional belief there are many gods, in reality there is only one (*see* MONOTHEISM).

**Antonia 1.** (b. 39 BC) Elder daughter ('maior') of Mark Antony and Octavia. She was the wife of L. Domitius *Ahenobarbus and the grandmother, through their son Gnaeus, of the emperor Nero.

**2.** (b. 36 BC) Younger daughter ('minor') of Mark Antony and Octavia, and wife of Nero Claudius Drusus (younger brother of the emperor Tiberius). Their children were *Germanicus, Livia (usually known as Livilla), and Claudius (later emperor). After her husband's death she refused to marry again, and brought up her grandchildren, including Gaius, the future emperor Caligula. He gave her many honours, including the name Augusta, but resented her criticisms and reputedly drove her to suicide (in AD 37). Claudius rehabilitated her memory.

**Antonines** A collective name for the Roman emperors Antoninus Pius (reigned AD 138–61), his adopted son Marcus Aurelius (161–80), and the latter's son Commodus (180–92). Antoninus' reign was proverbially peaceful and happy, and the period from AD 96 to 180, including also the reigns of Nerva (96–98), Trajan (98–118), and Hadrian (118–38), was famously described by Edward Gibbon in the third chapter of his *Decline and Fall of the Roman Empire*: 'If a man were called to fix the period in the history of the world, during which the condition of the human race was most happy and prosperous, he would, without hesitation, name that which elapsed from the death of Domitian (AD 96) to the accession of Commodus.' It was the time when the Roman empire reached its greatest extent and its peak of stability and prosperity. The whole period from 96 to 192 is sometimes called the age of the Antonines, although strictly speaking the name applies only to the last three of its six emperors.

**Antonine Wall** *See* BRITAIN 3 and ANTONINUS PIUS.

**Antoni'nus Pius** Roman emperor AD 138–61, born in 86 at Lanuvium in Latium in Italy (Città Lavinia) and named Titus Aurelius Fulvus Boionius Arrius Antoninus. His family had originated at Nîmes in Gaul but settled at Rome; both his father and grandfather had been consuls. He won fame for his integrity as proconsul of Asia and joined the circle of advisers of the emperor Hadrian, who adopted him as successor not long before his death. Antoninus maintained good relations with the senate and his long reign was peaceful and orderly, without striking incident. His policies were beneficent and mildly progressive, lacking extravagance, and his whole reign is marked by a general sense of well-being, aptly expressed in *Aristeides' oration 'To Rome', *Fronto's *Letters*, and the tribute in Marcus *Aurelius' *Meditations*. He married Anna Galeria Faustina. It was in his reign, *c.*142, that the wall of turf known as the Antonine Wall was built in Britain between the firths of Forth and Clyde by his lieutenant Lollius Urbicus. The reason why a new frontier was thought necessary so soon after the completion of his predecessor's wall is still discussed.

**Anto'nius, Marcus 1.** (143–87 BC) One of the greatest orators of his day, consul in 99, a member of the party of Sulla, and put to death by the supporters of Marius. He was grandfather of the famous Mark *Antony. He is one of the chief interlocutors in Cicero's *De oratore*.
**2.** *See* ANTONY, MARK.

**Antonius Musa** Doctor to the emperor Augustus, whom he cured of a serious illness.

**Antony, Mark (Marcus Antonius)** (*c.*83–30 BC) Eldest son of M. Antonius (Creticus) and Julia, sister of L. Julius Caesar, and grandson of the orator Marcus *Antonius (1). After serving under Aulus Gabinius in the East and under *Caesar (2) in Gaul, he was one of the tribunes in 49 BC, when he supported Caesar against the senatorial (republican) side, joined him before the crossing of the Rubicon, and held a command in the ensuing campaigns in Italy and Epirus. After Caesar's victory at the battle of Pharsalus (48) where he commanded the left wing, Antony remained in Italy as second-in-command during the lawless period of Caesar's absence. He was Caesar's colleague in the consulship when the latter was assassinated in 44. At the Lupercalia on 15 February 44 he had offered Caesar a diadem, but the latter refused this symbol of kingship. Antony's eloquence won over the people, so that he was in a favourable position to take over the leadership of the Caesarians, while remaining conciliatory towards the senate. However, his leadership was threatened by Caesar's heir Octavian (*see* AUGUSTUS), who sided with the republican senate in opposition to Antony. Civil war broke out between Caesarians and republicans. It was at this time that *Cicero ((1) 5) delivered his speeches against Antony known as the *Philippics*, and powerfully contributed to raising the republican opposition to him. Antony was defeated by the republican Decimus Brutus at the battle of Mutina in 43. At this time Octavian had joined forces with the senate, but after Mutina the differences between him and Antony were settled, and Octavian, Antony, and Lepidus were appointed as a triumvirate to rule for five years. *Proscriptions followed, in which Cicero and his brother were sacrificed to Antony's desire for vengeance. In 42 Antony, sharing the command with Octavian, defeated the republicans Marcus Brutus and Cassius at Philippi.

Afterwards a division of the Roman world was made, in which the East and Gaul were assigned to Antony, the West to Octavian. But hostilities soon broke out between the two leaders, temporarily settled by the treaty of Brundisium in 40 (whereby Antony surrendered

Gaul), and by the marriage of Antony to Octavian's sister Octavia (Antony's wife Fulvia having died in 40). This marriage interrupted his liaison with *Cleopatra, queen of Egypt, which had begun when he met her at Tarsus in Cilicia in 41. Their twins were born in 40; the liaison was resumed in 37 and a third child was born in 36. Both stood to profit by their association: Antony would have at his disposal the resources of Egypt to further his scheme of obtaining complete power over the East; Cleopatra would be confirmed in her rule over Egypt, which was none too secure. In 37 the triumvirate was prolonged for another five years. But the campaign which Antony undertook against the Parthians in 36 was unsuccessful, and the elimination of Lepidus from the triumvirate sharpened the rivalry between Antony and Octavian. After subduing Armenia in 34 Antony returned to Alexandria, the Egyptian capital, where he lived like an oriental ruler. He made donations of large parts of the eastern provinces to form kingdoms for Cleopatra, *Caesarion, and his three children by Cleopatra. On the last day of 33 the agreement between Antony and Octavian came to an end, and in the following year he divorced Octavia. At this point Octavian got hold of and published Antony's will, in which he allegedly left bequests to Cleopatra and requested burial in Alexandria. Antony, having alienated the sympathy of Rome, gave Octavian the opportunity to declare a national war against Cleopatra. He would now seem a traitor if he sided with the enemy. The result was decided by Octavian's victory in the sea-battle at *Actium in 31, when Cleopatra's sixty ships sailed away, followed by Antony himself. In 30 Octavian invaded Egypt; Alexandria capitulated, and Antony took his own life.

Shakespeare's play *Antony and Cleopatra*, based on Plutarch's Life of Antony, in which he is presented as a man who lost the world for love, may give a romantic and distorted view of events. Although the senate decreed a *damnatio memoriae*, letters from Antony survive in Cicero's correspondence. Through his daughters by Antonia he was the ancestor of Germanicus and of the emperors Caligula, Claudius, and Nero.

**Anū'bis** In Egyptian religion, the jackal-headed god who conducted the souls of the dead to the region of immortal life, identified by the Greeks of the Hellenistic period with *Hermes.

**A'nytē** Arcadian poet of Tegea who lived in the early third century BC. Some eighteen of her epigrams survive in the Greek *Anthology. They have great charm and are among the first pastoral descriptions of wild nature in Greek literature, and also include the first epitaphs for animals.

**A'nytus** One of the three accusers who brought Socrates to trial on a charge of impiety (*See* APOLOGY OF SOCRATES). A wealthy Athenian, and a democrat in politics, he was represented by Plato in the *Meno* as an enemy of the *sophists. He may have thought that by attacking Socrates he was acting in the best interests of Athens.

**Apatu'ria (Apatouria)** *See* PHRATRIES.

**ape'lla** The name sometimes given to the assembly of the people at Sparta. *See* ECCLESIA.

**Ape'lles** The most famous painter of antiquity, born at Colophon in Ionia in the first half of the fourth century BC. None of his works survives, but there are descriptions by several ancient authors. One of the most renowned was of Aphrodite Anadyomene, 'Aphrodite rising from the sea', wringing the sea-water from her hair. Apelles was court painter to Philip of Macedon and his son Alexander the Great and is known to have painted several portraits of Alexander, sometimes in allegorical situations. His work was renowned for its gracefulness.

**Aphai'a** *See* BRITOMARTIS.

**A'phobus, Against** Speeches by Demosthenes against his fraudulent guardian; *see* DEMOSTHENES (2) 1.

**Aphrodī'te** The Greek goddess of sexuality, beauty, and fertility, identified by the Romans with *Venus. She has two alternative genealogies: according to Hesiod she sprang from the foam (*aphros*) of the sea that gathered about the severed genitals of the god Uranus when he was castrated by his son *Cronus. To Homer she is the child of Zeus and Dione. There is no agreement about her origins, but Homer calls her 'the Cyprian', and the Greeks themselves thought of her as coming from the East. She is also called Cytherean, from the name of an island off the Laconian coast. Homer makes her the wife of *Hephaestus. When her amorous intrigue with *Ares was discovered, the pair were caught in a net by Hephaestus and exposed to the ridicule of the assembled gods (though the goddesses withdrew out of shame). Aeneas is her son by the Trojan *Anchises, and she always supported the Trojan cause against the Greeks (see TROJAN WAR). In later literature she is the mother of *Eros. For other legends about her see ADONIS and PARIS, JUDGEMENT OF. She had cults in every region of Greece, and was connected with fertility in every sphere. 'Black' Aphrodite shows her power over black earth as well as her connexion with the powers of the night. For Aphrodite 'in the Gardens' see ARRHEPHOROI. Her worship by prostitutes shows that through her seductive nature she was a protector of this profession. Although primarily a goddess of love, she was also a protector of sailors and of magistrates since she was a goddess of civic harmony. Two common titles of Aphrodite are Urania ('heavenly') and Pandemos ('[protector] of all the citizens'), cult names which Plato interpreted as symbolizing intellectual and sensual love. Thus Plato's account in *Symposium* (in the voice of a character Pausanias) of Aphrodite Pandemos as 'Common' (rather than 'of all the citizens') has no foundation in belief. She was sometimes shown as 'bearing arms', especially at Sparta, where she probably had a role as protector. The story of her love affair with Ares perhaps arose from the desire to reconcile two opposites, Love and War.

**Api'cius, Marcus Gavius** Gourmet of the reign of Tiberius (AD 14–37). His recipes were written down; but the work on cookery which bears the name of Caelius Apicius is thought to be a compilation of a later period, perhaps the fourth century. It is sometimes entitled *De opsoniis et condimentis sive de re culinaria libri decem*, 'Ten books on catering and seasoning, or on cookery'.

**Apocolocynto'sis** Title of a Menippean satire (a medley of prose and verse; see MENIPPUS) by *Seneca (2), formed from the words *apotheosis*, 'deification', and *colocynta*, 'pumpkin'. Manuscripts give the further title *Ludus de morte Claudii*, 'A joke about the death of Claudius'. It was written early in the reign of the emperor Nero (c. AD 54) in mockery of the deification of his predecessor Claudius; the pumpkin perhaps alludes to the latter's stupidity. It describes Claudius' arrival in heaven, the difficulty of finding out who he is because of his stammer, and the proposal of the deified

emperor Augustus that he should be deported to the Underworld because of the murders he has committed. Here he meets his victims and is brought for trial before *Aeacus. Following Claudius' own system, Aeacus hears the case against him and pronounces sentence without listening to the defence. Claudius is finally made clerk to one of his own freedmen. The work combines serious political criticism with literary parody.

**Apo'llō (Apollon)** Greek god, the son of *Zeus and *Leto, twin brother of Artemis. Seeming to many the most characteristically Greek of all the gods, he embodied youthful but mature male beauty and moral excellence. Though he had many different functions he was associated especially with the beneficial aspects of civilization, giving to Greek culture its ideal of the beautiful, athletic, virtuous (though not moralistic) and cultivated young man (see KOUROI and EPHEBOI). A young man's first cut hair when he came of age was dedicated to Apollo. His association with music (especially the lyre), poetry, and philosophy derives from his educational aspect; he is *Musagetes*, 'leader of the *Muses'. He was the god also of light (hence his title Phoebus, 'the bright'), and sometimes identified with the sun. A similar meaning is sometimes given for his enigmatic title Lykeios, but that is more generally connected with 'wolf'. Perhaps in this aspect he was also associated with the care of flocks and herds, acquiring the epithet Nomios, 'of the pastures'. His own song, the *paean, was understood in classical times as a healing song, and he was regarded as a healing god (until replaced from the fifth century BC onwards by *Asclepius) and so the god of purification, as in the case of *Orestes. He was also the god who sent plague, and he decreed that his statue should be set up to avert the Athenian plague of 430 BC. In Homer he was an enemy of the Greeks.

He was widely known as an oracular god, and not only at *Delphi. His shrines at Branchidae, Claros, and the holy island *Delos were notable. The Sibyls are usually described as priestesses of Apollo. His origins are much debated, and there is no certain occurrence of his name in the *Linear B tablets (but see PAEAN). In archaic and classical Greece Delphi was his supreme oracular shrine, having grown out of purely local worship in the eighth century BC. According to one myth he destroyed the dragon Python, the guardian deity of Delphi, and this story provides an explanation for his title Apollo Pythios, 'Pythian Apollo'. Apart from favouring Troy in Homer, his political oracles seem to have been on the whole impartial, though the Delphic oracle was suspected of supporting Persia in the Persian Wars and Sparta in the Peloponnesian War. Of his many loves, the most famous was that for Coronis, mother of Asclepius. Others loved by Apollo include Cassandra, Cyrene, Hyacinthus, and Marpessa.

Apollo was introduced into Rome on the advice of the Sibylline books (*see* SIBYL) during a plague in 433 BC. A temple, to Apollo Medicus ('the Healer') was built where there had already been a cult-place of the god. The emperor Augustus, perhaps because of the victory of the Caesarians in the name of Apollo at Philippi in 42 BC, made Apollo his particular god and had a second temple dedicated to him in 28 BC in celebration of his victory at Actium in 31 BC. It was built near Augustus' house on the Palatine, with a magnificent library attached. Apollo figures in Virgil as a healer but pre-eminently as the giver of oracles, and in the *Eclogues* as the patron of poetry and music. *See also* ARISTEAS.

**Apollodō'rus 1.** (*c.*394–after 343 BC) Elder son of the rich Athenian banker *Pasion. A minor politician at Athens, he was an indefatigable litigant, now credited with seven speeches wrongly attributed in the manuscripts to Demosthenes. He repeatedly quarrelled with his stepfather *Phormion about money. In the late 340s BC he prosecuted Neaira, a former prostitute, for illegally claiming Athenian citizenship, and his speech on that occasion is a rich source of information about some aspects of Athenian society.

**2. Apollodōrus of Athens** (*c.*180–after 120 BC) A very learned scholar and writer who worked with *Aristarchus in Alexandria and later lived in Athens. He wrote a rationalistic treatise *On the Gods*, which was frequently drawn on by later writers, and a *Chronicle* based on the researches of *Eratosthenes, covering the period from the fall of Troy (traditionally 1184 BC) to 144 BC. It was written in verse (trimeters) and so was easy to memorize. Only fragments survive. A spurious but famous work which does survive is the *Bibliothēkē* (Lat. *Bibliotheca*, 'Library'), a compilation of the first or second century AD which relates the stories

of Greek heroic mythology and is a valuable if uncritical source.

**Apollo'nius 1. Apollonius Dy'scolus** ('Bad-tempered'; second century AD) Alexandrian scholar and grammarian. He is our chief source of information for the history of grammatical studies from the second century BC to his own day. Four of his works survive, on the *Pronoun, Conjunction, Adverb*, and on *Syntax*. The *Syntax* does not expound a comprehensive system but deals in turn with the article, pronoun, verb, preposition, and adverb. He himself writes Hellenistic, *\*koinē*, Greek, as was suitable for handbooks, not the literary Attic, and he knew some Latin. He had great influence on later Greek and Latin grammarians, especially the late Latin grammarian *Priscian. He was father of *Herodian (1) who wrote on Greek accents.

**2. Apollonius of Pergē** (in Pamphylia; fl. 200 BC) Greek mathematician. He composed eight books on *Conics*, the study of cones, in Alexandria 'somewhat too hurriedly' and then wrote a revised edition. The first four books survive in Greek, the more specialized books 5 to 7 in Arabic, and the eighth is lost. Apollonius does not claim that his work is original but says that he expounds the fundamental properties 'more fully and generally' than his predecessors (who included *Archimedes). Book 5 in particular shows that Apollonius was in fact a highly original mathematician. His terminology and methods became standard, and earlier work on the subject lapsed. Most of his work on other topics, which included important work in theoretical astronomy, is lost. Also lost is a commentary on the *Conics* by *Hypatia.

**3. Apollonius Rhō'dius** ('of Rhodes') A literary figure of major importance at Alexandria in the third century BC. He was librarian of the *Alexandrian Library and tutor to the royal prince (later *Ptolemy III Euergetes). The ancient biographies make him a pupil of Callimachus, who was clearly an important influence. Some scholars believe the two disagreed about the value and style of epic, but Apollonius does not appear in the list of Callimachus' opponents, the *Telchines. His main work, which survives, is the *Argonautica*, a Greek epic which he deliberately shaped into four long books (5,835 lines) on the story of Jason and the *Argonauts, telling of the voyage of the *Argo* from Iolcus (in Thessaly) to Colchis by way of the Propontis and the Black Sea, the winning with Medea's help of the Golden Fleece so that Jason claims his rightful kingdom, and the return to Iolcus by the Danube, Po, Rhone, western Mediterranean, North Africa and Crete.

*Book 1.* The Argonauts set out for Colchis at the eastern end of the Black Sea (in modern Georgia), which is ruled over by the cruel *Aeëtes. Catalogue of Argonauts. The main events are: a year-long stay at Lemnos where the women have murdered all the men on the island, and welcome the Argonauts as an opportunity for procreation; description of Jason's cloak; Jason sleeps with *Hypsipyle; Heracles is lost from the expedition.

*Book 2.* A boxing match in which Amycus is beaten by Polydeuces; the Argonauts meet the blind prophet *Phineus and save him from the Harpies; he tells them of the voyage ahead. They sail through the Clashing Rocks (*Symplegades) and meet on the island of Ares the sons of Phrixus (*see* ATHAMAS), who fled from Greece on the ram with the Golden Fleece.

*Book 3.* Aeetes agrees to surrender the fleece to Jason on condition that he performs the seemingly impossible tasks of ploughing a huge field with fire-breathing bulls, sowing it with the teeth from Cadmus' dragon, and killing the warriors who spring up from them. Jason succeeds because he has used a magic salve given him by Medea, Aeetes' daughter, who has fallen in love with him at the instigation of the goddess Hera.

*Book 4.* Medea flees with the Argonauts, having drugged the serpent which guarded the fleece. They sail along a great river (the Danube) which is visualized as flowing from the Black Sea into the Adriatic. At the river's mouth Jason and Medea lure her brother Apsyrtus, who is commanding the pursuit, to his death. Zeus decides that they must be purified for this crime by Medea's aunt Circe who lives on the west coast of Italy. They reach her by way of the rivers Po and Rhone, which are thought of as linking north-east Italy and the Western Mediterranean. From there they sail to Corfu, Homer's Scheria, where Jason and Medea are married, and are then driven to the deserts of Libya, where the gods rescue them. They finally return to Iolcus by way of Crete, where Medea uses magic to destroy *Talos, who guards the island.

The *Argonautica* is an imaginative re-creation of Homeric epic. The language is Homeric, enriched by borrowings from the whole tradition of high poetry. Apart from Homer, important influences are Pindaric lyric and especially Pythian 4, which tells the story of the Argonauts in vivid snapshot style, and Euripides' tragedy *Medea*. Episodes such as the Catalogue of Argonauts and the description of Jason's cloak (both in book 1) point to their origins in comparable parts of Homer (the cloak corresponds to Achilles' shield in the *Iliad*). The voyage of the Argo in the Mediterranean in book 4 harks back to Odysseus' adventures at sea on his way home. Fantasy and magic play a larger part in the *Argonautica* than in the *Odyssey*, but that is inevitable with a character such as Medea. Very Alexandrian is the interest in cult and ritual and their origins. In recent years the *Argonautica*, though essentially an artificial creation, has become a serious study for readers who appreciate its originality, complexity, and sophistication.

**4. Apollonius of Tya'na** (in Cappadocia) Neo-Pythagorean philosopher and mystic, whose life reputedly spanned most of the first century AD. He led the life of a wandering ascetic, visiting far-off places, including India, and advising cities. After his death (he was supposedly carried up to join the gods) he became an object of cult. A fragment of his writings, *On Sacrifices*, survives. A perhaps unreliable biography of him was written by *Philostratus.

**5. Apollonius of Tyre** *See* NOVEL [Latin].

*Apology of Socrates* (*Apologia Sokratous*) ('Socrates' Defence') **1.** Plato's version of three speeches made by Socrates in 399 BC in the Athenian law-courts, answering the charge of impiety that was brought against him by Meletus on behalf of the poets, Anytus on behalf of the craftsmen and politicians, and Lycon on behalf of the orators. How far it represents Socrates' actual words is unknown.

In the first speech, the actual defence, Socrates distinguishes between previous vague accusations (that he speculated about questions of cosmology and physics, and made the 'worse cause'—or 'weaker argument'—appear the better) and the charge of impiety now being brought. On the former, he explains that he is neither a scientist nor a *sophist; his only wisdom consists in knowing that he knows nothing. At the instigation of the Delphic oracle, he has sought constantly to find a wiser man than himself, but has found none. He has gone to those who had a reputation for wisdom, and finding they had none has tried to convince them of this fact. Young men imitate these questionings and examine other people themselves. This has provoked popular enmity and given rise to these accusations. Socrates turns next to Meletus and cross-examines him on his specific charge, that he, Socrates, corrupts the youth and does not accept the city's gods. He then addresses the judges and declares himself unrepentant: he will persist in the practices complained of, for he must continue, in obedience to the god (of the Delphic oracle, Apollo), to preach the necessity of virtue. If they kill him, they will be injuring themselves, for he is the gadfly sent by the gods to stir Athens to life.

At the end of this defence the jury delivers its verdict: Socrates has been convicted and the penalty the prosecutors propose is death. Socrates replies to their proposal and assumes a more serious tone, though his argument is paradoxical (not to say highly provocative). Why should he propose an alternative punishment? As a benefactor of Athens he ought to be rewarded. Imprisonment, exile, a fine, would certainly be evils, but as for death he does not know whether it is good or bad. Nevertheless he suggests a fine of 30 minas, which his friends will guarantee since he himself has no money.

This proposal is put to the jury, who reject it, and Socrates is sentenced to death. There follows a brief third speech to the jury in which he prophesies that many will arise after his death to condemn his judges. He comforts his friends with regard to his own fate: death is either a dreamless sleep or a journey to a place of true justice, where he will be able to converse with Hesiod and Homer and the *heroes. Nothing evil can happen to a good man; if he is to die, it must be better for him. He forgives his accusers and judges. (Such an address after the conclusion of a case is otherwise unknown in Athenian law-suits.)

**2.** A brief account by *Xenophon of Socrates' defence in the same trial. At the time, Xenophon was taking part in the expedition of Cyrus (*see* ANABASIS), and he ostensibly relies on the authority of Hermogenes, a friend of Socrates who is mentioned in Plato's *Phaedo* as present at the death. This account is intended to bring out especially the self-confidence with which Socrates spoke and his willingness to die. His pleas are here stated with less elaboration than by Plato.

**apo'phradĕs** 'Impure' days in the Athenian *calendar when there was danger of incurring *pollution because of inauspicious events, e.g. those days when homicide trials were taking place in the Areopagus or the nights were moonless. Then temples were closed and important business avoided.

**aporia** In a philosophical discussion, the state of having no way to save an argument; being unable to proceed further in an argument for reasons of logic. *See* ELENCHUS.

**apotheosis** Elevation to divine status. It was commonly thought that the *Dioscuri, *Heracles (Hercules), and *Romulus were added to the gods because of their services to humankind on earth. *See* HEROES and RULER CULT.

**appeal** [Lat. *provocatio*] At Athens a court known as the *eliaia* may have been set up by Solon in the early sixth century BC to hear appeals against the verdicts of the archons. However, after *juries were set up by the mid-fifth century there was no appeal from their verdicts, though there were some occasions when a case was reopened or a decision set aside by the *ecclesia*.

At Rome, it was thought that from early times an appeal to the people (*plebs*) could be made against a judgement involving death (*see* HORATII). In the early republic it was probably possible to appeal to a *tribune against the action of a magistrate, whether he was using coercion or presiding over a lawcourt. The Valerian law (*lex Valeria*) of 300 BC made it a criminal offence for a magistrate to ignore an appeal, and Cicero believed that some sort of provision for appeal existed in the *Twelve Tables of *c.*450 BC. The protection of citizens increased in the second century BC and ultimately the grant of tribunician power to the emperor Augustus led to the establishment of appeal to the emperor rather than to the people. *Justinian in the sixth century reformed the system, making every judgement subject to the possibility of appeal except that of the *praetorian prefect.

***Appendix Virgilia'na*** Collection of short Latin poems mostly dating from *Virgil's lifetime or soon after, ascribed to Virgil in late antiquity but of very doubtful authenticity. The collection comprises the following:

*Catalepton* [Gk., 'On a small scale'], fifteen epigrams, perhaps identical with the *Epigrammata* attributed to Virgil by Donatus and

Servius; four poems dedicated to Virgil's friends are possibly authentic (especially, readers hope, *Cat.* 5). The title had been used earlier by Aratus for a collection of short poems.

*Ciris*, a hexameter *epyllion of Alexandrian inspiration relating the story of Scylla, daughter of *Nisus (1). Ciris is the mythical bird into which Scylla was changed. The poem contains Virgilian verses and phrases often inappropriately adapted to a new context. Not by Virgil.

*Cōpa* ('Dancing girl'), a short elegiac poem about a tavern girl who dances to castanets to entertain her customers. It contains phrases from Virgil and Propertius, and advocates drink as a remedy against thoughts of mortality. Not by Virgil.

*Culex* ('Gnat'), a poem in hexameters telling the story of a shepherd who kills a gnat which has stung him to warn him of a snake. The ghost of the gnat later appears to the shepherd, reproaches him, and describes the Underworld. Though this poem was widely believed in antiquity to be by Virgil it is a later pastiche of Virgilian phrases and Ovid's *Metamorphoses*.

*Dirae*, transmitted as one hexameter poem in the manuscripts but usually edited as two: *Dirae*, 'Maledictions', in which a farmer curses the soldiers who have dispossessed him of his farm, and *Lydia*, in which the poet laments in pastoral style his separation from his mistress. Neither is by Virgil.

*Elegies on Maecenas*, two elegies on *Maecenas' death, handed down in the manuscripts as one continuous poem.

*Moretum* ('The salad'), a realistic and only mildly mock-heroic poem in hexameters about a farmer's preparation of a meal, much in the spirit of the *Georgics*. It vividly describes the farmer rising at cock-crow on a winter morning, blowing the fire back to life, grinding his corn in a hand-mill, collecting from the garden the ingredients for his salad, all tantalizingly itemized including herbs and dressing, and completing his meal with the freshly baked bread, before starting for his day's work at the plough. Not by Virgil.

*Priapea*, three small poems ascribed to Virgil among a collection of eighty addressed to the god *Priapus, probably not by Virgil but made in the reign of Augustus.

*Aetna.

**A'ppian (Appianos)** (of Alexandria, d. soon after AD 160) Greek historian. He experienced the Jewish uprising against the Greeks in AD 116–7, became a Roman citizen, and practised as a lawyer in Rome. He compiled narratives in Greek of the various Roman conquests from the earliest times to the accession of Vespasian, in twenty-four books. The preface, books 6–9, and books 11–17 survive almost complete and there are portions of others. After the preface and book 1 on early Rome in the period of the kings the books are arranged mainly ethnographically, describing the individual peoples as Rome conquered them. Thus, book 2 describes Italians; 3, Samnites; 4, Celts; 5, Sicilians; 6, Iberians; 7, Hannibal; 8, Carthaginians (Libyans and Nomads); 9, Macedonians and Illyrians; 10, Greeks and Ionians; 11, Syrians (Seleucids) and Parthians. Book 12 deals with Mithridates VI; 13–17, the Civil Wars at Rome; 18–21, the wars in Egypt; 22, the first century AD up to the accession of Trajan in 98; 23, Trajan's campaigns against Dacians, Jews, and Pontic peoples; 24, Arabians.

The most valuable are books 13–17 describing the Civil Wars between 146 and 70 BC. As his sources Appian used a variety of Greek and Roman authors, including Julius Caesar and Augustus. Since many of his sources are lost, his information particularly on the Civil Wars is very valuable.

**Appian Way (*Via Appia*)** The principal road from Rome to the south.

**A'ppius Claudius** Roman consul in 451 BC; *see* CLAUDIUS (1).

**A'ppius Claudius Caecus** Famous Roman *censor (312–308 BC); *see* CLAUDIUS (2).

**Apple of Discord** *See* ERIS.

**Apule'ius, Lucius** (b. *c.*AD 125) Author of the only Latin *novel that survives entire. He was born at Madauros in Africa, where St Augustine received part of his education. On a journey to Alexandria, when a young man, he fell ill, was nursed by a rich widow named Aemilia Pudentilla, and married her. Her relations brought an action against him on the charge of having won her by the use of magic. His *Apologia* or speech for the defence survives. From this we learn that he had inherited a considerable fortune but had wasted it, that he was deeply interested in natural science, and that the accusation was founded on trivial grounds. However, the speech covers most usefully many aspects of magic; that Apuleius was in fact much interested in the subject appears from many passages of his novel, the *Metamorphoses* (see below). He was acquitted and subsequently settled at Carthage, from where he travelled among the African towns, making philosophical declamations in Latin. We possess a collection, perhaps made by a later admirer, of excerpts from these lectures under the name *Florida* ('Anthology'), which show evidence of wide learning. Two popularizations of Platonic philosophy are attributed to him, *De dogmate Platonis* ('On the beliefs of Plato'), probably spurious, and *De deo Socratis* ('On the god of Socrates'), as well as a free translation (*De mundo*, 'On the world') of the *Peri kosmou* attributed falsely to Aristotle.

The work for which he is famous is his *Metamorphoses* or *Golden Ass*, a Latin romance in eleven books. An epitome of the same story also exists in Greek, *Loukios e onos*, 'Lucius or the Ass', doubtfully attributed to *Lucian; both works may well derive from the *Metamorphoses* of an unknown 'Lucius of Patrae', known to Photius writing in Byzantium in the ninth century AD. This original was remodelled by Apuleius and enlarged by many incidental tales.

The romance takes the form of a narrative recounted in the first person by a young man named Lucius, a Greek, whose adventures begin with a visit to Thessaly, the reputed home of sorceries and enchantments. There, while being too curious about the black art, he is accidentally turned into an ass, falls into the hands of robbers, and becomes an unwilling and much-beaten partaker in their exploits. Some of the robber stories are excellent, but the most beautiful and famous of the stories embedded in the novel is the tale of Cupid and *Psyche, reminiscent of allegorical myth in Plato. After many vicissitudes, in the course of which he serves one of the strange bands of wandering priests of *Cybele, and becomes a famous performing ass, Lucius is transformed back into human shape by the favour of the goddess *Isis, and appears to become Apuleius the author himself. The last portion of the work refers to his initiation into the mysteries of Isis and Osiris and bears witness to the interest shown in his day to oriental religions. The many realistic details that he gives vividly illuminate the popular life of his time. The style of the novel resembles the exuberantly Asianic style of oratory (*see* ORATORY [Greek]), with vocabulary drawn from a variety of registers, archaic, poetic, Greek, and colloquial. The baroque effect is fascinating and moving.

**Apu'lia** Region of south-east Italy, modern Puglia. Its dry but fertile soil was excellent for sheep-rearing and Apulian wool was famous. The region was strongly influenced by Greek settlers. In the late fourth century BC it became subject to Rome and remained loyal against *Pyrrhus. In the *Punic and *Social Wars, however, many Apulians revolted and Apulia was much devastated in consequence.

**Aquae Sulis** Modern Bath, a Romano-British town associated with the Belgae in *Britain. The hot springs, perhaps used in Iron-age Britain, were developed from the second half of the first century AD and a temple to Sulis Minerva, or Sul Minerva, was built, of which fragments remain. Many inscriptions record the presence of visitors from Britain and abroad at this health resort. Some notable curse-tablets have also been found. In Saxon times the site was deserted.

**A'quilo** (Gk. Boreas) The north wind.

**Arabia** The name first applied to the desert region on the northern coast of the Arabian peninsula that lies east of the Nile delta and merges with Syria. Later it was extended to the whole peninsula. By the second century AD Ptolemy knew the later division of the peninsula into Arabia Felix ('fertile') in the south, and Arabia Deserta. The Greeks and Romans were familiar with the eastern shore of the Arabian Gulf, and their knowledge was increased after the exploratory voyages of Alexander's admirals in the later part of the fourth century BC. The interior however always remained unknown. Arabia was regarded by the ancients as the land of spices and proverbially rich. It had vast stretches of desert grass fragrant with aromatic herbs, which also provided pasturage for its famous horses, and the fruitful terraced districts near the west coast grew balsam, aloe, myrrh, and frankincense. But Arabia stood on many trade routes and many of her exports—spices and precious stones—came from India or lands further east. When Egypt came under Roman rule in the first century AD the Romans traded directly with southern Arabia and India, and the old 'incense route' to the north diminished in importance. In the seventh century AD occurred the movement that became the Arab conquest of the Near East,

Egypt, North Africa, and Spain, begun by Muhammad in 622, checked by the Arab defeat at Constantinople in 717 but not ceasing to be a political force until the tenth century. The flowering of Arab culture that accompanied the movement left a legacy in Europe, particularly in Spain, while the Arabs themselves absorbed much from Greek philosophy and played a part in its survival (*see* ARISTOTLE 5 and TEXTS, TRANSMISSION OF ANCIENT 3 and 7.)

**Ara′chnē** ('spider') In Greek myth, a woman of Lydia who challenged the goddess Athena to a contest in weaving. She depicted in her web the amours of the gods, and Athena, angered at her presumption and choice of subject, tore the web to pieces and beat the weaver. Arachne in despair hanged herself, but Athena turned her into a spider, compelled for ever to weave her webs.

**Aramaic** A Semitic language originating in Mesopotamia and spoken in the Middle East from early in the first millennium BC, in the Assyrian and Persian administrations and throughout the Roman period. There are many Greek–Aramaic bilingual inscriptions. One dialect form became 'Syriac', the main language of the Christian church in the Middle East.

**Ara Ma′xima** *See* HERCULES.

**Ara Pācis** ('Altar of Peace') An altar in the Campus Martius at Rome, constructed during the years 13–9 BC by order of the senate to commemorate the safe return of the emperor Augustus from the pacification of Spain and Gaul in the previous year. The walls surrounding it were covered with elaborate sculptures, most notably a representation of the procession on the day it was inaugurated (4 July 13 BC), with portraits of Augustus' family and other leading citizens. The whole monument has now been reconstructed (under cover) with most of its surviving sculptures incorporated.

**Ara′tus 1.** A Greek poet perhaps from Soli in Cilicia (*c*.315–*c*.240 BC), who studied at Athens. He subsequently spent part of his life at the court of *Antigonus Gonatas, king of Macedon; there he wrote hymns for the king's marriage. His best-known work, and the only one still extant, is a didactic poem, the *Phaenomena* ('Astronomy'), in 1,154 hexameters, describing with elegant clarity and little mythological allusion the relative positions of the chief stars and constellations, and their risings and set-

tings; it is based on a prose treatise of the same name by the mathematician and astronomer *Eudoxus of Cnidus. The last 400 lines of the poem, dealing with meteorology, were sometimes given the separate title *Diosemeia*, 'Weather signs'. This part was derived from a similar work, perhaps by *Theophrastus. The *Phaenomena* achieved immediate fame, and became one of the most widely read poems in the ancient world. Many commentaries were written on it, some criticizing the serious astronomical errors it contains. The commentary by the astronomer *Hipparchus is the only one of the latter's works to survive, because it was connected with such a famous text. The language of the poem is Homeric Greek but the thought is consistently Stoic, and the Zeus of the proem is the Stoic God. It was translated into Latin by Cicero in his youth, and the latter part of it also by *Germanicus and *Avienus. Cicero's translation is thought to have had considerable influence on the style of Lucretius. Other poems were ascribed to Aratus but have not survived. The apostle Paul, who also came from Cilicia, quotes from the *Phaenomena* when preaching to the Athenians (Acts 17: 28).

**2.** (Of Sicyon, third century BC) General of the *Achaean confederacy.

**Arca′dia** Region of Greece in the centre of the Peloponnese, very mountainous, especially in the north, and reaching the sea only in the south-west. The most prosperous parts were the eastern plains of Orchomenus, Mantinea, and Tegea which developed as independent states. Among its rivers were Alpheus, Stymphalus, and *Styx. It was a land of villages and so was of little direct importance in Greek politics, although *Mantinea and *Tegea were involved in Spartan expansion, particularly in the fifth century BC. Its chief strength lay in its manpower. Under *Epaminondas an Arcadian confederacy was formed in the fourth century BC against Sparta and it later joined the *Achaean confederacy. Arcadia's isolated geographical position is the reason for several of its distinctive features. Known Mycenaean sites are few but interesting, and the inhabitants regarded themselves as the most ancient people of Greece. Their dialect, which is not seen in extant literature and is known only from inscriptions, closely resembles that of Cyprus (and is consequently known as Arcado-Cypriot), and is markedly different from the other Peloponnesian dialects. This suggests that Arcadia, with its mountainous and inaccessible countryside, remained largely cut off (*see* GREECE). Arcadia also preserved remarkable myths and cults; the gods Hermes and Pan are particularly connected with the region. According to one tradition Zeus was born on Mount Lycaeon, and here also human sacrifice is attested. Anyone eating human flesh at the sacrificial feast was said to be changed into a wolf. Many gods in Arcadia are represented as half-animal in form, like Pan. The region is connected through *Evander with the origins of Rome. A famous and beautiful late fifth-century temple of Apollo was built at Bassae. Arcadians were notoriously poor, 'acorn-eaters' according to Herodotus. The idealized picture of the pastoral life of Arcadia is originally due to the Roman poet Virgil, who made it the notional setting of bucolic poetry (*see* ECLOGUES) because it was the home of the pastoral god Pan, and also perhaps because it was, to Virgil, more remote from the troubles of Italy than Theocritus' *Magna Graecia. However, the fame of 'Arcady' in relatively modern times, as a place of love and poetry where politics and the city rarely intrude, is derived from the Renaissance poets. The Latin tag familiar from seventeenth-century pastoral paintings, *et in Arcadia ego*, often translated as 'I too [have lived] in Arcadia', may more correctly mean 'I [am found] even in Arcadia', and refer to death.

**Arcesila'us (Arce'silas) 1.** The name of many of the ruling dynasty of Cyrene in North Africa, which ruled from the foundation of the colony (*c.*630 BC) for some 200 years.
 **2.** Head of the *Academy from *c.*268 BC.

**archaic age** Name given to one of the five periods of the Greek era (defined on the basis of pottery styles). It begins *c.*620 BC and ends in 480 BC. *Cf.* PROTO-GEOMETRIC; GEOMETRIC; ORIENTA-LIZING; CLASSIC. The term Archaic age is sometimes used more widely to describe the period from *c.*750 to 480 BC.

**Archelā'us** King of *Macedon *c.*413–399 BC.

**archetype** *See* TEXTUAL CRITICISM.

**Archias** *See* PRO ARCHIA.

**Archidamian War** Name given to the first ten years (431–421 BC) of the Peloponnesian War between Sparta and Athens. It comes

from the Spartan king at that time, Archidamus II, who led the first incursions into Attica. *See* PELOPONNESIAN WAR 3 and 4.

**Archidamus** The name of several kings of Sparta of the *Eurypontid (junior) branch.

**Archilochus** Greek poet from the island of Paros, who lived probably around the mid-seventh century BC: he mentions a total eclipse of the sun which was almost certainly that of 6 April 648 BC. He wrote short poems in a variety of metres, elegiac, iambic, and trochaic. Little is known of his life; he took part in the colonization of Thasos and fought there, and was reputedly killed in a battle between Paros and Naxos. He was the object of a cult described in an inscription of the third century BC by a certain Mnesiepes, discovered in 1949. His poetry survives only in the quotations of later writers and some papyrus fragments. Ancient tradition says that he repeatedly attacked a certain Lycambes, who had betrothed his daughter Neobule to Archilochus but later forbade the marriage, and Archilochus avenged himself with such detailed accounts of the sexual pleasure that he and others had enjoyed with Neobule and her sister that father and daughters hanged themselves for shame. Some lines of his verse seem to confirm the existence of Neobule; one poem recovered from a papyrus, the 'Cologne Epode' found in 1974, recounts the poet's rejection of Neobule and his seduction of her younger sister. Other fragments confirm his ancient reputation for being an innovator in metre, language, and subject matter (in relation to the convention of scurrilous abuse in *iambic poetry). His iambic poems in particular show a great variety of tone—mocking, enthusiastic, melancholic, abusive—as well as a mordant wit. His self-consciously anti-heroic epigram on throwing off his (hoplite) shield as he fled from battle had a considerable literary following (*see* AL-CAEUS and HORACE); a fragment suggests that the unwarlike *Anacreon had behaved in a similar way. Several elegiac fragments lament men drowned at sea. *See also* SYMPOSIUM and PARIAN MARBLE.

**Archimē'dēs** (*c.*287–212 BC) Greek mathematician, born at Syracuse, the son of an astronomer Pheidias. He was the greatest mathematician of antiquity, an astronomer, engineer, physicist, and inventor. He probably studied at Alexandria and subsequently lived at the court of Hieron II, tyrant of Syracuse, where he was killed at the capture of the city by the Romans under *Marcellus (1). He corresponded with *Conon (2) and *Eratosthenes. Popular history knew him as the inventor of machines for warfare which helped to postpone the fall of Syracuse (see Plutarch's Life of Marcellus), and other devices such as the screw for raising water and the compound pulley. It attributed to him the boast, 'Give me a place to stand, and I will move the earth', and the exclamation 'eureka' ('I have found it') when after observing in his bath the displacement of water by his body he realized how to test (by specific gravity) whether base metal had been introduced into Hieron's gold crown. He famously constructed two spheres, a planetarium and a star globe, which were taken to Rome.

Cicero, who was quaestor in Sicily in 75 BC, discovered the tomb of Archimedes near one of the gates of Syracuse, overgrown with brambles and forgotten. By Archimedes' own wish it had been marked by a column depicting a cylinder circumscribing a sphere, which recalled his discovery that their volumes were in the ratio 3 : 2.

In his breadth and freedom of vision Archimedes ranks as one of the greatest mathematicians of all time. In his work called the Sand-reckoner (counting grains of sand was proverbially impossible) he describes a system for expressing very large numbers verbally in Greek when the language stops at a myriad, 10,000: $10{,}000 \times 10{,}000$ becomes 'a second myriad' and so on. In effect Archimedes used a myriad as a base, showing that he understood the nature of a numerical system far better than anyone else in antiquity. The Sand-reckoner is also his only surviving work to touch on astronomy, and is the best source for the heliocentric system of *Aristarchus, whose surviving work is geocentric. Some of Archimedes' treatises survive on other topics including the circle, the sphere, and the cylinder. His work On Floating Bodies is a treatise on hydrostatics, a science which he invented. Already known in a Latin translation, the Greek text was discovered in 1906. Two of his works survive only in Arabic. The decipherment in recent years of the 'Archimedes palimpsest', a prayer-book written in the thirteenth century over texts copied in the tenth, has revealed seven short works by Archimedes, two of them hitherto unknown. No work by him survives on catapults, burning-mirrors, giant ships, or the other devices with which he is supposed to have kept at bay the Romans besieging Syracuse, which finally fell by treason.

See also TECHNOLOGY.

**architecture, orders of** There were three 'orders' or styles in Greek architecture, which were based on the form of the column.

**1. Doric.** The Doric order was the oldest, evolved during the seventh century BC and appearing first at Corinth, and it was the normal style of mainland Greece, Sicily, and Magna Graecia. The column had no base but rose directly from the floor, tapering slightly from about a quarter of the way up and having a ratio of height to maximum diameter in the region of five or six. It had wide, shallow flutings (usually twenty in number), and was surmounted by a capital consisting of a basin-shaped circular moulding and a plain, square slab.

**2. Ionic.** The Ionic order developed in Ionia and the Aegean islands in the late sixth century BC. The Ionic column was more slender than the Doric, with a ratio of height to maximum diameter of about eight or nine, and deeper flutes (normally twenty-four). It stood on a base, and the capital was decorated with volutes (spiral scrolls).

**3. Corinthian.** The Corinthian order was essentially a development of the Ionic. Introduced in the later part of the fifth century, the column retained the Ionic form but the capital had an inverted bell shape decorated with acanthus leaves. Imported to Rome, the Corinthian became the great imperial order.

To these three the Romans added in the early empire a fourth, the 'composite', a combination of Ionic and Corinthian.

**archons** ('rulers') The general Greek term for all holders of office in a state. The Athenians believed that when Athens ceased to be ruled by kings (supposedly in the eleventh century BC; see CODRUS), the government then devolved by gradual degrees upon three archons. These were elected from the aristocracy, at first for ten years but from 683 BC for one year only. The three were the archon basileus ('king archon') who was responsible particularly for religious ceremonies, and presided over the *Areopagus; the polemarchus ('war ruler') who commanded the army; and the archon who was the civilian head of state, sometimes called the eponymous archon (at least by the end of the fifth century) because his year of office was identified for calendrical purposes by his name. His legal duties were the widest and included the protection of all property and of the family; he also directed the festivals of the *Panathenaia and *Dionysia. At some time in the seventh century six *thesmothetai*, 'those who lay down the law', were added as additional archons whose duties were mainly legal, and who presided as chairmen over many types of law-suit and 'laid down the law' probably in the sense of pronouncing verdicts. In the fifth or fourth century BC a secretaryship was instituted so that a board of ten was established, one from each of the ten tribes of *Cleisthenes (2).

The political struggles of the seventh and sixth centuries centred upon elections to the office of eponymous archon, but after 487 BC the appointments were made first by lot from an elected shortlist, and from later that century entirely by lot. In the early fifth century only the two highest property classes were eligible, but in 457 eligibility was extended to the third class, the *zeugitae* (see SOLON), and no one of lower qualification was in practice excluded. After a year of office an archon became a member of the Areopagus for life, a fact which added importance to their office in earlier times but ceased to be significant when they were appointed by lot, because then the Areopagus too lost its political importance.

**Archȳ'tas** (first half of the fourth century BC) Philosopher from Tarentum with Pythagorean connections. He was a younger contemporary of Plato, and as a mathematician may have been visited by him in the early 380s. Archytas was reputed to have sent a ship to rescue Plato from Dionysius II in 361 BC. He was famous for his elegant solution to the problem of doubling the cube but little is known of him for certain, and only a few of the surviving fragments seem to be genuine. Most of his work seems to have been concerned with technical matters in mathematics and especially harmonics. Ptolemy regarded him as 'the most dedicated of the Pythagoreans to the study of music'. Archytas thought that 'correct calculation' (*logistike*) was required for the proper conduct of social and political life, and argued that the study of the sciences (*mathemata*)—astronomy, geometry, arithmetic, and, in the sense of harmonics, music (see SEVEN LIBERAL ARTS)—was crucial for understanding reality.

Archytas figures in an ode of Horace (1.28), where he is addressed as a 'sand-reckoner', but there is no evidence that he 'counted the sand' as *Archimedes did.

**Arcti'nus** *See AETHIOPIS*; EPIC CYCLE; *ILIUPERSIS*.

**Areopagiticus** A speech by the Greek orator *Isocrates advocating a return to a form of government where the *Areopagus would exercise, as formerly, supervision of all aspects of Athenian life. The English poet John Milton recalled this speech in his discourse of 1644, *Areopagitica*, in which he passionately advocates the repeal of a parliamentary order of 1633 by which press censorship was reimposed.

**Areo'pagus (Areios pagos)** The 'hill of Arēs' at Athens, north-west of the Acropolis and separated from it by a depression; also the name of the ancient council that met on it. According to legend, it was so called because there Ares was tried by the gods and acquitted of the murder of Halirrhothios, Poseidon's son, who had raped Ares' daughter at that place. Again according to legend, as found in the *Eumenides* of Aeschylus (see ORESTEIA), it was there that Orestes was tried for the murder of his mother Clytemnestra, the goddess Athena having referred the case to a tribunal of Athenian citizens.

Originally the council known as the Areopagus must have existed to advise the king, and was composed exclusively of *Eupatridae, nobles. Its influence increased as the monarchy declined until in the seventh century it was virtually the government. After the reforms of *Solon its membership was recruited from all ex-*archons, who remained members for life, and who now represented the wealthy as well as the nobly born, so that it became a less exclusive body. Its constitutional powers were perhaps redefined and to some extent limited by *Cleisthenes (2), but it remained powerful down to the Persian Wars. With the rapid advance of democratic institutions its great powers seemed out of place. It may have declined in prestige as it declined in political power after 487 BC, when the archons were first appointed by lot and recruitment was no longer based on political ability. In 462 *Ephialtes deprived it of its 'guardianship of the laws' and circumscribed its jurisdiction. It remained the court for murder trials but for a time lost all political importance. However, in the mid-fourth century BC Isocrates in his *Areopagiticus* represented it as part of Athens' past glory when it exercised authority, and from the 340s it was empowered to make reports on matters at the request of the assembly. After the battle of *Chaeronea it tried Athenian deserters, and it reported against Demosthenes in the Harpalus affair. It was still in existence in the fourth century AD.

The term *boule*, 'council', usually refers to a second body which was distinct from the Areopagus and dated from the time of Cleisthenes, although it has also been thought that Solon created a second council at the time of his reform of the Areopagus.

**Ārēs** In Greek myth, the war-god. He was the only son of *Zeus and his wife *Hera and, in the story told by Demodocus at the Phaeacian court (*Odyssey* book 8) the lover of Aphrodite, who gave birth to their daughter Harmonia. In literature he is identified with Enyalius, a different but marginal war-god. Compared with Athena, who fights to defend the city, Ares represents the destructive and least heroic side of war. In *Iliad* 5 Zeus tells Ares he is 'most hateful to him.' His name may occur on *Linear B tablets and if so may be Greek. The tradition was that he came from Thrace, thus being felt by the Greeks to have come from outside themselves, as befitted a god of strong emotions (*cf.* DIONYSUS).

The Romans identified him with *Mars, a god of greater dignity and importance. *See also* AREOPAGUS.

**Arē'tē** In Homer's *Odyssey*, the wife of Alcinous, king of the Phaeacians.

**aretē** Greek word commonly translated loosely as 'virtue'. It can denote moral 'goodness' and also 'excellence' of every kind, not necessarily moral. In early Greek the excellence denoted by *arete* was predominantly courage, a meaning that persisted later. In the fifth and fourth centuries BC *arete* commonly included the qualities required of (particularly) a man if he was to be well thought of, namely, as well as courage, wisdom (*sophia*), justice, and good sense (*sophrosyne*). By this time *arete* had also acquired the sense of 'reputation', 'success', 'power', so that it was quite reasonable for *sophists to claim it as a subject they could teach. For Plato the word has a narrowly moral sense. In Aristotle the word comes to denote the particular 'excellence' or quality that makes a thing what it is; human excellence is the power of reason, which only humans possess. *See* NICOMACHEAN ETHICS.

**Arethū'sa (Arethousa) 1.** One of the *Hesperides.

**2.** A spring on the island of Ortygia, in the harbour of Syracuse. According to legend *Alpheus, a river-god, fell in love with the nymph Arethusa when she bathed in his stream in Arcadia. She fled from him to Ortygia and was changed into a fountain (by Artemis, in one version); but Alpheus flowed under the sea to Ortygia to be united with the fountain. It was believed in antiquity that there was a real connection between the two and that a cup thrown into the river would be recovered from the spring.

**Argeiphontes** ('Argus-slayer', supposedly) Epithet of the Greek god *Hermes.

**Arginu'sae (Arginousai)** Small islands between Lesbos and the mainland of Asia Minor, off which in 406 BC the Athenian fleet heavily defeated that of Sparta, capturing or destroying seventy Spartan ships. The Athenians lost twenty-five ships whose crews were not rescued, allegedly owing to bad weather (*see* THERAMENES). It was thought at Athens that insufficient efforts had been made to take up the dead and save the wounded and drowning, and the blame was laid on the eight generals (*strategoi*) who had been present. Two of them fled; the remaining six were condemned to death by the assembly in a wave of popular anger, sentence being pronounced on all the accused together instead of each being judged, as was constitutional, separately. These were executed, including Pericles, son of the famous statesman, and Thrasyllus (*see also* THRASYBULUS (2)). Socrates, one of the presidents of the assembly at the time, opposed the illegality of the proceedings (*see* PRYTANY).

**Argo** *See* ARGONAUTS.

**Argonau'tica** *See* APOLLONIUS (3) and VALERIUS FLACCUS.

**A'rgonauts (Argonautai)** ('those sailing on *Argo*') The heroes of one of the earliest sagas of Greek mythology, the voyage of *Argo* to recover the Golden Fleece. They lived one or two generations before the Trojan War and most of them came from Thessaly, central Greece, and the Peloponnese. In surviving Greek literature their story is told mainly in Pindar's Pythian 4, the *Argonautica* of *Apollonius Rhodius, and *Apollodorus (1). Their leader was Jason, the son of Aeson (son of Cretheus and Tyro), who was the rightful king of Iolcus in Thessaly, but the throne had been usurped by Aeson's half-brother Pelias. Jason had been sent for safety and education to the Centaur *Chiron in Thessaly. Pelias had been warned by an oracle that he would be killed by a descendant of *Aeolus (2) who would come to him wearing only one sandal. This prophecy was fulfilled when Jason, grown up, returned to Iolcus to claim his inheritance, having lost a sandal while carrying an old woman (the goddess Hera in disguise) across a river. Pelias promised to restore the throne to him if he would first recover the Golden Fleece. This was the fleece of the ram that had carried away Phrixus and Helle (*see* ATHAMAS), and had been hung in the grove of Ares at Colchis, at the eastern end of the Black Sea, guarded by a dragon that never slept. Jason undertook the task, and embarked in *Argo* at Pagasae with some fifty of the chief heroes of Greece. These seem originally to have come from Thessaly, the home of the *Minyans (as the Argonauts are often called), but later storytellers added heroes from different times and traditions, such as Heracles. Heroes most generally said to have been on the expedition include Orpheus, Peleus, Telamon, the Dioscuri, Zetes and Calais, Idas and Lynceus, Tiphys the helmsman, Argus, who built the ship, Admetus, Augeas, and Neleus' son Periclymenus. Acastus joined at the last moment. Many of the stories concern dangers which are overcome by the particular virtue of one hero or another (e.g. Polydeuces by his boxing defeated Amycus, son of Poseidon). For other adventures *see* HYLAS; HYPSIPYLE; PHINEUS; SYMPLEGADES).

The expedition eventually reached Colchis, where the king *Aeētes expressed willingness to surrender the fleece if Jason would perform certain apparently impossible tasks (*Argonautica* book 3). With the help of the magic arts of Medea, the king's daughter, the tasks were successfully accomplished, and Jason and Medea and the other Argonauts returned to Iolcus with the fleece. The account of the expedition now divides into several main variants describing adventures in many parts of the Mediterranean and Black Sea areas. Some stories have the Argonauts returning to Greece by sailing west along the stream of Ocean (*see* OCEANUS), either to the north or the south, and entering the Mediterranean by the Pillars of Hercules. For the rest of Jason's story, *see* MEDEA. Jason was said to have died at Corinth, killed, according to one version, as he sat under the old *Argo* by a falling baulk of timber. For the subsequent adventures of Medea, *see* THESEUS.

The story of the Argonauts is one of the oldest Greek sagas, containing many elements from folk-tale including two of the most popular themes, that of sending a hero on a dangerous voyage to get rid of him, and that of confronting him with a series of difficult tasks in which he is helped to success by an unexpected ally. The scholars of antiquity saw it as reflecting the age of Greek colonization and expansion. Modern scholars have tended to see it as an expression of those qualities which the Greeks felt best represented them and defined their difference from other peoples.

**Argos** Greek city in the north-east Peloponnese 5km (3 miles) from the sea, on a site occupied since prehistoric and Mycenaean times. The name often signifies also the territory belonging to the city, sometimes called Argolis ('the Argolid'). In Homer the name is used to describe (i) the city, of which Diomedes was the king, (ii) the kingdom of Agamemnon, who was Diomedes' overlord, and (iii) by extension the whole of the Peloponnese, as opposed to Hellas, i.e. Greece north of the Isthmus of Corinth. Hence the name 'Argives' in Homer frequently means simply 'Greeks'. In the stories of the *Dorian invasion, Argos became the stronghold of Temenus, the eldest of the *Heracleidae. It probably retained leadership of the Peloponnese until challenged by Sparta in the seventh century BC. Argos defeated Sparta at the battle of Hysiae in 669, perhaps under the leadership of its king *Pheidon, a legendary figure to whom no certain date can be ascribed. However, the wide power which Argos won under Pheidon did not survive his death, and thereafter, largely influenced by jealousy of Sparta, Argos played a secondary and not always very glorious role in the history of Greece (*see also* CLEISTHENES (1)). For its defeat *c.*494 BC *see* TELESILLA. At the time of the *Persian Wars its unfaithfulness to the Greek cause was concealed under a mask of neutrality. A democratic government was introduced and Argos allied itself with Athens against Sparta in 461 BC. In the first part of the *Peloponnesian War it remained neutral. In 420, after the Peace of Nicias and as a result of the efforts of Alcibiades, it joined Athens and shared the latter's defeat at Mantinea in 418. Argos sided with Philip II of Macedon and was one of the last cities to join the *Achaean confederacy after a period of rule by tyrants.

The great Argive goddess was Hera, worshipped at the Heraeum some 10km (6 miles) north of Argos. Argive sculptors were outstanding in the early classical period, notably Polycleitus. For Argive myth *see* ADRASTUS.

**Argus 1.** In Greek myth, the herdsman that Hera set to watch *Io, given the epithet Panoptes because he had eyes all over his body; when Hermes killed him, Hera placed his eyes in the peacock's tail.

**2.** In Homer's *Odyssey* (17.292) the dog which recognizes its master Odysseus on his return and then dies.

**Aria'dnē** In Greek myth, daughter of *Minos and Pasiphae. When *Theseus came to Crete she fell in love with him and gave him the thread by which he found his way out of the labyrinth after killing the Minotaur. He then fled, taking her with him, but abandoned her on the island of Dia (Naxos). There the god Dionysus found her, married her, and made her immortal.

**Ari'cia** Ancient Latin town in a hollow of the Alban hills about 25km (16 miles) south-east of Rome. In a grove near the town was the famous temple of the goddess *Diana, whose ruins can still be seen in the woods surrounding Lake Nemi. The priest was a runaway slave who had murdered his predecessor (*see* GOLDEN BOUGH).

**Arimaspians** Legendary people of the far north who were one-eyed, and fought with griffins who guarded a hoard of gold. They were supposedly the subject of an epic by the poet *Aristeas of Proconnesus.

**Arī'on 1.** Greek lyric poet, perhaps of the seventh century BC, said to have been born at Methymna in Lesbos, but largely a figure of legend. He is reputed to have been a pupil of the lyric poet *Alcman and to have spent the greater part of his life at the court of *Periander, tyrant of Corinth. He visited Italy where he amassed much wealth. According to a story in Herodotus, on his return he was thrown overboard by the sailors, who wanted his treasure,

but a dolphin, charmed by the song he had been allowed to sing before his death, carried him to land. To Arion was attributed the change in the performance of the *dithyramb from an improvised song sung during a procession into one sung by a stationary chorus. Through this change he was said to be connected with the birth of tragedy, which perhaps means that his type of dithyramb helped eventually to produce tragedy. Nothing survives of his work.

**2.** Name of a legendary horse, the offspring of *Poseidon and Demeter. It belonged to the Argive hero *Adrastus and its speed enabled him to escape after the failure of his expedition against Thebes.

**Ariovi'stus** Chief of the Suebi, a Germanic people called into Gaul *c*.71 BC to assist a Gallic tribe in local warfare and then found impossible to dislodge. The Roman senate acquiesced in his conquests but he was eventually routed by Julius Caesar in 58 BC and died soon after.

**Aristae'us** In Greek myth, son of the god Apollo and the Thessalian nymph Cyrene, whom Apollo carried off to the region in North Africa which bears her name. Aristaeus was a god of various kinds of husbandry, including bee-keeping, and of hunting. He fell in love with *Eurydice, who while trying to escape from him trod on a serpent and died from its bite. The *dryads avenged her by killing all his bees. According to Virgil (*Georgics* 4.315), after this calamity Aristaeus, on his mother's advice, consulted the god Proteus, appeased the dryads and obtained new swarms from the carcasses of bulls. Aristaeus married Autonoe, daughter of Cadmus, and became the father of *Actaeon.

**Aristagoras** Deputy tyrant of Miletus during the absence of his kinsman the tyrant Histiaeus, both Greeks but loyal to Persia. For his own purposes he instigated the Ionian revolt against Persia in 499 BC. *See* PERSIAN WARS.

**Arista'rchus 1.** (of Samos, b. *c*.320 BC) An astronomer, famous for hypothesizing that the earth revolves about the sun, and that it rotates about its own axis. His only extant treatise, however, presupposes a geocentric universe. He is dated by his observation of the summer solstice in 280 BC.

**2.** (of Samothrace, *c*.215–143 BC) Head of the *Alexandrian Library from *c*.153 BC until he left

Alexandria for Cyprus *c.*145 BC. In scholarship he continued the tradition begun by *Aristophanes of Byzantium and was the first scholar to write numerous commentaries on classical Greek texts as well as the first to write about prose authors. He also produced treatises on particular topics, especially Greek grammar, scraps of which still survive in the ancient notes on classical authors which are found in some manuscripts (*see* SCHOLIUM). His most notable contribution to scholarship was his critical edition of Homer, followed by his editions of, or commentaries on, Hesiod, Archilochus, Alcaeus, Anacreon, and Pindar, the tragedians, and Aristophanes, and among prose writers, Herodotus. He adopted the admirable practice of interpreting a poet by the poet's own usage—'explaining Homer by Homer'—and avoided allegorical interpretation. His editions were accompanied by a full apparatus of critical signs (*see* TEXTS, TRANSMISSION OF ANCIENT 1).

**Ari'steas** (of Proconnesus, an island in the Propontis) A largely legendary Greek traveller of early times whom Herodotus knew as a performer of shamanistic feats and the author of a hexameter poem *Arimaspeia*. It told how, inspired by Apollo whose cult he promoted, he travelled among peoples in the far north beyond the Black Sea, including the fabulous Arimaspians. The poem was subsequently regarded as a source of geographical and historical information. Scanty fragments survive which are purported to come from it. *Cf.* ANACHARSIS.

**Aristei'dēs 1.** (d. *c.*467 BC) Athenian politician known as 'the Just', a cousin of *Callias. He was famous for his incorruptibility, moderation, and poverty, and was popularly contrasted with the opportunistic *Themistocles. He was said, perhaps wrongly, to have been a *strategos* at the battle of Marathon in 490 BC and was *archon in 489/8. He came into conflict with Themistocles when the latter rose to power, and as a consequence was ostracized in 482. According to a story told by Plutarch, who wrote his Life, an illiterate citizen requested the unrecognized Aristeides to write his name on a voting shard in favour of the ostracism; on being asked what harm Aristeides had ever done him, he replied, none, he did not even know the man, but he was sick of hearing him always called 'the Just'. Aristeides returned

from exile in 480, in the general amnesty issued under the Persian threat; he held a command at Salamis, and led the Athenian contingent at Plataea (for an anecdote *see* NYMPHS). After the Persian Wars he helped Themistocles get the Athenian city walls built without the Spartans finding out. His final achievement was in the apportionment of tribute by the *Delian League, when he fixed each member's contribution, a task entrusted to him on account of his justice and discretion. He was remembered as an Athenian patriot; a Life of him by Nepos survives as well as that by Plutarch.

**2. Aristeides, Publius Aelius** (AD 117–89) Greek rhetorician of the *Second Sophistic. Born in Mysia, he was educated at Pergamum and Athens, and spent most of his life in the intervals of illness writing and lecturing in Asia Minor. On a visit to Rome at the age of 26 he was struck down by an illness from which he suffered for the rest of his life. He sought a cure in the temple of *Asclepius at Pergamum, and left accounts ('Sacred discourses', *Hieroi logoi*) of instructions given to him in *dreams by Asclepius and of his own experiences in carrying them out. These are of great importance as a first-hand report of religious experience in the pagan world, and valuable as evidence for the practice of incubation. He left behind him a large body of work of various kinds, essays, addresses on public and private occasions, declamations on historical themes, and prose hymns to various gods. Fifty-five of his compositions are extant. His wide knowledge of ancient Greek literature, evident throughout his work, has made him an important figure in the transmission of the Greek heritage to later generations. His public address *To Rome* is an eloquent encomium on the Roman achievement; the comparable *Panathenaic Oration* on Athens gives a summary history of that city in the classical period. Two interesting polemical pieces on rhetoric and politics aim to answer Plato's criticisms of these in the *Gorgias*. He was known to the physician *Galen, who cited him as an example of one whose power of oratory had 'caused his whole body to waste away'.

**Aristi'ppus** (of Cyrene) A pupil (so-called) of Socrates, and allegedly the first of his associates to charge a fee for teaching. His writings, said to include dialogues, are entirely lost. *See* CYRENAIC SCHOOL.

**aristocracy** The Greek word *aristocratia* means 'rule of the best-born', and is not attested in Greek until the fifth century BC. The term is used in modern studies of early Greece to describe the governments of states by the noble families who had emerged from the *Dark age (i) with most land and political power. At Athens these were the *Eupatridae. They governed the state through a council (*see* AREOPAGUS) whose authority was diminished by the reforms of *Solon. Aristocracy in Greece often differed little from *oligarchy, and for a long time aristocratic families dominated political life. Sparta and Thessaly remained strongly aristocratic throughout the classical period. The poems of *Theognis (of Megara) show the views of an aristocrat alarmed by the effect of wealth in disturbing the old social and political order, while the odes of the Theban poet Pindar reflect some of the ideals of the aristocratic life. *See also* SYMPOSIUM. For aristocracy at Rome *see* ROMAN REPUBLIC and ORDERS.

**Aristodē'mus 1.** Legendary Messenian hero of the First Messenian War against Sparta (see MESSENIA). He killed his daughter in consequence of an oracle which said that the sacrifice of a maiden would ensure the preservation of Messenia. He became king and was at first victorious over the Lacedaemonians, but later, despairing of ultimate success, committed suicide over his daughter's grave.
**2.** The only one of *Leonidas' 300 Spartans to return home after the battle of Thermopylae (480 BC), having missed the fighting through sickness. He was disfranchised, and according to Herodotus (7.230), 'no man would give him a light for his fire or speak to him; he was called Aristodemus the coward'. At the battle of Plataea in the following year he redeemed himself by fighting recklessly to the death.

**Aristogei'ton** *See* HARMODIUS.

**Aristo'menēs** Legendary Messenian hero of the Second Messenian War against Sparta (perhaps *c.*650 BC), who was eventually defeated. *See* MESSENIA.

**Aristo'phanēs 1.** (b. between 460 and 450, d. *c.*386 BC) Athenian comic poet, writer of Old Attic Comedy (*see* COMEDY [Greek 3]). Virtually nothing is known of his life. Clearly he started his career early, and he feuded with Cleon from 426. He is confident enough to blame the Athenians for not appreciating the first version of *Clouds* (below), and in *Peace* (739–53) he professes to try to refine the coarse nature of Old Comedy. Using the chorus as his mouthpiece in the *parabases he claims to speak on behalf of the *city, although the citizen body as a whole is sometimes made to feel his lash. He describes his art as *trygōidia*, a coinage much discussed in antiquity and later, which seems to combine the words for 'tragedy' and 'wine-lees', perhaps indicating that a serious message underlies the buffoonery. He may have seen himself as writing in the spirit of *Solon, a poet with a serious political purpose. Eleven of his plays survive; we also have some 32 titles and many fragments. His plays may be dated as follows:

427   *Daitaleis* ('Banqueters', people of an imaginary deme of that name), now lost. Fragments of two speeches survive. The play won second prize in the dramatic competitions.

426   *Babylonians*, produced at the *Dionysia, now lost. Afterwards Aristophanes was apparently prosecuted by Cleon for ridiculing the magistrates 'in the presence of foreigners' (the audience at the City Dionysia would include visitors from abroad). No penalty seems to have been imposed.

425   *Acharnians*, produced at the *Lenaea, the first of his surviving comedies; it won first prize.

(These three plays were not produced by Aristophanes, but by a certain Callistratus, who may have been another comic poet; the reason is not known for certain, but it may have been that Aristophanes was under the customary age.)

424   *Knights* (Lenaea, first prize).
423   *Clouds* (Dionysia), ridiculing Socrates and the new learning. It won third prize (i.e. came last). It was rewritten by Aristophanes in the form we now have; we know that he substituted two scenes showing hostility to the new school. This second edition was not produced at either of the great festivals.
422   *Wasps* (Lenaea, second prize).
421   *Peace* (Dionysia, second prize).
414   *Birds* (Dionysia, second prize).
411   *Lysistrata*, produced by Callistratus, and *Thesmophoriazusae* (probably at the Lenaea and Dionysia respectively).

405   *Frogs* (Lenaea, first prize).
392   (probably) *Ecclesiazusae.*
388   *Plutus*, the second play of this name.
        The first, which has not survived, was
        produced in 408.

After these, Aristophanes wrote two comedies
which he gave to his son Araros to produce, but
which are now lost. One of them, *Kokalos*, we
are told started the type of New Comedy (*see*
COMEDY [Greek 6]), introducing romantic features which are characteristic of the plays of
Menander. Aristophanes' plays down to 421
show him as the chief representative of Old
Comedy, but from the *Birds* onwards he introduced significant changes in its structure.

Aristophanes' language is colourful and
imaginative, his lyric poetry subtle and varied
in tone. His subject matter is rooted in the
issues of the day at Athens, especially the Peloponnesian War. His humour lies largely
in exaggeration, parody, and satire, directed
against new movements in thought or
culture, and against prominent men who are
suitable for this treatment (in the spirit of invective)—the fawning politician Cleon, the useless
intellectual Socrates, the tragedian Euripides
with his ridiculous affectations. No group or
class is exempt, and as a result it is notoriously
difficult to decide what moral or political lesson,
if any, we are meant to derive from a play. The
sympathetic characters are in the main people
who wish to be left alone to enjoy their private
lives in a conventional way, untroubled by wars
and politicians, cultural change and intellectuals. They themselves, however, are often narrowly self-seeking, and no final decision is
made as to who, or which cause, is 'right'.
Plato in his *Symposium* represents Aristophanes as an agreeable and convivial drink-
ing-companion, happy in Socrates' company,
and puts in his mouth an amusing, original,
and insightful encomium of love. This is perhaps the light in which to regard much of his
work. The tenor of his plays does not appear in
fact to have affected the course of political
events: Cleon was elected *strategos* shortly
after Aristophanes won a prize for *Knights*, in
which he is pilloried.

**2. Aristophanes of Byzantium** Head of the
*Alexandrian Library *c.*194 BC. He was a scholar
of wide learning, the teacher of *Aristarchus,
who continued along the lines laid down by his
master. Aristophanes made critical editions
of several Greek poets, including Homer,

Hesiod's *Theogony*, Alcaeus, Alcman, Pindar,
and Aristophanes (1). He is said to have invented or regularized Greek *accents; and he
devised a set of critical signs to indicate passages in manuscripts suspected of being interpolations or otherwise noteworthy; *see* TEXTS,
TRANSMISSION OF ANCIENT 1 and CANONS.

**A'ristotle (Aristotelēs)** (384–322 BC) Greek
philosopher.

**1. Life.** Aristotle was born at Stageira in Chal-
cidicē, the son of Nicomachus, physician to
Amyntas II (father of Philip II), king of Macedon.
In 367 he came to Athens, and for the next twenty
years was a pupil of Plato, whose influence is
evident in all his work. After Plato's death in
347 he left Athens, perhaps for political reasons.
In the same year, his home town of Stageira
having been destroyed by the then king of Macedon, Philip II, Aristotle settled at Assos in the
Troad, where there was a small colony of philosophers from the *Academy. These were supported by Hermeias, the enlightened tyrant of
the neighbouring city of Atarneus, to whom Aristotle later wrote a poem of praise and whose
niece, Pythias, he married. He remained there
for three years, probably lecturing and writing,
until the philosophers were driven out after the
murder of Hermeias. Aristotle retreated to Mytilene in Lesbos (where he met *Theophrastus),
teaching there until 343/2. It was during his stay
at Assos and Mytilene that he conducted many of
his zoological researches. At the end of that time
he was invited by Philip to be tutor to his 13-year-
old son *Alexander (the Great). His teaching of
Alexander was probably mainly in Homer and
the dramatists (he was said to have prepared for
his pupil an edition of the *Iliad*), but the need for
some political education may have stimulated
Aristotle's own interest in politics (a lost work is
entitled 'Alexander, or On Colonization').

In 335, when Alexander had succeeded to
the throne and started on his expedition to
Asia, Aristotle returned to Athens and taught
there in a *gymnasium built in a grove sacred
to Apollo Lykeios and known (in the Latin form
of the name) as the Lyceum. Here he was said
to have lectured to his pupils in the morning
and the general public in the evening. The kind
of philosophy he and his successors taught
came to be known as the *Peripatetic, perhaps
owing its name to the covered court (*peripatos*)
or shady walks (*peripatoi*) where the students
strolled up and down. (Aristotle is said to have
called a lecture a *peripatos*. One source says

that Plato always walked about while teaching and his pupils adopted the same style.) Scholarly research of all kinds was carried on, literary, scientific, and philosophical. Aristotle collected manuscripts and maps, and formed the first considerable library of antiquity as well as a museum of natural objects. At some time during this period Pythias died; they had one daughter. Aristotle lived afterwards with a slave woman Herpyllis, by whom he had a son Nicomachus. After the death of Alexander in 323 it was probably anti-Macedonian feeling which forced Aristotle, who had obvious Macedonian connections, to entrust his students to Theophrastus and leave Athens. He said he was going away so as not to let the Athenians 'sin twice against philosophy' (the first time being the execution of Socrates). He died the following year at Chalcis in Euboea, of a digestive illness. His will, reproduced by *Diogenes Laertius, shows him as generous and thoughtful.

**2. The fate of his works in antiquity.** Aristotle left his books and manuscripts to Theophrastus, his associate and successor as head of the Lyceum. Only about a fifth has survived, but it is a considerable and representative sample. Some of his work became well known at the Lyceum and in the intellectual milieu of Alexandria. In the first century BC Cicero among others in Rome read and admired a number of published works (sometimes called 'exoteric', i.e. 'for the outside public') which are now lost. They were written in a fluent style for the general reader and were perhaps Platonic in their basic assumptions. Of the works we still have, the story, with variations, is that Theophrastus (d. 287) left the then unpublished manuscripts to a certain Neleus of Scepsis, whose heirs hid them in a cellar. Eventually they were sold to a certain Apellicon early in the first century BC and taken to Athens, whence Sulla shipped them to Rome as part of his war-booty after the Mithridatic War (89–85 BC). There they were edited, perhaps by Andronicus of Rhodes with other Peripatetic scholars, and their work is the basis of all our surviving manuscripts of Aristotle both in Greek and in other languages. Most of the works that were considered genuine and edited we still possess, surviving in manuscripts from the ninth century AD onwards. This edition was circulated and closely studied and commented upon, on the grounds that these works were more profound and original than the books already published; as a consequence the latter ceased to be read and were eventually lost.

There have been many investigations into the nature and origin of these surviving works, and the general agreement is that they are lectures written out by Aristotle himself, although the titles and some introductory and concluding material may be by later editors, and were never intended to be read as books. There are also editorial problems: some passages seem to be in note form only, others need to be transposed, some discussions occur in more than one place, and so on.

**3. The lost works.** The lost works of Aristotle fall into two classes:

(i) The early popular works of philosophy, mostly in dialogue form, which were published by Aristotle himself and of which only fragments preserved by quotation in later writers now survive. These include the *Protrepticus* ('Exhortation to philosophy') which served as a model for Cicero's *Hortensius*, itself now lost. These works were perhaps Platonic in their general assumptions.

(ii) Large collections of historical and scientific facts, made by Aristotle sometimes in co-operation with others and now mostly lost. They included lists of the victors at the Olympian and Pythian games (*see* CALENDARS) and the *didascaliae* (records of the dramatic performances at Athens), traces of which remain in our scholia to the extant Greek plays. The only work from this class to have survived almost entire is the *Athenaiōn politeia*, 'Constitution of the Athenians', the first in a collection of 158 such accounts of the constitutions of the Greek states, recovered from an Egyptian papyrus in 1890. Some believe it to be the work of a pupil.

**4. The surviving works.** Mostly philosophical and scientific, the surviving works comprise the following (the Latin titles are retained where they are commonly used):

(i) On logic: *Categories* (i.e. 'Predicates'); *De interpretatione* ('On interpretation'); *Prior Analytics* and *Posterior Analytics*; *Topics* (i.e. 'Forms of argument'); *De sophisticis elenchis* ('Refutations in the manner of the sophists'; *see* SOPHISTICI ELENCHI). In later times these six works came to be called the *Organon* ('Tool' or 'Instrument').

(ii) *Metaphysics*, a mixture of treatises or lecture notes from different periods, put together by Andronicus of Rhodes (2 above) and called by him *Metaphysica* because in his edition they came 'after the Physics' (Gk. *meta ta physika*).

(iii) On natural science: *Physica* (*'Physics'); *De caelo* ('On the heavens'), on the movement of terrestrial and celestial bodies; *Meteorologica* (*'Meteorology').

(iv) On biology: *De generatione et corruptione* ('On coming-into-being and passing-away'); *Historia animalium* ('Inquiry into animals', sometimes referred to as 'The history of animals'); *De partibus animalium* ('On the parts of animals'); *De motu animalium* ('On the movement of animals'); *De incessu animalium* ('On the progression of animals'); *De generatione animalium* ('On animal reproduction'). *See* ANIMALS, ARISTOTLE ON.

(v) Philosophy of mind: *De anima* ('On the soul'), a treatise in three books on the proposition that soul and body relate to each other as form to matter; *Parva naturalia* ('Short works on nature'), on such topics as sense perception, memory, and dreaming.

(vi) On ethics and politics: *Eudemian Ethics* (*see* NICOMACHEAN ETHICS); *Nicomachean Ethics*; *Politics*.

(vii) On rhetoric and poetry: *Rhetoric* and *Poetics*. Aristotle argues, against Plato, that rhetoric, which is persuasion through speech, can be a systematic branch of learning. For the Greeks rhetoric and the study of literature were closely connected. Both the *Rhetoric* and the *Poetics* include many ethical topics as well as touching upon the emotions.

Throughout his work Aristotle shows the strong influence of Plato even when, as often, he disagrees with him (as in the *Rhetoric* and *Poetics*). In principle, however, they were in agreement. Both believed that the acquisition of knowledge is a process which must be systematic and unified, and that it was structured by logic (which Plato thought of as *dialectic). Aristotle was familiar with mathematics but not a professional, and did not pretend to have advanced the subject. Undogmatic, he was an outwardly conventional polytheist, but it is clear that though there were 'gods' of a sort in his universe they were remote and impersonal abstractions, like the Unmoved Mover which is outside the universe and which imparts change to other things without changing itself.

**5. The influence of Aristotle.** The influence that Aristotle exerted on later generations of philosophers and scientists has been immense, by the stimulus he gave, by the instruments of investigation which he invented, and by his actual contributions to knowledge. The extraordinarily wide range of his learning inaugurated a beneficial tradition of universal knowledge. In western Europe in the early Middle Ages, down to about AD 1200, it was mainly his writings on logic (the *Organon*), and not all of these, that were known and studied and that imposed a structure of thought upon posterity. His writings on other areas of philosophy and on science, however, followed a different path. From about AD 800 onwards they were translated and expounded by the Arabs, first in the East and then, as a result of the Arab conquest (*see* ARABIA), in Spain. The Arab versions were then retranslated into Latin and these Latin texts made their way from Spain into the rest of Europe, where they had previously been unknown, at the beginning of the thirteenth century. At first the study of these new writings was prohibited, but they soon became the basis of a Christian philosophy which was a fusion of theology and Aristotelianism.

When at the end of the thirteenth century the Latin translations from Arabic were superseded by more accurate translations made directly from the Greek, Aristotle's authority in science and philosophy was absolute. It was particularly unfortunate that *astronomy, which, with alchemy, made up the entire scientific interest of the Middle Ages, was one subject in which Aristotle was influential but went astray: he believed the earth to be a stationary sphere and the universe geocentric (*see* EUDOXUS). Dante and Chaucer, for example, who both had a considerable knowledge of astronomy, exhibit the Aristotelian view. When Galileo (1564-1642) disputed the truth of it, it was against a very Aristotelian Christianity that he was offending. Galileo's English contemporary Francis Bacon (1561-1626), though contemptuous of the ancient philosophers in general, adopts Aristotle's division of the four causes as expounded in the *Physics*, and entitles part of his own work in Latin the *Novum organum* ('The new tool'). We still use concepts which Aristotle first introduced—genera and species, universal and particular, premiss and conclusion, subject and attribute, potentiality and actuality; there are many more. Even in the sphere of literature, his *Poetics* was regarded as an authority from Elizabethan days onward. In some areas of biology and in logic his work was not superseded until the early twentieth century. In philosophy he is still read as a current practitioner.

**Aristo'xenus** (of Tarentum, b. *c.*370 BC) Philosopher and especially a musical theorist, famous for his work on harmonics and on rhythmics. He studied under the Pythagoreans before becoming a pupil of Aristotle, who passed him over for headship of the *Lyceum in favour of Theophrastus. Substantial parts survive of three books of a treatise on musical scales known as *Elementa harmonica* ('Elements of harmonics'). The Pythagoreans had studied the mathematical relations of notes as physical variables. Aristoxenus regarded notes rather as points along a continuum perceptible to the ear. In his view the aim of the science of harmonics is to identify the components of melody and to investigate the principles governing their relationships, for only in this way can distinctions between melodic and unmelodic sequences be understood. This work was a strong influence for many centuries. Part of book 2 of a work known as *Elementa rhythmica* ('Elements of rhythmics') also survives, in which rhythm is regarded as a temporal structure imposed upon melody, and not inherent to it. Aristoxenus defines the rhythmic elements partly in terms of the ratio between *arsis ('upbeat') and *thesis ('downbeat').

Aristoxenus wrote biographies of at least four philosophers, Pythagoras, Archytas, Socrates, and Plato, the first two much used by later scholars. Though he regarded the Pythagoreans with favour, having originally been one himself, his views of Plato and especially Socrates are notably hostile. He was influential in his expressed preference for the pure styles of Greek music of the fifth century BC over later developments.

**Arminius** (b. *c.*19 BC) German war-chief who had previously served in the Roman auxiliary forces and had citizenship. In AD 9 he annihilated three Roman legions under *Varus, who had trusted him, and thwarted further Roman expansion in Germany in the following years. The historian Tacitus acknowledged that he preserved German freedom. In AD 19 he was killed by his own people.

**Arpi'num** Town in Latium, the birthplace of Marius and Cicero.

**arrhe'phoroi** ('basket carriers') In Greece, two or four girls between the ages of 7 and 11 chosen by the *archon basileus to serve the goddess Athena Polias and who took part in the Athenian festival of the Arrhephoria. Their task was to help in the weaving of the robe, *peplos*, offered to Athena at the *Panathenaea. As part of the rite of the Arrhephoria they carried on their heads covered baskets, containing unknown objects, to the shrine of 'Aphrodite in the Gardens', returning with other objects similarly unknown.

**A'rria 1.** The Elder, wife of the Roman A. Caecina Paetus. When her husband was condemned to death by the emperor Claudius in AD 42, she 'taught her husband how to die', stabbing herself and handing him the dagger with the words *Paete, non dolet* ('It doesn't hurt, Paetus').

**2.** The Younger, daughter of the above and wife of *Thrasea, a Stoic philosopher put to death by Nero in AD 66.

**A'rrian (Lucius Flavius Arrianus)** (*c.*AD 86–160) Outstanding Greek historian of Alexander the Great who modelled himself on Xenophon. He came from Nicomedia in Bithynia and studied philosophy in Greece with the Stoic *Epictetus, whose oral teachings he later published verbatim (allegedly having taken them down in shorthand) as *Diatribai*, 'Discourses'. Four books of these survive from an original eight, together with a summary, the *Encheiridion*, 'Manual'. While in Greece he attracted the notice of the emperor Hadrian who appointed him to the Roman senate. After holding office as *consul suffectus* he was appointed legate (governor) of Cappadocia (131–7). He retired to Athens, where he was archon in 145/6, and may have lived to see Marcus Aurelius become emperor (161). In his *Cynegeticus* ('The hunting man'), which aims to bring up to date Xenophon's treatise of the same name, he gives an engaging account of his own hare-coursing bitch Hormē ('Dash'), a hound of a breed unknown to Xenophon. He took more pleasure in the chase than in the kill. Other minor works which still survive are the *Periplous*, 'Circumnavigation' (of the Black Sea), *Tactica*, 'Essay on tactics', and 'The order of battle against the Alans', describing in the style of Xenophon's *Cyropaedia* Arrian's own tactics in 135 when he repelled the Alans, a tribe from north of the Black Sea who had invaded Cappadocia. His most important works concerned the life and times of

Alexander. 'The events after Alexander', covering the period after Alexander's death, 323–319 BC, survives only in fragments, but the *Anabasis* ['Expedition up-country', i.e. the campaigns] *of Alexander* in seven books survives in its entirety and is the author's masterpiece. It is completed by a short work, the *Indica*, describing India and Indian customs and recounting the voyage of *Nearchus from the Indus through the Persian Gulf to the Tigris, in order to join Alexander at Susa. In his opening sentence Arrian names his sources with a frankness rare among ancient historians: *Ptolemy (1) and a certain Thrasybulus; if they disagree he chooses the one who seems more reliable. On the whole these accounts were favourable to Alexander, and some stories were chosen for their entertaining detail. The result is a highly readable work in a simple and attractive style, but one in which the details cannot wholly be relied upon for accuracy.

**Arsacids** The royal dynasty of Parthia *c.*250 BC–*c.*AD 230.

**Ars amatō'ria** ('Treatise on love') A poem in three books of elegiacs by the Roman poet *Ovid. It is a mock-didactic poem on the art of seduction, its lack of serious purpose indicated by the rejection of the usual metre for *didactic poetry, the hexameter, in favour of the metre of love-poetry, *elegiac couplets. The first two books, written in about 1 BC, consist of instructions to men, although women are also addressed as readers; the third, presented as a sequel, advises women on how to entrap men, though the interests of men seem uppermost in the poet's mind. The social setting is the Rome of Ovid's own day, giving the reader glimpses of city life and manners—the circus, the theatre, the banquet. The poem was very popular: quotations from it have been found on the walls of Pompeii. With its sophisticated and knowing humour and its apparently cynical and frivolous attitude to sex wholly divorced from marriage it seems likely that it was the *carmen* ('poem') cited as one reason why the emperor Augustus subsequently banished the poet.

**Arsi'noë 1.** The name of several princesses among the ruling *Ptolemies of Egypt (who were of Macedonian descent). The most important was Arsinoe II (*c.*316–270 BC), daughter of Ptolemy I and Berenice, who married first Lysimachus, one of the generals and successors of Alexander the Great, and secondly after his death her half-brother Ptolemy Ceraunus.

Thirdly she married her brother Ptolemy II Philadelphus, thus becoming queen of Egypt. Her influence contributed to the brilliance of court life and the dynastic cult they introduced strengthened the monarchy. She and her husband were both deified in their lifetime. Her death was lamented in an elegy by Callimachus.

**2.** Greek settlement founded by Ptolemy II, and named for his sister-wife (1) above, in the Faiyum, an oasis some 80km (50 miles) south of Cairo in Egypt which was renamed the Arsinoite nome. Extensive ruins survive. It was the first source in modern times of papyri of Greek texts (*see* PAPYROLOGY).

**arsis** In metric, the up (or weak) beat. The metrical foot was divided between *arsis* (sometimes known as *anacrusis*) and *thesis*, the down (strong) beat. The terms are often confused and used in the opposite of these (original) senses.

**Ars poe'tica** The title by which *Horace's poetic *Epistle to the Pisos* has been known since Quintilian (*see* EPISTLES). The poem takes the form of a letter of advice on the pursuit of literature, addressed to a father and two sons whose identity is as uncertain (*see* PISO (2)), as is the date of composition: perhaps about 19 BC, after the composition of *Odes* books 1–3. It is in the tradition of Aristotle's *Poetics* and *Rhetoric*, though it does not make use of either. Its content is as follows.

*Lines 1–44:* a poem should be unified; a poet should avoid extremes and keep within the bounds of his competence;

*45–118:* a discussion of poetic vocabulary and appropriateness in style;

*119–52:* the choice of material and how to treat it, with examples from drama and Homer;

*153–294:* the rules governing drama; characters, action on stage, the rule of the Three Actors, the chorus, music, the satyr plays; metre and the history of Greek tragedy and comedy;

*295–476:* general rules and observations on writing poetry.

The purpose of the *Ars poetica* in the form Horace gave it has always puzzled critics. As a treatise, far from being systematic, it is impressionistic, allusive, and apparently expressed from Horace's personal viewpoint. Transitions from one subject to another are abrupt and the arrangement seems haphazard. Secondly, its concentration on epic and drama seems irrelevant to the contemporary Roman literary scene. An ancient commentator said that Horace selected his material from the similar treatise of Neoptolemus of Parium, a Hellenistic Greek writer of the third century BC, but the structure of the *Ars poetica* and Horace's practice elsewhere suggest rather that he used no one Greek source but selected from among several sources those precepts which agreed with his own views on poetic style and were suitable for imaginative poetic treatment.

The lively autobiographical approach of the *Ars poetica* and its expression of personal standards in literature make it unique as a work of criticism in the ancient world. Many of its apt phrases, the 'ridiculous mouse' (*ridiculus mus*) of bathos, 'in the middle of things' (*in medias res*) of an abrupt beginning, the 'purple patch' (*purpureus pannus*), and the reference to 'Homer nodding' (*dormitat Homerus*), have passed into common literary parlance. It exercised a great influence in later ages on European literature, notably on French drama through Nicholas Boileau's *L'Art poétique* (1674), written in imitation. It was translated into English (1640) by Ben Jonson.

**art, attitudes to** The Greeks had no general word for 'art' or 'artist' as in modern usage. They used the words *technē* and *technikos*, in the general sense of 'skilled craft' and 'skilled craftsman', or where appropriate the specific terms 'painter', 'statuary' etc. in the same way as they would 'potter' or 'shoemaker'. Those who produced art objects were viewed primarily as craftsmen. On the other hand outstanding practitioners of their craft were recognized as such and often became rich and prominent in society—artists such as the sculptors *Pheidias and Polycleitus in fifth-century Athens and the painters *Parrhasius and *Zeuxis. As early as the seventh century BC potters and painters began to sign their names on vases and in the sixth and early fifth century BC signatures on Attic vases became fairly common, though later they became rather rare. This may suggest a sense on the part of some practitioners that their names conferred an artistic value on their products.

Art in the classical Greek world was mostly public, either religious—cult images for example—or politically commemorative, in funerary monuments or paintings of famous battles. Private art fell mostly in the category of painted vases or jewellery, or perhaps even terracotta

statuettes such as those of Silenus described in Plato's *Symposium* (but unknown to archaeology). However, Plutarch's story about the efforts of Alcibiades to get his house decoratively painted suggests that wall-paintings were valued by the rich in fifth-century Athens. Certainly sculpture and painting entered the sphere of private art in the Hellenistic period.

In Rome, private patronage of the arts by the rich was much commoner than in classical Greece, undoubtedly stimulated by the huge amount of Greek sculpture and paintings captured by the Romans in the third and second centuries BC. To satisfy demand Greek artists even migrated to Rome in the late republic, thus helping to create an art-world with collectors and dealers and the first public art galleries. Public paintings and sculptures recorded important ceremonies and military successes (*see* ARA PACIS and TRAJAN). Rome made a significant contribution to the scope of art in portraiture which had been largely ignored by the Greeks except in the case of images (somewhat standardized) of important public figures—Pericles, Socrates, etc. By the time of the early empire it was commonplace for ordinary citizens to commission portraits of themselves which, when they survive, strike us at least as touchingly individual.

*See also* AESTHETICS and PLATO.

**Artaphe'rnēs 1.** Brother of Darius I, king of Persia. He took a leading part in suppressing the Ionian Revolt against Persia in 499 BC (*see* PERSIAN WARS).

**2.** Son of (1), who with Datis commanded the Persian expedition which was defeated at the battle of Marathon in 490 BC.

**Artaxe'rxēs** The name of several Persian kings of the fifth and fourth centuries BC.

**Artemidō'rus** (late second century AD) Author of the only surviving ancient Greek dream-book, *Oneirocritica* ('Interpretation of dreams'). He called himself 'of Daldis' (in Lydia), whose chief deity Apollo, he believed, instigated his work on predictive dreams. It was influential in the Arab world and in Europe from the Renaissance onwards. *See* DIVINATION.

**A'rtemis** In Greek myth an important Olympian goddess, worshipped throughout Greece, the daughter of Zeus and *Leto and the elder twin sister of Apollo. For the myth of her birth *see* APOLLO. The etymology of her name is uncertain. She is a virgin and a huntress: one of her Greek titles is Elaphabolos, 'Shooter of deer'. But she is also a protector of wildlife and a bringer of fertility, and is sometimes represented in art flanked by animals (a style which may show that this aspect of her divinity had a Minoan origin; *see* BRITOMARTIS). She is concerned with women, particularly at their transition to married life and at childbirth and during child-rearing, and with men at hunting and in certain aspects of war. Her festival at Athens included sacrifices in thanksgiving for victory at Marathon. In the Trojan War she, like Apollo, is on the side of the Trojans (and is beaten by Hera with her own bow and sent away weeping). And she sends sudden death to women as Apollo does to men. In Euripides' *Iphigeneia in Tauris* the goddess Athena orders Orestes to take the statue of Artemis to Athens and erect it in a shrine he was to found at Halai in Attica.

Artemis has a fairly slight mythology. With Apollo she killed the children of *Niobe and it was she who demanded the sacrifice of *Iphigeneia. *See also* ACTAEON; CALLISTO; HIPPOLYTUS; ORION. In Attica she had important cults at Brauron and Munichia (or Munychia), where little girls took part in a ritual (perhaps to mark puberty) in which they 'acted' as bears. Other divinities were sometimes identified with Artemis when they shared similar features, such as the Greek moon-goddess *Selene, *Hecate, and *Eileithyia, who were all associated with childbirth and, in the case of Hecate, with young animals. The closest and most notable identification was with the Italian goddess *Diana, originally a moon-goddess. Her cult at Ephesus (*see* Acts 19) included Asiatic elements: her image in the temple showed her with a head surrounded by a mural crown and a body covered with breasts.

The most important of her cults in Sparta was that of Artemis Orthia, at which youths undergoing the Spartan military upbringing, *agoge, tried to steal cheese from the altar on pain of a beating if caught.

**Artemi'sia 1.** (early fifth century BC) Daughter of Lygdamis, ruler of a Carian kingdom which included Halicarnassus, and after his death regent of his kingdom. With five ships she accompanied Xerxes on his invasion of Greece in 480 (*see* PERSIAN WARS), and is said by Herodotus (himself from Halicarnassus) to have tried to persuade Xerxes not to fight at

Salamis, but fought bravely herself and sank a ship on her own side in order to escape. (Xerxes is reputed to have said, 'My men have become women and my women men!')

**2.** Sister and wife of *Mausolus of Caria in whose memory she built the Mausoleum at Halicarnassus *c.*353 BC. She instituted a rhetorical funeral competition in which the most famous rhetoricians of the age took part, including Isocrates (perhaps not the famous orator) and Theopompus, who won the prize.

**Artemi'sium, battle of** *See* PERSIAN WARS.

**artists of Dionysus** *See* DIONYSUS, ARTISTS OF.

**arval brethren (arval brothers, arval priests)** (Lat. *fratres arvales*) The most ancient college of priests in Rome, already in existence under the early republic but perhaps ceasing to function later until they were restored by the emperor Augustus. They were so called from performing rites for the fertility of the fields (*arvum*, a ploughed field). The legend of their origin was that the nurse of Romulus had twelve sons and when one died Romulus took his place, calling them all the 'arval brethren'. Many of their records survive in inscriptions. The college had twelve members chosen for life from the most distinguished senatorial families; from imperial times they seem to have included the reigning emperor. Their most important ceremony, which seems to have included an ancient leaping dance, took place in May in honour of the agricultural goddess Dea Dia, in a grove on the Via Campana 8km (5 miles) from Rome. The famous hymn of the priests, the *carmen arvale*, sung during the sacrifice to Dea Dia, has been preserved on an inscription of AD 218; it dates originally from before the fourth century BC and is the oldest surviving specimen of Latin poetry. Other surviving inscriptions recording vows and offerings they were required to make are incidentally important for the history of Latin script in Rome and also for the chronology of the empire, since many events in the house of the reigning emperor were commemorated by the priests. *Cf.* SALII.

**Arverni** An advanced Gallic people occupying modern Auvergne who for a long time fought the Aedui for the supremacy of Gaul. In 52 BC Vercingetorix, the son of a former

Arvernian king, led the Gallic revolt against Julius Caesar (*see* COMMENTARIES 1, book 7).

**arx** ('citadel') At Rome, the north-eastern of the two summits of the Capitoline hill (*see* CAPITOL), the citadel proper. The temple of *Juno Moneta was here, also an augur's observation post and the Tarpeian Rock (*see* TARPEIA).

**Asca'laphus** In Greek myth, the son of *Acheron who revealed that *Persephone while in the Underworld had eaten some pomegranate seeds, obliging her to remain there for part of each year. According to Ovid, Persephone turned him into an owl for his betrayal.

**Asca'nius** (sometimes known as **Iūlus**) In Roman legend, son of Aeneas and, according to Virgil in the *Aeneid* and the historian Livy, the Trojan princess Creusa. He accompanied his father to Italy after the fall of Troy and eventually became king of Lavinium, near where Aeneas first landed in Italy. Livy also mentions an alternative version in which his mother was the Italian princess *Lavinia. The *gens *Julia* at Rome claimed descent from him; and his alternative name Iulus was said to have been given because he killed Mezentius (but *see* AENEID, book 10) when his beard was first sprouting (Gk. *ioulos*).

**asceticism** [from Gk. *askēsis*, 'training', 'exercise'] For the Greeks the term was associated with the philosophical life, indicating the exercise of self-mastery. For aspects of asceticism in antiquity *see* SOCRATES; ANTISTHENES; CYNICS; STOICISM; SPARTA; GYMNOSOPHISTS; NEOPLATONISM; PLATO.

**Asclēpi'adēs** (of Samos, b. *c.*320 BC, also referred to as Sicelidas) One of the earliest writers of the Greek literary *epigram, and in particular of the love epigram, in the Hellenistic age. He was a contemporary of Philetas and Theocritus, and a strong influence on Callimachus. Many of his poems survive in the *Greek *Anthology*. He gave his name to the 'asclepiad' metres, which had been used earlier by Sappho and Alcaeus, because he revived them.

**Asclē'pius** (Lat. *Aesculapius) The Greek god of healing. Strictly speaking he was a hero (*see* HEROES), the son of the god Apollo (himself a healing god) by a mortal, Coronis, daughter of Phlegyas. According to myth Apollo killed Coronis for being unfaithful to him in

marrying the mortal Ischys. (Regretting it afterwards, he turned the crow which had told him of her infidelity from a white bird into a black.) However, he saved his unborn child Asclepius, and entrusted him to the care of the Centaur *Chiron. From him Asclepius learned the art of medicine. Homer in the *Iliad* represents Asclepius as the father of Machaon and Podaleirius, the doctors of the Greek army at the siege of Troy. For his death *see* ADMETUS.

By classical times Asclepius had overshadowed other healing gods and heroes and was widely worshipped as a god and the founder of medicine. The most famous seat of his cult was at Epidaurus, where his first sanctuary was built *c.*500 BC. From there lesser shrines were founded in other places, notably at Athens in 420 and at Rome in 293 BC (*see* AESCULAPIUS). There is a tradition that the poet Sophocles played a prominent part in establishing the Athenian cult on the west slope of the Acropolis. Many inscriptions found at Epidaurus and at Athens describe successful cures, achieved perhaps sometimes through faith but also through normal medical treatment. In historical times the Asclepiadae were a clan (*genos*) which practised medicine as a hereditary skill, tracing their descent from Asclepius and perhaps deriving their science partly from the priestly cult. They seem to have admitted to membership doctors from other families (*cf.* HOMERIDAE). Most shrines of Asclepius contained a sacred snake, and some, like Epidaurus, sacred dogs as well. In instituting new shrines a sacred snake was always taken from the temple at Epidaurus. In art Asclepius is often shown bearing a staff, which is usually entwined with a snake, and is sometimes accompanied by a dog. *See also* ARISTEIDES (2).

**Ascō'nius Pediā'nus, Quintus** (probably AD 3–76) Writer of historical commentaries on Cicero's speeches, of which five survive, including one, now lost, on Cicero's speech during his candidature for the consulship in 64. Since he is close in date to Cicero his evidence is valuable.

**Asia**
**1. The continent.** When the Ionians produced the first maps in the Greek world before 500 BC (*see* ANAXIMANDER) they divided the land mass of the world into two roughly equal parts, Europe in the north and north-west, and Asia including *Africa (Libya) to the south and south-east. By the time of Herodotus in the

fifth century BC they had separated Africa from Asia and set the boundaries of the latter (very roughly speaking) at the Indian Ocean in the south and the river Tanais (Don) in the north. Herodotus saw Asia Minor as a peninsula jutting into the Mediterranean Sea. Asia extended east as far as India, beyond which the earth was unknown and thought to be desert, with the river Oxus apparently marking its northern boundary. Not until the expedition of Alexander the Great towards the end of the fourth century BC did the Greeks have any detailed knowledge of the eastern regions of the continent. The conquest by the Romans of Asia Minor and Syria and their wars with Mithridates and the Parthians in the first century BC greatly increased knowledge not only of western Asia but more especially of the Caucasian north, a region of which the Greeks were almost totally ignorant. The Romans' taste for luxuries such as silk and spices led to their exploration of the ancient trade routes and even to contact with Chinese merchants.

**2. The Roman province.** When Attalus III of Pergamum died in 133 BC he bequeathed his kingdom to the Romans. It included all of Greek Asia Minor; its eastern boundary was a line from Bithynia in the north to Lycia in the south and it later included Phrygia. It was rich in natural resources and had flourishing agriculture, industry, and trade. As a consequence of the rapacity of capitalists and successive Roman governors, it was ready to join *Mithridates VI, king of Pontus, who, seeking to extend his territory, occupied most of Asia Minor in 88 BC. However, he was forced by the Roman general Sulla to make peace in 84 and to give up all his conquered territory. Sulla reorganized the province and its system of taxation, but it continued to suffer during the late republic from periodic exactions. With the principate of Augustus Asia became a senatorial province governed by a proconsul, and the provincials, feeling hopeful that their life would improve, enthusiastically embraced the *ruler cult. Asia was essentially made up of many city-states, some of which remained nominally free under Roman rule. Their rivalries prevented any real sense of provincial unity but individual city-states were often enriched by the pride of their citizens and new cities were created. Ephesus replaced the old Attalid capital Pergamum in importance. During the first two centuries AD Asia enjoyed great prosperity, re-

flected in the panegyrics of the orator *Aristeides, for example. The coastal cities retained a sophisticated Greek society with their wealthy rhetors and sophists (*see* SECOND SOPHISTIC). Those of the interior however became Hellenized only gradually, and always retained something of their non-Greek background. In this region early Christianity flourished and most of the region seems to have been converted by the end of the third century. In the fourth century when Constantinople became the capital of the eastern Roman empire, Asian traffic was inclined to stop there, no longer passing on to Greece and Italy as it had for centuries. Thus Asia was deprived of the western influences which over these centuries had helped to mould its complex character. Only Ephesus, Sardis, and Aphrodisias retained something of their former glory.

**Asia Minor** The peninsula in the extreme west of Asia that now forms the greater part of Turkey from the Aegean to the Euphrates. The west and south coastal areas were part of the Mediterranean and Hellenic world; the interior retained much of its indigenous Anatolian culture. It is a largely fertile country which was inhabited from earliest times by a variety of tribes from Asia and Europe, and in the second millennium BC was the centre of the Hittite empire. Greek tradition said that as a consequence of the *Dorian invasion into mainland Greece many of those now dispossessed emigrated to the coast of Asia Minor and there planted the Greek language and customs: the north was colonized by Aeolians who reputedly came from Thessaly and Boeotia (*see* AEOLIS); to the south of them were the Ionians, said to have come from Attica, who were to be more prominent in history and whose part of the coast was called *Ionia; further south again were Dorian colonies from the Peloponnese and Crete. The actuality however was much more complicated: the settlers were of more mixed origin and the colonization may have extended from the tenth to the seventh century BC. The settlements quickly prospered. City life developed, first under kings and then under oligarchies, and trade in the Aegean, around the Black Sea and in the interior of Asia Minor itself, created further prosperity. Folk memories of heroic life in Mycenaean Greece flowered into epic poetry (*see* HOMER), and scientific thinkers speculated about the nature of the physical universe on the supposition that some underlying principle could be discovered (for Ionian philosophers *see* PHILOSOPHY [Greek]). Perhaps these developments were in part due to the influence of the Asiatic peoples: over the centuries the Greeks adopted the Asiatic modes of music, introduced eastern myths into their religion (*see* e.g. CYBELE), and were strongly influenced by Asiatic art, astronomy and mathematics, and technology.

In the seventh and sixth centuries BC great political changes came about in Asia Minor. In 612 BC the empire of *Assyria had been overthrown by the Medes under Cyaxares. They advanced into eastern Asia Minor and clashed with Lydia. After a battle in 585 a frontier was established between the two kingdoms at the river Halys. Gyges, king of Lydia in the seventh century BC, had brought the Greek cities in Asia Minor under Lydian control and by the time of Croesus (d. 546 BC), the last Lydian king, most of them paid tribute to Lydia; but they still retained considerable freedom and their trade prospered, no doubt helped by their adoption of the west-Asian invention of coinage (*see* MONEY AND COINS 1). Both Lydia and Media, however, were to fall to a new empire, that of the Persians, who lived in the hilly area north-east of the Persian Gulf. In the mid-sixth century, under the leadership of Cyrus I they conquered in succession the Medes, the Lydians, and the Babylonians, and under Cyrus' son Cambyses they conquered Egypt. Asia Minor was absorbed into the Persian empire; the Greek cities had to pay tribute, supply troops, and appoint tyrants acceptable to Persia. When Darius I became king of the Persian empire in 521 BC the Greeks in Ionia became increasingly discontented for political and economic reasons and decided in 499 to revolt (*see* PERSIAN WARS). This revolt was finally crushed by the Persians in 494 but the Ionians were not entirely without success, for the Persians now set up democracies in the Greek cities. From this point the history of Greek Asia Minor becomes bound up with that of Greece proper. *See also* MILETUS.

**Asianism and Atticism** Asianism was the name given to the artificially mannered style of Greek oratory which developed among the Greek orators of Asia Minor in the period after Demosthenes (d. 322 BC); *see* ORATORY [Greek]. Atticism describes the reaction against it in favour of using only the style and vocabulary of late fifth-century Attic oratory. Contro-

versy developed, which is satirized by *Lucian (second century AD) in his work *Sigma versus Tau*, an imaginary law-suit in which the conservative Atticists try to restore 'ss', as in speech before the fourth century BC, to words which subsequently had 'tt'. The distinction came to be applied to Latin oratory also, and Cicero, with his Greek education and showy style, was criticized as 'Asian'. Latin literature of the Silver age (*see* LATIN LITERATURE, PERIODS OF (iii)) could be seen as 'Asian', but in the eastern empire the Atticizing orators prevailed. *See* LATIN LANGUAGE and SECOND SOPHISTIC.

***Asina'ria*** ('The she-ass') Farcical Roman comedy by *Plautus. It is adapted from the Greek comedy of the same name, *Onāgros* (or *Onagos*) of Demophilus (author and title are named in the prologue but are otherwise unknown).

Demaenetus, an indulgent father, wishes to help his son Argyrippus to save the prostitute Philaenium from an old procuress, but he is tyrannized by his wife Artemona, who keeps tight control of the purse-strings. By a trick of one of his slaves he gets possession of twenty minae which were to be paid to Artemona's steward for some asses which have been sold (whence the name of the play), and father and son spend the evening banqueting with Philaenium. But a rival for the girl's favours, furious at finding himself anticipated, warns Artemona; she descends on the party, and with dire threats removes her husband.

The saying 'man is a wolf to man' (*homo homini lupus*) is taken from the play (1.495).

**Aspā'sia** (of Miletus, late 470s–*c*.400 BC, daughter of Axiochus) Mistress of the Athenian statesman *Pericles after he divorced his wife and one of the most talked-about women in Athens. It is not known what brought her to the city. The relationship began *c*.445 BC and continued until his death in 429. They had one son, also called Pericles, who was legitimated by decree after the death in the plague of 430 of Pericles' two sons by his wife. Aspasia became a natural target for the comic poets, who depicted her as Pericles' whore. Aristophanes in the *Acharnians* (425 BC) alleges (not very seriously) that one cause of the Peloponnesian War had been some Megarians' theft of two prostitutes from Aspasia (implying that she procured women for the lustful Pericles). She also had the reputation of having considerable intellectual ability. Plato in his *Menexenus* makes Socrates claim that she was his and Pericles' tutor in rhetoric, and Xenophon quotes her marital advice with approval. After Pericles' death Aspasia married the democratic leader and Athenian general Lysicles, who was killed fighting in 428. (This legal marriage to a citizen indicates that she was free-born.) Nothing is known of her later life.

**Asphodel, Plain of** In Homer's *Odyssey*, the place in the Underworld (*see* HADES) where all the dead dwell, leading a shadowy continuance of their former life in the world. The asphodel (whence 'daffodil') is a flowering plant of the lily family; in Hesiod it is given as an example of the cheapest and plainest food.

*Aspis* ('The shield') Greek comedy by *Menander, the first half of which has been recovered on a papyrus.

One of three brothers has died, leaving a son and daughter. The son Cleostratus goes off to the wars, leaving his sister under the protection of their uncle Chaerestratus. Cleostratus is reported dead, leaving his property to his sister. By Greek law the closest male relative of an heiress (within the permitted degree) was entitled to marry her. Chaerestratus was already planning to marry the girl to his stepson, but now his brother Smicrines tries to marry her for her money. A plot is laid to trick Smicrines into offering marriage to Chaerestratus' daughter instead, but Cleostratus, alive after all, returns. The play probably ended with the marriages of the cousins and the discomfiture of Smicrines.

The play is enlivened by the resourceful slave Daos who engineers the deception and must be typical of many such slaves who appeared in other plays of Menander, but are now known chiefly from Roman comedy.

**Assa'racus** Great-grandfather of Aeneas (for genealogy *see* TROS).

**assembly** (political) In Greece, *see* ECCLESIA. At Rome citizen assemblies, *comitia*, met in the *Comitium*, an area north of the Forum, or in the *Campus Martius; see* ROMAN REPUBLIC.

**assonance** The noticeable recurrence of a sound in successive words; *cf.* ALLITERATION.

**Greek.** The Greeks occasionally employed assonance for the sake of its aesthetic effect but took no pains to avoid it when no effect was intended, even when the repetition of sound seems to us displeasing. To judge from a comic fragment, fault was found with Euripides for excessive use of the letter sigma, but his extant plays are not noticeably more sigmatic than the rest of Greek literature. Punning assonance sometimes occurs, but not always for humorous effect; many Greek thinkers believed that there was a significant connection between similar-sounding words (*see* ETYMOLOGY). Hence phrases like *soma sema* ('the body is a tomb') acquired deeper meaning. There is little evidence for deliberate rhyming in epic or drama, though it occasionally happens at the end of a scene, or in a proverb. Prose writers avoided rhyme, except for conscious and mannered stylists like Isocrates and Gorgias.

**Latin.** The kind of assonance known as alliteration, often obtrusively employed in commonly repeated phrases or proverbs, is also a common feature of early Latin poetry. By the time of Virgil, however, it had come to be employed with great subtlety and with emotional effect. A similar development is seen in prose, Cicero using the device with more point and less obtrusiveness than his predecessors. Tacitus uses alliterative pairs of words with great effect. The Roman ear seems to have enjoyed the judicious repetition of similar terminations in the more impassioned parts of oratory, an aspect of assonance employed more subtly by the poets. This usage easily turns into a species of rhyme found occasionally in poetry of all periods, but used deliberately in the accentual hymns from the fifth century AD onwards and with great beauty in secular medieval lyrics.

**Assyria** A kingdom in the upper Tigris region in what is modern Iraq, powerful from 2000 BC. It eventually became the centre of an empire, which was finally destroyed in 612 BC by the Babylonians and Medes, who sacked its then capital Nineveh. Its patron deity was Ishtar, goddess of love and war.

**Aste'ria** In Greek myth, sister of *Leto and mother, by the Titan Perses, of Hecate. Being pursued by Zeus she turned into a quail, leapt into the sea and became Ortygia ('Quail island'), afterwards known as *Delos. (Several other places are also called Ortygia.)

**Astrae'a** ('Starry maiden', later applied as an epithet to Queen Elizabeth I of England) The constellation Virgo, identified by *Aratus with Justice (Gk. *Dikē*), the last deity to leave the earth. She was supposed to have lived among men in the *Golden age, retired to the mountains in the Silver age, and finally, during the wickedness of the Bronze age, fled to heaven.

**astra'galoi** (Lat. *tali*) Knucklebones, used in various games by Greeks and Romans. They were also used as four-sided *dice, since the four long faces were of different shapes, one flat, one irregular, one concave, and one convex, and these were given the respective values 1, 6, 3, and 4. The best throw was 'the throw of Venus', when four dice showed the four different numbers. The worst was 'the dog', when all four showed the number 1.

**astrology** The study of the positions of heavenly bodies and the conversion of these data into predictions about their outcome in human affairs. Astrology did not develop in the ancient Greek and Roman world until the Hellenistic age, deriving from the Babylonian cult of planetary gods and their astronomical observations and calculations for purposes of ritual and for divination (*see* BABYLON). Alexandria was an important centre for astrology. The belief underpinning it, common to educated people generally and to most philosophical schools (the Epicureans were the exception), was that the cosmos was a unity, and that whatever happened in the heavens was bound to affect or be reflected in events on earth. This was a theory known as 'cosmic sympathy'. As it was possible to predict the recurrence of celestial phenomena by observation of the heavenly bodies, so it might likewise be possible to predict terrestrial events by the same means. Astrology could therefore appeal for various scientific, religious, and philosophical reasons to the educated as well as the uneducated, and it came to be generally believed that the fortunes of an individual depended upon the aspect of the sky at the moment of birth, and that astrologers could give guidance accordingly.

It has been suggested that by the second century BC *Hipparchus' method for computing the positions of heavenly bodies contributed to the enormous expansion of this subject at that time. Astrology spread to Rome, and a vogue for it began when a number of manuals started to circulate widely. Cato and Ennius expressed hostility, but in the next century believers included Sulla, Poseidonius, and Varro (but not Cicero). Vitruvius, Propertius, and

Ovid all professed to believe, and Augustus published his own horoscope. From the first century AD onwards virtually everyone, Christians, pagans, and Jews alike, accepted the predictability of fate and the maleficent powers of the planets (*see* MANILIUS). Pliny the Elder was a notable exception. Ptolemy makes a well-reasoned case for astrology, arguing that it is merely the application of astronomy to the sublunary world. A few held out, usually with the argument advanced by Plotinus and Origen, that while stars, by reason of cosmic sympathy, may *indicate* the future, they cannot *determine* it. Rome particularly was sensitive to the potential political dangers, and at times of national crisis (e.g. 139 and 33 BC) banished all professional astrologers. However, no permanent ban was intended, and the emperors themselves frequently had recourse to horoscopes. Thrasyllus, the astrologer of Tiberius, acquired great influence. (But after Tiberius discovered a conspiracy against himself in AD 16 he banished astrologers and magicians.) It was not until the fourth century, with Augustine's emphatic denial of its validity, and with the advent of the Christian emperors, that the practice of astrology was officially banned. Nevertheless for the ordinary person it retained an axiomatic validity until the seventeenth century and beyond. *See also* TIMAEUS and PTOLEMY.

**astronomy** The science of astronomy (to which Rome contributed nothing) did not develop in Greece until the fifth century BC and, being for the Greeks essentially a system for describing and predicting the observed motions of the heavenly bodies by means of a consistent mathematical model, it covered only a part of what we understand by the term. In the pre-classical period—in Homer and Hesiod—interest was confined to observations of the solstice and equinox and of the rising and setting of the most obvious stars and constellations for dating the agricultural tasks of the seasons, for navigation by sea or land, and for establishing a *calendar. In *Odyssey* 5 Odysseus used the Great Bear constellation to steer east when leaving Calypso's island, and noted the rising and setting of Orion, Arcturus, and the Pleiads. This kind of astronomy no doubt goes back to prehistoric times. The fifth-century Athenian astronomer *Meton (*c.*435 BC) tried to correlate the lunar year with the solar year in a nineteen-year cycle derived from Babylonian astronomers (*see* BABYLON), but it seems that his system was not incorporated into the Athenian calendar, and he won immortality rather as the comic 'town-planner' in Aristophanes' *Birds*. It is very doubtful whether the Presocratic philosophers actually made the astronomical discoveries attributed to them (*see* THALES). Their theories were purely speculative although individuals reached some of the truths from which the science of astronomy could develop, such as that the earth is a sphere (believed by the Pythagoreans and by Parmenides, but *see* POMPONIUS MELA) and that the moon receives its light from the sun, found in Parmenides, Empedocles, and *Anaxagoras. The last two also understood the principles of *eclipses. *Philolaus may have been the first to include the earth as a planet. Not until the fourth century BC can we be sure that the Greeks identified the five planets known to the ancient world, Venus, Mercury, Mars, Jupiter, and Saturn (to give them their modern, Latin, names). *Eudoxus put forward a theory for their motion, but there were discrepancies between his theory and observable facts. Eudoxus' model was modified by *Callippus (an associate of Aristotle); it was this modified model that was accepted by Aristotle. It may have been at this point that *Aristarchus of Samos (*c.*280 BC) realized that the idea of a geocentric universe could be changed to a heliocentric one and as a consequence made that famous hypothesis. However, the idea was not taken up; nor was the suggestion of the fourth-century philosopher of the Academy Heracleides Ponticus, that the earth makes one revolution daily on its axis, west following east, at the centre of the cosmos.

Between 147 and 127 BC astronomy was transformed by the work of *Hipparchus, the only predecessor Ptolemy deigns to admire. Babylonian astronomy had been known, fitfully, at Athens from the time of Meton in the late fifth century, but Hipparchus appears to have had access to the large resources of the Babylonian archives, recording astronomical observations going back for centuries, and benefiting especially from their advanced arithmetical procedures. For the next 300 years we have to rely on the scanty evidence of papyri and on Indian texts based on lost Hellenistic Greek works, but it is clear that Hipparchus' successors continued along his lines, to the great benefit of astrologers who

needed to calculate the positions of the heavenly bodies for a given birth-time.

In the second century AD Ptolemy was able to crystallize the picture of the cosmos which had been accepted by Aristotle. He could calculate the position of all the known heavenly bodies at a given moment, predict eclipses, and foretell the appearance and disappearances of the planets and fixed stars. It was generally believed from the time of Eudoxus that at the centre of the cosmos was the earth, a globe divided into five zones, suspended in space and composed of the cold, heavy impurities of the universe, whose weight had taken it to the centre. The inhabited world comprised the upper or northern temperate zone; the questions of whether the southern temperate zone was inhabited and whether the sun rises there as it sets in the north were discussed by the Romans. The earth was surrounded by a system of concentric spherical shells, rotating at various speeds and about various axes. On these were carried the moon, the sun, the five planets, and the fixed stars. The terrestrial atmosphere reached as far as the moon. The outermost sphere, that of the fixed stars, was composed of the rarest thing of all, the aether, and revolved daily about the earth. Ptolemy in his *Almagest* gave canonical form to this view of the cosmos, and his work remained uncorrected except in small details throughout all antiquity until Copernicus (1473–1543) and Galileo (1564–1642). *See also* the names cited under MATHEMATICS.

**Asty'anax** (known also as Scamandrius) The son of Hector and *Andromache, born during the siege of Troy and thrown from the battlements by *Neoptolemus or killed by Odysseus after the capture of the city.

**Atala'nta (Atalantē)** In Greek myth, daughter either of Iasos, an Arcadian, or of Schoeneus, a Boeotian; in either case her mother was *Clymene. She was a huntress, loved by *Meleager with whom she took part in the Calydonian boar-hunt, but averse from marriage. She refused to marry any man who could not defeat her in a race, and any suitor whom she defeated was put to death. Hippomenes (or Milanion) took up the challenge, and on the advice of Aphrodite carried with him three golden apples which she gave him. He dropped these at intervals and, as Atalanta could not resist the temptation to stop and pick them up, won the race. Their son was Parthenopaeus. As a punishment for making love in a sanctuary during a hunt the couple were turned into lions.

**Ata'rgatis** (often known simply as 'the Syrian goddess') A fertility goddess, worshipped at Hierapolis (Bambycē) where her temple was the greatest and holiest in Syria. Her consort was Hadad. In the second century BC her worship spread to a number of Hellenic cities, and appeared sporadically in the West. *Lucian describes the cult in Syria, and *Apuleius the life of her Galli, wandering priests.

**Ātē** In Greek myth, the personification of blind folly or delusion (often translated as 'infatuation') in the grip of which the victim cannot distinguish between right and wrong, advantageous and disadvantageous courses of action. Homer makes her the daughter of Zeus, who expelled her from Olympus to bring disaster to individuals; Hesiod sees Ate impersonally, as punishment for *hubris.

**Ate'llan farces** (*fābulae Atellānae*) Named after the town of Atella in Campania, ancient dramatic performances of Italian low life (the only Oscan literary form known to us; *see* ITALY), apparently performed by masked actors. There were certain stock characters, Bucco the fool, Dossennus the hunchback (or the glutton), Maccus the clown, Manducus ('with champing jaws') the glutton, Pappus the greybeard, etc., who were probably introduced in ridiculous situations. Some of the later titles suggest burlesques of mythology. Atellan plays became popular at Rome, probably in the third century BC, and were acted in Latin, rather than Oscan, by amateurs. They were revived in more literary form, with the same stock characters but with a written plot in verse, by Pomponius of Bononia and Novius, who probably flourished early in the first century BC. These revivals, acted by professional comedians, were staged after the end of performances of tragedy, and seem often to have been tragic parodies. They continued intermittently until the end of the first century AD. According to Strabo, writing early in that century, they were performed at Rome in Oscan in his day. Only fragments survive.

**A'thamas** In Greek myth, king of Boeotian Orchomenos, son of Aeolus (2), husband of Ino, and father of Phrixus, *Helle, Melicertes,

and Learchus. Phrixus and Helle were the children of Athamas' first wife Nephele. Their stepmother Ino, daughter of Cadmus, plotted to kill them but they escaped death on a winged ram with golden fleece, provided by Hermes at Nephele's request. Helle became giddy and fell into that part of the sea which in consequence is called the Hellespont. Phrixus arrived safely in Colchis where the king Aeētes received him hospitably. The ram was sacrificed to Zeus and its golden fleece hung up in Colchis and guarded by a dragon. For the rest of the myth *see* ARGONAUTS, and for the fate of Athamas, Ino, and her two sons *see* DIONYSUS. Athamas settled in a country he called Athamania and married Themisto.

**atheism** The belief that no God or gods exist. The term *atheos* ('godless') in Greek usually meant a person hated by the gods; it was also applied to those who merely rejected traditional polytheism as well as to those who positively denied the existence of any kind of divinity, so the exact shade of meaning to be attached in any particular case is difficult to ascertain.

The societies of Greece and Rome were polytheistic. Throughout antiquity until pagan cult was banned in AD 391 (*see* CHRISTIANITY IN THE ROMAN WORLD) individuals and the state worshipped many gods. Out-and-out atheism as a serious belief, as opposed to the expression of thoughts of an atheistic nature, never attracted a following. Ideas akin to atheism emerged in the Greek world in the sixth century BC among the Milesian philosophers (*see* MILETUS), whose work marked the emergence of Greek rationalism. They rejected mythological explanations for the origin of everything, seeing the universe as operating naturalistically according to laws comprehensible to human reason. However they each believed in a first principle (Thales in water, Anaximander in an 'unbounded', and Anaximenes in cosmic 'air') which itself had no origin and was immortal and eternal, so that in those respects they were believing in something godlike.

Plato (in *Laws*) attests the existence of positive atheism when he states that there are those who think the world is governed not by a god but by nature or chance and furthermore that morality is a human invention. *Critias in his lost play *Sisyphus* has a character, perhaps Sisyphus himself, argue that gods were an invention of a 'wise law-giver' to deter secret crime. Unbelief of any degree did not seem to incur a penalty at Athens except when other issues, such as the survival of the city in time of war, raised anxieties about offending the gods. Thus Socrates, who questioned some traditional beliefs but had a strong religious sense and was scrupulous in religious observance, was charged by Meletus with atheism (*see APOLOGY OF SOCRATES*). But one who rejects the traditional gods is assumed to worship gods of his own choice; so Socrates in Aristophanes' *Clouds* is represented as worshipping Aer and Aether, Breath and Chaos. (In *Frogs* 892 Euripides' deity is Tongue.) The uncompromising atheist in fifth-century Athens, Diagoras (from Melos), was convicted of impiety but prudently fled. Anaxagoras, Critias, Prodicus, and Protagoras are often included on ancient lists of atheists but probably without sufficient justification (*see* AGNOSTICISM). Plato, Aristotle, and the Stoics (*see* STOICISM) all in their very different ways bypass polytheism but retain the divine (in some sense) as a first principle. Democritus, the Greek atomist philosopher of the fifth century BC, and his influential follower Epicurus were both listed as atheists by some. Epicurus expressly stated that the gods exist, but added that they take no interest in the lives of humans. He was accused, implausibly, by Cicero of wishing to abolish the gods but fearing public reaction if he did so.

At Rome Epicurus' much later follower the poet Lucretius believed that the names of the gods of mythology should only be used as symbols for natural objects, Ceres for corn, for example, or Bacchus for wine. Yet, like his mentor Epicurus, Lucretius believed that the gods existed, though they were impersonal and remote, and that imitation of their tranquil life might lead humans to lead similar lives. Under the empire Christians were accused of atheism when they refused to burn incense on the emperor's birthday (*see* RULER CULT). The Christian Tertullian observed, 'If the Tiber rises too high or the Nile too low the cry is "The Christians to the lion". All of them to a single lion?' *See also* EUHEMERUS.

**Athē'na (Athē'nē, Athenaia)** The patron goddess of Athens. In Homer she is generally called Athene, but in the Attic dialect of tragedy Athenaia. The (abbreviated) form Athena became common in the fourth century BC. She was worshipped in the *Parthenon, her great temple on the Acropolis at Athens, and throughout Greece, the islands, and the colonies. This verbal connection between city and deity is unique in Greece. Whether Athens is named after the goddess or the goddess after Athens is an ancient argument, but the latter is generally considered more probable. Her name is perhaps to be found on a *Linear B tablet from Cnossus, and in an earlier incarnation she may have been a palace-protecting Mycenaean goddess. She is sometimes known as Pallas Athene for reasons which remain obscure; Pallas was sometimes understood to mean 'maiden', sometimes 'brandisher' (of weapons). Equally obscure is the meaning of her name Tritogeneia, 'Trito-born', for which a number of explanations was given in antiquity. In classical times she was pre-eminently the city-protecting goddess of many Greek cities including Sparta, and despite the fact that she is the enemy of Troy, she is still the goddess of the Trojan citadel; *see* PALLADIUM. She remains a virgin and is par excellence a war-goddess, often the helper of a hero such as Heracles, and most frequently represented in art as armed. Nevertheless she is the patroness of all urban arts and crafts, especially spinning and weaving, and so she unites the characteristic skills of both sexes. She is also the inventor of the musical instrument the *aulos. Her principal myth relates to her birth. She was the daughter of Zeus and *Metis ('cunning intelligence'). Zeus swallowed the pregnant Metis through fear of a prophecy that she would give birth to a son stronger than himself. In due time the god Hephaestus (or Prometheus, it was sometimes said) opened Zeus' head with an axe and Athena emerged, fully armed and uttering her war-cry. Zeus gave Hephaestus leave to marry her, and from his unsuccessful attempt sprang the Athenian king *Erichthonius. She also competed with *Poseidon for possession of Attica, a contest in which she emerged victorious by producing the olive tree still to be seen in Pausanias' day. (For another myth *see* ARACHNE.) At the festival of the Greater *Panathenaea at Athens she was presented with a robe. She is generally represented as a goddess of severe beauty, in armour, with helmet, *aegis, spear, and shield (sometimes bearing the *Gorgon's head); she often has an owl sitting on her shoulder, especially in fifth-century Athens, in reference to her stock epithet *glaukōpis*, which appears to mean 'owl-faced' but could also be interpreted as 'bright-eyed'. *Cf.* MINERVA.

**Athenae'um** At Rome, the emperor Hadrian's famous institute for lectures and recitations by rhetors and other literary figures.

**Athenae'us** (of Naucratis, fl. *c.* AD 200) Greek author of the *Deipnosophistae* ('Scholars of the art of dining'), now in fifteen books with an epitome which covers some losses. About thirty learned men (some having the names of real persons, including Galen) are represented dining together at Rome over several days with their host Larensis, a Roman magistrate. Some of the guests may be Roman, but most are Greek-speakers from the eastern empire. They discuss, with innumerable quotations, the food as it is put before them, and a wide range of other tangentially related subjects. Rome, they agree, is the centre of the universe: all goods are available to her. Athenaeus was an industrious collector of excerpts and anecdotes, which are a fruitful source of information on the literature and usages of ancient Greece. The work belongs to the genre of *symposium literature, in which the conventions of the drinking-party (here, the preceding dinner as well) give structure to the composition.

**Athēnaiōn politeia** ('The constitution of the Athenians') **1.** Attributed from antiquity to Aristotle, the only treatise to have survived from a collection of comparative descriptions of the constitutions of, we are told, 158 states. It was recovered, with only the opening chapters lost, in 1890 from an Egyptian papyrus. Chapters 1–41 cover the history of the Athenian constitution up to the restoration of the democracy (after the fall of the *Thirty Tyrants) in 403 BC, and contain valuable information which is not found in any other text. The remaining chapters, 42–69, describe the workings of the constitution in the author's own day and appear to be based on personal knowledge of the 330s and 320s BC, when Aristotle was in Athens (from 335 to 323 BC).

**2.** Monograph attributed to an unknown writer, the *Old Oligarch.

**Athena Nike, temple of** *See* ACROPOLIS.

**Athenian empire** *See* DELIAN LEAGUE.

**Athens (Athenai)** (Lat. Athenae) The chief city of *Attica, in Greece.

**1. Topography.** In classical times the city stood about 5km (3 miles) from the sea at its nearest point, in the central plain of Attica, surrounded by mountains on all sides except the south. It is enclosed on the north-west by Mount Parnes, on the north-east by Mount Pentelicus, on the south-east by Mount *Hymettus, and on the west by Mount Aegaleus (less important). The citadel of Athens, the *Acropolis, sometimes called simply *polis*, is a roughly square rock rising steeply out of the plain. North-west of it is a second hill, the *Areopagus, and to the south-west a third, the *Pnyx. To the north-east and outside the city wall of Themistocles (built soon after the expulsion of the Persians in 479 BC) stands the peaked mountain of Lycabettus. To the east and west of the city flow the Ilis(s)us (joined by the Eridanus) and the Cephis(s)us.

The Themistoclean wall of the city was breached by a dozen gates, the most-used of which was the Dipylon in the north-west. Some 75m (80 yards) to the south was the Sacred Gate from which the Sacred Way led to Eleusis. Communication between Athens and her harbours Piraeus and Phalerum was protected by the Long Walls. The *agora established by Solon in the early sixth century BC and used for the next eight hundred years was north-west of the Acropolis and Areopagus, in the *Ceramīcus.

**2. Early History.** The Acropolis was the centre of the earliest prehistoric settlement at Athens, surrounded by a scatter of farms and dwellings. It became a Mycenaean stronghold, with rich tombs in the fourteenth century BC and in the later thirteenth century fortifications and a water supply system on the acropolis (*see* MYCENAE). According to Athenian tradition it was at this time that the hero Theseus amalgamated the various communities in Attica into one state with Athens as the capital city, but this 'synoecism' (Gk. *synoikismos*) is now generally dated around 900 BC after the *Dorian invasion and the Ionian migrations (*see* IONIA). The Athenians of the classical period flattered themselves that they were autochthonous, 'sprung from the soil', the original inhabitants, unlike the Dorians, who were invaders (*see* ERICHTHONIUS).

Legend had it that Athens, like other Greek states, was ruled in early times by kings. The last king was *Codrus, after whom from 683 BC Athens was governed by *archons elected annually from the nobility. The attempt by *Cylon to overthrow the aristocracy and become tyrant (*c.*632) failed. Despite the legislation of *Draco (621) the position of the nobility was not weakened until the reforms of *Solon in

594 BC. His economic and political reforms in the 590s made many more Athenian citizens eligible for the archonship, but these measures failed to prevent tyranny at Athens, and the popular leader *Peisistratus seized power in the mid-sixth century. The tyrannies of Peisistratus and his sons *Hippias (1) and *Hipparchus (1), lasting until 510 BC, were not oppressive. They saw a considerable increase in the city's material prosperity and cultural standing. After the expulsion of Hippias, the reforms of *Cleisthenes (2) established a political system that was the foundation for *democracy.

**3. The fifth century.** At the beginning of the fifth century BC Athens was a powerful state, but her intervention in the Ionian Revolt provoked Persia (see PERSIAN WARS). The first Persian invasion was defeated at Marathon (490) and a second ten years later at Salamis. Athens, under the influence of *Themistocles, had built a strong navy, and she emerged from the struggle with the city in ruins and her territory ravaged but with her fleet a force to be reckoned with, her prestige increased, and her position as leader of all the Ionian Greeks acknowledged. The war with Persia was effectively ended with *Cimon's victory at the river Eurymedon c.466. The Ionian Greek cities which had rebelled against Persia accepted the leadership of Athens, and this was the origin of the *Delian League (477). Under the guidance of Cimon and *Pericles, Athens became an imperial power, against a background of increasing tension with Sparta, now displaced as the leading power in Greece. Through the constitutional reforms of *Ephialtes and Pericles in the years before 457 (when the archonship became open to the lowest property class as defined by Solon) democracy reached its fullest development: the citizens were entirely self-governing, political offices were open to all, and the citizens were paid for undertaking their political duties, so that even the poorest could afford to exercise their rights.

The Athenian empire survived the so-called First *Peloponnesian War c.460–446. Aegina fell to Athens after a long blockade (457–456), but the Thirty Years Peace made with Sparta in 446 ended Athens' ten-year control of Boeotia when the Athenians were defeated at Coronea by a Boeotian rising in that year. The Delian League was being turned into an empire, by land as well as by sea; this was the period in which the first *cleruchies were established. Sparta, and not only Sparta, felt threatened by Athenian expansion in the early 430s, and the Second Peloponnesian War broke out in 431. It ended the *Pentekontaětia or 50-year period from the Persian Wars, the period of Athens' greatest glory, and lasted until 404 BC.

In the first ten years of the war, (431–21 BC, known as the *Archidamian War) the Spartans did not succeed in their professed aim to 'free' Greece from Athenian tyranny, and after defeat at Pylos made overtures for peace which Athens rejected. The failure of the *Sicilian Expedition (413) was the signal for revolt by many of Athens' subject-allies. The latter part of the war was marked also by the cooperation against her of Sparta and Persia (see also ALCIBIADES). The democracy was temporarily overthrown and an oligarchic council of *Four Hundred established in 411, but this was deposed within the year. After the defeat at Arginusae in 405 Athens sued for peace (see THIRTY TYRANTS). She became a dependant of Sparta, but despite all she soon regained her democracy (in 403) and her freedom. In 395 she joined Thebes, Argos, and *Corinth in their attempt to overthrow the Spartan supremacy, an attempt which failed in its object and was ended when friendly relations between Sparta and Persia were restored and the king of Persia imposed the pro-Spartan Peace of Antalcidas or *King's Peace (387/6). The king regained possession of the Ionian cities of Asia Minor and remained master of the Aegean Sea.

**4. The fourth century.** Political interest in early fourth-century Greece is focused on the rivalry between Sparta and Thebes, in which Athens played only a secondary role. In 378 Athens started to make alliances in order to protect herself against Sparta, and thus the Second Athenian League (or confederacy) was formed (the first, a century earlier, was the Delian League: above), composed of various islands and cities of the Aegean, Corcyra, and other states. Athens retained her commercial supremacy, and in 376 Chabrias (a professional soldier) won back her supremacy at sea by a decisive naval victory over Sparta near Naxos. The most prominent Athenian statesman of this period was Callistratus, whose general policy was based on harmony with Sparta and a balance of power between that city and Thebes. Thebes, led by *Epaminondas, was now aspiring to the leadership of Greece, and

Athens, having supported the Thebans until their victory over the Spartans at Leuctra in 371, was more influenced by jealousy of neighbouring Thebes than by the old rivalry with Sparta. In the ensuing struggle between these two, Athens was in alliance with Sparta. Meanwhile *Macedon was rising in importance and threatening the Athenian position in the north Aegean (see MACEDONIA and PHILIP (1)). Faced with the threat of Macedon, Athens had to decide whether or not to come to terms with Philip, with some loss of independence. The eloquence of Demosthenes in the cause of independence prevailed, and a final battle between Athens and Thebes on the one side and Philip on the other was fought at Chaeronea in 338. Athens was defeated, and was obliged to accept Philip's moderate terms (the loss of the Hellespont) and join the Hellenic confederacy which he organized. After the risings that followed the accession of Philip's son in 336 (see ALEXANDER (1)) Athens enjoyed a period of tranquillity. The death of Alexander in 323 appeared to give the Greeks an opportunity to recover their freedom, but in the so-called *Lamian War (323–322) Athens with the other Greek states was defeated at Crannon by *Antipater. Demosthenes took poison to avoid capture. The democrats were reinstated at Athens under the brief rule of Polyperchon, but *Cassander appointed *Demetrius of Phalerum as his governor at Athens in 317. His ten years' governorship was a period of peace for the city, yet when *Demetrius Poliorcetes captured the city from Cassander in 307 he was looked upon by the Athenians as a liberator.

**5. Later history.** The third century BC saw the end of the political importance of Athens. The *Chremonidean War (266–262) is notable as the last occasion when she took the lead against Macedon. Supported by Sparta and King Ptolemy Philadelphus of Egypt, she revolted against Antigonus Gonatas (see MACEDONIA), was besieged, and finally surrendered through famine. In 229, on the death of Demetrius II, son of Gonatas, Athens recovered her freedom and except for one attack by Philip V, grandson of Gonatas, had a peaceful existence as Rome slowly grew to power. After the defeat of the *Achaean league by the Roman consul Mummius in 146 BC Greece became a Roman protectorate (not a province until the time of Augustus), but neither Athens nor Sparta had to pay taxes to Rome. There was a revival of material prosperity, and

the great quadrennial festival of Athens at Delos was restored. This prosperous period came to an end with the Mithridatic War of 89–85, when Athens, which had sided with *Mithridates, was sacked and in part destroyed in 86 by the Roman general *Sulla though she retained 'free' status. Even greater ruin followed from the Roman civil wars of the first century BC, and endured until the emperor Augustus made Greece a Roman province in 27 BC.

In spite of her political decline Athens retained much of her intellectual prestige and remained pre-eminent for the study of philosophy (see HELLENISTIC AGE). She was patronized in the second century BC by the *Attalids of Pergamum, who adorned the city with colonnades (see STOA) and sculptures. It became fashionable for Romans to go to the philosophical schools of Athens as to a university. *Atticus lived there for many years; Cicero and his son and Horace were among those who studied in the city. Horace, and in a later age Lucian, appreciated the peaceful charm of Athens compared with the turmoil of Rome. Athens enjoyed some revival of her former glories in the second century AD under the emperor Hadrian and the Antonines, and in the fourth century Julian the Apostate was a lover of the city. It remained a centre for philosophy and above all *Neoplatonism until c.530. The end of Athens' period of intellectual eminence came in AD 529, when the Christian emperor Justinian caused the closing of her schools of philosophy and the Parthenon became a church.

**Athens, Constitution of** See ATHĒNAIŌN POLITEIA.

**athletics** [from the Greek root *athl-*, denoting 'struggle', 'conflict', or 'prize in a contest'] In Greece from Homeric times athletic contests were an essential part of the Greek way of life and the most important element in many religious festivals. The important contests in classical times were for men only, but there were separate competitions for women, especially at Sparta. From the first century AD onward women's events were included in general athletics meetings; they were chiefly running races but women's wrestling also featured. Greek male athletes were distinguished in one respect from other nationalities including Romans in that by the fifth century BC at the latest they generally practised and competed entirely naked. Women customarily wore a short tunic. The pattern of athletics competitions was strongly influenced by the Olympian games (*see* OLYMPIA), whose supremacy from 776 BC onwards resulted in their own rules and restricted programme becoming the norm. The usual events are listed below. The Greeks and Romans did not usually keep records of athletic performance, so we do not know what they achieved. One exception is the case of the famous Phayllus of Croton (early fifth century BC), who according to an epigram in the Palatine Anthology jumped 16.8m (55 ft.). This figure, almost twice the present world-record long jump, may result from error or deliberate exaggeration, or may refer to a multiple jump.

*Running.* The ancient race course was essentially a rectangle about 200m (220 yards) long with a starting line at each end and a turning post in the middle of each of these lines (*see* STADE, STADIUM). In the 'single' foot-race (*stadion*), the competitors ran the length of the track; in the 'double' foot-race (*diaulos*), they had to make an abrupt turn around the post and run back again (oddly enough there are no references in Greek literature to the possibility of foul play or falls during this manoeuvre). The long-distance race comprised twelve laps of the stadium (about 4,800m or 3 miles). By the middle of the fifth century BC races were started by a mechanical starting gate.

The race in (hoplite) armour, in time reduced to a symbolic helmet and shield, was introduced at the Olympian games of 520 BC and became less esteemed as time went on. Relay races were not held in the stadium in regular programmes of athletics but took place at separate festivals when the runners ran through the streets and handed on a lighted torch.

*Wrestling.* Classification in Greek wrestling was by age rather than weight, so fortune favoured big men, and in the important games professionalism crept in. At a lower level, wrestling was the most popular Greek sport and the *palaestra or wrestling school a feature of every Greek city for many centuries. All Greek athletes oiled themselves before exercise; wrestlers in addition dusted themselves with powder to ensure a good grip. A wrestling match was for the best of three falls; a fall was judged to be when a man's shoulders, or perhaps his knees, touched the ground.

*Boxing.* A boxing match was not divided into rounds but continued uninterrupted until a contestant was knocked out or raised a hand in acknowledgement of defeat. Boxing gloves took the form of soft leather wound round the wrists and knuckles both as a protection and to prevent cutting the opponent's face. The magnificent Hellenistic bronze of a resting boxer in the Terme Museum at Rome shows the details clearly. We do not know for certain what blows were permitted and what forbidden, but the rules were enforced by referees with forked sticks for stopping offenders. Men in training used ear-guards and softly padded gloves, and practised with a punch-ball as well as by shadow-boxing. (Boxing played a large part in the gladiatorial shows in Rome but then the gloves were loaded with lead and even spiked to draw blood. The emperor Augustus was said to have been particularly keen on boxing, but perhaps in its less violent Greek form.)

*The pancration.* A specialized form of all-in wrestling in which the aim was to get an opponent to admit defeat when he was in danger of strangulation or a broken limb. The only tactics we know to have been forbidden were biting and gouging out an opponent's eye. After the fourth century BC the event became increasingly professional and increasingly popular as it became more violent. Success in the *pancration* was highly esteemed.

*The pentathlon.* A combination of five events: long jump, foot-race, throwing the discus, throwing the javelin, and wrestling. We do not know its origin, nor how the victor was chosen. It is unlikely that the Greeks used any system of reckoning points since they were interested only in victory and not in second or third places. It seems that by a process of elimination only the two best competitors were selected for the final event, the wrestling. By the first century AD the pentathlon had declined in popularity compared with the other contests. *Eratosthenes had the nickname *pentathlos*, meaning 'all-rounder'.

*Javelin.* Distance was the aim in athletic javelin-throwing, but the javelin had to land on its point. The Greeks always threw with the help of a thong wound tightly round the shaft leaving a loop hitched over the fingers of the throwing hand, to increase the leverage of the throwing arm and so add to the speed of projection, and to impart spin so as to keep the javelin steady in flight and carry it much further. The competitor was allowed five throws, only the best counting.

*Discus.* Throwing a circular, slightly convex, plate of stone or metal was an event entered by heavy men. Surviving specimens of discus vary in weight between about 1.4kg and 8kg (3 to 18 pounds); the modern discus for men weighs 2kg. The method of throwing is illustrated by vase-paintings and statues, notably the *Discobolus* of Myron. The discus was held in the hand with the arm straight, then swung back and released with an underarm pull. The aim was to throw it from a fixed space to the greatest distance. As with the javelin, only the best of five throws counted.

*Long jump*. All we know about the Greek long jump is that the athlete always used jumping weights, from which it has been inferred that the contest was for a standing rather than a running jump (where weights reduce the distance covered). It is not known how many jumps each competitor was allowed.

The Etruscans practised most of the events in the Greek athletic programme, as their tomb-paintings show, although they did not follow Greek practice in competing naked. The Romans often experimented with Greek athletic events, but they never wholly accepted them as part of their way of life. The earliest Greek-style games in Rome took place in 186 BC at a time when the enthusiasm of some Romans for Greek culture was at its height. Other Greek games were promoted during the first century BC, but in general their appeal was only to the leisured and literary classes. During the Augustan period we hear of wealthy young Romans taking up Greek athletics for amusement (*see* SECULAR GAMES). They favoured running, boxing, horse-riding, and, after these activities, swimming in the Tiber. But on the whole, despite the support of some Roman emperors, notably Nero, the general Roman contempt for most things Greek prevailed in this sphere also. The *gymnasia were seen by many as hotbeds of vice threatening the traditional Roman methods of training for war.

**Athos** Headland on the most easterly of the promontories of Chalcidice, with a mountain nearly 2,000m (6,600 feet) high rising sheer from the sea, sacred to Zeus. To avoid the sea passage around Mount Athos when he was invading Greece, the Persian king Xerxes cut a canal through the isthmus (483–481 BC), still visible in places. Athos is now the site of several monasteries.

**Ath. Pol.** *See* ATHĒNAIŌN POLITEIA.

**atimia** The loss of some or all civic rights by a citizen of a Greek city in punishment for certain offences concerning the state. The loss of rights might be temporary or permanent.

**Atla'ntis** Huge mythical island or continent thought of as situated in the Atlantic outside the Straits of Gibraltar in prehistoric times, first mentioned in literature by Plato, who seems to be the originator of the idea, in his dialogues *Timaeus* and *Critias*. The name is derived from *Atlas. Its empire, once virtuous, degenerated into aggression but was defeated by the Athenians, the island being afterwards swallowed up in great earthquakes and floods. There has been speculation as to whether the myth embodied folk memories of, for example, the Minoan civilization of Crete or the eruption at Thera (Santorini).

**Atlas** In Greek myth, a *Titan, son of *Iapetus and Clymene; he married the *Oceanid Pleione. His name probably means 'he who endures'. In Homer he is the father of Calypso but usually his daughters are the *Pleiades, and sometimes the *Hyades and the *Hesperides too. He is the guardian of the pillars of heaven (which hold up the sky), and later as punishment for his part in the revolt of the Titans he had to hold the sky up himself. He became identified with the western part of the Atlas mountains in north-west Africa, and sometimes with the southern Pillar of Hercules. A later tale said that *Perseus had turned him into stone with the Gorgon's head. When Heracles was seeking the apples of the Hesperides (*see* HERACLES, LABOURS OF 11) Atlas offered to fetch them if Heracles would hold up the sky; he then refused to take back his burden until tricked into doing so by the hero.

**atomists** *See* DEMOCRITUS; LEUCIPPUS; EPICURUS; LUCRETIUS.

**Ato'ssa** Wife of *Darius I, king of Persia, and mother of Xerxes.

**A'treus** In Greek myth, one of the sons of *Pelops and grandson of *Tantalus; he was king of Mycenae, husband of Aerope, and father of Agamemnon and Menelaus. After Pelops was cursed by the dying Myrtilus, each generation of the family came to disaster. Atreus' brother Thyestes seduced Aerope who secretly gave him the golden lamb which entitled him to claim the kingship of Mycenae. As a consequence Zeus reversed the course of the sun as a sign of his anger. Atreus banished Thyestes, but afterwards pretended to be reconciled and invited him to a banquet at which he served up to Thyestes the flesh of his own sons before banishing him again. Later he married his own daughter Pelopia and became the father of Aegisthus, who was to be a further agent of the curse. The details of this story are variously told. *See also* PLEISTHENES.

**A'trium Vestae** ('Hall of virgins') Residence of the *Vestal Virgins, east of the forum at Rome. The remains now visible are of imperial times, but republican foundations have been discovered.

**A'tropos** ('Irresistible') One of the three *Fates. Her function, according to the poets, was to cut off the thread of life.

**A'ttalids** The ruling dynasty of Pergamum in the third and second centuries BC. When, after the death of Alexander the Great, his generals succeeded to his empire (*see* DIADOCHI) and divided it among themselves, a certain Philetaerus, son of an unknown Attalus, became ruler of Pergamum and founder of the dynasty. He was originally an officer of Antigonus, and later put in command of Pergamum, under the suzerainty of the general Seleucus (later Seleucus I; *see* SELEUCIDS). He was succeeded by his nephew Eumenes I (d. 241 BC) who secured Pergamum's independence from the Seleucid empire. He in turn was succeeded by his cousin and adopted son Attalus I who, by driving back and confining the Galatians to an area of Phrygia, obtained power and prestige and took the title of king. For a time Attalus was able to bring under his control nearly the whole of Seleucid Asia Minor. In 201 the Pergamenes and the Rhodians became embroiled with *Philip V of Macedon, and took the decisive step of asking Rome for help. This gave Rome the pretext for the Second Macedonian War and for intervention in Greek affairs.

In 189 BC, as the ally of Rome against Antiochus III at the great victory of Magnesia, Pergamum established its position as the leading state in Asia Minor, and received the bulk of the dominions ceded by Antiochus. In 172 Eumenes II, son of Attalus I, again incited Rome against Macedonia and provided the pretext on which war was declared against *Perseus (2) in 171. Eumenes' brother Attalus II succeeded him, and continued the Attalid policy of caretaking for Rome in the east. He was succeeded

in 138 by Attalus III, son of Eumenes II. The dynasty ended in 133 with the death of Attalus III, who bequeathed his dominions to Rome; these became the Roman province of Asia.

The Attalids ruled over what was constitutionally a Greek city-state, but they had wide powers of interference and ruled directly over the native population of the surrounding country. This country possessed natural resources including silver mines but its wealth, for which the Attalids were proverbial, lay in its agricultural produce and the dependent industries of wool and parchment (a word derived from Pergamum). The Attalids were devoted patrons of art and literature, and under their influence Pergamum became one of the most beautiful of all Greek cities, famous for its library and school of architecture.

**Atthis** (Gk. *Atthis historia*, 'history of Attica', pl. *Atthides*) Name given to a type of chronicle dealing with the local history of Athens and Attica. It was popular from c.350 to 250 BC out of nostalgia for the past glories of Athens. The pattern seems to have been set by *Hellanicus' history published soon after 404 BC. The contents of *Atthides* were traditional and concentrated on mythology, origins of cults, and descriptions of political institutions. The writers are referred to as 'atthidographers'. Only fragments of their works survive.

**Attic** (adj.) Relating to *Attica.

**A'ttica** The territory of *Athens (its chief city), a mountainous and largely arid area forming the south-east promontory of central Greece, about 2,500 sq. km (1,000 sq. miles) in extent. Attica is dominated by its four mountain systems, Aegaleus, Hymettus, Pentelicus, and Laurium, which divide the land into three plains, to the west the Thriasian plain with its chief town Eleusis, in the centre the Attic plain, and to the east the Mesogeia. The main rivers of Attica, which are full only in winter or after heavy rains, are the Cephi(s)sus and the Ili(s)sus. There are fertile upland valleys and damp lowland valleys. The mountain slopes are more or less barren but the plains are productive, though better for olives and figs than for corn. In ancient times grapes were cultivated but did not produce a notable wine. The honey was particularly fine, especially that of Hymettus. The country is too hilly and dry for horse-breeding, but sheep and goats flourished. Fish was plentiful in the coastal waters. Of natural resources, Attica was famous for its dazzling white Pentelic marble, and the grey, blue, and black marble from Hymettus. Its potters' clay was excellent, and there were silver and lead at Laurium. Attica originally consisted of many separate communities, traditionally twelve in the time of the king *Cecrops, which were later fused into a single Athenian state, an achievement attributed to *Theseus but in fact a gradual process probably lasting into the seventh century BC. Athens became the capital city, although local loyalties remained and even during the sixth century aristocratic families still lived independent lives in the countryside. It was the tyranny of *Peisistratus and even more the reforms of *Cleisthenes (2) which finally broke local ties and brought the whole of Attica under a centralized government at Athens.

**A'ttica, Pompō'nia** See AGRIPPA.

**Attic drama** See DRAMA; COMEDY; TRAGEDY.

**A'tticism** See ASIANISM AND ATTICISM; ORATORY [Greek]; SECOND SOPHISTIC.

**Attic Nights** See GELLIUS.

**Attic orators** In the Hellenistic period a canon of ten Attic orators was drawn up. It comprised Lysias, Isaeus, Hyperides, Isocrates, Deinarchus, Aeschines, Antiphon, Lycurgus, Andocides, and Demosthenes. Some lists exist showing slight variations. See ORATORY [Greek].

**A'tticus, Titus Pompō'nius** (110–32 BC, b. at Rome of an equestrian family) Intimate with *Cicero from boyhood, he was eventually his financial adviser and banker, his publisher, and his affectionate and tolerant friend. His sister married Cicero's brother Quintus. In 85 he sold his assets and left Rome for Athens, where he lived for many years (hence his *cognomen* Atticus, 'of Attica', i.e. 'the Athenian'). Highly cultivated in Greek and Latin, he adopted the Epicurean philosophy and took no active part in politics, but maintained an attitude of neutrality. He inherited a considerable fortune, and by judicious investment became very wealthy. He protected Cicero's wife Terentia when Cicero went into exile, and Antony's wife Fulvia and his lieutenant Volumnius at the time of *Mutina (43 BC). In consequence he was spared by Antony in the *proscriptions. He became the friend of the emperor Augustus, and his daughter Attica married M. Vipsa-

nius *Agrippa. (Their daughter Vipsania married Tiberius and was mother of the younger Drusus.) The series of Cicero's letters to Atticus begins in 68, and continues until Cicero's death. In both public and private life Cicero constantly turned to him for sympathy and advice. Atticus saw to the copying and circulation of Cicero's writings. His own works, including a chronological table of Roman history which helped to establish 753 BC as the official date of the founding of Rome, have not survived. In 32 BC when suffering from an incurable illness he committed suicide. We have a Life of him by *Nepos.

**A'ttila** (known as Etzel in medieval German saga) King of the Huns AD 435–53; he ruled an empire stretching from the Alps to the Caspian Sea. In 452 he invaded Italy and sacked several cities, but was persuaded to withdraw without entering Rome. While preparing to invade the eastern empire again, having ravaged it in the 440s, he died suddenly on his wedding night. See FALL OF ROME.

**Attis** In mythology, the youthful companion (or companion-god) of *Cybele, called at Rome the *Magna Mater*, 'Great Mother-goddess' of Anatolia (also known as Agdistis in Phrygia). The Phrygian version of his myth relates that he was the son of Nana, daughter of the river-god Sangarius (a river in Asia Minor). She conceived him after gathering the blossom of an almond-tree sprung from the severed male organs of Agdistis/Cybele who, born both male and female, had been castrated by the gods. When Attis wished to marry, Cybele, who loved him and was jealous, drove him mad so that he castrated himself and died. There are many variants of this myth, which, among other things, purports to explain why Cybele's priests, *Galli, are eunuchs. Attis appears only rarely in Greece, but with Cybele became an accepted deity at Rome under the emperor Claudius. For a poem on the subject of Attis *see* CATULLUS.

**A'ttius, Lucius** See ACCIUS.

**Au'fidus** River in Apulia (south Italy), on which stood Venusia, the birthplace of Horace, who refers in his poems to its swift and roaring current. It was on the banks of this river that Hannibal defeated the Romans at the battle of Cannae in 216 BC.

**Augē** In Greek myth, the mother by Heracles of *Telephus.

**Auge'as (Augeiās)** King of Elis whose stables Heracles was required to clean as one of his Labours (*see* HERACLES, LABOURS OF 6). *Trophonius and Agamedes, the legendary architects, are said to have built his treasury.

**augury** [Lat. *augurium*, 'portent', 'omen'] At Rome, augury or 'taking the auspices' (Lat. *auspicium*, 'watching the birds [*aves*]') was a form of divination to find out the intention of the gods. Augurs were members of a priestly college, the experts who maintained the procedures of augury in Roman public life and decided their validity or otherwise in particular cases. They were not concerned with prodigies nor with studying the entrails at sacrifices (*see* HARUSPICES); they observed mostly the behaviour of particular species of birds, including sacred chickens, but also that of some other animals, and they interpreted thunder and lightning and other unusual events. They did not normally take the auspices themselves (*see* PRIESTS); it was usually the city magistrates acting as political leaders, or generals in the field, who did so, although an augur might be present to approve the procedure. In early times the auspices might be taken by private individuals before a personal event such as a wedding. A magistrate had the power to reject the advice of the augurs if he so pleased. The auspices were valid for one day only, so it was possible to seek divine approval for the same action at a later date.

Auspices could be deliberately sought or casually chanced upon, unsolicited. Of the former the best-known example is the observation by the Romans of sacred chickens, carried by armies in the field. Food was given to these birds and if they ate it greedily so as to drop some from their beaks it was a good sign. When they refused to eat before the sea-battle of Drepanum between Rome and Carthage in 249 BC, the Roman admiral threw them overboard, saying, 'Then let them drink'; the Romans were, of course, defeated. If wild birds were to be observed, the augur indicated with a wand the part of the sky to be observed (the *templum*, the word also used for an area of ground consecrated for the augur's use), dividing it into left and right, front and back regions. He would stand facing south or east; the significance of a bird's flight or cry varied according

to the direction from which it came. A notable example of unsolicited auspices occurred on the morning of the battle of Lake Trasimene in 217 BC, during the Second Punic War, when the consul C. *Flaminius ignored the auspices with disastrous results. In the case of an unsolicited sign which was unfavourable, such an omen being considered binding, an augur had the right of making an announcement about it at a public assembly.

Cicero, although an augur himself, wrote *De divinatione* ('On divination') to disprove the possibility of divination. The emperor Augustus seems to have believed in the auspices.

**Augusta** *See* AUGUSTUS, THE.

**Augustan age** (of Latin literature) Term applied to the period following the *Ciceronian age, in which Augustus' personal influence on the literary scene as well as the imperial system which he created were formative. It spans roughly the time from the assassination of Julius Caesar in 44 BC to the death of Ovid in AD 17 (Augustus died in AD 14); its great authors were Virgil, Horace, Tibullus, Propertius, Ovid, and Livy. It started with the destructions of the *Civil War, saw the death of republican government after the battle of Actium in 31 BC (*see* ROME 4), and ended after the restoration of order following nearly a century of revolution. Political activity as it existed under the republic came to an end with the institution of the empire (*see* ROME 5); Augustus' ambition was to restore something of the spirit of the republic in its heyday, and to reinvigorate religious cults and civic ritual. However, real freedom of political and historical inquiry and expression were rather limited; hence the eclipse of oratory (*see* DIALOGUS DE ORATORIBUS) and perhaps of prose literature in general. The support in varying degrees given to Augustus' policy by the poets and historians of the time marks their literature in subtle and ambiguous ways. Support was often solicited by the emperor himself and by other patrons in high official positions, men such as *Maecenas and *Messalla. Augustan writing is in the main serious, often drawn from the moralizing tradition. The writers are enthused when they are concerned with historic Italy and Roman traditions. Even Ovid and Propertius, who appear often to ignore contemporary politics, show the pleasure they feel in the Italian scene. The poetry in particular is characterized by an increasing technical refinement and blend of Greek and Roman themes, and presupposes a sophisticated readership.

**Augustus** (63 BC–AD 14) First of the Roman emperors and the creator of many of the institutions of the empire and of the ideas which sustained it during the first three centuries AD.

1. He was born Gaius Octavius on 23 September, son of a *novus homo* C. Octavius, praetor in 61, and of the niece of Julius *Caesar, and was one of the latter's closest male relations. After his adoption by Caesar in 45 he was named C. Julius Caesar Octaviānus (Octavian; *see* NAMES [Roman]). After 27 BC he was known by his title Augustus. When Caesar was murdered in 44 and his will revealed that he had adopted Octavian and named him as his heir, Octavian at the age of 19 left Greece where he had been finishing his education and returned to Italy to avenge him. The comet that was seen in Rome after Caesar's death was regarded as signifying his apotheosis, but the Elder Pliny says that Octavian secretly thought it an omen for his own future. With political acumen he won the support over the next months both of Caesar's veterans and of moderate republicans who had been opposed to Caesar, including Cicero (*see* CICERO (1) 6). This brought him into conflict with Mark *Antony for the leadership of the Caesarian party. Antony was defeated at the battle of *Mutina and Octavian marched to Rome and made himself consul by force. He and Antony became reconciled and, with *Lepidus, formed the ruling *triumvirate in 43 BC. When (the dead) Julius Caesar was deified in 42 (*see* DEIFICATION) Octavian became *divi filius*, 'son of a god', and later took on a mediating role between gods and people (*see* RULER CULT).

2. The next years saw the land confiscations for army veterans and the *proscriptions in which he too participated. Differences between the triumvirs were reconciled by the treaty of *Brundisium in 40, and Antony married Octavian's sister Octavia, an event which some think occasioned Virgil's fourth *Eclogue. In the same year Octavian married *Scribonia in order to win over Sextus *Pompeius (her brother's son-in-law), but divorced her in 39 after the birth of his only child, Julia, in order to marry Livia Drusilla. He remained devoted to her throughout his life; there were no children of the marriage. In the following year he apparently took *Imperator as a first name (*praeno-*

*men*), denoting his supreme power and commonly used in that sense, and when in 36 he compelled Lepidus to retire from the triumvirate he was in sole control of Rome's western empire. Antony's liaison with the Egyptian queen *Cleopatra, which alienated him from Rome, strengthened Octavian's position still further. In 31 war was declared against Cleopatra; taking her side, Antony was defeated at the sea-battle of Actium and committed suicide. In this year Octavian had regularized his authority by being elected consul (he held the consulship every following year to 23 BC). He returned to Rome in 29, celebrated a triumph, dedicated important temples and closed the temple of *Janus. Now his ostensible duty was to restore the republic.

3. In 27 Octavian laid down his *de facto* dictatorship and reinstated the magistrates, senate, and people in their old constitutional roles, thereby formally restoring the republic. However, he retained the consulship, and Spain, Gaul, Syria, and Egypt as his provinces, together with command over the greater part of the army, and possibly other powers as well. He received many honours including, from the senate, the title of *Augustus (Gk. *sebastos*, 'venerable') which became the imperial title and set the holder above the entire state. By this title Octavian was thereafter known, together with the name Imperator. He also came to be designated, informally at first, as *princeps*, 'citizen of the first importance', a term often used under the republic, especially in the plural, to describe influential statesmen, former consuls, and the like. This was the title he preferred. In 2 BC the senate, on the proposal of *Messalla, conferred on him the ancient republican honorific title *pater patriae*, 'father of his country'. His actual authority was overwhelming. In 23 BC he had resigned the consulship but at the same time received for life (perhaps in three stages) the tribunician power (*see* TRIBUNES OF THE PLEBS), which in effect gave him complete control.

4. Over the years Augustus spent much of his time in the *provinces, where he had enormous authority. Since all holders of *imperium* ('power to command') had a great deal of independent authority it was necessary that Augustus' imperium should be *maius*, 'greater', and he achieved this end in 23. He made religious and moral reforms aimed at restoring the old Roman virtues of simplicity, hard work, and faithful and prolific marriages. In this aim

he was generally supported by the influential literary figures of the age (*see* AUGUSTAN AGE). The premature deaths of promising young men in his family thwarted plans for his successor and he was compelled to accept *Tiberius, son of Livia by a previous marriage. (For Augustus' plans for the succession *see* MARCELLUS (2); AGRIPPA (1) and (2); DRUSUS (3).) When he died in AD 14 it was decreed that he should be deified and accepted among the gods of the state. His life had been for the most part an exemplification of the virtues he preached. Republican government had been over before he came to power, but he tried to establish internal peace based on Roman traditions without offending sectional interests. In this his achievement was immense. However, he leaves behind an impression of a man in whom ideals were always subordinated to a ruthlessly practical end. He was notorious for keeping people guessing about his intentions: his seal-ring was engraved with a sphinx. *See also* APOLLO; BIOGRAPHY; *CARMEN SAECULARE*; PRINCIPATE.

**Augustus, the** [Gk. *sebastos*, 'venerable'] Title held exclusively by all the Roman emperors except Vitellius. When the emperor *Diocletian established a tetrarchy by dividing the empire among four rulers in AD 293, he established two nominally joint emperors who shared the title of Augustus to rule the eastern and western halves of the empire, each with a subordinate ruler, designated a 'Caesar', who might expect to succeed to the higher rank. By personal authority the senior Augustus could hope to remain in effect sole emperor. Although the system failed as a means of establishing the succession, the titles and their general application survived. The title 'Augusta' was bequeathed by the emperor Augustus to his wife Livia, and after Domitian was held by the wife of the reigning emperor.

**Aulis** Town of Boeotia in central Greece. It was celebrated as the place where the Greek fleet assembled for the expedition against Troy and where Agamemnon sacrificed his daughter *Iphigeneia to Artemis to allay the anger of that goddess, who was keeping the fleet windbound.

**aulos** In Greece, a musical pipe sounded with a reed, similar to the oboe. *See* MUSIC [Greek 4] and BOTANY.

**Aululā'ria** ('Pot of gold') Roman comedy by *Plautus, probably adapted from a Greek comedy by *Menander. The prologue is spoken by the *lar familiaris* who has been keeping safe the pot of gold of the title (*see* LARES).

Euclio, an old miser, has found a pot full of treasure buried in his house. He hides it and continues to pretend poverty, for fear that the treasure will be taken from him. His daughter Phaedria has been seduced, at a feast of Ceres, by Lyconides, a young man who is now repentant and wishes to marry her. But meanwhile his uncle Megadorus approaches Euclio with a view to marrying her himself. Euclio, thinking that Megadorus has designs on the treasure, takes it away from his house and hides it in one place after another. He is seen by a slave of Lyconides, who removes it. Euclio is in despair at its loss. (The end of the play is lost, but it may be supposed that Lyconides restores the treasure to Euclio, who in gratitude agrees to his marriage to Phaedria.)

**Aulus Ge'llius** *See* GELLIUS.

**Aure'lian (Lucius Domitius Aurelianus)** (*c.* AD 215–75) Roman emperor 270–5, a brilliant soldier who was successful against Gothic invasions, and a man of humble origin made emperor by the army. His most famous campaign was against Zenobia, queen of Palmyra.

**Aurē'lius, Marcus** (AD 121–80) Roman emperor from 161 to his death. He was born M. Annius Verus ('True'), of consular family; his father and grandfather had the same name. He received a careful education from tutors who included *Fronto (in Latin) and *Herodes Atticus (in Greek). While still young he won the favour of the emperor Hadrian (who nicknamed him *Verissimus*, 'Most true'). When Hadrian adopted *Antoninus Pius as his successor in 138, the latter adopted Marcus. In 145 he married Faustina, Antoninus' daughter (and his own cousin). His peaceful family life is mentioned with affection in his *Meditations*. He became emperor in 161, and shared the throne with Lucius Verus (who had also been adopted by Antoninus) until Verus' death in 169. His reign was dominated by warfare against invaders on all the important frontiers. His twelve books of *Meditations* (Gk. *Ta eis heauton*, 'Notes to himself') were written, in Greek, during the last ten years of his reign while he was on campaign on the frontiers of the empire. They were not published until after his death, by someone unknown. As a young man he had adopted *Stoicism through the influence of a tutor, but the *Meditations* are eclectic and include Platonic and Epicurean aspects. Except for the first book, in which he pays his debts of gratitude, the *Meditations* are arranged in no systematic order but appear just as he wrote them, in difficult Greek, as a series of entries in personal diaries, and record his thoughts about the meaning of world-order and the relationship to it of humankind. Hence they have an immediacy and intensity that impart a strongly personal feeling to Stoic moralizing. They show him to be disillusioned and despondent, seeking fortitude against the fear of death, the cares of this world, and the misdeeds and injustices of others. Thus he is more intimately known than any other Roman statesman or emperor since Cicero. Part of the correspondence between him and his tutor Fronto has survived. He was succeeded as emperor by his son *Commodus.

**Aurō'ra** *See* EOS.

**Ausŏ'nia, Au'sŏnes** Poetic names for Italy and Italians, in Latin and Greek; Ausonia was derived from *Ausones*, an ancient, perhaps originally Greek, name for the inhabitants of middle and south Italy, who have been variously identified. *See* CALYPSO.

**Ausŏ'nius, Decimus Magnus** (c.AD 310–c.393) Latin poet, the son of a physician of Burdigala (Bordeaux), educated there and at Tolosa (Toulouse). After teaching rhetoric at Burdigala for thirty years he was appointed tutor to Gratian, son of the emperor Valentinian I. With his pupil he accompanied Valentinian's expedition against the Germans in 368–9. When Gratian succeeded his father in 375 Ausonius received rapid official advancement, finally becoming consul in 379. After the murder of Gratian in 383 he returned to his family estate at Burdigala, where he appears to have spent most of the remainder of his life. The prayer embedded in the *Ephemeris* (below) suggests Christian belief (his patron Gratian was influenced by St Ambrose). However, he tried to dissuade his pupil Paulinus (later St Paulinus of Nola) from abandoning the world for a life of religion.

Ausonius wrote a great deal of verse in a variety of metres, showing great technical ability. There are over a hundred epigrams, some

of which are in Greek. He seems to have written on any theme that presented itself, such as the names of the days and months, or the properties of the number three. He particularly enjoyed composing verse catalogues: the professors of Burdigala, the famous cities of the world, the Twelve Caesars, the *Seven Sages. He delighted also in such feats of skill as the composition of a prayer in forty-two rhopalic hexameters beginning *spes deus aeternae stationis conciliator* ('God, | our hope | of haven | safe for ever, | uniter of all'). His more important and interesting poems are the *Ephēmeris* ('a day's events'), a description of a normal day in his life (when and where is not clear), his awakening, talking with his various servants, and so on; and the *Mosella*, a long hexameter poem describing in considerable detail the beauties of the river Moselle and the life that goes on around it. His prose writing includes a long *Grātiarum actio*, or thanksgiving for his consulship, addressed to Gratian.

**auspices** *See* AUGURY.

**auster** The south wind (Gk. *notos*).

**autobiography** *See* BIOGRAPHY.

**Auto'lycus** In Greek myth, a son of the god *Hermes and the father of Anticlea, mother of Odysseus. He was a master of trickery and thieving, who received from his father the gift of making himself and his stolen goods invisible, or of changing the appearance of the latter so as to escape detection. He was outwitted by *Sisyphus, another trickster.

**Auto'medon** In Homer's *Iliad*, the charioteer of Achilles, hence his name symbolized any charioteer.

**Auto'noē** In Greek myth, daughter of *Cadmus, mother of *Actaeon.

**A'ventine** The most southerly of the seven hills of Rome, and the setting of the story of Hercules and *Cacus, whose cave Evander showed to Aeneas (Virgil, *Aeneid* 8.184). Until the empire it was mostly occupied by the plebeians, and it remained outside the *pomerium* or city boundary until AD 49. A temple of Diana stood on the summit.

**Ave'rnus** A deep volcanic crater, now a lake near Cumae and Naples. Close to it was the cave by which Aeneas descended to the Underworld (Virgil, *Aeneid* 6). The name was sometimes used for the Underworld itself. It was supposed to be derived from the Greek *aōrnos*, 'without birds', and the lake was in consequence thought to have no bird life. *See* AGRIPPA.

**Avēs** *See* BIRDS.

**Avia'nus** (fl. *c*.AD 400) Roman poet, author of forty-two *fables (based on those of *Babrius) written in elegiac couplets, which were popular in medieval schools. Nothing is known of his life.

**Avie'nus, Postumius Rufius Festus** (fourth century AD) By his own account a native of Volsinii (Bolsena) and twice proconsul. He was the author of an extant astronomical poem in Latin hexameters, based on *Aratus, as well as of a 'Description of the world' (a translation of *Dionysius Periegetes) and a 'Maritime shore', an account of the coastal regions of the Mediterranean, written in iambics. Only part of the last survives.

**axō'nĕs** In the *Prytaneum at Athens, three- or four-sided wooden pillars revolving about a vertical axis on which were written the laws of Draco and of Solon. Small fragments were still in existence in the time of Plutarch.

**Ba'brius** Greek writer of *fables in verse who lived no later than the second century AD. Nothing is known about him. There are 144 fables in existence, written in the version of iambic metre known as choliambic in the ordinary language (*koinē*) of the time and based on the fables of *Aesop with some apparently original additions. They remained very popular in later centuries and were frequently paraphrased in Greek prose and verse.

**Babylonia** Region in southern Iraq stretching from Baghdad to the Arab–Persian Gulf. (Classical writers did not include Babylonia in Mesopotamia.) Through irrigation from the Tigris and Euphrates rivers its fertility was legendary. The first settlement was in the sixth millennium BC. From the sixteenth century BC Babylonia was a state with Babylon as its capital. From the late eighth century BC it was subject to *Assyria until, with the help of the Medes, it destroyed the Assyrian empire, taking the capital Nineveh in 612 BC. The most famous Babylonian king of this period was Nebuchadnezzar II (604–562 BC) who sacked Jerusalem and took the Jews captive to Babylon in 587 BC. The last Babylonian king was defeated by *Cyrus I, the Great, of Persia in 539 BC. He freed the Jews and created a single Achaemenid (Persian) satrapy out of the Babylonian territory.

Babylonia was associated with the study of *astronomy and *astrology in the minds of the Greeks and the Romans, who often referred to Babylonian scholars as 'Chaldaeans' (one of the Babylonian peoples). Babylonian mathematics and astronomy were an accumulation of rules for the solution of particular religious problems, above all the need to predict astronomical events so as to appease the gods who caused them. The thousands of surviving cuneiform tablets reveal the high level reached in their calculations and observations by *c.*1600 BC and persisting for the next thousand years. The question remains as to how much of this knowledge reached Greece. Some seems to have spread to Greece by way of Ionia in the sixth century BC, perhaps influencing Thales and Anaximander. *See* HIPPARCHUS.

**Bacchae** ('*Bacchants', female celebrants of the rites of Bacchus, also called Dionysus) A Greek tragedy by *Euripides probably written during the poet's stay in Macedonia and found after his death there in 406 BC. It was subsequently produced at Athens (probably in 405) by the poet's son (or nephew) also named Euripides, together with *Iphigeneia at Aulis* and *Alcmaeon in Corinth* (the latter now lost).

*Dionysus, divine son of Zeus and the Theban princess Semele, travelling through the world to make himself known to men as a god, comes to Thebes, where his divinity has been denied even by Semele's sister Agave, mother of Pentheus, king of Thebes. Dionysus has driven the women of Thebes to frenzy and compelled them to celebrate his rites on Mount Cithaeron. Pentheus is implacably hostile to the new religion in spite of the remonstrances of his grandfather Cadmus and of the seer Teiresias, and imprisons Dionysus (who claims to be not the god himself but a votary). Dionysus proves his power over material things by causing Pentheus to bind a bull in his stead and by making an earthquake destroy the palace. A messenger arrives and describes the behaviour of the Theban women on the mountains. Dionysus induces Pentheus to disguise himself as a woman in order to see for himself, and then engineers Pentheus' discovery by the women, who tear him to pieces. Agave, in her frenzy, bears his head triumphantly to Thebes. It is only when she recovers that she finds she has killed her son. The family of Cadmus is doomed to banishment from Thebes and the play ends with their departure.

The *Bacchae* is about a supposed historical event, the introduction into Greece of a new god and his worship. By Euripides' time both had long been accepted as part of Greek life, but worship of Dionysus offered an emotional religious experience different from any that might be found in the cult of the traditional Olympian gods, and its power to change the mood of his worshippers from blissful calm to exultant savagery is made shockingly evident in the play.

**Bacchanā'lia** Latin name for the fundamentally Greek religious rites of the god *Dionysus, derived from his alternative name of Bacchus. Livy in his history of Rome (39.14) gives an account of their wild excesses and subsequent suppression in 186 BC, after the rites had been introduced to Rome and Italy from Etruria and (Greek) south Italy. A surviving inscription records the senatorial decree which authorized their suppression. *See also* MYSTERIES.

**Bacchants (Bacchantēs, Bacchanals, Maenads)** Women inspired to ecstasy by the Greek god *Dionysus (sometimes called Bacchus), as described by Euripides in the *Bacchae*. They are depicted wearing the skins of fawns or panthers and wreaths of ivy, oak, or fir and carrying a thyrsus (a wand wreathed in ivy and vine leaves, topped with a pine cone). Freed from the conventions of normal behaviour they roamed the mountains with music and dancing and, according to myth, inspired by the god performed supernatural feats of strength, uprooting trees, catching and tearing apart wild animals, and sometimes eating the flesh raw.

**Bacchī'adae** Aristocrats in *Corinth who claimed descent ultimately from Heracles (*see* HERACLEIDAE) but more immediately from Bacchis, king of Corinth perhaps *c.*900 BC. The monarchy was overthrown in 747 (the traditional date) and thereafter the city was governed by a Bacchiad oligarchy until 657 BC when they were destroyed by *Cypselus, who made himself tyrant. The Bacchiadae supposedly laid the foundation for Corinth's greatness in colonization, maritime affairs, trade, and in particular pottery. Their flight to *Corcyra may have initiated the hostility between Corinth and that colony.

**Ba'cchidēs** ('Girls called Bacchis') Roman comedy by *Plautus, adapted from the Greek comedy of Menander *Dis exapatōn* ('The double deceiver').

The opening of the play is missing, but the situation is clear. A young man Pistoclerus is searching in Athens on behalf of an absent friend Mnesilochus for a courtesan Bacchis of Samos. He finds that she has visited her sister, also called Bacchis, and falls in love with the sister. When Mnesilochus arrives he is horrified to learn that his friend is making love to 'Bacchis'. The confusion about the supposed disloyalty is soon cleared up, but by then the young men's fathers have been informed. Finally, the sisters beguile the fathers into forgiveness and all ends happily.

**Bacchus** Alternative name, perhaps of Lydian origin, for the Greek god *Dionysus, and his usual name in Latin.

**Bacchy'lides** (*c.*520–450 BC) Greek lyric poet from the island of Ceos, nephew of the poet Simonides and contemporary of Pindar, whose great rival ancient scholars believed him to be. Although he was well known down to Roman times (Horace imitated him and the emperor Julian we are told 'enjoyed reading him') his works were lost in antiquity and only a few lines survived in quotation until, at the end of the nineteenth century, the British Museum acquired the remains of two papyrus rolls containing fifteen epinician odes (*see* EPINIKION) and six *dithyrambs. Since then more fragments have been found on papyri (*see* PAPYROLOGY), and some *scholia. Bacchylides seems to have been employed by the same patrons as employed his uncle Simonides and Pindar. He and Pindar both composed odes for at least two victories won in the great games by Hieron tyrant of Syracuse: thus Bacchylides' Ode 5 and Pindar's Olympian 1 both commemorate the horse-race at the Olympian games of 476 BC, and his Ode 4 and Pindar's Pythian 1 the chariot-race at Delphi in 470. The epinician odes of Bacchylides contain the same elements as Pindar's—central mythical narrative, passages praising the victor, his country, and the gods, passages of moralizing—but he lacks Pindar's profundity and brilliant imaginative gifts. His strength lies in his moving and dramatic narratives, as is also apparent in the dithyrambs. Ode 18 (Dithyramb 4) is unique among surviving choral lyric in being wholly a dialogue, between the leader of the chorus representing Aegeus, king of Athens, and, presumably, the remainder of the chorus who represent the people of Athens. Aegeus has heard the news of the imminent arrival of a young hero and in reply to questions elaborates on the deeds of the young man whom he does not yet know to be his son Theseus. Probably the form of the poem was influenced by contemporary drama, but it is tempting to see in this dithyramb's unparalleled dramatic style a survival of an older form of dithyramb which Aristotle believed to be the precursor of tragedy (*see* TRAGEDY 1). Bacchylides also wrote *hymns, *paeans, maiden-songs (*see* PARTHENEION), *hyporchemata, and encomia, very little of which survives.

**Baiae** A small place near Cumae on the Bay of Naples, perhaps originally its port, first famous for its volcanic warm springs containing a variety of minerals and then, from before the time of Cicero, a fashionable Roman resort. Lucullus, Pompey, and Caesar all had villas here, as did some later Roman emperors.

**Balbus** A common *cognomen* in several Roman *gentes* (*see* NAMES [Roman] and GENS).

  **Lucius Cornelius Balbus** was a native of Gades (Cadiz), who had Roman citizenship conferred upon him in 72 BC through Pompey's influence, for his services to Rome in the war against *Sertorius in Spain, and took a Roman name. He moved to Rome where, with Pompey's favour, he soon became a man of considerable importance, valued for his wealth and political sense. Prudently he cultivated Caesar's favour also, and partly brought about the coalition between Caesar, Pompey, and Crassus in 60 BC. His influence made him many enemies who engineered his prosecution in 56 for illegally assuming Roman citizenship, but he was successfully defended by Cicero in an extant speech, *Pro Balbo*. In the Civil War he was outwardly neutral while privately favouring Caesar, and subsequently Octavian. In 40 BC he became Rome's first foreign-born consul. His published diary has not come down to us, but a few of his letters to Cicero survive. (His namesake and nephew is also mentioned in Cicero's correspondence.)

**Balius** *See* XANTHUS.

**Bandu'sia** Italian fountain made famous by Horace in *Odes* 3.13. Its location is uncertain.

**barbarian** [Gk. *barbaros*] A non-Greek speaker, i.e. 'foreigner'; eventually, in a cultural sense, 'barbarian'. It is an onomatopoeic word derived from the Greek perception of sounds made by foreigners speaking their own language. Homer used the word (in a compound) only once, to describe the non-Greek speech of the Carians, from Asia Minor. In the *Iliad* he does not in any obvious way portray the non-Greek Trojans as different from the Greeks, and this is true of archaic literature in general. (The Homeric scholar *Heracleitus (3), however, assumed that the Greeks in Homer were superior to the 'barbarians' in intelligence.) At the beginning of the fifth century BC the monsters portrayed in Hesiod's *Theogony*, Typhoeus and the Giants and Titans, were often given allegorical significance: in Pindar the destruction of Typhoeus symbolized the defeat of the Carthaginians and Etruscans by the Greeks, barbarians overcome by civilization. (Public sculpture exploited the contrast: the victory of Attalus I over the Galatians some time before 230 BC was represented on the Altar of Zeus at Pergamum by the depiction of the Olympian gods defeating the Giants.) Also in the early fifth century, the time of the Persian Wars, 'barbarian' was used more specifically to denote the Persians (Herodotus, book 1). Classical Greek literature started to define a Greek identity, based on shared descent, language, religion, and customs, as Herodotus has it, and to contrast it with that of the Persians to the disadvantage of the latter, who then acquired the connotation of barbarian. In Xenophon's *Anabasis* the Greek mercenary army drawn from various Greek states consciously feels its common Greekness to be a strong bond in the face of hostile peoples in the countries of the Persian empire. Foreigners were excluded from the Olympian games and from participating in the *mysteries of Eleusis. As 'barbarians' they came to be characterized as lacking reason and self-control. They are seen as the natural enemy of Greeks, who should unite against them rather than fight each other. One factor contributing to the Greek attitude was the large influx of slaves, the result of almost incessant warfare on the fringes of the Greek world, who included non-Greek speakers like Illyrians, Paeonians, and Thracians (note the attempts at speaking Greek by the Scythian archers in Aristophanes' *Thesmophoriazusae*), and people like the Epirotes who spoke a dialect of Greek but were outside the orbit of the Greek city-state. Plato in the *Republic* opposed the enslaving of Greeks by Greeks. It became a commonplace that the barbarian was a slave by nature. Occasionally the natural unity of all humankind was emphasized instead, by intellectuals like the widely travelled philosopher Democritus ('for a wise man every land is open'), the sophist

Antiphon ('Greeks and foreigners/barbarians, we are all exactly alike in nature'), and the poet Meleager ('if I am a Syrian, what wonder? We all dwell in one country, the world; one Chaos brought all mortals to birth'). This seems to be a view endorsed by Euripides in *The Trojan Women*. But in his portrait of Medea (from Colchis) Euripides drew attention to her 'barbarian' nature, and in *Iphigeneia at Aulis* he is at pains to emphasize the superiority of Greeks to barbarians.

In the Hellenistic period the distinction between the two came to seem less important to some thinkers and especially to Stoics: *see* STOI-CISM. As the scholar *Eratosthenes wrote in the third century BC, 'Not only are many Greeks bad [*kakoi*, perhaps meaning here 'ill-bred', 'uncouth'], but many of the barbarians are civilized, notably the Indians and Arians [west of Afghanistan], and also the Romans and Carthaginians, who enjoy such admirable forms of government'. The Romans, barbarians themselves from the Greek point of view (which they sometimes adopted), drew on the concept to emphasize the 'barbarian' traits of dangerous foreigners like Cleopatra, who was Greek by race. The Romans adopted the word 'barbarian' and its general significance, but altered its reference to embrace everyone not Greek or Roman. The Roman comic poet, Plautus, whose plays were adaptations from the Greek, uses the word in the Greek sense for comic effect to describe a Roman or Italian. As late as the early third century AD a Greek-speaking guest in the *Deipnosophistae* of *Athenaeus objects angrily to the introduction of Latin words into the Greek conversation as a barbarism, even though the setting is Rome.

**basileus** *See* ARCHONS.

**baths** In Greece, bathing was not the social institution it became in Roman times. Public baths existed, where hot water was poured over bathers seated in hip-baths, but water was in quite short supply and frequent use of warm water was sometimes regarded as excessively luxurious, especially by the Spartans, except to relax the muscles after exercise. Athenian homes possessed basins on pedestals, but bathing seems to have been a luxury reserved for special occasions such as a party. A kind of soap was used as well as the strigil (a curved instrument made of metal or bone) to remove oil and dirt from the skin. After bathing both men and women anointed themselves with oil.

The Roman baths are one of the most characteristic of their institutions, found universally in the Roman world and enjoyed by all classes of society including some slaves, except the very poorest. During their earlier history the Romans bathed only for the sake of cleanliness. For most of their history they went out to bath. The earliest known public baths are found at Pompeii and date from the early first century BC. The process of bathing changed radically with the invention of the system for carrying hot air from a furnace through passages under floors (hypocausts), and through ducts embedded in room walls. With this providing warm water and hot air, by the middle of the first century BC the use of public and private baths had become general, and though public baths were intended at first for the poor they were soon made use of by all classes. Baths were communal, each being roughly the size of a small, shallow swimming-pool. The price of a bath was a *quadrans*, the smallest piece of coined money, virtually worthless. The essential rooms for public baths were the changing-room (*apodyterium*), the cold-bath room (*frigidarium*), an indirectly heated warm-room (*tepidarium*), and a strongly heated room (*caldarium*). Larger establishments might include a hot vapour bath (*laconicum*), a sweating-room (*sudatorium*), suites of recreational rooms, exercise grounds (it was usual to take exercise before bathing), and gardens. These buildings were the natural medium for the development of concrete vaulted architecture and comprised some of its most sophisticated examples. Those surviving strongly influenced the style of Renaissance architecture. Though mixed bathing was not unknown, women more usually had separate (and inferior) baths adjoining those of the men.

Public bathing at Rome declined as the aqueducts fell out of repair. In AD 537 the besieging Goths cut them off, and the city's baths never recovered.

**Bathy'llus** *See* PANTOMIME.

**Batrachomyoma'chia** ('Battle of the frogs and mice') A short Greek mock-epic poem in the style of Homeric epic, sometimes attributed to Homer in antiquity and difficult to date but perhaps of the fifth century BC. The story derives from a fable of Aesop; a mouse

Psīcharpax ('crumb-stealer') is invited by a frog Physignathos ('puff-cheek') son of Peleus to ride on his back to visit his watery kingdom. Unfortunately, at the sight of a water-snake the frog dives and the mouse is drowned. But the incident has been seen by another mouse, and a one-day Homeric war ensues between the mice and the frogs, in which the mice seem to be winning. At the request of Athena, Zeus intervenes, and having failed with thunderbolts sends crabs to quell the strife.

**Battiadēs** *See* BATTUS.

**Battus** Leader of a body of Dorian Greeks who left the island of Thera in about 630 BC at the bidding of the Delphic oracle, to colonize Cyrene in Libya (North Africa). Battus, like other founders of colonies, achieved semi-mythical status, and the stories told about him have a strong element of folk-tale. He was said to be a descendant of the ancient race of heroes known as the *Minyans and of the *Argonaut Euphemus. His strange name has been variously interpreted, as the Libyan word for king or as meaning 'stammerer' from a supposed speech impediment. His descendants ruled Cyrene for more than 200 years. The father of the poet Callimachus was a Cyrenaean of royal descent called Battus; hence the poet is often called 'Battiades' ('son of Battus').

**Baucis** *See* PHILEMON.

**beards** Men in both Greece and Rome wore beards in early times. During the fifth century BC men at Athens wore beards, but from the time of Alexander the Great (d. 323 BC), who was always portrayed beardless, Greek men shaved their chins. To judge from portraiture Greeks then tended to remain clean-shaven until the time of Justinian in the sixth century AD, except for philosophers and other intellectuals who chose to grow long beards. 'A long beard does not make a philosopher' became a Greek proverb.

Romans wore their beards uncut until 300 BC when a certain P. Ticinius Maenas brought over a barber from Sicily. A fashion for shaving soon developed, though some merely trimmed their beard. Scipio Africanus at the end of the second century BC was said to have been the first Roman to shave every day. For young men the first shave was an event to be celebrated (Nero put his first beard in a gold box set with pearls and dedicated it to Jupiter Capitolinus).

Most portraits of the Julio-Claudian emperors and their successors in the first century AD show them clean-shaven, but Hadrian (d. AD 138) revived the beard—a sign perhaps of his devotion to Greek culture—and this was an influence on later portraiture. Marcus Aurelius (emperor AD 161) wore the long beard of the philosopher, and the soldier-emperors of the late third century had what looks like curly stubble. Clean-shaving reappeared as a fashion with the emperor Constantine I (d. 337).

Shaving was mostly performed with a cut-throat style razor, kept in a razor-case. Those who could not face this used powerful ointments which destroyed the hair, or depilatory plasters. Stray hairs were removed with tweezers.

**Bē'driacum** The site of two decisive battles in AD 69, near modern Calvatone, midway between Cremona and Verona in Cisalpine Gaul. In the first, the forces of the Roman emperor Otho were defeated by the supporters of Vitellius, who succeeded to the empire. The latter's forces were defeated some months later by Vespasian's.

**Behistun** *See* BISITUN.

**Belgae** A population group occupying part of Gaul in Roman times. Their area was bounded in the south by the rivers Seine and Marne, in the west by the sea, and in the east and north by the Rhine. They boasted of German descent and were the fiercest inhabitants of Gaul. Julius Caesar says that some tribes passed into Britain from about 100 BC onwards and settled in the south and south-west, but there is no clear archaeological evidence of their settling then in that area, and Caesar's statement, if it is more than an excuse for invading Britain, may merely indicate close contacts between Britain and Gaul throughout the first century BC. However, many of the Belgae eventually settled in Britain, and the Romans established Venta (Winchester) as the Belgic *civitas* (citizen-community) there. Caesar subdued the Gallic Belgae in 57 BC but they continued to give trouble to the Romans for the next thirty years.

**Belle'rophon** (**Bellerophontēs**) In Greek myth, son of Glaucus (the son of Sisyphus) and Eurymede; in some accounts his father was said to be the god Poseidon. His grandson was Glaucus in the *Iliad*. He was an ancient Corinthian hero, and his adventures sound similar to those of Heracles and Theseus. He spent some time at the palace of Proetus, king of Tiryns, whose wife Anteia (sometimes called Stheneboea) fell in love with him. When he rejected her Anteia accused him to her husband of trying to seduce her. Proetus, unwilling to violate the laws of hospitality by killing Bellerophon in his house, sent him to Iobates, Proetus' father-in-law and king of Lycia, with a sealed letter requesting the king to execute Bellerophon. The king accordingly set him a number of tasks likely to prove fatal, killing the *Chimaera, defeating the Solymi and the *Amazons, but Bellerophon with the aid of the winged horse *Pegasus was always victorious. He became reconciled to the king and married his daughter. Afterwards he incurred the wrath of the gods by trying to ride Pegasus to Olympus, but the horse threw him. He ended his life a lonely outcast.

**Bellō'na** (older form, Duellona) The Roman goddess of war, sometimes thought of as the wife or sister of Mars. She had no *flamen and no festival, and virtually no mythology. Her first known temple was that vowed by Appius Claudius Caecus while fighting the Etruscans in 296 BC and built in the Campus Martius near the Circus Flaminius. Since the temple lay outside the *pomerium* or city boundary of Rome, it was used by the senate to give audience to foreign ambassadors and returning generals (*see* TRIUMPH) whom it was not considered prudent to admit into the city. Here also stood the pillar symbolizing the enemy's frontier over which the *fetialis* threw a spear when a declaration of war was made. The Greek equivalent of Bellona was recognized to be Enyo.

**Bellum Africum** ('The African war') A short record of Julius *Caesar's four months' war in Africa (47–46 BC) against the supporters of Pompey. The author is not known; the attribution to A. *Hirtius is impossible. The contents suggest that he was a soldier who took part in the campaign but was not in Caesar's confidence.

**Bellum Alexandrī'num** ('The Alexandrian war') A continuation of Julius Caesar's history of the Civil War (*see* COMMENTARIES 2), probably written by *Hirtius (the style is comparable with the *Bellum Gallicum* book 8, not written by Caesar but probably by Hirtius). It describes the war of 48–47 BC in Egypt, where Caesar, following his pursuit of Pompey, remained to settle the Egyptian succession by restoring *Cleopatra as ruler. It makes no mention of the liaison with Cleopatra or the birth of Caesarion, and ends with Caesar's victory at Zela in August 47 (*see* CAESAR (2)).

**Bellum Cīvī'le** ('The Civil War') **1.** History in three books by Julius *Caesar of the first two years of the Civil War between him and Pompey begun in 49 BC; *see* COMMENTARIES 2.
　　**2.** Title of an epic poem by the Latin poet *Lucan on the Civil War between Julius Caesar and Pompey, often known as *Pharsalia.*

**Bellum Gallicum** *See* COMMENTARIES 1.

**Bellum Hispanie'nse** ('The Spanish war') An account of Julius *Caesar's final campaign of the Civil War fought in Spain in 45 BC against Pompey's sons and Labienus, ending in Caesar's victory at Munda. The author is unknown but was probably a soldier in Caesar's army. The text, written in uneducated Latin—'the worst book in Latin Literature'—has not been accurately preserved.

**Bellum Pū'nicum** *See* NAEVIUS.

**Belus** (Gk. form of the god Baal, and Babylonian Bel) In Greek myth, king of Egypt, son of Poseidon and of Libya or Eurynome, twin-brother of *Agenor, father of Aegyptus and *Danaus. Through his sons he became the ancestor of several royal houses in Greece and Africa. Belus was also the name of *Dido's father.

**bematists** ('pacers') The surveyors of Alexander the Great who measured important distances in his empire. Their reports combined calculations of distance with observations of the flora and fauna of the empire, as well as of customs (of doubtful accuracy). Eventually they produced an archive which came into the possession of Seleucus I. The measurements gave *Eratosthenes a framework for his geography of Asia.

**Bendis** In Greek myth, a goddess originally worshipped in Thrace and identified with Artemis. Her cult was accepted officially at *Piraeus in 430–429 BC for the benefit of resident Thracians. Her festival, which included a torch-race on horseback, is the occasion of Plato's dialogue the *Republic.*

**Berenī'cē 1.** (b. c.340 BC) First the mistress and then the third wife of *Ptolemy I Soter, king of Egypt, and known as Berenice I. Their children were Ptolemy II Philadelphus and Arsinoē II, who married her brother as his second wife (his first wife being Arsinoe I). Idyll 15 of Theocritus concerns the Adonis festival in her honour.

**2.** (b. c.280 BC) Daughter of Ptolemy II and Arsinoe I and sister of Ptolemy III; she was married to Antiochus II, king of Syria. After his death she and her son were murdered by Antiochus' first wife.

**3.** Berenice II (b. c.273 BC) Daughter of the king of Cyrene, married to Ptolemy III Euergetes in 247. In 246 Ptolemy set out for Syria to support, too late, the claims of his sister's son to the throne of Syria ((2) above). On his departure, his wife Berenice dedicated to the gods a lock of her hair as an offering for his safe return. This lock mysteriously disappeared. Conon, the court astronomer, claimed flatteringly to have discovered it in a hitherto unnamed constellation, seven faint stars near the tail of Leo, thereafter known in Latin as *Coma Berenices* (Gk. *Berenikes plokamos*), 'the lock of Berenice'. This event was celebrated in an ingenious and entertaining poem by Callimachus, in which the lock of hair addresses the reader. Catullus' poem 66 is virtually a translation of it into Latin, and Alexander Pope based upon it his *Rape of the Lock* (1712).

**4.** (b. AD 28) Daughter of Agrippa I of Judaea (called Herod in Acts of the Apostles 12) and great-granddaughter of *Herod the Great. After the death of her second husband she lived with her brother Agrippa II, and to allay suspicion of incest married the king of Cilicia (AD 54). She soon left him, however, and returned to her brother, with whom she was living when the apostle Paul spoke his defence before them both (as in Acts 25, where she is called Bernice). She and her brother tried in vain to dissuade the Jews from rebelling against Rome in AD 66, and when war broke out they both sided with the Romans. When *Titus, the son of the Roman emperor Vespasian, was fighting in Judaea in 67–70, he fell in love with her, and after she visited Rome with Agrippa c.75 they lived openly together for three or four years. This liaison was unpopular and Titus was compelled to send her away when he succeeded to the throne in 79. Juvenal mentions her contemptuously in his Satire 6. She is the Berenice who was the

heroine of tragedies by the French playwrights Corneille (1606–84) and Racine (1639–99).

**Bērō's(s)us** Priest at Babylon in the third century BC who wrote a history of Babylon in three books in Greek, of which only quotations survive. Also ascribed to him were works on astronomy and astrology, which are known only from references in later writers.

**betrothal** In Athens, the initial stage of a marriage which was necessary to make it legal. It was a contract between the groom and the bride's *kyrios*, 'guardian' (usually her father; if he was dead, her nearest adult male relation), according to which the transfer was agreed of the bride to the groom for the procreation of legitimate children. An agreement would be made concerning dowry. The bride's consent was not legally required, nor need she be present or even of an age to understand. In the end the marriage might not take place, as in the case of Demosthenes' sister who was betrothed at the age of 5.

In the Roman republic, betrothal (*sponsalia*) was not a legal prerequisite for marriage. It consisted of reciprocal promises with the possibility of breach-of-promise actions if agreements were broken. In the course of time *sponsalia* came to be an informal agreement, celebrated by a party and by the prospective husband putting an iron ring on the third finger of his betrothed's left hand. *See* MARRIAGE CEREMONIES and MARRIAGE LAW.

**Bī'as** Brother of the Greek seer *Melampus.

**Bi'bulus, Marcus Calpu'rnius** Julius *Caesar's political opponent but colleague in the consulship of 59 BC. After being forcibly prevented from blocking Caesar's agrarian laws, which aimed at giving land to the poorest citizens, he shut himself up in his house for the rest of the year, ostensibly to watch for omens and so make Caesar's legislation technically invalid. This gave rise to the joke that it was the consulship of 'Julius and Caesar', not of Caesar and Bibulus. Upon the latter's proposal Pompey was elected sole consul in 52 BC. Bibulus was proconsul of Syria in 51 and commander of Pompey's fleet against Caesar in 49. He died in 48. His second wife was *Porcia, daughter of Marcus Porcius Cato of Utica, who subsequently married Marcus Brutus, one of Caesar's assassins.

**bilingualism** The knowledge of two languages by an individual, or the use of two languages in one community. In the former case, what is often denoted by the term in the ancient world is knowledge by an individual of both Latin and Greek. The Greek sense of the superiority of their own culture, including their language, apparently precluded them from showing much interest in other languages. Herodotus tells us that he needed an interpreter to translate an Egyptian inscription for him. The sources that describe the wide travels of famous Greek thinkers make no mention of the languages in which they conversed with other wise men. We are not told in what language the very widely travelled Democritus, for instance, communicated with 'men distinguished in every kind of science' in Asia and elsewhere, or whether Ionian Greek cosmologists were able to speak Aramaic to their Babylonian counterparts. Perhaps the assumption of the sources was that all foreigners worth speaking to could speak Greek. The exceptionally far-sighted Themistocles spent a year learning Persian (or perhaps *Aramaic) before arriving at the Persian court. It is to be expected that foreign residents, traders, and slaves as well as mercenary soldiers learned something of the languages of the people they mixed with. In Aristophanes' *Thesmophoriazusae* the Scythian archers speak mangled Greek. It was a literary commonplace that the natives of Italy who lived near the Greek cities there (*see* MAGNA GRAECIA) were bilingual in their own language and Greek (Horace disapproved of the satirist *Lucilius mixing his vocabulary in this way). One of the striking things about Xenophon's *Anabasis* is the ease with which the Greeks communicate, often at length, with the Persians and various other peoples. Interpreters are sometimes mentioned, but the interlocutors themselves seem to know enough of each other's languages to keep a check on what is said. The wily Seuthes, king of Thrace, brought along a personal interpreter to a crucial meeting, 'though he had a fairly adequate knowledge of Greek himself'. Thousands of inscriptions in Egypt and throughout Asia (as far east as Kandahar) are often bilingual, in both Greek and the local common language.

In Italy a variety of languages was spoken down to the first century BC, many of which were related to Latin. Classical Latin, the language of Latium and the written form of the Roman dialect, assumed its classical form from about 90 BC and was a product of several centuries of refinement. From the third century BC when the Romans became involved in the affairs of Greece the educated and ruling class at Rome had been impressed by and interested in Greek language, literature, and philosophy. Latin was not thought of as a language in which literature could be written. The first Roman historian, Q. *Fabius (3), wrote his history in Greek (*c.*200 BC), as much for literary as for political reasons. Rome's greatest enemy, the Carthaginian general Hannibal, was notable for being fluent in Latin and many other languages, using this skill to eavesdrop on his soldiers. Such was his fluency in Latin that he made an audacious attempt to gain entry to an enemy city by impersonating the Roman consul Marcellus, whom he had previously killed in battle. (The attempt failed because the city had been forewarned.) A stereotypical Carthaginian in Plautus' *Poenulus* also 'knows all languages'. Cornelius *Scipio Africanus (who captured Carthage in 146 BC) is represented by Cicero as one of a group of aristocrats enthusiastic about Greek literature and philosophy, sometimes referred to, misleadingly perhaps, as the Scipionic circle. All these people were at home in Greek, as was Cato the Elder (234–149 BC), whose *Origines* was the first Roman history to be written in Latin. However, he was hostile to what he saw as the corrupting effect of Greek culture, and though fluent in Greek he insisted when in Greece on addressing the Athenians through an interpreter. When Greek was spoken in the senate (as by Greek-speaking envoys) it was not always considered necessary to have an interpreter. Most Roman emperors were bilingual, to the extent that Marcus Aurelius wrote his *Meditations* in Greek. The poet Ovid was exceptional in learning during his exile the language of his neighbours the Getae and Sarmatians. He even wrote a poem in Getic (which has not survived) and recited it to the native speakers to much applause: they rattled their quivers. In his epitaph the Greek poet *Meleager (fl. 100 BC), who was born in Syria, lived in Tyre, and retired to the Greek island of Cos, bids farewell in the three corresponding languages.

In the West, Latin was the language of Roman law and administration, and of the army, as well as of those who wanted to make their way in the professions. In the

Greek-speaking East the administration under the Roman empire was mostly conducted in Greek and inscriptions were often in Greek; the abundance of bilingual inscriptions seems to indicate that there was no policy to impose Latin, and Greek speakers retained a reluctance to learn Latin. Plutarch (living in Boeotia in Greece) had a working knowledge of Latin but had no need to use it in conversation: all his Roman friends would have spoken Greek. Competence in both languages prevailed among the educated class until at least the fourth century AD, but when the seat of empire was transferred to Constantinople in AD 324 Latin was increasingly used in government and administration, and in the West, knowledge of Greek, even among the educated, declined. *See* BOETHIUS.

**biography** Biography is not a rigidly defined literary genre in the ancient world.

**Greek.** The term *bios* (Gk. 'life' in the sense of biography, 'a written life') covered, as in modern times, works of varying length and seriousness, and different degrees of sensationalism, truth, and bias. Greek origins may be seen in (sung) *dirges and (spoken) funeral orations commemorating the dead, but their contents are formal and do not extend to much if any detail about the lives of the deceased until about the fourth century BC. In the fifth century BC *Ion of Chios wrote a book of *Epidemiai* ('Visits', i.e. to the famous) in which he related his gossipy conversations with the great men of his day. Historians wrote thumbnail sketches of historical characters: Thucydides memorably describes Pausanias and Themistocles in book 1 of his history, and in the early fourth century BC Xenophon in his *Anabasis* writes succinct and deliberately contrasting accounts of the Greek generals Clearchus, Proxenus, and Menon, treacherously done away with by the Persian governor Tissaphernes. These character sketches of the main participants continued to be a part of history writing, in which the influence of human personality came later to be emphasized. They make clear one tendency of ancient biography, that is to regard a person's character as being fixed, and the function of biography to describe 'what a man is like', which involves examination of his virtues and vices. This method is followed without much regard to the subject's development over time even though the overall arrangement of a biography was chronological. Character assess-

ment of this kind is found in the *Evagoras* of *Isocrates. Xenophon's longer biographical works (*see* AGESILAUS; CYROPEDIA; MEMORABILIA) have more in common with the rhetorical genre of *encomia* ('speeches in praise' of individuals): the eulogistic *Cyropedia* has been compared to a modern historical novel that glorifies the main character at the expense of fact. Also influential in the development of Greek biography, however, were the many accounts of Socrates written by his pupils (the Socratics, so called), in which attention is drawn to Socrates' idiosyncrasies of behaviour as part and parcel of his mission of philosophical enquiry. This more psychological approach gains impetus from Aristotle and the Peripatetic philosophers, who taught that a man must live with his inborn nature (*physis*) but can train his moral character. The Hellenistic scholars valued biographical information about classical authors as a means of explaining their writings, but conversely and unfortunately also used the authors' imaginative writings to explain their lives. None of this work survives except in fragments. What we do possess is a Latin adaptation of Hellenistic 'lives of great men' in the *Viri illustres* ('Great Men') of Cornelius Nepos (below). These brief histories represent a tradition of portraying character. Over 200 years later Plutarch (second century AD) owed the form of his *Parallel Lives* (a Greek Life paired with a corresponding Roman) largely to his Hellenistic predecessors. To some extent his characters exemplify virtues or vices (notably ambition) in a rather simplistic way, but his understanding of the historical evidence and, quite often, of the complexity of character, far exceeded in scope and seriousness anything that had gone before. In the early third century AD *Diogenes Laertius wrote a compendium of the lives and doctrines of the Greek philosophers, but it is merely a synthesis of earlier compositions.

Autobiography appears patchily in the Greek world. Self-description and self-analysis go as far back as Greek lyric poetry (*see* e.g. SAPPHO). Xenophon, recounting in the *Anabasis* how he had found himself at the head of a large army in gravest danger of annihilation, writes vividly of his own feelings—and dreams—at such a crisis. The Jewish historian *Josephus (first century AD) wrote what he called his 'Life', but it was limited to a defence against his enemy Justus. Letters, particularly of self-exculpation, ascribed to certain famous authors but probably the work of others, purport to be genuinely autobiographical (*see* PLATO 1). The (genuine) *Meditations* of Marcus *Aurelius (AD 121–80) may be thought to be not so much autobiography as generalized reflections on human life.

**Roman.** Roman biography developed from a native tradition of funeral orations and sepulchral inscriptions which listed the achievements of the dead man in considerable detail. Many generals and politicians wrote accounts of their careers in order to justify their actions; Sulla, for example, wrote his memoirs in twenty-two books (now lost). Julius Caesar's *Commentaries* on his Gallic Wars and on the Civil War are subtly slanted to ensure that his own perspective on events and his role in them should survive. Cicero wrote about the high points of his career in both Greek and Latin (and in prose and verse), but little survives. The deaths of Cato (2) the Younger and Brutus (2) inspired a spate of works that were closer to ideological propaganda (for the republicans) than to biography. Caesar's hostile rejoinder to Cicero's panegyric of Cato was the *Anticato* (which does not survive). Under the empire memoirs were written by the emperor or members of his family, by Augustus and Tiberius, for example. Very few fragments survive. The most important surviving biographies are those of famous men, Greek and Roman, by Cornelius *Nepos (first century BC), of *Agricola by his son-in-law Tacitus (end of the first century AD), of the Twelve Caesars by *Suetonius (Tacitus' younger contemporary), and of the later emperors by the writers of the *Historia Augusta.* The *Agricola* has the self-serving aim of showing how a successful political life can be prudently conducted even under a tyrant. In Suetonius' *Lives of the Caesars* the purely historical content is much reduced and the focus is on character and behaviour instead. This was an influential innovation, to be followed in the *Historia Augusta.* It seems strange that the self-awareness found in much of late republican and Augustan poetry did not translate into biography; public figures continued to be treated without intimacy.

The only autobiography that reveals anything of the writer's own inner life and thought is the *Confessions* of St Augustine, written *c.* AD 397–400 (cf. the *Meditations* of Marcus Aurelius, above).

**biology** See ANATOMY AND PHYSIOLOGY; ANIMALS, ATTITUDES TO; BOTANY; GYNAECOLOGY; HUMOURS; MEDICINE; ARISTOTLE 4 (iv); EMPEDOCLES.

**Bion 1. the Borysthenite** (fl. early third century BC) Greek popular philosopher born in the Greek colony of Olbia in Scythia, near the estuary of the river Borysthenes (Dnieper). According to his own account his family was enslaved to a rhetorician but Bion received a good education and was eventually freed. He studied in the various philosophical schools in Athens but became an adherent of no one school. He seemed closest to the *Cynics, whose caustic wit and anti-authoritarian attitudes he shared. Most of his life he spent wandering from city to city, lecturing and teaching for money. He popularized the Greek *diatribē* ('spoken address') as a written sermon, so that it could reach a wider audience; and the connotation of abusiveness which the word has acquired in modern times derives from Bion's humorous but sharp attacks on human faults and weaknesses. His influence on the Latin satires of Lucilius and Horace was notable. He died *c.* 246 BC. Fairly extensive fragments of his writing survive.

**2.** (of Smyrna) The third Greek bucolic poet known to us after Theocritus and Moschus, to whom he is generally linked (*see* PASTORAL POETRY). He lived at the end of the second century BC. Virtually nothing is known of his life; according to the anonymous *Lament for Bion* (attributed to Moschus), he lived in Sicily and died by poisoning. He wrote in hexameters in the (literary) Doric dialect, and seventeen fragments of his poems (some may even be complete) survive. Since the Renaissance he has been credited with the *Lament for Adonis,* perhaps intended for recitation at a festival. The pastoral element in his work is slight, most of the poems being playfully erotic.

**Birds (Ornithes)** (Lat. *Aves*) Greek comedy by *Aristophanes which won second prize at the City *Dionysia in 414 BC. It is by far the longest of Aristophanes' comedies, and has the largest number of speaking parts (22). In 415 the Athenian fleet had set out on the Sicilian Expedition (*see* PELOPONNESIAN WAR), and its success was still in the balance. The *Birds* is a fantasy of wishful thinking in which two Athenians, Peisetairos ('Persuader') and Euelpides ('Optimist'), dissatisfied with life in Athens and its endless lawsuits, go to look for the mythical Tereus, king of Thrace (*see* PHILOMELA), who according to story was turned into a bird and might therefore know of a more agreeable place to live. Tereus suggests various countries, but there are objections to them all. Peisetairos now has a brilliant idea: let the birds all unite and build a great walled city in the air, and they will defy both men and gods; they will intercept the smoke from the sacrifices on which the gods are nourished. The chorus of birds (twenty-four named individual species), at first hostile, is won over, and the birds quickly set about building the city, to be called Nephelokokkygia ('Cloudcuckooland', from *nephele*, 'cloud', suggesting the insubstantial, and *kokkyx*, 'cuckoo', suggesting folly), under the direction of Peisetairos and Euelpides, who grow wings to suit their new condition. Then various unwelcome types arrive: a priest, a needy poet with a hymn in honour of the new city, an oracle-monger, *Meton the famous astronomer, now in the role of a town-planner (to lay out the streets), an official inspector, and a decree-seller. They are all appropriately dealt with. The new city is now finished, when a guard comes in with the news that a god has escaped the birds' blockade. The god, who turns out to be Iris, sent to enquire why sacrifices have stopped on earth, is seized and told that birds are now the gods, and finally goes off in tears to complain to her father (Zeus). Meanwhile people have become bird-mad and want wings. Further visitors arrive: a father-beater, because young cocks fight their fathers (he is reminded that young storks must feed their fathers); Cinesias the lyric poet, because he wants to soar on airy pinions; an informer (*sycophant), who would find wings useful for serving writs; and the god Prometheus, who hides from Zeus under a parasol while he tells of the food shortage among the gods and advises Peisetairos to make hard terms with them and insist on having Basileia ('Royal lady', 'Princess'), daughter of Zeus, to wife. Then come ambassadors from the gods, Poseidon, Heracles, and a god from the barbarous Triballians (democracy being in full swing among the Olympian gods, there must be barbarian gods also). Thanks to Heracles' reluctance to starve, gods and birds are reconciled, and Peisetairos gets the sceptre of Zeus as well as Basileia; he is hailed as the highest of the gods, and preparations are made for his wedding.

**birthdays** The birthdays of some important Greek gods were celebrated monthly on the dates assigned to them. Human birthdays seem not to have had particular significance for the Greeks except in the case of outstanding individuals (Plato and Epicurus for example) whose devoted followers annually marked their birth. In the Hellenistic period the birthdays of the Ptolemies, Seleucids, and Attalids were publicly fêted. The Romans from earliest times celebrated birthdays with presents and parties, and later the birthdays of emperors especially as well as members of the imperial families.

**Bisitun** (modern Bīsotūn, in Iran) A cliff 30km (20 miles) east of Kermanshah on which the Persian king *Darius I had a long trilingual inscription carved, in Elamite, Babylonian, and Old Persian, recording his victories over his enemies in the first year of his reign (522 BC), and added to in subsequent years. Copies were sent throughout the empire.

**Bithynia** A territory belonging to a people of Thracian origin in north-west Asia Minor. Originally limited to the peninsula of Chalcedon, the Bithynians expanded east to Paphlagonia and south across the Propontis. Bithynia had one of the richest territories of Asia Minor, with good harbours and important highways. Their kings promoted Greek culture and founded many cities. Becoming 'the province of Pontus and Bithynia' in 63 BC, the territory continued to flourish under the Roman empire. The correspondence between Pliny the Younger (as proconsul) and the emperor Trajan, as well as the speeches of Dio Chrysostom, illustrate life in the province in unusual detail.

**Bitōn** *See* CLEOBIS.

**Boadicē'a** *See* BOUDICCA.

**Bocchus I** *See* JUGURTHA.

**body** *See* ANATOMY AND PHYSIOLOGY; BEARDS; COSMETICS; HAIR; MEDICINE; NUDITY.

**Boeō'tia** A state of central Greece, on the north-west border of Attica. Its two main cities were (Boeotian) Orchomenus and Thebes, both standing in rich plains, good for breeding horses and growing wheat. It possessed the two famous mountains of *Cithaeron and *Helicon. In classical times much of the northern plain where Orchomenus stood was covered by the shallow Lake Copāis (now drained), famous for its eels, into which the waters of the Boeotian Cephisus and its tributaries flowed. The land was occupied from Neolithic times onward and was clearly important in the Bronze age. There were Mycenaean palaces at Thebes, Orchomenus, and the modern Gla (whose ancient name is unknown). *See* MINYANS.

Most Boeotian myth centres on the city of Thebes (*see* CADMUS; HERACLES; OEDIPUS), and the power of Thebes at any one time determined the importance of Boeotia's role in the history of the period. Thebes was never strong enough, however, to enforce its authority over all the cities of Boeotia and combine them into one state. The cities of Thespiae and *Plataea often figured in Boeotian politics. By the last quarter of the sixth century BC a confederacy of cities had been formed, probably under the leadership of Thebes. In the Persian Wars Boeotia played an equivocal part, if she was not actively disloyal to Greece. Plataea, Thespiae, and some groups in Thebes supported the Greeks, but after the Greek defeat at *Thermopylae only Plataea stayed loyal. As a consequence of the Greek victory in 479 Boeotia became politically unimportant. When Athens was seeking to extend her power in the mid-fifth century BC she invaded Boeotia and was defeated by an alliance of Spartans and Boeotians at Tanagra in 457 BC. However she defeated the Boeotians later in the same year at Oenophyta and compelled all the cities except Thebes to acknowledge her supremacy. The independence of Boeotia was restored ten years later when Athens was defeated at Coronea. Boeotia sided with Sparta in the Peloponnesian War, and Thebes laid siege to Plataea. A further defeat for Athens at Delium in 424 put an end to Athenian hopes of reconquering Boeotia. The fourth century saw the extension of Theban supremacy over the rest of Boeotia, particularly under the leadership of Epaminondas, and the Thebans' defeat of Sparta at Leuctra in 371 and again at Mantinea in 362. Like the rest of Greece, however, Boeotia could not resist the rise of Macedon under Philip II. After the defeat of Theban and Athenian forces at Chaeronea in 338 and the destruction of Thebes in 335 by Philip's son Alexander the Great, Boeotia rapidly declined. In Roman times nothing remained of most Boeotian cities except their ruins and their names. From 27 BC it formed part of the Roman province of Achaia, and its later society is represented in the works of Chaeronea's most famous son, Plutarch.

To the Athenians particularly the Boeotians seemed dull and thick-witted, a condition which Cicero and Horace ascribed to the dampness of the atmosphere. It seems true that Boeotia was backward artistically, but its contribution to music and literature was considerable: as well as Plutarch, the poets Hesiod, Corinna, and Pindar were all Boeotians. The dialect in the classical period was Aeolic, as spoken in Lesbos and Thessaly, but had some features in common with west Greek and a vowel-system peculiar to itself.

**Bōē'thius (Anicius Manlius Sevērīnus Boethius)** (*c.*AD 476–524) Latin philosopher and (Christian) theological writer, son of the consul for 487 and member of a family which had held many high offices of state in the fourth and fifth centuries. Boethius was himself appointed consul in 510 by the Ostrogothic king of Italy, Theoderic, who retained the Roman civil administration in Italy and made Boethius his *magister officiorum*, 'head of the civil service' (perhaps in 522). However, in 523 Boethius was implicated in a senatorial conspiracy, imprisoned, and put to death in 524. He was buried at Pavia and was regarded as a Catholic martyr (because Theoderic was an Arian, i.e. a heretic) and canonized as 'St Severinus'. His importance derives from his being the last Latin-speaking scholar of the ancient world to have a genuine mastery of Greek. After him no one in the West had first-hand acquaintance with Greek philosophy until the rediscovery of Aristotle in the twelfth century (*see* TEXTS, TRANSMISSION OF ANCIENT 7).

In his early life Boethius' declared aim was to translate and write commentaries upon all the writings of Aristotle and Plato in order to show that a harmony can be made out of the two philosophies. This huge task was never completed, but his translations of and commentaries on Aristotle's logical works and *Porphyry's Introduction (*Isagoge*) to the *Categories* of Aristotle as well as five logical works of his own played an influential role in medieval education and ensured that knowledge of Aristotle was never totally extinguished in the Western world. His handbooks of arithmetic, music, geometry, and astronomy (the *quadrivium*) were much used in medieval schools (the two former books survive). There also survive several Christian treatises. His literary fame depends on the enormously influential book he wrote in prison, the *Consolation of Philosophy*, a dialogue between himself and a personified Lady Philosophy. This work influenced the thought of the Middle Ages as much as any other. It consists of five books in prose interspersed with 39 short poems in thirteen different (and metrically accurate) metres in the style of Menippean satire (*see* MENIPPUS). Philosophy, who ousts the Muses, comes to console the prisoner; she reminds him of the sufferings of other thinkers such as Socrates, and invites him to lay bare his troubles. Boethius describes the ingratitude with which his integrity has been met, and laments the triumph of injustice. Philosophy reminds him of the mutability of fortune and the vanity of those things which the world esteems good. The only real good is God. Boethius asks how, under a beneficent God, evil can exist or pass unpunished (book 4), and is answered by a justification of divine government followed by a discussion on free will. It is a moving work, written from the heart, and it provided comfort to innumerable readers of the Middle Ages, as is shown by the hundreds of manuscripts of it which exist today, and the fact that it was translated into more European languages than any other book except the Bible. Its translators include King Alfred, Chaucer, and Queen Elizabeth I. Its tone, though theistic, is largely pagan and classical and it ignores the specifically Christian consolations, owing more perhaps to Stoicism and Platonism. Cf. Boethius' kinsman *Cassiodorus.

**Bona De'a** The Good Goddess, the title of an Italian fertility goddess (name unknown) worshipped exclusively by women, especially in Rome and Latium. Rites in her honour were celebrated annually at the house of the chief magistrate, under the leadership of his wife assisted by the *Vestal Virgins, and these were attended only by women. It was these rites that *Clodius violated in 62 BC by entering in female disguise.

**book illustration** An Egyptian tradition. In Greek, illustrated papyri are mostly scientific (*see* DIOSCORIDES) or mathematical. There are rare illustrated fragments of Homer and drama. Illustration became relatively common in the late Roman codex; *see* VARRO.

**books, Greek and Roman**
1. Writing had developed in Mesopotamia and Egypt at the end of the fourth millennium BC, for the purposes of accounting, millennia before the skill reached Greece. While clay tablets were used in the Near East (*see* AHHIYAWA), the Egyptians wrote on papyrus. The oldest surviving inscribed papyrus texts are

Egyptian and dated to the middle of the third millennium BC. In Crete strands of papyrus have been identified fire-baked into seals which apparently hung from papyrus documents as early as the second millennium BC. In late Bronze-age Greece a script known as *Linear B was used on clay tablets but as far as we can tell only for making official inventories and not for literary purposes, and it did not survive the collapse of this civilization in about 1150 BC. Homer makes one obscure reference to writing (*Iliad* 6.166 ff.), but otherwise his world seems to be illiterate and bookless. Although it is hardly conceivable that the complex structure of the *Iliad* and the *Odyssey* could have been achieved without writing, poetry continued to be primarily an oral art form throughout the archaic and classical periods.

The Greek name for papyrus was *byblos* (or *biblos*) which suggests that it may have been imported from *Byblos in Phoenicia (Lebanon), and the classical Greeks believed, probably correctly, that their alphabetic system of writing derived from Phoenicia (*see* ALPHABET and CADMUS). Archaeological and literary evidence suggests that writing became widespread in Greece between 750 and 650 BC. Pictures of book-rolls of papyrus first appear on Attic vases *c.*500 BC. Before then, according to Herodotus, when papyrus was scarce, the Ionians had used sheep- and goat-skins. It is reasonable to think that papyrus was in general use in Greece by the time of the poet Archilochus (*c.*680–640 BC), which is probably when poetry in general came to be written down, and that book-rolls must have contributed to the transmission of Greek poetry at this time.

2. In reference to classical texts the word 'book' is used ambiguously. In modern parlance Homer's *Iliad*, Virgil's *Aeneid*, and Thucydides' history of the Peloponnesian War, for example, would each be called a book. However, because of the use of papyrus rolls, each of these works is made up of many smaller 'books' in the ancient sense—twenty-four, twelve, and eight respectively (*see* EPHORUS). The *Alexandrian Library was probably responsible for introducing standardization in book production. Papyrus was bought in rolls, not sheets, usually about 10m (33 ft.) long. With writing of average size such a roll could contain a book of Thucydides, or two of the shorter books of Homer. The work was written in vertical columns of 5–10cm (2–4 in.) wide

throughout the length of the roll, with a margin between the columns and a broader margin at top and bottom. Scribes seem not to have been concerned to keep a regular number of lines to a column or of letters to a line. In the fourth and third centuries BC the minimum of help is given to the reader; *punctuation and spacing between words are non-existent or at best erratic; punctuation where it exists takes the form of a single point level with the top of the letter. Enlarged initial letters are not used. A short stroke under the line (*paragraphos*) often indicated where there was a pause in the sense or a change of speaker in dramatic texts (but the name of the speaker was hardly ever given). *Accents appear, if at all, only in poetic texts. These aids become more frequent during the Roman period.

Book titles were first employed with Attic drama, because the titles of plays had to be entered for the competitions. Plato refers to one of his dialogues by name, but lyric poetry and most prose works seem not to have had titles, beyond their opening words. Titles were written beside the opening line or at the end of a roll (the part least liable to damage); a roll was often identified by a label (Gk. *sillybos*, Lat. *titulus*) which hung from it as it lay on a shelf or in a pigeon-hole or box. A roller (Gk. *omphalos*, Lat. *umbilicus*) might be attached to the end of the papyrus, ornamented with projecting knobs. Some have been found in Herculaneum but none in Egypt. The rolls comprising a long work or the complete works of an author might be kept together in a cupboard (Lat. *armarium*) or bucket (Lat. *capsa*). A reader would undo the roll with his right hand, and roll it up, as he proceeded, with his left.

The alternative material to papyrus was vellum (Lat. *vellus*, 'skin', 'hide') made from the skins of cattle, sheep, and goats. The skins were scraped, rubbed with pumice, and dressed with alum. This material was later known as parchment, a name derived from the city of Pergamum which was famous for its manufacture. The story was told that in the second century BC a king of Egypt, jealous of the library at Pergamum, placed an embargo on the supply of papyrus to that city, where parchment was promptly invented. (In modern usage, parchment is made from the skin of sheep and goats, vellum from that of calves, lambs, and kids.)

3. Books to the classical Greeks were essentially a substitute for recitation. In antiquity reading generally meant reading aloud: Polybius in the second century BC included reading with the examination of witnesses when he wrote of 'learning through the ears'. However, readers when engrossed in intense study read silently (like Ambrose, when seen reading by an astonished Augustine). It is not until the fifth century BC at Athens that we find the beginnings of a book trade, fostered by the large number of prose books written by the *sophists for educational purposes. Plato has Socrates say that a book by Anaxagoras could be bought in the *orchestra* in the agora at Athens for a drachma or less. In the fourth century BC books became relatively common and the practice of reading seems to have become firmly established (*see* LITERACY and LETTERS). Aristotle and his school formed a large collection of books. The oldest surviving literary papyrus rolls date from the second half of the fourth century BC (*see* TIMOTHEUS). In the third and subsequent centuries the output of books greatly increased after educated slaves were employed as copyists and the production of papyrus and later of parchment was organized by the Hellenistic kings.

4. The Latin word for book, *liber*, 'bark', originated at an early time when books in Rome were written on bark, but the introduction of Greek literature into Rome in the third and second centuries BC propagated the papyrus roll. Very few papyrus fragments of Latin books have survived compared with Greek because the very dry and warm climate which allows survival is found in Egypt, a Greek-speaking area. On the other hand, Latin literature is much richer than Greek in information about books and the book trade. From the first century BC we hear of booksellers with their staffs of copyists. Cicero had his writings published by *Atticus, and Horace mentions the Sosii as booksellers. The demand for books increased and it became the fashion for rich Romans to have a library. The price of books seems to have been moderate. There was no law of copyright and authors did not profit directly from the sale of their books.

5. A papyrus roll (Lat. *volumen*, hence English 'volume') was not very convenient to use. It had to be manipulated by both hands and rewound after use. Athenian vase-paintings show readers getting into difficulties with twisted rolls, and they were easily torn. From Homer onwards sets of wooden tablets hinged on a ring or leather thong had been used for

notes or letters. The tablets were either whitened and written on in ink or, more usually, coated with wax and the writing scratched on with a stylus (the wax could be smoothed again with the blunt end); thus the Latin verb 'to write', *exarare*, meant originally 'to plough up', because the stylus furrows the wax like a ploughshare. From these tablets there slowly developed from the first century AD the book in modern form, known as a codex, made from folded sheets of papyrus or parchment, put together quire by quire (eight leaves, sixteen pages), stitched at the spine and bound with wooden boards. The codex had several advantages over the papyrus roll: it was very easy to consult, since the leaves could be turned forwards or backwards at will; both sides of the leaves could be written on; it could hold four or five times as much text as a roll; and it was longer-lasting. It is noticeable that the Christians adopted the codex form quite early, from the early second century onwards, perhaps because the sayings of Jesus were originally recorded in a parchment notebook of the kind used by lawyers and businessmen, perhaps also because the codex gave ease of reference. By the fourth century it had superseded the papyrus roll, and parchment was preferred to papyrus. From this and the following century come the earliest surviving manuscripts of classical authors. The roll form was retained for public documents through the Middle Ages to modern times. Paper was introduced from China by the Arabs in the ninth century, but its use did not become common until the twelfth century.

*See also* TEXTS, TRANSMISSION OF ANCIENT; EPIGRAPHY; OSTRAKA; VINDOLANDA TABLETS.

**Bo'reas** In Greek, the north wind (Lat. *aquilo*); in Greek myth, son of the *Titan Astraios ('Starry one') and Eōs ('Dawn'). His native land was said to be Thrace. He carried off as wife the nymph Oreithyia, daughter of Erechtheus, an early king of Athens, and was thus thought by the Athenians to be specially connected with them. They are said to have instituted a state cult for him after the north wind destroyed part of the Persian fleet at Cape Sepias as it accompanied the army along the coast to Thermopylae in 480 BC. The wind was attributed to the intervention of the god himself on the Athenians' behalf; soon afterwards the fleet was defeated by the Greeks at Salamis.

Boreas was the father of Zetes and Calăis, mentioned among the *Argonauts.

**Bory'sthenēs** A river of Scythia (south Russia), the modern Dnieper, and a principal route into the Scythian hinterland.

**Bo'sporus** (sometimes Bosphorus, supposedly meaning 'ox-ford') **1.** The Thracian Bosporus, the strait connecting the Sea of Marmara with the Black Sea, and separating Europe from Asia. According to Greek myth it was here that the heifer *Io crossed from one continent to the other (perhaps from Asia to Europe). The strong current and the winding channel made it dangerous to shipping.

**2.** The Cimmerian Bosporus, the straits connecting the Black Sea with the Sea of Azov. It also is said to derive its name from a crossing made by Io.

**botany** The scientific study of plants may be said to have begun with Aristotle, who considered the nature of plants in relation to other forms of life. When classifying living things in gradations of increasing complexity he put plants first as possessing the simplest form of life, demonstrating merely nutrition, growth, and reproduction. His work in this area was totally eclipsed by that of his successor as head of the Lyceum, *Theophrastus. Most of Theophrastus' botanical writings survive intact, and his *Historia plantarum* ('Researches on plants') in nine books, and the *De causis plantarum* ('Aetiology of plants') in seven books, of which the last is lost, are the origin of the subject in the West. The style is that of lectures given to a circle of fellow researchers, the sentences compressed, elliptical, and sometimes obscure. In the *Historia* Theophrastus starts as Aristotle did in his *Researches on animals* (*see* ANIMALS, ARISTOTLE ON) by first classifying and identifying plants and gathering information about them. He explains the main problem in classifying plants: it is difficult to define the essential parts because in many plants some or all of the parts are not permanent; they may die away annually. After describing the parts which belong to all plants alike (root, stem, leaves, flowers, seeds or fruit) Theophrastus proceeds to the various classes into which all plants may be divided— tree, shrub, under-shrub ('which rises from the root with many stems') and herb (i.e. potherbs or vegetables 'which come up from the root with their leaves'). Book 2 deals with the reproduction of plants, and book 3 with the ways in which trees and plants may originate. In connection with the latter he mentions spontaneous generation as the suggestion of natural philosophers but reminds the reader that this suggestion is 'somehow beyond the ken of our senses'. Book 4, dealing with trees and plants that will grow only in particular areas, has an enormous amount of information on Asia, among other things how *Harpalus, the friend of Alexander the Great and governor of Babylon, could not get ivy to grow in the gardens there. There is also exhaustive discussion of the reeds grown for making the music pipe the *aulos. Book 5 covers the timber of trees and its uses, and Book 6 deals with undershrubs, including the many varieties of roses (heavy pruning recommended), and has much to say about the highly prized silphium of Cyrene (similar to asafoetida, but now extinct). Book 7 is about herbaceous plants, pot-herbs and wild herbs, book 8 about cereals, pulses, and summer crops. Book 9, which covers plant juices and the methods of collecting them, has much fascinating herbal material, including a section on poisons. Here Theophrastus enters the territory of the herbalists ('root-cutters'), some of whose practices border on the magical. He rejects as fanciful such advice as to cut the peony at night or risk having your eyes taken out by a woodpecker, and as foolish and incredible the bizarre practices associated with cutting mandrake: 'praying, however, is perhaps not unreasonable.'

Much of this material is prefaced by 'They say that . . .'. It is likely that many of Theophrastus' sources were the observers Alexander the Great took with him into Asia. Having now gathered his information, Theophrastus proceeds in *De causis* to the distinctive functions of a plant: its sprouting, flowering, and fruiting, which is its goal. In books 2, 3, and 4 he covers the effects of the seasons on sprouting and fruiting, and the effects of agriculture. He sees his subject as falling into two distinct halves, one dealing with spontaneous phenomena in the plant world (unconnected with human activity or interference), and the other with the effects of human activity directed towards helping nature to achieve its goal. He moves on to the diseases and death of plants. Book 6 deals with natural flavours and odours from plants, and the lost book 7 dealt with manufactured flavours.

It is worth remembering when reading Theophrastus that he did not have the taxonomic terms of modern botany—class, genus, species, variety—nor did he have any artificial aid such as a hand-lens.

*See also* Dioscorides; Galen; medicine; Pliny (1).

**Bou'dicca** (incorrectly Boadicea) The wife of Prasutagus, king of the Iceni, a tribe living in East Anglia. When he died without a male heir, the Romans annexed and began to despoil his kingdom; Boudicca was flogged and her two daughters raped. While the Roman governor Suetonius Paulinus was campaigning in Anglesey Boudicca led a revolt (AD 61) during which the British sacked Camulodunum (Colchester), Londinium (London), and Verulamium (St Albans): according to Tacitus (*Annals* 14), about 70,000 Romans and pro-Roman Britons were killed. On his return the governor routed Boudicca's forces and she is said to have taken poison. Londoners like to think that her burial mound lies under King's Cross station.

**boulē** The general Greek name for 'council' in those states where the government was carried out by an assembly of citizens, the *ecclesia*, and a smaller executive body, the *boule*. The latter was a specially appointed body of citizens, which prepared business for the sovereign assembly, implemented its decisions and administered the day-to-day running of the state. In classical Athens the boule consisted of 500 (male) citizens over 30 years old, appointed annually by lot by the *demes* (acting as voting districts) of Athens and Attica, from those who were willing to stand and had survived a preliminary scrutiny. No one could serve on the boule more than twice in a lifetime. Hence a large proportion of the male population served at some time in their lives. The origin of the boule as it functioned in classical times lies in the reforms of *Cleisthenes (2) at the end of the sixth century.

**bouleutē'rion** At Athens, 'council-chamber'; *see* METROON.

**boustrophē'don** (lit. 'as the ox turns') In Greek *epigraphy, a term used to describe the script on early Greek inscriptions in which the lines of writing run alternately from right to left and from left to right, as the ox pulls the plough in successive furrows. The letters too are turned round to face the appropriate direction. *See also* ALPHABET.

**boxing** *See* ATHLETICS.

**Bra'sidas** (d. 422 BC) The most distinguished Spartan general in the early years of the *Peloponnesian War, receiving rare praise from Thucydides for his 'virtue' (*aretē*) and intelligence. In 424 he was sent north to damage Athenian interests in Thrace; there he gained possession of several important cities in alliance with Athens, including Amphipolis (*see* THUCYDIDES) and Torone. He continued operations in Thrace until 422, when he had to face without reinforcements a fresh Athenian army under Cleon sent to recoup the losses. The Athenians took back Torone but failed to recover Amphipolis, and in the battle both Cleon and Brasidas were killed. Brasidas was accorded the singular honour of burial within the walls of Amphipolis, and his tomb received yearly sacrifices as if for a hero. Thucydides records three speeches in his name and clearly admired his resourcefulness. He permanently damaged the Athenians' cause in a vital part of their empire.

**Brauron** (modern Vraona) On the east coast of Attica, one of the twelve early Attic townships traditionally united by Theseus into a single Athenian state. It was well known from ancient times for the worship of Artemis, who had an important temple there and in whose honour a festival, Brauronia, was held every four years. The cult was in some way associated with *Iphigeneia; local legend said that her sacrifice took place there rather than at Aulis, but that a bear was substituted for her. It was chiefly for women and is now thought to have been a rite of passage for pubescent girls. Its notable feature was that young girls between the ages of 5 and 10 wearing saffron dresses 'acted the she-bear', supposedly in atonement for the killing of a bear belonging to Artemis. (*Munychia seems to have had a similar ritual.) Originally, it seems, no girl might be married until she had performed this ritual bear-dance. By classical times the ritual was part of the Athenian state religion and was performed only by the daughters of noble families.

**Brennus** 1. The leader of those Gauls (or *Celts) who according to tradition invaded Italy *c.*385 BC, defeated the Romans at the river Allia, 19km (12 miles) from Rome, and then captured Rome apart from the Capitol. Legend relates that the Gauls massacred the priests and old patricians as they sat silently in their chairs of state in the porticoes of their houses. For the part supposedly played by the Capitoline geese in saving the Capitol, *see* MANLIUS. Legend also relates that, after six months' siege, when the gold which the Gauls accepted as the ransom of Rome was being weighed and a Roman tribune complained of false weights, Brennus threw his sword into the scale with the words, '*vae victis*', 'woe to the conquered'. Roman pride handed down the story that Brennus and his army were annihilated before they could leave Italy (*see* CAMILLUS). It has been suggested that the name Brennus was attributed to him in later times from the Gallic chieftain who invaded Greece in 280–279 BC ((2) below).

2. The leader of a Celtic people from Gaul who in 280–279 BC overran Macedonia and thence Greece. He was checked by a force of Athenians and others at Thermopylae, but finally turned their position as the Persians had outflanked the Greeks in 480 BC. He was defeated and wounded at Delphi and committed suicide in 278. The Gauls retreated northwards with great loss.

**brevis brevians** ('the shortening short') A phonetic tendency in popular Latin speech transferred to less formal kinds of Latin verse (e.g. comedy). A short syllable apparently shortens a following long syllable if the latter is preceded or followed by an accented syllable (e.g. *bŏ'nīs* might be scanned ⏑⏑). The term was invented in modern times.

**Bria'reōs** (Lat. Briareus) In Greek myth, the most conspicuous of the *hecatoncheires, three 'hundred-armed' giants, the sons of Pontos (Sea) and Gaia (Earth). Briareos was also called Aegaeon. He and his two brothers fought with Zeus against the *Titans and were rewarded by being set to guard the Titans imprisoned in Tartarus. When the other Olympian gods were about to put Zeus in chains, Briareos, who lived in the sea, summoned thence by Thetis, saved him. The 'hundred-armers' were often confused with the other Giants who were the offspring of the same parents.

**Briga'ntēs** Numerically the largest tribe in Britain, whose territory under queen *Cartimandua stretched from coast to coast and from Hadrian's Wall (and, in the west, beyond it) to as far south as a curved line between the Mersey and the Humber, taking in the Peak

District but excluding east Yorkshire. The territory was annexed by Rome in the seventies AD.

**Brīsē'is** In the *Iliad*, Achilles' captive slave-concubine taken from him by Agamemnon, when the latter, at the wish of Apollo, had to return his own concubine Chryseis to her father. Hence the anger of Achilles, which is the theme of the *Iliad*.

# Britain

1. Iron-age Celtic culture first appeared in Britain in the eighth century BC (*see* CELTS). The people were agrarian and lived in separate, self-governing tribal territories. From *c.*500 BC they shared an idiosyncratic art-style of great beauty and high technical achievement. The Greek sailor *Pytheas from Massalia (Marseilles) visited tin-miners in Cornwall and the tin-depot at 'Ictis' in the late fourth century BC (*see* CASSITERIDES). From the late second century BC trade with Transalpine Gaul increased and Britain began to receive goods such as amphorae of wine. British coins of this period are also found. Neither the branch of the Celtic language which we may refer to as British, spoken throughout almost the whole of Britain well before the Roman period, nor Latin, persisted after the Saxon incursions in the fifth century AD. (British survives in the remains of Old Welsh, Cornish, and Breton.)

The Celtic religion had several gods which became assimilated into the Roman tradition: thus Brigantia, the patron goddess of the *Brigantes, was identified by Caesar with the Roman goddess Minerva. A triad of gods, perhaps goddess, consort, and child, is frequently attested. The priesthood of the Druids was centred on Britain. Because Celtic was an oral culture little is known of their doctrine, but their religious rites which included human sacrifice became a byword for savagery for the Romans, who completely abolished druidism.

Julius Caesar had defeated the warlike *Belgae of Gaul in 57 BC. The migration of many of them to Britain gave him the pretext for invading Britain in 55. He may have felt that his conquest of Gaul was hardly secure without at least a show of Roman strength in Britain: rebellious Gauls sought refuge there and Britons fought in the Gallic armies. Total conquest may not have been his intention. The first invasion was in the nature of a reconnaissance, but the second in 54 was a more serious affair. Caesar crossed the river Thames (Tamesis or Tamesa) to attack the British commander *Cassivellaunus, king of the *Catuvellauni, the most powerful of the southern tribes. Cassivellaunus was forced to give hostages and pay tribute; Caesar then withdrew to Gaul (*see* COMMENTARIES (1) [books 4 and 5]).

2. Britain was now a recognized part of the Roman world. In the thirties and twenties BC the Latin poets Virgil and Horace sometimes speak as if (the later emperor) Augustus was on the verge of annexing Britain, but nothing came of it and it was the emperor Claudius who made the conquest after a period of inter-tribal war which alarmed Rome. In AD 43 Claudius sent a force of perhaps 40,000 men; he arrived in person for the capture of Camulodunum—Colchester—and celebrated a triumph in Rome. Claudius pursued the policy of having client kingdoms around the province: such were the *Iceni of Norfolk and the Brigantes in the north, though the latter felt themselves to be largely independent. An important client king was Cogidubnus, whose land centred on the Chichester area of west Sussex (the palace excavated at Fishbourne may have been built for his old age). The Romans called the province Britannia, a name which appears to be derived from the Greek *Prettania* and has no direct Celtic origin (*see also* ALBION). Aulus Plautius, who had led the invasion, was made governor with orders to secure the rest of the country and by 47, when his term as governor ended, the whole area south of the Humber and east of the Severn was under Roman control. Ostorius Scapula, governor from 47 to 52, made advances into Wales, and in 51 defeated Caratacus, who had become the leader of British opposition to Rome. Gaius Suetonius Paulinus, governor from 58 to 61, quashed the much more serious revolt of *Boudicca, ushering in a long period of stability in the south. In the 70s the whole of Wales was subdued, and *Agricola (governor 77/8–84) advanced into Scotland, reaching the line of the Forth and the Clyde in 81. In 83 he moved further north and in 84 inflicted a famous defeat on the Caledonians at Mons Graupius. Having sent a fleet around the north of Britain, he was able to confirm that it was an island (*see* THULE). However, by the end of the century, or soon after, under Trajan (emperor 98–117) there was a gradual retreat to the Tyne–Solway line and the opportunity never came again to embrace the whole island in one province.

The retreat was confirmed by Trajan's successor Hadrian (emperor 117–38), who built the most elaborate frontier in the Roman world, 'Hadrian's Wall'. It was begun after the emperor's visit in 122 and ran from Wallsend-on-Tyne in the east to Bowness-on-Solway in the west, 118km (74 miles) in all. It acted as a base for patrols, cut off raiders from the north, and produced settled conditions in the south in which the economy and the arts of peace could flourish.

3. Soon after Antoninus Pius became emperor in 138 he initiated a sudden change of policy. The governor of Britain, Q. Lollius Urbicus, advanced once more into southern Scotland and built a new frontier wall of turf—the Antonine Wall (see ANTONINUS PIUS)—across the line of the Forth and the Clyde, 60km (37 miles) long, less elaborate than Hadrian's Wall but of the same basic plan, with forts interspersed with smaller stations. The history of this period is confused, but the Antonine Wall seems to have been abandoned c.163. Not long after 180 what is described as the greatest war of the emperor *Commodus' reign occurred in Britain. Tribes from the north swept over Hadrian's Wall, ravaged widely, and destroyed a Roman force. A punitive campaign was successfully waged in 184, followed by withdrawal to the Wall. Roman influence was accepted in the Scottish lowlands but the tribes remained autonomous.

After the assassination of the emperor Commodus in 192, Clodius Albinus, governor of Britain, became a rival to the new emperor, Septimius Severus, and eventually claimed the throne. In 196 he crossed with an army to Gaul, where he was defeated by Severus in 197 and committed suicide. His withdrawal of troops from Britain gave the opportunity to those who hated Rome, especially those beyond the Wall, to vandalize and loot. In 208 Severus himself with his entire family arrived in Britain and directed a punitive expedition into Scotland; he was planning a further campaign when he died in 211. At some time in the early third century Britain was divided into two provinces, the upper (northern) having its centre at York and the lower (southern) at London. (A further division, into four, took place later under Diocletian.) For the rest of the century Roman Britain remained relatively undisturbed and moderately prosperous, untypically so if it is compared with the contemporary convulsions elsewhere in the empire.

4. In 287 Carausius, commander of the British fleet, declared himself emperor of Britain, making the island independent of the central government in Rome. Carausius was left in peace and his government was efficient and successful, but in 294 he was assassinated by his finance minister, Allectus, who himself seized the provinces of Britain. In 296 Constantius launched an invasion against Allectus, and the latter was killed in battle. Constantius thereby regained the provinces, which needed considerable reconstruction. In 306, when Constantius had become the *Augustus (emperor), he was joined by his son Constantine (the Great) for another invasion of Scotland, and won a great victory. Shortly after, he died at York and his son succeeded as Caesar. Constantine had soon to leave for Gaul, but during the first half of the fourth century Britain enjoyed peace and prosperity.

In 337 Constantine died and out of the ensuing chaos his son Constantine II emerged as senior Augustus with command over Britain, Gaul, and Spain. He invaded Italy, the domain of his brother Constans, in 340, and was killed in battle. Some unknown crisis brought Constans unexpectedly to Britain in 343, perhaps attacks by Picts and Scots beyond the Wall and by Saxon and Frankish marauders in the south. By 368 the threat to British security was alarming, and in that year a concerted attack was made by the tribes in the north, the west coast, and the south-east. The country was overrun and London threatened. It was two years before a military commander Theodosius (the Elder), a Spaniard, sent by the emperor Valentinian, could restore order. He drove out the invaders and again repaired the Wall. Once more Britain had a firm government and secure defences, but the growing power of invaders from outside the empire threatened all Europe and from 383 there were repeated withdrawals of troops from Britain to defend Italy. There was considerable decline in the later fourth century, and soon after 400 effective occupation of Hadrian's Wall had ceased. The cessation of Roman rule in Britain was rapid but perhaps not sudden—it may have been spread over several decades. By c.450 the invaders were in Britain to stay.

5. Local government in Britain under the Romans was based on tribal capitals, *civitates* (sing. *civitas*), which were autonomous citizen-communities formed from a local ethnic or social unit. Each *civitas* contained numerous

*oppida* ('towns', sing. *oppidum*). Sixteen *civitates* are known in Britain, and include Canterbury (home of the Cantiaci), Chichester (Regni), Dorchester (Durotriges), Exeter (Dumnoniae), St Albans (Catuvellauni), and Winchester (Belgae). By the fifth century AD they had declined to the extent of losing all their urban characteristics. Agriculture remained the main occupation: of a total population possibly exceeding three-and-a-half million, perhaps 90 per cent lived in the countryside (estimates vary considerably). Prosperity seems to have peaked in the earlier half of the fourth century, noticeable in the opulence of a number of villas at this time. After 450 there was a sharp decline in all aspects of material wellbeing—in buildings, pottery, and coinage for example, for all except the highest levels of society.

*Christianity seems to have been a significant force in some areas by the end of the fourth century, though the extent of its acceptance is disputed. Three British bishops are attested at the Council of Arles in 314. Eventually Christianity became the leading religion and gained influence through monasteries which developed also into centres of learning (*see* TEXTS, TRANSMISSION OF ANCIENT 5).

**Brita'nnicus (Tiberius Claudius Britannicus)** (AD 41–55) Son of the Roman emperor *Claudius and his wife *Messal(l)ina. He was displaced as heir by the young *Nero, after whose accession he soon died, perhaps by poison.

**Britoma'rtis** Cretan goddess of hunters and fishermen, frequently identified with the Greek goddess *Artemis after the introduction of the latter into Crete. Her name is said to mean 'sweet maiden'. *Minos, king of Crete, pursued her for nine months, and finally to avoid him she leaped over a cliff into the sea but was caught and saved by fishermen's nets—hence she is also called Dictynna (a name which the Greeks derived from their word for 'net'). She escaped to Aegina, where she was worshipped under the name of Aphaia, in a temple whose ruins still survive.

**Bro'mius** A name for the Greek god *Dionysus meaning 'the noisy, boisterous one', from the Greek noun *bromos*, 'loud noise'.

**bronze** Compound of copper and tin, typically in the proportion 9 : 1, that came into general use in the ancient world in the third millennium BC and remained so until replaced (though not entirely) by iron in the eleventh century BC. *See* BRONZE AGE.

**Bronze age** In mainland Greece, the period from *c*.2800 to *c*.1050 BC. In Crete and the Aegean islands it began a little earlier, *c*.3000 BC. It was followed by the Iron age, *c*.1050–850 BC (which mostly coincides with the Greek *Dark age). The periods of the Bronze age on the mainland are called Helladic, Early (EH), Middle (MH), and Late (LH); these are subdivided into EH I, II, etc. and further subdivided as need be (*see* MYCENAE). The periods of Bronze-age *Crete are known as Minoan and similarly divided into EM I, II, etc. For the *Cyclades the term is Cycladic, thus EC I, II, etc. In Italy the Bronze age was the period from *c*.1800 to *c*.1000 BC. In Gaul, Spain, and Britain it gave way to the Iron age in the eighth century BC.

**Bronze-age collapse** *See* MYCENAE.

**Brundi'sium** (modern Brindisi) The best harbour on the east coast of Italy, situated on the heel, and the nearest Italian town to the eastern Adriatic coast. It was made a Latin colony in 244 BC. Connected to Rome by the Via Appia, it was the regular port of embarkation for Greece and Epirus. It was from Brundisium that Cicero and Ovid set out on their respective exiles, and it is a journey to Brundisium in company with, among others, Virgil, that Horace describes in *Satires* 1.5. Here Virgil subsequently died, in 19 BC, on his way home from Greece. Lucan in the *Pharsalia* relates Pompey's departure from the same port, and Tacitus (*Annals* 3.1) the arrival there of Agrippina bringing home the ashes of Germanicus. The treaty of Brundisium was made in 40 BC between Mark Antony and Octavian, by which Antony surrendered Gaul, already occupied by Octavian, and married Octavian's sister.

**Brutus** The name of a Roman plebeian family of the *gens Junia*, the Junian clan, which traced its descent from L. Junius Brutus ((1) below) and included the Brutus ((2) below) who murdered Julius Caesar.

**1. Lucius Junius Brutus** The traditional founder of the Roman republic and probably a historical figure, although accounts of him in ancient sources contain legendary elements. He pretended to be an idiot (*brutus*) in order to escape the fate of his brother who had been murdered by their uncle, Tarquinius Superbus, the (last) Roman king. When *Lucretia was raped by Tarquinius' son, Brutus led an insurrection which ousted the *Tarquin family, and was elected the first consul (traditionally in 509 BC) with L. Tarquinius Collatinus (Lucretia's husband). He was famous for his strict justice and put to death his own two sons who were attempting to restore the Tarquins. He was killed fighting an Etruscan army which was engaged in the same attempt.

**2. Marcus Junius Brutus** (c.85–42 BC) Son of the similarly named tribune of 83 BC (executed after *Mutina) and Servilia, and the leading assassin of Julius Caesar. In 49 BC he joined in the Civil War on Pompey's side against Caesar, but after the former's defeat at Pharsalus he sought Caesar's pardon, which was granted, and became one of his protégés. About 45 he married Porcia, the daughter of M. Porcius *Cato whom he greatly admired and by whose republican sympathies he was influenced. In 44 Caesar appointed him as praetor, and he appeared to bear Caesar's dictatorship with equanimity, but *Cassius, a fellow praetor, prevailed upon him to lead a conspiracy to murder Caesar, playing upon his patriotic desire to follow his famous ancestor and restore the republic. It is related by Suetonius that Caesar gave up the struggle against his murderers when he saw Brutus among them, exclaiming in Greek, *kai su, teknon* ('even you, my child!'). The Latin version, 'Et tu, Brute!' ('you too, Brutus!') was made famous by Shakespeare. Soon after the assassination Brutus was forced to leave Italy through public hostility. He went to Greece, and with Cassius prepared to resist the army of the *triumvirs Antony, Lepidus, and Octavian. In the autumn of 42 Antony and Octavian defeated Brutus and Cassius at *Philippi in eastern Macedonia, and Brutus committed suicide.

In his youth Brutus acquired a love of learning which never left him. He had a reputation as an outstanding orator. He was not impressed by Cicero's style, calling it (according to Tacitus) 'effeminate and mincing'. Although he was one of Cicero's favourite literary adversaries, Cicero seems not to have liked him, having failed to win him over to his own way of thinking in oratory, philosophy, and politics. In his treatise *Brutus Cicero made him one of the speakers, and he dedicated to Brutus his *Orator*, *De finibus*, and *Tuscu-*

*lan Disputations*. In Cicero's correspondence with *Atticus some letters describe Brutus' financial dealings with the people of Salamis (in Cyprus); these and other similar stories give an interesting indication of his character: he lent money to the town at 48 per cent interest, and was prepared to go to any length to recover the debt.

**3. Decimus Junius Brutus** One of the assassins of Julius Caesar (not to be confused with Marcus Junius, (2) above, to whom he was only distantly related). As a young man he served under Caesar in Gaul and fought for him in the Civil War against Pompey. Caesar trusted Brutus so completely that he promised him the governorship of Cisalpine Gaul and allowed him to be his escort to the senate house on the day of his assassination. After Caesar's murder Brutus retired to Cisalpine Gaul and refused to surrender it to Mark Antony. The latter proceeded to besiege him and his republican forces in Mutina (43 BC), but Brutus and the city were saved when Hirtius and Octavian raised the siege. Later, however, finding himself deserted, Brutus tried to cross over to M. Brutus, (2) above, in Macedonia, but was betrayed and put to death by Antony's order.

**Brutus (*De claris oratoribus*)** Treatise by *Cicero ((1) 5) 'on eminent Roman orators'. Written in 46 BC with the purpose of defending Cicero's own oratorical practice, it gives interesting details of his early life and training as an orator and his gradual rise to the highest position. It purports to record a recent conversation between Cicero, M. Junius *Brutus, and *Atticus, in which Cicero ends an introductory section on Greek orators by referring to the Attic, Asianic, and Rhodian schools of *oratory, commending some of the qualities of the Asianists as well as of the Atticists. He reviews the long series of Roman orators up to his own times, starting from Brutus the Liberator, supposedly consul in 509 BC, but more particularly from Cethēgus, consul in 204 BC ('the marrow of persuasion' according to Ennius), giving a brief description of each. His requirements for an ideal orator are formidable: knowledge of literature, philosophy, law, and history; the ability to arouse emotion; to digress and expand where it is advantageous—and all to be done with wit and humour. Cicero regularly spoke last himself, so that he could leave the legal aspects to others.

**Būce'phalas** ('Ox-head') The black horse of Alexander the Great, his favourite for twenty years, which died probably of wounds at the battle fought against the Indian king Porus at the river Hydaspes (Jhelum) in 326 BC. In his memory Alexander founded the town of Bucephala (probably Jhelum on the west bank of the river in Pakistan) near the site of Bucephalas' last river crossing. The popular story was that the horse had proved unmanageable until the 12-year-old Alexander, observing that it shied at its own shadow, turned its head to the sun, soothed, and then mounted it.

**bucolic poetry** *See* PASTORAL POETRY.

**burial and cremation** *See* DEAD, DISPOSAL OF.

**Burrus** *See* SENECA (2) 1.

**Būsī'ris (Bousīris)** In Greek myth, a king of Egypt, son of Poseidon, who, in order to end a drought, on the advice of a seer, sacrificed to Zeus all strangers who arrived in his kingdom. The seer himself, being a visitor from Cyprus, was the first victim. Soon afterwards *Heracles arrived and killed Busiris and his son and all his attendants.

**Byblos** (Jbeil, in modern Lebanon) The principal port of ancient Phoenicia, believed by its natives to be the oldest city in the world. There is archaeological evidence for connections with Bronze-age Crete and Greece. The Greeks took its name as their word for papyrus, and so for *book.

**Byzantine age** Term describing Greek history and culture of the period from (at its widest) AD 330 until 1453, derived from the name of the capital of the eastern Roman empire, the Greek city *Byzantium. The period begins when the emperor Constantine the Great transferred his residence from Rome to Byzantium and renamed the city Constantinople. In AD 395, at the death of the emperor Theodosius the Great, the empire was divided between his two sons, Arcadius ruling from Byzantium/Constantinople in the East and Honorius from Rome in the West. Thereafter there was complete separation of administration and even of succession. When the western empire collapsed in the fifth century (*see* FALL OF ROME) relations between East and West declined. The last eastern emperor to use Latin as the official language of imperial government at Byzantium

was *Justinian, with whose reign (527–65) the Byzantine age (or Byzantine empire) is sometimes said to begin. Greek literature, no longer pagan, was now centred on Byzantium, and had lost its classical stamp under Roman, Eastern, and Christian influences. The Greek pronunciation had changed, syllables in Byzantine Greek having different quantities from classical Greek, with the result that after the second century AD it was no longer possible, except for a few deliberately archaizing poets, to write verse in the old classical metres. New literary genres appeared, such as Christian hymns and saints' lives. The kind of Greek used by authors varied widely, from the most ornate imitations of classical literary Greek to the very different near-vernacular. It was primarily an age of prose, of theology and history particularly; notable historians include *Procopius, Anna Comnena (1083–after 1148), and Michael Psellus (*c.*1019–*c.*1078) (the last two outside the scope of this book). Many writers were occupied with lexicons, abridgements of classical works, and commentaries on them, and played an important part in the preservation and transmission of the ancient authors. The period ended in 1453 with the fall of what was still officially the eastern Roman empire and the capture of Byzantium/Constantinople by the Ottoman Turks. *See also* SECOND SOPHISTIC and TEXTS, TRANSMISSION OF ANCIENT 2 and 3.

**Byzantium** Greek city by the Propontis (the Sea of Marmara), at the southern end of the Bosporus on the European side, later renamed Constantinople (below) and now Istanbul. It was magnificently situated, commanding the two opposite shores of Europe and Asia with the advantages of security and facility for trade. It was originally founded by Megarians in the seventh century BC, opposite Chalcedon (the 'city of the blind', so called by the Delphic oracle because its earlier Megarian founders had failed to choose the superior site of Byzantium). Ruled by Persia from 512 to 478 BC, then alternately under Athenian (*see* DELIAN LEAGUE) and Spartan dominion in the fifth and fourth centuries, Byzantium was a formal ally of Athens from *c.*378 to 357 BC, and then again when successfully resisting Philip II of Macedon in the famous siege of 340–339 BC. The help supposedly given by the goddess Hecate on this occasion was commemorated on Byzantine coins by her symbol of crescent and star (adopted by the Turks as their device after they captured the city in AD 1453). The city suffered severely from the Celtic (Gallic) invasions in the 270s BC and subsequently passed into the Roman empire, while remaining Greek in culture. It was chosen by the emperor Constantine for his new capital (AD 330), to be known thereafter in the West as Constantinople. When the Roman empire in the West finally collapsed in the fifth century under barbarian invasions (*see* FALL OF ROME) the eastern empire and its capital, firmly in the Greek world, flourished. The city's position as the capital of the eastern empire was interrupted in 1204 when it was captured by the French and Venetians (collectively known as Latins) during the Fourth Crusade, and became the seat of the Latin empire until restored to Greek possession in 1261. The last emperor, Constantine XIII, was killed when the city and empire fell to the Turks in 1453. *See also* BYZANTINE AGE.

# C

For Greek names beginning with C see also under K.

**Cācus** In Roman myth, a fire-breathing monster, son of Vulcan, inhabiting a hill at Rome (Aventine, according to Virgil) and who terrorized the country. As *Hercules was driving home to Greece the cattle he had stolen from the monster *Geryon, he rested at the site of the future Rome, where he was entertained by *Evander. Cacus stole some of the cattle and dragged them into his cave tail-first so that it was impossible to follow their traces. When the remaining cattle passed the cave those within began to bellow and so were discovered; Hercules then killed Cacus. Virgil may have invented this story. Cacus seems to have originated in Etruscan myth, where he was a seer on the Palatine.

**Cadmus 1.** In Greek myth, the legendary founder of the city of Thebes (in Boeotia). He was the son of Agenor, king of Tyre (in Phoenicia), who was sent to look for his sister Europa after she had been carried off by Zeus in the shape of a bull. Advised by the Delphic oracle to abandon the search, he was told that he would meet a cow which he should follow until it lay down, and there he should found a city. The cow led him to the site of Thebes, but when he sent his companions to fetch water for sacrifice from a nearby spring they were all killed by the dragon guarding it. Cadmus slew the dragon and at the instruction of the goddess Athena sowed half the dragon's teeth (Athena kept the other half for Aeëtes, king of Colchis, to give to *Jason). A crop of armed men sprang up whom he set fighting by throwing a stone among them, and they fought each other until only five survived. These five, the Spartoi ('sown men'), helped to build a citadel (the Cadmea) and in historical times were held to be the ancestors of the Theban nobility. Zeus gave Cadmus as bride Harmonia, the daughter of Ares and Aphrodite, and all the gods attended the wedding. Cadmus gave his bride as a present a necklace made by Hephaestus which subsequently was to play a fatal part in the Theban story (*see* AMPHIARAUS and ALCMAEON). Their daughters, all of whom met disaster, were Ino, Semele (mother of *Dionysus), Autonoē, and Agave (mother of Pentheus). Cadmus eventually abdicated in favour of his grandson Pentheus, but returned after the latter's death (*see* BACCHAE). He and Harmonia finally withdrew to Illyria, where they were changed into snakes and carried off by Zeus to Elysium. Cadmus was said to have civilized the Boeotians and taught them the art of writing 'with Phoenician [or palm-leaf] letters' (*see* ALPHABET). Because in Theban mythical history victory so often entailed disaster for the victors, a 'Cadmean victory' was proverbial in Greek (compare 'Pyrrhic victory'; *see* PYRRHUS).

**2.** Of Miletus, *see* LOGOGRAPHERS.

**Caeci′lius Stā′tius** (d. in the 160s BC) The chief Roman comic dramatist of his day. He was a Gaul from northern Italy, probably Mediolanum (Milan), taken to Rome as a slave and subsequently manumitted. He was a friend of the poet Ennius and came in point of time between the dramatists Plautus and Terence. He was still alive in 166 to pass judgement on the latter's *Andria*. No complete play of his survives. He wrote *fabulae* *palliatae* of which some forty-two titles are known, sixteen of them deriving from Menander, the Greek writer of New Comedy. Some fragments survive in quotations. *See* COMEDY [Roman].

**Cae′lius, Mons** The most south-easterly of the *seven hills of Rome, south of the Equiline.

**Cae′lius Rufus, Marcus** (b. *c.*87 BC, d. 48 BC) Roman with political ambitions, friend and pupil of Cicero from 66 to 63. He broke with Cicero and associated with *Catiline for a while but did not join his conspiracy. After a successful prosecution in 59 of Antonius, Cicero's colleague in the consulship of 63, Caelius became popular in fashionable circles and rented a house in the desirable Palatine quarter near *Clodia, perhaps supplanting the poet Catullus in her affections, if he is the

Rufus whom Catullus mentions. Their affair was over by 56, the year in which he was prosecuted (for involvement in a murder) by L. Sempronius Atratinus after he had himself unsuccessfully prosecuted the latter's father L. Calpurnius Bestia earlier in the year. He was defended by Crassus and also by Cicero in a notable speech which still survives (*see* CICERO (1) 4). Cicero depicted the prosecution as a plot by Clodia, and Caelius was acquitted. Clodia thereafter disappears from view. Caelius was tribune in 52, a supporter of *Milo and enemy of Pompey. In 51 Cicero went to Cilicia as governor, and during his year's absence Caelius kept him informed of home affairs in seventeen witty and politically acute letters which survive in Cicero's correspondence. In 49, as civil war became imminent, he declared for Caesar, but soon grew discontented and he joined Milo in raising a rebellion in south Italy. This was easily suppressed by Caesar, and Caelius and Milo were both killed.

**Caesar 1.** The name of a Roman patrician family of the *gens* *Julia*, one of the most ancient clans in Rome, which traced its origin back to Iulus, son of Aeneas (himself the son of the goddess Venus. The title 'Caesar' survived into modern times in the Russian 'Tsar' and German 'Kaiser'. Julius Caesar's great-nephew and adopted son Octavian (later the emperor Augustus), added 'Caesar' to his own name, as did his own adopted son, the emperor Tiberius, and his successors. Although the Caesarian branch of the Julian clan became extinct with the death of Nero, succeeding emperors tended to assume the name as a title, until 'Augustus' became the title of the reigning emperor, and 'Caesar' that of the emperor's designated heir or second-in-command (*see* AUGUSTUS, THE).

**2. Caesar, Gaius Julius** Roman general, politician, and dictator, b. 12 or 13 July 100 BC, assassinated 15 March (the *Ides) 44 BC.

**1. 100–62 BC.** Julius Caesar came of a patrician family without social equal, being supposedly descended from *Aeneas and the goddess Venus (his contemporaries privately exchanged jokes on the subject). He was the son of Gaius Caesar, who died before attaining the consulship, and Aurelia. His father's sister married Marius and in 83 he himself married Cornelia the daughter of Cinna (the opponent of Sulla), so from the beginning he was associated in politics with the popular party (*see* POPULARES). In 81 he served his first military campaign, in Asia, but he came to public attention as an orator by two (unsuccessful) prosecutions in Rome. He then retired to Rhodes to study under a Greek rhetorician (M. Antonius Gnipho, who also taught Cicero). On the way there, having been captured for ransom by pirates, he told them that on his release he would capture and crucify them. Soon after his release he was as good as his word. He returned to Rome in 73 and became a senator before 70, supporting *Pompey when the latter as consul repealed some of Sulla's revisions of the constitution. Before he went as quaestor to Hispania Ulterior (Further Spain) in 68 his wife Cornelia died, and on his return in 67 he married one of the Pompeian family, a granddaughter of Sulla, no doubt in order to cement an alliance. He also gave his support to Pompey's enemy *Crassus in various political schemes. When in 65 he was elected to the aedileship, an office whose holder was expected to spend lavishly on buildings and public entertainments, he was able to draw on Crassus' purse. In 63 he was prominent in the successful prosecution of Rabirius in order to challenge indirectly the authority of the *senatus consultum ultimum* (*see* CICERO (1) 2), and opposed Cicero's execution of *Catiline's supporters. In the same year he was elected *pontifex maximus*, a lifetime appointment of immense prestige, through lavish bribery it was said, and to the praetorship *suo anno* for 62 (*see* CURSUS HONORUM). The end of his praetorship was marked by the scandal arising from *Clodius' profanation of the Bona Dea mysteries in Caesar's house by appearing disguised as a woman in order, it was said, to meet Caesar's wife Pompeia in her husband's absence. Caesar, who thought it worthwhile to believe in Clodius' innocence, nevertheless divorced his wife Pompeia because, according to Plutarch, 'his wife must be above suspicion'.

**2. 61–50 BC.** Caesar's successful governorship of Further Spain in 61 established his reputation as a general, although he had hitherto had very little military experience. On his return he was elected consul for 59, also *suo anno*, together with *Bibulus whose vetoes he notoriously disregarded, and made an informal alliance with Pompey and Crassus (often called by modern scholars 'the first triumvirate'). His legislation satisfied the personal ambitions of Pompey and Crassus. In particular he carried a sweeping measure for the redistribution of land. As proconsul in 58 he took for himself the governorship of Illyricum (Dalmatia), Cisalpine Gaul (northern Italy), and the south part of Transalpine Gaul (southern France).

The next nine years were occupied in the conquest of the rest of *Gaul (the Gallic War), brilliantly described in his *Commentaries. In the early years there is no evidence of discord with Pompey, who in 59 married Julia, the daughter of Caesar by his first wife Cornelia. Caesar himself married as his third wife *Calpurnia (1), the daughter of L. Calpurnius Piso who was consul in 59. By 56 Caesar regarded the conquest of Gaul as complete, and spent 55 and 54 in sending expeditions to *Germany and *Britain. The compact with Pompey and Crassus had been renewed at Luca (Lucca) in 56; these two became consuls for 55 and renewed Caesar's command for a further five years. However, in 53 Crassus was killed fighting the Parthians, and Pompey and Caesar were left alone at the head of the state. Pompey's wife Julia, who had formed a bond between them, had died in childbirth the previous year. Sporadic revolts in Gaul in 53 culminated in a general rising in 52 under Vercingetorix, which Caesar put down after the most difficult fighting of his career. Large private fortunes were made by Roman speculators (mostly equestrians) from plunder in Gaul, which was devastated. By 50 Gaul was completely subdued. Meanwhile civil disturbances at Rome (see ROME 4) led to the appointment of Pompey as sole consul for 52, and his measures included a law that allowed Caesar to stand for the consulship when absent. Caesar's governorship expired in 49 and he therefore needed the consulship for 48 if he was not to become a private citizen, liable to prosecution by his political enemies in Rome. The senate wished to recall him before there could be any risk of his becoming consul while still at the head of his army, and the consul C. Marcellus proposed that he should lay down his command by 13 November. Pompey hesitated whether to give his support, but finally threw in his lot with Caesar's enemies.

**3. 49–44 BC.** On 7 January 49 the senate ordered Caesar, now at the river *Rubicon, the boundary between Cisalpine Gaul and Italy, to disband. On 10 January Caesar nevertheless crossed the Rubicon with his army, and the

Civil War was launched. Pompey was entrusted by the senate with the whole management of the war on behalf of the republic, but he was outmanoeuvred and crossed to Greece, and within three months Caesar was master of Italy with a large measure of popular support. He was prudently merciful to the defeated, in contrast with earlier Roman leaders and their *proscriptions. Rather than pursue Pompey to Greece he went to Spain, where in a brief and brilliant campaign he forced the surrender of the Pompeian army at Ilerda (Lerida). In 48 he followed Pompey to Epirus in Greece and suffered a reverse at Dyrrhachium from the latter's powerful army. However, Pompey withdrew to Thessaly, where he was persuaded to offer battle and was defeated at *Pharsalus. Caesar pursued him to Egypt, but on his arrival found him already murdered (48). After Ilerda, Caesar had been appointed dictator in order to hold the consular elections (in which he was elected consul) and pass some necessary legislation, but, that done, he had laid down the dictatorship. When news of his victory at Pharsalus reached Rome he was again nominated dictator, this time for a year. Throughout the winter of 48 he was occupied with a difficult war (the Alexandrian war; see BELLUM ALEXANDRINUM) to establish *Cleopatra VII, now his mistress, on the throne of Egypt; and he thereby gave the Pompeian forces time to regroup. Soon afterwards Cleopatra had a son (*Caesarion), claiming Caesar to be his father. Before returning to Rome, Caesar marched through Syria and Pontus aiming to defeat Pharnaces, king of Pontus and son of the famous Mithridates. This he did in 47 at Zela, a victory which he announced with his famous boast, veni, vidi, vici, 'I came, I saw, I conquered'. In Rome he was elected to his third dictatorship, but before the year ended he set out for Africa where he defeated the Pompeians (i.e. republicans) at Thapsus in 46 (the consequent suicide of *Cato (2) at Utica became an inspiration for later republicans). On his return to Rome he was consul for the third time and given the dictatorship yet again, for another ten years. In four magnificent triumphs he celebrated his victories over foreign enemies (not those over other Romans).

He now turned to legislation, using his amazing ability and energy to bring about many much-needed reforms, none of such long-lasting benefit as the reform of the calendar with the assistance of Sosigenes, the

Alexandrian mathematician (*see* CALENDARS 2). This (Julian) calendar remained in operation until it was further reformed in the sixteenth century. In the midst of these activities Caesar was called to Spain where a republican revolt had broken out, led by Pompey's two sons and Caesar's own former officer Labienus. They were finally defeated at Munda, Caesar's hardest-fought battle (45). Among the army and the people Caesar's popularity was enormous, and the senate granted him his fourth sole consulship and his fourth dictatorship as well as extraordinary emblems of monarchy. But although he attempted to conciliate powerful senators by merciful treatment of his enemies, his evident intention of putting an end to republican government for ever and keeping the supreme power within his own family led to a conspiracy against his life, led by *Cassius and *Brutus (2), and he was stabbed to death in the senate house in 44 BC. (Dante in the *Inferno* put these two with Judas Iscariot in the lowest circle of Hell.) For the aftermath of Caesar's murder *see* ROME 4 and AUGUSTUS.

Caesar had re-established order and had begun to restore the economic situation, he was lavish in granting citizenship to provincials and had abolished tax-farming in Asia and perhaps in other provinces (*see* PUBLICANI). He enlarged the senate to 900, even recruiting its members from outside Italy. He had many other projects in mind, such as that of codifying the law, and was planning an expedition to Parthia at the time of his death.

**4.** Caesar's *Commentaries* (i.e. 'Notes', 'Memoirs') on the Gallic War, and the (unfinished) three books on the Civil War are his only writings that survive entire. The title of the former was chosen deliberately to suggest that it was not history that was being written but rather a bald record of events jotted down in the third person, and therefore an objectively truthful account. Caesar wished, in fact, to create the impression that he was a simple soldier fighting necessary wars for the good of Rome, so as to refute the charges of his political enemies that he was fighting for his own autocracy. Nevertheless, despite its political purpose, the *Gallic War* is unique as a contemporary account of a foreign war written by a Roman general, in lucid, unrhetorical Latin. Each book seems to have been composed at the end of the year with which it deals, perhaps from a daily diary, and perhaps sent individually to Rome. Books 1–7 were published as a whole

probably in 51 BC (book 8 was a later addition by A. *Hirtius). The *Civil War* is rather more obviously a political pamphlet, with the theme that his enemies had forced war upon him, but the narrative is occasionally relieved by a human touch or a flash of sardonic humour. The *Bellum Africum*, *Bellum Alexandrinum*, and *Bellum Hispaniense* were written by members of Caesar's staff.

Caesar also wrote a number of other books which have not survived: a collection of jokes and sayings, later suppressed by Augustus as too frivolous; a grammatical work on declensions and conjugations, composed while he was crossing the Alps and dedicated to Cicero; an irritated reply, *Anticato*, to Cicero's panegyric of Cato (3 above), and a number of poems, of which a verse epigram to Terence survives. He was an outstanding orator, described by Cicero as the most eloquent of Romans (*see* ANALOGY AND ANOMALY). We have Lives of Caesar by Plutarch and Suetonius. Several portrait busts considered authentic show a clean-shaven, austere face, with hair combed forward in later life to conceal baldness, as Suetonius described him. He was tall, pale, with keen black eyes, and took pains over his appearance. It was related that he was born by being cut from his mother's womb, the so-called Caesarian section, but this story is also told of the first member of the Julian *gens* to take the name Caesar, in order to explain the name by deriving it from *caesus*, 'cut'.

For 'Caesar' as a title under the Roman empire *see* AUGUSTUS, THE.

**3.** *See* GAIUS CAESAR.

**Caesa'rion** ('little Caesar') The nickname given by the Alexandrians, and generally accepted, to Ptolemy XV (Ptolemaeus Caesar), the son of *Cleopatra VII, born in 47 BC and said by her to have been fathered by Julius Caesar. Mark Antony told the Roman senate that Caesar had acknowledged his paternity, and so tried to set him up as a rival to Octavian, Caesar's adopted son and heir. Octavian had him executed in 30 BC.

**caesū'ra** ('cut') The place in a metrical line where a break between words regularly occurs, dividing the line into two unequal parts.

**Calabria** In ancient times the heel of Italy. It did not acquire its modern designation, the toe, until AD 700. It was very fertile despite its dryness and its great heat in summer, and was famous for olives, fruit, wine, and horses. *Brundisium was its chief city.

**Ca'laïs and Zētēs** In Greek myth, sons of Boreas, the north wind. They were of human shape but had wings on their shoulders. They took part in the expedition of the *Argonauts to recover the Golden Fleece, in the course of which they saved *Phineus from the Harpies. On their way home they were killed in revenge by Heracles on the island of Tenos, because on the voyage to Colchis they had persuaded the other Argonauts to leave him behind on the coast of Bithynia (on the Propontis) when he was frantically searching for the lost *Hylas. Heracles erected two pillars over their grave, one of which moved whenever the north wind blew.

**Calchas** The seer of the Greek army in the Trojan War. At the opening of Homer's *Iliad* he reveals the reason for the plague in the Greek camp. After Homer he is introduced into several narratives relating to the capture of Troy, such as Agamemnon's sacrifice of his daughter *Iphigeneia and the construction of the Trojan Horse.

**Caledō'nia** The name used by Tacitus and other Romans to describe Britain north of the Firth of Forth. The name survives in modern Dunkeld, Rohallion, and Schiehallion. *Agricola defeated the Caledonians without conquering them.

**calendars** Virtually all peoples have used the lunar month as a measure of time, although, since this period comprises 29½ days, the months inaugurated by each new moon cannot contain a constant number of whole days. The succession of seasons is determined by the yearly cycle of the earth around the sun in roughly 365¼ days, that is, the solar year, which is about eleven days longer than twelve lunar months. Hence, when the solar year is divided into twelve months, the beginning of each month cannot in general correspond exactly with the appearance of the new moon. The agricultural year, punctuated by the beginnings and ends of seasons, when the appropriate agricultural tasks are carried out, is marked by the rising and setting of stars and constellations (*see* ASTRONOMY).

**1. The Greek calendar.** All Greek city-states had their own individual civil year of twelve months with 29 and 30 days alternately, each month beginning with the new moon. Since the year thus contained only 354 days, adjust-ment to fit the solar year had to be made, and the magistrates did this by adding ('intercalating') extra months or fractions of months as need arose. *See* METON.

The civil year at Athens began in July with the appearance of the first new moon after the summer solstice, and was named after the chief *archon (at Sparta, the senior *ephor). The first day of the Athenian month was 'the new moon'. The days within the Greek month or the prytany were sometimes divided into three periods of (mostly) ten days (decades) and the days within each decade denoted by number, but there were many variations. For ill-omened days *see* APOPHRADES. Thucydides (5.20) found the calendar of the seasons the best method for dating the Peloponnesian War so as to be universally understood.

In the fifth century BC some Greeks, to establish an era, had used the Olympian games, whose first recorded victor won in 776 BC and which recurred every four years. The numbering of *Olympiads (four-year periods) and the counting of years within an Olympiad probably goes back to the third century BC, and this system lasted until the Byzantine age. *See* HELLANICUS; HIPPIAS (2); TIMAEUS.

**2. The Roman calendar.** The original Roman calendar ran from March to December ('month ten', *decem*), with an uncounted gap in the winter when no agricultural work was possible. In 153 BC January was made the first month. By *Caesar's day the Roman year consisted of 355 days divided into twelve months, which corresponded with neither the sun nor the moon, and by 46 BC the civic and solar years were discrepant by about three months. On the advice of the mathematician Sosigenes Caesar gave the year 46 BC 445 days to remove the discrepancy, and from 1 January 45 made the year consist of 365 days, with the individual months having essentially the same length as in the modern calendar. He also introduced the leap year. In this Julian calendar the year is about eleven minutes longer than the solar year, and by the late sixteenth century the accumulated difference amounted to ten days. Accordingly Pope Gregory XIII omitted ten days from 1582 and suggested that three intercalary days be omitted every 400 years. Britain eventually adopted this Gregorian (i.e. the modern) calendar in 1752, but it is essentially the Julian calendar, which is still used for dates before 1582. By contrast the Greek and

Russian Orthodox churches have not adopted the Gregorian calendar and continue to use the Julian.

The Romans dated their year by the names of the consuls. We have a complete list of these from 509 BC (when the republic was founded and the consulship began) to AD 541, although the names for the first two centuries may be largely fictitious. The method of dating by magistrates is only effective if the series of names continues uninterrupted. Dating by eras, where the years are numbered consecutively from an agreed starting-point, has obvious advantages. (*See* HELLANICUS.) The Romans did not widely use the era *ab urbe condita* ('from the foundation of Rome', abbreviated to AUC), perhaps because the date we now accept as traditional, 753 BC, was disputed (*see* ATTICUS). The method of reckoning by indictions was introduced by the Roman emperor Diocletian and used up to the Middle Ages and beyond.

The system of dating by the years of the Christian era was introduced in the mid-sixth century by Dionysius Exiguus, a Scythian monk living at Rome, who erroneously put Jesus' birth in 753 AUC and made it year one. Year 0 does not exist: 1 BC is followed by AD 1, so the interval between a date in 5 BC and the same date in AD 5, for example, is nine years not ten.

For the Roman system of dating the days of the year *see* IDES; KALENDS; and NONES.

**Cali'gula** ('little boot') The popular name of the Roman emperor *Gaius Caesar, derived from the heavy hobnailed open boot (*caliga*) worn by Roman soldiers.

**Ca'llias** Son of Hipponicus, at Athens a rich and distinguished politician of the fifth century BC. He was said to have negotiated the 'Peace of Callias' *c.*450 BC which finally ended the wars between Athens and Persia (and was possibly a renewal of *Cimon's attempted peace). The omission of all mention of this treaty by Thucydides in his history has led some scholars to deny its existence, but hostilities between Athens and Persia ceased at this period until 413 BC. Callias was remembered for having married Cimon's sister (or half-sister) Elpinice for love and without a dowry.

**Calli'cratēs** Greek architect of the fifth century BC, associated with Ictinus and Pheidias in the building of the *Parthenon.

**Calli'machus** (b. between 310 and 305 BC in Cyrene, North Africa, d. *c.*240) Greek poet and scholar of the Hellenistic age. He is occasionally referred to as Battiades (i.e. son or descendant of *Battus). During the reign of Ptolemy II Philadelphus, king of Egypt 285–246 BC, he arrived at Alexandria and was commissioned by the king to prepare the great catalogue (*pinakĕs*) of all the books in the *Alexandrian Library. This enormous undertaking (the catalogue ran to 120 volumes) not only benefited the library but also influenced the poet's style: like other Hellenistic poets who combined poetry with scholarship he found in his researches material to be polished and incorporated in his verse. During this time Callimachus produced several prose works of scholarship which have not survived. Of his many poetical works the only ones to survive intact are the six Hymns and perhaps sixty-one short epigrams. The Hymns were modelled on the (so-called) *Homeric Hymns but were not, like the latter, intended for recitation at festivals. Rather they were complex literary compositions, designed to be recited to, or read by, a cultivated audience appreciative of an intriguing narrative and a learned and sometimes ironic imitation of an earlier form. Hymn 1 is to Zeus, 2 to Apollo, 3 to Artemis, and 4 to Delos; Hymn 5, 'The Baths of Pallas', is written in elegiac couplets, unlike the others which are in hexameters; Hymn 6, to Demeter, tells the gruesome story of the insatiable hunger of *Erysichthon. In the *epigrams Callimachus plays subtly with the conventions of this (relatively new) literary form. The epigrams which appeal most to us seem to reflect the poet's own experiences and emotions.

The rest of Callimachus' surviving poetry exists only in fragments, most of it on papyri discovered in the twentieth century; it includes the *Aitia*, the *Hecale*, the *Iambi*, a lyric poem called *Apotheosis of Queen Arsinoe*, and an elegiac poem, *Victory of Sosibius*. The *Aitia* ('Causes') was an elegiac poem in four books, comprising about 7,000 lines. The first two books have an elaborate framework: the poet is transported in a dream to Mount Helicon where (like the poet Hesiod) he is instructed by the Muses, in his case in the origins of all kinds of mythical lore connected with Greek history, customs, and religious rites. None of the stories except for one is known from earlier literature, and the sources appear to have been local histories. The style is learned and allusive but it is enlivened by dry humour and occasionally moving poetry. The third and fourth books, which were probably composed much later, do not have this framework, and are a collection of separate 'causes'. The first and last poems are in praise of the queen *Berenice II, the last being the famous *Plokamos* (Lat. *Coma*) or *Lock of Berenice*. This was later translated into Latin by Catullus in poem 66, which in its turn became the model for Alexander Pope's *Rape of the Lock* (1712). The *Aitia* was also imitated by Ovid in his *Fasti*. By way of introduction to the whole work Callimachus composed the *Answer to the *Telchines*, apparently his critics, who belittle his achievement because he has not written one long continuous poem on an epic theme. His reply is that the small-scale poem is more attractive; moreover Apollo himself has commanded the poet to 'cultivate a slender Muse' and 'tread an unworn path'. As he reputedly said elsewhere, 'a big book is a big evil'; poetry should aim at small-scale perfection. A late tradition relates that chief among his opponents was the epic poet *Apollonius Rhodius, who was thought to be the object of Callimachus' (lost) verse invective, *Ibis*, later translated and adapted to his own purposes by Ovid. (*See also* ANTIMACHUS.)

*Hecale* is an example of the kind of epic Callimachus approved, an *epyllion perhaps about a thousand lines long (now known only in fragments) in which the poet tells how Theseus was on his way from Athens to Marathon to fight the Marathonian bull when a storm arose and the hero took shelter in the hut of an old woman, Hecale, who prepares a simple meal for him (the source perhaps of a similar meal in the hut of *Philemon and Baucis in Ovid's *Metamorphoses*). When Theseus returns from killing the bull he finds that Hecale has died and men are digging her grave.

The fragmentary *Iambi* consist of thirteen short poems, in iambic and choliambic metres, which look back to the sixth-century vituperative poet *Hipponax; they are satirical in tone and often criticize contemporary literary attitudes.

Callimachus was a writer of astonishing output (reputedly 800 volumes) and remarkable originality and versatility, who aimed to be both a poet and a man of taste and erudition. His contribution to the development of a new literary taste in a new cosmopolitan society was very considerable (*see* HELLENISTIC AGE). His blend of sensitivity and detachment, elegance, wit, and learning, had a profound influence on later Roman poets, especially Catullus, Ovid, and Propertius (the last thought of himself as the Roman Callimachus), and through them on the whole European literary tradition.

**Callī'nus** (first half of the seventh century BC) The first Greek poet known to have written in elegiac couplets. He lived in the Greek city of Ephesus in Ionia on the coast of Asia Minor, and the few fragments of his poetry which survive refer to the barbarian invasions of '*Cimmerians and Trerians' from south Russia *c.*652 BC. In the only fragment of any length he exhorts his fellow countrymen to take up arms and defend their country.

**Callī'opē** ('Fair-voice') In Greek (and Roman) myth one of the *Muses. When, in later Greek literature and art, each Muse is made the patron of a particular branch, Calliope is represented as the Muse of epic poetry, with writing tablet and stylus. Orpheus was sometimes said to be her son.

**Callippus** (fl. 330 BC) Astronomer from Cyzicus, who associated with Aristotle at Athens. He proposed a year-length of 365¼ days, on which he based the 76-year cycle named after him. It was an improvement on *Meton's nineteen-year cycle.

**Calli'rrhŏē** ('Fair-flowing') **1.** Daughter of the god *Oceanus and mother of *Geryon.
 **2.** The famous spring at *Athens, later called *Enneakrounos*, 'Nine spouts'. *See also* PEISISTRATUS.

**Calli'sthenēs** Greek historian, born *c.*370 BC, a nephew of Aristotle under whom he studied at Stageira. All his works, including his history of Alexander the Great, are lost. He collaborated with Aristotle in the preparation of a complete list of the victors at the Pythian games from the earliest time. He accompanied Alexander on his expedition east as the historian of the campaigns; his biography of the king, which was widely read, extolled him as the champion of *panhellenism, claiming him to be the son of Zeus. However, he quarrelled with *Alexander (*see* (1) 5) over *proskynesis* (prostration before a ruler), was suspected of being involved in Hermolaus' conspiracy against him, and was put to death in 327. There is no evidence that the murder of Callisthenes earned for Alexander the strong hostility of the school of Aristotle, but Theophrastus, Aristotle's successor, mourned his death. Because of his adulatory and rhetorical style of history, Callisthenes' name became attached to an early version of the popular *Alexander Romance* (*see* ALEXANDER 8).

**Calli'sto** In Greek myth, nymph attendant upon the goddess Artemis. She was loved by Zeus and by him became mother of Arcas, the mythical ancestor of the Arcadians. She was changed into a bear, either by Zeus, to save her from the anger of his consort Hera, or by Hera or Artemis out of vengeance. In this form she wandered about until her son, now grown up, met her when out hunting and would have killed her with his spear. But Zeus turned both into constellations, the Great Bear and the Little Bear (Arctophylax, also known as Boötes).

**Calpu'rnia 1.** The daughter of *Piso (1) Caesoninus (the object of Cicero's speech *In Pisonem*), and the third wife of Julius Caesar, whom she married in 59 BC. Calpurnia's affection for Caesar survived his proposal, made in 54 after the death of his daughter Julia, Pompey's wife, that he should divorce her and marry Pompey's daughter to maintain the family connection, and she tried to keep him from the senate on the day of his murder. After his murder she gave his papers and 4,000 talents to Mark Antony.

**2.** Third wife of *Pliny the Younger, whom she accompanied to Bithynia.

**Calpu'rnius Si'culus, Titus** The otherwise unknown Latin author of seven *pastoral poems (an additional four appended and attributed to him in the manuscripts are by Nemesianus). He is usually thought to have been writing between AD 50 and 60. Three of the seven, Eclogues 1, 4, and 7, are courtly poems aimed to flatter the emperor Nero, while the remainder are more strictly pastoral. They are full of reminiscences of Augustan poetry and especially of Virgil's *Eclogues*.

**Calvus, Gaius Lici'nius** (82–*c*.47 BC) Son of the Roman annalist Licinius Macer (*see* ANNALS), a celebrated love poet in his day and a successful lawyer. He employed the austere Attic style of *oratory, and his speeches against Vatinius were still used as models of oratory a century later. He was also a friend of Catullus, the *salaputium disertum* ('eloquent dwarf') of the latter's poem 53 (and the recipient of poems 14, 50, and 96). The very scanty fragments of his

verse that survive—from epithalamia, a narrative poem, and satiric epigrams (attacking Pompey and Caesar)—at least show that his range was similar to that of Catullus.

**Ca'lydon** *See* MELEAGER.

**Caly'pso** In Greek myth, a goddess or nymph, the daughter of Atlas, who lived on the island of *Ogygia where Odysseus was washed up after being shipwrecked. She kept him there for seven years and promised to make him immortal if he would be her husband, but when Zeus sent Hermes to order his release, she gave him materials to make his own boat. Some stories make her the mother by Odysseus of Auson, the eponymous ancestor of the Ausonians of Italy.

**Cambȳ'sēs** King of Persia 530–522 BC, eldest son of *Cyrus the Great. His main achievement was the conquest of Egypt in 525 BC, which established Persian rule there for two centuries. Greek writers, perhaps following a hostile Egyptian tradition, represent him as impious and tyrannical. The revolt of his brother Smerdis forced Cambyses to leave Egypt in 522. He died in Syria and was succeeded by *Darius.

**Camē'nae** Italian goddesses of a spring outside the Porta Capena at Rome from which the Vestals drew water daily for their rites. They were identified with the Greek Muses after *Livius Andronicus invoked the Camenae at the beginning of his Latin translation of Homer's *Odyssey*.

**Cami'lla** [Lat. *camilla*, 'religious attendant'] A maiden-warrior of the Volsci, and ally of Turnus, known only from Virgil's *Aeneid* and perhaps a Virgilian invention. According to Virgil, when she was a baby her father Metabus, king of the Volscians, was driven out for his cruelty, and arrived with his baby daughter at the flooded river Amisenus. He tied her to a spear, dedicated her to the goddess Diana, and threw her across the river to safety. He then swam across himself. In the *Aeneid* she is killed by the Etruscan Arruns.

**Cami'llus, Marcus Fū'rius** (d. *c*.365 BC) Roman statesman and general. His exploits were greatly embellished in later times, and according to Livy he was 'the saviour of his country and second founder of Rome' after its occupation by the Gauls in the 380s BC. His most famous victory was the capture of the

Etruscan town of Veii in 396 BC when he had been appointed dictator, after which he built a temple to the Veientan Juno on the Aventine. In 394 Camillus reputedly captured another Etruscan town, Falerii. To this campaign belongs the story of the local schoolmaster who brought his pupils to Camillus' camp with the suggestion that they should be used as hostages to secure the town. Camillus, refusing to profit by treachery, returned the children safely, and the schoolmaster in chains. The citizens were so struck by this example of Roman justice that they surrendered.

According to tradition Camillus was accused of appropriating booty and went into exile, but was recalled as dictator when the Gauls captured Rome *c*.385 (*see* BRENNUS (1)). He is supposed to have annihilated the Gauls and later conquered the Volsci and the Aequi. He was a moderating influence during the civil strife between patricians and plebeians that ended in 367, and marked the return to peace by founding a temple to Concord built at the foot of the Capitoline hill. He was five times dictator, and a reform of Roman military organization is attributed to him.

**Campus Martius** ('field of Mars') At Rome, the park and recreation ground of the Romans. Situated outside and to the north-west of the city boundary, in early times it was used for exercising armies and for *athletics, and it was the meeting-place of the *comitia centuriata* (*see* ASSEMBLY). It took its name from an altar to Mars. Public buildings were gradually erected on it, and in 221 BC the censor C. *Flaminius constructed there the circus that bore his name. In 52 BC, Pompey built close to this the first permanent theatre in Rome. In the late republic and during the empire imposing buildings and colonnades were erected there, including the *horologium* of Augustus (*see* CLOCKS).

**Ca'nacē** In Greek myth, daughter of *Aeolus and Enarete. She fell incestuously in love with her brother Macareus, and for this reason was put to death by her father, or, according to some accounts, committed suicide.

**Candau'lēs** Last Heracleid king of Lydia, killed by *Gyges *c*.685 BC.

**candidā'tus** ('whitened') In Rome, a candidate for a magistracy, so called because candidates wore a white toga specially brightened with chalk when greeting electors in the Forum.

**canē'phori** ('basket-bearers') In Greece, maidens who bore baskets on their heads in religious processions; in particular, those from noble families who did so in the procession to the temple of Athena Polias at the *Panathenaea at Athens, and who were required to be chaste. To be rejected as unsuitable, as *Harmodius' sister was by Hipparchus, was a grave insult. The baskets contained all that was needed in the sacrificial ceremony.

**Canī'nius Re'bilus, Gaius** Roman senator who achieved fame when Julius Caesar appointed him consul at noon on the last day of the year 45 BC for the remainder of the day (the consul of that year having died on his last day of office). This was the consulship in which, according to Cicero's joke, no one breakfasted and the consul never slept.

**Cannae** Village in Apulia in Italy, the scene of a great defeat inflicted on the Romans by Hannibal in 216 BC. The consul Aemilius *Paullus and (it was said by Polybius) 70,000 Romans and their allies were killed in the battle. *See* PUNIC WARS.

**canons** Selective lists of Greek authors, dating from ancient times. By the mid-fourth century BC it was recognized at Athens that there were only three outstanding tragic dramatists, Aeschylus, Sophocles, and Euripides, who comprised the tragic canon, but the idea of compiling lists of the best authors in a particular genre was attributed by the Romans to the Hellenistic scholars, *Aristophanes of Byzantium and *Aristarchus, in the third and second centuries BC. These lists can only be reconstructed from later references and there was no unanimous agreement on their contents, but it seems clear that they named as the best *iambographers Archilochus, Hipponax, and Semonides; as the best epic poets Homer and Hesiod; as the best writers of Old Comedy Eupolis, Cratinus, and Aristophanes; and of lyric poetry Pindar, Bacchylides, Sappho, Anacreon, Stesichorus, Simonides, Ibycus, Alcman, and Alcaeus. Lists of orators, historians, and philosophers were subsequently compiled, although only that of the Attic orators rivalled in fame the lists of the poets. The ten best Attic orators were generally deemed to be Antiphon, Lysias, Andocides, Isocrates, Isaeus, Demosthenes, Aeschines, Lycurgus, Hypereides, and Deinarchus. The authors themselves were called in Greek, *hoi* *enkrithentes*, 'those selected', and in Latin, *classici*, i.e. 'of the first class' (*see* CLASSIC), but there was no term for 'selective list' until the German-Dutch scholar David Ruhnken in 1768 originated the use of 'canon' in this sense (Gk. *kanōn*—originally 'rod', then carpenters' 'rule', hence metaphorically 'standard of excellence'). 'Canon' is also applied to the books that came to be accepted for the Bible.

Nowadays literary criticism does not much concern itself with how far a work conforms to a notional standard of excellence.

**ca'ntica** In Roman comedy and particularly in Plautus, the parts that were sung or recited to a musical accompaniment. They were either continuous sequences of long lines delivered in recitative, or lyric passages in a variety of metres, a particular feature of Plautus. They appear to have been an invention of Roman comedy, since there is nothing like them in Greek New Comedy. *See* COMEDY [Roman 2].

**cantō'res Euphoriō'nis** *See* EUPHORION (2).

**Căpănē'us** In Greek myth, one of the *Seven against Thebes, and father of Sthenelus. He climbed the walls of Thebes boasting that not even Zeus would stop him, and was destroyed by Zeus' thunderbolt. His wife Evadne committed suicide by throwing herself on to his funeral pyre.

**Capitoline triad** At Rome, the gods *Jupiter, Juno, and Minerva.

**Capitō'lium (mons Capitōli'nus)** The Capitoline hill, the smallest of the hills of Rome; it had two peaks, the south-west summit known as the Capitol and the north-eastern one known as the *arx* ('citadel'). However, these two last terms are used indiscriminately by ancient as well as modern writers to signify the whole hill as well as one or other of the summits. There are traces of Bronze-age habitation but in historical times it was used as a citadel and a religious centre. The Capitol was the site of the temple to Iuppiter Optimus Maximus ('Jupiter best and greatest'), Juno and Minerva; it was therefore the most sacred part of Rome. According to tradition it was begun by the king *Tarquin and dedicated in the first year of the republic, 509 BC. Here sacrifice was offered by magistrates on taking office, and by victorious generals in a *triumph. It was destroyed by fire in 83 BC but subsequently rebuilt. On the Capitol also stood the ancient

temple of *Jupiter Feretrius. The pattern of hill with temple of Jupiter was reproduced in many cities of Italy and the provinces. For the legend of how the Capitol was saved from the Gauls by the cries of the sacred geese *c.* 385 BC *see* MANLIUS CAPITOLINUS.

**Captī'vī** ('Prisoners of war') Roman comedy by *Plautus, the Greek original of which has not survived. There are no women in the play and so, unusually, no love interest, and the characters are more high-minded than is usual in Plautus.

One of the two sons of Hegio has been taken prisoner by the Eleans; the other was kidnapped when a child by a slave and has not been heard of since. Some Eleans have now been taken prisoner in a war and Hegio has bought two of them, Philocrates and his slave Tyndarus, in the hope of effecting an exchange for his captured son. The slave is to be sent to Elis to negotiate, but he secretly changes identity with his master in order to release him. The trick is revealed unintentionally by an Elean fellow-prisoner and Hegio, thinking that he will not now recover his son, sends Tyndarus loaded with fetters to work in the quarries. Presently Philocrates returns bringing with him Hegio's captive son and the slave who stole his second son. The slave reveals that the boy had been sold to the father of Philocrates and is in fact Tyndarus. The dramatic ironies and the dignified behaviour of the two prisoners make this one of Plautus' most interesting plays.

**Ca'pua** The chief city of Campania, in western Italy. It was an Etruscan city, but after *c.*425 BC when it was captured by the Oscans it became one of the most powerful cities of *Italy. In 338 BC after the Latin War (*see* LATIN LEAGUE) Capua was granted citizenship (at first 'without the vote'). When the Romans were defeated at Cannae in 216 BC during the Punic Wars Capua went over to the Carthaginian side but was recaptured by Rome in 211, severely punished, and had direct government from Rome imposed. It regained its civic rights in 58 BC. Julius Caesar settled 20,000 colonists in its territory. According to the *Aeneid*, the founder of Capua was Aeneas' companion Capys.

**Caraca'lla (Marcus Aurelius Antoninus)** (AD 188–217) Emperor of Rome 211–17. His nickname Caracalla was the name of the long, hooded Celtic cloak which he introduced. He was the elder son of Lucius Septimius Severus (emperor 193–211) and *Julia Domna. His original name was Septimius Bassianus, but in 195 his father renamed him after Marcus Aurelius (emperor 161–80) and made him Caesar (for the title *see* AUGUSTUS, THE). In 198 Caracalla was made Augustus and his younger brother, Geta, Caesar. He accompanied his father to Britain, where they waged a joint campaign against the Caledonians. After his father died in 211 he had Geta killed. In the following year he granted citizenship to all free inhabitants of the empire, in the so-called Antonine constitution. He became mentally unstable, and was murdered in 217.

**Carmen arvale** *See* ARVAL BRETHREN.

**Carmen Saeculā're** Latin choral hymn in the sapphic metre written by *Horace in 17 BC at the command of the emperor Augustus. It was performed at the *Ludi saeculares* (*'Secular Games') by a choir of 27 boys and 27 girls. A marble inscription recording the games and the part played by Horace still survives. The hymn, sung first at the new temple of Apollo on the Palatine and then sung on the Capitol, is in the form of a prayer addressed to Apollo and Diana, and the achievements of Augustus are commemorated.

**Carme'ntis (Carme'nta)** In Roman myth, a prophetic goddess, mother of *Evander the first settler at Rome. She may have been a water-goddess, and she was certainly a goddess of protection in childbirth, worshipped by matrons. She came to be identified with the *Camenae and thus associated with poetry. A minor *flamen was assigned to her, and her festival, the Carmentalia, was on 11 and 15 January. It was said to have been inaugurated by the senate in the third century BC to mark the successful protest of Roman women who refused to have children until the senate restored their right, recently taken away from them, to ride in carriages. One of the gates of Rome near the foot of the Capitoline hill was named after her, the Porta Carmentalis.

**Carne'adēs** (of Cyrene in North Africa, *c.*213–128 BC) An important Greek philosopher, a *Sceptic whose headship of the *Academy at Athens marks the transition from the Middle Academy of Arcesilaus to the New Academy. He was already head of the Academy in 155 BC, when he was sent by Athens as one of three

philosophers on an embassy to Rome. There he won fame for giving, on two consecutive days, first a lecture in praise of justice and then another in which it was proved not to be a virtue but a civil compact to maintain society. After hearing him Cato the Censor demanded the expulsion of the Athenian philosophers in order to protect Roman youth from their influence. He followed the fashion of his Sceptic predecessors and published nothing, but his arguments were recorded by his pupils, notably by Clitomachus, through whom they have survived in the philosophical writings of *Cicero ((1) 5). His influence was considerable. He argued at length against the Stoic belief that knowledge about the world was attainable if it was based upon sense impressions which recorded the facts (or objects) correctly, and that the percipient could be sure that the sense impressions were correct through their complete conformity with the facts perceived. Carneades did not believe that the percipient could be sure; sense impressions have no particular characteristics by which one may distinguish those which are correct from those which are not. Therefore he thought, like *Arcesilaus, that knowledge was unattainable, but he allowed that some sense impressions are 'persuasive', i.e. seem probable, while others are not. For the purposes of life we have to assume the truth, or the falsity, of many sense impressions, but we should not assert either, because the truth about facts or objects may actually be quite different from our perception of them.

Carneades attacked many Stoic and Epicurean dogmas, exposing their improbabilities and the often shaky arguments on which they were based. The Stoics modified some of their theories in the light of his criticism. After Carneades the tradition of (moderate) Scepticism in the Academy was continued by Philon of Larissa (head of the Academy 109 BC). Cicero declared himself an adherent of the 'New' Academy which began after Arcesilaus, and particularly of Carneades and Philon.

**Carrhae** City in northern Mesopotamia, scene of the defeat of the Roman general M. Licinius *Crassus by the Parthians in 53 BC.

**Carthage** City occupying a strong strategic position on the Tunisian coast of North Africa. It was founded by colonists from Phoenician Tyre, traditionally in 814 BC though the earliest archaeological evidence dates from a century later. (For its foundation legend *see* DIDO.) It gradually outstripped other Phoenician cities in North Africa (Utica was the chief rival) and became the centre of a powerful empire whose wealth was based on agriculture and commerce. It carried on trade all along the coasts of the Mediterranean and maintained control of sea-routes to the west, especially the important tin-routes. Carthage eventually ruled all the islands of the Western Mediterranean, but it never achieved complete control over *Sicily, which Greeks and Carthaginians fought over for three centuries. In 480 BC a large Carthaginian expedition was defeated by the Sicilian Greek tyrants Gelon and Theron at Himera, reputedly on the same day as the Persians were defeated at Salamis. Carthaginian interests also came into conflict with those of Rome, leading to the *Punic Wars, which began in 264 BC. When they ended in 146 BC Carthage was utterly destroyed. Rome decreed that no house should be built nor crop planted, but the city was refounded by Julius Caesar in 44 BC and became the capital of the enlarged province of *Africa. By the second century AD Carthage had become the largest city in the west after Rome. Under the empire Carthage became first a famous educational centre, especially for law and rhetoric, and then a focus for Christianity in the west, especially in the time of Tertullian and Cyprian (second and third centuries AD). Carthage fell to the Vandals in 439 and became the capital of their king Gaiseric, but after the victory of the Romans in 533 it remained loyal to the Roman empire in the east until the Arab conquest in 697.

**Cartima'ndua** British queen of the *Brigantes whose treaty with the Roman emperor Claudius safeguarded the northern borders of Roman Britain. Her relationship with her husband Venutius was weakened when, in observance of her agreement, she handed over the fugitive Caratacus to Rome in AD 51. She subsequently divorced Venutius and married his officer Vellocatus, but in 68 Venutius defeated Cartimandua and regained the kingdom. In order to rescue the queen the Romans advanced further north, conquered Brigantia and incorporated it into the province.

**caryă'tids (karyātidĕs)** The Greek name for columns carved in the form of women in long drapery. They appear in Greece c.550 BC. The most famous are the six which supported the roof of the small porch on the south-west corner of the Erechtheum, one of which is now in the British Museum. The derivation of the name is unknown; one suggestion is that it means 'maidens of Caryae', a place in Laconia, and it is perhaps connected with the girl dancers who performed there in honour of Artemis.

**Casca, Servilius** Two brothers so named joined the conspiracy against Julius Caesar in 44 BC. One of them, Publius Longus, was the first to strike Caesar at his assassination. Both killed themselves after the defeat of the republicans at Philippi in 42 BC.

***Ca'sina*** Roman comedy by *Plautus, adapted from a play ('Men casting lots') by the Greek writer of New Comedy, *Diphilus.

An elderly Athenian and his son have both fallen in love (*cf.* MERCATOR) with Casina, a slave-girl who has been rescued from exposure as a baby and brought up in their household. The father wants to have her married to his bailiff, the son to his own attendant Chalinus, each for his own purpose, while the father's wife, aware of her husband's scheme, plots on her son's behalf. Lots are drawn to settle the matter and the father wins, but at the wedding the bailiff is fobbed off with Chalinus dressed as a bride, who beats both bailiff and father. Casina is found to be a free-born Athenian and marries the son.

**Cassa'nder (Kassandros)** (c.358–297 BC) Macedonian, son of the general *Antipater who helped Alexander the Great to succeed to the throne of Macedon after the death of his father Philip II. In 323 BC Cassander was sent to Alexander at Babylon in the last months of the latter's life; there seems to have been strong mutual dislike. After Alexander's death Cassander was involved in the power-struggles among the generals. He eventually gained control of Macedon and procured the deaths of Alexander's mother *Olympias, wife Roxane, and posthumous son *Alexander IV. He managed to establish himself as his father's successor and ruled over Macedon and most of Greece, being a leading figure in the war against *Antigonus I. By c.305 he had himself proclaimed 'King of the Macedonians' but spent the rest of his life trying to keep his territory. He founded the city of Thessalonika (Salonika) and rebuilt Thebes.

**Cassa'ndra** (also called **Alexandra**) In Greek myth, the prophetic daughter of *Priam, king of Troy, and Hecuba his wife. For Homer, who makes no mention of her prophetic gifts, she is the most beautiful of Priam's daughters. It was according to a later tradition that she promised herself to Apollo and was given the gift of prophecy, but when she broke her word he condemned her to the fate of always prophesying truthfully but never being believed. She appears in Greek tragedy in this role, vainly foretelling the disaster that Paris would bring on Troy, or warning against the Wooden Horse. When Troy was captured, Ajax the Locrian, son of Oileus, found her in the temple of Athena clinging to the sacred statue of the goddess (the *Palladium), dragged her away, and raped her. To expiate this sacrilege the Locrians were obliged to send two maidens to Troy every year to serve in Athena's temple. The Locrians maintained that this obligation was imposed for a thousand years. After the sack of Troy Cassandra was awarded to the Greek commander *Agamemnon as his concubine, but on their return to Mycenae they were both murdered by his wife Clytemnestra.

**Cassiodō'rus** (**Magnus Aurēlius Cassiodōrus**) (c.AD 490–c.585) Christian Roman politican, writer, and monk. Born in south Italy the son of a praetorian prefect (see PRAEFECTUS PRAETORIO) of Theoderic, king of the Ostrogoths, he too served Theoderic, was consul in 514, and pursued a public career until 538. He then retired to his estates to devote himself to scholarship and the Christian life, as a monk in the monastery he founded at Vivarium in Bruttium (Calabria). He published twelve books of his *Variae epistulae* ('Various letters'), the most important letters and edicts he had written for the Gothic kings to the notable personages of the day, and a valuable source to us for sixth-century history. Among his other writings were a *History of the Goths*, of which a summary survives, a brief history of the world down to AD 519, very popular in medieval times, and some grammatical works. His *Commentary on the Psalms* was intended to turn a scriptural work into an encyclopaedia of the *seven liberal arts, hitherto a pagan preserve. The chief literary work of his later life was the *Institutiones* ('Institutions'), a guide to the religious and secular education of his monks, the secular part being based on the seven liberal arts. It also gives instruction about the copying of manuscripts, in which Vivarium was very active, but not, as far as can be seen, in the area of classical Latin texts. Nevertheless Cassiodorus played a part in the transmission of a literate Christian and Roman culture to the western medieval world. Cf. his kinsman *Boethius.

**Cassiope'ia** (**Cassiepeia**) In Greek myth, wife of Cepheus, king of the Ethiopians. She boasted that her daughter *Andromeda (or possibly she herself) was more beautiful than the Nereids; in consequence Poseidon sent a sea-serpent to ravage the land, to which Andromeda was to be sacrificed until *Perseus saved her life. After their deaths Cassiopeia and her family became constellations.

**Cassite'rides** ('Tin islands') Name given by the Greeks, probably generically, to all the unknown lands in the north-west of Europe producing tin, including Britain. Herodotus in the fifth century BC knew that tin came to Greece reputedly from these islands, but did not know by what route or where the islands were to be found. *Pytheas, the Greek explorer from Massalia (Marseilles) of the late fourth-century BC, said he visited Belerium (Cornwall) and the tin depot at Ictis (St Michael's Mount or possibly Vectis, the Isle of Wight), but was not universally believed. The Phoenicians, from their colony at Gades (Cadiz) in Spain, or from Carthage, were probably the first to discover a sea-route to Cornwall in the eighth or seventh centuries BC, but they kept their sea-routes secret, hence Herodotus' ignorance. A Roman, probably P. Licinius Crassus, while governor in Spain c.95 BC, is credited with making the sea-route between Cornwall and Spain generally known.

**Ca'ssius, Gaius Longī'nus** One of the murderers of Julius Caesar in 44 BC. He was quaestor to M. *Crassus at the battle of Carrhae in 53 BC, where he succeeded in extricating a division of the Roman army from the disaster. He supported Pompey in the Civil War and was given a naval command, but on hearing of Pompey's defeat at Pharsalus in 48 BC, abandoned the war and later obtained Caesar's pardon. He was *praetor peregrinus* in 44 when he played a leading part in the conspiracy against Caesar. Following the assassination Cassius had to withdraw from Rome, and spent time campaigning in Asia. When Caesar's murderers were outlawed in the autumn of 43, Cassius joined Brutus in Thrace to meet the triumvirs. In the first battle of Philippi in 42 his camp was captured and he ordered his slave to kill him.

**Ca'ssius Dīo** (*c*.AD 164–235, also known as Dio Cassius) Author of a Roman history in eighty books, written in Greek. His family came from Nicaea in Bithynia but lived at Rome, where his father was a senator. He himself was consul twice, proconsul of Africa, and legate, first of Dalmatia and then of upper Pannonia. He wrote a small book on dreams and portents, and a history of the civil wars of AD 193–7 (both lost), but his major work was the history of Rome, from the landing of Aeneas in Italy down to AD 229. Books 36–54, covering the years 69–10 BC, survive complete, books 55–60 (9 BC–AD 46) have substantial gaps, and books 79–80 (AD 217–20), ending with his own retirement, survive in part. The rest of the history has to be pieced together from the summary descriptions by Byzantine historians of the eleventh and twelfth centuries. He is an important witness for contemporary events and a valuable commentator on the political aspects of history through his own experience, but he is unreliable about republican institutions and the style is coloured by his rhetorical training. He believed strongly in divine intervention, often intimated by portents which he frequently describes, and his accounts of events during the late republic are often shaped so as to prefigure later developments under the empire.

**Cassivellau'nus** King of a British tribe, presumed to be that of the *Catuvellauni, the most powerful of the southern tribes. He may have been the great-grandfather of Cunobelinus. He was commander of the British forces that resisted Julius Caesar's second invasion of Britain in 54 BC (*see* BRITAIN 1). When Caesar discovered and captured his stronghold, perhaps at Wheathampstead in Hertfordshire, Cassivellaunus was forced to make terms and pay tribute. After this Caesar withdrew to Gaul.

**Castā'lia** In Greek myth, the nymph who, when pursued by Apollo, threw herself into the spring on Mount Parnassus near Delphi. The spring Castalia was held sacred to Apollo and the Muses. All who wished to consult the Delphic oracle were required to purify themselves in its waters. It may still be seen a little to the north-east of *Delphi. To the Romans, 'drinking the waters of Castalia' signified poetic inspiration, since Apollo was the god of poetry.

**Castor and Pollux (Polydeukēs)** Twin sons of Leda, brothers to Helen of Troy. For their story *see* DIOSCURI.

**catalectic, catalexis** ('stops short') In metre, term describing a final metron of a verse in which a final or near-final syllable is omitted. The term 'acatalectic' describes a verse or metron which does not lack such a syllable, in cases where the distinction is needed.

**Catale'pton** See APPENDIX VIRGILIANA.

**Catalogue of Women (Ē(h)oīai)** (Lat. *Ē(h)oēae*) Greek hexameter poem ascribed to *Hesiod in antiquity, but probably too late, being not earlier than the sixth century BC, to be by him. It was a continuation of his *Theogony* in five books, containing accounts of the women who had been loved by the gods and become the mothers of *heroes. Some parts of the work survive in quotation and in papyrus fragments. The title was derived from the Greek words introducing each new group of heroines, *ē hoiai* ('or such as . . . ').

**Categories (Katēgoriai)** [Lat. *Categoriae*, 'predicates'] One of the six logical works which comprise Aristotle's *Organon* (*see* ARISTOTLE 4(i)). It is a treatise on the ten different types of predicate, or classes, into which the attributes of things may be divided. Aristotle distinguishes substance (thing) from quality, as in 'the box (substance) is small, round, wooden . . . ' (qualities). Within substance Aristotle separates a primary substance from a secondary, and argues that a primary substance is an individual thing, '*this* box', '*that* man *over there*'; the generic 'box' and 'man' are secondary substances because they have no real independent existence: the words merely signify two *kinds* of primary substance. Individual things are the basis on which everything else depends. Aristotle draws out the implications of this by considering many examples. The Neoplatonist philosopher *Porphyry wrote a short commentary on the text, which survives.

**catharsis** *See* POETICS.

**Ca'tiline (Lucius Sergius Catilīna)** (d. 62 BC) Roman patrician, but from a relatively obscure family. A legate of Sulla, he rose to political prominence in the 60s of the first century BC. He was praetor in 68, governor of Africa for the following two years, and on his return was prosecuted for extortion and so prevented from standing for the consulship until he was finally acquitted. He was defeated for the consulship of 63 by Cicero, who captured the vote of the *optimates*; they might otherwise have supported Catiline but were alarmed by what his intentions might be. He was exploiting the widespread unrest in Italy at that time among many classes of society and proposing the cancelling of debts, and was said to have the support of Julius Caesar and Crassus. Defeated for the consulship of 62 also, he laid plans for revolution, against which Cicero could not take action until he had frightened Catiline into leaving Rome to join forces with destitute veteran soldiers in Etruria, and had obtained written evidence to convince the senate of Catiline's intentions. The *senatus consultum ultimum* was passed late in 63 and the leaders of the conspiracy still in Rome were arrested and, after much debate and a vote in the senate, executed. Catiline was now in open rebellion against the state; the consul Antonius marched out with an army, and defeated and killed him early in 62.

Catiline's severest critics, Cicero and Sallust, credit him with bravery and qualities of leadership, but his actions were prompted by a desperate ambition. Cicero was hailed as the saviour of Rome but was open to the charge of having executed citizens without trial. *See also* CICERO (1) 2.

**Cāto, Marcus Po'rcius 1.** ('the Elder' or 'the Censor', 234–149 BC) A dominant figure in the political and cultural life of Rome in the second century BC. A *novus homo*, he was born at Tusculum, fought in the Second *Punic War as military tribune, and embarked on a political career under the patronage of L. Valerius Flaccus, subsequently his colleague as consul and censor. He was quaestor in Sicily in 204, and returning to Rome via Sardinia he is said to have found the poet Ennius there and brought him to Rome. He was praetor in 198 and consul with Flaccus in 195, when he unsuccessfully opposed the repeal of the Oppian law limiting women's finery. He was governor in Spain where he won a *triumph for his military operations. During the 180s Cato was prominent in attacking the *Scipios.

A constant champion of the traditional Roman virtues, he was hostile to their attempts to introduce Greek culture to Rome (*see* CARNEADES), although this did not prevent him from learning Greek himself in his later years (*see* BILINGUALISM). He was elected to the censorship in 184, an office he held with a severity which became proverbial. He applied himself to restraining the corrupting pursuit of wealth through trade by the Roman ruling class and checking the extravagance of the wealthy. His ideal was a return to the primitive simplicity of a mainly agricultural state. His son married a daughter of L. Aemilius *Paullus, a notable philhellene but also devoted to Roman religious tradition.

Late in life (153 BC) Cato went on an embassy to Carthage and was so impressed by the danger to Rome from her revived prosperity and military strength that, henceforth, when asked for his opinion in the senate, whatever the subject under debate, he always declared 'Carthage must be destroyed' (Lat. *Carthago delenda est*). He had the satisfaction of seeing the Third Punic War under way before his death.

Cato chose to educate his son himself rather than entrust him to the Greek teacher in his household, and gave him a tough upbringing. His instructions 'To his son' were collected in several books (a few fragments survive) and contained many strictures against Greek education. He wrote on a variety of subjects, and in so doing virtually became the founder of Latin prose literature. Previous Roman historians had written in Greek. Cato's *Origines* ('Beginnings') in seven books, begun in 168 BC and still being written at the time of his death, dealt with the foundation legends of Rome and the Italian cities (whence the title) and the history of recent wars. This discursive work, now lost, was the first of its kind in the Latin language (*see* HISTORIOGRAPHY [Roman]). He wrote with greater sophistication than is suggested by his precept, *rem tene: verba sequentur* ('stick to the meaning: the words will follow'). His *De agri cultura* ('On agriculture'), sometimes known as *De re rustica*, which in large part survives, is written with the professed aim of advising the owner of a medium-sized estate who is farming for profit. Cato only farmed seriously when he was young and poor. Plutarch observed that when Cato became keen on making money he treated an agricultural estate as a source of income, from such things as mining and pasturage and forestry that could not be ruined by the weather. Cato placed a high value on making money, and thought it honourable for a man at the end of his life to have more property than he had inherited. His advice to sell off a slave when he is too old to be profitable is notorious. Plutarch commented: 'For my part I would not sell even my draught ox simply because of his age, far less turn out an old man from his home.'

Cato was also a successful orator (150 of his speeches were known to Cicero) and he was a persistent litigant. The surviving fragments show shrewdness and wit. Nearly fifty prosecutions were brought against him, the last when he was 86. This was the occasion on which he said, 'It is hard for a man who has lived through one generation to have to defend himself before another.' He kept his vigour into old age, and Cicero makes him the principal interlocutor in his dialogue *De senectute* ('On old age'). For an anecdote concerning his views on divination *see* DE DIVINATIONE.

**2.** ('the Younger', of Utica, Lat. *Uticensis*, 95–46 BC) Great-grandson of Cato (1). He was a man of unbending Stoic principles and uncompromising integrity, who was impelled by his devotion to Roman tradition and his desire to emulate the virtue of his great-grandfather to support senatorial government and the republican cause. He was influential in persuading the senate to execute Catiline's fellow conspirators in 63 BC (*see* CICERO (1) 2), accusing Julius Caesar of being an accomplice, and was the chief antagonist of the so-called 'first triumvirate' of Caesar, Pompey, and Crassus in 60 BC. He was so much of an annoyance to them, obstinately opposing Caesar, that they arranged for Clodius to propose a law which sent him away to annex Cyprus. After his return Cato, his reputation intact, continued to oppose the triumvirs but, to the people's surprise, supported Pompey's unconstitutional sole consulship in 52 for the pragmatic reason that any government was better than none. When Caesar marched on Rome Cato advised that Pompey should be chosen as commander-in-chief, on the grounds that those who are responsible for bringing about a desperate situation should have the job of curing it. He resolutely followed Pompey and held Sicily for the senate. When Caesar's supporter Curio landed, Cato withdrew to join Pompey, but was holding Dyrrhachium during the campaign leading up to the republican defeat at Pharsa-

lus. He proceeded to Africa, where his march around the Great Syrtis (Gulf of Sirte) became famous as a feat of endurance. He became governor of Utica, where he heard of Pompey's death and, subsequently, of Caesar's victory over the senatorial party at Thapsus. All Africa, except Utica, surrendered to Caesar. Cato, after seeing to the safety of his friends, chose to refuse Caesar's pardon and committed suicide, having spent the previous night reading Plato's *Phaedo*. One letter of his survives in Cicero's correspondence, civilly refusing to use his influence in procuring Cicero a triumph. His death conferred its own nobility on the losing republican side (*see* PHARSALIA), to inspire Romans with a republican ideal long after republicanism was dead. Virgil in the *Aeneid* (book 8) makes him a judge in Elysium.

**Catu′llus, Gaius Vale′rius** (*c.*84–probably 54 BC) Roman poet, born in Verona, son of a wealthy man whose acquaintances included Julius Caesar. As a young man he went to Rome and joined the fashionable literary circle (*see* NEOTERICS) who were enthusiastic about Hellenistic Greek culture. He addressed poems to Cicero, Cornelius Nepos, and Hortensius among others, and freely insulted Caesar (with whom he was subsequently reconciled) and Mamurra. Very little is known of his life except what can be gleaned, with caution, from his poems: that he spent a year (57 to 56) with his friend *Cinna in Bithynia on the staff of the governor, Gaius *Memmius; that he saw his brother's grave in the Troad; that he returned from abroad to a villa at Sirmio on Lake Garda. Twenty-five poems are addressed to a certain Lesbia, a married woman of some social standing whose real name, Apuleius plausibly tells us, was *Clodia. These chronicle his love affair from an idyllic beginning to final disillusionment, and suggest that she deserted Catullus for a succession of partners, including, it seems, *Caelius.

Catullus died young, leaving behind 114 poems which fall into three groups, apparently arranged as they are for metrical reasons. 1–60 are short pieces, in hendecasyllables or other lyric metres (iambics, scazons, and in one case glyconics) and in elegiacs. They are very varied in subject and manner, embracing incidents of daily life, expressions of friendship, satires, political lampoons, love poems, even a hymn to Diana; poem 51 is a translation of an extant poem by the Greek poet Sappho.

The second group, 61-4, are longer poems: 61 is an epithalamium for a friend, 62 another wedding song, 63 an extraordinary metrical feat, a poem in the galliambic metre on the legend of *Attis, a young man who, in religious frenzy for the goddess Cybele, emasculates himself and lives to regret it; 64 is an *epyllion on the marriage of Peleus and Thetis (happy love), but consisting mostly of a digression on the story of Ariadne (unhappy love).

The first four poems of the third group, 65-8, are longer elegiac poems: after an introductory poem (65), 66 is a translation of Callimachus' poem, *The Lock of Berenice* (*see* BERENICE (3)), and 68 a poem of complex structure difficult to interpret. It is sometimes seen as a bridge between supposed Hellenistic Greek love elegy and the later love elegies of Propertius and Tibullus; 69-116 form a sequence of epigrams in elegiacs on a wide range of subjects. Like the first group, the third contains love poems expressing both happiness and disillusionment, as well as witty and malicious occasional poems which most characterize Catullus in the minds of his readers. Poems to some named individuals—Furius and Aurelius, Julius Caesar, and the young man Iuventius, with whom the poet professes to be in love, are scattered throughout the book.

Catullus was the leading figure among the new poets of the day who were looking for inspiration not to past Romans but to the Greeks, both to the learned, polished poets of the Hellenistic age and to the more direct lyric poets of earlier centuries, such as Sappho. Part of his appeal lies in his versatility, but it is as a love poet that he is chiefly remembered. He was the first ancient poet to describe the progress of one deeply felt love affair, and in this he exerted a wide influence on his successors, on Tibullus, Propertius, and Ovid and others whose works are lost.

We are fortunate to have his poems, for they nearly perished. The three fourteenth-century manuscripts in which they are preserved are copies of one earlier text, now lost. *See* TEXTS, TRANSMISSION OF ANCIENT 6.

**Ca'tulus, Quintus Lutā'tius** Roman consul in 102 BC with *Marius and joint victor over the Cimbri in 101 BC, also with Marius and helped by his legate Sulla. Catulus, resentful that Marius received most of the credit for the victory, became one of his chief opponents. When Marius and Cinna captured Rome in 87 BC he was prosecuted and committed suicide. He was a cultured man, a competent orator—Cicero introduced him into his *De oratore*—and a writer of epigrams, two of which survive. His son of the same name is an interlocutor in Cicero's *Academica*.

**Catuvellau'ni** The most powerful tribe in southern Britain at the time of Julius Caesar's invasions, ruled by *Cassivellaunus. Their capital was at Verulamium (St Albans). A later king was Cunobelinus.

**Caudine Forks (Furculae Caudīnae)** The defile of Caudium in Samnium where the Roman army in 321 BC was obliged to surrender to the Samnites without a fight—a notoriously shameful disaster for Rome. The site has never been certainly identified, possible places not fitting Livy's description.

**cavalry** *See* HIPPEIS and EQUESTRIAN ORDER.

***Cavalry Commander, The (Hipparchikos)*** A treatise by the Athenian *Xenophon on the duties of a cavalry commander, written perhaps c.357 BC. It deals authoritatively (from the author's long experience of cavalry) with all that is involved in commanding the Athenian cavalry. Some of the sections cover rather randomly various aspects of cavalry life, such as how to perform at festivals, but the most interesting parts concern the strategy and tactics of fighting with cavalry, including intelligence-gathering.

**Cēbēs** (of Thebes) An associate of Socrates who, with Simmias, is a main character in Plato's *Phaedo*. In the *Crito* he is one of those who are prepared to help Socrates escape from prison.

**Cecrops** A mythical king of Athens, regarded by the Athenians as their first king. He was sprung from the earth (i.e. autochthonous) and represented as serpent-shaped below the waist. The state of Attica was sometimes called Cecropia after him. By Aglaurus he had three daughters (for their story *see* ERICHTHONIUS). The contest between Athena and *Poseidon for possession of Attica took place in his reign, and in some accounts he was the judge, awarding the land to Athena.

**Ce'lĕus** *See* DEMETER.

**celibacy** *See* CHASTITY.

**Celsus 1. Aulus Cornelius Celsus** Roman encyclopaedist of whom very little is known. He lived in the reign of the emperor Tiberius (AD 14–37). Of his encyclopaedia, *Artes* ('Arts'), eight books, on *medicine, survive. After giving in the proem a brief history of medicine from Homer onwards, which is important for reconstructing Hellenistic doctrines, he surveys the whole field of medical science as it was known at Rome in his day, but without adhering to any one school. Consideration of diet and of the general principles of treatment is followed by a survey of diseases, classified as internal or external, and their treatment, and a discussion of pharmaceutical preparations. He gives a good account of medicinal plants. The final two books deal with diseases that are to be remedied by surgery, and with skeletal anatomy, perhaps the most interesting and advanced part of the work. Much of the practice described was not superseded until the nineteenth century. Celsus' book was unknown for centuries until it was rediscovered and printed in the fifteenth century, from which time it became immensely popular, in part because of the simple and elegant style of the Latin in which it was written.

**2.** Greek-speaking Platonist philosopher of the second century AD who wrote, probably between 175 and 181, the first comprehensive attack on Christianity. Large parts of it survive in Origen's reply, *Contra Celsum* ('Against Celsus'), written (in Greek) in the 240s.

**Celts** Term used by ancient and modern writers to describe a population group occupying in prehistoric and historic times lands mainly north of the Mediterranean, from the Spanish peninsula and the British Isles in the west, to what became known as Galatia in central Asia Minor. Its application to the Irish, Scots, and Welsh is modern. The unity of the Celts can be recognized from the fact that they had a common speech, evinced in place-names, and from a common and very idiosyncratic artistic style. It is generally thought that they spread from the region of the Upper Danube during the Bronze age, around the thirteenth century BC, and spoke an early form of Celtic (from which the later dialects of Old Welsh, Cornish, and Breton derive). Since the beginning of the twenty-first century Celts have become better-known through archaeology. From the eighth century BC the use of iron weapons, rather than bronze, may have enabled Celts to settle in Spain and Britain at that time. Those who settled in Gaul came to be known themselves as Gauls. The invaders of Italy who are said to have sacked Rome in the 380s BC (*see* MANLIUS CAPITOLINUS) and who entered the Balkans, raided Delphi in 279 BC, and crossed the Hellespont going east in 278 BC are referred to either as Celts or as Gauls. The latter settled in and gave their name to the territory of Galatia, where Celtic was still spoken in the fifth century AD. From the third century BC onwards the Celts in Europe were overrun by invading Germans crossing the Rhine and by the migrations of the Germanic Cimbri and Teutones soon after 120 BC, and so they withdrew westward from Bohemia and south Germany (*see* HELVETII). Those who settled in what is now France were also conquered by Rome in the Gallic War. The ancient writers acknowledged their fighting skills and noted the savagery of their religion (including human sacrifice), conducted by the priesthood of the druids, whose centre was in Britain.

**censors** Magistrates at Rome, two in number, who were elected every five years but held office for eighteen months only, in order to take the census. They made up the official list of citizens and at its conclusion carried out the solemn purification, *lustrum*, which gave its name to the interval of (usually) five years between each purification. The registration of citizens took place in a special building on the Campus Martius. The censors exercised a general supervision over the conduct of citizens; they lacked *imperium*, but their power and prestige derived from their duty of revising the roll of senators, removing those who had acted against law and morality and replacing them by others. They also had the duty of making contracts for public works and for the farming of taxes, and of leasing state lands. The office was established in 443 BC, and throughout the middle and late republic the censorship stood at the head of the *cursus honorum*, traditionally going to ex-consuls, but its authority was reduced by the legislation of *Sulla. After 22 BC the emperors took over the duties and the office disappeared.

**census** The register of adult male citizens prepared at Rome since the time of Servius Tullius for the purposes of taxation, voting rights, and military service. Details of the family property and occupation were included but not the names of women and children. The centuries of cavalry were registered separately, but the citizens were registered in tribes according to domicile, and in centuries according to property and age. Most of the centuries were then divided among five classes according to their wealth; each class was divided into *seniores*, those over the age of 45 and usually beyond military service, and *iuniores*. The poorest were registered as *capite censi*, 'counted by head'; *see* PROLETARII. A census was normally held every four (later five) years, but in the later republic the practice lapsed. It was revived by the emperor Augustus, who extended it to the provinces, the inhabitants supplying information about their property essential for the equitable levying of taxes. *See also* LUSTRATION.

**Centaurs** In Greek myth, a race of creatures with the body and legs of a horse but the chest, head, and arms of a man, said to be the offspring of *Ixion and Nephele ('Cloud'). They lived on Mount Pelion in Thessaly, and symbolized for the Greeks the appetites of animal nature (and perhaps barbarism, as on the Parthenon metopes, where they can be read as the Persians; *see* BARBARIAN. Similar meaning may be attached to the representation of Lapiths and Centaurs on the sandals of Athena's statue at Olympia). When their neighbours the Lapiths were holding a feast for the wedding of their king Peirithous with Hippodameia, the Centaurs were invited but, having tasted wine and got drunk, tried to rape Hippodameia and other women. They were routed and driven from Thessaly to the Pindos mountains. Some ancient authors locate the wedding feast in Arcadia. Individual Centaurs have myths of their own; *see* CHIRON; NESSUS; PHOLUS.

**centurion** The highest-ranking professional officer in the Roman army, who commanded a century. (*See also* LEGATI and TRIBUNI MILITUM.) Every *cohort had six centurions, and to be first centurion of the first cohort (*primus pilus*) was the highest honour for a professional soldier.

**Ce'phalas** *See* ANTHOLOGY [Greek].

**Ce'phalus 1.** In Greek myth, a famous hunter, the husband of Procris, daughter of Erechtheus. Eos ('Dawn') fell in love with him and bore his son Phaethon, which caused dissension between husband and wife. Artemis (or Minos) gave Procris a hound which always caught its quarry and a spear which never missed its mark, originally gifts from Zeus to *Europa which passed to Minos. Procris gave these to Cephalus and a reconciliation followed. But Eos made Procris jealous of the time Cephalus spent hunting. Procris hid in a bush to watch him and he, thinking that he heard an animal stir in the bush, hurled his spear and killed her. These two are the 'Shafalus' and 'Procrus' mentioned in the Pyramus and Thisbe playlet of Shakespeare's *A Midsummer Night's Dream*.

**2.** The old man in Book I of Plato's *Republic, the father of the Attic orator *Lysias.

**Cerami'cus (Kerameikos)** The potters' quarter at Athens, an area north-west of the Acropolis. When the Themistoclean city wall was built this quarter was divided into the Inner and Outer Ceramicus. The part outside the walls was used as a burial ground; the agora was included in the inner part.

**Ce'rberus** In Greek myth, the monstrous dog guarding the entrance to the Underworld (*see* HADES), the offspring of Typhon and Echidna. He had three (or fifty) heads and a mane or tail of snakes. As one of the labours imposed on him by Eurystheus, Heracles dragged Cerberus out of the Underworld, showed him to Eurystheus, and then returned him. Aeneas on his descent was told to drug him with a specially prepared cake: hence the expression 'a sop to Cerberus'.

**Ce'rcidas** (*c*.290–*c*.220 BC) Greek poet, lawgiver, and statesman from Megalopolis in Arcadia of whose poems only a few fragments survive. He was strongly influenced by the Cynic philosophers.

**Cercō'pes** In Greek myth, a pair of monkey-like dwarfs whose mother Theia told them to beware of a certain Melampyges ('Black-buttocks'). *Heracles caught them trying to steal his armour and slung them upside down from a pole borne across his shoulders. They found themselves staring straight at his buttocks, covered with black hair, and thus understood the warning. Their jokes at his hairiness so amused Heracles that he let them go.

**Cērēs** An ancient Italo-Roman goddess of growth, in classical times identified with the Greek *Demeter. In cult she was associated with *Tellus, the earth-goddess. Her worship at Rome was very ancient, as is clear from the existence of a *flamen cerialis* and the occurrence of the festival of the Cerialia (held on 19 April) in the calendars, but very little is known of it. Her most famous cult was that on the Aventine hill at Rome. The Sibylline books (*see* SIBYL) were consulted under the stress of famine *c.*496 BC and recommended the introduction of the worship of the Greek gods Demeter, Korē (*see* PERSEPHONE), and Iacchus, to be identified with the Roman Ceres, Liber, and Libera. The temple was completed in 493 and became a centre for the activities of the plebs (*see also* SECESSION). Games were instituted which became a prominent feature of the Cerialia.

***Certamen Homeri et Hesiodi*** ('The Contest of Homer and Hesiod') A prose work dating in its present form from the second century AD but telling a story known by the third century BC. Homer and Hesiod take part in a contest at royal funeral games at Chalcis in Euboea. First Hesiod recites a hexameter line incomplete in sense and Homer successfully supplies a capping line. Next Hesiod asks a series of one-line questions which Homer answers similarly. Finally each recites a part of his poetry he considers his best. Homer tells of war and Hesiod of peace; the audience applauds Homer but the king awards the prize to Hesiod for his praise of peace and husbandry. There is evidence suggesting that the original author was *Alcidamas.

**Cē'yx** In Greek myth, husband of *Alcyonē.

***Chae'reas and Calli'rrhŏē*** The title of a Greek *novel by Chariton.

The novel opens with Chariton naming himself as author and his city as Aphrodisias. Fragments found on papyri show that Chariton was writing not later than the mid-second century AD but he may have been writing a century or more earlier. The novel survives in a single manuscript now in Florence. It is given an historical setting: Syracuse in the late fifth century BC. The heroine's father is *Hermocrates, the (historical) victor over the Athenians in 413 BC during the *Syracusan Expedition. The narrator declares himself to be secretary to an orator Athenagoras (presumably the Syracusan orator mentioned by Thucydides as the political opponent of Hermocrates). The novel begins with the marriage of Chaereas and Callirrhoe, both very beautiful. Soon after Chaereas, made jealous by disappointed rivals,

kicks his pregnant wife, who appears to die and is buried. She comes to life in the tomb and is carried off by robbers to Miletus, where she is sold to the rich and educated Dionysius. Chaereas hears that she has been abducted and sets out to look for her but is himself enslaved. Callirrhoe marries Dionysius to safeguard herself and Chaereas' unborn child. The Persian satrap Mithridates is overcome by her beauty; he and Chaereas dispute their claims to her before Artaxerxes the Persian king, who is similarly smitten, and she and Chaereas meet again. After very many more incidents the couple, reunited, return to Syracuse, to live happily ever after.

**Chaeronē'a (Khairōneia)** City in north-west Boeotia commanding the route south through the valley of the river Cephissus on the border of Phocis. It was the scene of the defeat of the Thebans and Athenians by *Philip II of Macedon in 338 BC, it would seem commemorated by the erection of a large stone lion; by whom or when is not known. The lion was smashed in the Greek War of Independence (1821–2) and restored in the late nineteenth century. Nearby were found the bones of some two hundred and fifty-four men, perhaps of the *Sacred Band. Chaeronea was also the scene of the defeat of Mithridates VI of Pontus by Sulla in 86 BC, and the birthplace of Plutarch.

**Chāos** ('Gaping void', 'Yawning space') In Greek mythical cosmogony the first existing thing, an intangible void beneath the Earth, full of darkness. It was scarcely personified at all but was that out of which came the primordial deities Gaia (Earth), Erebus (Darkness), Eros (Love), and Nyx (Night). Ancient authors differ in their interpretation.

**character, concept of** Greek thinking about character, to judge from epic, tragedy, and comedy, and from discussion in Plato, and particularly in Aristotle's *Ethics*, is focused on the identifying of strengths and failings, virtues and vices. Where modern interest is in individuality and a person's distinctive mental, moral, and emotional make-up and perhaps (in the last century or so) in underlying psychological forces, ancient writers tend to assess a character morally, to decide whether it is good or bad. In imaginative literature, even when characters are sympathetically portrayed, it is still the limits of good and bad behaviour that are being explored. Even in the case of Socrates, whose individuality was perceived by contemporary writers clearly enough to be communicated to later times, the peculiarities of his behaviour were felt to be bound up with his moral imperative to teach. In Aristotle we see a rather narrowly ethical view of character. A person's nature, *physis*, leads him or her to develop a disposition, *hexis* (pl. *hexeis*). This disposition, influenced by beliefs and reason, leads to the person making decisions, and speaking or acting accordingly: it is speech and action that reveal a person's *ethos* or (ethical) character. The virtuous are conspicuously stable in character; the non-virtuous are deficient in being swayed by fluctuating passions (*see* CHILDHOOD). (One oddity, from a modern point of view, of the Greek view of character in the fifth century BC is their belief that *music had a moral effect on character and it was important that the appropriate style of music should be employed in the education of the young.)

The Greek view of character is evident in the Roman writers also: Horace's *Satires* and *Epistles*, Virgil's *Aeneid* (with refinements), Tacitus' works, and (in Greek) Plutarch's *Lives*. On the other hand, from the early Hellenistic period onwards, both art and literature showed an interest in depicting individuals who, deviating from a desirable Aristotelian norm, belonged to a recognizable type. Such characters appear in New Comedy—the harsh or the over-indulgent father, the wily slave, the generous prostitute, and so on—and this interest found particular expression in *Theophrastus' Characters. From a modern perspective there still seems to be an absence of interest in individuality, an absence which is most noticeable when the ancient writers turn to *biography. But the awareness of self which is apparent in the early Greek lyric poets (Sappho, Alcaeus, and also Archilochus) and in the very much later *Meditations* of Marcus Aurelius, shows an appreciation that the make-up of human character is complex.

**Characte'rēs** *See* THEOPHRASTUS.

**Chara'xus** Brother of *Sappho.

**Chārēs** (*c.*400–*c.*325 BC) Famous Athenian general and commander of naval operations, notably against Philip II of Macedon. His troops were mercenaries whose pay he had to find himself. He fought at *Chaeronea and continued to hold commands until his death.

**Chariclē'a and Theā'genēs** Alternative title of the novel *Aethiopica* by Heliodorus.

**Cha'rites** (sing. Charis) *See* GRACES.

**Cha'riton** Author of a Greek *novel, *Chaereas and Callirrhoe*.

**Cha'rmidēs** Title of an early dialogue by Plato. It is set in a gymnasium at Athens where Socrates has gone to see friends after returning from campaign at *Potidaea, which was under siege by the Athenians (432–30 BC). When the beautiful Charmides, the current idol of Athenian male society, enters with a crowd of followers, including his slightly older cousin *Critias, Socrates engages him in discussion. Charmides' attempts to define the Greek word *sōphrosynē*, meaning self-control or moderation, are rejected, and Critias takes over the argument, with no more success. A provisional but unsatisfying answer ends the dialogue, the purpose of which is difficult to understand.

Charmides, who would become Plato's uncle, was one of those accused of profaning the Eleusinian *mysteries. He took part in the oligarchic revolution of 404 BC and died with Critias fighting against the democrats under Thrasybulus in 403.

**Chāron 1.** In Greek myth, the ferryman who conveyed the dead in his boat across the river Styx, or the Acheron, to their final abode in the Underworld, provided they had received the proper rites of burial and paid the fare (an obol, placed in the mouth of the corpse). He is unknown to Homer, but is mentioned by Aeschylus, and plays memorable parts in the *Frogs* of Aristophanes and book 6 of Virgil's *Aeneid*.

**2.** Of Lampsacus, *see* LOGOGRAPHERS (1).

**Chary'bdis** In Greek legend, a whirlpool in a narrow channel of water, traditionally sited in the Straits of Messina. Homer (*Odyssey* 12) pictured it as a female monster, daughter of Poseidon and Gaia, who sucked in seawater and spewed it out three times a day. The equally dangerous *Scylla was on the opposite shore, so that Odysseus had to decide which to avoid as he sailed between them. The two have become proverbial to describe equally unpleasant alternatives.

**chastity** Some Greek goddesses and their Roman equivalents remained virgins, notably

Hestia (at Rome, Vesta) and Artemis (Diana), and some priestesses were required not to marry (*see* VESTAL VIRGINS and *also* ATTIS). However, as a possible attitude to adopt in real life the virginal devotion to Artemis shown by Hippolytus in Euripides' play of the same name was not depicted wholly sympathetically. In the ancient world marriage was the normal expectation. Hippocratic medicine recommended it as the cure for many ailments among girls, seemingly on the grounds that thereby it became possible for organs to function normally. However, the famous physician *Soranus (of the early second century AD) held the view that sexual activity, pregnancy, and childbirth were all debilitating and damaging to health, though he conceded the necessity for reproduction.

An ascetic attitude, which might lead to chastity, is found in Plato, who tends to see an opposition between senses, which are an unreliable guide to the truth, and the soul, the seat of the intellect, which alone can achieve true knowledge. In Socrates' speech in the *Symposium* Plato depicts a person being led towards knowledge of ultimate truth by a sublimated erotic love. This aspect of Platonism exerted some influence upon early Christian thought. The first generation or two of Christians were already inclined towards celibacy and chastity not only through Jewish roots and by the lives of John the Baptist and Jesus, but also through the expected coming of a new age in which the demands of the body would be incompatible with a perfect state of living. (See St Paul's compromise approach to the ascetic Corinthians in which marriage is tolerated but the celibate state extolled.)

To judge from stories in Roman legendary history, unchastity in daughters could be felt to merit death at the hands of fathers (*see* e.g. VIRGINIA). Augustus' law on adultery (15 BC) only permitted a father to kill both offenders, perhaps as a deterrent to killing at all.

**Cheiron** *See* CHIRON.

**Che'rsonese** [Gk. *chersonēsos*, 'peninsula']
**1.** Thracian Chersonese (Gallipoli), projecting into the north-east of the Aegean Sea, separated from Asia Minor by the Hellespont. It was important as a wheat-growing district and more especially because it lay on a main crossing route between Europe and Asia and so controlled the corn-supply from the Crimea.

It was settled by Greeks from Aeolis and Ionia in the eighth and seventh centuries BC, with Athenians arriving in the late seventh century. The elder Miltiades seemed to have had a private fiefdom there which was taken over by the younger *Miltiades in the late sixth century. In the fifth century BC when the Athenians took an interest in safeguarding the corn route a number of Chersonese cities joined the *Delian League. The Chersonese was threatened by *Philip II of Macedon, and this threat was one of the chief grounds of hostility between Athens and Macedon. It was finally ceded to Philip in 338 BC. After Alexander the Great it became part of Pergamum's domain and then passed into Roman possession (133 BC) and under Augustus became an imperial estate.
**2.** Tauric Chersonese, in the Black Sea, the modern Crimea, famous in Greek history as a source of grain.

**Chersonese, On the** Political speech by *Demosthenes (2) 2.

**chīa'smus** (from the form of the Greek letter chi, *X*) Figure of speech in which the terms in the second of two parallel phrases are in reverse order to the corresponding terms in the first; e.g. '*odit* populus Romanus privatam luxuriam, publicam magnificentiam *diligit*': 'The Roman people *hate* private luxury but public display they *love*.'

**childbirth** In the ancient world attendance at childbirth was a matter for women, probably friends and neighbours. Midwives existed—we are told that Socrates' mother Phaenarete was one—but are scarcely mentioned in the Hippocratic writings of the fifth and fourth centuries BC (*see* HIPPOCRATES). The uterus was thought of as a container rather than a muscle, from which, if all else fails, the baby may be extracted by instruments that in effect cause its death. *Herophilus in the third century BC practised dissection and was able to remove some of the mystery surrounding the female anatomy; in particular he stated that there is no fundamental difference in the constitution of male and female bodies although certain functions such as childbirth belong only to women (*see* GYNAECOLOGY). He wrote a treatise, *Midwifery*, which seems to have dealt with the whole subject from a scientific point of view. Our knowledge is greatly increased when we come to *Soranus, a Greek doctor practising at Rome in the late first century and early second century AD. His handbook, *Gynaecology*, expects the mother to be seated on a birthing-chair and describes a breathing technique to aid delivery. Warm clothes on the abdomen and sharp scents are supposed to ease the pain, and the midwife must reassure the mother. She performs all the usual functions of a midwife, but also lays the baby on the ground and assesses whether it is 'worth rearing'. Common superstitions are mentioned—that some midwives are reluctant to cut the cord 'with iron', or believe that there should be no tight cords or bindings in the delivery room.

For the Greeks childbirth polluted all those present in the house because blood was shed, hence it was not permitted to give birth on sacred ground. Purification was achieved by washing or sprinkling water, or by fumigation. At Athens the *amphidromia*, so-called because friends of the child's parents 'carried it around' the hearth, was the naming ceremony held on the fifth day after the birth. The Romans had various childbirth rituals (but it is uncertain how regularly these were carried out) such as the father lifting the baby from the earth or carrying it around the hearth (i.e. accepting it into the family). The important celebration was on the naming day, the *dies lustricus*, 'day of purification', usually ten days after the birth.

*See also* INFANTICIDE and CHILDHOOD.

**childhood** In Greece generally it was the father who decided at the birth of a child whether or not it should be brought up. At Rome there was reputedly a law of Romulus which stated that all male children and the first-born girl should be reared. (For exposure of infants *see* INFANTICIDE.) Those writing about the Egyptians, Jews, and Germans noted particularly that they reared all their children, which suggests that Greeks and Romans countenanced but were uneasy about disposing of their own unwanted babies. Girls and boys stayed together in the care of mother or nurse until they were about 6, when some sort of formal education began. Plutarch implies that *Cato the Elder was unusual in being present whenever possible when his baby was being fed or bathed, and in refusing to beat a child. Corporal punishment was not uncommon in the ancient world; the Roman *paterfamilias* (male head of a family) even had the power of life and death over his children, though that power was rarely exercised in the late republic and empire. For children's play

we largely rely on the archaeological evidence of toys found in tombs and written descriptions of board games. Plato in the *Laws* has the Athenian Stranger giving his prescriptions for an ideal upbringing in which children between the ages of 3 and 6 attend a kind of nursery where they play with toys or invent games but, the Athenian recommends, without too much variety or diversity, so as not to encourage the development of an inconstant and unstable personality.

Infant mortality was probably high. Literature reveals the practice of adoption to be widespread, probably reflecting the fact that children were necessary for the support of parents in old age. In Greece, though not in Rome, children were legally required to maintain parents who could no longer work.

**children** *See* CHILDBIRTH and CHILDHOOD.

**Chīlon** *Ephor at Sparta in 556 BC, one of the *Seven Sages of Greece. He was said to have 'yoked the ephors alongside the kings', a reference to the oaths exchanged each month between the two kings and the ephors to respect each others' powers. He may have helped to extend Spartan influence through the establishment of the *Peloponnesian league. After his death he was worshipped in Sparta as a hero.

**Chi'maera** In Greek myth, a fire-breathing monster with the head of a lion, body of a she-goat, and tail of a snake, the offspring of Typhon and Echidna. It was killed by *Bellerophon, mounted on the winged horse Pegasus.

**Chīron (Kheirōn)** In Greek myth, a *Centaur, but, unlike the others, the son of Philyra and Cronus. He owed his shape, half man and half horse, to the fact that Cronus assumed the shape of a horse when he approached Philyra so as to escape the jealous notice of his wife Rhea. In consequence Chiron's nature was different from that of the other Centaurs; he was wise and kind, and instructed by Apollo and Artemis he was skilled in medicine, music, hunting, and the art of prophecy. He became the tutor of some of the most famous of the Greek heroes, Asclepius, Jason, and Achilles. He was the grandfather (through his daughter Endeis) of Peleus, saving him by restoring his sword when he was abandoned weaponless by Acastus on Mount Pelion, the Thessalian home of the Centaurs. Chiron also helped him to win his bride Thetis. Like the other Centaurs he was driven out of Thessaly by the Lapiths. When Heracles came in pursuit of the Erymanthian boar (see HERACLES, LABOURS OF 3) and was involved in a fight with the Centaurs, one of his poisoned arrows scratched Chiron. Although immortal, Chiron suffered great pain and, wishing to live no longer, transferred his immortality to the Titan Prometheus. Zeus set him in the sky as the constellation Centaurus.

**Chloris** *See* FLORA.

**Chŏē'phoroe, Chŏē'phori (Khŏēphoroi)** ('Libation Bearers') The second tragedy in the *Oresteia* trilogy by Aeschylus.

**chŏes** *See* MEASURES 1.

**chōlia'mbic** (or scazon) In metre, the so-called 'limping iambic' line in which the penultimate syllable, short in an iambic line, is long.

**choral lyric** *See* LYRIC POETRY [Greek].

**chorē'gia** ('paying for a chorus') At Athens, a form of *liturgy or public service in which individual wealthy citizens were expected to fund a chorus for one or other of the various lyric and dramatic contests (at the *Panathenaea, Thargelia, *Dionysia, and *Lenaea), and hence were known as *choregoi* ('chorus-leaders', but here in a special sense; *see* CHORUS). The expense, which covered training, maintenance, and costuming, was considerable. The prize for the winning *choregos* in the *dithyrambic contest was a tripod which was then dedicated to the god; in Athens these dedications lined a street, consequently known as the 'street of the tripods' (*hoi tripodĕs*).

**chŏ'riamb** In metre, the metron – ∪ ∪ –.

**chorodida'skalos** In Athens, the trainer of a chorus performing in one of the various lyric and dramatic contests, usually the poet himself. *See* CHOREGIA.

**chŏrus (chŏros)** ('dance') In Greece the dance was a very important part of public religious ceremonies, performed by a troupe to whom the same name, 'chorus', was also given. By archaic times the chorus sang as well as danced in performances of choral *lyric poetry, usually under a leader. As well as this the chorus had a role in tragedy and comedy. Aristotle says in the *Poetics* that Attic tragedy had its origin in the kind of choral lyric

known as the dithyramb, sung and danced in honour of the god Dionysus (*see* TRAGEDY 1), and that comedy likewise developed out of the cheerfully insulting songs sung by bands of revellers as they accompanied the *phallus in Dionysiac processions (*see* COMEDY [Greek 2]). If this is the case, the fact that the chorus continued to play an important role in all fifth-century drama is natural. The chorus sings the lyric passages (which are themselves referred to as 'the choruses') to *aulos* accompaniment. Like the actors the chorus was masked (as in Dionysiac ritual). In tragedy it always performed in character as a group of people involved in the action; the chorus-leader, known as the *coryphaeus* or *hēgemon*, is sometimes made to converse briefly with the characters. Sophocles was said to have raised the number of the tragic chorus from twelve to fifteen, as it remained thereafter. The chorus entered the *orchestra* (*see* DIONYSUS, THEATRE OF) on the audience's right in quadrangular form, three or five abreast. The chorus-leader stood in the middle of the row nearest to the audience; sometimes this role was taken by the *choregos* (*see* CHOREGIA). The chorus in Old Comedy comprised twenty-four members and was of central importance, the characters represented often giving the play its name, e.g. *Frogs* and *Wasps*, and their entry being a high point in the play. They threw off their assumed character in part at least of the *parabasis* (*see* COMEDY [Greek 3]) and addressed the audience on behalf of the poet. After the fifth century the role of the chorus in tragedy and especially in comedy became much reduced: in Middle and New Comedy its role became entirely non-dramatic, and a song from a chorus (not included in the text of the play) became merely a device for dividing one act from the next. The Roman adaptations of Greek tragedy and the comedies of Plautus and Terence did not include a chorus.

**Chremōnidē'an War** The Athenian democratic politician Chremonidēs carried a decree in 268/7 BC, by which Athens joined the Peloponnesian anti-Macedonian coalition and led a revolt against *Macedon and its ruler Antigonus Gonatas. The coalition lost; Athens was besieged and surrendered in 262 BC. Chremonides fled to Egypt.

**Chrēstoma'thia** *See* PROCLUS.

**Christianity in the Roman world** Christians first became known to the Romans as a troublesome Jewish sect. Suetonius writing in the early years of the second century AD about the reign of the emperor Claudius (AD 41–54) describes them causing continuous disturbances in Rome. Tacitus earlier refers to the originator of their sect, Christus, a Greek translation of the Jewish term for the Messiah, God's chosen deliverer, being executed by Pontius Pilate in Tiberius' reign (AD 14–37). This is the only mention in pagan Latin literature of Pilate's role. The Jews had been allies of Rome since they had fought the *Seleucids together in the second century BC. Moreover the Jews were an ancient people, and for both reasons they were entitled to follow their national religion. Tolerance of their religion persisted, and was safeguarded by legislation even when relations between Rome and the increasingly nationalistic Jews deteriorated towards the end of the first century BC and became still worse after AD 6 when Judaea was made a Roman province. The Christians, first so called in Syrian Antioch in a hostile way, were regarded by the Romans as no different from the Jews. They benefited from this official tolerance, as shown in the Acts of the Apostles. But the Jews in general were implacably hostile to the Christians and anxious to embroil them with the authorities, and Christians came to see Judaism as just another non-Christian religion. After the burning of Rome in AD 64, Nero found the Christians convenient scapegoats for the fire. Although the official Roman attitude towards Jews and Christians underwent no change for another century, the mutual hostility between the two increased as well as that of the general pagan public to both, which resulted in intermittent persecution in various parts of Asia (reflected in the book of Revelation). It was from Bithynia in Asia in AD 112 that the Roman governor, the Younger Pliny, wrote his famous letter to the emperor Trajan asking how he was to deal with the Christians (*Letters* 10.96). It is clear that at this time Christians had to behave provocatively before official notice was taken of them, and also that some of them were not unwilling to be martyred. By the end of this century, however, thoughtful pagans saw Christianity not merely as a nuisance to the state but as a threat to its safety and stability. Christians seemed bound together by mysterious ties into secret societies to which they owed more loyalty than to the state. Since traditional Roman religion was in the nature of a contract between men and gods, by which the gods protected Rome as long as they received their due worship, some token participation in pagan religious ceremonies was one of the demands made of the Christians by the Roman government. By refusing to take part the Christians evinced not only that irritating 'obstinacy' for which they were notorious but also disloyalty to Rome.

During the latter part of the second century a coherent Christian creed was beginning to emerge, and a case for Christianity could be stated to pagan intellectuals. In the third century it seems that some pagans attempted to absorb the Christian god into their pantheon: the emperor Alexander Severus (Marcus Aurelius Severus Alexander, emperor AD 222–35) is said to have kept in his private chapel, and paid equal reverence to, statues of Orpheus, Abraham, Christ, and *Apollonius of Tyana. The end of his reign marked the end of a long period of official toleration of Christians. The emperor Decius (249–51) initiated the first systematic attempt to exterminate them, at a time when a united effort was needed to repel the barbarians pressing on the frontiers, the Christians were numerous, and the emperor believed that the restoration of state cults of the pagan gods was essential to preserve the empire. On the death of Decius in 251 this persecution collapsed, but subsequent emperors, Valerian and Gallienus, revived the attacks, the worst in the western empire being that of 258–9. The last serious attempt by the government to suppress Christianity was that of Diocletian in 303, but he forbade the killing of Christians; they were in any case too numerous in the countryside as well as in the towns for any measure he took to be successful. Persecution of Christians ended in the West with his abdication in 305, though it dragged on in the East until 311 when Galerius granted them religious toleration. In 313 Constantine issued certain regulations in favour of Christians, known as the Edict of Milan, and in 325 at the Council of Nicaea Christianity became in effect the religion of the Roman empire. The attempt by the emperor Julian (360–3) to restore paganism was short-lived, and the pious Theodosius I (emperor 378–95) gave the final endorsement to Constantine's espousal of Christianity. He listened with favour to petitions for the conversion of pagan temples to churches and turned a blind eye to attacks on them. The pagan rhetor *Libanius complained bitterly about the destruction of rural shrines around Antioch by bands of marauding monks. In 391 Theodosius laid a total ban on all pagan cult (though not on pagan belief). Afterwards, some Christians wondered why God had so soon seen fit to lay upon a Christian empire the scourge of the barbarians. Although for nearly a century after some still hoped that a pagan emperor might arise to restore the old religion, this ban was never lifted.

**chroniclers** For Greek, *see* LOGOGRAPHERS; for Roman *see* ANNALS.

**chronology** *See* CALENDARS.

**Chrȳsā'or** ('golden sword') In Greek myth, the (perhaps monstrous) son of Poseidon and the *Gorgon Medusa, and brother of the winged horse Pegasus. The brothers sprang from the blood spilt when *Perseus decapitated Medusa. Chrysaor married Callirrhoe and became the father of *Geryon and Echidna.

**Chrȳsē'is** In Homer's *Iliad*, the daughter of Chrȳsēs, priest of Apollo on the island of Chrȳsē near Troy. When the Greeks sacked the island they gave her to Agamemnon as his gift of honour. He took her as his concubine, declaring that he preferred her to his wife Clytemnestra, and refused the rich ransom offered by Chryses. Chryses prayed to Apollo, and after the Greeks suffered in consequence nine days of plague Agamemnon agreed to return Chryseis on condition that he should receive in compensation the girl Briseis who had been given as a prize of war to Achilles. Hence arose the anger of Achilles, one of the main themes of the *Iliad*.

**chryselepha'ntine** ('of gold and ivory') Term used to describe certain Greek statues made of wood overlaid with gold and ivory, such as *Pheidias' statue of Athena in the Parthenon.

**Chrȳsi'ppus** (of Soli, in Cilicia, *c.*280–207 BC) Greek Stoic philosopher, third and most influential head of the Stoa at Athens and its dominant intellect (*see* STOICISM). He was educated at the Academy in Athens under the *Sceptic Arcesilaus and then studied at the Stoa under Cleanthes, whom he succeeded as head in 232 BC after becoming a convert to Stoicism. At this time Stoic philosophy seemed about to break up into a number of different positions, but Chrysippus gave it coherence and logic, expressed in voluminous writings (now lost) which became recognized as Stoic orthodoxy.

**Chrȳsŏ'themis** *See* ELECTRA (1).

**Ci'cero 1. Marcus Tu'llius Cicero** (106–43 BC) Roman orator and statesman.

**1. Early life, 106–64 BC.** Cicero was born on 3 January 106 at Arpinum (Arpino) some 110km (70 miles) south-east of Rome, the elder of two sons of a wealthy *eques*, the family being distantly related to the general Gaius *Marius. His early promise suggested a career as advocate and politician, and he was sent to Rome to study law under the two great lawyer-politicians of the day, the *Scaevolas (3 and 4), as well as philosophy under Philon, the former head of the Academy at Athens, and Diodotus the Stoic. At the age of 17 Cicero saw military service in the *Social War, serving under Pompeius Strabo, the father of *Pompey the Great. Also serving under Strabo was the young *Catiline (see 2 below). During the turbulent eighties Cicero completed his forensic education. His earliest surviving speech is *Pro Quinctio* of 81, a complicated partnership case; the result is unknown, but we know that the opposing advocate was Hortensius, the greatest orator of the day. Cicero's reputation was established in the following year (80) by his successful defence of Roscius of Ameria (*Pro Roscio Amerino*) on a charge of parricide. Both speeches had a political aspect; in the latter Cicero courageously attacked Sulla's powerful freedman Chrysogonus. At this point (79) Cicero left Rome to spend two years abroad and pursued his studies under Greek masters of rhetoric and philosophy, who included at Athens the Epicurean Zeno and the Academic Antiochus. His companion at Athens was another young Roman, Titus Pomponius *Atticus, who was to become his lifelong friend and, since Atticus spent most of his life away from Rome, his most valued correspondent (see 7 below). He describes his student days in Athens most vividly in the introduction to book 5 of *De finibus*. In Rhodes Cicero met *Poseidonius, the great scholar and Stoic philosopher.

About 77 he married his wife Terentia. Perhaps to this period after his return belongs his defence of his friend the comic actor Roscius (*Pro Roscio comoedo*). In 76 he was elected quaestor for 75 at the minimum age (of 30), as with every subsequent office he held, and so qualified for membership of the senate, remaining a member until his death. He served his quaestorship at Lilybaeum (Marsala) in west Sicily; after his return to Rome in 74 he never willingly left Italy again (but see 4), refusing provincial governorships both after his praetorship and after his consulship. In the next few years he was occupied with legal work in the courts, particularly on behalf of the *equites*, through which he gained wealth and eventually political support. His reputation was unshakeably established in 70 with his brilliant prosecution for extortion of C. *Verres, the corrupt governor of Sicily from 73 to 71, at the request of the Sicilians. Verres was defended by the famous Hortensius, but the latter was never called upon to speak: after Cicero's first speech for the prosecution (*actio prima*) Verres threw up the case and retired into exile in Massalia (Marseilles). Cicero's immense labours in gathering evidence for this case were not to be wasted; he published as well as his first speech the five long sections that were to comprise the *actio secunda* ('second stage' of the trial), and they made his reputation as Rome's leading advocate and fearless opponent of corruption.

In 69 Cicero became aedile, and in 66 praetor at the minimum age of 40. In this year he delivered in public assembly his first purely political speech, *Pro lege Manilia*, in which he supported, against strong *optimate opposition, the proposal of the tribune Manilius that command of the war in the East against Mithridates should be transferred to Pompey. In this Cicero was to some extent motivated by self-interest: it would be invaluable to his political ambitions to have the backing of the powerful Pompey. Throughout his life Cicero was to remain a supporter of Pompey, seeing him as the one man who could save Rome from external enemies and internal lawlessness while preserving the republican constitution. His other important speech of this year was *Pro Cluentio*, in which he successfully defended the rich *eques* Cluentius on a charge of poisoning his stepfather.

During the years from 66 to 63 Cicero gradually moved away from his earlier reformist position and moved closer to the position of the conservative *optimates*, while men like Publius Crassus, Julius *Caesar, Gaius Anto-

nius, and Catiline (the last two Cicero's rivals for the consulship in 63) propagated populist schemes for radical social reform.

**2. 63–62 BC: Cicero's consulship.** In the elections of 64 Cicero, a *novus homo*, a 'new man' with no advantages of birth, stood for the consulship of 63 and came top of the poll, *consul prior*, at the earliest permissible age, 42, *suo anno*, 'in his own year'. In a poor field his candidature was successful partly because the *optimates* were alarmed by the revolutionary inclinations of the patrician Catiline, who might otherwise have been their candidate. His colleague in the consulship was Gaius Antonius, an ally of Catiline. As consul in 63 Cicero delivered the speeches *De lege agraria contra Rullum*, arguing successfully that the legislation proposed by the tribune of 63, P. Servilius Rullus, for the distribution of land was fraudulent. The speech *Pro Rabirio* of the same year was in defence of an elderly *eques* charged by the popular party (at the instigation of Caesar; *see also* LABIENUS) with having killed, thirty-seven years earlier, the tribune Saturninus after the emergency decree, the *senatus consultum ultimum*, had been passed by the senate. The prosecution was in fact questioning the validity of that decree and drawing popular attention to the possibility of its abuse. The trial was abandoned, but Cicero emerged as a moderate conservative, in opposition to Caesar and the popular party who had brought about the prosecution. At the elections held in 63 for the consulship in 62 Catiline was again a candidate, and the natural leader of those desperate for much-needed economic reform. Again he was defeated. He seems to have hoped for some sort of aid from Cicero's colleague Antonius, but Cicero won over the latter by offering him the governorship of a profitable province (Macedonia instead of Cisalpine Gaul). Catiline saw that his only chance of success lay in the violent seizure of power. Cicero discovered sufficient evidence of his plans to convince the senate of the imminence of an uprising to be followed by a massacre at Rome, and persuaded them to pass the *senatus consultum ultimum*. He still had no firm evidence against Catiline, however, and when he addressed the senate on 8 November 63 in the most famous of all his speeches, his first *In Catilinam*, Catiline was present (*see* JUPITER). Immediately afterwards Catiline left Rome for his army in Etruria (where he was defeated and killed early in 62). His departure was followed by Cicero's exposition of events to the people on 9 November (his second speech *In Catilinam*), and the arrest on 2–3 December of five prominent citizens, who were leading conspirators in treasonable correspondence with envoys of the Allobroges (a Gallic tribe). In a third speech Cicero explained the new developments to the people. The fourth was delivered in the senate (5 December) on the question of the punishment of the prisoners, a speech of studied impartiality. The consul designate Silanus proposed the death penalty; Caesar proposed life imprisonment, a novel penalty in Roman law (*see* PRISON). Marcus *Cato spoke powerfully in favour of the death penalty and in the panic of the moment carried the senate with him. Cicero had the sentence carried out at once, violating the citizen's right to a trial, and justified only by the passing of the *senatus consultum ultimum*. He never doubted that he had saved the state from grave danger, and he wrote of his action in prose and verse, in Latin and Greek (see 8 below), and invited others, including *Poseidonius, to do the same. At the height of the crisis Cicero found himself defending the second consul designate, L. Murena, on an ill-timed charge, brought by Marcus Cato, of bribery in the election. Had Cato succeeded in overturning the election it would have benefited Catiline's cause but Murena, a man of proved courage and military ability, was acquitted. In his speech *Pro Murena* Cicero almost condones electoral corruption provided the best man is elected consul, and jokes at the rigid creed of Stoics such as Cato.

**3. 62–58 BC.** Cicero never forgot, nor allowed anyone else to forget, the glory of 63, and Marcus Cato saluted him as 'father of his country' (*pater patriae*). But the legality of the executions was soon questioned by the popular party. Cicero had an idealistic but unattainable notion of a union of all sound and respectable men of property from both the senatorial and equestrian classes, a *concordia ordinum*, 'harmony between the *orders', but by the end of 61 it became clear that this was a delusion. In 62 he had delivered two speeches, *Pro Sulla* and *Pro Archia*. At the end of that year Publius *Clodius, who later emerged as a powerful popular leader, was detected while in disguise as a woman at the (female) mysteries of the

Bona Dea, and prosecuted. Although he obtained an acquittal by bribery, his attempt to set up an alibi was defeated by the evidence of Cicero, who thereby incurred Clodius' hatred. It appears that when Caesar, Pompey, and Crassus were about to form a political alliance in 59, Caesar made advances to Cicero with a view to including him in the alliance, but Cicero could not reconcile himself to Caesar's unconstitutional attitude and adopted a course of opposition. Cicero's only surviving speech of this year (59) was *Pro Flacco*, a defence on a charge of extortion in his province of one of the praetors of 63 who had brought about the arrest of the Catilinarians. In it Cicero took the opportunity to appeal to popular sentiment in his own favour. When Caesar renewed his overtures and Cicero again refused, Caesar seems to have allowed Clodius to get his revenge. As tribune for 58 Clodius brought in a bill aimed at Cicero, proposing to outlaw anyone who had put Roman citizens to death without trial. Cicero found himself without any obvious support; he therefore yielded to Clodius' threats and left Rome for exile in March 58.

Clodius now carried a decree exiling Cicero by name and confiscating his property. Cicero's magnificent house on the Palatine was destroyed (and part consecrated to *Libertas*, 'Liberty', an ironic touch by Clodius), and his villa at Tusculum badly damaged. He spent his exile in Macedonia, at Thessalonika in 58 with the quaestor Gnaeus Plancius, moving at the end of the year to Dyrrhachium. He was utterly crushed by his misfortune and consumed by self-pity. But Pompey lost little time in starting to bring about Cicero's recall, with the support of the tribune *Milo, who employed violence as freely as Clodius.

**4. 57–45 BC.** Cicero was recalled by a law of the people on 4 August 57 and reached Rome a month later, to an enthusiastic welcome. In the two speeches *Post reditum* ('After the return'), whose authenticity has been questioned, he thanked the senate and people for his recall. His speeches during the ensuing period arise out of his struggles to secure public compensation for the damage to his property (*De domo sua*, 'On his house', and *De haruspicum responso*, 'On the response of the diviners') and out of his support for those responsible for his recall. Thus in 56 he defended P. Sestius (*Pro Sestio*), a tribune who had exerted himself on his behalf, against a charge of rioting brought by Clodius. This speech, largely occupied with Cicero's own services and an attempt to rally aristocratic feeling against the triumvirs, contains some of the orator's most admired passages. The speech *In Vatinium* was an attack on Vatinius, one of the witnesses, a supporter of Caesar's who had tried to get Sestius convicted. The speech *Pro Caelio* succeeded in obtaining the acquittal of a fashionable young friend, M. *Caelius Rufus, on charges that included conspiracy to murder an Egyptian envoy and the attempted poisoning of Caelius' former mistress *Clodia, the sister of Clodius (and very probably the 'Lesbia' of Catullus). The attack on Clodia herself is Cicero's most brilliant *tour de force*. His wit made him many enemies.

Cicero hoped that the political manoeuvrings of 57 and 56, which took place against a background of increasing civil violence, would end in the break-up of the 'triumvirate', but in April 56 Caesar, Pompey, and Crassus renewed their political union and Cicero was forced to accept the situation and make his peace with Caesar, who always behaved with generosity towards him. Cicero's capitulation was evident in the speeches of 56, *De provinciis consularibus* ('On provinces governed by consuls') in favour of the prolongation of Caesar's command in Gaul, and *Pro Balbo*, a defence of the citizenship procured by Pompey for a rich Spaniard, *Balbus, who was also a friend of Caesar's. In letters to his close friends Cicero reveals the blow that his pride has suffered. He had some satisfaction in speaking against his old enemy L. Calpurnius *Piso (*In Pisonem*) when the latter had been recalled from the governorship of Macedonia largely as a result of Cicero's attacks on him in *De provinciis consularibus* (see above). In 54 he defended his friend Plancius, who had received him during his exile in Macedonia (see 3 above), on a charge of electoral corruption (*Pro Plancio*), and Rabirius, a partisan of Caesar, on a charge of extortion (*Pro Rabirio Postumo*) as well as M. Aemilius Scaurus, ex-governor of Sardinia, on a similar charge (of this speech we have only fragments). The worst humiliations came in 54 when, at the behest of the triumvirs, he was forced to defend his enemies, Vatinius for bribery (successfully), and (unsuccessfully) on a charge of extortion the hated Gabinius, who as consul in 58 had made no attempt to prevent Cicero's exile. He was mortified by his failure in 52 to defend Milo successfully when the latter was charged and condemned for the murder of Clodius, and had to content himself with sending to the exiled Milo the speech *Pro Milone*, often considered the finest of all his speeches. It is an elaboration of the one he tried to deliver when he lost his nerve, presented as he was with a courtroom packed with Clodian supporters and the hostile soldiers of Pompey. Milo is said to have congratulated himself that it was not delivered, otherwise he would have been acquitted and never have known the excellent seafood for which Massalia (Marseilles) was already famous. In 53 or 52 Cicero was somewhat comforted by being elected augur.

During the 50s, as he withdrew from the collapsing world of republican politics, he found some consolation in writing on philosophy and rhetoric, which he considered a poor substitute for active politics, and arguing against his literary antagonists, who were principally Julius Caesar, *Calvus, Marcus *Brutus, and Asinius *Pollio. By the end of 55 he had finished *De oratore*, a treatise in three books on rhetoric, designed to replace his early work on the same subject, *De inventione* ('On invention'), written before he was 25; it was followed, perhaps in the late 50s, by a briefer essay on rhetoric, *Partitiones oratoriae* ('Divisions of oratory'), in which Cicero answers his young son's questions on the orator's craft. From this period also comes the *De republica* (of which we have only parts, including the *Somnium Scipionis*), and *De legibus* ('On laws'), which seems to have been begun in 52, probably published after Cicero's death. There was to be a further outpouring of philosophical works between 46 and 44. Meanwhile Cicero was reluctantly obliged to govern the province of Cilicia from summer 51 to summer 50 under the new regulations of Pompey's law for the government of the provinces. He disliked leaving Rome but he carried out his duties honestly and efficiently, winning a victory over the brigands and returning to Rome with the *fasces* of his lictors wreathed in fading laurels. He found Rome on the brink of the Civil War, and when war did break out he left the city, with many of the senatorial party. Pompey had accepted the command of the republic's forces in Italy, but after he withdrew with them to Epirus in Greece Cicero was in deep perplexity. Caesar invited him to join the remnants of the senate in Rome, but this Cicero, with the greatest politeness, refused to do. His mind at last made up, he followed Pompey to Greece. After the defeat of the Pompeians at Pharsalus in the summer of 48 (at which battle he was not present because of illness), he returned to Italy. Suspense was ended in 47 when Caesar came to Italy and the two were reconciled. At last Cicero could return to Rome.

At first he remained detached from public life, attending meetings in the senate but not speaking, regarded with suspicion by both sides. But he began to entertain the faint hope that when the Civil War was finally over Caesar might perhaps set about restoring constitutional government. In 46, the year in which he wrote *Brutus*, he delivered his first important speech for five years, *Pro Marcello*, a speech of thanks to Caesar for pardoning M. Marcellus who as consul in 51 had launched the attack on him which ultimately precipitated the Civil War (see CAESAR (2)); it contains a famous sentence, 'I have lived long enough for the demands of nature or fame' (*satis diu vel naturae vixi vel gloriae*). In 45 he delivered *Pro Ligario*, a defence of Q. Ligarius, tried as an enemy of Caesar, a speech whose eloquence is said to have moved Caesar to acquit the accused; and in the same year he delivered the speech *Pro rege Deiotaro*, defending the tetrarch of Galatia on a charge of attempting to murder Caesar. Shortly after Cato's death at Utica (Utique) in 46, Cicero, at Brutus' suggestion, wrote a panegyric on him, now lost. It displeased Caesar, who replied to it in a work, also lost, called *Anticato*.

In 46 Cicero divorced Terentia, his wife of some thirty years, and shortly after married Publilia, who had been his ward. In 45 his beloved daughter *Tullia died, and Cicero was overwhelmed with grief (see CRANTOR). A famous letter of consolation (*Epistulae ad familiares* 4.5) was written to him by the jurist *Sulpicius. Publilia offended Cicero by her lack of sympathy, and this second marriage also ended in divorce. These personal blows were made harder to bear by Cicero's growing realization that Caesar was never going to attempt to restore the republican constitution, and he took what consolation he could in literary composition.

**5. Philosophical and literary writings.** Between 46 and 44 Cicero wrote *Brutus*, a history

of Roman oratory, *Orator*, a picture of the accomplished speaker, and other works on rhetoric, including the *Topica* ('Matters relating to commonplaces'), dealing with kinds of arguments, supposedly derived from Aristotle's work of the same name, and perhaps *De optimo genere oratorum* ('On the best kind of orators'), although that may have been written earlier, in 52. A preface to his (lost) translations of the two Greek orations *De corona* of Demosthenes and *Against Ctesiphon* of Aeschines may not be by Cicero. In 45 he wrote the *Consolatio* ('Consolation') on the deaths of great men, a work (of which fragments survive) occasioned by the death of Tullia; *Hortensius* (now lost), a plea for the study of philosophy which greatly moved St Augustine; *Academica*, on the views of the Athenian 'New' Academy, and in particular of *Carneades; and *De finibus bonorum et malorum*, on the different conceptions held by philosophers of the 'chief good'. After these works he wrote during 45 and 44 *Tusculanae disputationes* ('*Tusculan Disputations') on the conditions of happiness, the most intensely felt and expressed of all his philosophical works; *De natura deorum*, the views of different philosophical schools on the nature of the gods; *De fato* ('On fate', of which only fragments survive), a discussion of free will; the two essays on old age and friendship *De senectute* and *De amicitia*; *De divinatione*, the examination of Stoic belief concerning fate and the possibility of prediction, published soon after Caesar's murder; and his last work on moral philosophy, *De officiis*, finished in November 44 and written for the edification of his son. It was altogether a wonderful output for two or three years.

As a philosopher Cicero sometimes claimed to be a follower of the New Academy of Carneades, which held that certain knowledge was impossible and that practical conviction based on probability was the most that could be attained. But while his general attitude was that of the New Academy, he was an eclectic: he did not adhere to any one school, but picked from among the doctrines of the various Greek schools those which commended themselves to his reason; and in questions of morality he was inclined (e.g. in *De finibus*, the *Tusculan Disputations*, and *De officiis*) to accept the positive Stoic teaching. He believed in the existence of a divine being, and maintained that it is prudent to keep up traditional rites and ceremonies. He had no sympathy for Epicureanism, which he thought demoralizing. Finally, in *De fato* he shows his belief in the freedom of the will against Stoic determinism. He did not claim that his philosophical works were original but he popularized Greek thought and created a Latin philosophical vocabulary. The works *De senectute*, *De amicitia*, *De officiis*, the *Tusculan Disputations*, and the *Somnium Scipionis* (detached from the *De republica* which was ultimately lost) had considerable influence on the Fathers of the early Church. In the Middle Ages, when Cicero's political and oratorical works had yet to be rediscovered (*see* TEXTS, TRANSMISSION OF ANCIENT 8), these books were studied extensively, and handed on to the European world a knowledge of Greek philosophy which was not otherwise attainable.

**6. 44–43 BC: The *Philippics* and Cicero's death.** When Caesar was murdered in 44 by a heterogeneous collection of men, united only in their desire to put an end to despotic rule, Cicero was not invited to join them, although he greeted the news with delight. For several months he remained aloof from politics, but he still ardently desired to see the restoration of the republic. When, after several months of confusion, the political alignments were becoming clear, and Mark *Antony had left Rome for Cisalpine Gaul to lay siege to the republicans under Decimus *Brutus at Mutina, Cicero put himself at the head of what was left of the senatorial party. He gave full expression to his hatred of the Caesarian tyranny in fourteen surviving orations against Antony (at least three others have been lost) which he entitled *Philippics*, after the patriotic speeches delivered by the Athenian orator Demosthenes against Philip II of Macedon. The *First Philippic* was in fact delivered to the senate on 2 September 44, before Antony left for Cisalpine Gaul; the *Fourteenth Philippic*—the last of all Cicero's surviving speeches—was delivered on 21 April 43. It celebrated the defeat of Antony at Mutina, but the rejoicing was premature. Cicero was fooled by Octavian into believing that he intended to destroy Antony, but instead Octavian marched on Rome with his legions to demand the consulship, and obtained it on 19 August 43. He then proceeded to make his peace with Antony, rescinding sentences outlawing the latter and Lepidus, and at the end of October all three met to agree on a threefold division of power, the (second) triumvirate.

They were to prosecute the war jointly against Marcus Brutus and Cassius in the East, money and land were to be obtained to satisfy their troops, and old scores settled by widespread *proscriptions. On the first list sent to Rome Antony wrote Cicero's name and Octavian did not strike it out. On 7 December 43 his soldiers caught Cicero in a not very resolute attempt to escape by sea, and he bravely submitted to execution. His head and hands were displayed on the Rostra, the speakers' platform in the Forum.

**7. Letters.** Perhaps, ironically, to his detriment, Cicero is known to us more intimately than anyone else in the ancient world through his voluminous correspondence covering the period 68 to 43. Over 800 of his letters survive in which, with candour and more truth than one can generally expect from his speeches, he recorded his moods and actions. The first we hear of publication is in July 44 when he writes about making a small collection of his letters to *Tiro and Atticus (see also 1 above). Because he was closely involved in the politics of the period, and wrote to correspondents of the most diverse political views as well as to members of his household, the letters are an invaluable historical source. They have come down to us in four collections, which include some letters from his correspondents, and comprise: those written to Atticus (*Epistulae ad Atticum*) between 68 and 43 which were published by the time of the Younger Seneca (d. AD 65); those written to more than ninety other friends and relations (*Epistulae ad familiares*) including letters to him, published by Tiro before those written to Atticus; those to his brother Quintus (*Epistulae ad Quintum fratrem*; *see* CICERO (2)), written when the brothers were separated, chiefly between 59 and 54; and twenty-five letters written to Marcus Brutus (*Epistulae ad Brutum*), all written in 43. There are no letters for the year of Cicero's consulship (63) or the preceding year.

**8. Poems.** Cicero's very early poetry has perished but there survives a large part of the *Aratea* (469 consecutive hexameter lines and some fragments) from his translation of the *Phaenomena* of *Aratus, a Greek didactic poem; his philosophical works also contain snippets from Homer and the Greek tragedians in his own Latin version, and a few lines survive of an epic *Marius*. Little has survived of his famous autobiographical poems of self-glorification, the three books *De consulatu suo* ('On my consulship') written in 60, and, some five years later, the three further books *De temporibus suis* ('On my times'). There remain a passage of 72 lines on his consulship and the two notorious lines which aroused the derision of his contemporaries for their old-fashioned-sounding assonance and boastful expression, *cedant arma togae, concedat laurea laudi* (or *linguae*) ('Let arms submit to civil power, let military laurels yield to praise' or ' . . . to speech'), and *O fortunatam natam me consule Romam* ('O happy Rome, born in my consulship'). In general his poetry was at least competent.

**9. Cicero's influence on literature and thought.** Cicero's reputation was eclipsed in the two centuries after his death; his views on rhetorical education had little influence, and Latin prose style tended to avoid Ciceronian fullness and balance in favour of what was striking and epigrammatic. His letters were published in the course of the first century AD but aroused no particular interest, nor was his philosophy much read. Some Christians saw him as a symbol of the pagan culture which should be rejected, but his good sense and his style ensured that he was studied by Christian apologists needing an acceptable language to express their beliefs to a pagan audience, and sometimes needing the arguments too. Those books that seemed to prefigure or echo Christian wisdom were especially favoured in Christian reading and education: *Somnium Scipionis, De officiis, De amicitia, De senectute,* and the *Tusculans*. These works were the most popular in the Middle Ages, when the speeches and the oratorical works were almost forgotten. Cicero was rediscovered in the Renaissance, and his profound influence set up an ideal for that age of the civilized human being, as brilliant, humane, practical in the discharge of civic duties, and enjoying a refined leisure. Interest in his Latin style became less intense towards the end of the sixteenth century when taste turned to Seneca and Tacitus, and in any case the various vernaculars established themselves as respectable vehicles of composition, themselves much influenced by Ciceronian style. In England in the seventeenth century the language of John Milton and of the Authorized Version of the Bible shows their indebtedness. The eighteenth century with its cool rationalism felt a special affinity to Cicero, and in France (and America) his freedom from dogma and his open-minded speculations struck a chord among aspiring revolu-

tionaries. In the nineteenth century his reputation as a statesman collapsed; his philosophical writings too ceased to exert their previous influence and seemed unoriginal and excessively moralistic, and interest turned towards their Greek sources. For modern readers his close involvement in the politics of a momentous period of history makes his letters the most fascinating of his works.

**2. Quintus Tu'llius Cicero** (102–43 BC) Younger brother of the orator (*see* CICERO (1)), an able soldier and administrator, and similarly educated. He was praetor in 62, and governor of Asia 61–58, where he received from his brother two long letters of advice. He served as legate with Caesar in Gaul during 54–51, taking part in the invasion of Britain, and then joined his brother in Cilicia. He followed Pompey in the Civil War, was pardoned after Pharsalus, and took no further part in public life. He and his son died in the \*proscriptions of 43. He had wide literary interests but his works do not survive, except for four letters to his brother. His marriage to Pomponia, sister of his brother's friend \*Atticus, was not happy.

**3. Marcus Tu'llius Cicero** (b. 65 BC) Only son of the orator (*see* CICERO (1)) and his wife Terentia. He was taken out to Cilicia with his father in 51. He fought with a squadron of cavalry in Pompey's army in 49/8 and was pardoned after the battle of Pharsalus. He was sent to Athens in 45 to study under the Peripatetic Cratippus. After Philippi (42) he joined Sextus Pompeius, but took advantage of the amnesty after 39 to return to Rome. He was consul with Octavian for a brief period in 30; subsequently he governed Syria and after that we hear no more of him. An apologetic letter survives written by him to \*Tiro in response to letters from his father and \*Atticus which expressed displeasure at his idle life while a student in Athens. In it he gives a careful account of his reformed mode of life.

**Ciceronian age** (of Latin literature) Term sometimes used to signify that period in Latin literature that roughly coincided with the lifetime of Cicero (106–43 BC) including the last years of the republic. The writers of the period apart from Cicero include Lucretius, Catullus, Sallust, and Varro. Virgil (70–19 BC) is generally associated with the \*Augustan age. *See* LATIN LITERATURE, PERIODS OF.

**Cili'cia** Country on the eastern half of the south coast of Asia Minor. In Homer's *Iliad* the Cilices, after whom the country is named, lived in the Troad, but after the Trojan War some Greeks, under the leadership of Mopsus the seer, applied the name to this new region in which they settled. The western area was rough and mountainous, but the east consisted of a large and very fertile plain. In the second century BC it became a pirate stronghold and the Romans constituted it as a province *c.*80 BC to deal with the menace. The pirates were not suppressed until Pompey's campaign of 67 BC. Cicero was governor of Cilicia in 51–50 (*see* CICERO (1) 4). Its most important city, autonomous until annexed by Pompey in 66 BC, was Tarsus, the seat of a famous school of philosophy and birthplace of St Paul.

**Cimme'rians (Kimmerioi)** A people who belong partly to legend and partly to history. In Homer's *Odyssey* (book 11) they are a fabulous people living on the edge of the world by the shore of *Oceanus in perpetual darkness. Here Odysseus gained access to the spirits of the dead. In Herodotus they are a historical people driven from their home (the biblical Gomer) north of the Black Sea in the eighth and seventh centuries BC by nomadic Scythian tribes. In the early seventh century they overturned Midas' kingdom of Phrygia (at which Midas took poison), attacked Lydia, killing the king Gyges, and in *c.*644 BC, during the reign of his son Ardys, took the capital Sardis, except for the citadel. The Greek poets Callinus and Archilochus bear witness to the terror they inspired in Ionia. Then plague struck them and they retreated east. Some who remained were finally expelled about 600 BC by Alyattes, king of Lydia.

**Cīmon** (*c.*510–*c.*450 BC) Wealthy Athenian aristocrat, politician and soldier, renowned as a patriot. He was the son of *Miltiades and Hegesipyle, daughter of the Thracian king Olorus. The historian Thucydides, son of a certain Olorus, was probably a kinsman. Cimon's sister Elpinice married Callias. It seems to have been thought that he owed some of his features—his great height, shaggy hair, and slowness of wit—to his Thracian ancestry. Cimon entered politics shortly after 480. He was *strategos* in 478, thereafter held that office frequently, and from 476 to 463 was commander in nearly all the operations of the *Delian League. In 475 he conquered the island of Scyros, drove out the pirates, and brought back in triumph to Athens what were supposed to be the bones of the Athenian hero Theseus who was said to be buried there. Cimon's greatest military achievement was the defeat of the Persian fleet at the mouth of the Eurymedon, perhaps in 466. It is possible that at this time he tried unsuccessfully to negotiate a peace with Persia (*see* CALLIAS). Subsequently he reduced Thasos in 463 after a two-year siege when that island revolted from the Delian League. Cimon's benevolence towards Sparta was unpopular, however, leading to his *ostracism in 461. One tradition states that he was recalled before the full ten years of exile had elapsed in order to fight for Athens against Sparta at Tanagra in 457 (*see* PELOPONNESIAN WAR, FIRST). When he duly returned *c.*451 he arranged a five years' truce between Athens and Sparta. Cimon led a last campaign against Persia to recapture Cyprus and died there *c.*450.

**Cincinnā'tus, Lucius Quinctius** A legendary Roman hero who had been consul in 460 BC. According to tradition he was called from his farm to be dictator in 458, when the Roman army under the consul Minucius was blockaded by the Italian tribe of the Aequi on Mount Algidus. He defeated the enemy, resigned his dictatorship after sixteen days, and returned to his farm. He is often cited as an exemplar of old-fashioned Roman simplicity and frugality.

**Cinē'sias** Athenian *lyric (in particular, dithyrambic) poet who lived in the second half of the fifth century BC. Of his work nothing of interest survives. He was much mocked by his contemporaries, especially Aristophanes, for his new free style of music.

**Cinna 1. Lucius Cornelius Cinna** (late second to early first century BC) Member of a Roman patrician family but politically a supporter of the 'popular' party. He fought in the *Social War (2) and became consul in 87 BC, although opposed by Sulla. He was deposed and driven out of Rome by his colleague Cn. Octavius. Cinna gathered an army of veterans and after he had summoned Marius from Africa they both marched on Rome and captured it late in 87. Both were proclaimed consuls for 86, when Cinna tried to restrain Marius' indiscriminate massacre of his enemies. After Marius' death in 86 Cinna became consul again in 85 and in 84, when he died in a mutiny.

**2. Lucius Cornelius Cinna** Son of (1) above and brother of Julius Caesar's wife Cornelia. He was praetor in 44 BC after Caesar had reinstated the sons of those proscribed by Sulla. Cinna had republican sympathies and expressed approval of Caesar's murder. He may have died in the proscriptions of 43 BC. See also (3) below.

**3. Gaius Helvius Cinna** Roman poet and friend of *Catullus, with whom he was probably in Bithynia in 57 BC. His *epyllion *Zmyrna* was greatly admired by his contemporaries for its vast erudition in the Alexandrian manner. He also wrote erotic poetry in various metres, of which only very small fragments survive. The ancient sources identify him with the tribune of 44 BC who, at Caesar's funeral, was lynched by the angry mob in mistake for Cornelius Cinna (see (2) above) who had spoken publicly against the dictator on the previous day (or 'for his bad verses', according to Shakespeare).

**Ci'nyras** Legendary king of Cyprus and donor of Agamemnon's magnificent corselet (in the *Iliad*). Later he was proverbial for great wealth. He was the founder of the cult of Aphrodite at Paphos in Cyprus. Through an unwitting union with his daughter Zmyrna (or Myrrha) he became the father of *Adonis. He was regarded as a seer and musician, and sometimes said for that reason to be the son of Apollo. (*See also* PYGMALION.)

**Circē** In Homer's *Odyssey* (book 10), a goddess living on the fabulous island of Aeaea (later identified by the Romans with the promontory of Circeii in Latium), powerful in magic, who turned Odysseus' men into swine. Odysseus resisted her magic by means of the mythical herb moly. Circe was the daughter of *Helios and Perse, and the sister of Aeëtes; by Odysseus she was the mother of two or three sons, one of whom was *Telegonos. In *Apollonius' *Argonautica* she purifies Jason and Medea after they have killed Medea's brother Apsyrtus.

**circe'nsēs** At Rome, contests and other displays in the circus, including chariot-races. 'Bread and circuses' (*panem et circenses*) were, according to the poet Juvenal, the only things that the degenerate Roman people cared about.

**Ciris** *See* APPENDIX VIRGILIANA.

**Cirrha** Originally, it would seem, the port of *Crisa.

**Cisal'pine Gaul** *See* GAUL.

**Cistellā'ria** ('The casket') Roman comedy by *Plautus, regarded as one of his earlier plays, adapted from the New Comedy *Synaristōsai* ('Breakfasters') by the Greek poet *Menander. The plot turns on the discovery by means of a casket of the true parentage of a foundling girl, Selenium, who has passed into the care of a courtesan and become the mistress of a young man Alcesimarchus. She is found to be the daughter of a citizen, Demipho, and is thereupon married to her lover.

**citadel** *See* ARX.

**Cithae'ron** The westerly part of the mountain range that separates the north of Attica from Boeotia. The summit was sacred to Zeus, but the mountain was also sacred to Dionysus, and on one of the crests was a famous cave of the *nymphs. It was the scene of several myths and legends including the metamorphosis of *Actaeon, the death of Pentheus (*see* BACCHAE), and the exposure of *Oedipus.

**ci'thara** ('lyre') The most important stringed instrument for Greek music (*see* MUSIC [Greek 2 and 3]). Homer calls it a *citharis*; the form *cithara* does not appear until the fifth century BC.

**citizenship**
**Greek.** Citizenship meant full membership of a *city-state, the qualifications for which depended on its constitution (*see* ARISTOCRACY; DEMOCRACY; OLIGARCHY). In all constitutions citizenship was an exclusive right for a limited number; in Athens the qualifications changed with time as the constitution became more democratic (*see* SOLON and CLEISTHENES (2)), but there was always a section of the population who were not citizens (*see* METICS). Descent from full citizen parents, legitimately married, was the usual qualification, and in Athens from 451 to 338 BC was generally necessary; *see* PERICLES. (An exception was the admission to citizenship of those slaves who manned the ships at the battle of Arginusae in 406 BC.) At other periods the requirement was less stringent. Adult male citizens were members of the *ecclesia* and so shared in law-making and electing magistrates, and acted in the lawcourts and the *dokimasia*. Women's share in the privileges of citizenship was limited by their having

no political rights and being ineligible to own property. Only citizens were entitled to own land. Thucydides mentions grants of Athenian citizenship to a few individuals. It was an honour with practical advantages if the recipient claimed his full rights, including the coveted right to own land. *Lysias failed to acquire citizenship. The Plataeans had a form of Athenian citizenship from 427 BC at the latest, and perhaps earlier, but how fully is still an open question. In order to take up his citizen rights the Athenian male youth at the end of his eighteenth year was registered by his father or guardian as a member of the family *deme, after his qualifications had been scrutinized. The duties of a citizen were to obey the laws, worship the city's gods, and (for men) perform military service, make decisions on public matters, act as judges and administrators, and make financial contributions as required. Citizens also shared in public privileges, ownership of land, and distributions. Citizenship was lost by *atimia and *exile. From the fourth century BC onwards full participatory democracy declined and citizenship became more a matter of status; grants of citizenship to foreign individuals became increasingly common.

**Roman.** Full Roman citizenship, originally limited to the inhabitants of Rome, was in early times extended to the citizens of colonies set up in Roman territory and to the citizens of some Italian communities which, having surrendered their independence to Rome, had been fully incorporated into the Roman state. Citizenship was automatically conferred upon slaves when they were freed. The normal qualification for Roman citizenship was to be the child of two legitimately married Roman citizens or, in certain cases, of one citizen and one foreign parent; a grant of citizenship could be conferred by a decree of the people (or, later, the emperor). No Roman citizen could also be a citizen of another independent state. In the early (aristocratic) republic, citizens were divided into *patricians and *plebeians, of whom the former enjoyed more rights in the matter of voting, and a monopoly of office (*see* MAGISTRATES), while the latter had to struggle for political equality (*see* ROME 2). Entire Italian communities (*see* MUNICIPIUM) also became citizens of Rome, something that surprised Greek observers, with the rights and duties of citizenship and either with voting rights (*optimo iure*)

or without (*sine suffragio*). After the Social War (90–88 BC: *see* ROME 4), Roman citizenship was extended to all the Italian allies (*see* SOCII), so that Rome ceased to be a city-state and became more like a capital city. By that time all male citizens had voting rights in the various assemblies at Rome (*see* ROMAN REPUBLIC), the right to stand for office, and rights of trade and of intermarriage (*commercium* and *conubium*; *see* LATIN RIGHTS). Women had no political rights and were unable to own property.

Citizenship entailed certain duties for males, according to varying liability, notably in military service, the payment of direct taxes, and civil obligations such as the maintenance of roads and waterworks. For the poorest class whose only contribution to the state was their children, *see* PROLETARII. Under the empire the political rights of citizens became insignificant, but the rights of *commercium* and *conubium* remained valuable, as did the citizen's right of appeal to a higher magistrate, ending with appeal to the emperor, against a judgement in a law-court. Citizenship was granted to all free inhabitants of the empire in AD 212, by the emperor Antoninus Caracalla. *See also* SLAVERY.

**city-state** (Gk. *polis*, pl. *poleis*) In Greece, the characteristic unit of urban life which grew out of the village, the politically, legally, and militarily autonomous city controlling its own surrounding territory. Athens and Sparta possessed larger territories than other city-states. The city itself was of no great size (*see* POLITICS); its citizens might live in the city and work there or in the countryside, or might live and spend most of their time in the country (*see* DEMES). Its citizens were ethnically and socially homogeneous, and had a strong sense of community though they were constantly making leagues and alliances. For the Greeks, *polis* always meant 'the city-state': they did not have the concept of a city that was not politically independent (but *see* FEDERAL STATES). For the different cultural identities of the Greek people, Ionians, Dorians etc., *see* GREECE 2.

There were several hundred city-states in Greece and the colonies. All worshipped the same Olympian gods (*see* RELIGION [Greek]); their religious life focused on sanctuaries and their festivals, some inside the city, others, it has been observed, at its territorial boundaries. Each state consisted of the city, with its citadel (*acropolis*) and marketplace (*agora*), and the surrounding countryside. The government was entirely concentrated in the city, and in the hands of those citizens empowered by the constitution to govern (*see* ARISTOCRACY; OLIGARCHY; DEMOCRACY). It was carried on by an assembly (*see* ECCLESIA), council (*see* BOULE), and magistrates (*see* ARCHONS). Citizens had certain obligations towards the city: to worship the state gods and take part in their cult, perform military service, pay taxes, and obey the laws. There was also a large non-citizen population of slaves and perhaps of resident foreigners also (*see* METICS). Political struggles mostly centred on the kind of constitution the city possessed (e.g. between supporters of oligarchy and supporters of democracy) and on social and economic conditions; civil war (*stasis*) was frequent. The large number of independent city-states was the chief reason for the endless internal wars in Greece and the infrequency of any panhellenic action. The *poleis* lost much of their vital life when they lost their independence after the conquests of Alexander the Great and the emergence of the Hellenistic kingdoms in the late fourth century BC, but for Aristotle the *polis* 'belongs to the class of objects which exist by nature, and the human is by nature a social animal [*politikon zōon*]', i.e. one whose nature it is to live in a *polis* (*Politics* 1253a).

**civil war** (at Rome) Any one of three periods of civil war at Rome, first between Marius and Sulla from 88 to 82 BC; secondly between Julius Caesar on the one hand and Pompey and the republicans on the other, from 49 to 45 BC; thirdly between Caesarians and republicans, and in the latter stage between Antony and Octavian, from 44 to 30 BC.

***Civil War*** Commentaries by Julius Caesar; *see* COMMENTARIES 2.

**clan** *See* GENOS and GENS.

**classic, classics, classical, classicism** English terms derived from the Latin adjective *classicus* meaning 'of the highest class' (of the five classes of Roman citizens divided by king Servius Tullius on a property basis). *Fronto writing in the early second century AD and quoted by Aulus *Gellius seems to have been the first to use the adjective figuratively to describe a writer whose Latin vocabulary could be taken as authoritative, but Cicero had already taken the noun *classis* ('class') from its

political and military sphere and used it to describe a 'class' of philosophers (*see also* CANONS). Renaissance scholars writing in Latin adopted the adjective to describe Greek and Latin authors in general, and from this the modern usage is derived. The terms are sometimes used with a narrower, temporal meaning to describe what is thought to be the best period, in a cultural and artistic sense, of the Greek and Roman civilizations. In this sense the classical period of ancient Greece was most of the fifth and fourth centuries BC, roughly from the defeat of the Persians in 480 to the death of Alexander the Great in 323 BC, and that of Rome the first century BC and the following century up to the death of Augustus in AD 14, sometimes referred to as the Golden age. In modern usage classicism refers to the imitation of ancient styles over a wide range of topics.

**Claudian** (**Claudius Claudiānus**) (d. *c*.AD 404) The last great Latin poet in the classical tradition. He was born at Alexandria *c*.AD 370 and came to Italy before 395. Although a native Greek speaker, he turned to composing in Latin and became immediately successful as a court poet under Honorius, the young emperor in the West, writing in hexameters a number of eulogies of him and his ministers and, in particular, a series of panegyrics of the general and regent Stilicho. (The absence of any reference to Stilicho after 404 suggests that as the year of Claudian's death.) He also wrote poems savagely abusing Honorius' political enemies, mostly in the eastern empire (ruled by Honorius' young brother Arcadius), attacking in particular Rufinus, the guardian of Arcadius, and the eunuch Eutropius, Rufinus' successor. He wrote an (incomplete) *epyllion of 526 lines on the defeat of Gildo who led an uprising in Africa, and another on Stilicho's defeat of the Visigothic king Alaric at Pollentia (Pollenza). In these poems Claudian shows sincere enthusiasm for the Roman empire, great technical and rhetorical skill, and a vigour at times reaching high eloquence, although both his panegyric and his invective are extravagant. The best of his short poems is on a stay-at-home farmer, reminiscent of Virgil's Corycian gardener in *Georgics* 4. His most finished work, as it seems today, is *The Rape of Proserpine*, of which 1,100 lines survive; he tells with great charm the familiar story of Proserpine's abduction by Pluto in the field of Enna. Although Honorius' court was Christian, it is possible that

Claudian remained unconverted. The inscription from a statue of him has survived and is in Naples.

**Claudius** 1. **Appius Claudius Crassus** Roman consul 471 BC and patrician leader of the decemvirs (*decemviri*, commission of ten men) appointed in 451 BC to draw up a written code of laws, the *Twelve Tables, in response to the agitation of the *plebs*. The traditions concerning later events should possibly be rejected. They say that the decemvirs, when reappointed for a second year, appear to have become oppressive, and Appius' conduct towards *Virginia provoked their overthrow in 449. Appius was arrested but committed suicide before he was brought to trial (Livy 3.58), in the prison which he himself had built. To later Romans he came to symbolize aristocratic arrogance, particularly of the Claudii.

2. **Appius Claudius Caecus** ('blind') Famous Roman censor (in 312 BC), reputedly a proud and obstinate man with original and broad views. He used his censorship to extend membership of the senate to rich citizens of the lower classes, and even to the sons of freedmen. Their support as well as heavier taxation enabled him to build Rome's first aqueduct (Aqua Appia) and the *Appian Way. In 279/8 BC, when old and blind, he successfully attacked the proposals of *Pyrrhus for peace, in a famous speech still circulated in Cicero's day. He is the first Roman prose-writer whose name is known to us. Cicero says that he was a notable orator, and that some of his funeral orations were still read. He composed aphorisms in Saturnian verse of which a few have survived; they include 'a man is the creator of his own fortune', *faber est suae quisque fortunae*.

3. **Tiberius Claudius Nero Germa'nicus** (10 BC–AD 54) The Roman emperor Claudius, who reigned from 41 until his death. He was the son of *Drusus the Elder and Antonia, daughter of Mark Antony) Hampered by a limp, trembling, and a stammer, and the general belief that he was mentally deficient, he led a retired life and devoted himself to scholarship, producing various histories and an autobiography, none of which has survived. When the emperor *Gaius (Caligula) was murdered, Claudius was the only surviving adult male of the Julio-Claudian line, and was proclaimed emperor by the praetorian guard almost, it seemed, by accident, after being discovered in hiding, and against the wishes

of the senate who wanted to restore the republic. Claudius took part in the invasion of Britain in AD 43 and was present at the capture of Camulodunum (Colchester). In 48 he divorced for infidelity his wife *Messallina, by whom he had a daughter Octavia and a son Tiberius Claudius Caesar Britannicus, and married *Agrippina, daughter of his brother Germanicus, whose son *Nero he adopted. It was generally believed that his death four years later was caused by a dish of mushrooms poisoned by Agrippina. His subsequent deification was the subject of a satire by Seneca (2), entitled *Apocolocyntosis.

**clau'sula** ('sentence-ending') In Greek and Latin *rhetoric, the closing words of a sentence (or of a clause ending in a strong stop) are rhythmically very important and often follow a regular metrical sequence based on syllable length.

**Clea'nthēs** (of Assos in the Troad, c.331–c.232 BC) Successor of Zeno, the founder of *Stoicism, as head of that school of philosophy from c.261 BC to his death. He was said to have defined Zeno's instruction to 'live consistently' as meaning 'to live consistently with nature'. In his ethical teaching he stressed disinterestedness, saying that to do good to others with a view to one's own benefit was no different from feeding cattle in order to eat them. His Stoicism was pervaded by a religious fervour expressed in the 39 surviving hexameter lines of a hymn to Zeus, in which Zeus is envisaged as the spirit that permeates and rules the universe, and human beings as the only living things that have a semblance to him. Parts of the poem express the Stoic view that all events are the will of a perfect God, and that acceptance of this fact will bring peace of mind. The text and interpretation are much debated. Other small fragments of Cleanthes' works survive.

**Clei'sthenes** 1. Tyrant of Sicyon, a city in the north Peloponnese west of the isthmus, c.600–570 BC. His policy was consistently anti-Dorian and anti-Argive (Sicyon had originally been occupied by Dorians from Argos but retained a large pre-Dorian element in its population) and led to war with Argos. Earlier, Cleisthenes had taken a leading part in the First Sacred War of c.590 in support of Delphi against Crisa, which he destroyed. He won the chariot-race in the first Pythian games. His daughter

Agariste married the *Alcmaeonid Megacles and was mother of the Athenian Cleisthenes (2). For her marriage *see* HIPPOCLEIDES.

**2.** (d. after 507 BC) Grandson of Cleisthenes (1), tyrant of Sicyon, and an *Alcmaeonid through his father Megacles. He is regarded as the founder of Athenian democracy. He was *archon at Athens under the tyrant *Hippias in (perhaps) 525 but when later in Hippias' reign the Alcmaeonids went into exile they bribed the Delphic oracle to press the Spartans into overthrowing the tyranny at Athens. When Hippias was expelled by the Spartan king *Cleomenes I in 510 and those exiled had returned, there was a power-struggle between Isagoras, a leading citizen with ties to Cleomenes, and Cleisthenes. At this point Cleisthenes sought popular support with a programme of political reform. Eventually Isagoras retired to Sparta and Cleisthenes was able to enact far-reaching reforms which paved the way for democracy. He broke up what remained of the old political organization based on the Attic tribes and family groups, and substituted a new system based on topography. He divided the territory of Attica, including the city of Athens, into 139 *demes (*demoi*), local communities or parishes, and each citizen was to be a member of his local deme. Cleisthenes then grouped all the demes into ten new tribes in such a way as to ensure that no tribe had a continuous territory or represented a local interest; on the contrary, each contained groups of demes (*trittyes*, 'thirds') from the city region, from the coast, and from the interior. By these means groups of people in various parts of Attica were brought together and required to act in common, and the old parties acting out of purely local interest were abolished. Solon's council (*boule*) of 400 became a council of 500, with 50 members from each tribe. The organization of the army depended on the new tribes, each of which contributed a regiment of hoplites and a squadron of cavalry. Cleisthenes subordinated the *boule* and the *Areopagus to the supreme authority of the *ecclesia*, 'assembly' of all the citizens, which met regularly and might deal with any important state matter. He seems to have retained Solon's restrictions on eligibility for the higher offices of state. The archons could be chosen only from the two wealthiest classes of the population, and the *Eupatridae retained the monopoly of priestly offices. Cleisthenes seems also to have introduced the practice of *ostracism. At his death he received a public burial in the *Ceramicus.

**Cleitus** Brother of the foster-mother of Alexander the Great and commander of his *hetairoi*. He saved Alexander's life at the battle of the Granicus (334 BC), but was subsequently murdered by him in a drunken fury in 327. The story became a standard example of monarchical excess.

**Cle'obis and Bitōn** Sons of the Argive priestess of Hera, who were described by Solon to Croesus, according to a story in Herodotus (1.31), as having been among the happiest of men. When on one occasion the oxen for the priestess's chariot were not brought in time, her sons drew it the 8km (5 miles) to the temple. She prayed to Hera to grant them the greatest blessing possible for mortals, and the goddess caused them to die while they slept in the temple. Statues of the early sixth century BC found at Delphi have been tentatively identified as Cleobis and Biton on the basis of an inscription.

**Cleo'menēs 1. Cleomenes I** King of Sparta *c.*520–*c.*490 BC, of the *Agiad line. Having expelled the tyrant *Hippias from Athens in 510, in 508 he supported the aristocratic faction in the city, led by Isagoras, against *Cleisthenes (2), and by invoking the hereditary pollution incurred by Cleisthenes' father Megacles (*see* CYLON), compelled him and his supporters to retire. When Cleomenes arrived in Athens and attempted to set up Isagoras and his friends in a narrow oligarchy, there was a popular uprising; after being besieged in the Acropolis both were obliged to withdraw, and Cleisthenes was able to return. Later Cleomenes failed in attempts to restore first Isagoras and then the tyrant Hippias, obstructed in both cases by Demaratus, the other Spartan king. The latter also prevented him from punishing Aegina in 491, when that island was suspected of favouring Persia before the outbreak of the Persian War. He did not, however, support the Ionian Revolt. Earlier, in 494, he defeated Argos, an occasion on which the Argive women were armed to resist under the inspiration of the poet Telesilla.

**2. Cleomenes III** (b. *c.*260 BC) Agiad king of Sparta from *c.*235 to 222. Following the social ideals of his predecessor Agis IV, whose widow he married, he attempted to restore Spartan power by a series of idealistic reforms designed to rehabilitate the constitution of *Lycurgus. The ephorate was abolished on the grounds that it was pre-Lycurgan (but was later restored; see EPHORS). This was in 226–225, when Cleomenes had already built up a strong position in the state by his successful wars against the *Achaean confederacy. The reforms were in part carried out, but in 222 Cleomenes was defeated at Sellasia by the Achaeans under Aratus of Sicyon and fled to his patron Ptolemy III Euergetes in Egypt; there he committed suicide in 219. He was a nationalist and an idealist whose ideals lived on after him, but in practical terms he made no lasting gains.

**Clē'on (Klĕōn)** (d. 422 BC) Athenian politician prominent during the first part of the *Peloponnesian War, the son of a rich tanner. He was perhaps involved in attacks on *Pericles in 431 and 430. After Pericles' death in 429 he succeeded him as the most influential politician of his day. In 427 he proposed the decree (carried but rescinded the following day) to execute all the men of Mitylene after the suppression of its revolt. He favoured the ruthless pursuit of victory in the war, by any means so long as it brought power, glory, and wealth to the Athenian people. In 426 he attacked Aristophanes' *Babylonians* as a slander on Athens. After the Athenian victory at Pylos in 425 he thwarted the Spartan peace proposals. He attacked for incompetence the generals who were unsuccessfully besieging the Spartans on the island of Sphacteria, and when Nicias proposed to hand over the command to him he was forced to accept. With the help of the general Demosthenes, Cleon was able to make good his promise to take Sphacteria and bring home the prisoners within twenty days. He gained popularity with the people at this time by raising the pay for jury service from two to three obols, and would certainly have supported, if he did not originate, the measure greatly increasing the tribute paid by the allies (see DELIAN LEAGUE). In 423 he secured a decree for the destruction of Scione and the execution of its citizens (carried out in 421). After Athenian setbacks in Thrace he was elected *strategos* and commanded the expedition to that area, but after some successes he was defeated and killed at Amphipolis by the Spartan general *Brasidas, who was himself mortally wounded (422). His death and that of Brasidas removed the principal obstacles to the Peace of Nicias, which was concluded in 421.

A vivid but hostile picture of Cleon as a coarse and unscrupulous *demagogue is presented by Thucydides and by Aristophanes, and we have no independent witnesses who might give a less prejudiced view. He was not from the old aristocracy; his influence lay in his forceful style of oratory, and his appeal to the emotions and prejudices of the people. He seems to have aimed at short-term goals, but Athens' poor stood to benefit by his policies, at the expense of her allies.

**Cleopa'tra VII** (69–30 BC) Daughter of Ptolemy XII Auletēs, king of Egypt (d. 51 BC). She was appointed by him as his successor with her younger brother, Ptolemy XIII, to whom she was nominally married. (By Ptolemaic custom she could not rule alone.) She was expelled in 48 by her brother's party but reinstated by Julius Caesar (see CAESAR (2)), who was in Egypt in pursuit of Pompey. When in the consequent war (see BELLUM ALEXANDRINUM) Ptolemy XIII, who opposed Caesar, lost his life, Cleopatra married another younger brother, Ptolemy XIV, but was effectively sole ruler. Caesar besieged and captured the Egyptian capital Alexandria in 48–7, and by then she was his mistress. In 47 she gave birth to a son, *Caesarion, declaring that Caesar was the father. In 46 she followed Caesar to Rome, returning to Egypt after his murder. When Ptolemy XIV died soon after, perhaps poisoned by her, she made her son co-ruler. In the Civil War following Caesar's murder she naturally sided with the triumvirate against the murderers. In 41 she met Mark *Antony at Tarsus in Cilicia; he spent the winter of 41–40 in Alexandria, and she bore him twins, a son and a daughter. Another son was born in 36. After 37 she and Antony were in permanent association, and by 32, when Rome declared war on Cleopatra (alone), the association was seen as a threat to the Roman empire and to Octavian. After their defeat in the sea-battle at *Actium (31), Cleopatra and Antony sought peace terms from Octavian, but without success. Alexandria was surrendered in 30 and Antony committed suicide. Cleopatra was ordered to leave for Rome, and apparently committed suicide to avoid the shame of participating in Octavian's triumph. The story that she died by the bite of an asp (said to be painless) was accepted enthusiastically by the Romans as appropriate for a barbarian queen, and reported with some reservations by the historians.

Cleopatra was Greek by descent (the name is found in Homer), from Alexander's general Ptolemy Soter, and with her ended the Macedonian dynasty of the *Ptolemies in Egypt. She was reputedly the first of that dynasty to learn Egyptian. We do not know her true character behind the romantic tales, but she clearly had personal courage and magnetism, and she wielded sufficient power to be feared by the Romans.

**Clē'ophon** Athenian politician prominent in the latter part of the Peloponnesian War, and a leader of the people (*demagogue) after the restoration of democratic rule in 410 BC. He introduced a dole of two obols a day for poor citizens. His manner was as aggressive as *Cleon's, and he prevented the Athenians from accepting Sparta's peace offers in 410 and 405. He was prosecuted for treason and condemned to death by the *Thirty Tyrants in 404.

**cle'psydra** The water-clock, widely used throughout antiquity, consisting essentially of a vessel with a small opening at the bottom through which water was allowed to trickle. At Athens it was used to measure the time for which people were allowed to speak in the law-courts and appears to have been in common use from the second half of the fifth century BC at the latest (see LAW AT ATHENS 3). The clepsydra was introduced into Roman law-courts by Pompey during his third consulship (52 BC). As used in the courts the clepsydra did not measure time absolutely, but vessels of similar construction were used in ordinary life, during the hours of darkness for example. The vessel itself might be graduated, or there could be a graduated container to catch the outflow. Improvements to the basic clepsydra attributed to the Alexandrian inventor Ctesibius (third century BC) and others included devices to increase its accuracy by maintaining a uniform flow of water, and to indicate the time lapsed. Ctesibius is said to have designed a clock in which dripping water turned wheels, gradually elevating a small statue whose pointing stick indicated the passing hours. See CLOCKS.

**clēruch (klērouchos)** Athenian citizen who held an allotment (klēros) of land in a foreign country. A cleruchy (klērouchia) or group of such cleruchs differed from a colony in that the former retained their Athenian citizenship, did not create a new independent community,

and did not even necessarily reside on their allotted land. This kind of settlement on conquered territory (Greek and foreign) was introduced in the last years of the sixth century BC and was much developed in the fifth, when it became an important feature in the Athenian imperial system. It ensured a sort of permanent garrison in foreign territory and in that of the allies (see DELIAN LEAGUE), in addition to providing land for the poor. The leader of a cleruchy was known as the oecist (oikistes). Important cleruchies were in Chalcis (506, and again c.446), Naxos, the Thracian Chersonese, Lemnos, Euboea (446), and Aegina (431).

**client** [Lat. cliens] At Rome, from early republican times, a free man who entrusted himself to a powerful *patron to whom he rendered services and from whom he received protection. Clientship was a recognized social relationship which could be hereditary. *Freedmen became automatically clients of their former owners. The client would show his patron respect, particularly by greeting him in the morning, and attend him in the streets, and give him political support. In return the client would receive daily a dole of food or money (sportula). The extent to which clientship played a part in Roman political life is still debated. Under the empire the client became almost indistinguishable from the *parasite, the subservient hanger-on, familiar from the satires of Juvenal and Martial. Certain conquered foreign states are sometimes spoken of as 'clients' of Rome, and some individuals and families in Rome built up a large following from client states.

**client kings** Foreign rulers under the patronage of Rome (see FRIENDSHIP [Roman]). Hieron II of Syracuse was the first to be so described (c.263 BC).

**Clīo (Kleiō)** See MUSES.

**Cloā'ca Ma'xima** The 'main drain' at Rome, originally a stream draining north-east Rome through the Forum to the Tiber. Its canalization was attributed to the *Tarquins, and particularly to Tarquinius Superbus in the late sixth century BC. It was first enclosed in the third century BC, and much of the existing sewer is the work of *Agrippa c.33 BC, with later extensions. It still forms part of the drainage system of the modern city. (See CRATES (1).)

**clocks** *(hōrologia;* sing. Gk. *hōrologion,* Lat. *hōrologium)* In ordinary life the Greeks and Romans referred to the time of day in descriptive terms, 'first light', 'midday', etc. The hour, when used, was not a twenty-fourth part of the astronomical day but one-twelfth of the time from sunrise to sunset (or sunset to sunrise), and its length therefore varied with latitude and season. The clocks which were used to measure these hours in the ancient world were all variants of two basic kinds, the shadow-clock or sundial, and the water-clock (*\*clepsydra*). A simple clepsydra from the late fifth century BC has been found in the agora at Athens, and the later 'Tower of the Winds', still to be seen there, is believed to have contained a water-clock. Herodotus says that the sundial and the *gnomon* ('pointer'), and the twelve-part division of the day, were introduced into Greece from the Babylonians. The shadow-clock had disadvantages other than its dependence on sunshine: it required different scales according to latitude, and for dividing the period of daylight into equal parts it required, like the water-clock, seasonal correction. The first clocks brought to Rome, in the third century BC, were shadow-clocks in the form of sundials, *solaria,* erected in public view. The most famous was one captured in Sicily in 263 BC and set up on a column but not adapted to the latitude of Rome. In 159 BC, P. Scipio Nasica erected a public clepsydra which told the hours of day and of night. The *horologium* of Augustus in the Campus Martius was a magnificent *solarium,* measuring the length of days on a meridian line now restored, its *gnomon* an Egyptian obelisk. Clocks were also kept by private individuals (*see* HEROPHILUS); Cicero sent one to *Tiro. Clepsydrae were used by the Romans in their military camps to measure the four watches into which the night was divided.

**Clō'dia** (b. *c.*95 BC) In Rome, the second of the three sisters of P. *Clodius and wife of Q. Metellus Celer (consul in 60; d. 59 BC, allegedly poisoned by Clodia). She was notorious for her reckless way of life. Among her lovers was the poet *Catullus, who celebrated her as 'Lesbia' (the identification is sometimes doubted but remains highly probable). Her enemy Cicero paints a vivid picture of her in his letters and especially in his speech of 56, *Pro Caelio* (*see* CICERO (1) 4), which is instructive for the social background of Catullus. She may have been still alive in 45 BC.

**Clō'dius (Publius Clodius Pulcher)** (b. *c.*92 BC) Roman patrician of the famous Claudian *\*gens,* who, like his sister *Clodia and some other members of the *gens,* used the plebeian form of the name. His adoption into a plebeian *gens* was ratified in 59 BC, and in 58 he was elected tribune. His raft of measures included free corn for the plebs and a bill confirming the exile of Cicero. He helped to bring about the joint consulship of Pompey and Crassus in 55, and stood for the praetorship of 52, but before the election could take place, postponed because of riots, he was murdered by his enemy *Milo when the rival gangs of both sides met and fought. His supporters burned down the senate-house in revenge. Clodius was notorious for his vicious aggression and recklessness, and as the enemy of Cicero. For his profanation of the mysteries of the Bona Dea in 62 BC, his hatred of Cicero and its repercussions, and his violent death in 52, *see* CICERO (1) 3 and 4 and CAESAR (2) 1.

**Cloe'lia** According to Roman legend, one of the Roman hostages given to the Etruscan king Lars *Porsen(n)a in the course of his war with the newly founded Roman republic (510 BC). She escaped by swimming, or on horseback, across the Tiber to Rome, but was handed back to Porsenna; he freed her and other hostages, in admiration of her bravery, thus initiating a reconciliation between the two sides. An equestrian statue on the Via Sacra celebrated her action.

**closure** What constitutes a sense of finality at the end of a literary work is first and briefly considered by Aristotle in the *Poetics.* He defines an end as that which follows naturally from something else and from which nothing else follows. In a later chapter on drama he states that *genre determines what kind of ending is suitable. Study of the various genres of ancient literature reveals the existence of certain conventions of form and expression in endings, but the lack of obvious finality in the concluding parts of some notable literary works has led to doubt as to whether we do in fact possess the endings. This is particularly the case with Herodotus and Lucretius and, in lyrics, Catullus 51 and its equally problematic model by Sappho; *see also* IPHIGENEIA AT AULIS. The subject provokes much discussion.

**Clōtho** ('Spinner') One of the three Greek *Fates.

**Cloudcuckooland** *See* BIRDS.

**Clouds (Nephelai)** (Lat. *Nūbēs*) Greek comedy by *Aristophanes, ridiculing Socrates (then aged 46) as a typical *sophist and corrupt propagator of absurd new ideas among the young. The play was originally produced at the City *Dionysia of 423 BC but won only third (and last) prize, and Aristophanes, who seems to have thought it his best play to date, set about rewriting it. We have only the revised version dating from the period 418–416. The revision was never completed and the play never performed.

Strepsīades ('Twister'), an elderly dishonest farmer, has been financially ruined by his fashionable wife and horse-loving son Pheidippides, a young man in the cavalry. He has heard of Socrates, a man who can make the worse cause appear the better, and hopes that he will teach his son how to defraud his creditors. As his son refuses to enter Socrates' school (the *phrontisterion*, 'think-shop'), Strepsiades decides to go himself. He is told he must resign himself to hard work and simple living, and is introduced to the chorus of Clouds; they are the deities who produce thunder and rain (and not Zeus, as generally believed). But Strepsiades is too stupid and too much concerned with his debts to learn very much, and Pheidippides has to take his place as pupil. Socrates hands Pheidippides over to be instructed by Right (the Better Argument) and Wrong (the Worse Argument) in person. A contest between these two (one of the substituted scenes) follows, in which Wrong is victorious. Strepsiades, by the aid of what little he has learnt, fobs off and drives away his creditors. But the tables are turned when, as a result of the same learning, Pheidippides starts to beat his father (and threatens to beat his mother too), and proves that he is justified in doing so. Strepsiades, disgusted with the new education and repenting of his dishonesty, sets fire to Socrates' school and drives the inmates away.

**Cly'menē** ('Famous') Name of many women in Greek myth of whom the following are the most important.

**1.** Daughter of Oceanus and Tethys and wife of the *Titan Iapetus, by whom she became the mother of Atlas, Prometheus, and Epimetheus.

**2.** Daughter of *Minyas and wife of *Cephalus; as a result of her union with *Helios she became the mother of Phaethon. She was also the mother of Atalanta.

**Clytemne'stra (Klytaim(n)ēstra)** In Greek myth, daughter of Tyndareus king of Sparta, and Leda; sister of Helen (of Troy), Castor, and Polydeuces (Lat. Pollux). She married *Agamemnon king of Mycenae and became the mother of Iphigeneia (or Iphianassa), Chrysothemis, Electra (or Laodice), and Orestes. During Agamemnon's absence in the Trojan War she took Aegisthus (*see* PELOPS) as lover, and upon Agamemnon's return with Cassandra, his Trojan concubine, she killed them both, Agamemnon in the bath. When Orestes reached manhood he killed his mother and Aegisthus. The chief interest of her story for the authors who related it is the variety of motives it admits for the murder of Agamemnon, and the different characterizations of all the participants it therefore makes possible.

**Cn.** In Latin, abbreviation for the name Gnaeus; *see* ALPHABET [Latin].

**Cnossus (Knōsos, Knōssos)** The most famous city of *Crete in ancient times, situated near the middle of the north coast of the island about 6km (4 miles) inland. Its foundation was attributed to the legendary king *Minos who also built there the *labyrinth to contain the Minotaur.

**Coclēs, Publius Horā'tius** *See* HORATIUS.

**Cocy'tus** In Greek myth, one of the rivers of *Hades. It was also the name of a tributary of the Acheron in Epirus.

**cōdex 1.** *See* BOOKS, GREEK AND ROMAN 5 and JUSTINIAN.

**2.** (In the sense of 'legal code') By the fourth century AD in the Roman empire 'codex' had come to mean, in legal circles, a collection of imperial laws, a code of law. *See* JUSTINIAN.

**Codrus** In Athenian legend, king of Athens in the eleventh century BC. He was the son of Melanthus, descendant of *Neleus, and a member of the Messenian royal family. When the Dorians captured Messenia, Codrus came to Athens; there he became king at the time when the Dorians conquered the Peloponnese. When they invaded Attica (*see* DORIANS) they were told by an oracle that they would be victorious if they spared the king. Codrus, hearing this, entered the Dorian camp in disguise, provoked a quarrel, and was killed; the

Dorians then withdrew. One tradition said that because no one was thought worthy to succeed such a king, the monarchy was thereafter abolished, and *archons appointed instead. The first archonship was held by Codrus' son Medon. Another tradition made Medon king, and a later descendant the first archon.

**cognō'men** *See* NAMES [Roman].

**cohort** In the Roman army, the tenth part of a legion, nominally 600 men (six centuries or three maniples).

**coinage** *See* MONEY AND COINS.

**Cōlax** *See* KOLAX.

**Colchis** Country at the eastern end of the Black Sea, bounded on the north by the Caucasus, famous in Greek legend as the destination of the *Argonauts and the kingdom of Aeëtes, father of *Medea. It was also known as Aea. Its river, Phasis (the modern Rioni), was sometimes regarded as forming the boundary between Europe and Asia, its navigable waters taking sailors from the Black Sea as far east as they could go. It was regarded as the homeland of the 'Phasian bird', the pheasant.

**Colise'um** *See* COLOSSEUM.

**Colline Gate** At Rome, on the northeast side of the city, the scene of a battle in 82 BC in which *Sulla, after his return from the first Mithridatic War in the East, finally overcame the Marian forces and made himself master of Italy.

**cōlon** In Greek lyric poetry cola are the units into which the various metres are analysed (rather than into feet, for example). A colon is a metrical sequence of some twelve syllables with a recognizable, recurring pattern of long and short syllables.

**Colō'nus** A deme or district of Attica, about 2½km (1½ miles) north of the Acropolis at Athens, the legendary scene of the death of *Oedipus, and the birthplace of Sophocles.

**Colosse'um** The great *amphitheatre of Rome, begun by the emperor Vespasian and dedicated by his son Titus in AD 80. It stands on a site previously occupied by part of the *Golden House of Nero and the name derives from a large statue of Nero that stood nearby (*see* COLOSSUS OF RHODES). The Colosseum was capable of holding at least 50,000 people in three tiers with standing-room above. It was used for gladiatorial and wild-beast shows (not for burning Christians). At the inaugural 'hunt' 5,000 wild and 4,000 tame animals were killed. The arena could also be flooded for *naumachiae*, mimic seafights.

**Colo'ssus of Rhodes** [Gk. *kolossos*, 'statue; from the late Hellenistic period 'a more-than-lifesize statue'] A huge bronze statue of the Greek sun-god Helios, the patron of Rhodes. One of the *Seven Wonders of the ancient world, it was erected to commemorate the successful defence of the city against a siege in 305–304 BC by Demetrius Poliorcetes. It almost certainly stood overlooking the city on its eastern side, not astride the harbour as sometimes claimed, and was 70 cubits high (30–35m, 100–115 feet). It was completed *c*.280 BC and overthrown by an earthquake in 228 (or 226) BC. Its size gave a new meaning to *kolossos*.

**columbarium** *See* DEAD, DISPOSAL OF.

**Colume'lla, Lucius Junius Moderā'tus** A Spaniard from Gades (Cadiz) in Spain who served as a tribune of the Roman army in Syria. In about AD 60–5 he composed a treatise on farming, *De re rustica*, in twelve books which survive. He writes in the tradition of the Elder Cato's *De agri cultura* celebrating the secure agrarian basis of the early Roman state (up to mid-second century BC). The work deals with the layout of a villa, organization of slave-labour, arable cultivation, viticulture, livestock, fishponds, bees, and gardens, while the last two books expound the duties of the bailiff and his wife, and wine- and oil-processing. All the books are written in prose except for book 10, which deals with gardens in rather uninspired hexameters, in order to make his work appreciated by literary landowners. Columella writes as a practical farmer who is distressed by the decline of Italian agriculture, remedy for which he sees in knowledge, hard work, and interest on the part of the landowner. He is a warm admirer of the *Georgics*. His prose is dignified and stylish, without affectation. A shorter manual on agriculture, of which one book, *De arboribus* ('On trees'), is extant, may not be by him.

**comedy**
**Greek.** The only Greek comedy we possess is Athenian. For that reason it is also known as

Attic comedy (from the state of Attica, of which Athens was the chief city).

*1. Background.* Comedies at Athens, like tragedies, were produced under the auspices of the state and were a matter for competition (*cf.* TRAGEDY 2). They were first produced at the annual festival of the City *Dionysia in 486 BC and at the *Lenaea (another Dionysiac festival) shortly before 440 BC. It is likely that performances also took place in the late fifth century in theatres in the demes. Before and after the Peloponnesian War (431–404 BC) five comedies were performed annually at each festival; during the war the number is said to have been reduced to three for reasons of economy. Comic dramatists (often called comic poets because the plays were written in verse) who wished to have their plays performed 'applied for a *chorus' to the magistrate in charge of the festival, who chose the successful applicants. The duty of paying the expenses of a chorus fell upon rich citizens (*see* CHOREGIA). The dramatists, who received payment, usually presented only one play each, and were in competition for first prize, which may have been no more than a garland of ivy. At the Lenaea a prize seems also to have been given for the best comic actor, but not at the City Dionysia until the late fourth century. Ten judges were appointed by lot from among the citizens, according to an elaborate method designed to avoid corruption. It seems to be the case that no Greek wrote both tragedies and comedies; when, at the end of Plato's *Symposium*, Socrates presses *Agathon, who wrote tragedies, and *Aristophanes, who wrote comedies, to admit that the same man could write both, the admission was intended to be paradoxical (but *see* ION (2)).

*2. The origin of Greek comedy.* Aristotle in the *Poetics* theorized that comedy had its origin in phallic songs sung at festivals of Dionysus. Another tradition made *Epicharmus an influence on its development. The earliest comedy we possess, the *Acharnians* of Aristophanes, was produced in 425 BC; we do not know how it differed from the earliest comedies performed in Athens, nor how comedy started in the first place.

*3. Old Comedy (the comedy of Aristophanes).* The term 'Old Comedy' denotes the comedies produced in Athens in the fifth century BC. Of all these works the only complete plays surviving are eleven by Aristophanes, and of these the last two (*Ecclesiazusae* and *Plutus*) were written in the fourth century BC and are different in character from the rest, notably in the much-reduced role of the chorus. Our knowledge of Old Comedy therefore depends upon Aristophanes' other nine plays, all produced in the last quarter of the fifth century. However, there are sufficient resemblances between these plays, late in the tradition though they are, and the many citations from the other playwrights (see 4), to allow cautious generalizations about the nature and structure of Old Comedy.

A comedy required for its performance three or (more probably) four actors, occasionally with the support of supernumeraries, and a chorus of twenty-four members (all men); the lyric element of their songs is not always conspicuous. The role taken by the chorus was of primary importance; many plays took their titles from it (e.g. *Acharnians*, *Wasps*, *Birds*), and its costume and dances provided spectacle. The attitude of the chorus to the hero or heroine, hostile or well-disposed or inconsistent, contributes to the drama. The actors' costumes were an exaggeration of reality, with grotesque masks (which included hair) and body padding and, probably, a large phallus for male characters. The costume expressed the robust nature of Old Comedy, in which the jokes were much concerned with sex and excretion and the language uninhibited. The comedy took as its starting point a fantastic scheme on the part of the hero, the achievement of which, wholly impossible in real life, constituted the plot. A few prominent citizens were vilified, ridiculed or parodied; in some comedies they figure in major roles, either in their own names, e.g. Socrates in *Clouds*, Euripides in *Thesmophoriazusae*, or in thin disguise, e.g. Cleon as the Paphlagonian slave in *Knights*. Topical comment on personalities, events, and institutions of the day (e.g. the lawcourts in *Wasps*) was pervasive. The more extreme aspects of contemporary democratic politics, the more ridiculous developments in education, music, and literature, and the hardships of war, were seized upon and exaggerated for comic effect. A paragraph in the *Old Oligarch whose significance is debated (2.18) states that the people do not allow dramatists to mock the *demos* (the lower classes) unless an individual member has got above himself. Mythology and the gods, or certain gods, were similarly treated with irreverence, especially Dionysus, who appears in the *Frogs* as cowardly and none too intelligent. There is no question of disbelief; nothing ill-omened is said or done. It is all part of the ordinary person's protest against external forces which get in the way of self-indulgent enjoyment. It is difficult to see how far serious social comment lay behind the jokes. Altogether, Old Comedy was a humane (to modern taste) blend of religious ceremony and ridicule, satire and criticism (political, social, and literary), wit and foolery.

An Aristophanic comedy is elaborate in structure and is usually divided into the following named parts: prologue, parodos, agon, parabasis, epirrhema, episode, and exodus. (See the entry for each.)

4. *Authors of Old Comedy.* Of the authors of Old Comedy other than Aristophanes we know little. The two greatest after Aristophanes, as the Greeks thought, were *Cratinus and *Eupolis. Many quotations from their works survive. Within fifty years or so, taste had changed (see 5 for Aristotle's comment) and the audience became sensitive to what they saw as the crudity of Old Comedy. Plutarch five centuries later judged it unsuitable entertainment for parties. He and his contemporaries found the writer too much in earnest, the jokes coarse, and the people mentioned largely unknown: New Comedy (see 6) was altogether more agreeable.

5. *Middle Comedy.* 'Middle Comedy' is a Hellenistic term, used to describe Athenian comedy of the period c.400–c.323 BC (between Old and New Comedy), almost all of which is lost. It was a period of experimentation, and no single type of play can be said to represent it exclusively. The loss of confidence following Athens' defeat at the end of the Peloponnesian War (404 BC) was reflected in comedy by the evolution of a type that was cosmopolitan and less Athenian in character. Aristophanes' *Ecclesiazusae* (probably 393 BC) and *Plutus* (388) are thought of as typical early examples. The *parabasis*, when the chorus broke the dramatic illusion and addressed the audience directly, disappeared, and the role of the chorus declined sharply; the padded costume and the phallus were probably given up at this time. Aristotle, a contemporary, comments on this new kind of comedy that it prefers innuendo to coarsely explicit language. Plots based on mythology continued to be popular in the first half of the period, but political themes and comment gradually disappeared, to be replaced by satire of familiar types in society, the professional soldier and the courtesan, for example. Mythology too disappeared in time and emphasis came to be put on the realities of ordinary life, which provided the setting for plots about 'love affairs and the rapes of maidens' as ascribed to a certain Anaxandrides. We know the names of about fifty dramatists of this period, of whom the most famous (after Aristophanes) were Antiphanes, Eubulus, and *Alexis; but Aristophanes apart, no complete play survives, although we have a large number of fragments.

6. *New Comedy.* New Comedy is the name given to comedy composed mainly for first performance at Athens in the period c.323–c.263 BC, that is, from the death of Alexander the Great to the death of Philemon, the last great dramatist of New Comedy. The plays of New Comedy adhere to a recognizable pattern which is a final development from Old Comedy. They were divided into five acts, separated by irrelevant choral interludes performed by a chorus which took no other part in the play and whose songs have not survived. There was very little obscenity; padded costume and the phallus had been abandoned but masks were retained (Pollux describes forty-four types). In other respects the actors wore ordinary Athenian dress. The dramatists set their plays in Athens and were themselves based in Athens, but many of them were drawn there from other cities. Political comment was rare. Their plots were concerned with some perhaps stereotyped but relatively realistic episodes in the private life of the moderately well-to-do family, cosmopolitan rather than narrowly Athenian, but essentially bourgeois. Their success lay in the delineation of characters who found themselves in situations and family relationships which are universal and deeply felt. Love or infatuation (always heterosexual) was often the mainspring of the plot but not always the most interesting part, which often centred on social tensions between rich and poor, or town and country, or family members (parents and children, brother and brother). These characteristics gave New Comedy a wide and long-lasting appeal, and the plays spread rapidly (*see* DIONYSUS, ARTISTS OF) and enjoyed great popularity for many centuries in the Greco-Roman world. It is ironic therefore that the Attic Greek in which they were written, foreshadowing the international *koinē*, was

considered in the Byzantine age to be inferior to Attic speech of the fifth century BC, and thus unsuitable for the Byzantine schoolroom. As a result manuscripts of the plays were not circulated or copied after the seventh century AD and none has survived to the present day. However, a number of papyrus finds in the twentieth century (*see* PAPYROLOGY) has restored to us large parts of several plays of *Menander, and we have fragments of some other dramatists. More successful in his own day than Menander was Philemon (*c.*361–263 BC). He was probably born in Syracuse, but became an Athenian citizen. Sixty titles are known and over 200 fragments. His technique can be gathered from Roman adaptations of his plays by *Plautus and *Terence. Diphilus from the Milesian colony of Sinope on the Black Sea was another dramatist of the second half of the fourth century BC. Again, about 60 titles are known, and a few of his plays were adapted by Plautus.

## Roman

*1. Background.* Livy's version of the origin of drama at Rome, only one of several, was that it began with jests in roughly improvised verses similar to the *Fescennine verses (whatever these may have been) which Horace saw as the origin of comedy. Knowledge of Greek drama must have been widespread in South Italy (Magna Graecia) from the fifth century BC onwards, but *Livius Andronicus (*c.*284–204 BC), a Greek from Tarentum, was, according to Livy, the first to introduce plays with a plot: a translation of a Greek tragedy and a New Comedy at celebrations for the end of the First Punic War (240 BC). The first important Italian exponent of Greek comedy was *Naevius. We know the titles of more than thirty of his comedies, mostly translations of Greek New Comedy. He was followed by *Plautus, *Caecilius Statius (whose plays do not survive), and *Terence, all imitators and adaptors of New Comedy. Their plays were known in consequence as *fabulae *palliatae*, 'plays in Greek cloaks', and the actors almost certainly wore masks. By the middle of the second century BC comedies were being written with an Italian flavour although the structure was Greek. None of these so-called *fabulae *togatae* ('plays in togas') survives, except for short quotations. Lucius Afranius (b. *c.*150 BC) was the most famous of their authors. Roman comedy practically ceased to be written in the first century BC, supplanted by the more popular *mime, which

had no claim to literary merit. The last recorded revival at Rome of a comedy by Plautus, *Pseudolus*, was staged in Cicero's day.

*2. Performance of Roman comedy.* There had always been an audience at Rome for dramatic performances of one sort or another. From the third century BC days were set aside for stage performances at the public games, and besides regular festivals there were occasional performances at such events as the funeral games of distinguished men. Audiences were drawn from all social classes, but, in general, Roman audiences were less knowledgeable and appreciative than their counterparts in Athens, and had less respect for actors and for the occasion. Horace alleged that an audience will demand a bear or boxers in the middle of a play. Plautus in the prologue to *Poenulus* enumerates an amazing list of activities he would prefer the audience to refrain from, of which letting the baby cry is the least. Roman actors, it is assumed, were always men, except in mimes. There was no strict limitation upon the number of actors, as there was in Greece, and many plays require at least five speaking actors. Masks were worn in the native Atellan drama, and perhaps in *fabulae togatae*; there is some doubt about the comedies of Plautus. Though the texts of the plays of Plautus have been divided into five acts since the Renaissance, and those of Terence since ancient times, they were written to run continuously, and they did not employ a chorus, although they included parts that were declaimed or sung. The scenes of spoken dialogue were written in iambic senarii and are called *diverbia*. All other parts are called *cantica*.

*See also* PANTOMIME and SOCCUS.

## Commentaries (*Commentarii*) ('Notes',

'Memoirs') Memoirs on the Gallic War and on the Civil War, *Commentarii de bello Gallico* and *Commentarii de bello cīvīli*, by Julius *Caesar. They describe, respectively, his campaigns in *Gaul from 58 to 52 BC and the Civil War against *Pompey which culminated in the battle of Pharsalus in 48 BC.

### 1. The Gallic War

*Book 1.* After a brief geographical description of Gaul (which, as was famously known to schoolchildren, was divided into three parts), Caesar describes the migration of the *Helvetii into Gaul, and how the Romans resettled them in their old homes. He then records fruitless negotiations with the German king Ariovistus about German incursions into Gaul, and the battle north-east of Vesontio (Besançon) in which the Germans were routed (58).

*Book 2.* The Belgic tribes (*see* BELGAE), of German descent but living in Gaul, combine for war against Rome. In a critical battle against the Nervii (a Belgic tribe) the Romans virtually exterminate them, and the whole of Gaul is temporarily pacified (57).

*Book 3.* Armorican tribes (in Brittany) revolt, but are defeated by the makeshift Roman fleet and its unexpected tactics.

*Book 4.* Caesar responds to a German invasion by crossing the river Rhenus (Rhine) to demonstrate Roman power. He makes his first expedition to Britain, which had supported Gaul against the Romans. A small force lands in Kent in face of fierce opposition. Caesar's fleet at anchor is badly damaged by storm, and the British manner of chariot-fighting throws his troops into confusion. He withdraws his force from Britain in September (55).

*Book 5.* After a second invasion of Britain with a larger force, a storm again destroys many of the transports. Caesar reaches and fords the Thames, captures the stronghold of the chief Cassivelaunus, and obtains his surrender (*see* BRITAIN 2). Caesar takes hostages, fixes the tribute payable by Britain, and withdraws to the Continent (at this point the book includes a geographical description of Britain). During the winter the Gauls revolt, annihilate the Roman garrison at Aduatuca and then lay siege to the camp of Q. Cicero (*see* CICERO (2)), who is rescued by Caesar.

*Book 6.* Various punitive expeditions are made by the Romans chiefly against Ambiorix, who escapes. German horsemen cross the Rhine to plunder what they can, but the Romans drive them off (53). The book contains an account of the customs of the Gauls and Druids, and of the Germans.

*Book 7.* The disturbed state of Italy encourages the Gauls to a general revolt, and a coalition of the principal tribes is formed under Vercingetorix, leader of the Arverni (who gave their name to Auvergne), threatening Transalpine Gaul. Caesar hastens back from Italy, secures the province, and drawing Vercingetorix south to defend Auvergne gathers his troops together. He recaptures Cenabum (Orleans) and Avaricum, where in revenge for past sufferings the Romans butcher all the inhabitants. After some setbacks Caesar

rejoins *Labienus and the united army moves against Vercingetorix, who is again threatening the province of Transalpine Gaul. They follow him to his stronghold Alesia (Mont Auxois) and capture the stronghold as well as Vercingetorix after fierce fighting (52).

*Book 8.* A continuation of the others, but written by A. *Hirtius. Books 1–7 were published in 51 BC.

**2. The Civil War.** All the events of the first two books take place in 49 BC.

*Book 1.* The opening of the war, after the senate had voted that Caesar should lay down his military command and he, in defiance, had crossed the *Rubicon with his army (49 BC). Caesar rapidly overruns Italy, and Pompey, under pressure, retires first to the south Italian port of Brundisium (Brindisi) and then across to Epirus in north-west Greece, before Caesar can close the harbour. Caesar therefore turns west to Massalia (Marseilles), starting to lay siege to it, and then to Spain, where his strategy in the neighbourhood of Ilerda (Lerida) secures the surrender of Pompey's lieutenants Afranius and Petreius.

*Book 2.* The continuation of the siege of Massalia and its surrender, the conquest of western Spain, and the disastrous North African campaign of Caesar's lieutenant, C. Curio, whose rashness brings about the annihilation of his force by King *Juba (1).

*Book 3.* The operations of Caesar in 48 against Pompey in Epirus, the unsuccessful attempt to blockade Pompey at Dyrrhachium, Caesar's withdrawal to Thessaly where he is reinforced by fresh troops, the battle of Pharsalus where Caesar's veterans defeat Pompey's numerically superior forces, and Pompey's flight to Egypt, where he is murdered through the agency of the Egyptian king's advisers. The work ends with an account of the political situation in Egypt, Caesar's activities there, and the grave danger to which he and his forces are exposed.

**commercium and conubium, rights of**
*See* LATIN RIGHTS.

**Co'mmodus, Lucius Ae'lius Aurē'lius** (AD 161–92) Roman emperor from 180 to his death, elder twin son of Marcus *Aurelius, and the first emperor 'born in the *purple'. Late in his reign he became insane, renamed Rome Colonia Commodiana ('colony of Commodus'), and believed himself to be the reincarnation of Hercules. When he determined to appear in public as consul and gladiator, his ministers had him strangled by an athlete called Narcissus.

**commū'nes loci** ('commonplaces') In *rhetoric, 'arguments that can be transferred to many places', which were published in handbooks of rhetoric and practised in schools. According to Cicero they originated with the Greek *sophists Gorgias and Protagoras. Hence the modern term 'commonplace book', but in a different sense.

**companions** *See* HETAIROI.

**Concord, temple of** According to tradition the first temple of Concord at Rome was dedicated by M. Furius Camillus in 367 BC to celebrate the end of civil strife over the Licinian rogations (*see* LICINIO–SEXTIAN LAWS). It was restored by L. Opimius in 121 BC after the death of C. Gracchus and again by the emperor Tiberius in AD 10 from the spoils of his German campaigns. It stood overlooking the Forum from the slope of the Capitoline. The senate often met there and it was the setting for some of Cicero's great political speeches. It was there too that Sejanus was condemned to death.

**conco'rdia o'rdinum** ('concord between the classes') *See* CICERO (1) 3.

**concubinage** A recognized, stable union between a man and a woman without the customary pledges of a formal marriage. At Athens, the phrase 'for the purposes of producing children' is sometimes attached to descriptions of such a union, leaving it unclear whether or not the woman is a slave. A man could have a concubine as well as a wife, but his children by her were not legitimate. At Rome a concubine was a free woman cohabiting with a man without being his wife. Legal problems of inheritance were likely to ensue if a man had a concubine and a wife simultaneously. It was more honourable for a man to have his own freedwoman as concubine than as a wife. Later in the empire higher classes of citizens were forbidden to marry freedmen or freedwomen. The emperors Vespasian, Marcus Aurelius, and Antoninus Pius lived with concubines after they became widowers.

A great deal of uncertainty surrounds the relationship. *See also* LOVE AND SEXUALITY.

**confarreā'tio** At Rome, the oldest and most solemn form of marriage. *See* MARRIAGE CEREMONIES 2.

**conflict of the orders** *See* ORDERS, CONFLICT OF and ROME 2.

**Cōnon 1.** One of the Athenian commanders at the battle of Aegospotami between Athens and Sparta at the end of the *Peloponnesian War (405 BC). He escaped from the Athenian disaster with eight ships, and made his way to *Evagoras in Cyprus where he helped revive Persian sea-power. He was subsequently appointed with Pharnabazus to command the Persian fleet against Sparta, and in 394 defeated the Spartans at Cnidus, destroying their naval power and avenging Aegospotami. He returned to Athens and with the help of Persian money and mercenaries completed the rebuilding of the *Long Walls. He died shortly after his return to Cyprus, leaving his son *Timotheus (2) a wealthy man.

**2.** (of Samos, first half of the third century BC) Mathematician and astronomer, who settled in Alexandria. He is best known for his discovery (*c*.245) of the new constellation, the Lock of *Berenice (*see also* CALLIMACHUS), and is said to have worked on intersecting conics; nothing of his writings survives. He was a close friend of Archimedes, who writes of him with admiration.

**consentes, di** *See* DI CONSENTES.

*Constitution of the Athenians* *See* ATHENAION POLITEIA.

*Constitution of the Lacedaemonians* (*Lakedaimoniōn politeia*) Minor work of *Xenophon, written *c*.388 BC, a largely admiring account of the Spartan way of life. Xenophon attributes the power of Sparta to the traditional institutions of *Lycurgus which he describes: the marriage system, the physical training of both sexes, the unusual manner of educating the young (*see* AGOGE), the system of eating in public messes, the discouragement of private property, the preference for an honourable death to a disgraceful life, the army system, and the position and function of the kings. In ch. 14, perhaps written later, he laments the decline from Lycurgan values in the Sparta of his day. Of the actual Lacedaemonian constitution, in spite of the title, he tells us very little.

**consuls** [Lat. *consules*] At Rome under the republic, the chief civil and military magistrates, two in number with equal powers. Originally called *praetores*, *praetors, their power, originally that of a king, was in course of time reduced by the creation of new magistracies, notably the censorship (*see* CENSORS). Consuls were elected annually by the people, but as the candidates were required to be senators the choice was restricted (*see* SENATE). After 367 BC one consul was always *plebeian. In that year a third magistrate, designated as praetor, was created, and civil jurisdiction passed effectively to him from 366; from 244 there were two praetors. The chief functions retained by the consuls were those of military command. Later they received as 'proconsuls' an extension of their authority after the termination of their year of office, to enable them to carry on a military command or govern a province (*see* PROCONSUL). In the Roman *calendar the years were dated by naming the consuls. Under the emperors the consulship increasingly became a mainly honorary office; consuls were generally appointed for no more than two to four months, only those who entered office on 1 January giving their name to the year. They retained some judicial functions and introduced legal cases before the senate. *See* CURSUS HONORUM and IMPERIUM.

A *consul suffectus* was elected to succeed a consul unable to complete his term of office, or, under the emperors, appointed after the term of the *eponymous consul had expired.

**co'ntio** A public gathering at Rome, but one at which no legally binding decision could be made. It generally took place in the Forum.

**contraception** The ancient world had no effective means of contraception that was not mechanical. It is likely that the use of pessaries, as simple as sponges soaked in a spermicidal substance, oil or vinegar for example, was common. Some practices, like wearing amulets, clearly relied on magic, while others such as inserting cabbage leaves into the vagina after coition, rather than before, seem to verge on the magical, or are at least optimistic. There were drugs, taken by mouth, which were supposed to prevent conception. Drinking mint tea made from pennyroyal was always popular; drugs included the rather mysterious *misu* (sometimes spelt 'misy' in English), made from a copper ore, drinking which was thought to prevent conception for a year. Ointments were also used, applied internally to the mouth of the

womb or even to the man's penis. The possibility was known (and mentioned by Lucretius) of avoiding conception by the woman withdrawing somewhat at the moment of ejaculation (a form of *coitus interruptus*), but it is nowhere discussed, though it may be mentioned obliquely and metaphorically in a fragmentary poem by Archilochus. The Latin poets indicate that a woman engaging in intercourse with apparently passionate movements may merely be following a prescription for avoiding pregnancy. After coition has taken place, washing, sneezing, and drinking cold water are recommended. Anal intercourse was notoriously used by *Peisistratus when he married Megacles' daughter.

Tacitus in the *Germania* speaks approvingly of the Germans' refusal to limit the number of children in a family (or expose later-born infants). The Egyptians and the Jews famously reared all their children.

**Contra Rullum** ('Against Rullus') or *De lege agraria* ('On the agrarian law') Three speeches delivered by Cicero in 63 BC; *see* CICERO (1) 2.

**contrôve'rsiae** Latin rhetorical exercises in the oratory of the law-courts; *see* SENECA (1) and NOVEL.

**Cōpa** Short Latin elegiac poem doubtfully attributed to Virgil; *see* APPENDIX VIRGILIANA.

**Corax** (of Syracuse, first half of the fifth century BC) Said to have been the first Greek teacher of *rhetoric, including *Teisias among his pupils. He was interested in arguments from probability.

**Corcȳ'ra (Kerkyra)** (modern Corfu) Island in the Ionian Sea in north-west Greece, off the coast of Epirus, identified by the ancients with Scheria, the land of the Phaeacians in Homer's *Odyssey* (book 5). Colonized first by Eretrians, and then in 734 BC by Corinthians, it was, and is, an important port on the western sailing route between Greece and Italy. In consequence of a quarrel with Corinth in 435 BC (one of many in its history) it made an alliance with Athens in 433. Serious political strife between oligarchs and democrats in 427 resulted in wholesale massacre, memorably described by Thucydides (3. 69 and 4. 46–8). Corcyra remained an Athenian ally until 410, but rejoined the Athenian league in the fourth century BC.

**Corē** ('the maiden') In Greek myth, *Persephone.

**Cori'nna 1.** Greek lyric poet from Tanagra in Boeotia, thought in ancient times to be an older contemporary of her fellow countryman the poet Pindar, and thus of the second half of the sixth century BC. But her spelling of the Boeotian dialect and the lack of early references to her have led to the suggestion that she lived c.200 BC. The question is still unresolved. The fragments of her poetry which survive in quotation have been augmented by the substantial remains of two poems found in a papyrus (see PAPYROLOGY). One concerns a singing contest between the mountains Cithaeron and Helicon, each traditionally associated with the Muses and so with poetry (Helicon loses); the other is from the speech of a seer to the river-god Asopus explaining the disappearance of the latter's nine daughters. The poems are written in regular stanzas using simple lyric metres. According to an ancient anecdote Corinna criticized the absence of myth from one of Pindar's poems; when he thereupon went to the other extreme she remarked that one should 'sow by handfuls, not with the whole sack', an expression which became proverbial.

**2.** In Ovid, see AMORES.

**Corinth (Korinthos)** One of the most important cities of ancient Greece, mentioned in Homer's *Iliad*, where it is also referred to by the name Ephyre. Strategically situated on the Isthmus joining north Greece to the Peloponnese, between two important seas (the Ionian and Aegean), it was therefore destined to be a great maritime power. Commanding one of the three passes from the Isthmus to the Peloponnese, it was one of the three 'fetters of Greece', as Philip V called them; more importantly, it was situated on an east–west trade route. It was easier to drag small ships across the Isthmus (see CORINTH, ISTHMUS OF) or unload from ships on one side and reload on to different ships on the other, than to risk a long and stormy voyage around the Peloponnese. The territory of Corinth (Corinthia) was not fertile except for the coastal plain.

Corinth is connected with the early history of Greek literature through *Arion and *Eumelus. In myth it is associated with *Sisyphus and his descendants; *Medea and Jason fled there after the former contrived the murder of Jason's uncle Pelias. Intensive occupation developed from the late tenth century BC onwards. The tradition was that from 747 until 657 BC the city was ruled by the Dorian oligarchy of the *Bacchiadae, under whom Corinth founded the colonies of *Corcyra and Syracuse in 734, and remains found on the site attest the city's widespread foreign contacts. In 657 the Bacchiads were overthrown by the tyrant *Cypselus and under him and his son *Periander (c.625–585 BC) Corinthian power and prosperity reached their zenith. Three years after the death of Periander, who was succeeded by his nephew Psammetichus, the tyranny fell and was replaced by a narrow oligarchy. The city became a Spartan ally but then turned to Athens, alarmed perhaps by Spartan power (see CLEOMENES (1)). Corinth was one of the cities that fought with the Greeks in the Persian Wars. With the growth of Athenian imperialism in the second half of the fifth century (see ATHENS 3) relations with the Athenians deteriorated, and disputes between Athens and Corinth over Corcyra and *Potidaea (another Corinthian colony) contributed to the outbreak of the Peloponnesian War in 431. Corinthians were among the most active and persistent opponents of Athens throughout the war and joined in the successful defence of their colony Syracuse. After the war, however, Corinth joined Athens, Argos, and Boeotia to make war against the tyrannical rule of Sparta (the Corinthian War, 395–386 BC). That war ended with the *King's Peace, also known as the Peace of Antalcidas (a Spartan general), engineered with the aid of Persia. In the war against Philip II of Macedon, Corinth joined Athens in the cause of Hellenic freedom. After the defeat of the Athenians and Thebans at Chaeronea (338), it was at Corinth that Philip summoned a congress of Greek states to form the Corinthian league under Macedonian supremacy, Corinth becoming one of its principal strongholds. In 243 it was captured by Aratus, and joined the *Achaean confederacy. Afterwards Corinth passed into Macedonian control until Flaminius' victory over Macedon in 198–196 BC, when it was declared free like all other Greek cities and became the chief city of the Achaean confederacy. In the course of Rome's operations against the confederacy it was completely sacked by Mummius in 146 BC in revenge for the insults suffered by the Roman ambassadors, and its population slaughtered or enslaved. It was the extinction, as Cicero said, of 'the light of all Greece'. The *Greek Anthology* (9.151) contains a moving lament by a contemporary poet. After a century of desolation it was refounded by Julius Caesar as a colony (46 BC). When the apostle Paul visited it about a hundred years later it was the capital of the Roman province of Achaia, and a prosperous and populous city. It became notorious for luxury and excessive refinement; the adjective 'Corinthian' has been used in English with a similar connotation.

**Corinth, Isthmus of** The neck of land east of the city of Corinth, 6km (4 miles) wide at its narrowest. Across it merchandise was transported from one sea to the other and on occasion ships were dragged along a portage-road (*diolkos*), still visible in part, perhaps built by *Periander. It was also the site of the *Isthmian games. Octavian's fleet was dragged across in pursuit of Antony and Cleopatra after the battle of *Actium in 31 BC. The emperor Nero undertook the work of cutting a canal through the Isthmus (as others, from Periander onwards, had contemplated before him), and actually started it with his own hands and a golden pick-axe; but it was discontinued after a considerable amount of excavation had been done.

**Corinthian War** (395–386 BC) Corinth, Athens, Argos, Boeotia, and others against Sparta. *See* CORINTH.

**Coriolā'nus, Gnaeus Ma'rcius** One of the great legendary heroes of Rome, a general who according to tradition won his name (*cognomen*) from the capture of the Volscian town of Corioli in 493 BC (*see* VOLSCI). His arrogance towards the people during a corn shortage led to his prosecution by the tribunes on the charge of aspiring to become tyrant, and subsequent exile. He withdrew to his old enemies the Volscians, led them against Rome, and approached within five miles of the city. Moved by the pleas of his mother Veturia and his wife Volumnia (in Plutarch, Volumnia and Vergilia respectively), he withdrew his army and returned to the Volscian city of Antium (Anzio), where he was put to death by the Volscians. His story is told by Livy (book 2). Shakespeare's play *Coriolanus* depends upon the Life written by Plutarch.

**Cornē'lia** (second century BC) Mother of the *Gracchi, famous in her day and after as the ideal Roman matron, distinguished for her virtue and accomplishments. She was the second daughter of *Scipio Africanus, and married Ti. Sempronius Gracchus (d. 153). Of her twelve children only the two famous tribunes Tiberius and Gaius Gracchus, and a daughter Sempro-

nia who married Scipio Aemilianus, survived childhood. After her husband's death she devoted herself to the management of the estate and the education of the children. She remained an important influence on her sons. Tiberius was said to have been urged on to propose his laws by his mother's reproach that she was known as the mother-in-law of Scipio, not the mother of the Gracchi. Plutarch tells the well-known story that when a visitor asked to see her jewels she produced her sons, saying 'These are my jewels.' Two fragments of letters from her to Gaius appear to have survived in quotation but their authenticity is disputed.

**Cornē'lius Sevē'rus** Roman epic poet of the late first century BC; *see* EPIC 2.

**Corno'vii** British tribe which occupied what is now Staffordshire, Cheshire, and Shropshire, centred on Viriconium (Wroxeter) and later on Deva (Chester).

**Cornū'tus, Lucius Annae'us** Philosopher at Rome in the first century AD. *See* LUCAN and PERSIUS.

**Corōnē'a (Korōneia)** The scene of two battles in Boeotia.

**1.** In 447 BC, the Athenians, under Tolmides, were defeated by the Boeotians with Locrians, Euboeans, and others, and had to surrender the sovereignty they had exercised over Boeotia and central Greece for the previous ten years (*see* ATHENS 3).

**2.** In 394 BC the Spartans under *Agesilaus II defeated the Boeotians and their allies, including Athens. Xenophon, present at the battle, described it as 'unlike any other fought in our time'.

**Corō'nis** In Greek myth, the mother of *Asclepius.

**correption** In metre, the shortening of a long vowel or diphthong at the end of a word when the following word begins with a vowel. It occurs frequently in Homer, much less frequently in other poets.

**Coryba'ntēs** Male priests associated with various gods who had orgiastic cults such as Dionysus, and in particular the companions of the Asiatic goddess *Cybele, whom they followed with wild dances and music, inducing madness in others. They were often confused with the *Curetes, the attendants of Rhea.

**Cory'cian cave 1.** In Greece, a celebrated cave on Mount Parnassus above Delphi, sacred to *Pan and the nymphs. The Delphians used it as a refuge in 480 BC during the Persian invasion; it was the scene of one of the miraculous happenings that brought about the Persians' precipitate retreat from Delphi (Herodotus 8. 36).

**2.** A cave at Corycus in Cilicia (on the southern coast of Asia Minor), the reputed dwelling of the giant *Typhoeus (Typhon), and famous for its saffron-producing crocuses. Corycus was the home of Virgil's *Corycius senex*, 'old man of Corycus', the gardener of *Georgics* 4.125.

**coryphae'us** Chorus-leader; *see* CHORUS.

**cosmetics** Ancient literature gives the impression that although the Romans in the early republic scorned bodily enhancement, in the early empire they used make-up and perfumed oils far more enthusiastically than the Athenians. An Athenian husband, quoted by Xenophon, advises his wife to take exercise (some Greek women led very enclosed lives) to acquire a good colour rather than having recourse to paint or powder (a preparation of white lead) and rouge (from a variety of plants). The implication is that by wearing make-up she would look like a prostitute. She might also have lengthened her eyebrows by brushing on a preparation of soot and darkened her eyelids with powdered antimony. Women in comedy do these things to appear more attractive, and a wife is described by Lysias as having her cheeks whitened when she waited for a lover's visit, although she should still have been in mourning for her brother who had died 'not thirty days before'. Some Greek men may have used make-up, notoriously the pro-Macedonian governor of Athens, *Demetrius of Phalerum, who used a dye to colour his hair blond and put rouge on his cheeks. *Alcibiades, shortly before he was killed, had a dream in which his mistress was making up his face with rouge and white lead.

Compared with Athens, we know of a greater variety of ointments, oils, and salves used in imperial Rome by men and women. These gave the body and the hair a good colour as well as fragrance. (Cicero instanced scented hair-oil as effeminate.) Some anointed themselves two or three times a day, and perfume (associated with eastern royalty) was used lavishly. The trade in perfumes was huge: Capua,

a city much given to luxury, had one street entirely devoted to perfumiers. The Elder Pliny says that the emperor Caligula, who invented scented bath-oil, even had the walls of the baths washed with it. The Romans seem to have gone further than the Greeks in the use of facial cosmetics, emphasizing the blueness of the veins of the temple, and wearing patches on the face: the Younger Pliny mentions a distinguished lawyer and orator who moved his patch from eyebrow to eyebrow according to whether he was speaking for the prosecution or the defence. Preparations used by Romans for cleaning the complexion sound unappealing: oily wool from the rear-end of a sheep and, more exotically, powdered crocodile dung.

**cosmology** In the ancient world, branches of science which today are quite separate studies were treated as a unity. Speculation and investigation—virtually the same thing for the early Greek thinkers—embraced both the structure and composition of the universe and the origin and nature of life here on earth. *Presocratic philosophers explained the workings of the body in terms of what they individually thought was the original stuff of the universe (water, for Thales) or the *elements out of which it was made (most influentially earth, water, air, and fire for Empedocles). *See also* ASTRONOMY and METON.

**cothu'rnus (kothornos)** The 'buskin' or calf-length laced boot of soft leather with a thin sole and turned-up toes worn by actors playing heroic roles in Greek *tragedy, and hence the symbol of high tragedy. The famous tragic buskin with a sole several inches high was an invention of the late Hellenistic age. Since the boot could be worn on either foot, the word was used as a nickname for a politician prepared to support either side, a 'trimmer' (*see* THERAMENES). *See also* CREPIDATA and SOCCUS.

**Cottus** *See* HECATONCHEIRES.

**council** *See* BOULE.

**courtesans** *See* HETAIRAI.

**Crannon** Town in Thessaly, the home of the powerful family of the Scopadae (*see* SIMONIDES). The battle of Crannon in 322 BC was a Macedonian victory over the Athenians in the *Lamian War.

**Crantor** (of Soli in Cilicia, on the southern coast of Asia Minor, *c*.335–275 BC) A Greek philosopher belonging to the *Academy at Athens, who wrote a commentary on Plato's dialogue *Timaeus*. His work 'On grief' was much admired by later writers including Cicero, who used it as a model for his own (lost) 'Consolation' written to comfort himself on the death of his daughter Tullia (*see* CICERO (1) 4).

**crāsis** In Greek grammar, the running-together of a vowel or diphthong at the end of a word with a vowel or diphthong at the beginning of the next, the two syllables being thus joined together, with consequences for the spelling and, in verse, the scansion; e.g. *kai ego* ('and I') becomes *kāgo*. Cf. synizesis, where the spelling of the two words remains unaffected.

**Crassus 1. Lucius Lici'nius Crassus** (140–91 BC) The outstanding Roman orator of his day and chief exemplar for Cicero, who makes him the main speaker in his *De oratore* and praises him for his *gravitas*. He was a strong supporter of the aristocracy. His style was Asianic, but not excessively so. His speeches have not survived.

**2. Marcus Lici'nius Crassus** (115–53 BC) The so-called triumvir, the son of Publius Licinius Crassus (under whose consulship in 97 BC the senate prohibited human sacrifice). He was one of *Sulla's lieutenants, and had made a fortune in the *proscriptions. In 71 he put down the slave revolt led by *Spartacus, who had defeated the consuls in the previous year, but *Pompey took the credit. He was consul in 70 with Pompey whom he now felt to be his rival. They greatly modified Sulla's constitution and diminished the power of the senate. In the following years Crassus increased his fortune, and by helping suitably eminent or promising men in need (such as Julius *Caesar) he gained much influence. When Caesar returned from Spain in 60 BC, he, Pompey, and Crassus made an informal coalition, known in modern times as 'the first *triumvirate', with the purpose of enabling each man to achieve his particular aim. Crassus helped Caesar to become consul in 59. In 55 Caesar procured the consulship for both Pompey and Crassus, and arranged for Crassus to proceed afterwards to the province of Syria, which the latter reckoned to be the place to acquire wealth and military glory by a victory over the Parthians. In the event the Romans suffered an appalling defeat at Carrhae in 53 and Crassus was subsequently murdered by the Parthians. The Parthian king was celebrating the marriage of his son and entertaining the wedding party with a performance of Euripides' *Bacchae*, when a messenger arrived with the head and hand of Crassus. To the delight of the spectators the actors applied to Crassus' head the lines in the play referring to that of Pentheus.

**Cratēs 1.** Of Mallus, Greek scholar and grammarian of the second century BC. Visiting Rome as an envoy from Pergamum, probably in 159 BC, he broke his leg in the *Cloaca Maxima. The lectures he gave during his convalescence were said to have stimulated interest in Greek scholarship.

**2.** Of Thebes (*c*.365–285 BC), *Cynic philosopher and poet. Having gone to Athens as a young man he was won over by the example of *Diogenes (1) and became famous for the wholehearted way in which he embraced Cynic doctrine. Having renounced his large fortune, and restricting himself to absolute necessities, he achieved a high degree of self-sufficiency. Hipparchia, the daughter of a rich family, threatened suicide in order to persuade her parents to let her share his life. He was not as extreme or as intolerant as Diogenes, and he earned a reputation for reconciling enemies—being a 'door-opener'—and for kindliness—a 'good spirit'. Fragments of his poems show him to have been a witty reworker of passages from Homer and Solon in Cynic style. Crates originated the type of mendicant Cynic philosopher who wandered the Greek world with stick and knapsack, the frequent object of mockery. Cynic beggars of this kind suddenly proliferated in the first and second centuries AD, and still existed in the sixth; the contrast between them and true Cynic philosophers became a literary commonplace.

**Cratī'nus** Writer of Greek Old Comedy; *see* COMEDY [Greek 4].

**Cra'tylus** Dialogue by *Plato on the origin of language and on etymology, much of it written in a teasing style that makes interpretation difficult. The date too is hard to fix. Cratylus was a follower of the philosopher *Heracleitus, from whom Socrates learned that 'everything is in flux'.

In the dialogue, Cratylus claims that names of things in all languages have by their nature (*physis*) affinity with their objects, whereas Hermogenes argues that they are merely labels imposed by convention, *nomos*, and can be changed at will (*see* NOMOS–PHYSIS ANTITHESIS). Socrates disclaims any knowledge on the subject but joins in the discussion by asking questions of each of them in turn, producing himself a long series of incredible etymologies. The conclusion is that it is the absolutes, absolute beauty, absolute good, and so on (*see* PLATO 5 and PLATONISM) that we need to study, not the particulars and their names. *See also* ETYMOLOGY.

**cremation** *See* DEAD, DISPOSAL OF.

**Cre͞'mera** *See* FABIA, GENS.

**Cremū'tius Cordus, Aulus** Roman historian who wrote in the early first century AD a history from the civil wars to 18 BC or later, celebrating the republicans Cicero, Brutus, and Cassius. He committed suicide when prosecuted by the emperor Tiberius because, it was said, he called *Cassius (one of Caesar's murderers) 'the last Roman'. At his death his work was burnt.

**Crēon** ('ruler', 'prince') Name given to several figures in Greek myth; *cf.* CREUSA, 'princess'.
  **1.** King of Corinth, with whom Jason and Medea took refuge (*see* ARGONAUTS). Jason abandoned Medea in favour of marriage with the king's daughter, and in revenge Medea contrived the death of father and daughter.
  **2.** Brother of Jocasta, the wife of *Oedipus, king of Thebes. He ruled Thebes on three occasions: after Laius' death, after Oedipus' downfall, and again after the death of Oedipus' son Eteocles (*see* ANTIGONE). He gave his daughter Megara in marriage to Heracles (*see* HERACLES, MADNESS OF).

**crepidā'ta, fa'bula** Term applied to a Roman *tragedy on a Greek theme, such as the tragedies of Accius and Pacuvius; from *crepida*, the Latin word for the high boot, *cothurnus*, worn by Greek tragic actors.

**Crete (Krētē)** (Lat. Crēta) Mediterranean island to the south-east of Greece and the south-west of Asia Minor. Its position makes it a natural stepping-stone from Europe to Egypt, Cyprus, and the eastern Mediterranean. Holding therefore an intermediate position in early times between the ancient civilizations of the Near and Middle East and the western Mediterranean, it was well suited to become the site of the earliest European high civilization.

The British archaeologist Sir Arthur Evans, who began excavations on the island in 1899, named this *Bronze-age culture Minoan civilization, after Minos, the legendary early king of Crete. Evans divided it into three main phases, Early, Middle, and Late Minoan (EM, MM, LM), covering the period c.3500–c.1100 BC. Each was further divided into periods, I, II, and III. Further subdivisions have since been made, e.g. LMIIIA, LMIIIA1. Sometimes the periods are named with reference to the island's palaces (see below), so for example EM becomes pre-palace and LM late-palace or post-palatial. Absolute dates are established through connections with Egypt (which has an absolute chronology) and refined by radiocarbon and (where appropriate) tree-ring dating. The chief sites are at *Cnossus, Phaestus, Mallia, and Khania (in classical times known as Cydonia); other smaller sites have also been excavated.

The Early Minoan period (c.3500–2000 BC), which succeeded a long Neolithic age, was marked by a new style of pottery and a rise in population, indicating the arrival of some new settlers. Knowledge of bronze-working became widespread by c.2500 BC. In the centuries following, the evidence of burial sites indicates a social hierarchy and shows affinities to the centralized societies of the eastern Mediterranean. Cultural links with the Cycladic Islands also become apparent. The end of this period marked the start of the great period of Minoan civilization, c.2000–1470 BC (MMI–LMI), when the first palaces were built. These were structured to contain large storage rooms, the contents of which were recorded in two kinds of script, so-called Cretan hieroglyphic (chiefly at Cnossus and Mallia) which was pictorial and used on seals, and *Linear A at Phaestus. The language has not so far been identified. The palaces were also centres for the import of raw materials, copper from Attica, tin and ivory through Syria, which were used for works of fine craftsmanship. Contacts were maintained with Greece and the Aegean islands. Cult-sites were developed at this time, at caves, springs, and, most characteristically, at mountain tops. Population increased and spread around the palace sites. In MMIIA at about the end of the eighteenth century BC all three palaces were destroyed, probably by earthquake rather than war. Afterwards they were entirely rebuilt, in the period MMIIIA, sometimes known as the neo-palatial or second palace period. Contact with the Greek world, the eastern Mediterranean, and Egypt was maintained; notable frescos appear on the walls of the palaces and are seen most strikingly at Akroteri on the island of Thera, evidence of Minoan influence there. During this period a new type of settlement appears, the so-called 'villas', having many of the functions of the palaces though on a smaller scale and also using the Linear A script. The architectural uniformity of the palaces and the widespread use of Linear A have suggested to some that Crete might at this time be wholly under the dominion of one ruler or government located at Cnossus. This period came to an end in LMIB (roughly 1470 BC) with a series of destructions which included the palace at Phaestus but excluded Cnossus. Later, in the post-palatial period, Cnossus was finally destroyed. The date of this last event is controversial but may be as late as *c.*1200 BC; see below. However that may be, during the time of its destruction clay tablets appear at Cnossus written in *Linear B, the language of the Mycenaeans. One implication is that by the time Cnossus was destroyed Crete was being ruled by Mycenaean Greeks, whether in the fifteenth century BC or later, who may therefore have been responsible for destructions in the mid-fifteenth century.

In the second half of LMIIIB (*c.*1250–1200 BC) many settlements on Crete were abandoned or destroyed (*see* MYCENAE), as was the case in other parts of the Aegean world, and this may have included the final destruction of Cnossus. Some Minoan settlements, including Cnossus, were reoccupied during the following Iron age (from 1000 BC). Very few cult-sites were revisited, but Crete's strategic position ensured its continuing fame. Homer talks of 'Crete of the hundred cities' (more than half of which are known). In historical times Crete was predominantly *Dorian; it was governed by an aristocracy and its important cities were Cnossus (still), Gortyn, and Lyttos, and later Cydonia (Khania). It had a reputation for producing good slingers and archers, and also lawgivers. During the fifth and fourth centuries BC the island lay outside the main events of Greek history. By the late third century BC, the notoriety of Crete as a refuge for pirates rivalled that of Cilicia. The pirates supported *Mithridates VI, king of Pontus, against Rome, but those in

Crete were crushed in 68–67 BC by the Roman general Q. Metellus, who captured many cities and destroyed Cnossus. Thereafter Crete became a Roman province.

**Cretheus** Son of *Aeolus (2) and Enarete, father of Aeson (*see* ARGONAUTS).

**cretic** In metre the sequence - ⌣ -.

**Crĕū'sa** (Gk. Kreousa, 'Princess', the feminine form of *Creon) In myth the name of several heroines of whom the best-known are the following.

1. Daughter of Erechtheus, king of Athens, wife of Xuthus and mother, by Apollo, of *Ion (1).

2. Daughter of the Trojan king *Priam and his wife Hecuba, wife of Aeneas and mother of Ascanius. According to Virgil's *Aeneid* she died in the flight from Troy after its capture by the Greeks. Her ghost warns Aeneas of the adventures that lie before him.

**Crīsa** (or **Crissa** or **Cirrha**—whatever the original differences, the names were used interchangeably in classical times) A Mycenaean city in Phocis, whose territory included a fertile plain. The name is often used to denote Delphi, which was a few kilometres to the northwest.

**Cri'tias** (*c.*460–403 BC) At Athens, an extreme oligarch, from an aristocratic family, a cousin of Plato's mother. He played little or no part in the oligarchic revolution of the *Four Hundred in 411, but went into exile *c.*406, returning when Sparta defeated Athens at the end of the Peloponnesian War (404). Being an admirer of Spartan ways he became one of the *Thirty Tyrants; according to Xenophon he proposed the execution of his more moderate colleague Theramenes. He was killed fighting against Thrasybulus in 403 BC in the civil war that ended the tyranny of the Thirty. Like his friend Alcibiades he associated with the sophists and with Socrates. He wrote elegiac poems and tragedies, some fragments of which survive. Plato, who disapproved of the excesses of the Thirty, nevertheless honoured his memory in the dialogues *Protagoras*, *Timaeus*, and *Critias* (*see* PLATO 2). *See also* ATHEISM.

**Cri'tias** Unfinished dialogue by *Plato which contains the myth of *Atlantis.

**Crīto (*Kritōn*)** Dialogue by *Plato.

Socrates is in prison, awaiting the time when he must submit to the death penalty by drinking hemlock. His friend Crito comes to him and proposes a means of escape, urging his duty to his children. Socrates replies that the only question is whether an attempt at escape would be a just act. Suppose the laws of Athens should remonstrate with him and ask why he, who was born and has lived under them, should now try to overturn them? Moreover, how will he gain by a life of exile? The requirement of the laws is that he should first act justly, and only afterwards think of life and children: that is what the laws say to him. Crito admits that he has no reply.

**Croe'sus** The last king of Lydia, reigned c.560–546 BC, son of Alyattes and proverbial for his great wealth. He subdued the Greek cities on the coast of Asia Minor, but in general he showed favour to the Greeks, making rich offerings to Greek shrines, especially Delphi; he also contributed to the building of the great temple of Artemis at Ephesus. The rise of Persia as a rival power led him to seek a decisive battle, and emboldened by an oracle from Delphi which in the event proved ambiguous ('If you cross the Halys you will destroy a great realm') he crossed the river Halys, the boundary of his empire, in an expedition against the Persian king Cyrus. Croesus was defeated and his capital Sardis taken. Legends telling of his fate seem to have sprung up soon after: that he set himself on his own funeral pyre, but was miraculously wafted to the *Hyperboreans by Apollo out of gratitude for his gifts to Delphi; or that he was spared after being put on a pyre while still alive by Cyrus, who, hearing Croesus recall the warning of *Solon about the uncertainty of life, reflected on his own mortality and repented of his murderous intention. *See also* CLEOBIS AND BITON.

**Cronus** In Greek myth, the youngest and most important of the *Titans, the older gods who preceded the Olympian *gods. The Titans were the children of *Uranus and *Gaia, Heaven and Earth. On the advice of his mother Gaia, Cronus castrated his father Uranus, releasing the other Titans from inside Gaia where Uranus had forced them to remain confined. Cronus then took as wife his sister Rhea, and from them most of the race of the Olympian gods was born: Hestia, Demeter, Hera, Hades, Poseidon, Zeus (*see* LETO). Because Cronus knew he was fated to be supplanted by one of them, he swallowed them all at birth, but when *Zeus

was born Rhea handed Cronus a stone instead and hid the baby in Crete (*see* CURETES (1)). When Zeus grew up he made Cronus disgorge the stone and all the rest of his children (a stone set up at *Delphi is by tradition the one disgorged). Cronus and the other Titans (with the aid of the *Giants and *Typhoeus) waged war against Zeus and the new gods (who were helped by the *Cyclopes and the *Hekatoncheires), but the Titans were eventually overwhelmed and consigned to *Tartarus. The extraordinary narrative of this succession myth is paralleled by myths current among eastern peoples, notably the Phoenicians and the Hittites, in the second millennium BC, and it is likely that it reached Greece from these sources. The act of castration represents the separation of heaven and earth, a common motif in mythology from many parts of the world. The cruelty of this version is in sharp contrast with another group of stories which represent the period when Cronus ruled, after he had overthrown Uranus, as a *Golden age on earth. Cronus is mainly a figure of myth (rather than of religion) and so rarely the object of cult. The Romans identified him with *Saturn.

**Croton (Krŏtōn)** (Lat. Crŏtōna or Cortōna; modern Crotone) Achaean Greek colony on the toe of Italy, somewhat south of its rival Sybaris, settled by *Achaeans from the Peloponnese in 709 BC. It became a large and flourishing city, founding its own colonies, and famous for its doctors and athletes. It won a notable victory against Sybaris at the river Crathis in 510 BC (its army led by its most famous athlete, *Milo), reaching the height of its power as a consequence. Pythagoras settled there c.530 BC and founded his school, and for a while the Pythagoreans dominated the politics of the city. Croton was conquered by Dionysius I of Syracuse in 379 BC and suffered severely in the Roman wars against Pyrrhus and Hannibal. It is ironic that the Greek pastoral poet Theocritus chose it in Idyll 4 as the scene of tranquil country life at a time when it was being ravaged by war (first half of the third century BC). In 194 BC it was colonized by the Romans, but without lasting success.

**Crown, On the (Peri tou stephanou)** (Lat. *De corona*) Speech by Demosthenes in reply to Aeschines' general indictment of his policy. *See* DEMOSTHENES (2) 3.

**Ctē'sias** (of Cnidus in Asia Minor) Greek physician of the early fourth century BC, who lived for a number of years at the Persian court. He wrote a history of Persia in twenty-three books (*Persika*) and a geographical treatise as well as the first book to be devoted entirely to India (*Indika*). We possess a few fragments of these and synopses made by Photius (*Bibliotheca* 72), more entertaining than reliable.

**Ctē'siphon** *See* AESCHINES.

**cubit** A Greek unit of length. The normal cubit, the *pēchys*, was the distance from elbow to finger-tips, roughly 24 Greek 'fingers' (*see* MEASURES).

**Cu'lex** ('gnat') Latin poem in hexameters doubtfully attributed to Virgil (*see* APPENDIX VIRGILIANA).

**cult** Religious practice, the general term for the worship of a god or hero with ritual or rites in specially designated areas, which gives honour to its object. Believing in, respecting, or recognizing the gods was to both Greeks and Romans primarily a matter of observing their cult by traditional rites and rituals, of correct action irrespective of personal conviction or spirituality. The most important aspect of cult was making an offering to the god by *sacrifice, *libation, or dedication (i.e. the gift of an object). The offering was accompanied by prayer, on the principle of *do ut des*, 'I give [to you] so that you will give [to me]'. *See also* CHRISTIANITY IN THE ROMAN WORLD; RELIGION; RULER CULT.

**Cupid** [Lat. *cupīdo*, 'desire'] The Roman boy-god of love, son of Venus and Vulcan. He was an adaptation of *Eros, the childlike god of Hellenistic Greece with wings and a quiverful of arrows, and a figure of literature rather than of cult. He is familiar in the Latin poets, and especially in the first book of Virgil's *Aeneid* where Venus sends him to take the place of Ascanius, and to excite love for Aeneas in Dido. Later he appears in the fairy-story of Cupid and *Psyche, set in the narrative of the *Golden Ass*, a Latin novel of the second century AD by *Apuleius. Cupids appear on ancient coffins as a symbol of the life after death promised to initiates of the mystery religions (*see* MYSTERIES), and hence into churches as winged cherubs.

**Cupid and Psyche** *See* PSYCHE.

**Curcu'lio** ('Weevil') Name of the main character in this Roman comedy by *Plautus.

Phaedromus is in love with Planesium, a slave-girl, but lacks the funds to buy her from the pimp Cappadox. Curculio, a *parasite of Phaedromus, steals a seal-ring from the boastful soldier Therapontigonus, who has deposited with a banker a sum of money in order to buy Planesium for himself. By means of a letter sealed with this ring Curculio secures the girl for his master. Therapontigonus is furious at the fraud, but the ring reveals the fact that Planesium is his freeborn sister, and so he gets his money back and Phaedromus marries the girl.

**Cūrē'tēs 1.** In mythical times, young warriors who attended *Zeus and the goddess *Rhea. They were thought to be originally semi-divine people inhabiting Crete, to whom the infant Zeus was entrusted by his mother Rhea for protection against his father *Cronus; to conceal the child they danced around him, drowning his cries with the clashing of their weapons (*see also* AMALTHEA). They are often confused with the *Corybantes, who were properly the attendants of the Asiatic goddess Cybelē, because she was often assimilated to Rhea and to other mother-goddesses.

**2.** The name of an Aetolian tribe; *see* MELEAGER.

**cū'ria** Originally, one of the groups into which the Roman people was divided in the time of the kings, thirty in number, ten to each *tribe. They were the basis of the political and military organization of the state, such as it was. Each *curia* had its own meeting-place, and so the word came to mean 'a place of assembly', and in particular denoted the senate-house of Rome, situated on the north side of the Comitium in the Forum (*see* ASSEMBLY). This was known as the Curia Hostilia because its erection was ascribed to *Tullus Hostilius, king of Rome in the mid-seventh century BC. It was burnt down by the mob in 52 BC when *Clodius' body was placed on a pyre made up of its furnishings. A new curia was begun near the site of the old by Julius Caesar in 44 BC, and inaugurated by Augustus in 29 BC.

**Curiā'tii** *See* HORATII.

**Cu'rius Dentā'tus, Mā'nius** (d. 270 BC) Roman general, famous as epitomizing the Roman values of simplicity and severity. As consul in 290 BC he defeated the Samnites, bringing the Samnite Wars to an end. Consul for a second time in 275 he defeated *Pyrrhus at Beneventum (Benevento). His triumphal procession was adorned by four elephants, the first ever seen at Rome. He was consul for a third time in 274, and defeated Pyrrhus' Italian allies who were still in arms. When the Samnites tried to bribe him with costly presents, he replied that he preferred ruling over those who possessed gold to possessing it himself.

**cursive script** Name given to fluent, everyday handwriting and in particular to that used in the early centuries AD not only privately but by Greek and Roman scribes for official letters and documents. It was an influence in the development of the later book-hand known as minuscule (*see* TEXTS, TRANSMISSION OF ANCIENT 3 and 5). Some letter forms are unexpected; e.g. in Roman cursive E was written ||, N |||, and M ||||.

**cursus honō'rum** ('the sequence of magistracies', i.e. political offices) At Rome, a term signifying the order in which an individual held the various political offices. The *cursus* was determined by custom at an early date and first fixed by law in 180 BC. The customary pattern was service in the army followed by the increasingly responsible offices of quaestor (minimum age 30), praetor (40), consul (42), and censor. If the tribunate and the aedileship were held (which was not obligatory) they came after the quaestorship. Each office, except for the censorship (*see* CENSORS), was held for a year. The minimum interval between magistracies was set at two years, but this requirement varied at different times and was frequently ignored. To gain a magistracy 'in one's own year' (*suo anno*) meant at the earliest possible age (*see* CICERO (1) 2).

**Curtius** Hero of a Roman legend invented to explain a depression or pit known as Lacus Curtius ('Curtius' pond') in the Roman Forum, which had dried up and was paved over by the end of the first century BC. There were three versions of the legend: (i) a Sabine, Mettius Curtius, pursued by Romulus and the Romans, leapt with his horse into the swamp which covered the later site of the Forum; (ii) the consul Curtius in 445 BC had the area enclosed as sacred because it had been struck by lightning; (iii) (most famously) after a cleft had opened in the Forum (supposedly in 362 BC) and an oracle had said that the chief strength of Rome must be thrown into it before it would

close, a soldier Marcus Curtius, understanding the oracle's meaning, rode fully armed into the cleft.

**Cu'rtius Rufus, Quintus** Roman historian of the first century AD who wrote a history of Alexander the Great in ten books, of which the first two are lost. The extant books start in 333 BC with Alexander's march through Phrygia and the cutting of the Gordian knot. The narrative is dramatic and rhetorical, but founded on good sources though the detail cannot be relied upon. He lays stress upon Alexander's gradual moral deterioration.

**curule magistracies** In Rome, important magistracies which entitled the holders to use the *sella curūlis*, or 'chair of state', as a symbol of their authority. The 'chair' was in fact more like a folding stool, inlaid with ivory; it originated in Etruria, where it had been used in the royal chariot (Lat. *currus*) from which justice was administered. The entitled magistrates were censors, consuls, praetors, and the two 'curule' aediles. It was also the prerogative of a dictator and those immediately under him, and of the highest-ranking priest, the *\*flamen dialis*.

**Cy'belē (Kybelē)** (or in Lydian, Kybēbē) The great mother-goddess of Anatolia, associated in myth and cult with a young male companion *\*Attis*. Her fame spread all over the ancient world. The centre of her cult was on Mount Dindymus, at Pessinus in Phrygia, where she was called Agdistis, and where her image, of stone, was believed to have fallen from heaven. She was primarily a goddess of fertility, but also a goddess of wild nature, symbolized by her attendant lions. She was said to cure (and send) disease, and protect her people in time of war. Her worship often induced states of ecstasy and insensibility to pain in the worshippers. By the fifth century BC she was known in Greece and was soon identified with the local 'mother of the gods' and with Demeter. In 204 BC in the stress of the Second Punic War, and perhaps in accordance with a prophecy in the Sibylline books (*see* SIBYL) and advice from Delphi, the Romans sent a distinguished embassy to Pessinus on the delicate diplomatic mission of taking back to Rome the sacred black stone. On its voyage it had an escort of five quinqueremes. The temple built for the goddess's reception and dedicated in 191 BC (*see* PSEUDOLUS) stood on the Palatine, but the cult was kept under surveillance until the end of the republic. Except that they might join in her festival, the Megalesia, Roman citizens were forbidden to participate in her priesthoods and rituals. She was kept to her temple and served only by oriental priests (*see* GALLI) although processions of the priests were allowed (as described by Lucretius). In 186 BC the senate took steps to repress what they saw as a dangerous cult. These restrictions were lifted by the emperor Claudius. Worship of Cybele and Attis became part of the state religion, and one of the important mystery religions (*see* MYSTERIES) of the Roman empire. A belief in immortality was probably part of the appeal. Attis and Cybele came to be regarded as cosmic powers, and the soul may have been thought to return to them after death. Women in particular were attracted by the cult.

**Cy'clades** Archipelago of some 30 islands in the southern part of the Aegean Sea, so called because they form roughly a circle (*kyklos*). They include Delos, Ceos, Naxos, Paros, Andros, Tenos, and Thera, and offer a helpful route to sailors by which they can always be in sight of land. During the early and middle *Bronze age (a period which in the Cycladic region began *c.*3000 and lasted until *c.*1000 BC) they enjoyed an independent culture known as 'Cycladic'. From *c.*2000 BC cities developed, perhaps as a result of contact with Minoan *Crete, but later declined after the rise of Mycenaean Greece (*see* MYCENAE). In the eleventh century BC certain sites were fortified but later abandoned and destroyed. In about 1000 BC they were occupied by Ionic-speaking Greeks, with Delos as their cult centre. After the Persian Wars they joined Athens' *Delian League, and many joined the Second Athenian League after 377 BC.

**cyclic poems** *See* EPIC CYCLE.

**Cȳclō'pēs** (sing. Cyclops, 'Round-Eyed') According to Homer, one-eyed giants, living a pastoral life on a distant island without government or laws. Odysseus visited the cave of one of them, *Polyphemus. In Hesiod they were the sons of *Uranus (Heaven) and Gaia (Earth), three in number, called Brontes, Steropes, and Arges, who made the thunderbolts of Zeus and aided him in his war against the *Titans. They often appear as Hephaestus' workmen, and were credited with the construction of ancient walls, such as those of

Tiryns and Mycenae. In these cases they have little in common with the Cyclopes of the *Odyssey. See also* ASCLEPIUS and *CYCLOPS.*

**Cȳclops** Satyric drama by *Euripides, produced perhaps in 408 BC (*see* SATYR PLAY).

Hearing that the Greek god *Dionysus has been captured by pirates, Silenus has set out in pursuit, accompanied by his satyrs, and has fallen into the power of the Cyclops *Polyphemus. Odysseus and his crew arrive and bargain with Silenus for food in exchange for wine. Polyphemus returns and makes prisoners of Odysseus and his men. The blinding of the Cyclops and the escape of Odysseus are told much as in the *Odyssey. The whole subject is dealt with humorously.

**Cycnus** ('Swan') There are several figures of this name in Greek myth. The best-known are the following.

**1.** Son of Arēs, who robbed and killed travellers taking offerings to Delphi, and tried to build a temple to Apollo out of their skulls. He was killed by Heracles when the latter was on his way to fetch the apples of the Hesperides (*see* HERACLES, LABOURS OF 11, and *SHIELD OF HERACLES*).

**2.** Son of Poseidon, ally of the Trojans in the Trojan War, invulnerable to human weapons but strangled by the Greek hero Achilles when he tried to prevent the Greeks landing at Troy. The story is found in the **Cypria* but not in Homer.

**Cȳlon** Athenian noble who married the daughter of Theagenes, tyrant of Megara, and with his help seized the Acropolis at Athens with a view to setting himself up as a tyrant (perhaps in 632 BC). The Athenians under the archon Megacles laid siege to the Acropolis, and after Cylon and his brother managed to escape to Megara, killed their associates who had taken refuge at the altar of Athena. Those responsible for this sacrilege, especially Megacles and his family, the *Alcmaeonidae, were said to have incurred *pollution, and this was frequently invoked against them in later political disputes at Athens. Cylon was a winner at the Olympian games, perhaps in 640.

**Cynēge'tica** *See* OPPIAN.

**Cynēge'ticus** ('Treatise on hunting') A treatise by *Xenophon. Hunting was part of the traditional good life, enjoyed also by intellectuals, 'useful for reputation, life, and limb'.

After an exordium, exceptional in Xenophon's works, tracing the invention of hunting game with hounds to Apollo and Artemis, who handed it on to *Chiron, and he to a number of heroes, the author urges all young men to take up hunting, especially of hare on foot, with hounds. He begins by describing the necessary equipment, the nets, the hounds, and their points, but wanders on to the question of scent and the habits of the hare. He then returns to the trappings of the hounds, the proper way to fix the nets and call to the hounds, and the actual hunt; here Xenophon shows his enthusiasm. A passage follows on the breeding, training, and naming of hounds (47 names to choose from, all disyllabic for easy calling). The author next describes the hunting of deer (for which hounds and snares were used) and of wild boar (with hounds, nets, javelins, and spears), hazardous, but a matter of prestige, and gives a short chapter to the hunting of big game in foreign countries. He then enumerates the benefits of hunting to health, military prowess, and moral education. The treatise concludes with an attack on *sophists as useless and untrustworthy.

*Arrian also wrote a book on hunting, which still survives, in the style of Xenophon and as a supplement to his treatise.

**Cynics** [Gk. *cynikos*, 'dog-like'] In Greece, the 'dog-like' philosophers who followed the principles of the first Cynic philosopher *Diogenes of Sinope (but *see* CYNOSARGES). Diogenes had been given his nickname Cyōn, 'the dog', because, by applying his philosophy of 'living according to nature', i.e. living the life of a primitive human or an animal, in the most literal sense possible, his behaviour was as completely without shame as that of a dog. The Cynics developed no elaborate philosophical system. Cynicism was not so much a philosophy, since there was little scope for development of thought, as a way of life lived with varying degrees of strictness. The emphasis was on self-sufficiency. Diogenes' lifestyle was imitated, with some concessionary modifications, by *Crates, whose most famous disciple, *Zeno of Citium, the founder of Stoicism, made the link between the two philosophies.

The Cynics rejected *nomos* ('law', 'convention'; *see* NOMOS–PHYSIS ANTITHESIS) in all its forms—political and civic life, and authority; family ties; all distinctions based on gender, race, or social group (stemming from rejection of the city and the family); wealth; everything intellectual, educative, or cultural—material possessions, literature, music, and philosophy except for practical ethics: wisdom consisted in action rather than thinking. They were never organized into a school, so in practice they embraced a range of beliefs while maintaining as their central tenet that self-sufficiency could bring contentment in all the vicissitudes of life; virtue was supposed to be the natural consequence. This cast of mind led naturally to the mendicant life, and to mordant wit. The Socratic roots of Cynicism are evident in *Socrates' pursuit of wisdom in the marketplace rather than by founding a school like the *Academy, his ironic, and sometimes sarcastic, humour, his physical toughness as evidenced by his threadbare cloak and unshod feet, his outspokenness, and his belief that virtue was sufficient for happiness. Cynicism's own form of humanity, which derived from the belief that all people are equal, was philanthropy, concern for all fellow humans.

Cynics declined in number in the second and first centuries BC but Cynic beggars (*see* CRATES) proliferated in the next two centuries, and still existed in the sixth century AD. Christian ascetics were sometimes confused with Cynics, who were in fact a strong influence on them. Cynicism greatly influenced later philosophy, and Stoicism is a development of it. *See also* ANTISTHENES; BION (1); CERCIDAS; ONESICRITUS.

**Cynosarges** ('The place of the white dog') A gymnasium outside Athens where *Antisthenes taught. On this has been based an alternative explanation for the name *'Cynic'.

**Cynosce'phalae** In Thessaly, scene of the defeat in 197 BC of Philip V of Macedon by the Roman Quinctius *Flamininus which ended the Second Macedonian War. For an earlier battle there *see* ALEXANDER (4).

**Cynthia, Cynthius** Epithets given to the Greek gods Artemis (equivalent to the Roman Diana) and Apollo, derived from Mount Cynthus in their native island of Delos. 'Cynthia' was the name given by the Roman poet Propertius to his mistress (cf. Lesbia, the object of Catullus' love poems, named from the island of Lesbos, and *Delia).

*Cy'pria* (perhaps 'the epic composed in Cyprus') A lost poem of the Greek *Epic Cycle. It recounted, in eleven books, the events that led up to the point in the Trojan War at which Homer's *Iliad* begins, including the wedding of Peleus and Thetis, the Judgement of Paris, the abduction of Helen, the assembly of the Greek fleet, the rescue of Iphigeneia by Artemis at the moment of sacrifice, and the first engagements at Troy. The epic is sometimes ascribed to Stasinus of Cyprus or Hagesias of Salamis in Cyprus, hence the title (otherwise unexplained).

**Cȳprus** Economically and strategically important island in the north-east Mediterranean where copper has been extracted since prehistoric times. In the early *Bronze age it seems to have received settlers from Anatolia, and in later centuries traded with Egypt, the eastern Mediterranean, and *Crete. From *c.*1400 BC Mycenaean influence seems to have been dominant and by the thirteenth century Cyprus had become an urbanized society, to which trade in copper made a major contribution. During this Mycenaean period the Cypriots used a syllabic script derived from Cretan *Linear A, and now known as Cypro-Minoan, which was the ancestor of a syllabic script ('classical Cypriot'), related to Linear B and used from the seventh to the third centuries BC to write Cypriot Greek (*see* PHAESTUS). Cyprus shared in the turbulence of the late Bronze age (*c.*1200–1050 BC) but it also produced, briefly, a brilliant material civilization. Iron-age Cyprus possessed many city-kingdoms, which remained the pattern throughout antiquity. After 1050 settlers arrived, first Greek and later Phoenician, whose influence grew until in the fourth century BC much of central Cyprus was in Phoenician control. From the mid-sixth century BC Cyprus came under Persian rule, but it enjoyed a brief period of independence after the efforts of the philhellene *Evagoras in 411. In the late fourth century BC the island came under the control of the Ptolemies of Egypt for nearly two and a half centuries. It was annexed by Rome in 58 BC and attached to the province of Cilicia. The sanctuaries of *Aphrodite on the island, at Paphos and Amathus, were especially renowned, so that the goddess is often called simply 'the Cyprian' (Gk. Kypris, Lat. Cypria). According to one myth it was at Paphos that she was born from the sea-foam.

**Cy'pselus** Tyrant of *Corinth, who overthrew the aristocracy of the *Bacchiadae and founded a dynasty of tyrants, ruling himself from *c.*657 to 627 BC, when he was succeeded by his son *Periander. Under him Corinth grew in power and prosperity. His name was explained by a story, that his father Eëtion was of humble birth but had managed to marry a Bacchiad wife, Labda, because she was lame. As the result of an oracle prophesying their overthrow the Bacchiads tried to kill the son of the marriage, but his mother had hidden him in a box, *kypsele*, and he survived. A magnificent chest of cedar wood carved and decorated with figures in ivory and gold, purporting to be that of Cypselus, was dedicated by him or his son in the temple of Hera at Olympia and was seen there many centuries later by Pausanias. His description suggests that it was in the style of the seventh to sixth century BC.

**Cȳrenā'ic school** School of philosophy founded at Cyrene, probably not by *Aristippus but by his grandson. Its characteristic doctrine was that the present moment is the only reality, that immediate pleasure is the only end of action, and that knowledge is based on sensation. It was influential in the late fourth and early third centuries BC.

**Cȳropaedī'a (Kyrou paideia)** ('Education of Cyrus') Narrative by *Xenophon, in eight books, of the career of *Cyrus the Great, king of Persia, in which characters and historical facts are modified or invented to suit the author's didactic purpose. Writing roughly at the same time as Plato, who in the *Republic* argues for *his* conception of the education of an ideal ruler, Xenophon sets out his own idea of a political and military leader in the *Cyropaedia*, a work which strongly resembles a historical novel with a moral purpose. Cyrus himself is an idealized character, the perfect statesman, ruler, and general, drawn partly from the character of the younger *Cyrus (2) who was known to Xenophon and appears in his *Anabasis*. The constitution of Persia, and the method of education described, similarly represent Xenophon's ideals (based in part on the institutions of Sparta). The military precepts and the tactics described are Xenophon's own. There are numerous minor characters, kings, soldiers, and councillors, and among them the Indian tutor of the Armenian king's eldest son, Tigranes, unjustly put to death—a portrait intended to suggest Socrates. The tedium of the work (for most modern readers, though it was very popular in antiquity) is somewhat relieved by the romantic episode of the farewell of Abradatas (who is about to die in battle) to his wife Panthea. After the narrative of Cyrus' military campaigns is concluded with the capture of Sardis and Babylon, the work ends with a description of the organization of the Persian empire and the death of Cyrus. But by the time Xenophon came to write the end of the book it had become apparent that the Persian system was neither efficient nor progressive. The final chapter, describing the confusion resulting from Cyrus' death, was perhaps intended as a counterweight to the earlier admiration. *See* BIOGRAPHY.

**Cȳrus 1. Cyrus the Great** The founder of the Persian empire. He was the son of Cambyses I, of the Persian family of the Achaemenids, and when *c.*557 BC he became king of the small kingdom of Anshan in Persia he was subject to Astyages, king of Media. Beginning in 550 he conquered Media, Sardis, Lydia (capturing Croesus, king of Lydia), the Babylonian empire (thereby liberating the Jews from captivity; *see* BABYLONIA), Assyria, Syria, and Palestine. He administered a vast empire with wisdom and tolerance, being prepared to accommodate local rulers and local conditions while exerting tight overall control. To Xenophon he was an example of the ideal ruler (*see* CYROPAEDIA). His grave is at the Persian city of Pasargadae, near the place where he defeated Astyages. He was succeeded by his son *Cambyses II after his death in 530.

**2. Cyrus the Younger** Descendant of *Darius I, the second son of Darius II, king of Persia 424–405 BC. In 408 he held command in Asia Minor and being on friendly terms with the Spartan general *Lysander was able to attack the Athenians in Asia Minor effectively. When the Peloponnesian War ended he was at the coronation of his elder brother Artaxerxes II. He gathered together a mercenary army, which included Xenophon, ostensibly for an expedition against Pisidia, but in reality to oust his brother from the throne. A pitched battle was fought at Cunaxa in 401; Cyrus' army was defeated and he himself killed. The north-westward march of his Greek mercenaries to the Black Sea coast is the subject of Xenophon's *Anabasis.

**Cythē'ra** Island off the south coast of Laconia in the Peloponnese. Some Greek myths relate that Aphrodite landed there after being born from the sea-foam, hence she is sometimes called 'Cytherean' (but *see also* CYPRUS).

**Cythē'ris** *See* GALLUS.

**Cy'zicus** The scene of *Alcibiades' naval victory over the Spartans in 410 BC.

# D

**dactyl** [Gk. *daktylos*, 'finger'] In metre, the sequence – ◡ ◡.

**Dactyls, Idaean** (the 'Fingers' of Mount Ida) In Greek myth, magical smiths of small stature, the subject of obscure and conflicting stories. Located on either the Cretan or the Phrygian Mount *Ida, they were sometimes thought of as the beings in Crete to whom the infant Zeus was entrusted, and are then identified with the *Curetes; or they are confused with the *Corybantes. They may have originated in prehistoric times when the working of iron seemed a magical skill.

**Dae'dalus** ('Cunning worker') Legendary Greek artist-craftsman and inventor, thought of as living in the age of *Minos. Through his mechanical inventions the Greeks personified the development of sculpture and architecture; his impossibly ingenious devices provided the plot of many exciting stories. He was credited with the invention of the walking style for *kouroi, and it was said that his statues could move themselves. (His eponymous connection with the 'Daedalic' style in Greek sculpture is modern.) Being afraid that his nephew and pupil Talos would outdo him (for to the latter was ascribed the invention of the saw and the potter's wheel), Daedalus threw him down from the Acropolis (Pausanias saw his reputed grave at Athens in the second century AD) or into the sea (when Athena changed him into a partridge, *perdix*, by which name Talos was also known). Daedalus was condemned for his crime by the Areopagus and fled to Crete, where he constructed the *labyrinth for king Minos. (*See also* PASIPHAE.) Afterwards, Minos would not let him go; Daedalus then made wings for himself and his son Icarus out of wax and feathers, and they flew away. But Icarus flew too near the sun; the wax of his wings melted and he fell into the sea and was drowned. Daedalus landed on the island in the Sporades now called Ikaria and buried his son's body. He then escaped to King Cocalus in Sicily, where Minos followed in pursuit; enticed into Cocalus' palace, Minos was scalded to death in a bath of Daedalus' invention. Virgil at the beginning of book 6 of the *Aeneid* describes Daedalus arriving at Cumae in his flight from Minos and dedicating a temple there. Pausanias saw several statues said to have been sculpted by Daedalus, and accepted that he really existed.

**daimon** (pl. *dai'mŏnĕs*) In Greek, etymologically 'giver of share' or 'allotter' (of one's luck or destiny). The word is used loosely in Greek poetry to mean 'god' or 'the gods' or divine power generally without specifying any god in particular, and only occasionally designates an Olympian god. It is this power which gives people good or bad fortune at any time, so that they may feel that they have the *daimon* on their side, or else against them; thus *daimon* approximates in meaning to fate. (The philosopher Heracleitus declared that an individual's character is his *daimon*, perhaps asserting that destiny is determined by character, over which a person has some control.) The first *libation at a wine-drinking was made rather enigmatically in honour of the Good Daimon. Hesiod says that after death the men of the *Golden age were transformed by Zeus into wealth-giving *daimones*, able to confer prosperity on humankind. Perhaps this was one basis for honouring great and powerful men after death (*see* HEROES). In later literature and philosophy the *daimon* can represent an individual's personal fate. It came to be believed by some that a *daimon* accompanied each human life like a metaphysical guardian, a belief which Plato seems to adopt in *Phaedo*. In the myth of Er in the *Republic* he shows individual souls choosing their own *daimon*, fate in life, before rebirth, but more usually the Greeks believed that one's fate was allotted. The adjective *eudaimon*, 'fortunate and happy', described a person whose *daimon* was good. The notion of *daimones* as spiritual beings intermediate between gods and men may long have existed in popular superstition, but it is introduced into literature by Plato in the *Symposium*; Xenocrates, a pupil of Plato and head of the *Academy from 339 BC, extended the idea to include *daimones* who were evil spirits also, 'demons', and to relate them to the heavenly bodies. The view of the cosmos as populated by spiritual beings is that of the Stoics (and later the Neoplatonists) and is reflected in popular magic. *Empedocles refers to himself both as a god and as a *daimon*. For Socrates' 'divine thing' (*daimonion*, i.e. divine voice, sign, or power) *see* SOCRATES. *See also* FATE; DEMOCRITUS; PLUTARCH 3.

**damna′tio memo′riae** ('obliteration of the record') A Roman practice as punishment for a crime against the state, in which use of the condemned man's *praenomen* (*see* NAMES [Roman]) was forbidden in his family, every image of him destroyed, and all public mention of him erased.

**Da′moclēs** A courtier of Dionysius II, tyrant of *Syracuse in the fourth century BC. When he praised to excess the happiness of a tyrant, Dionysius invited him to experience it for himself. He placed Damocles at a banquet where presently the latter observed a naked sword hanging over his head by a single hair, symbolizing the precarious nature of such happiness.

**Damon** (fourth century BC) Pythagorean philosopher from Syracuse, proverbial for his friendship with Pythias (whose name in fact seems to have been Phintias). The latter, condemned to death, left Syracuse in order to arrange his affairs, leaving Damon to stand surety for him, and returned in time to redeem his friend. The ruling tyrant was so impressed by their friendship that he pardoned the criminal.

**Dana′ans (Dǎnǎoi)** One of the general names, along with Achaeans and Argives, for the Greeks in Homer and in later poets. More particularly, a Peloponnesian Greek people inhabiting the region of Argos in early times; thus the name Danaans sometimes signifies Argives. For their supposed origin *see* DANAUS.

**Dǎ′nǎē** In Greek myth, daughter of Acrisius king of Argos (brother of Proetus) and Eurydice. When an oracle foretold that Acrisius would be killed by his daughter's son, he imprisoned her. But Zeus descended on her in a shower of gold, and she bore a son Perseus. Acrisius

placed Danae and the child in a chest and cast them adrift in the sea (for a Greek lyric poem on the subject *see* SIMONIDES), but they landed on the island of Seriphos, where they were sheltered by Dictys, brother of Polydectes, the king of the island. For the conclusion of her story *see* PERSEUS (1).

**Da′naids (Dǎnǎidĕs)** In Greek myth, daughters of *Danaus.

**Dǎ′nǎus** In Greek myth, son of *Belus, king of Egypt, descendant of *Io, and brother of Aegyptus. The brothers' names show that they were regarded by the Greeks as the ancestors of the *Danaans and the Egyptians. Aegyptus had 50 sons, Danaus 50 daughters (the Danaids). These were betrothed to their cousins, but to escape this marriage fled with Danaus to Argos (the home of their ancestress Io), where they were received by the king Pelasgus. The sons of Aegyptus followed, and Danaus was forced to consent to the marriages, but he ordered his daughters to stab their husbands with daggers which he provided, on their wedding night. This they all did except Hypermnestra, who spared her husband *Lynceus. She was imprisoned and put on trial by her father, but the Argive court, perhaps through the intervention of Aphrodite, acquitted her. Pindar tells how Danaus, in order to select other husbands for his daughters, set these at the end of a race-course and let their suitors run for them. After their deaths the other Danaids were punished in the Underworld for their crime by having to try to fill leaky jars with water (apparently a Roman rather than a Greek motif). *See* SUPPLIANTS (1).

**dancing** In the ancient world, dancing, usually vigorous and often noisy, was a natural and inseparable part of many everyday activities, religious, social, and even military.

**1. In Greece.** The popularity of dancing is attested by the 200 or so names of dances which have come down to us. It is frequently mentioned in Homer as a natural entertainment: in the *Odyssey* the suitors of Penelope amuse themselves with music and dancing; Odysseus at the court of Alcinous is impressed by a display of especially skilful dancers. Entertainments of this sort, sometimes verging on the acrobatic (*see* the anecdote concerning *Hippocleides), sometimes including mimetic dances interpreting a story, might be provided at the end of a dinner-party (*symposium*) by professionals, slaves, or prostitutes hired for the purpose. Xenophon describes how, when he was on campaign, an evening's entertainment was concluded by a soldier's dancing girl performing a war-dance to amuse the Paphlagonian guests. Public religious festivals were accompanied by choruses singing and dancing with simple rhythmical movements (see CHORUS). Plato thought that all dancing should have this religious character. Dancing was also educative, associated with music and poetry in the art called *mousikē* which embraced all three elements and developed grace and beauty. The dances of the Ionians however, who were thought effeminate in classical Greece, came to be regarded as indecent. In a more bracing form dancing was a part of gymnastic training as a preparation for war, especially in Sparta; it trained soldiers in drill. Most celebrated of the war dances, usually performed with weapons, was the Pyrrhic dance, said to be of Cretan or Spartan origin. Its rapid body movements represented the way in which a soldier evaded blows and missiles.

Although people danced at social gatherings such as weddings, harvests, and victory celebrations, grown-up men and women did not dance together: the dances were for groups of people. One of the most famous was the Delian dance known as the *geranos*, invented according to tradition by Theseus and his companions when they stopped at Delos on the way back to Athens from Crete, its complicated figures commemorating the *labyrinth. Other distinctive dances were those of the Greek theatre, the stately *emmeleia* of tragedy, the lewd *cordax* of comedy, and the coarse and violent *sikinnis* of satyric drama.

**2. In Rome.** Dancing, though a common feature of life for country people, did not pervade Roman civic life to the same extent as in Greece. In early times it was common at religious festivals, the most famous dances being those of the *Salii and the *arval brethren. Military dances too existed among the Romans as among the Greeks: the *bellicrepa saltatio* ('dance to the sound of arms') was said to commemorate the capture of the Sabine women by Romulus. But by the second century BC the Romans in the city had a low opinion of dancing, and it was not engaged in by a citizen for purposes other than religious: Cicero observes in a speech that 'no sober man will dance unless he is mad'. In Terence's comedy

*Adelphoe*, Demea is shocked at the sight of his brother, the head of a household, dancing and singing at the prospect of his son's marriage. Hence the traditionalists' outrage when the emperor Nero danced in public was a natural Roman response. Mimetic dances, however, were developed to such a pitch that they became an independent art-form. See PANTOMIME.

**Daphnē** ('Laurel') In Greek myth, a nymph, daughter of a river-god (generally Ladon in Arcadia but also represented as Pēnēus in Thessaly). She was a huntress and wanted no lovers, but was pursued by Leucippus who joined her hunting companions disguised as a girl. When Daphne and her companions bathed after the hunt Leucippus was found out and killed. She also rejected the love of the god Apollo and fled from him, praying to the river-god Peneus for deliverance; she was thereupon changed into a laurel tree, the foliage of which became particularly associated with Apollo.

**Daphnis** Legendary Sicilian herdsman, a recurring figure of bucolic (i.e. pastoral) mythology, said to be the originator of bucolic song (see PASTORAL POETRY). His father was sometimes said to be the Greek god Hermes, his mother a nymph who exposed him under a laurel bush (*daphne*), from which his name is derived. He himself was mortal. He was loved by a nymph to whom he vowed eternal fidelity, but he was made drunk and seduced by a princess. Thereupon the nymph blinded him, and he consoled himself by inventing pastoral songs, or became himself the subject of the first bucolic poetry, composed by other herdsmen. There are variations on this story, notably in *Theocritus where Daphnis appears to die of love. Daphnis epitomizes the musician-shepherd, the ideal inhabitant of the idyllic pastoral world, his life and death powerfully signifying that even in such a world there is no escape from the pangs of unhappy love or from mortality.

**Daphnis and Chloe** Greek *novel of the late second or early third century AD in four books by Longus, of whom nothing is known other than that he appears to be from Lesbos, where the story is set. The distinctive feature of this romantic narrative is that the setting and atmosphere belong to the world of pastoral simplicity (see PASTORAL POETRY). The subject is the mutual love and sexual education of Daphnis and Chloe.

The story is presented as a description (*ec-phrasis*, which in this case becomes the background story) of a picture which Longus has seen. Found abandoned as infants, the hero and heroine are suckled by a goat and a ewe, and subsequently reared by their finders. When they grow up they look after herds and gradually fall in love with each other. Soon kisses and simple embraces fail to satisfy but they cannot discover how else to express their mutual passion. An experienced young wife from town observing their plight gives Daphnis a practical lesson, but he is too afraid of hurting Chloe to put his knowledge into practice, and in any case too poor to marry her. However, the Nymphs find money for him, rival lovers are defeated, the natural parents discovered, and the wedding leads to a happy pastoral life ever after. The innocent lovers were the inspiration for Bernardin de St Pierre's novel *Paul et Virginie* (1787).

**Da'rdanus** In Greek myth, son of Zeus and Electra, the daughter of the Titan *Atlas. The name is usually thought to be Illyrian. He was the ancestor of the kings of Troy, and was said to have lived in Samothrace (in the north Aegean), from where he went to Phrygia. The local king Teucer welcomed him and gave him part of his territory and his daughter as wife. Dardanus built a city on the slope of Mount Ida (south-east of the future site of Troy) and called it Dardania. Hence the Trojans are sometimes called 'Dardanians' (the name survives in the Dardanelles). In the Trojan War, the enmity of Zeus' wife Hera towards the Trojans in part originated from her jealousy of Electra for having won the love of Zeus.

**Darī'us (Dāreios) 1. Darius I** Son of Hystaspes, and king of Persia from 521 to 486 BC. He claimed to be, like Cyrus I (the Great), a member of the Persian *Achaemenid family; he succeeded to the kingdom after the death of Cyrus' son *Cambyses II by overthrowing a usurper who was impersonating Cambyses' dead brother. Restoring order after anarchy, he revised the boundaries of the provinces, creating twenty *satrapies, a system which was retained by later kings. He also built two new palaces, at Susa and Persepolis. About 514 Darius cut across Europe, marching through Thrace in a north-easterly direction in a show of force against the Scythians, and calling on the Ionian Greek cities to support him: these cities were his vassals, ruled by tyrants under the

general control of Persia. In 499 they revolted, but by 494 the revolt was suppressed. The cities of mainland Greece had been implicated and in 491 Darius sent envoys to Greece demanding submission. When this was not forthcoming he sent an army under his general Datis, which was defeated at Marathon in 490 (*see* PERSIAN WARS). Darius died four years later and was succeeded by his son *Xerxes, who continued the war against Greece. *See also* BISITUN.

**2. Darius III** (*c.*380–330 BC) King of Persia, descended from a collateral branch of the royal family. He was overthrown by Alexander the Great and died as the result of a plot.

**Dark age(s)** A term used to describe various turbulent periods of history when civilization was endangered and few records handed down. In the ancient world it refers to the following two periods.

(i) In Greece, the period from, very roughly, the twelfth to the ninth century BC. It begins with the upheavals that resulted in the final destruction of *Mycenae and ends with the emergence of Athens as a cultural force in Greece (*see* ATHENS 2 and GREECE 2).

(ii) In the later Roman empire, the centuries following the mainly Germanic invasions of the fifth century AD, very roughly from the fifth to the late eighth century. *See* ARABIA; BYZANTINE AGE; FALL OF ROME; LATE ANTIQUITY; TEXTS, TRANSMISSION OF ANCIENT 3.

**dates** *See* BRONZE AGE and CALENDARS.

**dead, disposal of** Correct disposal of the dead according to the custom of the time and place was always a matter of the greatest concern in the ancient world, and the idea of an unburied or uncremated corpse caused great unease. A symbolic scattering of three handfuls of earth on the corpse was sufficient to prevent pollution and to allow the spirit to enter the Underworld (*see* SOUL). It seems clear from Thucydides that men convicted of treason or sacrilege could be forbidden burial on home territory. Presumably the body would then be taken beyond the state boundary rather than be left to cause pollution. Except in earliest times burial took place in cemeteries outside the city, often in small grave plots lining the roads leading out of it. The forms of disposal in prehistoric Greece and Rome varied not only between cremation and inhumation but also in the kind of tombs or receptacles used. For a time in the late Bronze age on the Greek mainland rock-cut chamber-tombs were the norm, but regional variation returned in the following Dark age, with frequent change particularly noticeable at Athens. It is possible to generalize to the extent that in warrior burials the body was cremated and the ashes placed in a bronze urn, Homeric-style, and infants were usually buried inside jars. From the sixth century BC at Athens burials became simpler (perhaps as a result of sumptuary laws). Grave goods accompanying the dead seem to have been symbolic rather than seriously intended to equip them for an after-life, and the tradition of adding a coin to pay *Charon the ferryman, or lamp and shoes for the journey, was not always observed. From the fourth century BC expenditure increased in the rest of Greece on vaulted tombs in the so-called 'Macedonian' style, the name derived from the late fourth-century royal tombs at *Aegae. Cicero says that *Demetrius of Phalerum, governor of Athens, banned lavish tombs there (probably in 317 BC). Under Roman rule inhumation was the norm throughout the Greek East.

In prehistoric Italy burial customs were as varied as in Greece. Burials at Rome (until c.100 BC) were simple and have left few traces, in contrast with the Etruscans who built chamber-tombs which often contained cremations in urns and rich grave-goods. In Campania many fine Etruscan tomb-paintings have survived. In the third century BC cremation was on the increase and by the first century BC it was usual, though Varro mentions that in the late republic accommodation for mass burial in pits was made for the urban poor. At the same time the Roman nobility were beginning to create very elaborate tombs for themselves, a fashion the emperor Augustus abruptly ended. After c.AD 40 the *columbarium* became popular as providing decent burial for the less wealthy. (The name is a modern usage of the Latin for 'dove-cot', coined to describe the niches arranged in rows to contain the ashes of cremations in urns.) In the first and second centuries at Rome and throughout the western empire cremation was the norm (in contrast with the inhumation practised in the Greek culture of the eastern Roman empire). Fashion then changed, and from the second century AD and throughout the third century inhumation spread across the west. Although not connected, the change in practice was in accord with Christianity which in general opposed cremation. From the beginning of the fourth century AD at Rome there was

a movement in favour of burial in the catacombs and within basilicas.

Death was a polluting event to the Greeks and the Romans; anyone coming into contact with a dead body incurred *pollution, and would keep apart from other people and from sacred places for eight clear days. *See* DEATH, ATTITUDES TO.

**De agri cultū'ra (De re rustica)** ('On agriculture') Treatise by M. Porcius *Cato ('the Censor') written c.160 BC and the oldest piece of Latin prose of any length to survive. It is a concise, practical handbook for the owner of a medium-sized estate in Latium perhaps or Campania, dealing with the cultivation for profit of vines, olives, and fruit, and with cattle-breeding. Cato discusses the purchase of a farm; the duties of owner, overseer, housekeeper, and slaves; the tilling of the soil; the care of livestock; and a few minor matters, such as a prescription for treating a sick ox, recipes for curing hams and making cheese-cakes, and religious and superstitious formulas. The work is written in a curt, abrupt style, without much organization of material, but it was widely read and quoted from in antiquity. It was composed at a period when there was a vast increase in wealth at Rome with consequent social change. The preface expresses admiration for the traditional peasant farmer who becomes a hardy soldier in time of war. But throughout the work Cato is instructing the contemporary Roman absentee landlord in modern investment farming and the exploitation of slave labour, which will put an end to traditional farming.

**De amīci'tia** (in full **Laelius de amicitia,** 'Laelius on friendship') Dialogue by *Cicero ((1) 5) composed in the autumn of 44 BC and addressed to *Atticus. The dialogue is supposed to take place in 129 BC a few days after the death of *Scipio Aemilianus. The interlocutors are *Laelius, the intimate friend of Scipio, and his two sons-in-law, C. Fannius and the augur Quintus Mucius *Scaevola. Cicero in his youth had received instruction in the law from Scaevola and had heard him, he tells us, repeat the conversation. Laelius in his discourse discusses the nature of friendship and the principles by which it should be governed. The conclusion is that friendship is founded on, and preserved by, virtue; for it owes to virtue the harmony, permanence, and loyalty that are its essential features. This is one of the most admired of Cicero's dialogues for its dignity and calm and for the melodious quality of its polished prose.

It was one of the two books in which Dante found consolation for the death of Beatrice.

**De anima** ('On the soul') Treatise by *Aristotle, in three books, on life and living. Aristotle criticizes materialist views of the *soul and Plato's dualistic view—the idea of the soul as something that dwells in a body. Instead his proposition is that the soul of any living thing relates to its body as form to matter. Thus the soul, which is the life force, does not survive the death of the body though Aristotle seems also to say that the human soul possesses a portion of 'active reason' which is immortal and eternal, and perhaps akin to God. He proceeds to more biological accounts of how living things feed themselves, reproduce, perceive, and think.

**De architectū'ra** ('On architecture') Treatise in ten books on building and architecture, written towards the end of the first century BC by Julius Caesar's military engineer *Vitruvius. It is the only ancient work of its kind to have survived.

### death, attitudes to

**Greek.** An unequivocal acceptance of human mortality pervades Greek literature. The general Homeric idea that after death every soul, good and bad alike, continued to have a shadowy existence in a dark Underworld (*see* HADES and SOUL) seems to have persisted in some form throughout antiquity. However, in the first book of Plato's *Republic* the old man Cephalus describes how ideas about an Underworld with punishment there for wrongdoing (not a Homeric notion except for certain special offenders) may trouble the mind in old age whereas in youth such stories were laughed at. Plato at the end of *Gorgias* tells a myth which assumes a judgement of the dead. There seemed to exist a vague belief that there might be *post-mortem* reward and punishment for certain individuals. In the treatise *On Cheerfulness* by the atomist philosopher Democritus (which survives only in fragments), he includes advice on achieving contentment and avoiding fear of death. Yet a happy after-life promised to initiates of the mystery cults of Eleusis and Orpheus (and an unpleasant fate for the rest) seems to have been one of their attractions. On the whole the Greeks of the fifth and fourth centuries BC doubted whether the dead had any perception of what happens among the living, although as occasion required someone might suggest that a dead parent will rejoice at a child's success. It was possible to speak of bringing glory or shame upon one's ancestors. The necessity for burial rites is universally felt (*see* DEAD, DISPOSAL OF), and is a matter in which the gods take an interest. Tomb-*cult seems to have been little practised in early times, but in the fifth century BC women visited family graves with offerings of cakes and libations of pure water. Curses written on lead tablets are sometimes found in graves (and in wells and other places with a supposed entrance to the Underworld) because the dead were thought to have access to the gods of the Underworld, who might fulfil the curse.

**Roman.** From the sixth century BC, and perhaps earlier, Greek religious beliefs and philosophical speculation were a strong influence in Italy, and so the idea of an underworld is commonplace in classical and Augustan Latin literature, as is debate about the possible immortality of the soul. It was a Stoic idea that philosophers and statesmen might enjoy a divinely-appointed after-life together (*see* POSEIDONIUS and *SOMNIUM SCIPIONIS*). There were various views of death, but a specifically Roman belief was that the dead joined the *di *manes*, spirits of the dead, a kind of collective divinity in which the individual dead were undifferentiated. However, Romans could also refer to the *manes* or *di manes*, 'soul' or 'spirit', of an individual. Official state cult did not specify the fate of individuals after death. Graves received regular cult at the festivals of the Feralia, Parentalia, and Lemuria, as well as on the deceased's birthday; it was these celebrations that ensured that person's 'survival'. The Lemuria was held in order to propitiate the *lemures*, the spirits of the unburied dead which would come to haunt the houses of the living, having no resting place of their own. *See also* DEIFICATION and SOUL.

**De be'llo cīvī'li** and **De be'llo Ga'llico** *See* COMMENTARIES.

**De caelo** ('On the heavens') Treatise by *Aristotle on the movement of the earth and heavenly bodies. Aristotle knew that the earth was spherical but concluded that it was situated unmoving at the centre of the universe. *See* EUDOXUS; ARISTARCHUS; ASTRONOMY.

**Decelē'a (Dekeleia)** An Attic *deme northeast of Athens near the pass east across Mount Parnes. It was about 22km (14 miles) from Athens and visible from there; ships entering Piraeus were in its view. Its occupation by the Spartans from 413 to 404 BC, during the Peloponnesian War, at the suggestion of the

Athenian Alcibiades, put a stranglehold on Athens for the rest of the war and was one of the chief reasons for the decline of Athenian power according to Thucydides. The term 'Decelean War' is sometimes used to describe this last period, from 413 to 404. *See also* SLAVERY.

**decemviri (decemvirs)** ('ten men') In Rome the name was given to several boards of ten men set up for particular purposes. The most famous were the *decemviri legibus scribundis* (an early form of the classical Latin *scribendis*), 'decemvirs for writing down the laws', appointed in 451 BC with Appius *Claudius as their leader. Before that time the laws at Rome remained unpublished and inaccessible to the people, and it was thus easier for the ruling patricians to manipulate justice to their own advantage. *Decemviri stlitibus* (an early Latin form of *litibus*) *iudicandis* were 'decemvirs for judging cases'; they acted as a jury to decide whether an individual was a slave or free.

**Dĕ'cius Mus, Publius** One of the Roman consuls in 340 BC during the war with the Latins. According to legend he gained the victory for Rome by 'devoting' himself and the enemy to the gods of the Underworld (*see* DEVOTIO), and then charging into the enemy ranks to his death. His son of the same name played a similar part in 295 BC at the battle of Sentinum (Sassoferrato) against the Samnites. The latter instance of *devotio* is more likely to be historical (*see* FABIUS (1)).

**declamation** (Gk. *meletē*) In Roman *oratory under the empire (but originating with the Greek *sophists of the late fifth century BC), the chief means employed to teach young would-be orators in the rhetorical schools. These pupils were required to deliver a speech arguing on one side of an invented law-suit—a *controversia* ('argument')—or a deliberative speech arguing for a course of action in an historical or mythical situation—a *suasoria* ('speech of persuasion'). *See* ANTIPHON [*Tetralogies*]; GORGIAS [*Helen* and *Palamedes*]; SENECA (1); *see also* SECOND SOPHISTIC.

**De corō'na (Peri tou stephanou)** ('On the crown') Title of a speech by *Demosthenes ((2) 3).

**decuriones** ('councillors') Members of the local councils which ran local government in the Roman and Latin colonies and municipalities (*see* MUNICIPIUM). They held office for life

as long as they met the criteria of free birth, age, wealth, and reputation.

**De dīvinātiō'ne** ('On divination') Dialogue in two books by Cicero composed as supplement to his *De natura deorum* and published in 44 BC soon after Caesar's murder (*see* CICERO (1) 5). The Stoics accepted divination as part of their philosophic system, believing that the nature of the gods is adapted to reveal their will through prophecy. Cicero rejects their view but affirms his belief in a divine being. The dialogue takes place at Cicero's villa at Tusculum, between his brother Quintus and Cicero himself (Marcus). Quintus expounds, with a wealth of illustration and quotations from the Stoics, especially *Poseidonius (and also from Cicero's own writings), his reasons for believing in certain forms of *divination. Marcus explodes the belief in divination in general by this dilemma: future events are either at the mercy of chance or are foreordained by fate. If the former, no one, not even a god, can have foreknowledge of them; if the latter, there is no use in divination (i.e. investigation into the future in order to avoid unpleasant events) because what is foreordained cannot be avoided. Marcus thinks that divination on state matters by official augurs should be maintained for reasons of prudence but ridicules its absurdities, quoting in passing the saying of Cato (the Censor) that he wondered how a soothsayer (*haruspex; see* HARUSPICES) could meet another soothsayer without laughing. Marcus recognizes an art of *augury, but denies a science of divination. He similarly demolishes other methods of prediction based on dreams, omens, astrology, and 'inspired' prophecy. The work contains the much-quoted observation, 'there is nothing so ridiculous that some philosopher won't say it' (*nihil tam absurde dici potest quod non dicatur ab aliquo philosophorum*).

**De do'mo sua** ('Concerning his house') Speech delivered by *Cicero ((1) 4) in 57 BC to the College of Pontiffs (*see* PONTIFICES).

When Cicero was exiled in 58 BC, *Clodius had his house on the Palatine destroyed, consecrated the site, and erected on it a monument to Liberty. Cicero asks the College of Pontiffs to annul the consecration on the grounds that Clodius' tribunate was irregular, that his law banishing Cicero was unconstitutional, and that the dedication was unjust. The College decided in Cicero's favour.

**De falsa lēgātiō'ne** (*Peri tou pseudous symbaseōs*) ('On the false embassy') Speech by *Demosthenes ((2) 2).

**De fī'nibus bono'rum et malo'rum** ('About the ends of goods and evils'; often simply *De finibus*, 'On ends') An ethical work by *Cicero ((1) 5) consisting of three dialogues, in five books, addressed to M. *Brutus and written in 45 BC. In this work, on the different conceptions of the chief good and evil, Cicero presents the theories of each of the leading philosophies of his day, Stoic, Epicurean, and Academic, with the criticisms that might be made of each. By the date of composition the imagined interlocutors, friends of Cicero's youth, were all dead. The first dialogue, occupying books 1 and 2, deals with the ethics of Epicurus, which are refuted from the Stoic viewpoint; the second, in book 3, expounds Stoic ethics, which are criticized by Cicero in book 4 from the standpoint of the 'Old' *Academy of Antiochus of Ascalon; the third, in book 5, goes back in time to 79 BC when Cicero and his friends were students in Athens; the ethics of Antiochus are expounded by Piso, a friend of Cicero, and afterwards criticized by Cicero from the Stoic point of view. Piso is given the last word.

**deformity** *See* INFANTICIDE.

**Dēianei'ra** In Greek myth, the wife of *Heracles.

**de'i conse'ntēs** *See* DI CONSENTES.

**Dēidamī'a (Dēidameia)** In Greek myth, the mother of Neoptolemus by *Achilles.

**deification** Elevation of an exceptional individual to the status of a god. Although it became a Roman practice, it may have been Greek in origin, derived from Hellenistic Greek beliefs (*see* RULER CULT). But some legendary Romans of early times, such as Romulus, later acquired god-like status, and perhaps it is possible to speak of a spectrum between the human and the divine. During the republic Roman governors and other distinguished figures received divine honours in Greek cities, including T. Quinctus *Flaminius the 'liberator' of Greece. Cicero, under the influence of Stoicism, believed that deserving individuals might become divine after death. There is a strong possibility that Julius Caesar received divine honours shortly before his assassination, but

at any rate after his death the triumvirs, supported by popular demand, constrained the senate to accept his deification in 42 BC as 'The Divine Julius' (*Divus Iulius*). Augustus was deified after his death. Following these precedents deification became customary for the Roman emperors and some members of their families.

**De impe'rio Cn. Pompeii** ('Concerning Pompey's command') Alternative title for Cicero's speech *Pro lege Manilia in support of the proposal in 66 BC to extend Pompey's command in Asia.

**Deina'rchus** (*c*.360–*c*.290 BC) A distinguished Greek orator, Corinthian by birth, who lived in Athens. Not being an Athenian citizen he was debarred from addressing the assembly, but he composed a large number of speeches for others, including a speech *Against Demosthenes* connected, like his other two surviving speeches (*Against Aristogeiton* and *Against Philocles*), with the Harpalus affair (*see* DEMOSTHENES (2) 4). Three other speeches surviving in the manuscripts of Demosthenes have sometimes been attributed to Deinarchus: *Against Boeotus II*, *Against Theocrines*, and *Against Mantitheus*.

**De interpretātiō'ne** ('On interpretation') A work on logic by *Aristotle. It deals mainly with the logical properties and relationships of various kinds of statement. The introductory chapters define the terms 'name', 'verb', 'sentence', 'statement', 'affirmation', and 'negation', and are important for later theories of grammar and meaning. Some topics are developed further in Aristotle's *Prior Analytics*.

**De inventiō'ne** ('On invention') An early work (*c*.84 BC or even earlier) on oratory by *Cicero ((1) 4). It explains how the subject matter should be chosen and arranged, how the speech should be divided into sections, and what kind of treatment is appropriate to each section. It is obscurely but intriguingly related to *Rhetorica ad Herennium*.

**Deiotarus** (first half of the first century BC) Hellenized ruler of Galatia. After being attacked by *Mithridates VI he became a loyal Roman ally and in 51 BC put his troops at the disposal of Cicero and Bibulus, who were governing Cilicia and Syria respectively at the time. He followed Pompey initially in the Civil War but went over to Caesar after the latter's defeat of Pompey at Pharsalus in 48 BC. When in 45 BC he was accused before Caesar of trying to murder him Cicero spoke in his defence in a surviving speech (*Pro rege Deiotaro*). When Caesar was murdered Deiotarus joined Brutus and the republicans but deserted to the triumvirs after Brutus and Cassius were defeated at Philippi in 42 BC. He died peacefully in 40 BC.

**Dēi'phobē** Name of the Cumaean *Sibyl in Virgil's *Aeneid*.

**Dēi'phobus** In Greek myth, son of *Priam, king of Troy, and of Hecuba. He took a prominent part in the fighting at Troy. After the death of Paris he married Helen and was subsequently killed at the fall of Troy. His body disappeared, but Aeneas erected a cenotaph to him on Cape Rhoeteum; on his visit to the Underworld Aeneas heard the story of his death from Deiphobus himself (*Aeneid* book 6).

***Deipnosophi'stai*** Title of a literary work by *Athenaeus.

***De lau'de Pīsō'nis*** ('In praise of Piso') Latin verse panegyric in 261 hexameters by an unknown author sometimes thought to be *Calpurnius Siculus. The Piso of the poem may be Gaius Calpurnius Piso who was executed for plotting against Nero in AD 65.

***De lē'gibus*** ('On laws') Dialogue by *Cicero ((1) 4), a sequel to *De republica*, probably begun about 52 BC. The date of its completion (if it ever was completed) is unknown; Cicero seems not to have published it. Most of the first three books survive.

The interlocutors are Cicero, his brother Quintus, and Atticus; the scene is Cicero's estate at Arpinum.

**Dē'lia** Name of the woman celebrated in his poems by the Roman poet *Tibullus. (*Cf.* CYNTHIA.)

**Dē'lian League** The modern name given to the alliance of Greek states against the Persians created in 478 BC after the expulsion of the Persian invaders from Greece. The alliance comprised mainly Athens, the Ionian Greek cities on the coast of Asia Minor, the Hellespont, the Propontis, and most of the islands in the Aegean. At the request of the allies, who pleaded Pausanias' behaviour (*see* PAUSANIAS (1)) and Ionian kinship, Athens took over the leadership. The island of *Delos, sacred to Ionians everywhere, was the venue for meetings of the league and provided the treasury for league funds (removed to Athens in 454 BC). Some states with strong navies, e.g. Chios, Samos, and Lesbos, contributed ships; the remainder paid tribute (money). At first the league undertook military operations against the Persians, thereby extending Greek control along the whole coast of Asia Minor, but its character changed to become an alliance of cities controlled by Athens, i.e. her empire. With the defeat of Athens in the Peloponnesian War (404) the league came to an end. (For the Second Athenian League *see* ATHENS 4.)

**Dēlos** Small solitary island, 3 sq. km (1.2 sq. miles) in area, in the Aegean Sea, in the middle of the Cyclades. According to Greek myth it was the birthplace of Artemis and Apollo (*see* LETO) and this was the basis of its importance in historical times. The Homeric Hymn to Apollo attests that already from the eighth century BC Delos was the scene of an Ionian festival to the god, with song, dance, and games, attracting Ionians (including Athenians) from the islands and coasts of the Aegean. In later times it was said that the Athenians instituted the festival to commemorate the safe return of Theseus and his companions from Crete. Every year, reputedly since the days of Theseus, the Athenians sent a sacred embassy to Delos. During the absence of the state ship on this mission Athens was kept in a state of ceremonial purity, when no criminal might be executed. (It was this which delayed the execution of Socrates.) In the late sixth century the Athenians purified the island by removing burials, and in 426 BC carried out a second purification, when those about to give birth or die had to leave the island. Delos was also chosen as the meeting place and treasury of the *Delian League.

Athenian domination lasted until the late fourth century BC. From the early third century BC Delos started to become a commercial centre, attracting foreign banks and traders. It lost its independence again after 166 BC when Rome, putting Delos under Athenian control, made it a free port (i.e. abolished all duties on the movement of goods) in order to damage the trade of Rhodes, a free city and an object of Roman jealousy. It became the most important market for the slave trade. The island was sacked in 88 BC by soldiers of Mithridates of Pontus, sacked again by pirates in 69 BC, and went into decline. Before the end of the first century BC trade routes had changed; Delos was replaced by Puteoli as the chief focus of Italian trade with the East, and as a cult-centre too it was eclipsed. Its rapid decay became a commonplace of Latin moralizing literature.

**Delphi (Delphoi)** City in the Greek mainland state of Phocis, the site of the famous sanctuary and oracle of Apollo and the site also of the *Pythian games. It was situated on the southern slopes of Mount *Parnassus, above the Gulf of Corinth. Little is known of its history until the eighth century BC. On the road from Thebes to Delphi is the crossroads where Oedipus was said to have murdered his father Laius.

Inside the wall surrounding the sanctuary and oracle stood the many monuments dedicated by successful athletes in the Pythian games, and also the so-called treasuries built by various Greek cities to hold their most valuable vessels and their offerings to Apollo. The treasury of the Athenians, dating perhaps from the 490s, still stands (rebuilt using the original stones), and the remains of about twenty others have been excavated. Also in the sanctuary was the main temple of Apollo, in front of which, in the open air, stood the great altar of the god. In 480 BC the Persian invaders fled when he 'defended his own' with thunderbolts and rock falls. The earliest temple for which there is evidence dates to the second half of the seventh century BC; it was destroyed by fire in 548 BC. A new temple was built with help from the Athenian family of the *Alcmaeonidae, then in exile at Delphi; this was destroyed by earthquake in 373 BC and a third temple replaced it. On the front of the temple were engraved the maxims ascribed to the *Seven Sages, 'know yourself' (*gnōthi sauton*), i.e. know your human weakness in contrast with the power of the gods, and 'nothing in excess' (*mēden agan*); also set up was the Greek letter E, the exact significance of which remains obscure (*see* PLUTARCH 3).

Inside the temple was the hearth beside which the priest of Apollo was said to have killed *Neoptolemus, and beside it the iron chair of the poet Pindar, from which he reputedly sang his hymns to Apollo. On the hearth burned a perpetual fire. Further inside was the *omphalos*, the half-egg-shaped navel stone supposed to mark the mid-point of the earth, determined by Zeus as the place at which two eagles met, after flying one from the eastern and one from the western boundary of the world. Another story makes the *omphalos* the tomb of the serpent Python: *see* DELPHIC ORACLE.

In Aeschylus' tragedy *Eumenides* the Pythia (prophet of Apollo), passing through the temple to the inmost sanctuary (the *adyton*), catches sight of Orestes seated by the *omphalos*. (The marble stone, a man-made object which was seen by Pausanias, has possibly been recovered.) In the *adyton* the Pythia gave oracular responses to those who came to consult her.

North of the temple, still in the sanctuary, was the tomb of Neoptolemus, and beyond it the stone which, according to Greek belief, *Cronus swallowed in place of his son Zeus. Here also was the spring (where Apollo slew Python), which watered the sacred grove of myrtles and laurels and perhaps provided water for the *adyton*. To the west of this area lay a small theatre where the musical contests in the Pythian games were held, and a little further north the Lesche or public room (dedicated by the Cnidians), famous for its two large paintings by *Polygnotus, *The Fall of Troy* and *The Descent of Odysseus into Hades*, both crammed with incident. About 10km (6 miles) north-east of Delphi was the *Corycian cave.

The temple of the fourth century BC survived until Roman times. It was repaired by the emperor Domitian in AD 84 and the cult was revived under Trajan and Hadrian in the early second century AD. In 391 the sanctuary of Apollo was closed for ever along with all other pagan temples by the Roman emperor Theodosius, in the cause of Christianity.

Excavations at the site have revealed the remains of several famous memorials: the base of the Serpent Column commemorating the Greek victory over the Persians at Plataea in 479 BC (the bronze serpent itself was taken by Constantine the Great to Constantinople, where it still survives); the bases of the statues dedicated by the Spartan general Lysander after he destroyed the Athenian navy at Aegospotami in 405 BC; the bases of the gold tripods dedicated by Gelon and his brother Hieron, tyrants of Syracuse in the early 470s; the bronze charioteer probably dedicated in 474 BC by Polyzelos, tyrant of Gela; and many notable finds of sculpture.

*See* AMPHICTYONY.

**Delphic oracle** The oracle of the god Apollo at *Delphi, in historical times the most important oracle in Greece. According to fifth-century myth Apollo was not the original owner of the oracle but a latecomer, preceded by the oracular cult of Gaia (or Themis, or Poseidon), whose serpent, Python, he killed before ousting the goddess. The oracle seems to have come into existence at the end of the ninth century BC, when it became very influential in the formation of Greek cities and the foundation of colonies. In Apollo's temple the priestess, known as the Pythia, speaking under the inspiration of the god, answered questions put to her by enquirers. The Pythia was over the age of 50 when she was appointed for life, and thereafter lived chastely; how she was selected is never explained. When prophesying the Pythia, wearing a crown of laurel, sat on a tall tripod similar in style to the cooking utensil (i.e. three metal legs supporting a bowl), said in Hellenistic times to be placed over a chasm from which fumes were exhaled but for which there is no archaeological or classical evidence. Plutarch records that in early times the Pythia gave oracles only on rare occasions, and not during the three winter months which the god spent with the *Hyperboreans. The day had to be declared auspicious by the priests of the temple, and the sacrifices favourable. It seems that the enquirer addressed his question to the Pythia directly in the *adyton*, though perhaps she was out of sight; she became possessed by the god and prophesied under divine inspiration. Her utterances were interpreted by a *prophētēs* ('interpreter', 'expounder') who put them into coherent form, sometimes in verse, though usually in prose, and often ambiguously. (For Greeks ambiguity was the hallmark of prophecy.) With this the consultation ended. The impressiveness of the wild scenery at Delphi as well as of the ritual no doubt contributed to the importance of Apollo's oracle. Its religious authority was for many centuries supreme, especially in the areas of pollution and cult, and it was consulted by questioners from all over the Mediterranean world. The Roman historian *Fabius Pictor was sent to consult it in 216 BC after Rome's defeat at Cannae.

The oldest written evidence for the Delphic oracle and cult is the third *Homeric Hymn (of the archaic period) in which Apollo is said to give his oracles 'from the laurel tree', an obscure statement which some think refers to the laurel tree said to grow in the temple. The Delphic oracle was administered by the *amphictyony, whose duties included overseeing the *Pythian games. The amphictyony fought and defeated Crisa in the first Sacred War, after

which, in 582 BC, games were added to the festival of Apollo, so inaugurating the Pythian games in the form in which they were known in historical times.

In Hellenistic times the Delphic oracle began to decline in significance. It enjoyed a brief revival under the emperor Hadrian, but by the time of the fervently pagan Julian (emperor AD 360-3) it was beyond resuscitation, as its last message to the emperor, reported by a later historian, makes clear: 'Tell the emperor that the finely wrought hall is fallen to the ground; no longer has Phoebus his shelter, nor his prophetic laurel, nor his babbling spring; the water of speech is dried up.' In 391 the sanctuary of Apollo was closed for ever along with all other pagan temples by the Roman emperor Theodosius.

**Dē'madēs** (*c.*380–319 BC) Athenian politician and orator whose career was devoted to implementing his realization that, in order to survive, Athens must come to terms with Macedonian power. After the Athenian defeat by Philip II of Macedon at Chaeronea in 338 BC he secured an honourable settlement for Athens and in 335 he succeeded in dissuading Alexander the Great from demanding the surrender of Demosthenes and other advocates of revolt against Macedonian rule (*see* HYPEREIDES). However, when in 322 BC Antipater, the governor of Macedonia, defeated a Greek coalition at Crannon (*see* LAMIAN WAR) which had been supported by Demosthenes, Demades secured by decree the deaths of the politicians opposed to peace with Macedon, Hypereides and (indirectly) Demosthenes. In 319, caught in the political intrigues after the death of Antipater, he was himself executed by *Cassander.

Demades had no formal training in rhetoric and published no speeches, but a few of his striking phrases were remembered and survive. He was famous for his wit and for being able to speak on the spur of the moment (unlike Demosthenes, who had to prepare his speeches). *See* DEMOSTHENES (2) 1 and 4.

**de'magogue (***dēmagōgos***)** ('leader of the people'). This term to describe a leader of the people arose in Athens in the late fifth century BC, not originally or necessarily in the pejorative sense of an unprincipled mob orator. For the most part demagogues did not hold magistracies, so that they could not be called to account if any of the policies they advocated miscarried. The most notable of them at

Athens were *Cleon, *Hyperbolus, *Cleophon, and Androcles.

**Demara'tus** Father of Tarquinius Priscus, the fifth king of Rome (*see* TARQUIN (1)). He was a *Bacchiad refugee from Corinth who fled to Tarquinii in Etruria to escape the tyranny of Cypselus.

**demes (*dēmoi*)** Local communities or parishes in Athens and the Attic countryside, numbering 139. In the reforms of *Cleisthenes (2), they replaced kinship groups as the basis of the democratic constitution in Athens (*see* GENOS and PHRATRIES). Cleisthenes arranged the demes into ten tribes (*phylai*) and each tribe into three *trittyes* (*see* TRITTYS); in each tribe one *trittys* comprised demes from the city region, another demes from the interior, and the third demes from the coast. In this way each tribe was made representative of the whole. Each deme had its own finances and its demarch (deme leader), elected by its assembly (*agora*) which dealt with local affairs. After Cleisthenes, membership of a deme was hereditary and did not change with change of residence. On reaching the age of 18 every male Athenian citizen was registered in his family deme. Membership of a deme was a guarantee of citizenship, indicated by deme name (a 'demotic', usually in an adjectival form, e.g. *Acharneus*, meaning 'from Acharnae'). Deme membership was hereditary for men, irrespective of where they actually lived.

**Demē'ter** In Greek myth, daughter of Cronus and Rhea, sister of Zeus, a corn-goddess, patroness of agriculture in general and so sustainer of life for people and animals. By Zeus she was the mother of *Persephone (Lat. Proserpina), called simply Kore, 'Girl', and by *Iasion the mother of *Plutus. The Romans identified her with the Italian goddess of the corn, *Ceres. Most of the myths concerning her relate to the abduction of Persephone by her uncle Hades, god of the Underworld. Demeter sought her daughter all over the world, fasting, with hair untied, and carrying torches. In her wanderings Demeter came to Eleusis where, in the guise of an old woman, she was hospitably received by the king, Celeus, and his wife Metaneira, and tended their newborn son Demoph(o)ōn (or *Triptolemus). She was discovered holding the child in the fire, to make it immortal by purging away its mortality. She explained her action by revealing her divinity, and promised Demo-

phon heroic honours after death. Then, having ordered the Eleusinians to build her a temple and altar, she withdrew to the temple, leaving the earth barren. To appease her Zeus forced Hades to release Persephone in Eleusis, which he did; but she had eaten a pomegranate seed and so was compelled to return to the Underworld for a third of the year. This myth has always been interpreted as an allegory of nature: Persephone, like seed, must descend into the earth so that the new corn may eventually spring up. The Athenian festival of Demeter and Persephone, the *Thesmophoria, took place in autumn near to sowing time. The two goddesses are the *Thesmophoroi*, 'bringers of law', of settled, agricultural, life.

At Eleusis the goddesses were celebrated by a 'mystery' cult (*see* MYSTERIES) in which initiates learned secrets which offered them prosperity in life (personified by Demeter's son Plutus, 'wealth') and a happy fate after death. The island of Sicily was also specially sacred to the goddesses, with many festivals; in Hellenistic and Roman times Persephone's abduction was located in the centre of the island, in a meadow near Enna.

*See also* ERYSICHTHON and IAMBE.

**Dēmē'trius 1. Demetrius of Phalērum** (*c*.350–*c*.283 BC) Athenian statesman and *Peripatetic philosopher. He was pro-Macedonian and favoured *Cassander's succession to the throne of Macedon. When most of the Greek states including Athens surrendered to Cassander in 318, the latter made Demetrius governor of Athens, where he ruled as an enlightened tyrant for ten years. He went into exile when the Macedonian Demetrius Poliorcetes (see (2) below) took Athens in 307, and later joined the Egyptian court of Ptolemy I Soter at Alexandria. Having been a pupil of *Theophrastus at Athens, it is probable that it was in this capacity that he advised Soter about the foundation of the *Alexandrian Library and possibly about the *Museum too. He is thus partly responsible for their being organized in the Peripatetic fashion and spirit, which may account for the nature and trend of much of the intellectual life of Alexandria. After Ptolemy II Philadelphus became sole ruler in 283 BC Demetrius was exiled to Upper Egypt where he died. He was an outstanding orator and the author of many scholarly works of which only fragments survive. *See also* FABLE.

**2. Demetrius Poliorcē'tēs** ('The Besieger', 336–283 BC) Macedonian general, son of Antigonus I. In 307 BC he liberated Athens from the regime of Demetrius of Phalerum (above) and in 306 defeated the fleet of Ptolemy I and captured Cyprus. In 305–304 his famous year-long siege of Rhodes for possession of its fleet and dockyards earned him his nickname. The siege was ended by negotiation, and from the sale of his siege engines the Rhodians financed the *Colossus. After many changes of fortune Demetrius reappeared in Greece, and *c.*295 was invited to intervene in the affairs of Macedon. He murdered the young king Alexander V, seized the throne himself, and reigned until 287. He had grandiose schemes for regaining his father's empire but he was expelled from Macedonia and finally surrendered to Seleucus. He died after two years in captivity.

**3.** Greek author of a treatise 'On Style' (*Peri hermeneiās*), traditionally said to be Demetrius of Phalerum (above), but the style and contents suggest a date at least a century later, and the work perhaps belongs to the first century BC. The author analyses style (*charactēr*) under four headings (rather than the more usual three; *cf* ORATOR): plain (*ischnos*), grand (*megaloprepēs*), smooth (*glaphyros*), and forceful (*deinos*); the last category is a novelty in this kind of criticism. His discussion of humour and charm under the heading of the 'smooth' style is interesting. He also gives an account of style in letter-writing (*see* LETTERS), a literary genre usually ignored by other ancient critics.

**democracy, Athenian** [Gk. *dēmokratia*: 'rule', *kratos*, 'of the people', **demos*] Demos means the whole body of citizens (although when used by critics of democracy, Plato for instance, it can carry the implication 'the common people', 'the city poor'). Athenian democracy, from the political reforms of Cleisthenes (2) in 508 BC until Athens lost her independence in 322 BC, became the best-known example of a 'direct' democracy, which was more fully participatory than a 'representative' democracy. The degree of equality in the second half of the fifth century BC was remarkable: all male citizens should have an equal opportunity to participate in politics (*isonomia*) and to speak in political assemblies (*isegoria*) and all should be equal before the law. All political decisions were made by the majority vote of an assembly of citizens (**ecclesia*), its business prepared and decisions executed by a council

(**boulē*) and officials. After c.462 BC, under the influence of *Ephialtes and *Pericles, measures were introduced to bring about a radical (i.e. thoroughgoing) democracy. These were to ensure that all decisions were kept in the hands of the people, and to prevent power falling into the hands of those holding office. Thus all offices were decided by lot (*see* SORTITION), except for those few requiring special experience, in practice the generalship (*see* STRATEGOS); the term of office was brief and not generally open to re-election; officers underwent an examination of suitability before taking office (**dokimasia*), and were called to account at the end of their tenure (**euthynae*); and the property qualification, where it still existed, was minimal (*see* SOLON). Similarly with the law-courts: all legal cases were decided by juries drawn by lot from the citizen body. Payment was made by the state to all who might be excluded by poverty from performing their civic duties, including jury service and even, in the fourth century BC, to those attending meetings of the assembly. There were no political parties as such (but *see* STASIS). It was a feature of Athenian democracy that considerable power to influence decisions was wielded by individuals, skilful orators (*rhētors*; *see* ORATORY) or the *politeuomenoi*, 'those who take an active part in politics'. These constituted the small groups of active citizens who throughout the Athenian democracy were the politicians. Though unpaid they initiated policy in a more or less professional manner and tried to persuade the assembly to vote with them. By eloquence and personal influence they sometimes managed to dominate the assembly for long periods, as Pericles did from 443 until his death in 429 BC, and Demosthenes from 341 to 338 BC. *See also* DEMAGOGUE.

For the constitution of Rome, *see* ROMAN REPUBLIC and *POLITICS*.

**Demo'critus** Greek philosopher, with *Leucippus founder of the Greek atomic theory. He was born in Abdera (in Thrace) in 460 BC and reputedly lived to a very great age, dying *c.*357. In his early years he is said to have travelled very widely in Asia. Plato never mentions him by name, but Aristotle refers to him frequently and in several connections, always with respect. Little has survived of his copious writings on natural sciences, mathematics, mechanics, grammar, music, and philosophy, and the few surviving fragments deal mostly with ethical and political ideas. However, there are many ancient accounts of his physical theories. Since the works of Leucippus, who was said to have been his teacher, have also perished, it is impossible to separate the contribution of each to the atomic theory. These atomists' arguments aim to explain the perceptible world as it appears to the senses, containing multiplicity and diversity as well as motion and change.

Those earlier philosophers who are known as the *Eleatics had argued that 'what exists' (i.e. the cosmos and all that it contains) is homogeneous, indivisible, and unchanging, despite appearances to the contrary: the opposite to 'what exists', namely 'what is non-existent', their argument ran, is nothing, and what is nothing cannot exist. The atomists thought that in order to account for the world we perceive there must be plurality and motion. They argued that 'nothingness' exists and is as real as 'a thing', and might separate parts of 'what exists' from other parts. 'What exists', they thought, is indeed homogeneous, indivisible, and unchanging, but it is in the form of particles, indivisible small solids (*atoma*, 'things which cannot be divided'), differentiated from each other only in shape and size, randomly moving for ever in limitless 'nothingness', i.e. the void. All worlds—ours is not unique—first came into being through randomly colliding atoms causing a rotary movement in which atoms became attached to each other; different arrangements of atoms form different compounds, hence the variety of the world as we perceive it. Our world like every other came into being by accident and developed by necessity; its intelligibility does not depend upon its having been created by some sort of divine intelligence. The gods, if they exist, though superior to the human race are still creatures which have come into being and will eventually perish. People's consciousness and perception are entirely physical, to be accounted for by the arrangements of atoms which are by themselves not capable of consciousness. Consciousness resides in the *soul (which is also the cause of life) because the soul is made of particularly fine atoms, though it is as perishable as the body. Perception comes about through the impact made on the soul (and mediated through the sense-organs) by fine films emanating from the objects perceived.

In his prose treatise *On Cheerfulness* (*Peri euthymiēs*) Democritus states that to achieve cheerfulness the atoms forming the soul must be protected from violent disturbance, thus

expressing for the first time the idea (later developed by *Epicurus) that men should aim at the happiness which derives from peace of mind, itself based on knowledge of the physical basis of life. 'The only *daimon* you need is in your own mind'. Most later Greek philosophers, Plato, Aristotle, and the Stoics, did not take up the atomic theory of matter; Democritus' most influential followers were Epicurus and (the Roman) *Lucretius. A tradition in the Latin writers represented Democritus as 'the laughing philosopher' unable to restrain his mirth at the spectacle of human life (in contrast with the melancholy Heracleitus, 'the weeping philosopher').

**Demoph(o)ōn 1.** In Greek myth, son of Theseus, brother of Acamas, who succeeded his father as king of Athens. In his reign the *Palladium came to Athens; his sanctuary was part of the Palladian complex.

**2.** In Greek myth, Eleusinian hero, son of Celeus and Metaneira whom *Demeter attempted to make immortal. His role as young boy in the triad of Demeter, Persephone, and youth was taken over by Triptolemus.

**dēmos** In Greece, 'the people'. At Athens the term sometimes denoted the whole citizen body (and its assembly), sometimes only the common people in contrast with the upper classes. *See* DEMOCRACY.

**Dēmo'sthenēs 1.** (d. 413 BC) Prominent Athenian general during the Peloponnesian War. After earlier successes in the war his occupation of Pylos in 425 BC led to the capture of a body of Spartan hoplites on the neighbouring island of Sphacteria (*see* CLEON). In 413 after less successful campaigning he was sent with reinforcements for Nicias in Syracuse (*see* SICILIAN EXPEDITION). He failed to persuade that general to withdraw from the city until the Athenians lost control of the sea and had to attempt an escape by land. In that retreat he commanded the rearguard but was forced to surrender to the Syracusans and Spartans and was subsequently executed.

**2.** (384–322 BC) The greatest of the Athenian orators.

1. When Demosthenes was seven his father died, leaving the management of his estate to his two brothers and a friend. These so mismanaged the property that Demosthenes at 18 found himself almost without resources. He now prepared to sue his guardians, and

for three years tried unsuccessfully to obtain restitution, studying rhetoric and legal procedure, perhaps under *Isaeus. At 21 he brought a successful action against his guardians (*Against Aphobus*), but probably recovered little. In the political sphere, his early attempts to address the assembly at Athens were said not to have been a success. He thereupon made strenuous efforts to improve his delivery (practising with pebbles in his mouth). He also became a speech-writer (*logographos*) for those who had to plead private suits in the lawcourts. His growing reputation brought him employment for public trials also. *Against Androtion* is Demosthenes' earliest speech in a public prosecution, in 355. Androtion had proposed that crowns be awarded to the outgoing members of the council (*boulē*); Demosthenes supports a certain Diodorus in raising objections, on the grounds that the navy has not been increased during the year. In *Against Timocrates* (353) Demosthenes again supports Diodorus, in an embezzlement case (Timocrates was an associate of Androtion). *Against Aristocrates* (352) is an attack on the politician Charidemus for his dealings in Thrace. All of these were delivered by other speakers, but in 354 a speech *Against Leptines* was delivered by Demosthenes himself, perhaps because he was personally opposed to the policy advocated by Leptines, that in view of the financial difficulties of the state, all hereditary exemptions from taxation granted as a reward to benefactors of the state should be abolished. Demosthenes argues that the proposal is contrary to good policy and that the saving will be negligible. This would be consistent with his attitude in the speech *On the Taxation Groups* (*Symmoriai*), also in 354, in which he opposes the allocation of financial surpluses to the *theoric fund and urges against rashly rearming, as more likely to provoke the Persians to war.

In his speech *For the Megalopolitans* (352), Demosthenes advocates alliance with Megalopolis, the capital of the newly confederated Arcadia, recently founded with Theban help. While Thebes was occupied with the Sacred War against Phocis, Sparta was trying to regain her former control over Arcadia. Some of the Athenian assembly, out of hostility to Thebes, did not wish to take any action unfavourable to Sparta. Demosthenes urges the maintenance of a balance of power between Sparta and Thebes: if Sparta reduces Arcadia she will become too strong. His speech *On the Liberty of*

*the Rhodians* in 351 was in response to Rhodes' secession from the Athenian league; oligarchs were in control there and the leading democrats in exile. Demosthenes urges the Athenians to restore the democrats and follow their traditional role of liberators.

Sixty-one speeches have come down to us under the name of Demosthenes, but the authenticity of some of them, particularly among the speeches relating to civil cases, has been doubted. The private speeches cover many subjects, including bottomry loans, mining rights, forgery, and trespass. For speeches on behalf of Phormion (350) and against Stephanus (349) concerning the wealthy banker *Pasion, whose chief clerk Phormion was, *see* APOLLODORUS (1). A speech *Against Boeotus* (348) attempts to prevent an illegitimate son from claiming the name of his legitimate half-brother and so implying his own legitimacy (but *see* DEINARCHUS). *Against Conon* (341) is a brilliant and entertaining speech for the prosecution of Conon and his rowdy sons, for assault upon a virtuous young man. The speech *Against Callicles*, of uncertain date, alleges with touches of humour that the defendant has caused the plaintiff's land to be flooded by blocking a watercourse.

2. Demosthenes became prominent as a politician by constantly urging resistance to the encroachments of *Philip II of Macedon on the rest of Greece. His first oration against Philip, the so-called *First Philippic*, advocating a vigorous policy of resistance, was delivered in 351. In 349 Philip attacked *Olynthus, a city which had made overtures of friendship to Athens. Demosthenes delivered three orations urging help (the *Olynthiacs*) and attacking *Eubulus. But a faction inside Olynthus betrayed the city to Philip in the following year and it was destroyed. At the Dionysia of 348, a supporter of Eubulus, Meidias, publicly slapped Demosthenes' face and was prosecuted by him. The case was settled out of court and the surviving speech *Against Meidias* never delivered. In mid-348, before the fall of Olynthus, Demosthenes successfully defended Philocrates against the charge that the latter's proposal to open negotiations with Philip was illegal. His friendship with Philocrates continued and he took part in the two embassies that resulted in the Peace of Philocrates between Philip and Greece in 346. Demosthenes played a leading part in its

acceptance, but on the two embassies to Macedon he got on badly with his fellow ambassadors. After the return of the second embassy it became known that Philip and his army were at Thermopylae (which carried the main pass from northern to central and southern Greece), and that *Phocis could not be saved. Demosthenes was convinced that Philip did not want peace and set about undoing the settlement, but advised caution in his speech *On the Peace* in 346. Soon after that Philip extended his conquests in Thrace, subdued the Phocians, and secured a place on the Amphictyonic Council (*see* AMPHICTYONY). Demosthenes, who subsequently did all he could to repudiate the Peace, considered that for the time being resistance was impossible and in this speech advises a pacific policy.

In 344 Demosthenes persuaded the assembly to refuse Philip's offer to renew the Peace. Philip had resumed his interference in Greece, strengthening his position in Thessaly, and in the Peloponnese supporting the Argives and Messenians against Sparta. Demosthenes went on an embassy to those cities to warn them of the dangers of consorting with Philip, who promptly protested. The *Second Philippic* is his speech in reaction to Philip's protests. He exposes Philip's designs for empire and proposes a reply to him (the text of which has not survived). In the following year his speech *On the False Embassy* relates to the disagreements between Demosthenes and his fellow ambassadors when the Peace of Philocrates was made. The terms of the Peace were that Athens and Macedon should each retain the territories they possessed to date. As Philip was constantly engaged on fresh conquests it was urgent, when once Athens had accepted the terms, that the second embassy sent to receive Philip's oath of ratification should act with all speed. In spite of Demosthenes' protests the embassy delayed and Philip delayed further, so that by the time the Peace was ratified Philip had subdued Thrace. Moreover, on the embassy's return to Athens Aeschines gave so favourable an account of Philip's intentions that the assembly voted to extend the treaty to Philip's descendants, allowed him to occupy Thermopylae, and left Phocis, whose appeal for help Athens had earlier answered, to surrender to him. By 343 feeling at Athens had been roused by Philip's continuing aggressions, and *On the False Embassy* is Demosthenes' speech prosecuting *Aeschines

for the delays which had resulted in Philip's intervention in Phocis, and for giving false reports, suggesting that bribery was the cause of his pro-Macedonian stance. Aeschines' reply (which we possess), together with the support of Eubulus and Phocion, secured a decision in his favour by a narrow majority.

In 342 Philip intervened more directly in the affairs of Greece and Demosthenes tried to organize a Greek alliance against him In 341, in his speech *On the Chersonese*, Demosthenes sought to end the Peace by persuading the Athenians that Philip has already broken it; Philip was in Thrace, in dangerous proximity to the Chersonese and projecting an attack on *Byzantium. After the Peace of Philocrates Athens had sent settlers to the Chersonese under the general Diopeithes. The town of Cardia refused them admission, and Philip sent an expedition for the town's protection. Diopeithes, ill-provided with funds by Athens, made piratical raids in various directions, among others into Philip's Thracian territory, and Philip sent a protest to Athens. In this speech Demosthenes urges that Diopeithes should be vigorously supported. The speech is distinguished by the passion with which Demosthenes expresses his feelings about Philip's fundamental and implacable ambition.

A few months later, the threat to the Chersonese and Byzantium was closer and Philip was also interfering in Euboea. Demosthenes wants to unite the Greek cities against Philip and, trying to rouse the Athenians to the imminence of their danger, proposes in the *Third Philippic* the immediate dispatch of forces. This is one of the finest of Demosthenes' speeches, marked by gravity and deep anxiety; in one notable passage he contrasts the ancient spirit of Athens with her present degeneracy. (The *Fourth Philippic*, if genuine, would have been delivered soon after the *Third*.)

3. When Philip's activities in Thrace reached Byzantium, Athens, anxious for the security of her corn-route, sent aid to the Byzantines, and open war with Philip was begun; Demosthenes was the most influential voice in Athens at this time. In 339 Philip moved south and was at Elatea in Phocis before the end of the year. Demosthenes procured an alliance with the Thebans, and both sides met at Chaeronea in autumn 338, Philip winning a decisive victory. Demosthenes was present at the battle and returned so quickly to organize the city's

defences that Aeschines could accuse him of running away. This was his great moment, and he delivered the funeral oration over the dead, a speech which has not survived. There was no need for Philip to impose a direct political settlement on Greece: in most cities pro-Macedonian politicians and policies naturally came to the fore. Despite the defeat at Chaeronea, a battle which Demosthenes had actively sought, his friend Ctesiphon proposed soon afterwards that he should be honoured with a gold crown at the Great *Dionysia for his service to the city. Aeschines charged Ctesiphon with the alleged illegality of the proposal, but because of the events of the next few months the case was allowed to lapse until 330. In 336 Philip was murdered and Demosthenes hoped that that was the end of Macedonian domination in Greece. However, Philip's son and successor Alexander (the Great) quickly marched south to secure Greece, and Demosthenes had to accept the new order. He seems to have pinned his hopes on Persia defeating the Macedonians, but when the Persians were overwhelmed by Alexander at the battle of Gaugamela in 331 and Athens seemed isolated in opposition to the Macedonians, Aeschines resumed his attack on Demosthenes through Ctesiphon in 330. In his speech *Against Ctesiphon*, Aeschines reviewed Demosthenes' career and blamed on him all the recent misfortunes of Athens, but the latter's reply, *On the Crown*, was a masterpiece. It is Demosthenes' greatest oration, rebutting the attack of his rival and defending in detail his policy from the Peace of Philocrates in 346 to the defeat at Chaeronea in 338. He maintains that his advice has always been in accordance with the honourable traditions of Athens which has 'never preferred an inglorious security to the hazardous vindication of a noble cause'. Demosthenes includes a virulent attack on Aeschines, ridiculing, perhaps without strict regard to truth, his humble origins, and endeavouring to prove from the facts of his career that he was a traitor, bribed by Philip's money. Two passages are especially famous: the description of the confusion at Athens when the messenger came with the news that Philip was at Elatea (in Phocis) and so on Athens' doorstep (ch. 169); and the invocation of the Athenians who had fought the Persians at Marathon, Salamis, and Plataea a century-and-a-half earlier (ch. 206). Demosthenes secured an overwhelming vote in his favour; fewer than one-fifth of the jury voted for Aeschines (who then retired to Rhodes, where he died). Meanwhile, Alexander had made it clear that he did not intend to let Greece slip from Macedonian control.

4. Demosthenes remained to the fore in public affairs, but the later part of his career was clouded by the affair of Harpalus, the fugitive treasurer of Alexander the Great, who decamped to the coast of Attica in 325 with a vast sum of money. Demosthenes seems to have proposed first that Harpalus should be kept prisoner and his money stored on the Acropolis, and later, after Harpalus had escaped, that the *Areopagus should investigate the disappearance of some of it. Demosthenes' actions and motives are by no means clear, but he was accused and found guilty of appropriating a large sum from it for himself and was fined 50 talents (see DEINARCHUS and HYPEREIDES). He retired into exile, but after the death of Alexander in 323 he was active once again in stimulating concerted Greek resistance to Macedon, and returned to Athens in triumph. When the defeat at *Crannon in 322 led to the break-up of the Greek alliance, each state made its own separate peace with Antipater, Alexander's successor. The terms for Athens were that the chief agitators against Macedon should be surrendered; Athens refused, but when the Macedonians marched upon the city Demosthenes and his supporters fled. *Demades' proposal that they should be sentenced to death was carried. Rather than be taken alive from the temple on Calaureia (an island off the east coast of Argolis) where he had sought refuge, Demosthenes took poison. The Greek traveller Pausanias who visited Athens in the second century AD summed up his life: 'Demosthenes loved the Athenians too much, and this is what came of it. It seems to me a true saying that a man who devotes himself unsparingly to his country's affairs and trusts his people never comes to a good end.'

Demosthenes' claim to greatness rests partly on his oratorical brilliance (below) but also on the heroic role he chose to play in the tragedy of the Greek *city-state and on the sincere patriotism he showed throughout his life. The problem that the Greeks faced was how to counter the aggressive military power of the new nation-state, Macedon, which was so much greater than the power that any single city-state, Athens, say, or Thebes, could muster. The answer was to present a united front in a Common Peace as, to a very limited extent, the Greeks had done a century-and-a-half earlier when facing the Persian invasion. Demosthenes' political opponents seem to have supported this policy (Demosthenes himself seems never to have used the term). Internal dissension among the city-states, however, was too deep-seated and involved to be overcome. Demosthenes' argument that the Athenians (alone) should concentrate their military effort in arresting Philip's advance in northern Greece had much to recommend it, but Demosthenes himself seems to have made unrealistic assessments about the possibility of an Athenian army perhaps with the assistance of one or two other cities defeating the Macedonians in the field.

5. Demosthenes' speeches are marked by a passionate earnestness expressed in a great variety of tones: anger, irony, sarcasm, invective. Pathos and humour rarely appear. He writes in pure Attic Greek, with bold metaphors rarely but aptly placed, and likes vivid examples: the Athenians in their warfare with Philip are like barbarians boxing: 'Hit one of them, and he rubs the place; hit him on the other side, and there go his hands; but as for guarding, or looking his opponent in the face, he neither can nor will do it' (*Philippics* 1.40). The speeches were most carefully prepared but the style aims to conceal this fact, long, periodic sentences often being followed by short, pithy statements, which gives an impression of spontaneity. In all his speeches Demosthenes deliberately avoided hiatus (the placing of a word ending in a vowel before a word beginning with a vowel) except in unavoidable cases, such as those involving the use of 'or' (*ē*) or 'and' (*kai*); in his early speeches he was strict in the observance of this rule. As a further aid to euphony he avoided as far as possible a run of more than two short syllables. (For length of syllables *see* PROSODY.)

The oratorical method of Demosthenes was much studied by subsequent orators, especially *Cicero ((1) 6), who used the name 'Philippics' as the title of his own speeches against Mark Antony; hence it was adopted as a general title for speeches of political invective. *Quintilian thought that Demosthenes' speeches should not only be examined but learned by heart by students of rhetoric; *Longinus admired his intensity and sublimity.

**demotic** *See* DEMES *and* ROSETTA STONE.

**De nātū'ra deo'rum** ('On the nature of the gods') Philosophical dialogue in three books by Cicero, written in 45 BC after the death of his daughter, in which he sets out the theological tenets of the three principal Greek schools of philosophy in his day, the Epicurean, Stoic, and Academic. The attacks on Epicureanism and Stoicism in books 1 and 3 reproduce the arguments of the Academic *Carneades. For practical purposes Carneades accepted a belief in God as more or less probable and useful. Cicero seems also to have accepted the Stoic proofs for a god or gods who exercise a providential control over the world. The work is addressed to M. Brutus. (*See* CICERO (1) 5.)

**Dentā'tus, Mā'nius Cu'rius** *See* CURIUS DENTATUS.

**De offi'ciis** ('On [moral] duties') By Cicero, his last work on moral philosophy, finished in November 44 BC (CICERO (1) 5), in the form of a letter to his son Marcus then studying philosophy at Athens. It consists of three books of moral advice on a variety of problems of conduct, based on Stoic precepts and, in the first two books, on the teaching of *Panaetius; the third is based on that of *Poseidonius and others.

The first book deals with the four cardinal virtues, wisdom, justice, fortitude, and temperance, develops the various duties that devolve from these, and passes on to their application to individual people who vary in age, position, abilities, etc. The second and third books discuss the application of the above principles to the pursuit of success in life: the reconciliation of expediency with virtue. The two are shown to be in reality identical, even in cases of apparent conflict; for material gain cannot compensate for the loss of the sense of honour and justice. Cicero's doctrine is illustrated throughout with examples from Greek and Roman history. Noteworthy are the highly practical character of his precepts, his condemnation of abstention from public activities (in opposition to the Stoics), and his insistence on the social character of a man and the duty of men to their fellow human beings, something beyond patriotism. This work received high praise in later ages and was a pervasive influence in its exposition of the virtuous political life.

**De o'ptimo ge'nere ōrātō'rum** ('On the best kind of orators') An introduction by Cicero (of doubtful authenticity) to his intended translation of the Greek orations *De corona* of Demosthenes and *Against Ctesiphon* of Aeschines (*see* CICERO (1) 5). The translation itself may not have been done. Cicero argues that Demosthenes, who wrote in Attic Greek, had such a command of every oratorical style that it is inappropriate to use the term Atticism to describe a plain style of *oratory.

**De ōrātō′re** ('On the orator') A work in three books by *Cicero (*see* (1) 4), one of his three major treatises on the theory of Latin rhetoric (the other two are *Brutus* and *Orator*). It was completed in 55 BC after his exile and addressed to his brother Quintus. The dialogues which it comprises are supposed to take place in 91 BC and the chief interlocutors are the eminent lawyers L. Licinius *Crassus and M. *Antonius; Q. Mucius *Scaevola, another great lawyer, is also present; and after the first dialogue Q. *Catulus, consul with the general Marius, and C. Julius Caesar Strabo the orator. The scene of the dialogues is the villa of Crassus at Tusculum. Cicero's aim is to describe the principles underlying the practice of oratory. His ideal orator closely resembles the ideal statesman depicted soon after in *De republica.

**De re eque′stri (Peri hippikēs)** ('On horsemanship') Treatise by *Xenophon, the earliest surviving Greek work of its kind. Xenophon considers only the use of horses in war and writes accordingly, and out of long experience, about how to choose and train a horse for that purpose. His observations and general instructions are still pertinent.

**De repu′blica** ('On the state', often referred to as the *Republic*) Dialogue in six books on political science by *Cicero ((1) 4), begun in 54 BC and published by early 51 BC. The chief interlocutors are P. Cornelius *Scipio Aemilianus and C. *Laelius, and the discussion is supposed to take place over three days in 129 BC in Scipio's garden. We possess the greater part of the first three books and fragments of the others, including the *Somnium Scipionis*, 'Dream of Scipio', which formed the conclusion of the work and is preserved mainly in a commentary by *Macrobius. The dialogue, modelled to some extent on Plato's *Republic*, concerns the composition of the ideal state; Cicero favours a combination of monarchy, oligarchy, and democracy, and looks for a wise counsellor. He emphasizes the Stoic view of the individual as part of the cosmos and the natural order of things.

**De rerum nātū′ra** ('On the nature of things') Philosophical poem by *Lucretius.

**De re ru′stica** ('On farming') 1. Treatise on farming written in dialogue form by M. Terentius *Varro when his eightieth year (37 BC) admonished him 'that he must be packing his baggage to depart this life'. It is in the tradition of the *De agri cultura* of the Elder Cato, with a preface celebrating the virtues of the agricultural basis of the early Roman state (up to the mid-second century BC). The treatise is in three books and takes the form of conversations, to some extent in a dramatic setting: the first conversation is interrupted by news of a murder, and the third by incidents in an election. Book 1 deals with the farm itself, its buildings and equipment, and the agricultural year in general; book 2 with cattle- and sheep-breeding; book 3 with the smaller livestock on a farm, aviaries, poultry, bees, game preserves, and fishponds. The work is enlivened by touches of wit and a feeling for the country life.
2. Treatise by *Columella.

**De senectū′te (Cato Maior de senectute)** ('The Elder Cato on old age') Dialogue by *Cicero ((1) 5), probably written just before Julius Caesar's murder in 44 BC. The work is dedicated to *Atticus. The conversation is supposed to take place in 150 BC, when M. Porcius *Cato (the Elder) was in his eighty-fourth year. At the request of his young friends *Scipio Aemilianus and *Laelius, Cato expounds how the burden of old age may best be borne; he describes its compensations and consolations, drawing illustrations from his own experience, from reminiscences of old men he has known, and from his reading (notably of Plato and Xenophon). He concludes with a reasoned statement of his belief in the immortality of the soul. The early part of the dialogue is imitated from the conversation of Socrates and Cephalus in book 1 of Plato's *Republic.

**Deuca′lion** In Greek myth, the son of *Prometheus. When Zeus was so angry at the crimes of mortals that he decided to destroy them by a flood, Deucalion, warned by Prometheus, built a boat for himself and his wife Pyrrha, daughter of Epimetheus. They floated in it until the water subsided and they grounded on Mount *Parnassus. Advised by an oracle to throw their mother's bones over their shoulder, they realized that this meant the stones of the earth and did so, those thrown by Deucalion becoming men and those thrown by Pyrrha women. The new race was called the Leleges. Subsequently Deucalion and Pyrrha became the parents of *Hellen, the eponymous founder of the Greeks. The ancients had no other universally accepted account of human origins.

**de'us ex ma'china** ('a god in a machine') *See* THEATRE [Greek].

**dēvō'tio** ('vowing to death') If a battle was going against a Roman general it was open to him to dedicate himself and the enemy army to 'Tellus and the Manes', i.e. the gods of the Underworld, by a fairly elaborate ritual. He then sought to be killed among the enemy, on the understanding that if the gods accepted his 'dedication' of himself they must also accept the enemy army. *See* DECIUS MUS.

**Dia'dochi** ('Successors') The name given to the Greek rulers who succeeded to various parts of the empire of Alexander the Great from his death in 323 BC until the beginning of the third century BC. *See* MACEDON.

**Dia'goras 1.** Famous boxer of Rhodes, from a family of athletes. Pindar's seventh Olympian Ode celebrates him.
**2.** Lyric poet from Melos, living in Athens towards the end of the fifth century BC. He was notorious for being 'godless' (*see* ATHEISM) and left Athens after being convicted of impiety for revealing and ridiculing the Eleusinian *mysteries in 415 BC. (He was not connected with the profanation of the mysteries in the same year.)

**dialectic (***dialektikē***)** Term of Greek philosophy, derived from the verb meaning 'to converse', 'to discuss'; in Plato (who possibly coined the term) and others, a method of philosophical inquiry conducted by question and answer. The inventor of dialectic was said to have been the philosopher *Zeno the Eleatic, whose characteristic method was to take an opponent's hypothesis and deduce from it two contradictory conclusions, thereby rendering it absurd. The dialectical method of Socrates, as it appears from the dialogues of Plato, was a further development (*see* ELENCHUS). It had as its aim the testing of the truth of a proposition by question and answer, in a

manner roughly resembling ordinary conversation. It was destructive rather than constructive, in that it demonstrated flaws in a suggested proposition without arriving at a better substitute, but it had some positive value in clearing away mistaken ideas. Plato's own dialectic is a development from that of Socrates and he saw it as a method for distinguishing sound argument from persuasive speech. At its simplest it starts from an assumption taken to be true by both parties or all (as did Zeno's), and proceeds through question and answer (as did Socrates') in a methodically rigorous way until a conclusion seems to be reached, perhaps not to the satisfaction of all participants. It seemed to Plato that this cooperative investigation made it possible to acquire knowledge, and provide explanations for what is known, positively and systematically. For Plato, although it might signify a particular method, dialectic in general seemed to be the only way to reach the true end of philosophy, knowledge of the Good, and sometimes signified philosophy itself rather than simply a philosophical method. His pupils in the *Academy engaged in rigorous dialectical exercises, attacking and defending set theses in formalized argument. This training was a valuable propaedeutic for Aristotle, for whom, unlike Plato, dialectic was related to rhetoric. In Aristotle's logical works, dialectic, though still the means of reaching knowledge, differs from a scientific 'demonstration' because it describes reasoning from a hypothesis based merely on *endoxa*, 'reputable opinions, held by all or most people, or by the wise', and it is thus inferior to deduction, which starts from premises known to be true. Training in dialectic came to include mastery of debating skills, including the informal arguments that rely on probability, analogy, etc. (*see* TOPICA).

In modern usage, which is sometimes at a considerable remove from the ancient meaning, the term often describes the general arguments or ideas of an author.

**dialogue** Literary genre, Greek in origin, in which characters, usually real but sometimes imaginary, conduct a conversation, pursuing a single theme but admitting some of the digression and inconsequence found in normal conversation. The *mimes of Sophron of Syracuse (fifth century BC) are an example, said to have been admired by Plato, whose Socratic dialogues may have taken their form from the mimes while their content was based on the actual question-and-answer conversations of Socrates. Many of Socrates' circle wrote similar dialogues, including Xenophon and Aristotle, the latter's dialogues surviving only in fragments. Unlike Plato, who never appears as a character in his dialogues, Aristotle seems to have played a leading role in his. This literary form reappeared in the second century AD in the dialogues of *Plutarch and *Lucian. These were modelled on Plato's but in the case of Lucian served satirical rather than philosophical ends and were a witty and biting form of entertainment.

In Roman literature the first known writer of literary prose dialogue was Marcus Junius *Brutus, the father of Caesar's assassin (who had the same name). Cicero says that the elder Brutus wrote a work on civil law in the form of a dialogue with his son. However, the chief Roman examples of the dialogue are to be found in Cicero's political, rhetorical, and philosophical treatises (*see* CICERO (1) 5) and in the *Dialogus de oratoribus* of Tacitus. In these it is the usual pattern for the leading role to be taken by one interlocutor (sometimes the author himself), who expounds his view at length, the other characters' parts being conspicuously less important. Varro, Cicero's contemporary, used the dialogue form in *De re rustica*. Some of Seneca's philosophical essays are called 'dialogues' in the manuscripts but they contain no actual dialogue (*see* SENECA (2) 2).

**Dia'logus de ōrātō'ribus** ('Dialogue on orators') Dialogue by *Tacitus. It is dedicated to Lucius Fabius Justus, consul in AD 102, and so was probably published in that year or soon after. The claims of oratory against other branches of literature are discussed, and the reasons why oratory has declined since Cicero's day. Following the fictional style of Cicero's *De oratore*, Tacitus too recalls a conversation heard in his youth c.AD 75 in the house of Curiatius Maternus, a poet. The other interlocutors are Marcus Aper, Julius Secundus (both distinguished orators of Gallic birth and both teachers of Tacitus), and Vipstanus Messalla, an aristocrat. The first 27 chapters are introductory. Aper, a pragmatic lawyer, maintains the superiority of oratory over poetry, for the rewards it brings. Maternus, a meditative idealist, disdains wealth and power and prefers a quiet life and the companionship of the Muses. Aper admits no decline

in oratory. Messalla, a champion of former times, criticizes the modern speakers. At the request of Maternus he passes to the causes of the alleged decline (ch. 28), which for the purposes of the discussion is to be assumed. These causes Messalla finds in the lax education of the young, contrasted with the careful methods of former days; and in the defective training given to orators in the schools of rhetoric. After this there is a gap of several pages in the manuscript. When the text resumes someone else (probably Maternus) is speaking. He argues that the decline in oratory is due to the changed conditions of public life. Oratory flourished under the republic in times of disorder and revolution, when orators were inspired by political enthusiasm. The calmness of political life under the emperors has removed these incentives, although it has brought compensations. Tacitus leaves the reader to decide on the reasons for the decline.

**Dia'na** Perhaps originally a moon-goddess, the Italian goddess of woodland and wild nature, protector of women, identified with the Greek *Artemis. Her cult was widespread in Italy. From very early times she had a temple at Rome on the Aventine, traditionally founded by the king Servius Tullius (578–535 BC). Catullus' poem 34, *Hymn to Diana*, describes her role. Her most famous cult was at *Aricia, on the shore of Lake Nemi in the Alban hills. Her shrine there stood in a grove, an old religious centre of the Latin league, where she was worshipped in association with *Egeria and with a male god of the forest named Virbius, later identified with the Greek Hippolytus. The priesthood of this shrine was given to a runaway slave, called *rex* ('king'), after he had broken off a branch from a certain tree in the grove (*see* GOLDEN BOUGH) and killed his predecessor. From being worshipped (like *Hecate) at crossroads she derives her title 'Trivia' (*trivium*, 'place where three roads meet').

**diatribe** [Gk. *diatribē*, 'spoken address', 'lecture'] Name given to a short, ethical discourse, particularly of the kind composed by Cynic and Stoic philosophers (*see* EPICTETUS). These popular moral lectures were often polemical in tone, and 'diatribe' soon acquired the modern sense of 'invective'. Many Roman writers produced diatribes, as did Christian polemicists. Two or three of Horace's *Odes* as well as some satires owe their tone to the diatribe as much as to the Greek iambographers (*see* IAM-BIC POETRY).

**Dicaea'rchus** (of Messana in Sicily, third to second century BC) Greek polymath and pupil of Aristotle, whose works are lost. He wrote biographies of earlier Greek writers as well as philosophical, political, and geographical works. His most interesting was a treatise on life in Greece (*Bios Hellados*), which was the first universal history of culture from the (imagined) *Golden age to Dicaearchus' own day, taking account of the contribution from the Chaldaeans (*see* BABYLONIA) and Egyptians, and also including a description of the known world. He was an important influence upon *Eratosthenes, Cicero, Josephus, and Plutarch. Cicero admired him greatly, and took him as exemplar of the 'practical life' (*see* DE OFFICIIS).

**dicasts (*dikastai*)** In Athenian law-courts, the members of the jury (*see* JURIES).

**dice** (Gk. *kyboi*, Lat. *tesserae*) In antiquity dice had, as now, six numbered sides; three such dice were used in play. (Cf. four-sided *astragaloi*, knucklebones, used in fours.) In Aeschylus' *Agamemnon* there is a mention of three sixes as the highest throw.

**di conse'ntes** (perhaps 'the gods that are') In Roman religion, the twelve great gods, six male and six female; according to two hexameter lines of the poet Ennius,

Juno, Vesta, Minerva, Ceres, Diana, Venus, Mars, Mercurius, Jovi', Neptunus, Volcanus, Apollo.

Jovi' stands for Jovis, i.e. Jupiter (*see* ELISION).

**Dicta Catōnis** ('the sayings of [Marcus] *Cato [the Elder]') A collection of Latin moral maxims in prose and (mostly) verse, an immensely popular schoolbook in the Middle Ages, translated into several European languages. The maxims included probably date from the third century AD and are drawn from both pagan and Christian sources, Greek and Latin. From the sixteenth to the nineteenth century editions of the work have called the author, erroneously, 'Dionysius Cato', an attribution which perhaps acknowledges Cato the Elder's role as the first Roman moralist.

**dictator** At Rome, the dictatorship was an emergency office, admitted to the Roman constitution soon after the expulsion of the kings in 509 BC to allow supreme authority to be entrusted temporarily to one individual in times of grave crisis. The dictator was appointed by the nomination of a magistrate with *imperium* on the senate's proposal. His function was to command the army or deal with a civil emergency; he had supreme judicial authority, which was not subject to appeal, and he could not be called to account for his actions. The dictator, who was also known as *magister populi*, 'master of the infantry', immediately appointed as his assistant a *magister equitum*, 'master of the horse'. The other magistrates remained in office but were subordinate to the dictator, who held office for six months at most. This time-limit meant that the office was of little use outside Italy, and for that purpose specially chosen proconsuls were used instead. However, in 82 BC Sulla was appointed dictator 'to restore the republic', i.e. for an indefinite period. Similarly, Julius Caesar was appointed dictator first in 49 BC for the specific purpose of holding the elections for 48; secondly in 48, perhaps for a year; thirdly in 46 for ten years; and finally in 44, for life. These dictatorships were obviously different in intention from the original office. After Caesar's murder the dictatorship was formally abolished, and Augustus refused to revive it.

**didactic poetry** Poetry designed to give instruction. The Greeks did not recognize didactic poetry as a separate literary *genre. Since, like epic, it was usually written in hexameters they regarded it on the basis of their own criterion of metre as a form of epic poetry. For early examples of didactic poetry *see* HESIOD; EMPEDOCLES; PARMENIDES. In Greece this kind of composition which aimed to put the subject of the poem in a firm moral or philosophical context died out in the fifth century BC with the rise of prose literature. It was revived in the Hellenistic age but as a form of virtuosity, with the poets displaying their ability to deal with specialized and obscure topics in verse. *See* ARATUS and NICANDER, and for later works *see* DIONYSIUS PERIEGETES and OPPIAN.

Didactic poetry found favour in Rome quite early: *Ennius seems to have written at least two lengthy didactic works, including one on gastronomy (of which eleven lines survive). In the first century BC Lucretius in *De rerum natura* claims to be the first to write didactic poetry in Latin, perhaps wrongly, but he is certainly the first whose work harks back to the serious moral didacticism of Hesiod, as do Virgil's *Georgics*, whose subject is ostensibly farming. There follow in the early first century AD Ovid's *Fasti* and the quasi-parody of a didactic poem, the *Ars amatoria*, the *Astronomica* of *Manilius (2), and the *Aetna* of an unknown author. *See also* COLUMELLA [book 10].

**didasca'lia** At Athens, the 'teaching' of a *dithyramb, comedy, or tragedy to the chorus and actors who were to perform it, by the dramatist (or his representative). The word came to be used to describe the official record of a dramatic performance, giving the name of the festival at which the work was produced and that of the *eponymous archon; in the case of drama, the names of the dramatists in order of success (Greek drama was always a matter for competition; *see* TRAGEDY 2), and of the plays which each dramatist entered; the names of the protagonists, the best actor, and the *choregos* of the winning play (*see* CHOREGIA); in the case of the dithyrambic competitions, the name of the victorious tribe (each of the ten tribes provided a chorus) and the best *aulos*-player. This information has in some cases survived on inscriptions. Aristotle in the fourth century BC compiled a book of *didascaliae* which has not survived but which was used by Hellenistic scholars, some of whose records found their way into the manuscripts of extant plays, providing valuable information concerning dates and names.

**Dīdo** Legendary daughter of a king of Tyre called Belus by Virgil. She is said to have had the name Elissa at Tyre, but subsequently, at Carthage, Dido. She was married to her uncle Sychaeus, who was murdered for his great wealth by her brother Pygmalion when the latter was king of Tyre. Dido fled with some followers to Libya and founded the city of Carthage: Iarbas, a local king, had given her as much land as might be covered by an ox-hide; this she had cut into strips and stretched to enclose a large area. To escape marriage with Iarbas she built a pyre as though for an offering and threw herself on to the flames. For Virgil's adaptation of her story *see* AENEID.

**Di'dyma** Oracular shrine of Apollo in Asia Minor, about 16km (10 miles) south of Miletus. After being important in the sixth century BC it was destroyed by Darius I of Persia in the early fifth century and not refounded until 331 BC. One of the most important oracles in Asia Minor under the Roman empire, in AD 303 it was held responsible, at least by Christians, for giving the emperor Diocletian an oracle which instigated their persecution throughout the empire. A few years later, with the official establishment of Christianity under the emperor Constantine I, the oracle was closed for ever.

**Di'dymus** (of Alexandria, first century BC) A notable Greek scholar, nicknamed *Chalcenteros* ('Brazen-guts') on account of his enormous industry (he was said to have written 4,000 books). None of his works has survived entire, though some fragments have turned up on papyrus, yet the results of his labours can be seen in the learned notes (*scholia) on ancient texts which are found in some manuscripts, in the lexica and etymologies compiled by scholars in later centuries, and in the collections of out-of-the-way learning represented by works such as the *Deipnosophistai* of *Athenaeus. As a compiler and abstracter of earlier researches Didymus has been invaluable in preserving some of the Hellenistic scholarship of the previous two-and-a-half centuries which would otherwise have been lost. Perhaps his most important commentaries were on Homer and on Attic comedy, the contemporary background of which needed elucidation, but he also wrote on Pindar, Bacchylides, the tragedians Aeschylus, Sophocles, and Euripides, and the orators, especially Demosthenes. His many important monographs included one on the classification of Greek lyric poetry and another on proverbs.

**di'es fasti, nefa'sti** At Rome, 'lawful' and 'unlawful' days for conducting public business. In the Roman calendar, a day marked F for *fastus* was a day 'of speaking', when it was permitted to transact legal business by speaking the formal words necessary; conversely, the sign N indicated a *dies nefastus*, 'day of not speaking', when for religious reasons the courts were not open. *See* FASTI.

**Die'spiter** Archaic Latin nominative form of *Jupiter, generally replaced by the vocative Iuppiter.

**di i'nferi** 'Gods of the Underworld' in Roman religion.

**Dikē** ('Justice') In Greek myth, the personification of Justice, daughter of Zeus and Themis. *See* ASTRAEA.

**di mānēs, pare'ntēs** *See* MANES.

**dǐ'meter** Metrical line containing two metra or metrical sequences.

**Dī'narchus** *See* DEINARCHUS.

**Dindymē'nē** Name of the goddess *Cybelē, from Mount Dindymon in Phrygia, where stood one of her early shrines.

**dining** *See* SYMPOSIUM.

**Dio** *See* DION.

**Dio Chrysostom** (Gk. *Chrysostomos,* 'Golden-mouthed'; properly Dio(n) Cocceiānus, *c.* AD 40–after 111; also known as Dio Prūsius, 'of Prusa' in Bithynia) Greek orator and popular philosopher. A member of a wealthy family from Prusa, he came to Rome and fell under the influence of the Stoic philosopher *Musonius Rufus. Banished from Rome and Bithynia because of opposition to the emperor Domitian, he travelled widely through Greece and Asia Minor preaching Stoic-Cynic philosophy. He was highly thought of by the enlightened emperors Nerva (who succeeded Domitian in AD 96) and his successor (in 98) Trajan. Some of his 80 or so surviving speeches are genuinely political, dealing with real situations in Bithynia, but the rest are 'display pieces' typical of the *Second Sophistic, on a variety of popular themes, delivered to inform, improve, and entertain a variety of audiences while he was on his travels. He aims at the style and language of Attic Greek, in the easy manner of Plato and Xenophon, and his philosophy reflects conservative values of virtue and charity towards others. His speeches give a vivid picture of his life and times.

**Dīocle'tian (Gaius Aurēlius Valērius Dioclētianus)** (originally named Dioclēs, d. *c.* AD 312) Roman emperor AD 284–305. He was a Dalmatian of humble birth, elevated to emperor by the army. His genius was for administration, and many of his measures lasted for centuries. He made the empire into a tetrarchy (i.e. he divided the rule into four), in order to make government more effective and to bring about an ordered succession to the throne (*see* AUGUSTUS, THE). Many provinces were divided so as to become smaller administrative units, the frontiers were strengthened by fortifications and the size of the army was greatly increased. Diocletian's anxieties for the unity of the empire made him favour what he perceived as Roman tradition and discipline, and

it was probably this which led to his notorious persecution of the Christians, begun in 303 and felt particularly in Palestine and Egypt. As a consequence the Coptic and Ethiopian Churches reckon the years of the Christian era from the accession of Diocletian in 284 ('era of the martyrs'). Late in 303 Diocletian visited Rome for the only time in his life, but returned to Nicomedia where he abdicated in 305. Galerius succeeded him as Augustus in the West. *See also* DIDYMA.

**Dio (Dion) Cocceianus** *See* DIO CHRYSOSTOM.

**Diodō'rus Si'culus** Sicilian Greek historian of the first century BC, contemporary with Livy, who wrote a world history (*Bibliothēkē,* 'Library') in forty books, centred on Rome, from mythological times to 60 BC. Books 1–3 comprise the ancient legends of Asia and North Africa, books 4–6 those of Greece and Europe. All these books are fully preserved except for 6, which is fragmentary. Of particular interest are the descriptions of Egypt in book 1, based on *Hecataeus, and of India in book 2. Books 7–17 cover the period from the Trojan War to Alexander the Great; 7–10 survive in fragments, 11–17 are fully preserved and cover the period 480–302 BC. Books 18–40 cover the period from the Diadochi (successors of Alexander) to Julius Caesar (54 BC); 18–20 survive in their entirety, 21–40 survive in fragments. The work is an uncritical compilation, and confused when Diodorus changes sources, but valuable for preserving the evidence of these sources: for example, his evidence is very important when, for the events in Greece around 400 BC (his books 13 and 14), he uses *Ephorus who himself drew on the *Hellenica Oxyrhynchia* (*see* OXYRHYNCHUS HISTORIAN). He also used *Hieronymus of Cardia, *Timaeus, and *Poseidonius. In the early books he is a useful source of mythological information. (*See also* EUHEMERUS.)

**Dio'genēs 1.** (of Sinōpē, *c.*412–324 BC) The first so-called *Cynic philosopher. After his arrival in Athens, he seems to have adopted a way of life prefigured by the austere character and lifestyle of *Antisthenes, who was often said by later writers to have been the real founder of Cynicism. Diogenes became the subject of many anecdotes because of his fanatical espousal of 'living according to nature'. While in Athens he was supposed to have lived in a tub (of earthenware) belonging to the *Metröon (temple of the Mother of the gods). His later life was reputedly spent in Corinth, where he is said to have met Alexander the Great and asked him to move aside and not block the sunshine. Nothing has survived of his writings, composed despite the Cynical disparagement of literature. It may have been in a book, the *Republic*, that he expounded his famous belief in cosmopolitanism, in which gods, human beings, animals, and the natural world are embraced in an ultimate unity. For him, happiness consisted of satisfying one's barest natural needs for things outside oneself, for food and shelter for example, in the cheapest and easiest way, and for the rest living on one's own natural endowments, renouncing all possessions and relationships. This self-sufficiency could be achieved by physical and mental self-discipline, and by losing the conventional sense of shame. It was supposed to be on account of this last characteristic that Diogenes was nicknamed 'dog'. He illustrated his principles in his way of life and in caustic utterances: Plato called him a 'mad Socrates'; Diogenes thought Plato's philosophy absurd. His disciple *Crates promulgated the Cynic way of life.

**2.** Of Oenoanda, *see* EPICURUS.

**3. Diogenes Lāe'rtius** (i.e. of Laertē in Cilicia) The Greek author of *Lives and Doctrines* [dogmata] *of Eminent Philosophers* (generally known as *Lives of the Philosophers*). He probably lived in the first half of the third century AD, but about his life nothing is known. His work, in ten books, purports to give an account of the principal Greek thinkers (including in the term such men as Solon, the Athenian poet and reforming politician, and Periander, tyrant of Corinth), 82 in number, from Thales (*c.*600 BC) to Epicurus (fourth century BC). Diogenes was industrious, but he compiled his book from the works of earlier biographers and epitomizers of philosophical doctrines, so that he is often at several removes from the works of the philosophers themselves. Fortunately, he usually names his sources, and thus it is to some extent possible to tell when his evidence may be relied upon. He is most valuable in his preservation of the maxims and three epistles of *Epicurus, and he preserves the epigram of *Callimachus upon the death of his friend Heracleitus. Diogenes also wrote (rather bad) poetry, some of which he quotes in the *Lives*.

**Diomē'dēs** (in pre-twentieth-century English often Dio'mede) **1.** In Greek myth, a Thracian, son of Arēs and a nymph Cyrenē, king of the Bistones, whose man-eating horses Heracles captured as one of his Labours (*see* HERACLES, LABOURS OF 8).

**2.** In Greek myth, son of *Tȳdeus and of Dēḯpyle, daughter of Adrastus. He took part in the expedition of the *Epigoni against Thebes, and was leader of the men of Argos and Tiryns in the Trojan War. With the help of Athena he wounded Aphrodite and even the war-god Ares, and killed a number of Trojan warriors, but behaved chivalrously to his guest-friend *Glaucus of Lycia although he was on the enemy side. He and Odysseus raided the Trojan camp and killed Dolon and Rhesus. He plays an important part in the poems of the *Epic Cycle which describe what happened to the Greek heroes after the fall of Troy. With Odysseus he brought *Philoctetes from Lemnos and stole the *Palladium from Troy. When on his return home from Troy he found that his wife Aigialeia had been unfaithful to him, he left again and wandered to Italy where he founded various towns in Apulia; on his death he was buried on one of the 'Islands of Diomedes' (*Diomedeae insulae*; modern Tremiti Islands) near the Apulian coast. In *Aeneid* 11 he is represented as refusing to join in the resistance to Aeneas.

**Dīon (Dio) 1.** Ruler of *Syracuse (*see* PLATO 1).
**2. Dio(n) Ca'ssius** *See* CASSIUS.

**Diō'nē** Consort of Zeus at Dodona, the only seat of her cult, and by him the mother of *Aphrodite. The name is the feminine form of Zeus.

**Diony'sia** Name given in Greece to festivals of the god Dionysus, which were often characterized by ritual licence and revelry as well as dramatic performances (*see also* LENAEA). Attica celebrated five festivals annually dedicated chiefly to Dionysus, the Oschophoria, Lenaea, and Anthesteria, and two which included his name, the Rural (or Rustic) Dionysia in the month Poseideon (December), whose procession is imitated by Aristophanes in the *Acharnians*, and the Great (or City) Dionysia at Athens itself in the month Elaphebolion (end of March), known as 'Great' because of its importance. This latter festival was instituted, or at any rate considerably augmented, in 534 BC by the tyrant Peisistratus, who brought the cult to Athens from Eleutherae (on the border between Attica and Boeotia, north of Eleusis). The god's image was placed in the old temple of Dionysus within the precinct of the theatre (*see* DIONYSUS, THEATRE OF). A day or two before the festival began the image was taken from its temple to another outside Athens near the *Academy, so that by escorting it in a torchlight procession back to the theatre the Athenians might re-enact its original arrival in the city from Eleutherae; it was thus present throughout the dramatic performances staged in the god's honour. The Great Dionysia proper began on the tenth day of Elaphebolion with a spectacular religious procession (in which one conspicuous element was the carrying of phalluses in honour of the god) leading up to the sacrifices and libations poured by the ten *strategoi* in the precinct of Dionysus' temple. The procession included the *choregoi* (*see* CHOREGIA) of the various dramatic performances, dressed in their robes. Except for the period of the Peloponnesian War the festival seems to have lasted for five days, when five comedies were performed, one on each afternoon, preceded on two days by dithyrambic competitions and on three days by tragedies and satyr plays, the activities beginning at daybreak. During the war, to save expense and time, the festival was curtailed by one day and the number of comedies performed reduced to three.

At the time of the Great Dionysia, when the winter was over, the seas were navigable and there might be many visitors in Athens (as there were not at the earlier Lenaea in winter). The festival thus became for Athenians a patriotic display of the cultural and political superiority of their city. Children whose fathers had died fighting for Athens paraded in the theatre, and during the existence of the *Delian League it was the time when the allies brought their tribute to Athens to be displayed in the *orchestra* of the theatre.

***Dionysiaca*** *See* NONNUS.

**Dionȳ'sius 1. Dionysius I** and **II** Tyrants of *Syracuse.

**2. Dionysius Thrax** ('Dionysius the Thracian', of Alexandria, *c.*170–*c.*90 BC) A pupil of *Aristarchus and later a teacher of grammar and literature at Rhodes. His only surviving work is *Technē grammatikē* a Greek grammar (it does not cover syntax), which remained a standard work for many centuries. The form in

which Latin grammar was set out was derived from this Greek model, and through Latin most modern grammars of the European languages are indebted to it. Its influence spread beyond Europe through Syriac and Armenian adaptations, and a large body of comment gradually accumulated, which then accompanied the text. The Greek verb *typtō* ('I beat') was used to exemplify voices, numbers, and persons, but the full paradigm with all possible moods and tenses was introduced later.

**3. Dionysius of Halicarnassus** Greek *rhetor and historian who lived at Rome for many years from 30 BC. As a literary critic of good judgement he wrote (in Greek) a number of treatises: criticism of the Greek orators Lysias, Isocrates, Isaeus, and Demosthenes, showing in the introduction his preference for the Attic style of rhetoric over that of the Asianic school (*see* ORATORY [Greek]); some minor works on Deinarchus, Demosthenes, and (more importantly) Thucydides, whose prose style he found 'obscure' and 'contorted', and a letter on Plato, of whose 'dithyrambic' style Dionysius was also very critical; and, the most interesting of his works, a treatise *On the Arrangement of Words* (*Peri syntheseōs onomatōn*), the only surviving ancient work on word-order and euphony. To this we owe the best-preserved text of Sappho's 'Ode to Aphrodite' and the fragment from the *Danae* poem of Simonides. As a historian Dionysius had a great enthusiasm for Rome, expressed in the twenty books of his *Roman Antiquities* (*Rōmāikē archaiologia*), of which books 1–9 and large parts of 10 and 11 survive. It went from mythical times down to the outbreak of the First Punic War (264 BC), the point at which the history of Polybius begins, but the surviving part breaks off in 441 BC. It is a painstakingly detailed composition made from the Roman annalists, and a valuable supplement to Livy. It contains the observation, much repeated since the writer's day, that the style is the man (1.1.3).

**4. Dionysius the Areo'pagite** An Athenian converted by the apostle Paul (Acts 17: 34) and for long supposed to be the author of four treatises and some letters which in fact belong to the early sixth century AD. Their true author, now known as pseudo-Dionysius, seems to have been aiming to achieve a synthesis of *Neoplatonism and Syrian Christianity. He represents the cosmos as a revelation of divinity which through love draws all rational creatures into harmony with an unknowable

God. The symbolism combines Neoplatonic and Christian elements in a way that made the works immensely popular throughout the Middle Ages. Although their authenticity was challenged by some, in general they were accepted as the work of Dionysius and the texts commented upon by a succession of eminent theologians. They were translated into Latin by Eriugena in the ninth century and became one of the bases of medieval theology, second only to the writings of St Augustine. Their authenticity was not finally disproved until the nineteenth century.

**5. Dionysius Periēgē'tēs** ('the guide', probably second century AD) The Greek author of a *Description of the World,* a didactic poem in 1,185 hexameters, repeating the views of the Hellenistic scholar *Eratosthenes, and taking little account of later geographic discoveries. It enjoyed great popularity in later times. Eustathius in the twelfth century wrote a valuable commentary on it.

**Dionȳ'sus** In Greek myth, the god of wine and of ritual madness or ecstasy, son of Zeus and Semele, the daughter of *Cadmus, king of Thebes. When Semele was made pregnant by Zeus, his jealous wife Hera, in human disguise, persuaded her to pray to Zeus to visit her in all the splendour of a god. This he did and she was consumed by his lightning; but he rescued her unborn child from the ashes and placed him in his thigh, from which in due time he was born. The child was entrusted to Ino, sister of Semele and wife of *Athamas, but Hera, still jealous, punished them by driving them mad, so that Athamas killed his son Learchos and Ino leaped into the sea with her other son Melicertes. Ino was transformed into a sea-goddess Leucothea, and Melicertes became the sea-god Palaemon. Dionysus was now handed over to the nymphs of Mount Nyssa (located in various parts of Asia and Europe), where he was worshipped, and where he introduced the cultivation of the vine. He was persecuted by those who refused to recognize his divinity, but overcame them and extended his conquests far into Asia and into India. The most famous of these persecutions was that of Pentheus, king of Thebes, which forms the subject of the *Bacchae* of Euripides. The daughters of Proetus (*see* BELLEROPHON), king of Argos, also opposed him and were driven mad, their madness cured by the intervention of the seer *Melampus. For another, similar legend *see* MINYAS.

Dionysus is represented as accompanied on his conquests by a host of votaries, male and female, *satyrs, *sileni, *maenads, Bassarids, dancing about him, intoxicated or possessed. They were known as *Bacchi* (fem. *Bacchae*), sharing with the god his cult name, Bacchus. The seventh *Homeric Hymn relates how pirates found and kidnapped him, tying him up on shipboard; but the bonds fell off him, a vine grew about the mast, and the captive turned into a lion. The pirates in terror jumped into the sea, whereupon they were transformed into dolphins. For another myth about Dionysus *see* ARIADNE.

Dionysus scarcely appears in Homer, and this fact, combined with the stories of his coming to Greece from Thrace and having to overcome resistance before being accepted, led to the belief in relatively modern times that he was a new god, accepted late into the Greek pantheon of Olympians (*see* GODS [Greek]). However, his name has been found in Greece on *Linear B tablets from Pylos and Crete dated c.1250 BC, perhaps even in connection with wine, and a spectacular find of terracotta statues seems to suggest that he was worshipped in Ceos from the fifteenth century BC onwards. Moreover, the oldest Dionysiac festival of wine, the Anthesteria, pre-dates the Ionian migrations (in about the tenth century BC). This evidence seems to indicate that his name and cult may be Mycenaean in origin. He is a god of an essentially different type from the Olympian deities, a giver of joy and a soother of cares (the latter described by his epithet Lyaios), experienced by the worshipper through the ambivalent gift of wine. He is also experienced through ecstasy, which had nothing to do with alcohol but was felt as intensified mental power and the surrender of everyday identity. The Dionysus of myth had another aspect, known by the account of his ecstatic worshippers seizing a wild animal and tearing it apart in order to eat it raw (the act known as a *sparagmos*), believing, as in Euripides' *Bacchae*, that they were then incorporating in themselves the god and his power. This side of Dionysiac possession, though depicted in art and myth, never appears in actual cult. While men as well as women could 'go mad' for Dionysus, men could not join the bands of (female) maenads who notionally followed the god to the mountains every other year in many Greek cities. Maenadism was never practised in Attica; Athenian maenads went to

Delphi in Phocis to join the Delphic Thyiads (Dionysus-inspired women) on the slopes of Mount Parnassus.

Dionysus is also connected with death and with beliefs about the after-life among both Greeks and Romans. Tombs were sometimes decorated with carved Dionysiac figures, maenads, and ivy; see DIONYSUS ZAGREUS and ORPHEUS. Characteristic of the cult of Dionysus is the mask, symbol of the surrender of identity, and a means of transforming identity. At its simplest his image consisted of a mask on a column draped with a piece of cloth. Important in connection with his worship were the *dithyramb (a variety of Greek choral lyric poetry), tragedy, and comedy, all of which were performed at his festivals (see DIONYSIA). Dionysus is frequently represented as a rather effeminate youth, with luxuriant hair, reclining with grapes or a wine-cup in his hand, or holding the *thyrsos*, a rod wreathed in ivy and vine-leaves, topped with a pine-cone. Hellenistic Greeks connected him with the Egyptian god Osiris (ruler of the Underworld and the god who renewed life), and the Romans with their wine-god Liber, also called Bacchus. See also IACCHUS and BACCHANALIA.

**Dionysus, artists of** The general name for the guilds into which the troupes of itinerant Greek actors and musicians formed themselves from the third century BC onwards.

**Dionysus, theatre of** An open-air theatre at Athens situated in a hollow on the southern slope of the Acropolis. It was within the precinct of an old temple of the god Dionysus Eleuthereus ('Dionysus the Liberator'), who thus gave the theatre its name and whose image watched over the dramatic performances of the Great *Dionysia and of the *Lenaea. An altar of the god (*thymele*) stood in the centre of the dancing-floor (*orchestra*); the *aulos-player who accompanied the chorus of the play may have stood on its steps. The oldest remains of buildings on the site go back perhaps to the sixth century BC (see THEATRE [Greek]).

**Dionȳsus Zagreus** The myth of Dionysus Zagreus played an important role in the beliefs of the Greeks who practised the mysteries of *Orpheus. Zagreus was the son of Persephone and Zeus, who came to her in the form of a snake. He gave the rule of the world to the child, sat him on a throne and had the *Cory-

bantes guard him. At the instigation of the jealous Hera (wife of Zeus) the *Titans distracted the child's attention with toys, then seized him, tore him to pieces, and devoured him, all but the heart; this Athena saved and took to Zeus. From the heart Zeus remade his son and implanted him in Semele (see DIONYSUS), from whom was later born a new Dionysus Zagreus. He punished the Titans by striking them with his lightning, and from the rising soot sprang the human race, rebels against the gods but having in them some portion of the divine. This story is known only from writers of the Hellenistic age, but it seems to have been current earlier. The association of Dionysus with the Underworld is significant in the mystery religions (see MYSTERIES) which were primarily concerned with judgement after death, freedom from punishment, rebirth, and eventual blessedness. Another myth tells how Dionysus descended to the Underworld to rescue Semele from Hades and transfer her to Olympus.

**Diosco'ridēs (Dioskouridēs)** (first century AD) Greek physician from Cilicia who travelled widely in order to identify medicinal plants accurately by seeing them growing. He also investigated animal products and even minerals. He wrote up the results in a *Materia medica* (Peri hȳlēs iatrikēs, 'Drugs used in medicine') in five books in which he described the medicinal properties of some 700 plants and over a thousand drugs. Dioscorides is a careful observer and unsuperstitious. His method was to combine first-hand observation with the work of previous authorities on the subject, and to arrange his material in categories—animal, mineral, and plant products, the last subdivided into kinds of plant—and within each category to arrange the drugs according to their effect on the body. This careful arrangement was confused by later copyists who tried to introduce an alphabetic system; nevertheless the work was widely used, in Greek, Latin, and Arabic, until the sixteenth century, and the original illustrations continued to be copied.

**Dio'scūri (Dios kouroi)** ('sons of Zeus') In Greek myth, Castor and Polydeuces (Lat. Pollux). They were native to Sparta, where they were worshipped. In Homer and in Hesiod they are the twin sons of Tyndareus and *Leda, and the brothers of Helen (of Troy). Later, Polydeuces is represented as the son of

Zeus, and immortal. When Castor, the mortal son of Tyndareus, is fatally wounded (below), Polydeuces chooses to share his immortality with his brother, so that they both spend half their time below the earth at Therapne near Sparta and the other half with the gods on Mount Olympus. Other accounts make them both sons of Zeus, born like Helen from an egg. They occur in three mythical stories. When *Theseus carried off Helen as a child they made an expedition to Attica, recovered her, and took Theseus' mother Aethra as well to be Helen's slave. Helen's place of concealment had been revealed by the hero Akademos (*see* ACADEMY), whose land was always spared in consequence by invading Lacedaemonians. In another story they took part in the voyage of the *Argonauts, Polydeuces distinguishing himself in the fight against Amycus. Finally they carried off the two daughters of a certain Leucippus, Hilaeira and Phoebe, who were betrothed to their cousins Idas and Lynceus. In the ensuing fight (or, in some versions, in a cattle raid) Castor and both opponents were killed. It was on this occasion that Polydeuces gave Castor a share of his immortality (above). The Dioscuri are often identified with the constellation Gemini (the Twins). They were commonly regarded as protectors of sailors, to whom they appeared during storms (in Christian times as the lights of St Elmo's fire). They were also notable boxers and horsemen, frequently called 'riders of white horses', and therefore the patrons of athletes and athletic contests.

In Roman religion the worship of Castor and Pollux was introduced in early times, Castor always being the more popular. Their temple at Rome (nearly always known as the temple of Castor) was vowed by the dictator Aulus Postumius during the battle of the Romans against the Latins at Lake Regillus (496 BC). The story was that they then fought at the head of the Roman army and after the battle brought the news of the victory to Rome; they were seen watering their horses at the Lacus Iuturnae ('Pool of Juturna', a fountain in the Forum) and their temple was erected on that spot, beside the shrine of Vesta. According to another story, Publius Vatinius (grandfather of the famous tribune) informed the senate that he had met two youths on white horses who told him of the capture of Perseus of Macedon on that day (168 BC); he was thrown into prison until his statement was confirmed by dis-

patches. The Roman *equites* regarded the brothers as their particular patrons. The common oaths *mecastor* and *edepol*, based on their names, are evidence of their popularity. *See also* SIMONIDES.

**Dioscū'ridēs** *See* DIOSCORIDES.

**Dioti'ma** Priestess of Mantinea, real or fictitious, who figures in Plato's *Symposium* as Socrates' teacher in the mysteries of love.

**Di'philus** Greek poet of New Comedy (*see* COMEDY [Greek 6]), born in the mid-fourth century BC in Sinope, who lived most of his life in Athens. He won three victories at the *Lenaea. No complete play survives but there are interesting fragments. Plays by him were the originals of Plautus' *Rudens and *Casina.

**Dīrae (Furiae)** The Roman counterparts of the Greek Erinyes or Eumenides; *see* FURIES.

**Dīrae** ('Furies') Latin poem in hexameters attributed to Virgil; *see* APPENDIX VIRGILIANA.

**Dircē** In Greek myth, wife of Lycus, regent of Thebes. She was killed by the sons of *Antiope in revenge for her treatment of their mother; they tied her to the horns of a bull and she was dragged to death. After her death she was changed into the stream that bore her name, symbolic of Thebes in Greek literature: for example, the 'swan of Dirce' signifies the poet Pindar.

**dirge** (Gk. *thrēnos*) In Greek literature, lyric poem of lament sung over the dead. The dirges of Simonides and Pindar were famous, but only a few fragments survive. Cf. the funeral dirges (*naeniae*) of hired mourners at Rome.

**Dis (Dis Pater)** ('Father Dis') In Roman religion, the ruler of the Underworld, the equivalent of the Greek god Pluto (another name for *Hades). The name Dis (i.e. Dīvēs, 'rich') is perhaps the Latin translation of Pluto. During the Punic Wars foreign religious rites were from time to time introduced at Rome by order of the senate to hearten the people. In 249 and 149 BC the senate appointed special festivals of appeasement to the Roman equivalents of the Greek Underworld deities Pluto and Persephone, namely Dis and Proserpina (*see also* SECULAR GAMES). In classical Roman literature Dis has become merely a symbol of death.

**Discord, Apple of** *See* PARIS, JUDGEMENT OF.

**disease** For chronic and endemic diseases in the ancient world the Hippocratic Corpus (*see* HIPPOCRATES) and *Galen are good sources of information which can be supplemented to a limited extent by paleopathology (the study of diseases found in human skeletal remains). Much less information has come down to us concerning epidemic diseases. The most prominent diseases in the medical literature are malaria (recognized if not understood) and tuberculosis, the latter affecting mostly young adults. Heart disease is not prominent. Childhood diseases are hardly mentioned, but the high infant mortality observed in cemeteries was probably due to enteric diseases, and the diseases of malnutrition such as anaemia and rickets were common. There is no certain evidence for measles, and cholera is not attested. The common cold was certainly present but perhaps not influenza. Leprosy may have existed in the Near East in the Bronze age and spread slowly westwards, probably occurring sporadically. Some sexually transmitted diseases existed, such as genital herpes and the contagious trachoma, which seems to have been the main cause of blindness. Certain cancers are mentioned frequently; according to Galen breast cancer was common.

**Dis exapatō'n** ('Twice a swindler') Greek comedy by *Menander, very probably the original of Plautus' *Bacchides*. A papyrus fragment from the play is clearly the source of lines 494–562 of *Bacchides*, and is the first passage in Menander of any length which has been found to correspond to a later Roman adaptation.

**dissection** *See* ANATOMY AND PHYSIOLOGY.

**di'thyramb (***dithyrambos***)** In Greek, a form of choral lyric (*see* LYRIC POETRY) sung in honour of the god Dionysus; the word is of unknown origin, almost certainly not Greek. Its development from a simple cult song into a literary genre was the work of the poet *Arion in Corinth in the last quarter of the seventh century BC. From Corinth it was brought to Athens by *Lasus of Hermione, and in 509 BC it became a subject for competition at the festivals of Dionysus (*see* DIONYSIA). Simonides, Pindar, and Bacchylides all wrote dithyrambs; of the first two only fragments exist, but several of Bacchylides' survive almost entire. The dithyrambic chorus did not wear masks; they danced and sang in a circle in the *orchestra* (*see* DIONYSUS, THEATRE OF). Narrative plays a large part in these poems, but its subject matter is not particularly connected with Dionysus. At the Great *Dionysia at Athens each tribe entered two choruses for the dithyrambic competitions, one of boys and one of men, each under the charge of a *choregos* (*see* CHOREGIA) chosen from the tribe. Lots were drawn to determine the order for selecting poets and flute-players; the *choregos* also needed the services of a good chorus-trainer. The inscriptions preserving the lists of victors in the dithyrambic contests at Athens (*see* DIDASCALIA) preserve the names of the victorious tribes and their *choregoi* but not the names of the poets, no matter how famous. The successful *choregos* received, as the representative of his tribe, a tripod (a three-legged cooking cauldron given as a gift of honour), which he erected at his own expense upon a monument, with an inscription. After Bacchylides the musical component of the dithyramb seems to have increased in importance at the expense of the words, but since no music has survived it is hard to discern what happened. Up to this time the dithyramb had been composed in regular form in *strophes and antistrophes, but now this correspondence was abandoned in favour of a freer style of composition, with solo songs, and the language became far-fetched and artificial. The names chiefly associated with these changes are Melanippides of Melos (flourished *c*.480 BC) who introduced lyric solos, Philoxenus of Cythera (*c*.436–380) who introduced in his *Cyclops* a solo sung to the lyre, *Cinesias of Athens, and *Timotheus of Miletus. After the fourth century BC it seems that the dithyramb was no longer an important form of literary composition, although the competitions survived into the time of the Roman emperors.

**dīver'bium** Name given to dialogue in a Roman comedy, as distinct from *cantica*, the parts declaimed by the actors to a musical accompaniment.

**divination** The practice of interpreting certain signs as omens, i.e. divinely sent indications of future events, and fundamental to religion in the ancient world. To question their validity as the Greek chorus do at one desperate moment in Sophocles' *Oedipus Tyrannus* is to question belief in the gods themselves. Even the rationalistic Greek historian

Thucydides notes that the period covered by his history of the Peloponnesian War was rich in natural calamities, generally thought to be significant, though he is sparing in recording them (*see* NICIAS). The Greek historian and soldier Xenophon in his account of the dangerous retreat to the Black Sea in the *Anabasis* displays the attitude of a pious man in a difficult situation towards signs from the gods, when he tries to find out the intention of the gods in several ways: by questioning an oracle, through examining the organs of sacrificed animals, by observing birds, by interpreting dreams and chance events as significant—an opportune sneeze, a meaningful word casually spoken. At one point he keeps the army in suspense for several days because omens are interpreted as unfavourable. These forms of divination are found in Homer, except for divination by sacrifice which probably came to Greece from the Near East in the early archaic period. (According to *Arrian, lobeless livers from a sacrifice presaged the death of Alexander the Great.) Dreams might need a professional interpreter, or the dreamer could consult a dream-book (*see* ARTEMIDORUS). As the result of a dream the father of the young *Galen directed his son to the study of medicine. The Roman emperor Marcus *Aurelius was thankful to have received advice in a similar way on how to cure his ailments. In the practice of incubation a sick person would deliberately seek to have a dream which would suggest a cure, by sleeping in the temple of a healing god, usually *Asclepius. Another form of natural divination is prophecy from the speech of someone acting as the mouthpiece (*prophētēs*) of a divine power which possesses him. This kind of divination became institutionalized, with a succession of prophets, at the great oracular sites of Delphi, Dodona, Oropus, Ammon, and the various Sibylline sites. Collections of oracles were made and circulated by 'oracle-mongers', who often ascribed them to famous mythical seers such as the *Sibyl. These seers were frequently mocked by their contemporaries (as was the unjustly maligned *Meton in Aristophanes' *Birds*). The attitudes of philosophers to divination seem to have varied with the individual. Cicero's *De divinatione* is an important source of our knowledge on the subject. Some philosophers denied its possibility, like Xenophanes and the Epicureans and the Sceptic *Carneades; others, in the Aristotelian tradition (Peripatetics), accept-

ed that there could be inspired prophecy such as that of the Delphic oracle, and significant dreams. Stoics, by the tenets of their philosophy concerning the interconnectedness of everything, believed in prophecy generally.

For the Romans, the observation and interpretation of signs understood to refer to the state were part of their religion. Divination as practised at Rome was largely of the kind called by Cicero 'artificial', i.e. based on external observations of animals, plants, or objects; the best known form is *augury, observation of the behaviour of birds, which at Rome was entrusted to a college of augurs. Widely used also was observation of the entrails of sacrificial animals (*see* HARUSPICES and SACRIFICE 4). Predictions were sometimes based on certain involuntary human actions, a twitch or a sneeze for example. Exceptional plant growth might also be meaningful. Divination by throwing dice or drawing lots was common, and localized at certain sites. In later times, random consultation of the works of famous poets was favoured, perhaps because they were considered divinely inspired: hence the *sortes Homericae* and *Virgilianae* ('Homeric, Virgilian consultations'); *see* VIRGIL. Unusual meteorological phenomena were considered significant at all times (*see* ECLIPSES), and at Rome were recorded in the *annales maximi* (priestly records; *see* ANNALS). *Astrology became very popular after the conquests of Alexander the Great towards the end of the fourth century BC increased contact with what had been the Babylonian empire. (*See also* HIPPARCHUS.) Necromancy, calling up the spirits of the dead, was practised at all periods and is exploited for excitement in imaginative literature, but never acquired respectability. Prophecy by inspired utterance was more acceptable.

Most people accepted the forms of divination that had become established by their own day but looked with suspicion upon any new forms. Early Christian writers saw pagan divination as the work of evil demons and oracular sites as infested by them. The edict of the emperor Theodosius in AD 391, banning all forms of pagan cult, put a formal end to the practice.

**division of the Roman empire** (into eastern and western halves in AD 395) *See* BYZANTINE AGE.

**Dīvitiā'cus** (first century BC) Pro-Roman druid and chief of the Gallic tribe of the

Aedui, who appealed for Roman help against the invading Germans led by *Ariovistus. He assisted Caesar in his operations in Gaul (*see* COMMENTARIES 1 [books 1 and 2]). Both Caesar and Cicero based on him their views of druidism.

**divorce** *See* MARRIAGE LAW.

**Dōdō'na** The oracular sanctuary of Zeus, in Epirus, rivalling *Delphi in claiming to be the oldest Greek oracle. It is mentioned in Homer's *Iliad* and *Odyssey*. According to Greek tradition the oracles were extracted in some manner from a sacred oak-tree, perhaps by the rustling of its leaves or by doves perching in the tree (later Roman legends say by the sound of a sacred spring or brazen gong), and interpreted by priests known as Selloi (or Helloi), 'of unwashed feet and sleeping on the ground', according to the *Iliad*. By the middle of the fifth century BC the oracle was operated by three priestesses, later called 'the doves', who gave answers (a simple 'yes' or 'no') while in a trance-like state. The enquirer scratched his question on a lead tablet, many of which survive. The sanctuary was pillaged by the Romans in 167 BC.

**dokima'sia** (Gk., 'scrutiny') At Athens, the examination of successful candidates for political office by the *thesmothetai* (*see* ARCHONS) to ascertain their eligibility. In the main they were examined as to their being Athenian citizens aged 30 or over, innocent of serious wrongdoing, and holding political views acceptable at the time (e.g. not being anti-democratic).

**Dolabe'lla, Publius Cornēlius** (*c.*80–43 BC) Husband of Cicero's daughter *Tullia (against her father's wishes), a dissolute and debt-ridden aristocrat. They were divorced in 46. A legate of Julius Caesar in the Civil War, nominated by Caesar before his death to stand in for him as consul during his absence in Parthia, Dolabella seized the consulship and briefly turned republican for his own advantage after Caesar's murder, but reverted. He was finally defeated by the republican Cassius in Syria and committed suicide.

**Dōlon** In Homer's *Iliad* (book 10) and the *Rhesus* of Euripides, a Trojan spy killed by Odysseus and Diomedes.

**Domi'tian (Titus Flāvius Domitiānus)** (AD 51–96) Roman emperor from 81, when he suc-

ceeded his brother Titus, until his death. He was the younger son of the emperor Vespasian, and the last of the Flavian emperors. Tacitus and Pliny the Younger write about him in a hostile manner, probably representing the feelings of the senate at that time; Suetonius, though still hostile, gives a more balanced view, but one far removed from the flattery of Statius and Martial. Domitian was the first emperor since Claudius in 43 to go on military campaigns in person, in his case mostly on the Danube, where there were a number of incursions eventually contained by the emperor himself. In Britain at this time *Agricola continued his advance in Scotland, and his recall to Rome in 84 may reflect military need rather than Domitian's jealousy (as Tacitus implies in *Agricola*). At home Domitian promoted moral rectitude, to the extent of executing three Vestal Virgins for breaking their vows of chastity, and burying alive the chief Vestal. He was also diligent in the administration of the law, and tried to suppress corruption; he seems to have been an efficient financial administrator. Many public buildings were executed or restored: Domitian was the last to rebuild the Capitol, and he added the complex substructure to the arena of the Colosseum and further palace buildings on the Palatine. However, his autocratic behaviour angered the senate, and he became more ruthless in his treatment of those he considered to be his enemies. He executed at least twelve ex-consuls and expelled philosophers. After the execution in 95 of his cousin Flavius Clemens, whose sons were his heirs, a conspiracy was formed against him, possibly including his wife Domitia, and he was murdered in September 96. The senate decreed a *damnatio memoriae*.

**Donā'tus 1. Ae'lius Donatus** (fourth century AD) Latin grammarian, teacher of Jerome. He wrote two books of Latin grammar which remained in use throughout the Middle Ages, to the extent that 'donat' or 'donet' was used generally to mean 'textbook'. He dominated grammatical learning in Europe until the re-emergence of *Priscian in the twelfth century. He also wrote a commentary on Terence which survives in an abridged version, combined with the notes of other commentators, in the *scholia on that author; and most valuably a commentary on Virgil. Of this only the dedicatory epistle and the Life (derived from Suetonius), with an introduction to the *Eclogues*, survive entire, but it was extensively used by *Servius in his commentary.

**2. Tiberius Claudius Donatus** (late fourth century AD) The author of a rhetorical and stylistic commentary in twelve books on Virgil's *Aeneid*, which has no connection with the commentary of Donatus (1). He believed that the *Aeneid*'s main purpose was praise of Augustus.

**Do'rians, Dorian invasion** According to Greek myth, it had been the will of Zeus that Heracles should rule over the country of Perseus at Mycenae and Tiryns. After Heracles' death, however, the tradition was that these cities came into the hands of the descendants of *Pelops, and at the time of the Trojan War Agamemnon, not one of the Heracleidae, ruled at Mycenae. The Greeks believed as historical fact the legend that two generations after the Trojan War, *c.*1100 BC, a new Greek-speaking people known as Dorians (for the name *see* DORUS) entered Greece from the north-west. They accompanied the sons or descendants of Heracles (*see* AEGIMIUS and HERACLEIDAE), who were returning to the Peloponnese to claim their father's inheritance, first the city of Tiryns and then, by conquest, the whole Peloponnese. By this legend some historical events were explained, notably how the Dorians took possession of the Peloponnese by their dialect and culture. When in the 1950s the *Linear B script was found to be an early form of Greek, some thought the legend of a 'Dorian invasion' could reflect the arrival of Greek-speakers in the Balkan peninsula in the early part of the second millennium BC. However, it is more likely that the Greek language evolved in Greece itself, over time, through the mingling of *Indo-European and the indigenous population. The destruction of the Mycenaean cities in the twelfth century BC has also been seen to indicate a possible Dorian invasion. But there is no archaeological evidence to identify a people who might have destroyed the Mycenaean cities, and no positive signs of an influx of new people. The break in the pottery record at Sparta comes *c.*950–900 BC, rather too late for the mythical date. It has also been argued that there was in fact no Dorian invasion, that different groups of Greeks had been present in Greece since the beginning of Mycenaean culture, and that the destructions were caused by spasmodic raids or local uprisings of a suppressed population. However, a strong sense of cultural discontinuity following the destructions, as well as the legends themselves, seems to favour invasion.

**Dō'richa** The Egyptian courtesan loved by *Sappho's brother. Her nickname was *Rhodope.

**Dōrus** In Greek myth, son of *Hellen, the eponymous ancestor of the Hellenes (Greeks), himself the son of *Deucalion. Hellen became, by the nymph Orses, the father of the mythical ancestors of the three great branches of the Greek race, Aeolus (of the Aeolians), Xuthus (of the Achaeans and Ionians), and Dorus (of the Dorians). *See also* AEGIMIUS.

**drachma** In Greece, a coin worth six obols (*see* MONEY AND COINS 1). The word dates back to the days when Greece had a primitive iron currency; it means 'a handful', i.e. of obols (*oboloi*, 'spits').

**Drāco (Drăkōn)** An Athenian legislator, who received special authority to organize and codify the laws in 621 BC, the first time the Athenian laws were put in writing. Details of his legislation are not now known, but the laws were notoriously harsh (hence the adjective 'Draconian'), with nearly all offences (including idleness) punishable by death. When asked why he decreed death as the penalty for most offences he said that small offences deserved death and he knew of no severer punishment for great ones. All his laws were repealed by *Solon except those dealing with homicide (which restricted liability to individuals and entrusted trials for murder to the *Areopagus). No one at Athens in the fifth and fourth centuries BC doubted that the homicide laws then in force were those of Draco, but it cannot be assumed that in fact they had remained unchanged. The constitution attributed to Draco by Aristotle (*Athenaion politeia*, ch. 4) is now rejected as a later compilation.

**drama** *See* CHOREGIA; CHORUS; DIDASCALIA; DIONYSIA; DIONYSUS, THEATRE OF; DRAMATIC COMPETITIONS; THEATRE; TRAGEDY; COMEDY; MIME; PANTOMIME.

**dramatic competitions** At Athens, from the late sixth century BC onwards, tragedies and comedies were performed at festivals, under state supervision, by dramatists in competition with each other to win the prize for the best play or set of plays. *See* TRAGEDY 2 and COMEDY [Greek 1].

### Dream of Scipio *See* SOMNIUM SCIPIONIS.

**dreams** (Gk. *oneiroi*, Lat. *somnia*) Dreams are frequently personified in Greek and Latin literature; according to Hesiod, they are the daughters of Night. In Homer's *Odyssey* they live beyond *Oceanus, near the gates of the sun. Later poets wrote of a god of dreams, Morpheus (hence 'morphia', etc.), who made human shapes (*morphai*) appear to dreamers. Virgil says (in *Aeneid* 6) that the spirits of the dead send dreams to men from the Underworld, those that are true through a gate of horn, false dreams through a gate of ivory. He thus adapts what Homer says, very similarly, in *Odyssey* 19. The symbolism of horn and ivory, though exhaustively studied, remains obscure.

Belief in meaningful dreams and deceitful dreams is as old as Homer. Aristotle thought most people believed that dreams were sent by the gods, though he himself seems to have preferred a naturalistic explanation. The Persian Artabanus, as reported by Herodotus, tries to argue against King Xerxes that dreams are merely 'what is left of the day's thoughts'. Socrates professes in *Crito* to believe what was told him in a dream, that he would be put to death two days hence. Epicureans thought dreams were of no significance, and Romans seem to have been sceptical, except in times of crisis. With the growth of Christianity belief that dreams could foretell the future became common. Events revealed to a sleeper by an apparition were very common in ancient times but died out in early modern times. For reports of actual dreams (less bizarre than those in modern experience) *see* ARISTEIDES (2); ARTEMIDORUS. *See also* DIVINATION.

**Drūsus** For the various members of the Roman family of the Livii who bore this name (*cognomen*) see below and *see also* GERMANICUS.

**1. Marcus Li'vius Drusus** Tribune of the plebs in 122 BC, a supporter of the aristocracy against C. Sempronius Gracchus.

**2. Marcus Livius Drusus** Son of (1), grandfather of *Livia, the wife of the emperor Augustus, tribune of the plebs in 91 BC, who proposed, besides various democratic measures, to give the franchise to the Italian allies. His various enemies combined against him, and he was assassinated. His proposals and the consequent upheavals brought about the *Social War.

**3. Nero Claudius Drusus** (38–9 BC) Drusus the Elder, second son of Ti. Claudius Nero and *Livia. He was born about the time of Livia's second marriage, to Octavian (later the emperor Augustus). Thus he became the latter's stepson. His older brother was Tiberius (Augustus' successor as Roman emperor). He was commonly known as Drusus the Elder to distinguish him from Tiberius' son Drusus the Younger (below). He married Antonia Minor (daughter of Mark Anthony and Octavia), and was the father of Nero Claudius Germanicus and of the emperor Claudius. He was brilliantly successful in a series of campaigns against Germany during the years 12–9 BC, but died in the latter year from injuries received in a fall from his horse. After his death he was given the cognomen Germanicus; it is rarely used to describe him, but the name passed to his descendants.

**4. Drusus Julius Caesar** (*c*.13 BC–AD 23) Drusus the Younger, son of Tiberius (later emperor) and his first wife Vipsania Agrippina, daughter of *Agrippa. His original name, before the adoption of his father by Augustus, is not known. After the death of Germanicus, in AD 19, he became his father's principal collaborator and appears to have been designated to succeed him, but he died in 23, poisoned, it was later suspected, by his wife Livilla, who had been seduced by *Sejanus (Tiberius' ambitious minister).

**drȳads** *Nymphs of trees.

**duoviri** ('two men') At Rome, religious officials in early times whose duties included charge of the Sibylline books (*see* SIBYL).

**Dy'skolos** ('The bad-tempered man') Greek comedy by *Menander, produced at the *Lenaea of 317 BC and awarded first prize.

During a hunting-party a rich young man Sostratos catches sight of a country-girl praying to Pan and the nymphs at a shrine, and immediately falls in love and decides to marry her (this happens by the will of Pan, as the god himself reveals in a prologue). The girl's father Cnemon is misanthropic, the *dyskolos* of the title, and lives a deliberately solitary life with only his daughter and a servant for company, out of disgust at human vice. His harsh nature has driven his wife to leave the house, and she has gone to live on the next farm with her son by a previous marriage, Gorgias. Sostratos now asks him for his help. Gorgias tells him that the only kind of son-in-law Cnemon will contemplate is one like himself. Sostratos tries to impress Cnemon with his hard work on the farm but Cnemon does not see him. Sostratos' mother has a bad dream and proposes a sacrifice at the shrine of the nymphs and Pan. At this juncture Cnemon falls down a well, is rescued by Gorgias, with the help of Sostratos, and emerges cured to some extent of his dislike of human company. He takes back his wife and entrusts his property and daughter to Gorgias, who bestows the daughter on Sostratos. The latter then persuades his father to give his sister to Gorgias as wife, and the play ends with the teasing of Cnemon to make him join the feast.

**ecclē'sia** The assembly and sovereign body at Athens, comprising all the adult male citizens over the age of 18, all equally entitled to address the assembly and to vote. It normally met forty times a year on the *Pnyx, with extra sessions as required, and was presided over by the chairman of the **boule* (executive council) who had been chosen by lot for the day. Voting was by simple majority and generally by show of hands. The assembly elected the **strategoi* (military commanders) and served as a law-court in the matter of grave crimes threatening the safety of the state, but its chief work was the passing of decrees (*psephismata*) dealing in detail with every sphere of government, including foreign affairs, finance, naval and military operations, and the corn supply. The agenda for meetings were prepared by the boule and any citizen might submit a matter for inclusion. No motion might be debated unless it appeared on the agenda and had been duly advertised: snap decisions were thus avoided. The only restraint on the powers of the assembly was that of the laws. If a motion proposed was illegal or even inexpedient, the proposer was liable to prosecution. Since the number required to attend the assembly to decide on certain kinds of business was at least 6,000, it would seem that something approaching that number could be generally expected. Soon after 403 BC, to ensure that every citizen could exercise his political rights, payment of one obol to those attending was introduced, the rate becoming more liberal in the course of time. During the fifth and most of the fourth centuries the assembly functioned in a fully democratic way (given that women, slaves, and *metics were excluded). The boule exercised no control, and the initiation of policy lay entirely in the hands of the citizens. Continuous policy was achieved only when one man, or a group of men, holding the confidence of the people over a period of time, was repeatedly elected to the office of *strategos*. These semi-professional politicians were sometimes aristocrats, sometimes men of no family who were skilled orators, occasionally accepting fees from others in return for promoting certain measures in the assembly. They were the men who by and large proposed motions, and they wielded considerable influence in the assembly.

At Sparta the assembly (sometimes referred to in modern times by the Laconian term *apella*), comprising all Spartan male citizens, held regular meetings presided over by the *ephors. The ephors had strong executive powers but the assembly had the final right of decision. Control over resolutions brought before the assembly was exercised by a council of elders (*see* GEROUSIA). Voting was by acclamation (which Aristotle described as 'childish').

*See also* DEMOCRACY; DEMAGOGUE; SOLON; CLEISTHENES (2); PERICLES; CLEON; DEMOSTHENES (2); EUBULUS.

***Ecclēsiazū'sae (Ekklēsiazousai)*** ('Women at the assembly') Greek comedy by *Aristophanes produced probably in 392 BC (the **didascalia* has not been preserved). The theme of the play, women taking over the running of the city (from which they were in reality excluded; *see* ECCLESIA and DEMOCRACY) and introducing community of property, has something in common with *Lysistrata*. Both plays depict the women of Athens seizing the political and social initiative under the guidance of a powerful female character, here Praxagora. A remarkable feature of the play, foreshadowing the way drama was to develop in the fourth century, is the greatly reduced role of the chorus, who do not sing a song until the end (*see* COMEDY [Greek 5]). It is likely that the comic poet was no longer writing his own lyric passages, and these were not now integral to the drama but served simply as entertainment at breaks in the action. There is no *parabasis*, no boisterous attack on politicians, and there is a new style of quiet witty dialogue of the kind found later in New Comedy. The similarity between Praxagora's reforms and Plato's intention for the ruling class in his ideal republic (see REPUBLIC), that they should not possess any private property, has suggested the possibility that Aristophanes is satirizing Plato, but this is unlikely on chronological grounds and in view of the lack of evidence in the text.

As a result of a conspiracy of women led by Praxagora, she and her fellow conspirators, disguised as men, pack the assembly, and carry by a large majority a motion transferring control of the affairs of state from men to women. Praxagora, having been appointed head of the new government, returns to her husband, who has been put to great inconvenience by finding that she has borrowed his clothes. She explains the new social system that is to be introduced: community of property, community of women and children; a fair share in sexual relations for the old and ugly, men and women alike, to be secured by legislation. Then she goes off to the agora to arrange for the reception of all private property and administer the drawing of lots for dinner. A law-abiding citizen hastens to hand in his property; a sceptic waits to see what will come of the new system. The sexual consequences become immediately apparent. A young man arrives to find his girl, but three old women assert their prior rights to him, and one succeeds in carrying him off. The play ends with the chorus hurrying away to a communal dinner (where one of the dishes has a name seven lines long).

**Echi'on** One of the surviving Spartoi (see CADMUS). He married Agave and was the father of Pentheus.

**Echo 1.** Nymph unsuccessfully wooed by the god Pan; in revenge he sent madness upon the local shepherds so that they tore her to pieces and only her voice survived.

**2.** Nymph who was punished by the goddess Hera for engaging her in talk when the goddess wanted to spy on the amours of Zeus, her husband, with other nymphs. She was deprived of speech except for repeating the last words of her interlocutor. Having fallen in love with *Narcissus and been rejected by him, she wasted away to a voice.

**eclipses** In the ancient world eclipses of the sun and moon were widely believed to be bad omens (see DIVINATION and SICILIAN EXPEDITION). Some 250 eclipses are mentioned in the an-

cient sources, making it possible to date some historical events accurately and to follow the deviations of the Roman pre-Julian calendar. In the course of the fifth century BC the Greeks acquired the concepts for understanding eclipses. (It is highly improbable that *Thales could have predicted, as tradition has it, a solar eclipse as early as 585 BC.) What was known in Athens in the fifth century BC is most clearly expressed in a later account of the cosmology of the Presocratic philosopher Anaxagoras, who believed that the stars, sun, and moon are carried round the stationary earth by the rotation of the aether. He understood that eclipses of the moon (which he knew received its light from the sun) occur when the full moon is screened from the sun by the earth, while eclipses of the sun (much harder to predict) occur when the new moon screens the sun from the earth. See ARCHILOCHUS.

**eclogue** [Gk. *eklogē*, 'selection'] An occasional poem or passage 'selected' from a larger collection or work; in the plural the word was used to describe any short poems and in that sense was applied to Virgil's *pastoral poems (see ECLOGUES) although having itself no pastoral connotation. Since this title was also given to the later pastoral poems of *Calpurnius and *Nemesianus, it was appropriated by the poets of Charlemagne's court to describe their own pastoral poems written in imitation of Roman models and thence applied to the Latin pastoral poems of the Middle Ages and the Renaissance. However, in the manuscripts Virgil's whole collection of eclogues is entitled *Bucolica*, 'bucolic poems'.

***Eclogues*** (Lat. *Eclogae* or *Būcolica*; for the meaning of the title see ECLOGUE) Ten unconnected *pastoral poems written by *Virgil in imitation of the pastoral Idylls 1–11 of *Theocritus, at the suggestion of *Pollio, Virgil's literary patron at the time. *Eclogues* seems not to have been the title used by Virgil, who apparently called the book (and the poems) *Bucolica*. The ancient authorities state that Virgil began the *Eclogues* when he was 28, i.e. in 42 BC, and that he spent three years in their composition. At the end of the *Georgics* Virgil declares that the *Eclogues* were written when he was 'bold in youth'. Universal agreement on dates cannot be reached, but Virgil was certainly engaged in the composition of the *Eclogues* from 43 to at least 37, and they probably circulated among the poet's friends before publication: the pattern of dedicatees and addressees is complex, but *Gallus and Pollio are the most prominent. Suetonius says that they won such immediate success that they were performed frequently on stage by professional singers. Their present arrangement is not chronological but governed by artistic considerations of symmetry and contrast. The odd-numbered poems are dialogues, the even-numbered are narratives for only one speaker.

*Eclogue 1* is about a shepherd, Meliboeus, whose farm has been confiscated for the settlement of Octavian's veterans (*see* GALLUS). Another shepherd, Tityrus, made the journey to Rome while under the threat of eviction and was rewarded by being allowed to keep his farm through the intervention of 'a young man' (often but not necessarily identified with Octavian); his good fortune is contrasted with the enforced exile of Meliboeus who had stayed quietly at home. Virgil perhaps lost his own farm in the confiscations, which are also central to Eclogue 9. But the poem, if coloured by the poet's own experiences, is not autobiographical: his concern is a general one for the sufferings inflicted by war.

In *Eclogue 2* the shepherd Corydon laments that his love for the boy Alexis is unrequited. This theme, of 'the passionate shepherd to his love', and much of the detail, are taken from Theocritus (Idylls 3 and 11). *Eclogue 3* is also indebted to Theocritus for its form and characters—an exchange of aggressive banter between two rival shepherds, Damoetas and Menalcas, leading to a singing match (*see* AMOEBOEAN VERSE)—and some of the content: the two pairs of cups, for example, offered as the stake in the contest, recall the description of the cup of Idyll 1.

In *Eclogue 4*, which owes nothing to any Greek predecessor, the poet looks forward to the birth of a child who will inaugurate a new era. This poem has been more discussed than any other short poem in Latin. Throughout the Middle Ages it was accepted as a Messianic prophecy of the birth of the Christ-child given under divine inspiration. St Jerome was exceptional in expressing disbelief. Several contemporary children have also been suggested as the subject: a child of Pollio, a child of Octavian and Scribonia, even Octavian himself. The poem can be dated to 40 BC, near the time of the treaty of *Brundisium between Antony and Octavian, sealed by the marriage of Antony to Octavian's sister Octavia. It may well be that the child is for Virgil simply the symbol of a messianic hope, drawing perhaps on oracles of the time, that some power or person would bring about the dawn of a new age.

In *Eclogue 5*, rich in echoes from Theocritus, two shepherds celebrate in song the death and deification of *Daphnis. The shepherd Menalcas reveals himself as the composer of Eclogues 3 and 4 and the way is thus open to see Daphnis too as an allegorical figure, concealing an identity relevant to Virgil's own times. Since after the assassination of Julius Caesar in 44 BC it had been decreed that divine honours should be paid to him as if he were a god, some scholars, from antiquity onwards, have thought that Daphnis represents Caesar, if not in particular at least in general terms.

*Eclogue 6* remains obscure to us because we know little of its literary background in the Greek and Hellenistic poetic tradition. It opens with Virgil, in the character of Tityrus, about to sing of kings and battles when Apollo tweaks his ear and tells him that sheep should be fat but poems slim (*see* CALLIMACHUS). The poem does not have much to do with pastoral and bears little resemblance to Theocritus. It consists of a song sung by *Silenus in which he recounts the creation of the world in the style of Lucretius as a prelude to some allusively narrated myths. The narrative is interrupted by a description of Virgil's friend and fellow-poet Gallus accepting his vocation as a poet, in language reminiscent of Callimachus in the *Aitia*.

*Eclogue 7*, of uncertain date, describes a singing match between Corydon and Thyrsis, two Arcadian herdsmen (the first reference to Arcadia in connection with pastoral poetry); by staging this on the banks of his native river Mincius, Virgil demonstrates the detachment of his pastoral world from any specific landscape. The poem is notable for the grace and beauty of the pastoral songs.

*Eclogue 8* is dedicated to an unnamed person, usually thought to be Pollio, the campaigns referred to taken to be those of 39; *Servius, however, says that the dedicatee is Octavian, and it has been suggested that the campaigns are his of 35. The Eclogue is modelled mainly on Idylls 1 and 2 of Theocritus, and consists of a singing match between Damon and Alphesiboeus: the first sings a lament for his faithless mistress, the second relates the incantations and magic by which a girl hopes to win back her lover.

*Eclogue* 9 depicts a situation similar to that of Eclogue 1. Two countrymen fall into conversation on the way to town; Moeris has just been evicted, and Lycidas recalls how Menalcas, a poet (*see Eclogue* 5), tried to save the district by his poetry but failed.

*Eclogue 10* has Gallus as the subject, represented as dying of hopeless love for his absent mistress Lycoris, in the manner of later Roman love elegy (*cf.* PROPERTIUS). This is the boldest juxtaposition of the Arcadian and the real world that Virgil attempts, and one that was to have great influence on the style and content of later pastoral poetry (below).

Virgil's *Eclogues* became the models of pastoral poetry and the inspirers of pastoral romance and drama in later ages (for the *Idylls* of Theocritus were little read until the Renaissance). Unlike Theocritus in general (whose *Idyll* 7 is the exception) he allowed elements of contemporary reality to intrude into his Arcadian world (*see* ARCADIA), and used myth and symbolic imagery to allude to recent history. The degree to which this happened is a matter of scholarly debate, but he provided a precedent for the introduction of elaborate *allegory into the genre (below).

Virgil created a simple world by using pastoral vocabulary and pastoral names. It is an image of life but distinct from it, an idealized retreat into peace, the countryside, love, and art away from the horrors of civil war in contemporary Italy. The *Eclogues* derive their haunting quality from the implicit comparison of the two states, and Virgil's empathy with both. *Calpurnius (first century AD) and *Nemesianus (third century) enlarged the scope of this literary mode by using it more enthusiastically than had Virgil as a vehicle for panegyric, and in this they were followed by the eighth- and ninth-century poets of Charlemagne's court. Generations of commentators interpreted the *Eclogues* as allegory, and as a result allegory was thought to be an essential feature of the mode. The richness of English Renaissance pastoral, exemplified by the poets Sir Philip Sidney, Edmund Spenser, Michael Drayton, and Shakespeare, springs from the successful blending of the Virgilian and the vernacular traditions, as well as the poets' own belief in the mode as one that could be taken seriously. But by the eighteenth century English pastoral had lost its vitality, to be partially and uniquely recaptured in 1896 by A.E. Housman's *A Shropshire Lad*.

**e'cphrăsis** ('description') A motif of poetry which originated in the description of the shield of Achilles in Homer's *Iliad*. It then became a type of rhetorical exercise taking the form of an elaborate prose description of an object, real or imaginary; most often this was a work of art. The earliest extant collection of ecphrases is the *Eikones* ('Images') of *Philostratus (*see* (iii)), probably dating to the third century AD.

## education

**1.** Alphabetic writing was introduced into Greece in the second half of the eighth century BC (*see* ALPHABET and BOOKS, GREEK AND ROMAN 1), but we have no evidence until later for schools being set up to teach children the rudiments of reading, writing, and counting. Tradition said that the Spartan poet Tyrtaeus, who lived in the mid-seventh century BC, was a schoolmaster, and that the Athenian Solon introduced laws for the regulation of schools in 594 BC.

**2. In Sparta.** At some time in the seventh century BC Sparta adopted a militaristic form of education which subjected Spartan boys to a regime of military training and obedience. From the age of 7 they were entirely under the control of the state, living in barracks away from their families. Priority was given to their physical education so that they might become efficient soldiers, though they were also taught reading, writing, and music (*see* DANCING). Girls too were educated, especially in gymnastics, as befitted the future mothers of Spartan soldiers. *See* SPARTA 2 and 6.

**3. In classical Athens.** The first evidence for general *literacy in Athens is the institution of *ostracism (which required a citizen to scratch a name on a potsherd), and this is thought to have been introduced by *Cleisthenes (2) in 508 BC. By the fifth century the ability of the average male citizen to read and write is taken for granted. For evidence of Greek literacy in the writing of Ionian Greek soldiers *c*.600 BC *see* EGYPT. The ancient historians refer to schools in existence by the beginning of the fifth century. Education was not compulsory. Schoolteachers had to be paid by the parents, and teachers as a class were not highly esteemed. (Demosthenes taunted Aeschines with a social distinction, 'You taught reading and writing, but I went to school'.) Plato in the *Laws*, setting out an ideal education for children, girls included, prescribes what cannot have been too far removed from the traditional Greek education, and which he considers a necessary training for war, domestic business, and civil administration: as well as physical education, reading and writing were necessary for all, then arithmetic, music, and astronomy (see Hippias' educational programme, below).

Well-to-do boys, who were generally accompanied to school by a slave known as a *paidagogos* (*see* PAEDAGOGUS), naturally received more education than the rest. Elementary education began at the age of 7 and was in the hands of the *grammatistes*, who taught reading, writing, and, probably, arithmetic (with the help of the abacus), and required his pupils to learn by heart and recite passages from the poets, especially Homer, selected for their moral content. (For the early part of the fifth century Athens was still virtually a bookless society; literature was oral and books merely a substitute for recital; *see* BOOKS, GREEK AND ROMAN 3.) This constituted the minimum of education for Athenian children. The two other main branches for older boys were *music and formal physical training. Music played a substantive role in Greek society, and was also considered to have an educative value. Not only was it the case that every educated man was expected to be able to play the lyre and sing, skills which he learned from the *kitharistes* ('lyre-player'), but also that certain styles ('modes') of music were believed to foster moral virtue, particularly virtues of the traditional kind. Physical education, directed mainly towards military prowess but also cultivated for its own sake, was taught by the *paidotribes* ('trainer'; *see* GYMNASIUM and PALAESTRA). The *Old Oligarch comments on the hostility of the common people (*demos*) to 'those who train in the wrestling schools and learn music'. To judge from vase-paintings, girls too might sometimes take part, but to a lesser extent. (By the end of the fourth century BC it was established that young men of 18 should spend two years in physical and military training; *see* EPHEBOI.)

In the case of young men seeking education in specialist subjects like *medicine and *rhetoric the pupil had to seek out an expert in the field who was prepared to teach him. In fifth-century Athens there was no organized form of higher education, and this in part accounts for the success of the *sophists, who charged high fees for teaching a variety of subjects, including the new geographical and scientific topics which the recent expansion in knowledge had thrown up. The sophist *Hippias is alluded to in Plato's *Protagoras* for the inclusion in his educational programme of arithmetic, geometry, music (a mathematical subject in its theoretical aspect of *harmonics), and *astronomy (necessary for understanding those aspects of life dependent on the calendar, like farming). This combination, often referred to as the 'four sciences', was taken up by Plato and subsequently had a long history until it acquired the name *quadrivium* (*see* SEVEN LIBERAL ARTS) nearly a thousand years later (4 and 6 below). Most sophists, however, concentrated on literature and especially on language, with the aim of making the pupil expert at public speaking. Thus they fulfilled their claim to teach men how to succeed in political life by equipping them with the skill most needed by politicians in a fully democratic state where power lay with the assembly. Rhetorical teaching was always the area in Greek education where pedagogic skill was most highly developed.

In the fourth century BC schools of higher education came into existence, notably *Isocrates' school of philosophy and rhetoric at Athens founded in the late 390s, Plato's *Academy at Athens founded *c.*385, and Aristotle's *Lyceum founded outside Athens in 335. Plato, at least in his early days, was strongly opposed to rhetoric and literature on moral grounds, and though he later allowed rhetoric to be taught in the Academy his curriculum was mainly scientific, mathematical, and philosophical. Most philosophical instruction at the Academy was by Plato's favoured dialectical method (*see* DIALECTIC), and study of the exact sciences was the necessary propaedeutic to dialectic. According to a later commentator he had on his door the inscription 'without knowledge of geometry no one may enter', *ageōmetrētos mēdeis eisitō*. Plato aimed to produce what he saw as true politicians, men trained by dialectic to have philosophical insight who could therefore be just legislators and advisers to those in positions of power. Aristotle's Lyceum, by contrast, was more in the nature of a research institute. Isocrates aimed to train (the few) able students in morality (through philosophy) and in the political skills, and so produce politicians capable of leading and persuading the people. Poetry was purely cultural, dialectic and mathematics were purely disciplinary; his emphasis was on composition in literary prose. For Isocrates rhetoric was the basis of education and it was his programme which ultimately became the norm throughout the ancient world.

**4. Hellenistic education.** The pattern established somewhat incompletely by Athens was formalized in the Hellenistic period. Elementary education remained unchanged in form but was extended by benefactors, and a scheme of secondary education now emerged. Most cities had at least one gymnasium, associated with a public library, where literature, philosophy, and music were taught as well as physical training. The gymnasium was supervised by a *gymnasiarchos*, a state official elected for a year only. The curriculum now included literature, mathematics, and science, thus forming the ancient ideal of 'general education', the *enkyklios paideia* (the origin of the word 'encyclopaedia'), a system ultimately derived from the sophists through Isocrates and eventually becoming the seven liberal arts of the Middle Ages (see 5 and 6 below). For serious study youths who could afford it went to the great centres of learning—Alexandria, of course, then Athens, Pergamum, and Rhodes for philosophy and rhetoric, and Cos, Pergamum, and Ephesus for medicine. This pattern of education remained largely unchanged until medieval times. *See also* SECOND SOPHISTIC.

**5. Roman education.** The codification of the laws, the *Twelve Tables, in 451 BC points to literacy being by that time a part of everyday life, and by the end of the fourth century BC it must have been general for the senatorial class at least. At this time boys' education consisted of parental training and, in noble families, political apprenticeship. A father taught his son to read, write, and use weapons, as well as grounding him in manners, morals, religion, knowledge of the law and, at least in the case of the Elder *Cato, of the history of Rome. The son accompanied his father to all religious ceremonies and social occasions and even, if his father was a member, to the senate. At the age of 16 a youth of noble family was attached to some prominent figure to gain political experience, and from 17 spent the campaigning season with the army (*see* CURSUS HONORUM). In some families this kind of education persisted into imperial times. Livy, perhaps anachronistically, attests the existence of elementary schools at this early period, and in the third and second centuries BC under the influence of Greece (and particularly after the conquest of

Greece, when Greek slaves became plentiful), education could be had from schools, developed on the Greek models, or from tutors (*see* LIVIUS ANDRONICUS and ENNIUS). The *litterator* or *ludi magister* (elementary teacher) taught reading, writing, and arithmetic to both boys and girls aged about 7 to 11. Girls in Rome had a greater share in education than in Greece. The employment of a *paidagōgos* was adopted in imitation of Greek practice (3 above), and he sometimes taught his pupil Greek (*see* BILINGUALISM). Secondary education from 12 to 15 was in the hands of the *grammaticus*, who taught literary subjects in Latin and Greek both as a general education and as a preparation for rhetoric. Towards the end of the first century BC Cicero's works on oratory made an important contribution to teaching rhetoric in Latin, and the works of Virgil and other contemporary poets were introduced as suitable subjects for study.

Teachers of Greek rhetoric appeared at Rome in the second century BC (*see* CRATES (1) and SUETONIUS (2)) and were regarded with suspicion; some were expelled from Rome in 161 BC. The study of Latin rhetoric began early in the first century BC with the foundation of a Latin rhetorical school and like their Greek predecessors some teachers were expelled from the city, in 92 BC. The Latin equivalents of Greek rhetorical handbooks are known in the first century BC (*See* DE INVENTIONE and *RHETORICA AD HERENNIUM*). Conservative Romans like the Elder Cato looked with disfavour upon the introduction under Greek influence of, in their view, morally dubious subjects such as music and dancing (*see also* PHILOSOPHY [Roman] and PAULLUS). The Romans also paid far less attention than the Greeks to physical education, except when it was directly aimed at training future soldiers. When under the empire the practice of political oratory declined with the loss of political freedom, the rhetorical schools prepared boys for the career of advocate, again along Greek lines, or for administration in the public services. The themes that boys expounded in their public declamations (*see* DECLAMATIONES) have been criticized for their unreality and irrelevance to life, but they encouraged ingenuity and a facility of mind and speech which were valuable assets to an advocate. *Quintilian (1.10.1) eloquently pleads for the practical and moral value of a general education, which he calls *encyclios paedia* in imitation of the Greek term (4 above), as a preliminary to specialized study. Pupils who wished to pursue their studies further usually went to Athens or Rhodes. Caesar, Cicero, Octavian, and Horace all studied abroad. The emperors and other benefactors sometimes founded professorships and public municipal schools. However, the Roman state never instituted special officials to supervise schools comparable with the Hellenistic gymnasiarchs. No philosophical schools were founded in Rome until the third century AD (*see* PLOTINUS and PORPHYRY). Under the empire professorships of Greek and Latin rhetoric were endowed by the emperors. Quintilian was the first to hold the Latin chair at Rome.

**6.** Education in both Greece and Rome—the Greek tradition being borrowed and continued by the Romans—was based largely on the humane study of traditional literature and of the two languages in which it was written, with the aim, constant from beginning to end, of producing informed, cultivated, able, and effective public speakers. The *quadrivium* (as *Boethius called it), derived from Hippias (3 and 4 above), preceded by the *trivium* of grammar, rhetoric, and dialectic (or logic) derived from the sophists and Isocrates, formed the curriculum of the Middle Ages, designated the seven liberal arts by Martianus Capella.

**Ēge'ria** In Roman religion, Italian water-nymph, to whom pregnant women sacrificed to secure easy delivery. She was worshipped with the goddess *Diana at Aricia in Latium, and with the *Camenae outside the gate known as the Porta Capena at Rome. She was said to be the consort and adviser of *Numa Pompilius, legendary second king of Rome, at whose death she moved to Africa.

**Egypt** (Gk. Aigyptos, Lat. Aegyptus) For much of its history Egypt was divided into Lower and Upper Egypt, the former being the delta region, the latter the area south from the delta to Syenē (Aswan). Upper Egypt itself was often divided, the area north from Syene to Hermopolis Magna (El Ashmunein) being known as the Thebaïd, and that north from Hermopolis to the delta as Middle Egypt. Among the most ancient and important cities of Egypt was Thebes, the capital of Upper Egypt; modern Karnak and Luxor are on part of its site. It was a city of impressive size; according to Homer in the *Iliad* it had 100 gates and 200 war-chariots for each gate. Another ancient city was Mem-

phis, near modern Cairo, the first capital of the united kingdom of Upper and Lower Egypt. It declined in importance after the foundation of *Alexandria (below). Syene, the southern frontier town of Upper Egypt a little north of the first cataract, was believed in antiquity to be situated on the Tropic of Cancer, where the sun is vertically overhead at the summer solstice (*see* ERATOSTHENES (2)).

Archaeological evidence testifies to the existence of trading relations between Egypt and the Greek world in Mycenaean times (second half of the second millennium BC). Literary evidence becomes available in the eighth and seventh centuries and Homer tells the story of Menelaus' visit to Egypt (*Odyssey* 4). With the establishment of Greek settlements on the North African coast in the seventh century, it was not long before the Greeks secured a foothold in Egypt. They were profoundly impressed by the great antiquity of the country, as well as by its religion, monuments, and customs. They thought that Egypt above all other lands was the repository of ancient wisdom and many Greeks proverbial for their wisdom were supposed to have visited the country in the seventh and sixth centuries (some are known to have done so in fact). Solon is said to have visited the pharaoh Amasis, Thales to have 'invented' geometry after studying 'land-measurements' in Egypt. Herodotus travelled widely in Egypt in the mid-fifth century and devoted the second book of his history to giving an account of the country. In 462 a large Athenian fleet assisted in an unsuccessful Egyptian revolt against Persian rule (*Cambyses had conquered the country in 525), and when the hated Persian monarchy was finally overthrown in 332 BC by Alexander the Great (a Macedonian Greek), the change was not wholly resented. The Macedonian kings who thereafter ruled Egypt were known as the *Ptolemies (and Egypt under their rule as Ptolemaic Egypt). In their time the city of Alexandria which Alexander founded became a centre of Greek culture. The Greeks were at first the dominant race there, and the native Egyptians were not regarded as full citizens. Later the Greek element became Egyptianized; the official language was Greek, but Egyptian persisted, to emerge in the Christian period as Coptic. (*See also* ROSETTA STONE.) The Greek gods were known only as names for local deities.

Greek rule was in turn brought to an end by the Roman annexation of Egypt in 30 BC (after the battle of *Actium) when the country became a province of peculiar status, being governed by the emperor through an equestrian prefect rather than, as in all other important provinces, a senatorial legate. This special status indicates the value Augustus put upon the province and his appreciation of the temptation it presented to a governor ambitious for wealth and independence. No senator was allowed to set foot in Egypt without the emperor's permission. The first prefect was, disastrously for him, the soldier-poet *Gallus. Egypt with the rest of North Africa was the granary of Rome, eclipsing Sicily in that respect. It had a monopoly in the production of papyri (*see* BOOKS, GREEK AND ROMAN 1), and was the starting-point for trade with India. It had also become a country of great social and cultural complexity. A general survey of the Nile valley was made by the Romans and to this we owe the accurate description of it that appears in book 17 of Strabo's *Geography* (first century AD). The only serious revolt against Roman rule lasted from AD 162 to 166 before being finally put down. In the reign of Caracalla (early third century) Egyptians entered the Roman senate for the first time, and the worship of the Egyptian goddess *Isis was publicly sanctioned at Rome. Nevertheless, the province was never Romanized, and Greek and native Egyptian elements were united in opposition to Roman government. The Roman era came to an end with the Arab conquest of Egypt in 640.

**Ēhoe'ae, Ēhoiai** *See* CATALOGUE OF WOMEN.

**Eileithyī'a(e)** The Greek goddess of childbirth, sometimes referred to in the plural (*cf.* PAN and SILENUS) She was a lesser deity, not one of the twelve Olympian gods (*see* GODS [Greek]). Her name may mean the 'coming', i.e. of the child. Hesiod makes her the daughter of Zeus and Hera, who was herself a goddess of birth and therefore is sometimes given this title. She was a Minoan birth-goddess in origin; excavations at her cavern-sanctuary in Crete at Amnisos, mentioned by Homer and appearing on the *Linear B tablets from Cnossus, have revealed continuous cult from Neolithic to Roman times. She has no myth of her own but appears in various stories of birth, often in association with Artemis and Hera. The Romans identified her with Lucina (*see* JUNO).

**ekkle'sia** *See* ECCLESIA.

**e'kphrasis** *See* ECPHRASIS.

**E'lea** (Lat. Velia) Greek colony in Lucania on the west coast of south Italy. It was founded by Phocaea (in Ionia) soon after 540 BC, when most of the population left that city at the threat of Persian conquest and finally settled in Italy. Elea is chiefly famed for its school of *Eleatic philosophers.

**Eleatic philosophers** (Eleatics) Greek philosophical school based in Elea in south Italy, which originated with *Parmenides of Elea at the end of the sixth century BC. The earlier philosopher and poet *Xenophanes was called the founder by Plato and the doxographers, but this is less plausible. Parmenides believed that 'what is', the essential matter of the universe, is single, indivisible, and unchanging, and this monistic theory was subsequently defended by *Zeno (1) and by *Melissus, who lived in the mid-fifth century BC and was the last important member of the school.

**Ele'ctra 1.** In Greek myth, daughter of *Agamemnon and Clytemnestra. She does not appear in epic, but in the tragedies of Aeschylus (notably *Choephoroe; see* ORESTEIA), Sophocles, and Euripides she becomes a heroic figure in the story of the House of Atreus (*see* PELOPS), represented as implacably hostile to Clytemnestra and her lover Aegisthus, faithful to her father's memory, and devoted to her brother Orestes, whom she supports in the vengeance he takes on Clytemnestra and Aegisthus. She eventually marries Orestes' faithful friend Pylades. Her supposed tomb was shown in later times at Mycenae.

**2.** In Greek myth, daughter of the Titan *Atlas, mother by Zeus of Dardanus (*see* TROY).

**Ele'ctra 1.** Greek tragedy by *Sophocles. We have no evidence at all for the date; a possible suggestion puts it between 418 and 410 BC. It is disputed whether it preceded or followed Euripides' *Electra* ((2) below), itself of uncertain date. For the myth on which it is based *see* PELOPS.

Orestes arrives at Mycenae, accompanied by Pylades and an old man, Orestes' childhood attendant (*paidagōgos*), to avenge the murder of his father Agamemnon, in obedience to the *Delphic oracle. The old man is sent on to tell Orestes' mother Clytemnestra that Orestes has been killed in a chariot-race, and the others prepare to follow in disguise, taking with them an urn supposed to contain his ashes. Meanwhile Clytemnestra, having had a dream of bad omen, has sent her daughter Chrysothemis to pour libations on the tomb of Agamemnon, the husband she has killed. Her other daughter Electra, who is living a wretched life, bullied by Clytemnestra and Aegisthus on account of her constant mourning for her murdered father, meets Chrysothemis and persuades her to substitute for the offerings, doubtless polluted, of Agamemnon's widow and murderer other more personal offerings from his daughters. Clytemnestra appears and abuses Electra, who retorts in kind, but they are interrupted by the arrival of the old man, who delivers a brilliant but false 'messenger' speech describing the chariot-race in which Orestes is supposedly killed. Clytemnestra receives the news with scarcely concealed joy; Electra, on the other hand, is reduced to despair. The announcement of Chrysothemis that she has found a lock of hair on Agamemnon's tomb which is clearly Orestes' seems only to mock her sorrow. Since the expected help of Orestes is lost, she determines to kill Clytemnestra and Aegisthus herself. The more prudent Chrysothemis refuses to share in the murder and departs. Orestes and Pylades in disguise now approach with the ashes in an urn, and Orestes tells Electra by degrees who he is. He and Pylades enter the palace, and the cries of Clytemnestra are heard as they kill her. Aegisthus then approaches. He is lured into the palace to see what he supposes to be the corpse of Orestes, but finds to be that of Clytemnestra. He is driven at the point of a sword to the hearth where Agamemnon met his death and there killed. The chorus of Mycenaean women rejoice at the final passing of the curse which has rested on the house of Atreus.

The greater complexity of plot and situation open to the Greek tragedians after the introduction of the third actor (*see* TRAGEDY 2) is very apparent in *Electra*, especially in the three-cornered scene where the messenger's false narrative about the death of Orestes has very different effects upon Clytemnestra and Electra, and the action preceding the recognition scene where Sophocles is able to portray Electra faced by a rapid progression of people and events. It has seemed to many readers that Sophocles has chosen to ignore the moral issue, which is so important to Aeschylus and Euripides, as to how far the matricide is justi-

fied. The last few words of the chorus are problematic and the ending extraordinarily abrupt.

**2.** Greek tragedy by Euripides, often dated to 413 BC because of a supposed reference to the *Sicilian Expedition, but perhaps a few years earlier (see the suggested dates of Sophocles' *Electra*, (1) above).

The theme of the play is the same as that of (1), but there are marked differences of detail. Aegisthus has married Electra to a poor farmer living in a cottage on the borders of Argos so that no son of hers may aspire to lay claim to the kingdom of Mycenae. This farmer, though poor, is of noble descent and decent character, and refuses to consummate the marriage, considering that her marriage to him is beneath her dignity. Orestes and Pylades make their way there and recognition ensues. Aeschylus' treatment of the recognition scene in his *Choepheroe* was famous: it has been thought that here Euripides mocks his predecessor's simple-minded acceptance of the tokens which lead to recognition. Others have doubted whether the lines (518–44) are really by Euripides. The plan for vengeance is made and carried out, with Electra playing a vital part. Orestes first kills Aegisthus at a rural sacrifice. Clytemnestra is told that Electra has had a child and comes to visit. After a bitter exchange with Electra she enters the cottage, where she is killed; brother and sister emerge covered in blood. It was an act of justice but morally horrifying. Finally the *Dioscuri appear: Electra will marry Pylades and Orestes will be acquitted before the court of the *Areopagus.

Plutarch relates that after the Spartan capture of Athens in 404 BC, the Spartan admiral Lysander was moved to spare the city by hearing a Phocian singing the opening chorus of *Electra*.

**Ele'ctryon** In Greek myth, a son of Andromeda and *Perseus, whom he succeeded as king of Mycenae. He became the father of Alcmena (later the mother of Heracles), and six sons. He was accidentally killed by his nephew Amphitryon to whom he had betrothed Alcmena. By a Phrygian woman Midea he was the father of a seventh son Licymnius, according to some accounts.

**elegī'acs** Verses written in the elegiac metre (*see* ELEGY), a term applied particularly to verses in Latin.

**elegy** In Greek and Latin literature, any poem written in elegiacs (also called elegiac couplets), that is, in alternate lines of hexameter and pentameter. The word is derived from Greek *elegos*, a sung lament which was presumably in this metre. In antiquity the elegiac metre was used for a variety of poems, and the earliest elegiacs we possess, written in Greece at the end of the eighth century BC, bear no resemblance to lament. Elegiac poetry was the medium for expressing personal sentiments (as distinct from narrative): for description, for exhortation to war or to virtue, for reflection on a variety of subjects, serious and frivolous, for epitaphs and laments, and at Rome for love-poems. The use of elegiacs for inscriptions to commemorate the dead (epigrams) seems to have become popular in the middle of the sixth century BC and persisted throughout antiquity; those attributed to Simonides are the most famous, especially his poem on the battle of *Plataea and other fragments of personal poetry. Among the principal early elegiac poets of Greece were Tyrtaeus, Mimnermus, Solon, Phocylides, Callinus, and Theognis. Cheerful sympotic elegies were written by Archilochus. It is debated whether the Hellenistic poets used this form for love-poetry; they certainly introduced a number of metrical refinements. *See also* EPIGRAM.

The elegiac couplet was introduced into Latin by Ennius (four of his epigrams survive). It was developed at Rome in the first century BC, perhaps under Greek influence, chiefly as a medium for love poetry. The Romans gave elegy a new direction by using it for a cycle of short poems centred on the poet's relationship with a single mistress. Almost every individual feature of Latin love-elegy is derived from Greek models, but as far as the evidence allows us to judge the whole effect is of something completely original. The principal Roman poets of love-elegy were Catullus, Cornelius *Gallus (whose work is almost entirely lost), Tibullus, Propertius, and Ovid. Ovid also refined the already strict metrical rules for Latin elegiac still further, and extended the range of subjects to be treated in this metre: 'personal' *Amores*, the *Heroides* in letter form, didactic *Ars amatoria*, aetiological *Fasti*, and lamenting *Tristia*. After Ovid, the metre was used chiefly for short occasional poems and for epigrams. Martial is the most famous prac-

titioner of the epigram and he sometimes rivals Ovid in metrical virtuosity.

Only in comparatively modern times, since the sixteenth century, has the term elegy come to denote specifically a poem of lament for an individual or a poem of serious, meditative tone. Several famous elegies in English literature are written using the conventions of *pastoral poetry, one of the earliest being Edmund Spenser's *Astrophel*, on the death of Sir Philip Sidney (1586). The origin of the pastoral lament or elegy is to be found in *Theocritus' first Idyll; however, this poem, being written in hexameters and not in elegiacs, is not, in classical terms, an elegy.

**element** Defined by Aristotle as the primary constituent of something, whatever that thing may be. In early Greek thought (*see* PRESOCRATIC PHILOSOPHERS) an element was one of the fundamental constituents of the physical world. Empedocles thought there were four elements, which he called 'roots': earth, water, air, and fire (in order of decreasing density; the *aether, the rarest thing of all, compounded of air and fire, rose highest). This became a commonplace belief in the ancient world. The Roman poets Lucretius (in book 5) and Ovid (in the *Metamorphoses*, book 15) both eloquently describe, though from different philosophical positions, the coming-into-being of the cosmos from these elements. The term 'quintessence' (Lat. *quinta essentia*, 'fifth substance') describes a fifth element, believed by some (including medieval) philosophers to constitute the heavenly bodies and to be latent in all things. This was the quintessence that some alchemists tried to extract.

**ele'nchus** ('cross-examination') A term used to describe *Socrates' method of philosophical inquiry. In his search for knowledge it was his practice to ask a respondent for a definition ('what is courage? goodness?' etc.) on the grounds that if one could define or give an account of e.g. goodness one would have clearer ideas about the good life and a basis for further investigation. The definition was then submitted to rigorous testing by means of question and answer (*elenchus*). This, however, turned out to be a negative process: the definition was found to be inconsistent with the respondent's other assumptions, and was thus revealed as defective or inadequate, while no satisfactory alternative could be arrived at to take its place. The respondent was refuted and left in a state of helplessness, *aporia*, but his gain was that he now knew the extent of his ignorance. The method was further developed by Plato, who uses the term *dialectic to describe it.

**Eleusi'nian mysteries** *See* MYSTERIES.

**Eleusi'nion** At Athens, a temple below the Acropolis on the north side, east of the Panathenaic Way, dedicated to the goddesses Demeter and Persephone, dating from the time when Eleusis was finally amalgamated with Athens, perhaps at the end of the seventh century BC. Here were kept the sacred objects of the Eleusinian *mysteries.

**Eleu'sis** The most famous *deme in Athens after Piraeus, situated about 20km (12 miles) north-west of Athens near the sea. It remained independent of Athens until perhaps as late as the seventh century BC. The myth of *Erechtheus may reflect the Athenian conquest. According to ancient tradition it was at Eleusis that Persephone, who had been snatched away by Hades, god of the Underworld, was restored to her mother *Demeter. Eleusis owed its fame to the annual festival of the *mysteries traditionally instituted by Demeter herself and celebrated primarily in her honour. These attracted visitors from all over Greece and were much venerated. An important theatre of Dionysus stood there, and there also was the sanctuary of Demeter and Persephone. The magnificent *telesterion* ('hall of initiation'), the largest public building of its time in Greece, was erected under Pericles. There was much building in Roman times, including the great Propylaea ('Gateway') finished by Marcus Aurelius (emperor AD 161–80). The sanctuary ceased to function after AD 395. *See also* ELEUSINION and SACRED WAY.

**Eleven, the (*hoi hendeka*)** At Athens, magistrates appointed by lot for the care and management of the public prison. They were also responsible for seeing that sentences, including the judicial torture of slaves, were carried out.

**Elgin Marbles** *See* PARTHENON.

**ēliai'a (**often, but less correctly, **hēlia'ia)** At Athens, a law-court, in the sense either of citizens selected by lot to try a case or of the

building in which trials took place. The name may have originated with Solon's establishment of trials by citizens in the early sixth century BC. In the fifth century it was the name of one particular large court building (whose location remains uncertain). A juror at Athens could be called a *hēliastēs*.

**elision** In Greek and Latin speech and writing, the 'thrusting out', i.e. dropping, of a vowel at the end of one word before a vowel at the beginning of the next; in Greek this feature was confined mainly to the short final vowels α, ε, ο, and sometimes ι; in Latin it extended to the dropping of long final vowels also, and of syllables ending in m; early Latin writers sometimes elided final s. In Latin poetry the elided vowels are printed but dropped in scansion (*cf.* CRASIS).

**Eli'ssa** Name by which *Dido, queen of Carthage, was said to have been known at Tyre, where her father was king.

**Elpē'nōr** In Homer's *Odyssey*, companion of Odysseus who fell from the roof of Circe's dwelling and was killed and left unburied. His is the first shade Odysseus meets in the Underworld; Odysseus grants his request to be buried and to have his oar planted on his grave.

**Elpinī'cē** Daughter of the younger *Miltiades and wife of *Callias.

**Elysium (Elysian Fields, Elysian Plain)** Described first by Homer as a place in the far West beyond the stream of Ocean (*see* OCEANUS) where certain favoured heroes are sent by the gods to enjoy a blissful after-life instead of entering the Underworld. In later myth Elysium was represented as a special part of the Underworld ruled over by *Rhadamanthys (and Cronus). That is where Virgil locates it in *Aeneid* 6; there, in a passage recalling Plato's myth at the end of *Republic* 10, it is the place where certain souls temporarily rest before being reborn. *Cf.* the very similar ISLES OF THE BLEST.

**Ema'thion** *See* EOS.

**E'mathus** In Greek myth, son of Macedon and brother of Pierus, from whom Emathia (the Homeric name for *Macedonia) was believed to have derived its name. The daughters of Pierus, the Pierides, are sometimes called Emathides. 'The Emathian' is Alexander the Great.

**Embassy, On the False** (*De falsa lēgā-tiōne*) Political speech by Demosthenes. *See* DEMOSTHENES (2) 2.

**embo'lima** *See* TRAGEDY 3 (iv).

**emmelei'a** *See* TRAGEDY 2.

**Empe'doclēs** (*c*.492–*c*.432 BC) Greek *Preso-cratic philosopher whose genius showed itself in many areas: he had the reputation (perhaps derived from his poetry) of being a statesman, healer, philosopher, mystic, and wonder-work-er. He was born of aristocratic family at *Acra-gas in Sicily, and after the fall of the tyranny in *c*.468 BC was offered but declined the kingship, being an ardent democrat. Political upheavals led to his exile, and he travelled to south Italy and Greece. He was an accomplished orator, credited by Aristotle with the invention of rhet-oric; *Gorgias is said to have been his pupil. He also won fame as a scientist and healer; *Galen called him the founder of the Sicilian school of medicine. Later reports say that he encouraged the belief that he was a god, and according to tradition he met his death by leaping into the crater of Mount Etna to confirm this belief. However, it is as a thinker of far-reaching im-portance that he is chiefly known, and like *Parmenides, by whom he was strongly influ-enced, he expressed his thought in hexameter verse, much read until late antiquity. Only some 450 lines survive, in quotation in other authors, supplemented by papyrus fragments published in 1999, but this is enough to give an idea of his lines of thought. Two poems are ascribed to him, *On Nature* and *Purifications* (*Katharmoi*), but there is little general agree-ment about which fragments belong to which poem and in recent years suspicion has strengthened that these are alternative titles for one and the same poem. In his verse Em-pedocles attempts to explain the world on sci-entific and rational grounds.

He accepts the thesis of the *Eleatics that 'what exists' cannot come into being nor pass away, but against Parmenides he argues that 'what exists' is not single and unchanging. Em-pedocles claims that there are four 'roots' or eternally persisting elements from which all other things are formed and into which they can be resolved, namely earth, water, air, and fire (he uses the names of traditional Greek gods in referring to them). The rearrangement of these elements under the influence of Love and Strife gives rise to change; Empedocles uses as analogy the painter's depiction of a great variety of objects by mixing a limited number of pigments. (He regularly relies on metaphor and analogy to clarify his explana-tions.) His principles, Love and Strife, are also eternal, but have no perceptible qualities of their own and are apprehended only by their influence on the elements. The universe is under their alternate domination: Love main-tains a homogeneous whole, but Strife dis-solves this whole into its constituent parts which war against each other; the universe is thus recurringly brought together and then fragmented in cosmic cycles. Strife, Empedo-cles believed, was increasing at the time in which he lived. Part of his work is devoted to cosmogony, the gradual development of the present world, the evolution of animals, and many topics in biology. He explained percep-tion by stating that effluences from objects perceived entered the pores of the sense or-gans, an idea which proved influential. At cer-tain points he refers to himself both as a god and as a *daimon*, a 'divine spirit', which, like other divine spirits according to his belief, has been condemned to a series of mortal, includ-ing animal, reincarnations, because of some initial sin involving bloodshed. It is possible, he says, for the *daimon* to regain its divinity after 30,000 years. It is not clear whether he believes that the *daimon* survives for ever or only until the end of the current cosmic cycle. His ideas on reincarnation remain very ob-scure but have something in common with Pythagorean teaching and the Orphic poems (*see* PYTHAGORAS and ORPHEUS).

Empedocles' theory of four elements pre-vailed for the rest of antiquity. The Roman poet *Lucretius was inspired by him to com-pose his own scientific poem, *De rerum natura*, 'On nature', in which he praises his predeces-sor for 'the songs of his godlike heart'. *See also* COSMOLOGY; MEDICINE; HUMOURS.

**emperors, empire, Roman** *See* ROME 5; ROMAN EMPIRE; PRINCIPATE; BYZANTINE AGE; FALL OF ROME.

**empire, Athenian** *See* DELIAN LEAGUE.

**Endy'mion** In Greek myth, a beautiful young man, famed for his eternal sleep on Mount Latmus in Caria. He was the son of Calyce, daughter of Aeolus, and Āethlius or Zeus, and was king of Elis. He was especially loved by *Selene (Moon); according to one tradition he came from Elis to Mount Latmus and while he was sleeping in a cave Selene came down to him (presumably during the dark phase of the lunar month). His eternal sleep is variously explained, one version being that Selene sent it upon him, wishing to embrace him unobserved. One of his children (not by Selene) was Aetolus, the eponymous hero of Aetolia.

**E'nneads** See PLOTINUS.

**E'nnius, Quintus** (239–169 BC) One of the greatest and most versatile of the early Roman poets, born at Rudiae in Calabria in the heel of Italy where the inhabitants, the Messapii, spoke their own pre-Roman language until the first century BC. He seems to have been in Sardinia (perhaps as a soldier) when he met *Cato the Elder, quaestor there in 204, who took him to Rome. There he won a reputation in the 190s for writing tragedy. In 189 he accompanied M. Fulvius Nobilior on his Aetolian campaign (probably in order to celebrate his patron's achievements) and on his return had Roman citizenship conferred on him. He lived in modest style on the Aventine, teaching and writing. Anecdotes told by Cicero connect him with *Scipio Africanus, *Scipio Nasica, and Ser. Sulpicius Galba. It was at this time that he began the *Annales* ('Annals'), which, with his tragedies, constituted his principal work. Ennius also wrote comedies, of which only four separate lines survive; *fabulae *praetextae*; *saturae* (*see* SATIRE), four books of mixed verse of which seventy lines are extant; *Epicharmus*, a poem on the nature of the universe; the *Hēdyphagētica* ('of sweet eating'), a mock-heroic poem on gastronomy; and a poem in special celebration of Scipio Africanus. The *Euhēmerus* was a prose work which adopted the rationalist theory of *Euhemerus on the origin of the gods. Of his tragedies some twenty titles are known, of which perhaps twelve are derived from Euripides, perhaps three from Aeschylus, and one from an obscure contemporary of Euripides. The fragments remaining allow interesting comparison with the Greek originals, particularly in the case of *Medea*. The natural ease of the Greek has been replaced by a rather grand and high-flown style, but Cicero's admiration for it is understandable.

The *Annales*, an epic poem chronicling Roman history in fifteen books, occupied Ennius up to the time of his death. Fewer than 600 lines survive, which do no more than indicate the general scope of the work. The poem inaugurated a new era in Roman literature, being composed not in the Saturnian metre used by *Naevius and *Livius Andronicus but in the Latin version of the hexameter of Greek epic. To emphasize the connection with Greek poetry Ennius begins his work by recounting a dream in which he has been told by Homer that he is the latter's reincarnation. The *Annales* presented the history of Rome from the fall of Troy to the wars of the poet's own day, including a series of descriptions of great Romans. The First Punic War was omitted, having been dealt with by Naevius. The events of living memory seem to have occupied the last six books of the work. It was from reading Ennius that Roman schoolboys learned about the heroes of old and the Roman virtues. The famous line on Fabius Maximus Cunctator: *unus homo nobis cunctando restituit rem*, 'one man by his delaying restored the situation for us', was much quoted. Clumsy though the hexameters are, the style is grave and sonorous and suited to the poet's grand conception of his subject. Ennius was regarded by the Romans as the father of their literature; Lucretius and Virgil were considerably influenced by him, Cicero admired and quoted him. He reputedly composed his own epitaph:

> *nemo me lacrumis decoret neu funera fletu*
> *    faxit. Cur? volito vivo' per ora virum.*

('Let no one honour me with tears or attend my funeral with weeping. Why? I fly, still living, on the lips of men.')

The poet *Pacuvius was his nephew and heir.

**Enya'lius** In Greek myth from Homer onwards a war-god identified with *Ares. The name appears in *Linear B at Cnossus. The two gods had separate cults.

**Ēoe'ae (Ēoïai)** See CATALOGUE OF WOMEN.

**Ē'ōs** In Greek myth, the dawn-goddess (Lat. Aurora), who figures in myth rather than in cult. She was the daughter of *Hyperion and Theia (Ovid calls her a daughter of Pallas the Titan or Giant), and sister of Helios (Sun) and Selene (Moon). She carried off several youths celebrated for their beauty: *Tithonus, by whom she became the mother of Emathion and *Memnon; *Orion, whom Artemis killed; Cleitus, son of Mantius; and *Cephalus the husband of Procris.

**Epamino'ndas (Epameinōndās)** (d. 362 BC) Theban general and statesman who, with his friend *Pelopidas, raised Thebes to be for a time the most powerful city in Greece. When Sparta invaded Boeotia in 371, the Thebans, under Epaminondas' brilliant command, won a decisive victory at *Leuctra, bringing to an end Sparta's long supremacy on the battlefield and making Epaminondas famous. He invaded the Peloponnese in 370 to help the Arcadians throw off Spartan control (*see* MEGALOPOLIS), and he established the independence of *Messenia. He invaded again in 369 and in 366, when he put an end to Sparta's 300-year-old Peloponnesian league, and in 364 he even challenged Athens' naval supremacy at sea. In 362 he invaded the Peloponnese once more in order to reassert Theban influence there, but this time the Thebans found themselves fighting former allies, like the Athenians, now in alliance with Sparta. The armies fought at *Mantinea and the Thebans were in fact victorious, but the victory turned into defeat when it was known that Epaminondas had been killed. His creation of independent Arcadia and Messenia survived him, but he left behind no constructive policy for Thebes or Boeotia which others could continue, and he had no successors. His nobility of character as well as his tactical brilliance made him one of the greatest generals of antiquity, and his tactical innovations were studied by Philip II of Macedon and his son Alexander the Great. For his vegetarianism *see* ANIMALS, ATTITUDES TO. *See also* SACRED BAND.

**Epaphrodī'tus** Freedman and secretary of the emperor Nero. He received military honours for helping him to expose the Pisonian conspiracy (*see* PISO (3)) and he accompanied Nero in his final flight and helped him to commit suicide. He was subsequently secretary to the emperor Domitian, by whom he was killed in AD 95. The philosopher *Epictetus was his slave.

**Epei'os** Maker of the *Trojan Horse.

**epeiso'dion** *See* EPISODE.

**ephē'boi** ('youths') In Greek, boys who had reached puberty, and a term used to describe the age-class of boys between 15 and 20. On coming of age at 18 the Athenian ephebe swore an oath of loyalty and obedience to Athens. In the fourth century BC the term was used specifically to denote the young men of 18 to 20 who underwent a compulsory military training, a system which spread rapidly throughout the Greek world and lasted as long as the Greek *polis*. In their characteristic dress of dark mantle and broad-brimmed hat they were during their existence a graceful feature of the Athenian scene. Military service ceased to be compulsory in 305 BC and was reduced to one year in 282 BC. As a result the ephebate became a largely educational interlude for a wealthy elite and by the end of the second century BC had been remodelled into a school, especially of literature and philosophy.

***Ephesi'aca*** *See* EPHESIAN TALE.

***Ephesian Tale, An (Ephesiaca)*** Greek *novel, in five books as we now have it, by a virtually unknown Xenophon of Ephesus, probably dating to the mid-second century AD. Its full name is 'An Ephesian tale of Antheia and Habrocomes', and Xenophon is thought to be imitating Chariton's *Chaereas and Callirhoe*. The hero and heroine meet at the festival of Artemis in Ephesus and both waste away with love until their parents consult an oracle of Apollo, who tells the pair to marry but adds ominous pronouncements about their future. After the marriage they voyage to Rhodes but are captured by pirates and then seized by a robber-chief to be sold in Tyre. The couple are separated and are driven in different directions by various fates and many would-be lovers, attracted by their outstanding beauty. Habrocomes is often imprisoned, and Antheia at one point takes a sleeping draught in the belief that it is poison. She is carried off to Alexandria by pirates looking for tomb-offerings. Habrocomes is twice rescued by divine intervention from crucifixion and live incineration. Eventually, supported by faithful slaves, they arrive separately at Rhodes, are reunited and with their slaves return to Ephesus, where 'the rest of their life together was one long festival'.

**Ep(h)ia'ltēs 1.** Of Trachis, the Greek traitor said to have shown Xerxes the path by which the Persians outflanked Leonidas at Thermopylae (*see* PERSIAN WARS).

**2.** An Athenian who became the leading politician on the democratic side after about 465 BC and the opponent of the aristocratic *Cimon. He resisted (unsuccessfully) the sending of help to the Spartans during the helot revolt of 462 on the grounds that Sparta was the rival of Athens for power. He took advantage of Cimon's absence in Sparta to put into effect a number of radical reforms—depriving the *Areopagus of its main powers—necessary for the institution of democracy. In this he was supported by the young Pericles. The *Eumenides* of Aeschylus, performed in 458, testifies to some extent to the thoughts and feelings aroused by the new measures (*see* ORESTEIA). Cimon was ostracized, but Ephialtes was murdered in 461.

**ĕphors** At *Sparta a body of magistrates, by the late fifth century BC five in number, elected annually by the citizens and exercising general control over the kings' conduct; two ephors always accompanied a king on campaign. The senior ephor gave his name to the year (*see* CALENDARS). The ephors wielded great power: they controlled the general administration, convened and presided over the assembly, and had certain judicial functions; they could even sentence the kings to be fined or imprisoned, recall generals, mobilize and dispatch the army, and negotiate foreign treaties. The ephorate survived until at least the third century AD. *See also* CLEOMENES (2).

**E'phorus** (of Cyme, *c*.405–330 BC) One of the most influential Greek historians of the fourth century BC, the author of a history of the cities of Greece and Asia Minor in thirty books, and the first author known to have divided his work into books himself. Although the history no longer survives it was known to Polybius and used extensively by Strabo and Diodorus Siculus. It began with the 'return of the *Heracleidae' (i.e. the *Dorian invasion *c*.1100 BC) and continued to the siege of Perinthus by Philip II of Macedon in 341 BC, including myths and legends, geography and ethnography, political and military history. Ephorus consulted numerous authorities now lost to us. *See also* OXYRHYNCHUS HISTORIAN.

**epic** [from Gk. *epē*, 'hexameters']
**1.** The ancient definition of epic was entirely metrical, as 'verse in hexameters', and this included the didactic poetry of Hesiod and the bucolic poems of Theocritus. From a literary perspective, a Greek or Latin epic is a hexameter narrative poem on the grand scale concerning the exploits of a hero engaged in some serious endeavour. Homer's *Iliad* and *Odyssey* establish the norms. The hero, who belongs to the world of mythology (*see* HEROES), is distinguished by his strength and courage,

and is restrained only by a sense of honour. The subject matter of epic includes *myth, legend, history, and perhaps elements of folk- or fairy-tale. It is usually set in a heroic age of the past and embodies its country's early history and expresses its values. Battles and perilous journeys play a large part, as do gods, the supernatural, and magic; scenes are often set in the Underworld or in heaven. Certain formal features are conspicuous: the omniscient narrator vouches for the truth of his story; there are invocations, elaborate greetings, long speeches, detailed similes, digressions, and the frequent repetition of 'typical' elements, for example the stock adjectives or formulae (*see* HOMER 4), and stock scenes such as the hero arming for battle. Epic expresses a delight in the physical world, shown by painstaking descriptions of such things as arms, clothing, or ships.

**2. Greek epic.** Epic poetry in the shape of the *Iliad* and *Odyssey* of Homer is the earliest surviving form of Greek literature; the origins of these poems are lost, but they probably go back to Mycenaean times. From the incident of Odysseus asking the bard Demodocus (*Odyssey* 8) to sing of the ruse of the Trojan Horse it is clear that there was a corpus of sagas on which a bard could draw. What the bard recited (or rather chanted, to the lyre) would be a story taken from an existing body of myth but with no fixed text (and before literacy with no written text at all); rather it was an improvisation made up for each occasion with the help of stylized elements of phrasing or formulae, previously memorized, developed by a long succession of bards. The relationship between the early type of oral epic narrative and the Homeric poems as they now exist is still far from clear, but it is commonly thought that with the advent of alphabetic writing into the Greek world in the second half of the eighth century BC the Homeric poems were committed to writing in something like their present form, perhaps by a bard called Homer. It is at least clear that they embody traditional material of a much earlier date.

Greek epics which postdate the *Epic Cycle include the *Heraclea*, 'deeds of Heracles', written by Panyassis, a kinsman of Herodotus, who flourished in the early fifth century BC. By the end of the fifth century Greek epic writing had lost its spontaneity and was becoming allusive and even pedantic, as is clear from the sparse fragments of Antimachus of Colophon and Choerilus of Samos (the latter noteworthy in having composed an epic, the *Persica*, on a historical subject, the Persian Wars). Some later epic still survives. In the third century BC the Hellenistic poet *Apollonius Rhodius wrote the *Argonautica* in four books; in the fourth century AD *Quintus of Smyrna wrote the *Posthomerica* in fourteen books, to fill the gap between the events of the *Iliad* and of the *Odyssey*, and in the fifth century AD *Nonnus wrote the *Dionysiaca* in forty-eight books.

**3. Roman epic.** Epic was introduced at Rome in the third century BC in a Latin version of Homer's *Odyssey* rendered in the native Saturnian metre by *Livius Andronicus. It seems from the remaining fragments to have been an adaptation rather than a translation of Homer, but it became a famous and influential work. *Naevius in the late second century BC undertook an entirely original piece of work by composing an epic also in Saturnian metre on the Punic Wars. The *Annales* of *Ennius, an epic in eighteen books on the history of Rome, was a work in which the dactylic hexameter was applied to Latin epic for the first time. The greatest Roman epic was the *Aeneid* of Virgil, who was influenced in its composition not only by the Homeric Greek epics but also by Ennius and other Latin hexameter poets. In the Silver age Latin epic became rhetorical in character and seems written with the intention that it should be declaimed. The best epic of that age was Lucan's *Pharsalia*. Other epic poets of the empire whose works survive in part were *Silius Italicus, *Valerius Flaccus, *Statius, and *Claudian. Among those whose works are lost were Cornelius Severus (praised by Ovid and Quintilian) who wrote historical poems, and Albinovanus Pedo, author of a *Theseid* and a poem on the campaigns of Germanicus.

**Epic Cycle** Name given to a collection of Greek epics (excluding the *Iliad* and *Odyssey*), of which only some 120 lines now survive, written by various poets in the seventh and sixth centuries BC, which could be arranged so as to make a chronological narrative extending from the beginning of the world to the end of the heroic age. Some of these poems were occasionally ascribed to Homer. They seem to have been well known in the fifth and fourth centuries BC but little read later; a writer of the sixth century AD declares that they are no longer to be found, and our knowledge of their contents derives in part from summaries made in late antiquity by *Proclus. The epics known

to have comprised it are the *Cypria* (covering the preliminaries of the Trojan War), *Aethiopis, Little Iliad (see ILIAD, LITTLE), *Iliupersis (sometimes written *Iliu Persis*, 'The Sack of Troy'), *Nostoi ('Home-comings' of the heroes), and the *Telegonia* (concerning Telegonus, son of Odysseus by Circe). There was also a Theban cycle, the narrative of the legends of *Thebes, which included the *Thebaïs*, the *Oedipodeia*, and a Trojan cycle covering events at Troy leading to the war. These formed the storehouse from which Greek dramatic and lyric poets drew many of their subjects.

**Epicha'rmus** Greek writer of comedy from Sicily, who was active perhaps in the late sixth and certainly in the early fifth centuries BC. He was at the court of *Hieron of Syracuse in the 470s. No play survives, but many titles are known, and quotations and papyrus fragments give some idea of the contents. He seems to have enjoyed writing mythological burlesque, with Odysseus and Heracles the favourite heroes. It would appear that he also introduced various types of character, e.g. the *parasite, the sightseer, the philosopher, and an ancient writer asserts that he was the first to bring a drunkard on to the stage. Some of these characters were to appear later in literary *mime as well as in Attic comedy. The plural titles of some plays suggest that he employed a chorus, but there is no firm evidence in the fragments that he did so, nor do we know how many actors he employed, nor how long the plays were. His language is Sicilian Doric, used as wittily as the Attic of Old Comedy (*see* COMEDY [Greek 3]). Many of the comic aspects of language familiar from Aristophanes are present: parody, wordplay, the coining of long words, and the rattling-off of lists of things good to eat. There is no evidence that he used a variety of metres and there are no lyrics among the extant fragments. In antiquity Epicharmus was regarded as the author also of a number of philosophical and quasi-scientific works, but these are no longer thought to be genuinely by him.

**Epictē'tus** (of Hierapolis, in Phrygia, AD c.50–c.120) Stoic philosopher (*see* STOICISM), born a slave, owned and later freed by Epaphroditus, freedman and secretary of the emperor Nero. He attended the lectures of *Musonius Rufus at Rome and then gave lectures there himself. After Domitian banished the philosophers c.89 he migrated to Epirus in Greece where he spent the rest of his life. His lectures there were attended by the historian *Arrian, who took careful notes of what he said and published them; four books of *Diatribai* ('Lectures' or 'Discourses') survive (*see* DIA-TRIBE). Later Arrian published a summary of Epictetus' philosophy, the *Encheiridion* ('Manual'). These works strongly influenced the emperor Marcus *Aurelius. The *Manual* is a rather formal statement of Epictetus' views but the *Diatribai*, which are his comments on various Stoic writings, have a vivid informality, enlivened by anecdotes and imaginary conversations, and Arrian reproduces the *koinē* Greek in which Epictetus spoke. Epictetus emphasizes that learning is of little value for its own sake: it should be used to improve moral character. Unlike many Stoics he taught for the many and the humble, rather than for those few to whom Stoicism had an intellectual appeal, thereby continuing a tradition of popular preaching which began with the *Cynics in the fourth century BC. Only those who knew their own weakness and misery, he said, could benefit from philosophers. But like the other early Stoics he wanted to make men independent of their circumstances and of the vicissitudes of life: 'wealth consists not in having great possessions but in having few wants.' Having experienced slavery himself, he lays emphasis on that part of a man over which no one else has control, his mind. He is said (by Aulus *Gellius) to have preached that people should take to heart two imperatives, *anechou* and *apechou*, 'endure' and 'abstain'. He believes strongly in divine providence and the need to harmonize one's will accordingly. He also shows a robust faith in the power of the human will to surmount trials, and is more positive than Marcus Aurelius, with whom it is natural to compare him.

**Epicū'rus (Epikouros)** (341–270 BC) Greek philosopher of the Hellenistic age and founder of the Epicurean school of philosophy. He was born in Samos, the son of a schoolteacher who had Athenian citizenship. In his youth he was impressed by and studied the atomist philosophy of *Democritus, and established his own philosophical circles at Mytilene and Lampsacus. He settled in Athens in 307 and bought a house with a garden (*kēpoi*), which gave its name, the Garden, to the school of philosophy which he set up in it. At his death

he bequeathed this property to his successor Hermarchus. (In 51 BC Cicero wrote to *Memmius in Athens on behalf of the Epicureans there asking him not to demolish what was left of Epicurus' house.) Epicurus resembled Socrates in the affection and respect he inspired among his friends, who sought out his company. His school, perhaps better called a community, consisted of a group of like-minded people, including women and slaves, who lived with him in austere seclusion (*see* LEONTION). It attracted ridicule and accusations of self-indulgence and vice because of its communal life and Epicurus' philosophical hedonism (below), the serious aspects of which were ignored. Although Epicurus wrote prolifically most of his work is lost. *Diogenes Laertius preserves three important letters summarizing his teaching, together with a collection of 40 aphorisms, *Kyriai doxai* ('Principal doctrines'); some 80 further aphorisms survive in a manuscript. Of the 37 books of his great work *Peri physeōs* ('On nature'), fairly substantial fragments have been recovered from carbonized papyrus rolls found in a villa excavated at *Herculaneum. For our knowledge of his thought we also depend largely on the poem of *Lucretius, *De rerum natura*, which expounds Epicurus' physical theory and to some extent his moral theory too.

Epicurus accepted from Democritus that the world consisted of (unchanging and indestructible) atoms and void, change being brought about by the rearrangement of atoms. He gives a strictly mechanistic account of all phenomena: the universe is infinite; it came into being through random collisions of atoms in their natural downward path, and will eventually dissolve again through their dispersal. Atoms move naturally downwards because of their weight, at constant and equal speed. The fact of motion proves the existence of a void in which atoms can move. Sometimes they swerve (for unexplained reasons) and so collide. This swerve (Lat. *clinamen*) not only accounts for the existence of the cosmos and everything in it but also for the possibility of free choice of action by human beings and animals. Secondly, since knowledge is based on the evidence of the senses, appearances are never wrong; falsehood arises only in the opinion (*doxa*) which the mind (also made of atoms and void) forms about them. The soul too is composed of (extremely small) atoms which are dispersed at death. Gods exist, atomic compounds like everything else, but have no part in the processes of nature and take no thought for this or any cosmos. Men should respect and admire them for their eternal life of ideal happiness.

However, Epicurus' aim was not to investigate the physics of the universe but to make atomism serve a moral purpose: how to attain happiness through the wise conduct of life, by knowledge based on the evidence of the senses, and by eliminating superstition and belief in supernatural intervention. For Epicurus happiness consists in attaining tranquillity of mind (*ataraxia*, literally 'freedom from disturbance'), an attainment achieved by a proper understanding of nature. His moral theory is summed up in a sentence from one of his letters: 'The beginning and end of living happily we say is pleasure.' In his view pleasure is identical with the good. It is in the nature of people to seek pleasure; pain, which is a disturbance of the natural state, is caused by unsatisfied desire, and pleasure is experienced when the natural state is restored. Therefore one must satisfy desire, and this is pleasure. But some pleasures bring pain in their wake. Therefore one must satisfy desires that are natural and necessary, but accept as the limit of pleasure the onset of pain. Hence pleasure may lie in limiting desire. (Epicurus is perhaps uniting under the term 'pleasure' both positive enjoyment and the absence of pain.) Pleasure of the soul, which consists mainly of contemplation or the expectation of bodily pleasure, is more valuable than physical pleasure, and is found in *ataraxia*. This can be achieved in three ways: by learning the nature of the universe and of death, which removes fear of the supernatural, by withdrawing from the turmoils of public life, which frees us from jealousy and failure, and by avoiding emotional commitments.

The chief difficulty with Epicureanism is that it cannot easily include among its virtues concern for justice and the well-being of other people. Yet the Epicurean communities were famous for the friendship and unity of their members. The meaning given in modern times to the word 'epicure' (a gourmet or person devoted to sensual pleasures) represents widespread hostility to and misunderstanding of Epicurean philosophy. Particular antagonism was felt by the Stoics (*see* STOICISM). Nevertheless Epicureanism spread, first to Antioch and Alexandria, then into Italy, and for a brief time during the late republic it won the adherence of men like Calpurnius *Piso, *Cassius, and Cicero's friend *Atticus. Naturally the early Christians regarded Epicureanism with abhorrence because it stated that there was no providential God and no survival after death, that the universe had been created by accident, and that the aim of life was pleasure. A remarkable testimony to the continuing vitality of the philosophy was a very large public inscription (of which fragments survive) erected in AD 200 at Oenoanda in the interior of modern Turkey by a certain Diogenes, giving passages of Epicurean doctrine together with a concise summary of Epicurus' teaching. *See also* PHILODEMUS.

**Epidau'rus** Small Greek state on the Argolis peninsula in the north-eastern Peloponnese. Its best-preserved ancient monument is the theatre, but it is chiefly famed for its sanctuary of *Asclepius. This contained several public buildings, mainly built in the fourth century BC, of which substantial remains survive. Many inscriptions from the sanctuary also survive, attesting cures brought about by incubation (sleeping in a dormitory attached to the temple) and by following the prescriptions of the priests. The sanctuary revived in the second century AD and survived until the fourth.

**epidei'ctic (epidictic) oratory** The oratory 'of display' (Gk. *epideixis*), that is, speeches for delivery at festivals (panegyrics), and funeral orations; epideictic is distinguished from forensic oratory (of the law-courts) and deliberative (symbouleutic) or political oratory. *See* RHETORIC.

***Epi'dicus*** Roman comedy by *Plautus. The complicated plot turns on the deceits of the trickster slave Epidicus. He tricks his old master out of money, first to pay for a harp-girl to whom the old man's son has taken a fancy; then to pay for a captive girl whom the son, who has gone off to the wars and transferred his affections, has bought with borrowed money. The fraud is discovered, but as the captive turns out to be the old man's lost daughter, Epidicus is forgiven and freed.

**Epi'goni** ('Successors') In Greek myth, the sons of the *Seven against Thebes who, under the leadership of *Adrastus, the only survivor of the original Seven, drove the Cadmeans out of Thebes and put Thersander on the throne, an event supposed to have occurred shortly before the Trojan War. Their names (with some variations in the sources) were usually given as Alcmaeon and Amphilochus, sons of Amphiaraus; Aegialeus, son of Adrastus and the only one of the Epigoni to be killed in the expedition; Diomedes, son of Tydeus; Polydorus, of Hippomedon; Promachus, of Parthenopaeus; Sthenelus, of Capaneus; and Thersander, of Polyneices. The term Epigoni was also applied to the generation of rulers after that of the *Diadochi, officers of Alexander the Great who 'succeeded' to his empire.

**epigram** [Gk. *epigramma*, 'inscription'] A verse inscription. In Greece, epigrams were written at first in hexameters, later in elegiacs. The early epigrams (of the seventh century BC) were placed on gravestones or votive tablets, composed so as to suggest that the dead person or the dedicator was directly addressing the reader, giving him the bare facts in a severely laconic style which became the artistic hallmark of the epigram. The first famous epigrammatist was *Simonides of Ceos, to whom many anonymous epigrams have been falsely attributed. The few which we have reason to believe are genuinely his combine intensity of feeling with great simplicity of expression. Quite a few Greek epigrams purport to survive from the classical period attached to famous names, among them Euripides, Plato, and Aristotle, but they are almost certainly spurious. It was not until the fourth century BC that epigrams were written simply as literature (though real inscriptions in verse were still being composed) and the term was extended to mean a brief poem suggested by a single event, serious or trivial. Thus *Callimachus' epigram on the death of his friend Heracleitus, well known in English poetry through the nineteenth-century translation of William Cory, 'They told me, Heraclitus...', is a direct address by the poet to the dead man, in which he voices his personal sorrow in a manner very different from the impersonal style of the classic inscriptional epigram. *Asclepiades was one of the earliest and most influential of the Hellenistic epigrammatists, as was, in a different manner, *Leonidas of Tarentum. The subjects they treated were very varied, but generally the themes of love and wine predominated. Whatever the subject matter, brevity and elegance of expression were essential. In the first century BC *Meleager compiled the

first large anthology of epigrams written during the previous five centuries, the *Garland*, which was supplemented by later anthologists (*see also* ANTHOLOGY [Greek]). Marcus Argentarius in the first century AD introduced that final refinement of the epigram which is now considered its characteristic feature, an unexpected twist—a pun or a paradox—in the last few words. Epigrams continued to be written in Greek throughout the Byzantine period, sometimes upon Christian themes but often in a markedly pagan spirit; the poets best remembered are *Palladas, Paul the Silentiary, and *Agathias.

The Romans had their own tradition of funerary epigrams written in Saturnians in the third and second centuries BC, and Ennius wrote a few in elegiac couplets. The first Roman literary epigrams, written in the late second century BC in elegiacs, were Greek in inspiration and were all on the theme of love. *Catullus wrote epigrams of both love and hate, and after him epigrams were said to have been written by most of the prominent men of the late republic and early empire, but very few have survived. The literary form of the Latin epigram culminated in the work of *Martial, who cultivated especially the witty, paradoxical ending that is imitated by modern writers of epigrams.

**epigraphy** The study of inscriptions in respect of both their form and their content, an inscription being taken to mean any writing cut, scratched, or impressed on any durable material such as stone or metal, either in official form or casually by an individual (in the latter case known as a graffito). Coins are excluded, their inscriptions being within the province of the numismatist, and painted or incised inscriptions on pottery and vases are the province of vase experts as well as epigraphists.

**Greek.** The earliest surviving Greek inscriptions are dated to the middle of the eighth century BC and consist merely of names or brief personal comments scratched on pots. By the early seventh century inscriptions are of a more formal nature—dedications to gods or names of the dead on gravestones. Like the Phoenicians the Greeks originally wrote from right to left (retrograde); if a second line of writing was required, it was often written underneath the first line but proceeding in the opposite direction, a pattern of writing known as *boustrophēdon ('as the ox turns') which was helpful for the inexperienced reader whose eye could then continue to read without interruption at the end of a line. It sometimes seems from the inscriptions of the seventh and sixth centuries that the lines of writing need not even be horizontal: the words could apparently be as easily read when written vertically. It was not until the Greeks set up formal inscriptions, after 650 BC, of laws and lists of officials, as opposed to using words merely to identify, say, figures on a vase, that they adopted a consistent left-to-right direction. In the sixth century the Greeks, and notably the Athenians, adopted a style of inscription which suited their feeling for symmetry and uniformity, in which the letters were exactly aligned both horizontally and vertically (the *stoichēdon*, 'in a line', style). This persisted until the end of the fourth century BC, but had disappeared almost entirely by the end of the third. In the archaic and classical periods there was a great diversity of local alphabets, but from the end of the fifth century BC an increasing uniformity.

Greek inscriptions survive in their tens of thousands. Because there are so many inscriptions of a standard pattern (e.g. dedications or decrees in formulaic language) it is often possible to restore the text even when an inscription is weather-worn or a stone has parts missing. But there are also many uniquely worded inscriptions, including the hundreds of poems of various kinds which would otherwise be unknown to us. They immeasurably enrich our knowledge of Greek history, thought, and speech by being first-hand, contemporary records, in the authentic language of the time, of every aspect of Greek life. In recent years close study of the lettering of a cache of inscriptions from one location has shown that it is sometimes possible to identify the hands of individual stone-cutters, and this in turn has made it possible to date—and redate—a number of important historical inscriptions. Similar work is also being done for sculptors by studying the funerary reliefs from particular workshops. Among the more important Greek historical inscriptions are the Athenian *tribute lists, the law-code of Gortyn in Crete, and the chronological table known as the *Parian Marble.

**Latin.** Latin inscriptions earlier than the third century BC are rare, and unfortunately so, since those we have provide valuable evidence of linguistic usage at a period earlier than that of most surviving Latin literature. (The earliest inscription was at one time thought to be a craftsman's label on a gold fibula (brooch) from Praeneste dated to the late seventh century BC, but this is now believed to be a forgery.) Latin inscriptions were done on stone or, usually only in the case of public enactments or decrees, on bronze. (The latter are comparatively rare, many having been melted down in later times.) Most date from the early empire, but they continue beyond the collapse of Rome in the fifth century AD. Inscriptions from the provinces of the empire are of particular historical value. The Latin script was originally very like that of the early Greek alphabet used by the Greek settlers at Cumae (on the coast near Naples, founded *c*.750 BC), from which the Latin alphabet was ultimately derived. By the first century AD the cutters had developed the beautiful Roman capital lettering, seen at its best on the base of Trajan's Column. Latin inscriptions, like Greek, are an invaluable supplement to written history in the matter of politics and laws, treaties and legal contracts, military administration, and local government. We learn about the multifarious aspects of social life in many communities: the exemplary careers of otherwise unknown individuals, the activities of clubs, the amenities of public baths, the continuing importance of Roman religion in civic life. Christian inscriptions throw light on the development of Christian society and religious thought. Important Latin historical inscriptions include the so-called Monumentum Ancyranum, the emperor Augustus' official autobiography, written in both Latin and Greek (*see* RES GESTAE).

**Epime'nidēs** Semi-legendary Cretan poet, prophet, and wonder-worker, variously dated to between 600 and 500 BC, and credited with remarkable longevity, with wandering out of the body, and with a miraculous sleep of 57 years (*cf.* ARISTEAS). He is supposed to have visited Athens in about 600 BC to purify the city after the murder of Cylon's associates (*see* ALCMAEONIDAE). Tradition ascribed to him a theogony and other poems of a mystical nature. The quotation in the apostle Paul's Epistle to Titus 1: 12, 'Cretans are always liars', is said to be from his work.

**Epimē'theus** ('Afterthought') In Greek myth, brother of *Prometheus.

**epini'kion (epinician ode)** (Lat. *epinīcium*)
A form of Greek choral *lyric composed in the
grand manner in honour of a victory in one of
the great games in Greece, and publicly performed usually upon the victor's return to his
city. The principal epinician poets whose odes
are still largely extant are *Pindar and *Bacchylides. Of *Simonides' epinicians only a few
lines survive. Virtually all the odes adhere to a
standard pattern: they are usually written in
*triads, they eulogize the victor and his family
and city, they narrate a myth, and they relate
the victory to life in general, often by means of
moral reflections and exhortations which may
seem sombre in the context of victory and
celebration.

**epirrhē'ma** ('what is said afterwards') In
Greek Old Comedy, passage spoken by the
*coryphaeus* (chorus-leader) after the chorus
has sung a short lyric at the end of the *parabasis*. *See* COMEDY [Greek 3]. It often satirizes
various Athenians or admonishes the audience. The metre is trochaic.

**episode (*epeisodion*)** In Greek tragedy, the
action that takes place between two choral
odes, corresponding to the modern 'act' (*see*
TRAGEDY 3). In Old Comedy, episodes are the
brief scenes following the *parabasis*, separated by choral songs and illustrating the consequences of the hero's achievement of his aim
(*see* COMEDY [Greek 3]).

**epistemology** That branch of philosophy
which deals with the problem of knowledge:
what knowledge consists of, how we know (if
we do) what we think we know, and what
grounds we have for thinking that it is possible
to have knowledge of anything.

**Epistles (*Epistulae*)** ('Letters') Two books of
Latin hexameter poems by *Horace, of a reflective nature and written ostensibly as letters to
friends, a literary genre which had no obvious
antecedent in Greek or Latin. It is a matter of
debate whether the *Epistles* are real letters sent
on particular occasions to particular persons,
or fictions, the form merely providing a convenient framework for composition. (The published letters of the Greek philosophers,
especially of Epicurus, and, in poetry, Pindar's
third Pythian ode are possible influences.)
There are obvious advantages to Horace in
adopting this literary form: each epistle has a
starting point and a subject, and is patently a

unity; moreover, change of addressee from one
epistle to another permits different aspects of
the writer's thought or personality to emerge to
suit the situation of the recipient. The first book
was probably published in 20 or 19 BC; in the
opening poem Horace professes to have abandoned lyric poetry (books 1–3 of *Odes* were
published probably in 23 BC) and to have
turned to philosophy. This philosophy is not
that of the professionals, which he treats with
irony and humour (describing himself as 'a
hog from the sty of Epicurus'). Instead he concentrates on questions of how to lead one's
life—the contentment to be found in a simple
life, the dangers of avarice, and the advantage
of moderation in all things.

Book 1 contains twenty epistles, and many
lines have proved memorable: comparing the
man who puts off the hour of right living with
the countryman who waits for the river to flow
by, 'he who has begun his task has half done it;
have the courage to be wise' (*dimidium facti
qui coepit habet: sapere aude*, 2.40); describing
the folly of men who look for peace of mind in
a new place, 'it is the sky they change but not
their state of mind' (*caelum non animum mu-
tant*, 11.27); 'anger is a short madness' (*ira
furor brevis est*, 2.62); 'you may drive nature
out with a pitchfork but she will return every
time' (*naturam expellas furca, tamen usque
recurret*, 10.24); the 'by-ways of a quiet life'
(*fallentis semita vitae*, 18.103). Epistle 4 is interesting as addressed to the poet Tibullus;
Epistle 6 is a series of reflections on peace of
mind, 'to wonder at nothing' (*nil admirari*,
the *ataraxia* of Epicurus); Epistle 9 is a letter
introducing a friend to the young Tiberius, the
future emperor; Epistle 16 contains a description of the poet's farm.

Book 2 is usually dated to 12 BC on the basis
of historical allusions. It contains only two
epistles (but see below), the first to the emper-
or Augustus, written perhaps in 15 BC, and the
second to Julius Florus, a young companion of
Tiberius with literary aspirations, written in 19
or 18 BC. Both concern literature; in the first
Horace surveys the development of Latin poetry and defends the refinement of contemporary poetry under the influence of Greek
literature; in the second Horace gives his reasons for abandoning lyric poetry in favour
of philosophy. There are other interesting autobiographical passages and some literary
doctrine; unsparing self-criticism in an author
is especially recommended. For a third epistle

*see* ARS POETICA, a name it has been known by since Quintilian. *See also* LETTERS.

### Epistle to the Pisos (Epi'stula ad Pisōnēs)
*See* ARS POETICA.

**Epi'stulae ex Ponto** ('Letters from the Black Sea') Four books of elegiac poems written by *Ovid in the latter years of his exile at Tomis. Books 1–3 were published in AD 13; book 4 probably appeared after his death in AD 17. Like the poems of books 3–5 of the *Tristia*, these describe the rigours of his exile and plead for leniency; 'writing a poem you can't read to anyone is like dancing in the dark', he complains to a fellow poet. They differ only by being addressed to individuals by name. Ovid's hopes seem to rest on the genial character of Germanicus, nephew and adopted son of the emperor Tiberius, who is addressed or mentioned in several places.

**epitaphs** *See* EPIGRAM.

**epithala'mium** *See* MARRIAGE SONGS.

**epithets, divine** Particular epithets or adjectives are often applied to Greek and Roman gods, especially in *epic poetry. Many of these are purely ornamental or poetic, often joining with the proper name to form a convenient metrical unit, but others are known to have been used in cult. It can be difficult to decide to which category a particular epithet belongs. Some obviously indicate the place where the deity is worshipped: Apollo Dēlios is Apollo of Delos; others more interestingly, sometimes more importantly from a historical point of view, indicate an association with another deity, as in the case of Apollo Carneius. The largest class of epithets refers to the functions of the deity. Thus Zeus has many titles referring to his function as a weather god; he is the cloud-gatherer, loud-thunderer, rain-sender, the god 'who descends' (in lightning and the thunderbolt). Sometimes the epithet refers not to the characteristics of the god but to those of the worshipper. In one place Hera was addressed as 'maiden', 'wife', and 'widow' because she was worshipped by women of all ages and conditions. More rarely deities are described by an epithet referring to their moral or civic qualities (e.g. Apollo Archēgetēs, 'Founder', Apollo in his role as the god who approved schemes of colonization).

For Homeric epithets *see* ORAL POETRY.

**Epitrepo'ntes** ('The arbitrants') Greek comedy by *Menander, of which half is preserved intact on several papyri and a further sixth in fragments.

During the absence of her husband Charisios, Pamphile has borne a child five months after her marriage, and has exposed it with the help of her old nurse Sophrone. Charisios, told of this by his slave Onesimos, leaves home to stay with a friend Chairestratos and invites the harp-girl Habrotonon to join him, to the great indignation of Pamphile's unpleasant father Smikrines. A shepherd Daos finds the child and gives it to a charcoal burner Syriskos whose wife has lost her own baby, but Daos and Syriskos dispute possession of some trinkets found with the child and agree to submit to the arbitration of a passer-by. This chances to be Smikrines, who judges that the trinkets, being evidence of parentage, should accompany the child. Onesimos recognizes one as being his master's ring, and thus Charisios, already repenting of his priggish self-righteousness, is eventually revealed as having himself seduced Pamphile at a festival before their marriage and being the father of her exposed child. With the kindly help of Habrotonon all are reconciled and the play ends with the discomfiture of the objectionable Smikrines who, unaware of the turn of events, arrives determined to remove his daughter.

Terence's *Hecyra* resembles the *Epitrepontes* in plot.

**e'pode** ('sung after') *See* TRIAD.

**Epodes** Seventeen short Latin poems by the Roman poet *Horace, in various lyric metres, worked on in the 30s BC and published *c*.30. Some were written before Horace met *Maecenas. Referred to by Horace as *iambi*, 'iambics', they were professed imitations of *Archilochus. Eleven are in iambic metre and six in a combination of iambics and dactyls. Among other meanings their name denotes the line of a couplet, and thence the term is applied to short poems written in couplets of this form. The theme of Greek iambi was invective, but only seven of Horace's epodes engage in personal attack (4, 5, 6, 8, 10, 12, and 17) and even then not against well-known figures. Two, 7 and 16, are in the form of direct warnings to the Romans on the fatal nature of civil war. Horace addressed four to Maecenas, 1, 3, 9, and 14, in the early days of their acquaintance;

1 and 9 are written as to a friend in the context of the decisive battle of *Actium, 3 is a joke about garlic, and 14 a self-deprecating excuse. Epodes 11 and 15 are in the style of love-elegy, 2 is an ironic form of pastoral, and 13 anticipates a theme of the *Odes*, that in rough weather it is good to enjoy the pleasures of wine with friends.

**eponymous** ('that gives his or her name') Term used both of those who gave their names to places, as Alexander the Great to Alexandria or Antiochus to Antioch, and of the chief magistrate of a city (in Athens the principal archon, in Rome the two consuls) who gave his name to the year in which he held office, thereby identifying it. The latter was known as the eponymous magistrate (*see* CALENDARS). When *Cleisthenes (2) divided the Athenians into ten tribes, the Delphic oracle chose ten Attic heroes to be their eponyms (*epōnymoi*).

**epy'llion** [Greek diminutive of *epos*, 'epic'] In Greek and Latin literature, a very brief epic, i.e. a narrative poem a few hundred lines long, in hexameters, usually on the subject of the life and especially the loves of a mythical hero or heroine. It is characteristic of an epyllion to inset a lesser story within the main narrative. This genre was popular from the time of the Hellenistic poets Callimachus (*Hecale*) and Theocritus (Idyll 24) to Catullus (poem 64). The word is also used to describe self-contained episodes in longer poems, such as the Aristaeus episode in Virgil, *Georgics* 4, and the individual stories in Ovid's *Metamorphoses*. As a descriptive term it is modern.

**equestrian order (equitēs)** (pl. of Lat. *equēs*, 'knight') An important social class of Roman citizens, originally enrolled, according to tradition, by the kings of Rome to form the cavalry section of the army; each was given a horse from state funds (the so-called 'public horse') and the insignia which later became the distinctive attire of patricians, magistrates, and senators, i.e. the tunic with the *clavus*, the purple vertical stripe, and the *trabea*, a short embroidered cloak. For the political rights of the equites *see* ROMAN REPUBLIC. In the late second century BC they were enrolled by the *censors from all non-senators who possessed a minimum property of 400,000 sesterces (were of 'equestrian census') as well as being physically and morally worthy, and the term

'equestrian order' thus came to denote a wealthy social class. During this century the original *raison d'être* of the equites gradually disappeared when the cavalry contingents, if needed at all, were raised outside Italy. From this time on the military function of the equites changed to service as staff officers. (Cicero served for two years in the Social War.) In addition, eligibility for magistracies at Rome belonged only to those of equestrian census at least, since those holding public office were unpaid; hence military and civil offices were held by the same class. But it was various legal measures passed in the late second century BC which effectively gave political significance to the equites by handing over to them state responsibilities, such as the manning of certain juries which had been the prerogative of the senatorial class (*see* LAW, ROMAN). After the enfranchisement of Italy at the beginning of the first century BC the equestrian order was augmented by men of similar background from the colonies and *municipia*. In social standing the equites were almost equal to senators and shared with them both landed and business interests. They were capable of exerting considerable political force, and were particularly influential in the time of Cicero, who, himself the son of an *eques*, tried to unite them with the senate in a *concordia ordinum* ('concord between the classes'); *see* CICERO (1) 3. But although both classes were often united on an important issue, the equites were too disparate in their views and insufficiently interested in politics to form a stable political group. By the end of the republic the term 'equites' denoted all well-to-do citizens, *publicani*, bankers, businessmen, and administrators, who were of equestrian census and who did not belong to the senatorial class. Under the empire the order ceased to be a political force, but individual equites continued to be of importance in the civilian and military administration. When the rights of citizenship were extended to the Roman provinces, many of their wealthiest citizens qualified for and were enrolled in the equestrian order and were thus enabled to take up administrative duties in the empire. By the end of the third century AD almost all the higher military and administrative posts were held by equites. But in the following century the wide diffusion of honours among officials blurred the distinctions of class, and the equestrian order ceased to be a recognizable element in the state.

**era, dating by** *See* CALENDARS 2; ARCHAIC AGE; BRONZE AGE.

**Erasi'stratus** (of Ceos, third century BC) Famous physician who may have practised at Alexandria, often linked with *Herophilus. Both were said to have practised human dissection and to have vivisected condemned criminals as well as animals. Erasistratus saw the body as a mechanism, and was the first to expound a complete physiological scheme of the body. Mechanically, his view was that if matter is emptied from one place other matter will enter that same place, since emptiness is impossible; on this basis he not only gave a fairly accurate description of heart valves but also showed how their mechanism ensured that the blood could not flow through them backwards. Unlike Herophilus whose anatomical and physiological investigations he continued, Erasistratus abandoned the Hippocratic doctrine of *humours as an explanation of the origin of disease. Instead he postulated several causes for diseases, all ultimately stemming from the various parts of corporeal matter (blood, 'vital pneuma', etc) becoming mixed up in some way. He did not believe that there were diseases peculiar to women, and was opposed to drastic methods of treatment, such as blood-letting, for which *Galen criticized him. It was his view that the heart is the centre and source of both the arterial and the venous systems and that there are very fine interconnections between arteries and veins. In that respect he was not far from the conception of the circulation of blood, which was not accurately described until 1628 by the English physician William Harvey. His writings were still being read in the fourth century AD, but survive today only in quotation.

**E'rato** *See* MUSES.

**Erato'sthenes 1.** At Athens, one of the *Thirty Tyrants, prosecuted by *Lysias.

**2.** (of Cyrene, *c.*285–194 BC) The most versatile scholar of his time, who after spending several years in Athens became head of the *Alexandrian Library. He was styled *pentathlos*, 'all-rounder' (properly, in athletics), and *beta* because he was next best to the leading (*alpha*) specialist in every subject (for these last terms *see* ALPHABET). From *philologia*, 'love of learning', he coined to describe himself the word *philologos*, 'scholar'. It is apt for one who was literary critic, philosopher, mathematician, astronomer, chronographer, geographer, grammarian, and poet. Some small extracts of his work survive in scattered quotations. Of his critical works the most interesting was his twelve books (at least) *On Ancient Comedy*, but his most important works were the *Chronographies* (for which he was indebted to *Timaeus), the *Geographica*, and *On the Measurement of the Earth*. The *Chronographies* presented in the form of tables a reasonably clear and accurate chronological system of Greek history, as free from myth as he could make it, beginning with the fall of Troy and ending with the death of Alexander the Great (323 BC). Greek authors give different dates for the Trojan War, from *c.*1280 to 1184 BC and even later. Eratosthenes dated the fall of Troy to 1184 by working backwards from the established date of the first Olympian games, 776 BC, using the genealogies of the Spartan kings. This gave him 1104 for the *Dorian invasion, which according to tradition happened two generations, i.e. 80 years by one standard reckoning, after the Trojan War.

The three books of the *Geographica* were the first complete description of the inhabited world, and the work was completed by a world map of tolerable accuracy. (*See also* BARBARIAN.) In *On the Measurement of the Earth* he used an ingenious method to make a remarkably accurate calculation of the earth's circumference. His calculations were based on observations of the angles of the sun's rays at Alexandria and Syene (Aswan), which were (almost) on the same longitude and a known distance (about 800km) apart. He concluded that the distance from Syene to Alexandria must be 1/50th part of the earth's circumference, and on some estimates of the unit of distance (the 'stade') used by Eratosthenes, his result is within 1 per cent of the modern figure (40,075km). One poem which survives is on the duplication of the cube, an interesting topic in view of his statement that the aim of poetry is to entertain not to instruct. *See also* BEMATISTS.

**E'rebus (Darkness)** *See* CHAOS.

**Ere'chtheus** A figure of cult worshipped in the Erechtheum, often thought of as an early king of Athens. He is sometimes confused with the hero *Erichthonius, and like him said to have sprung from the earth and to have been nurtured by Athena. According to

Homer, Athena installed him in her temple, the Erechtheum, at Athens and made him her companion. The chief myth concerning him relates that when the Eleusinians and Eumolpus the Thracian, son of Poseidon, invaded Attica, Erechtheus, having enquired of the Delphic oracle and been told that victory would be his only if he sacrificed one of his daughters, performed the sacrifice and duly defeated the Eleusinians, killing Eumolpus. Poseidon in anger caused the death of Erechtheus and all his house. The story was the subject of a popular tragedy by Euripides, now lost. Like Cecrops, Erechtheus was the ancestral figure of all Athenians, who may be called, poetically, Erechtheids.

**Erichtho'nius** Attic hero and mythical king of Athens, usually said to be the son of *Hephaestus, whose semen fell upon the earth as he struggled to rape Athena. Gaia (Earth) gave birth to the child and Athena took him and hid him in a chest which she gave to the daughters of *Cecrops, king of Athens, to guard, instructing them not to open it. They disobeyed, and terrified by what they saw (either the child in serpent-form or attended by serpents), leaped from the Acropolis to their deaths. Erichthonius became king of Athens and was later worshipped in the form of a serpent. In some stories his son and successor is *Pandion.

**Eri'nna** Greek poet of the island of Tēlos near Rhodes, probably of the fourth century BC, who died at the age of 19. Three epigrams in the Greek *Anthology are ascribed to her. She was famous for a poem of 300 hexameter lines, The Distaff (Ēlakatē), which has not survived except for a few quotations and papyrus fragments; it was written in memory of her friend Baucis from whom she had been separated by the latter's marriage and death.

**Erī'nyes** See FURIES.

**Eriphȳ'le** In Greek myth, sister of Adrastus and wife of *Amphiaraus.

**Eris** ('Strife') In Greek myth, the goddess personifying strife (see PARIS, JUDGEMENT OF). Hesiod, in Works and Days, says there is not simply one strife but two: a bad one who promotes war and a good one who promotes productive competition. See also EMPEDOCLES.

**Eros** In Greek myth, the god of love, the Roman Cupid. He does not appear in Homer,

but Hesiod includes him as one of the first created gods (see CHAOS), signifying the power of sexual love over gods and men. Eros in this cosmogonic sense sometimes figures in the thought of the early Greek philosophers (see EMPEDOCLES). In the lyric poets however he is the personification of strong sexual desire, which comes as an external force affecting body and mind. This Eros is cruel and unpredictable, but embodies those qualities that inspire love, and hence is young and beautiful. He is the companion, often called the son, of Aphrodite. His bow and arrows, first mentioned by Euripides, and later his torch, figure prominently in his role of mischievous boy assigned to him by the Hellenistic poets and artists. Quite often he is expanded into a plurality of Erōtes. Eros was not, however, simply a literary conceit; he was also the object of a few ancient cults (notably at Thespiae) and much individual worship. See also IRIS and LOVE AND SEXUALITY.

**Erysi'chthon** In Greek myth, man who cut down a grove sacred to Demeter, by whom he was punished with insatiable hunger which ruined all his household. See CALLIMACHUS [Hymn 6].

**E'squiline** (Lat. Esquiliae or later Mons Esquilinus) One of the *seven hills of Rome, on the eastern side of the city, from early times used as a cemetery. It gave its name to one of the four regions (with the Suburbana, Collina, and Palatina) into which the republican city was divided.

**E'teoclēs** In Greek myth, the elder son of *Oedipus and Jocasta, brother of Polyneices, Antigone, and Ismene.

**Ether** See AETHER.

**Ethics** See NICOMACHEAN ETHICS.

**Etna** See AETNA.

**Etrū'ria** In Italy, the country of the *Etruscans.

**Etruscans** (called Tyrrhēnoi or Tyrsēnoi by the Greeks, Tusci or Etrusci by Latin speakers) A pre-Roman people of *Italy and the most important of their time, historically and artistically. Etruscan culture came into being in the ninth and eighth centuries BC, apparently as a development from that of the early Iron age Villanovans, but the origin of the Etruscans was already a subject for antiquarian specula-tion in the middle of the first century AD when the emperor Claudius wrote their history (which has not survived). The Greek historian Herodotus thought they came from Lydia in Asia Minor (and the language might well be Anatolian); but others (including Dionysius of Halicarnassus) have thought them indigenous to Italy. Politically the Etruscans made up a loose confederation of independent cities, and may not have possessed the ethnic unity which their name suggests. At the height of their power, from *c.*620 to *c.*500 BC, they con-trolled most of Italy including early Rome. The Roman king Tarquinius Priscus was said, prob-ably rightly, to have come to Rome from Etruria (*see* DEMARATUS). After the expulsion of the Tarquins from Rome in 510 BC, the Etrus-cans gradually lost their southern territory, suffering a famous defeat at Aricia *c.*504, and had perhaps already surrendered their north-ern lands to invading Celts. Their naval su-premacy was destroyed in a sea-battle off Cumae in 474 when they and the Carthagin-ians were defeated by a fleet of Cumaeans and Syracusans under Hieron, tyrant of Syracuse. By the end of the third century BC Rome held the whole of Etruria.

In the seventh century BC the Etruscans ac-quired luxury goods from the eastern Mediter-ranean in return for their own mineral resources, and thus were opened up to outside influences. The Euboean traders at Pithecusae (Ischia, in the bay of Naples) brought the Greek alphabet which was modified to fit spoken Etruscan (in its different forms, varying accord-ing to location). The Etruscans are known to us chiefly through their tombs, shaped like houses, dating from the seventh century on-wards, magnificently decorated with wall-paintings of their occupants at their cheerful everyday pursuits—banquets, games, hunt-ing—or with sculptures of lifelike immediacy, and containing portraits of the dead realistical-ly modelled. Their metalwork was outstanding and widely exported. The Capitoline Wolf and the Chimaera of Arretium (Arezzo) are both Etruscan bronzes. The Etruscans were celebrated in antiquity for the way in which every aspect of their public and private life was regulated by a code of religious practice, the so-called *Etrusca disciplina* ('Etruscan sys-tem'). They were particularly famed for their skill in augury based on scrutiny of the entrails, especially the liver, of sacrificial animals (*see* HARUSPICES). In this as in art, architecture, and engineering, Rome was deeply indebted to Etruria. No Etruscan literature has survived, but there exist thousands of inscriptions writ-ten in a Greek alphabet, mostly epitaphs, dat-ing from the seventh century BC to the time of the emperor Augustus. Etruscan is not related to any other well-known language nor is it entirely understood, although large parts of the vocabulary are known and the grammar com-prehensible. The only language so far shown to be related is the pre-Greek speech of Lemnos (in the Aegean Sea), itself extant in very few texts. This may connect with Herodotus' view that the Etruscans originated in Asia Minor.

**etymology** The study of words, their forma-tion and meaning. The chief interest of etymol-ogy in the ancient world concerned the ultimate origin of language: was the sound of a word merely an agreed convention (Gk. *nomos*), or was there a relationship between name and object indicating the nature (Gk. *physis*) of that object? In general it was as-sumed that the name revealed in some way the truth (Gk. *etymon*) about the object. Thus the name of Helen (of Troy) was associated with the verb *helein*, 'to destroy'. The argument was taken up by the sophists and is the subject of Plato's *Cratylus*. The thesis there is that language evolves, starting from simple sounds which are associated with particular ideas; the *l* sound is associated with smoothness, and the *rh* sound with motion, for example. Alexandri-an literary critics used this kind of etymology, among other things, to explain the meaning of rare words in early poetry. Aristotle saw words simply as signs whose meaning is established by convention. The Stoics, on the other hand, regarded etymology as elucidating the true na-ture of things, a view which proved very influ-ential. Stoic influence is apparent in the etymologizing of the gods' names in Cicero's *De natura deorum* and throughout Varro's *De lingua Latina*. The implicit belief was that names were originally given by name-givers to things in accordance with the nature of these things, and others continued the process. In contrast, Lucretius reflected the Epicurean view that sounds for things arose naturally but were later converted into words adopted by convention. For Rome as for Greece the lasting importance of etymology lay in its use-fulness, first for understanding obsolete words, and secondly for explaining and coining precise terms in technical writing, such as in law and medicine.

**Eubū'lus (Euboulos)** (*c*.405–*c*.335 BC) An important Athenian statesman who greatly influenced Athenian financial policy to the city's advantage between 355 and 342 BC. By getting a law passed which led to a financial cutback for military ventures he was able to devote money to civic purposes. He also aimed to unite all Greeks against Philip II of Macedon and even after Philip had broken the terms of the Peace of Philocrates in 346 BC (*see* DE-MOSTHENES (2) 2) still tried to maintain it. By 342 the war party led by Demosthenes was in control. No more is heard of Eubulus after the Greek defeat at Chaeronea in 338. *See also* ISOCRATES 5.

**Euclid (Eukleidēs)** Greek mathematician, who lived in Alexandria between *c*.325 and 250 BC, but of whose birthplace and life nothing reliable is known. His fame rests on his great textbook, *Stoicheia* ('Elements'): books 1–4 and 6 on plane geometry, 5 on proportion, 7–9 on arithmetic and the theory of rational numbers, 10 on irrationals, 11–13 on solid geometry. Books 14 and 15 are not by Euclid. This work caused the name 'Euclid' to become almost synonymous with 'geometry'. One of the few anecdotes told about him says that when Ptolemy I of Alexandria asked him if there was a shorter way to understand geometry than that of the *Elements*, he replied that there was no 'royal road' to geometry. His work drew extensively on the discoveries of his predecessors, particularly *Eudoxus, and restated them, but its great value lies in its rigorous exposition of the geometrical knowledge acquired by the Greeks from the time of Pythagoras, arranged systematically and in logical sequence. As soon as it was published Euclid's textbook became the subject of study and comment, and the edition (or reworking) by *Theon (in the fourth century AD) was widely used; most valuable is the commentary of *Proclus (fifth century AD) on book 1.

In western Europe Euclid's work suffered the common fate of Greek science and mathematics, being known only to the Arabs until in the first half of the twelfth century an Englishman, Adelard of Bath, translated the Arabic version of the *Elements* into Latin (*see* TEXTS, TRANSMISSION OF ANCIENT 7). The original Greek was not generally known until a text was printed at

Basle in 1533. The vernacular translations date from the middle of the sixteenth century. Although in Europe textbooks of geometry gradually incorporated modern advances in the subject, in Britain the *Elements* held their ground more or less unadulterated until the end of the nineteenth century. Euclid seems to have been the source of the words put at the end of mathematical proofs, 'which was to be proved' (Gk. *hŏper edei deixai*), usually known by the initials of the Latin version, *q(uod) e(rat) d(emonstrandum)*. He wrote a number of other mathematical works, some of which survive in Greek and others in the Arabic translations only. He may possibly have written two treatises on music, still extant.

**Eudē'mus** (second half of the fourth century BC) Friend and pupil of *Aristotle. His writings survive only in quotation. He used to be regarded as the author of the *Eudemian Ethics*, preserved among the works of Aristotle, but this work is now usually attributed to Aristotle himself (*see* NICOMACHEAN ETHICS).

**Eudo'xus** (of Cnidus, *c*.390–*c*.340 BC) Outstanding mathematician and astronomer in the half-century before *Euclid, a younger contemporary of Plato and his associate in the Academy. He is also said to have worked with the Pythagorean Archytas. His writings are lost but their contents are fairly well known from later writers. He is largely responsible for extending the theory of proportion to incommensurables (covered by Euclid in *Elements*, book 5) and for removing the check given to geometry when irrational numbers were discovered, by showing that a proportion could be established between any magnitudes. In solid geometry he showed that the volume of a pyramid was one-third of that of a prism of equal height on the same base, and correspondingly that the volume of a cone was one-third that of its containing cylinder. In astronomy his work marks the beginning of a new epoch, for he was the first to give a mathematical account of the movements of the heavenly bodies that tried to explain the fact that the planets (of which Eudoxus knew the five that were identified in the ancient world; *see* ASTRONOMY) occasionally appear to interrupt their movement eastward, relative to the fixed stars, along the zodiac, and for a time to move backwards from east to west (retrogression). Eudoxus suggested that the paths of the sun and moon and planets were produced by the rotation of concentric spheres, at different speeds and about different axes, with the earth at rest at their common centre. The system showed great mathematical skill and managed to account fairly successfully for a wide variety of phenomena. It was modified by *Callippus to remove the most obvious inconsistencies with observable fact, and in this form it was accepted by Aristotle (*see* ARISTOTLE 5). Eudoxus' astronomical calendar of the risings and settings of the constellations, in which there is some evidence of Babylonian influence, formed the basis of *Aratus' astronomical poem the *Phaenomena*. His geographical work (in several books), *Circuit of the Earth*, was important in giving a mathematical component to descriptive geography. More generally he taught, according to Aristotle, that pleasure is the good.

**Euhē′merus (Euēmeros)** (of Messene) Author, *c.*300 BC, of a fantasy travel novel in Greek, *Sacred Scripture* (*Hiera anagraphē*), now surviving only in fragments, but influential in its day. In it he describes an imaginary voyage to an island Panchaia in the Indian Ocean where he found a golden column (the 'Sacred Scripture' of the title) on which it was written that the gods of mythology were originally great kings, deified by their grateful people, a theory known to the modern world as 'euhemerism'. The idea was very relevant to the contemporary Hellenistic world where rulers like the Ptolemies of Egypt might, by demanding worship from their subjects (*see* RULER CULT), suggest to some that gods had once been human. *Ennius wrote in Latin a prose work *Euhemerus* based on the *Sacred Scripture*, impugning the majesty of Jupiter Optimus Maximus. That likewise has not survived. It seems that the theory of Euhemerus did not excite much attention.

**Eumae′us** In Homer's *Odyssey*, the faithful swineherd of Odysseus, who entertained Odysseus in his hut ignorant of his identity when the latter returned to Ithaca (*Odyssey* 14) and afterwards helped him to destroy the suitors.

**Eumē′lus** (of the aristocratic Bacchiadae of Corinth) Greek epic poet of the second half of the eighth century BC, author of an epic on the mythical and heroic history of Corinth (and perhaps other epic poems). He also wrote a famous *prosodion* (procession-song; *see* LYRIC POETRY [Greek]) for the Messenians to sing at the festival of Apollo at Delos. The small fragment which survives in quotation is, if genuine, interesting as a very early specimen of lyric.

**Eu′menes** The name of several rulers of Pergamum. *See* ATTALIDS.

**Eume′nidēs** ('Kindly ones') Euphemistic name for the *Furies and the title of a Greek tragedy by Aeschylus (*see* ORESTEIA).

**Eumo′lpus** ('Fair singer') In Greek myth, a Thracian, the son of Poseidon, who while in exile from Thrace as punishment for rape visited Eleusis where he founded, or became connected with, the Eleusinian *mysteries. He succeeded to the throne of Thrace, but was sent for by the Eleusinians to help them against *Erechtheus, king of Athens, in which campaign he was killed. He was the eponymous ancestor of the clan of the Eumolpidae, who officiated at the mysteries.

**eunomia** (Gk. 'good order') A term which seems to have meant originally 'obedience to the laws' (whether good or bad) as promoting good order. Aristotle thought *eunomia* should denote not merely obedience to the laws but 'well-enacted laws which people obey'. For *eunomia* as applied to the Spartan constitution *see* LYCURGUS (2); SPARTA 3; TYRTAEUS.

**Eunū′chus** ('The eunuch') Roman comedy by *Terence adapted from a Greek comedy of the same name by *Menander, with the characters of the *parasite and the soldier added from Menander's *Kolax*. It was performed in 161 BC with great success, well-earned by its varied action and lively dialogue.

Phaedria, a young Athenian, is in love with the courtesan Thāis, who is also loved by the boastful soldier Thraso (always attended by the parasite Gnatho). Thraso wants to give her as a bribe a young slave-girl bought in Rhodes whom Thais, knowing her to be of Athenian birth and stolen in childhood, wishes to own so as to restore her to her family. She therefore persuades Phaedria to let her pretend to give in to Thraso. Phaedria, meanwhile, has himself bought a present for Thais of a eunuch, but his brother Chaerea, having seen and fallen in love with the Rhodian slave-girl on her way to Thais' house, exchanges clothes with the eunuch and assumes his character in order to gain access to her. In this he succeeds, and when Thais reveals the girl's Athenian birth they are betrothed. Thraso, repulsed by

Thais as soon as she has gained possession of the slave-girl, tries unsuccessfully to carry her off, but a compromise is reached by which both he and Phaedria share her favours.

The prologue contains a line which subsequently became well known, 'nothing is said which has not been said before', *nullumst iam dictum quod non dictum sit prius.*

**eupa'tridae** ('the well-born') In general an informal term for the nobility at Athens, i.e. those born into one of the sixty or so named *genē*, 'clans' (*see* GENOS), which each claimed descent from a heroic ancestor who was himself the son of a god. They were generally rich landowners who could muster political support from their own territory. Until the end of the sixth century BC (*see* SOLON) they monopolized the offices of government, and even when the city became more democratic they were still influential.

**Eupho'rion 1.** Son of the Attic tragedian *Aeschylus, who is said to have won victories in the drama festivals with tragedies written by his father but not produced in his lifetime. In 431 BC he defeated both Sophocles and Euripides (one of whose plays was *Medea*), but with what plays is not known.

**2.** Of Chalcis in Euboea, a Hellenistic Greek poet of the third century BC who lived most of his life in Antioch in Syria, where he was librarian. The scantiness of his surviving work makes it difficult to assess, but he seems mostly to have written epic-style poetry on mythological subjects, his learned style reminiscent of Callimachus. He exercised a considerable influence on later poets; at Rome his *epyllia were greatly admired by Catullus and his contemporaries (hence Cicero's description of these poets as *cantores Euphorionis*, an obscure phrase perhaps meaning 'those who sing the praises of Euphorion'). He also influenced Gallus and Virgil. Perhaps the *Ciris* (*see* APPENDIX VIRGILIANA) reproduces his manner most closely.

**Eu'polis** One of the trio of famous Athenian poets of Old Comedy, the others being Cratinus and Aristophanes (*see* COMEDY [Greek 4]). He was contemporary with the latter, producing his first play in 429 BC and dying at some time after 415. He won three victories at the *Lenaea and at least one at the *Dionysia. None of his plays survives in manuscript, but we have nineteen titles and numerous quotations as well as some papyrus fragments. His comedies are similar in subject matter and style to those of Aristophanes. In *Marikās* (a non-Greek word meaning 'catamite') he attacked *Hyperbolus much as Aristophanes did Cleon in *Knights*; in *Demoi* ('Demes') great Athenians of the past were brought up from the Underworld to give the city good advice, and in *Taxiarchoi* ('Corps-commanders') he represented the god Dionysus undergoing hard military training under the Athenian general Phormion, recalling themes in Aristophanes' *Frogs* and showing that he and Aristophanes, as well as being rivals, were imitators of each other's work.

**Euri'pidēs** (*c.*485–406 BC) The youngest of the three great Athenian tragedians. We have little reliable information about his life, most of the anecdotes told about him being ultimately derived from the hostile jokes of the comic poets, such as the references to his mother selling herbs in the market. The story that he wrote his plays in a cave on Salamis confirms other reports of his solitary disposition, and he was not prominent in politics. He was associated in people's minds with the *sophists, whose influence is discernible in his work, and was said to be acquainted with Anaxagoras, Socrates, and Protagoras; it was supposed to have been at his house that Protagoras gave the first public reading of his sceptical work *On the Gods*. Euripides won the dramatic competitions with the trilogy containing *Hippolytus in 428, and posthumously with the trilogy containing *Bacchae and *Iphigeneia at Aulis, produced probably in 405, and on only two other occasions. In about 408, supposedly embittered by his unpopularity, he withdrew from Athens to the philhellenic court of Archelaus, king of Macedon. There he died, not long before the *Dionysia of 406, at the *proagon of which Sophocles marked his death by presenting his own tragic chorus ungarlanded.

We possess nineteen of the 92 plays Euripides is said to have written, and know the titles of about 80. The plays we possess are of two classes:

(i) a selection of ten plays perhaps made *c.* AD 200 and transmitted in manuscripts with *scholia, consisting of *Alcestis (438, second prize), *Medea (431, third prize), *Hippolytus (428, first prize), *Andromache (date not known; *c.*426), *Hecuba (date not known; *c.*424), *Trojan Women (415, second prize), *Phoenician Women (*see* PHOENISSAE; 409),

*Orestes* (probably 408), *Bacchae* (between 408 and 406; the scholia are lost), and *Rhesus* (perhaps not genuine);

(ii) part of an alphabetic arrangement of his work comprising plays whose (Greek) titles begin with the Greek letters E to K, namely, *Helen* (412), *Electra* (date not known; c.416), *Children of *Heracles* (*Heracleidae*) (date not known; c.430), *Madness of *Heracles* (date not known; c.414), *Suppliant Women* (*see* SUPPLIANTS 2; date not known; c.422), *Iphigeneia at Aulis* (between 408 and 406, produced with *Bacchae*); *Iphigeneia in Tauris* (date not known; c.413), *Ion* (date not known; c.410), and *Cyclops* (a satyr play, probably c.408). In this second group we therefore have some plays of Euripides that may be considered a representative selection of his work rather than plays selected for a purpose, such as a school curriculum. We also have sizeable fragments mostly from papyri of (in probable chronological order) *Telephus, Cretans, Cresphontes, Erechtheus, Phaethon, Alexander, Oedipus, Hypsipyle, Archelaus*.

Euripides' tragedies derive their characteristic tone from the author's departure from the orthodoxies of the time: he gives prominence to unconventional and untraditional views and to socially problematic people like women and slaves, and reappraises old stories in the light of late fifth-century scepticism. His mythical heroes and heroines, clothed in garments appropriate to their sufferings—the Athenians never forgot that in the *Telephus* he depicted the hero dressed in rags—describe their misfortunes in contemporary language and human terms, while a slave may reveal an inherent nobility of mind apparently at odds with his status. Aristotle, in the *Poetics*, quoted in this connection Sophocles' saying (not wholly clear) that he, Sophocles, represented people as they should be, Euripides as they are. Ancient critics noted Euripides' naturalistic treatment of human psychology, particularly that of women, and censured him for making his women unnecessarily bad. He was clearly attracted by the dramatic possibilities in stories of violent and bizarre passion—Phaedra falling incestuously in love with her stepson Hippolytus, Medea taking vengeance on her husband by murdering their children, Heracles' madness; but what interested him also was the conflict that arose in the minds of these people. Nineteenth-century critics liked to call him a rationalist because of his sceptical attitudes to

traditional religion and morality; in the twentieth century he was called, no less justly, an irrationalist, because he depicts people struggling with powerful irrational forces within and, from a Greek perspective, outside themselves which they cannot understand. In construction the plays sometimes seem awkward. Characters occasionally speak what may seem in a general way rhetorically appropriate to the situation or may fit the thought or events in late fifth-century Athens, but does not fit the character as portrayed up to that point. Some critics have seen in this tendency not a failure on Euripides' part to present a character as a consistent personality, but his awareness that personality is inherently a fragmented thing, different aspects being displayed at different times. Euripides is associated with painful portrayals of suffering: the Trojan women as victims of war, Orestes driven mad by guilt, Hecuba losing her humanity by multiple suffering.

Euripides was an innovator, especially in musical composition (an aspect comically parodied by Aristophanes). The distinction between the spoken parts of the actors and the songs of the chorus become blurred, as actors increasingly sing opera-like arias or duets at moments of high emotion, often in a metrically free, astrophic form (*see* STROPHE) and with a correspondingly loose syntax. At the same time the role of the chorus declines in importance. Confrontation between the main characters is often played out in a form which has come to be known as an *agon* ('confrontation' as between two opposing participants in a law-suit), in which the issue at stake is argued for and against in symmetrical and highly rhetorical speeches, with great formality. Another dramatic device employed by Euripides is the 'god in a machine' (*deus ex machina*: *see* THEATRE [Greek]), by which no fewer that eleven of his plays are brought to a conclusion.

Aristophanes parodied Euripides brilliantly in *Frogs*, and to a lesser extent in *Acharnians* and *Thesmophoriazusae*. Aristotle called him 'the most tragic of the poets' (i.e. best at arousing pity and fear; *see* POETICS). It was said that some Athenian prisoners after the *Sicilian Expedition won their liberty by reciting passages from his plays. (*See also* ELECTRA (2).)

**Eurō'pa** ('Broad-browed') In Greek myth, daughter of Agenor, king of Tyre (in Homer, daughter of *Phoenix (2)). Zeus loved her and so took the form of, or sent, a beautiful bull which swam to the seashore where she was playing and seemed so mild that she climbed upon its back. Thereupon it swam away with her to Crete. There she bore to Zeus *Minos, *Rhadamanthys, and, in post-Homeric accounts, *Sarpedon. She was then married to Asterius, king of Crete, who adopted her sons. The bull became the constellation Taurus. *See also* TALOS and CEPHALUS.

**Eury'alus** In Virgil's *Aeneid*, the friend of *Nisus (2).

**Euryclei'a** In Homer's *Odyssey*, the old nurse of Odysseus.

**Eury'dicē** The name of several women in Greek myth, including the wife of Creon, king of Thebes (*see* ANTIGONE). The best-known was a nymph and the wife of *Orpheus. While pursued by Aristaeus she was bitten by a snake and died. Orpheus followed her to the Underworld where the charms of his lyre suspended the tortures of the damned and persuaded Hades to allow him to bring her back, provided that he did not look round at her before he reached the upper world. He broke this condition and thus lost her forever. Through Virgil (*Georgics* 4.453) and Ovid (*Metamorphoses* 10.1) the story became well known to the Middle Ages. The story was sometimes given a happy ending, as in Gluck's opera where Eurydice was restored by the gods' forgiveness. The theme easily lent itself to a variety of symbolic interpretation, in ancient as well as modern times.

**Eurypo'ntid** The name of the junior branch of the royal house at Sparta, descendants of Eurypon, grandson of Procles (*see* HERACLEIDAE). (The senior branch was the *Agiad.)

**Eury'stheus** In Greek myth, king of Tiryns in Argos, son of Sthenelus and Nicippe, a descendant of *Perseus. When Zeus swore on oath that the first descendant of Perseus to be born on a certain day would rule the surrounding peoples, intending that it should be his son Heracles, Hera in jealousy contrived that Eurystheus was born first. In the usual version of the myth, after Heracles in madness had killed his wife and children, the oracle at Delphi ordered him to live at Tiryns and serve Eurystheus for twelve years in expiation. Eurystheus imposed upon him many dangerous tasks, known later as the Twelve Labours (*see* HERACLES, LABOURS OF). Even after Heracles'

death Eurystheus pursued his descendants (*see* HERACLES, CHILDREN OF).

**Euthydē'mus** Title of one of the earlier Greek dialogues of *Plato, taken from the name of the sophist of Chios.

Socrates narrates to his friend Crito, who is pondering how best to educate his son, a recent debate in the wrestling school, in which Cleinias, an aristocratic Athenian youth in danger of being corrupted unless properly educated, is presented with two opposing principles of education, the sophistic (*see* SOPHIST), represented by Euthydemus and Dionysodorus, and the Socratic. The sophists would teach 'virtue', *aretē, understood as meaning success in public life; Socrates expresses doubt as to whether *arete* can be taught at all. Crito, reinforced by an anonymous bystander who concluded that philosophy was worth nothing, doubts whether he should entrust his son to any of them.

**euthy'nae** ('straightening') At Athens, the examination conducted by the public auditors, *logistai*, of the accounts of every magistrate at the end of his term of office. It was primarily an examination of the officer's handling of public money, but complaints of other kinds could be brought against him.

**Eu'thyphrō** (*Euthyphrōn*) Title of an early Greek dialogue by *Plato.

Socrates, awaiting his trial for impiety, meets outside the court house Euthyphro the seer, who some years earlier had prosecuted his own father for unintentional homicide in order to clear himself of the pollution attendant on being connected with a murder. Socrates asks him for a definition of piety, but can only elicit the answer that piety is what is pleasing to the gods, and this turns out to be a matter of asking the gods for things and giving things to them. The dialogue satirizes a very inadequate conception of religion.

**Eutro'pius** Roman historian who published during the reign of the emperor Valens (AD 364–378) a survey of Roman history (*Breviarium ab urbe condita*) in ten books, from the time of Romulus to the death of the emperor Jovian in 364, ending with events of which the historian had personal knowledge. The early books are based on the epitome of Livy. The work is concise, well-balanced, and impartial.

**Eva'dnē (Euadnē)** In Greek myth, wife of Capaneus, one of the *Seven against Thebes, who threw herself on his funeral pyre. She appears in Euripides' tragedy *The *Suppliants*.

**Eva'goras (Euagoras)** (*c.*435–374 BC) King of Salamis in Cyprus, reputedly descended from *Teucer (2). He was friendly towards Athens and received many Athenian exiles at the end of the Peloponnesian War. His Hellenism brought him into conflict with the Persians, by whom he was finally defeated. He died by assassination in a palace intrigue.

**Eva'nder** [Gk. Euandros, 'good man'] In Greece probably a minor deity associated with Pan and Arcadia; he is mentioned as a son of Hermes and a nymph, identified with the Roman goddess Carmentis. In Roman legend he was regarded as having fled Arcadia and after landing at the site of Rome being allowed by *Faunus to make a settlement with his Arcadian followers on the Palatine (the name supposedly derived from his home at Pallantion in Arcadia). There he instituted the festival of the Lupercalia, connected with the worship of Faunus, in reminiscence of the Arcadian festival of the Lycaea, which was connected with Pan. Hercules visited him on one occasion and killed the monster *Cacus. In commemoration Evander established the cult of *Hercules at the Ara Maxima. Virgil in the *Aeneid* represents Evander as still alive when Aeneas arrives in Italy and as forming an alliance with him against the Latins. His son Pallas was killed fighting Turnus; it was to avenge him that Aeneas refused to spare Turnus. The story of Evander illustrates how the Romans created a connection in legend between Greece and Rome which included place-names and cults.

**exile** Long-term removal from one's native place, a form of penalty for criminal offences used in Athens and Rome. In Athens it was imposed for homicide, largely to get rid of a source of *pollution; it was permissible to go into voluntary exile in order to escape the death penalty. *Ostracism, which meant banishment for ten years, was a political expedient and not a penalty for an offence. Exile could be augmented by other penalties—the loss of property and of the right to be buried in Attic soil, the destruction of one's house, for example—but most of those who had committed unintentional homicide could keep their property and live abroad in freedom provided they avoided the great religious festivals and games, so as not to be a pollution. If a man suffering penal exile was found in Attica, he ran the risk of imprisonment and perhaps execution. Exile was for a fixed period or for life unless the sufferer obtained pardon.

In Rome, as in Athens, a defendant on trial for a capital crime might choose to go into exile (*exsilium*) before judgement was pronounced. However, in the last century of the republic exile became a substitute for the death penalty when magistrates were obliged to allow a condemned person time to escape before executing sentence, after which he was deprived of all legal protection and threatened with death ('denied fire and water') if he returned. There were varying degrees of voluntary and prescribed banishment, from the mild *relegatio* up to the severe *deportatio* (introduced by the emperor Tiberius), a perpetual banishment to a certain place, confiscation of property, and loss of citizenship. The term 'exile' came to be applied to them all.

**e'xodos** In Greek drama, the final scene. In *tragedy, it is the action following the final *stasimon* (choral ode); in Old Comedy it is the final rejoicing following the last *episode.

**exo'rdium** In *rhetoric, the introduction (or proem) of a speech.

**exposure of infants** *See* INFANTICIDE.

**Fa'bia, gens** One of the most ancient patrician *gentes* ('clans'; *see* GENS) at Rome, which traced its origins to *Hercules and *Evander. Its fame derives from an exploit in 479 BC when the *gens* offered to pursue the war against the Etruscan town of Veii entirely on its own; 306 men advanced from Rome and built a fortress on the Cremera (Fosso Valchetta), a small stream which falls into the Tiber a few miles above Rome. They were caught in an ambush and all killed with the exception of one youth, from whom all later members of the *gens* were descended. The later Roman defeat by the Gauls at the river Allia in 390 BC was believed to have occurred on the same day of the year (18 July, a.d.XV Kalendas Sextiles), subsequently regarded as a day of ill-omen.

**Fa'bius 1. Quintus Fabius Ma'ximus Rulliā'nus** (fourth century BC) Roman general of the Samnite wars, five times consul, dictator in 315 BC and perhaps again in 313, censor in 304. He celebrated *triumphs over Samnites (*see* ROME 2), Etruscans, and Gauls. Livy's account of his numerous exploits in books 8–11, based on Fabius Pictor and the later annalists, is untrustworthy and introduces incidents from the life of his grandson (or great-grandson), Fabius Cunctator (below). When consul for the fifth time in 295 he and his colleague P. *Decius Mus defeated an alliance of Samnites, Etruscans, Celts, and others at Sentinum (Sassoferrato) in the decisive battle for the supremacy of Italy. He may be the 'Q. Fabios' depicted in a military scene in a tomb on the Esquiline.

**2. Quintus Fabius Ma'ximus Verrucō'sus, Cunctā'tor** (*c.*275–203 BC) Roman general and consul during the Second Punic War. He was dictator in 221 and again in 217 after Hannibal destroyed the consul Flaminius and the Roman army at the battle of Lake Trasimene. During the six months of his second period of office he fought a war of attrition against Hannibal (*see* PUNIC WARS), and was called in consequence Cunctator, 'Delayer', by dog-

gedly following Hannibal's movements while avoiding a pitched battle which he thought the Romans could not win. After Rome reverted to a traditional encounter at Cannae in 216 and was disastrously defeated, Fabius' evasive strategy had to be resumed. The name derisively given to him took on an honourable connotation, and was incorporated in a famous line by the poet Ennius: *unus homo nobis cunctando restituit rem* ('one man by his delaying restored the situation for us'). In 213 he may have served as legate to his son. Fabius was consul (and leader of the senate, *princeps senatus*) for the fifth time in 209 when he recovered Tarentum (Taranto) from the Carthaginians. In 205 he strenuously opposed the plans of *Scipio (Africanus), who had recently driven the Carthaginians out of Spain, to take the war into the enemy's country by invading Africa, believing that it was an unnecessary risk. He died in 203, at about the time of Hannibal's departure from Italy, before the favourable conclusion of the war. Fabius was rightly called the Shield of Rome and was admired by later generations for his courage and old-fashioned patrician virtues. In British politics 'Fabianism' describes a socialist policy of cautious advance, as opposed to immediate revolution.

**3. Quintus Fabius Pictor** The earliest Roman historian, whose work survives only in quotations in later writers. (The family name Pictor, 'painter', derives from his grandfather who painted a temple *c.*302 BC.) He was a senator who fought in the Second Punic War (218–201 BC), and was sent to consult the Delphic oracle after the Roman defeat at Cannae in 216. His history of Rome, which dwelt at length with its foundation (dated by him to 748 BC) and continued to his own day, was written in Greek partly because Latin prose was not yet a literary medium but also with the purpose of justifying Roman policy to the Greek world. His work probably used pontifical records (*see* FASTI) and lists of magistrates. He was reliable, and frequently used by Livy and

Polybius, the latter for his account of the First and Second Punic Wars; Livy thought that his history was distorted by family pride in the Fabii.

**fable** In literature, a short story with a moral in which the characters are generally animals behaving as humans. The fable was a popular literary genre in Greece, as in other countries, at all times. Quintilian observes that it appeals particularly to the simple and uneducated. It is first found in Hesiod (*see* WORKS AND DAYS) and *Archilochus. By the end of the fifth century BC such fables in prose were generally attributed to *Aesop. A collection of 'Tales of Aesop' was made by *Demetrius of Phalerum. The earliest surviving collection of fables is that of *Babrius, probably of the second century AD, which enjoyed wide popularity. They were written in choliambic verse.

Latin authors frequently refer to fables which we know from Aesop. The earliest Latin collection was that of *Phaedrus, of the first century AD, written in iambic verse.

**Fabri'cius Luscī'nus, Gaius** [Lat. *luscinus*, 'one-eyed'] A hero of the Romans' war with *Pyrrhus (280–272 BC), a *novus homo who was twice consul, in 282 and 278, and was admired in later times for his old-style virtues of austerity, high principle, and incorruptibility. He refused bribes from Pyrrhus when he was sent as ambassador by the Romans in 280 to negotiate an exchange of prisoners; in the campaign of 278, when he was consul and in command of the Roman forces, he sent back to Pyrrhus the latter's treacherous doctor who had offered to poison him. Fabricius was a notably strict censor in 275. At his death he left no money to provide his daughters' dowry, which was given by the senate.

**fā'bula** ('story') The general Latin word for 'drama', 'play', frequently combined with an adjective defining the subject. The commonest types were the *fabula* *Atellāna*, farce, *f.* *crĕpidāta*, Roman tragedy on a Greek theme, *f.* *palliāta*, adaptation of a Greek comedy, *f.* *praetex(ta)ta*, a serious play on a Roman historical subject, and *f.* *tŏgāta*, a Roman comedy with a native theme concerning low life in Rome.

**Fali'sci** An Italian Iron-age people closely related to the Latins, who lived on the right bank of the Tiber north of Latium. Their principal city was Falerii, which the Romans captured in 241 BC.

**fall of Rome** No single event brought about 'the fall of Rome' or 'the decline of the Roman empire'. In any case, the decline of the empire in the West has to be dissociated from the happier fate of the Roman empire in the East, where culture flourished into the late sixth century AD and beyond. (For the division of the empire into two halves, East and West, *see* BYZANTINE AGE.)

Between AD 395 (when the Visigothic leader Alaric began to ravage inside the Roman imperial frontiers in Thrace and Macedonia) and 493 (when Theoderic the Great, king of the Ostrogoths, was proclaimed king of Italy), the Roman empire in the West was no longer capable of resisting Germanic incursions. Italy, Gaul, and Spain were gradually occupied by Germanic tribes, themselves migrating mostly under pressure from the advancing Huns, a Mongolian nomadic people. In 401 and again in 403 Alaric invaded Italy but was forced to withdraw by Stilicho, regent for the emperor Honorius. After Stilicho's death in 408 there was no general able to defeat the Visigoths, and on 24 August 410 after Honorius refused to negotiate they entered Rome and sacked it. It was the first time the city had fallen to a foreign enemy since its capture by the Gauls *c.*385 BC. In 452 the Huns devastated parts of Italy, but their king *Attila (known as the 'Scourge of God') was persuaded by Pope Leo I, the Great, to withdraw without entering Rome. Three years later the city fell to Gaiseric, king of the Vandals (another Germanic people from the Black Sea area), who stayed for a fortnight in the city to plunder its treasures. The last Roman emperor in the West was the young Romulus Augustulus, who reigned briefly 475–6. He was deposed and banished by Odoacer, Germanic follower of Attila and commander of the imperial guard, who was proclaimed king of Italy by the army and accepted the emperor in the East as his overlord. With him the Roman empire in the West came to an end (but *see* JUSTINIAN). Odoacer was murdered by Theoderic (above) who then established his own independent rule.

**fascēs** ('bundle of rods') Rods about 1.5m (5 feet) long, bound together by red thongs and carried on their shoulders by *lictors before important Roman magistrates as a symbol of their legitimacy and power. The practice seems to have been Etruscan in origin. Under the kings each bundle enclosed an axe, symbolizing the king's right to scourge and execute, but from the early republic onwards only dictators were allowed axes in Rome; other magistrates retained the axe when outside Rome and at the head of an army. In the case of a general who had won a victory and been saluted as Imperator by his soldiers, his *fasces*, which included the axe, were always crowned with laurel. The absence of the axe symbolized the citizens' right of appeal against capital punishment. From fascio, Italian for fasces, the twentieth-century Italian Fascist party took its name, with the *fasces* as its symbol.

**fasti** The name given to the old Roman *calendar which originally indicated *dies fasti and *nefasti*, the days on which it was or was not permissible to transact legal and public business. Later the word 'fasti' came to include other lists, of consuls (*fasti consulares*), of priests (*fasti sacerdotales*), and records of triumphs. They were published in 304 BC by Gnaeus *Flavius. Some fragments survive in inscriptions. From *c.*300 BC the records appear to be accurate. (*Cf.* ANNALS.)

*Fasti* ('Calendar') *Ovid's witty verse account, in elegiacs, of the Roman year, with its various observances and festivals. It was incomplete at the time of his exile in AD 8, and we have only the first six books (January to June), partially revised at Tomis. Ovid's models were Hellenistic poems, for astronomy the *Phaenomena* of *Aratus, and for his explanations of the origins of Roman history and religion the *Aitia* of *Callimachus, though he may have also been influenced by *Propertius' last book of elegies which contains a large number of Roman legends.

Ovid's design, as stated in the preface to the poem, is to study the calendar in the light of old annals, and to show what events are commemorated on each day and the origins of the various rites. He accordingly records day by day the rising and setting of the constellations (not without mistakes), and explains the perceived origins of the fixed festivals and the rites noted in the calendar, such as the Lupercalia on 15 February. He also relates the legends connected with particular dates, such as that of the founding of Rome on 21 April, and of the expulsion of the Tarquins on 24 February. Much of what he describes is not Roman at

all but imported Greek myth, such as the tale of Proserpine; and for disquisitions on a multitude of customs and beliefs, such as those connected with New Year's Day, the unluckiness of marriages in May, and the casting of straw men into the Tiber every year for uncertain reasons. The work is valuable as a source for the religious ideas of Ovid's own time, but not reliable for the remote Roman past.

**fate** In European thought the notion of fate as something inevitable, above all death, is often expressed. Greek nouns for 'fate' have the original meaning of 'a share', 'a portion', which falls to everyone at birth and which cannot be avoided. This idea is prominent in Homer: Zeus in the *Iliad* contemplates saving his warrior son Sarpedon from death but Hera persuades him not to rescue one 'long doomed to fate'. There is no sense of conflict between fate and the gods: what is contrary to fate does not happen. Nevertheless, within the bondage of fate human actions bring their own consequences: fate says that Odysseus will return home from Troy after twenty years, but when he fails to stop his men slaughtering the cattle of the Sun, against divine warning, he loses his ship and men and his fated homecoming is dismal. 'That which is fated cannot be fled', warns Pindar. For the Stoics fate is an unbroken chain of cause and effect which is also the working-out of the providential plan of the divine *Logos* (Reason) (*see* STOICISM). The place of human action and moral responsibility in this scheme of things was much debated by them and formed part of their argument with philosophers of the *Academy.

At Rome, most people (Stoics excepted) did not commonly have a strong sense of fate as a universal power (for *Parcae see* FATES). In literature fate, *fatum*, reflected Greek ideas. *See also* FORTUNA and DAIMON.

**Fates** (Gk. Moirai; Lat. Fāta or Parcae) The Greek figures of myth, the Fates, to which the Latin Parcae (so called from *pario*, 'I bring forth') were in all respects assimilated, were represented from Homer onwards as old women spinning, three in number according to Hesiod, the children of Nyx (Night) or, somewhat allegorically, of Zeus and *Themis. The three were called Klōtho ('Spinner'), who held the distaff, Lachĕsis ('Apportioner'), who drew off the thread, and Atrŏpŏs ('Inflexible'), who cut it short, Milton's 'blind Fury with th'abhorred shears'. The Parcae were named Nōna, Decuma, and Morta, meaning respectively, a nine-months' birth (premature, by Roman inclusive reckoning), a ten-months' (full-term) birth, and, it is presumed, a stillbirth. They could have been in origin birth-goddesses who became abstract powers of destiny only later. Their spinning could be thought of as completed at the moment of birth or continuing throughout life until all the thread is drawn off the distaff. (In either case they determine the time of one's death, and so can be associated with Underworld deities.) They may also weave; the images in the poets are various. They are present at all great beginnings, as at the marriage of *Peleus and Thetis, where they also sang. The Moirai could be worshipped as birth-goddesses—Athenian brides offered them locks of hair, and women swore by them.

**Faunus** In Roman religion, a divinity somewhere between gods and men, denizen of the wild forests and the source of the mysterious sounds heard in them which were thought prophetic, the protector of flocks, worshipped in long-standing local cults. In myth he was said to be one of the early kings of Latium, son of Picus or Mars, or else one of the gods of *Evander. In the *Aeneid* he is the father of Latinus, king of the Latini. He was also an oracular god, with the title Fātŭus, 'the speaker' (*see* ORACLES). When his first temple was built on the Tiber in 193 BC he came to be identified with Greek Pan, whose traits he took over to the extent of being visualized as having the legs and horns of a goat. He was thought to be connected with the Lupercalia; his own festival was on 5 December. As in the case of the Arcadian god Pan, the idea grew up of a plurality of Fauni (fauns), who were identified with the Greek satyrs but usually thought of as more gentle. Faunus seems to have been a favourite god of the poet Horace.

**Favō'nius** In Latin, the west wind, also known as Zephyrus, and associated with springtime.

**Favorī'nus** (*c.*AD 85–155) Sophist philosopher and teacher of Greek rhetoric (*see* SECOND SOPHISTIC). Born at Arelate (Arles) in Gaul he learned Greek probably in Massalia (Marseilles), and seems always to have written and spoken it in preference to Latin. Two of the speeches handed down in the works of *Dio Chrysostom (37 and 64) are probably by him,

and a fragment of his treatise *On Exile* survives. His powers of oratory and his philosophical knowledge—he professed the sceptical views of the 'middle' *Academy—brought him high distinction in Greece and Rome, and for a time he enjoyed the favour of the Roman emperor Hadrian. He may have been banished to Chios *c.*130, but was restored to favour under Hadrian's successor Antoninus Pius and remained at Rome until his death. He used to boast of three things: that being a (natural) eunuch he had been charged with adultery, that being a native of Gaul he wrote and spoke Greek, and that he continued to live despite having offended the emperor.

**federal states** Those states in Greece which comprised a geographical (or ethnic) region, such as *Boeotia, in which the individual cities sometimes came together to make common cause, in a war for example, while for most local purposes retaining their separate citizenship and autonomy (*see* CITY-STATE). In 519 BC Plataea refused to be incorporated into a Boeotian federal state dominated by her enemy Thebes, and gained the protection of Athens. *See also* ACHAEAN CONFEDERACY; ARCADIA; THESSALY.

**Fēlī'citās** The Roman goddess of good luck, unknown until the mid-second century BC, when L. Licinius *Lucullus dedicated a temple to her; another was planned by Julius Caesar and erected after his death. She was important in official cult under the emperors and appears frequently on coins. *See also* SULLA.

**fē'riae** Latin term for a festival or holiday which involved visiting temples and making sacrifice to the gods. Holidays were either public, observed by the state, or private, observed by a family to celebrate e.g. a birthday. Abstention from work, including legal and political business, was obligatory during public holidays (which were thus *dies nefasti*; *see also* FASTI), so that the sacred time should not be polluted. There exist interesting decisions made by the pontiffs as to what kind of work might be permissible; the pontiff Scaevola permitted any work in which delay might cause injury or suffering, such as rescuing an ox which had fallen into a pit. An important component in several public festivals was the accompanying games. Most festivals were held either on fixed dates or on days appointed annually by priests or magistrates. Special festivals were held as the occasion arose because of a specific event—a disaster or a victory, for example. *See* FERIAE LATINAE; LIBER; SATURNALIA; VESTA. *See also* RELIGION [Roman].

**fē'riae Lati'nae** ('Latin festival') A joint religious celebration of the Romans and the Latins in honour of Jupiter Latiāris, in his role as god of the *Latin league, held on the Alban Mount annually, usually at the end of April. It dated back to the period when *Alba Longa and not Rome was the chief city of Latium. The flesh of the sacrificial victim (a white heifer) was eaten in a communal meal by representatives from all the cities of the league. It was an important occasion, attended by all the magistrates; the festival was still celebrated in the third century AD.

**Fērō'nia** An Italian goddess of widespread cult in central Italy; of her functions and the etymology of her name nothing is known. Her temple already existed at Rome in 217 BC. Her chief cult was in the grove of Capena near Mount Soracte.

**Fesce'nnine verses (*versus fescennīni*)** In Latin, one of the earliest kinds of Italian poetry, ribald songs of abuse in extempore verse, produced for amusement at weddings; they were of the same nature as the abusive songs sung by soldiers at *triumphs and the term was used of scurrilous verse in general. Livy and Horace thought the original Fescennine verses were a crude form of metrical repartee exchanged extempore between rustics, and the origin of Italian drama; perhaps they were drawing on Aristotle's theory of the origin of drama in Greece (*see* COMEDY [Greek 2] and TRAGEDY 1). The name is derived from Fescennia, a town in Etruria (which presumably specialized in this entertainment).

## festivals
**Greek.** In Greece, festivals (heortai) were religious occasions pleasurably celebrated on fixed days every year, or every two or four years, by whole communities from the village to the city state, sometimes drawing people from further afield. In general the participants expected a reassuring ritual which honoured a god or gods and maintained their relationship with them, good company, food and drink, and entertainment, often of specific kinds. The festivals at Athens are best known. Some, like the City *Dionysia, extended over five or six days, while others lasted for one day only. It has been calculated that at Athens at least 60 days a year were given up to annual festivals, 'more than

any other Greek city' observes the *Old Oligarch. Some would celebrate legendary events or achievements in Athenian history, but others would be those of the villages the city had absorbed and subsequently administered. There was large variety in the form the festivals took, but the following are well-known types:

(i) Athletic festivals where the games had become of major interest. These consisted of a procession, sacrifice, contests (which might include music, dancing, and drama) and a banquet. *See* OLYMPIA; ISTHMIAN FESTIVAL; NEMEA; PYTHIAN GAMES; PANATHENAEA.

(ii) Festivals concerned with human, animal, and crop fertility, occurring at critical times in the farming year. These were often celebrated by women only and in secret, and as a result not much is known about the rituals. *See* THESMOPHORIA and MYSTERIES.

(iii) Annual festivals of initiation marking the passage of adolescents into adult society; these underwent rituals of separation from the community, transition, and reintegration with different status.

For individual festivals, *see also* the following. For Athens: LENAEA. For Apaturia (Ionian): PHRATRIES. For Sparta: GYMNOPAEDIAE.

**Roman.** *See* FERIAE.

**fētiā'lēs** At Rome, a college of twenty *priests, selected for life from among the nobles, who represented the people in their dealings with other nations. The origin of their name is uncertain, but it may be connected with words meaning 'ordinance'. They were concerned particularly in the rituals of making a treaty and declaring war, so that a war should both be and be seen to be a 'just war', *bellum iustum*. In the former case a fetial would pronounce a curse on Rome in the event of the Romans breaking the treaty first, and would confirm it by killing a pig with a flint; in the latter case the fetial cast a specially hardened spear across the border into the offending country, if it was a neighbour, or into a special piece of land near the temple of Bellona that by a legal fiction was constituted as enemy territory. The fetials were still being consulted in the second century BC. It is possible that the office lapsed in the last century of the republic but it was in existence, though perhaps 'revived', under Augustus.

**fire-brigade** *See* VIGILES.

**First Athenian League** *See* DELIAN LEAGUE.

**Five Thousand** (at Athens) *See* FOUR HUNDRED.

**flamen** (apparently meaning 'priest' or 'sacrificer') At Rome, a priest appointed to the service of one particular god (though able to join in the worship of others) from among the most ancient Roman deities. Fifteen in number, the flamens were part of the college of pontiffs under the authority of the *pontifex maximus*. They were distinguished by an epithet derived from the god's name. The most ancient and dignified (*maiores*) were the *flamen dialis* of Jupiter, *martialis* of Mars, and *quirinalis* of Quirinus, serving the three most important gods of early Rome and all chosen from among the patricians; the rest (*minores*) were plebeian. They were nominated by the people and elected for life. After the deification of the emperors, starting with Julius Caesar in 42 BC, flamens were appointed in Rome and in the provinces to superintend their worship also.

**Flāminī'nus, Titus Qui'nctius** (*c*.229–174 BC) Roman statesman and general, consul in 198 BC. In 197 he was sent to Macedonia where Rome was engaged in the Second Macedonian War against Philip V of Macedon. Flamininus won a pitched battle against him at Cynoscephalae in Thessaly, and by this victory the Romans found themselves responsible for the settlement of a newly liberated Greece. When Flamininus in a spectacular ceremony announced the liberation of the Greeks in Europe to the crowds gathered at Corinth for the Isthmian games of 196, he was hailed as a saviour. In 194 he and all Roman troops left Greece; in Rome they celebrated an unparalleled three-day triumph. However, peace was short-lived (*see* MACEDONIA). In his philhellenism Flamininus was comparable with *Scipio Africanus.

**Flami'nius, Gaius** The only politician before the *Gracchi who mounted serious opposition to the senate on behalf of the people. The literary sources (Polybius and Livy) are mainly hostile to him and it is difficult to arrive at the truth. He was tribune in 232 BC and succeeded in getting Italian territory which had been confiscated from the Gauls distributed to impoverished Roman citizens, against opposition led by Q. *Fabius (2). As consul in 223 BC

he led the first Roman army to cross the river Po (*Padus*) and defeated a powerful Gallic tribe, not reading until after the victory a letter from the senate ordering the consuls to abdicate because their election was ill-omened. (Stories about him frequently refer to his ignoring unfavourable omens.) As censor in 220 he constructed the Via Flaminia and the Circus Flaminius. Hannibal outwitted him in the Second Punic War and inflicted a heavy defeat at the battle of Lake *Trasimene, where Flaminius was killed with 15,000 of his men. The defeat was attributed to his neglect of the auspices.

**Flavian emperors** The emperors of Rome from AD 71 to 96 who belonged to the *gens* ('clan') *Flāvia*; they were *Vespasian (71–9), his elder son *Titus (79–81), and his younger son *Domitian (81–96).

**Flā'vius, Gnaeus** Secretary to Appius Claudius Caecus (censor 312 BC; *see* CLAUDIUS (2)), aedile in 304 BC. He was famous in the annals of Roman law for having been the first to publish or in some way make known to the people the rules of the calendar (*see* FASTI) which determined what legal acts might be done on which days, and probably also the *formulae* or form of words which in law had to be used to state a claim or make a defence. At any rate he made available to the people legal knowledge which had previously been available only to patricians, and the patricians were indignant to see it revealed.

**Flōra** An Italian goddess of flowers and spring whose antiquity is proved by the assignment to her of a *flamen floralis*, but who was not given a temple until 238 BC. At this temple, near the Circus Maximus, cheerful and boisterous celebrations in her honour were held every April, reaching their climax on the first of May. Ovid tells the story of Chloris who, when pursued by Zephyrus, changed into Flora and breathed out flowers which spread over the countryside; this myth is depicted in Botticelli's *Primavera*.

**Flōrus** Author of the Latin history known as the 'Epitome of all the wars during seven hundred years', an abridgement of Roman history up to the age of Augustus with special reference to the wars, and designed as a panegyric of the Roman people. Some manuscripts describe it as an epitome of Livy, but it is sometimes at variance with that historian while it draws on the work of Sallust and Caesar and perhaps Virgil and Lucan. The style is markedly rhetorical, and the author is sometimes brief to the point of obscurity. Florus' identity and other names are not known for certain, though he is commonly called Lucius Annaeus. He lived in the second century AD and is variously identified with the Florus who was poet-friend of the emperor Hadrian and with the author of a dialogue, only partly preserved, entitled 'Was Virgil an orator or a poet?'

**Forms, Platonic** See PLATO 4 and 5 and PLATONISM.

**formulae, Homeric (formulaic verse)** See HOMER 4.

**Fortū'na (Fors Fortuna)** Italian goddess, perhaps originally the 'bringer' of fertility (Lat. *ferre*, 'to bring'), but identified with the Greek *Tȳchē and so the goddess of chance or luck. She had an ancient temple in the Forum Boarium at Rome. Her cult was said to have been introduced into Rome by *Servius Tullius; she was not, therefore, one of the most ancient deities, a fact confirmed by her not having a *flamen. She was worshipped at Antium and at Praeneste, where she had an oracular shrine. At Rome her festival on 24 June was a popular holiday, and large crowds including slaves flocked to her shrine, near the river Tiber about 2km (roughly a mile) downstream from the city, to witness the sacrifices. The Romans addressed her by a variety of epithets expressing either particular kinds of good luck or the kinds of people to whom she granted it.

**Forty, the** At Athens, the magistrates (four picked by lot from each of the ten tribes) responsible for deciding private law-suits if the amount of money involved did not exceed ten drachmas.

**Four Hundred, the** At Athens, a revolutionary oligarchic council (*see* OLIGARCHY) which ruled Athens for a short time in 411 BC. The movement started in the fleet at Samos in 412 when *Alcibiades offered to obtain help from the Persians if an oligarchy were established. This initiative failed, but nevertheless an oligarchy was established through murder and intimidation by the *hetaireiai. It restricted the franchise to a relatively wealthy 5,000 citizens, and the assembly was coerced into selecting a council of four hundred which ruled for three months. But the democrats regained the ascendancy in the fleet at Samos and the oligarchy was overthrown. After the Athenian navy under Alcibiades defeated the Spartans at Cyzicus in 410 the democracy was fully restored, with its old council (*boule) of 500. *See* THERAMENES and ANTIPHON.

**fratres arva'les** See ARVAL BRETHREN.

**freedmen, freedwomen** (Lat. m. *liberti*, *libertini*; f. *libertinae*) Slaves who had been emancipated ('manumitted') by their masters, a class of people who figured much more prominently in Roman society than in Greek. Freedmen in Rome have been regarded as almost comprising a social class in the society of the late republic and early empire, and they included many people of intelligence, energy, and ambition although still legally barred from the *curule magistracies (*see* NARCISSUS (2)). In Athens manumission required no formal procedure; a manumitted slave was registered as a *metic (resident alien) with his former owner as sponsor. This meant that he was not a citizen and could not normally become one, but merged with other free non-citizens.

It was an extraordinary feature of Roman law that a slave manumitted in proper legal form by a Roman citizen owner became himself a Roman citizen, though, however rich, ineligible for high rank because he was not himself free-born (which his children would be). A freedman whose former owner or owner's children still lived owed obligations to the family which were enforceable at law (*see* CLIENT). Freed slaves became active in trades and crafts. The most prominent were usually those freed by the upper classes. Romans liked to think of the relationship between freedmen and patron as filial, and certainly bonds of affection could exist, as for example between Cicero and his family and their freedman *Tiro.

By the end of the republic freedmen constituted a large proportion of the Roman citizen body; the distinction between citizens of servile birth and those of free birth became blurred, and was replaced by the distinction between the rich and the poor. *Petronius' imaginary freedman Trimalchio is an extravagant satire on the characteristics of the class. Many of the higher posts in the bureaucracy during the first century AD were held by freedmen. These men often came to exercise great power, and incurred widespread hatred.

# friendship

**friendship** (Gk. *philia*, Lat. *amicitia*)
**Greek.** In Homer, heroic friendships, befitting the dignity of epic, are firm bonds—of personal attachment, as between Patroclus and Achilles, and of guest-friendship, as between Glaucus and Diomedes in *Iliad* 6. (*See also* ACHATES.) Loyalty rather than utility is of paramount importance.

Greek has no words which specifically mean 'friend' or 'friendship' in the English sense of the words. *Philia* is a wider concept. An Athenian felt that his duty was first to his parents, secondly to his wider family, and thirdly to his friends and others with whom he has ties of obligation and expectation in which affection need play no part. All these, family or associates, may be termed *philoi*, loosely, 'friends'. These are the people to call upon for help in a wide range of day-to-day needs as well as emergencies: for money, advice, help with children, borrowing, accommodation, including most of the matters that are usually dealt with nowadays by professional providers of services. Friends were usually equal in status to oneself, people with whom one exchanged equal favours. It was good to take the initiative in giving, to have the balance to one's advantage: Greeks valued highly the ideal of self-sufficiency. It was universally an ancient principle of conduct to help friends and harm enemies. Socrates says of Xenophon that he believed it to be the mark of a virtuous man not to be outdone in helping friends and harming enemies. The Roman general Sulla applied the maxim to himself and had it engraved on his tombstone.

There could be conflict between personal obligations. In Aristophanes' *Frogs* Dionysus, having to judge who is to succeed to the throne of poetry, is unwilling to decide between the claims of Aeschylus and Euripides because they are both his friends and he does not want to become an enemy of either. (Athenians did not disguise their hatreds.) More seriously, there could be conflict between friendship and patriotic duty, and whichever way an individual decided, he was likely to be blamed by one party or another. A speaker pleading for just treatment of the Athenian generals in 406 BC (*see* ARGINUSAE) declares that he has no intention of putting the interest of his relation (the younger Pericles) above that of the city. Friendship became an important topic in Greek ethics. It was discussed in Pla-

to's *Lysis* and, most influentially, analysed in the *Nicomachean Ethics* of Aristotle, for whom it is a necessary component of happiness. Aristotle identifies three different kinds of friendship, concluding that the primary kind, which is the richest, is that of mutual esteem based on virtue. He describes a friend of this kind as one's 'other self'. Such friendship, which extends beyond the quest for self-sufficiency, is glimpsed occasionally in the dialogues of Plato, in the warm intimacy between Socrates and the intelligent, well-to-do men whose society he is part of. The other kinds of friendship are based on utility and pleasure. For Plutarch in the *Erotikos* ('Book of Love'), sexual love between man and wife is the foundation of a special kind of *philia*, one which comprises all three Aristotelian classes.

All of the above concerns only men. Female friendship is known, insofar as it is known at all, almost entirely from early *lyric poetry (monody especially; *see also* SAPPHO) which attests emotional interdependence and intensity, reflecting the seclusion of women's lives.

Guest-friendship, *xenia*, was a bond of trust, imitating kinship between 'guest-friends', *xenoi*, who lived in different city-states or countries. It was a very important social institution for the well-to-do in Greece and Rome (where it was called *hospitium*), established as early as Homer (above). In Homeric times guest-friendship operated as a personal alliance which could if required operate between the rich and powerful to ensure mutual protection as well as the reciprocal supply of food, men, and arms, before the existence of political and military alliances between city-states. In later times in Greece the relationship persisted (*see* PROXENOS), on the assumption of its perpetuity, and could be taken up after a long lapse of time. Many stories were told of the origin of such friendships, and of their continuance over many generations. Guest-friendship was initiated ceremoniously, with solemn declarations and an exchange of gifts. *Xenoi* often had responsibility for each other's children: after his father's murder Aratus, the general of the *Achaean confederacy, was brought up by his *xenoi* at Argos. At Rome, Cicero sent his children to the court of his guest-friend (Lat. *hospes*) Deiotarus, king of Galatia.

*See* HETAIREIAI, 'bands of friends', for the social and political associations of upper-class young men in late fifth-century Athens. *See also* DAMON.

**Roman.** As Cicero makes clear in *De amicitia*, his treatise 'On friendship' (and by example in his other dialogues and his letters to Atticus, his friend of many years), ideal friendship is between individuals, and is based on trust, affection, common interests, and common values. The poet Horace, like the earlier Catullus, shows in his poems to friends some of the attitudes also found in Cicero's letters—sympathetic affection laced with humour and gentle teasing. *Amicitia* could also be a political term, describing a relationship between Rome and another (dependent) state or individual such as a so-called 'client king' (a modern term), who was a foreign ruler recognized by the senate as a 'king, ally, and friend'. In political life a prominent man would have *amici*, 'friends' whose main role was that of advisers, people who might offer professional legal or political advice, perhaps from a subordinate position, and give political support. Although *amicitia* suggests equality of status it could cover a position of dependence. During the republic upper-class Romans instituted bonds with prominent non-Romans, but Livy attributed *hospitium* with the Latins (permanent ties of hospitality; compare *xenia* in Greece) to the Roman king Tarquinius Superbus. Both Cicero and Caesar defended Italians in the law-courts and *hospitium* became a factor in the Romanization of well-to-do provincials. Under the empire the 'friends' of the emperor constituted his court.

***Frogs (Batrachoi)*** (Lat. *Rānae*) Greek comedy by *Aristophanes which won the first prize at the *Lenaea in Athens in 405 BC and earned its author a crown of olive, as well as a second production 'because of [the advice he gave in] the parabasis'. It gives expression to the city's literary attitudes and political plight at that time. The great tragic poets, Aeschylus, Sophocles, and Euripides, are all dead, the last two only recently; Athens, despite her victory in the sea-battle at Arginusae the previous year, is exhausted; she badly needs sound advice such as might be given by the best poets. The play opens with the patron god of tragedy Dionysus, characterized as possessing the human failings of the Athenian people—he is weak, conceited, credulous, and has a passion for Euripides—setting off for Hades disguised as Heracles in order to bring Euripides back from the dead. The journey in Charon's boat across the lake is accompanied by the croaking of a (secondary) chorus of frogs, who give their name to the play; the main chorus comprises initiates in the Eleusinian *mysteries. After arriving in Hades Dionysus has various adventures in consequence of being mistaken for Heracles, but is finally identified and asked to judge a dispute between Aeschylus and Euripides for possession of the throne of tragedy, Sophocles having relinquished his claim in favour of Aeschylus. Aeschylus represents his plays as superior in grandeur and moral purpose, Euripides his as more realistic and human, but each produces telling criticism of the other. Both agree that the duty of the poet is to make men better; Aeschylus says his heroes were models to be imitated, Euripides that he made the audience think; but Aeschylus objects that Euripides' depraved characters are the cause of the decline in morals. The poets then attack the construction of each other's plays, their language, metre, and music. The final test in which each poet speaks a line into a pair of scales to determine whose poetry is the weightier is easily won by Aeschylus. Dionysus, still unwilling to decide, asks each for advice on how to save the city. Euripides makes a characteristically enigmatic reply, and Dionysus chooses Aeschylus as representative of the old Athenian spirit.

**Frontī'nus, Sextus Julius** (*c*.AD 30–103) Consul in 72 or 73, after which he was sent as governor to Britain, where he subdued the Silures in south-east Wales. Of his writings there survive the *Stratēgēmata* ('Stratagems'), a manual of Greek and Roman strategy for the use of officers, in four books, in the first three of which he discusses techniques of military command using examples from the past and the contemporary campaigns of Domitian in Germany; fragments of a work on land-surveying; and his most famous work, *De aquis urbis Romae* ('On the waters of Rome'), in two books written after he was appointed superintendent of aqueducts (*curator aquarum*) in 97 (*see* TEXTS, TRANSMISSION OF ANCIENT 6). In this last he describes for the benefit of his successors the aqueducts and their history, the regulations governing them, and technical details concerning the quality and distribution of supply. Frontinus' writings have a straightforward style in keeping with their subject matter. Pliny called him one of the two most distinguished men of his day.

**Fronto, Marcus Cornelius** (*c.* AD 95–*c.*166) The leading Roman orator of his time. He was born in North Africa, but lived most of his life in Rome. His political importance was negligible although he was suffect consul (*see* CONSULS) in 142 (with *Herodes Atticus the Greek sophist). As a literary figure, however, he was influential, and was appointed tutor by Antoninus Pius to the future emperors Marcus *Aurelius and Lucius Verus. Very little of his work was known until a collection of his rather long-winded letters (partly in Greek) was discovered in 1815 at Rome and Milan. Disappointing as historical sources, despite being written to and including letters from the leading figures of the day, they are more revealing on personal and literary matters. A cordial friendship between Fronto and M. Aurelius is apparent, although the latter ultimately rejected *rhetoric as being unworthy of serious pursuit. Fronto's interest in rhetoric is largely confined to matters of language and style, and he was attracted by archaic and recondite Latin words. He is a frequent interlocutor in Gellius' *Noctes Atticae*. His most admired models of life and speech were the old Romans Cato the Censor, Plautus, and Ennius, down to Cicero and Sallust; he disliked Lucan and the younger Seneca. The few declamations and fragments of speeches which survive are in a vigorous and straightforward Latin.

**funeral games** Homer's account of the funeral games for Patroclus, in book 23 of the *Iliad*, is the earliest description we have of Greek athletic contests. The eight events there consisted of chariot-racing, boxing, wrestling, foot-race, javelin, fencing, throwing the weight, and archery. The deaths of great men were similarly marked in early historical times. At such an occasion the poet Hesiod won a tripod in a competition for a funeral song. At Rome, the comedy *Adelphoe* of Terence was performed in 160 BC at the funeral games held for L. Aemilius Paullus.

**Funeral Oration** See PERICLES.

**Fu'riae (Dīrae)** Roman equivalent of the Greek Erinyes or Eumenides (*see* FURIES).

There is no proof that they were ever the object of cult in Italy.

**Furies** (Gk. Erīnўĕs, also known by the propitiatory names of Euměnidĕs, 'Kindly ones', and Semnai, 'Holy ones') In Greek myth, spirits of punishment avenging without pity wrongs done to kindred and especially murder within the family. A prehistoric origin for the name Erinys (sing.) is indicated by its occurrence on a *Linear B tablet. According to Hesiod they were the daughters of Gaia (Earth), conceived from the drops of blood spilt when Cronus castrated his father *Uranus (Heaven), i.e. they were born of a crime committed by a son against a father. Sources differ as to their parentage, but they are always represented as more ancient than the Olympian gods and not under the rule of Zeus, although they honour him. They also punished perjurers and those who had violated the laws of hospitality and supplication, and came to assume the character of goddesses who punish crimes after death and seldom appear on earth. They were represented as carrying torches and scourges, and wreathed with snakes. Later writers make them three in number with the names Tīsiphŏnē, Megaera, and Allecto. Their cult was rare, but they had a sanctuary at the foot of the Acropolis.

**Fūrī'na** See FURRINA.

**Fu'rius Cami'llus, Marcus** See CAMILLUS.

**Furrī'na (Fūrīna)** Ancient Italian goddess whose nature and function had, by Cicero's day, become a matter of conjecture. Nevertheless she possessed a grove on the slopes of the Janiculum near the Pons Sublicius, a *flamen, and an annual festival (Furrinalia, 25 July), although in classical times this was celebrated only by the priests connected with the cult. It was in the grove of Furrina that C. Sempronius Gracchus had his slave kill him in 121 BC (*see* GRACCHI). The site became an important place of cult for Syrian gods in the later Roman empire.

**Gaia (Gē)** In Greek myth, the Earth, a primordial goddess, the daughter of *Chaos, the mother and wife of *Uranus, Heaven; their offspring included the *Titans and the *Cyclopĕs. On the advice of Gaia, Cronus, the youngest of the Titans, castrated his father; fertilized by the blood, Gaia became the mother of the Giants and the Furies. Later she bore Typhon to her son *Tartarus. Her cult can be traced in many places in Greece, but for the most part it was superseded in classical times by that of later gods; at *Delphi she seems to have been thought of as the original holder of the oracular shrine, before Apollo seized it by killing the serpent Python. Her characteristic function was to be a witness to oaths, as one who knows all that is done on earth. *See* ERICHTHONIUS.

**Gaius Caesar (Gaius Julius Caesar Germanicus)** (popularly known as Caligula, AD 12–41) Roman emperor, the son of *Germanicus and *Agrippina the Elder. In AD 14–16 he was on the Rhine with his parents, where he was nicknamed Caligula ('Little boot') because of the military-style boots he wore. After the death of his brother Drusus in 33 he became next in succession to the Principate, being the only surviving son of Germanicus. Soon after his accession in 37 at the death of Tiberius, he fell seriously ill; *Philo the Jew, who went on an embassy to Rome in 40, suggests that the illness affected his mind. At any rate his behaviour afterwards became increasingly despotic and mad, marked by wild extravagance, arbitrary executions, and aspirations towards deification. He was murdered in 41, together with his (fourth) wife and daughter.

**Galatē'a (Galateia)** (perhaps 'Milk-white') Greek sea-nymph, daughter of *Nereus and Doris. The story of her wooing by the ugly Cyclops *Polyphemus was frequently told by the bucolic poets. Ovid tells how she loved a young shepherd Acis but her love was discovered by Polyphemus who hurled a rock at him.

As it fell Galatea turned Acis into a river which henceforth bore his name. A later story made her bear a son to Polyphemus who became the eponymous ancestor of the Gauls.

**Galba, Se'rvius Sulpi'cius** (3 BC–AD 69) Roman emperor for about six months in 68–9 in succession to Nero. He came from a patrician family and had enjoyed the favour of previous emperors. After a distinguished military career he was from AD 60 governor of eastern Spain, until Vindex, governor of western Gaul, rebelled against the emperor Nero in 68 and invited Galba to replace him. Vindex was soon defeated, but then the praetorian guard (*see* PRAETORIANS), after bribery, deserted Nero and declared for Galba. Encouraged, he took the title of Caesar and slowly marched to Rome with Otho, governor of Lusitania, who hoped to be named as Galba's heir. Disappointed in this hope, Otho took advantage of the unpopularity Galba had incurred by his execution of opponents and his meanness, to conspire with the praetorian guard, and they murdered him in AD 69 and proclaimed Otho emperor. Tacitus describes Galba's career and character in book 1 of his *Histories*: 'In everyone's opinion he was capable of being emperor if only he had never ruled', *capax imperii nisi imperasset*.

**Galen (Gălēnos)** (of Pergamum, AD 129–99) Greek physician, whose outstanding influence on medicine in ancient and modern times has not been equalled. After a traditional education in rhetoric and philosophy he studied medicine in Smyrna and Alexandria, settling in Rome in 169 and becoming physician to the emperor Marcus Aurelius, his son Commodus, and Septimius Severus. He was the most polymathic scientist of his day, satisfying the popular taste with anatomical displays and lectures, and was in many ways typical of the cultural life of his time (*see* SECOND SOPHISTIC and ATHENAEUS). His later fame depends on his voluminous writings, much of which still survives, written in elegant if somewhat long-winded Greek. In his day the medical profession was divided into several mutually antagonistic sects, dogmatists and empiricists, but Galen was eclectic and deplored limitation; he preferred to take from each what seemed to be true, and aimed not to ignore any one part. He was a profound admirer of *Hippocrates, Plato, and Aristotle, probably in that order, and wrote a treatise entitled 'That the best physician is also the best philosopher'. He drew from Stoic theory as well, holding like Stoics a teleological view of the world as well as of the body. Like Hippocrates he believed that sound diagnosis depended on very close observation of every detail, and recommended that doctors should listen carefully to the patient. He confined his dissections to animals—pigs, sheep, goats, and the Barbary ape and Rhesus monkey who most closely resemble humans—and avoided human dissection (unlike *Herophilus and *Erasistratus), sometimes to the detriment of his conclusions. Galen adopted from Hippocrates' treatise *On the Nature of the Human Being* the view that disease was caused by imbalance of the four *humours (for Galen, blood, phlegm, yellow bile, and black bile) which affected the three main organs, heart, brain, and liver, and he used Stoic ideas of mixture to explain changes in the humours. His medicines and dietary regimens were based on the work of earlier specialists (*see* e.g. DIOSCORIDES). Like Aelius *Aristeides, he appears to have felt himself personally in touch with the healing god *Asclepius. He wrote several works on his own career and on his books, lost in a fire in 192. In a late work, 'On my own opinions', he lists what he knows for certain, what he knows as plausible, and what he does not know, which includes the nature of the soul.

Galen's writings formed the basis of all later medical works. After the ninth century, and the translation of his works into Arabic, he became the standard of medical perfection. His fame in Europe in the Middle Ages probably derived from the influence of the Arabic medical writers, and his opinions and his name were universally invoked even when his writings were little read. Much of his work still requires scholarly attention.

**Galli (Galloi)** The itinerant eunuch servants of the goddess *Cybele, who supposedly castrated themselves in imitation of the act of *Attis, Cybele's cult-partner. The origin of their name, variously explained in antiquity, is unknown.

**Gallic** *See* GAUL and CELTS.

**Gallic War(s)** The campaigns in which Julius Caesar completed the conquest of Gaul between 58 and 51 BC, and the name by which his commentary on the conquest (in seven books) is commonly known. The narrative is one of the best examples we have of unadorned Latin prose (*see* COMMENTARIES 1).

**Gallus, Gaius Cornelius** (*c.*69–26 BC) Soldier and poet, friend of the emperor Augustus and of Virgil. Born at (probably) Forum Julii (Fréjus), he went to Rome at an early age and was known to Cicero and Asinius *Pollio in 43. He fought in the civil war on Octavian's side and was one of the commissioners appointed by him in 41 to confiscate land in Transpadane Gaul (in Italy north of the river Po) and distribute it among his veterans, a confiscation which affected Virgil's family farm. Octavian made him the first prefect of the new province of Egypt in 30 BC but after four years he was recalled in disgrace for an offence which remains obscure but seems to be connected with self-aggrandisement; Octavian (now called Augustus) formally renounced his friendship, and Gallus was driven to commit suicide in 27/6 BC. Virgil is said, probably wrongly, to have rewritten the latter half of the fourth Georgic which had formerly contained a eulogy of Gallus.

Gallus' poetry, of which only one pentameter line and tiny papyrus fragments survive, included four books of elegies, probably entitled *Amores*, centred on his mistress, the famous actress Volumnia Cytheris (former mistress of Mark Antony), under the pseudonym Lycōris. The fragments, few as they are, are seen by some to confirm that love-elegy was a genre which he appears to have originated (*see* ELEGY). His poetry was influenced by the Hellenistic Greek poets Callimachus and Euphorion, and the Roman *'neoterics', so-called. Virgil in his tenth Eclogue worked some of Gallus' own lines into his poem.

**games, public** *See* FESTIVALS [Greek]; FERIAE.

**Ga'nymēde (Ganymēdēs)** In Greek myth, son of Tros (or Laomedon), king of *Troy, carried off to Olympus by the gods or the eagle of Zeus or Zeus himself because of his beauty, to be the cup-bearer of Zeus, who gave in exchange to his father a pair of divine horses. In later times he was thought to be immortalized as the zodiacal sign Aquarius. From the Latin version of his name (Catamītus) is derived the word 'catamite'. For the Middle Ages he typified homosexual love, but during the Renaissance his ascent to Zeus symbolized for some the soul's ascent to the absolute.

**Garden, the** *See* EPICURUS.

**Gates of Dreams, The** *See* DREAMS.

**Gaugamē'la** Small village east of the river Tigris in Assyria (Iraq), the scene of the final victory of Alexander the Great over Darius III, king of Persia, in 331 BC.

**Gaul (Gallia)**
**1. Cisalpine Gaul.** This is the name which the Romans before 42 BC gave to the region of north Italy that lies between the Apennines and the Alps, denoting 'Gaul this side (i.e. south) of the Alps' (as opposed to Transalpine Gaul, or 'Gaul beyond (i.e. north of) the Alps'). The Romans gave the name Galli to the Celtic invaders (*see* CELTS) who, originating perhaps in the Upper Danube, moved westwards across Europe in the eighth and seventh centuries BC and passed into north Italy during the sixth to fourth centuries BC; in the early fourth century they had displaced the Etruscans from the Po valley. Their marauding bands terrorized the country and *c.*385 BC even sacked Rome, or so tradition said (*see* ALLIA). They were a constant menace to Italian security until in the latter part of the third century BC, after a particularly dangerous incursion, Rome decided to put an end to the threat by annexing Cisalpine Gaul. This was largely achieved by the campaigns of 224–222 but the area was mostly lost again through Hannibal's invasion of 218. It was regained in the 190s and by 150 few Gauls remained in the Cisalpine plain. The name Gallia Togata ('Gaul with togas') was often applied to this area, indicating the numerical superiority of the *togati* ('those who wear the toga', i.e. Romans) over the Gallic population. By contrast, Gallia Comātā, 'Gaul with long hair', was applied to the rest of Gaul. The part of Cisalpine Gaul north of the river Padus (Po) was sometimes known as Transpadane Gaul and its inhabitants, mostly Celts, as the Transpadani. Cisalpine Gaul was constituted a Roman province by Sulla in his settlements of 82 BC, with the river *Rubicon as its southern boundary. In

42 BC the province was incorporated into Italy. Under the emperor Augustus the tribes of the Alpine foothills were conquered, and the Alps thus became the frontier of Italy.

**2. Transalpine Gaul.** This is the area that is commonly denoted by the single word 'Gaul', i.e. modern France. It was predominantly Celtic in culture but did not include the Celts from the Upper Danube and northern Italy (1 above). It contained Iberians and Ligurians in the south, and Germanic peoples in the north-east. Gaul first came into contact with the Mediterranean civilization through the foundation in about 600 BC of the Greek colony of Massalia (Marseilles). Rome's first interest in Transalpine Gaul arose from the need to secure communications with her trading ally Saguntum (Sagunto) in Spain. Communication was usually safeguarded by Massalia but when, in the second century BC, that city was threatened by neighbouring tribes, the Romans themselves fought and defeated them. These campaigns gave Rome possession of the Gallic territory between the Alps and the Rhone as far north as Geneva; in 121 it was formed into a province, at first called simply Provincia (modern Provence). Its territory was subsequently extended westwards and was then called Gallia Narbonensis (Narbonese Gaul); the Romans thereby commanded the road into Spain through the eastern Pyrenees. The capital Narbo (Narbonne) became a commercial rival to Greek Massalia, which remained nominally independent.

Devastating incursions of Northmen (*see* GERMANY) at the end of the second century BC were finally ended by Marius in 101, after which there was no great movement of peoples until 58 BC. In this year Julius Caesar, after the expiry of his consulship in 59, obtained Cisalpine and Narbonese Gaul for his province at a time when Transalpine Gaul had already suffered an invasion of Germanic peoples under Ariovistus, and an invasion from the Helvetii was threatening. For the events of the next few years *see* COMMENTARIES 1. By 51 Caesar had finally subjugated (with enormous destruction and loss of life) the whole of Transalpine Gaul, a country twice as large as Italy, and given it the structure of a province. He divided the country into three parts (excluding Narbonese Gaul, a fourth), namely Aquitania, Celtica, and Belgica. The final settlement of Gaul was the work of Augustus: between 27 and 13 BC Narbonese Gaul became a senatorial province; the other three parts, collectively Gallia Comata, became one imperial province which was eventually redivided into three. Romanization, which had begun two centuries earlier, was from now on very rapid: the Latin language became dominant, the Greco-Roman city developed, agriculture flourished and villas in the form of working farms were numerous. The population has been calculated at about ten million. An extensive road system and use of the navigable rivers facilitated trade.

From the late third century AD Germanic invasions began from across the Rhine. During the fourth century although the frontier was occasionally breached it was always restored. However, after the division of the empire in 395 the Roman frontier on the Rhine was neglected and there was growing encroachment across the river by Franks, Burgundians, and Visigoths, all Germanic peoples. After the middle of the fifth century high-ranking Gauls increasingly worked for the Germanic kings. It seemed that Gaul would be dominated by the Germanic Visigoths until late in the fifth century Clovis, the Frankish ruler of the Merovingian family (also Germanic), drove them into Spain and eventually became ruler of the whole of Francia (*see* FALL OF ROME).

In the late empire Gaul produced several interesting Latin writers, including *Ausonius, Paulinus of Nola, and Sidonius.

**Gē** Alternative form of *Gaia.

**geese, sacred** *See* MANLIUS CAPITOLINUS.

**Ge'llius, Aulus** (b. between 125 and 128 AD) The (Latin) author of *Noctes Atticae* ('Attic nights'), published *c.*180 in twenty books, of which all survive except the beginning of the preface, the end of book 20, and book 8 (for which we have chapter headings). His birthplace is unknown, but he passed most of his life at Rome. He spent at least a year in Athens where he visited *Herodes Atticus. His work is a random collection of short essays, based on the Greek and Latin books he had read and the conversations and lectures he had heard, and deals with a great variety of topics: philosophy, history, law, but above all grammar, including literary and textual criticism. He began collecting his material during the winter nights in Attica and arranged it in later life for the amusement and instruction of his children. It contains thousands of curious and interesting passages from works no longer extant, and is a

mine of information on Greek and Latin authors; we are particularly indebted to him for the preservation of many passages from early Latin literature—he is better read in Latin than in Greek—and, among many good stories, for that of Androclus and the lion (5.14).

**Gelon** (*c.*540–478 BC) Tyrant of Gela (*c.*491–485), after seizing the tyranny on the death of the tyrant Hippocrates, to whom he had been Master of Horse. He was subsequently tyrant of *Syracuse (485–478), in (Greek) Sicily. His brother Hieron succeeded him at Gela and later, after his death, at Syracuse. During Gelon's tyranny Syracuse became the strongest single Hellenic power of the time; the mainland Greeks sought his aid against Persia (in the Persian Wars), but that was frustrated by the Carthaginian invasion of Sicily. (The story was that the Greeks refused his condition that he should have supreme command.) In alliance with *Theron, tyrant of Acragas, he defeated the Carthaginians at Himera in 480, traditionally on the day on which the Greeks defeated the Persians at Salamis.

**gē'nius** (literally 'the begetter') In Roman belief, the spirit comprising the inherited traits of a *gens ('clan') which is born and dies with the male head of a family (*paterfamilias). It was the object of cult, though usually only among aristocratic families, and was thought of as a divine part of the paterfamilias, his 'double'. At some time during the republic the idea developed that a woman too had a 'double', the *iuno*, and generally that everyone had his or her own *genius*. However only the *genius* of the paterfamilias was the object of family cult at the household shrine of the *lares. Worship of the *genius* of the emperor Augustus, the 'double' of the living person, became an important part of Roman *ruler cult. The concept was extended to include places and corporations, any of which could be thought of as having a *genius* which summed up the totality of its characteristics; we hear of the *genius* of the Roman people and the *genius* of Rome itself. For educated Romans the *genius* was seen as resembling the Greek *daimon*.

**gĕnos** (pl. *genē*) In the Greek social system, a 'clan' or group of families who claimed descent in the male line from one ancestor and described themselves by using a collective plural name. A *genos* was narrower than a *phratry, and not all citizens belonged to one. Naturally most is heard about noble families whose ultimate ancestor was reputedly a hero or god, and their family *names were usually in patronymic form, meaning 'the descendants of . . .'; but the Athenian *gene* were probably not entirely aristocratic. Powerful *gene* at Athens were the Philaidae (the clan of Miltiades and Cimon) and the *Alcmaeonidae. A *genos* could come together as a body for common cult and religious ceremonies. *See also* EUPATRIDAE.

**genre** In literature, a type or category of literary work—epic, tragedy, lyric, and so on—and its subdivisions e.g. (of lyric) paean, dithyramb, dirge, etc. The distinctions between the different genres in the matter of topics and style were originally determined by the occasion which prompted each work. These formal features included vocabulary, metre (in poetry), and dialect (in Greek literature). There was very little theorizing in antiquity about what has nowadays come to be called genre. Plato in the *Republic* distinguishes three genres of poetic presentation (dramatic, descriptive, and 'mixed'); Aristotle in the *Poetics* covers in detail the genre of tragedy; Horace in *Ars poetica* speculates about the origins of tragedy and pastoral poetry. In Hellenistic and Roman times, when poetry in particular was written to be read and was not tied to performance as it mostly was in classical Greece, certain generic features no longer seemed binding. Ovid in the *Metamorphoses* strains epic conventions to the limit (in the matter of topics particularly), as he also strains conventions in the ostensibly didactic *Ars amatoria*. In *Heroides* he even claims to have invented a new genre. (*See also* GALLUS.) Though an excessive emphasis on genre as a tool in literary studies may be limiting, recognition of the form and function of a literary work can prevent misplaced criticism.

**gens** (pl. *gentēs*) In the Roman social system, a 'clan' or group of families bearing a common name or *nomen* (*see* NAMES [Roman]) and supposedly descended in the male line from one ancestor of that name. Originally the *gentes* were noble, *patrician families, but in early times the wealthiest *plebeian families organized themselves also into *gentes* and some probably gained admission to the patrician *gentes*. From the late republic membership of a *gens* was thought to be based not on kinship but on possession of the same name. A *gens* had certain common property (including a burial ground), held meetings of its members, and performed religious rites in common. Under the empire ties based on the *gens* gradually disappeared.

**geocentricity** *See* ASTRONOMY.

**Geogra'phica** *See* STRABO.

**geography** (*geōgraphia*) ('description of the earth') For Homer and Hesiod the earth was a plane circular land mass around the Mediterranean basin, surrounded by the stream of Ocean, and the first world maps drawn by Anaximander (early sixth century BC) and Hecataeus (fl. 500 BC) are largely in accordance with this view. By the early fifth century BC the Greeks knew of three continents, Europe, *Asia, and *Africa (Libya), but of none of them fully. It was generally believed that the distance from east to west was twice that from north to south, but the northern boundary of Europe was not known. The southern boundaries of Asia and Africa had reportedly been rounded by *Scylax and the Phoenicians according to Herodotus (4.42), who did not believe it. (For knowledge of the earth's sphericity *see* ASTRONOMY.) During the fifth century works of descriptive geography began to be written. Herodotus' *Histories* contain much geographical and ethnological material. *Ctesias wrote a geographical treatise and the first separate work on India. Two fourth-century historians, *Ephorus and *Timaeus, devoted several books to descriptive geography. The work of the mathematician and astronomer *Eudoxus in the fourth century BC made it possible to understand the nature and size of the earth in a realistic way. By 300 BC the Greeks knew that the 'inhabited earth' of which they felt a part occupied only a small area of the northern hemisphere. The conquests of Alexander the Great in the late fourth century BC and the opening up of western Europe by the Romans in the second and first centuries BC resulted in many treatises being written. The most notable work of descriptive geography to survive is that of the Greek *Strabo (first century BC to first century AD) who combined physical, historical, political, and mathematical geography. *Eratosthenes (c.275–194 BC) established mathematical geography as a science and *Ptolemy applied its principles in the first half of the second century AD. Unfortunately the scientific geographers did not oust the traditional and erroneous beliefs of older writers, which were perpetuated in the compilations of late antiquity. (*See also* POMPONIUS MELA.)

**geometric age** Name given to one of the five periods of the Greek era (based on the differences in pottery styles), denoting very roughly the period 875–750 BC. (*Cf.* PROTO-GEO-METRIC; ORIENTALIZING; ARCHAIC; CLASSIC.

**geometry** *See* MATHEMATICS.

**Georgics** [Gk. *gĕōrgica*, 'husbandry'] *Virgil's didactic poem, in four books and over 2,000 hexameter lines, dedicated to his patron *Maecenas. The most obvious model is the archaic Greek poet Hesiod, author of the *Theogony*, on the genealogy of the gods and the origin of cosmic order, and of the *Works and Days*, on the routine of the agricultural year which is the human contribution to order. Virgil spent seven years (36–29 BC) on its composition; he read the complete poem to Octavian on the latter's return from the battle of Actium. The *Georgics* are more sophisticated in thought and in technique than Hesiod, and owe something to the polished versification of the later Greek didactic poets *Aratus of Soli, *Nicander, and above all Callimachus. The poet derived some factual information from Varro's prose handbook *De re rustica* ('On farming') published in 37 BC (and he was perhaps also influenced by its moral and patriotic tone). However, Virgil resembles Hesiod in that his intention is not to compose a handbook of instruction for those who wish to be farmers; rather he is presenting a picture of the relationship between human life and the natural world: it is a world frugal and harsh, not especially hostile but prone to setbacks and not free from suffering. The fruits of the land are obtained only after unremitting effort. However, if life is lived in harmony with nature and with the divine scheme of things (a largely Stoic idea), it is morally and philosophically satisfying and it brings the reward of peace and contentment (2.458 ff.); it is also the basis of Italy's greatness. This is Virgil's reply to *Lucretius' *De rerum natura* and that poet's too great confidence in the power of reason. He recalls Lucretius not only in phrasing and in style but also in the passion with which he expounds his subject. The *Georgics* are a rebuttal of Lucretius' Epicureanism which asserted that the gods did not intervene in the world; Virgil reasserts divine providence, and dwells affectionately on the gods of the countryside. Nevertheless, for Virgil, as for Hesiod, hard work, *labor improbus*, is essential; he sees the individual as an oarsman rowing upstream who will be carried downstream by the current if he slackens his effort (1.199). It was Virgil's deep sympathy for all living things and his sense of the need for men to cooperate with nature that led his English translator John Dryden (1631–1700) to call the *Georgics* 'the best poem of the best poet'. Much of the pleasure of the *Georgics* lies in the digressions from didactic instruction, the descriptive or reflective passages, such as the famous 'praises of Italy' (below). The concluding section of each book is memorable, in particular the *'epyllion' that closes book 4. Ancient critics soon observed that Virgil's aim was to give pleasure rather than instruction.

Book 1 deals with ploughing and the raising of crops and the signs of the weather, ending emotionally with a description of the horrors suffered by Italy as a consequence of the murder of Julius Caesar; book 2 covers the growing of trees, chiefly the olive and the vine, and also contains glowing praise of Italy (136 ff.); book 3 deals with the rearing of cattle (concluding with a description of the cattle-plague in the Alps). By contrast, book 4 is about bees and bee-keeping. In it Virgil apologizes for not treating gardens at greater length, recalls an 'old Corycian gardener' whose bountiful produce from an unpromising plot included the first honey, and describes the bees with affectionate irony as exemplars of the ideal citizen body, 'little Romans', *parvi Quirites*. The work ends with the episode of *Aristaeus together with the story of Orpheus and Eurydice in which the success of Aristaeus in acquiring new bees from the carcass of a bullock is contrasted with Orpheus' grief for his wife Eurydice, a typically Virgilian theme of effort ending in loss and failure. We are told by Servius, although it is generally thought improbable, that Virgil originally wrote here a panegyric of his friend the poet *Gallus, which he removed after Gallus' suicide in 26 BC

**Geō'rgos** ('The farmer') Greek comedy by *Menander, a fragment of which has been recovered from a papyrus. The plot revolves around two neighbours, one a poor widow, Myrrhine, with a son and a daughter, the other a rich man with a son by a previous marriage, and a daughter. The rich man's son wishes to marry Myrrhine's daughter, who is already pregnant by him, but his father is arranging to marry him to his half-sister. The farmer of the title, Kleainetos, apparently also wishes to marry the widow's daughter. We may presume that in the end it is the rich neighbour's son who succeeds in doing so.

**Germā'nia** ('Germany') The name commonly given to an ethnographical monograph by *Tacitus on the origin, geography, institutions, and tribes of the Germans (*see* GERMANY), published in AD 98. It describes the various tribes: their appearance, political and social customs, and dress; the organization of their army; their land tenure and religion (their human sacrifices are regarded with abhorrence); their sloth alternating with warlike activity; their drunkenness and gambling; the exemplary morality of their family life (contrasted by implication with the laxity prevailing at Rome). Tacitus then passes on to the geography of the area and the particular characteristics of the several Germanic tribes (including the Swedes and ending with the Finns), arguing that the Germans are racially pure and indigenous on the basis that no one would live there if it were not his native place. As an ethnological work *Germania* is somewhat incoherent and some of the material was out of date when Tacitus wrote it, but there may have been other motives underlying its composition—a desire to point out the corruption of Rome by contrast with the purer morals of the barbarian, and to emphasize the threat Germany posed to Rome's security: 'Germany has afforded more triumphs than victories to Rome.'

**Germa'nicus** The *cognomen* (*see* NAMES [Roman]) borne by various members of the Julio-Claudian family at Rome. It was originally bestowed by the senate as a title of honour upon Nero Claudius *Drusus (b. 38 BC) and his descendants for his victories over the Germans (an achievement destroyed by *Varus in 9 BC). He was the second son of Tiberius Claudius Nero and *Livia (later the wife of the emperor Augustus), and younger brother of the future emperor Tiberius; he is usually known as Drusus the Elder: *see* DRUSUS (3).

The name Germanicus by itself commonly designates Nero Claudius Germanicus (15 BC–AD 19), the elder son of Drusus the Elder and Antonia Minor (daughter of Mark Antony and Octavia), who was adopted by his uncle Tiberius in AD 4 when Tiberius was himself adopted by Augustus. Germanicus thus became a member of the Julian *gens, in line to succeed to the imperial throne, and took the name Germanicus Julius Caesar. Emulating his natural father he too waged successful wars against the Germans and won his troops' affection, on which he was able to rely when he quelled the mutiny of the Rhine army in 14. Although Germanicus claimed that one more campaign would finally subdue the Germans, Tiberius refused. He was granted a triumph and given *maius *imperium to reorganize the eastern provinces. However Tiberius (who perhaps feared his popularity) appointed Cn. Piso as governor of Syria with the open intention of having him as a restraining influence on Germanicus. The two quarrelled and Germanicus ordered Piso to leave his province. Soon after, Germanicus died in mysterious circumstances and his friends accused Piso and his wife Plancina of having poisoned him with the connivance of Tiberius. The death of so admired and popular a leader—he was commonly compared with Alexander the Great—caused widespread grief and resentment in Rome. By his wife *Agrippina (the Elder) he had nine children who included the future emperor *Gaius (Caligula) and Agrippina (the Younger), the mother of the emperor Nero. He had literary tastes; he is said to have written comedies in Greek, but all are lost; fragments of his Latin translation of the *Phaenomena* of *Aratus still survive, with a few Greek and Latin epigrams. *See also* EPISTULAE EX PONTO.

**Germany** For the Romans, an undefined area east of the Rhine (Rhenus) and north of the Danube (Danubius or Ister). In the north it comprised what are now Denmark, Sweden, and Norway. It is generally thought that the German language and culture originated in south Scandinavia, Denmark, and north Germany, and from about 500 BC spread southwards and westwards. According to Tacitus one of the tribes was called Germani, and this name was first used by the Gauls to designate the whole race. Movement of peoples led to the gradual withdrawal of the Celts and to Germanic expansion into the Mediterranean world. It was not until shortly after 120 BC that the Germans entered Roman history, when the tribes of the Cimbri and the Teutones, invading south-east Gaul and, later, northern Italy, inspired great terror at Rome; they were finally destroyed by Roman armies under Marius. The same period probably saw the establishment of the ancestors of the Goths and Vandals in the east of modern Germany. Early in the first century BC another German tribe, the Suebi, moved to the area of the upper Rhine. Their inroads into Gaul in 58 BC led Julius Caesar to drive them back across the Rhine (as related in the first book of Caesar's *Gallic War*), which river became a frontier and the main line of Roman defence for the western empire. Later, under Augustus, Roman invasions of German territory were systematically undertaken, but Roman ascendancy in this region was brought to an end in AD 9 when *Varus and his army were destroyed by the German chief Arminius. After this disaster Augustus abandoned attempts to establish a western frontier beyond the Rhine.

During the first century AD the Germans lived in a developing Iron-age society in small communities without proto-urban settlements (unlike the Celts). They lived on their own agricultural products and traded raw materials for Roman imports. Political power lay in the hands of clan chiefs. In time of war they chose a battle-leader in assembly; having no large settlements to defend, and being formidably strong fighters who knew well their forested and boggy territory, they proved to be an elusive and virtually invincible enemy.

Around AD 90 Domitian formally established the two provinces of Germania Superior (Upper Germany) in the south and Germania Inferior (Lower Germany) in the north. During the reign of Marcus Aurelius (AD 161–80) there occurred a dangerous invasion across the Danube by the Marcomanni, a German tribe who advanced even into Italy and besieged Aquileia (near the coast at the head of the Adriatic Sea). The resulting war continued to the end of the emperor's life, and his successor Commodus had to make a compromise peace with the Germans. During the next three centuries the German tribes, especially the Alemanni and Franks, harassed Gaul by frequent invasions and finally crossed in great numbers over the Rhine, the Danube, and the Alps, conquering Gaul, Italy, and Spain and even penetrating into Africa. Other tribes such as the Angli and the Saxons had by that time crossed over into Britain. Nearly the whole of western Europe was thus overrun by German tribes. (*See also* FALL OF ROME.)

**gerou'sia** At *Sparta, the council of elders composed of the two kings and 28 other members over 60 years of age, elected for life from the leading families by measuring the acclamation of the citizens (a method which Aristotle thought childish). As a deliberative body they prepared business for the assembly (*see* ECCLESIA); as a judicial body they heard cases involving death, exile, or disfranchisement and, it was said, could even put the kings on trial.

**Ge'ryon (Gēryōn, Gēryonēs, Gēryoneus)** In Greek myth, son of *Chrysaor and Callirrhoē, a three-headed or three-bodied giant living in the far West on an island, Erytheia, in the stream of *Oceanus beyond the Pillars of Hercules; there he pastured a herd of magnificent cattle, aided by his herdsman Eurytion and his dog Orthrus. It was one of the labours of Heracles to steal the cattle and drive them back to Greece (*see* HERACLES, LABOURS OF 10).

**Giants (Gigantēs)** In Greek myth, monstrous beings of vast size, according to Hesiod sons of Gaia (Earth), conceived from the blood of *Uranus that fell upon the earth when he was castrated. In post-Homeric legend they rebelled against Zeus and the Olympian gods, who, learning that the Olympians would not win unless they were assisted by a mortal, called in Heracles. The Giants were defeated at Phlegra (Pallēnē, the westernmost prong of Chalcidice), and were believed to be buried under volcanoes in various parts of Greece and Italy. The Battle of Gods and Giants was a very popular myth in Greece, especially among sculptors, and was sometimes thought of as symbolizing the fight of civilization against barbarism (*see* BARBARIAN). The events of the three attacks on the Olympian gods made respectively by the *Titans, the Giants, and *Otus and Ephialtes were often confused by the poets. *See also* HECATONCHEIRES.

**Glau'cia, Gaius Servi'lius** Roman politician. As tribune (101 BC) and praetor (100) he cooperated with Marius and *Saturninus, and passed a law restoring the *repetundae* court to the equites. He hoped to be consul for 99 BC but his candidature was disallowed. He fled with Saturninus, but the senate had them arrested and they died in prison.

**Glaucus** In Homer's *Iliad*, a grandson of Bellerophon and leader (after *Sarpedon) of the Lycian allies of the Trojans. During the battle he confronted the Greek Diomedes, but when they found that their grandfathers were bound by ties of hospitality they exchanged armour, Glaucus giving Diomedes his equipment, made of gold and worth a hundred oxen, and receiving the other's of bronze, worth nine. He was killed by Ajax, son of Telamon.

**gnō'mē** (Gk., 'maxim', 'aphorism'; literally 'expression of opinion') Term used to describe the pithy expression of an acknowledged truth. The most famous *gnomai* are those inscribed on the temple at *Delphi, *gnōthi sauton* ('know thyself') and *mēden agan* ('nothing in excess'). They play an important part in Greek literary expression and are frequent in the poetry of Hesiod and Euripides. Gnomic poetry, usually written in elegiacs and embodying popular wisdom, can be traced back to *Phocylides and *Theognis in the mid-sixth century BC.

**gods** *See also* RELIGION.
**Greek.** The Greeks thought of their most important gods as living on Mount *Olympus and numbering twelve. The number was fixed, although some slight variation of names was possible. The Olympian gods who appear as the central group on the east frieze of the Parthenon are Zeus, Hera, Poseidon, Athena, Apollo, Artemis, Aphrodite, Hermes, Demeter, Dionysus, Hephaestus, and Ares. It is likely that Hestia was originally one of the canonical twelve and was replaced by Dionysus. Lesser gods who were sometimes important in cult include, among others, Asclepius, Cybele, Eileithyia, Enyalius, Eros, Hades, Hebe, Hecate, Helios, Leto, Muses, Pan, Titans, and various sea-gods (Nereus, Pontus, and Proteus). For each of these, see under the name; *see also* LINEAR B.

**Roman.** *See* ANNA PERENNA; CERES; DIANA; FLORA; FORTUNA; HECATE; HERCULES; INDIGETES; JANUS; JUNO; JUPITER; LARES; MAGNA MATER; MAIA; MANES; MARS; MERCURY; MINERVA; JUVENTAS; NEPTUNE; NUMEN; PENATES; POMONA; QUIRINUS; ROBIGUS; SABAZIOS; SATURN; SILVANUS; TELLUS; TERMINUS; VENUS; VESTA; VULCAN.

**gods, household** In Greece, household cult to ensure the security and prosperity of the house was concerned mostly with the ritual: the gods receiving the cult might vary. Thus a first-fruits offering would be placed on the hearth sacred to *Hestia at mealtimes, and before drinking wine *libations poured on the floor. Small offerings might also be made to particular gods for the protection of the house (*see* HERMS).

Roman household cult was similarly focused on the hearth (*Vesta). *See also* LARES and PENATES.

**Golden age** The Greek poet Hesiod, in *Works and Days*, was the first to describe earlier races or generations of humankind who lived in happier times than the present, and the earliest, whose life was most idyllic, was the Golden race, who lived at a time when the ruling god was not yet Zeus but his father *Cronus (Saturn at Rome). This race was succeeded by progressively inferior races, those of silver, bronze, and iron, the last being our own; the deterioration was interrupted by the race of *heroes (those who fought in the Theban and Trojan wars) who immediately preceded us. The Roman poets Horace, Virgil, and Ovid all borrowed the idea, but the Romans, in translating the Greek word *genos*, 'generation' or 'race', by the Latin *saeculum*, incidentally introduced the additional meaning of the latter, namely 'age' or 'long period of time'. Hence there came about the idea of a Golden age.

For the so-called 'Golden age' of Latin *see* LATIN LITERATURE, PERIODS OF.

**Golden Ass** *See* APULEIUS.

**Golden Bough** In Virgil's *Aeneid*, book 6, Aeneas is told by the Cumaean *Sibyl that he must find and pluck a bough of actual gold, resembling mistletoe, for Proserpine before he can enter the Underworld. This idea seems to be an invention of Virgil's own; *Servius, the fourth-century commentator on Virgil, associated it with the cult of the goddess *Diana at Aricia, where there was a sacred tree from which a branch had first to be broken off by the runaway slave who wished to kill the priest and take his place. From this starting-point Sir James Frazer developed his work on the evolution of religious beliefs and institutions, the *Golden Bough* (1890–1915).

**Golden Fleece** The fleece of the ram which had carried away Phrixus and Helle, sought by Jason and the *Argonauts. When the ram arrived at Colchis, kingdom of Aeētes, Phrixus sacrificed it to Zeus and then gave the fleece to Aeetes, who fastened it to an oak tree in a grove of Ares. The quest for the fleece was devised by *Pelias, the usurping king of Iolcus, to bring about the destruction of Jason, the rightful heir to the throne.

**Golden House (Domus Aurea)** The vast palace built by the emperor Nero in Rome after the great fire of AD 64, covering, it is calculated, about 50 hectares (125 acres) in the centre of Rome between the Palatine and Esquiline hills; the centrepiece was an ornamental lake in the valley later occupied by the *Colosseum.

**Good, the** *See* PLATO 5.

**Gordian knot** Alexander the Great, on his arrival at Gordium in Phrygia, found in the acropolis there an ox-cart of which the pole was fastened to the yoke by a knot of cornel-bark. According to legend, in ancient times a Phrygian peasant called Gordius, his wife, and son Midas chanced to arrive in this cart at an assembly of the Phrygians, who had just been told by an oracle that a cart would bring them a king to put an end to the civil disturbances. The Phrygians at once made Gordius king, and he dedicated to Zeus in the acropolis at the town subsequently named Gordium his cart and the yoke to which the oxen had been fastened. A further oracle declared that whoever could untie the knot, which had defeated all attempts to undo it, should reign over Asia. Alexander cut the knot with his sword and applied the oracle to himself. 'To cut the Gordian knot' thus signifies drastic and irretrievable action to solve a difficulty.

**Go'rgias** (of Leontini in Sicily, *c.*485–*c.*380 BC; ancient evidence gives him an extremely long life) One of the most influential of the Greek *sophists. His particular expertise was the teaching of rhetoric, based less upon systematic treatment of the subject matter than upon mannered, poetic, and effective expression. He made his pupils learn typical passages by heart. He has also acquired a reputation for thinking seriously about the power and also the limitations of words, appearing in one or two of Plato's dialogues (*see* GORGIAS), where he is treated with a certain amount of respect (although Agathon's speech in the *Symposium* is a telling parody of his style). The speeches he delivered in Athens in 427 when he headed an

embassy from his home-town stunned the Athenians with the brilliance and novelty of their style (*see* RHETORIC). His extant *Encomium of Helen* and *Defence of Palamedes* illustrate both his confidence that the well-taught orator can with ingenuity find arguments to support any case, however unpromising, and also his remarkable prose style, with its short symmetrical clauses, rhythmically balanced antitheses, verbal echoes, and play on words. Part of a funeral oration also survives, and a fragment on the paradoxical theme that 'nothing exists': even if anything existed it could not be known or communicated by one person to another. The seriousness of this thesis is much debated. Gorgias later travelled about Greece giving lectures, dying at a great age at Larissa in Thessaly. His influence has been detected in Antiphon, Thucydides, and especially in the speeches of *Isocrates.

**Go'rgias** Dialogue by *Plato named after the famous sophist. Socrates opens the dialogue by asking *Gorgias to define rhetoric. The latter replies that it is the most important of human concerns because successful statesmanship depends not upon knowing what should be done and advising accordingly, but upon having the knack of persuasive speech. A successful orator can therefore act as he pleases, justly or unjustly. When Gorgias retires his pupil Polus takes up the subject; against his will he has to concede to Socrates' argument, that it is better to suffer injustice than to do it, and that when one has done evil it is better to be punished than to go unpunished. When Polus retires his place is taken by a certain Callicles (otherwise unknown to us), who in a manner foreshadowing Nietzsche argues that virtue and happiness are to be found in the exercise of lawless self-will, for those whose nature is capable of it (*see* NOMOS–PHYSIS ANTITHESIS). The issue of the dialogue is suddenly seen to be the choice a man has to make between a life of action of the kind Callicles stands for and a life of philosophy represented by Socrates. Socrates reinforces his own choice of philosophy with a passionate denunciation of the supposedly 'great' Athenian statesmen of the past, Pericles, Cimon, and Miltiades, and emerges himself as the only true statesmen because he alone improves his fellow citizens. At the climax of the dialogue there is a myth, the earliest it would seem in Plato, of the judgement of the soul after death, perhaps as an additional incentive to avoid injustice.

**Gorgons (Gorgŏnĕs)** In Greek myth, female monsters. Homer seems to know only one Gorgon: in the *Iliad* her head adorns the *aegis of the goddess Athena and inspires terror. According to Hesiod there were three Gorgons, Sthenno ('Mighty'), Euryalē ('Wide-wanderer'), and Medusa ('Queen'), living in the far West, by the stream of Ocean, daughters of the sea-deities Phorcys and his sister Ceto, and sisters of the Graiae. They are often given monstrous features such as serpents in their hair and glaring eyes. Medusa, who alone was mortal, and whose head was so fearful that anyone who looked at it was turned to stone, was loved by Poseidon and pregnant by him when *Perseus killed her. At the moment of her death she gave birth to Pegasus and Chrysaor ('Golden-sword'). The head of Medusa was said to be buried under a mound in the agora of Argos, where it was probably thought to have apotropaic power, and the representation of the head, called a Gorgoneion, was often carved as a protective figure on armour and walls. In the art of the fifth century BC the head is humanized, and later is often shown as beautiful in death.

**Gracchi, the** Two brothers who were Roman statesmen and social reformers in the second century BC. They were among the twelve children of Tiberius Sempronius Gracchus, censor in 169, a man of high character and liberal thought, famous for his austerity. He married *Cornelia, the daughter of Scipio Africanus, and died in 154 BC.

**1. Tiberius Sempronius Gracchus** (*c.*164–133 BC) Like his father, he served with distinction in Spain, winning popular acclaim by negotiating a peace with the victorious Numantine army (later repudiated by Rome) which saved many Roman lives. In 133 he was elected tribune, and—alarmed by the concentration of land and wealth in the hands of a few—proposed a law aimed at alleviating poverty by redistributing public land. The law was passed, but in haste and by unconventional means which included deposing a hostile tribune, M. Octavius. When Tiberius further proposed that the property of Attalus III of Pergamum, bequeathed to Rome, should be used to finance the new allotment-holders, and when he unconstitutionally sought re-

election, the senate was persuaded that he was aiming at a tyranny. His cousin *Scipio Nasica led a mob of senators and their clients against Tiberius, killing him and many of his supporters on the Capitol. Tiberius' tribunate marks the advent of violence upon the Roman political scene, 'the Roman Revolution', and the beginning of the disintegration of the senate's power under the attacks of its own members who supported the people.

**2. Gaius Sempronius Gracchus** (*c.*153–121 BC) The younger brother of Tiberius, who was with Scipio Aemilianus in Spain in 133 when news of Tiberius' murder arrived. He returned to Rome, where he was already a member of the agrarian commission, but he seems not to have been very active in public life until he gained the quaestorship in 126 and was sent to Sardinia. After two years there he returned to Rome and was elected tribune for 123 and again for 122. The first laws he proposed were aimed at taking vengeance on his brother's enemies; he then passed a series of laws aimed at alleviating poverty as well as winning the support of the people. Other laws were aimed at limiting the power of senators. He proposed to establish a number of colonies, mainly in Italy, but including one on the site of Carthage (which had been ritually cursed), and early in 122 set out for Africa to supervise the settlement of this. During his absence the tribune Livius Drusus (who enjoyed senatorial support) managed to turn the people against him. Gaius failed to obtain re-election for 121, and violence broke out between the Gracchans and their enemies. The senate declared a public emergency (the first recorded use of the *senatus consultum ultimum*), and Gaius, finding himself cut off, ordered a slave to kill him (*see* FURRINA).

Gaius was an astute politician and an impassioned orator (some fragments of his speeches survive) and the more ambitious of the Gracchi. He recognized the need for the Roman people to benefit from the profits of empire without excessive exploitation of the subject peoples. He also believed that the senate and magistrates should continue to govern and administer but within constitutional bounds. These ambitions were nullified by his enemies' success. The consequences of the civil violence were disastrous for Rome, leading to the civil wars of the next century.

**Graces, the** (Gk. Cha'ritĕs, Lat. Gratiae) In myth, minor goddesses, usually said to be daughters of Zeus and to be three in number, called by the Greek poet Hesiod Euphrosyne ('Joy'), Aglaia ('Radiance'), sometimes said to be Hephaestus' wife, and Thalia ('Flowering'). They are the personification of the grace and beauty that enhance the enjoyment of life. Thus they accompany the *Muses, and the most perfect works of art are called the work of the Graces; they give wisdom its charm, they moderate the exciting influence of wine, and they accompany Aphrodite and Eros. For later Romans they were also the symbols of gratitude. They had cults of their own in various parts of Greece (notably an ancient one at Orchomenus in Boeotia), and are often made attendants on other gods. In early times the Graces were portrayed clothed, but later they were always shown naked.

**Gradi'vus** A title often applied to *Mars, perhaps signifying 'he who marches forth'.

**Graeae** In Greek myth, sisters of the *Gorgons, the personification of old age, grey-haired from birth, with one eye and one tooth between them. *Perseus stole their eye and so made them tell him where to find the Gorgons.

### Greece

**1. Topography.** In the ancient world Greece comprised an area of the Balkan peninsula comparable with that of modern Greece. It may be divided into three parts: (i) the peninsula south of the Isthmus of Corinth, known as the Peloponnese; (ii) the land north of the Isthmus roughly as far as the Ambracian Gulf in the west and the river Peneius in the east, which includes Thessaly and is in many contexts known as Greece proper (or mainland Greece); and (iii) the northern regions comprising Epirus, Macedonia, and Thrace, whose inhabitants were regarded as scarcely Greek by the states in the southern regions. For the main ethnic divisions of the Greek people in historical times, *see* HELLEN. To a large extent the north of Greece was cut off from the rest by the mountain ranges in that area, and Greece itself from the rest of Europe by the high mountain chain which runs from Thrace to Italy. Greece is a land dominated by mountains, which have been held to be the reason for the political development of the country into a scatter of independent territories each centred on a pocket of arable land.

**2. Language and Prehistory.** The Greeks had a tradition that their country was inhabited by a pre-Greek people, the *Pelasgians, and Herodotus said that he did not know what language these people spoke. The origins of Greek, an Indo-European language, go back to migrations into Greece of an Indo-European people *c.*2000 BC. In later centuries the formative influence on this people, the Mycenaeans (*see* MYCENAE), was the advanced culture of the Minoans in Crete, who were a non-Greek-speaking people (*see* LINEAR A). From the second half of the second millennium BC the Mycenaeans had a written form of their language, *Linear B, an early form of the Greek language. There is essential continuity from the most ancient form of Greek to that of modern times.

The Mycenaean civilization had finally collapsed by *c.*1100 BC. The Greek historian Thucydides, describing early Greece at the beginning of his History of the Peloponnesian War, had only oral tradition and his own observations to rely on, and mostly lacked archaeological evidence. Like all other Greeks he had no knowledge of the Minoan and Mycenaean civilizations, which were undiscovered until revealed by archaeologists of the late nineteenth century. The Homeric epics gave the Greeks a picture of an earlier, more glorious age, but it is now becoming apparent that the realistic details belong to the post-Mycenaean period, the so-called Dark age, lasting from *c.*1100 to 776 BC, with great impoverishment from *c.*1050 to *c.*900 BC. Of this period Thucydides seems to know nothing. At this time Linear B disappears and no other form of writing is in evidence. (It was perhaps then that early oral poetry on heroic themes began to take shape.) Archaeology shows that communities had very little contact with each other, and surviving material goods are of a low level. There are exceptions: excavations at Lefkandi on the coast of Athens' island neighbour Euboea have revealed a lavish burial of the tenth century BC with rich grave-goods and other evidence of contact between east Greece and Cyprus and the eastern Mediterranean, and similar finds have been made at the somewhat later site of Eleutherna near Mount Ida in Crete. Surviving legends, in particular 'The return of the sons of Heracles' (*see* HERACLEIDAE), and the evidence of the various Greek dialects suggest that around this time separate waves of Greek-speaking invaders (the first such invaders, according to those who believe that Linear B is not Greek) arrived in Greece: Ionians, Arcadians, and Cypriots *c.*1200 BC, and the Dorians, who perhaps precipitated the final collapse, *c.*1100 BC (*see* DORIANS, DORIAN INVASION). Another Greek tradition was that *c.*1000 Greeks made migrations eastwards and settled for the first time in an unofficial and unorganized way along the central coast of Asia Minor in what was later to be called *Ionia. Similarly the northern part of the coast from Tenedos southwards became known as *Aeolis.

By 800 BC the population of Greece was already distributed much as it was going to be in the classical age, and in communities that were somewhat different in organization from those of Mycenaean Greece, being small independent cities, which owed no allegiance to a higher authority (*see* CITY-STATE). The conventional date separating Greek prehistory from history proper is 776 BC, the date which Hippias of Elis made canonical as that of the first Olympian games. The alphabet was adopted from an eastern source, colonization was promoted in a more organized way, and there was a resumption on quite a large scale of communication and trade with the East. Greece was now about to enter the period for which written sources exist. For her subsequent history *see* ATHENS; SPARTA; THEBES; MACEDONIA; HELLENISTIC AGE.

**3. The archaic and later periods.** Despite the fact that Greece was made up of a large number of independent territories which occasionally fought each other (*see* e.g. LELANTINE WAR and PELOPONNESIAN WAR), the Greeks formed a single people, with one and the same civilization. Herodotus (8.144) described Greekness as based on shared descent, language, customs, and religion (*see* HELLAS and BARBARIAN). There was a broad similarity in their political institutions (government in city-states, normally under oligarchic or democratic constitutions); they had a common religion and respected the same oracular shrines; they had a common heritage of literature from Homer and Hesiod onwards and their art, despite certain diversities, had unity; many of the Greek colonies were founded in common by emigrants from more than one state. The social unity of Greece manifested itself in the common festivals and games; and some political unity was shown in the combined resistance to Persia. But they did not necessarily see themselves as a unity, and what we see as attempts to consolidate always collapsed before the jealously independent spirit of the different states.

The Greeks called their country Hellas and themselves Hellenes (originally the name of a tribe in south Thessaly). Graii, the local name of a tribe in west Greece, became the Latin name for the Greeks in general; Latin *Graeci* and *Graecia* ('Greeks' and 'Greece') are derivatives from Graii. It has been suggested that the Graii took part in the colonization of Cumae, the oldest Greek colony in Italy, and from them the name was applied more widely. When the Romans created the province of Greece in 27 BC they called it Achaia.

The phrase 'Greek world' describes that part of the world at the time in question in which Greek was, or had become, the principal language, or was the language of the rulers and the administration. Apart from mainland Greece and the Peloponnese, together with Epirus, Macedonia, and Thrace, it might include Magna Graecia and Sicily (during the Greek classical period; afterwards both were slowly Romanized), Egypt and Cyrenaica, Asia Minor, and to a varying extent lands to the east and south: Syria, north Arabia, and even Mesopotamia (Iraq) and beyond. Rome began to take over the Greek world in the second century BC and had done so before the end of the first century BC.

**griffin (gryphon)** (Gk. *gryps*) Fabulous animal with the body of a lion and the head and wings of an eagle, supposed to dwell in the far north between the *Hyperboreans and the one-eyed *Arimaspians, guarding the gold of the north. The conception would seem to be eastern in origin.

**groma'tici** Roman land-surveyors (Lat. *groma*, a measuring rod). During the empire several Latin authors wrote on surveying, including *Frontinus and *Hyginus; the treatise of the former is known to us only in extracts.

**gryphon** *See* GRIFFIN.

**guest-friendship** *See* FRIENDSHIP [Greek].

**Gygēs** King of Lydia, *c.*680–*c.*645 BC. He founded the dynasty of the Mermnadae by killing the king Candaules (called Myrsilus by the Greeks). According to Herodotus he was the favourite officer of Candaules who was so proud of his wife's beauty that he insisted Gyges should see the queen naked while remaining himself hidden. The queen, however, sensed his presence, and later summoned Gyges to offer him the choice of dying himself or murdering the king and taking the kingdom, with her as his queen. He chose the latter course. Plato in

*Republic*, book 2, tells the story that Gyges won the queen and the kingdom by means of a magic ring of invisibility, to illustrate the view that men are not virtuous when they need not fear the consequences of their actions. 'Gyges' ring' subsequently became proverbial, as did 'the riches of Gyges'. He reputedly sent rich gifts to Delphi in gratitude for an oracle which established his right to the throne. He was the first Lydian king to try to extend his rule over the Greek cities of the Ionian coast. His tomb has been identified in the royal cemetery at Bin Tepe.

**Gyli'ppus** Spartan general sent in 414 BC to help the Syracusans against the Athenians during the Peloponnesian War. Under his leadership the Spartans utterly destroyed the Athenian fleet and army. He was convicted at Sparta in 405 of embezzling public funds and went into exile.

**gymna'sium** [Gk. *gymnos*, 'naked'] In Greece, a (gymnastic) school, its name derived from the practice among Greek boys and men of exercising naked (*see* NUDITY). Education to the Greeks entailed a training for the *epheboi*, 'youths', which was both intellectual and physical (in preparation for war), and the gymnasia catered for both (*see* EDUCATION 3). While intellectual training ceased after youth, gymnastics were practised at all ages. In Sparta there were no gymnasia since all male citizens from the age of 7 were engaged exclusively in military training. At Athens, on the other hand, three gymnasia, the *Academy, *Lyceum, and *Cynosarges, became famous schools of philosophy. By the Hellenistic age the gymnasium had become an essential element of Greek life, and a hallmark of Hellenism. *See also* PALAESTRA.

**Gymnopae'diae** An annual festival 'of the naked youths' at Sparta which foreigners were allowed to attend. It was held over several days in the heat of July, and included displays of gymnastics and dancing by boys and men; hymns were sung in honour of the gods and Spartan heroes. Xenophon in the *Hellenica* memorably describes the self-control shown by the Spartans when the appalling news of the defeat at Leuctra arrived in the city on the last day of the Gymnopaediae in 371 BC. *See* THALETAS.

**gymnosophists** ('naked sages') Hindu ascetics who became famous in the Greek world after Alexander the Great met and talked to them in India (as reported by Plutarch; *see also* ONESICRITUS). They practised an extreme form of asceticism, leading solitary lives of contemplation in wild places, disdaining all appetite. They wore little or no clothing, ate only wild fruits, and had no sexual relations. They were religious rather than philosophical ascetics; Strabo divided them into those who did and those who did not admit the caste system. Their aim was to enter a state of pure being, above all by self-combustion on a pyre. Gymnosophists appear at the end of the Greek novel *Aethiopica* (despite the Ethiopian setting) as holy and prophetic priests who protest at the imminent sacrifice of the heroine, believing that all living sacrifice is wrong and unacceptable to the gods. *See also* PYRRHON

**gynaecology** Medical authorities in the ancient world disagreed as to whether there were diseases specific to women or merely different conditions to cause problems and different organs to become diseased. Some Hippocratic texts (*see* HIPPOCRATES) apply the same principles to the diseases of women as of men, and the famous Hellenistic Greek physicians of the third century BC, *Erasistratus and *Herophilus, did not believe that there were diseases specific to women. However, also found in the Hippocratic writings is the theory that women require a separate branch of medicine because their physical nature differs from men's: women's flesh is wet and spongy because they absorb more moisture from their food, losing the excess in menstruation (*see* HUMOURS). If too much remained in the body it would press on other organs and cause disease or even death. A missed period therefore required treatment, using irritant pessaries or other methods. The end of a menstrual period was thought of as the best time for conception, since the womb was clearly open. Since there was no menstruation during pregnancy it was believed that the foetus was formed out of the blood. The menopause was thought to occur when women became 'drier' as a result of ageing. *See also* TIMAEUS.

*Soranus in the second century AD wrote a much-studied book on gynaecology which survives in the original Greek as well as, in part, in a Latin translation. He too believes that though some conditions are specific to women their diseases are not generally different (and *Galen similarly). The book deals with female anatomy, conception, childbirth, pathology and surgery, and drugs, as well as listing the qualities of the ideal midwife. Only Galen's gynaecological work was more influential.

# H

**Hādēs** (Haidēs, Ăidēs, Ăidōneus) (in popular etymology meaning 'the unseen one'; also known as Plūto, the Latin form of the Greek Ploutōn, 'the wealth-giver'; or as Dis, the contracted form of Latin *dives*, 'rich') In Greek myth, the god of the Underworld, one of the three sons of Cronus and Rhea, and brother of Zeus and Poseidon. When the three cast lots for their domains (*see* ZEUS), Hades obtained the Underworld. He and his wife *Persephone are the rulers of the dead and Hades could even be regarded as death personified. Although he is therefore a grim and dreaded god, he is not an enemy to humankind, nor to his brothers. Plato observes that out of fear people prefer to call him by the euphemistic name of Plouton because all metals (i.e. wealth) are found under the earth. The etymology of Hades is uncertain; the name in Greek nearly always designates the god, not his kingdom, to which it was later extended by natural usage: the dead were said to go 'to [the house of] Hades'. His kingdom was thought of as underground (Homer seems to visualize it below a flat earth and sea), despite the tendency of Greeks to locate the abode of the dead in the West. The two ideas were reconciled by supposing the entrance to be at some locality in the far West. In Homer's *Odyssey* (24) it is in the far West beyond the stream of Ocean (which was believed to encircle the earth; *see* OCEANUS). Later it was thought to be approached by various natural chasms. Details in descriptions of the realm of Hades vary. The 'gates of Hades' are guarded by the dog *Cerberus, who prevents the dead from leaving and the living from entering. The souls of the dead, it was commonly believed, would not be admitted if their bodies had not received the rites of burial (*see* DEAD, DISPOSAL OF). Once inside, the souls dwelled in vast, dark, and sunless halls. The heroes *Aeacus, *Minos, and his brother *Rhadamanthys are named as 'judges' in the Underworld, although their function varies in the sources. There is no judgement of

ordinary souls; only those are condemned to eternal punishment who have seriously sinned against the gods, the mythical trio *Tantalus, *Tityus, and *Sisyphus (*see* TARTARUS). Conversely there are great heroes who are admitted to a blissful after-life in *Elysium (in Homer) or in the *Isles of the Blest (in Hesiod and Pindar).

The Underworld was intersected by four rivers: Acheron, Cocytus, Phlegethon or Pyriphlegethon ('Fiery one'), and Styx; and in Latin poetry by a fifth, *Lethe. Black sheep were sacrificed to Hades but he had very little cult, and few statues of him exist. He figures little in myth except for the story of *Persephone. *See also* DEATH, ATTITUDES TO.

**Hadrian** (Publius Aelius Hādriānus) Roman emperor AD 117–38. He was born in 76 in Spain, and when left fatherless entered the household of Trajan, his father's cousin. He won favour and held significantly high offices, being designated for a second consulship in 118, but when he was adopted by the childless emperor Trajan on the latter's deathbed it was a surprise which displeased some; nevertheless the senate sanctioned his succession in 117. He passed the years 120–31 in touring the provinces, visiting *Britain in 121 or 122 and spending at least two years in Athens, a city he greatly loved. While he was in Egypt in 130 his favourite companion *Antinous, then a young man of about 20, was drowned and Hadrian remained inconsolable. His travels reinforced his intention to aim at peace and sound defences in his foreign policy—hence the Wall across Britain; he renounced those eastern conquests of Trajan which could not be secured. A revolt in Judaea, 132–5, was the only serious war of his reign.

Hadrian was the most intellectual and cultivated of all the emperors, and a generous patron. His portraits show him bearded, as befitted a philosopher (*see* BEARDS), but according to Plutarch he grew a beard to hide facial scars. Most places he visited benefited from his liberality. In Rome he founded the Athenaeum, an institute for lectures and recitations, built the *Pantheon, the temple of Venus and Rome, and his mausoleum (modern Castel Sant'Angelo) together with the bridge, Pons Aelius, by which it was approached. He also built an extensive villa at Tibur (Tivoli), which has been a rich source of art treasures. His attitude towards Christianity was tolerant as far as was consistent with good order. Before his death he chose as his successor Antoninus Pius (and caused him to adopt in turn his nephew Marcus Aurelius). The story is that Hadrian died with a poem addressed to his own soul on his lips, 'dear little restless, agreeable soul . . .' (*animula, vagula, blandula*). His other works, which include speeches, letters, and an autobiography, are lost. His policy in the matter of frontiers and his Hellenism left their mark on the empire.

**Hadrian's Wall** *See* BRITAIN.

**Haedui** *See* AEDUI.

**Haemon** Son of Creon; *see* OEDIPUS.

**hair** Homer's Achaeans were given the conventional epithet 'long-haired', and wore their hair uncut even in battle. The Spartans continued the tradition in classical times, priding themselves on combing and dressing their hair before going into battle (according to Herodotus, to the great surprise of a Persian spy before the battle of Thermopylae). Spartan men and women alike tied their hair in a knot on top of the head. The fashion for Athenian men to wear their long hair in a topknot, fastened with gold clasps in the form of grasshoppers, had passed by the time Thucydides was grown up in the fifth century BC. From that century Greek men cut their hair short. Athenian males cut off their long hair at puberty, with considerable ceremony, and as *epheboi* wore it quite short. Women sometimes wore their hair tied up in a coif of net-work or of a closely woven material, otherwise their hair was braided and fastened behind in a knot. Greeks mostly had dark hair, but fair hair was more desirable (see below). In Homer Achilles and Odysseus among other heroes were fair.

In classical times Roman men wore their hair short. They associated long, uncombed hair with antique virtue, hence Horace's praise of *Curius Dentatus 'with unkempt hair'; careful combing was thought to be effeminate.

Roman women in republican times wore their long hair simply braided and knotted, like the Greeks, but in the early empire their hair was arranged in a complicated structure on top of the head. Ovid's *Remedia amoris* describes some fashionable styles. False blond hair was worn by both Greeks and Romans, and blond hair-colouring used. Slaves had their hair cut short as a mark of their servile status. *See also* BEARDS and COSMETICS.

**halcyon** *See* ALCYONE.

***Halieu'tica*** 1. Latin poem wrongly attributed to *Ovid, of which a fragment survives.

2. Greek didactic poem in five books of hexameters by *Oppian.

**hamadrȳ'ads** *Nymphs of trees, whose lives were coterminous with their trees.

**Hami'lcar** 1. (fifth century BC) Carthaginian general who invaded Sicily but was defeated and killed by *Gelon, tyrant of Syracuse, in alliance with Theron, tyrant of Acragas, at the battle of Himera (480 BC). He was the first to organize the Carthaginian army.

2. **Hamilcar Barca** (d. 229 BC) Father of *Hannibal, and the general appointed at a young age to command the Carthaginian forces in Sicily during the First *Punic War against Rome in 247 BC. He seized Heircte on the north coast of Sicily in the midst of enemy territory and held it for three years while raiding the Italian coast as far as Cumae. In 244 he abruptly left and took the town at the foot of Mount Eryx, where he defied the Romans for another two years. After the Carthaginian naval defeat at Aegates Insulae in 241 he negotiated the terms of peace and resigned his command. In 237 he went to Spain, perhaps intending to form there a new empire for Carthage, to compensate for the loss of Sicily and Sardinia, and to provide wealth and manpower for a new onslaught against the hated Romans. He was drowned during the siege of a Spanish town, leaving three sons, Hannibal, *Hasdrubal (2), and Mago, all of whom distinguished themselves in the Second Punic War. *See also* HASDRUBAL (1).

**Ha'nnibal** (247–183/2 BC) Eldest son of *Hamilcar Barca and the great leader of the Carthaginians against Rome in the Second *Punic War. Hamilcar took him to Spain in 237, after making him swear eternal hatred to Rome, a story told by Hannibal himself and not implausible. When *Hasdrubal (1) was assassinated in 221, the army elected Hannibal commander-in-chief. For two years he extended Carthaginian power in Spain and then in 219 besieged Saguntum, a city in alliance with Rome, thus, as he expected, precipitating war with Rome. In 218 he reached Italy after an arduous winter journey over the Alps, during which many of the war-elephants and large numbers of men perished. After fifteen years of continuous warfare in Italy he was ordered in 203 to withdraw his undefeated army to Africa to defend Carthage from the invading Romans. Finally defeated by *Scipio Africanus at Zama in 202, he escaped to Carthage and urged an immediate peace. When his enemies alleged to Rome that he was conspiring with Antiochus III of Syria, who was on the verge of war with Rome, Hannibal left to join Antiochus. He was defeated in a naval engagement at Side, and subsequently fled to Crete and thence to king Prusias I of Bithynia. The Romans were uneasy as long as Hannibal remained alive, and eventually demanded his surrender. Seeing all ways shut to him, he took poison in 183 or 182. Acknowledged to be one of the world's greatest soldiers, Hannibal inspired the utmost loyalty in his troops (even in defeat and hardship) and dread among his enemies. He lived on in the imagination as the archetypal enemy of Rome, and Roman mothers frightened their children with the nursery threat: 'Hannibal is at the gates' (*Hannibal ad portas*). *See also* BILINGUALISM.

**Harmo'dius and Aristogei'ton** A pair of lovers who killed Hipparchus, the younger brother of the Athenian tyrant *Hippias (1), at the festival of the Panathenaea in 514 BC. The story was that Hipparchus had arranged a public insult to Harmodius' sister after he had made advances to Harmodius and been rejected. They seem to have intended to kill Hippias and overthrow the tyranny but failed and were killed themselves. The tyranny lasted until 510 BC, but they were later honoured by the Athenian people as if they had succeeded. Bronze statues to them by Antenor were carried off as booty by Xerxes in 480 BC and replaced by others in 476; an epigram by Simonides was inscribed on the base, fragments of which have been found. *See* ALCMAEONIDAE and PEISISTRATUS.

**Harmo'nia, necklace of** In Greek myth, a necklace made according to some sources by the god Hephaestus, and given as a wedding present to Harmonia, daughter of Ares and Aphrodite, by her husband *Cadmus. It did harm to all who subsequently possessed it. (*See* AMPHIARAUS and ALCMAEON).

**harmonics, harmony** 'Harmony' combines the ideas of musical concord and the numerical ratios between musical intervals. *See* ARCHYTAS; ARISTOXENUS; HARMONY OF THE SPHERES; MUSIC [Greek 5]; PYTHAGORAS; EDUCATION 3.

**harmony (music) of the spheres** A concept attributed to *Pythagoras, harmony having cosmic significance for the Pythagoreans. It seemed to them, as to others, that the heavenly bodies must, like other large bodies moving at speed, produce a sound as they whirl through space; since the bodies move at different speeds they must produce different notes, but together these are harmonious. Plato's poetically describes this idea in the Myth of Er (*Republic*, book 10); he has it that on each of the eight concentric spheres in which the bodies rotate stands a *Siren uttering a note of constant pitch, the eight notes together making up a scale. As the Pythagoreans said, the octave 'has the Sirens in it'. (For the number eight *see* ASTRONOMY.) Because the sound is with us constantly from birth and there is no contrasting silence we are unaware of it; only Pythagoras, it was said, could detect it.

**ha'rmosts** [*harmostai*, 'regulators'] Name given to Spartan military governors abroad, especially to those sent to the cities occupied by Spartans after they had defeated Athens at the end of the Peloponnesian War in 404 BC.

**Ha'rpalus** Unreliable treasurer of Alexander the Great; *see* DEMOSTHENES (2) 4 and DEINARCHUS.

**Harpies** [Gk. *harpūiai*, 'snatchers'] In Greek myth, the daughters of Thaumas (son of Pontus, Sea) and Electra (daughter of *Oceanus). They appear to have been regarded by Homer and Hesiod as personifications of violent winds which carried off the daughters of Pandareus, Cleothera and Merope, to be slaves to the Furies. Among their names were Aello ('Storm-wind'), Ocypete ('Swift-flying'), Podarge ('Fleet-of-foot'), and Celaino ('Dark'). They are represented as birds with the faces of women. In the story of *Phineus the Harpies carry off or defile all his food. Virgil in *Aeneid* 3 makes Aeneas encounter them at the islands of the Strophades.

**haru'spicēs** ('diviners'; sing. *haruspex*) Name given in Rome to Etruscan diviners, believed to be interpreters of the will of the gods, as conveyed through the state of the entrails (*exta*) of sacrificial animals, and most importantly the liver. The gods' will was also conveyed through *monstra*, 'prodigies' (unusual births or growths), or *fulgura*, 'lightning', these two categories being considered to be sent as warnings. Haruspices possessed no religious authority at Rome but came to rival the augurs. *See* DIVINATION and AUGURY.

**Ha'sdrubal 1.** Carthaginian general and son-in-law of *Hamilcar Barca, upon whose death in 229 BC he became the commander in Spain. He extended the Carthaginian empire there to the boundary of the river Ebro, but in 221 was murdered by a Celtic slave, and was succeeded in the command by *Hannibal, his brother-in-law.
  **2.** Son of *Hamilcar Barca and younger brother of *Hannibal, left in command of the Carthaginians in Spain when Hannibal invaded Italy in 218 BC (Second *Punic War). From 218 to 208 he fought in Spain against the Roman generals Publius Cornelius *Scipio and his son Scipio Africanus. Having evaded the Roman army he then marched to Italy to the relief of Hannibal (207), but he was intercepted in the valley of the river Metaurus, defeated, and killed, in a significant victory for the Romans.

**Heau'ton timōrū'menos** ('The self-tormentor') Roman comedy (with Greek title) by *Terence, adapted from a Greek comedy of the same name by *Menander, and produced at Rome in 163 BC.
  The self-tormentor is an Athenian father, Menedemus, who imposes hardships on himself in penitence for the harshness which has driven his son Clinia out of the country on account of his love for Antiphila, supposed to be the daughter of a Corinthian woman of small means. His neighbour Chremes, perplexed by his behaviour, intervenes: *homo sum; humani nil a me alienum puto* ('I am a man; I reckon nothing human to be foreign to me'), he says in explanation, and lectures Menedemus on a parent's duty of indulgence. Clinia returns to Athens, making his home with

his friend Clitipho, son of Chremes, who, unknown to his father, is spending his money on the prostitute Bacchis. It is arranged that Bacchis will come to the house of Chremes, in the character of Clinia's friend, bringing with her Antiphila as a companion. By a trick of the slave Syrus, Chremes is cheated out of some money for the benefit of his son's extravagant mistress, and when Chremes discovers this and what has been going on in his house, he angrily disinherits the boy, repudiating his own doctrine of parental duty. His wife intercedes for their son, and Clitipho is let off on condition of a suitable marriage (not, however, with 'the red-headed, cat-eyed girl' first proposed to him). Meanwhile Clinia has been restored to his repentant father, and Antiphila has been discovered to be the daughter of Chremes, who gives her in marriage to Clinia. As in *Adelphoe*, the play revolves around the question of openness between fathers and sons.

**heaven** *See* ELYSIUM; ISLES OF THE BLEST; OLYMPUS; URANUS.

**Hēbē** In Greek myth, daughter of Zeus and Hera, the cup-bearer of the gods and wife to *Heracles after his death and translation to Olympus. She is the personification of the Greek word for youth; the Roman goddess Juventas was identified with her. She is occasionally the object of cult.

**He'calē** *Epyllion by the Hellenistic Greek poet *Callimachus, describing how Theseus was once hospitably entertained by a poor old woman of this name while on his way to kill the bull of Marathon. The poem was intended to explain the name and cult of the Attic deme of Hecale.

**Hecatae'us** (of Miletus, an Ionian Greek city in Asia Minor, fl. 500 BC) The most important of the Ionian Greek prose-writers known as *logographers, who wrote a pioneering work on the geography, ethnography, and mythology of the Mediterranean world. Known as the *Periēgēsis* (or *Periodos gēs*, 'Guide') it was in two books, covering Europe and Asia (which included Africa; *see* GEOGRAPHY), written from the perspective of a traveller voyaging clockwise around the Mediterranean and Black Sea, starting from the Straits of Gibraltar and taking in Scythia, Persia, India, Egypt, and Ethiopia. It is unclear how many of the places he describes Hecataeus actually visited himself.

Many fragments of this work survive in quotation, mostly too short to be illuminating. He also constructed (the second) map of the world (*see* ANAXIMANDER), showing a flat, circular earth with a hole in the middle, representing the Mediterranean, and the stream of Ocean (*see* OCEANUS) running like a river around the outside. Makers of this style of map were derided by Herodotus for their ignorance and simplicity. Herodotus refers to Hecataeus several times, once concerning his opposition to the Ionian revolt (*see* PERSIAN WARS) for geopolitical reasons. If he made use of the *Periegesis* he did so without acknowledgement. Hecataeus also wrote a work entitled the *Histories* or *Genealogies*, the few surviving fragments of which show a rationalizing approach to the claims of those families (including, apparently, his own) who claimed a god or hero as their ultimate ancestor. The first sentence is famous for embodying a new critical approach: 'I write what seems to me true; for the stories of the Greeks are many and in my opinion ridiculous.'

**He'catē** An ancient and somewhat mysterious Greek goddess, unknown to Homer, but according to Hesiod the daughter of the *Titans Perses and Asteria (sister of Leto). Hesiod in the *Theogony* described her as the source of innumerable blessings for men—wealth, victory, wisdom, good luck to sailors and hunters, and so on, and as uniquely honoured among the Titans for being allowed to keep her powers after Zeus became ruler of the gods. She was frequently confused with Artemis (at Rome, Diana), whose functions overlap hers to some extent. Hesiod makes no mention of the Underworld, but generally in Greece she was associated with the ghost world, an attendant upon *Persephone, queen of the Underworld, and she guarded its gates. In Virgil's *Aeneid* (book 6) she gives the Sibyl a view of Tartarus. At night she sent ghosts and demons into the world, and wandered about with the souls of the dead, her approach signalled by the howling of dogs. She was associated with witchcraft and black magic, and is invoked by Medea in Euripides' play and by Simaetha in the second Idyll of Theocritus. She was worshipped at crossroads (i.e. wherever one road meets another), where dishes of food were put out for her at the end of every month as a purificatory rite to mark the rising of the new moon; the usual sacrifice to her was of puppies. In statues she was often represented in triple form (perhaps looking along three roads).

**he'catomb** In Greece, a sacrifice of several animals. The word appears to denote the sacrifice of a hundred oxen (*hekaton bous*); the term came to be used even in Homer of any great sacrifice of animals. *Hekatombaion* was the name of a month at Athens, 'the time when hecatombs are offered'.

**Hecatonchei'res** ('the Hundred-handers') In Greek myth, three monstrous *giants, Briareus, Cottus, and Gyēs, sons of Uranus (Heaven) and Gaia (Earth), who helped Zeus in his war against the *Titans.

**Hector** In Greek legend, the eldest son of *Priam, king of Troy, and of his wife Hecuba, the husband of Andromache and father of Astyanax, the leader and the bravest of the Trojans during the siege of Troy. In the early books of the *Iliad* he takes a prominent part in the fighting and arranges the single combat between Paris and Menelaus. In book 6, having left the fighting to advise the Trojan women to supplicate the gods, he sees Andromache and Astyanax for the last time in a memorable scene of farewell. After his return to battle his challenge to single combat is taken up by Ajax, son of Telamon, who is his superior though the fight is inconclusive; they part with an exchange of gifts. In the battles that follow, while Achilles is absent from the field, Hector plays the leading part in the Trojan successes which culminate in his slaying of Patroclus. When Achilles returns to battle and the Trojans are routed, Hector alone awaits Achilles before the walls of Troy. Achilles pursues him around the city but eventually Hector halts, deceived by the goddess Athena into thinking that his brother Deiphobus has come to his aid. When he realizes the deception he knows that he must die. Achilles kills him and mutilates the body by dragging it behind his chariot to the Greek ships. In a moving scene Priam calls upon Achilles in order to ransom his son's body. The body is ransomed and an eleven-day truce agreed. Hector's funeral ends the *Iliad*.

**He'cuba** (Gk. Hekabē) In Greek legend, the (chief) wife of Priam, king of Troy, and daughter of Dymas, king of Phrygia. She was the mother of nineteen children including Hector, Helenus, Troilus, Paris, Cassandra, Creusa, and Polyxena. In the *Iliad* she remains in the background fulfilling the role of the bereaved queen destined to survive the sack of Troy and the loss of her husband and all her children. In Greek tragedy this latter part of her life becomes a favourite subject, being rich in dramatic possibilities. In the *Trojan Women* of Euripides she is allotted as spoils of war to Odysseus, and has to endure the sacrifice of her daughter Polyxena on Achilles' tomb and the murder of Hector's only son Astyanax. In the *Hecuba*, also by Euripides, she avenges the murder of her last remaining son Polydorus, and the prophecy is made that she will be metamorphosed into a bitch. Later legend elaborated upon this topic.

**He'cuba** Greek tragedy by *Euripides written perhaps in 424 BC.

Troy has fallen to the Greeks, the women of Troy have been apportioned to the victors, but the return home of the Greek fleet is delayed by contrary winds. The ghost of the Greek hero Achilles has demanded the sacrifice to him of Polyxena, daughter of Hecuba and Priam, king of Troy. The Greek hero Odysseus comes to lead her away. He is unmoved by Hecuba's despair and by her reminder that he once owed his life to her. But Polyxena, a striking figure, prefers death to slavery, and willingly goes to her sacrifice. As Hecuba prepares for the burial, she suffers a further sorrow. Her youngest son Polydorus had been sent for safety to Polymestor, king of the Thracian Chersonese (where the Greek fleet is now detained), with part of the treasure of Priam. When Troy fell, Polymestor had murdered the boy in order to secure the treasure for himself, and had thrown his body into the sea. It has now been washed up and is brought to Hecuba. She appeals to the Greek leader Agamemnon for vengeance; but he, though sympathetic, is timid. Hecuba thereupon takes vengeance into her own hands. She lures Polymestor and his sons to her tent, where her women put out his eyes and kill the sons. Agamemnon orders the blinded king to be left on a deserted island; he then prophesies that Hecuba will turn into a bitch, and that the site of her tomb will be commemorated by the name Cynossēma ('Dog's tomb') on the east coast of the Thracian Chersonese).

**He'cyra** ('The mother-in-law') Roman comedy by *Terence adapted from the Greek

original by Apollodorus of Carystus, a writer of New Comedy (*see* COMEDY [Greek 6]). The plot also resembles that of Menander's *Epitrepontes*. The *Hecyra* lost its audience at its first two productions, first in 165 BC to the rival attractions of rope-dancers and a boxing match, and secondly in 160 to a gladiatorial combat, and was successfully performed only at its third attempt in the same year. It has never been a popular play.

Pamphilus has been reluctantly persuaded by his father to give up the prostitute Bacchis and to marry. Soon after the marriage he is sent away by his father on business. During his absence his wife leaves her mother-in-law's house on a pretext and returns to her own mother's house. There she gives birth to a baby conceived before her marriage, having been seduced by an unknown man under cover of darkness. This man had taken from her a ring, subsequently discovered in the possession of Bacchis. With the latter's help it is discovered that the wife's seducer was Pamphilus himself, who is after all the father of his wife's child. Pamphilus, who had reluctantly felt that he must separate from his wife, therefore returns to her. It is made clear, for those who wish to see it that way, how women are treated by men. The title of the play is derived from the carefully drawn characters of the two mothers-in-law.

**Helen** In Greek myth, Leda, the wife of Tyndareus king of Sparta, bore four children, the twins Castor and Polydeuces (the *Dioscuri), Clytemnestra, and Helen; Helen's father was Zeus. According to the usual story, Zeus visited Leda in the form of a swan; Leda then laid an egg, and from this Helen was hatched. Helen and her brothers were worshipped as important deities in Sparta, but in the literary tradition, starting with Homer, she is the entirely human wife of King Menelaus of Sparta, the younger brother of Agamemnon, the latter being married to Helen's sister Clytemnestra. Of outstanding beauty, Helen was said to have been carried off in her youth by Theseus to Attica; but during Theseus' absence in the Underworld her brothers rescued her and took her back to Sparta together with Theseus' mother Aethra. She was subsequently wooed by all the leading men in Greece; at the suggestion of Odysseus she was allowed to choose whom she pleased, and the rest swore to abide by her choice and support her husband's rights. She married Menelaus and bore him a daughter Hermione, but while he was absent in Crete Paris arrived in Sparta, and either persuaded Helen to flee with him or carried her off by force to Troy. (The goddess Aphrodite had promised him the most beautiful woman in the world as his wife; *see* PARIS, JUDGEMENT OF.) On his return Menelaus and his brother Agamemnon raised an expedition against Troy. Another tradition, apparently as old as the poet *Stesichorus (sixth century BC), has it that Helen was carried for safe-keeping to King Proteus of Egypt, while the gods Zeus and Hera allowed only a phantom resembling her to accompany Paris to Troy (*see* HELEN). This provided a pretext for the Trojan War, which Zeus had already decreed should take place so as to reduce the numbers of people and their wickedness. After the war Menelaus found Helen in Egypt and took her home. A story much illustrated on Greek vases is that Menelaus, finding her in the ruins of Troy, intended to kill her but dropped his sword when he saw her breasts.

In the *Iliad* Helen is a tragic figure, compelled by Aphrodite to be the wife of Paris, ashamed of her position at Troy, and aware that her wrong-doing has caused suffering for everyone. Though her responsibility in the matter is not clear, she reproaches herself but is not generally reproached by the Trojans and never, as she says, by Priam (who blames the gods) or Hector. In a scene on the battlements of Troy (*Iliad* 3) the old men, seeing her, observe that such beauty puts her beyond blame (though they wish she would depart). In the *Odyssey* she lives peacefully in Sparta reconciled with her husband, but is an enigmatic figure (*see* TROJAN HORSE). Later writers, Greek and Roman, were generally hostile to Helen, and the speeches in her defence composed by *Gorgias and *Isocrates are little more than rhetorical demonstrations of how to defend the patently guilty.

**Helen** Greek tragedy (with a happy ending) by *Euripides, produced in 412 BC. The plot is based on the legend that it was not the real Helen but her phantom which accompanied Paris to Troy (*see* HELEN).

Helen herself has been magically conveyed by the god Hermes to the court of Proteus, king of Egypt, where she awaits the return of her husband Menelaus from Troy. But Proteus is now dead, and his son Theoclȳmenus is trying

to force her to marry him. She has taken refuge at the tomb of Proteus. The Greek hero Teucer, the brother of Ajax, arrives and tells her of the fall of Troy seven years previously, and of the probable death of Menelaus. While she is lamenting, Menelaus himself appears. He has been shipwrecked on the Egyptian coast, has left the 'Helen' whom he was bringing from Troy in a cave, and has come to the palace for help. A curious scene of reconciliation follows, for Menelaus is puzzled by the two Helens and is convinced of the reality of the 'Egyptian' Helen only when he learns that the other has disappeared into the air after revealing the deception. Helen now devises an escape for both of them from Egypt, a difficult matter, for Theoclymenus not only is determined to marry her, but will kill any Greek he finds in the land. With the help of Theonoē, a priestess and the sister of the king, Theoclymenus is fooled with a pretence of a funeral ceremony at sea for a supposedly dead Menelaus, and Menelaus and Helen escape on the ship provided for that purpose. Castor and Polydeuces, Helen's deified brothers (*see* DIOSCURI), appear at the end to avert the king's wrath against Theonoe for her complicity. The chorus consists of Helen's attendants, captured Greek maidens.

The poet does not fail to point out the grim humour of the situation: the ten years' siege of Troy has all been for nothing; and the lore of seers is not worth much, for *Calchas and *Helenus gave no indication whatsoever of the deception.

**Helen, Encomium on** See GORGIAS and ISOCRATES.

**He'lenus** In Homer's *Iliad*, son of Priam, king of Troy, and his wife Hecuba, and a warrior gifted with prophecy. According to Sophocles' *Philoctetes* (but not in Homer) he was captured by Odysseus and revealed that the Greeks would take Troy only if *Philoctetes was brought there with his bow and arrows. After the fall of Troy, Helenus became the captive of Neoptolemus, and after the latter's death married Andromache and became king of Chāonia, a part of Epirus. When *Aeneas, in the course of his wanderings, visited him there, Helenus made a prophecy about Aeneas' future ordeals.

**hēliai'a, hēliastēs** See ĒLIAIA.

**He'licon** Largest mountain of Boeotia in Greece, sacred to the Muses (their other haunt is Pieria) who had an ancient sanctuary there. On its slope was the village of Ascra, the home of the poet Hesiod, who tells how he met the Muses while tending sheep on the mountainside. The fountains of Aganippe and Hippocrene on the mountain, which supplied the streams Olmeios and Permessos, were believed to inspire those who drank from them; see PEGASUS.

**Hēliodō'rus** (of Emesa in Syria) Author of the Greek novel the *Aethiopica* (or *Theagenes and Charicleia*). Nothing certain is known of his life, which is dated variously in the third and fourth centuries AD.

**Hē'lios** In Greek myth, the Sun, personified as a god, son of the *Titans Hyperion and Theia, brother of Selene (Moon) and Eōs (Dawn), and the father of Aeētes, Circe, and *Phaethon. (Homer occasionally calls him Hyperion, a practice imitated by other poets.) He is generally represented as a charioteer driving daily from east to west across the sky, and floating back to the east during the night in a golden cup on the stream of Ocean, the cup which Heracles once borrowed (see HERACLES, LABOURS OF 10). He had cattle and sheep in the island of Thrinacia (see ODYSSEY [book 12], and SICILY). He received little actual cult but was always treated with respect, sometimes prayed to at rising and setting, and often appealed to as a witness because he sees and hears everything. This aspect perhaps contributed to his occasional identification with Apollo, the all-knowing god, after the fifth century BC. In Rhodes, however, he appears to have been the chief national god, who chose the island as his own before it rose above the surface of the sea. The famous statue, the *Colossus of Rhodes, erected by the harbour entrance, represented him.

**Helladic** See MYCENAE.

**Hellanī'cus** (of Mitylene in Lesbos) A Greek *logographer of the fifth century BC. He was a prolific writer, of whose important works comparatively few fragments survive. One of his aims was to establish consistency and coherence for the various traditions of Greek myth and history, above all in the matter of chronology. Accordingly he composed systematic genealogies for the heroes and their families.

He was one of the first to use the several lists which were in existence—of the annual succession of named magistrates, victors at the (Dorian) Carnean games, priestesses of the temple of Hera at Argos (also used by Thucydides), and so on—to establish a common chronology for Greek history. He also wrote a wide range of ethnographic works on people and places in Greece and abroad (work probably eclipsed by Herodotus), most importantly two books on the local history of Attica (see ATTHIS), from its beginning to the end of the Peloponnesian War, based on his arrangement of the mythical kings of Athens and the list of eponymous *archons.

**Hellas, Hellenes** Names used by the Greeks in classical times to denote Greece and the Greeks. Homer (who did not have a comprehensive name for the Greeks, calling them Achaeans, Argives, or Danaans) used these names in the *Iliad* to denote a small region of south Thessaly and its inhabitants. In the *Odyssey*, 'Hellas' seems to denote central and northern Greece, as opposed to the Peloponnese. Hesiod, however, uses Hellas in the general sense of Greece, and from about the seventh century onwards the Greeks called themselves and their country by these names, deriving them from a mythical ancestor *Hellen. In classical times the name Hellas embraced all lands inhabited by Hellenes, including not only the mainland of Greece, the Peloponnese, and the Greek islands, but also the colonies and the Greek cities on the coast of Asia Minor. From the fourth century AD onwards the Greeks of the eastern Roman empire called themselves *Rhōmaioi* ('Romans'); by that time the name 'Hellenes' denoted pagans. See GREECE.

**Hellē** In Greek myth, sister of Phrixus. While she and her brother were flying through the air on the back of the ram with the Golden Fleece to escape from their father *Athamas and stepmother Ino, Helle fell off into the sea and drowned. In consequence the sea was called the Hellespont, 'sea of Helle'.

**Hellēn** In Greek myth, the eponymous ancestor of the Hellenes, usually described as the son of Pyrrha and *Deucalion. He was the father of Dorus, Aeolus, and Xuthus, whose sons were Ion and Achaeus, the ancestors of the Dorians, Aeolians, Ionians, and Achaeans.

**Hellē'nica 1.** A seven-book history of Greece from 411 to 362 BC by *Xenophon (1), who lived through the events he describes. The work was not conceived as a unity, but was written in at least two instalments the second of which, from 2.3.10 to the end, was composed late in Xenophon's life, in the 350s. Since the publication of the fragments of the *Oxyrhynchus historian it has been realized that Xenophon's account makes some surprising omissions, particularly in the campaign of Agesilaus in 395 BC (books 3 and 4). It is nonetheless an indispensable source for the period. Xenophon begins his narrative at the point in the Peloponnesian War where Thucydides' history stops, and books 1–2 cover the years 411 to 403, up to the rule and overthrow of the Thirty at Athens. After leaving a gap for the events of 402–400, he covers the years 399 to 379 in books 3–5: the Spartan war against the Persians (399–387); the attempt of various Greek states to check the growing power of Sparta (the Corinthian War, 394–387, ended by the King's Peace); the rivalry of Sparta and Thebes. The second half of book 5 and books 6 and 7 take the reader from 379 to 362, and cover the triumph of Thebes at the battle of Leuctra (371) and her supremacy under the general Epaminondas (although his name is not mentioned in the description of Leuctra), ending with his death at the battle of Mantinea in 362.

**2.** History by *Theopompus, of which only fragments survive.

**Helle'nica Oxyrhy'nchia** See OXYRHYNCHUS HISTORIAN.

**Hellenism, Hellenization** Hellenism is generally understood to refer to the ideas and culture associated with ancient Greece, and Hellenization to the active promotion of those ideas and that culture or to the absorption of them by other cultures. The significance of these terms to their users has been the subject of debate, particularly in respect of Alexander the Great's intentions towards Asia. Similar questions arise in connection with the term 'philhellenism' as applied to attitudes towards Greece among educated Romans in the last three centuries BC, when the question might arise whether or not to accept cultural Hellenism. The culture of the Greek city (see CITY-STATE) survived into the Roman empire, and it was in fact by spreading the somewhat Romanized *polis* throughout the Greek east that

Rome imposed her own values and authority. See GREECE 3 and CATO (1).

**Hellenistic** Term used to denote the history and civilization, language, art, and literature of the Greek world from the late fourth to the late first century BC. (For the term 'Greek world' see GREECE; for the term 'classical' referring to the fifth and fourth centuries BC in Greece, see CLASSIC.) See also HELLENISTIC AGE.

**Hellenistic age** The period of Greek culture which may be said to start from the death of Alexander the Great in 323 BC and end with Rome's absorption of Greece and the Greek East in the latter part of the first century BC (the conventional terminal date is either put at 31 BC—the date of the battle of Actium—or 27 BC, when Augustus became the first Roman emperor). Before Alexander, Greek culture had little influence outside *Hellas; after his conquest of the Persian empire, important centres of Greek civilization and economy were to be found in Egypt and Asia, and the dominant culture of the Middle East was Greek. The new city of Alexandria in Egypt was its focus, hence the period is sometimes known as the Alexandrian age, but the cities of Pergamum (north-west Asia Minor), Antioch (in Syria on the river Orontes), and Athens were cultural rivals.

After Alexander the Great died his empire was divided among his generals, the *Diadochi ('Successors'). Though each attempted to seize more land and power than the rest, the Seleucids of Syrian Antioch were ultimately the most successful, followed by the Attalids of Pergamum. At the end of the third century BC Rome began to expand into the Greek world, and Roman conquest was completed within the next two centuries.

What remains of Hellenistic literature is only a small and unrepresentative fraction of the vast amount produced by the age. Out of hundreds of histories only five books of Polybius survive entire; important histories such as those of *Timaeus, *Hieronymus of Cardia, and *Poseidonius survive only in fragments. Such literature as survives is largely in verse. Even so, almost nothing remains of the scores of tragic poets, not even of the so-called Pleiad (see PLEIAIDES). Comedy retained its vigour at Athens in the early years of the Hellenistic age, in the New Comedy of Menander and Philemon (see COMEDY [Greek 6]); although it cannot be said to have survived in manuscript to the present day, our knowledge of it has been considerably enhanced by substantial papyrus discoveries made in the twentieth century (*see* PAPYROLOGY). Among other poetry which has perished are the works of poets who considerably influenced later Latin literature, like Philetas of Cos and Euphorion; but they seem to have resembled, in small scale and exquisite refinement, the surviving works of their contemporaries Callimachus and Theocritus. By contrast Apollonius of Rhodes wrote an epic about the voyage of the Argonauts (which survives), and there is a tradition that Callimachus quarrelled violently with him over his use of this genre, outdated in its large scale. Didactic poetry was popular on a variety of topics such as geography, astronomy, and fishing; the *Phaenomena* of Aratus is the chief example of the class. A novel Greek literary form, the mime, came to light when eight of these miniature dramas by Herodas turned up on a papyrus discovered at the end of the nineteenth century.

The Hellenistic age saw a striking advance in scholarship and scientific knowledge, the Library and Museum at *Alexandria being great centres of study and research. The leading names in this area were Zenodotus, Aristophanes of Byzantium, and Aristarchus of Samothrace. Hellenistic achievements in the fields of mathematics, astronomy, biology, and medicine are known to us mainly through the works of later writers. The great names in mathematics and astronomy are Aristarchus of Samos, Archimedes, Hipparchus, Euclid, and the polymaths Eratosthenes and Poseidonius. In biology and medicine the two great names were Herophilus and Erasistratus.

In the second and first centuries BC the rise of Rome, accompanied by constant wars and widespread destruction in the Greek world, brought about the decline of science and literature. But early in the first century BC the poet Meleager published an anthology of epigrams dating from the time of Archilochus (seventh century BC) to his own day, called 'the Garland' (*Stephanos*), the first large critical *anthology of poems of which we have knowledge; each of the fifty or so poets represented was likened to a flower. By now the oratory of the city-state, which largely depended on political stimulus, had died (with the exception of a few political speeches), but rhetoric, outliving it, had become the chief tool of education. It flourished in Greek Asia, where particularly exaggerated

importance was attached to form and to a mannered and florid style ('Asianism'; *see* ORATORY [Greek] and ASIANISM AND ATTICISM) against which later Greeks, and some Romans, were to react.

With the decline of the city-state and the loosening of the bond which united its citizens, philosophies arose that gave support to people as individuals, one may suppose, and aimed to bring them peace of mind. The Hellenistic age saw the rise of two new systems, that of Epicurus and that of Zeno and the Stoics; the doctrine of the latter exerted an immense influence not only on the Greek world but later on Rome and ultimately on Christianity. The other schools of philosophy occupied from now onwards a secondary position. After Aristotle's death (322 BC) the Peripatetics under Theophrastus and his successor Strato (d. 269 BC) continued his interest in problems of natural science, but their importance thereafter came to an end. Plato's Academy was likewise eclipsed, until under Arcesilaus and Carneades it resumed some prominence by its adoption of Scepticism.

**He'llespont** The Dardanelles, the strait which connects the Aegean Sea in the northeast to the Propontis (Sea of Marmara), and divides Europe from Asia. For the name *see* HELLE.

**helots** (Gk. *heilōtĕs*) Word of uncertain derivation but probably meaning 'captured', applied to the serfs at *Sparta. They had no political rights and were kept in subjection, but the fact that they were Greek and could live in normal family groups suggests that their status was somewhere between that of chattel slaves (*see* SLAVERY) and free people. However, helots could be killed by their masters with impunity.

**Helve'tii** Celtic tribe from southern Germany which in the first century BC tried to move from its territory through the Roman province of Narbonese Gaul to settle in Gaul proper. They were halted by the Romans and the remnants driven back to their old territory. See COMMENTARIES 1 [book 1].

**Helvi'dius Priscus** (first century AD) A member of the Stoic and republican opposition to the emperor Nero and son-in-law of P. Clodius *Thrasea Paetus, whose political views he shared. He was exiled in AD 66, but returned to Rome two years later. He became violently opposed to the emperor Vespasian perhaps on the issue of Vespasian's insistence that his son would succeed him, and on the role of the senate, and after being again exiled was put to death (perhaps in 75). Helvidius' son (of the same name) by his first marriage was a friend of Tacitus and Pliny the Younger, and was executed c.93.

**Hēphae'stion 1.** Macedonian noble, son of Amyntor, military commander and closest friend of Alexander the Great. He died suddenly in 324 BC. A famous story tells how the mother of the defeated Persian king Darius mistook him for Alexander (a scene painted by Veronese).

**2.** Of Alexandria, second century AD, a Greek metrist. He was the author of a treatise on Greek metres in forty-eight books, of which only an epitome survives; he analysed metres into feet and cola. Much of his value to literature lies incidentally in his quotations from many otherwise lost Greek poems.

**Hēphae'stus** Greek god of fire and of crafts, particularly those in which fire is employed. His origin, like his name, may be non-Greek, and perhaps Asian. In Greek myth he was the child of Zeus and Hera, or of Hera alone, and because he was lame from birth Hera threw him out of Olympus. He fell on Lemnos, an important centre of his cult. According to another version, he intervened on his mother's side in a quarrel between Zeus and Hera, whereupon Zeus seized him by the foot and hurled him down to earth. Hephaestus took his revenge on Hera by ensnaring her in an ingeniously constructed throne where she had to remain until Dionysus made him drunk and brought him back to Olympus to release her. This episode became a favourite subject for vase-painters. With a net of his own devising he also trapped his unfaithful wife Aphrodite with the god Ares. His many famous works of craftsmanship include the armour of Achilles and the necklace of *Harmonia. Hesiod has him create the first woman, Pandora. In Athens, where he was the father of the first king *Erichthonius and so in a sense the ancestor of the Athenians, he had a special cult and a temple above the *Ceramicus, where the shops of the smiths and braziers (as well as the potters) were to be found.

**Hēra** A major figure in the Greek pantheon, the daughter of *Cronus and Rhea, and the sister and wife of Zeus, from which position she derived her authority as queen of the gods. She appears, with Zeus, on a Mycenaean tablet. Her children by Zeus were Hephaestus, Arēs, Hebe, and Eileithyia. She is essentially the goddess of marriage and of married women; but she is never invoked as a mother and never represented as a mother with a child. At Stymphalus in Arcadia she was called simultaneously 'child', 'wife', and 'widow', thus embracing the life of a woman in all its stages. Her depiction in myth is often as the jealous wife outraged by her husband's infidelities and pursuing with vindictive hatred his children by other mothers, e.g. Dionysus and Heracles, as well as the other women he loved, e.g. Io. For her part in the Judgement of Paris see PARIS, JUDGEMENT OF. Her principal temples were at a sanctuary between Argos and Mycenae, and at Samos, where she was said to have been born. But she was worshipped all over Greece, and many important Greek temples are dedicated to her. She was later identified with the Roman Juno.

**Heraclei'dae** The children or the descendants of *Heracles, who fathered by Deianeira several sons, the eldest of whom was Hyllus, and one daughter, Macaria. For their story see HERACLES, CHILDREN OF. The phrase 'Return of the Heracleidae' was often used by the Greeks to refer to the *Dorian invasion; the Dorians claimed connection with Heracles through their kings who were descended from him, and his son Hyllus became a Dorian by adoption: see AEGIMIUS. Hyllus consulted the Delphic oracle to ask how he and his brothers should claim their father's kingdom of Tiryns in Argos (or, according to the Dorians, the whole Peloponnese; in this way they legitimized the Dorian invasion). He was told to await 'the third fruit'. Mistakenly interpreting this to mean the third harvest he duly made his attack on Tiryns three years later but failed and was killed in single combat by Echemus the Tegean. It was subsequently learnt that 'third fruit' meant 'third generation', and when this was reached Temenus and the other Heracleidae conquered the Peloponnese. The territory was divided into three portions: Cresphontes took Messenia, Temenus took Argos, and the sons of Aristodemus, Eurysthenes and Procles, received Lacedaemon, thus founding the dual kingship of Sparta; the Agiad line of the elder twin Eurysthenes, named for his son Agis, had seniority and greater honour. The Spartan kings traced their ancestry back in the male line through Heracles to *Perseus (whose father was Zeus). Perseus' mother was *Danaë, descendant of the Egyptian Danaus. Herodotus (6.52) speaks as if the Egyptian element was well known.

**Heracleides Ponticus** See ASTRONOMY.

**Heraclei'tus 1.** (*c.*540–*c.*480 BC) *Presocratic Greek philosopher who was born and lived his life at Ephesus. Though he could therefore be considered an Ionian philosopher he stands outside the various 'schools' of Greek philosophy. He came from a royal family but surrendered his hereditary privileges to his brother. He was notorious for holding the mass of humanity in contempt, and poets and philosophers fared no better: 'Having much learning does not teach wisdom. Otherwise it would have taught Hesiod and Pythagoras, Xenophanes and Hecataeus . . .' Although Heracleitus is said to have written a book entitled *On Nature* which he deposited in the temple of Artemis, many of the hundred or more fragments that survive in quotations suggest a collection of aphorisms or perhaps short sections rather than a continuous narrative. As they stand they are striking and paradoxical, but, lacking a context and an argument and being rather oracular in style, are difficult to interpret. The Greeks themselves complained of the obscurity of his writings: Aristotle comments on the difficulty of punctuating Heracleitus when it is not clear whether an adverb goes with what precedes it or what follows it (*see* PUNCTUATION). Yet *Diogenes Laertius found occasional brilliance: 'the brevity and weight of his expression are incomparable.'

Heracleitus believed that it is impossible to comprehend fully the reality of things and that appearances are unreliable, but nevertheless that some sort of knowledge is attainable: 'I went in search of myself.' His central concept is of *logos*, a Greek word which can be translated in a variety of ways and which seems to be used by him to denote the 'rationality', i.e. the underlying coherence and unity, of the world, the way in which it functions as a meaningful whole which few understand: 'this *logos* is the case'. But the unity is in a constant process of change: 'all things are in a state of flux (*panta rhei*)'; 'it is impossible to step into the same river twice.' Nature is compared with a taut bowstring, pulled simultaneously in opposite

directions: 'the way up and the way down are one.' The essential stuff of the universe is pure fire, of which some is always being kindled and some being extinguished to form sea and earth; the soul too is composed of fire (Heracleitus is the first Greek philosopher to have a theory, albeit enigmatically expressed, about the functioning of the living *soul: 'it functions best when dry and it is death to become water'). After death the souls of the virtuous join the cosmic fire. In Roman times Heracleitus became known as 'the weeping philosopher', weeping at the spectacle of human life (in contrast with 'the laughing philosopher' *Democritus).

**2.** Of Halicarnassus, a poet and friend of the Hellenistic poet *Callimachus, who wrote a famous epigram on his death.

**3.** Greek grammarian, author of *Homeric Problems*, a work of criticism, which has been tentatively dated *c.*AD 100. In this Heracleitus argues that an allegorical interpretation of the gods in the *Iliad* and *Odyssey* disposes of the problems raised by Homer's apparently mistaken and immoral descriptions of their behaviour. *See* ALLEGORY and BARBARIAN.

**He'raclēs (Hēraklēs)** (Lat. Herculēs) Most famous of the Greek heroes. He was the son of Zeus and Alcmena, whose husband was Amphitryon, grandson of *Perseus. (To beget such a hero Zeus required 'the length of two nights in one'.) His name has been interpreted as meaning 'glorious through Hera', resembling that of an ordinary man in that it has meaning and incorporates the name of a god. But naming him for Hera is inexplicable: she was the wife of Zeus and, always roused to jealousy by his union with other women, human or divine, persecuted the child. In his cradle Heracles strangled two snakes which Hera had sent to kill him, and she pursued him with implacable anger throughout his life. Through his mother Heracles too was descended from Perseus and through Perseus' mother *Danaë from *Danaus. His exploits were known and his cult was observed throughout the Greek world. Famous for his strength, courage, endurance, good nature, and compassion, he was also known for his appetites, gluttony, and lust. Since he was considered the universal helper, he was invoked on every kind of occasion, and commonly called *Alexikakos*, 'averter of evil'. He later became an ideal of human behaviour: as the noble ruler who acts for the good of human-kind and is finally elevated to the gods (Alexander the Great stamped the image of Heracles on his coins), and as the ordinary mortal who, at the end of a life of toil, may hope to join after death the company of the gods. The Stoics and Cynics saw him as an exemplar of fortitude, to the neglect of his other qualities. At all times he caught the popular fancy, and myths, some of them transferred from lesser-known heroes, accumulated about him, including those of the Labours (*see* HERACLES, LABOURS OF). For the story of his birth at Thebes *see* AMPHITRYON.

Heracles was instructed in the various arts by all the greatest experts: by Eurytus, grandson of Apollo, in archery; by *Autolycus in wrestling; by Polydeuces (*see* DIOSCURI) in the use of arms; by *Linus in music. When Linus tried to correct him, Heracles killed him with his own lute. Amphitryon then sent Heracles to tend his flocks on Mount Cithaeron, and there, when 18, he killed a huge lion. Cithaeron was also the setting of 'The Choice of Heracles': as he was pondering which course of life to follow, two women appeared before him, Pleasure and Virtue, one offering a life of enjoyment, the other a life of toil and glory; he chose the latter (*see* PRODICUS). On his return to Thebes, he relieved the city of a tribute it had been forced to pay to Orchomenus, and *Creon, king of Thebes, in gratitude gave him his daughter Megara to marry. Creon's younger daughter married Iphicles (Heracles' twin brother), who already had a son, Iolāus. The latter became Heracles' faithful companion and charioteer. After some years Hera sent a fit of madness upon Heracles, so that he killed Megara and his children under the delusion that they were his enemies (*see* HERACLES, MADNESS OF). After this calamity he went into exile and sought advice from the Delphic oracle on how he might be purified. He was told to go to Tiryns and serve Eurystheus, king of that city, for twelve years, and win immortality by performing the labours which Eurystheus imposed.

There are many different versions of the events of Heracles' life: Euripides' version of Heracles' madness, for example, makes it come upon him after the performance of the Labours; and various reasons are given why Heracles served Eurystheus. Eurystheus is sometimes represented as a coward who would take refuge in a bronze tub when Heracles returned with some monster or other.

Subsequently Heracles married Dēianeira, daughter of Oeneus of Calydon, winning her by defeating the river-god Achelōus in wrestling. When he and Deianeira departed, they came to the flooded river Evenus (in Aetolia). A Centaur, Nessus, carried Deianeira across and tried to rape her, whereupon Heracles shot him with a poisoned arrow. As he lay dying the Centaur advised Deianeira, apparently with friendly intention, to keep some of his blood, which, smeared on a garment, would win back the love of Heracles if he was ever unfaithful to her; this Deianeira did (below).

The following are only a few of the adventures ascribed to Heracles. He accompanied the *Argonauts (*see also* HYLAS) on the early part of their voyage. He rescued Alcestis, wife of *Admetus, from Death. He fell in love with Iole, daughter of Eurytus, king of Oechalia, but her father and brothers would not give her to him. One of these brothers, Iphitus, who had come to Tiryns in search of some lost cattle of his father's, was thrown by Heracles, in a fit of madness, from the walls of the city. For this murder the Delphic oracle sent him into slavery for a year, and he was sold to Omphale, queen of Lydia. There he was set to do a woman's work, in woman's dress, while Omphale took over his lion's skin and club. When his period of servitude was over he led an expedition against *Laomedon, king of Troy. Poseidon at an earlier time had sent a sea-serpent against Troy, and Laomedon had promised Heracles his famous horses if he would kill it, but when the feat was done had refused the reward. Heracles now gathered an army, which included Telamon (father of Ajax) and Peleus (father of Achilles), attacked the city, and captured it. Heracles gave Laomedon's daughter Hesione to Telamon, by whom she became the mother of Teucer.

Finally Heracles attacked Oechalia and carried off Iole. Deianeira, to win him back, followed the advice of Nessus and sent Heracles a robe smeared with the Centaur's blood (above). But this blood had been poisoned by the blood of the Hydra, in which Heracles had dipped his arrows (*see* HERACLES, LABOURS OF 2); the robe clung to Heracles' flesh and caused terrible suffering. To escape from it he had himself carried to the summit of Mount Oeta and placed on a pyre. He gave Iole to his son Hyllus (*see* HERACLEIDAE) and persuaded Poias, father of *Philoctetes, by the gift of his bow and arrows, to light the pyre. He was then carried up to Olympus, reconciled to Hera, and married to her daughter Hebe.

Among the numerous opponents of Heracles at one time or another were Cycnus, a son of Ares, who robbed Apollo of the hecatombs intended to be sacrificed to him at Delphi (the subject of the poem The *Shield of Heracles* attributed to Hesiod); Busiris, king of Egypt, who in order to avert a drought sacrificed strangers who came to his country and attempted to sacrifice Heracles too while the latter was on his way to the Hesperides (*see* HERACLES, LABOURS OF 11); and Eryx, the legendary king of the mountain of that name in Sicily, whom Heracles wrestled with and killed while searching for one of Geryon's cattle which had wandered into his territory. *See also* PROMETHEUS; ANTAEUS; CHIRON; CERCOPES.

The legends of Heracles connected him with both Thebes and Tiryns. For the claim of his descendants to the latter (then extended to the whole Peloponnese) *see* HERACLEIDAE.

**Heracles, Children of** (*Hērakleidai*) Greek tragedy by *Euripides, perhaps produced in the early part of the Peloponnesian War (i.e. *c.*430 BC), possibly intended to remind the audience of the gratitude due to Athens for saving the children of Heracles (the founders of the Dorian race) from the persecution of *Eurystheus, king of Argos.

Heracles is now dead, and his children, together with his nephew and former comrade-in-arms Iolaus, now an old man, have taken refuge from the unremitting persecution of Eurystheus at the altar of Zeus at Athens. The herald of Eurystheus demands their surrender, and, on the refusal of Demophon, king of Athens and son of Theseus, declares war. The soothsayers announce that the sacrifice of a nobly born maiden is necessary to secure the success of the Athenian army, and Macaria, daughter of Heracles, voluntarily offers herself as the victim and is sacrificed. As the army of Eurystheus approaches, Hyllus, eldest son of Heracles, comes to the aid of Athens, and Iolaus, miraculously made young again, joins in the fight and captures Eurystheus. The captive is brought before Alcmena, mother of Heracles, is reviled by her, and ordered off to his death.

**Heracles, Labours of** The number of Labours seems to have been canonized as twelve by the scholars working at Alexandria in the third century BC, but Euripides had already spoken of twelve, and twelve were depicted on the metopes of the temple of Zeus at Olympia (mid-fifth century BC). They were imposed on Heracles by *Eurystheus and according to the most commonly accepted list were as follows.

**The Peloponnesian Labours**

*1. The Nemean Lion,* an invulnerable monster, the offspring of Echidna and Typhon or Orthrus, sent to Nemea in Argos by Hera, to destroy Heracles. Heracles choked the monster in his arms, and clothed himself with its skin, using the beast's own claws, by which alone the skin was penetrable, to separate it from the body.

*2. The Hydra,* the offspring of Echidna and Typhon; it was a poisonous water-snake which lived in the marshes of Lerna near Argos. It had numerous heads; when one was cut off another grew in its place. Moreover Hera sent a huge crab to help it, hence the proverb 'Not even Heracles can fight two', spoken by the hero as he summoned his comrade-in-arms Iolaus. The latter, as Heracles cut off the heads, seared the stumps with burning brands. Heracles then dipped his arrows in the Hydra's blood, which made their wounds incurable (fatally for himself, as it proved; *see* HERACLES). The crab, which Heracles killed by crushing it under foot, became the constellation Cancer.

*3. The Erymanthian Boar.* Heracles' labour in this case was to catch alive the boar that lived on Mount Erymanthus in Arcadia. He drove it into a snowfield, tired it out, and caught it in a net. It was while searching for the boar that he was entertained by Pholus the Centaur, to whom he gave wine. The other Centaurs, lured to the cave by the smell of wine, got drunk and attacked Heracles, who killed many of them.

*4. The Cerynitian Hind.* In the usual version Heracles captures the hind alive after a year-long chase which takes him to the land of the *Hyperboreans. Though female and therefore by nature hornless, this creature was said to have gilded horns and to be sacred to Artemis.

*5. The Stymphalian Birds,* which infested the woods round Lake Stymphālus in Arcadia. Various reasons are given about the need for their destruction. Heracles scared them by means of a bronze rattle (made by Hephaestus), then shot some and drove the rest away.

*6. The Augean Stables.* Augeas, king of Elis, had enormous herds of cattle, like his father Helios.

Heracles, required to clean in one day their stables, which had never been cleaned before, diverted the river Alpheus so that it flowed through the yard. See MOLIONES.

## Labours outside the Peloponnese

*7. The Cretan Bull,* either the bull with which Pasiphaē (*see* MINOS) fell in love, or the one which bore *Europa to Crete. Heracles caught it alive, showed it to Eurystheus, then let it go. It finally settled down near Marathon (*see* THESEUS).

*8. The Horses of Diomedes.* Diomedes, the son of Ares and a nymph Cyrene, and king of the Bistones in Thrace, fed his horses on human flesh. Heracles killed Diomedes and fed his body to the horses, whereupon they became tame and Heracles brought them to Argos.

*9. The Girdle of the Amazon.* Heracles was sent to procure (for the daughter of Eurystheus) the girdle given to Hippolyte, queen of the Amazons, by her father Ares. In the ensuing battle Heracles killed Hippolyte and removed the girdle from her dead body.

*10. The Cattle of Geryon.* In order to obtain the cattle Heracles had to travel to the extreme west where they were pastured on the mythical island of Erytheia ('Red island') in Ocean (*see* OCEANUS). Helios (Sun) so much admired Heracles' boldness in drawing his bow on him when annoyed by the heat that he gave him his golden cup in which to sail to Erytheia. At the end of the journey Heracles erected two pillars (Calpe and Abyla), the Pillars of Hercules, one on each side of the Straits of Gibraltar. Having reached the island Heracles killed the dog Orthrus, the herdsman Eurytion, and lastly Geryon himself, who was a three-headed ogre, and brought away his cattle either in the golden cup, or by a long overland route through Spain, France, Italy, and Sicily, reaching even the Black Sea, and thus having opportunity for many more adventures (*see* CACUS) before he reached home safely.

*11. The Golden Apples of the Hesperides* (daughters of Night). Heracles had to bring back the apples given by Gaia to Hera as a wedding present, and grown on a tree in a garden at the edge of the world. Having forced *Nereus to give him directions he killed Ladon, the dragon guarding them. According to another version he induced *Atlas to fetch the apples, holding up the sky in his place while he did this. Some say that Atlas then refused to resume his burden, and had to be tricked into doing so.

*12. The Descent to the Underworld for *Cerberus* (Heracles' last labour and the only one explicitly mentioned in Homer). Heracles, after preliminary initiation into the Eleusinian *mysteries, and with the help of the gods Hermes and Athena, descended to the Underworld near Cape Taenarum in Laconia. While there he freed Theseus, but was unable to free Peirithous. (*See also* HERACLES, MADNESS OF) This may have been the occasion on which Heracles wounded Hades himself with an arrow, as Homer mentions. Heracles captured and bound the dog Cerberus, brought him to Eurystheus, and then returned him to the Underworld. This myth perhaps suggests that by conquering death Heracles earns his final immortality (*see also* ALCESTIS).

For the Roman Heracles *see* HERCULES.

## Heracles, Madness of (*Hēraklēs mainomenos*) (Lat. *Hercules furens*) Greek tragedy by *Euripides, of uncertain date but perhaps produced *c.*414 BC. It was originally called simply *Heracles.*

Heracles, engaged on the last of his twelve labours, has gone down to the Underworld to bring up the dog *Cerberus. During his long absence Lycus, supported by a faction of Thebans, has killed Creon, king of Thebes and father of Heracles' wife Megara, and seized power. He threatens with death Megara and the three young sons of Heracles (fearing their vengeance in the future) and Heracles' reputed father the now aged Amphitryon. They have taken sanctuary at the altar of Zeus, but Lycus threatens to burn them to death there, and they prepare themselves. At this point Heracles returns, rescues his family, and kills Lycus. But his persistent enemy the goddess Hera sends Lyssa ('madness') who reluctantly seizes on Heracles and drives him to kill his own children (he is under the impression that they are the children of Eurystheus) as well as his wife. Upon recovering from his madness, Heracles is in despair. Thereupon Theseus (whom Heracles brought back from the Underworld in his final Labour) arrives upon the scene, helps to restore his courage, and takes him away to Athens to be purified. Seneca (2) also wrote a Latin tragedy on the subject; *see* HERCULES FURENS.

**He'raclids** The children or descendants of Heracles. *See* HERACLEIDAE and *HERACLES, CHILDREN OF*.

**Heracli'tus** *See* HERACLEITUS.

**Herculā'neum** Ancient Italian town built on a spur projecting from the lower slopes of the volcano Vesuvius and to the west of it, about 8km (5 miles) south-east of Naples. In the first century AD it was a small and wealthy residential town. Like *Pompeii, it was destroyed by the eruption of Vesuvius on 24 August AD 79, but the volcanic matter which flowed over Herculaneum was different. It hardened to form a tufa-like rock, and as a result, although the buildings are more collapsed than at Pompeii, the remains, especially wood and papyrus, being completely sealed in, are better preserved but much more difficult to excavate. The modern town of Resina is built on top of the ancient town. Excavation, or rather treasure-hunting, began in the mid-eighteenth century. More systematic excavation has been carried out since 1987. In one of the luxurious villas nearby, excavated in the eighteenth century, and now known as Villa of the Papyri, a fine collection of sculpture was found (now in Naples museum) and a considerable library of carbonized papyrus rolls containing works on Epicurean philosophy, mainly by *Philodemus of Gadara (fl. 75–35 BC), the influential Epicurean teacher of philosophy. These are now being painstakingly unrolled and deciphered. *See* PISO (1).

**He'rculēs** The Roman name for the Greek hero *Heracles (from *Hercles*, the Italic pronunciation). His was the earliest foreign cult to be brought to Italy, reputedly by Evander but perhaps by the Greek colonists of Magna Graecia. At Rome his altar, the Ara Maxima ('Greatest altar'), stood in the Forum Boarium ('cattle market'); here he was worshipped as the god of victory and of commercial enterprise, and tithes of business profits were offered at the altar. It was here that Aeneas found Evander sacrificing (*Aeneid* 8). The *gens *Fabia* traced its origin to Hercules. His cult had many interesting and unique features.

**Hercules furens** Roman tragedy by *Seneca (2), based on Euripides' play *Heracles* (*see* HERACLES, *MADNESS OF*). There are differences of detail: Lycus, instead of threatening to kill Heracles' children, demands his wife in marriage; and Heracles' murder of her and the children forms part of the on-stage drama.

**Hercules Oetae'us** ('Hercules on Mount Oeta') Roman tragedy by *Seneca (2) (though the authenticity has been doubted), based on the *Trachiniae* of Sophocles. The play is of great length and shows variations from the original, presenting Deianeira not as a gentle and attractive figure but as fiercely jealous, and adding a scene showing Heracles' death and deification on Mount Oeta in Thessaly.

**Here'nnium, Rheto'rica ad** Latin treatise on oratory; *see* RHETORICA AD HERENNIUM.

**Hermae** *See* HERMS.

**Hermaphrodī'tus** In Greek myth, son of Hermes and Aphrodite, who was loved by Salmacis, the nymph of the fountain in which he bathed, near Halicarnassus (Bodrum). She closely embraced him and prayed to the gods to make them one body, which they did. He was worshipped as a god at Athens from the fourth century BC. In art Hermaphroditus is accordingly portrayed as a combined body, a beautiful youth with developed breasts and a soft physique. An inscription at Halicarnassus celebrates Hermaphroditus as 'founder of marriage bonds'. For the Romans the birth of a hermaphrodite was a prodigy of ill-omen, and there are several recorded instances which had to be dealt with by ritual.

**Hermēs** In Greek myth, son of Zeus and *Maia. He was born on Mount Cyllene in Arcadia. By noon on the day he was born he had left his cradle, killed a tortoise, and by using its shell as a sound-box invented the lyre. On the same day he drove off fifty cows belonging to Apollo, making them walk backwards so that they should not be traced, and then returned to his cradle. When Apollo, informed by an old man, arrived in a rage, he was mollified by the gift of the lyre and allowed Hermes to keep the cattle he had stolen and gave him in addition various divine powers. This story is told in the fourth *Homeric Hymn. Hermes is not a major figure in the Greek pantheon but he is already attested as a deity in *Linear B tablets. He seems not to have any original connection with the marker stones, the *herms, as used to be thought, though the Greeks themselves connected the two words. He has no recognized wife, but *Pan is sometimes said to be his son. He was the god of roads and boundaries, the messenger or herald of the gods, and conductor of the souls of the dead to the Underworld, *psychopompos*; he was also Priam's guide to Achilles' tent in the ransoming of Hector's body. He has magical traits: his sandals erase footprints and he knows how to put the enemy camp to sleep. Furtiveness and trickery were his attributes as well: he was the god of luck, particularly in the matter of making money, the patron of merchants and thieves; every lucky find was a *hermaion*, gift of Hermes. He was the patron of athletics, and his statue was commonly erected in gymnasia. In many parts of Greece he was the god of herdsmen and of the fertility of herds. Successful communication with enemies and strangers was due to Hermes, hence the Greek word for interpreter, *hermēneus*; and he gives his name to the art of interpretation, 'hermeneutics'. For this reason he was regarded as the patron of oratory, with an interest in literature generally. He is represented with wings on his sandals, a winged cap or the traveller's broad-brimmed felt hat, and the herald's staff (*kērykeion*, Lat. *cādūcus*) on which two serpents are twined in a broken figure-of-eight shape. His cult was widespread in the Peloponnese, and he had a particularly ancient cult on the Acropolis.

Hermes was identified by the Romans with their god *Mercury. *See also* HERMES TRISMEGISTUS and HERMAPHRODITUS.

**Hermēs Trismegi'stus** ('Thrice-greatest') The Greek god Hermes in Hellenistic times, his identity altered by assimilation to the Egyptian god of magic Thoth, the father and protector of all knowledge. Under this name he was believed to be the author of a collection of Greek and Latin mystical and philosophical ('Hermetic') writings, including astronomy and alchemy, dating probably from the first to the third centuries AD. The aim of this mystical teaching, an aim which can be traced back to Plato, was the deification of humankind through knowledge of God (*gnōsis*).

**Hermī'onē** In Greek myth, daughter of Menelaus and *Helen (of Troy), wife of *Neoptolemus and later of *Orestes.

**Hermo'cratēs** Syracusan politician and general who contributed to Athens' defeat in the *Sicilian Expedition of 415 BC. *See also* CHAEREAS AND CALLIRRHOE.

**Hermo'genēs** (of Tarsus, b. *c.* AD 160) Greek rhetorician, said to be the author of several surviving treatises on rhetoric, the most important of which is *Peri ideōn* ('On types of style'). He finds that orators have many different qualities of style, and distinguishes between seven types with considerable subtlety. They are clarity, grandeur, beauty, rapidity, character, sincerity, and forcefulness. The orator Demosthenes, in Hermogenes' view, is the outstanding exemplar of all these qualities. *Cf.* DEMETRIUS (3) and *LONGINUS ON THE SUBLIME*.

**herms** At Athens most commonly (but also elsewhere in Greece), quadrangular stone or bronze pillars bearing an erect phallus and surmounted by a bust of the god *Hermes (later other gods as well) depicted with old-style pointed beard (*see* HAIR), set up as boundary-marks at crossroads, by the roadside, near public buildings, and in front of houses; some acted as signposts. They replaced the heaps of stones which were the customary ancient boundary marks. Being phallic they were intended to be apotropaic, i.e. to avert evil influences. At Athens some were set up *c.*520 BC by *Hipparchus (1), son of the tyrant Peisistratus, with moral maxims engraved on them. They were regarded with reverence; hence the indignation and alarm felt at Athens when in the course of a night shortly before the departure of the *Sicilian Expedition in 415 BC the herms were mutilated on the face and phallus. *See* HETAIREIAI.

**Hero 1.** Heroine of a love-story known to us from Ovid but perhaps of Hellenistic origin. For her story *see* LEANDER.
   **2.** *See* HERON.

**hero-cult** *See* HEROES.

**Herod** (Gk. and Lat. Hērōdēs, *c.*73 BC–4 BC) Herod the Great, king of Judaea (a Roman protectorate since 63 BC), whose rule was established when Jerusalem was captured from the Parthians by the Romans in 37 BC. He ruled Judaea on the lines of a Hellenistic kingdom, built and adorned cities, gave peace and prosperity, and was a benefactor to the empire at large. But he was tyrannical and unscrupulous, and though he retained Augustus' confidence for many years by his loyalty, his high-handed behaviour and cruelty to his family—he put to death his wife, her two sons, and, just before his death, his own eldest son and heir—lost him Rome's support. Not even his magnificent rebuilding of the Temple won him the affection of the Jews, who hated him for being a foreigner, among other things (he was born in Idumaea, south of Judaea, and became a Roman citizen in 47 BC). He is said to have ordered the slaughter of all the male children in Bethlehem in order to procure the death of the infant Jesus. After his death the kingdom was divided between his remaining sons. His title 'Great' comes from *Josephus.

**Hērō'das** (perhaps **Herondas**) mid-third century BC) A Greek writer of literary *mimes, *mimiambi*, in the Ionic dialect and in scazons (*see* HIPPONAX). He probably lived in Alexandria. Only a few fragments existed in quotation until the publication in 1891 of a papyrus found in Egypt to which other fragments were later added. There now exist mimes 1–7 complete, 8 in a fragmentary state, and scraps of others. These are short, dramatic vignettes; there is no agreement as to whether they were intended for private reading or for solo performance or for a troupe: the form is essentially artificial. They present with lively characterization and humour, and in sophisticated language, scenes typical of mime, drawn from city life: the procuress, the pimp, the schoolmaster, the women worshippers, the jealous mistress, the private conversation about buying a dildo, the shoemaker (who also makes dildoes), the dream, women entertaining.

**Hērō'dēs A'tticus (L. Vibullius Hipparchus Tiberius Claudius Atticus Herodes)** (AD 101–77, the traditional dates) Athenian *sophist and rhetorician, benefactor of Greek cities, born at Marathon of the ancient family of the Aeacidae (descended from Aeacus). He was consul at Rome, with *Fronto, in 143 (by this time an honorary position conferred by the emperor). His fame as an orator, teacher, and public benefactor won him the friendship of powerful men: he enjoyed the support of the emperors Hadrian and Antoninus Pius, and was a tutor of the emperor Marcus Aurelius and his co-emperor Lucius Verus. He claimed descent from Miltiades and called his eldest daughter *Elpinice. With prodigious generosity he endowed public buildings on a grand scale, including at Athens the Panathenaic stadium (in Pentelic marble), the Odeum, and a temple to Fortune. Aulus *Gellius has left an account of pleasant days spent with him at his villa

among the woods of Cephissia (in Attica), which was a literary centre. Virtually none of his writings has survived. His burial site, in the stadium at Athens, has been tentatively identified.

**Hērō'dian 1.** Aelius Hērōdiānus, son of *Apollonius Dyscolus the Greek grammarian. He lived at Rome under Marcus Aurelius (emperor AD 161–80) and wrote in Greek on a number of grammatical subjects. His principal work was a treatise on Greek accents in twenty-one books, of which only epitomes survive. Only one other work is extant, on anomaly. He rejects his father's support of analogy (*see* ANALOGY AND ANOMALY).

**2.** Of Syria (fl. *c.* AD 230). He wrote in Greek a history of the Roman emperors in eight books, from the death of Marcus Aurelius in AD 180 to the accession of Gordian III in 238, being a contemporary observer. His authority is generally preferable to that of the *Historia Augusta*.

**Hero'dotus** (*c.*490–*c.*425 BC) Greek historian, author of the 'Histories' (*Historiai*, 'Inquiries') of the *Persian Wars. He was the son of Lyxes, of a distinguished family in Halicarnassus in Caria, at that time a city of Ionian Greek culture, and a kinsman (nephew or cousin) of the epic poet *Panyassis. As a result of political troubles Herodotus withdrew, or was exiled, to Samos and then travelled widely in the Greek world, including (it would appear) the shores of the Black Sea, south Russia, Babylon, Tyre, Egypt (along the Nile as far as Elephantine), Cyrene, and the coast of Asia Minor. He had no information about the far west of Europe or the Tin Islands (*see* CASSITERIDES). In the mid-440s he visited Athens, and is said to have become acquainted with Pericles there, before reputedly joining the Athenian colony at Thurii (founded 443) near Sybaris in south Italy. He mentions Greek events of the early 420s but none later, and is presumed to have died before 420.

Herodotus has been called by Cicero and others 'the father of history' because in his account of the Persian Wars he was writing on a scale and with a comprehensiveness that had never been attempted before, and with a grasp of the importance these wars had for the future of the Mediterranean world. His History covers a period of some 70 years and extends over most of the known world. Its scope is described in the opening sentence: 'It is an inquiry, *historiē*, undertaken so that the great achievements of Greeks and *barbarians [i.e. non-Greeks, in this case the Persians] may not be forgotten, and in particular, to show how they came to fight one another.' Herodotus may have seen his purpose as akin to that of Homeric epic, namely to record what heroic men have achieved, both Greek and non-Greek, before their achievements are obliterated by time. He was writing a generation after the Persian Wars, and facts were hard to come by. For the most part his sources for the war were not written down; he himself emphasized that his work was based on what he had seen and heard and the conclusions he had drawn. He sought out those who had the information he needed: aristocrats who preserved their family history (information particularly liable to distortion for political or other reasons), and priests and officials who had access to written records; but in foreign countries where he did not know the language he had to rely on interpreters. He was open-minded about the differences between races and peoples. He saw that the ways of the Egyptians were opposite to the ways of everyone else—even the Nile floods in high summer rather than in winter—while the Scythians, who are nomads, are described dispassionately although in most respects he 'cannot admire them'. His History was shaped by many influences. Sometimes, he says, it is impossible for him to decide what is a true record: he has no obligation to believe what he is told. Herodotus understood that the events of history are directly related to earlier events and actions and he sometimes summed them up or indicated their significance by stating a general truth as he saw it, a *gnomē, e.g. 'in everything one must look to the end'. The effect is reassuring. Painful events are narrated without being given a tragic interpretation but Herodotus sees pathos in the brevity and chanciness of human life. He tells the story of Xerxes at Abydos on the eve of his invasion of Greece reviewing the great array of his forces, first congratulating himself and then, astonishingly, bursting into tears at the thought that in a hundred years no man in all that host would still be alive.

The gods intervene in human affairs; their enigmatic communications with mortals in oracles, dreams, and omens cannot be disregarded. But Herodotus understood that on a different, non-religious level, cause and effect operated. His search for explanations of events and his interest in natural causes reveal the

influence of earlier Ionian scientists and *logographers (1), 'writers of tales', especially *Hecataeus, whom he mentions several times. Herodotus' digressions from the main theme of his History, ranging from mere anecdotes to a whole book on Egypt, for example, may be in the manner of such writers, but the boundless curiosity they display is entirely his own. These digressions diversify the work so that parts of it are, in our terms, studies in anthropology, ethnography, and archaeology rather than history.

The History covers the struggle between Greece and Asia from the time of Croesus (mid-sixth century BC) to Xerxes' retreat from Greece (478 BC). It has been regarded as unfinished but it is not clear that Herodotus intended to cover events later than the capture of Sestus from the Persians, which concludes the ninth and last book. It is an abrupt end, but some readers have detected a final ring in the last anecdote; *see* CLOSURE. The division of the work into nine books, each named after a Muse, is probably the scheme of Alexandrian editors; Herodotus himself divided his work into *logoi*, 'episodes'.

To some later Greeks, like Thucydides, Herodotus was a mere storyteller. To others, so improbable did some of his stories seem, he had the reputation of being a liar. Plutarch accused him also of unfairness and uncharitableness (Plutarch came from Boeotia, whose chief town, Thebes, was the bitter enemy of Athens). In modern times Herodotus' attempts to use oral tradition in describing other societies have been better understood, although his veracity is still a matter of dispute. His style is simple, clear, and graceful, and his narrative makes engrossing reading. He wrote in his native Ionic dialect, including archaic and poetic forms; the manuscripts, however, attest forms that it seems unlikely Herodotus could ever have written, the text having been compiled perhaps by later Greek editors ignorant of the correct usage. The following are the principal subjects of the several books:

*Book 1.* What caused the war between Greeks and Persians? After rejecting the abduction of various princesses as the cause, Herodotus gives his view that the story cannot be taken back earlier than Croesus, king of Lydia, whose attack on Cyrus of Persia destroyed his own kingdom (545 BC) and brought Persia into contact with those Greek communities on the Aegean coast of Asia Minor (the Ionians) which

Croesus had absorbed and which were then forced to submit to Persia. Cyrus had already annexed the kingdom of the Medes and continued his expansionist policy until he was killed in battle in 530 BC.

*Book 2.* The next object of Persian expansionism continued by Cyrus' son and successor, Cambyses, was Egypt, to which Herodotus devotes the whole book, writing about its geography, customs, and history.

*Book 3.* The story of Cambyses' conquest of Egypt, continued down to his death in 522 BC after a failed attempt to invade Ethiopia. Herodotus describes the turmoil that followed, with the story of the Persian usurper who impersonated Cambyses' murdered brother Smerdis, and the eventual emergence of the new king Darius I. There are anecdotes of Polycrates, tyrant of Samos, and his seal-ring, the self-mutilation of Zopyrus, and the resultant capture of Babylon by the Persians.

*Book 4.* The unsuccessful attempt of Darius to subdue the nomadic Scythian tribes who lived north and east of the Danube and across south Russia, and Persian north-African expansion in Libya, with geographical and ethnographic accounts of the peoples concerned.

*Book 5.* Persian expansion has now reached the boundaries of Greece. The Persian general Megabazus attacks the Thracians, who are described. The Greeks of Asia Minor attempt to throw off Persian control—the *Ionian revolt. Athenian support for that revolt was to prove fateful. In 498 BC the Ionians burn Sardis, the former capital of Lydia, now under Persian rule.

*Book 6.* The Persians suppress the Ionian revolt and determine to take revenge for Athenian interference. The Persian general Mardonius in 492 BC successfully marches an army to Macedonia but suffers heavy losses. The fleet accompanying them is largely wrecked off Mount Athos, and the Persians retreat. In 490 a seaborne expedition is launched by the Persians under Datis and Artaphernes, and their army is defeated at Marathon. Pheidippides runs from Athens to Sparta. In Herodotus' account events on the Persian side are alternated with events at Sparta and Athens.

*Book 7.* The death of Darius; preparations by Xerxes, his son and heir, for the invasion of Greece; defeat of the Greeks at Thermopylae.

*Book 8.* Victories of the Greeks at Artemisium and Salamis; the withdrawal of Xerxes.

*Book 9.* The victory of the Greeks at Plataea and the retreat of the Persians to the north; the victory of the Greeks at Mycale (on the Asian coast opposite Samos); the capture after siege of Sestus (previously held by the Persians).

**heroes** (Gk. *hērōĕs*) In archaic and classical Greece the Greeks thought that in times past there was living in Greece a race of men and women who were bigger, stronger, braver, and more beautiful than the men and women of their own day. These were heroes and heroines, the offspring or descendants of unions between gods and mortals, but still essentially human. The age in which they lived, the Heroic age, was quite short, embracing no more than two or three generations, and not wholly remote; it was the period of the Theban wars (*see* SEVEN AGAINST THEBES) and the siege of Troy, the latter roughly dated to the early twelfth century BC by the Greeks, who believed both events to be historical. The exploits of the heroes at Thebes and Troy was the stuff of epic poetry, often called in consequence 'heroic' poetry. The fact that Greek myths are dominated by stories about them even more than about gods makes them different from the myths of other cultures, giving them their human scale and interest. It is this aspect of Greek myth that influenced the direction taken by epic and tragedy. The close association of heroes and gods and the gods' interventions in the heroes' lives often give a moral significance to heroic myths and to the characters of the heroes. From the eighth century BC onwards, when the Homeric epics became widely popular (*see* HOMER), some ancient burial sites, or what were thought to be so, came to be regarded as the graves of Homer's heroes, and, since the latter had been superhumanly powerful, sacrifices (though perhaps of lesser value than to a god) were performed at the graves in the hope that in return for cult the heroes would actively defend their own locality, rising from the dead when the need arose. Only *Heracles, exceptional in this as in other respects, was both hero and god, his apotheosis following upon his death. Any community would be glad to have its own hero; aristocratic clans often claimed descent from one. The poet Hesiod, in his myth of the five ages of humankind (*see* WORKS AND DAYS and GOLDEN AGE), described the heroes as constituting the glorious race that existed before this present sadly degenerate age of iron. In practice, however, not all so-called heroes belonged to the Heroic age or were the offspring of gods: ordinary men who were outstanding in some way were sometimes paid heroic honours after death as being the possessors of power that might be channelled to good use: the tyrannicides *Harmodius and Aristogeiton, and the Spartan general *Brasidas, among others, were so honoured after death.

The Romans had lists of their heroes in the sense of 'great men who saved the state'; they included the Decii, Marius, Camillus, the Scipios, Curius, and Fabricius.

**Heroic age** *See* HEROES.

**heroic poetry** *See* HEROES and EPIC POETRY.

***Hērō'idēs*** ('Heroines', perhaps originally *Hērōidum epistulae*, 'Letters of heroines') Latin amatory poems in elegiacs by *Ovid, in the form of letters purporting to be addressed by heroines of legend to their lovers or husbands, though they read rather like dramatic monologues. In the first fourteen letters women address men (the authenticity of the fifteenth letter, from Sappho to Phaon, is doubted); letters 16–21 are in pairs, the woman answering the man's letter. It used to be thought that this last group was not by Ovid. The first group was published between the two editions of the *Amores*, i.e. towards the end of the first century BC; the second group perhaps in the earliest years of the first century AD, before Ovid's exile in AD 8. He claimed that they constituted a new literary form, invented by him.

The letters of the heroines are studies of love from the woman's point of view, based perhaps on Ovid's own observation but also on the rhetorical study of character-drawing; the sentiments and moral standpoint are those of Rome in Ovid's day. Applied to the tragic women of mythical times, this technique occasionally adds piquancy and touches of humour to their ingenious arguments. Euripides was clearly a source. The heroines are represented in various situations: betrayed or deserted (Deianeira, Phyllis, Medea, Ariadne, Oenone, Dido), neglected (Briseis), bound in a hateful marriage (Hermione), punished for their love (Hypermnestra, Canace), the victim of unlawful passion (Phaedra), or anxious for

their husbands' safety (Penelope, Laodamia). *Cf.* CATALOGUE OF WOMEN.

**Heron** (Lat. Hero; of Alexandria, first century AD) Greek engineer, inventor, and mathematician. It is likely that he drew on the work of his predecessors Ctesibius and *Archimedes. Of his many inventions some seem to have been mainly for interest or entertainment rather than practical application. His surviving written work (some of it only through Arabic) includes the following: *Automata*, on a variety of mechanical devices; *Catoptrica*, on optics and mirrors; *Mechanica*, in three books, on devices for lifting and transporting heavy weights; *Metrica*, in three books, on calculating the properties of geometrical figures, including Heron's formula for the area of a triangle; *Pneumatica*, in two books, on devices using the motive power of air, steam, or water. They include the so-called aeolipile (a primitive turbine driven by the reaction from steam jets), water-organs, siphons, and a coin-operated water dispenser.

**Hērondas** *See* HERODAS.

**Hēro'philus** (from Chalcedon, fl. first half of the third century BC) One of the great founders (with *Erasistratus) of Greek medicine at Alexandria. He made his mark primarily by his study of human anatomy based on human dissection; he is alleged by *Celsus to have practised vivisection on convicted criminals. His writings (which survive only in quotation) included a reasonably accurate account of the liver; he correctly opposed the orthodoxy of his day that the veins originated there. His dissections of the genital organs, the eye, and the brain were famous; his names for some of the main sections and chambers of the brain still survive, in their Latin form. The term 'duodenum' is his also, a translation of the Greek *dōdekadaktylos ekphysis*, 'twelve fingers in length'. He established that the brain and not the heart was the centre of the nervous system (as in his way did the Hippocratic author of *On the Sacred Disease*; *see* HIPPOCRATES (1) and ANATOMY AND PHYSIOLOGY 1), making for the first time the distinction between motor and sensory nerves. The vascular system was not understood by the physicians of his day, and no connection was seen between heartbeat and pulse-beat. Herophilus probably accepted that the arteries contained blood (not air, as was generally thought), and certainly believed that pulse-beat was caused by the normal contraction and dilation of the arteries, though he did not understand that the blood circulated through the arteries because of the pumping action of the heart. He invented a portable water-clock (*clepsydra*) to measure pulse-rate. He also increased the use of drugs, coining the happy description of them as 'the hands of the gods'. His pathology, however, showed no advance on that of his predecessors; having no knowledge of bacteria, he believed, as did almost everyone else, that disease was caused by an imbalance of *humours. In his treatise *Midwifery* he made clear his belief that although certain conditions are experienced by women there is no disease peculiar to them (*see* GYNAECOLOGY). The information about him that survives attests a man of great intellectual ability, wisdom, and humour.

**Hērōs** ('Hero') Greek comedy by *Menander, of which small fragments survive.

**Hē'siod (Hēsiodos)** (lived *c.*700 BC) One of the earliest-known Greek poets and, with Homer, representative of early Greek *epic poetry. He tells us himself something of his life: his father gave up his livelihood of sea-trading as being unprofitable and moved from Cyme in Aeolis (on the coast of Asia Minor) to Ascra in Boeotia, where Hesiod was born, to become a farmer. As Hesiod was tending the sheep on Mount Helicon he heard the *Muses calling him to become a poet and sing of the gods (*Theogony* 22). He once took part in a poetic contest at funeral games at Chalcis in Euboea and won a tripod. On his father's death the estate was divided between Hesiod and his brother Perses; the latter claimed more than his share and a dispute ensued in which Perses bribed the authorities to favour him. Hesiod is said to have died in Locris, but his tomb was shown at Orchomenus in Boeotia. The story of his meeting and contest with Homer (*see* CERTAMEN HOMERI ET HESIODI) is certainly untrue. Two genuine poems of his survive, the *Theogony* and the *Works and Days*. A third short poem, the *Shield of Heracles*, is not genuine. The *Catalogue of Women*, thought by the ancient Greeks to be by Hesiod, exists only in fragments. Among other works attributed to him, of which only small fragments survive, are the *Precepts of Chiron*, the *Melampodia* (stories of famous seers), and an *Astronomy*. In the *Works and Days* Hesiod sought his subject from outside the field of myth (*see* DIDACTIC POETRY), and much of the poem seems to derive from his

own experience and to reveal his own character. He wrote in the same oral tradition as Homer, using the epic dialect, but perhaps at a later stage of its evolution.

**Hespe'ria** [Lat., 'the western land', from Gk. *hespera*, 'west'] For Greeks, a term often denoting Italy; for Romans, Spain.

**Hespe'rids** In Greek myth, the daughters (numbering from three to seven) of Night (Nyx) and Darkness (*Erebus) who lived in the extreme west beyond the Atlas mountains, on the edge of Ocean (*see* OCEANUS), guarding a tree which produced golden apples (*see* HERACLES, LABOURS OF 11), a present from Gaia to Hera at her marriage to Zeus. The tree was also watched by the dragon Ladon (whom Heracles killed before taking the apples). From the same tree came the apples thrown down before *Atalanta.

**He'sperus** (Gk.; Lat. Vesper) The evening star.

**He'stia** ('Hearth') In Greek myth, the virgin daughter of *Cronus and Rhea, goddess of the hearth and symbol of the home and family. In Mycenaean times the hearth was the centre of the king's throne-room. Since the goddess never left the house she was hardly anthropomorphized, and has virtually no mythology; Homer never mentions her. When a new baby, bride, or new slave was accepted into the family various rituals centred on Hestia marked the initiation. A hearth with ever-burning fire was consecrated to her in the chief public building (*prytaneum*) of every capital city (and at Delphi and Olympia); fire from this was taken to every new colony of that city. Sacrifices began with libations to Hestia and she was mentioned first in prayers; the beginning of a meal was marked by small offerings being thrown on to the fire. The Romans worshipped her as *Vesta. *See* GODS.

**Hēsy'chius** (probably fifth century AD) Alexandrian Greek lexicographer, author of a work on rare words now known only from one badly preserved fifteenth-century manuscript, itself a considerable abridgement of the original work. Even so it is a valuable aid for the study of Greek poetry and dialects, and it often preserves correct readings which have been replaced in Greek literary texts by easier synonyms.

**hetai'ra** (pl. *hetairai*, 'female companions') In Greece, a euphemistic name for women paid for sexual favours. The term is usually taken to indicate a higher class of prostitute than that denoted by *pornē* (a female slave bought for prostitution), implying beauty and some degree of accomplishment and culture offering the opportunity for sophisticated entertainment (the model in modern eyes is Pericles' mistress *Aspasia). They associated with men outside the brothel, in society. The various stories told about the famous *hetairai* credit them with wit and character. Some were foreign women who, at Athens after the law passed in 450 BC, could not marry Athenian citizens (*see* NEAIRA), but most would have been slave-women of promise who bought or otherwise acquired their freedom. Those who associated with Neaira included the orator *Lysias and the general Chabrias. The *hetairai* acquired social distinction themselves and conferred similar distinction on the men they chose to associate with, in return for large sums of money. We learn about fictitious *hetairai* from Greek New Comedy (*see* COMEDY [Greek 6]), where they inspire infatuation in rich young men, have hearts of gold, and turn out to be marriageable when revealed to be of citizen birth but carried off by war, pirates, or brigands. For individual *hetairai see also* LAÏS; LEONTION; PHRYNE; THAÏS.

**hetaireiai** At Athens, clubs, associations of *hetairoi*, 'comrades', usually young men of the upper class linked by social and political ties. The mutilation of the *herms in 415 BC was said to be the work of a *hetaireia* to which *Andocides belonged.

**hetairoi** The 'Companions' of the Macedonian kings who personally selected them as officers of state and as their own cavalry bodyguard. Alexander the Great called all the cavalry, not merely an elite unit, 'Companion Cavalry'.

**heterosexuality** *See* LOVE AND SEXUALITY.

**hiā'tus** ('gap') In Greek and Latin poetry, a break in a line when a vowel at the end of one word is not elided before a vowel at the beginning of the next, as it would be by normal scansion (*see* ELISION). If the earlier vowel is long it may retain its length or be shortened. Hiatus is common in Greek epic verse (*see* CORREPTION), rare in Latin epic. In Greek prose

there is a tendency to avoid hiatus on the part of some writers—Plato in his later works, Demosthenes, and, to an amazing extent, Isocrates (Dionysius of Halicarnassus could not find a single example in the *Areopagiticus*).

In Latin poetry hiatus occurs occasionally in Plautus, and also in Virgil at a caesura or strong sense-break. Horace in the *Odes* avoids hiatus even at the ends of lines, and from Ovid onwards hiatus is rare. In Latin prose it was unnecessary to avoid what looks like hiatus because the tendency was to run vowels together when speaking.

**Hī'eron, I and II** (unrelated) Rulers of *Syracuse.

**Hi'eron** One of the minor works of the Athenian *Xenophon (428–c.354 BC). It is an imaginary dialogue between Hieron I, tyrant of Syracuse, and Simonides the poet, in which the lot of the tyrant is compared with that of the private citizen; Hieron points out the disadvantages of the former, while Simonides shows how a tyrant, by ruling well, may make himself popular and so acquire happiness.

**Hiero'nymus** (of Cardia, third century BC) The contemporary and apparently trustworthy Greek historian of the period from the death of Alexander the Great (323 BC) to the death of Pyrrhus, king of Epirus, in 272 BC, or perhaps as late as 263. He served as general and statesman under Eumenes of Cardia, c.361–316 BC (who had himself wielded considerable power first as secretary to Philip II, and then Alexander, and held high military command under the *Diadochi). He then went to the court of Antigonus I (one of Alexander's generals), his son Demetrius Poliorcetes, and his grandson Antigonus Gonatas, and thus had first-hand knowledge of the events he related. Although his history is largely lost it is the most important source behind Arrian and Diodorus Siculus (books 18–20), and was used by Plutarch for his Lives of Eumenes, Pyrrhus, and Demetrius, as well as by *Justin.

**Hī'mera** Greek city on the north coast of Sicily, founded c.648 BC by colonists from Zancle in the east of the island, itself a colony of Euboea founded in the previous century. Its most famous citizen was the poet Stesichorus. It was the scene in 480 BC of a spectacular defeat of a Carthaginian expedition (aiming to restore a tyrant) by Gelon, tyrant of Syracuse, and Theron of Acragas. In 400 BC Carthage took revenge and obliterated it.

**Hīme'rius** (AD *c*.310–*c*.390) Greek rhetorician from Bithynia, twenty-four of whose ceremonial speeches survive. They are incidentally valuable for their quotations from Greek lyric poetry otherwise lost. Himerius' pupils at Athens included the Christian Fathers St Gregory of Nazianzus and St Basil.

**Hippa'rchia** *See* CRATES.

**Hippa'rchus 1.** Younger son of *Peisistratus, tyrant of Athens, who was closely associated with his brother *Hippias (1) when the latter ruled Athens after the death of their father in 527 BC. Known particularly as a patron of literature and art, he was murdered by *Harmodius and Aristogeiton in 514 BC.
  **2.** (*c*.190–after 126 BC) Reputedly the greatest of ancient astronomers, who transformed Greek *astronomy from a theoretical science to one based on observation. He was a Greek born at Nicaea in Bithynia but later living in Rhodes. His only surviving work is a three-book commentary on the *Phaenomena* of *Eudoxus and *Aratus, and most of our knowledge of his other work comes from the *Almagest*, the astronomical textbook of *Ptolemy (second century AD). He made extensive observations of the positions of stars, and may have produced the first known catalogue; his recorded observations date from 147 to 127 BC. His investigations included calculating both the distance of the moon (combining observation with a mathematical understanding of parallax) and the length of the year. This latter seems to have led to a most notable achievement, the discovery of the precession of the equinoxes, i.e. the slight change in the timing of the equinoxes in each successive year due to the changing angle of the earth's axis. It may also be the case that he was the first to construct a table of chords, thus making possible the solution of problems in trigonometry. He is the first Greek astronomer to show considerable knowledge of Babylonian astronomical records and to use extensively their arithmetical procedures (*see* BABYLONIA), as well as being perhaps the first in Greece to make it possible properly to predict both lunar and solar eclipses. Hipparchus also wrote on *astrology, and his much more accurate calculations of the positions of the heavenly bodies may well have contributed to its subsequent expansion in popularity.

**hippeis** ('knights', 'the cavalry') At Athens, one of the names of the top social class; under *Solon, the second of his census-classes, those sufficiently wealthy to keep a horse. Before the fifth century BC most cavalrymen probably rode their horse to battle and then fought on foot. The Athenian cavalry became a properly organized force of a thousand horse only after the Persian Wars (and the Spartans not until 424 BC). They were not a battle-winning contingent, as the Macedonian cavalry became, because their weapon was the throwing javelin. The Macedonians instituted the thrusting lance which made it possible to break up infantry. For Aristophanes' play *see* KNIGHTS.

**Hi'ppias 1.** Eldest son of *Peisistratus, tyrant of Athens, and himself tyrant from 527 to 510 BC, in association with his brother *Hipparchus (1). Hipparchus was assassinated in 514 (*see* HARMODIUS AND ARISTOGEITON). At first a mild ruler, Hippias became harsher as his reign progressed. During his reign the Spartans under *Cleomenes I invaded and were repulsed, but a second invasion in 510 forced him to withdraw from Athens to the colony of Sigeum and thence to the court of the Persian king Darius. He was with the Persian forces when they were defeated by the Greeks at Marathon in 490 BC. The Attic coinage stamped with the owl probably began in his reign, as did the building of several notable temples.
  **2.** Of Elis, a *sophist of the later fifth century BC, a contemporary of Socrates, whose vast range of learning included grammar, poetry, mathematics, and astronomy. He is vividly depicted in two of Plato's dialogues, *Hippias Minor* and *Major* (the latter less certainly by Plato). He is commonly said to have compiled a list of victors at the Olympian games for chronological purposes. None of his voluminous works survives. *See* SEVEN LIBERAL ARTS.

***Hippias Major*** Dialogue attributed to *Plato although inconsistencies of Greek style and argument make it hard to date and have led some scholars to doubt its authenticity. *Hippias of Elis, the sophist, is presented for humorous effect as stupid and self-satisfied. Socrates engages with him, on behalf of a difficult friend, in an enquiry into 'the beautiful'. This search for a definition ends in failure.

***Hippias Minor*** Dialogue of *Plato in which Socrates shows the sophist *Hippias of Elis, by a sophistic argument, that one who does evil intentionally is less blameworthy than one who does it unintentionally.

**hi'ppikēs, Peri** See HORSEMANSHIP.

**Hippoclei'dēs** Athenian who won immortality through an anecdote in Herodotus. He had become the favourite with *Cleisthenes (1), tyrant of Sicyon, to marry the latter's daughter. At the feast at which Cleisthenes' choice was to be made known Hippocleides ordered the *aulos*-player to play a dance and 'probably danced to his own satisfaction', concluding by standing on his head and gesticulating with his legs, but he gravely displeased his intended father-in-law. 'Son of Teisandros, you have danced away your marriage', he was told; his reply, 'Hippocleides doesn't care', became proverbial. (The daughter Agariste later married Megacles of the family of the Alcmaeonidae: their son was *Cleisthenes (2), the great reformer of the Athenian constitution.)

**Hippo'cratēs 1.** The first famous figure in Greek *medicine, a contemporary of Socrates (b. 469 BC), born in the island of Cos. He is said to have died at Larissa (in Thessaly). Scarcely anything is known about his life; yet the attitudes apparent in the writings that go under his name as well as the medical practice they describe are attributed to him personally. The former still express the ethical ideal of a doctor, and the latter too has exerted a very strong influence until comparatively recent times. He is mentioned several times by Plato, who quotes his obscure claim that one cannot understand the nature of the body without understanding the nature of the whole. The large collection of medical writings known as the Hippocratic Corpus consists of some sixty treatises, all in the Ionic Greek dialect, most of which were compiled between c.430 and 330 BC and gathered together in the third century BC. There is no evidence that Hippocrates wrote any of them personally. They may represent the contents of the library of the Hippocratic school of medicine associated with the healing shrine of the god *Asclepius on Cos. The works cover surgery, epidemiology, pharmacology, embryology, and anatomy, including treatises on prognosis and general health-care, in some cases propounding widely differing medical doctrines. Hippocrates seems to have believed in the four *humours, based on *Empedocles' theory of the four elements.

Of two fifth-century works which Hippocrates could have written himself, *On Airs, Waters and Places* and *On the Sacred Disease* (epilepsy), the former discusses the effect of climate, water supply, and region on people, and compares the geophysical conditions of life in Europe and Asia. The latter attacks popular superstitions about the disease, condemning supposed remedies that employ magic and *purifications, and demonstrates (by examining the brain of an epileptic goat) that, no differently from any other disease, epilepsy, 'the sacred disease', arises from natural causes. The *Epidemics* contain the interestingly detailed case-book studies of over 40 patients with serious illnesses (of which most of the patients died); books 1 and 3 appear to date from the fifth century. The *Aphorisms* or collection of medical sayings contain the famous dictum: 'Life is short, science (*technē*) long, opportunity fleeting, experiment dangerous, judgement difficult.' The Hippocratic Oath, in which the doctor swears, among other things, never to administer poison, use the knife, abuse his patients, or break their confidences, seems to have originated in a particular group of medical practitioners, but most of the ideals it expresses are common to all. In the Middle Ages 'Ypocras' became a favourite subject with European storytellers in tales of magic and intrigue, as was 'Bokrát' among Arabic writers, who represented him as studying in a garden near Damascus.

**2.** (of Chios, c.470–400 BC) The first Greek mathematician of whose work, at Athens in the late fifth century BC, we have evidence. His writings are lost, but he would appear to have been the first to collect together an *Elements of Geometry* (the forerunner of Euclid's *Elements*), which probably contained the propositions known to the Pythagoreans. He was an early contributor to the classical problems of doubling the cube and squaring the circle. The latter is referred to by his contemporary Aristophanes in the *Birds*, so these problems must have become familiar by Hippocrates' time.

**Hi'ppocrēne (Hippokrēnē)** Fountain sacred to the Muses on Mount *Helicon in Boeotia (*see* PEGASUS), supposedly with the power to inspire with poetry those who drank from it.

**Hippodamei'a 1.** In Greek myth, daughter of Oenomaus of Pisa in Elis and wife of *Pelops.

**2.** In Greek myth, wife of Peirithŏus, king of the Lapiths (*see* CENTAURS and THESEUS).

**Hippoda'mus** (of Miletus, fifth century BC) The most famous Greek town-planner. In the mid-fifth century he planned the town of *Piraeus around the original sea-port, substituting broad straight streets intersecting at right angles in place of crooked, narrow streets. He was also the architect of the Athenian colony of Thurii (near Sybaris) in 443 BC and may have been responsible for its rectangular plan. According to one tradition he planned the city of Rhodes, founded in 408 BC.

**Hippo'lytē (Hippolyta)** In Greek myth, queen of the Amazons, sometimes called Antiopē; *see* HERACLES, LABOURS OF 9 and THESEUS.

**Hippo'lytus** In Greek myth, the son of *Theseus and the Amazon queen Hippolyte; after the latter's death Theseus married *Phaedra, the sister of Ariadne. During his absence Phaedra fell in love with Hippolytus who rejected her advances. Moreover, as a devotee of the goddess Artemis he led a life of perfect chastity. Phaedra subsequently hanged herself, after writing a letter to Theseus denouncing Hippolytus as her seducer. Theseus, not believing his protestations of innocence, banished him, and also used against him one of the three curses which he had been given by the god Poseidon. As Hippolytus drove away from the palace along the shore a monster or bull sent from the sea by Poseidon terrified the horses; Hippolytus was thrown from the chariot and dragged to his death. Theseus learned of his error from Artemis too late. Hippolytus had a cult at Troezen (north-east Peloponnese), the scene of his death, which included laments for him and offerings of hair from girls about to marry. Virgil and other authors relate that Hippolytus was brought back to life by *Asclepius and was conveyed by *Diana (the Roman equivalent of Artemis) to the grove of the nymph Aricia at Nemi in Latium, where under the name of Virbius (*vir bis*, 'a man twice') he lived out his days. His son by Diana, also called Virbius according to Virgil, was among the heroes who resisted the settlement of Aeneas in Latium.

**Hippo'lytus** Greek tragedy by *Euripides produced in 429 BC. For the story *see* HIPPOLYTUS. Euripides makes Phaedra a virtuous woman trying to resist her passion, her feelings betrayed to Hippolytus by her nurse. The false accusation Phaedra makes in the letter to Theseus was motivated, according to Euripides, by shame and anger at Hippolytus' scorn. *See also* PHAEDRA, the Roman tragedy by Seneca (2).

**Hippŏ'nax** (of Ephesus, mid-sixth century BC) Greek poet of satirical, often scurrilous, verse which survives only in quotation or papyrus fragments. He invented his own version of the iambic trimeter, making it end with a spondee, the so-called 'limping iambic' or scazon. Banished from Ephesus he moved to Clazomenae, another Ionian city, where according to one of his poems he lived in great poverty. Although the poems we have are few and fragmentary, enough remain to show his mordant wit, realism, and vigorous use of earthy Greek laced with colloquialisms and words from local dialects. He attacked his enemies with gusto. The best known (apocryphal) story about him relates his quarrel with the sculptor Bupalus and his brother Athenis, who made a statue caricaturing the features of the poet. He retaliated with such offensive verse that they both hanged themselves. Hipponax is sometimes credited, not impossibly, with the invention of parody.

**Hi'rtius, Aulus** One of Julius Caesar's lieutenants in Gaul. He was praetor in 46 BC and governor of Transalpine Gaul in 45. In 43 after Caesar's assassination he was consul with Vibius Pansa; in the subsequent fighting Cicero persuaded him to take arms against Mark Antony, who was besieging Mutina. The two consuls, together with Octavian, raised the siege but were both killed (*see* BRUTUS (3)). Hirtius added the eighth book to Caesar's *Gallic War* (*see* COMMENTARIES 1) and probably wrote the *Bellum Alexandrinum* as well.

**Hispa'nia** *See* CAESAR (2)1.

**Histiae'us** Greek tyrant of the Ionian Greek city of Miletus who accompanied the Persian king *Darius on his expedition to Scythia, c.514 BC. Darius, having rewarded him for loyal service with a district in Thrace where he built the strategically important city of Myrcinus, grew distrustful of him, especially when he failed to prevent the Ionian revolt (*see* PERSIAN WARS). He had no part in the battle at Lade. Histiaeus took to piracy, at one time occupying Byzantium. In 494/3 he was captured by the Persian satrap Artaphernes and crucified, having been unjustly held responsible for fomenting the Ionian revolt. It is difficult to make sense of his reported manoeuvrings.

**Histo'ria anima'lium** ('Inquiry into animals'; the usual English title is 'History of animals') Treatise by Aristotle; *see* ANIMALS, ARISTOTLE ON.

**Histo'ria Augu'sta** Name given by the Swiss scholar Casaubon in the early seventeenth century to a collection of biographies of Roman emperors, and certain heirs and claimants to the empire, from Hadrian to Numerianus (AD 117–284, with a gap between 244 and 259). The biographies are attributed to six authors: Aelius Spartianus, Julius Capitolinus, Volcatius Gallicanus, Aelius Lampridius, Trebellius Pollio, and Flavius Vopiscus, who, according to the manuscripts, lived in the time of Diocletian and Constantine I. Nothing is known of the authors. It was long assumed that the biographies were written in the reigns of these emperors in the early fourth century, and they are our only continuous account of the history of the emperors in the second and third centuries (and so used by Edward Gibbon in *Decline and Fall of the Roman Empire*). However, study of the style has led some to believe that the collection is the work of only one author, perhaps writing at the very end of the fourth century. It is now clear that the documents cited in the *Historia* are mostly forgeries, and the author's purpose in compiling the collection has been variously described, as intended to entertain readers with sensational stories or even as a veiled pagan attack on Christianity. The historical value of the narrative is doubtful, but research is leading to an understanding of how the text can be used as a historical source.

## historians

**Greek.** All of those named below wrote in Greek (some on Roman history) and have their own entries: Apollodorus, Appian, Arrian, Callisthenes, Cassius Dio, Ctesias, Diodorus Siculus, Dionysius (3) of Halicarnassus, Ephorus, Eratosthenes (2), Eusebius, Herodian (2), Herodotus, Josephus, Onesicritus, Plutarch, Polybius, Poseidonius, Theopompus, Thucydides, Timaeus, and Xenophon; *see also* LOGOGRAPHERS (1).

**Roman.** The following wrote in Latin: Ammianus Marcellinus, Caesar, Cremutius Cordus, Curtius, Eutropius, Festus, Florus, Hirtius, Jerome, Justin, Livy, Nepos, Orosius, Sallust, Si-senna, Suetonius, Tacitus, Trogus, Valerius Maximus, and Velleius Paterculus.

*See also* ANNALES; ANNALS; HISTORIA AUGUSTA; HISTORIOGRAPHY.

**Histories, The** (*Historiae*) A work by the Roman historian *Tacitus. Originally twelve or fourteen books long, it dealt with the period AD 69–96, from Galba to Domitian, but only the first four books and part of the fifth survive, covering the events of the 'Year of the Four Emperors', 69, and the first nine months or so of 70. The books were published, perhaps in instalments, between AD 105 and 108, and were written before the *Annals*. Portions were revised by the Younger Pliny, who sometimes furnished Tacitus with material, e.g. the account of the eruption of Vesuvius in AD 79 which caused the death of Pliny's uncle and namesake.

*Book 1* opens with a survey of how, after the prosperous security of the *Julio-Claudian dynasty, the empire is shaken by palace conspiracies, sudden murders, the armies moving on Rome from the frontiers, the frontiers themselves overrun by barbarians, the times 'rich in tragedies, terrible with battles, torn by civil strife'; even the Capitol is set on fire by citizens. It describes the brief reign of Galba, his adoption of Piso Licinianus, and the intrigues of Otho with the military which brought about the murder of Galba and Piso and Otho's own accession in 69. Tacitus brilliantly portrays the emperor Galba, his mediocrity, 'rather free from vices than endowed with virtues', the stinginess which was his undoing, his high birth and military reputation thanks to which he would have been judged 'equal to the imperial office had he not held it' (for the Latin *see* GALBA). The narrative passes to the mutinous conduct of the legions in Germany, their adoption of Vitellius as emperor, the movement of his forces under Valens and Caecina, the negotiations between Otho and Vitellius, the shifting allegiances of provinces and legions, and the outbreak of civil war.

*Book 2* turns to the important role that the commanders Vespasian and Titus were playing in the East, where, except for the resistance of Jerusalem, the war against the Jews had been concluded. Vespasian and Mucianus, governor of Syria, decide to await developments. Tacitus then returns to events in Italy, the fighting around Bedriacum (on the road between Verona and Cremona), and the suicide of

Otho, death seeming the only honourable course open to him. The reign of Vitellius is described, the emperor's sloth and gluttony, the disorder in the legions, the wasteful administration, and the threat of the advance of Vespasian's forces under Mucianus.

*Book 3* describes the operations of Vespasian's generals against Vitellius, the siege and the terrible sack and burning of Cremona, the fighting in Rome between partisans of the opposing forces, which leads to the burning of the Capitol, the final capture of the city, and the end of Vitellius, discovered wandering forlornly in the deserted palace and put to death (December 69). The author's gift for sombre depiction is seen at its most powerful in this book.

*Book 4* and the surviving portion of book 5 are occupied with the reign of Vespasian, the rising of the Batavians under Civilis, and the expedition of Titus against Jerusalem (the account of the siege is lost).

## historiography

**Greek.** Greek prose history was first written in the late sixth century BC in Ionia. Coinciding with the development of early science and philosophy in that part of the Greek world, a rational and systematic approach was applied not only to local traditions and the more broadly spread myths of epic poetry, but also to the information gathered by seafaring people about the coastline and harbours, people, customs, and local history of the Mediterranean. These historians were the so-called *logographers, 'prose writers', of whom the most influential was *Hecataeus of Miletus (c.500 BC), but their work survives only in fragments. They wrote both local and general (not necessarily Greek) history. Local histories continued to be written throughout the fifth and fourth centuries; those of Attica for example (*see* ATTHIS) form much of the basis of Aristotle's *Constitution of the Athenians* (*see* ATHENAION POLITEIA). Lists of annual magistrates and similarly regular recurrences were also compiled with the aim of establishing a chronological framework, e.g. of eponymous archons at Athens, priestesses of Hera at Argos, and victors in the footrace at Olympia. (*See* TIMAEUS.)

Greek history proper begins with the full-scale *historiai*, i.e. 'inquiries', of Herodotus (b. c.490 BC); the word soon acquired its more restricted meaning. Herodotus' work established the large scale of history, and his all-embracing curiosity, which made him include in his work, as well as history in its restricted sense, what we would now term archaeology, ethnography, geography, religion, and a fair amount of anecdote, might well have established also its scope. His rejection of myth was important, as was his limiting his work to historical time and to what could, up to a point, be checked. His intellectual successor is in some sense Aristotle, writing treatises over a wide range of historical and scientific subjects. Thucydides (b. c.460 BC) writing later than Herodotus, and choosing to write on contemporary history in which he himself had played some part, was able to apply much more rigorous standards of factual accuracy than had been possible for Herodotus. He criticizes his immediate predecessors (left unnamed, but certainly including Herodotus) for writing what is merely entertaining to listen to for the moment, rather than what is true and has permanent value. He not only aimed to relate what actually happened; his passion for generalization led him to write on such large matters as the underlying cause, *aitia*, of the Peloponnesian War, the behaviour of oligarchs and democrats, and the dynamics of imperialism. His influence narrowed the scope of history, turning it in the direction of war and politics almost before it had set off along the path Herodotus had indicated. Thucydides' combination of generalization with (apparent) factual accuracy was difficult to sustain, and no later Greek historian made the attempt. By including speeches he, like Herodotus, was imitating Homer, and initiating a historical style that would have a long following. His analytical style was more difficult for others to imitate; Polybius (b. c.200 BC; below) came closest to it.

The Hellenistic age witnessed both the vast conquests of Alexander the Great and his successors (the *Diadochi) and then the passing of these conquests and Greece itself into Roman control, and the consequent expansion of information and knowledge required historians to explain the new complexity of the world. Their work was made possible by the growth of libraries and facilities for scholarship in Alexandria and Pergamum, and later at Rome. Most of their writing is now lost, but the fragmentary remains of around a thousand histories quoted by later authors are still being sifted and studied to produce a clearer picture of their content. The classical historians Herodotus, Thucydides, and Xenophon as well as the later Theopompus and Ephorus were still closely read, in part for reasons of prose style. Rhetoric, particularly that of *Isocrates, was a strong influence on the last two, who were the first to aim at universal history, a genre which was to prove significant. As Polybius writes in his Introduction, after the Second Punic War history became a unified whole: the affairs of Italy and of Africa are connected with those of Asia and Greece, as the Romans consciously reached out to these places in aiming for universal dominion. Historians also helped to develop a general interest at the time in outstanding individuals, and ultimately in the development of *biography.

In this respect too Isocrates was influential, as also in the development of what is sometimes called 'tragic history', an emotional style aimed at entertaining readers. Polybius, the only Hellenistic historian whose work survives at sufficient length for us to appreciate his aim and how far he achieves it, rejected the style of tragic history. For him the value of history lies in its revealing the causes of what actually happened, enabling those facing similar problems to apply solutions known to have succeeded in the past.

**Roman.** Roman historiography aimed to tell the history of the Roman state. The past was seen very much from the perspective of the present, and was usually shaped to offer precedents for contemporary events or described in terms which brought to mind the politics of the present. Sallust, Livy, and Tacitus all expressed a wish that their work should inspire contemporary politicians.

The earliest Roman historians wrote in Greek, both because they wished to glorify Rome and justify her institutions and policy to the Hellenistic world, and because Latin prose had not yet developed as a literary medium. *Fabius (3), working at the beginning of the second century BC, is the most celebrated. The Greek Polybius (above) explored the rise of Rome, and this aim was further pursued by *Cato (1) in his *Origines*, who for the first time in a work of this kind wrote in Latin, between 168 and 149 BC. This great work, which survives only in fragments, included the Italian cities and inspired further historical study in Rome. The 'old' annalists (*see* ANNALS), Cassius Hemina and Calpurnius Piso (censor in 120

BC), began the systematic study of Roman institutions which led to the publication after 130 BC of the *annales maximi* ('the most important records'). Later writers who depended on this work for their chronological framework also tended to follow its method, describing events as they happened year by year. This basic form was elaborated by historians of the early first century BC, including Valerius Antias and Claudius Quadrigarius, who established in Rome the moralistic tone and especially the rhetorical style of writing history that harked back to Isocrates: a tendency to argue from probability and to see an overall picture which allowed them to impose structure on annalistic material; this was the style accepted by Livy. On the whole the Romans concentrated on imposing literary merit on their histories: the material available did not lend itself to accurate reporting.

The various other kinds of historiography current in Hellenistic times had taken root in Rome by the beginning of the first century BC (see above). This was the background against which Sallust and Cicero wrote, and the same tradition was later followed by Tacitus. Sallust's political thought is intensely moralistic, in the Isocratean manner, but his chief exemplar was the Greek historian Thucydides whose severe style he imitated. Sallust's portraits of individuals also go back through the biographical tradition to Thucydides. He was influenced too by the concise and abrupt manner of Cato, and he rejected the rhetorical amplitude of his own day. Tacitus (b. *c.*AD 56) resembled Sallust in style and content; and both have been criticized for political bias and inaccuracy. Tacitus, however, united the various traditions of historical writing into work of great power. The biographical tradition was continued with the *Lives* of *Suetonius (b. *c.* AD 69) in which it was dominant, but degenerated after him into the *Historia Augusta* (fourth century AD). Tacitus' history was continued (from AD 96) and imitated by *Ammianus Marcellinus (b. *c.*AD 330), a Greek writing in Latin for Roman readers. He is considered accurate in general and relatively free of bias, but his work was done in isolation. This was the age of epitomes and outlines of history, and, with the addition of Jewish history to that of Greece and Rome (*see* JOSEPHUS), the start of a tradition of Christian chronicles.

**Homer (Hŏmēros)** (probably eighth century BC) Greek *epic poet.

1. Homer was regarded in antiquity as the author of two sovereign works, the *Iliad* and the *Odyssey*. Other *epic poems were sometimes attributed to him, most popularly *Margites* and *Batrachomyomachia*, but the best authorities rejected these. The Greeks themselves knew no certain facts about his life; Herodotus dated him to about 850 BC. Modern scholars generally date the poems to the second half of the eighth century, the *Iliad* c.750, the *Odyssey* c.725, long after the events of the Trojan War and its aftermath, which they describe. Each of the poems is made up of 24 books, the divisions sometimes, but not always, representing distinct episodes in the plot. The *Iliad* is longer than the *Odyssey* by about a third.

2. Some Hellenistic scholars, known as the 'separatists' (*chōrizontĕs*), argued that the author of the *Iliad* was not the same poet as the author of the *Odyssey*, and since the eighteenth century some scholars (the 'analysts') have doubted that either poem was written in its entirety by only one poet. Nowadays greater understanding of the nature of *oral poetry has caused most scholars to see each poem as the work of one author only, although it remains uncertain whether a single poet wrote both poems or whether there were two poets. The poems have very many common features, but separatists point to the use of different words for the same common objects, and to two somewhat different views of the gods. Whether there are two poets or one, the predominantly Ionian form of the mixed dialect (6 below) suggests that both poems were composed in the east Aegean, as do some geographical details. Many cities in that part of the Mediterranean claimed to be Homer's birthplace, most plausibly Smyrna and Chios, the home of the *Homeridae. The ancient Greeks thought of Homer as a blind minstrel, suffering poverty and hardship in the course of a wandering life before his eventual death and burial on the Aegean island of Ios.

3. Homer lived later than the heroes of his poems, who to him belong to an earlier and superior generation. The assumed date of the Trojan War (*see* TROY) is towards the end of the Mycenaean age in Greece, around 1200 BC, the approximate time when the Mycenaean palaces in Greece were destroyed. Homer was looking back from a distance of perhaps more than 400 years, and years without records, at a heroic world (*see* HEROES) conceived of as infinitely grander than his own. His kind of poetry probably had its origins in the Mycenaean age, and it still contains small nuggets reminiscent of that age, but overall it is the product of the following Dark age during which it developed and spread.

4. Epic poetry was sung or chanted, the poet accompanying himself on the lyre. The metre of the poems is the dactylic hexameter, which has strict and intricate rules of scansion. A striking feature of the composition is the repetition of lines and phrases ('formulae'), a style recognized in the twentieth century as a feature of oral composition. In an illiterate society bards would entertain an audience by relating some heroic event in verse which they composed more or less as they performed, having learned in their apprenticeships a repertoire of traditional formulae, lines and half-lines, and even blocks of lines, out of which a variety of stories could be composed without a great deal of forethought. Formulae may vary in length from a noun plus adjective—'swift-footed Achilles', 'wily Odysseus'—to several lines, such as those describing a hero arming for battle. (*See also* EPITHETS, DIVINE.) As well as formulae the bards also made use of traditional descriptions of scenes—scenes of arrival and departure, of sacrifice, and of fighting, for example, which could all be adapted to fit a given context. Thus quite a long narrative could be delivered, on request, more or less extempore, by practised bards. The discovery of this technique in the twentieth century transformed modern understanding of Homeric epic. It is clear from the complexity of these poems that Homer came towards the end of a long tradition of oral composition. The question remains whether he, being illiterate but living when writing was available, dictated the poems to a scribe, or whether he wrote down the poems himself, keeping the oral technique but taking advantage of the refinements writing made possible. The resulting poems were intended for oral delivery; on the other hand the continuous narrative shows that they were designed to be heard in their entirety, the *Iliad* in particular being difficult to break up into episodes. Their length, however, precludes their being performed at a sitting: uninterrupted recitation of the *Iliad* would take roughly twenty hours, and

perhaps would only have been possible at one of the great festivals. It is therefore probable that in general the poems were sung in excerpts by *rhapsodes.

5. The indications, then, are that each of the two poems was conceived as a unity and composed by an individual poet (or two poets) working in the Ionian tradition of oral composition. It is generally felt that the cohesion and subtle artistry that each poem shows could not have been achieved by mere editorial activity. Aristotle in the *Poetics* singles out Homer's grasp of artistic unity for special praise. Moreover, ancient Greek unanimity about the existence of 'Homer' should not be discounted. A story of doubtful authenticity tells how the sixth-century Athenian tyrant *Peisistratus, finding the Homeric texts in confusion, was responsible for having them put in order and recited at the Panathenaic festival (*see also* ONOMACRITUS). The Athenian element in a few episodes, and perhaps even traces of the Attic dialect, indicate that at some stage Athens played a part in the transmission of the text. Indeed, an Athenian version of the text would appear to be the source of all our manuscripts of Homer; it may even be the origin of the division of the poems into 24 books each. At the end of the sixth century BC quotations from and references to Homer begin to appear in fair quantity. From these and subsequent quotations, as well as from papyrus fragments, it is clear that texts at that time contained considerable if superficial variations. For some centuries there was probably an oral transmission maintained by the rhapsodes as well as a written transmission. However, it is upon the editorial labours of the scholars at Alexandria from the third century BC onwards, *Zenodotus, *Aristophanes of Byzantium, and above all *Aristarchus, that the modern text is based.

6. *Dialect*. The language of the Homeric poems is a mixture of forms found all over the Greek world, never spoken in its entirety at any one place or at any one time. On the surface it seems to be Ionic, as spoken on the east Aegean islands and the coast of Asia Minor. Attic forms, although Attic is a branch of Ionic, are rare. Next in prominence after Ionic is Aeolic, the dialect of north Greece and the northern Aegean islands such as Lesbos. Remaining embedded in these later dialects are features of ancient Arcado-Cypriot, perhaps Mycenaean survivals. What all this implies for the history of Greek epic is not at all clear, but it would seem that the language, and so epic poetry itself, developed over a long period.

7. The world of the *Iliad* and the *Odyssey* is not self-contained; it is part of a much larger world of Greek heroic legend with which, it is assumed, audiences are already familiar. The main characters in the epics are never introduced; they are already known, and their fates also. Had it not been so the emotional effect of the foreshadowing of later events, so frequent and powerful a device in the *Iliad*, would have been lost. Homer's most striking quality is his humanity. His understanding of his characters, their motives frequently revealed in speeches, is most apparent in the *Iliad*. Though the ancient commentators thought he was 'always on the side of the Greeks', he does not obviously favour their cause or express hostility to the Trojans. The Trojans provide him with some of his most sympathetic characters; apart from the hero Hector he draws touching portraits of the Trojan mothers Hecuba and Andromache, and, most subtle of all, Helen. As a narrator he is omniscient. In the *Iliad* he knows what is happening in the Greek camp and at Troy and among the gods on Mount Olympus. In the *Odyssey* he keeps track of the travels of Odysseus and Telemachus and the situation at Ithaca, and brings all three together at the end. The *Odyssey* is a romantic epic of adventure, with elements of folk- and fairy-tale. As a result the characters are good or bad, and we rather callously take sides accordingly.

In Homeric epic there is no randomness; every event has a divine or human cause, or both. Herodotus believed that Homer and Hesiod gave the gods their titles, prerogatives, and powers. At any rate Greek literature after Homer reflected the characters and attributes of the gods as we meet them in his poems. There is a difference, however, between the two epics in the portrayal of the gods. In the *Iliad* the gods as well as men are closely involved in very similar ways. They take sides and actively intervene in the fighting, helping and protecting their favourites, moved by the same emotions as the mortals, loving and hating. Zeus, the supreme god, is not very different from the others in these respects. Gods and men alike, however, are governed by *fate which sets a limit to the lives of men and of cities—Troy must fall—and which the gods will not alter. In the *Odyssey*, where different subject matter requires different treatment, the family of gods present in the *Iliad* is largely replaced by Poseidon, Odysseus' enemy, and Athena, his helper. Most significantly the concept of Zeus is different. He now directs the world according to moral principles, and mortals can expect wrongdoing to be punished and justice to be rewarded.

The aristocratic style of life which underlies Homeric society, based on the ethos of the warrior band, never entirely disappeared from Greek society, nor did its morality, with emphasis on competition and on excelling. The influence of the aristocratic clans, with their ramified bases of power, is seen in the success of such families as the *Alcmaeonidae at Athens; the comradeship of the Homeric feast survives in the *symposium of classical Athens, and the gifts of guest-friendship in the reciprocal ties of obligation that bound Greeks to each other in later times (*see* FRIENDSHIP).

8. The Homeric poems have been read continuously, first in Greece and then in Europe generally, ever since their creation. Homer was regarded with reverence by most Greeks, the source (with Hesiod) of their knowledge of the gods, the formulator of the heroic code of conduct, a touchstone of wise behaviour. Aristotle in his *Poetics* regarded him as 'in the serious style the poet of poets', 'unequalled in diction and thought', and he was constantly quoted. Passages were frequently imitated or translated by Latin poets (e.g. Lucretius and Virgil); the *Odyssey* was translated into Latin Saturnians by *Livius Andronicus. A striking and much-imitated feature of Homeric narrative is the poet's use of long and elaborate similes, especially so because they are very rare in Hesiod and the *Homeric Hymns. Homer uses them in order to compare an event in the narrative with something within the experience of the audience. Once the point of comparison is made the simile develops into an independent vignette; it may be descriptive or it may have an emotional effect or relieve tension, particularly in the *Iliad* where it often introduces into an epic of war a glimpse of ordinary, peaceful life. Many similes are concerned with the weather, or with hunting, or herding domestic animals and defending them against wild animals. But more seem to express danger or a struggle to survive, a glimpse of the reality of a later world (*see* HESIOD) intruding into the heroic or the fairy-tale.

**Homeric Hymns** A collection of thirty-three Greek hexameter poems in *epic style composed during the period from the eighth to the sixth centuries BC. They were addressed to gods and minor deities, and were commonly attributed to Homer in antiquity but denied Homeric authorship by the Alexandrian scholars. It is not known when the collection was put together. The authors were evidently *rhapsodes; the author of the third Hymn describes himself as 'a blind man living in rocky Chios' (thus suggesting Homer). Many of the Hymns are only a few lines long and are preludes to the recitations from epic often given at festivals. The Hymn to Delian Apollo was recited at his festival. Others narrate at length some episode relating to the god. The most notable are: the Hymn to Demeter (hymn 2), which relates the famous myth of the seizing of *Persephone by Hades and Demeter's search for her, and ends with the founding of the Eleusinian *mysteries; the Hymn to Apollo (3, attributed to Homer by Thucydides and Aristophanes), the first part of which describes the god's birth on Delos and the second the establishment of his oracle at Delphi (the whole may be constituted out of two hymns); the Hymn to Hermes (4), a lively and amusing account of the god's achievements as a baby; the Hymn to Aphrodite (5), which depicts the goddess of love herself yielding to the power of love and marrying Anchises; and the Hymn to Dionysus (7), which briefly tells the story of the god's capture by pirates and the miracles he subsequently performed.

**Homeridae** ('sons of Homer') The name, from the sixth century BC if not earlier, of a clan (*genos*) of *rhapsodes in Chios who claimed descent from Homer and the prerogative of reciting Homer's poems 'by right of succession'. They also told stories about his life. Later they developed into a guild by admitting rhapsodes not claiming to be related to Homer.

**homosexuality** *See* LOVE AND SEXUALITY.

**Horace (Quintus Horātius Flaccus)** (65–8 BC) Roman poet, all of whose published work survives. A great deal is known about his life from a biography by *Suetonius and the poet's own testimony. He came from Venusia (Venosa, near the river Aufidus in Apulia, south Italy). His father had once been a slave, perhaps as a result of being captured in the Social War; he was an auctioneer and provider of credit, and had acquired a small estate.

He gave his son the best education available, first at Rome under *Orbilius, and later at Athens. The civil war following Caesar's murder in 44 BC broke out while Horace was in Greece; in 44–42 he served in Brutus' army (the republican side) as military tribune, and fought on the losing side (and, he says, ran away) at the battle of Philippi in 42 BC. After that he returned to Italy, lost his father's estate but received a pardon from the victors, and obtained an influential secretaryship in the office of a quaestor. He achieved or resumed equestrian status. About 38 BC he was brought into contact with Virgil and *Varius Rufus who introduced him to *Maecenas. He may have seen something of Octavian's war against Sextus Pompeius c.36 BC, and may have accompanied Maecenas at the battle of Actium in 31 BC. Around 33 BC Maecenas had given him a property in the Sabine hills beyond Tivoli which was to be the source not only of income and leisure but of much happiness, and which he often celebrated in his poetry. Later, Augustus offered him a post as private secretary, but this offer was politely refused.

During the thirties Horace wrote *iambi*, usually known as the *Epodes, published c.30 BC, and the *Satires (Lat. *Sermones*); the two books of the latter were published by 30 BC, the latest dateable reference. After this Horace turned to lyric poetry. The first three books of his *Odes, composed gradually in the course of some ten years and reflecting the political events of 33–23, were probably published together in 23 (some argue for separate publication). The *Carmen Saeculare is a long ode, which we know was sung to music, written for the Secular Games of 17 BC and commissioned by Augustus, a sign of continuing imperial favour. Book 4 of the *Odes was published in perhaps 13 BC. By this time Horace had returned to hexameter poetry and to the conversational style of the Satires in *Epistles book 1, published perhaps in 20 or 19 BC. The Epistles take the form of letters in verse addressed to a variety of recipients. A second book, made up of two literary letters, followed by the *Ars poetica or Epistle to the Pisos, are generally assigned to the last years of the poet's life, but their exact date is uncertain: Epistle 2.1 may be dated to c.16 BC, and 2.2 and the Ars poetica are sometimes placed as early as 19 BC. Horace died in 8 BC, a few months after Maecenas, with whom he had maintained a friendship of thirty years. He was never married. Suetonius describes him as short and stout; Horace speaks of himself as grey-haired.

Horace's position as one of the greatest of Roman poets rests on the perfection of form shown by the *Odes* and on the depth and detail of his self-portraiture throughout his work. This latter is enigmatic. To some readers he seems to adopt different masks, under which they find it impossible to discern the real man. Other readers perceive no self-contradiction but a diversity of qualities, through which they find in him a consistent attitude towards life, a rounded display of humanity, realism, urbanity, and dry humour, all tempered by irony. He was a lover of the simpler good things in life, a lover of his country and particularly of its countryside. Many of his poems are concerned with friendship in some aspect, a topic taken very seriously in the ancient world (*see* FRIENDSHIP and, especially, EPISTLES). In the *Odes* his gentle irony and subtle choice of words caused Petronius to refer to his 'studied felicity', *curiosa felicitas*; Quintilian called him 'most felicitously bold in expression', *verbis felicissime audax*. He has been the most quoted of Latin poets, giving lovers of the apt phrase a multitude to choose from. In his lifetime his works were appreciated by his fellow-countrymen, and the *Odes* had become a school textbook before he died. They have proved inimitable. The *Odes* found particular favour in the Renaissance (as did the *Ars poetica*, accepted as a complete guide to poetry) and again in the eighteenth century, when Horace's philosophy of moderation had particular appeal. *See also* LYRIC POETRY.

**Horae** *See* SEASONS.

**Horā'tii and Curiā'tii** According to Roman legend, the struggle between Rome and *Alba Longa (in Latium) in the reign of king Tullus Hostilius (seventh century BC) was decided by the single combats of three Roman brothers, the Horatii, against three Latin brothers, the Curiatii. Two of the former were killed and all three of the latter. As the survivor returned victoriously to Rome he met his sister weeping for the death of one of the Curiatii whom she was to marry. He stabbed her to death, was tried for murder, and eventually acquitted when allowed to appeal to the people. The story offered a precedent for the right of appeal on a capital charge.

**Horā′tius (Publius Horatius Coclēs)** ('One-eyed') The legendary Roman hero of the sixth century BC, from the same family as the *Horatii. He is the subject of the best-known of the *Lays of Ancient Rome* (1842) by Thomas Macaulay. With two companions, Sp. Lartius and T. Herminius, Horatius held at bay the whole Etruscan army under Lars *Porsenna while the wooden Sublician bridge over the Tiber into Rome was being cut down behind them (*see* PONS SUBLICIUS). At the moment of its collapse he sent back his two companions and held the position single-handed, finally jumping into the river and swimming back to the city.

**Horatius Flaccus** *See* HORACE.

**Horsemanship (*Peri hippikēs*)** (Lat. *De re equestri*) Treatise by *Xenophon. The author, himself a keen and experienced horseman, gives advice to his younger friends on the management of horses, under the following heads: buying a colt, the points, beginning with the feet and working upwards; breaking a colt; buying a horse that has already been ridden; age, mouth, behaviour, etc., of the animal; stable and yard; duties of a groom; instructions to the rider, mounting, seat, exercises, jumping, dismounting; treatment of a spirited horse; bits; horses for parade; armour for man and horse and arms for the rider. *See also* Xenophon's treatise the *CAVALRY COMMANDER*.

**horse-races** In Greece, races for single horses with riders, a feature of festivals and often of funeral games, were introduced at the Olympian games in 648 BC. They were held, like the chariot-races, at the hippodrome, and the horses raced for one lap (about 800m or half a mile). Pindar's most famous ode (Olympian 1) celebrated a victory in such a race, by the tyrant Hieron I of Syracuse (but as owner, not as rider), and a relay torch-race on horseback features at the beginning of Plato's *Republic*. Horses were unshod and the riders rode bareback without stirrups.

**Horte′nsia** Daughter of Quintus *Hortensius Hortalus, famous as having made in 42 BC a speech in the Roman Forum, contrary to custom for a woman, against a proposal of the triumvirs to impose special taxation on the property of wealthy women. Her plea was successful.

**Horte′nsius** Title of a lost dialogue by *Cicero (*see* (1) 5), composed in 45 BC after the death of the orator for whom it was named (*see* HORTENSIUS HORTALUS). It was an introduction and an exhortation to the study of philosophy, which Cicero defended against Roman prejudices. Very influential in late antiquity, it was based on the *Protrepticus* of Aristotle (of which only fragments survive).

**Horte′nsius Ho′rtalus, Quintus** (generally known as Hortensius, 114–49 BC) Distinguished Roman orator, consul in 69 BC, eight years older than Cicero and the latter's chief rival in the law-courts. He won fame on his first appearance in 95 BC pleading on behalf of the province of Africa which was accusing a Roman governor of corruption. He was eclipsed by Cicero as the leading orator of the day after Cicero's success in 70 BC at the trial of Verres, whom Hortensius was to defend (*see* CICERO (1) 1); he had no opportunity to speak since Verres prudently retired after Cicero's opening attack. Hortensius was consul-designate at the time. After Cicero's own consulship of 63 BC he and Hortensius were friends rather than rivals, though Cicero never quite trusted him, and avoided dedicating a work to him until the latter was dead; he praises Hortensius' oratory during the latter's lifetime in *De oratore* (53 BC), and after his death in *Brutus* (about 45 BC). Many stories are told of Hortensius' wealth and of his flamboyance, which extended to his oratorical performances in 'Asianic' style (*see* ORATORY): the pains he took in arranging his toga, and his theatrical deliveries (so that he was called Dionysia after a well-known dancer of the day), were keenly observed by the tragic actors Aesopus and Roscius. He also possessed a prodigious memory.

**Hōrus** Egyptian god, the child of *Isis, usually called by the Greeks Harpocrates, corresponding to the Egyptian Harpechrat, i.e. 'Har (or Horus) the child'. After the death of his father Osiris he succeeded in overcoming many obstacles and killing the wicked Set (Typhon to the Greeks). He became popular in Hellenistic times, and is represented as a child holding a finger to his lips, taken to indicate mystery and secrecy; among the Romans he was regarded as the god of silence. Herodotus identified him with Apollo, others with Heracles and Eros.

**Hostilius, Tullus** The sixth king of Rome, who traditionally reigned from 672 to 641 BC. To his reign are attributed the duel of the

*Horatii and Curiatii in the course of Rome's war with Alba Longa, the destruction of that city, and the incorporation of its citizens into the Roman state. The first Roman senate-house, the Curia, and the Comitium date from this time.

**Hours** *See* SEASONS.

**household gods** *See* GODS, HOUSEHOLD.

**hubris** English transliteration of Greek *hybris*, commonly denoting aggressive behaviour aimed at humiliating the victim, which in Athens was an offence punishable at law. 'Doing or saying things at which the victim feels shame, simply for pleasure', is how Aristotle describes it in the *Rhetoric*. Its present-day English meaning of excessive confidence, pride, or arrogance is based on a misunderstanding, in particular of the nature of the protagonist in Greek tragedy whose character was interpreted by some critics as flawed because of inordinate pride or passion, leading to divine punishment. *Hybris* denotes action rather than a state of mind. A famous instance was Meidias' slapping of Demosthenes' face on a public occasion (*see* DEMOSTHENES (2) 2).

**humours** [Gk. *chumoi*, 'juices'] In the Greek world, at least since the Hippocratic writings, it was common (but not universal; *see* ERASISTRATUS) to attribute diseases to an imbalance of certain fluids, humours, in the body, evacuation during illness indicating an excess of one or another. The idea corresponded in some accounts to the four *'elements' of Empedocles, earth, water, air, and fire, which were often interpreted as the cold, the wet, the dry, and the hot. There was no general agreement as to which body fluids were involved in diseases, but bile and phlegm predominate. However, the physician *Galen of the second century AD favoured as humours yellow bile, black bile, phlegm, and blood (corresponding respectively to fire, earth, water, and air), and as a consequence these acquired canonical status.

**Hundred-handers** *See* HECATONCHEIRES.

**hunting** *See* CYNEGETICUS.

**Hyaci'nthus** In Greek myth, a beautiful youth of Amyclae (an ancient city near Sparta). He was loved both by the god Apollo and by Zephyrus (the west wind), and preferred Apollo. Zephyrus, out of jealousy, blew a discus

thrown by Apollo so that it struck and killed Hyacinthus. From his blood sprang a flower bearing his name, perhaps a kind of iris, with markings interpreted as reading *aiai*, 'alas, alas'.

**Hy'adĕs** In the constellation Taurus, to the ancients a cluster of five stars between *Orion and the *Pleiades. With their last visible rising or setting before sunrise they marked the period May to November and hence the three chief events of the Greek agricultural year: reaping in May and ploughing and sowing, followed by the vintage, in late October and early November. The name Hyades seems to derive from the Greek verb meaning 'to rain' (the season of rainy weather began in November), and they were said to have been sisters who cried themselves to death when their brother Hyas was killed. They were also said to be the nurses of Dionysus.

**hybris** *See* HUBRIS.

**Hyda'spēs** River of the Punjab ('land of five rivers'), probably the modern Jhelum, where Alexander the Great defeated Porus. The name is used by poets to indicate the distant and romantic East.

**Hȳdra** *See* HERACLES, LABOURS OF 2.

**Hygiē'ia** The Greek goddess of health, daughter of *Asclepius and associated with him in cult.

**Hygī'nus, Gaius Julius** (*c*.64 BC–AD 17) Spanish freedman of Augustus, librarian of the Palatine library, friend of Ovid, and one of the greatest scholars of his day. His writings, now lost, covered a wide range of subjects, including a commentary on Virgil, a treatise on agriculture, historical and archaeological works, and works on religion. Under his name, though not in fact by him, two Latin works have survived, a handbook of mythology, *Genealogiae* or *Fabulae*, compiled from Greek sources probably in the second century AD, and a manual of astronomy, also based on Greek sources. A work on land-surveying and the laying-out of camps, probably of the third century AD, is attributed to a certain Hyginus Gromaticus (*see* GROMATICI).

**Hȳlas** In Greek myth, son of the king of the Dryopēs. Heraclēs, having killed the father, carried off the son to accompany him on the expedition of the *Argonauts. When the Argo touched at Cios on the coast of Mysia (Heracles having broken his oar), Hylas was sent for water. The water-nymphs, falling in love with him, drew him into the spring and he was lost. The Argonauts went on their way, but Heracles remained to look for him. The Mysians held a ritual search for him every year, in obedience to Heracles' orders, even in Hellenistic times.

**Hyllus** Eldest son of *Heraclēs by Dēianeira; *see also* HERACLEIDAE.

**hymenae'us** See MARRIAGE SONGS.

**Hyme'ttus** Mountain in Attica south-east of Athens, near the coast, famous for its honey and its marble. The honey is mentioned by Strabo and Pausanias; the marble is of a bluish-grey colour. It was when the glow of sunset appeared on Hymettus that Socrates drank the hemlock.

**hymns** In Greece, songs sung in honour of a god or hero, though in poetic usage any song may be termed a 'hymn'. In earlier times the word had not acquired its later specialized meaning and included hexameter poetry that was mainly narrative, e.g. the *Homeric Hymns. Of true cult hymns, written for public performance, very little remains; there are a few fragments of those by Alcman, Alcaeus, Pindar, and Bacchylides. The clearest indications of their style are given by some of the choruses in tragedy which are hymnal in form. The cult form consists of an invocation of the god under his several names and titles (clearly the aim was to be comprehensive), and a recital of his deeds, followed by a short prayer. The Latin hymns of Catullus (see poem 34) and Horace were modelled on Greek hymns and probably written to be read rather than performed (but *see* CARMEN SAECULARE). Horace's hymn to a wine-jar (*Odes* 3.21) is parody. The greatest Latin hymn, in effect if not in form, is the invocation to Venus at the beginning of *De rerum natura* of *Lucretius.

**Hȳpā'tia** (now pronounced thus in English, but from Gk. Hypatei'a; d. AD 415) Alexandrian Greek mathematician and Neoplatonist philosopher, daughter of the mathematician Theon. In an atmosphere of hostility to paganism she was murdered by a Christian mob. *See* NEOPLATONISM.

**Hype'rbolus** (d. 411 BC) An Athenian *demagogue during the Peloponnesian War,

sneered at in comedy for his origins (he was reputedly a lamp-maker), detested by Thucydides and the butt of the comic poets. After the death of *Cleon in 421 he became a leader of the people. A few years later, perhaps in 417 BC, an *ostracism took place in which he expected to secure the removal of *Nicias or *Alcibiades, but they joined forces against him and he was ostracized himself. He went to Samos, where he was murdered by revolutionary oligarchs.

**Hyperbo'reans** ('dwellers beyond the north wind') A fabulous people believed by the Greeks to live a blessed existence in the distant north, accessible only to a Heracles or Perseus. They were worshippers of Apollo, who traditionally spent the three winter months with them. It was thought that those specially favoured by the gods might spend their afterlife with the Hyperboreans. Herodotus tells us of offerings to Apollo at Delos, wrapped in wheat-straw, which pass from the Hyperboreans, city to city and hand to hand, until they reach the temple.

**Hyperei'dēs** (389–322 BC) Brilliant orator and distinguished Athenian politician and supporter of the cause of Greek liberty against *Macedon. The ancients ranked him second only to Demosthenes as an orator. Longinus (*see* LONGINUS ON THE SUBLIME) compared him with the pentathlete who wins the whole competition by being second-best in every particular contest. At first he was a professional speech-writer, but becoming involved in politics he made a name as an accuser of prominent men, most notably by his successful prosecution of Philocrates in 343 BC which presaged future opposition to Macedon. After the defeat of Athens at Chaeronea in 338 he took on a leading role and successfully urged the Athenians to resist Alexander the Great's demand in 335 (after he had put down the Theban revolt) for the surrender of Demosthenes and others. However, in 324 he was the leading prosecutor of Demosthenes and those accused of embezzling money deposited by Harpalus. He was one of the principal promoters of the war of revolt against Macedon (the Lamian War) after the death of Alexander the Great in 323 BC and pronounced the funeral oration (much of which survives) on the Athenian dead. After the defeat of the Greek alliance, when the Macedonian ruler demanded the surrender by Athens of those hostile to

Macedon, he was seized, with others, and put to death (Demosthenes committed suicide).

Hypereides' works were lost in antiquity and virtually nothing was known of them until in the mid-nineteenth century papyri were discovered containing extensive remains of six speeches, including fragments of *Against Demosthenes* of 324. Parts of two speeches have been found in the *Archimedes palimpsest. He was a pupil of *Isocrates but in general avoids his florid and rather artificial style, resembling *Lysias rather in the grace and simplicity of his language, and using a slightly colloquial vocabulary. One of the best-preserved speeches is *Against Athenogenes*, which was found in a papyrus of the second century BC and is therefore one of the most ancient of all classical manuscripts. This speech was praised in the treatise *Longinus on the Sublime*. In it Hypereides makes a lively and urbane speech for a client about a contract for the purchase of a perfumery (in order to free a slave, a youth with whom the client was in love). In his speech *For Euxenippus* (which survives complete) he defends a man accused of reporting a dream falsely after he had slept in the shrine of Amphiaraus in order to ascertain from a god-sent dream the ownership of a piece of land. Among his lost speeches was one in defence of the famous *hetaira* Phryne (he was one of her lovers) when she was accused of profaning the Eleusinian *mysteries. It is said that at the climax of his speech he had her uncover her breasts, and the jury was so moved by her beauty that she was acquitted.

**Hȳpe'rion** In Greek myth, a *Titan, husband of his sister Theia and father by her of *Helios (Sun), Selēnē (Moon), and Eōs (Dawn).

**Hyperm(n)e'stra** In Greek myth, one of the daughters of *Danaus.

**Hypnos** In Greek myth, the god of sleep, the (fatherless) son of *Nyx (Night) and brother of Thanatos (Death) with whom he is usually linked, especially in vase-paintings. He lives in the Underworld, but is kindly to men. Throughout antiquity he is thought of as a winged youth who pours sleep-inducing liquid from a horn, or touches the tired with a branch.

**hyporchē'ma** ('dance-song', pl. *hyporchemata*) Form of Greek choral *lyric in which dance, with mimetic movements, was prominent. The very few surviving fragments of *hyporchemata* by Pindar and Bacchylides give little indication of form or content.

**hypo'theses** The ancient term used to describe the introductory notes found in the manuscripts of Greek tragedy and comedy. These notes are derived ultimately from Alexandrian scholarship and give basic information about the plays, the outline of the plots, and details of production. *See* DIDASCALIA.

**Hypsi'pylē** According to Greek myth, the women of the island of Lemnos neglected the rites of Aphrodite and as a consequence the goddess inflicted on them a foul smell. They were then deserted by their husbands, who took concubines from Thrace. The women jealously killed all the men on the island, except that Hypsipyle spared her father, King Thoas, son of the god Dionysus, and aided his escape. When the *Argonauts came to Lemnos they spent a year there and married the women, fathering the next generation of Lemnians. Hypsipyle bore twin sons to Jason, called Euneōs and Thoas. Later, when she had been driven away from Lemnos after it was discovered that she had saved her father, she was captured by pirates and sold to Lycurgus, king of Nemea. When the Seven were marching against Thebes (*see* SEVEN AGAINST THEBES) and their army halted near Nemea, Hypsipyle, who was nurse of the king's infant son Opheltes (or Archemorus), laid the child on the ground in order to lead them to a spring. During her absence the child was killed by a serpent. The Seven gave him a splendid funeral and founded the Nemean games in his honour. Hypsipyle was saved from the anger of Lycurgus by the army and finally rescued by her sons who arrived and recognized her. The story is told in the *Thebaïd* of Statius.

I

**Ia'cchus** A supposed Greek deity, invoked by the cry *Iacch' O Iacche* during the procession of the initiates from Athens to Eleusis to celebrate the Eleusinian *mysteries. Iacchus was probably a personification of a ritual cry (*cf. Hymenaeus*; *see* MARRIAGE SONGS). Later stories made him the son of Demeter, or of Persephone, the goddesses of the Eleusinian mysteries. The name Iacchus, like Bacchus, was also used to refer to Dionysus, who had nothing to do with these mysteries.

**Ia'mbē** In Greece, a girl after whom the iambic metre is supposedly named. According to the second *Homeric Hymn, to Demeter, her scurrilous jokes made Demeter laugh when she was mourning Persephone. *See* IAMBIC POETRY.

**Ia'mbic poetry** [Lat. *ĭambi*, 'iambics'] Poetry written in the 'iambic' or a closely associated metre. The name comes from *iambos*, a word connected with scurrilous joking and verbal abuse which had a place in certain Greek religious festivals (*see* IAMBE). In Ionia in the seventh century BC poems by Archilochus were published which gave literary form to this type of entertainment, which the term 'iambic poetry' comes to describe. The three principal archaic writers of iambics ('iambographers') are Archilochus (the most versatile), Semonides of Amorgos, and Hipponax; the *Margites*, attributed improbably to Homer, may be included in this category. In the Hellenistic period iambic poetry was written by, among others, Asclepiades, Callimachus, and Herodas. Callimachus imitated the dialect and diction of Hipponax but Herodas went further and created a new genre, the *mimiambos*, by writing *mimes (dialogues or monologues) of low-class urban life in the language of Hipponax. The iambic metre was also available (as well as the hexameter or elegiac couplet) for more serious literary forms, for inscribed or literary epigrams. The metre seems also to have suited the requirements of Archilochus, Semonides, and Solon when they wrote their reflective and political poems. It was adopted as the natural metre for the dialogue and monologue parts of Attic tragedy and comedy.

At Rome iambics connoted abusive poetry and so Lucilius was sometimes called an iambographer although he wrote mostly in hexameters. Catullus and Horace both wrote iambics. Horace (in the *Epodes*) claims to have been the first in Latin to imitate Archilochus and invokes also the spirit of Hipponax, though the earlier Catullus and his contemporaries wrote vituperative iambi which they aimed at contemporary politicians. The *Epodes*, however, are both broader in theme (like Archilochus' iambics) and less savage than the poems of Catullus. The *Catalepton* (attributed to Virgil; *see* APPENDIX VIRGILIANA) includes several poems in iambic style.

**iambo'graphers** Greek writers of *iambic poetry.

**Ia'mus** In Greek myth, son of the god Apollo and the mortal Evadne, the mythical ancestor of the prophetic clan of the Iamidae in Greece. Seers from this clan made prophecies from the evidence of the sacrifices on the altar of Zeus at *Olympia. The famous seer Teisamenus of Elis, employed and given citizenship by the Spartans during the Persian Wars, was one of them. The clan continued at Olympia well into the third century AD

**Ia'petus** In Greek myth, a *Titan and father, by Clymene the daughter of *Oceanus, of Prometheus, Epimetheus, and Atlas. From the Renaissance he was identified with Japhet, son of Noah.

**Ia'sion** In Greek myth, brother of Dardanus and lover of *Demeter. He met Demeter at the wedding of Cadmus and Harmonia, and lay with her 'in a thrice-ploughed field'; the offspring of this union was the god *Plutus (Gk. Ploutos, Wealth).

**Ībē'ria (Hibēria)** One of the ancient names for Spain.

**Ībis** According to an ancient story, the title of an abusive poem by *Callimachus, addressed to a certain 'Ibis' who was supposed to have been the poet Apollonius Rhodius. Only very small fragments of the poem survive. The Latin poet Ovid, while in exile at Tomis, also wrote a curse-poem, in elegiacs, with this name, directed at an unknown enemy, in which he expresses indebtedness to Callimachus' 'brief poem'. Ovid's poem is, untypically, full of abstruse mythological learning.

**I'bycus** Greek lyric poet of the sixth century BC from Rhegium (in south Italy). Little is known of his life, and his dates are uncertain. It is said that he refused to become tyrant there and withdrew to Samos, where he worked at the court of the tyrant *Polycrates. The Alexandrian scholars arranged his works in seven books. They believed that his work consisted largely of narrative choral *lyric in the style of *Stesichorus, and also of encomia of which an interesting specimen, to Polycrates, has turned up on papyrus, and personal love-poems. The small fragments of his poems that have survived in quotation show that he had a taste for the colourful and picturesque, and wrote vividly on the power of love.

According to legend, Ibycus was attacked and killed by robbers. A flock of cranes was passing overhead and Ibycus exclaimed, 'Those cranes will avenge me'. Soon after, one of the robbers in a crowded theatre, seeing a flock of cranes hovering overhead, said to his companion, 'There go the avengers of Ibycus'. This was overheard, and the murderers were brought to justice.

**I'carus** See DAEDALUS.

**Ice'nī** A British tribe inhabiting East Anglia; see BOUDICCA and BRITAIN.

**Ichneu'tae** See SOPHOCLES.

**Ictī'nus** Greek architect who worked at Athens in the time of Pericles. In collaboration with Callicrates he designed the *Parthenon. He was also one of the architects who worked at Eleusis on the Telesterion.

**ictus** A term in metric, 'beat' or stress. *See also* ARSIS.

**Īda (Idē) 1.** Range of mountains in southern Phrygia, the southern boundary of the Troad. It was there that the Trojan *Paris was said to have been exposed and brought up by shepherds, and to have fallen in love with Oenone. From its summit Zeus watched the Trojan War.

**2.** Mountain in the centre of Crete. In a cave on this mountain (or on Mount Dicte) Zeus is said to have been born.

**Idae'an Dactyls** See DACTYLS, IDAEAN.

**Īdas** See LYNCEUS and MARPESSA.

**Ideas, Platonic** See PLATO 4 and PLATONISM.

**Ides** In the Roman *calendar the days of the month were reckoned in relation to three named days, the *Kalends, the *Nones, and the Ides. The date was calculated by counting backwards, inclusively, from the next named day. The Ides occurred on the thirteenth day except in March, May, July, and October, when they fell on the fifteenth. Thus 15 March was the Ides, Id(ibus) Mar(tiis), while 12 March, for example, was 'the fourth day before the Ides of March', *ante diem quartum Idus Martias*: in brief, a.d. iv Id. Mar.

**Īdo'meneus** In Greek myth, son of Deucalion, grandson of *Minos, and leader of the Cretans at the siege of Troy. In a storm on his way home he vowed to sacrifice to Poseidon the first living creature that met him, if he returned safe. This proved to be his son. He fulfilled, or tried to fulfil, his vow; in consequence a plague broke out and he was driven into exile by the Cretans (and settled, according to Virgil, on the south coast of Italy).

**idyll** [apparently from the Greek *eidyllion*, meaning in this context 'little scene', 'vignette'] The name given perhaps in Roman times to the poems of *Theocritus, which describe some episode or scene from life. Since several of his scenes were of pastoral life, 'idyllic' came to describe an idealized state or scene of tranquil happiness, particularly of a pastoral nature.

**Īleithyī'a** See EILEITHYIA.

**Ī'lia (Rhea Silvia)** In earliest Roman legend, the daughter of Aeneas and the mother by Mars of *Romulus and Remus. In later stories she is equated with Rhea Silvia, who is occasionally called Ilia, the daughter of Numitor (a later descendant of Aeneas), niece of Amulius, and a Vestal Virgin. Amulius had her and her two sons thrown into the Tiber (or Anio). The river-god made her a goddess and married her.

**I'liad (Īlias)** ('the Trojan poem') Greek epic poem by *Homer in twenty-four books. The division into books, which does not always correspond very clearly with episodes in the plot, seems to have been made later than the original composition. It is generally agreed that the poem we have is as originally composed, with the possible exception of book 10 where there is a strong possibility that it was a later addition. The title is derived from Ilion, another name of *Troy, which comes from Ilus, its legendary founder.

The unitary theme of the whole work is the 'wrath of *Achilles', arising from an affront to his standing committed by *Agamemnon, leader of the Greek army at the siege of Troy, and the tragic consequences of his anger. This is an episode in the history of the siege, occupying in books 2 to 22 merely four days of fighting separated by two days of truce in the tenth and final year of the war, yet this action in effect encapsulates the whole war. The poem ends with the death of the Trojan hero *Hector, symbolizing the fall of Troy which will soon follow. The gods in Olympus are divided in their sympathies and intervene on one side or the other, or fight among themselves. Their mixture of sublimity and frivolity makes a powerful contribution to the character of the *Iliad*. A bare outline of events is as follows.

*Books 1–8.* A plague has broken out in the Greek camp, and the seer Calchas declares that it has been brought about by the anger of Apollo on behalf of his priest whose daughter, Chryseïs, has been taken prisoner and given to Agamemnon as a gift of honour; if Agamemnon surrenders her the plague will cease. Agamemnon angrily consents but takes in her place Briseïs, a slave-concubine belonging to Achilles. The latter, wrathful at this high-handed act, retires to his tent, and with his Myrmidons (*see* Aeacus) and his friend Patroclus refuses to take further part in the fighting. The Greek army, deprived of his powerful support, suffers serious losses and is driven away from the plain of Troy and back to the camp.

*Book 9.* Being now hard pressed, Agamemnon recognizes the wrong that he has done, and sends an embassy to Achilles offering to make handsome amends if he will lay aside his anger. But Achilles has been nursing his grievance and is disillusioned with war and fame; he rejects Agamemnon's offers and announces that he will not fight until Hector fires the Greek ships.

*Books 10–17.* As a result, he sees the Greeks suffer further losses. His friend Patroclus is stung to shame and regret by their reverses, and obtains Achilles' permission, when the Trojans are actually setting fire to the Greek ships, to join in the fight; moreover Achilles, himself moved by the danger to the Greeks, lends his armour to Patroclus and summons the Myrmidons. The Trojans are driven back, but Patroclus is killed by Hector, and retribution for his anger thus comes to Achilles.

*Books 18–22.* Achilles, maddened by grief, puts aside his anger with Agamemnon and reveals himself unarmed to the Trojans, who retreat from Patroclus' body. His mother Thetis brings him new armour forged by the god *Hephaestus, and he goes out to avenge the death of his friend. He kills Hector and treats the dead body with gross outrage, tying it by the heels to his chariot and dragging it through the dust.

*Books 23–4.* The body of Patroclus is then buried and the event marked by funeral games. Priam, the aged king of Troy, comes to Achilles to beg the body of his son Hector and save it from the threatened fate of being thrown to the dogs. Achilles feels his common humanity with Priam, pities him, and returns the body, but his passion is not wholly spent; he accepts a ransom but his anger threatens to break out again. The poem ends with the funeral of Hector.

Side by side with this tragedy we have a picture of life in Troy under the shadow of impending disaster: *Helen, conscious of her guilt and the trouble she has brought on Troy, despising Paris, wishing that she had died at birth, and kindly treated by Hector, Priam, and the other Trojans (books 3 and 6); Hector talking to his wife *Andromache, his helmet frightening their young son (book 6); Priam and *Hecuba bereaved of many of their sons, and finally mourning their dearest, Hector (book 24).

A host of other warriors are presented, some of them sharply characterized (*see* entries for Aeneas; Ajax; Diomedes; Menelaus; Odysseus; Nestor; Sarpedon; Glaucus). Notable passages are the following: the Catalogue of Greek ships,

2.484–785; the Catalogue of Trojan forces, 2.786–877; the *Teichoscopia* (the 'viewing from the walls' of the Greek chiefs by Helen and Priam), the duel of Menelaus and Paris to settle the war and decide who will have Helen, and the ending of the truce when Paris is snatched away to his bedroom by Aphrodite, book 3; the *Epipōlēsis* (Agamemnon's 'tour of inspection' of his forces), 4.223–421; the exploits of Diomedes ending with the wounding of the god Ares, 5.239–909; the meeting and recognition of Diomedes and Glaucus, 6.119–236; Hector's farewell to Andromache, 6.370–529; the duel between Hector and Ajax, 7.206–282; the *Doloneia* (the night expedition of Odysseus and Diomedes, the slaying of the spy Dolon and of the Thracian *Rhesus, and the capture of the latter's horses), book 10; the *Dios apate* ('deception of Zeus' by Hera), 14.153–362; the forging of the arms of Achilles, 18.468–617; the fight of Achilles with the river Scamander, 21.211–382; the funeral games for Patroclus, 23.257–897.

***Iliad, Little*** (*Ilias parva*) Title of a lost poem of the *Epic Cycle, attributed to Lesches of Pyrrha or of Mitylene in Lesbos, a sequel to Homer's *Iliad*, in four books. The events it is said to cover are the awarding of the arms of Achilles to *Odysseus; the madness and suicide of *Ajax; the ambushing of *Helenus and his prophecy about the capture of Troy through the agency of *Philoctetes, who kills Paris; the arrival at Troy of *Neoptolemus (Achilles' son); the secret entry of Odysseus into Troy and his stealing of the *Palladium; and the entry of the Wooden Horse. The last part overlaps the *Iliupersis.

**Ī'lium** *See* TROY.

***Iliūpe'rsis*** (*Īliou persis*) ('Sack of Troy') **1.** Title of a lost poem of the *Epic Cycle attributed to Arctinus of Miletus or Lesches, a sequel in two books to the *Little Iliad*. The events are said to be the following. The Wooden Horse enters Troy; two snakes destroy *Laocŏon and one of his sons; Sinon (*see* TROJAN HORSE) signals to the departed Greek army to return to Troy, and the Greeks take the city; *Neoptolemus kills Priam, Menelaus finds Helen, and *Ajax son of Oileus tries to carry off Cassandra, pulling over the statue of Athena in the attempt; Odysseus murders *Astyanax, son of Hector, and Neoptolemus takes Hector's wife *Andromache as prize; the Greeks set fire to the city, sacrifice *Polyxena at the tomb of Achilles, and sail home, with the goddess Athena planning vengeance for Ajax's violation.

**2.** Title of a poem by *Stesichorus.

**illustrated books** *See* BOOK ILLUSTRATION.

**Īlus** *See* TROS.

**Īlȳthyī'a** *See* EILEITHYIA.

**imitation** *See* MIMESIS.

**imperā'tor** (Gk. *autocratōr*) Originally a Roman military title, 'commander', it became a title of honour given by acclamation of the soldiers to a general after his victory. He kept the title after his name until he celebrated his *triumph. The first properly attested *imperator* in this sense was L. Aemilius *Paullus in 189 BC. The increasing importance of the army in the late republic made the title the symbol of military authority, and Julius Caesar used the title permanently. After 38 BC Octavian (later the emperor Augustus) used the title as a *praenomen* (*see* NAMES [Roman]), i.e. Imperator Caesar, not Caesar Imperator. Thus it came to signify the supreme power of the emperor. The use of the title as *praenomen* did not prevent its being applied in the original manner, after the emperor's name, when he had won a victory. The formula *imperator Caesar* was sometimes extended to members of the imperial family who shared the emperor's power (*cf.* AUGUSTUS, THE). Under Vespasian *imperator*, 'emperor', became the ruler's title.

**impe'rium** In the Roman constitution, 'power to command', the supreme administrative authority vested in certain individuals, involving command in war and originally the interpretation and execution of the law (including the power to impose the death penalty); later, Roman citizens could not be executed without trial, and had the right of *appeal to the people (*see* HORATII). *Imperium*, originally the authority of the king, was possessed under the republic by consuls, military tribunes with consular power, praetors, dictators, and *magistri equitum* ('masters of the horse'), and by proconsuls and propraetors in their provinces. Sometimes a private citizen was granted imperium for a specific purpose. When Octavian resigned the consulship in 23 BC, his imperium as proconsul was made *maius*, 'superior' to that of anyone else.

**impiety** *See* AGNOSTICISM and ATHEISM.

**I'nachus** *See* Io.

**indi'getes (indigites)** At Rome, 'invoked deities', apparently nameless, who were secondary to the important gods whose functions they supported.

**Indo-European** It has long been recognized that many past and present languages including Greek, Latin, and Sanskrit (the literary language of India) share common features which show that they are the related descendants of an unattested parent language. They are now called Indo-European to indicate their geographical spread in early historical times. The parent language, which must have been spoken before writing was invented, is also known as Indo-European or as Proto-Indo-European. The earliest recorded examples of an Indo-European language date to the second millennium BC and include Hittite and *Linear B. The many peoples who spoke these languages are often referred to, in a linguistic sense, as Indo-Europeans. Scholars have often tried to find a homeland where the Indo-European languages could be said to have originated, but the complexities of trying to establish the social and linguistic processes that led to the dispersal of Indo-Europeans in prehistoric times have so far defeated all attempts. *See* GREECE 2.

**infanticide** Although exposure of babies is a frequent motif in Greek and Roman myth and legend, and sometimes in the Greek novel and New Comedy (*see* e.g. *EPITREPONTES*; *PERIKEIROMENE*; *AETHIOPICA*) it is impossible to know how much it occurred in real life, nor do we know whether the victims were more usually female. The Gortyn code allowed infanticide in certain circumstances, and a Roman father, who by right of *patria potestas* had the power of life and death over his children, was instructed by the *Twelve Tables to kill a seriously deformed baby. The Egyptians and Jews and, according to Tacitus in the *Germania*, the Germans, reared all their children. Aristotle says that 'the ordinance of custom' forbids exposing babies simply because a family had enough children (and recommends instead early abortion). In Sparta the law required the abandonment of deformed babies, and Aristotle also proposes that the law should forbid the rearing of a crippled child. The Greek physician and gynaecologist Soranus in the second century AD lists criteria for deciding whether a newborn baby should be reared. Notable individuals raised despite deformity, it would appear, are the Spartan king *Agesilaus II (who was lame: his opponents drew attention to an oracle warning against a 'lame reign at Sparta') and the Roman emperor Claudius. Attitudes changed with the official acceptance of Christianity: a law of AD 374 treated infanticide as murder.

**i'nferi, di** (Lat., 'gods of the Underworld') Term used in Roman religion.

**inhumation** *See* DEAD, DISPOSAL OF.

**Inō** In Greek myth, a daughter of *Cadmus and Harmonia, and wife of *Athamas. (*See also* DIONYSUS for her death and transformation into a sea-goddess.) It was she who saved Odysseus when his raft was wrecked, giving him her scarf to keep him afloat (Homer, *Odyssey* 5).

**inscriptions** *See* EPIGRAPHY.

**interce'ssio** ('interposition') At Rome, the veto which a magistrate might impose upon a motion carried by another magistrate of equal or lower rank. The tribunes of the people acquired the right to veto not only motions of all other magistrates but also the enactments of the senate and the *comitia* (*see* ASSEMBLY). Only the *dictator could not be obstructed by a veto since he had no equal or superior.

**interpolation** *See* TEXTUAL CRITICISM.

**interpreters** *See* BILINGUALISM.

**interrex** At Rome, originally an individual appointed by the senate at the death of a king to hold temporary power until a new king was appointed. Under the republic, if both consuls should die or resign, two *interreges*, who had to be senators and patricians, were appointed until new consuls were elected. The last known example of such an event was in 43 BC when both consuls were killed at *Mutina.

**Īō** In Greek myth, daughter of Inachus, mythical first king of Argos. When Zeus fell in love with her she suffered disturbing dreams. Inachus, in response to oracles he had consulted, then turned her out of the house. Zeus (or his wife Hera) changed her into a white heifer, for purposes of deception; Hera set the herdsman Argus, who had eyes all over his body, to watch over her, and sent a gadfly to sting her continuously, so that she would not rest long enough for Zeus to find and make love to her. Zeus sent

Hermes to kill Argus, but Io, now constantly haunted by the herdsman's ghost, was forced by the gadfly to wander far and wide. Part of the Adriatic Sea was thenceforth called Ionian (Gk. Ĭŏnios, apparently not derived from Ĭōnia, for which *see* ION (1)), and the Bosporus, 'oxford', was named after her crossing. When she passed by *Prometheus bound to his rock he prophesied to her what was to come. Eventually she reached Egypt, where Zeus changed her back to human form, touched her with his hand, and thus begat his son Epaphus ('he of the touch'). According to one version she was worshipped there as the goddess *Isis (Epaphus being identified with the bull-god Apis). Epaphus was the ancestor of Aegyptus and *Danaus, who would return to Argos with his daughters the Danaids.

**Ioca'stē** *See* JOCASTA.

**Iolā'us** *See* HERACLES and *HERACLES, CHILDREN OF.*

**Ī'olē** *See* HERACLES and *TRACHINIAE.*

**Ĭōn 1.** Eponymous ancestor of the Ionian Greeks (Gk. Iōnes or Iānes). According to Greek myth (as preserved by Euripides; *see* ION (1)) Crĕūsa, daughter of *Erechtheus, king of Athens, was loved by the god Apollo and bore him a son Ion, whom for fear of her father's anger she left in a cave under the Acropolis. Hermes carried the child to Delphi, where he was reared as a servant of the temple. Creusa afterwards married Xuthus (*see* HELLEN), but as they remained childless they went to Delphi to ask for offspring. At the order of Apollo, Xuthus accepted as his son the first person he met on coming out of the shrine, and this was Ion. Creusa, angered at the adoption of one whom she supposed to be a bastard son of her husband, attempted to kill the boy, but being detected, and in danger of death, took refuge at the altar of Apollo. By the intervention of the priestess, who produced the swaddling-clothes in which the infant Ion had been wrapped, Creusa recognized her child, and the goddess Athena revealed what had happened. Ion returned to Athens with Xuthus and Creusa to become, according to Athena's prophecy, the ancestor of the Ionian race.

**2.** Of Chios (b. in the 480s BC, d. before 421) Greek poet famed chiefly for his tragedies, which were studied and admired by the Alexandrian scholars and by *Longinus on the Sublime*.

None of them has survived. He also wrote lyric and elegiac poetry. It is possible that he wrote comedy as well as tragedy, thus being the exception to the rule that no Greek wrote both (*see* COMEDY [Greek 1]). Interesting anecdotes link Ion with many of the famous names of the fifth century: he heard Cimon speak in the assembly, met Aeschylus at the Isthmian games and Sophocles when he was *strategos* in 441/40, and was defeated in the tragic contests at the Great Dionysia of 428 when Euripides won with *Hippolytus*. A long quotation by *Athenaeus (*Deipnosophistai* 603), from Ion's prose work *Epidemiai* ('Visits'), in which he vividly describes an evening spent with Sophocles, gives cause for regret at the loss of his writings.

**Ĭon 1.** Greek tragedy (with a happy ending) by *Euripides, probably written a year or two after 412 BC. It deals with the story of *Ion (1). The essential features of the plot—a woman seduced, her child exposed, the subsequent recognition, and happy consequences—became typical of New Comedy (*see* COMEDY [Greek 6]; *also* MENANDER).

**2.** Very short dialogue by *Plato named after a *rhapsode of that name. Shown to possess no knowledge of his art, he is the object of genial mockery. This slight work gives Plato's view of literary critics, 'interpreters of interpreters'.

**Ĭō'nia, Ionians** The country of Ionia comprised the central portion of the west coast of Asia Minor, roughly from Smyrna to Miletus (in the south), as well as the adjacent islands, and was inhabited by Ionian Greeks who had migrated there from mainland Greece *c.*1000 BC. Ionians as a Greek people are mentioned once by Homer, the Ionian cities not at all. Ionia was the region in which early Greek literature and *philosophy were principally developed (*see also* HOMER 2 and HISTORIOGRAPHY [Greek]). For the legendary origin of the name *see* ION (1). The Ionians, who traced their origin from the city of Athens and kept the festival of the Apaturia (*see* PHRATRIES), had particularly close ties with Athens. Although Athens could not claim to be the mother-city of all Ionians, she may have some claim to have organized the first migrations to Ionia (*see* GREECE 2): the four ancient tribes of Attica, the Geleontes, Aigikoreis, Argadeis, and Hopletes (supposedly named after the sons of Ion) are found among the Ionians also. In the fifth century BC the

Athenians came to think of the Ionians as soft and given to luxurious living, in contrast with the hardy and austere Dorians.

**Ionian philosophers** See THALES; ANAXIMANDER; ANAXIMENES; see also PHILOSOPHY.

**Ionian Revolt** (499 BC) See PERSIAN WARS.

**Ionian Sea** An alternative name for the Adriatic Sea. See IO.

**I'ophon** Athenian tragic poet, the son of Sophocles. Aristophanes in the Frogs of 405 BC seems to imply that Iophon (if he can write without his father's help) is the best surviving tragic poet now that Sophocles and Euripides are dead. He won first prize at the Great *Dionysia in 435 BC.

**Īphiana'ssa** The name under which *Iphigeneia appears in Homer.

**Ī'phiclus** In Greek myth, son of Phylacus. He imprisoned for a year the seer *Melampus, who discovered the reason for Iphiclus' childlessness and cured him. Iphiclus subsequently became the father of Podarces and *Protesilaus.

**Iphigenei'a** In Greek myth, a daughter of *Agamemnon and Clytemnestra, whom Agamemnon was forced to sacrifice. The Greek fleet, when about to sail to Troy, was held wind-bound at Aulis (on the coast of Boeotia). The seer Calchas declared that Artemis required the sacrifice of Agamemnon's daughter (authorities vary on the reason), and Agamemnon sent for Iphigeneia on the pretext that she was to be married to Achilles. In Aeschylus' *Oresteia the belief is that she was actually killed; the version of the *Cypria (followed by Euripides in *Iphigeneia in Tauris), describes how, when she was about to be sacrificed, Artemis carried her off to be her priestess in the land of the Tauri (the Crimea), substituting a deer for her at the altar. The Tauri had a savage rite by which strangers coming to their land were sacrificed to Artemis, and Iphigeneia was required to consecrate the victims.

Iphigeneia's brother *Orestes, in order to expiate the blood-guilt incurred by his murder of Clytemnestra, was ordered by Apollo to secure the image of Artemis of the Tauri and bring it to Attica. He had been separated from Iphigeneia since he was a child and believed her dead. He and his friend Pylades were captured by the Tauri who ordered them to be sacrificed, but Iphigeneia discovered her brother's identity and was persuaded to escape with him from the country, carrying off the image of the goddess. The latter was set up in a temple in Attica—both Halae and Brauron in historical times claimed the distinction—where Iphigeneia became the perpetual priestess of Artemis. Other stories tell that she was married to Achilles on Leuce or in Elysium.

**Iphigenei'a among the Taurians (Īphigeneia hē en Taurois)** (Lat. Iphigeneia in Tauris) Greek tragedy by Euripides, produced probably in 413 BC. The play deals with that part of the legend of *Iphigeneia which relates to her life in the land of the Tauri as the priestess of Artemis. The heroine is represented as a woman who has long brooded over her grievances, bitter towards the Greeks who sought to murder her, but longing for home. The coming of Greeks to the Tauric Chersonese (Crimea) for the first time during her priesthood and the discovery that she is required to sacrifice her own brother arouse her natural affections. A plan of escape is devised. Thoas, king of the Tauri, is fooled; Iphigeneia, Orestes, and Pylades escape with the image of the goddess.

**Iphigenei'a at Aulis (Īphigeneia hē en Aulidi)** (Lat. Iphigeneia Aulidensis) Greek tragedy by *Euripides, produced posthumously, perhaps in 405 BC. The text may have been completed by others after Euripides' death; much of the ending is not by Euripides. The play deals with the story of the sacrifice of *Iphigeneia at Aulis. The poet has Agamemnon wavering and in despair. After sending for Iphigeneia, on the urging of his brother Menelaus and on the pretext of her marriage to Achilles (of which the latter knows nothing), he cancels the summons, but the second messenger is stopped by Menelaus. Clytemnestra and Iphigeneia arrive. Menelaus repents of his interference and offers to give up the expedition, but in vain; Agamemnon now dreads the anger of the army if the expedition is called off. Achilles learns that he has been used in a deception and boldly tries to save the girl. But Iphigeneia, after pleading for her life, changes her mind; resolving to be sacrificed in order to save the Greek expedition, she acquiesces.

The tragedy is concerned almost exclusively with the interplay of the various characters, and the role of the chorus is insignificant.

**Ī'phitus** *See* HERACLES.

**Īris** In Greek myth, the goddess of the rainbow. She was the daughter of Thaumas (son of Pontus, Sea) and Electra (daughter of Oceanus), and consequently sister of the *Harpies ('Snatchers', i.e. storm-winds). Iris is not only a personification of the rainbow but also a messenger of the gods, particularly of Hera. In Virgil the rainbow is the path along which she travels. According to the early Greek poet Alcaeus she is the mother by Zephyrus of Eros. She had no cult.

**Iron age** The period succeeding the *Bronze age. In *Greece it began *c.*1050 BC; *see also* DARK AGE; ORIENTALIZING AGE; PROTO-GEOMETRIC; GEOMETRIC. In *Italy it began *c.*1000 BC. Iron-working spread to Greece from Anatolia *c.*1000 BC; iron ore was found in Macedonia, Euboea, Attica, the Peloponnese, the Aegean islands, and Crete.

**Īrus** In Homer's *Odyssey*, book 18, the beggar with whom Odysseus fights.

**Īsae'us** (*c.*420–after 353 BC) An Athenian orator of whose life little is known. He is represented as either Athenian or Chalcidian by birth, a pupil of *Isocrates and a teacher of *Demosthenes. He was a *logographos* (*see* LOGOGRAPHERS (2)): all his speeches were composed for others to deliver, and he took no part in political life. Of some fifty speeches with which he was credited, eleven and part of a twelfth have survived. The eleven all deal with cases of inheritance and are important as illustrative of Athenian testamentary law and of social history. He was considered 'clever in devising pleas for the worse cause', according to Dionysius of Halicarnassus. He is comparable with *Lysias in plainness and simplicity of language but more elaborate in setting out his (sometimes complex) logical proofs combined with emotional appeal, and more vigorous in controversy. In these latter characteristics it may be thought that he influenced Demosthenes.

**Īsagō'gē** ('Introduction') *See* PORPHYRY.

**Īsis** Great Egyptian goddess, sister and wife of Osiris and mother of Horus. She was a creative and nurturing force, the bringer of the Nile flood, and the promoter of fertility and abundance. She was therefore equated with many similar divinities—Venus, Minerva, Magna Mater; Herodotus identifies her with Demeter—and acquired a universal appeal in Greco-Roman Egypt as protector of women, maternity, and marriage, a healer and deliverer. She thus became the focus of something akin to a personal religion for many people. She also, with Osiris, ruled in the Underworld. In Greece, her worship was established in Piraeus by the fourth century BC, by Egyptians living there. Her cult, which in some respects resembled a mystery religion (*see* MYSTERIES and APULEIUS), spread to Rome in the second century BC and became popular in the early centuries AD.

**Isles of the Blest** In Greek myth, islands in the stream of Ocean (*see* OCEANUS) in the fabulous far West beyond the Pillars of Hercules (*see* HERACLES, LABOURS OF, 10), where after their death specially favoured mortals, notably the *heroes and the first generation of humans, of the so-called *Golden age, spent a blissful after-life. They were ruled over, it was often said, by *Cronus. Plato thought his philosopher-kings would join their numbers. Many other mythical beings were thought to live in the far West: Chrysaor, Callirrhoe, the Gorgons, the Hesperides, the Hecatoncheires, and the Sirens (see individual entries; *see also* ELYSIUM).

**Ismē'nē** *See* OEDIPUS and ANTIGONE.

**Īso'cratēs** (436–338 BC) Athenian orator, of great importance for his influence on later education, oratory, and writing. He has been admired by some for his prescience in ushering in the Hellenistic age with its new political attitudes and values, and condemned by others as a sycophant more concerned with his own well-being than that of his country.

1. Physically weak, Isocrates played no direct part in the politics of his city, but his written speeches aimed to influence public opinion and they provide a valuable commentary on the issues of the day. He was the son of a wealthy Athenian, Theodorus, and fell under the influence of Socrates. (Plato in the *Phaedrus*, writing when Isocrates had become famous, represents Socrates at an earlier period prophesying with delicate irony the young man's future greatness either as an orator or as a philosopher.) Having studied under *sophists and critics of democracy Isocrates appears to have fled from the *Thirty Tyrants to Chios, where he taught rhetoric, and to have returned to Athens on the restoration of

democracy. For a time he wrote speeches for others to use in the courts (*see* LOGOGRAPHERS (2)). Orations 16–21 belong to this period. In about 392 he began to train others in rhetoric. He opened a school at Athens the aim of which was to inculcate in its pupils, under the name of philosophy, the right moral and political attitudes, judging himself to be a philosopher and an authority on politics (see EDUCATION 3, and 4 below). It was this aspect that seemed to Plato no better than the education offered by the sophists and rhetors of the late fifth century which he so vehemently opposed. The subjects studied had an intellectual basis, if not of the Platonic kind (for which *see* PLATO 3), including Isocrates' own works, and the pupils were trained to write, speak, and argue about them. Thus they received a more practical training than was offered by the highly theoretical Plato, whom Isocrates characterizes (without mentioning him by name) as offering 'astronomy, geometry, and the like' which are 'no help in the present either in our speech or in our actions but are rather a gymnastic of the mind and a preparation for philosophy'. The school became famous, and pupils from all parts of the Greek world came to it, including the historians *Ephorus and *Theopompus, Androtion the atthidographer (*see* ATTHIS), the orators *Hypereides and *Isaeus, and the politician *Timotheus (2).

2. He also began to write political discourses, chiefly devoted to the cause of Greek unity. The *Panegyricus* ('Festival oration'), published in 380 after ten years of composition, was his version of a familiar topic, a plea for the union of the Greek city-states under the joint hegemony of Sparta and Athens. The long period devoted to its composition suggests that it was intended as an enduring summation of the ideal (*see* PANHELLENISM). When this appeal met with no success, his panhellenism took another form: he sought a strong man to assume the leadership of a united Greece in an expedition against Persia. His chief hope lay in Philip II of Macedon, but he began to address similar pleas to other leaders, Agesilaus II of Sparta and Dionysius I of Syracuse, for instance, but without noticeable effect. Some purported speeches that he wrote at this time—*To Nicocles* (*c.*372), *Nicocles* (*c.*368), and *Evagoras*—read more like rhetorical exercises. *On the Peace* (Lat. *De pace*), written

shortly before the *Social War (1) ended in 355 with Athens' failure to retain her league, is a denunciation of an imperialist policy as a way to bankruptcy. The speech is inspired by strong feeling, and is the most vigorous of Isocrates' speeches. In the *Areopagīticus*, probably written in 355 or 354, Isocrates advocates a return from the degenerate Athenian democracy of his day to the earlier democracy of Solon and Cleisthenes, with particular reference to the function, formerly exercised by the *Areopagus, of being the supervising authority of public morals. This uncharacteristic outburst on the ills of Athenian democracy may have been occasioned by the financial and moral impoverishment of Athens after the Social War. (John Milton's *Areopagitica* of 1644 deals with state censorship of publications.)

3. By 353 he had become a very rich man, liable to heavy taxes in the form of frequent trierarchies (*see* LITURGY). In that year he was challenged to an *antidosis* and defended himself in the courts unsuccessfully. His speech *On the Antidosis* is a defence of his life, modelled on Socrates' *Apology*, in the course of which he gives an account of what he believed and expressed in his own educational system, the chief source of our knowledge of it.

Between the Peace of Philocrates in 346 BC (*see* DEMOSTHENES (2) 2) and Philip's intervention in Phocis which followed, Isocrates wrote his most important political work, the *Philippus*, calling on Philip to lead the Greeks in a campaign against 'the barbarians'. He had no success. In 342, when he was 94, he began his last great work, the *Panathenaicus*, completed three years later. It was a defence partly of himself and partly of the deeds and constitution of Athens, to the disadvantage of Sparta.

Isocrates died at a great age in 338 BC, shortly after Philip defeated the Athenians at Chaeronea, it is said by starving himself to death when his third appeal to Philip failed. He was the first orator of significance to treat rhetorical prose as a work of art (*cf.* GORGIAS). His rhetoric is of a literary character rather than practical oratory. The sentences are long and flowing, the periods complex and highly wrought so that clarity is sacrificed to form; his avoidance of *hiatus and of dissonance is almost total. This is Attic prose at its most elaborate. Owing to the popularity of his school, his influence on literature, Latin as well as Greek, was long-lasting, extending to Cicero. Nine letters (some of which may not be genuine) and twenty-one of his speeches survive.

4. Of the *epideictic pieces, the *Busiris* (c.390) and the *Encomium of Helen* (written in the 380s) are criticisms of the works of other rhetoricians, in which he shows how he thought these well-worn themes should be handled; the *Evagoras* is an encomium on the king of Salamis (in Cyprus; see EVAGORAS), a loyal supporter of Athens who was assassinated in 374. Isocrates' second essay on education, after the *Antidosis*, is *Against the Sophists* (391 or 390), a protest against the education given by the sophists (among whom he would have included Socrates and Plato) and an exposition of his own principles.

**Issus** Town in south-east Cilicia near which the battle so named took place in 333 BC, when Alexander the Great defeated Darius III of Persia.

**Isthmian festival, Isthmian games** A Greek festival of athletic and musical competitions held every two years in honour of the god Poseidon at his sanctuary on the Isthmus of Corinth. The prize in classical times was a wreath of wild celery. It was at these games in 196 BC that *Flamininus proclaimed the independence of Greece from Philip V of Macedon.

**Italian philosophers** A term covering Greek philosophers who lived and worked in Italy (*Magna Graecia). They are Pythagoras and the Pythagoreans, Empedocles, and the Eleatics Parmenides and Zeno (but not *Melissus, strictly speaking).

**Italy (Italia)** A name perhaps meaning 'land of calves' (as if from Vitelia; Lat. *vitulus*, 'calf'); it appears to have been originally applied to the southern half of the toe of Italy. By 450 BC it meant all of the south-west peninsula (now Calabria), subsequently inhabited by the Bruttii, and by 400 BC it also included Lucania (the mountainous district of south Italy north of Calabria). By the third century BC it meant the whole Italian peninsula south of Liguria and Cisalpine Gaul. After the death of Julius Caesar in 44 BC Cisalpine Gaul too became part of Italy.

At the end of the sixth century BC, the Italian peninsula as a whole was inhabited by a variety of races: *Celts in the north, *Etruscans south of these, Greeks in the south of the peninsula

(see MAGNA GRAECIA), and in the centre an agglomeration of kindred tribes, Umbrians, Sabellians, Oscans, and Latins. These peoples differed from one another to a greater or lesser degree in race, language, and culture. The physical characteristics of the country are no less varied, from the Apennines and other mountain ranges, which produced a hardy, frugal mountain people, to the warm southern seaboard, where Greeks led an easy and luxurious life, e.g. at Sybaris and Croton. The achievement of *Rome during the republican period was to conquer and absorb all the inhabitants of the peninsula, receiving from them in return influences which are clearly reflected in Roman literature.

For the languages of Italy see ETRUSCANS and LATIN LANGUAGE.

**I'thaca (Ithakē)** In Homer, the homeland of Odysseus and the capital of his kingdom. It has usually been identified with modern Ithaca, a small narrow island between Cephallenia and Leucas off the west coast of Greece in Acarnania. Because the modern topography does not always match Homer's description some scholars reject the identification. Ithaca played no part in classical Greek history.

**Ithō'mē, Mount** Isolated and easily fortified mountain in the plain of *Messenia (in the Peloponnese), the rallying point of the Messenians in their struggles for independence against Sparta. In the Third Messenian War, after the great earthquake of 464 BC, the Messenians, having revolted, took refuge there. They were blockaded but did not surrender for a number of years. In 369 BC, when Messenia recovered its independence with the help of the Theban general Epaminondas, a new capital Messene was founded on the slopes of Mount Ithome.

**I'tylus** See AEDON.

**Itys** See PHILOMELA and AEDON.

**Iūlus** Also known as *Ascanius, the son of Aeneas. At Rome the *gens Iulia*, the Julian clan, to which Julius Caesar belonged, claimed him as their eponymous ancestor (see JULIA, GENS).

**iuvenes** See AGE QUALIFICATION.

**Ixī'ōn** In Greek myth, a Thessalian, the ruler of the Lapiths, who married Dia, daughter of Dēïoneus (or Ēïoneus); their son

# Ixion

was Peirithŏus (*see* CENTAURS). He was by tradition the first Greek to murder a kinsman. When his father-in-law came to fetch the bride-price that had been promised, Ixion contrived that he should fall into a pit of burning coals. For this murder he could obtain purification only from Zeus. When Zeus invited Ixion to Olympus for the rite, Ixion tried to seduce Zeus' wife Hera. Hera complained to Zeus who, to trap Ixion, formed a cloud in the likeness of Hera, and by this cloud, Nephele, Ixion became the father of the Centaurs (or of Centaurus, a monster, who mated with the mares on Mount Pelion to produce the Centaurs). As a punishment for his crime Zeus had him bound to a fiery wheel, constantly revolving, in the Underworld.

**Jāni'culum** The ridge on the west bank of the river Tiber opposite Rome (but not one of the seven hills); the name is connected with the god *Janus, and from early times it was a defensive outpost of Rome. A red flag was flown when *comitia* were held in the *Campus Martius, to be dropped if an enemy approached. The grove in which C. Gracchus died was on the Janiculum (*see* GRACCHI).

**Jānus** In Roman religion, the god of gates and doorways (Lat. sing. *ianua*, 'door') and subsequently of beginnings in general. The word properly means an archway or gateway, free-standing rather than set in a wall, and used originally for ceremonial purposes. In early times Janus was one of the principal Roman gods: the 'god of gods' in the hymn of the *Salii, the first to be named in any list of gods in a prayer, even before Jupiter, and the first to receive a portion of the sacrifice. The first month of the Roman calendar was named after him, and his priest was the *rex sacrorum*. His symbol was a double-faced and bearded head, looking in opposite directions. A statue of Janus Bifrons ('with two faces') stood with that of Saturn in the palace hall of King Latinus (Virgil, *Aeneid* 7.180). In Rome his temple was a small shrine in the Forum, the Janus Geminus, 'double Janus', probably a four-way arch. The doors were closed only in time of complete peace. Livy records that from the time of Numa, who founded it, to his own day the shrine had been closed only twice, after the First Punic War (241 BC) and after the victory of Octavian at Actium (31 BC). The emperor Augustus in the Monumentum Ancyranum (*see* RES GESTAE) says that it had been closed on three occasions in his Principate. Janus rarely figured in myth. According to one Roman tradition he was an early king of Latium; his son Tiberinus was drowned in the river Tiber, so giving it his name.

**Jāson** (Iāsōn) **1.** In Greek myth, son of Aeson and Alcimede, and leader of the *Argonauts.

**2. Jason of Pherae** (*c.*385–370 BC) Tyrant of the Greek Thessalian town of Pherae, who sought control over the whole of *Thessaly; he achieved his object in 374 BC, winning over the last important city, Pharsalus, by diplomacy. Ancient sources have suggested that he may have aimed at becoming the dominant power in Greece and even at leading a Greek expedition against Persia. In 370 he alarmed Greece by his plan to display the strength of his army at the next Pythian festival, and to preside at the games, but he was assassinated before he could carry out his plans and his further intentions remain unknown. He is often compared with Philip II of Macedon.

**Jews** *See* ANTI-SEMITISM; JOSEPHUS; PHILON (2).

**Joca'sta** (Iokastē) (Epikastē in Homer) The mother and wife of *Oedipus.

**Jōsē'phus, Flāvius** (AD 37–after 93) Jewish priest and historian, who wrote in Greek. He visited Rome in early adulthood, returning to Jerusalem in 66 on the eve of the Jewish Revolt against Roman domination (Judaea having been a province since AD 6). He tried to persuade the nationalist leaders that war with Rome could lead only to disaster, but without success. When the revolt broke out in the same year, Josephus was given command of Galilee by the Sanhedrin (the supreme council in Jerusalem). He survived the siege of Jotapata and was captured; he claims that his life was spared when he prophesied to the Roman commander Vespasian that the latter would become emperor, but he was kept in captivity until his prediction was fulfilled in 69. After the fall of Jerusalem in 70 he did what he could to help his Jewish friends. Subsequently he settled in Rome, where he received Roman citizenship, a house, and a pension. His first work, *Bellum Iudaicum* ('History of the Jewish War against the Romans'), in seven books, was originally written in Aramaic for the Jews in Mesopotamia and later translated into Greek. The rest of his works are in Greek (Jerome called him 'the Greek Livy'). The first part of the *Bellum Iudaicum* deals with the history of the Jews during the 200 years or so before the revolt; the rest is devoted to the events of the war, many of which he witnessed in person. It ends with the capture of Masada. His next work was *Antiquitates Iudaicae* ('Jewish archaeology') in twenty books, a history of the Jews from Adam to AD 66, giving a fuller account than the *Bellum Iudaicum* of the events covered by the latter work. Josephus' third work was his *Vita* ('Life'), not a full autobiography but a reply to the allegations of his enemy, Justus of Tiberias, that he had instigated and organized the Jewish Revolt in Galilee, a dangerous charge against one who lived in Rome by the favour of the emperor (Domitian at this period). His last work, in two books, was entitled 'Concerning the Antiquity of the Jews' but widely known under the title given it by Jerome, *Contra* (or *In*) *Apionem* ('Against Apion', an Alexandrian Greek scholar); this is an eloquent defence of Jews, their religion, law, and customs, against anti-Semitic detractors personified in Apion (*see* ANTI-SEMITISM).

**Juba 1.** King of Numidia in North Africa from 60 to 46 BC, notorious for his cruelty. He sided with Pompey in the Civil War and defeated and killed Caesar's general Gaius Scribonius Curio in 49 BC. He escaped after the republican defeat at Thapsus in 46, but, rejected by all sides, committed suicide.

**2. Juba II** Son of Juba (1), who while still an infant was led in Julius Caesar's triumph in 46 BC. He was brought up in Italy, and when grown up reinstated in Numidia, receiving in addition the kingdom of Mauretania. He married Cleopatra, the daughter of Mark Antony and the Egyptian queen Cleopatra, and died c.AD 23, being succeeded by his son Ptolemy. Juba was a man of great learning who sought to introduce Greek and Roman culture into his kingdom, and made a remarkable collection of artistic treasures. He wrote many books, in Greek (all lost), which are frequently cited by the Elder Pliny: they include a treatise on the medicinal plant euphorbia, which he discovered growing on the slopes of Mount Atlas and named after his physician Euphorbus (brother of Antonius Musa, physician to the emperor Augustus). He was the first to explore the Canary Islands thoroughly.

**Judgement of Paris** *See* PARIS, JUDGEMENT OF.

**Jugu'rtha** (d. 104 BC) Grandson of *Masinissa and king of Numidia from 118 BC. In 112 BC, when attacking a rival for the throne, Jugurtha sacked the city of Cirta, and in doing so massacred many Italian businessmen, which led to agitation at Rome to declare war. In spite of Jugurtha's lavish bribery (according to *Sallust), the Romans decided to crush him. After two unsuccessful campaigns (111–110) Metellus, consul of 109, was sent against him. Metellus repeatedly defeated Jugurtha, but found it impossible to subdue him. His legate *Marius, profiting by this, gained the consulship in 107, on the promise of a quick end to the war. Success eluded him too, but the war was ended when Sulla, Marius' quaestor, persuaded Bocchus, king of Mauretania and Jugurtha's father-in-law, with whom Jugurtha had taken refuge, to surrender him to the Romans. He was executed after Marius' triumph in 104. The story of the war, with its many exciting incidents, is vividly told in the *Bellum Iugurthinum* ('Jugurthine war') of Sallust.

**Jū'lia** Some of the famous women of the *gens* *Julia* (who therefore had this name; *see* NAMES [Roman]) were the following.
 **1.** Wife of Marius and sister of Julius Caesar's father.
 **2.** Sister of Julius Caesar and mother of Atia, who was the mother of the emperor Augustus.
 **3.** Daughter of Julius Caesar and his first wife Cornelia, and wife of Pompey. She died in childbirth in 55 BC. On the people's insistence she was buried in the Campus Martius, where Caesar held games partly in her honour in 46 BC. *See* GLADIATORS.
 **4.** Daughter and only child of Augustus and Scribonia; she married her cousin, Augustus' nephew, M. Marcellus, in 25 BC, and after his death in 23 married in 21 M. Agrippa, by whom she became the mother of Gaius and Lucius Caesar, Julia, Agrippina, and Agrippa Postumus. Her third marriage, after Agrippa's death, to Tiberius, took place in 11 BC. In 2 BC Augustus finally learned of her adulteries and banished her to a small island; in AD 4 she was allowed to move to Rhegium. Scribonia, who had been divorced from Augustus since 39 BC, voluntarily shared her exile. She died in AD 14.
 **5.** *Livia, the wife first of Ti. Claudius Nero and afterwards of Augustus. Under the latter's

will she was adopted into the Julian *gens* and renamed Julia Augusta.

**Jū'lia Domna** (of Emesa in Syria) The second wife of Septimius Severus, Roman emperor AD 193–211, and mother of *Caracalla. She was reputedly a woman of great intelligence and character who gathered about her a circle of cultivated and learned men, including *Galen and *Philostratus. After Severus' death she tried unsuccessfully to reconcile her two sons Caracalla and Geta (Caracalla stabbed Geta to death in her arms). She died or committed suicide at Antioch in 217 on learning of Caracalla's assassination by his successor Macrinus.

**Jū'lia, gens** Distinguished patrician *gens* ('clan') at Rome, perhaps originally from *Alba Longa, which claimed descent from Iulus (Ascanius) the son of Aeneas, and through them from the goddess Venus. To this *gens* belonged Julius Caesar and the emperor Augustus (distantly through his grandmother, Julia (2), properly through being adopted by Caesar and made his heir).

**Julio-Claudian emperors** At Rome, the Julio-Claudian dynasty, the immediate successors of the emperor Augustus who were related by blood or adoption: Tiberius (reigned AD 14–37), Caligula (properly known as Gaius, 37–41), Claudius (41–54), and Nero (54–68).

**Jūno** In Roman religion, the wife of *Jupiter. She was an ancient and important Italian goddess, resembling the Greek *Hera with whom she was identified from the second century BC, and closely associated with the life of women, hence sometimes connected with the moon, with fertility, and with the sanctity of marriage. She had many distinctive names indicating her various attributes, e.g. Lucīna, 'she who brings [the child] to light', as the goddess presiding over childbirth, or Opigena, 'who brings help to women in childbirth'. But she also became a goddess of the state; as Juno Regina ('Queen') she forms one of the Capitoline triad with Jupiter and Minerva. She had one Roman myth related by Ovid: being annoyed at the birth of *Athena without a mother, she determined to produce a child without a father; at the touch of a herb produced for her by Flora, she became pregnant and bore Mars, the god of war. (In Greek myth Hera, the wife of Zeus, is also the mother of Ares, the god of war, but Zeus is the father; the child she produces without male assistance is Hephaestus.) The Roman story may have been invented to explain the important festival of the Matronalia, when husbands gave presents to wives on the first of March, the month dedicated to Mars. 'Moneta' was another of her titles, thought of as being derived from *monere*, 'to remind', and meaning 'one who reminds'. The temple of Juno Moneta stood on the northern summit (*arx*) of the Capitoline hill; it had been vowed during a war in 345 BC and dedicated in the following year, and was said to have replaced an older shrine where the sacred geese had been kept (the geese perhaps being originally kept for divination); see MANLIUS CAPITOLINUS. An adjoining building contained the Roman mint: thus from *moneta* is derived the word 'money'. See also LIBRI LINTEI. There was a temple to Juno in the Campus Martius and another on the Aventine. The latter was dedicated in 392 BC by M. Furius Camillus, the conqueror of Veii, who placed in the temple a wooden statue of Juno brought from the captured city. For Juno in the sense of a woman's tutelary spirit see GENIUS.

**Jū'piter** (Lat. Iuppiter) The sovereign god of the Roman pantheon, supreme in rank and power. Originally the Italian sky-god, the name probably derived from *dyew-pater* the first part of which is etymologically equivalent to Greek Zeus, and signifies 'bright sky' (*see* DIESPITER). As sovereign deity he was associated with the sky and responsible for the weather, especially rain and lightning. His symbol was the sceptre, signifying power. No political action could be taken without his prior favour revealed by *augury.

The Etruscan kings were thought to have introduced the cult of Iuppiter Optimus Maximus (i.e. the 'best and greatest' of all Jupiters) in which the god, in his temple on the Capitol said to have been founded by the *Tarquins, was associated with Juno and Minerva, the three together known as the Capitoline triad. This was Jupiter in his aspect of god of the Roman state. In his temple the magistrates offered sacrifices on entering their year of office, and generals brought their spoils after victorious campaigns. Here every year the first meeting of the senate was held, including that at which Cicero delivered his first oration against *Catiline.

Jupiter Feretrius was also worshipped in the first temple built in the city, by Romulus. The derivation of the epithet is uncertain; it seems likely that it was connected with Jupiter Lapis, 'Stone'. The temple had no cult statue but a sceptre and the famous *silex*, 'flint', used in the ritual connected with the declaration and conclusion of wars and the most solemn oaths. He seems also to be connected with Fides, the personification of 'good faith'. The special priests of Jupiter were the *flamen dialis* and his wife, and he had his own augurs.

For the worship of Jupiter as Jupiter Latiaris *see* FERIAE LATINAE.

## juries
**At Athens.** In the fifth century BC a system of courts manned by citizen juries was set up. We know most about juries after the mid-fifth century, when every year a list of 6,000 volunteer jurors (called 'dicasts') for that year was drawn up from male citizens aged over 30. Pericles introduced payment of two obols a day for jury service, later raised by Cleon to three obols. Since this was less than a normal day's pay for a working man one effect, to judge from Aristophanes' *Wasps*, was that men too old for normal work were more inclined to volunteer. The number of jurors trying a case varied according to its importance, but was normally several hundred (it is very plausible that the jury at Socrates' trial numbered 500). A complicated system of drawing lots to allocate jurors to try particular cases was introduced at the end of the fifth century in order to prevent bribery. Each trial was presided over by a magistrate—archon, basileus, polemarch, etc. In rare circumstances a case was tried by the *boule* or the *ecclesia*. Homicide cases were dealt with by the *Areopagus according to its own procedure.

**At Rome.** In 149 BC the first permanent (as opposed to *ad hoc*) court was set up, to try cases of extortion by provincial governors. The jury consisted of senators until 122 BC, when C. Gracchus transferred the membership to the *equites* (*see* EQUESTRIAN ORDER). Voting was secret, by tablets dropped into an urn. The verdict was decided by majority vote. In the following forty years several other permanent courts were instituted for particular crimes, and Sulla in 81 BC increased their number further, but these courts were composed entirely of senators. In 70 BC juries were empanelled equally and by lot from senators,

*equites*, and the property class below, known as the *tribuni aerarii*, 'tribunes of the treasury', the size of the jury varying with the importance of the case. The emperor Augustus added a fourth jury panel of members of a still lower property class. This type of law-court disappeared by the third century AD, and its functions were taken over by other officers. Both during the republic and under the empire many minor cases must have been dealt with by local magistrates.

**Justin** (Marcus Juniānus Justīnus) Roman historian of uncertain date (second, third or even fourth century AD), who wrote in Latin an abridgement of the universal history of *Trogus (*Historiae Philippicae*, 'Philippic Histories', now lost). It consists of largely unaltered (or apparently unaltered) excerpts joined together by colourless résumés; there are a few striking passages, such as the description of the multitude of Athenians pouring out to see Alcibiades on his return from exile, and of Brennus and his army of Gauls at Delphi. Since Trogus' work has not survived, Justin's book is valuable for the history of Macedon and the Hellenistic kingdoms. It was widely read in the Middle Ages.

**Justi'nian** (Flavius Petrus Sabbatius Justiniānus) (*c.*AD 482–565) Emperor of the *Roman empire in the East, ruling at Constantinople AD 527–65, He was the nephew of the Justin who became emperor in 518 and whom he succeeded. After 523 he married the actress and courtesan Theodora despite the scandals of her early life. He made her an equal and independent colleague in his imperial office, and remained devoted to her until her death. Justinian was determined to restore the Roman empire by recovering the lost provinces of the West, by codifying and rationalizing the legal system, and by reforming the administration. All this, he thought, depended upon God's favour, and this he resolved to win by legislating for orthodoxy, although he also sought to win over the Monophysites and unite the Church. His first aim was achieved through his great general Belisarius, who recovered Africa from the Vandals, invaded Italy, occupied Rome (535–6), and overthrew the Ostrogothic kingdom in Italy; finally, part of Spain was freed from the Visigoths.

Justinian's famous reorganization of Roman law came in three stages. The first was the completion, by a commission of ten, of the *Codex Justinianus* ('the Justinian *Codex', or 'code'), which contained in twelve books all imperial laws that were still in force, including the more recent, the *novellae* ('new laws'); all earlier codices were then repealed. This was completed within fourteen months in 529, and is a major achievement. Only the second edition of 534 survives. The second stage dealt with the works of the 'old lawyers of antiquity'. This work consists of an excerption from the original sources (some 1500 books) of what was still valid, and its condensation into 50 books, called *Digesta* ('Abstracts') or *Pandectae* ('Encyclopaedia'). The work was done under the supervision of Tribonian, a member of the earlier commission, and completed in three years. Ulpian was responsible for two-fifths of the *Digesta*. The whole project was completed by the reform of law-teaching. Tribonian and two other professors were told to edit and update the law lectures of *Gaius, the *Institutions*, making use of other elementary but authoritative textbooks. This work was published at the same time as the *Digesta*, in 533, and still survives. Despite Justinian's being the emperor of the Greek-speaking lands the codification was written entirely in Latin, and its impact was therefore limited. In the East few could make proper use of it, but in parts of the Latin-speaking West Justinian's laws were in force until the Arab invasions of the seventh century. From the eleventh century onwards his codification became the basis of European law.

Justinian carried out many reforms of the provincial administration, ridding it of numerous abuses. He kept a careful watch on financial expenditure, but was also a great church-builder, the chief memorial of his reign being the rebuilt church of Hagia Sophia (532–7) in Constantinople, the supreme masterpiece of Byzantine architecture. The original building had been destroyed, with much of the city, in the Nika riot of 532 (so-called from the participants' battle-cry meaning 'Conquer!'). This had broken out as a result of the mutual hatred of the Blues and the Greens, the two rival factions in the chariot-races, representing different political and social interests (Justinian himself was a Blue), and it was suppressed with great difficulty. In his pursuit of religious orthodoxy throughout the empire and the suppression of paganism, and to put an end to *Neoplatonist doctrines, in 529 Justinian closed all the famous philosophy schools of Alexandria and Athens.

Theodora died in 548. Justinian died childless and had failed to groom a successor. He was succeeded by his nephew, Justin II. *See* PROCOPIUS.

**Jutu'rna** An Italian goddess of fountains. It was at her spring in the Roman Forum that Castor and Pollux were said to have watered their horses after the battle of Lake Regillus (*see* DIOSCURI). A temple was dedicated to her at Rome in the Campus Martius by C. Lutatius Catulus, vowed in 241 BC during the notable sea-battle off Sicily in the First *Punic War. She is said to have been loved by Jupiter, who rewarded her with immortality and with rule over springs and rivers. Virgil in the *Aeneid* makes her the devoted sister of *Turnus, who disguised herself as his charioteer Metiscus, and restored to him his lost sword made by Vulcan. She was compelled by a Fury, sent from Jupiter, to give up her brother to his fate, and returned lamenting to her spring.

**Ju'venal** (Decimus Junius Juvenālis) (fl. early second century AD) The greatest of Roman satirical poets. He was probably a native of Aquinum (on the Via Latina in Latium) but beyond that fact very little is known of his life. Two inscriptions from that town were found (but are now lost) which may possibly have referred to him, and if so may indicate that he served in the army (as the first step on an official career) and held a local magistracy. The poet Martial, his elder contemporary, addressed three epigrams to him but the Younger Pliny does not mention him at all. The various ancient Lives of Juvenal which survive are of late date, somewhat contradictory, and probably not reliable. They mostly agree in referring to a period of banishment, in consequence of an offence to a favourite (the actor Paris) of the emperor Domitian; it is also stated by one that he practised declamation until middle age (Martial calls him *facundus*, 'eloquent'). If what Juvenal says in his *Satires* is literally true he was at one time poor, but later acquired a farm at Tibur (Tivoli), he could offer hospitality in his house at Rome, and he had visited Egypt. His sixteen satires, of which the last breaks off short, are arranged in five books. Internal evidence suggests they were published between *c*.110 and shortly after 127, in the peaceful reigns of Trajan and Hadrian which followed Domitian's death in 96.

The *Satires* are notable for their bitter, ironical humour, power of invective, grim epigrams, sympathy with the poor, and a narrow pessimism. They suggest that Juvenal was xenophobic, and disliked ostentatious women and cliquey homosexuals. He claims Lucilius and Horace as his masters, but he has none of the latter's humour or irony. The extravagance of his wholesale hatreds and condemnations is effective as rhetoric, but need not be taken as the expression of personal feelings. His gift is for the vivid evocation of scenes of (no doubt exaggerated) Roman life with a few economical and memorable phrases. (For a résumé of each satire *see* SATIRES (2).)

The *Satires* survive in more manuscripts than most classical texts, but only one is fairly reliable, so the text is doubtful in many places.

**Juve'ntas** The Roman goddess of youth, identified with the Greek *Hebe.

For Greek names with initial K see also under C.

**Kalends** In the Roman *calendar the name given to the first day of the month, one of the three named days in each month, together with the *Ides and the *Nones. A date was calculated by counting backwards, inclusively, from the next named day. Thus, 1 June was Kal (endis) Jun(iis) and, for example, 28 May was 'the fifth day before the Kalends of June'; in full, *ante diem quintum Kalendas Junias*, or a.d. v Kal. Jun.

**kalos ka'gathos** (pl. *kaloi kagathoi*, 'fine and good') Greek adjective of aesthetic and moral approval in which the moral sense predominates, used to describe men (and actions), rarely women. It may also have social connotations, implying that a man so described not only has good looks and is expected to be honourable and brave, but is quite rich, educated, and of good family, 'brought up in wrestling-schools and dancing and music', as the chorus in Aristophanes' *Frogs* describes him.

**kanephoroi** ('basket-carriers') In Greece, young women who carried baskets or vessels in religious processions, such as at the *Panathenaea. They had to be of good family and reputation, and unmarried: hence the saying 'to be fit to carry the basket'.

**Kēres** In Greece, undefined bringers of ills or the ills themselves, old age, disease, and death. The singular, *kēr*, often has the sense of 'fate'.

**kings of Rome** Later generations of Romans believed that the city had been ruled by kings from its foundation by Romulus in 753 BC (a date fixed by *Varro (1)) until 509 BC, the date conventionally accepted for the beginning of the republic. The canonical number of these was seven: Romulus, Numa Pompilius, Tullus Hostilius, Ancus Marcius, Tarquinius Priscus, Servius Tullius, and Tarquinius Superbus, who was expelled in 510. (The monarchy was not hereditary but elective, by the patricians.) Apart from the inherent improbability of such long reigns, archaeology does not support the achievements attributed to them.

**King's Peace** The Peace of Antalcidas, arranged by King Artaxerxes II of Persia to end the Corinthian war in 386 BC. It guaranteed the autonomy of the Greeks in return for recognition that the Greek cities in Asia and the island of Cyprus should belong to Persia. It was the first properly so-called 'Common Peace' in Greece, based on the principle of autonomy. Antalcidas was an influential Spartan (probably related to King Agesilaus II) who forced the Athenians and their allies to agree to the terms.

**knights** At Rome, *see* EQUESTRIAN ORDER; at Athens, *see* HIPPEIS.

***Knights*** (*Hippeis*) (Lat. *Equites*) Greek comedy by *Aristophanes, produced at the *Lenaea of 424 BC and awarded first prize. It was the first occasion on which Aristophanes produced one of his plays himself. The demagogue *Cleon, the object of attack, was at the height of his fame after his victory at Pylos the previous year. The play is in some sense an allegory; the master of the house is called Demos ('the people'), and his slaves Demosthenes and Nicias (named for the Athenian generals) are terrorized by a new slave, a Paphlagonian (i.e. Cleon; cf. *paphlazein*, 'to splutter').

Demosthenes and Nicias are lamenting their ill-treatment at the hands of the Paphlagonian, a spying flatterer of their master, and contemplating desertion as the only remedy. They learn from a collection of oracles that the Paphlagonian is to be ousted from favour by a sausage-seller. One of this trade appears on his way to the market, is told of his destiny to rule over the whole Athenian empire, and has his terror at the prospect of conflict allayed by the assurance that the knights (*hippeis*) will support him against the Paphlagonian. The latter enters threateningly, but the chorus of knights is called and comes charging on to the stage uttering their battle-cry, *paie, paie*

('Strike! Strike!'). The Paphlagonian and the sausage-seller contend with each other for the favour of Demos by flattery, bribes, interpretation of oracles, and mutual abuse. Then they both go off to the *boule* ('council') to do the same there, the sausage-seller returning to announce his victory. He is immediately followed by the Paphlagonian, and the competition in flattery of Demos continues. The sausage-seller is preferred in this, and in the competition of oracles, and in the final competition to settle who does more for Demos. After this the Paphlagonian discovers that the sausage-seller fits the description of the man fated to overthrow him, and retires in despair; the sausage-seller wins the day, and it is revealed that his name is Agorakritos, 'choice of the assembly', and that he is to be the reformer and saviour of the state. Demos confesses his past gullibility and promises to behave better in future.

**koinē** The common, simplified Attic Greek dialect of the Greek-speaking world during the Hellenistic period (from *c.*300 BC); the language of Menander, Polybius, and the Greek New Testament.

***Kōlax*** ('The flatterer') Greek comedy by *Menander, which, together with his *Eunouchos*, was made use of by Terence for his own *Eunuchus*. Some fragments of *Kolax* have been recovered from papyri but it is difficult to reconstruct the plot beyond the fact that it concerned an arrogant Greek professional soldier.

**kommos** In Attic *tragedy, lyric dirge or lament sung by the chorus and one or more of the actors alternately.

**kōmos** In Greece a band or procession of revellers who might be celebrating someone's victory in the games or proceeding noisily through the streets after a *symposium, singing and dancing. Aristotle in the *Poetics* records a tradition that comedy originated in the *komos*.

**Korē** ('daughter') *See* PERSEPHONE.

**kouroi, korai** ('youths', 'maidens') Names given to life-size archaic Athenian sculptures of the whole body combining detailed physical observation with refined beauty.

**Krypteiʹa** At Sparta, the equivalent of a secret police force in which selected young Spartan men were authorized by the *ephors to patrol the Laconian countryside and murder any supposedly dangerous *helots. It has been suggested that it was the rationalization of an ancient initiation rite for young men approaching manhood (*cf.* EPHEBOI at Athens). Aristotle ascribed the institution to *Lycurgus.

**Labe'rius, De'cimus** (*c.*105–43 BC) Roman knight and a famous writer of *mimes. According to *Macrobius, his outspoken criticism of Julius Caesar brought upon him the humiliation (perhaps in 45 BC) of being required to appear on stage in his own mimes in competition with *Publilius Syrus. Several anecdotes are told of this famous occasion. It is said that at one point all eyes turned towards Caesar when a character said, 'He needs must fear many whom many fear'.

**Labie'nus, Titus** (*c.*100–45 BC) Julius Caesar's most senior and trusted officer during a great part of the former's campaigns in Gaul from 58 to 49 BC. He had been tribune of the people in 63 (the year of Cicero's consulship), and in order to please Caesar had prosecuted Rabirius, who was defended by Cicero (*see* CICERO (1) 2). At the outbreak of civil war in 49 he joined Pompey and fought against Caesar until he was defeated and killed at the battle of *Munda in 45.

**labyrinth** (*labyrinthos*) The complicated building or maze, from which no one could escape, said to have been built by *Daedalus for King *Minos of Crete to contain the Minotaur which was fed on human victims (*see* THESEUS). The word, found in *Linear B, may be of pre-Greek origin, perhaps derived from *labrys* which, according to Plutarch, is the Lydian word for 'double-headed axe', the royal or religious symbol frequently found represented in the palace remains of Minoan Crete. The complicated figures of the Greek 'crane dance' were supposed to represent the convolutions of the labyrinth. The maze-like design is found on artefacts in Crete and may be a religious symbol.

**Lacedae'mon (Lakedaimōn)** (Lat. Lacōnica, or Lacōnia) The ancient Greek name for the territory in the south-east Peloponnese. Its capital city was *Sparta. In classical times the Greeks commonly applied the term 'Lacedaemonian' to the whole free population, including both Spartan citizens and the *perioikoi. In English, however, the name 'Sparta' is usually applied to the city and the territory and all its inhabitants ('the Spartans') without reference to their citizen status. Later Greek writers often called the territory Lakōnikē (from *Lakōn*, a shortened form of *Lakedaimonios*, 'Lacedaemonian').

**Lacedaemo'nians, Constitution of the** A work by Xenophon; *see* CONSTITUTION OF THE LACEDAEMONIANS.

**Lachēs** Dialogue by *Plato, named for the Athenian general killed at Mantinea in 418 BC. He and *Nicias, another general, ask Socrates for his views on military training for their sons. Courage is needed for fighting: what is it? It is agreed to be part of virtue but it emerges that a man possessing courage would also possess all the other parts of virtue. So it remains unclear what courage itself is.

**La'chesis** *See* FATES.

**Lacō'nia, Lacōnica** (Gk. Lakōnikē) The Latin name for *Sparta. *See* LACEDAEMON.

**La'dē, battle of** *See* PERSIAN WARS.

**Laelius** *See* DE AMICITIA.

**Lae'lius, Gaius** Consul at Rome in 140 BC, and close friend of *Scipio Aemilianus. He was a good soldier and led the decisive assault on Carthage as a legate under Scipio in the Third Punic War (149–146 BC). He was a prominent member of the intellectual, philhellenic circle; Cicero (in *Brutus*) considered him the outstanding orator of his day, and he was given the name Sapiens, 'the wise', for his wide learning and philosophical attainments (or, according to Plutarch, for dropping his proposal for agrarian reform in the face of senatorial opposition). It was said that the comedies of Terence, who was also a friend of Scipio, owed much to Laelius. Cicero makes him the principal speaker in *De amicitia*, and an interlocutor in *De senectute* and *De republica*. In *De oratore* Cicero tells how Laelius and Scipio liked to go on holiday to the seaside, 'where they became incredibly childish and used to collect shells and pebbles on the beach'.

**Lāe'rtes** In Homer's *Odyssey*, the father of Odysseus.

**Laestrygo'nians** Cannibal giants in Homer's *Odyssey* (book 10).

**Laïs** There seem to have been two famous Greek *hetairai* of this name whose separate identities it is impossible to disentangle. The elder came from Corinth and was celebrated as the most beautiful woman of her day (end of the fifth century BC). Laïs dedicating her looking-glass to Aphrodite is a frequent subject of epigrams in the *Greek *Anthology*. The younger Laïs, who was said to be a contemporary and rival of *Phryne, was loved by the painter *Apelles.

**Lā'ius** In Greek myth, legendary king of Thebes, father of *Oedipus, son of Labdacus, and great-grandson of *Cadmus. *See also* ANTIOPE.

**La'machus** (d. 414 BC) Athenian general of the time of the *Peloponnesian War; he had been *stratēgos* c.435 BC and so was well known by 425 when he was caricatured by Aristophanes in his comedy *Acharnians*. In 415 he was appointed with Alcibiades and Nicias to command the *Sicilian Expedition, and he pursued an energetic policy until killed in a skirmish there in 414. After his death Thucydides and Aristophanes treated him with respect.

**La'mian War** (323–322 BC) The war which followed the revolt of the Greek states against Macedonian rule after the death of Alexander the Great. Athens joined with the states of northern Greece, and under the Athenian general Leosthenes the Greeks were successful for a time and besieged *Antipater (1), regent of Macedonia, in Lamia, a Thessalian town. But after Leosthenes was killed the war ended with a Macedonian victory at the battle of Crannon. The Macedonian fleet played an important part in the war and put an end to the sea-power of Athens. Antipater placed a Macedonian garrison at Piraeus and demanded the surrender of *Demosthenes (2).

**Lāo'coön** Trojan prince, brother of *Anchises, and priest of Apollo or Poseidon. For his story *see* TROJAN HORSE. Laocoön is best known through his depiction with his two sons in a statuary group (in the Vatican) carved by three sculptors from Rhodes—Hagesandros, Athanodoros, and Polydoros—probably in the first century AD. In Rome, it was exhibited in the palace of Titus and seen by the Elder Pliny, who ranked it as the greatest work of art in the world; his description enabled it to be recognized when it was found in the ruins on the Esquiline hill (possibly from Nero's *Golden House) in 1506. The German critic Lessing made this sculpture the basis of his book *Laokoon* (1766) analysing the different potentialities and limitations of poetry and the visual arts.

**Lāo'medon** In Greek myth, king of *Troy, father of Priam. When the gods Apollo and Poseidon were doomed to serve a mortal for wages (a punishment for revolting against Zeus), Laomedon employed them to build the walls of Troy; when they had finished, however, he refused to pay them. Apollo then sent a plague and Poseidon a sea-monster against Troy, the danger from which could be averted only if Laomedon sacrificed his daughter Hesione to the monster. Heracles happened to arrive at Troy and undertook to kill the monster if Laomedon would give him his famous horses (originally a gift from Zeus in exchange for *Ganymede), but Laomedon defrauded him as well. After many years Heracles returned with an army, captured the city, killed Laomedon and all his sons except Priam, and gave Hesione to *Telamon, who had helped in the attack. There was a story that Laomedon was buried above the Scaean Gate at Troy, and ensured the safety of the city as long as he was undisturbed (the gate was dismantled to admit the *Trojan Horse). When the Trojans were called 'sons of Laomedon' it was a hint at possible teachery.

**Lapiths** In Greek myth, a Greek tribe inhabiting the north of Thessaly; Peirithous, son of *Ixion, was their king. *See* CENTAURS.

**lārēs** In Roman religion, spirits associated with a particular place. There are two theories about their origins. One is that the *lares* were originally deities of the farmland, invoked (in the words of Tibullus) to 'give good crops and wine', and that the household *lar* *familiaris* ('of the servants') was introduced into houses at a later time by the farm-slaves. The other theory is that the *lares familiares* were the deified spirits of dead ancestors, good and beneficent so long as they were treated with respect. By classical times the *lares familiares* were guardian spirits who had the special care of the house and household. Every household had its shrine, often like a cupboard, containing small images of the *lares*, set up in the *atrium*. The *lares familiares* had their counterpart in the *lares praestites* ('guardians') of the state. These had a temple at the head of the Via Sacra; the figure of a dog stood between their images, symbolic of their faithful guardianship. In later times the *lares* were identified with the *Dioscuri. They have no mythology. *See also* AULULARIA; GENIUS; PENATES.

**Lars Po'rsena** *See* PORSENA.

**larvae** *See* LEMURES.

**Lāsus** (of Hermione in Argolis, b. *c*.548 BC) An early Greek *lyric poet, celebrated as the founder of the Athenian school of dithyrambic poetry (he instituted the dithyrambic contests at Athens; *see* DITHYRAMB) and as the teacher of Pindar. He also wrote the first book about music. He was a contemporary of Simonides, and like him he lived at Athens under the patronage of Hipparchus (brother of Hippias the tyrant). According to Herodotus, he revealed *Onomacritus as the forger of an oracle supposedly by Musaeus. Virtually nothing of his poetry survives.

**late antiquity** A term which came into use in the late twentieth century meaning the period from roughly the mid-third century to the end of the eighth century AD, concluded by the coronation of the Frankish king Charlemagne as Christian emperor of the West in 800. The term is perhaps preferable to 'early Middle Ages' and is useful to describe the thought-world of that period, which saw the revival and the end of Platonic philosophy in the form of *Neoplatonism, and the rise and ultimate triumph of *Christianity and Islam, with consequent changes of attitude to fundamental aspects of human life. However, this characterization is in some opposition to the more traditional view of the later Roman empire in the West as one of violent invasion and disintegration in the fifth century leading to the

collapse of civilization in Europe and a *Dark age (the eastern empire flourished for another century, some parts even later; *see* JUSTINIAN). Perhaps both views of the period need to be kept in mind. *See also* PRINCIPATE.

**latifu'ndia** 'Large estates', which Pliny the Elder in the first century AD famously declared 'have ruined Italy'. What exactly the term means and why they ruined the rural economy have long been subjects of debate. They have been thought to originate in distributions by lease, from the third century BC, of large tracts of *ager publicus* ('state-owned land') given over to grazing, or to have been large oil- and wine-producing properties staffed by slaves under the supervision of bailiffs, *vilici*, and centred on a villa, as described by Cato the Elder. When slave-labour ceased to be so plentiful in the first century BC the *vilici* continued to cultivate the home farms but leased the other farms to *coloni*, tenant farmers, and collected their rent. On many *latifundia*, especially in the south of Italy, stock-rearing or cultivation of the vine and olive were seen to be more profitable than arable farming. The introduction of new farming machinery from Gaul, suitable for working large areas, has also been seen as fundamental to their establishment. The effect in any case was to drive small farmers from the land, thereby depriving Rome of sturdy independent people with the physical and moral toughness upon which, it was felt, her greatness depended. It would seem that for Rome this loss was more significant than the economic advantages of these estates. Archaeology and literary references seem to support the view that all over Italy and in the provinces estates were amalgamated, particularly in the early empire.

**Latini, Latins** The name of an ethnic group in Italy who from *c*.1000 BC had a common material culture, religion, and language, and similar social and political institutions. In the early *Iron age they occupied the southern part of the lower valley of the river Tiber (between, to the south, the Greek culture of Magna Graecia and, to the north, the Etruscan culture of Etruria). They gave their name to this territory, *Latium. The Latins traced their descent from *Latinus (the father-in-law of Aeneas) who after death became Jupiter Latiaris (*see* FERIAE LATINAE), the god of the *Latin league worshipped from remotest times on the Alban mount. For a later use of the name 'Latins' *see* BYZANTIUM. *See also* LATIN LANGUAGE.

**Latin language** Latin was the language of the city of Rome and the territory of *Latium to the south from 800 BC or earlier. Latin spread with the power of Rome until it became the common language first of Italy, then of the western Mediterranean and the Balkan regions of the Roman empire. It is known to have been one of several related dialects which formed the Italic group in the *Indo-European family of languages, but it is markedly different from the other major branch of Italic, Osco-Umbrian (Oscan and *Umbrian; *see also* ITALY) and it is not at all close to Greek, although the latter is also Indo-European.

To judge from inscriptions the Romans were probably literate before 600 BC. Early legal and religious texts, records, and (Saturnian) verse were written in a refined form of Latin. The illiterate majority in Rome, Italy, and the provinces spoke what is now known as Vulgar Latin, which eventually evolved into the Romance languages (see below). Scholars of the late republic and early empire did not find early Latin easy to understand or attractive (*see* SALII and TWELVE TABLES). Polybius, writing in the second century BC of 'the first Carthaginian treaty' (perhaps 509 BC), says that even the best scholars after much study had difficulty in interpreting some of it. However, these early written forms, modified from the mid-third century BC by the influence of Greek literature (*see* LIVIUS ANDRONICUS) led eventually to a generally accepted written form of the Roman dialect, the 'polite speech' (*sermo urbanus*), i.e. classical Latin. The terms 'spoken' or 'colloquial' Latin cover the easy 'everyday speech' (*sermo cotidianus*) of educated people. The plays of Plautus and Terence provide the best evidence for this style, but also important are the letters of Cicero, especially those to his intimate friend Atticus, with their very free syntax. Similar in effect although poetic are Horace's *Satires* and *Epistles*, and parts of Catullus. Interesting in this respect is the *Satyricon* of *Petronius, with its range of registers from the urbane to the coarse. The other Italic dialects played no part in Latin literary culture (in contrast with the situation in Greece).

The term 'classical Latin' describes the written language used by authors from *c*.90 BC to *c*.AD 120. It is an artificial creation, deviating considerably from what should be considered mainstream Latin, the Vulgar Latin of speech.

Common usage and the informal converse of writers (as in e.g. Cicero's letters) provided the link for centuries between the most refined literary forms and the plain language of the law and of technical works. Vulgar Latin is known from inscriptions and especially graffiti, a few texts such as the *Satyricon* of Petronius, and the early development of the Romance languages. It is marked by slurred or confused pronunciation, a standardization of originally diverse word forms, a breakdown of declensions leading to an increased use of prepositions, a much simpler syntax, and a more natural word-order. Gradually the literary tradition incorporated Vulgar elements of syntax and vocabulary and well before the end of the first millennium AD became medieval Latin, the main form of communication at the time. It was during this time that regional variations in spoken Latin developed into the Romance languages, which would have been incomprehensible to a classical Roman.

**Latin league** In Italy, the association of Latin towns, from the seventh century BC onwards, for, among other things, the joint worship of deities widely recognized among all the Latins (*see* LATINI). Most important was the celebration of the festival of the Latin Jupiter (Jupiter Latiaris) on the Alban Mount (*see* FERIAE LATINAE). *Alba Longa traditionally led a Latin league, but the leadership allegedly passed to Rome when she destroyed Alba *c*.600 BC. After the Latin War of 340–338, in which the Romans were completely victorious, the Latin league was dissolved and the individual cities had to accept Rome's terms, of incorporation into the Roman state for some (the smaller), and of becoming Roman (subject) allies for the rest.

**Latin literature, periods of** The following terms are sometimes used to describe the successive periods of Latin literature:

(i) *Early Latin*, up to about 90 BC.

(ii) The Latin of the *Golden age*, from about 90 BC to the deaths of Livy and Ovid in AD 17. The literary activity of Cicero and Caesar gives special importance to the years 81–43 BC, sometimes called the *Ciceronian age. The years following that are known as the *Augustan age (the emperor Augustus died in AD 14). *See also* VELLEIUS PATERCULUS.

(iii) *Silver Latin*, from AD 17 to about AD 150, felt to mark a falling off from the literature of the preceding Golden age. It is characterized by the development of *rhetoric, which sometimes led to a striving for novelty, variety, and effect, and is marked by exaggerated emphases, antitheses, and epigrams, seen clearly in the prose of Tacitus and the poetry of Lucan.

(iv) *Late Latin*, from AD 150, which merges into medieval Latin.

**Latin rights** (Lat. *ius Latii*) Rights held by Latin cities that remained unincorporated in the Roman state (such as Tibur and Praeneste) and by Latin colonies. The Latins by their origin (*see* LATIUM) and special position among Rome's allies (*see* LATIN LEAGUE) occupied from the Roman point of view an intermediate position between Romans and other Italian allies; they shared many material privileges with Roman citizens including the important rights of *commercium* (the right of transacting business and conducting law-suits at Rome on the same footing as Roman citizens) and *conubium* (the right of intermarriage with Romans). In 89 BC, after the *Social War (2), the Latins were granted Roman citizenship along with all the Italian allies.

**Latins, the** *See* LATINI.

**Latī'nus** In Roman legend, eponymous hero of the Latins, king of *Latium and, according to Virgil, son of the god *Faunus and of the nymph Marica; thus through Faunus' father *Picus he was descended from Saturn. In the *Aeneid* (book 7) he is the father of Lavinia and, in accordance with an oracle to marry her to a stranger, offers her hand to Aeneas (whom she later marries); his queen Amata prefers *Turnus and with him declares war on Aeneas. Latinus survives the war and peace is promised if, as happens, Aeneas is victorious (books 7-12). A certain Latinos was known to the Greek poet Hesiod, who makes him a son of Odysseus and *Circe.

**Latin War** *See* LATIN LEAGUE.

**La'tium** Originally a small area of land in western Italy around the Alban mount (about 20km or 13 miles south-east of Rome), lying between the Apennines and the Tyrrhenian Sea, whose boundaries were gradually extended north to the river Tiber and south to Sinuessa. In historical times Latium was inhabited by *Latini.

**Lātō'na** Latin name for the Greek goddess *Leto.

**Laus Pisō'nis** *See* DE LAUDE PISONIS.

**Lausus 1.** In Virgil's *Aeneid* (book 10), the son of *Mezentius. While trying to save his father he is killed by Aeneas.

**2.** Name of a son of Numitor, king of *Alba Longa, killed by his uncle Amulius.

**Lavi'nia** In Virgil's *Aeneid*, daughter of *Latinus; she is betrothed to *Turnus (book 7) but her father pledges her in marriage to Aeneas.

**Lavinium** (modern Pratica di Mare) According to tradition the first city Aeneas founded in Italy. His son Ascanius became king, before moving his government to Alba Longa. The *penates from Troy were said to have come to Rome from Lavinium. It had direct links with the Greek world and may have played a part in transmitting Greek culture to Rome. Its Trojan associations were always important to Rome. *See* VENUS.

**law, natural; law, universal** (Lat. *ius naturale* and *ius gentium*, the 'law of nations') Natural law is a concept expressing the belief that certain laws are rooted in principles of nature which are found everywhere and are therefore universally valid. Aristotle divided law into natural and man-made, and at Rome the idea of natural law was taken up by the Stoics and often found in Cicero. During the third and second centuries BC, when large numbers of foreigners were drawn to Rome by the expansion of her power, there developed the idea of a 'universal law', based on the notion that a common element was to be found in the laws of all nations. In a practical sense the universal law came to be found especially in the law of contract, which was presumably based on the universal customs of the Mediterranean peoples and came to be applied everywhere. In philosophical discourse natural law became erroneously identified with universal law. However, the Roman lawyer *Gaius observed that according to natural law all people are born free, whereas by universal law some might be enslaved. The Roman jurist Ulpian seems to have regarded natural law as being concerned with the instincts which humans share with animals. The concept of human rights (as contrasted with the narrower citizen rights) was not developed until the twentieth century. *See also* NOMOS–PHYSIS ANTITHESIS.

**law, Roman** Romans regarded their legal system as beginning with the promulgation *c.*450 BC of the *Twelve Tables, a codification of existing law which eventually became obsolete but was never abolished. Roman life and thought are permeated by the law to an exceptional degree, and the body of material relating to it is vast.

In the early republic new laws originated in proposals made by the senate which then had to be ratified by the political *assembly of the people, the *comitia centuriata*. Private law (civil law in its limited sense) was confined to Roman citizens and was an area in which the state very largely did not interfere. The male head of the Roman family possessed considerable legal power over his family, including the power of life and death (*see* PATERFAMILIAS). At this period the law employed formulaic expression to a remarkable degree, which made it inaccessible to many citizens: fixed words and phrases had to be used in legal transactions with complete exactitude (*see* FLAVIUS, GNAEUS). In the third and second centuries BC change came about because of Roman expansion through conquest and trade. Laws hitherto governing relations between citizens had to be adapted to cover transactions with foreigners. Only those provincials who had gained Roman citizenship, for example, conformed to Roman private law, whereas under Roman rule the provinces from the beginning had the right to organize their own legal affairs according to their own laws.

In *c.*242 BC a second *praetor, in addition to the 'city' praetor, was created, the *praetor peregrinus*, 'praetor for foreigners', who is credited in some sources with having some jurisdiction over legal cases involving foreigners. The city praetor, like other magistrates, on entering office published an edict for the year explaining how he proposed to exercise his jurisdiction. By this means, during the last century of the republic, the law came to be gradually reformed and developed by the introduction of flexible procedures more relevant to the cases actually being tried than the old formulaic system. Thus was the civil law, in the words of the later jurist Papinian, 'supported, supplemented, and corrected'. This model was followed in imperial times: the emperors issued edicts, judged cases, replied to appeals and petitions, and so on, and their judicial decisions or replies on points of law were grouped together and considered to have the force of law beyond the case in point.

A civil trial usually took place before a single magistrate acting as judge, who was bound to apply the law but otherwise could take the advice of anyone else he chose. For this reason men of standing with legal knowledge came into prominence, e.g. *Scaevola (4) under the republic. At the end of the trial the judge had to announce a verdict, unless he took an oath that the outcome 'was not clear to him', when a retrial before another judge would take place. Under the republic no *appeal from a judgement in civil law was possible but in the early empire appeal to the emperor was allowed.

In Rome's early days criminal law was not distinguished from civil law; only gradually did the state take over from private action, first in the matter of crimes which threatened public interest and then in those offences which affected private property or interest. (By the time of *Justinian in the sixth century AD the state had absorbed nearly all criminal law.) There was intense legislation during the late republic, covering crimes by senators and magistrates, as well as homicide and violence. (Tacitus later observed that when the state was most corrupt, then there were most laws: *corruptissima re publica, plurimae leges*.) Criminal jurisdiction in the republic was in the hands of the magistrates who had *imperium. From time to time, when a serious case arose, the senate set up a special court (*quaestio*) whose members were senators. The first permanent court was set up in 149 BC to try cases of extortion by provincial governors, and in 122 BC C. Gracchus changed the composition of the jury from senators to equites (*see* EQUESTRIAN ORDER). In the following years several other permanent courts were set up, and under Sulla in the late 80s BC many more, all composed of senators, and all found by 70 BC to be unsatisfactory. As a consequence panels of senators, equites, and *tribuni aerarii* were established from which juries were chosen by lot, varying in number according to the importance of the case. Voting, by tablets placed in an urn, was secret. There was no public prosecutor, prosecutions being undertaken by private individuals as at Athens or in political cases by tribunes. The defendant might have an advocate (*patronus*) to speak on his behalf. As at Athens the length of speeches was regulated by a water-clock, *clepsydra, and the jury gave its verdict by majority vote. The death penalty was rarely inflicted in practice, being usually replaced by exile. Executions were the result of exceptional circumstances, e.g. a *senatus consultum ultimum* (*see* CATILINE). Fines were the commonest penalty; a later punishment was deportation to some desolate island.

When Roman citizenship was extended by the emperor *Caracalla in AD 212 to all freeborn subjects of the empire, Roman law applied to a great variety of nations to some of which, having well-established institutions of their own, it was not suited, and the law was modified to accommodate them. After the emperor Constantine transferred the centre of government to Constantinople in AD 330, Roman law was subjected to Greek as well as Christian influences. As expressed in its final form, the 'Body of Law' (*Corpus Iuris*) of Justinian, it includes the effect of non-Roman influences but is nevertheless the creation of Roman minds.

The later spread of Roman law was brought about chiefly by peaceful diffusion, radiating from two centres, Italy and Constantinople. After the Dark ages a great impulse to its extension was given by the revival of legal study at the University of Bologna towards the end of the eleventh century. Thence the study of Justinian's *Corpus* spread to the universities of France, England, Spain, and Germany. The development of canon law for the regulation of ecclesiastical affairs, based largely on Roman law, was a further stage in this diffusion. Whether by formal adoption or by the codification on Roman principles of local customs, much of Europe is still governed by what is essentially Roman law.

*See also* THEODOSIAN CODE.

**law at Athens** For legislation at Athens before the fifth century BC *see* DRACO and SOLON.

Once democracy was established by *Cleisthenes (2) in 508 BC, laws were made by a vote of the *ecclesia* ('assembly'). If they were general and permanent they were called *nomoi*; if for a particular occasion, they were 'decrees', *psephismata* (literally 'votings'), but in the fifth century BC there seems to have been no hard-and-fast distinction. From the end of that century all existing laws were inscribed on stone; no decree could override a law. The framing of new laws became the responsibility of *nomothetai*, 'law-makers', citizens specially appointed for the purpose. For the workings of the jury system *see* ELIAIA and JURIES [at Athens]. The main distinction made in the matter of offences was between public actions for offences affecting the whole city and private actions affecting only an individual, who alone could initiate the action. In the case of homicide the victim's relations were required to prosecute the killer. Any citizen could bring a public action on behalf of the state, and was encouraged to do so by receiving some reward for a successful prosecution. The unintended result was the rise in the number of malicious prosecutions by *sycophants, and penalties had to be imposed.

At a trial the presiding magistrate did not act like a modern judge: he gave no guidance or summing-up to the jury. The prosecutor spoke first, and if the litigant was a woman or child the nearest adult male relation spoke for them. Each litigant had to speak for himself, though he might deliver a speech written for him by a *logographer (2) and might call on friends to testify on his behalf. He could also call witnesses. A slave's evidence was only permissible if it was extracted under torture. Speeches were limited in length, varying with the nature of the case, and timed by a water-clock (*see* CLEPSYDRA). As soon as the speeches ended the jury was required to vote, by placing a pebble or shell in one of two urns, for acquittal or conviction. This system was further refined in the fourth century BC to preserve secrecy and prevent corruption. A single majority decided the case; a tie was treated as acquittal (*see* ORESTEIA [*Eumenides*]). For some offences the penalty was laid down by law; in other cases the jury decided (*see* APOLOGY OF SOCRATES). A just verdict required alertness and clear-sightedness on the part of the jurors, and might not be arrived at when a powerful speaker was pleading. But the juries were composed of men as nearly as possible the equals of the defendant, and in respect of fairness and equality their establishment was a notable achievement.

**Laws (*Nomoi*)** Dialogue by *Plato, his last and longest work (in twelve books), left unrevised at his death. It lacks the vigour and charm of the earlier dialogues; the style is tortuous and the sentences very long. The interlocutors are three elderly men, an unnamed Athenian, Cleinias a Cretan, and a Spartan Megillus. The dramatic situation is fully revealed only at the end of book 3. The Cretans have decided to refound a deserted city, and the task has been entrusted to ten commissioners, of whom Cleinias is chief. Cleinias and Megillus have met an Athenian and are walking on a midsummer's day from Cnossus to the cave and temple of Dicte, the traditional birthplace of Zeus. Their conversation turns to the merits of the traditional lawgivers of Sparta and Cnossus, Lycurgus and Minos, whom the Athenian criticizes for directing their laws towards superiority in war, whereas peace not war is the business of the legislator. The Athenian stranger seems to have had experience of life in a city under a tyrant, and to represent the views of an organized group of scientific thinkers (such as Plato's *Academy at Athens), being knowledgeable about jurisprudence and constitutional theory. The conversation therefore develops into a complete outline of a constitution and code of laws for the new city, and the Athenian lays down for Cleinias the number of its citizens and their distribution, its organization in respect of magistrates, marriage, property (including slaves), and the material conditions of life generally, education, festivals, and other regulations. The three last books are mainly concerned with criminal offences and their expiations. Plato's judgements seem governed by examples more from history and experience, and less from theoretical considerations than in the *Republic*. Perhaps the work is a product of the times, when the Academy was sometimes called upon to assist in drawing up a written constitution and laws for a newly founded city.

**Lea'nder (Leandros)** Youth of Abȳdus (on the Asiatic side of the *Hellespont) who, according to legend, was in love with Hero, the beautiful priestess of Aphrodite at Sestus on the opposite (Greek) shore. Leander used to swim across to Hero every night, his course guided by a light in a tower. One stormy night the light was extinguished and Leander was drowned. When his body was washed up Hero, in despair, threw herself into the sea. See MUSAEUS (2).

**Lēda** In Greek myth, daughter of Thestius, king of Aetolia, the wife of Tyndareus, king of Sparta, and mother of *Clytemnestra, *Helen of Troy, and of Castor and Polydeuces (the *Dioscuri). She was loved by Zeus, who approached her in the form of a swan (a favourite subject in ancient art). Stories vary as to which children

were fathered by Zeus; usually Helen is so described, and either both the Dioscuri, or Polydeuces alone. Leda is often said to have laid an egg, from which Helen (or Helen and Polydeuces) was hatched. Homer does not mention the egg, and later Greeks disbelieved the story or made fun of it.

**Lefkandi** See GREECE 2.

**legā'ti** During the late Roman republic, members of a provincial governor's staff having senatorial rank, often made military commanders of a detachment or legion. See also TRIBUNI MILITUM.

**legend** See MYTHOLOGY.

**Lelantine War** A Greek war fought in the late eighth century BC in Euboea between its two most important cities, Chalcis and its neighbour Eretria, for possession of the Lelantine plain. The issues remain obscure to us, but the war itself is cited by Thucydides as the only other concerted Greek action known to him (apart from the Peloponnesian War) whose main parties enlisted the aid of so many other Greek states.

**lemma** In ancient manuscripts, a word or phrase repeated from a text as the heading for a marginal comment (*scholium*) on it. See TEXTS, TRANSMISSION OF ANCIENT 1.

**Lēnae'a** At Athens, festival in honour of *Dionysus Lenaios, the epithet meaning 'of the *lēnai* ('maenads')'. It was celebrated on the twelfth day of the month named Lenaion among the Ionian Greeks, from the festival, but known as Gamelion at Athens, January–February. There was a procession, but very little is known of the rites. Its chief importance for us lies in the dramatic competitions held in the theatre of Dionysus which were inaugurated *c.*440 BC and in which comedy, arranged as at the *Dionysia, was more important than tragedy (only two tragic poets competed, with two tragedies each).

**Leo'nidas 1.** *Agiad king of Sparta *c.*490–480 BC, who succeeded after the death of his half-brother Cleomenes, and was commander of the Greeks at the battle of Thermopylae in 480 BC (see PERSIAN WARS). Leaving behind the rest of the Spartan men temporarily by their obligation to celebrate the *Carnea, Leonidas marched to Thermopylae with an advance party of 300 Spartans he had picked himself, 'all fathers of living sons', and some other allied troops. When, after two days of successful defence, the Persians had reached his flank, Leonidas dismissed the main body of his army. The Spartans with the Thespian contingent (from Boeotia) and some others remained to fight. The Spartans died to a man (but *see* ARISTODEMUS (2)) The corpse of Leonidas was mutilated by the Persians but later his remains were brought back to Sparta and he was declared a hero, with a cult established in his honour (*see* HEROES).

**2.** Of Tarentum (first half of the third century BC) Greek writer of *epigrams, one of the most popular poets of the Greek *Anthology. His verse is highly finished, densely expressed, and often melancholy.

**Leontion** The follower and lover of Epicurus, whose impertinence as a mere courtesan in writing an attack on Theophrastus is deplored by Cicero (*De natura deorum* 1.93), although he concedes that she wrote it in good Attic Greek.

**Leōsthenēs** The Athenian general in the *Lamian War (323–322 BC), whose death ruined Greek hopes of victory over Macedon. His funeral oration was delivered by *Hypereides (oration 6).

**Le'pidus, Marcus Aemi'lius** (d. 13 or 12 BC), Roman politician and *triumvir. As praetor in 49 BC he supported Julius Caesar, and was consul in 46 and Caesar's *magister equitum* in 46–44. After Caesar's death he joined forces with Mark Antony, who contrived his appointment as *pontifex maximus*, and left to govern the provinces assigned to him by Caesar, Narbonese Gaul and Hither Spain. In 43, despite assuring Cicero of his loyalty to the republic, he planned the triumvirate with Antony and Octavian. He held a second consulship in 42 and was in charge of Rome and Italy during the campaign of Philippi. However, his importance to the triumvirate gradually diminished: in 36 his troops left him for Octavian, and he was compelled to retire to an Italian municipality. He kept his title of *pontifex maximus* until his death. His wife Junia was a sister of M. *Brutus.

**Leptinēs, Against** Speech in a public prosecution by *Demosthenes ((2) 1).

**Lernae'an Hȳdra** *See* HERACLES, LABOURS OF 2.

**Le'sbia** *See* CATULLUS.

**lesbianism** The earliest apparent reference to the island of *Lesbos being associated with lesbianism in the modern sense is in a poem by Anacreon, where he concludes by saying that he is spurned by a girl from Lesbos who is 'gaping after another' (the last word being in the feminine gender). Different interpretations of the last two lines have been offered, and it may be that at that time in the mid-sixth century BC Lesbos did have the reputation that has been supposed. A few fragments of the poems of Sappho (from Lesbos), nearly a century earlier, indicate erotic love between her and other young women, but this is not commented upon until Hellenistic times. References in classical times show that Lesbos could connote sexual shamelessness in general, and Lesbians were supposed to have invented fellation in particular. The first fairly explicit references connecting the island with female homosexuality occur in Augustan Rome, from Horace and Ovid. Why Catullus chose to call his mistress Lesbia remains an open question. *See* LOVE AND SEXUALITY.

**Lesbos** Largest of the Greek islands off the coast of Asia Minor. Of its five cities the most important were Mytilene and Methymna. Its Aeolic dialect may be due to the earliest Greek settlers (perhaps in the tenth century BC). The poets Terpander, Arion, Sappho, and Alcaeus were born there. The poet Anacreon (mid-sixth century BC, a generation after Sappho) seems to allude to the island in a way which suggests that it was already known for the practice of female homosexuality, to which it has given its name (*see* LESBIANISM).

Lesbos formed part of the *Delian League, but Mytilene revolted from Athens in 428 BC during the Peloponnesian War. Methymna did not support the revolt, which was subdued by an Athenian expedition in 427. Under the influence of *Cleon the assembly at Athens voted that the whole population of Mytilene should be put to death or enslaved. On the following day the matter was reopened, and on the proposal of Diodotus the edict was revoked and a fast trireme sent to overtake the one already sent to carry out the decision. It arrived at Lesbos just in time to prevent the massacre; only the leaders of the revolt were put to death, and the territory of the island (except for

Methymna) was distributed among Athenian *cleruchs.

**Leschēs** (seventh century BC) Epic poet, known as the author of the *Little Iliad* or the *Iliupersis* (*see* EPIC CYCLE).

**Lēthē** ('Forgetfulness') In the Greek poet Hesiod the personification of forgetfulness, the daughter of Eris (Strife); in later Greek literature a place of oblivion in the Underworld. In the myth at the end of Plato's *Republic* Lethe is a plain bounded by a 'river of unmindfulness' (*amelēs potamos*) from which the souls drink before rebirth so as to forget the past; but is not itself a river. In the Latin poets however it is one of the five rivers of the Underworld (*see* HADES); in Virgil's *Aeneid* 6 its water is drunk by souls about to be reincarnated. Ovid, in *Metamorphoses* 11, has it as a river flowing around the Cave of Sleep where its murmuring induces drowsiness. The name was borne also by a spring in the oracular cave of the god *Trophonius.

**Lēto** (Lat. Latōna) In Greek myth, goddess, one of the *Titans, daughter of Coeus and Phoebe. She is one of the few Titans to have had cult at several sites in Greece in historical times. Her chief importance is as the mother of the twin gods Apollo and Artemis, whose father was Zeus. For fear of the anger of Zeus' wife Hera, no land would receive Leto when the time of their birth approached, until she came to the island of Ortygia (identified later with *Delos), then a floating island which Zeus secured to the seabed. There she gave birth to the twins, after some delay because Hera would not allow *Eileithyia (goddess of childbirth) to go to her. While giving birth she leaned against Mount Cynthus, or a palm tree (later identified and regarded as sacred).

**letters**
**Greek.** The earliest reference to a written message, 'baleful signs inscribed in a folding tablet', is in Homer's *Iliad* (book 6). The earliest actual (but brief) correspondence is that mentioned by Herodotus (book 3) between *Polycrates and Amasis of Egypt in the 520s BC. Letter-writing seems not to have been a widespread practice before the fourth century BC, but is mentioned by *Euripides in his Iphigeneia plays. Letters attributed to famous Greeks which have survived from ancient times are almost all spurious. The most important are those attributed to *Isocrates,

*Plato, and *Demosthenes. It is likely that none is genuine.

Official Greek correspondence from Hellenistic times onwards is found preserved on papyri in Egypt in profusion, together with some private letters. It is known that Aristotle's correspondence was collected and published by the *Peripatetic philosopher Artemon, together with notes on the art of letter-writing. The next sets of letters known and still preserved are those of the Roman emperor Julian (in Greek), followed by those of *Libanius. 'Open' letters, meant for the public at large, include those giving moral or philosophical advice (as by Epicurus and his followers), or consolation (as by Plutarch to his wife on the death of their longed-for daughter), or exhortation (epistles of St Paul). There are also scholarly essays which were given superficial epistolary form, such as those of *Dionysius of Halicarnassus on Thucydides and Plato.

There is a broad literary category of wholly fictitious letters (composed from the first century BC), which comprises a literary genre of its own, and one which *Demetrius (3) (*On style*) gives an account of, using some observations of Artemon (above): 'no genre so fully reveals *character (*ēthos*) as the letter'; it is an 'image of the writer's soul (*psyche*)'. Wholly absent from Greek literature (apart from a few short poems of invitation in the Greek *Anthology*) is the verse epistle, though Pindar's Pythian 3 has seemed to some an exception to this generalization.

**Latin.** The Romans were great letter-writers, and important men in Cicero's time had among their slaves couriers (*tabellarii*) to deliver and collect letters, who might cover 50 Roman miles (almost 80km) a day. Cicero's voluminous correspondence seems to have been preserved in various ways. *Atticus, Cicero's most intimate friend, to whom he wrote in his own hand, kept the letters he received, as did Cicero's brother Quintus. His secretary *Tiro appears to have kept copies of the letters Cicero sent to his various other friends, and these copies were collected and published, perhaps after Cicero's death (*see* CICERO (1) 7). Nearly 100 letters received by Cicero have also been preserved, providing an interesting contrast of styles. Most of the letters of *Pliny the Younger, of which we have ten books, are more self-consciously composed for publication.

The Greek philosophical letter as written by Epicurus (above) is represented in Latin by

Horace's *Epistles* to some extent, and particularly by the younger *Seneca's large collection of *Epistulae morales* ('Moral epistles'), which are addressed to a friend and written informally and from a personal standpoint, but are not a genuine correspondence. The poetic epistle is richly represented in Latin literature. Apart from Horace's *Epistles* there are Ovid's poems of exile, *Tristia* and *Epistulae ex Ponto*, and the *Heroïdes*, a genre invented by the poet. Modern interest in literary and sub-literary self-presentation has made ancient letters a fruitful subject of study. *See also* LITERACY.

**Leuci'ppē and Clei'tophon** Greek *novel in eight books written in the late second century AD by Achilles Tatius. To judge from the number of surviving papyrus fragments it was very popular. The story is narrated to the author by Cleitophon himself. Cleitophon falls in love with his visiting cousin Leucippe against his father's wishes and they elope to Alexandria. They are shipwrecked, picked up, but then attacked by bandits. Cleitophon is rescued but Leucippe is apparently sacrificed before his eyes by disembowelling. However, this turns out to have been an illusion contrived by using stolen stage properties. Leucippe goes mad after taking a love potion from a lovesick soldier but recovers. She is carried off by pirates and Cleitophon again sees her murdered. Months later a letter from his father reaches Cleitophon, which should have arrived before they eloped, consenting to the marriage. It is apparently too late, but Leucippe is not dead, and after several amorous intrigues with others including one night of love for Cleitophon with a married woman, and Leucippe's apparent murder for the third time, the lovers are united. The narrative is occasionally interrupted by digressions (e.g. on the phoenix, on the elephant, and a debate on the rival advantages of homosexual and heterosexual love), as well as dramatic descriptions of paintings (*see* ECPHRASIS).

**Leuci'ppus 1.** (second half of the fifth century BC) Greek atomist philosopher, later than Parmenides. *See* DEMOCRITUS.

**2.** In Greek myth, son of Oenomaus; *see* DAPHNE.

**Leuctra** Village in the territory of Thespiae in Boeotia. It was the scene of a battle in 371 BC, in which the Thebans under Epaminondas defeated the Spartans, thus bringing to an end the period of Spartan hegemony in Greece which had followed the Peloponnesian War, and two centuries of Spartan supremacy on the battlefield.

**Liba'nius** (of Syrian Antioch, AD 314–*c*.393) Greek rhetorician. He studied at Athens (336–40), and afterwards taught rhetoric at Constantinople (until 346) and at Nicomedia (in Bithynia, on the shores of the Propontis). Having declined a chair of rhetoric at Athens, in 354 he accepted instead a chair at Antioch, and remained there for the rest of his life. Although he remained a pagan, deeply attached to old ways, he had many distinguished Christian pupils, including John Chrysostom, and perhaps Basil the Great and Gregory of Nazianzus. Among his voluminous writings, his 64 speeches, which include his autobiography (oration 1) and his funeral oration on the emperor Julian (whom he corresponded with and greatly admired), and some 1,600 letters, are of considerable historical importance.

**Libation Bearers (Choephoroe)** *See* ORESTEIA.

**libations** (Gk. *loibai* or *spondai*, Lat. *libationes*) Offerings to the gods, *heroes, or the dead, usually of unmixed wine, but sometimes also of milk, honey, oil, or pure water, poured on the ground. At the beginning of a drinking-party (*symposium*), a little unmixed wine was poured on the floor to the Good *Daimon. The wine was usually mixed in three wine-bowls (*craters*), and in Athens at least a libation was poured from each, to Zeus and the Olympian gods, to the heroes, and to Zeus Soter ('saviour'). This third cup became a symbol of good luck, hence the saying 'third time lucky'.

**Līber** Italian god of fertility and of wine, commonly identified with the Greek god Dionysus. He had no temple in Rome but an important cult on the Aventine hill with his female counterpart Libera and with Ceres, founded in 493 BC. His festival, the Liberalia, was on 17 March, characterized by a procession with phallus and by crude songs and, according to Virgil in *Georgics* 2, the use of masks, apparently hung on trees. This festival was a popular time for boys to assume the *toga virilis* ('man's toga'). The Romans connected his name with *libertas* ('liberty').

**liberal arts** *See* SEVEN LIBERAL ARTS.

**Libitī'na** Italian goddess of funerals, which were registered in her grove on the Esquiline at Rome, where those who disposed of the dead kept their equipment (*see* DEAD, DISPOSAL OF).

**libraries** The first considerable collection of books of which we are reliably informed is that of Aristotle, although the tyrant Polycrates of Samos was said to have collected books, and the Athenian tyrant Peisistratus is most improbably said to have founded a public library at Athens. Euripides is also credited with a collection of books. It was apparently the arrangement of Aristotle's library that provided a model for the *Alexandrian Library, founded in the third century BC, and the *Pinakes* ('Catalogues') of *Callimachus made the books accessible. The Attalid kings of Pergamum also formed a great library at about this time, said to have contained, when Mark Antony presented it to Cleopatra, 200,000 rolls (five rolls would be very roughly equivalent to a modern book). The Seleucid king Antiochus the Great (223–187 BC) had a library at Antioch of which the poet *Euphorion had charge. Perseus of Macedon (king 179–168 BC) also possessed a library at Pella. Athens did not have a public library until the second century BC, the gift of a Ptolemy. This Ptolemaion, as it was called, was visited by Cicero and Pausanias.

At Rome we hear of private libraries formed by Aemilius *Paullus, who secured the Macedonian royal library, Sulla, who acquired Aristotle's books (*see* ARISTOTLE 2), and *Lucullus, who captured the books of the Pontic kings. Private libraries became fashionable: Cicero and his friend *Atticus both had considerable collections of books. Julius Caesar had the intention of setting up a public library at Rome, and of placing *Varro in charge of it, but the credit for achieving that seems to belong to C. Asinius *Pollio, in the reign of the emperor Augustus. It contained Greek and Latin books, was adorned with portraits of authors, and was housed in the Atrium Libertatis ('Hall of Liberty'). There followed Augustus' library on the Palatine, the Bibliotheca Ulpia ('Ulpian Library') of the emperor Trajan (AD 98–117), and others by Caracalla and Diocletian. Under the empire the gift of a library to a provincial town was a recognized form of public munificence. *See also* BOOKS, GREEK AND ROMAN, and TEXTS, TRANSMISSION OF ANCIENT. For a private library *see* PISO (1) and LUCULLUS.

**libri linte'i** ('books written on linen') Lists (now lost) of magistrates at Rome from 509 BC, the foundation of the republic, onwards, although they seem upon occasion to have been defective. Supposed to have been of great antiquity, they were probably not compiled before the mid-second century BC. They were stored in the temple of *Juno Moneta, to be consulted by historians and others who were interested. *See* LIVY and MACER (1).

**Libya** *See* AFRICA.

**Licinio-Sextian laws (Licinian rogations)** In Roman history, according to tradition, proposals originally made in 376 BC by the tribunes of the plebs P. Licinius Stolo and L. Sextius Lateranus and after a long struggle passed in 367 BC, enacting that one consul might be a *plebeian and reducing in other areas the political inequalities between *patricians and plebeians.

**Licinius Macer, Gaius** *See* MACER (1).

**lictors** (*lictorēs*) Attendants who always walked before Roman magistrates having *imperium*, and before certain priests; they proceeded in single file, each carrying the *fasces on his left shoulder, symbolizing the magistrate's right of arrest, summons, and, in early times, execution. The number of lictors varied with the importance of the office: a dictator had twenty-four; consuls had twelve.

**Linear A** Script found in Minoan *Crete and in Minoan settlements in the Cyclades from *c.*1750 to *c.*1450 BC, used for writing the Minoan language. It seems to have developed from a pictographic form of writing found on seals, and to have been a syllabary written on a variety of objects. Most surviving texts are on clay tablets and are clearly identifiable as allocations of commodities. The tablets are relatively few in number, compared with *Linear B, and no suggested decipherment has yet won general acceptance, though some features of the grammar have become clear. The language itself, whether Semitic, *Indo-European, or indigenous, remains unknown.

**Linear B** A later form of the *Linear A script, used to write what is now generally accepted to be an early form of Greek. Many of the regular signs of Linear A are also found in Linear B, perhaps indicating that many Minoan words were retained. Linear B survives on several thousand clay tablets found on the Greek mainland, chiefly in excavations at the palaces of *Mycenae, Tiryns, Thebes, and Pylos, and at Cnossus and Cydonia (Khania) in *Crete. Most of these tablets date to *c.*1200 BC though a significant number may be *c.*1375 or earlier; the dating is controversial. The identification of the language as Greek is supported by the presence of characteristic sound changes, inflections, and vocabulary including specifically Greek words (both *Indo-European and otherwise). The script consists of about 200 signs, monosyllabic signs with phonetic values and ideograms (i.e. signs pictorial in origin) used to signify totals of commodities, including people and animals. This syllabary is not well adapted to show Greek noun inflections, with the result that the cases are sometimes ambiguous; there are also many words which cannot be matched with words known in later Greek. Numbers are decimal-based, with characters representing one, ten, one hundred, and one thousand repeated up to nine times to indicate numbers up to 10,000 if need be. The script was adequate for the day-to-day accounts and inventories which are all that the clay tablets so far discovered seem to record. The tablets are valuable for the light they throw on economic conditions and the nature of the administration. Of particular interest is whether the administration in (part of) Crete was in the hands of Mycenaean Greek-speakers from the Greek mainland, and when. Those tablets concerned with temple property are interesting because of the gods they name, including Zeus, Hera, Poseidon, Paian (*Paean), Hermes, Athena, Dionysus, *Eileithyia, Erinyes (*Furies), and Anemoi (Winds). *See also* ALPHABET and BOOKS, GREEK AND ROMAN 1.

**Linus** In Greek literature, an ancient and apparently mournful song containing the refrain *ailinon, ailinon* which was interpreted as *ai, Linus* or 'alas for Linus!' The history of Linus was variously told in different parts of Greece. According to one version, he was a music-teacher killed with his own lyre by Heracles, whom he had reprimanded. The 'song of Linus' was also sung, cheerfully, at harvest and vintage time from Homeric times onward.

**literacy** It is impossible to determine how many people in the ancient world could read and write, and difficult to define what that ability meant in practice. At Athens one might

scratch a few letters on a potsherd so as to vote in an *ostracism without being able to read properly. The evidence of literature indicates that in the classical periods of Greece and Rome the educated classes attained a very high degree of literary sophistication, which presupposes the skill to read from and write on a papyrus roll. Yet in Rome particularly much of the reading and writing was done by slaves. The Spartans had little use for written records and were considered illiterate by other states, an impression confirmed by their terseness (*see* SPARTA 5). Reading aloud, rather than silently to oneself, was the common practice, and so one that could be shared. At Athens from the fifth century BC onwards books must have been relatively plentiful, to judge from the number of works of all kinds that we know to have existed. Socrates in the *Apology* enquires if his accuser supposes the jury to be so ignorant of 'letters' (meaning literature) as not to know about the kind of ideas found in Anaxagoras' book. No doubt there is irony here, but we are told that the book cost no more than the day-wage of an ordinary working man (a drachma). There were incentives to read: legislation and political decrees were publicly displayed. The Sausage-seller in Aristophanes' *Knights* confesses to having had no proper education except for 'letters' (here meaning elementary reading and writing), and being very bad at that. But in Euripides' *Hippolytus* Phaedra writes a suicide note. In the Hellenistic period and under the Roman empire there was provision in the cities for elementary education, and the indications are that there was widespread literacy of a practical kind. Electoral posters and advertisements for gladiatorial shows dating from the first century AD are frequently found at Pompeii but it is the graffiti there which give the best indication that ordinary people in the city at that time had some command of reading and writing. *See* ALPHABET; EDUCATION 3 and 5; LETTERS.

### literary criticism, Greek and Roman
*See* AESTHETICS; *ARS POETICA*; DEMETRIUS (3); DIONYSIUS OF HALICARNASSUS; *LONGINUS ON THE SUBLIME*; ORATORY; PLATO 1; *POETICS*; QUINTILIAN; RHETORIC; *RHETORIC*.

### *Little Iliad* See ILIAD, LITTLE.

**liturgy (*leitourgia*)** At Athens in the fifth and fourth centuries BC, a public service involving considerable expense compulsorily required of the richer citizens and *metics. Exempted were *archons and members of the *boule during their year of office, and descendants of *Harmodius and Aristogeiton. There were some sixty liturgies a year in Athens alone, apart from the rest of Attica. One of the most costly was the *choregia (provision of a chorus) for one or other of the various lyric and dramatic contests. Others included the *gymnasiarchia,* the management (with nine others) of the *gymnasia and everything connected with them, and the *architheoria,* the leadership of a public embassy to one of the panhellenic festivals. In addition to these there was the occasional charge of the *trierarchia,* for the equipment and maintenance of a trireme (i.e. a warship) for a year. This was imposed only or principally in time of war, and only on the wealthiest citizens (*see* e.g. ISOCRATES). *See also* ANTIDOSIS.

**Lī'via 1. Livia Drusilla** (58 BC–AD 29; later known as Julia Augusta) The wife, first, of Tiberius Claudius Nero (Cicero's first choice as husband for his daughter Tullia), and mother by him of the emperor Tiberius and of Nero Claudius Drusus, father of the emperor Claudius. In 39 BC, when she was pregnant with her second son, her husband was obliged to divorce her because Octavian, later the emperor Augustus, having divorced his first wife Scribonia, wished to marry her himself (which he did). Although she had no children by Augustus she retained his affection and high regard throughout their long marriage. She was a woman of intelligence, dignity, great beauty, and tact, and she ruled over an orderly, well-regulated household. It is impossible to tell how much influence she exerted in matters of state, but Augustus valued her counsel, and she won the reverence of the Roman people. Under Augustus' will she was adopted into the Julian *gens* (*see* JULIA, GENS) and renamed Julia Augusta; she was the link between the Julian and the Claudian houses in the *Julio-Claudian dynasty. After the accession of her son Tiberius, discord arose between them. At her death he refused to execute her will or allow her to be deified (as Julius Caesar and Augustus were deified after their deaths); the emperor Caligula (Gaius) later carried out the former, and her grandson Claudius, when emperor, the latter. Some believed her to have acted ruthlessly to promote her own wishes (such as the succession of her son Tiberius) and to have

had a hand in the deaths of *Marcellus and of Augustus' grandsons C. and L. Caesar (*see* JULIA (4)), as well as of *Agrippa (2) and of her grandson *Germanicus (son of Claudius Drusus).

**2. Livia Julia** (or Claudia, often called Livilla; b. *c*.13 BC) Daughter of Nero Claudius Drusus (the younger brother of the emperor Tiberius and son of Livia (1)) and sister of Germanicus. She was the wife first of Gaius Julius Caesar (the son of Augustus' daughter Julia) and after his death of Drusus Julius Caesar, the only surviving son of Tiberius. By him she became the mother of Tiberius Julius Caesar Nero (whom the emperor Caligula (Gaius) later put to death). Her husband Drusus died suddenly in AD 23, and in 25 *Sejanus allegedly asked Tiberius for permission to marry her, but without success. When Sejanus was executed in 31 she was accused of adultery with him and others, and of having poisoned Drusus; she too was put to death.

**Lī'vius Andronī'cus, Lucius** (*c*.284–204 BC) A *freedman of the Livii, regarded as the first to write poems of the Greek type in Latin, and thus the father of Roman literature. He was probably by origin a Greek of Tarentum, taken as a prisoner of war, after the fall of that city, to Rome in 272 BC. (An alternative chronology in antiquity made him come to Rome in 209 after the Romans had to recapture Tarentum from Hannibal.) He probably became tutor to the family of M. Livius Salinator, consul in 207, from whom he took his name when he was freed. He seems to have wanted to introduce Greek literature to the Romans, and translated Homer's *Odyssey* into the long-established Italian Saturnian metre, giving the gods and heroes Latin names. His translation remained a school textbook for more than two centuries; 46 lines of it survive. He is credited by Livy with introducing plot into the hitherto plotless Roman stage performances (*see* COMEDY [Roman 1]); he did so for the first time in 240 (according to the earlier chronology), producing a tragedy and a comedy, probably based on a classical Greek tragedy and a play of New Comedy (*see* COMEDY [Greek 6]), for the *Ludi Romani* ('Roman Games'), celebrations to mark the end of the (First) Punic War. He continued as a playwright; the titles of ten tragedies are known, but very few lines; even less is known of the comedies—three titles survive. In 207 BC he was commissioned to compose a 'maiden-song' to Juno (*see* LYRIC POETRY [Latin]). This does not survive; Livy considered the words too 'unpleasing and graceless' to quote, though good enough for the time at which they were written. As reward the temple of *Minerva on the Aventine was set aside as a place where writers and actors might meet and make dedications as a *collegium* ('guild'). His work was regarded by Cicero as antiquated and not worth reading, but his historical importance is considerable; he introduced to Roman literature Greek epic, drama, and lyric. Horace tells us that he used to learn Livius' *Odyssey* by heart, under threat of beating by *Orbilius. Livius is not included among archaic poets thought to have been models for Virgil.

**Livy (Titus Līvius)** (59 BC–AD 17) Roman historian. He was born and died at Patavium (Padua) in north-east Italy, probably of a well-to-do family, but little is known of his life. The evidence suggests that he did not come to Rome until his adulthood. There he gave readings of his work, and won and retained the friendship of the emperor Augustus, who respected his republican sympathies, and encouraged the young future emperor Claudius in his historical studies. Livy appears never to have held any public office, but to have devoted his life to literature and history, also writing philosophical dialogues which have not survived. He began his immense 'History of Rome from its Foundation' (*Ab urbe condita libri*) in or shortly before 29 BC, and published it in instalments; it immediately brought him fame. He survived Augustus by three years.

The history consisted of 142 books, of which the last twenty-two dealt with the events of his own day from the death of Cicero in 43 BC. An epitome of it was written as early as the first century AD, and from this were compiled *periochae* or short abstracts of each book, of which there were perhaps two versions. Of the original work there survive books 1–10, 21–45 (41 and 43–5 with gaps), and a palimpsest fragment of book 91. The epitome is lost except for the parts covering books 37–40 and 48–55, which have been found on an Egyptian papyrus (the so-called Oxyrhynchus Epitome) in the twentieth century. The *periochae* survive for all the books except 136 and 137. Books 1–5 describe the legendary founding of the city, the period of the kings, and the early

republic down to its conquest by the Gauls *c.*385 BC. Books 6–15 deal with the subjugation of Italy (the Samnite Wars) before the conflict with Carthage, 16–30 with the first two Punic Wars; 31–45 with the Macedonian and other eastern wars down to 167. Of the subsequent books, now lost, 46–70 covered the succeeding period to the outbreak of the Social War; 71–90 to the death of Sulla; 91–108 to the Gallic War; 109–16 the civil war to the death of Caesar; 117–33 to the death of Antony; 134–42 the rule of Augustus down to 9 BC. The whole survived into the sixth century, but the Middle Ages knew no more books than are known today.

The work opens with an introduction in which Livy explains his purpose: to commemorate the deeds of the leading nation of the world, to describe the men and the mode of life that had raised Rome to greatness, and the decline of morals which brought about the troubles of the first century BC, so that his readers might thereby learn important lessons. His general purpose is thus ethical and didactic. His methods were those of the fourth-century Greek Isocrates (*see* HISTORIOGRAPHY): it is the duty of the historian to tell the truth and be impartial, but the truth must be elaborated and given literary form. Livy's attitude to the early legends which he relates is that he neither affirms nor denies their truth, but regards it as of no great importance: if the legends are not true, they resemble the truth. They illustrate those aspects of Roman character which led to Rome's imperial greatness, as well as the true traditions to which Livy hoped, in the early Augustan period, that Rome might return from the moral decay, luxury, and indiscipline of the recent past. Livy used as his sources the earlier annalists, then *Polybius for events in the East (in books 31–45), and for the latest books *Poseidonius, Julius Caesar, and Augustus' own *Memoirs*. He relied on written histories and did not feel obliged to consult original records, nor does he treat his source material critically. He has been criticized for not consulting the *libri lintei* in person when he had found conflicting reports in his sources. He lacked the scientific method and the insight of Thucydides and Polybius, and sometimes misunderstands the latter. His inexperience of military affairs makes his descriptions of battles unrealistic, and he throws little light on economic conditions or social life in Rome. He sometimes confuses his sources so that his narratives are inconsistent; they are often given an anachronistic or implausible slant because of his ignorance of conditions at different times and in different places, e.g. in early Rome or in the East. He makes mistakes in his dating, sometimes because he has to fit Polybius' Olympiads to the Roman system of consular years (*see* CALENDARS). But significant events are treated dramatically and memorably: the action is set against what Livy imagines its background to be in time and place; previous deliberations, changes of mind and heart, the characters of the protagonists, all such circumstances are explored and explained, so that the reader is presented with a story fully comprehensible in the way in which Livy wishes it to be comprehended, whatever its relation to actuality. Livy's prose is eloquent, clear, orderly, and full, developed from that of Cicero. Asinius *Pollio saw in it an element which he humorously called 'Patavinity', which might suggest provincialism.

Livy was no doubt a supporter of Augustus' Principate, but not sycophantically so. A. *Cremutius Cordus, prosecuted by the emperor Tiberius for disloyalty, was said by Tacitus to have claimed in defence that Livy praised the republicans Brutus and Cassius without damaging his friendship with Augustus. Livy was much praised by his immediate successors, Tacitus, the Senecas, and Quintilian, and drawn upon by Plutarch and Lucan. He is little heard of in the Middle Ages, but the Renaissance adopted him with enthusiasm 'who errs not'. Among the many famous narratives found in the extant books are the following:

*Book 1.* Romulus and Remus (chapters 4–7); the rape of the Sabines (9–13); the fight of the Horatii and Curiatii and the death of Horatia (24–6); the coming of Lucumo (Tarquinius Priscus) to Rome (34); the accession of Lucius Tarquinius and the crimes of Tullia (46–8); the rape of Lucretia by Sextus Tarquinius and the revenge of Brutus (57–60).

*Book 2.* The execution of the sons of Brutus by their father (5); 'how Horatius kept the bridge' (10); Mucius Scaevola's attempt to kill Porsena (12); Cloelia swimming the Tiber (13); Menenius Agrippa and the parable of the belly and the other body parts (32); the meeting of Coriolanus and his mother outside Rome (40); the 306 Fabii marching out against the Veientes (49).

*Book 3.* The summoning of Cincinnatus from his farm to be dictator (26); Appius Claudius and Verginia (44–58).

*Book 4.* The fight between Cossus and the Etruscan king, in which the former won the *spolia opima (19).

*Book 5.* The Roman siege and sack of Veii; the defeat of the Romans at the *Allia (38) and the capture of Rome by the Gauls.

*Book 6.* The execution of M. *Manlius Capitolinus (20).

*Book 7.* M. Curtius leaping into the abyss to expiate an omen (6).

*Book 8.* T. Manlius Torquatus ordering the execution of his son who, in defiance of orders, had fought and killed an enemy chief (7); P. Decius Mus 'devoting' himself to death (*see* DEVOTIO) for the victory of his army (9); the anger of the dictator L. Papirius Cursor against his *magister equitum,* Q. Fabius Maximus Rullus (30).

*Book 9.* The disaster of the *Caudine Forks (1); the unexpected digression on what would have happened had Alexander the Great encountered the Romans (17)—he would have been defeated: his empire, unlike Rome's, was not the result of hard-won, gradual expansion.

*Book 21.* The character of Hannibal (4), the siege of Saguntum (12), Hannibal's crossing of the Alps (30), and his victory at the battle of the river Trebia (52).

*Book 22.* The defeat of the Romans at Lake Trasimene (4); the conflict of Q. Fabius Maximus (grandson of the Fabius in book 8) with his impetuous *magister equitum,* Minucius (14); the defeat of the Romans at Cannae (44); Maharbal's criticism of Hannibal's delay, that he knew how to conquer but not how to use his victory (51).

*Book 23.* Hannibal at Capua, the debilitating effect of Capuan luxury on his army (45), and the turning point of the war.

*Book 24.* The siege of Syracuse by the Roman general Marcellus and the defensive devices of Archimedes (34).

*Book 25.* The capture of Syracuse (24) and the death of Archimedes (31).

*Book 26.* Hannibal's approach within three miles of Rome (10; the land on which his camp stands is sold in the city at its full price,

11); Scipio Africanus appointed commander in Spain at the age of 24 (18), and capturing Nova Carthago (46); his generosity and restraint in the treatment of a beautiful Spanish captive (50).

*Book 27.* The interception of Hasdrubal at the Metaurus; his defeat and death (48).

*Book 30.* The romantic story of Sophonisba, Syphax, and *Masinissa (15); defeat of the Carthaginians at the battle of Zama (32).

*Book 33.* The defeat of Philip V of Macedon at Cynoscephalae (7); the notable speech of Flamininus on making peace with a defeated enemy (12); the proclamation of Greek freedom at the Isthmian games (32).

*Book 34.* The repeal of the Oppian sumptuary law (1).

*Book 35.* The conversation at Ephesus between Scipio and Hannibal, with Punic subtlety, about great military commanders (14).

*Book 38.* The proud reminder by Scipio Africanus when tried for embezzlement that the day was the anniversary of his victory at Zama (51).

*Book 39.* The discovery and suppression of the Bacchanalian orgies (8–22); the character of Cato the Censor (40); the suicide of Hannibal (51).

*Book 44.* The Roman victory over the Macedonians at Pydna (40).

**locus amoenus** (Lat., 'a charming place') Phrase used in modern times to refer to the literary description of a landscape with typical recurring features—shady trees, running water, a grassy meadow, and a cooling breeze. This commonplace (or *topos*) goes back to the grotto of Calypso and the garden of Alcinous in Homer's *Odyssey*, and it is the background to the *pastoral poetry of Theocritus and Virgil, as well as, later, to Roman wall-paintings and Roman gardens themselves.

**logo'graphers** [Gk. *logographos*, 'prose writer'] **1.** Term used to describe the early writers of Greek history, the predecessors or contemporaries of Herodotus who were forerunners of historians proper (*see* HISTORIOGRA-PHY [Greek]), and who lived mostly in Ionia (Greek Asia Minor) in the sixth and fifth centuries BC. None of their works has survived, but there are numerous references to them and quotations in later authors. Their histories in-cluded mythological as well as historical events and as a consequence they were disparaged by later writers. The earliest are said to have been Cadmus and Dionysius, both of Miletus, but very little is known of either. *Hecataeus, also of Miletus, was one of the most famous. Pherecȳdes of Athens, active in the first half of the fifth century BC, wrote *Histories* (i.e. 'inquiries') in ten books, both mythical and genealogical. Charon of Lampsacus, Xanthus of Lydia, and *Hellanicus of Lesbos were a little earlier than, or contemporary with, Herodotus. Of these, Hellanicus, who outlived Herodotus, was the most influential and prolific. His *Atthis* was criticized by Thucydides for its inadequate chronology of the fifth century.

**2.** Name given at Athens to persons who were hired to write speeches for litigants to deliver in a court of law. *Antiphon was said to have been the first of these; *Lysias and *Demosthenes (2) were also very successful at this practice. Since many trials were political, speech-writing sometimes laid the foundation for a later political career.

**Longī'nus, Ca'ssius** (*c*.AD 213–73; to be distinguished from the supposed author of the treatise *Longinus on the Sublime*) An eminent Greek rhetorician and philosopher. A *Neoplatonist, he taught at Athens, and was the teacher of *Porphyry. In the last few years of his life he became the principal counsellor of Odaenathus and Zenobia, the rulers of Palmyra. For his loyal support of Zenobia he was executed when the city fell to the Roman emperor Aurelian. Fragments of his works survive.

**Longī'nus on the Sublime** (*Peri hypsous*) Greek literary treatise (a third of which is lost) of unknown authorship and date. Manuscripts attribute it to 'Dionysius Longinus' or 'Dionysius or Longinus', and until the nineteenth century it was generally believed to be by Cassius *Longinus. This tradition is contradicted on chronological grounds by internal evidence indicating a date in the first century AD. The author says that his work is a reply to a similarly entitled treatise of the first century BC by Caecilius of Calacte, who gave what 'Longinus' considers to be an inadequate account of 'sublimity', failing in particular to attach sufficient importance to the emotional element in this concept. It is addressed to a friend, Postumius Terentianus (of whom nothing is known, but who is presumed from his name to be

Roman), and is on the subject of what constitutes sublimity in literature. It has greatly appealed to later readers by its enthusiasm, sage criticism, apt examples (mostly from Greek literature), and clarity of expression. The author analyses the constituents of sublimity, and finds them in elevated thought ('sublimity is the echo of a noble mind', 9.2); strong emotion; certain kinds of figures of thought and speech; nobility of diction ('truly beautiful words are the very light of the spirit', 30.1); and composition, i.e. word-order, rhythm, euphony. He lists the faults to be avoided: turgidity, puerility, false emotion, frigidity; discusses the part played by imagination and various figures of speech; and illustrates his points by a wealth of quotation. There are interesting observations on successful and unsuccessful ways of representing supernatural beings and of exciting awe, and comparisons of Homer's *Iliad* and *Odyssey*, and of Demosthenes and Cicero, which are very rewarding. The author finds the chief examples of sublimity of style in Homer, Plato, and Demosthenes, of whom he speaks with appreciative enthusiasm. At one point (in a section on selection and organization of material) his quotation preserves an ode of *Sappho, translated by the Roman poet Catullus (see his poem 51). There is a notable passage (9.9) in which the author points out, as an instance of grandeur in representing the divine, the first verses of Genesis. No other pagan writer uses the Bible in this way, and one must presume that the author had, unusually, both Roman (in the case of his addressee) and Jewish contacts.

This is a critical work of timeless importance; the writer is able to see beyond the rhetorical tradition in which he worked and contribute to our understanding of true literary greatness.

**Longus** *See* NOVEL.

**Long Walls** At Athens, the two Long Walls connecting Athens with her ports at Piraeus and Phalerum, built between 461 and 456 BC. Around 445 BC a third wall was built parallel to the Piraeus wall and south of it, the original Phaleric Wall being allowed to fall into ruin. The two walls to Piraeus were each about 6km (4 miles) long. The main road from Athens lay outside these parallel walls, the road between them being primarily military. The effect of the walls during the *Peloponnesian War was to turn the whole territory between Athens and

the ports into a fortress, victualled from the sea. After the Spartan victory at the end of the Peloponnesian War (404 BC) the walls were dismantled, to the sound of pipe music. They were rebuilt by *Conon after his victory at Cnidus in 394 BC, but were in ruins when Philip V of Macedon attacked Athens in 200 BC. Today there is virtually no visible trace of them.

**Lotus-eaters (Lōtophagoi)** In Homer's *Odyssey* 9, a fabulous people visited by Odysseus, in ancient times located in North Africa. They live on the lotus-fruit, whose property is to make those who eat it forget their home and desire to remain for ever in Lotus-land.

## love and sexuality

1. Marriage was regarded in the ancient world as an institution for the procreation of legitimate children who would inherit property, take on family responsibilities, and become full members of their community (*see* MARRIAGE LAW). It was an important way of promoting social stability (see Plutarch in the *Erōtikos*, below). The assumption was that virtually all men and women would marry, and marriages were arranged for prudential reasons. Men's sexual activity was not expected to be limited to marriage. Greece and Rome were societies in which slaves as well as prostitutes were always available, and *hetairai* and their Roman equivalents provided more sophisticated entertainment. Women in Greece of some social standing, on the other hand, were generally secluded from men outside the family and had few opportunities to meet them; at Rome an attempt to seduce a free-born young woman (or youth) was a criminal offence. (Young men might visit young women for other reasons, as for example in the Greek novel *Leucippe and Cleitophon*, to enjoy their skills in music.) It is therefore unlikely that a girl would have had much say in the choice of a husband, and in Greece, unlike Rome, her consent was not required. (For a rebellious daughter *see* CRATES.) Nevertheless Greek wives might fall in love with their husbands. According to a speaker in Plato's *Symposium*, it was the *eros*, passionate love, of *Alcestis for her husband that moved her to die in his stead, and Euripides in his tragedy *Alcestis* gives her the strongly expressed line, 'I did not choose to live torn away from you'. Male writers more often attest the love of wives for husbands than the reverse. But pleasing ways

could make even plain women lovable; 'habit wins love', says the Roman Lucretius tersely.

2. It is assumed in Greek literature of the classical period that a woman feels pleasure in sex and it was a popular belief that all women would be promiscuous, given the chance. Lucretius also admits that there can be joint pleasure in sex, and he acknowledges the female orgasm (as does Ovid). But, he adds, 'wives have no need for lascivious movements', and 'none of this is necessary for our wives'. Perhaps Lucretius is not a reliable witness, believing as an Epicurean that love is a mental delusion (*De rerum natura*, book 4), and should be avoided, or desire satisfied in the least troublesome way. Romantic love is, however, prominent in the poetry and, it would appear, also in the life of Catullus, in ways that seem very familiar to modern readers, and the theme of passionate love, if not for wives then for women with whom the poet is in love, is continued by the elegiac poets (*see* e.g. GALLUS and PROPERTIUS). Marriages made for love were known in life as well as in literature. The Greek Plutarch, in an essay *Conjugal Advice* offered to a young couple at the end of the first century AD, says that marriage between those in love is a more intimate union than between those who marry for dowry or for children, but a wife should not be so immodest as to make the first sexual approach (*see also* MUSONIUS). In his *Erotikos* he sees sexual love as giving rise to a special harmony and contentment between marriage partners, and praises Solon's supposed enactment to the effect that husbands should make love to their wives at least three times a month to wipe away accumulated differences and restore unanimity, as cities renew mutual peace-treaties. In classical Athens *Cimon's sister or half-sister Elpinice, who was too impoverished to marry, reputedly lived with Cimon as his wife until the very rich *Callias fell in love and married her without a dowry. Cimon himself was deeply attached to his wife Isodice and inconsolable when she died. Demosthenes, in a speech for a client, describes an individual in the case as being in love with his wife. The Roman Sulla was notably uxorious. After the death of his wife Metella he fell in love with, married, and became equally devoted to Valeria, who bore their daughter after his death. Pompey too was dearly loved by his wives Julia and, after her death, Cornelia. Perhaps Homer encapsulates two

possible attitudes when he shows Agamemnon making recompense to Achilles for appropriating the latter's concubine Briseis in *Iliad* 9. He offers the wrathful hero seven women from Lesbos, 'surpassing womankind in beauty', and free choice of twenty Trojan women captives. Achilles' response is incredulity. 'Do only the sons of Atreus love their bed-partners? Surely any man who is good and sound of mind loves his own and cherishes her even as I loved mine with all my heart, though she was only the captive of my spear.'

3. The ancient world did not have words equivalent to English 'heterosexual' and 'homosexual'; sexuality was not categorized so precisely. The Greeks took it for granted that to a normal male the sight of an attractive youth could be as sexually pleasurable as the sight of an attractive girl. Although Aristophanes' speech in Plato's *Symposium*, among other evidence, shows recognition of the fact that people varied in their sexual orientation, there was in general no feeling that a sexual response to the beauty of someone of the same sex was unnatural or undesirable. Homosexual love was a more conspicuous feature of life throughout Greece from the archaic period onwards than in other societies of the ancient world, including Rome, and the reasons for this are by no means clear. Pederasty, the love of a man for a youth, was particularly favoured by the educated upper-class Athenian male. Even when Plato at his most prescriptive (in the late work *Laws*) states that in his constitution he would legislate for sex only between legally married heterosexual couples and would ban all male homosexual association, he recognizes that his proposals 'are no more than a pious hope'. The ideal pattern of a pederastic relationship projected by the Greeks was that between a well-to-do lover (*erastes*), usually fairly young himself, and a virtuous, intelligent, handsome 'beloved' (*erōmenes*), about the age of puberty, and of good family. The relationship is entered into by persuasion on the part of the lover; he feels passionate love for the youth and the beneficial purpose of the relationship is to educate the beloved in learning and in manly virtues; the youth feels only affection and admiration for the man. The lover shows self-restraint and the youth remains chaste; the pair will not engage in intercourse, towards which the professed general attitude seems to have been disapproval but toleration. The convention was that the

beloved did not experience physical pleasure; if he did he was liable to be regarded as either a prostitute or in some way perverted (see Aristotle and Ovid below).

It is clear that the reality departed from the ideal, and well-to-do fathers put 'tutors' (*see* PAEDAGOGUS) in charge of their under-age sons in order to protect them from would-be lovers. But in general the pursuit of a youth by a man was part of pre-marriage behaviour; the Roman poet Tibullus loses his 'beloved' Titius to a wife. Aristotle concedes that if a relationship produces a similarity of character it may end as lifelong friendship (as perhaps in the case of *Agathon and Pausanias). Homosexual attractiveness was thought to fade with maturity, and the Greeks tended to disapprove of homosexual behaviour that continued beyond the usual time-span, and most particularly if an individual always adopted a passive role. Passivity in an adult male was thought to be disgusting and womanish, and a good subject for abuse in Attic Old Comedy. Aristotle thought that there was something wrong with the nature of such a man, or that he had perhaps been badly treated when young; in either case it was a defect, but one for which he could not be blamed.

4. Aristophanes' speech in Plato's *Symposium* contains the only reference there seems to be to female homosexuality in classical Attic literature, which is otherwise silent on the subject. It is perhaps surprising that the topic is not exploited for humour in Old Comedy. The strongest expression of women's love for other women is found in the fragmentary poems of Sappho of Lesbos in the early sixth century BC (*see also* LESBIANISM), and similar if less passionate sentiments seem to be expressed in the near-contemporary *Partheneia* ('songs for choruses of maidens') of the slightly earlier (male) Spartan poet Alcman. According to Plutarch, Spartan women enjoyed such relationships. For Latin erotic poetry written by women in the early empire *see* SULPICIA.

5. In New Comedy and Roman comedy the setting is that of the comfortably-off conventional household, and since the assumption was that all men married, the love interest is correspondingly almost entirely heterosexual. Although the *novel embraces a wide variety of settings the plots of the Greek novels known to us concern a chaste pair of heterosexual lovers (but see the Latin *Satyricon*). The Greek novel *Leucippe and Cleitophon* actually includes a debate between proponents of heterosexual and homosexual love, but in general homosexuality was not seen as an exclusive preference. Among Romans and Greeks alike the adulterous pursuit of a married woman was disapproved of. Traditionally-minded Romans also disapproved of homosexuality (Cato the Elder was predictably hostile), but with Rome's growing acquaintance with Greek culture from the mid-second century BC the Romans acquired a taste for the *palaestra, the *symposium, and pederasty. A century later Cicero's downplaying of the behaviour of the youthful *Caelius indicates that homosexual behaviour was at least tolerated by those listening to his speech. At this time pederastic love was one of the motifs of Hellenistic Greek erotic poetry which the Roman poets had no reluctance in using (and even on occasion applying to themselves): Catullus in his Iuventius poems, Horace in the *Odes*, Virgil in the *Eclogues*, and so on. Ovid is the exception, saying in the *Ars amatoria* (with reference to the passive 'beloved'), 'I hate unions which do not exhaust both partners; this is why I am not so keen on love with a boy' (for a boy's supposed lack of feeling see above). At Rome the passive homosexual grown-up male was the butt of invective.

6. For the philosophically inclined, the attitude to love was mediated through Epicureanism or Stoicism. Since the Epicurean ideal is the avoidance of pain, and nothing, including love, is god-sent, falling in love with the risk of attendant failure and jealousy will be avoided by the wise. (For an Epicurean, *friendship was the important thing.) The Stoic view of love was more benign. For Stoics who veered towards Cynicism it was immaterial whether one made love to a girl or a boy as long as one's need was satisfied, and if it was, then it was of no consequence whether one was loved or not. For the un-Cynical Stoic, love can be a positive incentive to virtue, but in any case Stoics downplayed the passions and the emotions. *See also* CONCUBINAGE.

**Lūcan (Marcus Annaeus Lucānus)** (AD 39–65) Silver Latin poet, born at Corduba (Cordoba) in Spain. He was the grandson of Seneca the Elder, and his father was the brother of Seneca the Younger (and the brother of Gallio of Acts 18). He was educated at Rome, studying philosophy under the Stoic Cornutus, whose tuition he is said to have shared with the satirist *Persius. He continued his studies at

Athens but was recalled by the emperor Nero, who admitted him to his circle, made him quaestor and augur, and greatly admired him for a time. In AD 60 at the first celebration of the games called Neronia he won a prize for a poem in praise of Nero. In 62 or 63 he published three books of his epic now surviving in ten books, *De bello civili* ('On the civil war [between Caesar and Pompey]'; *Pharsalia* is an alternative title). However, hostility arose between him and Nero, for which various reasons are given; it is possible that the emperor was jealous of Lucan's literary success, having himself some claim to being a poet. Lucan was forbidden to write further poetry or to plead in the courts. He took to lampooning the emperor and even joined the conspiracy of *Piso (3) (64–5). When this was discovered Lucan, in spite of confessions and abject pleas, was compelled to commit suicide (as were his father and both uncles). His death is described in Tacitus' *Annals* 15. There is a biography of him by Suetonius.

Lucan was a voluminous and precocious writer, but all his works apart from the unfinished *Pharsalia* are lost, among them an address to his much-loved wife Polla Argentaria. The *Pharsalia* is the greatest Latin epic after the *Aeneid*, and Lucan's brilliant style won him the admiration of his contemporaries. One of them, Quintilian, while recognizing its qualities, adds that it is 'a safer model for orators than for poets'.

**Lu'cian (Loukiānos)** (Lat. Lūciānus, b. *c.* AD 115 at Samosata on the Euphrates in Syria, d. after 180) The author (in Greek) of some eighty prose pieces in various forms: essays, speeches, letters, dialogues, and stories, mainly satirical in tone. His native language was probably Aramaic, but he received a good Greek education in rhetoric and became first an advocate and then, like many of his day, a travelling lecturer, although he was a satirist rather than a sophist (*see* SECOND SOPHISTIC). The details of his life are known only from his own writings; no contemporary or near-contemporary mentions him. He travelled through Asia, Greece, Italy, and Gaul, but in middle age he moved to Athens and abandoned rhetoric for philosophy. It may have been after that that he developed the dialogue form (familiar from Plato) which made him famous, although it is impossible to date his works securely. His writings were influenced by Greek iambic poetry, Attic Old Comedy, the dialogues of Plato, and especially the satires of the Cynic *Menippus, and he scathingly, if humorously, indicts the follies of his day. In later life he was appointed to a minor post in the Roman bureaucracy in Egypt.

*Lucius or the Ass* (*Lucius sive asinus*) is a short novel included in the manuscripts of Lucian but unlikely to be by him. If, as is possible, the story originated before his day, it is unlikely that the surviving version is his. Several episodes are found also in *Apuleius' Metamorphoses* (or *Golden Ass*) which could have come from the original pre-Lucianic version. In the story a young businessman finding himself in Thessaly (notorious for witchcraft) witnesses his host's wife's transformation into an owl. He tries to transform himself likewise but is changed into an ass. Before he can change back into a man, by eating roses, he is stolen by bandits and undergoes a series of misfortunes before he manages to snatch some roses at a public spectacle and regain his human form. He then sails home to Patras.

Among Lucian's writings on literary and quasi-philosophical subjects are the following:

(i) *The Vision* or the *Life of Lucian* (*Somnium* or *Vita Luciani*), a chapter of his early life, telling how he abandoned sculpture (to which his parents had apprenticed him) for learning.

(ii) *Nigrīnus*, which contains an interesting picture of the simplicity and peace of contemporary Athens contrasted with the turbulent and luxurious life of Rome.

(iii) *The Literary Prometheus* (*Ad eum qui dixerat, 'Prometheus es in verbis'*: 'To him who said, "you are like Prometheus in your language"'), in which he describes the basis of his satires, namely a blend of comedy and Platonic dialogue.

(iv) *The Way to Write History* (*De historia conscribenda*), an entertaining criticism of the eccentricities of contemporary historians, followed by an acute exposition of the qualities required in a history and its author.

(v) *Demonax*, an account of the character of that Cynic philosopher, Lucian's teacher, praised for his austere virtue.

(vi) *Imagines* (Gk. *Eikonĕs*), a dialogue with interesting references to the chief works of some of the great Greek artists, Pheidias, Praxiteles, Polygnotus, and Apelles.

(vii) *True History* (*Verae historiae*), a parody of travellers' tales, including Homer's *Odyssey* and *Ctesias' *Indica*, which Lucian begins with the assertion that he tells the truth only when he says that it is all lies. The adventures related are of the most extravagant and ingenious kind, involving a voyage to the moon and to the Isles of the Blest, where the travellers meet Homer and hear him condemn his critics, and assert, among other things, that he began the *Iliad* with the anger of Achilles merely from chance, without any settled plan. When the travellers arrive at the Underworld they find Herodotus and Ctesias there paying the penalty for their falsehoods.

Lucian's satirical dialogues are numerous, and together with his fantastic tales are his most characteristic works, showing his wit and inventiveness as well as his hatred of cant, hypocrisy, and fanaticism, especially in religion and philosophy. Among the best-known of these dialogues are the following:

(i) *Dialogues of the Gods* (*Deorum dialogi*) and *of the Sea Gods* (*Marinorum dialogi*), short dialogues making fun of the myths about the gods.

(ii) *Dialogues of the Dead* (*Mortuorum dialogi*), short dialogues set in the Underworld. Death shows up the vanities and pretences of living men (including the arguments of philosophers). The irony, at the expense of all humankind, is grim and tinged with melancholy.

(iii) *Menippus* (also called *Necyomantia*). Menippus, the Cynic philosopher, exasperated by the contradictions of philosophy, visits the Underworld to consult Teiresias as to the best life to lead, and is told merely to do, with smiling face and taking nothing too seriously, the task that lies to hand. Similar themes are treated in the *Charon*, where Charon, the ferryman from the Underworld, visits the upper world to see what life is like and what it is that makes men weep when they enter his boat (i.e. life seen from the point of

view of death); this is the most poetic of Lucian's dialogues, with its comparisons of cities to beehives attacked by wasps, and of human lives to bubbles. The whole is a picture of the pettiness of mankind; Charon himself observes, 'This is all laughable'.

(iv) *The Dream* or *The Cock*, concerning Micyllus the cobbler, who threatens to kill a cock which has woken him from a happy dream of riches. The cock reveals himself to be Pythagoras, in one of his incarnations (a previous one had been *Aspasia), and argues that Micyllus is much happier than many rich men. To prove the point the cock and Micyllus, rendered invisible by the former's magic tail feathers, visit the houses of several rich men and observe their miseries and vices.

(v) *The Sale of Lives* (*Vitarum auctio*), in which the chief proponents of various philosophic creeds are put up for sale, Hermes being the auctioneer: Diogenes the Cynic goes for two obols, useful as a house dog; Heracleitus is unsaleable; Socrates (apparently identified with Platonic philosophy), after considerable ridicule, fetches the enormous sum of two talents, bought by Dion of Syracuse; Pyrrhon the Sceptic is disposed of last, and even after he is in the hands of the buyer is still in doubt as to whether he has been sold or not.

(vi) *Icaromenippus*, resembling Aristophanes' *Birds*. Menippus (see (iii) above), disgusted with the disputes of the philosophers, resolves to visit the heavens himself to find out the truth, cutting off the wings of an eagle and a vulture as a mechanical aid. He finds *Empedocles in the moon, carried there by the vapours of Aetna. He is civilly received by the gods, and watches Zeus receive human prayers, through ventholes in the floor of heaven; he attends a banquet and hears the gods decide to destroy all philosophers as useless drones. Returned to earth Menippus hastens with malicious pleasure to the *Stoa Poikile to announce to the philosophers their impending doom.

(vii) *Dependent Scholars* (*De mercede conductis*), written to dissuade a Greek philosopher from accepting a place

(viii) *Peregrine's death* (*De morte Peregrini*), a satirical narrative of the career of a fanatical Cynic and apostate Christian (a historical character) who, in pursuit of notoriety, had himself burnt alive on a pyre.

(ix) *Lover of lies* (*Philopseudēs*), description of a \*symposium at which ten stories of magic and ghosts are told, the last being the prototype of 'The sorcerer's apprentice.'

**Lūcī'lius, Gaius** (c.180–102 BC) Latin satirical poet, born at Suessa Aurunca in Campania of a senatorial family, a friend of eminent Romans of that time including \*Scipio Aemilianus and Laelius, and famous as the creator of Roman poetical satire. Lucilius wrote in various metres but finally established hexameters as the standard metre for the genre. Of his thirty books numbers 26–30 are the earliest, in a mixture of metres; in the later books, 1–21, he adopts the hexameter. Books 22–25, in elegiacs, probably consisted of epigrams and epitaphs. In the style of Archilochus, Lucilius writes uninhibitedly in the first person, attacking his enemies by name. He covers incidents in the lives of himself and his friends, travels, literary subjects, public and private morality, and popular philosophy, especially Stoicism (and is warmly praised for his philosophy by the Younger Seneca). Some of his satires included outspoken criticism of authors and men in public life. Of these works some 1,400 lines survive, but no single substantial passage. The satires served as a model for later satirists, especially Horace, whose celebrated 'Journey to Brundisium' (\*Satires 1.5) was modelled on one, and they were read well into imperial times.

**Lūcī'na** *See* JUNO.

*Lucius or the Ass* *See* LUCIAN.

**Lucrē'tia** The wife of L. Tarquinius Collatinus, great-nephew of Tarquinius Priscus, fifth king of Rome. According to legend she was raped by Sextus, son of Tarquinius Superbus, seventh and last king, and having revealed this to her husband took her own life. After her death Collatinus conspired with Junius \*Brutus to overthrow Superbus, and they both became the first consuls in 509 BC, when the Romans expelled the Tarquins from Rome. However, Collatinus as a member of the Tarquinian *gens* was forced to go with them. The story is told by Livy and Lucretia is the subject of Shakespeare's poem *The Rape of Lucrece* (1594).

**Lucrē'tius** 1. Titus Lucretius Cārus (*c*.99–*c*.55 BC) Roman poet and Epicurean philosopher, author of *De rerum natura* ('On nature'), his only known work. Of his life virtually nothing has come down to us. Jerome, in his translation of the *Chronica* of Eusebius, states that he was born in 94 BC, was poisoned by a love philtre, wrote in the intervals of madness some books which Cicero later 'emended', and took his own life at the age of 44. \*Donatus (1) states in an aside that he died in 55. The poem, though in a finished state, may not have been finally completed. Among other problems, the prologue to book 4 occurs also in book 1; Lucretius may have intended to substitute another passage in 4. Though the prologue to book 6 states that this is the final book, the ending is abrupt and textually corrupt (*see* CLOSURE). The poem may have been published as it stood after the author's death. It is dedicated to the aristocrat C. Memmius, the patron of Catullus and Cinna (whom Catullus accompanied to Bithynia during Memmius' propraetorship of 57). The description Lucretius gives of Memmius in the proem to Book 1, as excelling in all graces and helping his country in her hour of need, is likely to antedate the latter's disgrace and banishment in 53 for corrupt practices in the elections of 54.

*De rerum natura* is a \*didactic poem in six books of hexameters (some 7,400 lines), and is the fullest exposition we possess of the physical system of \*Epicurus, in which Lucretius was a convinced and ardent believer. His immediate sources are unknown, and seem not to include directly Epicurus' own great work, *On Nature*; but the poem owes something to other scientific works, such as Plato's *Timaeus* and the Hippocratic corpus (*see* HIPPOCRATES). The purpose of the poem is to free men from a sense of guilt and the fear of death by demonstrating that fear of the intervention of gods in this world and of punishment of the soul after death are groundless: the world and everything in it are material and governed by the mechanical laws of nature, and the soul is mortal and perishes with the body. Thus most of the poem is devoted to an exposition of the atomic theory which Epicurus had adopted from the philosophers *Democritus and *Leucippus: that an infinite number of atoms moving about in infinite space collide and combine with each other to bring into existence the world in all its variety, and there is nothing in the world that is not material. However, Lucretius allows that men possess free will, and accounts for it by stating that atoms occasionally swerve from their path out of their own volition. He also touches upon Epicurus' moral theory that pleasure is the aim of life.

Each book is a unity both in structure and subject matter, with prologue and concluding section.

*Book 1* opens with a famous invocation of Venus, goddess of creative life, to grant to the poet inspiration and to Rome peace. It then starts with the proposition that nothing comes to be out of nothing, and proceeds to the demonstration that the universe consists of void and small particles of matter, atoms, which are solid, indivisible, and indestructible. In passing Lucretius refutes the physical systems of *Heracleitus, *Empedocles, and *Anaxagoras, and demonstrates that the universe is infinite in extent.

*Book 2* starts with a passage on the blessings of philosophy. It then deals with the motion and shape of the atoms which, endlessly falling through space by their own nature, may swerve a little from their path (the swerve being Epicurus' rejection of a determinist universe) and, colliding with other atoms, form into masses; from these masses the universe is built up by chance arrangement. The book concludes with the important Epicurean doctrine that the universe contains an infinite number of other worlds and the connected proposition that our world has both a birth and a death.

*Book 3* starts with praise of Epicurus and then proceeds to a demonstration that the soul too is made of atoms, of an extremely rarefied nature, and, with a long series of proofs, that it is mortal. The book ends triumphantly with an eloquent exposition of the foolishness of fearing death.

*Book 4* deals mainly with the Epicurean theory of vision, sensation, and thought, and with various biological processes, digestion, sleep, and the meaning of dreams, and ends with a vigorous denunciation of the physical passion of love, seen as a mental delusion which destroys the Epicurean ideal state, peace of mind.

*Book 5* begins with an extravagant eulogy of Epicurus, holding him to be partly divine because of his godlike peace of mind. Lucretius attacks the theological view of the world. He shows how the world had a beginning and will have an end, and discusses some problems of astronomy. He then traces the origin on earth of plant and animal life, including human life, and in the most famous part of the poem he describes with remarkable insight the development of primitive humans and the birth of civilization.

*Book 6*, whose introduction is one more laudation of Epicurus, is the loosest in composition. It deals with those phenomena most likely to lead to false belief in the gods—thunder, earthquakes, volcanoes, the magnet, etc., concluding with the aetiology of disease and a horrific account derived from Thucydides of the plague at Athens in 430 BC (*see* PELOPONNESIAN WAR).

Beyond his aim to enlighten there is no specific treatment of the subject of moral conduct, but it is clear that Lucretius accepted the view of Epicurus. He believes that pleasure and pain are the only guides to conduct, but by pleasure he understands the calm that proceeds from absence of pain and desire, and freedom from care and fear. He is deeply moved at the thought of Epicurus' great contribution to the alleviation of human suffering, and he speaks of the philosopher with religious awe. Much of the subject matter does not lend itself easily to poetic treatment, and there are parts that make for tortuous reading, and others where the versification is heavy and clumsy. His hexameters have weight and dignity, though admitting metrical practices that later poets preferred to avoid. He had a wide range of literary models, and his style shows the influence of the old Latin poets, *Ennius (particularly), *Naevius, *Pacuvius, and *Accius. He freely uses alliteration, assonance, and even rhyme, as well as repetition, and archaic forms and constructions; and he does not hesitate to invent new words, complaining of the poverty of his native tongue. By recalling the examples of *Parmenides and *Empedocles as philosophical and scientific poets Lucretius made his own blend of poetic form and scientific content seem traditional. His main model is Empedocles' poem *On Nature*, chiefly because this work too was offering an important scientific explanation of the world to its audience. His great success both as a poet and as a scientist lies in the exactness of his imagery, which makes clear the complexity of what he is expounding. But perhaps a long-perceived conflict between the poetry and the philosophy still remains. After all, Aristotle in the *Poetics* did not think that using Homer's metre made Empedocles write like Homer: he remained a scientist. But poetry is important as the 'honey on the rim' of the cup containing the bitter draught of philosophy.

Lucretius aroused the admiration of Virgil ('happy the man who was able to understand the causes of things', *felix qui potuit rerum cognoscere causas*; see *GEORGICS*), of Statius (who speaks of 'the towering frenzy of the learned Lucretius', *docti furor arduus Lucreti*), even of Ovid. But he appears to have been almost completely forgotten in the Middle Ages; the text is based upon only two primary manuscripts. It is through Lucretius that the atomic theories of Epicurus are best known today.

**2. Quintus Lucretius Vespi'lio** Consul at Rome in 19 BC, who was concealed by his wife Turia during the *proscriptions of 43–42 BC until his pardon was obtained. He has been thought to be the author of the remarkable *Laudatio Turiae* ('Eulogy of Turia'), an encomium, preserved in an inscription, describing how faithfully and bravely his wife looked after him.

**Lūcu'llus, Lucius Lici'nius** (*c.*114–57 BC) Roman general and politician. He was *Sulla's most reliable officer, entrusted with the diplomatic side of his dealings in the East, and became his literary executor. He governed Africa as propraetor in 77 with honesty and humanity. Consul in 74, he obtained the command against *Mithridates, king of Pontus, and carried out a series of brilliant campaigns in the Third Mithridatic War until his troops, kept under strict discipline, began to mutiny. He settled the taxation of Asia fairly, thereby offending business interests at Rome, and in 66 he was replaced by Pompey under the Manilian law (*see PRO LEGE MANILIA*) and returned to Rome, where he had to wait until 63 for a *triumph. He divorced his wife, the sister of *Clodia, for adultery. He led the senate's opposition to the eastern settlement of his rival

Pompey, but after unpleasant experiences of Caesar's consulate (59) retired and gave himself up to the indulgence of his hedonist tastes, having acquired great wealth in Asia. His luxury became proverbial: 'Lucullan' has been applied as an epithet to good food. He was an ardent philhellene, a lover of literature and the arts, and a friend of the philosopher Antiochus of Ascalon (*see ACADEMY*). The books of the Pontic kings, booty from the war, remained his private property, but he was always ready to lend them, and his library became a centre for literary Greeks at Rome (*see LIBRARIES* and *PRO ARCHIA*). He wrote a (lost) history in Greek of the Marsian War (90–89 BC). He lapsed into insanity before his death.

**lustration** Ceremony of purification at Rome, a circular procession with torches and sacrificial animals, accompanied by music and dance. At the end the animals were sacrificed and their entrails inspected. The ceremony marked a new beginning. The most important lustration was carried out at the end of the *census.

**Lycā'on** In Greek myth, son of Pelasgus and king of Arcadia, who founded the cult of Zeus Lycaeus and sacrificed a child on the altar. Some sources say he entertained Zeus to a feast and having offered him the child's flesh was turned into a wolf (*lykos*). From that time onwards, every time sacrifice was made at that altar a man turned into a wolf; the creature might revert to human shape in the ninth year if it had not tasted human flesh. Another story said that when Zeus and Hermes visited Arcadia, Lycaon, to test Zeus, served him human flesh. Zeus as punishment struck down all Lycaon's sons except one, turned Lycaon into a wolf, and sent a great flood (*see DEUCALION*). The story seems to represent a belief that Zeus, as weather-god, could be moved by human sacrifice.

**Lycē'um (Lýkeion)** Grove and gymnasium near Athens, sacred to Apollo Lyceius, where Aristotle taught. The name is sometimes used to signify the philosophy school of Aristotle and his successors. The Lyceum lay to the east of the city near the river Ilissus.

**Lý'cophron** Hellenistic poet of the third century BC, from Chalcis in Euboea. When a young man he went to Alexandria and became one of the Pleiad of tragic poets (*see PLEIADES*). To him has been attributed the *Alexandra*, a dramatic monologue in 1,474 lines of iambic trimeters in which the slave set to watch Alexandra (i.e. *Cassandra) reports her prophecies to her father Priam, king of Troy. They concern the destruction of Troy and the crime of *Ajax (2), the return of the Greeks and their fate, Aeneas' arrival in Latium, the eventual struggles between Europe and Asia, and the rise of Roman power as exemplified in the victory of the Roman Flamininus at *Cynoscephalae in 197 BC. These last passages, which probably concern events later than Lycophron's own lifetime, raised doubts even in antiquity as to whether he could really be the author. The whole poem is written in an extremely obscure and allusive style.

**Lycō'ris** *See* GALLUS.

**Lycu'rgus (Lykourgos) 1.** Mythical king of the Edones, a Thracian people; he persecuted the youthful *Dionysus when he came with his nurses seeking refuge, and was consequently struck blind, or driven mad, so that he killed his family; he was then eaten alive by wild horses.

**2.** Legendary legislator of *Sparta, about whom nothing certain is known, not even when (or if) he lived: various centuries have been suggested, starting from the ninth BC. Plutarch tells how Lycurgus brought back from the Delphic oracle a *rhētra*, 'verbal agreement', to be a compact between him and the Spartan people, and the foundation of the Spartan constitution and the social and military systems. *Eunomia*, 'good order', is the name usually applied to these. It is generally accepted that this was essentially a work of conscious design but not of a single legislator. It is perhaps significant that Lycurgus is not mentioned by *Tyrtaeus when he writes of the *eunomia* in the seventh century BC.

**3.** (*c*.390–*c*.325 BC) Distinguished Athenian orator and statesman, pupil of Isocrates, and a member of a noble family. Lycurgus was in charge of Athens' finances from the time of her defeat by Philip II of Macedon at Chaeronea in 338 BC until 326. The increase in the size of the navy at this time is attributed to his raising the revenue, and he embarked on an extensive building programme, including the reconstruction in marble of the theatre of *Dionysus. He won the confidence of his fellow-citizens to such a degree that they refused to surrender him to Philip's son Alexander the Great in 335

when the latter demanded the arrest of those hostile to Macedon. Lycurgus had statues erected of the tragic dramatists Aeschylus, Sophocles, and Euripides, and an official copy made of all their works (later borrowed by Ptolemy II Philadelphus, king of Egypt, for the library at Alexandria and never returned). Of his fifteen orations known to the ancients one survives, the indictment for treason of a certain Leocrates, for having allegedly fled from Athens at the news of the defeat at Chaeronea. It was said that after his death Lycurgus was accused of having left a deficit in the city treasury, and that when his sons were unable to repay the money they were imprisoned, in spite of a defence by *Hypereides; after an appeal by Demosthenes they were released.

**Lycus** *See* ANTIOPE and *HERACLES, MADNESS OF.*

**Ly'gdamus** *See* TIBULLUS.

**Ly'nceus 1.** In Greek myth, son of Aphareus, king of Messenia, and the younger brother of Idas. The two brothers were inseparable, and both sailed with the *Argonauts. Lynceus' eyesight was so keen that he could see for great distances and even through the earth. In a fight with Castor and Polydeuces (*see* DIOSCURI) both brothers were killed, as also was Castor.

**2.** In Greek myth, a son of Aegyptus, the only one to be spared by his bride, Hypermnestra, on their wedding night (*see* DANAUS). He became king of Argos and was succeeded by his son Abas.

**lyre** *See* TERPANDER and MUSIC [Greek 1 and 3].

## lyric poetry

**Greek.** Lyric poetry, meaning poetry 'sung to the lyre', existed in Greece from earliest times. Although it was, strictly speaking, song, the words were of primary importance and are now all that remain, knowledge of the accompanying music having been lost in antiquity. The Alexandrian scholars of the third century BC drew up a *canon of nine great lyric poets, the earliest dating from the archaic age: Alcman, Sappho, Alcaeus, Stesichorus, Ibycus, Anacreon, Simonides, Pindar, and Bacchylides. Some added a tenth, Corinna. Lyric poetry is also found in the Attic drama of the fifth century BC, in the choruses (so-called; *see* CHORUS), but towards the end of the fifth century the chorus was relegated to a subordinate role (*see* COMEDY [Greek 5]). In relatively modern times, Greek lyric poetry outside drama has been divided into two kinds, choral lyric, sung by a choir (also known as choral odes), and monody (Gk. *monōdia*, 'solo song'). Both kinds of lyric were written in a great variety of metres. Elegy and iambic poetry, written in their own particular (non-lyric) metres, are both occasionally included with lyric poetry (strictly speaking erroneously and despite incompatibility of metre) when the subject-matter seems to suggest this grouping, as for example in love elegy.

Choral lyric was sung and danced by a chorus (or by a leader answered by a chorus) to a musical accompaniment usually played on the lyre, occasionally on the pipe (*aulos). In ceremonial choral lyric, as in drama, the elaborate dress of the choir contributed to the spectacle. The choir speaks with a collective voice, seeming to represent the public voice of the community. Although in the odes of Pindar the voice is that of the poet himself it has a similar public quality. Lyric was composed probably from earliest times, certainly from the seventh century BC, and throughout Greek history for public religious ceremonies. To this fact are attributable the predominantly elevated tone and the inclusion of myth and moralizing. Homer mentions many varieties of choral lyric: *dirges, *hymns, *hyporchemata, maiden-songs (*see* PARTHENEION), and *marriage songs. The procession-song (*prosodion*) is another very ancient form. Later developments were the *dithyramb (accompanying the worship of Dionysus), the *nome, and the encomium and *epinikion, the two last written in praise of men, and indicative of the increasing secularization of this form of poetry. The earliest choral odes of which substantial parts survive are *partheneia* by Alcman (seventh century BC) which seem to be composed in metrically corresponding stanzas known as *strophēs and antistrophēs. In later choral lyric the form became triadic (*see* TRIAD), reputedly the innovation of Stesichorus, and of an increasing metrical complexity which reached its culmination in the odes of Pindar. The content of a choral ode was relatively standardized and included praise of the gods, mention of the occasion and the personalities involved, moral maxims, and mythical narrative, this last providing the main subject matter. The charm of lyric lies in the freshness, vigour, and clarity of the language.

The development of choral lyric is associated with the Doric-speaking Peloponnese, especially Sparta, and with the names of *Thaletas, *Eumelus, and *Arion, whose works are virtually all lost. The association is indicated by the ancient convention that choral lyric was written in the Doric dialect; Doric elements were retained even in the choral lyric of Attic tragedy. The great poets of choral lyric, some of whose work survives, are Alcman, Stesichorus, Ibycus, Simonides, Pindar, and Bacchylides. For choral lyric as an element in Attic drama *see* CHORUS; TRAGEDY 1; COMEDY [Greek 3].

Of monody relatively little remains. It was sung to the accompaniment of a lyre. The intimate nature of the subject matter—friendship, love, and hate—suggests that it was performed by a single individual on private occasions, for example after a banquet among friends (*see* SYMPOSIUM and SCOLIA). The surviving lyric of Sappho, Alcaeus, and Anacreon is mostly monody. The fact that a poem is triadic in form is usually taken as an indication that it is a choral rather than a monodic ode; monody is generally simpler than choral lyric in form, metre, and expression. Attic tragedy contains a small amount of monody in the lyrics occasionally sung by individuals (rather than by the chorus). *See also* ARCHILOCHUS.

**Latin.** Comparatively little lyric poetry was written by the Romans. There exist in Latin some fragments of folk-songs, hymns, and religious incantations which indicate the existence in early times of an indigenous lyric poetry, but the earliest Latin lyric deserving of the name was modelled on Greek forms, mostly the simpler forms of monody, and it has been assumed to be a literary product, not rooted in social practice, intended to be read and not sung. Two notable exceptions are, first, the maiden-song composed for Juno at a time of crisis in 207 BC by *Livius Andronicus, based presumably on Greek models; and secondly, Horace's elegant *Carmen Saeculare* (17 BC). Laevius was another early writer of lyrics (probably at the beginning of the first century BC), but only fragments of his work have survived. However, Cicero at least liked to believe that the old Romans used to hold dinner parties at which songs were sung which did not survive to his own day, 'and which Cato mentioned in the *Origines* as sung by guests in praise of famous men' (*Brutus* 19). Varro said something similar. The two chief writers of literary lyric were Catullus and Horace. Catullus experimented with lyric metres in poems of great verve (11, 17, 30, 34, 51, and 61), and wrote other equally lively poems in hende-casyllables and scazons which it is natural to regard as lyrics, even if the metres are not strictly speaking those of song (see above); their style and subject matter both recall the manner of Greek monody. Horace in the *Odes uses a fair variety of the lyric metres found in Greek monody, frequently combining lines of different metres into couplets or four-line stanzas. He regarded music as an accompaniment to lyric poetry, but it is generally believed that he accepted the primacy of words over music, as the influential contemporary philosopher *Philodemus argued should be the case. Horace also expresses a range of sentiments, from deep seriousness in Pindaric vein (though not attempting the complexities of Pindar's triadic structure), to love-poems and drinking-songs in a more subjective style (written with technical refinement learned from the Hellenistic poets, but lacking the spontaneity of early Greek monody). The iambic metres of the *Epodes do not strictly belong to lyric, although the subject matter in most cases makes them close to it. Horace's technical mastery seems to have deterred later poets from attempting to follow him, and lyrical subjects tended to be treated in the elegiac metre. Statius' *Silvae include two lyrics (4.5 and 4.7), Martial occasionally used lyric metres, and *Seneca (2) included choral lyrics in his tragedies. The note of true inspiration is not heard again until the Christian hymns of Prudentius and Ambrose (to which should perhaps be added the emperor Hadrian's poem to his soul).

**Lȳsan'der (Lȳsandros)** (d. 395 BC) Spartan naval commander towards the end of the *Peloponnesian War (431–404 BC), who won a great victory over the Athenian fleet at Aegospotami in 405. At Samos he was subsequently worshipped as a god, perhaps the first living Greek to be so honoured (*see* RULER CULT). He blockaded Piraeus and after the surrender of Athens in the spring of 404 BC supported the establishment of the *Thirty Tyrants. He subsequently became estranged from the Spartan government and lost power and influence. At the outbreak of the Corinthian War (395–386; *see* CORINTH), in which an alliance of Greek states opposed Sparta's tyrannical rule, he invaded Boeotia but was killed there at the siege of the city of Haliartus in 395. He was among the ablest Spartan leaders, but perhaps be-

cause of this unpopular with his coevals. His Life was written by Nepos and Plutarch.

**Ly'sias** (b. *c*.458 BC according to the biographical tradition, but perhaps some fifteen years later; d. *c*.380) Attic orator, son of Cephalus, a wealthy Syracusan, whom Pericles persuaded to settle as a *metic (resident alien) in Athens; brother of Polemarchus and Euthydemus. The family owned a prosperous shield-making business; it is the house of Polemarchus, the eldest son, at Piraeus, that provides the setting for Plato's *Republic, in which Cephalus and Polemarchus take part in the opening discussion. At some time Lysias went with his brother Polemarchus to *Thurii in south Italy and is said to have studied rhetoric under *Teisias of Syracuse. They were expelled as Athenian sympathizers after the defeat of the *Sicilian Expedition in 413 BC and returned to Athens. In 404 the two brothers were among the wealthy Athenians arrested by the *Thirty Tyrants; Lysias escaped to Megara but Polemarchus was put to death and their property was seized. While in exile Lysias spent what was left of his fortune in aiding the democracy; as a consequence, on his return in 403 an attempt was made to confer citizenship upon him, but it was defeated as unconstitutional. Being now rather poor he became a professional speech-writer (*see* LOGOGRAPHERS (2)) and proved outstandingly successful, reputedly composing over 200 forensic speeches. As a metic he could not appear in court in person. However, the first speech of his career he delivered on his own behalf, perhaps to a court of inquiry. The speech was *Against Eratosthenes* (speech 12), the defendant being allegedly the murderer of Lysias' brother, and it contains a vivid description of the writer's experiences under the Thirty.

Of the speeches attributed to him thirty-five survive, only twenty-three entire, and some (perhaps many) are spurious. They include a funeral oration (*epitaphios*) on those who died in the Corinthian War (395–386; *see* CORINTH) and a fragment of an epideictic ('display') speech delivered at the Olympian festival of 388 (*Olympiakos*), in which he urges the Greeks to end internal discord and unite against the two great enemies, the Persian king and Dionysius, tyrant of Syracuse. Lysias' speeches cover a range of cases, from murder and treason to adultery and embezzlement. Among the most interesting are: *For Man-*

*titheus* (a young man accused of having served in the cavalry under the Thirty); *For the Cripple*, a defence of a man charged (perhaps justifiably) with receiving a state pension under false pretences; *Against Alcibiades* (son of the famous Alcibiades), for dereliction of military duty; *On the Murder of Eratosthenes* (speech 1, not to be confused with 12; see above), a speech for a husband who had murdered his wife's seducer, fascinating for its glimpse of the life and conversation of an ordinary Greek household.

Lysias was admired in antiquity for the simplicity and naturalness of his style. His precise use of language, avoidance of all affectation and extravagance, and moderation of tone—he is rarely passionate, and pathos is not his strong point—could lead to monotony, but this is avoided by his gift of putting himself in his client's place and preparing for him a persuasive speech such as only he could have made according to his own circumstances, age, and temperament. Without resort to rhetorical devices, the speeches are clear and vivid, and orderly in arrangement (preface, narrative, proof, conclusion). It is said that he wrote a defence for Socrates to speak at his trial, but that Socrates refused it. The *Phaedrus* of Plato contains what purports to be a speech by Lysias on love, but is probably a Platonic parody.

**Lȳsis** Dialogue by Plato which (like *Euthyphro*, *Laches*, and *Charmides*) aims at defining a single concept, in this case *friendship, and like these others ends in apparent failure. Socrates enters into conversation with two boys (aged about 13), Lysis and Menexenus, who are close friends, in order to discover how a person becomes a friend to another. The arguments are involved and confusing, and Socrates seems to get entangled in verbal ambiguities. Friendship, it appears, is always for some end, never for the enjoyment of the relationship itself. Even if we have a natural affinity to and arrive at the ultimately lovable, our friendship still implies a lack on our part (Aristotle in the *Ethics* will later deny that). The dialogue ends when the *paidagogoi* appear to take their charges home. Friends though they all are, they still do not know what a friend is.

**Lȳsi'strata** (**Lȳsistratē**) ('Disbander of armies') Greek comedy by *Aristophanes, produced by Callistratus in the spring of 411 BC (probably at the *Lenaea rather than the Diony-

sia; it is not known whether the play won first prize). This was an alarming time for Athens: the *Sicilian Expedition had ended in disaster in 413 BC, a large part of her empire was in revolt, and her enemy Sparta had made an advantageous alliance with the Persian satrap Tissaphernes. Yet though Athens was seriously weakened there was no immediate danger of collapse; for the time being she could hold on. The play is an expression of a natural desire for peace, so long as it can be achieved by compromise, without putting Athens in real danger. It contains no *parabasis, and in this represents the beginning of a change in the form of Old Comedy (*see* COMEDY [Greek 3]). It is worth noting that in 411 the priestess of Athena Polias, the highest sacred office for a woman at Athens, was one Lysimache, 'disbander of battles'.

The men having failed to bring the war to an end, it occurs to Lysistrata that the women should take over control of affairs and force a peace, first by refusing sexual relations, and secondly by getting possession of the Acropolis and the state's reserve of money in the Parthenon, without which the Athenian war-effort would collapse. She gets the women together, including Lampito from Sparta and women from other enemy states. After some reluctance they fall in with her scheme and swear to carry it out. The foreigners depart to their own countries and Lysistrata with the Athenian wives occupy the Acropolis, which has already been seized by a band of old women. A chorus of old men tries to recapture it, but is driven off by a second chorus of old women with pails of water. An elderly *proboulos is also routed, together with his band of Scythian archers (the Athenian police force). In place of a *parabasis* the two choruses exchange insults. Then Lysistrata has to encourage the women, who are trying to slip away, to keep to their resolve. A frustrated husband Cinesias arrives to recover his wife Myrrhine, is tantalized by her, and finally cheated as she returns to the Acropolis. A herald from Sparta, similarly distressed, arrives to announce his country's intention to sue for peace, and a conference of both sides follows. Lysistrata scolds them all and urges reconciliation; peace is made, and Athenians and Spartans go to the Acropolis for a banquet, followed by the re-pairing of husbands and wives.

It is interesting that an analogy Lysistrata makes (lines 567 ff.) of women unravelling the war as they deal with matted wool is used also by Plato in the *Statesman*.

# M

**Macedon, Macedonia** In general the former is used to describe the political entity, the latter the geographical area. Geographically, Macedonia occupies a central area between the Balkans and the Greek peninsula, a largely mountainous region with strong natural defences. Politically, the kingdom of Macedon was said to have been founded, probably in the mid-seventh century BC, by Perdiccas I, who came from Argos and claimed descent from the mythical Temenus, king of Argos (and the eldest of the *Heracleidae). His capital was at Aegae (Vergina).

During the reigns of Amyntas (late sixth century) and his son and successor Alexander I, considerable territorial gains were made, and friendly relations were established with Athens. Although some Greeks persisted in saying that the Macedonians were *barbarians rather than full Hellenes, Alexander's claim to be a Temenid (see above) was recognized at Olympia and he was allowed as a true Hellene to compete in the games. He gained more territory after the Persian retreat in 479 BC. The question of the origin of the Macedonian language has not been answered definitely, largely because of the lack of early written evidence. On the whole it seems to be a dialect of Greek related to north-west Greek, but some think it is an independent *Indo-European language of the Balkans.

Alexander's successor Perdiccas II (king c.452–413) played a shifty role in international politics, vacillating between Athens and Sparta during the Peloponnesian War. He was succeeded in 413 by Archelaus, portrayed by Plato in the *Gorgias* as a monster of cruelty. Nevertheless, he did most to ensure that his country was part of Greece proper by making his new capital at Pella a centre for Greek artists and poets, entertaining among others Euripides, Agathon, Choerilus of Samos, Timotheus, and Zeuxis. Many Macedonian customs which seemed un-Greek, like tattooing, had lapsed by this time, but one or two lingered; by the mid-fourth century BC it was no longer traditional for a Macedonian who had not 'killed his man' to wear a cord round his waist, but until a very late date no one was permitted to recline at table (having instead to sit upright) who had not killed a wild boar without nets. (At the age of 35 *Cassander was still sitting up to the table.) The country was wild, and as late as classical times contained lions and bears.

Macedon assumed a central role in Greek history under *Philip II (reigned 359–336 BC), whose expansionist policy roused Athens and Thebes to war against him. When he defeated them at Chaeronea (338) he became master of Greece. Under Philip's son and successor *Alexander the Great, Macedonian power reached its zenith. At his death in 323 he left an empire stretching from the Adriatic to the Punjab, and from north Afghanistan to Libya. However, there was no competent successor in the family and there followed for nearly half a century a complicated power struggle among Alexander's generals for fragments of his empire. Cassander achieved control of Macedonia itself, and other generals founded dynasties in various parts of the empire—the Antigonids in Asia, the *Attalids in Pergamum, the *Ptolemies in Egypt, the *Seleucids in Syria. With the death in 281 BC of Seleucus, the last survivor of Alexander's generals (the *Diadochi), the possibility of the union of the empire under one ruler came to an end.

In 279 Macedonia was invaded by a Celtic people known as Gauls (or Galatians), but they were defeated by *Antigonus Gonatas (grandson of one of Alexander's generals), who established the Antigonid dynasty of Macedon and proved a vigorous, successful, and cultured ruler (277–239).

After Gonatas, the most prominent of the Antigonids was his grandson Philip V (221–179), a man of remarkable energy and ambition, who precipitated two wars with Rome—the First and Second Macedonian

Wars (214–205 and 200–197). The first war was inconclusive; in the second Philip was defeated by Q. *Flamininus at Cynoscephalae in Thessaly in 197, and in the following year Flamininus made his famous announcement at the Isthmian games that Greece was free of Macedonian domination. Philip V's son *Perseus (2) was the last Macedonian king. In the Third Macedonian War (172–168/7) his army was practically annihilated at the battle of Pydna (168) by the Roman consul Aemilius *Paullus; this was followed by the dethronement of the Antigonids and the break-up of the Macedonian kingdom into four federal republics. The end came twenty years later, when an attempt by a pretender to reunite Macedon was defeated by the Roman general Caecilius Metellus, and the country became a Roman province (146). Those cities, like Athens and Sparta, which had taken Rome's side, remained Roman allies; the rest were made subject and tributary. Greece became a Roman protectorate (not a province until the time of Augustus).

**Macedonian Wars** (of Rome) *See* MACEDONIA and FLAMININUS.

**Macer 1. Gaius Lici'nius Macer** (d. 66 BC) Roman annalist (*see* ANNALS), father of Catullus' friend and fellow-poet *Calvus. His history of Rome (in at least sixteen books) has not survived, but was used by Livy for his books 4 and 5, and also by Dionysius of Halicarnassus. He claimed to have consulted original authorities and in particular the *libri lintei*. Praetor in 68, he was convicted of extortion in 66 and committed suicide.

   **2. Aemi'lius Macer** Roman poet of Verona, d. 16 BC, the author of Latin didactic poems, *Ornithogonia* on birds, and *Theriaca* on snakebites. Only a few fragments survive. Ovid heard him reciting in his old age.

**Machā'on and Podalei'rius** In Homer's *Iliad*, sons of *Asclepius and Epione and doctors to the Greek army at Troy as well as fighting themselves.

**Macrō'bius, Ambro'sius Theodo'sius** (fl. *c.* AD 400; known to his contemporaries as Theodosius) Roman writer and philosopher. He is generally identified with the praetorian prefect of Italy in 430, but little else is known of his life.

   Macrobius wrote the *Saturnalia* ('Festival of Saturn'), dialogues in seven books dedicated to

his son; it is supposed to represent conversations at a banquet during the *Saturnalia festival between a number of eminent Romans, at the house of Vettius Praetextatus, praetorian prefect in 384 and the leading pagan intellectual of his time. In form the work is very similar to the works of *Athenaeus and of Aulus *Gellius (who is used as a source, though nowhere mentioned). Among those who are purported to be present are Avienus (identity uncertain), Symmachus (the orator and administrator), *Servius (the later Virgilian commentator), and a certain Euangelus, sceptical and rather bitter, who speaks disparagingly of Virgil and Cicero. Macrobius himself plays no part. The discussion covers a multitude of subjects, but the central topic is criticism of Virgil. He is discussed from various points of view which cover his knowledge of ritual, his power of expressing emotion, his debt to Homer and other Greek authors, and his debt to Ennius and other ancient Romans; and he is gradually built up to be the unique scholar and poet in a way which foreshadows the medieval view of him as a wonder-working magician. This section throws light on the history of Virgilian scholarship at the time.

   The *Commentarii* ('Commentaries'), also dedicated to his son, consist largely of a commentary on Cicero's *Somnium Scipionis* ('Dream of Scipio'). The 'Dream' comprises a section at the end of Cicero's De republica ('On the state'). Since Macrobius set out the text in successive paragraphs before commenting on each in turn, this part of the De republica was preserved when most of the rest was subsequently lost. He writes the commentary from a Neoplatonist perspective; his source is mainly *Porphyry's (Greek) commentary on Plato's Timaeus, but he shows knowledge of Plotinus also and praises the 'Dream' for uniting all branches of philosophy. He examines the enigma of the soul and its destiny in the light of *Neoplatonism and of the astronomy and mathematics of the day (incidentally covering many topics including music and geography), and tends to reinforce the doctrine of the 'Dream', of the immortality and divine quality of the soul, from a pagan standpoint. Macrobius' commentary was attentively studied in the West during the Middle Ages, thereby transmitting much ancient science and Neoplatonic thought.

   Macrobius also wrote a grammatical treatise which in large part survives, comparing the Greek with the Latin verb.

**Maecē'nas, Gaius** (d. 8 BC) The most famous Roman literary patron, descended from Etruscan kings, according to Horace and Propertius, an equestrian by birth (*see* EQUESTRIAN ORDER). He was one of Octavian's earliest supporters—he arranged his marriage with Scribonia—and his intimate and trusted counsellor. He was influential precisely because he never held a political office or even became a senator. Between 31 and 29 BC, when Octavian was away from Italy, he was in complete control of Roman affairs. He was also the enlightened patron of a literary circle which included Virgil and Horace particularly, Propertius to some extent, and *Varius Rufus. The rewards for these protégés were great: Horace owed his Sabine farm and Virgil his independence to him, and both poets addressed him in terms of admiration and gratitude; they made a substantial return by supporting the imperial regime in their poetry. Maecenas is said to have suggested to Virgil the subject of the *Georgics* (3.41). Only fragments survive of his own poetry and prose. He wrote a *Prometheus*, perhaps a Menippean satire (*see* MENIPPUS), and a *Dialogue*. Seneca regarded him as typical of the adage that the style is the man, perhaps indicating a complex personality. After the conspiracy and execution of his brother-in-law Varro Murena in 23 BC a coolness developed between Maecenas and Augustus and his political career came effectively to an end. He was a man of luxurious tastes and habits (he is said to have introduced heated swimming-baths at Rome), and spent the closing years of his life in the enjoyment of a cultivated leisure. *See also* AUGUSTAN AGE.

**maenads (*mainaděs*)** ('mad women', also referred to as *bacchae* and *thyiaděs*) In Greece, women inspired with ecstatic frenzy by the god *Dionysus. *See* BACCHANTS.

**Maeo'nidēs** Name sometimes applied to Homer, either because Maeonia was an ancient name for Lydia where, according to some, Homer was born, or because he was said to be the son of one Maeon.

**magi'ster e'quitum** *See* MASTER OF THE CAVALRY.

**magistrates** Name given to officers of state in Greece and Rome. For Athens *see* ARCHON; POLEMARCH; STRATEGOS. For Rome *see* AEDILES; CENSORS; CONSULS; CURSUS HONORUM; CURULE MAGISTRACIES; DICTATOR; PRAETOR; QUAESTORS.

**Magna Graecia** (Gk. Megalē Hellas) The coastal region of southern Italy colonized by Greeks from the mainland and from the Greek cities of Asia Minor. It stretched roughly from Cumae, north of the bay of Naples, to *Tarentum on the 'instep' of south Italy. Some accounts include *Sicily. The cities, founded between 740 BC (Cumae) and 433 BC (Heraclea) became prosperous through trade and the fertility of their land, and developed a flourishing culture and even their own schools of philosophy (*see* PYTHAGORAS and ELEA). Mutual hostility brought about the destruction of Sybaris by *Croton, and decline set in *c.*400 BC. By 300 BC most of the cities needed Roman protection against other Italian peoples, and the Roman wars against Hannibal and Pyrrhus completed their ruin. By 89 BC all the surviving cities were Roman colonies or *municipia. See also* THURII.

**Magna Mater** ('Great Mother') A mother-goddess worshipped in Asia from ancient times and introduced into Greece; *see* CYBELE.

**Maia 1.** In Greek myth, eldest of the *Pleiades, daughters of the Titan *Atlas; she was the mother by Zeus of the god Hermes, to whom she gave birth in a cave on Mount Cyllene in Arcadia.
**2.** Obscure Italian goddess associated with Vulcan; on 1 May the *flamen volcanalis* sacrificed to her. She seems to have been connected with the growth of living things, and the name of the month is probably derived from her name. By confusion with (1) she was associated with Mercury, the Roman equivalent of Hermes.

**maiden-song** *See* PARTHENEION.

**majuscule script** *See* UNCIALS.

**Ma'mertines (Māmertīni)** ('Mamers' is the Oscan form of the Roman god Mars; *see* ITALY) Italian mercenaries from Campania, settled in *Syracuse by the tyrant Agathocles who had hired them to fight for him against Carthage. When he died they seized Messana (between 288 and 283 BC), and terrorized north-east Sicily. After a defeat *c.*265 by Hieron II of Syracuse, they requested the Carthaginians to install a protective garrison in Messana, but at virtually the same time they also asked Rome for help. When Rome acceded the Mamertines expelled the Carthaginian garrison and a Roman force arrived. The resulting clash of interest between Rome and Carthage precipitated the First *Punic War.

**Māmu'rra** (of Formiae) Caesar's chief engineer in Spain and Gaul, where he acquired much wealth and was the first at Rome to face his mansion with marble. He is prominent in Catullus' invectives against Caesar.

**mānēs** In Roman thought, the spirits of the dead (the singular does not exist) named, probably euphemistically, the 'kindly ones', from the old Latin adjective *mānus*, 'good'. From a sense of their collective divinity they were worshipped as the *di manes* ('the divine dead') at the festivals of the Feralia, Parentalia, and Lemuria. By extension the name *manes* was applied by the poets first to the realm of the dead, the Underworld, and secondly to the gods of the Underworld (*di inferi*), Dis, Orcus, Hecate, and Persephone. Later the *di manes* were individualized and identified with the *di parentes*, the 'family dead'. Graves were originally dedicated to the dead collectively and were inscribed 'sacred to the divine dead', *dis manibus sacrum*. The individual tomb led to the conception of each dead person having an individual spirit, and *manes*, although a plural noun, came to be used of an individual's soul. Under the empire it became customary to add the name of the dead person, as if the meaning was 'sacred to the divine soul of so-and-so'.

**Ma'netho 1.** Priest of Heliopolis in Egypt in the third century BC who wrote in Greek a history of Egypt from mythical times to 323 BC, claiming to have consulted the chronological lists of kings. Portions of his history have been preserved by later writers such as Eusebius and are of great value in establishing biblical as well as Egyptian chronology.

**2.** (second to third century AD) The name claimed by the author of six books of Greek hexameter verse on astrology.

**Mānī'lius 1. Gaius Manilius** Tribune for 67/6 BC, who carried a law conferring on *Pompey the command against Mithridates, with *imperium* over all the provinces of Asia Minor.

**2. Marcus Manilius** (fl. beginning of the first century AD) Stoic author of the *Astronomica*, a Latin didactic poem in hexameters in five books on astrology. It is clear that it was completed during the last years of Augustus'

Principate and the succession of Tiberius. Unlike the Epicurean poet Lucretius, Manilius sees design and 'heavenly reason' in the organization of the universe (*see* STOICISM). Book 1 describes the creation and the arrangement of the stars in the heavens (influenced by *Aratus); book 2 the twelve signs of the zodiac, and their relation to human life; book 3, a different system of twelve 'lots' (Lat. *sortes*) of human experience, and the calculation of the horoscope at birth; book 4, the influence of the zodiac at birth, and the partition of the world under its signs; book 5 describes the risings of signs, other than those of the zodiac, and their effect on children born under them. (There is a gap in the text at 709.) The work closes with a description of the magnitudes of the stars, comparing them with human society.

**maniple** In the Roman army, a tactical unit of a legion, containing two centuries.

**Ma'nlius Capitōlī'nus, Marcus** According to Roman tradition, a commander who held the Capitol against the Gauls when they sacked Rome *c*.385 BC (*see* CAPITOLIUM). It is said that, awakened by the cackling of the sacred geese while sleeping in his house on the Capitol, dogs having failed to give warning, he summoned the guards and repulsed a surprise attack by the Gauls. Thereafter the feeding of the sacred geese was a charge on the state. In an annual commemoration geese were carried on litters with purple and gold cushions, and dogs were crucified on stakes of elder (a ritual which survived into Christian times). In the political crisis that followed the withdrawal of the Gauls, Manlius, though a patrician, is said to have supported the poor who were suffering under the stringent laws of debt. He was accused of attempting to make himself tyrant and was thrown to his death from the Tarpeian rock (*see* TARPEIA). After his death and disgrace no other member of the family was given the name Marcus (*see* DAMNATIO MEMORIAE).

**Ma'nlius Torquā'tus (Titus Manlius Imperiōsus Torquātus)** Roman hero who reputedly, in resisting an invasion of Gauls in 361 BC, killed in single combat an enormous Gaul and earned his *cognomen* (*see* NAMES) by taking from him an ornamental neck-chain, *torques*. He also exemplified Roman *pietas* ('dutifulness') in saving his father from prosecution for maltreating him. In the Latin War of 340 BC the consuls, of whom Torquatus was one, forbade single combats with the enemy. When the son of Torquatus nevertheless engaged and killed a Latin champion his father had him executed for disobedience. In later times the expression *Manliana imperia*, 'Manlian orders', became proverbial for commands of extreme severity.

**Mantinē'a** Small city-state in the south-east of Arcadia, north of Tegea, created by the unification of four or five villages *c*.500 BC. It was at first friendly to Sparta, but during the *Peloponnesian War entered into alliance with Athens, Argos, and Elis (*c*.420). It was the scene of a decisive Spartan victory in 418 BC in a battle against Athenians and Argives. In the fourth century BC Mantinea was attacked by Sparta and broken up into the original villages (385). After the battle of *Leuctra (371) the city was restored and took part in the pan-Arcadian confederacy founded at this time. It was the scene of another battle in 362 BC between Sparta and Thebes (in which Thebes was victorious but Epaminondas killed. Gryllus, the son of Xenophon, fighting with the Athenian contingent on the Spartan side, was killed in a cavalry engagement at Mantinea shortly before the main battle.

**Ma'ntua** (modern Mantova) Town on the river Mincius in Cisalpine Gaul, seldom mentioned in ancient literature but famous as the town near which the Roman poet Virgil was born. It was also the home town of 'Mantuan', a late fifteenth-century Carmelite monk who wrote Latin eclogues in a very easy Latin which consequently became a popular book in schools.

**maps** *See* ANAXIMANDER and PTOLEMY.

**Ma'rathon** Large Attic *deme on the north-east coast of Attica, commanding a long fertile plain lying along a deep bay, sheltered at its northern end, and connected with Athens by a main road running south of Mount Pentelicus. It was the scene of a defeat inflicted by the Athenians and Plataeans under Miltiades on the invading Persians in 490 BC. (*See* PERSIAN WARS and, for the Marathon race so-called, PHEIDIPPIDES.) *Herodes Atticus was a native of Marathon; traces of his estate are still visible.

**Marathon, battle of** *See* PERSIAN WARS.

**Marce'llus, Marcus Claudius 1.** (d. 208 BC) Roman general. As consul in 222 BC he

campaigned successfully against the Gauls, winning the *spolia opima* by killing the Gallic chief in single combat. He fought with distinction in the Second Punic War, showing great determination after the disaster at Cannae in 216 BC, and capturing *Syracuse in 211 after a long siege. He was killed in an ambush by Carthaginian forces when consul for the fifth time.

**2.** (b. 42 BC) Son of Gaius Claudius Marcellus and of *Octavia (1), sister of the emperor Augustus. In 25 BC he was married by Augustus' wish to the latter's daughter Julia, and in 24 Augustus showed favour towards him, rather than *Tiberius, as possible heir by accelerating his progress through the magistracies (*see* CURSUS HONORUM). In 23, as aedile, Marcellus celebrated particularly magnificent games, but died later that year. He was a young man of great promise, and was lamented by Virgil in a famous passage of the *Aeneid* (6.860–87), the reading of which so affected Octavia that she fainted.

There were several other distinguished Romans of this name.

**Marcus Aure'lius** *See* AURELIUS.

**Mardo'nius** Nephew and son-in-law of the Persian king Darius I; *see* PERSIAN WARS.

**Margī'tēs** ('Madman') Title and hero of a lost Greek narrative poem, apparently of the seventh or sixth century BC and unknown authorship, but attributed to Homer in antiquity. It was written in hexameters irregularly interspersed with iambic trimeters. Margites was an ancient Simple Simon, proverbial for his stupidity. He could not count beyond five, nor did he know whether his father or his mother had given birth to him. A few papyrus fragments survive, one describing his wedding night. Aristotle, who believed the author to be Homer, saw in *Margites* the germ of comedy, as the same poet's *Iliad* and *Odyssey* seemed to him to contain the germ of tragedy.

**Mā'rius, Gaius** (*c*.157–86 BC) Roman general and statesman born near Arpinum (Arpino, birthplace also of Cicero) to a family of equestrian status. As a soldier he served with distinction at Numantia under *Scipio (2), who was a family connection. He was quaestor *c*.123 and tribune, with the help of the Metelli, in 119 but he later opposed the consul Metellus (*see* METELLI (2)). After a period as governor in Further Spain he returned and married Julia, a patrician and aunt of Julius Caesar. He was elected consul in 107 (as a *novus homo) despite the hostility of the Metelli, and subsequently superseded Metellus as commander in Numidia. He remedied the long-standing manpower shortage in the old Roman citizen army by the radical step of abolishing the property qualification and recruiting a volunteer army of all classes including the *proletarii. This was a measure designed for the moment, but without realizing it he created a new type of client-army, dependent on its general for its reward, paving the way for *Sulla and the political domination of successful generals, and ultimately for the creation of the empire.

In 104 he celebrated a *triumph for the defeat of *Jugurtha (actually brought about by the diplomacy of Sulla), and in 100 became consul for the sixth time. He further improved the army, and his victories over the German invaders in north Italy brought him immense popularity (*see* ROME 4). He accepted the help of the tribune Saturninus in providing land for his veterans, but he did not trust him or his supporter *Glaucia and no doubt had a hand in their deaths. He now began to lose senatorial support, and when Metellus was recalled from exile Marius left for the East 'to fulfil a vow'. By 92 he seems to have made alliances with the *equites* and to have organized opposition to the tribune *Drusus (2), but by this time the senate was supporting Sulla. Marius was not given supreme command in the *Social War (2), but in 88 he secured by devious means and with the help of the tribune *Sulpicius (1) the command of the war in the East against *Mithridates. Sulla, who had already been given the command by the senate, responded by seizing Rome with his army and having Sulpicius killed, to the shock of his own supporters and the unprepared city. Marius fled to Africa, having many dramatic adventures (later much embroidered). When Sulla departed for the East early in 87 Marius returned to Italy, joined the popular leader *Cinna (1), marched on Rome, and captured it late in 87. Fulfilling, it was said, a prediction he became consul for the seventh time in 86. He then embarked on an indiscriminate massacre of all those who might be considered his enemies, until Cinna intervened. His health failed and he died before he could take up the Eastern command which had been voted to him. Marius had no positive policies, but his enmity with the senate gained him a reputation as a friend of the people.

Julius Caesar, his widow's nephew, won public favour by restoring to the Capitol his trophies, which Sulla had removed.

**Mark Antony** *See* ANTONY, MARK.

**Māro** *Cognomen* of the poet Virgil, by which he is occasionally called (*see* NAMES [Roman]).

**Marpe'ssa** In Greek myth, daughter of the river-god Evenus. She was loved by Idas (*see* LYNCEUS) and carried off by him in a winged chariot given him by the god Poseidon (in some accounts his father). They were pursued by Apollo, who also loved Marpessa, and Idas prepared to fight the god, but Zeus intervened and asked the girl to choose: she chose Idas, since, being mortal, he would grow old with her. Marpessa had a daughter Cleopatra who married *Meleager (in consequence Idas and Lynceus took part in the Calydonian boar-hunt). After Idas died Marpessa killed herself; his father Aphareus, king of Messenia, being left without an heir, bequeathed his kingdom to Nestor of Pylos (or Nestor's father Neleus).

**marriage ceremonies** Marriages in the ancient world were often, but not always, accompanied by ritual but very rarely by any religious ceremony (the exception is Roman *confarreatio*; see 2 below and MARRIAGE LAW).

**1. In Greece.** The favourite time for marriage was in winter, the month Gamelion (January/February) deriving its name from *gamos*, 'marriage'. This was the time in the agricultural cycle when tasks were at their lightest. Ceremonies differed somewhat from place to place in Greece, but those best-known, at Athens, seem typical. Our knowledge is derived from ancient literature, in which the ceremonial is probably idealized. The goddesses concerned were Artemis, presiding over the girl's transition to womanhood, Hera (Teleia), the goddess of the institution of marriage, and Aphrodite, the goddess of sexual attraction. After sacrifices and offerings and the bride's ritual bath in water from a particular source (in Athens, the spring *Callirrhoe) the bride was adorned. There was a banquet at the home of the bride's father, the bride's unveiling, and in the evening the procession to the groom's house, on foot or by carriage, accompanied by the groom's best friend, the bride's mother carrying torches (*see* MARRIAGE SONGS). The bride was welcomed at her husband's house with a shower of dried fruit and nuts, and the couple then retired to the bridal chamber while their friends sang marriage songs outside. On the day after they were sent wedding gifts.

**2. At Rome.** The favourite month for marriage was June. On the previous day the bride put away her *toga praetexta (if she wore it) because she had come of age. Her dress and appearance were prescribed by custom. Her hair, divided by the point of a spear, was arranged in six locks, bound with woollen bands. Her dress was a white woven tunic, fastened at the waist with a 'knot of Hercules' to be untied later by her husband, and a veil and shoes of flame-colour. Friends gathered in the bride's father's house, both bride and groom spoke words of consent and their hands were linked by the matron of honour. The bride was conducted to the husband's house by three boys; she herself carried a distaff and spindle with wool. She was carried over the threshold and greeted with fire and water, perhaps a symbolic welcome, before being taken to the bedchamber. Outside the door the usual *marriage songs were sung, and on the following day there was probably an entertainment for friends.

There could be many variations in the form of the marriage, but there was no religious ceremony except in the case of marriage by *confarreatio* when a sheep was sacrificed and its fleece spread over two chairs for the bride and groom to sit on, a solemn prayer offered, and another sacrifice made. The ceremony took its name from the use of a cake made of spelt (*far*) offered in sacrifice to Jupiter. The chief *flamens (priests) had to marry in this way and to have parents so married.

**marriage law** Greece and Rome were monogamous societies. At Athens a legal marriage began with betrothal, which was a formal statement by the woman's father or guardian granting her to her husband. Plato seems to indicate that a girl would marry at 16, a man at 30 (but *see* AGE QUALIFICATION). From 450 BC marriage between an Athenian citizen and a foreigner was forbidden. At marriage a woman became part of her husband's household but might return to her natal home if there was a divorce. It may have been possible for a father to terminate his daughter's marriage. A husband owed no fidelity to his wife; he could also have a concubine (*pallakē; see* CONCUBINAGE), but his children by her were not legitimate. A wife, on the other hand, owed fidelity to her husband,

otherwise she might introduce a bastard into the family. A marriage could be ended by mutual agreement. A husband could divorce his wife simply by dismissing her, the wife returning to her father's house, free to marry again, but he was obliged to return any dowry she had brought. If a wife wanted a divorce she had to plead her case in person before the *archon. (There was no equivalent in Athens to the Roman *paterfamilias.) A husband could arrange in his will for his widow's future marriage: Pasion bestowed his wife on *Phormion.

A full Roman marriage could take place only between Roman citizens, or between them and those who had the right to marry Roman citizens (*see* LATIN RIGHTS), and no prior betrothal was legally necessary. Marriage was possible when puberty was reached. Both partners were required to consent to the marriage, and the fathers also if the couple were still under their control. By the end of the republic it was unusual for marriage to affect the wife's property rights; she remained either under 'the power of her father' (*patria potestas; see* PATERFAMILIAS) or independent. Divorce came about without legal intervention through the will of one or both partners; the dowry was usually returned to the wife. In the late republic divorce and remarriage became quite common. To give or take back the household keys could constitute a divorce. Cicero divorced his wife of thirty years, Terentia, married a much younger woman, and then divorced her too. A marriage by *confarreatio* could not be dissolved.

*See also* ADULTERY and LOVE AND SEXUALITY.

**marriage songs** In Greece the marriage song is mentioned by Homer at the wedding depicted on the shield of Achilles (*Iliad* 18). Alcman was the earliest lyric poet to be known for his marriage songs. Sappho's wedding songs probably made up book 9 of her poems, but apart from one surviving hexameter passage describing the wedding of Hector and Andromache very little survives; the songs seem to be for several singers. In Greece and Rome marriage songs were sung on two occasions during the wedding day. First was the *Hymenaios* (Lat. *Hymenaeus*), sung by the bride's mother and attendants as the bride was taken in procession to the bridegroom's house in the evening. The name was derived from the custom of calling out during the procession *Hymen o Hymenaie*, supposedly an invocation to a deity, Hymen or Hymenaios, who presided over weddings. Afterwards epithalamia (Gk. *epithalamios* '[song] sung at the bedroom') were sung by young men and women outside the bedroom. Theocritus' Idyll 18 and, in Latin, Statius' *Silvae* 1 and 2 are epithalamia. Catullus' poem 61, written for a real wedding, is a lyric poem which takes the reader through the wedding day until the bedroom door is shut. Catullus 62, in hexameters, is written as if to be sung at the end of the wedding banquet and perhaps during the bride's procession to her new home.

**Mars** Italian god of war and the most important god after Jupiter, equated with the Greek god \*Ares and consequently regarded as the son of Juno (who corresponded to the Greek goddess Hera). Mars was also connected with agriculture; the Elder Cato, in his handbook on agriculture, quotes an elaborate prayer to be addressed to Mars by the farmer at the \*lustration of his fields. Since the month named after the god, March (originally the first month of the Roman year), saw both the rebirth of the agricultural year and the start of the campaigning season, it may be that his combination of functions was natural to an agricultural people often engaged in war. Mars had his own priest at Rome, the \**flamen martialis*; his altar was in the Campus Martius, and his sacred animals were the wolf and the woodpecker. A succession of festivals in March was dedicated to Mars as god of war and the protector of growth, including, on 15 March, horse-racing in the Campus Martius, and on 23 March the purification of the sacred trumpets, originally used in war (the Tubilustria). On several days in March the Salian dancers (*see* SALII) performed a sort of war-dance, suggesting preparations for war, and there were similar occasions in October, marking the fact that this is the time of year when farmers and soldiers lay aside their tools and weapons.

A temple of Mars, probably dedicated during the Gallic invasion of *c.*385 BC, stood on the Appian Way outside the city. Here the victory of Lake Regillus was celebrated annually. The emperor Augustus promoted the worship of Mars in the god's capacity as father of Romulus, founder of Rome, and under his title of Ultor ('Avenger'). As early as 42 BC Augustus vowed a temple to Mars 'in vengeance of his father' (i.e. Julius Caesar), and again in 20 BC he ordered a temple of Mars Ultor to be built in the Forum: it was eventually dedicated in 2 BC.

Here were laid the standards lost by Crassus and Antony and recovered by Augustus from the Parthians. Both Horace (*Odes* 1.2) and Ovid (*Fasti* 5.561) glorify the new cult. Mars' love for Venus was early established as a favourite subject for artists.

**Marsian War (Marsic War)** Alternative name for the \*Social War (2), from the central Italian tribe the Marsi who precipitated the war by taking the initiative in demanding Roman citizenship.

**Ma'rsyas** In Greek myth, a \*satyr or silenus associated with the river of that name (a tributary of the Maeander in Asia Minor), who picked up the \**aulos* (musical pipe) which the goddess Athena had invented but had thrown away because it distorted the player's face. He became so proficient a player that he challenged Apollo to a musical contest (Apollo playing the lyre), with the Muses as judges. It was agreed that the victor should do what he pleased to the other, and when Apollo was judged victor he tied Marsyas to a tree and flayed him alive. The river sprang from his blood or the tears of his mourners. *See also* MIDAS.

**Ma'rtial (Marcus Valerius Martiālis)** (*c.*AD 40–103/4) Roman poet, given his *cognomen* to commemorate his birth on 1 March (*see* NAMES). He was a native of Bilbilis in Spain and claimed Iberian and Celtic ancestry. In 64 he went to Rome, where his association with his fellow Spaniards Seneca the Younger and Lucan was cut short by their deaths as a result of the conspiracy of \*Piso (3). Little of his early career is known and that mostly depends on what he tells us himself. He was poor and lived in a third-floor lodging, but later had a cottage at Nomentum (in Latium, about 20km or 13 miles from Rome) and a small house on the Quirinal hill at Rome. He wrote poetry for his living, depending on the sale of his books and on patrons who did not make very generous return for his complimentary verses. Gradually his reputation, if not his wealth, increased, but he took no part in public affairs. His first known work was a *Liber spectaculorum* ('Book of spectacles') to celebrate the opening in AD 80 of the Colosseum; of this work thirty-three epigrams survive, interesting for what they reveal of the shows given on that occasion. In 84–5 were published the collections of elegiac couplets which later appear as books 13 and 14 of the

*Epigrams* (see below): they consist of mottoes to accompany *xenia*, guest-gifts (mostly of food and drink), or *apophoreta*, gifts taken home from banquets at the festival of the \*Saturnalia (which are of the most varied kind, stationery, clothing, furniture, toys, works of art, food, pets, even slaves).

Martial's more important work, the first twelve books of the *Epigrams*, began to appear in 86. Between that year and 98 eleven of these books were issued. In 98 he returned to Bilbilis (his travelling expenses paid by the Younger Pliny), to a quiet country life on a farm given him by a patroness. From there he issued his twelfth book of epigrams in the winter of 101. The Younger Pliny in a letter of 104 mentions his death. Among Martial's friends, or addressees at least, besides Pliny (who speaks of him as 'talented, subtle, penetrating, witty, and sincere') were Juvenal, Quintilian, Silius Italicus, and Valerius Flaccus. The fact that he does not mention Statius, nor Statius him, is usually understood to indicate that the two disliked each other (and perhaps competed for the same patrons).

The *Epigrams*, which number well over 1,500, are short poems each expressing concisely and pointedly some single idea. By far the most are written in elegiac couplets; about a sixth are in hendecasyllables, some eighty in choliambics, a few in iambics and hexameters. Many consist of a single couplet; the rest rarely exceed twenty lines. Several of the books are preceded by an interesting preface in prose defending the author's work against criticism, actual or anticipated. The epigrams are for the most part addressed to some individual, but the name may be imaginary; Martial does not give the real names of those he satirizes: 'spare the sinner but denounce the sin', *parcere personis, dicere de vitiis*, is his aim. He depicts with realistic detail the most diverse characters of contemporary Rome, fortune-hunters, gluttons, drunkards, debauchers, hypocrites of various kinds; he includes a few devoted wives, faithful friends, true poets, and honest critics. Many of the pieces are complaints about the meanness of patrons, or requests for gifts or loans. Some are invitations to a simple hospitality, some take leave of a parting guest or greet his return. Many give vivid glimpses of the Roman scene: the vendor of hot sausages on his round, the Gaul who has sprained his ankle in the street and gets a lift home on a pauper's bier, the far-from-perfect guest who arrives too late for breakfast and too early for lunch. Those addressed to the emperor Domitian are markedly adulatory and often frigidly contrived; adulation was no doubt necessary for survival, and his role as suppliant for patrons' favours does not appear to have struck Martial as humiliating. Many are obscene (Martial defends this in the preface to book 1 and in 1.35, appealing to the precedent of Catullus, among others), but none of these are in book 5, addressed to *matronae puerique virginesque* ('mothers, youths, and maidens'), or book 8. As a rule he feels amusement rather than indignation at the vices he reveals, a trait which has been better received at some periods than at others.

Against this may be set his pride in his Spanish homeland, his admiration for the heroism of Romans in the days of the republic, his delight in country life, his affection for his friends, his occasional tenderness. His poems include some \*epigrams in the original sense of the word (i.e. 'inscriptions'), some touching epitaphs, including three laments for the poet Lucan, and notably that for the young girl Erotion on whom he bids the earth press lightly, 'for she pressed light on thee': these lines were parodied by the English divine and poet Abel Evans (1675–1737) in his mock epitaph on Vanbrugh, the architect of Blenheim Palace,

> Lie heavy on him, Earth! for he
> Laid many heavy loads on thee!

Martial generally writes straightforwardly and without mythological allusion. By giving his poems wit and pointedness, and especially by putting the sting in the tail, he changed the form of the epigram, giving that term the meaning which it bears in modern times, in marked contrast with the Greek epigram, which did not aim to have a pointed conclusion. But he does not merely aim at wit; his view of life is essentially humorous. Some of his lines have become well known, such as that frequently seen on sundials, *soles ... qui nobis pereunt et imputantur* ('the days that perish and are charged to our account'). A plea that his epigrams are more serious than some authors' tragedies ends with the line, *laudant illa, sed ista legunt* ('*Those* they praise, *these* they read'). A couplet (1.32) directed against a certain Sabidius acquired a wide circulation in English translation by the satirist Thomas Brown (1663–1704), 'I do not love you, Dr Fell ...'.

**Masini'ssa** (238–148 BC) Successful Numidian king who in alliance with Carthage helped his father defeat the western Numidian king Syphax *c.*213 BC. He crossed to Spain and fought for the Carthaginians before defecting to Rome. In 203 Syphax was finally defeated and taken captive by the Romans with his Carthaginian wife Sophonisba. The Roman historian Livy tells the romantic story of how Masinissa fell in love with her at first sight but was forced by a promise to her to allow her poison so that she might not appear in a Roman triumph. When the Romans decisively defeated the Carthaginians at Zama in 202 to end the Second Punic War, Masinissa commanded the Numidian cavalry on Scipio's right. His subsequent crafty statesmanship generally brought him the support of Rome for his expansionist policy in North Africa. He died peacefully at the age of 90 and bequeathed his enlarged kingdom to his sons.

**master of the cavalry** (Lat. *magister equitum*) At Rome, the assistant of a *dictator.

**mathematics** Arithmetical and algebraic problems were known to the Babylonians (*see* BABYLONIA), as were the facts of elementary geometry, including *Pythagoras' theorem and formulae for calculating the properties of some plane and solid figures. How and when this knowledge reached Greece is not known, nor whether the Greeks made their own independent discoveries. Greek tradition ascribed the invention of geometry to the Egyptians and its introduction into Greece to *Thales and Pythagoras. The first Greek mathematician of whose work there is clear evidence is *Hippocrates (2) (late fifth century BC). *See also* (in roughly chronological order): PHILOLAUS; ARCHYTAS; EUDOXUS; ERATOSTHENES; EUCLID; ARCHIMEDES; APOLLONIUS (2); HIPPARCHUS (2); PTOLEMY; THEON; HYPATIA. *See also* NUMBERS.

**Mātū'ta** In Roman religion, a goddess of the dawn, having some connection apparently with young growth. She developed into a protectress of childbirth, and was worshipped at the Matralia. Later she was identified with the Greek goddess Ino, also called Leucothea.

**Mauso'lus (Maussōllos)** Native of Caria (in south-west Asia Minor) who in 377 BC succeeded his father Hecatomnus as ruler of that country and was recognized as its satrap by the king of Persia. However, he ruled in virtual independence of Persia and extended his rule over the Greek cities of the coast and over Lycia, moving his capital to Halicarnassus. Plotting to get control of the neighbouring islands he fomented the revolt of Rhodes, Cos, and Chios from the Athenian league in 357 BC (*see* SOCIAL WAR (1)) in order to bring them under his control. In this he was successful; but he died in 353 and was succeeded by his widow (and sister) Artemisia. His tomb, the Mausoleum, regarded as one of the *Seven Wonders of the ancient world, included the over-life-size statues of Mausolus and Artemisia, now in the British Museum. It stood until the fifteenth century.

**measures** (In what follows the left-hand column gives the plural of the unit names.)

**1. Capacity**

*Greek.* The basic unit is the *cotyle*, which usually measures either 240 or 270ml (8½ or 9½ fluid ounces, or just under half an imperial pint).

(i) *Dry measures* (for corn and similar)

| | | |
|---|---|---|
| 4 cotylai | = | 1 choinix |
| 48 choinikes | = | 1 medimnos |

At Athens the *choinix* was a day's corn ration for a man. In eighteenth-century England 2½ pounds per day was reckoned for a man.

(ii) *Liquid measures*

| | | |
|---|---|---|
| 12 cotylai | = | 1 chous (roughly 3l, or between 5 and 6 pints) |
| 12 chôĕs | = | 1 metrētēs (or wine-amphora, about 36l, 7½–9 gallons) |

*Roman.* The basic unit is the *sextarius*, measuring 546ml, 0.96 of a pint or 19.2 fluid ounces.

(i) *Dry measures*

| | | |
|---|---|---|
| 8 sextarii | = | 1 semodius (about one gallon) |
| 16 sextarii | = | 1 modius (two gallons, or one peck) |

(ii) *Liquid measures*

| | | |
|---|---|---|
| 2 hēmīnae | = | 1 sextarius |
| 6 sextarii | = | 1 congius |
| 8 congii | = | 1 amphora |

A ship's burden was measured in amphorae.

**2. Length**

*Greek.* Units of length were based primarily on parts of the human body, with the foot as the fundamental unit. Fractions of a foot and a few longer measures were reckoned in fingers (*daktyloi*) as follows:

| | | |
|---|---|---|
| 16 fingers | = | 1 *pous* (foot) |
| 24 " | = | 1 *pēchys* (cubit, elbow to fingertips) |
| 27 " | = | 1 'royal' cubit |

Multiples of feet were:

| | | |
|---|---|---|
| 2½ feet | = | 1 *bēma* (pace) |
| 6 " | = | 1 *orguia* (a stretch of both arms, a fathom) |
| 100 " | = | 1 *plethron* |

(An area 100 feet square, the Greek 'acre', representing the amount of land which could be ploughed in one day in Greece, was also known as a *plethron*.) The later Greek unit the *stadion* (*stade) is equivalent to 600 Greek feet; the *parasang (*parasangēs*), consisting of 30 stades, was adopted from Persia.

There were many forms of the Greek foot in existence, varying from town to town. As used in building it measured between 270 and 360mm. The Olympian foot (as used in the running track at Olympia) was 320mm (12.6 inches; the modern foot is 305mm). The stade, which measured 600 feet regardless of the length of the foot, may therefore be taken to be somewhere around 190m or 200 yards.

*Roman.* The Roman foot (*pes*, pl. *pedēs*) measured 296mm (11.6 inches). It was sometimes divided into 16 fingers (*digiti*), as in the Greek system, but more usually into 12 inches (*unciae*, 'twelfth parts'). The other units were:

| | | |
|---|---|---|
| 5 feet | = | 1 *passus* (pace) |
| 125 paces | = | 1 *stadium* (stade) |
| 1,000 paces | = | *mille passus*, 1 (Roman) mile |

The Roman mile measured 1,480m (about 140 yards less than the modern statute mile of 1,760 yards).

*See also* WEIGHTS.

**Mēdē'a (Mēdeia)** In Greek myth, granddaughter of *Helios (Sun), daughter of Aeētēs, king of Colchis, and like her aunt *Circe an enchantress. The Greeks derived her name from *medesthai*, 'to devise', and saw her as typifying the cunning foreign 'wise-woman'. When Jason and the *Argonauts arrived at Colchis in pursuit of the Golden Fleece, Aeetes consented to surrender it to Jason if the latter

would perform certain apparently impossible tasks. These included the sowing of a dragon's teeth from which armed men arose whose fury was turned against Jason. With the help of Medea's magic the tasks were successfully accomplished, and Medea finally enabled Jason to take the fleece by killing or drugging the serpent that guarded it. She engineered the Argonauts' escape from Aeetes; in one version of the story she murdered and cut into pieces her young brother Apsyrtus, scattering the fragments so that her father might be delayed in his pursuit of the Argonauts by gathering up the body. In other versions Apsyrtus is grown up and leads the pursuit until Medea contrives his murder. At Iolcus Medea took vengeance on Pelias (Jason's uncle) for the wrong done by him to Jason's family. First she restored Jason's father Aeson to youth by boiling him in a cauldron with magic herbs, and then persuaded the daughters of Pelias to submit their father to the same process. But on this occasion she deliberately gave them ineffective herbs, and the daughters were unwittingly the cause of their father's death. Acastus, their brother, then drove Jason and Medea from Iolcus and they took refuge in Corinth. For the rest of the story, *see* MEDEA. When Aegeus' son *Theseus came to Athens from Troezen Medea recognized him and tried unsuccessfully to have him killed.

Medea was the subject of tragedies by Aeschylus, Sophocles, and Euripides, but only that of Euripides survives. Seneca the Younger and Ovid also wrote tragedies about her (*see* MEDEA (2) and (3)); she receives a more romantic treatment by Apollonius Rhodius, and by Ovid in *Heroides* and *Metamorphoses*.

***Mede'a 1.*** Greek tragedy by *Euripides, produced in 431 BC. Despite its later fame it won only third prize in the dramatic competition. It deals with the later part of the story of Jason and *Medea. These two have fled to Corinth after Medea has murdered Pelias for Jason's sake. Jason, ambitious and insecure, has arranged to marry the daughter of Creon, king of Corinth, for prudential reasons he alleges, but Medea thinks he is tired of her, his troublesome foreign wife. The desertion and ingratitude of her husband arouse her savage anger which she openly expresses. Creon, fearing her vengeance, pronounces instant banishment on Medea and her two children. Medea coaxes him into allowing her one day's respite, and by a poisoned robe and diadem contrives the deaths of the king and his daughter, Jason's intended bride. Then she kills her own children, partly to make Jason childless, partly because, since they now must surely die, it is better that it should be by her hand than by that of her enemies, who would otherwise triumph over her. Finally, taunting Jason in his despair, she escapes to Athens where she has secured asylum from king Aegeus in return for her earlier promise, made to him at Corinth, to cure his childlessness.

2. Roman tragedy by *Seneca (2), based on that of Euripides, with variations of detail. Medea's children are not sentenced to banishment; she asks for them to be allowed to accompany her into exile, but Jason's love for them prevents it. Medea thus learns where Jason is vulnerable and kills them to revenge herself on him. The play contains a famous passage in which Seneca seems to prophesy the discovery of a New World (374 ff.):

> *venient annis*
> *saecula seris quibus Oceanus*
> *vincula rerum laxet, et ingens*
> *pateat tellus Tethysque novos*
> *detegat orbes, nec sit terris*
> *ultima Thule.*

(In later years a new age will come in which Ocean shall relax its hold over the world, and a vast land shall lie open to view, and Tethys shall reveal a new world, and *Thule will not be the last country on earth.)

3. Roman tragedy by *Ovid, of which only two lines have survived. It was praised by *Quintilian.

**Medicā'mina faciē'i fēminē'ae** ('Cosmetics for the female face') Latin poem in elegiacs by *Ovid; only 100 lines survive.

**medicine** A large body of medical literature survives from the ancient world, most of it preserved in the Hippocratic Corpus (see HIPPOCRATES (1)) and the writings of *Galen (second century AD), based on both theory and practice. The treatment of disease in classical antiquity was conventionally classified into three types: regimen and diet, drugs, and surgery (see e.g. the proem to his work On medicine by the Roman encyclopaedist *Celsus). The different approaches were a response to a variety of attitudes towards illness. Physicians interested in regimen and diet were themselves divided into two groups, theoreticians

(sometimes called 'dogmatists') and empiricists. The former concentrated on the causes of disease, while the latter, who included gymnastic trainers, paid more attention to treatments based on experience than to research into causes. (The historian Polybius, who favoured experience, thought that, like doctors, historians also fell into similar classes.) Many doctors also thought that good health was a matter of achieving a correct balance in the body between *elements or *humours (blood, phlegm, and bile). Drugs were important from Homer onwards, and no doubt before that. Silphium was the great panacea (see BOTANY), but the ancient world eventually had available a huge collection of drugs derived from plants, spices, animal products—honey, beeswax, fat and blood from various creatures—and oils extracted from seeds of all kinds: opium was the most important narcotic, and rose-oil was a favourite. *Theophrastus (see *Enquiries into plants*, book 9) even included myrrh and frankincense, which must have arrived in Greece along a trade-route from south Arabia. The Elder *Pliny's *Natural History* attests the wide range of drugs available by the first century AD (see also NICANDER and DIOSCORIDES). The opium poppy and its very many derivatives and the autumn crocus (for gout and bronchitis) were then, as now, in everyday use.

In the matter of surgery most doctors would have had skill of at least a basic kind. Galen certainly had such expectation, and also assumed that a doctor would be able to deal with the after-effects of surgery. The Hippocratic works On Fractures, On Dislocations, and Wounds of the Head (compiled c.400 BC and still used in Europe in the mid-eighteenth century) can sound surprisingly modern when treating the subject of cleanliness and the proper preparation of the operating room. Archaeological finds of surgical instruments (especially at Pompeii) increasingly reveal their refinement and variety. Celsus reports on operations which must have been very delicate—removing a deeply embedded arrow-head, even a cataract. The Greeks excelled in ophthalmology, perhaps because of the prevalence of eye disease in the Mediterranean world. Until the eighteenth century in Europe operations on the eye and the treatment of eye disease had not advanced much beyond what was practised by the Hellenistic Greeks. The anatomy of the eye was almost completely understood, although their theory of vision was mistaken and the explanation of disease based on belief in the humours. Treatment was usually by eye-salve and special diet.

Several treatises on veterinary medicine survive, mostly concerning the horse. Livestock was well-tended: studies of animal bones show high levels of nutrition, good health, and signs of simple remedies knowledgeably applied. Sheep-dipping, for example, was practised. Surgery used procedures still in use, including obstetrical operations and eye-surgery, with specialized instruments. *See* PALLADIUS.

*See also* ASCLEPIUS; HEROPHILUS; ERASISTRATUS; ARISTEIDES (2); SORANUS; ANATOMY AND PHYSIOLOGY; DISEASE; GYNAECOLOGY.

**medieval Latin** *See* LATIN LANGUAGE.

**Medū'sa** In Greek myth, one of the three *Gorgons, the only one who was mortal. Anyone who looked at her head, even after her death, was turned to stone. She was killed by *Perseus.

**Me'gaclēs** Name of several prominent members of the aristocratic *Alcmaeonid *genos* at Athens.

**1.** Archon, 632/1 BC, responsible for the murder of *Cylon.

**2.** Grandson of (1), married perhaps in 575 BC to Agariste, daughter of Cleisthenes (1), tyrant of Sicyon. Peisistratus married his daughter.

**3.** Nephew of *Cleisthenes (2) who was the founder of Athenian democracy (and who was himself the son of (2) above), ostracized in 486, winner of the chariot-race at the Pythian games in the same year, and celebrated in Pindar's seventh Pythian Ode. He was the uncle of Pericles.

**Mega'rian school** The Socratic school of philosophy founded by Eucleides of Megara (fl. *c.*390 BC), an associate of Socrates. It adopted the doctrines of the *Eleatic philosophers. Its members developed a reputation for skill in dialectical argument (*cf.* ZENO (1)).

**Mēla, Pompō'nius** *See* POMPONIUS.

**Mela'mpus (Melampous)** In Greek myth, famous seer, son of Amythaon (a grandson of *Aeolus), and supposed ancestor of the prophetic clan of the Melampodidae, who produced famous seers in historic times. He took care of some young serpents whose parents had been killed by his servants, and these one day licked his ears while he was sleeping. Thereafter he understood the language of all creatures. His brother Bias sought to marry Pero, daughter of *Neleus, but the latter demanded as bride-price the cattle which *Iphiclus had taken from Neleus' mother. Melampus undertook to get them for Bias but was caught and imprisoned. Hearing from the woodworms that the roof was about to fall in, Melampus warned the gaoler. When Iphiclus found out he was so impressed he promised to hand over the cattle if Melampus could tell him why he was childless. This Melampus was able to do by questioning a vulture, and Bias was thus enabled to marry Pero. Another of his feats was curing the daughters of *Proetus of their madness. According to Herodotus it was Melampus who introduced the name of the god *Dionysus into Greece. Among his mythical descendants who were also seers were *Amphiaraus and Theoclymenus in *Odyssey* 20.

**Meleā'ger (Meleagros) 1.** In Greek myth, the hero of the Calydonian boar-hunt. Son of Oeneus, king of the Aetolians of Calydon, and his wife Althaea, he married Cleopatra, daughter of Idas and *Marpessa. The *Fates appeared at his birth and declared that he should live as long as a brand that was on the fire was not consumed. Althaea snatched the brand from the fire and carefully preserved it. Later, when Meleager was a young man, Oeneus omitted to sacrifice to Artemis and the goddess in anger sent a great boar to ravage Calydon. Oeneus collected a band of heroes to attack the beast, offering the boar's skin to whoever should kill it. *Atalanta, the virgin huntress, was the first to wound it, and when Meleager finally killed it he gave her the spoils, being in love with her. During the war between the Aetolian Calydonians and the *Curetes, Meleager killed his mother's two brothers. When Althaea heard of their death she took out the brand and burned it, and Meleager died. In the version of the myth recounted in Homer (*Iliad* 9), he is cited as an example of a valiant but misguided warrior of a past generation who refused to aid his people when they were attacked by the Curetes because he was angry (having been cursed by his mother for killing her brothers). Although he was finally persuaded and drove off the enemy, he received no reward because he changed his mind too late. He was sometimes said to have been one of the *Argonauts.

Later writers add that after his death the women who mourned him were turned into guinea-fowl (*meleagrides*). The hunt of the Calydonian boar, Meleager leading, was a favourite subject in art.

**2.** Of Gadara in Syria, Greek poet who lived *c*.100 BC. He wrote short elegiac poems on love and death, about a hundred of which survive in the *Greek \*Anthology*. They are technically very accomplished and often moving. His chief claim to fame is as the compiler of an early anthology of poetic epigrams from the preceding two centuries (which has not survived intact), called the 'Garland' (*Stephanos*) and likening each poet to a flower.

**Mele'tus** Nominal accuser of Socrates in 399 BC, though \*Anytus was the real antagonist. He was perhaps the son of the tragic poet of the same name who is mocked by the comic poets; it is also possible that he was the Meletus who prosecuted \*Andocides for impiety in 400 (and the real author of the sixth speech of \*Lysias). The name is very common.

**Mēlian dialogue** In \*Thucydides 5.84 ff., the debate between Athenian envoys and the magistrates of Mēlos, a (Dorian) Greek island in the south-west Cyclades. During the \*Peloponnesian War Melos remained independent and refused to surrender to Athens. The dialogue took place in 416 BC when the Athenians proposed to subdue the island, and the speeches of the Athenians are an exposition of their ruthless imperial policy. Melos was taken by the Athenians shortly afterwards; the men were put to death and the women and children enslaved. *See* TROJAN WOMEN (1).

**Melice'rtēs** *See* DIONYSUS. According to Greek myth, the body of the drowned Melicertes was carried ashore by a dolphin on the Isthmus of Corinth. He was deified and known as Palaemon, and the \*Isthmian games were said to have been founded to commemorate him. There was a temple of Palaemon at Corinth.

**Meli'ssus** (of Samos) The commander of the Samian fleet which defeated the Athenians in 441 BC, but remembered more as the last important member of the \*Eleatic School of philosophy. He wrote in prose a defence of \*Parmenides' view that the universe is homogeneous, indivisible, unchanging, and everlasting, and often expounds with greater clarity

matters which Parmenides deals with more obscurely. Some modern interpreters think that he was the first Eleatic to hold the view that void must exist for there to be motion.

**Mēlos** *See* MELIAN DIALOGUE.

**Melpo'menē** The Muse of tragedy; *see* MUSES.

**Me'mmius, Gaius** Dedicatee of \*Lucretius' poem *De rerum natura*, minor poet and orator, and patron of poets; nothing of his work survives. Catullus and Helvius \*Cinna accompanied him to Bithynia where he was propraetor in 57 BC. In 53 he was banished for dishonesty in the elections of the previous year and he went into exile in Athens in 52. He was married to \*Sulla's daughter, who later married Milo, and died before 46 BC.

**Memnon** In Greek myth, son of Tithonus (brother of Priam) and Eos (Dawn), and brother of Emathion, king of Egypt. He was the black king of the Ethiopians, and fought on the Trojan side at the siege of Troy wearing armour made by Hephaestus. Memnon killed Antilochus and was later killed by Achilles. His story was related in the *Aethiopis* (by Arctinus), a poem of the \*Epic Cycle, according to which Zeus made him immortal. His final battle and his body carried away by his mother are favourite subjects for vase-painters. A tradition arose that a colossal statue, supposedly of Memnon, which stood before a temple in Egyptian \*Thebes (2) used to sing when struck by the first light of dawn, in greeting to his mother (the statue is in fact one of a pair of colossi of an Egyptian king).

**Memorabi'lia (***Apomnēmoneu'mata***)** 'Reminiscences [of Socrates]' by \*Xenophon, in four books, which describe his character and some of his opinions, chiefly by means of more or less imaginary conversations between Socrates and various persons (including Xenophon himself).

The first part is a refutation of the particular charges on which Socrates was tried and sentenced to death (that he did not believe in the gods of the state, but introduced other new deities, and that he corrupted the youth); the work consistently presents him as respecting the gods and helping his fellows. Xenophon illustrates the character and opinions of Socrates, his support for his friends, his piety, and his views on education and various philosophical questions, probably derived in part from Xenophon's own recollections, in part from other sources. The opinions attributed to Socrates, for example on the good and the beautiful, do not always accord with those attributed to him by Plato. The work concludes with a peroration on Socrates' virtues.

**Menae'chmi** Roman comedy by *Plautus. A merchant of Syracuse had indistinguishable twin sons. One of these, Menaechmus, was stolen when seven years old. The other, Sosicles, had his name changed to Menaechmus in memory of his lost brother. When he is grown up Sosicles-Menaechmus sets out in search of his brother, and finally arrives at Epidaurus where his brother is living. Comic misunderstandings arise when he successively encounters the lost brother's mistress, wife, and father-in-law. Wife and father-in-law conclude that he is insane, but owing to a further confusion it is the original Menaechmus, their real husband and son-in-law, whom they attempt to lock up. Finally the twins confront each other and the puzzle is solved.

Complaints about the duties of a *patron are a rare comment on an exclusively Roman problem in this Greek-based literary form. The play, directly or indirectly, furnished the main idea for Shakespeare's play on mistaken identity, *The Comedy of Errors*.

**Mena'nder** (Menandros) (*c*.342–292 BC) The greatest writer of Attic New Comedy (*see* COMEDY [Greek 6]). He was said to have studied under the philosopher Theophrastus and the comic poet Alexis (*see* COMEDY [Greek 5]), and to have been a companion in youth of another philosopher, Epicurus. He was also a friend (and fellow pupil) of *Demetrius of Phalerum, the pro-Macedonian governor of Athens. According to tradition he died by drowning in the harbour of Piraeus. Nearly 100 titles of his plays are known, although some may be alternatives. The plays themselves were lost in the seventh and eighth centuries AD, but in the twentieth century numerous finds of papyri brought to light one complete play, *Dyscolus*, and sizeable fragments of *Aspis*, *Epitrepontes*, *Misumenos*, *Perikeiromenē*, *Samia*, and *Sicyonios*. There are shorter fragments of many others including *Geōrgos*, *Dis exapatōn*, *Heros*, Theophoroumenē ('A girl possessed'), Kitharistēs ('The harp girl'), Phasma ('The apparition'), Karchedonios ('The Carthagi-

nian'), *Kōlax*, Koneiazomenai ('The drugged women'), and Perinthia ('The girl from Perinthus'). Orgē ('Anger'), which has not survived, is said to have been his first play, and some authorities say that it won the dramatic competition. On the whole Menander was unlucky at the competitions, winning only eight victories. *Quintilian commented that he enjoyed more fame after his death than in his lifetime, and the Latin poet Martial has the line (5.10), 'the theatre applauded Menander but he rarely won the crown', *rara coronato plausēr̆e theatra Menandro*. The number of papyri found of his works is exceeded only for Homer and Euripides (*see* PAPYROLOGY). The loss of his plays through neglect may be partly due to their exclusion from the Greek school curriculum of the fifth and subsequent centuries AD because they were written not in classical Attic Greek but in the *koine*.

Before the discovery of the papyri Menander was known from a large number of quotations, many of them highly sententious, so that a false impression was given of moral earnestness. Even St Paul quoted him (1 Cor. 15: 33), 'Evil communications corrupt good manners'. In fact many of these famous lines are now seen to have been spoken ironically: 'Whom the gods love die young', to an old man; 'I am a human being, and I think nothing that is human to be outside my interest', by a busybody (quoted by *Terence).

His plays are set in contemporary Greece, usually in Athens or the surrounding countryside. The plots are concerned with the private lives of well-to-do families, with a love-entanglement as an important but not always central feature: thus in *Dyscolus* Cnemon and his misanthropy are more important than his son's love-affair. The plays contain many features that were commoner in the theatre of the time than in real life: abandoned or kidnapped children, recognitions by means of trinkets, seductions of well-brought-up girls at night festivals (where it was too dark to see their faces), amazing coincidences. Characters too are often conventional, the talkative, self-important cook, the bragging soldier, the angry father, the cunning but cowardly slave, the kind-hearted prostitute. Yet they are given other traits that conventional portraits lack and consequently seem more lifelike. Their speech, too, is apt and appropriate. The plots are often complicated but always skilfully put together and exciting, and the dialogue is fast-moving, often pointed and witty. A frequently cited apostrophe from the Alexandrian scholar *Aristophanes of Byzantium, 'O Menander and Life, which of you copied the other!' indicates that for all their contrivance the actions and the characters seem natural, and the underlying sentiments real. Menander's attitude to his creations is one of sympathy and gentle irony; resolution of the difficulties is achieved through the virtues of generosity and understanding.

The plays are written in verse, for the most part in iambic trimeters, which contrive to give the effect of natural speech. The Roman rhetor Quintilian warmly recommended the study of Menander's plays even to students of rhetoric, regarding him as supreme among the writers of New Comedy. Through the adaptations of the Roman comic writers *Plautus and Terence he deeply influenced the development of European comedy, notably in Molière, the Restoration dramatists, and Sheridan.

**Menelā'us (Menelāos, Meneleōs)** In Greek myth, king of Sparta (though Aeschylus in *Agamemnon* has him rather oddly sharing Agamemnon's palace in Argos before the Trojan War). He was the son of Atreus, younger brother of Agamemnon, and husband of *Helen, whom *Paris carried off to Troy, thus bringing about the Trojan War. In Homer's *Iliad* he agrees to settle the war by a duel with Paris and would have killed him but for the latter's rescue by Aphrodite. Menelaus acquits himself well in the fighting over the body of Patroclus, but he is usually overshadowed by Agamemnon, the leader of the Greek army, and subtly depreciated. He reappears in the *Odyssey* living at Sparta having returned there after the war, reconciled with Helen, and visited by Odysseus' son Telemachus. Tragedy represents him less favourably; he appears in Sophocles' *Ajax* and Euripides' *Helen, Andromache, Orestes*, and *Trojan Women*.

**Mene'xenus** Dialogue by *Plato in which Socrates delivers to Menexenus impromptu a funeral speech over the war dead which he says was taught him by *Aspasia. He alleges that Aspasia coached Pericles in the latter's Funeral Oration (Thucydides, book 2) and has let him, Socrates, have some phrases which were left over. The speech abounds in rhetorical commonplaces but also contains senti-

ments which seem to be Plato's own, making interpretation of the whole dialogue difficult.

**Meni'ppus** (of Gadara in Syria, third century BC) *Cynic philosopher who satirized (in Greek) the follies of men and philosophers in a serio-comic style, using a mixture of prose and verse. His writings are lost, but they were imitated in Latin by *Varro in his *Saturae Menippeae*, who introduced to Latin the mixture of prose and many verse forms which goes by the name of Menippean satire. Menippus himself figures frequently in Lucian's 'Dialogues of the Dead', and one of Lucian's satires bears his name.

**Mēno (Měnōn)** Dialogue of *Plato. Socrates is represented as conversing with a young Thessalian aristocrat Meno on the question of whether virtue can be taught. When attempts to define virtue meet with no success, the origin of knowledge is discussed; Socrates propounds his theory that knowledge is acquired before birth by the soul, which is immortal, and that knowledge is in fact recollection, which it is the purpose of teaching to bring out. Socrates demonstrates how this can be done by eliciting from Meno's slave, through careful questioning, the solution to a geometrical problem. If virtue is knowledge and therefore teachable, there ought to be teachers of it. But there are no teachers of virtue; it is not teachable after all; good men, who care that their sons should share their virtues, fail to teach them virtue, which is at most 'true belief' (*orthē doxa*) and will become knowledge only if it is 'tied down by a chain of reasoning'. Socrates illustrates the difference between the two by contrasting the man who knows the way to Larissa because he has been there, with one who happens to know the way correctly. It cannot be stated with certainty how virtue arises until it is known what exactly virtue is.

The historical Meno was a Thessalian general in the expedition of the Ten Thousand, whose treacherous conduct is related by Xenophon in the *Anabasis.

**Mentor** In Homer's *Odyssey*, an old Ithacan friend of Odysseus, to whom the latter, when he left Ithaca for Troy, gave charge of his house. He acts as an adviser to Telemachus, Odysseus' son; hence the use of his name to describe a trusted counsellor.

**Mercā'tor** ('The merchant') Roman comedy by *Plautus adapted from a Greek comedy by Philemon (*see* COMEDY [Greek 6]). A young man, sent abroad on a trading venture by his father, falls in love with a girl at Rhodes and brings her back to Athens, pretending that she is a present for his mother. His father discovers her and himself falls in love, with consequent complications.

**Mercury (Mercurius)** In Roman religion, son of *Maia and Jupiter, the god of trade (*merx*), particularly of the corn-trade, introduced at an early date from a Greek or Greco-Etruscan source and identified with the Greek god *Hermes, whose attributes he shared. His temple was on the Aventine overlooking the Circus Maximus; its traditional date of dedication was 495 BC. He was the god of travel, movement, and commerce, including the exchange of speech. Like Hermes he was the god of eloquence and was often represented carrying a herald's staff, *caduceus*, with two entwined snakes, and winged hat and shoes. His name was later given to the element mercury (quicksilver) because of his imagined quickness of movement. He was also seen as mediator between the divine and the human. The fact that he does not have a *flamen indicates that he was not a deity worshipped at Rome from earliest times.

**Mesopotamia** ('[Land] between rivers'; modern Iraq) Region of the Middle East between the rivers Tigris and Euphrates which includes the ancient kingdoms of *Assyria and *Babylonia. In classical times Mesopotamia usually excluded Babylonia (south of Assyria, southern Iraq).

**Messal(l)ī'na, Statilia** Third wife of the emperor Nero, whom she survived.

**Messal(l)ī'na, Vale'ria** (d. AD 48) Greatgranddaughter of Octavia, the sister of the emperor Augustus. She married in AD 39 or 40 her second cousin the emperor Claudius, then aged about 50, as his third wife, and bore him two children, Claudia Octavia (later the first wife of the emperor Nero) and Britannicus. She was notorious for her promiscuity (pilloried by Juvenal in *Satires* 6 and 10), to which Claudius alone was blind. In AD 48, though still apparently married to Claudius, she went through the formalities of a marriage with the consul-designate C. Silius. While Claudius was still irresolute his freedman Narcissus sent an executioner, and encouraged by her mother she committed suicide.

**Messa'lla Corvī'nus, Marcus Vale'rius** (64 BC–AD 8) Roman patrician and distinguished orator, soldier, and patron of literature. He fought on the republican side at Philippi (42 BC) and then supported Antony, but disillusioned by the latter's conduct with Cleopatra transferred his allegiance to Octavian, fighting against Sextus Pompeius and taking part in the defeat of Antony at Actium in 31. He was employed in Roman administration, and proposed the title 'Pater Patriae' ('Father of his country') for the emperor Augustus (2 BC). He was a great patron of poets (*see* AUGUSTAN AGE), notably of Ovid, Tibullus, and his own niece *Sulpicia, and gained fame as an orator; he was also famous for his linguistic knowledge. For the *Panegyric on Messalla see* TIBULLUS.

**Messā'na** (modern Messina) City on the north-east tip of Sicily opposite the toe of Italy, founded as Zancle by Euboean colonists *c.*730 BC (Zancle itself colonized Himera in 648). In 486 BC it received immigrants from Messenia in the Peloponnese who changed its name to Messana. In 288 BC it was seized by the *Mamertines. After 241 BC Messana became a prosperous city in alliance with Rome.

**Messē'nē** City founded in 369 BC by *Epaminondas to be the capital of an independent *Messenia in the Peloponnese. *See also* ITHOME, MOUNT.

**Messē'nia** South-west region of the Peloponnese. In mythology it was the kingdom of Aphareus who gave refuge, and later bequeathed his kingdom, to *Neleus, when the latter was driven from Thessaly. Subsequently it was ruled over by Neleus' son Nestor. After the *Dorian invasion Messenia was ruled by Cresphontes, one of the *Heracleidae, and then by his youngest son Aepytus, who gave his name to the Messenian royal line. After the First and Second Messenian Wars against Sparta, perhaps in the eighth and seventh centuries BC (*see* ARISTOMENES and TYRTAEUS), the land was seized by the Spartans and the Messenians reduced to the status of *helots or *perioikoi. (Much of what we thought we knew about the Second Messenian War has been shown to be derived from an epic poet

Rhianus of the third century BC.) The Messenians' bid for independence after the earthquake of 464 BC, the Third Messenian War, ended with the surrender of their stronghold at Ithome after a long siege. During the Peloponnesian War they were encouraged by the Athenians to revolt, and the threat increased the anxieties of the Spartans. In 369 BC Messenia achieved independence through the efforts of the Theban general *Epaminondas. In the second century BC it came with the rest of Greece under Roman control.

**Metamorphō'sēs** ('Transformations')
**1.** Latin poem, epic in scope, in fifteen books of hexameters by *Ovid, his longest and only surviving work in this metre. (It is longer than Virgil's *Aeneid*.) It seems to have been composed from *c.*AD 2 onwards, and had not been finally revised when the poet was banished in AD 8. Myths of metamorphosis were a Hellenistic taste; *see* NICANDER and PARTHENIUS. The model for this kind of composition was to some extent the influential *Aitia* of *Callimachus, but there the stories are unconnected. In the opening lines Ovid proposes 'a continuous song from the beginning of the world to my own day', and there is a chronological progression starting with the transformation of Chaos into the ordered universe. The poem is essentially a collection of stories from Greek and Roman myth and legend, but includes the Near Eastern tale of the Babylonian lovers Pyramus and Thisbe. Although it purports to tell of the characters undergoing miraculous transformations into another form, these are sometimes of minor importance to the stories, which are linked together by devices of association and contrast, often tenuously and in contrived transitions (specifically censured by *Quintilian). After a succession of stories about gods and heroes drawn from Greek mythology the subject matter passes to what was thought of as history, Aeneas and Dido, Numa and Egeria, the doctrines of Pythagoras, and to Ovid's own times, ending with the death and deification of Julius Caesar. However, there is comparatively little sense of linearity; instead, patterns of thematic association between stories seem to emerge, giving a deeper meaning and more significant unity to the work than can be explained merely by the poet's desire to entertain.

This poem is the work to which Ovid pinned his hopes of immortal fame. The brilliance of the poet's imagination and power of expression put the final stamp on many myths. The reader is both touched by the characters' sufferings, improbable as they may be, and impressed by the poet's artistry. However interpreted, it is a work of enormous inventiveness, charm, and originality. Favourite narratives include: (book 2) Phaethon driving the chariot of the sun; (book 3) Echo and Narcissus; (book 4) Pyramus and Thisbe, Perseus and Andromeda; (book 5) the rape of Proserpine; (book 6) Pallas Athena and Arachne; (book 7) Jason and Medea, Cephalus and Procris; (book 8) the flight of Daedalus, Philemon and Baucis; (book 10) Orpheus and Eurydice, Venus and Adonis; (book 11) Midas, Ceyx, and Halcyone; (book 13) Polyphemus and Galatea; (book 15) the discourse of Pythagoras.
**2.** *See* APULEIUS.

**Metanī'ra (Metaneira)** *See* DEMETER.

**metaphysics** Philosophical enquiry into ideas about being and knowing which seem to be beyond what is empirically knowable. The Scottish empiricist Hume denied its validity, believing that we can know only what is perceived by the senses. *See* METAPHYSICS.

**Metaphysics** (for the origin of the title *see* ARISTOTLE 4(ii)) A philosophical work put together after Aristotle's death from his lecture notes and treatises written at various times. Its thirteen books are now known by the first thirteen letters of the Greek alphabet; the two parts of the first are *A* and *α*, and the remaining twelve books are *β* to *ν*. The work is an investigation into 'what is' or 'being' (*to einai*) i.e. into what constitutes basic reality, which Aristotle also refers to as *ousia*, 'substance'. 'The question which is continually posed now and has been in the past, and is continually puzzled over, is this: what is being? And that means, what is substance?' (For examples of the answers given by Aristotle's predecessors *see* e.g. ELEATIC PHILOSOPHERS and DEMOCRITUS.) This is an investigation which Aristotle calls 'first [i.e. primary] philosophy' since it concerns the primary form of being, substance, focusing on what is meant by identity and by change. In the matter of identity Aristotle regards the question as two-pronged: what are the basic constituents of the world, and what is it that makes a thing the very thing it is. In considering whether there is an eternal, non-perceptible, unchanging substance he examines the

Platonic Forms (*see* PLATONISM) and mathematical objects (and lists 23 objections to the theory of Forms). As metaphysics is primary philosophy it is identified with theology, on which everything else is dependent. What Aristotle here calls God operates as a final cause, the changeless source of change in others (commonly known as the Unmoved Mover; *see* SOUL); it is through the existence of God that the motion of the stars comes about, and this causes the change of seasons and consequently change in everything else (*see also* PHYSICS). The topics covered in the *Metaphysics* are many and complex, and contain much that is difficult to interpret. It is a work that has been studied and commented upon by generations of scholars, Greek, Arabic, and Christian, and has been enormously influential on later thought.

**Mete'lli** Name of a noble family at Rome, belonging to the plebeian *gens Caecilia*. The Metelli first came to prominence in the First Punic War and thereafter were one of the most distinguished of the Roman families, always supporting the *optimate cause. Members include the following.

   **1. Lucius Caeci'lius Metellus** Consul 251 BC, *pontifex maximus* 243, died 221. In 250 BC, during the First Punic War, he won a notable victory against the Carthaginians in Sicily, capturing many war elephants, hitherto considered invincible. As a consequence the elephant was the symbol used on coin-issues of later members of the family. In 241 he reputedly rescued the *Palladium when the temple of Vesta was on fire, and lost his sight as a result.

   **2. Quintus Caecilius Metellus Numi'dicus** Consul in 109 BC at a critical time in the war against *Jugurtha. His immediate success earned him his *cognomen* Numidicus, 'of Numidia', but he failed to bring the war to a conclusion and was superseded in 107 by his former subordinate C. *Marius. In 100 he was the only senator not to swear to observe an agrarian law of *Saturninus, and went into exile. His recall (probably in 98) was a victory for the senate. He died *c.*91.

**metempsychosis** *See* PYTHAGORAS; ORPHEUS; REPUBLIC [book 10].

**meteorology** In the ancient world the study of not only what we would call meteorology but also the supposedly related phenomena of

tides, earthquakes, and volcanoes. Aristophanes in the *Clouds* satirizes 'meteorosophists' for their silly speculations, the premises of their subject being mostly undemonstrable. Aristotle's *Meteorology* includes accounts not only of comets and meteors but of the weather, earthquakes, the origins of seas and rivers, and the formation of minerals. Theophrastus also wrote a *Meteorology*, parts of which survive in a Syriac version. The Epicureans aimed to dispel fear by explaining the nature of those aspects which terrify most (*see* LUCRETIUS, book 6). *Poseidonius' work in some part survives in the Younger Seneca's *Natural Questions*, and treats the subject in Stoic fashion as part of the workings of the whole cosmos.

**metics (*mĕtoikoi*)** In the Greek city-states, voluntary resident aliens who had acquired a recognized status in the community; those at Athens, where very large numbers were resident, are best known. Metics enjoyed full civil rights (as opposed to political rights, which they did not possess; *see* e.g. DEINARCHUS) except that they could not own land or contract legal marriages with citizens. As a class they concentrated on commercial and industrial activities, and carried on important businesses as bankers, shipowners, importers, and contractors. Some were physicians, philosophers, sophists, and orators (e.g. Aristotle, Protagoras, Lysias); the comic poets Antiphanes and Philemon were metics.

**Mētis** ('Counsel') The divine personification of intelligence. In Greek myth she was the daughter of *Tethys and *Oceanus, the first wife of Zeus and the wisest of gods. Zeus was warned by Gaia and Uranus that his children by Metis would be dangerously clever. He therefore swallowed her when she became pregnant, and the goddess *Athena was subsequently born from Zeus' head. By swallowing Metis, Zeus also acquired her wisdom.

**Mēton** Athenian astronomer of the fifth century BC, dated by his observation of the summer solstice in 432. He suggested a system of regularly intercalating lunar months (seven in a period of nineteen years, giving 235 months in all, the Metonic cycle) to correlate the lunar month and the solar year, with the purpose of providing a fixed system of reckoning for astronomical observations (the civil calendar, it appears, remained unaffected). Since, by Meton's system, the sun and the moon were out of step by one day after 76 years, the nineteen-year cycle was superseded a century later by the corrected 76-year system of Callippus (fourth century BC), which was used by *Hipparchus (2) and *Ptolemy. Meton appears in Aristophanes' *Birds* (414 BC) as a comic 'town-planner'.

**Mētrō'on** At Athens, the sanctuary of the Mother (*mētēr*) of the gods (*see* CYBELE), in the agora. The original small temple may be dated to the beginning of the fifth century BC. After the destructions of the Persian invasion of 480 BC (*see* PERSIAN WARS) this temple was not rebuilt, and the cult seems to have been transferred to the neighbouring (old) Bouleuterion, council-chamber of the *boule*. After the new Bouleuterion was built at the end of the fifth century the old building came to be called the Metroon. The building served also as a public record office. In the precinct stood the large earthenware tub in which Diogenes the *Cynic philosopher is said to have lived.

**metropolis** *See* HESTIA.

**Mēze'ntius** In Virgil's *Aeneid*, a cruel atheistical tyrant, of Caere in Etruria (the name is Etruscan), who has been expelled by his people and joins *Turnus in opposing Aeneas and the Trojan settlement in Italy. In contrast, his son Lausus is made an attractive figure. Both are killed by Aeneas, Lausus in defence of his father. Mezentius has a horse called Rhaebus. Mezentius and Turnus both figured in the Aeneas legend as told by *Cato the Censor in the *Origines*.

**Mīdas** Legendary king of Phrygia who, having hospitably entertained *Silenus, the companion of Dionysus, when he had lost his way, was given a wish, and wished that all he touched might turn to gold. On discovering that this applied to his food also he asked to be relieved of the gift. He was told to wash in the river Pactolus, which ever since has had sands containing gold. Midas is also said to have captured Silenus, who used to visit his garden, and curious to learn his wisdom made him drunk by mixing wine with the water of the spring. What he told Midas seems to have been a matter of conjecture among the ancients, but according to one version he said that it was best for a man not to be born at all, or once born to die as soon as possible.

On another occasion, having to judge a musical contest between Apollo and *Pan (or *Marsyas), Midas had the indiscretion to decide against Apollo, who thereupon gave him ass's ears to indicate his stupidity. These Midas concealed with his headdress but was obliged to tell his barber. The latter, unable to keep the secret but afraid to reveal it publicly, whispered the news into a hole in the ground which he then filled up. But reeds grew over the hole and repeated the story whenever the wind blew.

**Middle Platonism** The philosophy deriving from the work of Plato in the period from the time of Antiochus of Ascalon (d. 68 BC) to *Plotinus (b. AD 205). Following Antiochus in rejecting the Scepticism of the New *Academy, it turned towards a positive philosophy that included doctrines from the Platonic, Aristotelian, and Stoic schools and led eventually to *Neoplatonism.

**Mīlēs glōriō'sus** ('The boastful soldier'), Roman comedy by *Plautus; there is reason for thinking it was produced *c.*204 BC and is therefore an early work. It is uncertain from what Greek comedy it was adapted; Plautus gives the name of his original as *Alazon* ('Boaster').

The boastful captain Pyrgopolynices (a name recalling Polyneices from the Greek myth of the *Seven against Thebes, with the addition of *pyrgos*, 'tower') carries off the girl Philocomasium from Athens to Ephesus while her lover Pleusicles is absent at Naupactus. Pleusicles' slave sets off to inform his master but is captured by pirates and given as a present to Pyrgopolynices at Ephesus. The slave then writes a letter to Pleusicles, who comes to Ephesus and takes up residence with an old family friend next door to the soldier. By the ingenuity of the slave and the kindness of Pleusicles' host, Pleusicles and Philocomasium meet by passing through a hole in the party wall between the two houses. It is given out that the girl's twin sister has arrived, and this explains Philocomasium's appearance now in one house, now in the other. Pyrgopolynices is fooled into believing that Pleusicles' host has a young wife who is dying for love of him; he is therefore induced to dismiss Philocomasium in order to pursue this new love, and is lured into the neighbouring house, where he is well beaten as an adulterer, while Pleusicles and his mistress sail off to Athens.

The *miles gloriosus* was a stock character in Roman comedy (see the prologue to Plautus' *Captivi*); he is the prototype of Ralph Roister Doister and Bobadill and other swaggering soldiers of the English Elizabethan stage.

**Milesian philosophers** *See* Miletus.

**Milē'sian Tales (Milēsiaka)** By Aristeidēs of Miletus (Greek, second century BC), short stories of love and adventure. Only one fragment survives, but the type may be seen in the tale of the Ephesian widow in the *Satyricon* of *Petronius Arbiter. They were translated into Latin by L. Cornelius Sisenna. Their generally erotic and titillating character may be inferred from the fact that the Parthians were greatly shocked by a copy found among the spoils after the Roman defeat at Carrhae in 53 BC. They were forerunners of such medieval collections of tales as the *Gesta Romanorum*, the *Decameron* of Boccaccio, and the *Heptameron* of Marguerite of Navarre. 'Milesian Tales' became the generic name for this kind of literature.

**Milē'tus** Southernmost of the great Ionian Greek cities of Asia Minor and originally Carian, with a fine harbour near the mouth of the river Maeander. During the seventh and sixth centuries BC Miletus founded many colonies on the Black Sea and was an important sea-power. It attained great brilliance at the end of the seventh century, under the tyrant Thrasybulus, and during the sixth century it produced the philosophers *Thales, *Anaximander, and *Anaximenes, and a little later *Hecataeus the logographer and *Phocylides the poet. *Histiaeus was tyrant at the time of the first Persian expedition into Europe. Later his son-in-law Aristagoras ruled in his place, and both seem to have promoted from Miletus the Ionian Revolt of 499 against Persia (*see* Persian Wars). Miletus was captured after a siege and burnt by the Persians in 494; its inhabitants were carried off to the Persian capital Susa (*see* Phrynichus (1)). It was refounded in 479, joined the *Delian League, and revolted against Athens in 412, becoming the main Spartan naval base in the region. Famous Milesians of this period were *Aspasia, the *hetaira* of Pericles, *Hippodamus the town-planner of the Piraeus, and the poet *Timotheus. In the fourth century Miletus came under the control of *Mausolus, but in 334 it was captured and liberated by Alexander the Great. It was a manufacturing town and the centre of the wool industry, its wool being regarded in antiquity as the finest in the world.

**Mīlō, Titus A'nnius** (d. 48 BC) Roman political agitator, tribune of the people in 57 BC and notorious as the rival of *Clodius. Between 57 and 52 Milo and Clodius organized street violence against one another with rival gangs of hired gladiators, thereby contributing to the general collapse of law and order at this time. In 52 Milo killed Clodius in one of their affrays and was brought to trial by Pompey. He was to be defended by Cicero (whose return from exile Milo had promoted against Clodius' opposition), but Cicero was intimidated and withdrew. His speech for the defence, which survives, was published later. Milo was condemned and exiled. In 48 he joined M. *Caelius Rufus in an abortive rebellion against Caesar and was killed in south Italy. *See* Cicero (1) 3 and 4.

**Miltī'adēs** Name held by several members of the noble (*Eupatrid) family of the Philaidae at Athens. The so-called younger Miltiades (*c.*550–489 BC) was sent out to the Thracian Chersonese *c.*524 to regain possession of the dominion of his uncle the elder Miltiades when it had fallen into Thracian hands. Later he became a vassal of the Persian king Darius and after the suppression in 494 of the Ionian Revolt (*see* Persian Wars), which he had supported, he returned to Athens in 493, perhaps fearing the Persians. He survived a prosecution for 'tyranny over Greek subjects' in Thrace and became an influential politician in spite of the opposition of the *Alcmaeonidae. Elected *strategos* ('military commander') for 490–89 under the polemarch Callimachus it was he according to tradition who persuaded the Athenians to adopt his strategy at Marathon and was therefore the architect of that victory. An unsuccessful attempt to capture Paros in 489, for which the Athenians had entrusted him with 70 ships, led to his being impeached (on the accusation of *Xanthippus) and fined 50 talents. Soon after he died in prison of wounds received in the attack, and his son *Cimon eventually paid the debt.

Miltiades married Hegesipyle, a Thracian princess, who became the mother of Cimon and (probably) other children, including *Elpinice.

**Milvian bridge (Pons Mulvius)** Near Rome, site of a battle in AD 312 when the emperor Constantine I defeated Maxentius.

**mime** (Gk. *mīmos*, Lat. *mīmus*). Originally a Greek word meaning 'a mimic', the term came to be applied in Greece to a dramatic sketch presenting a scene from daily life ('The quack doctor') or myth ('Dionysus and Ariadne'). In the fifth century BC Sophron of Syracuse wrote mimes in some kind of rhythmic prose and popular (Doric) language; a papyrus fragment and some quotations survive. His mimes were described as 'to do with men' or 'to do with women'. Sophron, who was perhaps the first to give mime a literary form, probably influenced *Herodas and *Theocritus, particularly in Idylls 2 and 15, and was admired by Plato. We are told that the philosopher slept with Sophron's mimes under his pillow, and had his hand on them when he died. Mime in the ancient world should not be confused with 'mime' in the modern sense, which signifies a play in which the parts are performed by gesture and action alone, without words, and to the accompaniment of music. For this *see* PANTOMIME.

At Rome the name was applied to a kind of dramatic performance introduced there before the end of the third century BC, perhaps from *Magna Graecia. The actors included both men and women, who acted in bare feet and without masks scenes from everyday life or from romance, spoken in prose. Mime gradually ousted the *Atellan farce as a tail piece or finale (*exodium*) after tragedies. It developed into licentious farce, with stock characters of husband, faithless wife, her lover, and the maid. A popular feature of the ludi Florales was the appearance of actresses, *mimae*, naked. The actress Cytheris was the mistress of both Mark Antony and the poet Gallus. The mime took a literary form in the first century BC. The principal writers then were D. *Laberius and *Publilius Syrus, who included elements of social and political criticism. Under the empire, mimes contributed to the decline in stage performances of comedy, being patronized by the emperors (*Justinian's empress was a mime actress) and highly popular with the people, who loved their farcical nature, indecency, and topicality. The Christian Church denounced them in vain, but they were finally suppressed in the Roman world in AD 502.

**mimē'sis** [Gk., 'imitation'] Term used by Plato and Aristotle when discussing art in general to describe one of art's functions, namely the copying of external appearances, or the representation of life in drama. *See* AESTHETICS and *POETICS*.

**Mimne'rmus** (of Colophon in Ionia, second half of the seventh century BC) Greek poet. He wrote chiefly love-poems in elegiacs which were collected in two books, one of them called *Nanno* after the *aulos-girl he is said to have loved. His most memorable poems are concerned with the pleasures of youth and love and the horrors of old age, but he seems also to have written a *Smyrnēis* or historical poem on Smyrna's victory over *Gyges of Lydia. Other fragments suggest that he wrote on a variety of themes: a description of the Sun sailing in his cup over the Ocean through the night to his rising (*see* HELIOS), and an account of the foundation of Colophon. He is admired for the musical qualities of his verse, and for his expression of melancholy.

**Mine'rva** Italian goddess of crafts and trade guilds, probably a native deity rather than an early borrowing from Greece, her name perhaps connected with *meminisse*, 'to remember'. She was one of the three great Capitoline deities, the 'triad', together with *Jupiter and Juno. She was worshipped in a shrine on mons Caelius and also had a temple on the Aventine, outside the city wall. Here the guild of tibia-players held a festival on the Ides (13th) of June, in the evening of which they dressed in masks and long robes and roamed the streets (*see* LIVIUS ANDRONICUS). Minerva's festival was the Quinquatrus, on 19 March, the date of the dedication of the temple. She was identified with the Greek goddess Athena and seems to have taken over the martial characteristics of Athena Promachos ('Champion'). Certainly her worship spread at the expense of that of Mars, the Quinquatrus having originally been his festival. Virgil presents her both as a goddess of handicrafts and as a goddess of war.

**Mīnō'an** *See* MINOS and CRETE.

**Mīnos** In Greek myth, a king of *Crete who lived two generations before those who fought in the Trojan War. The stories told about him faintly reflect the historical importance of the Bronze-age Cretan civilization called after him

Minoan. He is represented in the *Odyssey* (book 11) as Zeus' favourite of mortal kings, a just ruler who became a judge of the dead in the Underworld (together with, in later authors, his brother *Rhadamanthys and the hero *Aeacus). Minos, Rhadamanthys, and *Sarpedon were the sons of Zeus and *Europa, whom Zeus carried off by assuming the form of a bull. To settle the question of who should be king of Crete, Minos prayed to the sea-god Poseidon to send him a victim he might sacrifice, and the god sent a bull from the sea. Thus Minos took the kingdom, but he could not bring himself to kill the magnificent bull. Poseidon thereupon caused Minos' wife *Pasiphaē to fall in love with it, and the result of their union was the Minotaur ('Minos' bull'), which had the body of a man with a bull's head. The *labyrinth, a maze in which to hide it, was constructed by *Daedalus (who was himself imprisoned there).

Minos is said to have been close to his father Zeus, who received him every nine years in his cave on Mount Ida and gave him laws to impose on his Cretan subjects, the first laws mortals received. In the course of his reign he made war on Megara and Athens. For the story of the former conflict *see* NISUS (1). In Athenian legend he is made the villain of a story in which *Theseus is the hero. Minos laid siege to Athens in the time of King Aegeus because of the city's involvement in the death of his son Androgeos, and for its deliverance the city had to agree to pay an annual or nine-yearly tribute of seven youths and girls, who were shut up with the Minotaur. One year Theseus, King Aegeus' son, contrived to be included, and succeeded in killing the Minotaur. Herodotus (7.170) relates that Minos met a violent death during his pursuit of Daedalus, who had escaped to Sicily. By Pasiphae Minos was the father of many children, including *Phaedra, *Ariadne, and *Deucalion (and through Deucalion the grandfather of Idomeneus, who fought at Troy). *See also* BRITOMARTIS.

**Mī'notaur** *See* MINOS.

**minuscule script** *See* TEXTS, TRANSMISSION OF ANCIENT 3 and 5.

**Mi'nyans (Minyai)** An ancient Greek people believed by the Greeks of the classical age to have lived in the Heroic age (*see* HEROES). Their chief branches appear from the *Iliad* to have lived at Orchomenus in Boeotia and Iolcus in Thessaly as well as the south-west Peloponnese. As most of the *Argonauts were descended from the Minyans they are often called by that name. *See* MINYAS.

'Minyan' ware, so-called by the nineteenth-century German archaeologist Heinrich Schliemann (who first excavated *Mycenae) when he found it at Orchomenus, is a fine monochrome burnished pottery, originally thought to signify the arrival of a new people in Greece in the early *Bronze age but now known to have evolved in Greece.

**Mi'nyas** Legendary ancestor of the *Minyans and founder of Orchomenus in Boeotia. He was the father of *Clymene (2) and other daughters. Of these it is told that they resisted the cult of Dionysus, were driven mad, and tore in pieces Hippasus, the son of Leucippe, one of their number. They were turned into bats.

*Misū'menos* ('The man she hated') Greek comedy by *Menander; in antiquity it was very popular but only a fragment of it survives from a papyrus, and not sufficient to reconstruct the plot. Thrasonides, a professional soldier, holds captive a girl Crateia, with whom he is madly in love, but refuses to force himself upon her because of her hatred for him. Her father Demeas seems to have ransomed her; more than that cannot be ascertained. The chief interest of the play must have lain in the relationship between Thrasonides and Crateia, both of whom are made sympathetic.

**Mithridā'tēs VI Eu'pator** (reigned 120–63 BC) King of Pontus on the south shore of the Black Sea, during his lifetime Rome's most formidable antagonist in the East and a permanent threat to her control over client kingdoms in Asia Minor. The kings of Pontus were from the Persian nobility, claiming descent from *Darius, but perhaps their more immediate descent was from local rulers on the Propontis. The majority of the population was only lightly Hellenized. After murdering his mother and brother, Mithridates married his sister Laodice, and proceeded to extend his power around the Black Sea area. He fought three wars, the Mithridatic Wars, against Rome: in 89–85, 83–82, and 74–63. During the first, when he annexed Bithynia and Cappadocia and quickly overran most of Asia Minor, on a set date in 88 he had Roman and Italian residents there put to death (the 'Asian vespers'; the number killed was said to have been 80,000). He failed to take Rhodes but took

Athens in 86. In the same year his army was twice defeated by *Sulla and he was allowed to retire to Pontus. In the second war Mithridates was attacked by L. Licinius Murena, proconsul of Asia, but easily repelled the attacks and again Sulla made peace. Mithridates opened the third war by invading Bithynia, which had been bequeathed to Rome by its ruler Nicomedes IV in 75. He was defeated and driven back from his conquered territory first by Lucullus, then by Pompey, and took refuge eventually in the Crimea. Here he failed to raise a new fleet and army, and a revolt against him was led by his son Pharnaces. He preferred death to captivity, but found that, having taken so many antidotes, he was immune to poison, and had to get a slave to stab him (63 BC).

**Mityle'nē** (officially **Mytilēnē**) *See* LESBOS.

**Mnēmo'synē** In Greek myth, a *Titan goddess, a personification of Memory, and the mother, by Zeus, of the *Muses.

**Moirae** *See* FATES.

**Molio'nes** In Greek myth, the twin sons of Actor (or Poseidon) and Molione, named Eurytus and Cteatus; in some accounts (but not in Homer) conjoined twins. They were enemies of the Pylians, and also took part in the Calydonian boar-hunt (*see* MELEAGER). They fought against Heracles on behalf of their uncle Augeas (*see* HERACLES, LABOURS OF 6), killing Heracles' brother Iphicles; later they were themselves ambushed and killed by Heracles.

**Monē'ta** *See* JUNO.

### money and coins

**1. In Greece.** Coinage in the sense of marked metal pieces of standard weight is now generally agreed to have been first used in western Asia Minor, in the second half of the seventh century BC, and by the end of the sixth century BC many Greek states had adopted a coinage, mostly based on silver.

Before coinage proper, the Greeks had a primitive currency based on the iron cooking-spit, *obelos*; from this derived the names and equivalences of the Greek silver coinage (*see* DRACHMA). (In Sparta, spits continued to be the only permitted currency long after all other states had coinage.)

Greek money values may be summarized as follows:

| | | |
|---|---|---|
| 6 obols | = | 1 drachma |
| 2 – 4 drachmas | = | 1 stater |
| 100 drachmas | = | 1 mina |
| 60 minas | = | 1 talent. |

At Athens at the end of the fifth century BC a building-worker or a rower on a trireme would receive one drachma a day, but would be unlikely to earn more than 300 drachmas in a year. He could feed himself, on bread and 'relish' (i.e. meat, fish, vegetables, or fruit), for a little over a drachma a week. Fifty minas was regarded as a large sum to pay for a house; a mean dwelling could have been bought for three.

The coinage of Philip II of Macedon and, especially, of his son Alexander the Great had world-wide circulation. Alexander and his successors were the first rulers to introduce portraits of themselves, some of them very fine, on their coins.

**2. At Rome.** The cities of Magna Graecia in south Italy issued splendid series of silver coins as early as the sixth century BC, and in Etruria, to the north of Rome, coinage began in the fifth century BC. However, Rome under the kings and in the early republic did not have a coinage. The Latin word for money, *pecunia*, is probably derived from the use of livestock, *pecua* (pl.), as units of exchange. In the fourth century BC Rome issued a bronze and a silver coinage but for the most part managed without until the war with Pyrrhus (third century BC), from which time a coinage was issued down to the end of the empire in the West. At first a cast bronze coinage was put into circulation, each piece known as an *aes* or *as* (pl. *asses*) and weighing a Roman pound (12 Roman ounces, about 330g). The huge expense of the Second Punic War (from 218 BC) led to a new coinage with a much reduced metal content. In 211 BC the silver *denarius* was introduced, the main Roman silver coin for the next four centuries, worth ten asses. By this time the as weighed about two ounces. Growing prosperity at Rome in the second century BC led to an increase in silver coinage, and the enhanced position of Rome in the world led to the omission of the identifying word 'Roma'. In 141 BC bronze coinage was devalued and the denarius made equivalent to 16 asses. Towards the end of the first century BC, as most of the Mediterranean region came under direct Roman rule, the use of Roman coinage spread throughout the world. The large quantity of gold brought as booty from Gaul and Britain following Julius Caesar's conquests was turned into a massive issue of gold coins, *aurei* (sing. *aureus*), in 46 BC, on Caesar's own authority. He was the first to put his own head on Roman coins. When Octavian came to power (*see* AUGUSTUS), authority for minting passed to the state. One aureus was worth 25 denarii. The Romans commonly expressed even large sums of money in so-called *sestertii*. The word *sestertius* (sing.) is a contraction of *semi-tertius*, 'the third time, half', i.e. two and a half times the unit; in this case, the as. From the time of Nero's reduction in the weight of gold and silver coinage in AD 64 there was a gradual debasement under the empire. Towards the end of the third century AD the denarius ceased to be minted. The emperor Diocletian at the beginning of the fourth century AD attempted to restore the value of the currency and introduced a gold coin known as the *solidus* (sixty to the Roman pound in weight). Under the emperor Constantine the Great the solidus was reduced in weight, but it remained standard for many centuries.

**monism** (monistic theory) *See* ELEATIC PHILOSOPHERS.

**monody** (monodic poetry) *See* LYRIC POETRY [Greek].

**monotheism** Writers in classical antiquity sometimes seem to express belief in one god only, when they occasionally ascribe a state of affairs to the will of 'god' instead of 'the gods', apparently indiscriminately. This usage is not true monotheism; it merely expresses a feeling natural to humans that a power outside themselves is at work beyond their control. For most people of classical and early Christian times (apart from Jews and Christians) it would have seemed highly unlikely that there was only one god. For more genuinely monotheistic belief among the Greeks *see* ANTISTHENES; XENOPHANES; GALEN; STOICISM.

During the first three centuries of the Roman empire adherents of Judaism or Christianity, or of the cults of Isis and Mithras, recognized only their particular god, but it is difficult to distinguish between those who believed their deity to be the only one and those believing theirs to be the most powerful, and to say whether they could properly be called monotheistic. Even the Christians related God the Father in different ways to the Son and the Holy Spirit, while traditional Romans continued to believe that though Jupiter was supreme there were other gods to be worshipped. *See also* NEOPLATONISM.

**Monume'ntum Ancȳrā'num** *See* RES GESTAE.

**Mōrā'lia** *See* PLUTARCH.

**Morē'tum** ('The salad') *See* APPENDIX VIRGILIANA.

**Mo'rpheus** Son of Hypnos (Sleep), the Greek god of *dreams. Later authors use the name also for the god of sleep.

**Moschus** (fl. *c*.150 BC) Greek poet of Syracuse whose extant poems include five hexameter pieces, one of which is bucolic (comparing the pleasures of the countryman with the hard lot of the fisherman), and an *epigram on Eros as a ploughman; there are also an *epyllion *Europa* in 166 hexameters on the rape of Europa by Zeus, and the *Megara*, a hexameter dialogue between Heracles' wife (who gave her name to the poem) and his mother Alcmena, who bewail their misfortunes caused by Heracles' long absence. Also attributed to Moschus, but improbably since *Bion (2) lived at least a generation after him, is the beautiful (bucolic) *Lament for Bion*. (*See also* PASTORAL POETRY.)

**Mostellā'ria** ('Ghost') Roman comedy by *Plautus, possibly adapted from a Greek comedy (*Phasma*, 'Apparition') by Philemon (*see* COMEDY [Greek 6]).

The plot depends on the effrontery and resourceful lying of the slave Tranio. Philolaches, during his father's absence abroad, purchases from a pimp and then frees a girl whom he loves, borrowing money for the purpose from a moneylender, and brings her to live in his father's house. The father returns unexpectedly. Tranio, to prevent him entering the house and discovering what is going on, pretends that the house is haunted by the ghost of a murdered man and has consequently been vacated. But the moneylender appears and demands his money. Tranio tells the father that Philolaches has borrowed it to buy the house of their neighbour Simo, and Simo is induced by further lies to allow it to be inspected. In the end Tranio's lies are exposed, and the father is appeased.

**Mother-goddess** *See* CYBELE.

**mou'sikē** *See* DANCING 1.

**Mucius, Quintus** *See* SCAEVOLA (4).

**Mu'lciber** [from Lat. *mulcet*, 'he mitigates'] Name of the Roman god *Vulcan, who may have been worshipped originally as 'the averter of fires'. In classical times he was identified with the Greek god *Hephaestus.

**Mu'mmius, Lucius** Consul 146 BC. He succeeded Metellus as the Roman commander against the *Achaean confederacy in that year, and was responsible for the sack of *Corinth, and for shipping Corinth's art treasures to Italy. He celebrated a triumph and became censor with *Scipio Aemilianus in 142; he died soon after.

**Munda** Town in Spain, and scene of a battle won by Julius *Caesar in 45 BC, after a republican revolt by Pompey's sons and Labienus (Caesar's own former legate in the Gallic War). Caesar is reported to have said it was his hardest victory.

**mundus** According to Plutarch, a pit in Rome (traditionally in the *Comitium*; *see* ASSEMBLY dug by Romulus in which he put first-fruits and clods of earth from each territory from which his followers came, afterwards filling it up and putting an altar on it. This pit seems to have been called *mundus Cereris* or *Cerealis*, 'pit of Ceres'. *Mundus* was also the name of another pit dug in Rome, probably not identified with the first, which supposedly gave access to the Underworld. The latter *mundus* was closed with stone except for three days of ill omen, 24 August, 5 October, and 8 November, when *mundus patet*, 'the pit is open'.

**mūnici'pium** ('municipality') Term describing originally the towns of Etruria, Latium, and Campania, and indicating their status. The inhabitants had the duties of Roman citizenship, including serving in the army and paying taxes, but only the private rights of Roman citizens, not the public rights: they had *civitas sine suffragio*, 'citizenship without the vote [at Rome],' though full rights might be acquired by moving to Rome. After the *Social War (2) (90–88 BC) all Italian communities had the right to vote and their inhabitants became full Roman citizens. Henceforth *municipium* meant an Italian borough, usually governed by magistrates called the *quattuorviri*, 'the fourteen'.

**Mūny'chia (Mounychia, Munichia)** The acropolis (citadel) of *Piraeus and a small harbour adjoining it.

**Mūsae'us (Mousaios)** ('he of the Muses') 1. Mythical Greek poet, said to have come from Eleusis or to be an immigrant from Thrace and to have been a pupil of *Orpheus; a collection of oracles was attributed to him. *See also* ONOMACRITUS.
2. Greek poet of uncertain date but perhaps late fifth century AD; a learned Christian and Neoplatonist, he wrote a short epic poem on the love of Hero and *Leander.

**Muses (Mousai)** (Lat. Musae) In Greek myth, daughters of Zeus and *Mnemosyne (Memory), the goddesses of literature, music, and dance, later of all knowledge. Upon these depended the poets, and later other creative artists including philosophers, for the inspiration to create their works. The early Greek poet Hesiod is the first to name them (and perhaps coined their names himself). According to him they were nine in number, and his famous description at the opening of the *Theogony* of their gift to him of song and knowledge of the past influenced later poets when they came to give an account of how they were inspired to compose poetry. The original seats of the Muses' worship were Pieria, near Mount *Olympus in Thessaly, and Mount *Helicon in Boeotia (whence they are often spoken of as Pierian or Heliconian), but smaller cults existed throughout Greece. In late Roman times each Muse presided over one particular art: Calliope, epic poetry; Clio, history; Euterpe, flute-playing (and lyric poetry accompanied by the flute); Melpomene, tragedy; Terpsichore, (choral) dancing (and the song that goes with it); Erato, the lyre (and the lyric poetry, often erotic, accompanied by it); Polyhymnia, hymns to the gods, and later, pantomime; Urania, astronomy; Thalia, comedy and bucolic poetry. Their numbers, names, and attributes vary at different times. A few myths are associated with them: the Thracian poet *Thamyris competed against them and lost his sight and power of song; the *Sirens competed against them, but were defeated, lost their wings, and jumped into the sea; in one version of the story describing the contest between Apollo and *Marsyas, the Muses are made the judges. Artists of all kinds felt a personal bond with the

Muses, who seemed to them to be the source of their gifts. *See* MUSEUM.

**musē'um (mouseion)** In Greece, originally a place connected with the *Muses, sometimes in a religious sense but more usually as a place where the arts and learning were cultivated. Thus 'museum' came to mean a place of education, connected with the Muses. Euripides describes the places where birds sing as *mouseia*. The most famous museum was that of *Alexandria in Egypt, founded by Ptolemy I Soter (ruled 323–283 BC) possibly on the advice of the Athenian *Demetrius of Phalerum. It was distinct from the Library, and housed scholars engaged in research who were supported by the Ptolemies and, after Egypt came under Roman control, by the emperors. There is no evidence that there was provision for formal teaching, but lectures were given and there were many discussions which even the kings might attend; Cleopatra, the last independent ruler of Egypt, is reputed to have done so. Scholars at the Alexandria Museum stabilized classical texts, which became the source for the spread of standardized versions (*see also* ALEXANDRIAN LIBRARY). After the foundation of Constantinople in AD 324 many of the Museum scholars are said to have retreated there to avoid the theological controversies of Alexandria. The last of its scholars to be mentioned explicitly is Theon the mathematician, father of *Hypatia, *c.* AD 400. Dinners with clever conversation were a characteristic institution of the Museum; a poet of the third century BC described it as the 'hen-coop of the Muses'. Museums as buildings housing collections of objects did not exist as such in the ancient world, but collections of material goods, dedications, and old weapons were kept in temples in ancient Greece.

**music** [Gk. *mousikē*, 'art of the Muses']
**Greek.** Music was an integral feature of Greek life, an essential ingredient of all public religious occasions and of banquets and social gatherings at all levels. It was also inseparable from song and dance because all three parts came together in religious ceremonies and civic occasions.

1. Nearly every form of Greek poetry was traditionally accompanied by some form of music: the Homeric epics were chanted or recited to the lyre; elegiac poems were sung to the accompaniment of the *aulos (Lat. *tibia*), 'pipe'; monodic '*lyric' poetry, which was composed in more elaborate metres, was accompanied by the singer himself on a lyre (or even a harp), on occasions such as symposia. Choral lyric survives for us only as poetry, but for the Greeks it was a great spectacle created from a blend of poetry, melody, and dance. *Dithyramb and *tragedy, again known to us only as dramatic poetry, had their origin in the singing and dancing of choruses to the accompaniment of *auloi*. In classical times instruction in singing and playing the lyre (and less often the aulos) was part of every well-brought-up boy's education. In the home women too played music. Thus a Greek city had many people who could participate in civic and religious musical performances, thereby expressing communal identity and values.

2. The principal musical instruments were the lyre or *cithara, of which there were several forms and names, and the aulos, which is often, but misleadingly, translated as 'flute'; see below. The lyre was used mostly to accompany lyric poetry; Pindar's lyric odes, however, were sometimes accompanied by the aulos as well. The latter was the usual instrument for accompanying the dithyramb and for the choruses of tragedy and comedy. It was the main instrument for worship of Dionysus and in the enactment of the mysteries. It was also played at banquets, sacrifices, and funerals, and was used to mark time for dancers. But the lyre was considered the superior instrument both socially (playing pipes distorted the face) and for education, and it was also important in military music. Both were used in religious music.

3. The lyre had vertical strings of equal length (thereby differing from the harp) which were plucked with the fingers or, more usually, with a plectrum, bowed instruments being unknown until the Middle Ages. Pitch was regulated by the tension, and perhaps the thickness, of the strings. The strings of gut or sinew stretched upwards from a tail-piece or holder, over a bridge, to a cross-bar at the top of the instrument, which joined the two slender, curved, side pieces of horn or wood. At the cross-bar there were pegs for tuning. The sound-box at the bottom of the lyre was originally provided by the shell of a tortoise (*see* HERMES), often replaced by a similarly bowl-shaped open box, with a piece of ox-hide stretched over its concave side. This quieter

instrument was used at home and in school. The player rested the instrument against his body as he played, plucking the strings with one hand and perhaps using the other to silence them as required. The exact function of each hand is not clear. There were several varieties of lyre, and the names for them overlap in usage. Homer calls the same instrument both a *phorminx* and a *citharis*; Pindar calls his instrument a *lyra* or a *phorminx*. The *barbitos* appears to describe an instrument slightly different from these. The lyre used in public performance by professional musicians had a more substantial wooden square-based sound-box. Several types of harp (which had many more strings of very different lengths, struck with the fingers) were also known, one being the *psalterion*, but they were never in common use. Early lyres probably had only four strings, but the standard number in classical times was seven or eight (*see* TERPANDER). Strings on lyres and harps were not normally stopped but were played open.

4. The translation 'flute' for Greek *aulos* is misleading since the instrument, having a reed, was more akin to the clarinet or oboe. The pipe, made of reed, wood, bone, or ivory, was nearly always cylindrical but occasionally slightly conical, to judge from surviving fragments and illustrations. It was pierced with holes, as many as sixteen by the late fifth century BC. The player generally played two pipes at once (the 'double' aulos), often held in position by a head- and cheek-band; each was fingered by one hand. It is not known whether the two pipes, which were of equal length, were played separately and provided an extended scale or whether they were played together, making a rudimentary harmony; possibly both techniques were used. The aulos was notable for expressing strong emotions, particularly religious frenzy in Bacchic and Corybantic cults. In the hands of a great player it could charm and soothe (but see 6 below). The *syrinx* (or pan-pipes; *see* PAN), the characteristic instrument of herdsmen, generally consisted of around seven pipes bound together and blown directly without the aid of a mouthpiece. In Greece the pipes were of equal length but were stopped internally; the *syrinx* with a 'stepped' shape, familiar in art, is the Etruscan and Roman variety.

5. Greek music was primarily melodic, and based on one of many possible 'attunements',
*harmoniai* (sometimes called 'modes' or 'tunings'), which roughly resembled modern octave scales (*see* ARISTOXENUS). The *harmoniai* differed from each other in the sequence of musical intervals. Fundamental to any *harmonia* were the concords – the octave, and the intervals the fifth and the fourth. Greek music also used many small intervals which modern western music has lost. Classical writers refer to the different *harmoniai* by ethnic names: Mixolydian, Lydian, Phrygian, Dorian, Hypolydian, Hypophrygian, Hypodorian. (Different names are found in later writers.) Each represents an octave rising from seven successive starting notes. Further names were used to indicate the pitch (*tonos*) of a scale, i.e. how high or low it was. In the case of the lyre, each *harmonia* probably required its own tuning. *Harmonics became an important discipline.

6. For the Greeks music had an ethical dimension. Plato thought that music not only aroused the emotions temporarily but influenced character, and he admits only the Dorian and Phrygian modes into his ideal state. The aulos he banned altogether. Aristotle too accepts that different rhythms and modes are imitations of different ethical characters and have corresponding effects on the listener's soul, in contrast with Philodemus in his *De musica*; *see* AESTHETICS. For education (though not for relaxation, for which all kinds of music are suitable) Aristotle would admit only the Dorian mode. He too would not have citizens learn to play the aulos.

7. Music as an art integrated with poetry and dance started to change in the fourth century BC with the decline of tragedy and with changes in religious and civic tradition. Several dozen small fragments of Greek musical scores survive on papyri, almost all from the Hellenistic period or later, and some scores survive as inscriptions on stone. A few late pieces are found on manuscript. There are allusions to musical practice in *Athenaeus and the treatise *De musica* falsely attributed to Plutarch (*see* PLUTARCH 4). Also surviving are some technical treatises on musical theory, though we cannot be sure how far these relate to actual practice (*see* e.g. ARISTOXENUS). It is apparent that the Greeks used two kinds of alphabetic notation, one for the voice and another for musical instruments. Interpretation of the fragments is very uncertain.

*See* TIMOTHEUS (1) and CINESIAS.

**Roman.** In contrast with Greece, at Rome music did not figure as an essential part of an aristocratic education, and on the whole music as an art, and musicians, were regarded with mild contempt, the latter organizing themselves into guilds (*collegia*) at an early stage for mutual protection. Nonetheless, singing at dinner-parties, *convivia*, to stringed instruments and pipes, as at Greek *symposia*, is widely attested as going back to the second century BC. Varro says that boys used to sing in praise of the ancestors, sometimes with unaccompanied voice, and Quintilian adds that the lyre used to be passed around. Suetonius notes that at his dinner parties Augustus not only had various recitals but also actors and performers as well as story-tellers. Music on the *tibia* (see above) accompanied prayers, sacrifices, triumphal marches to the Capitol, processions to the Circus Maximus, and funeral processions. Phrygian pipes provided music for the sung portions of drama (*cantica*) and are often depicted in Roman art. Etruscan influence probably accounts for the use of horns and trumpets in ritual connected with the dead. The trumpets, *tubae*, were 'purified' at the annual festival of the Tubilustria on 23 March (*see* MARS). Under the empire musical recitals of all kinds became a regular feature of entertainment for those with educated tastes. *See also* LYRIC POETRY.

**music of the spheres** *See* HARMONY OF THE SPHERES.

**Mūsō'nius Rūfus, Gaius** Roman Stoic philosopher of the first century AD who probably taught in Greek. Among his pupils were Pliny the Younger, Epictetus, and Dio Chrysostom. He was banished by the emperor Nero for being involved in the conspiracy of *Piso (AD 65), but subsequently returned. He was again banished by Vespasian and returned under Titus. Some of his sayings have been preserved by a pupil, and these show him to have been a humane and attractive figure. They include the remark that marriage is a very good thing, and even a philosopher should accept it gladly. Musonius believed that girls and boys should receive the same kind of education. *See* STOICISM.

**Mu'tina** (Modena, near Bologna) Prosperous town of Cisalpine Gaul famous for its successful resistance to *Pompey in 78 BC and to *Antony in 43 BC (the *bellum Mutinense*, 'war of Mutina'). On the latter occasion it was held by the republicans under D. *Brutus.

**My'calē** Mountainous promontory in Asia Minor, opposite the island of Samos, the scene of the last battle of the *Persian Wars (479 BC), where the Greeks destroyed the Persian army and fleet.

**Mycē'nae (Mȳkēnai, Mykēnē)** An ancient Greek city situated around a rocky hill in the north-east corner of the plain of Argos in the Peloponnese. According to Greek myth it was founded by *Perseus (1) and was subsequently the kingdom of the Homeric hero *Agamemnon who led the Greek army during the Trojan War: Homer calls it 'rich in gold'. In 468 BC, however, Mycenae was destroyed by Argos and never successfully reinhabited. The very considerable ruins were visited in the second century AD by *Pausanias (2), who commented upon the graves, the massive walls, and the Lion Gate, all still to be seen today.

All reliable knowledge of the people who had built this remarkable city had disappeared long before the classical period, and the prominence of Mycenae in Homer is not supported by other legends, which give first importance to Argos. Late *Bronze-age Mycenae was first revealed to the world by the excavations in 1876 of Heinrich Schliemann, a wealthy German merchant and archaeologist, who wished to prove that it was indeed the city of Agamemnon. Schliemann discovered the tombs of kings who reigned some 400 years or more before the commonly accepted date for the fall of Troy (1184 BC; *see* ERATOSTHENES), and in so doing he revealed a splendid civilization, which perhaps became the background and basis of later stories of the Heroic age (*see* HEROES and HOMER 3). The term 'Mycenaean' is now applied particularly to late Bronze-age culture on the mainland of Greece. For purposes of dating the term 'Helladic' is used; the Mycenaean period *c.*1600–*c.*1125 BC is known as Late Helladic (LH), following on from Middle Helladic (MH) and subdivided as follows:

| | |
|---|---|
| LH I | *c.*1600–1500 |
| LH II | *c.*1500–1400 |
| LH III | *c.*1400–1125 |

Further subdivisions can be indicated by the addition of letters, e.g. LH IIIB. LH I was essentially a continuation, without noticeable break, of the previous period MH III.

Corresponding systems for *Crete and the Cyclades are known as Minoan and Cycladic respectively.

At Mycenae rulers appeared in the sixteenth century BC with wealth and power that are not easy to account for. They appear to belong to the prevailing mainland Helladic culture and there is no firm evidence that they are invaders. Their wealth is visible in the contents of the shaft graves of that time and even more so in the *tholos* ('round') tombs of the fifteenth and fourteenth centuries, with their treasures in gold and other precious materials; the finest of these are known as the 'Tomb of Clytemnestra' and the 'Treasury of Atreus'. Apart from Mycenae itself, the major mainland cities of the time included Athens, Thebes, Orchomenus, Pylos, and Tiryns. Extended palaces, resembling on a smaller scale those of Minoan Crete, and fortifications were built in these and other places in the fourteenth century. The palaces were the site of all administration as well as of craft workshops and storage, and the focus of some religious ceremonial. There was considerable influence, particularly in craftsmanship, from Crete.

It has been suggested that the destruction of Troy VI, perhaps c.1270, is the reality behind Homer's *Iliad* and the myth of the Trojan War, and that the siege of Troy by the Greeks under Agamemnon, king of Mycenae, was the last united effort of the Mycenaean Greek world. Hittite references to a foreign country *Ahhiyawa (though without mention of a war) cover nearly 200 years (c.1400–1220), but the tempting identification with Achaean (i.e. Mycenaean) Greece is disputed. Similarly, it is often held that Mycenaean invasion brought about the collapse of the Minoans c.1450 BC and the subsequent expansion of Mycenaean influence in Crete, but hard-and-fast evidence is elusive. Mycenaean power peaked during the fourteenth century, extending over the south Aegean and along the coast of Asia Minor. In the closing years of the thirteenth century the last phase of fortification building was undertaken at Mycenae, Tiryns, Athens, and elsewhere. *Linear B tablets from Pylos seem to indicate defensive action from some threat.

The end of the Mycenaean civilization, the so-called Bronze-age collapse, poses many problems. In about 1200 BC Mycenae, Pylos, and other cities in southern Greece were burned; none of the Mycenaean palaces survived. Athens continued to be occupied, but within a more localized sphere. There appears to have been serious depopulation in the Peloponnese. Suggested external causes have included the *Dorian invasion, the 'sea peoples' mentioned in Hittite and Egyptian sources, apparently engaged in piracy, disrupting the trade on which the palace economies depended, natural disasters, wars between states, or invasions from the north, perhaps facilitated by newly developed weapons, long-swords and javelins. Other explanations include instability in an increasingly complex society; Greek myths about Atreus, Heracles, Proetus, Diomedes, Oedipus, etc. suggest internecine war between Mycenaean centres of power. Whatever the reason, the period c.1200–1125 is one of upheaval, destruction, and decline. The Hittite empire collapsed also and the capital Hattusa was destroyed; Egypt too lost her Asian empire and former brilliance. Some areas, notably Attica, seem to have suffered less (*see* ATHENS 2), but eventually they too declined into the *Dark age.

For the Mycenaean language *see* LINEAR B.

**My'rmidons** *See* AEACUS.

**Myrrha (Smyrna)** *See* ADONIS and ZMYRNA.

**My'rsilus 1.** Name by which Candaules, king of Lydia, was known among the Greeks; *see* GYGES.

**2.** Tyrant of Mytilene; *see* ALCAEUS.

**My'rtilus** Charioteer of Oenomaus; *see* PELOPS.

**Myrtis** Boeotian poet, said to have been the teacher of *Corinna and Pindar. Corinna, in a surviving fragment from one of her poems, reproves her for competing with the far more brilliant Pindar, which may indicate her date to be the fifth century BC. Apart from the summary Plutarch gives of one of her poems, nothing of her work survives.

**mysteries, mystery cults** [Gk. *myein*, to initiate; *mystes*, an initiate; *mysteria* (pl.), Lat. *initia*, 'the mysteries', the whole proceedings] Devotees of mystery religions believed that certain truths about the universe could be revealed only to those initiated by special ceremonies into a virtually secret society of worshippers which brought them into close contact with their god. In addition, initiates usually had the promise of a better time in the after-life. It was possible to be an adherent of several mystery religions at once, and to continue in the usual worship of the gods. Several mystery cults are known to have existed in Greece, of which the most famous by far and the most complex was that of *Eleusis, near Athens. It was more extensively documented throughout its thousand-year history than any other Greek cult, and attracted initiates from the whole Greek-speaking world. The earliest testimony appears in the *Homeric Hymn to Demeter, usually dated to the seventh century BC, and the cult survived until its suppression by the Roman emperor Theodosius in AD 393. Three years later the sanctuary at Eleusis, which had been a sacred site since Mycenaean times, ceased to function. Most, but not all, Athenians seem to have been initiated.

The Eleusinian mysteries were celebrated in the month Boedromion (September–October), at the time of sowing. The priest opened the festival by declaring that those should keep away who 'are not of pure hands and speak an incomprehensible tongue', i.e. murderers and *barbarians. Those participating, having gathered at Athens, bathed in the sea for purification, and then each sacrificed a piglet. After the ceremony for new initiates in the *Eleusinion above the agora, the sacred and secret objects, which had been brought a few days earlier by *epheboi from Eleusis to Athens and placed in the Eleusinion, were taken back to Eleusis in a great procession of initiates along the *Sacred Way. The ritual re-enacted in part the myth of *Demeter and Persephone. The rhythmic shout of Iakch' o Iakche (see IACCHUS) was also regularly raised during the procession; it was regarded by many as referring to the god Dionysus. Before *Salamis the Persians heard a phantom procession, presaging their defeat (Herodotus 8.63). In the Telesterion ('Hall of initiation') at Eleusis, built to hold several thousand people, the initiating priest showed the sacred objects to the initiated. The details are not known: it appears that after the hall had been in darkness for some time, a bright light suddenly shone, the birth of a divine child (his identity uncertain) was announced, and gloom gave way to general rejoicing. Demeter and Kore ('Daughter', i.e. Persephone), Iacchus-Dionysus, Pluto, and *Triptolemus, the mythical hero of agriculture, all had their role. The ceremony ends with a proclamation of the happiness of those who have gained enlightenment, as well as the goddesses' favour in this world and the next.

Bacchic, or Dionysiac, mysteries, orgia, associated with *Bacchus (Dionysus) are also very ancient in Greece, although direct evidence is available only for the later periods. They seem not to have been associated with particular cult-sites but appeared wherever adherents might be found, who were mainly but not entirely, it would seem, women (Herodotus has a story of the Scythian king being initiated, and Euripides in the Bacchae has the aged King Cadmus and the seer Teiresias joining in the rites). Liberation and surrender to Bacchic frenzy in order to achieve a sense of freedom and well-being seem to have been the aim of the Bacchic mysteries, but initiates were also given promises about the after-life. Other mysteries were associated with the name of *Orpheus over which Plato in the Phaedrus has Dionysus preside, and which were apparently performed according to the writings of Orpheus. They too aimed to free from guilt and give better hopes for the after-life to those who practised their rites, and were based on the myth of *Dionysus Zagreus. The goddess *Cybele was associated with mysteries in Hellenistic times; apart from *Attis having a prominent role little is known about these. See also ISIS and SABAZIOS.

**mythology** Term used to denote either the study of myths or, loosely, myths themselves. Myths are traditional tales. Their plot remains roughly the same whenever or however they are told and they have become traditional because they possess some significance or enduring quality. When stories of this general kind are based on some great historical or purportedly historical event (the Siege of Troy, the Return of the Children of Heracles) they are often described as saga. On the other hand, when they are short narratives which are fictional but attached to a real person or place and given a fairly realistic setting, as for example the stories of the early kings of Rome, they may be termed legends. Myths of these two kinds constituted all the Greeks and Romans knew of their early history; in the case of Greece myth pervaded all aspects of their life. A third variety of myth is folk-tales, simple narratives of adventure, often containing elements of ingenious trickery and of magic, perhaps involving superhuman creatures, e.g.

monsters and giants; they are characterized by recurring features of character and plot, lost sons seeking their rightful inheritance, princes slaying monsters to win princesses. The stories of *Perseus (1) contain many such. Myth can include any of the features of saga, legend, or folk-tale, but its particular characteristic is that it is a serious story about the gods (and in Greece about *heroes too) and, especially in Attic tragedy, their relations with one another and with men and women.

There is no touchstone to enable one kind of myth to be clearly distinguished from another, nor can the characteristics of myth be isolated: the same elements may occur in all types, and a given narrative may be categorized differently by different critics. There are myths which explain the origin of the earth, natural phenomena, human (and animal) behaviour, religious practices (see MYSTERIES, concerning the myth of Demeter and Persephone), and human institutions in general. Myth was originally conceived in an oral society, leading to another feature of mythical narrative, its fluidity, and its admitting of endless variations on a general storyline (see HELEN). But Greek myths in general, as we meet them written down in poetry from Homer to Attic tragedy and beyond, are stories of some complexity and subtlety, and they are the form in which the poets choose to express their ideas. A striking thing about Greek myth is the importance attached to it by the Greeks up to the end of the fifth century BC. But in the course of that century, writing became widespread and the medium for serious thought came to be prose. Out of the mythical genealogies of gods and heroes arose the concept of history (see HISTORIOGRAPHY [Greek]). Similarly, the cosmogonical myths shaped the speculations that led eventually to the rise of science and philosophy (see COSMOLOGY; PHILOSOPHY [Greek]; PRIMORDIAL DEITIES). Myth continued to be of significance in poetry and art as long as it was of religious importance for cult and ritual, but as Greece moved into the *Hellenistic age it became more of a deco-

rative element and less intellectually and emotionally charged.

It is noteworthy that many of the principal Greek myths are connected with Mycenaean centres (see MYCENAE), e.g. the stories of Perseus and Atreus with Mycenae itself, that of Oedipus with Thebes, that of Heracles with Thebes and Tiryns, a fact which suggests that the stories are of great antiquity. The sources of our knowledge of Greek myths are in the first place Homer and Hesiod, then the classical Greek poets, in particular Pindar and the dramatists. Further material is provided by the Hellenistic poets, notably Callimachus, and by compilers such as *Diodorus Siculus and the author of the *Bibliotheke* attributed to *Apollodorus (2); also by the Roman poets, especially Ovid (see METAMORPHOSES). Finally the scholiasts, in their commentaries on the classical authors (see SCHOLIUM), frequently furnish mythological information. Naturally the stories drawn from these various sources do not always agree, local traditions and perhaps the fancies of the narrators being freely incorporated.

Roman and Italian myths which antedate contact with Greek literature can hardly be said to exist. That of *Romulus is the best-known (see also CACUS). The old Italian gods are vague personalities, and barely anthropomorphic; they are not actuated by human motives, they do not marry or fight or have love affairs with mortals. The myths that the Roman poets and antiquarians attached to them were borrowed from Greece (e.g. by the process of identifying Roman deities with Greek), or invented, largely under Greek influence. Since educated Romans regarded such myths as *fabulae*, 'fictional stories', it is difficult to see what role myth played in Roman society. Such native Italian traditions as there were have been lost or, where they survive, lack imaginative richness: imagination comes into play only to explain some old custom, ritual, or name. (See also FASTI).

**Mytile'ne (Mitylene)** See LESBOS.

# N

**Nae'vius, Gnaeus** (*c.*270–190s BC) Roman tragic and comic dramatist and epic poet from Campania. He fought in the last year of the First Punic War (264–241 BC), and started producing his own plays in 235, but he seems to have written nothing after 204. As well as writing tragedies on themes taken from Greek originals he wrote on subjects drawn from Roman history, *fabulae *praetextae*, and was the first Roman to do so. Of these, very few fragments or titles survive. However, it seems to have been in comedy that he excelled. Again, the surviving fragments are very scanty, but some thirty titles are known. These seem to have been based on models from Greek New Comedy, *fabulae *palliatae*, but it is possible that Naevius also wrote comedies with an Italian setting, *fabulae *togatae*. His outspokenness offended the powerful family of the *Metelli: one line in particular became notorious (written in iambics, the metre of spoken drama, and so presumably delivered in a play), *fato Metelli Romae fiunt consules* ('by fate the Metelli become consuls at Rome'), implying lack of ability. Naevius may have gone into exile as a consequence; he is said to have died at Utica in North Africa. He is supposed to have composed his own epitaph, claiming that the Latin language died with him. It is quoted by Aulus *Gellius (1.24.2.) but may not be authentic. His most important work, written in old age, was the epic *Carmen Belli Poenici* ('Poem on the Punic War'), written in Saturnian metre and later divided into seven books, but only about sixty lines survive. The work seems to have contained mythological digressions, including descriptions of the departure of Aeneas from Troy, the founding of Rome, and perhaps that of Carthage also. It survived at least until the time of Horace. Borrowings from it were detected by early scholars in Virgil's *Aeneid*.

**nai'ads (naiadĕs)** *Nymphs of springs, rivers, and lakes.

## names, personal

**Greek.** One personal name only was the rule, given at birth for men and women alike; women did not change their name upon marriage. There was a very wide variety of names, many of which were compounds of two common nouns with a flattering meaning; Megacles, for example, means 'of great fame'. Others incorporated the name of a god, e.g. Apollodorus, 'gift of Apollo', or reflected personal characteristics (Plato, 'broad-shouldered'), or circumstances (Didymus, 'a twin'). Choice of name was entirely free, although it was quite customary for the eldest son to be named after his paternal grandfather. In Homer it is common for a hero to be called on occasions not by his own name but by a form of his father's name, his 'patronymic': thus Agamemnon is sometimes called Atreides, meaning 'son of Atreus'. By classical times the patronymic had ceased to be used in its original sense; a name in patronymic form, e.g. Miltiades, was sometimes chosen as an ordinary personal name; occasionally a patronymic was added to indicate the subject's *genos (clan); for example, someone called additionally 'Philaides' would belong to the *genos* of the Philaidai, the descendants of Philaios. If an additional name was necessary to aid identification, the father's name was added in the genitive case: thus 'Cimon, [son] of Miltiades'. In some contexts indication of the person's *deme is added, in adjectival form: thus 'Cimon, [son] of Miltiades, Lakiades' (from the deme of Lakiadai), or 'Pericles, [son] of Xanthippus, Cholargeus' (from the deme of Cholargos). These additional names were not used as a form of address. It is the practice of the historians Herodotus and Thucydides to identify a person by adding the father's name; in Aristophanes' comedies, on the other hand, characters introduce themselves by name and deme, and this is usually the practice in the fourth-century orators.

**Roman.** Among the Italian peoples, including the Etruscans, every freeman and woman had two basic names, the *praenōmen*, 'forename' or personal name, of which there were relatively few, and (more importantly) the *nōmen*, the 'name' of the *gens* or clan. In addition they usually had a *cognōmen* (see below). The *praenomen* was commonly written in abbreviated form as follows:

| | |
|---|---|
| A. | Aulus |
| Ap(p). | Appius |
| C. | Gaius (*see* ALPHABET [Latin]) |
| Cn. | Gnaeus (*see* ALPHABET [Latin]) |
| D. | Decimus |
| L. | Lūcius |
| M. | Marcus |
| M'. | Mānius |
| N. | Numerius |
| P. | Publius |
| Q. | Quintus |
| Ser. | Servius |
| Sex. | Sextus |
| Sp. | Spurius |
| T. | Tītus |
| Ti. | Tiberius |

For Roman women, at least in the upper classes, the *praenomen* was virtually abandoned, and they were usually known by the feminine form of their *nomen* or clan name, e.g. 'Cornelia', 'Claudia'. A person's *nomen* was the same as that of the (legal) father; women did not change their name upon marriage. The *nomen* very often ends in -*ius* (Cornelius, Claudius); the (masculine) endings -*a*, -*as*, -*anus*, and -*enus* are characteristic of names from the north of Italy.

The *cognomen* was an extra personal name added after the *nomen*, and functioned originally rather like a nickname, indicative of the bearer's personal characteristic: Balbus ('stammerer'), Rufus ('red-head'), Brutus ('idiot'), Naso ('big-nose'), Pictor ('painter'), Scipio ('stick', originally given to a Cornelius who acted as a 'stick' to his blind father). Often, as in the case of Scipio, the *cognomen* was also handed down from father to son, and thus came to designate a sub-division within the clan, a family. Some clans, even distinguished ones such as that of the Antonii, admitted *cognomina* only rarely (Mark Antony, for example, had no other name; and cf. C. Marius, whose lack of *cognomen* has sometimes been attributed to alleged humble origins). Extra *cognomina* could be added (often called *agnomina*; sing. *agnomen*): thus the Cornelii Scipiones Nasicae were a subdivision of the Cornelii Scipiones.

An adopted son took his adoptive father's names but might add as *cognomen* the adjectival form of his own original *nomen*: thus the elder son of L. Aemilius *Paullus, when adopted by P. Scipio, became P. Scipio Aemilianus; C. Octavius, when adopted by C. Julius Caesar, became C. Julius Caesar Octavianus (Octavian). Slaves were usually called by their own (single) name. Freedmen took their original owner's *praenomen* and *nomen*, adding their own (slave) name as a *cognomen*: thus Cicero's faithful slave *Tiro became M. Tullius Tiro.

In informal surroundings a man might be addressed intimately by his *praenomen*; by friends he might be called by his *nomen* or his *cognomen* alone. In formal circumstances he was addressed by *praenomen* and *nomen* (and perhaps *cognomen* as well).

Under the empire, with the use of a plurality of names and reversal of the usual order, the system broke down, and there was eventually a return to the ancient use of a single name.

**Nanno** *See* MIMNERMUS.

**Na'rbonese Gaul** *See* GAUL.

**Narci'ssus 1.** In Greek myth, a beautiful youth, son of the Boeotian river god Cephisus and the nymph Liriope. The nymph *Echo fell in love with him, but was rejected. Aphrodite punished him for his cruelty by making him fall in love with his own image reflected in water. After fruitless attempts to approach his beautiful reflection he despaired and wasted away to death. The gods changed him into the flower that bears his name.

**2.** Freedman and private secretary to the emperor Claudius (d. AD 54), who exercised great political influence and gained enormous wealth. He did not favour Claudius' marriage to Agrippina (mother of Nero), and after the emperor's death and the accession of Nero he was arrested and compelled to commit suicide. *See also* MESSAL(L)INA, VALERIA.

**narratology (narrative, narration)** The study of 'story', focusing both on the story as event, 'what happened', and on its representation, 'how it is told'. It could be said that the subject started with the *Poetics* of Aristotle, who gave primary importance in tragedy to *mythos*, 'plot', and required it to have organic unity. Dramatic texts, however, function within the constraints of performance. As far as classical texts are concerned it is fictional narrative in epic and the novel that is mostly the subject of study. Topics arising include the *order* in which events are narrated (linearity, flashback, abrupt entry into the plot), *duration* (scenes with dialogue, which is representation, contrasted with summaries of events, which is narration), and the *mode* in which information is conveyed (focalization from the point of view of one of the characters). The ancient *novel, slow to develop its technique from linear narrative to much greater complexity, e.g. by including the device of a story within a story (as in the *Odyssey*), has proved a fruitful area of study. So too has the application of narratology to the writing of history.

**Nāso** Cognomen (*see* NAMES [Roman]) of the Roman poet *Ovid, by which he always refers to himself. It is derived from *nasus*, 'nose', and probably means 'big nose'.

***Natural History** See* PLINY (1).

**Nau'cratis** Greek town in the Delta of Egypt, about 50km (30 miles) from the sea on the Canopic (western) branch of the Nile. Naucratis was the principal port of Egypt until the foundation of Alexandria in 332 BC by Alexander the Great. It was famous for its prostitutes, who included *Rhodopis (Doricha), with whom Sappho's brother Charaxus fell in love when he travelled there on business, and a certain Archidice, said by Herodotus to be 'known by song the length and breadth of Greece'. It was the birthplace of *Athenaeus and Julius *Pollux.

**Nausi'căa (Nausicā'a)** In Homer's *Odyssey* (book 6) the daughter of the Phaeacian king, Alcinöus, and his wife Arete. On the night on which Odysseus' raft is wrecked off Scheria, the goddess Athena, appearing to her in a dream, tells her to go down to the river-mouth next day and do the household washing. This she does, with her maids, and they all play ball. Odysseus, woken by their cries, emerges almost naked from some bushes, frightening away the maids. Nausicaa receives him with dignity, gives him food, clothing, and oil, and after he has washed and dressed offers to show him the way to the city, requesting him to walk the last part alone so as to avoid giving rise to gossip. The hero is then entertained and sent on his way by Alcinous, who, like Nausicaa herself, had rather hoped that Odysseus might prove a suitable bridegroom for her, but he longs to return home to Penelope. The episode was dramatized in the lost *Nausicaa* of Sophocles.

**Neai'ra** Included among Demosthenes' speeches is one (59) delivered by *Apollodorus (1), son of Pasion the Athenian banker, against Neaira, the woman who lived as the wife of an Athenian citizen, Stephanos. She is accused of having usurped Athenian citizenship (*see* PERICLES) and of pretending that her daughters were citizens. The speech includes a graphic account of Neaira's early career as a *hetaira*.

**Nea'rchus** (of Crete) Friend of *Alexander the Great (see (1) 6 and 8). Nearchus wrote an account of his voyage along the coast from the mouth of the river Indus to the Persian Gulf, of which only fragments survive. *See* ONESICRITUS.

**nectar** *See* AMBROSIA AND NECTAR.

**Nēleus** In Greek myth, a son of the god Poseidon and *Tyro, and king of Pylos (*see* MESSENIA). He married Chloris, the only daughter of *Niobe to survive. *Heracles, after he had killed Iphitus, sought purification from Neleus, who refused it. Thereupon Heracles killed him and all his sons except *Nestor, the youngest.

**Ně'měa** Valley in Argos, legendary scene of Heracles' encounter with the Nemean Lion (*see* HERACLES, LABOURS OF 1). It was the site of the sanctuary of Zeus and the Panhellenic Nemean games, an athletic festival held every two years (from 573 BC) in the second and fourth years of each Olympiad. The games were said to have been founded by Adrastus in memory of the child Opheltes killed there by a snake during the expedition of the *Seven against Thebes (or by Heracles).

**Ně'měan Lion** *See* HERACLES, LABOURS OF 1.

**Nemesiā'nus (Marcus Aurelius Olympius Nemesiānus)** North African Latin poet of the third century AD, author of four *pastoral poems in hexameters, long ascribed to *Calpurnius Siculus, who, with Virgil, was a strong influence on his verse. He also wrote *Cynegetica*, a hunting manual in verse which breaks off after 325 not very informative lines, at the beginning of the hunt, though we learn that the animals to be hunted include mongoose, polecat, and hedgehog.

**Ne'mesis** ('Retribution') In Greek myth, a daughter of *Nyx (Night) and the personification of righteous anger or punishment, especially that of the gods at human presumption. According to some versions she and not *Leda was loved by Zeus and laid the egg out of which Helen (of Troy) was hatched. She provides one of the rare instances where an apparent personification of an abstract quality is the object of an ancient cult. She was worshipped at Rhamnus in Attica, where a magnificent temple was built for her in the late fifth century BC, replacing a sixth-century temple destroyed by the Persians.

**Neobu'lē** See ARCHILOCHUS.

**Neopla'tonism** A modern term describing *Plotinus' version of Platonic philosophy (see PLATONISM) which dominated the ancient pagan world from the mid-third century AD to the closing of the schools of philosophy at Athens (because they were pagan) by the Christian emperor *Justinian in AD 529. It exerted a strong influence on medieval and Renaissance thought. Plotinus is the greatest philosopher of Neoplatonism and is usually considered to be its founder. Recent writers see his thought as a logical development from earlier Greek philosophy, Platonic, Aristotelian, and Stoic, and from other thinkers nearer to his own time who were working to produce a systematic philosophy based on Plato. Plotinus aimed at a comprehensive Greek philosophy, one which incorporated into a new synthesis the collected wisdom of the ancient world. But Neoplatonism was not only a philosophy; it also met a religious need of its age by showing how the individual soul might reach God. Thus it presented with traditional Greek rationalism a scheme of salvation comparable with those schemes offered by Christianity and the mystery religions (see MYSTERIES). No one before Plotinus could either achieve the desired philosophical synthesis or convey as he did the inner mystical experience of the merging of the self into some larger life. His profound metaphysical ideas gave his successors much material for further thought.

Plotinus' central doctrine was that all forms of being, material or mental, temporal or eternal, are created as the result of an 'overflow' from the One, which is therefore the cause of all existing things. The One can be identified with the Form of the Good in Plato, and therefore it is also the source of all values. The 'overflow' may be visualized as a series of concentric circles gradually removed from the One. The outermost circle represents Matter, the limit of reality. Between the One and Matter lie, in descending levels of reality, three creative principles, the World-mind (Gk. *nous*), the World-soul (Gk. *psyche*), and Nature (Gk. *physis*), the lowest of them. Human beings contain all three, and have the potential to achieve through intellectual discipline, though rarely, the ecstatic experience of unity with the One.

After Plotinus and his pupil *Porphyry the next notable Neoplatonist was the early fourth-century *Iamblichus who founded an influential school in Syria. He introduced into Neoplatonism the idea that the unity of the soul with the One could be achieved not by a person's own mystical efforts but by acts of magic correctly performed and by the power of symbols comprehensible only to the gods. The intellectual content of Plotinus' brand of mysticism was thus rejected for good.

During the fourth century Neoplatonism became the favoured pagan creed; Latin Neoplatonists included *Macrobius. It also began to influence Christian thinkers, notably Augustine. It was widely taught, but its intellectual centres were Athens and also Alexandria, where the mathematician *Hypatia and her pupil the poet and orator Synesius of Cyrene were both Neoplatonists. The last important Neoplatonist at Athens was *Proclus (AD 411–85), born at Constantinople. Many Neoplatonists carried metaphysical speculation into the realm of fantasy, mingling magic and superstition. Demonology in particular was highly developed by them, and a complete hierarchy was devised of good and evil demons (see DAIMON) who were thought to pervade the universe and were the object of semi-religious, semi-magical rites. The teaching of Neoplatonism, ended at Athens by Justinian in 529, continued at Alexandria, perhaps through an understanding with the Church, until the end of the sixth century. Neoplatonism was a strong influence on later thought.

**Neopto'lemus** In Greek myth also named Pyrrhus ('red-haired'), son of *Achilles and Dēidamīa. Odysseus was sent as messenger to summon him to the siege of Troy from Scyros after his father's death because his presence was one of the conditions necessary for taking the city. He went also with Odysseus to bring *Philoctetes to the siege. He was one of the warriors concealed in the Trojan Horse, and it was he who killed the Trojan king Priam, in some versions incurring the wrath of Apollo thereby (and as a consequence being himself killed later, by attendant priests at Delphi; however, various accounts are given of his death). He also killed the Trojan princess Polyxena at the tomb of his father Achilles. His prizes from the sack of Troy were Andromache, widow of Hector, and Helenus, Andromache's brother. In Homer Neoptolemus returned home safely, and Menelaus sent his own daughter Hermione to marry him. There was another tradition which said Neoptolemus accompanied by Andromache went to Epirus to rule over the Molossians. The kings of Epirus claimed descent from him and were often named after him (*see* PYRRHUS). In the *Andromache* of Euripides, Neoptolemus marries Hermione but is murdered by Orestes, who carries off his widow.

**neote'rics** [Gk. *neoterikos*, 'modern'] Greek term often used to describe a postulated 'modern school' of poets at Rome, in imitation of Cicero, who, writing in 50 BC, referred to some of them sarcastically in Greek as *hoi neōteroi* ('the young ones'); elsewhere he referred to probably the same people as *poetae novi*, 'new poets'. His mention of *cantores Euphorionis*, perhaps meaning 'singers praising Euphorion', is likely to be a similar reference. Of their writings only the poems of *Catullus survive. They avoided epic and drama as old-fashioned, and turned for their models to *Callimachus and the Hellenistic Greek poets (*see* EUPHORION), aiming at perfection in miniature, and experimenting with new metres, different kinds of language, new words (often Greek), new themes (romantic, exotic, some bizarre), and a mannered style. As well as Catullus the neoterics would have included *Calvus, *Cinna, Bibaculus, and Cornificius. Virgil felt their influence but their style lived on chiefly in the works of the elegiac poets Cornelius *Gallus, Tibullus, Propertius, and Ovid, and to some extent in Virgil and Horace. *See also* PARTHENIUS.

**Nēpos, Cornēlius** (*c.*100–*c.*25 BC) Roman biographer, the earliest whose work survives; his *praenomen* is unknown. He was a native of Cisalpine Gaul like Catullus who dedicated his book of poems to Nepos (*see* CATULLUS, poem 1), with a touch of irony at the expense of the latter's 'laborious and learned' universal history in three books, *Chronica* (which has not survived). Nepos was also a friend of Cicero and, more especially, *Atticus. His writings included love poems, a book of anecdotes and other information (*Exempla*), and a series of 'Lives of famous men', *De viris illustribus*, in at least sixteen books, of which one survives on foreign generals (nineteen of them Greek). The Lives include Themistocles, Miltiades, Epaminondas, Pausanias, Hannibal, Hamilcar, and Datames the Persian. They are biographical sketches designed to eulogize their subjects and point a moral rather than relate the historical events of their lives. From a historical point of view they are marked by many inaccuracies and omissions and by lack of proportion (the battle of Leuctra, for example, is barely mentioned in the biography of Epaminondas). Of the Greek Lives the most interesting character portrayal is that of Alcibiades. There also survive a short Life of the Elder Cato, and a longer one of Atticus, of whom Nepos can speak with intimate knowledge, and whose stance of political neutrality Nepos understood and shared. Both of these Lives show greater acumen.

**Neptune (Neptūnus)** Ancient Italian god of water, of whom in his original form hardly anything is known. The etymology of his name is uncertain. He was worshipped at the festival of the Neptunalia on 23 July; of the ritual we know only that arbours of foliage were erected, and the object may have been to obtain sufficient water at this hot and dry time of year. Under Greek influence he became a sea-god and was identified with *Poseidon. Owing to Poseidon's connection with horses, and because horses were associated with the Roman god Consus, the latter was identified with Neptune.

**Nē'reïds** *See* NEREUS.

**Nē'reus** In Greek myth, a sea-god, represented as very old, the son of Pontus, husband of the Oceanid Doris (*see* OCEANUS), and father of the Nereids, the sea-maidens. He is praised by Hesiod and Pindar for his benevolent justice, and like other 'old men of the sea' he had great wisdom and the gift of prophecy (*see* HERACLES, LABOURS OF 11), and could transform himself into various shapes (*cf.* PROTEUS). Two of the Nereids were famous, Thetis (*see* PELEUS) and *Galatea.

**Nēro** (AD 37–68) Roman emperor 54–68, son of Cn. Domitius *Ahenobarbus and *Agrippina (3) the Younger. His mother was later the fourth wife of the emperor Claudius, who adopted Nero as son and heir. Originally named Lucius Domitius Ahenobarbus, he assumed on his adoption the name of Nero, a *cognomen* in the Claudian *gens* (*see* NAMES [Roman]) first held by a son of Appius *Claudius Caecus the Censor, from whom the emperor was descended. (In order to strengthen his rather remote claim to the throne much was made of his connections to the deified Augustus.) The name is said to be a Sabine word meaning 'brave and energetic'. Nero was only 16 when he succeeded in 54 and the first five years of his reign ran smoothly under the guidance of his mother and his former tutor *Seneca the Younger. All witnesses attest that this was a golden period. In 59, however, he had his mother Agrippina murdered, his barren wife Octavia (daughter of Claudius) suffering the same fate in 62 to facilitate his marriage to his pregnant mistress Poppaea Sabina. The baby, a girl, died at four months. Nero's reign swiftly degenerated. He pursued his genuine artistic enthusiasms with greater freedom, and he encouraged the upper classes to take lessons in *dancing and singing. Having introduced quinquennial public games in the Greek manner to Rome in 60, he gave a musical performance himself at their second celebration in 65, to the disgust of the senatorial class. In 64 a large part of Rome was destroyed in a disastrous fire; Nero took advantage of the ruin of his own house to build himself a magnificent palace, the Domus Aurea (*Golden House), and it was rumoured (probably unjustly) that the fire had been started on his orders. He made the Christians the scapegoats and savagely persecuted them (according to tradition St Peter and St Paul suffered martyrdom at this time). In 65 a plot was discovered, to assassinate him and make C. Calpurnius *Piso (see (3)) emperor. Many distinguished men were executed or forced to commit suicide, among them Seneca the Younger, Petronius, and the poet Lucan.

Despite another conspiracy at Beneventum Nero set out in 66 for Greece to perform at all the Greek games. In November 67 at a special celebration of the *Isthmian games at Corinth he announced the liberation of Greece from Roman administration and taxation. He returned to Rome in March 68 and was faced with revolts in the provinces. When the praetorian guard deserted (*see* PRAETORIANS), Nero fled Rome and committed suicide. His last words are reputed to have been, 'What an artist dies in me!' (*qualis artifex pereo!*). Suetonius describes him as having pleasant features but a spotty complexion, yellow hair, spindly legs, and a prominent belly, and as being careless of his appearance.

**Nerva, Marcus Cocce'ius** (AD 30?–98) Roman emperor AD 96–8. He was distantly connected with the Julio-Claudian family, and had come to the fore while aiding Nero in the suppression of the Pisonian conspiracy in 65 (*see* PISO (3)). Nero also admired his poetry. Despite this he was chosen by the emperor Vespasian as his colleague in the consulship of 71, and again by the emperor Domitian in 90. He appears to have taken no part in the plot to murder Domitian, but after the latter's assassination in 96 the senate chose him as emperor and he aimed in every way to contrast with his predecessor. He did much to justify the aspirations expressed on his coinage: 'freedom', 'salvation', 'equity', 'justice'. Tacitus observed that he combined two incompatible qualities, liberty and imperial rule. The army, however, which had admired Domitian, was hostile and there was rebellion among the praetorian guard (*see* PRAETORIANS). At this critical time in October 97 he adopted Trajan as his heir. He died in January 98. Having been born of a family from the old Latin colony of Narnia (modern Narni) he was the last strictly Italian Roman emperor.

**Nessus** *See* HERACLES.

**Nestor** In Greek myth, youngest son of *Neleus and king of Pylos. He lived to a great age, and in Homer's *Iliad* is represented as having outlived two generations, while retaining considerable mental and physical vigour. He fulfils the role of an elder statesman; though full of long-winded advice and inclined to be anecdotal, it is he who suggests the Embassy to Achilles in *Iliad* 9. In the *Odyssey* he is shown as having returned safely from Troy to Pylos, where he entertains Odysseus' son Telemachus. For the death of his son *see* ANTILOCHUS. The Mycenaean vase of beaten gold known as the 'cup of Nestor' (National Museum, Athens) is so called because it resembles (in simpler form) the great gold cup, brought by Nestor from Pylos, described in *Iliad* 11. Nothing is known about his death.

**Nica'nder (Nikandros)** (of Colophon, an Ionian Greek city in Asia Minor) Hellenistic Greek *didactic poet of the second century BC, of whose numerous works there survive only two didactic hexameter poems, the *Theriaca* ('On poisonous creatures') and the *Alexipharmaca* ('Antidotes to poison'). He also wrote the *Georgica*, on farming, which had some influence on Virgil, and a mythological poem (*Heteroioumena*, 'Metamorphoses') which appears to have been an influence on Ovid when the latter composed his *Metamorphoses*. His poems became standard works on toxicology, and with their blend of magic and *medicine contain some interesting and out-of-the-way pieces of folklore.

**Ni'cias** (*c.*470–413 BC) Athenian politician and general admired by his contemporaries, including Thucydides, for his virtuous and upright life. After the death of Pericles at the beginning of the *Peloponnesian War, he became one of the political leaders at Athens in opposition to Cleon; his opinions were moderate and he aimed for peace with Sparta as soon as possible on terms favourable to Athens. He was largely responsible for the Peace of 421 that bears his name, short-lived though it proved to be. Despite his disapproval of the ambitious *Sicilian Expedition, he was appointed one of its generals, with Lamachus and Alcibiades, in 415. Its disastrous outcome may have been in part the result of his irresolute leadership, shown by his fear of condemnation at Athens if he withdrew from Sicily after a defeat, and his yielding to the soldiers' unwillingness to march away for 27 days after an eclipse of the moon; Thucydides says that he was 'too much given to divination', and Plutarch that he kept his own domestic seer. The Athenians refused to relieve him of his command despite his illness. During the final battle Nicias surrendered to prevent further slaughter and was put to death, 'a man who of all the Greeks of my time', wrote Thucydides, 'least deserved such a fate, because throughout his life he had practised every virtue'. His great wealth was derived from the Laurium silver mines, but he spent generously on *liturgies.

**Nicomachean Ethics** [Gk. *ēthika*, 'matters of character [*ēthos*]'] One of two treatises by *Aristotle on ethics, and the one commonly referred to simply as Aristotle's *Ethics*. It is in ten books and is named for Aristotle's son Nicomachus, who may have edited the text. The other treatise, known as the *Eudemian Ethics* (named for *Eudemus, a friend and pupil of Aristotle), covers much the same ground. Its books 4, 5, and 6 are the same as books 5, 6, and 7 of the Nicomachean, which is usually thought to be a revision of the other although some differences of view between the two remain. Their relationship is still debated.

For Aristotle, acquiring a good character is a practical matter. 'We are engaging in this enquiry not in order to know what goodness is but in order to become good people.' To discover the end to which conduct should be directed Aristotle accepts, as most people do, that the aim of human activity is happiness (Gk. *eudaimonia*), a word which in Greek means something like 'flourishing', 'doing well'. Aristotle wants to show how a person can lead a flourishing life. He argues that everything possesses its own particular 'excellence' (Gk. *arete*), the quality or qualities that make it peculiarly what it is. One can talk about the 'excellence' of an axe or of a horse. Human excellence is reason and intellect, which are found in the soul. If humans are to flourish they must exercise the distinctively human faculty of reason. It therefore emerges that *eudaimonia* is 'an activity of the soul in accordance with excellence'. The excellence in accordance with which a person must act includes the intellectual virtues—knowledge, (practical) wisdom, good judgement—but humans can also distinguish between good and bad, so *eudaimonia* requires them to have the virtues of character which we think of as moral virtues—courage, generosity, fair-mindedness, and so on. Action is under the control of reason but it responds to the stimulus of desire. Aristotle believes that correct response in a person requires a disposition to choose a mean, intermediate between too much and too little action, e.g. between asceticism and yielding to temptation—what Horace was to call the 'Golden Mean', something precious and hard to find (*Odes* 2.10.5). Aristotle also regards *friendship as a kind of excellence by which he sets great store, and on which he writes interestingly.

Among the many topics raised originally by Plato and then treated more systematically by Aristotle is that of *akrasia* (Gk., 'incontinence', weakness of will'), first considered by Socrates and Plato, which manifests itself in acting against one's own best judgement and especially in knowingly doing what is bad for oneself, i.e. being unable to resist temptation. Socrates argued that such a state was impossible; apparent incontinence was in fact ignorance of what is best. Aristotle, observing that this is not what most people think, considers the problem at some length in book 7.

In the last book of the *Ethics* Aristotle seems to go further: human intellect is now 'the divine within us, our sovereign and best element', and he goes on to praise the life that is devoted to 'contemplation of the eternal'. There seems to be an incompatibility here between this advocacy of the contemplative life and the aim of achieving 'flourishing' which is the subject of the rest of the work.

Aristotle's *Ethics* are related to his *Politics*: the latter too has a practical purpose, and the investigation of happiness is part of politics, since law-givers must frame laws in accordance with human aims.

The *Ethics* had an impact upon later philosophy from soon after Aristotle's death in 322 BC, affecting the establishment of *Stoicism (c.300 BC) and the thought of *Epicurus (d. 270 BC). It has continued to be the subject of commentary, exegesis, discussion, and argument from late antiquity to the present day.

**Nīco'machus** Son of *Aristotle; according to an ancient source, Aristotle dedicated to him the *Ethics* that bear his name (see NICOMACHEAN ETHICS), but perhaps the work is so called because he edited it.

**Night** See NYX.

**Nigrī'nus** See LUCIAN.

**Nīkē** The Greek goddess of Victory, said by Hesiod to be the daughter of the Titan Pallas and of (the river) Styx who like Nike herself helped Zeus to victory against the *Titans. She was the goddess of athletic as well as military victory. She became especially common on vases after the Greek victory at Marathon in 490 BC, and was often depicted with two or four wings.

**Nī'obē** In Greek myth, daughter of *Tantalus and wife of Amphion, mother of six children (according to Homer; the number varies later). She boasted of them to the goddess *Leto, who had only two children, Apollo and Artemis. Thereupon Apollo and Artemis killed all Niobe's sons and daughters with their arrows (but see NELEUS). Niobe wept for them until turned into a column of stone on Mount Sipylus in Lydia (visited by the traveller *Pausanias (2) in the second century AD, and still to be seen).

**Ni'reus** After Achilles, the best-looking Achaean in the Trojan expedition, who became a standard literary example of male beauty.

**Nīsus** 1. In Greek myth, son of Pandion and king of Megara, whose life and his city's safety depended on a lock of red (or purple) hair on his white head. His daughter Scylla cut it off so that the city would fall to the besieging general *Minos, for a bribe or for love. Minos, horrified, drowned Scylla (or she drowned herself). Nisus was turned into an osprey, Scylla into the bird *ciris* pursued by him. The port of Nisaea was named after him. Megareus, the husband of Nisus' daughter Iphinoe, gave his name to the city. (See APPENDIX VIRGILIANA [*Ciris*]).

2. Companion of Aeneas in Virgil's *Aeneid*, presented as the devoted lover of the young and headstrong Euryalus. He helps Euryalus win the foot-race in book 5 and dies avenging him in a night-sortie from the Trojan camp in Italy (book 9).

**nō'bilēs** 'Nobles', i.e. the 'well-known'; at Rome, those families, whether *patrician or *plebeian, whose members had held *curule magistracies (later, the consulship only), and were therefore allowed to have images (*imagines*) of their ancestors. They enjoyed high status. At all times it was possible, though rare, for a man not of a noble nor even of a senatorial family to achieve the consulship, usually with the backing of noble families; if he succeeded he was known as a *novus homo*, 'new man', 'recruit'. Under the empire the word still chiefly described the descendants of republican consuls, but most of the noble families had died out by the middle of the second century AD.

**Noctēs A'tticae** See GELLIUS.

**nome** [Gk. *nomos*] In Greek music, said to have been a style of song written to a prescribed 'tuning' (see MUSIC [Greek 5]) and with a definite rhythm. There were seven types which could either be played on the lyre or on the *aulos. When the 'new style' of music came into fashion in the late fifth century BC (see TIMOTHEUS) nomes took new forms.

**nōmen, cognō'men,** etc. *See* NAMES [Roman].

**nomos–physis antithesis** [Gk. *nomos*, 'law', 'norm', 'convention', seen in opposition to *physis* 'nature'] In late fifth-century Athens a particular argument of the *sophists concerned whether the widely accepted if mostly unwritten norms of political and ethical behaviour existed by nature or by convention, and so whether they operated everywhere at all times or applied only to people and if so only to particular countries or even particular individuals (see PROTAGORAS). If, as Hesiod says, Zeus gave justice (*dikē*) to all humans as a norm, *nomos*, for behaviour (*Works and Days* 276), then *Antigone for example is justified in obeying these 'unwritten laws' and burying her brother's corpse, as she does in Sophocles' tragedy of that name. But if belief in the gods is questioned then the enforcement of uncodified moral norms is also questionable. Support for nature, *physis*, as opposed to *nomos* gave rise to ideas of equality between individuals and nations and of human kinship: distinctions of race, class, wealth etc could then be thought of as existing merely by convention. On the other hand, support for *physis* also produced men like Callicles in Plato's *Gorgias who argued that laws exist only for the benefit of the weak, who are thereby able to curb nature's intention that might is right. In the atmosphere of revolution in Athens at the end of the fifth century BC (see OLIGARCHY) this argument was seen to have political implications. *See also* ANALOGY AND ANOMALY; ANTIPHON; *CRATYLUS*; CYNICS; LAW, NATURAL.

**Nones** [Lat. *Nōnae*, the 'ninth day [before the Ides]'] One of the three named days, with the *Kalends and the *Ides, used to reckon dates in each month of the Roman *calendar. The Nones fell on the fifth day except in March, May, July, and October, when they fell on the seventh. Thus 2 April, for example, was by Roman inclusive reckoning 'the fourth day before the Nones of April', *ante diem quartum Nonas Apriles*, or in brief, a.d. iv Non. Apr.

**Nonnus** (fifth century AD, from Panopolis in Egypt) Author of a Greek epic poem *Dionysiaca*, in forty-eight books (the longest ancient poetic text), on the antecedents of Dionysus' birth, the birth itself (in book 8), and his struggle to obtain recognition as a god against the enmity of Hera. Books 13–48, which deal with Dionysus' expedition against the Indians, are Nonnus' equivalent of the *Iliad*. His elaborate and metrically strict style is of interest to metricians. The poem contains a large fund of mythological learning which marks the author as a 'learned' poet in the manner of Callimachus. Nonnus may also be the author of a translation of St John's Gospel into Homeric hexameters.

**Nostoi** ('Homecomings') Lost poem of the *Epic Cycle in five books ascribed to Homer, Agias, or Eumelus. It describes the various returns of some Greek heroes from Troy and ends with the murder of Agamemnon, the revenge of his son Orestes and the homecoming of his brother Menelaus. A work with the same title was written by Stesichorus.

**Notus** (Gk. Notos, Lat. Auster) The south wind.

**novel** Romantic narrative in rhetorical prose. **Greek.** Five complete novels survive (together with two summaries and a number of papyrus fragments): *Leucippe and Cleitophon* by Achilles Tatius; *Chaereas and Callirrhoe* by Chariton; *Aethiopica* or *Theagenes and Chariclea* by Heliodorus; *Daphnis and Chloe* by Longus; and *An *Ephesian Tale* by Xenophon of Ephesus. The novel as a literary genre seems to have developed in the Hellenistic age, but flourished especially from the second century AD onwards. It was poor in characterization but strong in plot, typical themes being the separation of two lovers, hair-breadth escapes from a series of appalling perils and adversities, and final reunion and a happy ending. Virginity and preserving the chastity of the heroine, are of vital importance. *See also* LUCIAN, for *Lucius or the Ass*, and PSEUDO-CALLISTHENES.

**Latin.** The *Satyricōn* ('[Tales] of satyrs') by *Petronius (d. AD 66) is the first Latin work we have that can properly be called a novel; enough survives to show that it contained a continuous narrative of considerable length. It is itself partly a parody of romantic novels. In about the middle of the second century AD appeared *Apuleius' *Metamorphoses* (also known as *The Golden Ass*), a series of tales attached to the hero's adventures in the form of an ass. This novel has a surprising and serious ending in the description of the hero's initiation into the *mysteries. Apart from these two very little is known about the Latin novel. The *Milesian Tales* were an influence on both. The anonymous *History of Apollonius, King of Tyre*, may have been written originally in Greek in the third century AD; in about the sixth century it was translated into Latin and given a Christian slant. It is the ultimate source of Shakespeare's *Pericles*.

**No'vius** *See* ATELLAN FARCES.

**novus homo** ('new man', 'recruit'), term used at Rome to describe the first man in a family to obtain a *curule magistracy, and in particular the consulship. *See* NOBILES.

**nudity** In Greece in classical times male nudity in the *gymnasium and in the games was normal, and Greeks thought that their willingness to appear nude in public distinguished them from the *barbarians. When training in the gymnasium athletes rubbed olive oil over their bodies to preserve their skin from damage through the grit and dust which enabled wrestlers to get a grip. In a famous passage Thucydides (1.6.5) states that the Spartans were the first to strip naked and rub themselves with oil in athletic exercises, though the ancient custom (observed at the Olympian games) was to wear loincloths, until 'not many years ago'. An ancient epigram identifies the first athlete to run naked in the Olympian games as Orsippos of Megara in 720 BC.

**Numa Pompi'lius** In legendary Roman history, successor of Romulus as second king of Rome. He had, according to tradition, a long and peaceful reign (715–673 BC), regarded in later times as a sort of golden age. Many distinguished Roman families claimed descent from him, and the Romans attributed to him many of their religious institutions: festivals, sacrifices and other rites, all recorded in the ritual calendar as days for public business or religious observance; the priesthoods of Jupiter, Mars, and Quirinus; and the *pontifices*, the Vestal Virgins, and the Salii. He also founded the temple of *Janus. Later legends say that he received counsel from the nymph *Egeria, and make him a disciple of the Greek philosopher and mystic *Pythagoras (in defiance of chronology) to account for similarities between early Roman religion and Greek cults in south

Italy, where Pythagoras lived. Most of the reforms attributed to him were probably the result of a long process of cultural development and religious change.

## numbers

**Greek.** The Greek names for the numbers 1 to 10 are: *hēīs, duo, trēīs, tessarĕs* (or *tettares*), *pentĕ, hex, hepta, octo, ennĕa, deka*. Neither Greeks nor Romans had the equivalent of zero but *see* PTOLEMY. The system commonly found in papyri and manuscripts for writing numbers is based on the *alphabet and is as follows:

| | |
|---|---|
| 1–5 | $\alpha$–$\epsilon$ |
| 6 | ς (stigma, a small-letter version of the digamma) |
| 7–9 | $\zeta$–$\theta$ |
| 10–80 (by tens) | $\iota$–$\pi$ |
| 90 | ϙ (koppa, not in the Attic Greek alphabet) |
| 100–800 (by hundreds) | $\rho$–$\omega$ |
| 900 | ϡ (sampi, in the Carian alphabet, equivalent to $\sigma\sigma$ or $\tau\tau$) |

It is customary to add a tittle to each character for numbers up to 999, thus: $\alpha'$, $\beta'$, etc. Higher numbers are written as follows:

| | |
|---|---|
| 1,000–9,000 (by thousands) | ,$\alpha$–,$\theta$ |
| 10,000 | M |

Multiples of 10,000 are indicated by writing the multiplier on top. Thus (e.g.):

$$21,527 \quad \overset{\beta}{M},\alpha\phi\kappa\zeta$$

(For Archimedes' system of expressing very large numbers *see* ARCHIMEDES.)

**Roman.** The Latin names for the numbers 1 to 10 are: *unus, duo, tres, quattuor, quinque, sex, septem, octo, novem, decem*. Roman numerical signs, originally special characters, gradually developed into letters of the alphabet as follows:

I = 1; V = 5; X = 10; L = 50; C = 100; D = 500; M = 1,000.

Horizontal lines were often used to denote thousands; thus $\overline{V}$ = 5000. A notation was constructed by conventions for adding or subtracting according to the following rule: when two figures stand side by side, if the right-hand figure is the larger, the left-hand figure is to be subtracted from it; if the left-hand figure is the larger, the right-hand figure is to be added: e.g. IX = 9; XI = 11; MCM = 1,900. When, as in this last example, a smaller numeral occurs between two larger, it is subtracted from the numeral on the right.

**numen** In ancient Roman religion, the 'expressed will of a divinity'. The word is derived from *nuĕrĕ* 'to nod' (a god is thought to nod to indicate his will). The *numen Augusti*, the will of the emperor Augustus, received a cult expressing awareness of the exceptional power of the ruler.

**Ny'cteus** See ANTIOPE.

**nymphs** [Gk. *nymphē*, 'maiden'] In Greek myth, female personifications of various natural objects, rivers, trees, mountains; they were vague beings, young and beautiful, fond of music and dancing, long-lived but not immortal, usually gentle, occasionally formidable. They possessed some divine gifts, such as that of prophecy. The nymphs of trees, especially oak-trees, were called dryads (*drys*, originally 'tree', but commonly 'oak-tree'). Hamadryads were tree-nymphs whose life depended on that of their tree. Nymphs of springs, rivers, and lakes were naiads; those of mountains oreads. Before the battle of Plataea against the Persians (479 BC), the nymphs of Mount Cithaeron were among the deities to whom the Athenian commander *Aristeides was told to pray by the Delphic oracle. Most nymphs are benevolent, but they punish those who do not respond to their offers of love, as in the case of *Daphnis.

**Nyx** Night, in Greek myth, a *primordial deity, one of the earliest to come into existence, emerging out of *Chaos. Her children included Death (Thanatos), Sleep (*Hypnos), and the three *Fates.

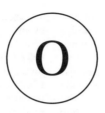

**o'belos (o'bolos)** (Lat. *obelus*) **1.** At Athens, an obol, an iron spit, used also as currency in early times; from the sixth century BC a small silver coin of equivalent value, one-sixth of a drachma. An obol was also used as a small measure of weight; *see* MONEY AND COINS 1 and WEIGHTS [Greek].

**2.** Critical sign used in the annotation of texts by Alexandrian scholars of the Hellenistic age, a horizontal stroke in the left-hand margin, originally indicating a spurious line in Homer; *see* ZENODOTUS. The modern equivalent is the obelus, 'dagger'.

**Ōce'anus (Ocean)** In Greek myth, a *Titan, son of Uranus (Heaven) and Gaia (Earth), husband (and brother) of Tethys; his daughters are the Oceanids and his sons the river-gods. Like Uranus and Gaia he also has a cosmological significance in early Greek thought as the wide river encircling the whole plain of Earth (*see* GEOGRAPHY). All the rivers of the earth are thought of as having their origin in Ocean through subterranean connections and his waters are therefore fresh. Everything in the world that is strange and fabulous is situated by the 'stream of Ocean', the Aethiopians, Cimmerians, and Pygmies, Geryon and the Gorgons, and the Gardens of the Hesperides. The sun and stars rise and set in the Ocean; a fragment of a poem by *Mimnermus describes the sun sailing along the stream of Ocean from west to east during the night.

**Octa'via 1.** (d. 11 BC) Sister of Octavian, later the emperor Augustus; she was married first to C. Claudius Marcellus by whom she had three children including a son, M. Claudius Marcellus, who married Augustus' daughter Julia (*see* MARCELLUS (2)). In 40 BC her husband died and she was married at once to Mark *Antony to seal the treaty of Brundisium. She was divorced by him in 32 BC but brought up not only their two daughters but also all his surviving children by Fulvia and Cleopatra, as well as her three children by Marcellus. Her

Roman virtues of nobility and loyalty as well as her kindness won her general admiration. One of her daughters by Antony was the mother of the emperor Claudius; the other married Lucius Domitius *Ahenobarbus (consul 16 BC) and their son Gnaeus was the father of the emperor Nero.

**2.** b. AD 40, daughter of the emperor Claudius by his third wife *Messalina, and sister of Britannicus; she married the future emperor *Nero in 53. Nero divorced her in 62 for sterility, banished her, and had her murdered soon after. She is the subject of the only surviving *fabula *praetexta*, *Octavia*.

**Octa'via** Roman tragedy, the only surviving *fabula *praetexta*, a dramatization of the fate of the emperor Nero's first wife (*see* OCTAVIA (2)). It has been handed down in the manuscripts of the plays of *Seneca the Younger, who is included as a character to protest against Nero's cruelty, but it cannot be by him: the 'prophecy' uttered by the ghost of Nero's mother about her son's fate is so true to fact that it shows the play was written after Nero's suicide (and Seneca's own death) in AD 68. The true author is unknown. The play contains too much lamentation and mythological display to be dramatically successful.

**Octa'vian** *See* AUGUSTUS.

**ode** [Gk. *ōdē*, 'song'] In Greek or Latin, a *lyric poem in stanza form (*see* STROPHE and TRIAD).

**Odes** By Horace, short Latin poems in various lyric metres. For the dates when they were written and published *see* HORACE.

Horace declares that his models for the four books of *Odes* are the early Greek lyric poets Sappho and Alcaeus. Books 1–3 comprise eighty-eight poems; book 4, published later, comprises another fifteen. Thirty-seven poems are in the alcaic metre, twenty-five in the sapphic, and the rest in a variety of asclepiads and other forms. The first six odes of book 3 are sometimes referred to as the

Roman Odes, written in stately alcaics in elevated style on patriotic themes. These grander
odes owed something to the inspiration, if not
the form, of the Greek poet Pindar, who also
had to evolve a style in which he could address
powerful rulers intimately. There are many
odes which touch on political themes, as did
the lyrics of Alcaeus. They reflect the transition
of Roman feeling from anxiety for the safety of
the state to security and triumph under the
guidance of Augustus, whose achievement
Horace admired.

Overall the *Odes* cover a variety of subjects,
private as well as public, incidents in the poet's
own life or the lives of his friends, their departures on voyages or happy returns, their love
affairs and his own, the changing seasons, the
joys of the countryside and of wine; the poet
sometimes treats these last subjects as symbolic of the brevity of human life with its ephemeral pleasures. Mostly the poems address
individuals, as did early Greek lyric poetry, or
start out with a personal reference. Many of
them show Horace's keen sense of situation
and his sharp observation of the human comedy; the moderation and urbane good sense they
express, in an often ironic and self-deprecating
tone, often with a surprise at the end, have
endeared them to readers of all periods. The
*Odes* are the product not of immediate, intense
emotion, but of meditation, not lyric in a modern sense nor yet in the original Greek sense (*see*
LYRIC POETRY). They are characterized by faultless
economy of phrasing, perfect control, balance
and harmony of thought and expression; their
euphony and intricate word-order have proved
inimitable. Horace saw them as his monument,
never to be surpassed or forgotten. He had no
successors in this field.

**ōdē'um** (Gk. *ōdeion*, Eng. odeon) In Greece,
a theatre built for musical performances and,
unlike other Greek theatres, provided with a
roof supported by pillars. A famous odeum was
built by Pericles *c*.444 BC east of and near to the
theatre of Dionysus at Athens, supposedly in
imitation of the tent of Xerxes, for concerts and
the musical contests of the *Panathenaea. The
*proagon* also took place here. The Athenians
themselves set fire to this odeum before the
invasion of Sulla in 86 BC so that the enemy
would not find in it a ready supply of wood for
the siege of the Acropolis. Another odeum was
built in the agora *c*.15 BC by M. Vipsanius
*Agrippa, but by AD 150 it had ceased to serve

its original purpose and a third was built between 160 and 174 by *Herodes Atticus.

**Ody'sseus (Ulyssēs)** (Lat. Ulixēs) In Greek
myth, hero of Homer's *Odyssey*, the son of
Lāertes, king of Ithaca, and Anticleia, daughter
of the cunning *Autolycus. Odysseus was one
of the suitors of *Helen but had no hope of
being chosen because he was poor and from
an obscure kingdom. It was he who advised
Helen's father Tyndareus to make the suitors
swear to support the chosen bridegroom. He
then married Penelope, daughter of Icarius,
king of Sparta. When Helen was carried off to
Troy, Odysseus, bound by oath like the other
suitors, joined in the Greek expedition to recover her, having failed to escape his obligation by pretending to be mad (*see* PALAMEDES).
Odysseus figures prominently in Homer's
*Iliad*, good in counsel no less than in battle,
cool, energetic, tactful, and at times cunning.
Several stories lay great emphasis on this last
trait. He behaves notably in the embassy to
Achilles (book 9) and the night expedition
with Diomedes (book 10). After the death of
Achilles a quarrel arose between Ajax, son of
Telamon, and Odysseus in the contest for
Achilles' armour (*see* ILIAD, LITTLE). Since Odysseus was much the better speaker he easily
persuaded the army that he had best served
the Greek cause, and won their vote. Ajax,
mortified, committed suicide. It was Odysseus
who with Neoptolemus brought *Philoctetes to
Troy from Lemnos. The *Odyssey* relates his
adventures on the way home to Ithaca from
Troy. His dealings with the Phaeacians and
especially with Nausicaa show tact and understanding. After his safe return to Ithaca, and his
killing of the suitors of Penelope who had
thought him dead, he appeased his last
enemy the god Poseidon, founding a shrine
in his honour so far inland that an inhabitant
mistook the oar he was carrying for a winnow-
ing-fan. There he fixed the oar in the ground,
and sacrificed a ram, a bull, and a breeding
boar to Poseidon. According to the *Telegonia*
(*see* EPIC CYCLE) Odysseus met his death at the
hands of Telegonus, his son by *Circe, who had
come to Ithaca to make himself known to his
father and killed him unwittingly. See also PAL-
LADIUM and TROJAN HORSE.

In the *Odyssey* his chief characteristics are
his longing for home, his endurance of
suffering in order to get there, and his self-
control until the moment is ripe for him to

destroy Penelope's suitors. The epithets 'much-enduring' and 'cunning' in both epics refer more appropriately to his story after the Trojan War. He is less favourably depicted in some of the Attic tragedies; Euripides in particular makes him heartless and unscrupulous.

**O'dyssey (*Odysseia*)** Epic poem by *Homer, divided into twenty-four books (for this division *see* HOMER 5). It is the story of the return of *Odysseus from the siege of Troy to his home in *Ithaca, and of the vengeance he took on the suitors of his wife *Penelope. Various indications in the text suggest that the *Odyssey* is a later work than the *Iliad* (*see also* HOMER 1 and 2), but that they both belong to the same general period. The gods do not take sides, as in the *Iliad*, though Poseidon and Helios exact punishment for offences committed against them personally; Athena, hostile to the returning Greeks in the early stage of the story, later protects Odysseus and takes an active part in promoting his return. The events of the poem occupy six weeks.

When the story opens, ten years have elapsed since the fall of Troy to the Greeks. All the Greek leaders have returned to their homes, or are dead, except Odysseus, who is in the island of *Ogygia where the goddess *Calypso has detained him for seven years. Odysseus' wife Penelope has had no news of him but, hoping that he is still alive, has put off choosing a second husband from her many suitors among the island princes, by insisting that she must first finish weaving a shroud for Odysseus' father Laertes; but each night she has secretly unravelled what she had woven during the day. The trick has now been discovered and she must come to a decision. Meanwhile the suitors are staying at Odysseus' palace lavishly entertaining themselves at his expense. In the hope of hearing news his son Telemachus goes to visit Nestor at Pylos and Menelaus and Helen at Sparta; the suitors plot to ambush and kill Telemachus on his way home (books 1–4). Calypso is ordered by Zeus to release Odysseus; the latter builds a raft and sails on it for seventeen days until within sight of Scheria, the land of the Phaeacians. The god Poseidon, who hates Odysseus because he has blinded the god's son *Polyphemus, raises a storm and destroys the raft. Odysseus, after two days in the sea, buoyed up by a scarf given him by the sea-goddess Ino, is washed up on the shore of Scheria (book 5). He

is found by *Nausicaa, daughter of the Phaeacian king Alcinous, and by her help is hospitably received in the palace (books 6 and 7). Here he is entertained by the songs of the bard Demodocus (which include the quarrel of Odysseus and Achilles, book 8, 75–82; the love of Ares and Aphrodite, 266–366; the Trojan Horse, 499–520) and by the athletic contests of the Phaeacians.

Odysseus reveals his name and tells of his adventures since leaving Troy, first of his piratical raid on the Cicŏnes at Ismarus (on the south coast of Thrace), then of his visit to the land of the Lotus-eaters, and afterwards to that of the Cyclopes, where he encountered Polyphemus (book 9). Next he tells of his entertainment by *Aeolus and the gift of the bag containing the adverse winds (which his companions released), of his adventures with the Laestrȳgŏnes, cannibal giants who destroyed eleven of his twelve ships, and of his coming to the island of Aeaea, where the enchantress Circe turned his companions into swine; he himself was protected by the herb moly, given him by the god Hermes, and he obtained the restoration of his companions. After a year Circe released him and directed him to consult *Teiresias in the Underworld (book 10). Odysseus recounts his visit there, where he saw the ghosts of many dead heroes, their wives and daughters, and conversed with some of them, including his mother Anticleia; Teiresias then prophesied to him the manner of his return (book 11). Odysseus tells of his sailing past the *Sirens and between *Scylla and *Charybdis, and of his coming to Thrinacia, where, in spite of Teiresias' warning, his company killed the cattle of the sun-god Helios. This sacrilege brought about the destruction by Zeus' thunderbolt of the ship and its crew. Odysseus alone was carried on the wreckage to Ogygia, where Calypso received him kindly but refused to let him go (book 12). This brings him to the situation at the opening of the first book.

After finishing his tale (which became proverbial among later Greeks for a long story) Odysseus is carried in a Phaeacian ship to Ithaca. (On its return to Scheria the ship is turned into a rock by the god Poseidon.) The goddess Athena disguises Odysseus as an old beggar (book 13). He learns of the insolent and extravagant behaviour of Penelope's suitors from the faithful swineherd Eumaeus. He reveals his true identity to Telemachus, when the latter returns safely from Sparta, having escaped the ambush. Together they plot the destruction of the suitors (books 14–16). Odysseus now goes to his house where he is recognized by the old dog Argus, but in his beggar's disguise is beaten and insulted by the goatherd Melanthius and the suitors Antinŏus and Eurymachus, and fights with the beggar Irus (books 17 and 18). Odysseus is recognized by his former nurse Eurycleia, who is ordered to keep her knowledge secret. Penelope reveals her decision to marry the man who the next day will string the bow of Odysseus and shoot an arrow through a line of twelve axe-heads (book 19). The seer Theoclymenus has a vision of the doom of the suitors (book 20). Odysseus alone is able to bend and string the bow, and he shoots an arrow through the axes. He then shoots Antinŏus, and aided by Telemachus, Eumaeus, and another faithful servant, kills the rest of the suitors. Those women servants who have been their lovers are hanged. Penelope is at last convinced, by the hero's knowledge of the peculiar construction of the bedstead, that he is her husband (books 21–3). Odysseus makes himself known to his father Laertes. The relatives of the suitors attempt revenge, but are repulsed, and the goddess Athena stops the blood-feud (book 24).

**Oecono'micus** ('Household management') Treatise by *Xenophon on the management of a household and estate, in the form of a dialogue between Socrates and Critobulus, in the course of which Socrates recounts an earlier conversation (occupying most of the work) which he had with a certain Ischomachus (who seems to represent Xenophon). Chapter 4 describes the horticultural activities of the younger *Cyrus (the Persian king), and the latter's conversation with the Spartan general Lysander on the subject of gardens (imitated by Cicero in *De senectute, ch. 17). The conversation with Ischomachus is an interesting and humane account of the latter's relations with his wife, married very young so that he can train her as he will, of the wife's notionally equal and significant role in marriage, and of the running of a house. This is an intriguing work, potentially valuable for social history but hard to evaluate.

**Oe'dipus (Oidipous)** ('swollen-foot') In Greek myth, the son of *Laius, king of Thebes. What follows is pieced together from many sources: see EPIC CYCLE; for the kernel of the

story Sophocles' tragedy *Oedipus Tyrannus became the definitive account. When Amphion and Zethus gained possession of Thebes (see ANTIOPE), Laius had taken refuge with *Pelops, but had carried off his host's son Chrȳsippus. The god Apollo warned him that, as punishment, if he fathered a son that son would kill him. Laius recovered his kingdom after the death of Amphion and Zethus, and married Jocasta (Epicaste in Homer). Accordingly, when a son was born, he was given to a servant to expose on Mount Cithaeron, his feet having been transfixed by a spike. Instead the servant gave the baby to a shepherd who brought him to Polybus, king of Corinth, and Merope, his queen. These two, being childless, brought him up as their own son, naming him Oedipus from the deformity of his feet.

When Oedipus was grown up, being taunted with being no true son of Polybus, he went to Delphi to enquire about his parentage. He was told only that he would kill his father and marry his mother. Deciding therefore never to return to Corinth he wandered in the direction of Thebes and by chance encountered Laius (whom he did not know) at a place where three roads met. A quarrel ensued in which Oedipus killed Laius. He went on to Thebes, which was at that time terrorized by the *Sphinx, a monster who destroyed those who could not answer the riddle she posed. Creon, brother of Jocasta and regent of Thebes, offered the kingdom and Jocasta as wife to whoever should overcome this pest. Oedipus guessed the answer to the riddle and the Sphinx killed herself. He married Jocasta and they had two sons, Eteocles and Polyneices, and two daughters, Antigone and Ismene.

According to Homer, when it was discovered that Oedipus had married his mother, the latter hanged herself (before the birth of children), but Oedipus continued to rule in Thebes. In *Oedipus Tyrannus*, discovery was precipitated by plague and famine, and the pronouncement of the Delphic Oracle that these could be averted only if the killer of Laius was expelled from the city. Oedipus' attempts to discover the truth revealed that he himself was Laius' son and killer; Jocasta hanged herself and Oedipus blinded himself. Oedipus was deposed and went into retirement, at first shut up in Thebes. Later he went into exile, wandering, attended by Antigone, to Colonus in Attica, where he was protected by *Theseus and where he died (see

OEDIPUS AT COLONUS). His sons having quarrelled about who should succeed to the throne, Oedipus before he died put a curse on them that they should each kill the other. When they first took the throne they agreed to divide the inheritance, ruling in alternate years. Eteocles ruled first, but when his year of kingship had elapsed he refused to make way for Polyneices. The latter had spent his year of absence from Thebes at the court of Adrastus, king of Argos, and had married his daughter Argeia. Adrastus supported his son-in-law and gathered an army, headed by seven champions, the *Seven Against Thebes. Each champion was posted to one of the seven gates of Thebes, and Eteocles similarly assigned a Theban defender to each gate, deciding to confront Polyneices himself. The Argive army was routed and all the champions killed except Adrastus. The brothers Eteocles and Polyneices killed each other.

Creon, now king of Thebes, ordered that the bodies of the enemy, including that of Polyneices, should not be buried (see DEATH, ATTITUDES TO). What followed is variously told. One version is given by Euripides in the *Suppliants*. Sophocles, in *Antigone*, tells how Antigone, rebelling against Creon's decree, contrived secretly to perform the burial rite for her brother. For this Creon had her placed alive in a stone tomb, although she was to marry his son Haemon. There she hanged herself, and Haemon stabbed himself beside her body. The story was related in the lost poem of the Epic Cycle *Thebaïs*. See also EPIGONE; *PHOENISSAE* (2); THEBAID.

## Oe'dipus

Roman tragedy by *Seneca (2), based on Sophocles' play *Oedipus Tyrannus*, but with long descriptions of the plague at Thebes, and of necromantic and sacrificial rites. Jocasta's suicide takes place on stage.

## Oe'dipus at Colō'nus (Oidipous epi Kolōnōi)

(Lat. *Oedipus Colōneus*) Greek tragedy by *Sophocles written not long before his death in 406/5 BC, produced in 401 BC by his grandson Sophocles the Younger, and winning a posthumous victory.

*Oedipus, blind and banished from Thebes, has wandered, attended by his daughter Antigone, to Colonus, a deme of Attica a little north of Athens. He is warned by the inhabitants to leave, but having learnt that this is the locality foretold in an oracle as the place where he will

die, refuses to go. Theseus, king of Athens, is appealed to, and assures Oedipus of his protection and of a burial place on Attic soil; in this way his spirit will be a protection to Athens (see HEROES). Oedipus' second daughter Ismene arrives and tells him of the quarrel between his sons Eteocles and Polyneices for the throne of Thebes (see SEVEN AGAINST THEBES), arousing his anger against them. Creon, regent of Thebes and brother of Oedipus' dead wife Jocasta, arrives to seize Oedipus so that Thebes and not Athens may have his body; his guards carry off Ismene and Antigone, and Creon himself is about to lay hands on Oedipus when Theseus intervenes and rescues him and his daughters. Meanwhile Polyneices has arrived and with professions of repentance asks for his father's favour in his struggle with Eteocles. Oedipus turns on him with bitter anger and places on his sons a curse that they may die by each other's hand. Peals of thunder warn Oedipus that the time of his death is approaching. He withdraws, and a messenger reports that he blessed his daughters, withdrew to a lonely spot, and in the presence of Theseus alone met his end, the exact form of which remained unknown to the messenger.

## Oe'dipus Tyra'nnus (Oidipous Tyrannos)

(Lat. *Oedipus Rex*, 'Oedipus the king') Greek tragedy by *Sophocles, of unknown date; some tenuous indications suggest it may have been written in the years following 430 BC. The tetralogy (see TRAGEDY 2) of which it was part is reputed to have come only second in the dramatic competition, yet *Oedipus Tyrannus* itself is regarded by many as Sophocles' masterpiece, and was particularly admired by Aristotle (in the *Poetics*). It deals with that portion of the story of *Oedipus in which he is king of Thebes and husband of Jocasta.

The events of the play are as follows. Oedipus learns from the Delphic oracle that a plague which has fallen on the city is due to the presence there of the murderers of king Laius. He calls upon all who have any knowledge of the matter to come forward. Teiresias, the blind seer, is first summoned. He knows the truth but at first refuses to divulge it. Accused by Oedipus of plotting with Creon, Jocasta's brother, against him, Teiresias then reveals the truth, rather cryptically, but it sounds too far-fetched for Oedipus to entertain it. Oedipus next turns against Creon whom he charges with trying to oust him from the throne. He is deeply disturbed by Jocasta's description of the scene of Laius' death and of the retinue he then had with him, which matches the circumstances in which Oedipus himself had once killed a man. On one point he seems now to receive enlightenment: a messenger comes from Corinth to announce the death of the king Polybus and the election of Oedipus to succeed him, and Oedipus, still dreading that he may unwittingly marry his mother in fulfilment of the oracle, expresses reluctance about returning to Corinth. But the messenger then reveals that Oedipus is not in fact the son of Polybus; he himself had given Oedipus as a baby to the king and his wife Merope, having received the baby from a shepherd on Mount Cithaeron (near Thebes). Whose son then is he? Jocasta guesses the truth and retires. An old shepherd who has been sent for as the only surviving member of Laius' retinue at the time of the latter's death now completes the disclosure. It was he who had carried the infant Oedipus, son of Laius and Jocasta, to Cithaeron, and had from pity given him to the Corinthian. Oedipus rushes into the palace, to find that Jocasta has hanged herself, and blinds himself with her brooch. Creon takes over the government and Oedipus, though begging to be sent away from the city, remains in Thebes.

**Oeneus** *See* MELEAGER.

**Oeno'mäus** In Greek myth, king of Pisa in Elis and father of Hippodamīa; *see* PELOPS.

**Oenō'nē** In Greek myth, nymph of Mount Ida near Troy, who was loved by *Paris before he knew that he was a Trojan prince. Later she tried to persuade him not to sail to Greece, where the beautiful *Helen lived, having prophetic powers and foreseeing the outcome. Failing to persuade him she promised to heal him if he was wounded. When, towards the end of the Trojan War, he was wounded by *Philoctetes with one of Heracles' poisoned arrows, he sought her help but she refused because he had deserted her. Soon after she repented, but he had already died; in her grief she hanged herself.

**Ogy'gia** In Homer's *Odyssey*, the island of *Calypso. It is described by Homer as being far away to the west beyond Scheria (generally identified in antiquity with Corcyra), and as the

'navel of the sea'; but it is not clear whether it was thought of as being in the Mediterranean or in the Ocean further west.

**Old Oligarch** The name given in modern times to the author of a short monograph (of three chapters) on the Athenian constitution of the fifth century BC, *Athenaion politeia* (2), one of two works with this title. He is so named because he appears to be an Athenian of oligarchic sympathies (*see* OLIGARCHY) critical of the contemporary democracy. The monograph has survived among the works of *Xenophon (1) but was written too early, probably in the 420s, to be by him. The evidence it provides for democratic practices and attitudes in fifth-century Athens is valuable, or would be if the reader could be sure that the text was intended to be read straightforwardly. Since no contemporary author refers to it and nothing else in this style and of this period is known, it is difficult to be sure about its purpose and literary genre. If as is generally assumed it is a serious work of its apparent date then it provides glimpses of how democracy actually worked at Athens at this time. Most acutely it emphasizes the link between the people (*demos*) and Athens' sea-power: 'it is right that it should have more power...because the *demos* mans the fleet.' *See also* COMEDY [Greek 3].

**oligarchy** [Gk. *oligarchia*, 'rule of the few'] One of the three basic categories of political constitution (with monarchy and *democracy) defined by the Greeks from the fifth century BC onwards. In oligarchy political power was limited to a section of the community, such as a few families or individuals (the oligarchs). It was characteristic of oligarchs that they possessed greater wealth and influence than the rest of the community; high birth was not a necessary condition (*cf.* ARISTOCRACY), but in Greece it commonly happened that the oligarchs were a section of the old nobility which had excluded from power the poorer nobles. Even during the second half of the fifth century BC, when Athenian ascendancy promoted democratic forms of government, there were still many oligarchic states in Greece, the most notable perhaps being at Corinth and at Thebes. Sparta, though not typical of oligarchies, set itself up as their champion. Various kinds of oligarchy are discussed by Aristotle in the *Politics*. Revolution in Athens at the end of fifth century BC resulted in the oligarchic regimes of the *Four Hundred and the *Thirty Tyrants. The government at Rome under the republic is often described as 'oligarchical'. It was certainly government by the rich. *See* NOBILES and ROMAN REPUBLIC.

**Oly'mpia** The main panhellenic sanctuary of Zeus in Greece, in the state of Elis near the west coast of the Peloponnese on the north bank of the river Alpheus. (The location is quite separate from Mount *Olympus, which is some 275km or 170 miles to the north in Macedonia.) Olympia was on a well-watered site in a fertile region among gentle hills, a fairly unusual landscape for Greece and particularly appealing to Greek sensibility. It was in marked contrast with its rival in religious importance, the main sanctuary of Apollo in the dramatic setting of *Delphi. There is archaeological evidence of prehistoric settlement at Olympia and of Mycenaean tombs. The sacred precinct of Zeus, a walled enclosure, was known as the Altis (the local dialect form of *alsos*, 'precinct'). In the early sixth century BC permanent buildings began to be erected, first the famous temple of Hera, built c.590 BC in the precinct. The temple of Zeus himself was built mid-fifth century BC on a vast scale (covering about twice the area of the *Parthenon in Athens). It housed *Pheidias' great seated statue of the god, one of the *Seven Wonders of the ancient world. Its appearance is now known only through small reproductions on coins and gems, but a good deal of the superb sculptural decoration of the temple survives (in the Olympia Museum).

As well as the temples, the precinct contained very many statues of athletes and racehorse owners who had been successful at the Olympian games, the most important part of the festival held from the early eighth century BC every four years in August or September in honour of Zeus. It was the major athletic competition of the ancient world, and the forerunner of the modern Olympic games. The original contest was the *stadion*, 'foot-race' of about 200m (*see* STADE, STADIUM); other contests were added over time, and by the fifth century the festival lasted for five days. During the month of the festival all warfare stopped. In 420 BC Sparta was excluded after she had sent an armed force against Elis during the Olympian truce. Because of their prestige the Olympian programme and rules were accepted for

games everywhere, and the four-year period between festivals, known as an *Olympiad, was used by the Greeks as a dating system. According to Pindar, the games were instituted by Heracles, although an alternative tradition ascribed the foundation to *Pelops after his victory over Oenomaus. The games were held without a break from 776 BC until at least AD 261, and finally suppressed as a pagan cult by the Christian Roman emperor Theodosius in AD 391 or soon after. In the sixth century the whole site was covered with debris from an earthquake, an event to which is owed the burial and hence preservation of many objects. *See also* ATHLETICS and HORSE-RACES.

**Oly'mpiad** (Gk. *hē Olympias*) The four-year period between two Olympian festivals (*see* OLYMPIA). Greek writers of the post-classical era often date an event by ascribing it to a particular Olympiad, each Olympiad being numbered in sequence from the first recorded games of 776 BC. The first list of Olympian victors, which such a dating system presupposes, was published by the sophist *Hippias (2) in the late fifth century BC. The numbering system seems to have been introduced by *Timaeus, who identified Olympiads by the name of the winner in the foot-race, and taken over by *Eratosthenes. The years within an Olympiad were numbered (first perhaps by Eratosthenes) one to four. Thus by this reckoning the battle of Marathon (490 BC) occurred in Olympiad 72, 3 (for strict accuracy it must be remembered that the Olympian year, like the Attic year, began in the summer). From Eratosthenes onwards all Greek dating was based on, or synchronized with, Olympiads. There was some difficulty in Roman times in relating Olympiads to the Roman consular year, which from 153 BC began on 1 January and so included parts of two Olympian years.

**Olympian gods** *See* GODS [Greek].

**Oly'mpias** Wife of *Philip II of Macedon and mother of Alexander the Great. In 331 BC, rejected by Philip in favour of another wife, she retired to her native Epirus, which she virtually ruled for a number of years; after Alexander's death in 323 she returned to Macedon, where she made Alexander's posthumous son Alexander IV sole king. Her murderous violence brought back *Cassander, who condemned her to death, and she was finally killed by the relations of those she had murdered.

**Olympic games** *See* OLYMPIA.

**Olympië'um (Olympieion)** Name given to the temple of Zeus Olympius (Olympian Zeus) at Athens, situated south-east of the Acropolis. The first temple was begun by the architects of *Peisistratus at the end of the sixth century BC. With the fall of the Peisistratid tyranny in 510 BC, work on the temple was discontinued and was not resumed until 174 BC when Antiochus IV Epiphanes, the *Seleucid king of Asia (176–165), undertook to rebuild it at his own expense, but it was again left unfinished at Antiochus' death and remained so for three centuries. In 86 BC Sulla removed some of the columns to Rome. It was finally completed by the emperor Hadrian in AD 132, making it one of the largest of Greek temples. Fifteen of its Corinthian columns are still standing.

**Oly'mpus** (not to be confused with *Olympia) The highest mountain in Greece, nearly 3000m (about 10,000 ft.) in height. It is situated at the eastern end of a chain of mountains which forms roughly the northern boundary of Greece proper, overlooking the Vale of Tempe. In Greek myth it was believed to be where the twelve Olympian *gods had their houses, built for them by the god Hephaestus, with Zeus' house occupying the summit. (The gods could also be thought of as dwelling in the heavens above Olympus.)

**Oly'nthiacs** Three political speeches by *Demosthenes (see (2) 2).

**Oly'nthus** Greek city north of Potidaea on the peninsula of Chalcidice. It was a city of mixed race, and after 433 BC became the capital of a Chalcidian confederacy. Sparta, suspicious of its power, captured it in 390 and disbanded the confederacy, which was re-formed after the Spartan defeat at Leuctra in 371. When Amphipolis fell to *Philip II of Macedon in 357, Olynthus and the confederacy went over to him, but becoming alarmed by his increasing power turned to Athens. Athens, however, failed to save the city. It was betrayed to Philip in 348 and completely destroyed.

**omens** *See* DIVINATION.

**O'mphalē** *See* HERACLES.

**o'mphalos** *See* DELPHI.

**One, the** *See* PARMENIDES; *PARMENIDES*; *SOPHIST*; PLOTINUS.

**Onēsi'critus** Greek historian with Alexander the Great in India, who with *Nearchus explored the sea-route from the mouth of the Indus to the Persian Gulf. The longest surviving fragment from his narrative of Alexander's Indian campaign describes an interview between the author and some Indian *gymnosophists. His reputation in antiquity was of being a great liar.

**Onoma'critus** An Athenian who lived at the court of the tyrant *Peisistratus and his sons at Athens in the late sixth century BC. He was engaged to collect and edit the oracles of *Musaeus and is said to have been detected by *Lasus of Hermione in inserting a false one (that the island of Lemnos would disappear into the sea). When the Peisistratids had been overthrown, they employed him to give oracles to the Persian king Xerxes which favoured his planned invasion of Greece.

**onomatopoe'ia** The formation and use of words to imitate sounds. A famous example occurs in a line of the early Roman poet Ennius: *at tuba terribili sonitu taratantara dixit* ('the war-trumpet with terrifying sound blew *taratantara*'). The word is used also, in a wider sense, of the formation of whole phrases or sentences which suggest in sound what they describe, such as Virgil's dactylic hexameter, *quadrupedante putrem sonitu quatit ungula campum* ('the horses' hooves with fourfold beat shake the crumbling plain'). For an interesting ancient discussion see *Dionysius of Halicarnassus, *De compositione verborum* 14–20.

**O'ppian (Oppiānos)** (late second century AD, of Cilicia in south-east Asia Minor) Writer of Greek *didactic poetry in hexameters. His *Halieutica* ('On fishing') is in five books; the *Cynegetica* ('On hunting', a popular topic in Greek prose), in four books, is also ascribed to him but seems to be the work of a different poet, a native of Syria, though perhaps of the same name. Both poems contain descriptive passages of power and beauty.

**Ops** Roman goddess of abundance. Her festivals, Opalia on 19 August and Opiconsivia on 25 August, were close to festivals of Consus, the god of the granary. Her oldest place of worship was a small shrine in the *Regia and she also had a temple on the Capitol.

**optimā'tēs** ('the best class') In Roman politics, until the time of the *Gracchi (*c.*133 BC) there was no serious challenge to the overwhelming predominance of the noble families in the ruling oligarchy (*see* NOBILES). In response to the rise of the *populares*, i.e. political leaders 'on the side of the people', the Roman upper class called themselves *optimates*, understanding the term both socially and morally on the model of the Greek *kaloi kagathoi*. Thus in the late republic the name was applied to the senatorial party and their supporters, those who acted in the interests of the *optimi*, the 'best men'.

**oracles** An oracle (Gk. *manteion, chrēstērion*, Lat. *orāculum*) was an answer given by a god or hero (*see* HEROES) to an individual's question (the answer usually taking the form of a command or a prediction or a statement of fact). The term may also mean the shrine itself where the answers were given. In each of the many oracular shrines in the ancient world the god was consulted in his own particular way. The most famous were those of Zeus at *Dodona in Epirus, and of Apollo at Delphi (*see* DELPHIC ORACLE). Zeus had another oracular shrine at Olympia (*see* IAMUS). Apollo had many oracles in Greece and Asia Minor of a type similar to that of Delphi. The healing god *Asclepius had a shrine at Epidaurus particularly famed for sending curative visions to the sick through incubation. The shrine of the hero *Amphiaraus at Oropus was credited with similar healing properties. One of the most famous hero-oracles was that of *Trophonius in a cave at Lebadea in Boeotia. Among foreign oracles that of Zeus *Ammon at Siwa in the Libyan desert, consulted by Alexander the Great, had a high reputation among the Greeks. Very many oracular responses to questions are known, usually on everyday matters, 'whether to marry or to sail or to lend', says Plutarch, and mostly they direct the questioner to which particular religious act is acceptable or to which particular god. It seems probable that the famous replies said to have been given on notable historical occasions (as from the Delphic oracle to the emperor Julian) are not in fact genuine. From at latest the sixth century BC collections of oracles were made and peddled (*see* ONOMACRITUS).

There were no oracular shrines in Italy comparable in importance with those in Greece. During the Roman republic oracles, apart from the Sibylline books (*see* SIBYL), were not consulted by the state. However, under the empire, and with the increased worship of Greek and oriental divinities, more attention was paid to oracular predictions. As in Greece, the collection of oracles at Rome must have begun quite early. In 213 BC at a critical time in the Second Punic War the senate made the praetor Acilius seize and suppress several collections in circulation. With the similar purpose of arresting panic the emperor Augustus had 2,000 books of prophecies burnt. The most important oracle in Italy was at Cumae, where the Sibyl's cave was situated under the temple of Apollo. At Praeneste there was an ancient and famous temple of Fortune (*see* FORTUNA), where oracles known as *sortes*, 'lots', were given: tablets, each inscribed with its own oracle, were shuffled by a child who drew one and gave it to the questioner. *Faunus was regarded as a prophetic god, as was the nymph *Carmentis (mother of Evander); both are referred to by Virgil. At the temple of Faunus at Tibur incubation was practised; a sheep was killed and the enquirer slept in its skin. The use of oracles as an aid to decision-making became particularly apparent in the second century AD with the popularization of the *sortes Virgilianae* (*see* VIRGIL), a practice said to have originated with the emperor Hadrian, by which the enquirer opened Virgil's works and chose a line at random to be a guide to the future. Copies of the *Aeneid* were deposited in temples for that purpose.

**oral poetry** Poetry composed and transmitted without the aid of writing. The term is usually applied to narrative poetry which was composed orally in pre-literate societies. The Greek epic poems of *Homer, the *Iliad* and *Odyssey*, are generally believed to be in origin oral compositions. In the 1930s the extemporizing 'guslars', the oral poets of Yugoslavia, became a point of comparison. It is characteristic of orally composed narrative poetry that it contains 'formulae' (*see* HOMER 4), repeated words, especially 'stock' epithets and phrases, even whole lines and paragraphs describing typical scenes, which enable the poet who has already committed them to memory to deliver a poem extempore when required. It is often felt that if a poem is the product of oral composition, disproportionate significance should not be given to, for example, epithets which fit the metre but not the context, or slight discrepancies between one typical scene and another. *See* EPIC.

**Ōrā'tōr** Latin treatise by *Cicero ((1)5) written in 46 BC and dedicated to M. *Brutus, which describes the ideal orator and outlines a scheme for his education. He must be a master of the three styles, the plain, the grand, and the middle. *See also* ORATORY [Roman].

**oratory** Although in general usage the two terms oratory and *rhetoric are virtually synonymous, in what follows a distinction is made between them: rhetoric is taken as the theoretical art of speaking, oratory its practical application. Both were exhaustively studied in the ancient world, for mastery of the spoken word was the key to success in the fields of politics and law, and successful careers in either field (though the two careers were generally associated) brought power, prestige, and wealth. For the classification of oratory *see* EPIDEICTIC.

**Greek.** Attic Greek oratory, in its period of splendour (from *c.*460 BC until 322 BC when Athens finally lost her freedom to Macedon; *see* ATHENS 4), produced a large number of people who professed to be able to teach it, known as rhetors (*see* RHETORIC). As is clear from Homer, effective speakers existed long before a theory of rhetoric was developed, and the early plays of Euripides show that oratory was already a well-understood art in Athens before the famous arrival of the sophist *Gorgias in 427 BC. As well as the political assemblies (*see* ECCLESIA) the large *juries made it vital for orators to be able to sway a crowd. The careers or even the lives of clients often depended on the skill of speechwriters (*see* LOGOGRAPHERS (2)). The orators *Lysias and *Demosthenes (2) both wrote speeches for others.

No speech by any of the great political figures of the fifth century survives, though the Funeral Speech of Pericles as it is reproduced by Thucydides (2.35–46) may give some idea of his elevated style. The earliest and only truly fifth-century Attic orator whose speeches in part still exist is *Antiphon (*c.*480–411 BC); he was followed by *Andocides (at the very end of the fifth and beginning of the fourth century), and the great fourth-century orators Lysias, Demosthenes, and *Aeschines. The speeches of *Isaeus and *Isocrates were all written for others to deliver. Of the remaining Attic orators

the most important were *Lycurgus (3), *Hypereides, and *Deinarchus (*see* CANONS). After the end of the fourth century BC the political situation in Greece did not give much scope for the practice of political oratory. However, from the beginning of that century important questions were being raised about the value and aims of rhetoric, particularly in education, not merely by the philosopher Plato (*see* GORGIAS and *PHAEDRUS*) but also by Isocrates. Its importance in education continued to rise, and it became the principal tool in the spread of Greek culture in Asia Minor and at Rhodes and Pergamum, where oratory of a rich, exuberant, and declamatory kind developed. This was the so-called Asianic style, in contrast with the simple lucid Attic style modelled on Lysias (*see* ASIANISM AND ATTICISM). The former term arose, according to a grammarian, when the Greek language spread into Asia (from the late fourth century BC) and the Asians used Greek circumlocutions when they did not know the precise words. Quintilian's view is that the style reflected the bombastic and boastful nature of the Asians, compared with Attic speakers who despised vapid and redundant speech. *See also* DIO CHRYSOSTOM and ARISTEIDES (2).

**Roman.** At Rome, as in Greece, the importance of oratory was recognized from early times. Even in the fourth century BC Appius *Claudius Caecus the Censor had a high reputation as an orator. In the survey that Cicero gives in his *Brutus* of the great Roman speakers, the principal names are those of *Cato the Censor, the *Gracchi (especially Gaius, described by Cicero as wise, lofty, and weighty, but lacking the final polish), M. *Antonius (grandfather of Mark Antony), L. Licinius *Crassus (consul in 95 BC, whose speeches were deliberately built up in accordance with the rules of Greek rhetoric), Julius *Caesar, C. Licinius *Calvus, an exponent of the pure Attic style, and *Hortensius, noted, on the contrary, for his luxuriant Asianism. Cicero found himself under attack as an Asianist by admirers of Calvus who thought his periodic and rhythmical style over-elaborate; he defended himself in the *Brutus* and *Orator*.

From the second century BC onwards Roman orators were a product of Greek schools (*see* ISOCRATES) or of Greek teachers who had migrated to Rome (*see* HELLENISM). Handbooks such as the *Rhetorica ad Herennium* were based on Greek models. But Greek theory was subordinate to Roman practice: it was the institutions of the law-courts and above all the senate, where affairs of state were debated before an intelligent, educated, and trained audience, that moulded the dignified Roman oratorical style. Of this wealth of eloquence only the speeches of Cicero survive.

As in Athens in the late fourth century BC, so in Rome under the empire oratory as a living art declined when the political decisions were taken by the emperor and no longer followed public debate (*see DIALOGUS DE ORATORIBUS*). But rhetoric still remained the fundamental element in *education, though now it was taught only for the law-courts or display purposes, and exercised in consequence a strong influence on all forms of literature. Professorships of rhetoric were set up in all the large cities of the empire, and for as long as the empire lasted higher education was almost entirely rhetorical. *Quintilian was the first professor of rhetoric at Rome and, like Cicero, saw rhetoric as providing the finest literary discipline. Orators or teachers of rhetoric in the West included many of the greatest figures of their time, e.g. St Augustine, St Ambrose, and *Ausonius. In many areas of classical literature and ancient literary criticism, understanding depends upon awareness of the large role rhetoric and oratory played in ancient life and culture.

**Orbi'lius Pupi'llus, Lucius** (of Beneventum, *c.*112–*c.*17 BC) A grammarian, famous as the schoolmaster at Rome of Horace, who calls him *plagosus*, 'whacker', from beatings inflicted during lessons on *Livius Andronicus' version of Homer's *Odyssey*. There is an account of him in Suetonius.

**orchestra** ('dancing-floor') *See* DIONYSUS, THEATRE OF.

**Orcus** In Roman religion Orcus is apparently a synonym of *Dis, the god of the Underworld, or the Underworld itself.

**orders** [Lat. *ordines*] At Rome in the early republic, the two hereditary estates or broad social divisions of the Roman people, namely *patricians (the rich) and *plebeians, (plebs, the poor). There was probably a distinction of birth as well as wealth at some periods. In early times the plebeians were excluded from the magistracies (political offices), the senate, and the (religious) colleges, and from intermarriage with patricians. By the third century BC the practical distinctions between patricians and

plebeians had disappeared; *see* ORDERS, CONFLICT OF. During the later republic the adjective 'plebeian' acquired the sense of pertaining to the lower social class. In the first century BC the term 'order' denotes only the senatorial or *equestrian order. Cicero's *concordia ordinum*, 'harmony of the orders', was the union of senators and equestrians; *see* CICERO (1) 3.

**orders, conflict of** At Rome, the political struggles during the early republic at the end of which the plebs achieved near political equality with the patricians (*see* ORDERS), and the wealthiest plebeians achieved their aims. The stories relating to this period form an important part of the tradition of early republican history, but probably depart some way from the reality of the situation. Debt and shortages of food and land fuelled the grievances of the plebs, which included the facts that the chief religious offices were the prerogative of the patricians, that political decisions of the popular assemblies needed patrician assent, and that most, if not all, consuls were patrician. The plebs proceeded to organize its own assemblies and appoint its own officers (first *tribuni plebis*, 'tribunes of the people', later *aediles) and achieved inviolability for them. The plebeians also kept their own records (in temples on the Aventine). *Secession was a tactic first used successfully in 494 BC, and finally in 287 BC. On this last occasion the decisions of the plebs were made binding without needing patrician approval (*see* ROME 2). From this time the plebs was no longer significantly disadvantaged, and the conflict was deemed to be over. *See also* TWELVE TABLES.

**orders of architecture** *See* ARCHITECTURE, ORDERS OF and VITRUVIUS.

**o'rĕads** (Gk. *oreiadĕs*, Lat. *orēades*) *Nymphs of the mountains.

**Orestei'a** The collective name given to the three Greek tragedies (a trilogy; *see* TRAGEDY 2) by *Aeschylus on the story of *Agamemnon, Clytemnestra, Electra, and Orestes, produced at Athens in 458 BC when it won the dramatic competition. It is the only trilogy to survive complete. The plays are *Agamemnon*, *Choëphoroe* ('Libation bearers'), and *Eumenides* ('Kindly ones', a euphemism for the *Furies).

The story is taken from the mythical history of the descendants of *Atreus in which crime led to further crime through several generations. The

*Agamemnon* opens in an atmosphere of hope mingled with foreboding, as the watchman on the roof of Agamemnon's palace in Argos looks out for the signal beacon to announce the fall of Troy. After the signal is seen, the news is confirmed by the arrival of a herald. Agamemnon's wife Clytemnestra appears jubilant, but the chorus of Argive elders recall Agamemnon's sacrifice of his daughter *Iphigeneia to enable the Greek fleet to set sail, and brood over the possible consequences. Agamemnon arrives, bringing with him the captured Trojan princess *Cassandra, his concubine. Clytemnestra treacherously welcomes him and then leads him into the palace. Cassandra, who has not spoken up to this point, is now moved to frenzied prophecy, foreseeing Agamemnon's murder and her own, as well as having a vision of the past crimes of the house, and utters a lament. She too enters the house, knowingly going to her death. The cries of the dying Agamemnon are heard. The interior of the palace is revealed, with Clytemnestra exulting over the bodies of the two victims. She answers the elders' reproaches by citing as justification Agamemnon's sacrifice of Iphigeneia. Aegisthus, her lover, appears, and subdues the elders with threats of force. The latter can only hope that one day Agamemnon's son Orestes will avenge him.

In the *Choephoroe*, Orestes, the son of Agamemnon, after years of exile, returns to Argos with his friend *Pylades, to avenge his father on the god Apollo's instructions; he comes to his father's tomb and dedicates on it a lock of his hair. The two draw aside while Electra, Orestes' sister, and a chorus of Argive women approach to pour libations on the tomb by order of Clytemnestra, who has been disturbed by ominous dreams. Electra recognizes the lock of hair and footprints nearby as strikingly similar to her own; her brother reveals himself and a reunion takes place (a scene thought by some to be mocked by Euripides in the very similar scene in his *Electra*). Electra and Orestes join in an impressive invocation of their father's dead spirit, calling upon his aid in their pursuit of vengeance. Orestes and Pylades, disguised as travellers bringing news of the former's death, enter the palace. Aegisthus is summoned and on his arrival is killed by Orestes. Clytemnestra pleads with her son for her life, and for a moment Orestes falters; but Pylades, in his only speech, reminds him of Apollo's command, and Orestes drags her into the palace and

kills her. While he is justifying his action he sees avenging Furies arrive to haunt him, and flees from them.

*Eumenides* opens to show Orestes as suppliant at the shrine of Apollo in Delphi. The Furies, forming the chorus, are asleep around him. Orestes is promised protection by Apollo, who tells him to go to Athens to seek justice from the goddess Athena. After he leaves, the ghost of Clytemnestra stirs up the Furies to pursue him. The scene changes to the front of Athena's temple on the Acropolis at Athens. Athena, acting as presiding *archon, having heard the pleas and justifications of the Furies and of Orestes, refers the judgement to a tribunal of Athenian citizens (i.e. the historical *Areopagus court for judging cases of homicide, of which this episode was the legendary foundation). The Furies prosecute, and Orestes defends himself. Athena votes last, after the other judges, and the votes are found to be equally divided. Athena therefore declares that in future, when the votes are equal the defendant is to be acquitted, as was Athenian practice at this time. (There are different interpretations of what exactly happens at this point.) The Furies are indignant at Orestes' escape, but are conciliated by Athena's promise of a permanent home in her city and honour in their new role as beneficent powers.

For the poem *Oresteia* see STESICHORUS.

**Ore′stēs** In Greek myth, son of *Agamemnon and Clytemnestra, and brother of Iphigeneia and Electra. For his story *see* PELOPS; *ORESTEIA*; *ORESTES*; *ELECTRA*; *IPHIGENEIA AMONG THE TAURIANS*. For his marriage to Hermione (daughter of Menelaus and Helen) *see* NEOPTOLEMUS.

**Ore′stēs** Greek tragedy by *Euripides produced probably in 408 BC. For the background *see ORESTEIA*.

Orestes, having killed his mother Clytemnestra and her lover Aegisthus, has been driven mad by the Furies and is being tenderly nursed by his sister Electra. The citizens of Argos are about to pass judgement on them for their crime, and a sentence of death is expected. At this point Agamemnon's brother *Menelaus appears, on his way home to Sparta from Troy, together with his wife Helen, but is too cowardly to help, although Orestes appeals to him. Sentence of death is passed on Orestes and Electra who now, urged on by Pylades, plan to kill Helen, the source of all their troubles, and to seize Menelaus' daughter Hermione as a hostage. Helen mysteriously disappears. They then threaten to kill Hermione unless Menelaus intervenes to save their lives. However, in this confused situation Apollo appears and dictates a general pacification, explaining that Helen has been carried off to heaven, and that it is Orestes' destiny to be brought to trial at Athens and, after being freed, to marry Hermione and become ruler of Argos.

**O'rganon** ('Tool') Collective name given by later commentators to Aristotle's six surviving works on logic, and so-called because logic was thought to be not merely one particular branch of philosophy but a method for thinking which was useful as a tool in all enquiries. For the titles of the individual works *see* ARISTOTLE 4 (i).

**orientalizing age** Name given to one of the five periods of the Greek era (based on the differences in pottery styles), denoting very roughly the period from 720 to 620 BC (*cf.* PROTO-GEOMETRIC; GEOMETRIC; ARCHAIC; CLASSIC). The adjective is also applied more widely to ancient art in general when it appears to adopt features of Eastern art. For example it can be applied to Etruscan metalwork and pottery, or to some of the details of Hadrian's villa, which are said to copy features found on Alexander the Great's booty from Persia.

**Orī'on** In Greek myth, a giant and a hunter of Boeotia, already in Homer identified with the constellation of that name, and the subject of various stories. He pursued the *Pleiades, and both he and they were turned into constellations. He was deprived of sight by the god Dionysus, or killed by Artemis (either because he challenged her to throw the discus against him or from jealousy because he was loved by Eos, Dawn), or stung to death by a scorpion sent by Gaia (Earth), because he boasted that he would kill all wild beasts. Ovid (*Fasti* 5.495) relates the curious story of how he was created from the urine of three gods (based on the false derivation of his name Orion from Gk. *ouron*, 'urine').

**O'rpheus** In Greek legend, a pre-Homeric poet, dated by the Greeks to a generation before the Trojan War and associated with the expedition of the *Argonauts, who were helped by his singing to resist the lure of the *Sirens.

He was said to be a Thracian, a follower of the god *Dionysus, the son of Apollo (or Oeagros) and a *Muse, perhaps Calliope, and so marvellous a player on the lyre that he could charm wild beasts and make even trees and rocks move by his music. His story is well known from the Roman poets Virgil and Ovid. He married Eurydice, a *dryad. While being pursued by *Aristaeus, Eurydice trod on a snake, was bitten and died. Orpheus went down to the Underworld to recover her and by his music induced the goddess *Persephone to let her go, but on condition that he should not look back at her as she followed him. He forgot, looked back, and Eurydice immediately vanished for ever. Later Orpheus was torn to pieces by women, either Thracians who were jealous of his love for Eurydice, or by *maenads because he did not honour their god Dionysus (this story was the subject of a lost play *Bassarae* by Aeschylus). His severed head, floating down the Thracian river Hebrus, and in some versions still singing, reached the island of *Lesbos, the home of lyric poetry, where it gave prophecies before being buried.

From perhaps the middle of the sixth century onwards the authorship of several poems that referred to mystery cults was attributed to Orpheus (*see* MYSTERIES). These poems dealt with purifications and initiations; secret rites that were supposed to free participants from ancient guilt, and impart to them better hopes for the after-life, were performed according to the books of Orpheus and Musaeus (*see also* ONOMACRITUS). The term Orphism is sometimes used to describe the beliefs and practices of those who took part in mystery cults based on the poems attributed to Orpheus, or who engaged in ascetic practices. However, it is uncertain to what extent Orphism can be thought of as a unified spiritual movement. Hexameter poems ascribed to Orpheus survive and an entire corpus of hymns, but the main texts are theogonies, the earliest dating to the first half of the fifth century BC. Gold tablets have also been found, intended to accompany the soul's journey to the Underworld. Interesting information has come from the Derveni papyrus, which contains an ancient commentary on the theogony of Orpheus. Orphic myth, now known mostly from references in Plato and especially the Neoplatonists, explained the mixture of good and evil in human nature by the myth of *Dionysus Zagreus. It departed from normal Greek beliefs by making the guilt and punishment of the individual after death the centre of its doctrine (*see* DEATH, ATTITUDES TO); it would seem that, according to Orphic myth, men bear the guilt for the death of Dionysus Zagreus, and they have to pay the penalty after death to Persephone before she allows them to rise to higher existence. It also taught the transmigration of souls (having much in common with Pythagoreanism); after the soul has been reincarnated three times and has each time lived a virtuous life, it dwells in the *Isles of the Blest for ever. But as well as a virtuous life, ritual purity and correct knowledge as prescribed by Orphic doctrine are necessary. Evildoers, and the uninitiated, risk punishment after death. The high ethical tone and ascetic practices of some of the followers of Orpheus became debased by the superstition and charlatanism of others, and although Pindar and Plato were attracted by some of the doctrines, to others of the fifth century BC 'Orphic' was a term of contempt. There was a revival of belief under the Roman empire.

**Orphism** *See* ORPHEUS.

**Orsippos** *See* NUDITY.

**Orth(r)us** In Greek myth, the dog of *Geryon and the offspring of the monsters Typhon and Echidna. *See* HERACLES, LABOURS OF 10 and SPHINX.

**Orty'gia** *See* LETO.

**Ossa** Mountain in Thessaly; *see* PELION and OTUS AND EPHIALTES.

**o'stracism (*ostrakismos*)** At Athens in the fifth century BC, an institution traditionally attributed to *Cleisthenes (2) in 508 BC whereby a prominent but unpopular citizen might be banished without loss of property for ten years. Each year the *ecclesia* voted on whether an ostracism should be held that year. If an ostracism was agreed upon, every citizen who wished to vote scratched on a potsherd (*ostrakon*; *see* OSTRAKA) the name of the person whose banishment from the state seemed to him necessary for public well-being. Provided there was a total of 6,000 votes cast in all, the person whose name appeared most often was banished. Prominent men known to have been ostracized are *Xanthippus, *Aristeides (1), *Themistocles, *Cimon, and *Thucydides son of Melesias. Ostracism existed in a few other Greek states. At Syracuse the institution was

called 'petalism' because the names were written on olive-leaves (*petala*).

**o'straka** ('potsherds') Broken fragments of pottery used as writing material, especially in Egypt after the Greek conquest at the end of the fourth century BC. Ostraka were not greatly used for writing in Greece except as voting tablets (*see* OSTRACISM). Latin ostraka have been found near Carthage.

**Otho, Marcus Sa'lvius** (AD 32–69) Roman emperor briefly in AD 69 in the chaos that followed Nero's death. He was a friend of Nero and the husband of *Poppaea Sabina, with whom Nero fell in love and later married after her divorce. Otho was sent to Lusitania as governor in 58 and remained there until Nero's death in 68. He organized a conspiracy among the praetorian guard (*see* PRAETORIANS) and was hailed as emperor on 15 January 69, but he was decisively defeated in battle by *Vitellius and committed suicide on 16 April.

**Ōtus and Ephia'ltēs** In Greek myth, giant sons of Alōeus (whence they are called Alōīdae), or of Poseidon and the wife of Aloeus. They attacked the gods and tried to pile Mount Ossa on *Olympus, and Mount Pelion on Ossa, in order to reach the heavens themselves and attack the gods there. They were destroyed by Zeus. A passage in Homer's *Iliad* tells how they imprisoned Ares, the god of war, in a bronze jar for thirteen months, where he would have perished if Hermes had not released him. A different tradition makes them beneficent *heroes who founded cities and the worship of the Muses. Ephialtes was also the name of the demon of nightmare among the Greeks. *See also* GIANTS.

**Ouranos** *See* URANUS.

**ovā'tio** *See* TRIUMPH.

**Ovid (Publius Ovidius Nāso)** (43 BC–AD 17) Roman poet. He was born at Sulmo, in a valley of the Apennines east of Rome, on 20 March. He tells the story of his life in one of his own poems, *Tristia* 4.10. His family was of *equestrian rank, and he was educated at Rome; by his father's wish he studied rhetoric with a view to practising law, but his taste for poetry asserted itself. According to the Elder Pliny, he applied himself to the emotional rather than the argumentative side of rhetoric. He travelled, and visited Athens, Asia Minor, and

Sicily. For a time he held some minor judicial posts in Rome, but soon abandoned public life for poetry. He was one of the group of poets around *Messalla and stood slightly apart from the Augustan circle centred on *Maecenas. Horace and Propertius were among his friends, but his warmest feelings were expressed in his elegy for *Tibullus (*Amores 3.9), also a member of Messalla's circle. Virgil he only saw. He was three times married and had one daughter, probably by his second wife. His third wife remained devoted to him, and loyal during his exile.

Ovid's poetry had made him a leading figure in the social and literary circles at Rome, when in AD 8 he was suddenly banished by Augustus to *Tomis on the western shore of the Black Sea and his books removed from the public libraries. (He suffered only *relegatio*, 'relegation', which meant that he retained his property and civic rights at Rome, not the more severe *exsilium*, 'exile'.) According to Ovid himself the grounds for this sentence were two, a poem and a blunder, *carmen* and *error*; the poem was the *Ars amatoria* but, since this was published eight years before, the *error* is likely to have been the greater cause. This Ovid refers to only obliquely, but insists it was not *scelus*, 'a crime', and was connected with the Julian family to which Augustus belonged (*see* JULIA, GENS). Ovid seems to have been present when something culpable was done, perhaps being involved in one of the adulteries of Augustus' daughter *Julia (4), who had been banished some years earlier in 2 BC, or of his granddaughter, also called Julia, who was also banished, like Ovid, in AD 8. The *error* must have provided the occasion for the emperor to satisfy his resentment at the poem, which ran counter to his moralistic legislation. Ovid has described in a famous poem (*Tristia* 1.3) his last sad night at Rome and the hardships of his voyage to Tomis, and many of the poems of the *Tristia* and the *Epistulae ex Ponto* attest the tedious years of boredom, deprivation, and even danger he had to endure in that supposedly bleak place (it is now a seaside resort). There he died after ten years of unbroken exile. He eventually became reconciled to its inhabitants: they were kind and considerate and won his esteem. Though the city was a Greek foundation, half the population was Getic and either spoke Greek with Getic accent or used the local language. Ovid not only learned the language but wrote in it a poem (which has not survived) in honour of Augustus and Tiberius.

The order in which Ovid wrote his works is difficult to establish but is roughly as follows. The first edition of the *Amores*, which we do not have, may have appeared as early as 20 BC. We possess the second edition, published later, perhaps much later, than 16 BC. The 'single' *Heroides* ('Heroines') was published between the two editions of the *Amores*, i.e towards the end of the first century BC, the 'double' nearer the time of the poet's exile. *Medicamina faciei femineae* was written before the third book of the *Ars amatoria*, and perhaps before 1 BC; the first two books of the latter were published not before 1 BC, and the third book purported to be a sequel; *Remedia amoris* between 1 BC and AD 2; *Metamorphoses* and *Fasti* contemporaneously, from AD 2 onwards; *Tristia*, AD 9; *Ibis*, c. AD 11; *Epistulae ex Ponto* 1–3, AD 13 (book 4 probably appeared posthumously). A tragedy, *Medea*, was praised by Quintilian and Tacitus, but only two lines survive. (The poems *Halieutica*, of which only a fragment survives, *Nux*, and *Consolatio ad Liviam*, all attributed to Ovid, were probably not by him.) All his poems except *Metamorphoses* were written in elegiac couplets.

Ovid was born in the year after the murder of Julius Caesar, too late to experience the horrors of civil war and so to welcome the policies of the Augustan regime. He was single-mindedly devoted to poetry, and his virtuosity, linguistic as well as metrical, was considerable. He refined even more strictly the rules of composition for the elegiac couplet. His wit and inventiveness make him the most consistently entertaining of the Roman poets, and a brilliant, perhaps over-exuberant, epigrammatist. Frivolous and irresponsible his poetry may sometimes seem, but when, as often happens, his imaginative sympathy is aroused, he can write movingly and simply, without artificiality or straining for effect. He is a gifted storyteller, skilful at focusing upon the telling scene or significant moment in a narrative, and with a sensitivity to natural beauty rare in the ancient world. The Elder Seneca has preserved a story illustrating Ovid's fondness for verbal extravagance. He was once asked by his friends if they might choose three lines to be excised from his works. He agreed, on condition that he might also choose three lines that were on no account to be sacrificed. The choice in each case turned out to be the same three lines. One of them was (of the Minotaur), 'a man half bull and a bull half man', *semibovemque virum semivirumque bovem.*

As a storyteller and guide to Greek myth and Roman legend Ovid was very influential on later Roman writers and was read, quoted, and adapted during the Middle Ages. He was the favourite Latin poet of the Renaissance. Shakespeare seems to have been well acquainted with Ovid in Latin as well as in Arthur Golding's English translation of the *Metamorphoses* (1564–7).

**Oxyrhy'nchus (El Bahnasa)** Place in Upper Egypt, south of the Faiyum and west of the Nile, the richest source of ancient papyri in Egypt through excavations of the town's rubbish dumps carried out in the late nineteenth and the twentieth centuries (*see* PAPYROLOGY). Papyri of the Roman and Byzantine periods have been preserved by the hot and dry atmosphere, but unfortunately the earlier Hellenistic papyri lay below the water table. The sites are now worked out. Many papyri have been of considerable literary importance (*see* e.g. ME-NANDER and OXYRHYNCHUS HISTORIAN), but also of great interest is the light thrown on the social and economic life of the town in Roman times by the survival of thousands of apparently ephemeral and personal documents and letters.

**Oxyrhy'nchus historian** Greek historian, unknown by name, fragments of whose work were first discovered at *Oxyrhynchus in 1906. Two sets of papyrus fragments, both from the second century BC, found separately, proved to belong to the same history (sometimes referred to as the *Hellenica Oxyrhynchia*, 'the Greek history from Oxyrhynchus') which was probably composed in the first half of the fourth century BC. One set gives an outline of events towards the end of the Peloponnesian War, and the other covers the naval war between Athens, under the command of the admiral *Conon (1), and Sparta in 397–6 BC. This work is valuable in that it covers the same events as Xenophon in his *Hellenica* but is independent. It was used by *Ephorus and is the basis of books 13 and 14 of *Diodorus Siculus. It has been greatly admired for being based on sound research and the author's own observations, and being written in a sober and factual style. There have been many attempts to identify the author from among those known to have written on the period. Cratippus is one possibility.

# P

**Pactō'lus** Tributary of the river Hermus in Lydia. *See* MIDAS.

**Pacu'vius, Marcus** (220–*c*.130 BC) Of south Italian birth, Latin writer of tragedies and nephew of the poet Ennius. There exist the titles and fragments of twelve tragedies, based on Greek originals, and of one *fabula* *praetexta* (a drama having its subject in Roman history) on Paullus (probably L. Aemilius *Paullus). Of the titles, only *Antiopa* (Gk. *Antiope*), his most famous work, indicates an original by Euripides; the original of *Niptra* ('The foot-washing', of Odysseus by his old nurse Eurycleia in *Odyssey* 19) was probably by Sophocles; other titles suggest post-Euripidean originals. The poets *Lucilius and *Persius ridiculed certain peculiarities of his diction, especially compound adjectives, but his work showed command of pathos and passion, and impressive character-drawing. He was known as *doctus*, 'learned', a term of high praise, probably on account of his Grecisms and his familiarity with lesser-known stories of Greek legend. Varro and Cicero looked upon him as the greatest of Roman tragedians; the latter in his *De amicitia* testifies to the popular enthusiasm with which a scene in Pacuvius' *Orestes* was received.

**Paean (Paiān, Paiōn).** In two passages in Homer, Paian (Paieon) appears as the name of a healing god, and it is found as a name among the gods at Mycenaean Cnossus (*see* LINEAR B). Also in Homer, and in later Greek literature, the name is given to the Olympian god *Apollo in his aspect of a god of healing who drives out pestilence, averts evil, and brings about victory. The cult hymn of Apollo is called a paean, from the cry *iē, ie Paian*, which came to be used as a refrain. Paeans were sung at religious festivals, at a time of plague, after a military victory, and by guests at a *symposium after the libations. Later the paean could be addressed to other gods also: Sophocles is said to have composed one to *Asclepius, and Xenophon in his *Anabasis* describes the Greeks singing a paean to Zeus. Several paeans by Pindar have been discovered, in a rather fragmentary condition, on papyri.

**paedagō'gus** In Greece, a slave employed to take boys of well-to-do families to and from school or the *gymnasium. *See* LOVE AND SEXUALITY.

**Paetus** *See* ARRIA.

**pāgā'nus** ('pagan') The inhabitant of a *pagus*, 'hamlet', the smallest division of the community in the Italian countryside. By the first century AD it had acquired the contemptuous sense of 'one who stays at home' (i.e. a civilian, in contrast with a soldier), and hence, in Christian writers, 'one who is not a soldier of Christ', 'a heathen'. It has also been suggested that its last meaning is derived from the sense of 'rustic', 'unsophisticated'.

**palace society** *See* CRETE and MYCENAE.

**Palae'mon** In Greek myth, a sea-god. *See* DIONYSUS.

**palaeo'graphy** The study of manuscripts or their equivalent (e.g. papyri and wax tablets) in respect of their handwriting, including the study of variations in the latter which help to establish date and place of writing. It is also concerned with the layout of the writing on the page and with the form of the book. *See also* BOOKS, GREEK AND ROMAN.

**palae'stra** ('wrestling school') In Greek cities, the place where boys (more usually of the upper classes) were instructed in wrestling and athletics. It was often in private ownership (in contrast with the municipally owned *gymnasium) and provided the opportunity for pederastic relationships (*see* LOVE AND SEXUALITY).

**Palamē'dēs** In Greek myth, a proverbially ingenious hero, son of Nauplius, said to have invented some of the letters of the alphabet and the games of draughts and dice. When

*Odysseus tried to avoid his obligation to join in the expedition to Troy by pretending to be mad, Palamedes exposed his deceit. In revenge Odysseus forged a letter purporting to come from King Priam of Troy arranging for Palamedes to betray the Greeks in return for gold. Palamedes, in whose tent Odysseus hid some gold, was consequently stoned to death by the army. Nauplius avenged his son by luring the Greek fleet, returning from Troy, on to the rocks of Euboea by false beacons.

**Pa'latine (Palātīnus mons)** Chief of the *seven hills of Rome and traditionally the site of the first Roman settlement there. Traces of Iron-age occupation have been found. It was here that Aeneas was shown by Evander (*Aeneid*, book 8) the cave of Lupercal. From 330 BC at the latest many famous Romans chose to build their houses on the hill, including in their day *Hortensius, Cicero, Crassus, Milo, and Mark Antony. The house of Hortensius was acquired by the emperor Augustus and became the nucleus of a group of buildings known as *palatia* ('on the Palatine'), from which the English word 'palace' is derived.

**Pa'latine Anthology** See ANTHOLOGY [Greek].

**pa'limpsest** [Gk. *palimpsestos*, 'scraped again'] Manuscript in which the text has been written over an effaced earlier text. The practice of writing on the renovated surface of old parchment was frequent among the monks of the Middle Ages, and since perfect removal of the original writing was seldom achieved, it has proved possible to recover valuable old texts of e.g. the Bible, Cicero, and Plautus. *See also* ARCHIMEDES and GAIUS.

**Palinō'dia** See STESICHORUS.

**Palinū'rus** In Virgil's *Aeneid* (books 5 and 6), the helmsman of Aeneas, who, overcome by the god of sleep, fell overboard, was washed up on the shore of Italy and there murdered by the inhabitants. Aeneas, visiting the Underworld, met his ghost; it had not crossed the river Styx because his body remained unburied. A tomb was subsequently erected to him at the site of his death, and Cape Palinurus (on the west coast of Italy) named after him.

**Pa'lladas** Greek writer of *epigrams who lived at Alexandria in the fourth century AD. About 150 of his poems are in the *Greek *An-*

*thology*. He was a schoolmaster embittered by poverty, living in an age of expanding Christianity although it is impossible to discover his own beliefs. His bitterness, vigorously expressed, and his cold pessimism recall the manner of classical Greek poetry, but sound a wholly individual note.

**Pallā'dium** A small wooden image of the Greek goddess *Pallas Athena, identified by the Romans with Minerva, said to have been sent down from heaven by Zeus to *Dardanus, the founder of Troy (or to his son Ilus). Since Troy could not be captured while it contained this image, legend related that the Greek heroes Diomedes and Odysseus carried it off and thus made it possible for the Greeks to sack Troy. It is variously said to have found its way to Athens, or Argos, or Sparta, or Rome. The Romans believed that an image in the innermost part of the temple of *Vesta, thought to have saved Rome from the attack of the Gauls c.385 BC, was the Palladium, which either arrived eventually at Rome after Aeneas brought it to Lavinium (Diomedes having succeeded in stealing merely a copy) or which was surrendered by Diomedes. When the temple of Vesta caught fire in 241 BC the image was rescued by the *pontifex* L. Metellus (*see* METELLI (1)) but at the cost of his eyesight. Whatever its origin, it seems clear that such a talismanic object was kept in Rome and was still there in AD 191 according to Herodian (2).

**Palla'dius (Palladius Publius Rutilius Taurus Aemilianus)** Author in the fifth century AD of a Latin treatise on agriculture (*De re rustica*) in fourteen books, with an appendix in elegiacs on grafting trees. The first book contains general directions on the choice of a site, on farm buildings, the management of poultry, and agricultural implements. The next twelve books deal with the work to be done on the farm in each month. The fourteenth book is on veterinary medicine. The work was quite well known in later times and a translation was made into Middle English.

**Pallăs** Title of the Greek goddess *Athena (who is often called Pallas Athena); suggested meanings include 'maiden' and 'brandisher' (of weapons). A late source says that Pallas was the friend of Athena whom the goddess accidentally killed, or the name of a giant she overcame. *See* PALLADIUM.

**Pallās** In Greek myth, the son of Evander, who accompanies Aeneas to war against the Italians and is killed by Turnus.

**palliā'ta, fā'bula** ('drama in a Greek cloak [*pallium*]') In Latin literature, term applied to the type of comedies written by Plautus and Terence which were adaptions or imitations of Greek comedies. *Cf.* PRAETEXTA.

**Pan** Greek god of shepherds and of flocks, for whose fertility he is responsible. Native to *Arcadia, where gods part human, part animal occur, he was born on Mount Lycaeus (*see* LYCAEON) with human torso and arms but the legs, ears, and horns of a goat. He is generally thought to be the son of *Hermes (the only other Arcadian god of importance), but his mother is variously named; she is usually a *nymph, often *Callisto, but an odd Arcadian tradition makes *Penelope his mother, by Apollo or Hermes. Pan has little mythology; a late story tells how he invented the musical pipe of seven reeds which he named *syrinx* in honour of the nymph of that name whom he loved and who was changed into a reed in order to escape from him. Other stories describe how he also loved the nymphs Pitys and Echo, who when they fled from him were changed respectively into a pine tree and a voice that can only repeat the last words spoken to her. Generally he haunts mountains, caves, and lonely places; he was reputed to be the cause of sudden groundless fear, 'panic', which may be felt in remote surroundings or in an army. His cult began to spread beyond Arcadia in the early fifth century BC. Herodotus (book 6) tells how in 490 BC Pan appeared to the Athenian runner *Pheidippides and promised help against the Persians, as a consequence of which the Athenians, after their victory at Marathon (490 BC), gave him a cave-shrine on the Acropolis.

A famous story in Plutarch tells how, in the reign of the Roman emperor Tiberius (AD 14–37), the passengers in a ship sailing along the west coast of Greece heard a great voice shouting from the direction of the islands of Paxi that the god Pan was dead. In Christian legend this story was associated with the death and resurrection of Christ, which entailed the death of the pagan gods. Since his name is also the Greek word 'all', and the classical Greeks themselves sometimes understood the name to have this meaning, in later times speculations concerning a universal god, the All, were attached to his name. Sometimes a collection of Pans is found, the god's individuality submerged in a generalized representation of pastoral nature. By the Romans he was identified with *Faunus.

**Panae'tius** (of Rhodes, *c.*185–109 BC) Greek Stoic philosopher (*see* STOICISM). In *c.*144 he went to Rome and joined the circle of P. Cornelius *Scipio Aemilianus, whom he accompanied on a mission to Egypt and Asia. After his return *c.*138 he divided his time between Rome and Athens; in 129 he succeeded *Antipater as head of the Stoic school in Athens, and there he died. He adapted Stoic doctrine to fit Roman ideals, dwelling on the active virtues of magnanimity and benevolence rather than the passive virtues of indifference to misfortune and danger and of avoiding wrongdoing; he emphasized the subordination of private ambition to the good of the state, conformity to the same standard of virtue in public and private life, and the suppression of self-indulgence. Unlike earlier Stoics he had reservations about *astrology and *divination. The most important of his works was *On Duty* (now lost), on which Cicero modelled books 1 and 2 of his own *De officiis*. He was a powerful influence on Roman thought.

**Panathēnae'a** Ancient Athenian festival supposedly founded in the time of *Theseus in honour of the birth of Athena, the patron goddess of the city, and held every year at the end of July. For three out of four years it lasted for two days and was called the Lesser Panathenaea, but starting from the archonship of *Hippocleides in 566/5 BC it was celebrated with particular splendour every fourth year, when it lasted for seven days and was called the Great Panathenaea. The augmented festival included games, horse-races, and musical contests, to which the Peisistratids added poetical recitations by *rhapsodes. The equestrian events were held on that part of the Panathenaic Way (from the Dipylon Gate to the Acropolis) which crossed the agora. Pericles extended the musical contests and built a special theatre, the *Odeum, for them. The prizes at the athletic contests were of money, or highly decorated *amphorae (some of which still survive, the earliest dated 570–560 BC) filled with olive oil; as many as 140 of them were given as the principal prize. The festival culminated on the last day in a magnificent procession along the Panathenaic Way and up to the Parthenon, in which Athena's new robe, a *peplos*, was carried to her statue. This was a costly garment, woven by Athenian girls of good family to include scenes from the battle of Gods and *Giants; it was a signal honour for a girl to be thought 'worthy of the peplos'. It was carried on a great ship on wheels, followed by girls known as *arrephoroi*, 'basket-carriers', by groups of boys bearing pitchers and old men with olive branches, by chariots, and finally by a cavalcade of young men on horseback (as depicted on the frieze of the *Parthenon). The feast was completed with a *hecatomb of oxen, the flesh distributed among the people. In the fifth century BC the allies of the *Delian League were required to take part, and so the procession became a symbol of Athens' imperial status.

**Panathēnā'icus** Late work by *Isocrates in praise of Athens.

**pancra'tion** An event in Greek athletic *festivals. It was a popular kind of all-in wrestling in which victory brought considerable prestige. *See also* ATHLETICS.

**Pa'ndarus** In Homer's *Iliad*, son of *Lycaon and leader, in the Trojan War, of the Trojans who lived about the foot of Mount Ida. He breaks the truce (*Iliad* 4) and wounds Menelaus with an arrow, and is eventually killed by Diomedes. The story of his relations with Troilus and Cressida as told by Chaucer and Shakespeare is derived ultimately from the work of Dictys Cretensis and Dares Phrygius. His name survives in the English 'pander'.

**Pandī'on** Legendary king of Athens, variously described as grandson or great-grandson of *Erechtheus, or son of Erichthonius. He was father of *Philomela and Procne.

**Pandō'ra** In Greek myth, the first woman; *see* PROMETHEUS.

**Panegy'rici** A collection of eleven complimentary speeches in Latin by rhetoricians, ranging in date from AD 289 to 389, in honour of the emperors of this time, chiefly Maximian, Constantius, Constantine I and II, Julian, and Theodosius. The collection also contains the Younger Pliny's panegyric of Trajan on which the later speeches were modelled. Composed in the rhetorical schools of Gaul, they have little literary interest beyond being examples of pure Pliny-like Latinity, but they throw light on the history of fourth-century Gaul.

**panhe'llenism** The idea that what the Greeks have in common is significant and should unite them against foreigners, especially Persia. The idea was promoted by *Gorgias and *Lysias, but most especially by *Isocrates.

**Paniō'nium** The meeting-place and religious centre of the Ionian league (mainly Ionian cities in Asia Minor), a temple dedicated to Poseidon Heliconios at Mount Mycale (in Asia Minor, between Ephesus and Miletus).

**Panthe'on (Pa'ntheon)** At Rome, a magnificent temple consecrated, as the name implies, to all the gods, built by Hadrian (emperor AD 117–38) to replace that of M. *Agrippa built 27–25 BC in the Campus Martius. It consists of a huge domed rotunda with a pedimented portico, and the basic structure (although not the decoration) has survived virtually intact. It was dedicated as a Christian church by Pope Boniface IV in AD 609.

**pantomime** Form of dramatic entertainment among the Romans in which a single actor/dancer (*pantomimus*, 'one who imitates everything') mimed a story in dumb show, playing all the parts himself, supported by a chorus and musicians. The stories chosen were almost entirely mythological. Pantomime in this form was introduced to Rome in 22 BC by Pylades of Cilicia (in south-east Asia Minor) and Bathyllus of Alexandria; hitherto in Rome dumb shows had been enacted by individuals, but it was Pylades' innovation to introduce a more serious style with chorus and musicians. Bathyllus, who favoured the comic and lewd, became so popular in this form of drama that his name came to be used for any pantomime actor. Performances took place both on the public stage and privately. The actor wore a graceful silk costume and a mask with closed lips. The songs of the chorus were of minor importance; surviving fragments are in Greek. Pantomime and *mime, the seriousness of the former contrasting with the coarseness of the latter, came to dominate the Roman stage, and contributed to the decline of serious drama there. Despite the opposition of the Church to its pagan ethos pantomime still flourished in the sixth century.

**Panya'ssis** (of Halicarnassus) Older kinsman of Herodotus and the last great epic poet of archaic Greece (i.e. of the period before 480 BC). He lived in the early part of the fifth century and was put to death for his political activities by Lygdamis, tyrant of Halicarnassus, in the 460s or early 450s. He wrote two works: on Heracles, the *Heracleia* (9,000 lines in fourteen books), of which a few fragments remain, and on the Ionian colonial settlements, the *Ionica* (7,000 lines, and perhaps written in elegiacs, of which nothing survives). Panyassis' language appears to be basically Homeric, but includes some unusual words. The fragments of the *Heracleia*, though few, provide valuable information about Greek myths and legends.

**papyro'logy** The decipherment and elucidation of anything written on papyrus, and the study of the papyrus roll as a form of book. For the manufacture and uses of papyrus *see* BOOKS, GREEK AND ROMAN 2. Most papyri discovered in modern times come from Egypt, where the rainless climate favours their survival. Serious excavations there began in the nineteenth century, and at *Oxyrhynchus in particular. Outside Egypt Greek papyri have been found at *Herculaneum, in Palestine, and one at Derveni in Greece. The earliest papyrus book we have, the *Persae* of *Timotheus, dates from the fourth century BC. Since many of the papyri are of school texts, and the education available was the traditional Greek one (Egypt was conquered by Alexander the Great in 332 BC), more than half of the several thousand surviving literary papyri are of Homer. Of the rest, fragments of works hitherto unknown slightly outnumber the fragments of works already familiar. New texts discovered include several plays of Menander (mostly incomplete), much of Bacchylides, some poems of Sappho, Pindar, Stesichorus, and other lyric poets, much of Callimachus, the mimes of Herodas, the *Ichneutae* of Sophocles, and several other sizeable fragments of tragedy; and, in prose, Aristotle's *Athenaion politeia*, the *Hellenica Oxyrhynchia* (a history continuing that of Thucydides), and several speeches of Hypereides. Other papyri contain fragmentary scientific and medical texts, and works on astrology and magic, important as social documents. Discoveries of Christian literary papyri have been equally important, adding further testimony to works already known, most valuably in the case of the New Testament text, and revealing hitherto unknown works, for example the *Sayings of Jesus* (part of the gnostic *Gospel of Thomas*).

Most of the papyri discovered, however, are simply documentary: private letters and accounts, legal and administrative documents. A great deal has been learnt from these about the Greek language at various periods, in its most educated and in its semi-literate forms; in particular, the language of contemporary documents has thrown new light on the syntax, vocabulary, and idiom of the New Testament.

Latin papyri have been found in Egypt and a few other places but are comparatively rare. Most date from after the late third century AD, when the emperor Diocletian opened up Egypt, making it equal in status to the rest of the empire and encouraging all the eastern provinces in the use of Latin. The many military documents have considerably increased our knowledge of the Roman army. Nearly all papyrus fragments of Latin literary texts belong to prose works, but there are important papyri of Juvenal and of Terence's *Andria*. In recent years papyri of Artemidorus of Ephesus (a geographer of the first century AD), perhaps a forgery, the Greek epigrammatist Poseidippus (third century BC), and *Sappho have been found.

**para'basis** In Greek Old Comedy, the 'coming forward' of the *chorus after the *agon ('debate') between the two main adversaries, when all the characters have left the stage. The chorus-leader addresses the audience directly on behalf of the poet, in verse of a particular metre (anapaestic tetrameters), on subjects that have little to do with the plot but are of topical interest. The anapaests end in a long sentence to be spoken in one breath (*pnīgos*, 'the choke').

**pa'raloi (para'lioi)** ('coastmen') *See* PEISISTRATUS.

**parasang** Persian unit of distance, equivalent to 30 stades, or roughly 5km (3 miles). The *stathmos*, 'stage', a normal day's march, was about five parasangs.

**parasite** [Gk. *parasītos*, 'sponger', originally 'fellow-diner', 'guest'] A stock character of Greek and Roman comedy. At first he was called *kōlax*, 'flatterer', one who earns a meal by flattering and humouring his socially superior host. Sometimes he makes a pair with his patron, a boastful soldier, whose vanity he flatters in return for being kept. The names of notorious parasites in real life appear in some comedies. *See* COMEDY [Greek].

**Parcae** *See* FATES.

**parchment** *See* BOOKS, GREEK AND ROMAN 2.

**Parian Marble (Parian Chronicle)** (Lat. *Marmor Parium*) An inscribed marble slab originally set up in the Greek island of Paros and containing a chronological table of events from the beginning of the reign of Cecrops, the mythical first king of Athens (taken to be 1580 BC), down to 263 BC, presumably the date or near-date of compilation. Two substantial fragments survive, one in the museum on Paros, the other in the Ashmolean Museum, Oxford. The events are dated by the number of years separating them from 263 BC and by the name of the Athenian king or *archon then in office. Those selected for inclusion are a mixture of political, military, religious, and literary history. Other inscribed tablets found in the nineteenth and twentieth centuries on Paros, relating events in the life of the local poet *Archilochus, are not included under this name.

**Paris 1.** (also called Alexander, Gk. Alexandros) In Greek myth, a son of *Priam king of Troy and his wife *Hecuba. He was exposed when he was born because his mother had dreamed that she would bear a firebrand (the story told in Pindar's Paean 8) which would destroy the whole city, and a seer foretold that he would bring destruction on Troy. However, he was rescued and brought up by shepherds, and passed his youth pasturing sheep on Mount Ida, loved by the nymph *Oenone. He had a favourite bull which Priam's servants carried off to be the prize at some funeral games. Paris, determined to win back the animal, entered for the games and won several events. Priam's daughter *Cassandra recognized him and he was restored to the family although Cassandra prophesied disaster. Priam sent Paris on an embassy to Menelaus, king of Sparta, whose wife Helen fell in love with him (*see* PARIS, JUDGEMENT OF). They fled together to Troy, thus bringing about the Trojan War, in which Paris, a skilful archer, took part. Homer represents him as affectedly bold and self-consciously martial in appearance, but unable to withstand the onslaught of Men-

elaus. In the single combat between the two, to decide the war, Paris was dragged off by Menelaus and had to be rescued by Aphrodite. He then makes love to Helen. It was his arrow, guided by Apollo, which finally killed Achilles (Homer does not recount this event); *see* ILIAD, LITTLE. At the fall of the city he was fatally wounded by a poisoned arrow from *Philoctetes' bow (which had belonged to Heracles) and sought, in vain, a cure from the nymph *Oenone whom he had deserted.

**2.** The name of two popular *pantomime dancers, one of whom was executed by order of the emperor Nero (AD 67), the other by Domitian (AD 87). For one of them the poet *Statius wrote his libretto *Agave*.

**Paris, Judgement of** In Greek myth, at the marriage feast of *Peleus and the goddess Thetis, Eris (Discord) threw down a golden apple (the 'apple of Discord') inscribed 'for the most beautiful'. The goddesses Hera, Athena, and Aphrodite all claimed it, and they applied to Paris, the most handsome of mortal men, then a shepherd on Mount Ida near Troy, to settle the dispute. Each goddess offered him a reward in return for the apple: Hera greatness, Athena success in war, and Aphrodite the most beautiful woman in the world as his wife (compare the 'choice of *Heracles'). Paris awarded the apple to Aphrodite, and with her help carried off *Helen. It was ultimately this judgement which brought about the Trojan War, but it is not an aspect of the story used by Homer: he retains the hostility of Hera and Athena for Troy, but leaves it unexplained.

**Parme'nidēs** (*c*.515–after 450 BC) Greek *Presocratic philosopher from the Greek colony of Elea in south-west Italy. He is said to have given laws to his city. According to tradition he was a pupil of, but did not follow, the Ionian philosopher *Xenophanes, preferring to associate with Pythagoreans. He is said to have visited Athens in his sixty-fifth year (*c*.450 BC) and to have met Socrates (he appears as one of the chief interlocutors in Plato's dialogue *Parmenides*). Founder of the so-called *Eleatic school of philosophy, he was the first Greek philosopher whose work, a philosophical poem in hexameters, survives in large fragments. This consists of a prologue and two sections called the *Way of Truth* and the *Way of Seeming* (or *Opinion*).

The prologue describes how the unnamed narrator, escorted by the daughters of the Sun, was carried in a horse-drawn chariot to the gates of night and day. He is met by a goddess who proceeds, in the *Way of Truth*, to tell the narrator the truth of things as they really are. She begins by defining the two possible ways of enquiry, each contrary to the other: either a thing 'is, and cannot not-be'; or it 'is not, and must not-be'. The latter way is rejected on the grounds that it is impossible to conceive of the non-existent: one can only think or speak about 'what is'. Ordinary mortals, deluded by their sense perceptions, mix up the two paths and believe that a thing both is and is not: that 'what is' can become something different, i.e. what it hitherto was not, by means of change. This belief is rejected, on the grounds that it is self-contradictory. Once the premiss 'a thing is' is established by elimination as the only possibility, Parmenides (in the person of the goddess) deduces what follows from it. (It is difficult to be sure of the exact meaning Parmenides attached to 'is', with the result that the details of the argument are disputed at every stage by modern scholars.) 'What is' is not subject to birth or decay; it is single and not divisible (what is entailed by this is not clear: is there no plurality, motion, or time?); it is complete in itself and unchanging. This unity is sometimes referred to as 'the One', as in e.g. Plato's *Parmenides*. All of these conclusions are reached by verbal reasoning alone, neither appealing to experience nor admitting any connection between the world of the intellect and the world of the senses. Because of this, Parmenides is often seen as the first true Western philosopher.

In the *Way of Seeming* the goddess sets out a false cosmogony, presumably because Parmenides thought this was the simplest way to demonstrate how human misconceptions arise and operate. Cosmogony, the science of the evolution and development of the cosmos, had been rejected in the *Way of Truth* because if 'what is' had a beginning in time there must have been a reason for that beginning, and there could be no reason if nothing at all existed. Since Parmenides believes only in the *Way of Truth* it hardly matters that the text of the *Way of Seeming* is too fragmentary to permit reconstruction. The mutually exclusive nature of the two *Ways* indicates that Parmenides

considered the world of verbal reasoning and the world of the senses to be utterly different and unrelated constructions, only the first one representing reality. His views were developed further by his followers *Melissus and *Zeno (1). Parmenides was the most influential of the Presocratic philosophers; he had shown that even what people regarded as fundamentally true was not beyond question, and he showed that 'what is' can be deduced not from experience or from the senses but entirely from the logic of the verb 'to be' and its relationship to objects of thought and speech. Not until Plato's late dialogue *Sophist* is an answer given to the problem of talking about the non-existent. (For the answer of the atomists to Parmenides *see* DEMOCRITUS.)

**Parmenides** Dialogue by *Plato, tentatively dated to between 370 and 367 BC, the first of a group of four which he intended to be read in conjunction; the others are *Theaetetus*, *Sophist*, and *Statesman*. The scene is set at a time soon after 400 BC: a group of philosophers from Clazomenae (the home-town of Anaxagoras) has come to Athens to hear at second hand an account of a meeting some fifty years earlier between a 'very young' Socrates, the middle-aged *Zeno (1), and the elderly *Parmenides. Such a meeting could have happened, but it is unlikely. Also present is a young Aristoteles (the Greek form of the name 'Aristotle', but not in this case the famous philosopher). Against Parmenides' questioning Socrates defends 'his' (i.e. Plato's) theory of Forms (*see* PLATONISM), which links the world of the senses with the world of the intellect, a connection denied by Parmenides. The theory was rooted in Parmenides' work, but in this dialogue it is found to be inadequate and Socrates is told that he cannot proceed further unless he submits to some tedious dialectical exercise. From this point onwards the dialogue changes in style from a narrative to direct question and answer, with Aristoteles as respondent, on the subject of 'the One', i.e. Parmenides' unity, and it provides an example of dialectical argument. The meaning of the work as a whole remains controversial.

**Parna'ssus** In Greece, a spur running southeast a few miles north of Delphi, rising to about 2,460m (8,070 ft.). The towns of Phocis lie on its eastern flank, and the plain of Crisa with the high valley of Delphi is on the south.

On it were the *Corycian cave and the Castalian spring (see CASTALIA), and the whole mountain, as well as the spring, was sacred, associated with the worship of Apollo and the *Muses. The two peaks between which the Castalia flows were sometimes spoken of as the two peaks of Parnassus, but the summit is in reality hundreds of metres above them.

**pa'rodos** In Greek tragedy and Old Comedy, the 'entry' of the *chorus into the orchestra near the beginning of a play, including the song which the chorus sings to reveal its character and, often, the situation at the start of the action.

**parody** Burlesquing serious poetry for comic effect was known in Greek literature from very early times. It might have been possible to see the *Margites (perhaps c.700 BC) as a parody of Homeric epic had more of it survived. One tradition ascribes the invention of parody to *Hipponax (mid-sixth century BC); Aristotle in the Poetics attributes its invention to Hegemon of Thrace, who was later than Hipponax and may have been the first to win contests at Athens for parodies. In surviving Greek literature the most notable parodists are Aristophanes, Plato, and Lucian. The first produces outstanding parodies of Aeschylean and Euripidean lyrics in Frogs, but mostly parodies tragic style in general and that of Euripides in particular, exploiting the latter's idiosyncracies of style and thought. Plato's parodies, of the style and manner of his interlocutors, are more subtle and have more than humorous ends in view. Those of the participants in the Symposium are the most obviously funny; and scholars still debate whether the speech purportedly by *Lysias in Phaedrus really is by him or by Plato. Lucian's parodies, often at the expense of the Olympian gods as they are depicted in mythology, are funny in an obvious way.

In Latin literature Roman comedy burlesques in the Aristophanic manner the linguistic pomposities of Ennius and Pacuvius, but to a much lesser degree. A rare example of the only sustained and obvious Latin parody is in the tenth poem of the Catalepton (see APPENDIX VIRGILIANA), in which Catullus' address to his yacht (poem 4) is turned into an address to an officious magistrate. In modern studies critics detect parody when any imitation of a higher literary genre appears in a lower, such as satire.

Thus in Horace, Satires 2.5, the conversation between Ulysses and Teiresias may be read as parody of Homer, Odyssey 11, and much of Ovid approaches parody (e.g. of Virgil's Aeneid in Metamorphoses 13 and 14). Petronius' Satyricon is now taken as parodying a wide range of literature. On the whole, though, in Latin literature the boundaries and degree of parody are difficult to discern. See also HYMNS.

**Parrha'sius** (of Ephesus) Famous Greek painter who lived c.400 BC and practised mostly at Athens. The story of his contest with the younger painter *Zeuxis in producing illusion is well known. Zeuxis painted some grapes so naturalistically that birds came to peck at them, and victory seemed to be his. He then asked Parrhasius to draw back the curtain concealing the latter's picture, but the curtain turned out to have been painted by Parrhasius. Zeuxis declared himself defeated; he had succeeded in deceiving the birds, but Parrhasius had succeeded in deceiving him. Xenophon in the *Memorabilia represents Socrates as discussing with him aspects of facial expression.

**parthenei'on** ('maiden song') Form of Greek choral *lyric, a processional hymn sung by a choir of girls, upon a religious, but not a solemn, occasion. Partheneia were composed by Alcman, Simonides, Bacchylides, and Pindar. Fairly substantial fragments of some by Alcman and Pindar have been found on papyri.

**Parthe'nius** (of Nicaea, first century BC) Greek poet and scholar taken as a prisoner-of-war by the Romans and sent to Rome in 73 BC. Subsequently freed, he is thought to have influenced the Roman poets of the day such as *Cinna and *Gallus, and his Metamorphoses would have been a source for Ovid and the author of Ciris (see APPENDIX VIRGILIANA). According to *Macrobius he was Virgil's tutor in Greek. His poetry, mostly in elegiacs, was highly thought of, but very little of it survives. Extant are the prose outlines he made (in Greek) of love stories found in Greek poetry and fictional literature, ostensibly intended for use by his poet friend Gallus to ornament either epic or elegy; they provide evidence about the Greek *novel.

**Pa'rthenon** ('Temple of the Maiden') The temple of Athena Parthenos built on the highest part of the *Acropolis at Athens, probably as a thank-offering for the successful conclusion of the Persian Wars. It was begun under the administration of Pericles in 447 BC and dedicated in 438. A temple had been begun on the site after the Persian invasion of 490, and its foundations were used for the new building. The architect was Ictinus, assisted by Callicrates, and the work was supervised by *Pheidias, who made the great cult statue of the goddess in gold and ivory for the interior. The temple measures about 70×30m (230×100 ft.) with seventeen columns along each side and eight at each end. Its adornment with sculptures continued, almost certainly under the direction of Pheidias, until 432. These sculptures were more elaborate, more relevant to the cult, and more unified in theme than most temple sculptures. They were apparently coloured; traces of blue pigment have been found on what survives. The ninety-two metopes (decorative slabs above the colonnade), represented in high relief on the east the battles of the Gods and the Giants, on the west the victory of the Greeks over the Amazons, on the south the struggle of the Centaurs and the Lapiths (these now the best-preserved), and on the north the Trojan War, the common theme being the glorification of the Greek victory over Persia, and especially the Athenian contribution. The pediments showed the birth of Athena from the head of Zeus (east end), and the contest of Poseidon and Athena for the possession of Attica (west end). These figures are carved in the round. The frieze, in low relief, 160m (525 ft.) long, which ran high around the inner building, is unique in apparently showing a contemporary scene, the procession at the *Panathenaea. The suggestion is that it commemorates the young Athenians who died at Marathon.

In the late sixth century the Parthenon was converted into a Christian church (the dedication—to Holy Wisdom—perpetuating an attribute of Athena), and after Athens was captured by the Turks in 1458 it became a mosque. It remained almost intact until 1687 when, in the course of a siege by the Venetians, it was partially destroyed by an explosion of gunpowder stored there by the Turkish garrison. Most of the surviving sculpture (together with some other pieces, including a *caryatid from the Erechtheum) was acquired by the seventh Earl of Elgin when he was envoy to Constantinople (1799–1803) and sold (at a loss) to the British Government in 1816. They are in the British Museum and known as the Elgin Marbles.

The Parthenon today is partly a reconstruction of the 1920s. More accurate restoration began in 1986.

**Pa'sion** (*c.*430–370 BC) In Athens, at the time of his death the richest banker and manufacturer of his day. He began his career as a slave working for bankers in the Piraeus, acquired his freedom and became a citizen, and eventually owned the bank. Several speeches attributed to Demosthenes (*see* APOLLODORUS (1)) and a speech by Isocrates, *Trapeziticus* ('Speech against the banker'), give much information about his business dealings.

**Pāsi'phāē** In Greek myth, wife of *Minos king of Crete, daughter of Helios (Sun), mother of Ariadne and Phaedra. When Minos refused to sacrifice a fine bull to Poseidon, as he had promised, Poseidon punished him by inflicting on Pasiphae a passion for the bull. Enabled by the help of *Daedalus to satisfy her passion she became the mother of the Minotaur, part bull and part man.

**pastoral poetry** What we call 'pastoral poetry' the Greeks knew as 'bucolic', a term derived from the Greek word for herdsmen, *boukoloi*. 'Bucolic' was first used to describe this type of poetry by the Greek poet *Theocritus, who invented the genre and wrote what are now called *idylls. These were imitated by the Greek poets *Bion and *Moschus, and later and most notably by the Roman poet Virgil (in the *Eclogues; *see also* CALPURNIUS SICULUS). It was Virgil who originally gave the genre its location (*Arcadia in Greece), its static form, and many of the motifs subsequently used by later European pastoral poets (though Arcadia's pastoral fame in more modern times is perhaps due rather to the poets of the Renaissance). In the typical pastoral poem the herdsmen-poets suffering from the noonday heat sing of themselves, their loves and quarrels, and their music in a stylized Greek landscape with *Daphnis, *Pan, and the *nymphs. At its best the artful simplicity of pastoral poetry conceals a subtlety of composition that mostly appeals to a sophisticated taste prepared to appreciate its studied remoteness from the realities of a shepherd's life. Many of its features are found in John Milton's poem *Lycidas* (1637). Because of its limited subject matter and easily recognized conventions pastoral poetry came to be used as a vehicle for *allegory or veiled social and political comment as early as Virgil, if not Theocritus. *See also* GENRE and ELEGY.

**paterfami'lias** At Rome, the male head of the family. In the early republic the Roman family was an exclusive unit, and legal power known as *patria potestas*, 'power of a father', was concentrated in the man who was its head. In the relations between him and his family the state scarcely interfered. He was the sole owner of the property, including his wife's dowry, and he had complete power over his children including that of life and death, not merely at birth, to decide whether they should live or not (as in Greece; *see* INFANTICIDE), but at any time. By the late republic adult sons were often 'emancipated', i.e. freed from the absolute power of the paterfamilias, and adult women, though still after marriage nominally in the power of a paterfamilias who might be a guardian, were allowed considerable freedom in the management of their property. *See also* GENIUS.

**Pater Pa'triae** ('Father [i.e. saviour] of one's country') Honorific title given at Rome to those who had shown outstanding service to the state. Cicero was so addressed in the senate after his consulship of 63 BC, and likewise the emperor Augustus in 2 BC (*see* MESSALLA CORVINUS).

**patrēs conscri'pti** *See* SENATE.

**patria potestas** *See* PATERFAMILIAS.

**patri'cians** At Rome, members of certain families, a privileged class, distinguished from the *plebeians (plebs), the rest of the citizen body. Their name is probably connected with *patres*, 'fathers', a collective term for patrician members of the *senate. If, as may be the case, the right to membership of the senate became hereditary in early times, perhaps under the kings, that would have distinguished certain families from the rest of the citizen body. In the patriciate itself a distinction was made between the 'lesser clans' (*gentes minores*) and the 'greater clans' (*gentes maiores*), explained as the result of 'new men' being made patrician by the kings. Until 445 BC patricians were not allowed to marry plebeians. Under the early republic they held the magistracies and the important religious offices: only a patrician could become *rex sacrorum, *interrex, and perhaps *princeps senatus*. Their political strength began to be challenged in the fourth century BC by powerful plebeians, but until 172

BC one of the two consuls was always a patrician. Their numbers also declined: about fifty patrician clans are known in the fifth century, but only fourteen at the end of the republic. Patricians could renounce their status by a special public act or simple adoption (*see* CLODIUS). Julius Caesar and Octavian admitted new members to the patriciate. *See* ORDERS and ORDERS, CONFLICT OF.

**Patro'clus** (**Patroklos, Patrokles**) In Homer's *Iliad*, son of Menoetius and the favourite companion of Achilles. When young he killed a playmate and sought refuge with Achilles' father Peleus, who made him the slightly younger Achilles' personal attendant. For the rest of his story *see* ILIAD.

**patron** (Lat. *patrōnus*) At Rome, a powerful man who agreed to protect another by making the latter his *client. In the early republic the custom grew up of poor citizens attaching themselves to rich and influential men who gave them financial and legal assistance in return for their political support and social attentions. It became a matter of prestige for a patron on his public appearances to be attended by a crowd of respectful clients. The relationship between the two was felt to be a binding obligation. Slaves who acquired their freedom became the clients of their former masters, who retained certain legal rights over them. Sometimes Roman commanders exercised a general patronage over the peoples they conquered which was transmitted to their descendants. Pompey's son Sextus was able to get support from his father's clients in Spain and Asia.

**patronage, literary** In Greece, literary patronage was exercised among others by the tyrants of Corinth (*see* CYPSELUS), Athens (*see* PEISISTRATUS), Samos (*see* POLYCRATES), and Sicily (*see* HIERON), who supported at their courts as a matter of prestige the poets Alcman, Anacreon, Bacchylides, Pindar, and Simonides. Archelaus, king of Macedon at the end of the fifth century BC, invited Agathon, Timotheus, and Euripides to his court. In the same century the city of Athens itself with its musical festivals and commissions for temple decoration and other works of art offered the advantages of patronage, and there were wealthy Athenian aristocrats giving hospitality to philosophers and teachers (*see* SOPHIST). Similarly, in the Hellenistic age the kings of Egypt, the

Ptolemies, were great supporters of all the arts, rivalled by the Attalids, kings of Pergamum.

At Rome, literary patronage was an extension of the relationship between *patron and client, and even included Greek writers. When the book trade became important in the first century AD Augustus and then many later emperors were patrons of literature in order that their achievements might be immortalized, as were wealthy individuals such as Pollio, Maecenas, Messalla, and the Younger Pliny. Among those benefiting were Virgil, Horace, Statius, and Martial, who could feel like Pindar and Bacchylides before them that patronage fell within the conventions of *friendship.

**patrony'mic** *See* NAMES.

**Paullus, Lucius Aemi'lius** (*c.*230–160 BC) Roman general and statesman, given the *cognomen* Macedonicus because of his victory at Pydna in 168, which brought the Third Macedonian War to an end (*see* MACEDON). When Epirus was sacked on instructions from the senate the enormous proceeds of the booty were scrupulously paid into the Roman treasury. Paullus kept for himself only the books which had belonged to the Macedonian king Perseus, thereby forming the first private *library at Rome. The triumph that he celebrated at the end of 167 BC (marred by the death of his two young sons) was the most spectacular that Rome had until then seen. Paullus combined the traditional Roman virtues of integrity and devotion to duty with admiration for the culture of ancient Greece, and was a strong influence on his circle of friends as well as on Roman public life. His two elder sons had been adopted and became Q. Fabius Maximus Aemilianus and P. Cornelius *Scipio Aemilianus. (*See also* PACUVIUS.)

**Pausa'nias 1.** (d. 467/6 BC) Spartan general in the Persian Wars, son of the king Cleombrotus I and nephew of *Leonidas. He commanded the Greek land forces that defeated the Persians at Plataea (479) and the allied fleet that captured Byzantium (478), but he was suspected of treasonable negotiations with the Persian king Xerxes. He was twice acquitted of the charge, but was later suspected of fomenting a revolt by the *helots (the Spartan serfs). To escape arrest he took refuge in a sanctuary on the Spartan acropolis, where he was walled up and left to starve. At the point of death he was taken out, to die on unconsecrated ground so as to avoid pollution (467/6 BC).

**2.** (fl. *c.* AD 160) Greek traveller and geographer, the author of an extant 'Description of Greece' (*Periegesis Hellados*), who appears from passages in it to have been born in Lydia. The work is in ten books, namely: 1, Attica and Megara; 2, Corinth and Argolis; 3, Laconia; 4, Messenia; 5 and 6, Elis (with Olympia); 7, Achaea; 8, Arcadia; 9, Boeotia; 10, Phocis (with Delphi). Pausanias generally outlines the history and then the topography of important cities, followed by their religious cults and mythology. He is most interested in objects and places of historical and religious interest, and especially in artistic monuments of the archaic and classical periods; indeed his work is the most important literary source for the history of Greek art (what he tells us is based on his own travels and his general accuracy is attested by the extant remains of the monuments he describes). Only occasionally does he refer to the scenery and natural products of the regions he describes, nor is he much interested in objects later than 150 BC. He is honest about reputed marvels, such as the spotted fish of the river Aroanius; these he admits did not, as was supposed, sing like thrushes, although he waited by the river till sunset. Of the two stories accounting for the presence of a pickled Triton (perhaps some sea-creature) in a temple at Tanagra, he thinks it more credible that the creature was lured ashore by a bowl of wine and decapitated as it lay drunk on the beach, than that it was killed in single combat by the god Dionysus. His style is simple and plain.

**Pax Augusta, Pax Romana** ('The Augustan [or Roman] Peace') Pax, the Roman personification of peace, was adopted by the emperor Augustus as a cult to signify his maintenance of order and security within the Roman empire. Its most famous monument at Rome was the Altar of the Peace of Augustus (*Ara Pacis Augustae*). The term *Pax Romana* became a slogan of the period, though Ovid complains that his part of it at *Tomis saw precious little peace.

**Peace (*Eirene*)** (Lat. *Pax*) Greek comedy by *Aristophanes, produced at the Great *Dionysia in 421 BC, where it came second in the dramatic competition.

The *Peloponnesian War between Sparta and Athens is in progress; the Athenian demagogue and general *Cleon and the Spartan general *Brasidas have been killed in the summer of 422 at Amphipolis, and Aristophanes anticipates the successful outcome of negotiations for the Peace of *Nicias (concluded some ten days after the performance). Trygaios, an Attic vine-grower, who with his family is suffering from the food shortage, decides to imitate the mythical hero *Bellerophon on his winged horse Pegasus, and ride to heaven on a dung-beetle, fattening it up to gigantic size for the purpose. The voyage is successfully accomplished, but Hermes who answers the door tells him that Zeus and the other gods have moved house so as to be further away from the war down below, and War (Polemos) is in charge; he has cast Peace into a deep cave, from which, perhaps, she will never emerge, and is preparing to pound all the states in a mortar. While War looks for a pestle (failing to borrow one from Athens or Sparta because their 'pestles of war', Cleon and Brasidas, are lost), Trygaios and the Attic farmers (the chorus) whom he has summoned, having bribed Hermes with extravagant promises of festivals and a gold cup, draw Peace out of the cave with her two attendants Opora ('Harvest') and Theoria ('Holiday'; literally, 'attendance at festivals'), and return with them to Greece. General jubilation follows (except on the part of arms manufacturers), and preparations are made for the wedding of Trygaios and Opora.

**Peace, On the** Title of speeches by *Isocrates and *Demosthenes ((2) 2).

**Peace of Nicias** See NICIAS and PELOPONNESIAN WAR.

**Pe′gasus** In Greek myth, a winged horse who, with his brother Chrysaor, was sprung from the blood of the *Gorgon Medusa, pregnant by Poseidon, when she was killed by Perseus. The fountain Hippocrene on Mount Helicon in Boeotia, sacred to the Muses, was said to have been produced by a stamp of his hoof. With the help of Athene or Poseidon *Bellerophon was able to catch this horse when it was drinking at the fountain Peirene in Corinth, and bridle it. Mounted on it he succeeded in killing the *Chimaera, but was thrown when he attempted to fly to Olympus on its back. Pegasus appears on a handsome series of Corinthian coins, symbolizing the city.

**Peirae′us** See PIRAEUS.

**Peirē′nē** Celebrated fountain at Corinth; see PERIANDER and PEGASUS.

**Peiri′thŏus** See CENTAURS and THESEUS.

**Peisistra′tidai** ('Peisistratids') Hippias and Hipparchus, the sons and successors of *Peisistratus.

**Peisi′stratus** (c.600–527 BC) Tyrant of Athens, three times. He claimed descent from the Neleids of Pylos (see NELEUS) and from a Peisistratus who was *archon at Athens 669/8 BC. During the struggles for political power that developed between the 'plainsmen' and the 'men of the coast' following the reforms of *Solon in the early sixth century, Peisistratus (a relation of Solon) emerged as leader of a third faction, the poorer 'hillsmen' (diakrioi or hyperakrioi). In about 560 he seized the *Acropolis and made himself tyrant. The other two parties eventually united to drive him out of Athens, but he soon returned (in the mid-550s), accompanied in his chariot by a tall and beautiful woman whom he had dressed up as the goddess Athena. He said she had come to restore him to the city and she was received with acclamation. Although he was soon forced into exile again, Peisistratus returned in 546 with a force of mercenaries, defeated his opponents at the battle of Pallene, and remained in power for the rest of his life. His eldest son Hippias succeeded him, and associated his brother Hipparchus in the tyranny. Hipparchus was unpopular because of his dissolute arrogance, and in 514 was killed by *Harmodius and Aristogeiton. After this the rule of Hippias became harsher. His fall was brought about chiefly by the Alcmaeonids (see CLEISTHENES (2)), who induced Sparta to invade Attica. Hippias, besieged in the Acropolis, capitulated and retired to Sigeum in 510. Here he negotiated with the Persians in order to secure their help in his restoration. His hopes frustrated, he subsequently died at Lemnos.

Tradition said that Peisistratus was a benevolent and law-abiding ruler. It is not always possible to distinguish his work from that of his sons. He created a citizens' property tax which provided subsidies to poor farmers, enabling them to avoid debt (which Solon had failed to achieve). Under him the commercial importance of Athens greatly increased; her wine, oil, and pottery reached all the surrounding countries. Under his sons better roads were built between the city and country demes, and lawsuits in the demes were heard by travelling judges, so that country people did not need to travel to the city to have their cases heard. Athens was provided with a good water-supply; water was brought by aqueduct from the Ilissus valley, and the famous spring-house (*Enneakrounos*, 'nine-jets') was built in the agora, the water channelled in clay pipes from the spring Callirrhoe. The Peisistratids beautified the city with new temples (remains of the buildings have been found on the Acropolis, as well as many marble statues) and they encouraged art and literature: for instance, Simonides of Ceos and Anacreon of Teos were invited to Athens. The *Panathenaic festival was celebrated with greater splendour from 566 onwards, with the addition of contests in athletics, music, and poetry; recitals of Homer by rhapsodes were said to have been introduced by the Peisistratids (*see* HOMER 65). Peisistratus is also credited with the creation of the state festival of the City *Dionysia in 534, and with encouraging the cult of Demeter at *Eleusis.

**Pelasgians** A people who figure in Greek mythical history, thought of by the Greeks as the original pre-Greek inhabitants of *Greece and the Aegean area, with whom they sometimes included the Tyrrhenians (Etruscans). Since the Athenians claimed to be autochthonous they too were 'Pelasgian' (*see* ATHENS 2). *See also* PELASGUS.

**Pelasgus** Early king of Argos, father of *Lycaon. He was king at the time when *Danaus and the Danaids arrived, and welcomed Demeter when she came in search of *Persephone.

**Pēˈleus** In Greek myth, son of *Aeacus (mythical king of Aegina) and Endeis; he became king of Phthia in Thessaly. His name may mean 'man of Pelion' (a mountain in Thessaly). When he and his brother *Telamon killed their half-brother Phocus, Aeacus banished them; Peleus went to Phthia, where the then king Eurytion purified him of his crime and gave him his daughter in marriage and a share of his kingdom. Peleus took part in the Calydonian boar-hunt (*see* MELEAGER), where he accidentally killed Eurytion and was again banished. He went to Iolcus in Thessaly where Acastus, son of Pelias, purified him, and he took part in Pelias' funeral games where he wrestled with *Atalanta. Acastus' wife, Astyda-

meia, fell in love with Peleus. When he rejected her she sent a message to his wife saying that he was about to marry another woman; at that his wife hanged herself. Astydameia told her husband that Peleus had made advances to her; Acastus then took Peleus hunting on Mount Pelion, hid his sword as he slept, and left him to be attacked by the Centaurs. The Centaur *Chiron, however, restored his sword; Peleus then captured Iolcus and took his vengeance on Astydameia by killing her and marching his army between the pieces of her severed body. He was given as wife the goddess Thetis (*see* NEREUS). Zeus had previously fallen in love with her, but when told by Prometheus that she was fated to bear a son more powerful than his father, decided to give Thetis to a mortal so that her son should be mortal also. Peleus had to wrestle with her while she changed into various shapes in order to win her. At their wedding feast, which was attended by the gods, the Apple of Discord was thrown down (*see* PARIS, JUDGEMENT OF). Thetis' child was Achilles, whom Peleus took to Chiron to be brought up. On his death Peleus was reunited with Thetis and made immortal.

**Peˈlias** In Greek myth, son of Poseidon and *Tyro, and the usurper king of Iolcus in Thessaly, the rightful king being his half-brother Aeson, father of Jason; *see* ARGONAUTS, and for his death *see* MEDEA.

**Pēˈlion** High wooded mountain in (Magnesian) Thessaly, famous as the home of the Centaur *Chiron. In Greek myth, the Giants *Otus and Ephialtes, in an attempt to scale the heavens and overthrow the gods, piled Pelion upon Ossa (another Thessalian mountain) and Ossa upon Olympus.

**Pella** Capital of Macedonia c.400–167 BC (i.e. from the time of King Archelaus until the conquest by Rome), on the river Lydias, which is navigable from Pella to the sea. It became the largest Macedonian city until overtaken by Thessalonika in 146 BC. Pella was later a Roman colony. The ancient city has been extensively excavated.

**Peloˈpia** Daughter of Thyestes and mother of Aegisthus. *See* PELOPS.

**Peloˈpidas** (c.410–364 BC) Theban general, who with his friend and colleague *Epaminondas brought *Thebes to the zenith of her power. In 379 BC, with six confederates dressed as women, he killed the pro-Spartan generals who, with the support of a Spartan garrison, were tyrannizing Thebes. At the battle of Leuctra in 371 BC Thebes drove the Spartans out of central Greece. Pelopidas won great fame for his leadership of the *Sacred Band both at this battle and at his earlier defeat of the Spartans at Tegyra (375 BC). He accompanied Epaminondas on his first invasion of the Peloponnese (370/69), but after that looked northwards to Thebes' other enemies, *Alexander of Pherae (in Thessaly), and Macedon. In 364, in an expedition against Alexander of Pherae, Pelopidas, although victorious, was killed at the battle of Cynoscephalae.

**Pe'loponnese (Peloponnesos)** ('island of Pelops') The southern part of Greece, connected with central Greece by the Isthmus of Corinth. Its chief political divisions were Argos, Laconia (Sparta), Messenia, Elis, Achaea, and Arcadia.

**Peloponne'sian league** The earliest and longest-lived Greek alliance, dating from the reign of Cleomenes I (sixth century BC) when Sparta negotiated treaties with Peloponnesian states whereby she could expect the support of all members in war if a majority vote favoured such a course, each state having one vote. *Chilon, one of the *Seven Sages, is credited with its creation. The term is modern; ancient authors would refer to 'the Spartans and their allies'. The league was dissolved in 366 BC.

**Peloponne'sian War** (431–404 BC) A war between Athens and Sparta—the two leading Greek city-states—and their respective allies. A number of sources of friction sparked it off, notably Athenian intervention in a quarrel between Corinth (Sparta's ally) and her colony Corcyra, but the real reason for the conflict, according to the Athenian historian *Thucydides, was the rise of Athens to greatness, which made the Spartans fear for their own position. Athens was morally the aggressor, but it was Sparta who declared war. Sparta's army was far superior in quality and quantity, but the Athenians had an even bigger advantage at sea. The defences of Athens were strong and the city could not be starved into surrender, as it was connected to the port of Piraeus by the *Long Walls and could import supplies almost with impunity. It had sufficient finances to buy supplies and pay the fleet (and army). This was the assessment of the situation made

by *Pericles, the Athenian leader, and his strategy was based upon it. He persuaded the country population to move themselves and their possessions into the city and into the space between the Long Walls, temporarily sacrificing their farms.

The first ten years of the war, known as the Archidamian War from the name of the Spartan king who led the incursions into Attica, were indecisive. The Peloponnesians who invaded and ravaged Attica in 431 found it deserted, and after about a month returned home; this was to be, in general, the pattern for the next six years. In 430 a devastating plague broke out in Athens and the city lost more than a quarter of her population. Pericles died as a result of it in 429, his death depriving Athens of the only man who could impose a single policy on the Athenians. Nevertheless the Athenians won a number of victories on land and at sea in the next few years, notably the capture of *Pylos in 425, and Sparta gave up her annual invasions of Attica and made overtures for peace. *Cleon, who had succeeded Pericles as the most influential politician in Athens, persuaded the Athenians to reject the Spartan offers, but both he and the outstanding Spartan general *Brasidas were killed at *Amphipolis in 422, and thus the two chief opponents of peace were removed (the 'pestles of war' as they were called in Aristophanes' *Peace*). The Peace of *Nicias was concluded in 421. It was in the main a victory for Athens, especially since she kept her empire intact while her enemies were divided, Corinth and Boeotia refusing to sign the Peace.

The truce was unstable and broke down completely in 415, when Athens, under the influence of *Alcibiades, sent a great fleet to attack Syracuse—the *Sicilian Expedition. The expedition was a disaster, ending in 413 with the defeat of the Athenian fleet and army and the exhaustion of their finances. The period 413–404 is sometimes known as the Ionian or Decelean War. Sparta was developing a good fleet of her own, financed by Persia. The war at sea continued to go Athens' way for several years, but in 405 the Spartan commander *Lysander destroyed the Athenian fleet at Aegospotami. Besieged by land and sea, without money or allies, Athens capitulated in April 404 and became virtually the subject-ally of Sparta, impoverished, her population severely depleted, all her overseas possessions lost, and her fleet reduced to twelve ships. Sparta imposed an oligarchy on the city, and for eight months in 404–403 Athens was ruled by the *Thirty Tyrants. Thereafter she regained her democracy and her freedom.

The principal literary authority for the Peloponnesian War up to 411 is Thucydides; for 411 to the end, Xenophon in the *Hellenica; see also DIODORUS SICULUS and OXYRHYNCHUS HISTORIAN.

**Peloponne'sian War, First** Modern name for the period of intermittent warfare in central Greece between Athens, Boeotia, Aegina, and Corinth (and occasionally Sparta) from 460 to 446 BC, ended by the *Thirty Years' Peace. During the Persian Wars elements in Boeotia had favoured the Persians (contrast *Plataea) and their defeat had weakened Boeotia, leaving her threatened by Athenian expansion. Athens abandoned her alliance with Sparta in favour of Argos and Thessaly (a change perhaps reflected by the prominence of Argos in Aeschylus' Oresteia of 458) and won some successes against Sparta's allies Corinth and Aegina. In 457 Boeotia allied herself to Sparta. These two defeated Athens at Tanagra in 457 (see CIMON), but a few months later the Athenians defeated the Boeotians at Oenophyta. This gave Athens control of Boeotia except for Thebes. However, in 447 the Boeotians defeated the Athenians at Coronea, killing the general Tolmides. As a result the Athenians withdrew from Boeotia and entered into the Thirty Years' Peace. *Aegina remained tributary to Athens but her autonomy was guaranteed. (See ATHENS 3.)

**Pelops** In Greek myth, son of the Lydian king *Tantalus; his mother is usually said to be Dione, daughter of Atlas. He was the founder of the Pelopid family after whom the Peloponnese is named. According to the usual story he was expelled from Sipylus in Lydia by Ilus, an early king of Troy, and brought his great wealth to Pisa in Elis, where he became king. Pelops has two main stories: in the first, his father Tantalus killed him when a child and served his flesh to the gods at a banquet, to see if they could tell it from that of some animal. *Demeter, absorbed in her grief for Persephone, ate part of the shoulder; but the other gods detected the nature of the dish, brought Pelops to life again, and replaced the missing shoulder with one of ivory. Tantalus was subsequently punished in Hades. The other story tells how Pelops, grown up, sought to marry Hippoda-

meia, daughter of Oenomaus king of Elis. The condition of winning her was that he should outdistance Oenomaus in a chariot-race. If he was caught, Oenomaus would spear him. Pelops bribed Myrtilus, the king's charioteer, to take out the lynch-pin of a wheel on his master's chariot; the wheel fell off, Oenomaus was thrown and killed, and Pelops carried off his bride. But he refused to give Myrtilus the promised reward and threw him in the sea (hence, perhaps, the name of the Myrtoan Sea, east of the Peloponnese). The dying Myrtilus (or Oenomaus) cursed Pelops, which is the origin of the curse upon his house. For the time being Pelops flourished and fathered six sons. Pindar speaks of his burial near the great altar at Olympia, where he was worshipped as a hero and sometimes said to be the founder of the Olympian games.

Two of Pelops' sons were Atreus and Thyestes, in whom the curse was manifested. Atreus became king of Mycenae, and Thyestes seduced his brother's wife Aërope; thereupon Atreus banished Thyestes but later recalled him on pretence of being reconciled and prepared a banquet for him consisting of the flesh of his two sons. When Thyestes realized what he had eaten, he fled in horror, calling down a curse on the house of Atreus. He now became, by his own daughter Pelopia, the father of Aegisthus, who was exposed at birth by his mother but brought up by shepherds; when Atreus heard of the boy's existence he sent for him and brought him up as his own child. When Aegisthus was grown up, Atreus sent him to kill Thyestes, but the latter recognized him as his own son and the two contrived the death of Atreus instead. Atreus was the father of *Agamemnon and Menelaus. When Agamemnon led the Greek expedition to Troy and left the kingdom of Mycenae in the care of his wife Clytemnestra, his cousin Aegisthus seduced her and joined with her in murdering Agamemnon on his return. Later, Agamemnon's son *Orestes, with the help of his sister *Electra, avenged their father by killing Aegisthus and Clytemnestra. The curse on the house was not finally expunged until the purification of Orestes. (See also ORESTEIA.)

Most of this legend is not known to Homer, for whom the kingdom passes naturally from Pelops to Atreus, Thyestes, and Agamemnon.

**penalties, legal** See EXILE; LAW AT ATHENS; LAW, ROMAN; PRISON.

**penā'tēs, di** In Roman religion, 'the gods dwelling in the store cupboard' (*penus*, 'provisions'), who had their images in the atrium of every Roman house and were regarded together with the *lares as protectors of the house. There were also state *penates* (*penates publici*, protectors of Rome); their cult was attached to the temple of *Vesta. According to Virgil, Aeneas had brought these to Italy from Troy. For Virgil, not only Rome and Troy had their *penates* but even Carthage, the city of a hated enemy; similarly in the fourth Georgic the bees, the most human-like of the animal creation, 'have their *penates* and their fixed abode'. The worship of the domestic *penates* centred on the family meal: a portion was set aside and thrown on the flames of the hearth for the gods, and the table always held a salt-cellar and small offerings for them. A member of the family, returning after an absence, would greet the *penates* as living members of the household, the traveller's stick perhaps hung up beside their images.

**Pēne'lopē (Pēnelopeiā)** In Homer's *Odyssey*, daughter of Icarius and wife of *Odysseus. She faithfully awaits her husband's return during his twenty years' absence (ten years at the siege of Troy, ten years in his wanderings afterwards), although wooed by numerous suitors among the local nobles. She pretends she cannot remarry until she has woven a shroud for Odysseus' father, Laertes. This she unravels every night, so that the work is never completed, but her deception is revealed by one of the maids and she is compelled to finish it. She then promises to marry the suitor who can string the bow of her absent husband and perform a feat of archery. Odysseus returns in disguise at this juncture, wields the bow against the suitors and, when he reveals to her his knowledge of the construction of their bed, is finally accepted by Penelope as her husband.

In the *Telegonia* Telegonus marries Penelope after Odysseus' death. *See* EPIC CYCLE and PAN.

**pene'stae** *See* THESSALY.

**penta'meter** In Greek and Latin, line of verse containing five metrical units (*metra*) or feet. In practice the term almost always refers to the elegiac pentameter.

**pentāthlon** An event in the Greek athletic *festivals. Competitors in this event had to enter five contests: long jump, foot-race, throwing the discus, throwing the javelin, and wrestling. Victory in three events seems to have been sufficient for overall victory, but not necessary. It is not known how victory was decided if no competitor won three events. *See also* ATHLETICS.

**penteco'nter** The Greek warship of the archaic period, from the late seventh century BC, a long ship rowed by fifty (*pentekonta*) oarsmen, each pulling a single oar. The ships were equipped with masts and linen sails for long journeys, and they were steered by a helmsman from a raised platform at the stern, using one or two steering oars. From the late sixth century BC the penteconter was largely but not entirely superseded by the *trireme.

**Pentēkontaĕ'tia** In Greek history, the 'Period of fifty years' (roughly) between the end of the Persian and the beginning of the Peloponnesian Wars (479-431 BC). It was described (but not so called) by the historian Thucydides (1.89-118), with some omissions and some doubtful chronology. This was the period in which Athens developed her empire (*see* ATHENS 3 and DELIAN LEAGUE) and produced some of her greatest works of art and literature. It was the age of the statesman Pericles, the tragedians Aeschylus and (for the first half of their productive lives) Sophocles and Euripides, the philosopher Anaxagoras, the sophist Protagoras, and the artists Polygnotus and Pheidias; the Parthenon was built during this time, and Socrates, Thucydides, and Aristophanes grew up. Thucydides represents Pericles as describing the Athens of his day as 'the school of Greece'. In other parts of Greece it was the period of Pindar, Bacchylides, Herodotus, Parmenides, Zeno, Empedocles, and Polycleitus.

**Penthesilē'a (Penthesileia)** In Greek myth, queen of the *Amazons who came to the aid of Troy after the death of Hector. She fought with distinction, according to the *Aethiopis*, but was eventually killed by Achilles, who grieved over her body.

**Pentheus** In Greek myth, son of Echion and of Agave, daughter of *Cadmus king of Thebes. *See* BACCHAE.

**Pe'rdiccas** Name of several notable Macedonians. The king Perdiccas II was active in
the Peloponnesian War, changing allegiance
several times in his own interest. Another
Perdiccas was second-in-command to Alexander the Great and became in effect regent
of the empire after Alexander's death;
soon after that he was killed in a mutiny. *See*
MACEDON.

**Perdix** *See* DAEDALUS.

**Peria'nder (Periandros)** Tyrant of *Corinth
from about 627 to 587 BC, who succeeded his
father *Cypselus and brought Corinth to the
height of fame and prosperity. Periander was
probably a stern ruler, and is reputed to
have killed his wife and quarrelled with
his sons. Herodotus tells how he was advised
to deal with rivals by the tyrant *Thrasybulus,
who walked him through a field of corn,
lopping off the tallest heads. A powerful and
energetic man, his practical good sense led
to his being included by some among the
*Seven Sages of Greece (his court is the
scene of Plutarch's dialogue the *Banquet of
the Seven Sages*). He was a patron of the
arts (*Arion the dithyrambic poet stayed at his
court) and he was probably responsible for
the construction of the *diaulos* or portage way
across the Isthmus of Corinth (*see* CORINTH,
ISTHMUS OF).

**Pe'riclēs** (*c*.495–429 BC) Athenian statesman,
an *Alcmaeonid, son of *Xanthippus and Agariste, niece of *Cleisthenes (2). In politics he
supported the *democracy and came into political prominence as one of the state prosecutors of *Cimon in 463. In 462/1 he and
*Ephialtes joined in reducing the powers of
the *Areopagus, and after Ephialtes' murder
and Cimon's *ostracism, both in 461, he became the most influential man in Athens. From
this time until his death he dominated Athenian politics, and he has given his name to the
most brilliant period of Athenian history, 'Peri-
clean Athens' standing for a high point of
Greek civilization. Athens' imperialistic policy
was developed under his guidance, and the
*Delian League, created to keep the Persians
out of Greece, was converted into an Athenian
empire. Also attributed to Pericles is the introduction of jury pay (*see* JURIES) and the law
restricting Athenian citizenship to those
whose mothers as well as fathers were Athenian citizens (*see* MARRIAGE LAW).

Athens' imperialism brought her into conflict with Sparta, which was involved in hostilities against Athens from 460 to 446 (*see*
PELOPONNESIAN WAR, FIRST). The Thirty Years'
Peace which followed gave Pericles the opportunity to carry on a great building-campaign,
most notably of the *Parthenon. When war
broke out again with Sparta in 431 (the *Peloponnesian War), Pericles dictated a policy for
Athens calculated to neutralize Spartan superiority on land, but it involved considerable
hardship for the population of Attica. Nevertheless his authority was undiminished until
the ravages of the plague in 430 broke Athenian morale. He was then removed from office,
tried for embezzlement, and fined. Soon after
he was reinstated, but he too had caught the
plague, and he died six months later. No other
Athenian ever achieved Pericles' unchallenged
ascendancy. The historian Thucydides, his
great admirer, says that under him Athens,
though nominally a democracy, was in
fact ruled by its first citizen. He was a man of
powerful character, incorruptible, grave
and reserved in manner, dignified in speech.
He associated with the intellectuals of the
day, Pheidias, Anaxagoras, Sophocles, Herodotus. Some of them, including his mistress
*Aspasia, were attacked by his enemies, who
could not impeach the man himself. The
Funeral Oration which he delivered over
the Athenian dead after the first year of the
Peloponnesian War (Thucydides 2.35–46) expresses his high concept of Athens and
the Athenian democracy, although his ideals
included undisguised imperialism. *See also*
PERSIANS.

**Peri hy'psous** *See* LONGINUS ON THE SUBLIME.

**Perikeiro'menē** ('The girl with shorn
hair') Greek comedy by *Menander, of
which about half has been discovered on papyrus.

A poor merchant Pataecus has exposed his
twin children, a boy and a girl (*see* INFANTICIDE).
The boy Moschion is adopted by a rich woman
who subsequently marries Pataecus, and the
latter adopts Moschion, not knowing that he is
really his own son. The girl Glycera, now the
mistress of a soldier Polemon, is discovered
kissing Moschion, whom she knows to be
her brother, although Moschion himself is
still ignorant of this fact. In jealousy Polemon
cuts off her hair (hence the title of the play),

whereupon she takes refuge in the house of the now wealthy Pataecus. Some trinkets left with her when she was exposed reveal her identity, and Moschion also discovers his identity by eavesdropping. Thus all are reconciled and Glycera is able to marry Polemon.

**Pe'rillus** *See* PHALARIS.

**Pe'riochae** ('Summaries') *See* LIVY.

**perioi'koi** ('dwellers around [Sparta]') In Laconia (the south-east territory of the Peloponnese), the free inhabitants of such small towns and villages as were not subjugated to *Sparta. Their origin is unclear. They were under Spartan supervision, however, served in the army and paid taxes on a par with Spartan citizens although they had no political rights in the Spartan state. They carried on what industry and commerce there was, from which Spartans were excluded.

**Peripate'tic School** The Aristotelian school of philosophy in Athens (*see* ARISTOTLE 1). Aristotle taught in the groves and gymnasium of the *Lyceum, where there were paths and walks, *peripatoi*, from which the school derived its name. Another ancient explanation for the name was that Aristotle was accustomed to 'walk about' (*peripatein*) while lecturing. Peripatetic philosophy is the kind taught by Aristotle and his successors (in contrast with the Academic philosophy of Plato; *see* ACADEMY).

**peripetei'a** In Greek tragedy, a 'sudden reversal' of circumstances; *see* POETICS.

**Persa** ('The Persian') Roman comedy by *Plautus. The subject is the deception of a pimp, to whom a Persian sells a beautiful Arabian captive. But the Persian is in fact the *parasite Saturio and the captive is his daughter; he has agreed to the deceit for the sake of a good meal.

**Persae** 1. Greek tragedy by Aeschylus; *see* PERSIANS. **2.** A nome by *Timotheus (1).

**Perse'phonē** (Lat. Prōse'rpina; also known as Kore, 'daughter') In Greek myth, the daughter of Zeus and Demeter, snatched away to be queen of the Underworld by *Hades while she was picking flowers in the meadows of Enna in central Sicily. For Demeter's search for her daughter *see* DEMETER. Zeus yielded at length to her lamentations, but Persephone could not be entirely released from the Under-

world because she had eaten some pomegranate seeds (as was revealed by Ascalaphus, son of Acheron, river of the Underworld, whom Demeter thereupon turned into an owl). It was arranged that she should spend eight (or six) months of the year on earth and the remainder with Hades. The myth is told in the *Homeric Hymn to Demeter, by Ovid in his *Fasti* and *Metamorphoses*, and by *Claudian in *De raptu Proserpinae*. Persephone was understood in ancient times to symbolize the seed-corn that must descend into the earth so that from seeming death new life may germinate; she later came to symbolize death. Cicero visited Enna and tells in his Verrine orations (*see* CICERO (1) 1) how he found the priestess and inhabitants grief-stricken because Verres had stolen their statue of Demeter. *See also* DIONYSUS ZAGREUS and ORPHEUS.

**Perse'polis** In Persia, the residence and the burial-place of the Achaemenid kings (Cyrus, Darius, Xerxes, etc.). In 331 BC it was sacked and the palaces burned by Alexander the Great.

**Pe'rseus** 1. In Greek myth, the son of Zeus and Danae. *See* DANAE for the story of his birth, of the prophecy that he would kill his grandfather Acrisius, and of the casting away of mother and child and their arrival on the island of Seriphos, where Polydectes was king. Polydectes fell in love with Danae, but his love was not returned. Perseus was now a young man, and Polydectes, finding him an obstacle to his designs on Danae, persuaded him to undertake the dangerous venture of obtaining the head of Medusa (*see* GORGONS), thinking that he would be destroyed. But the gods favoured him: although accounts vary as to which gods gave him which gifts, they commonly say that Pluto lent him a cap of darkness which would make him invisible, Hermes wings for his feet, Athena a mirror (so that he need not look directly at Medusa, whose gaze turned people to stone), and the nymphs a wallet to put the head in. Directions for finding Medusa were given him by the *Graeae. On his return, having killed Medusa, Perseus rescued *Andromeda from where she was chained to a rock, and married her, after turning another suitor, Phineus, to stone when he attempted to carry her off. It is also said that with the Gorgon's head he turned *Atlas into a mountain, because Atlas had been inhospitable to him on his travels. Perseus then returned to Seriphos, just in time to save Danae from the violence of Polydectes, whom he also petrified. Leaving his brother Dictys there as king, Perseus now went to his native Argos, but found that his grandfather Acrisius had gone to Larissa in Thessaly. There Perseus, taking part in some games, accidentally killed him when throwing a discus and thus fulfilled the prophecy. He refused to take his grandfather's kingdom himself, to which he was heir, but withdrew to Asia, where his son Perses became ruler of the Persians, supposedly named after him; or, according to another version, took Tiryns in exchange for Argos and founded Mycenae.

**2.** King of Macedon 179–166 BC, elder son of Philip V. He devoted his energies to consolidating Macedonian power and prestige in Greece at a time when Greece, while nominally independent, was under the protection (and will) of Rome. He was defeated by Aemilius *Paullus at Pydna in the Third Macedonian War (*see* MACEDON) and taken to Rome, where he died.

**Persians (Persai)** (Lat. *Persae*) Greek tragedy by *Aeschylus, produced in 472 BC eight years after the Persian defeat at Salamis, which it celebrates. Pericles was *choregos. The play was modelled on the (now lost) *Phoenissae* of *Phrynichus.

The chorus of Persian elders express their anxiety for the fate of Xerxes' expedition against Greece in 480 BC (*see* PERSIAN WARS), and Atossa, mother of Xerxes, tells of ominous dreams and portents. A messenger arrives and announces the disaster of Salamis, giving a vivid account of the battle and the destruction of the Persian fleet. Atossa and the chorus call up the spirit of the dead Darius (father of Xerxes), who sees in the catastrophe the accomplishment of oracles and the punishment by the gods of the Persians' excessive ambition. He tries to console the queen and chorus but foretells the defeat at Plataea. Xerxes himself arrives, his robes torn, and the play ends in general lamentations. The author displays a certain compassion for the vanquished, mingled with pride in the great victory of the Greeks. This is the only surviving Greek tragedy based on a contemporary event.

**Persian Wars** A series of conflicts between the Greek states and the Persian empire. For the early history of the Persian empire *see* CYRUS (1); CAMBYSES; and DARIUS.

The wars can be said to have begun in 490 BC, when the Persian king Darius invaded mainland Greece; they effectively ended in 479 BC when his son Xerxes, having suffered comprehensive defeats on land and at sea, was forced to withdraw from the Aegean (although peace was not agreed for another thirty years). However, conflict between Greeks and Persians really originated in 499, when the Greek colonies of Ionia, which were under Persian rule, were encouraged to revolt by Aristagoras, deputizing for *Histiaeus, the absent Greek tyrant of *Miletus who was loyal to Darius. Histiaeus seems to have realized the hopelessness of the Ionian cause in the face of the great resources of the Persian empire (*see also* HECATAEUS), but he failed to subdue the revolt, and too frightened to return to Darius he retreated to his stronghold in Thrace. Aristagoras did not obtain help from Sparta but won support at Athens and Eretria (in Euboea). After a number of successes the Ionians were defeated at Lade (an island off Miletus) in 494. The Persians sacked Miletus and other Greek cities of Ionia (*see* PHRYNICHUS) but then allowed them democratic local government.

Darius decided to punish Athens and Eretria for the help they had given the Ionian colonists. In 492 the Persians conquered Thrace and Macedonia, but the Persian fleet was wrecked in a storm, bringing the expedition to an end. Two years later the Persians attacked again; they destroyed Eretria and landed an army in Attica in the Bay of Marathon. The Athenians appealed to Sparta for help (*see* PHEIDIPPIDES), but the Spartans arrived too late and the Athenians, numbering some 10,000, had to face a far stronger enemy with help only from Plataea, who sent all her hoplites (heavy infantry), a thousand men. Led by *Miltiades, the Greeks won a great victory, attributed largely to the Athenians, utterly routing the enemy. According to Herodotus, 6,400 Persians were killed, and only 192 Athenians. This was the end of the First Persian War, in reality a minor affair aimed only at Athens and Eretria, but in popular estimation soon acquiring mythical status. For Aristophanes and others sixty years later the 'men who fought at Marathon', *Marathonomachai*, epitomized the stubborn virtues of the old soldier. The epitaph of Aeschylus the tragedian claimed as his only glory that he had fought in the battle.

Darius at once set about measures for a new invasion. He died in 486, but his son and successor Xerxes carried on the preparations on a huge scale and in 480 attacked by land and sea. The numbers given by Herodotus for the size of the Persian forces are fantastic; modern estimates are 100,000 men for the army and 600 ships for the navy. The route of the Persian army lay through the narrow pass of *Thermopylae, which was held by the Spartan king *Leonidas. For two days he and his contingent of 6,000–7,000 men held back the Persians and inflicted heavy losses on them. Then a traitor showed the Persians a mountain path by which they could outflank the Greek position. When Leonidas heard what had happened he dismissed his allies but remained with his 300 Spartans to die heroically in an impossible last stand (for their epitaph see SIMONIDES). During these three days the Greek fleet was holding its own against the Persian fleet at Artemisium (a promontory on the north-east coast of Euboea) and the Greeks were technically the victors when the news of Thermopylae reached them; they and the Persians broke off, both sides battered by storms. Nevertheless this battle was regarded as a victory for the Greeks in which, according to Pindar, the Athenians, who provided the largest contingent, 'laid the shining foundation of freedom'. The Persian army now advanced into Attica, and Athens, which had been evacuated in response to an enigmatic Delphic oracle telling the Athenians to 'trust to their wooden wall', was captured and burned in September 480. At sea, however, the Athenians remained strong, and within days of the sack of Athens the Greeks won a brilliant and crushing victory over the Persian fleet at Salamis (see BOREAS). Xerxes, who had watched the battle from a throne on the mainland shore, returned to Persia, leaving a picked force to winter in Thessaly and continue the campaign by land. In the following year (479) the Greeks won a decisive victory near Plataea, largely through the 'Dorian spear' of Sparta, and the Persian commander Mardonius was killed. Meanwhile the Greek fleet had gone on to the offensive, and on the same day (it was said) as the battle at Plataea won another victory at Mycale on the Ionian coast. These two victories ended the Persian threat, and until hostilities were formally ended by the Peace of *Callias, the Greeks were on the offensive.

As a result of the Persian Wars, Greeks in general, becoming increasingly conscious of their common nationality, acquired a sense of superiority, and the Athenian city-state in particular gained enormously in pride and self-confidence. Our knowledge of these wars is derived mainly from Herodotus. Of contemporary evidence there are inscriptions, some epigrams of Simonides, and Aeschylus' tragedy the *Persians*. The Persian side of the story is largely unknown.

**Pe'rsius Flaccus, Aulus** (AD 34–62, known generally as Persius) Latin satirical poet. Born at Volaterrae in Etruria, he belonged to an equestrian family and was a relation of the famous *Arria, wife of Paetus. He was educated at Rome, and became the pupil of the Stoic Cornutus, who exercised a strong influence on him (see STOICISM); a fellow pupil was the Roman epic poet Lucan. He joined the group of Stoics around *Thrasea Paetus, the senator who was married to the younger Arria. He bequeathed his books and a part of his large fortune to Cornutus, who accepted the books but not the money. Persius is said to have been a modest and gentle man. He took no part in public life, died young, and left only a small amount of literary work: six satires (650 hexameter lines) modelled on *Lucilius and Horace. The prologue is in the scazon metre, 'limping iambics' so-called; satire is only a semi-poetic genre. Except for the first, these poems are homilies rather than satires in the strict sense, preaching an uncompromising Stoic morality as it could be applied to private life, and only incidentally touching on public life. Persius uses a mixture of styles and voices which are sometimes difficult to disentangle, and his language is obscure, but his moral sincerity is unforced.

In Satire 1, which has the form of a conversation between Persius and a friend, he attacks the artificiality of modern poetry which has corrupted Persius' own plain style (perhaps quoting from the poems of the emperor Nero himself). Like *Midas he entrusts a secret to the ground: all Romans have asses' ears. Satire 2 is concerned with the right use of prayer, mocking those who ask for external goods rather than virtue. Satire 3 is obscure in form. It seems to be a dialogue between a lazy student and his Stoic tutor; the student is forgetting all the virtues he has been taught but should reform before it is too late. Satire 4 is a dialogue between the young *Alcibiades, ambitious to be a politician, and Socrates, who urges virtue and self-knowledge. Satire 5 is a eulogy of Cornutus the philosopher, describing the simple and studious life the poet leads when in the former's company; its subject is the rarity of true freedom—we are all the slaves of our passions or superstitions. Satire 6 is addressed to Caesius Bassus (a lyric poet commended by Quintilian) who edited Persius' satires after his death and is said to have died in the eruption of Vesuvius in AD 79 (*see* POMPEII); Perseus meditates on the small legacy he will leave his heirs, and expounds the wisdom of living comfortably, but not covetously.

**persuasion** *See* SOPHIST.

**Perusine War** (42–40 BC) Campaign by Mark *Antony's wife Fulvia and brother Lucius Antonius against Octavian while Antony was in Egypt. Octavian attacked Lucius partly because the latter championed the Italian cities against the settlement of Octavian's veterans. Lucius took refuge and was besieged in the Etruscan hill-city of Perusia (Perugia) during the winter of 41/40 until starved into surrender. Octavian executed the Perusine senate but forgave Lucius, who died later in Spain.

***Pervigi'lium Ve'neris*** ('Eve of Venus') A poem preserved in the *Latin *Anthology* written in trochaic tetrameters catalectic, 93 lines long. The author and date are unknown, but it was written after the second century AD, perhaps as late as the fourth century. The setting is Sicily, on the eve of the spring festival of Venus; the poem celebrates the triumph of spring, the resurgence of life in the world, and the next day's festival, its spirit summed up by the passionate refrain, *cras amet qui nunquam amavit, quique amavit cras amet* ('he who has never loved and he who has loved—tomorrow let them both love'). The poem ends on a poignant note: *illa cantat; nos tacemus; quando ver venit meum?*) ('[the nightingale] sings; we are silent; when will my own springtime come?'). The poem is unique in Latin for its sensuous beauty, here enhanced by the strong beat of the trochaic rhythm and by assonance, both characteristic of later Latin accentual poetry.

**Petrō'nius A'rbiter** (d. AD 66) Latin satirical writer, author of the *Satyricōn* ('[Tales] of satyrs') or *Satyrica*. Although it cannot be proved, he is usually assumed to be the voluptuary of that name at Nero's court, whose life and death are memorably described by Tacitus (*Annals*, 16.17–20). He was at one time governor of Bithynia and later a consul, and was subsequently admitted by the emperor Nero to the inner circle of his intimates and chosen by him, in Tacitus' words, as his 'arbiter of taste', *elegantiae arbiter*, a play on his name. *Tigellinus, prefect of the praetorians, whose jealousy he aroused, falsely accused him to the emperor as implicated in the conspiracy of Piso (*see* PISO (3)); he was forced to commit suicide, but not before he had smashed a valuable wine-ladle to prevent it falling into the emperor's hands, and written a letter detailing the latter's vices. Tacitus describes Petronius as devoted to the refined pursuit of pleasure, indolent in his ordinary life, but energetic in public affairs.

Of the *Satyricon*, a long picaresque novel with affinities to the Greek Hellenistic *novel, only parts of books 14, 15, and 16 survive. The title alludes to the influence of satire, and perhaps, with irony, to the unsatyric sexual incapacity of Encolpius. It is in prose interspersed with verse, like the Menippean satires (*see* MENIPPUS), and describes the disreputable adventures of the homosexual pair Encolpius (the narrator) and the younger Giton around the bay of Naples, fashionable with philhellenic Romans, and in the low haunts of the semi-Greek cities of southern Italy. They encounter a number of characters, including the unscrupulous Ascyltus. The three are completely devoid of morals but have a quick intelligence which sees them through their escapades, narrated with dispassionate realism. The principal episode in book 15 is the *Cena Trimalchionis*, 'Trimalchio's dinner-party' (it appears in only one manuscript, not found until 1650). Trimalchio is a freedman, a vulgar *nouveau-riche* to whose dinner-party the adventurers obtain admission. He and his wife Fortunata present an ostentatious display of wealth in the decoration of the house and in the profusion of fantastic dishes set before the guests; there are grotesque incidents during dinner—a drunken brawl and a dog-fight—and ridiculous conversation; Trimalchio's absurd conduct as he becomes more and more drunk finally reaches a maudlin stage in which he describes the contents of his will and his future monument. Two good ghost stories round off the episode, one about a werewolf, the other about witches substituting a changeling made of straw for a boy. The whole is told with vitality and panache.

A further character in the remaining incidents is a lecherous poet named Eumolpus with whom the adventurers travel to Croton in south Italy to advance their fortunes by fraud. The sea-voyage ends in shipwreck, and the extant portion of the work ends with various amorous adventures and misfortunes sometimes reminiscent of the *Odyssey*. In the course of these Eumolpus expounds his views on epic poetry (in chapter 118 he refers, in a phrase that has since become famous, to *Horatii curiosa felicitas*, 'Horace's studied felicity'). As illustration of the kind of inspirational poetry of his own day that he deplores, he recites sixty iambics on the fall of Troy and some 300 hexameters on the Civil War of 49 BC. It is Eumolpus who, at an earlier stage (111), relates the story of the widow of Ephesus who, watching inconsolably in the vault where her recently dead husband has been laid, is induced by a kindly soldier to take food, and presently to accept him as her lover. This is a story very similar in type to the *Milesian Tales*. Petronius' characters, while thoroughly disreputable, are not wholly unlikeable. The racy, vivid, colloquial Latin in which the *Satyricon* is written reveals a great deal about the popular speech of the time, and about tastes and attitudes that appear to fit the Neronian court. A few lyric and elegiac poems by the same author have also survived.

**Phaeā'cians (Phaiākes)** In Homer's *Odyssey*, the magical seafaring people of the island of Scheria on which Odysseus was cast ashore (book 5). Their king was Alcinöus.

**Phaedo (Phaidōn)** (b. *c.*418 BC, an aristocrat of Elis in the north-west Peloponnese) Founder of the philosophical school at Elis. Said to have been a prostitute in his youth, he came to Athens as a young man, perhaps as a prisoner of war, and became one of Socrates' most devoted pupils. Plato named after him the dialogue in which Socrates' last hours are described. After the latter's death Phaedo returned to Elis.

**Phaedo** Dialogue by *Plato in which *Phaedo narrates the discussion that took place between Socrates and his friends during the last hours of his life, and the manner of his dying. The dialogue starts from the remark of Socrates

that the true philosopher 'practises for death' (67) because it is his affirmation of the principles by which he has lived; the philosopher will be convinced that after his death the soul of the just man will be under the care of good and wise gods no less than before—and perhaps in the company of the best men of the past; moreover, death is the release of the *soul from the body, and it has been the philosopher's aim to make the soul independent of bodily vicissitudes. (Plato's phrase inspired Nietzsche to denounce him as the enemy of life-affirming Hellenism.) Cebes' objection that the soul may not survive death leads to the series of arguments which make up the core of the dialogue and are intended to vindicate Socrates' belief in the immortality of the soul. One argument is that learning is recollection of knowledge possessed in a former existence (an argument prominent in *Meno also), so the soul must have existed before its present incarnation. The reader meets the theory of Forms or Ideas (*see* PLATO 4) by which, for example, a thing is beautiful when it partakes of the Form of beauty. It is also argued that the soul, which imparts life to the body, cannot admit death, and is therefore immortal. Socrates introduces this last section by giving an account of his intellectual history, describing his difficulties with the kind of explanation of the physical world offered in the natural sciences (including that of *Anaxagoras) and the evolution of his own method of enquiry based on *elenchus. The argument is rounded off with a myth which gives a speculative picture of the afterlife and the judgement of departed souls. Belief in 'either this or something like it' is said to be a noble risk. The dialogue ends with the moving description of Socrates' fearless acceptance of the cup of hemlock. This is the work from which *Cato (2) is said to have drawn strength on the night before he committed suicide.

**Phaedra** In Greek myth, daughter of *Minos, king of Crete, and Pasiphaē, and sister of Ariadne; she married Theseus, king of Athens. For her story *see* HIPPOLYTUS.

**Phaedra** Roman tragedy by *Seneca (2), based on the *Hippolytus* of Euripides, with certain variations. Here it is Phaedra herself (not the Nurse on her behalf) who declares her love to her stepson Hippolytus; she then in person (not in a posthumous letter) slanders him to Theseus; and finally it is she herself who discloses her guilt, before she dies (not the goddess Artemis after her suicide).

The play opens with Hippolytus preparing for the hunt. After his departure Phaedra complains to the Nurse about the perpetual absence of her husband Theseus, and admits her passion for her step-son Hippolytus. The Nurse counsels self-control and reminds Phaedra of Hippolytus' vow of chastity. To Hippolytus the Nurse later recommends sexual experience in general terms, but he reaffirms his rejection of all women. Phaedra enters and faints; Hippolytus catches her. Phaedra seizes her opportunity and asks Hippolytus to satisfy her passion but he rushes away horrified, dropping his sword as he goes. This the Nurse picks up, realizing it can be used as evidence against him. Theseus suddenly returns, to a palace in confusion, and the Nurse tells him Phaedra intends suicide. When Theseus makes threats in order to extract the truth, Phaedra says that the owner of the sword has tried to rape her by force. Theseus recognizes the badge on the sword and curses Hippolytus, who subsequently is killed by a bull from the sea (*see* HIPPOLYTUS). Phaedra enters with a sword, confesses that she has lied to Theseus, and stabs herself. Hippolytus' remains are brought in, which Theseus prepares for a funeral pyre. Phaedra's body is to be buried deep in the ground.

***Phaedrus*** Dialogue by *Plato in direct speech between Socrates and his Athenian friend Phaedrus, an apparently young member of Socrates' circle, on the banks of the river Ilissus a little outside Athens. Socrates claims (perhaps ironically) to be moved by the beauties of nature, and ascribes to that the exalted tone of his second speech. Phaedrus reads a speech purporting to be by the Attic orator *Lysias (*see also* PARODY) expounding a paradoxical view of love, that it is better for a boy to accept as a lover a man who is not truly in love with him than to accept one who is, which Socrates counters with a cleverer speech on the same theme. Socrates is then prevented from departing by his 'divine sign' (*see* SOCRATES), which convinces him that he has been blasphemous to associate love only with physical passion: he recants in another speech. The true lover is worthy of respect; he is mad with a madness that comes from the gods. To understand this it is necessary to understand the nature of the soul, and Socrates first establishes that the soul

is immortal. He then describes its nature and destiny by the analogy of a charioteer driving a pair of winged horses. These represent the three parts of the soul, in which reason controls both a person's spirited side and their sensual appetites. The true lover may be at first attracted physically to a like-minded person, but if his love is reciprocated, and the sensual appetite overcome, both lovers may leave behind love of physical beauty for the common pursuit of that beauty which is to be finally found only in the Form (or Idea) of the Good (*see* PLATO 5). The conversation returns abruptly to a prosaic discussion of *rhetoric based on the three speeches just made; rhetoric should be a true *techne*, having as its foundation knowledge of the truth, which can be obtained only by those passionate in its pursuit (*see* RHETORIC). Only living speech, not books, can produce knowledge. Plato first describes here a technique for reaching a definition by 'collection and division'—collecting a general field and then dividing it to distinguish the particular thing to be defined. The ancients debated whether this dialogue was concerned primarily with love or with rhetoric. Phaedrus appears also in Plato's *Protagoras* and *Symposium*.

**Phaedrus, Gaius Julius** (*c.*15 BC–*c.* AD 50) Thracian slave who came to Rome and became a freedman in the household of Augustus, the author (in Latin) of a collection of *fables in five books containing some hundred stories, published probably in the thirties of the first century AD. There is an appendix of another thirty-two fables, probably also by Phaedrus. The collection includes fables proper, a number of anecdotes (e.g. about Aesop, Socrates, and Menander), and defences of the author against detractors. The fables are based on *Aesop and other collections as well as the author's own experiences. They are written in verse, in iambic senarii, and their object is to give advice and to entertain. They are generally serious or satirical, dealing with the injustices of life and social and political evils, but occasionally they are light and amusing. In general they express patient resignation. Phaedrus observed in the prologue to the third book that the fable was invented so that a slave might say obliquely what he dared not speak openly. Many of the stories are well known to us, having been handed down (often through the Greek collection of *Babrius) through medieval times to the present day. They include 'The Wolf and the

Lamb', 'The Fox and the Sour Grapes' and 'King Log and King Water-snake'. Phaedrus is the source of the expression 'adding insult to injury', *iniuriae qui addideris contumeliam* (5.3.5).

**Phaeno'mena** Astronomical poem of *Aratus.

**Phaestus** Ancient city of south Crete, the site of a Minoan palace (*see* CRETE) destroyed in about 1400 BC. The fired-clay tablet found there in 1908, known as the Phaestus disc, apparently dates from the middle or late Bronze age (second millennium BC) and is inscribed on both sides with pictographic writing, otherwise unknown but generally thought to be syllabic, running clockwise towards the centre. The script does not seem to relate to *Linear A or *Linear B, and it is not known whether the disc originated in Crete or what its purpose was. As a body of text employing reusable signs it is unique, and possibly a forgery.

**Phā'ethon** In Greek myth, son of *Helios (Sun) and *Clymene (2). When he grew up he sought out his father, who recognized him and offered him his choice of gift. Phaethon asked to be allowed to drive his father's chariot for one day. In spite of Helios' warning he attempted to do so, but soon proved unequal to controlling the horses. They bolted from their course and the earth was in danger of being burnt up, when Zeus intervened and hurled a thunderbolt at Phaethon, who fell into the river Eridanus. His sisters wept for him until they were turned into alder-trees; their tears, oozing from the trees, hardened into amber.

**Pha'laris** Tyrant of Acragas in Sicily in the mid-sixth century BC, soon after the foundation of that city (*c*.580 BC). He was remembered for his cruelty, supposedly roasting his enemies to death in a brazen bull with a fire underneath, their cries sounding like the roar of the bull. This was the invention of a certain Perillus, who was its first victim. The so-called 'Letters of Phalaris' were proved by the English scholar Richard Bentley (1662–1742) to be a forgery. The real author was a sophist of perhaps the second century AD.

**Phalē'rum** (modern Phaleron) The principal harbour of Athens until the early fifth century BC, i.e. before the Persian Wars and the development and fortification of *Piraeus, which lies

to the west. It is an open roadstead, offering little protection to ships. For the Long Wall connecting it with Athens *see* LONG WALLS.

**phallus** Model of the male genital organ, the symbol of fertility carried in procession in many ancient religious ceremonies in order to stimulate the fruitfulness of the earth, the flocks, and the people, and so prevent weakness of the race. In Greece the phallus was especially associated with the worship of Dionysus, the god of fertility (hence its connection with comedy; *see* COMEDY [Greek 1 and 2]); of Hermes, the god of pastures, crops, and herds (*see also* HERMS); of Pan, the protector of flocks; and of Demeter, the earth-goddess. Occasionally a god Phales was invoked, the personification of the phallus. In the Roman festival of the Liberalia (comparable with the Greek *Dionysia) the phallus was similarly carried in procession (*see also* PRIAPUS).

**pharmacology** *See* BOTANY and MEDICINE.

**Pharos** *See* ALEXANDRIA.

**Pharsā'lus, Pharsā'lia** In Thessaly, the scene of the decisive defeat of Pompey by Caesar in the summer of 48 BC. Pharsalus was the name of the city, Pharsalia of its territory.

**Pharsā'lia** Latin epic poem by *Lucan (AD 39–65) in ten books of hexameters, on the civil war between Pompey and Julius Caesar (the title in the manuscripts is *De bello civili*, 'On the civil war': the name *Pharsalia* comes from *Pharsalia nostra* at 9.985). The poem was apparently not completed and ends abruptly in the tenth book with Caesar at war in Egypt. Lucan probably intended to continue the narrative to the death of Caesar, if not further. It was not his purpose to give a full, historical account of the war (for which *see* CAESAR (2)), and apart from omissions there are a few notable departures from historical truth, as when he portrays Cicero haranguing Pompey on the eve of the battle of Pharsalus: in fact Cicero missed the battle because of illness. The poem may be seen as an inversion of the vision of Rome's triumphant development in Virgil's *Aeneid* book 6, an anguished portrayal of the self-destruction of the Roman republic, 'an imperial people turned their victorious right hands against their own breast' (1.3). There is no hero: rather there are two protagonists, with Cato the Younger as a third.

*Book 1.* The sources of the war; a sketch of the characters of the two leaders; Caesar's crossing of the river Rubicon into Italy. Caesar is confronted by the spirit of Rome, which challenges his right to advance. The flight of citizens and senators is described, together with the many hostile portents.

*Book 2.* Events in Italy (with a long digression on the massacres of Marius and Sulla); the resolution of Cato (2) and (Marcus Junius) Brutus to resist Caesar; the episode of the resistance of Corfinium (under the command of the senator Lucius Domitius Ahenobarbus); Pompey's withdrawal to Brundisium and his escape to Epirus.

*Book 3.* Caesar's occupation of Rome and the fighting on land and sea around Massalia; a description of the sacred Druid grove in the neighbourhood of the town, which Caesar had felled. The book ends with the description of a sea-battle.

*Book 4.* Caesar's campaign in Gaul. Confrontation in Illyria (north-west of Greece) including the incident of the attempted escape of some Caesarian soldiers on three rafts; one of these is stopped by the Pompeians and the soldiers on board, Gauls from Opitergium (Oderzo), kill each other rather than surrender. The expedition of Curio, Caesar's commander, to Africa, and his defeat and death at the hands of Juba; the legend of Hercules and Antaeus.

*Book 5.* The most interesting parts describe Appius, a Pompeian, consulting the *Delphic oracle, although it had been closed for many years, and receiving an ambiguous reply; and Caesar's attempt to cross the Adriatic Sea in a small boat on a stormy night.

*Book 6.* The fighting around Dyrrhachium (Epidamnus, in Illyria) and Caesar's withdrawal to Thessaly; the fight to the death of Caesar's centurion Scaeva (in reality he survived, with, according to Caesar, 120 holes in his shield). To Lucan's disgust, Sextus Pompeius (Pompey's younger son) consults the Thessalian witch Erichtho, who employs necromancy to foretell the destiny of the Pompeians.

*Book 7.* Pompey's deceptively happy dream before the battle of Pharsalus; omens all over the world presaged disaster. The battle itself is described, and the ensuing scenes.

*Book 8.* Pompey's flight first to Lesbos to join his wife and then to Egypt, and his murder there by the order of the royal council and of Ptolemy XIV.

*Book 9.* Pompey's spirit is borne to heaven and Cato pronounces a panegyric on the dead leader. Cato resolves to continue the war and marches with his troops to Mauretania (in North Africa). Confident in his Stoic faith and in the rightness of the course that he has chosen, he refuses to consult the oracle of Ammon. This book is largely praise of Cato. There is a digression on Egyptian serpents, their legendary origin in the blood of Medusa, the Gorgon, and their varieties. The Egyptians present Pompey's head to Caesar, who hypocritically laments his fate.

*Book 10.* Caesar's actions in Egypt, and his affair with Cleopatra. He is besieged by the troops of Pothinus and Achillas. At this point the poem ends abruptly.

Lucan had a difficult task in writing epic about events only a century before his own day. He discarded the epic convention of interventions by the gods to direct human actions, substituting an impersonal and negative Fate, through which the future is hinted at by a constant stream of portents and dreams. He introduced a number of digressions, which strike some readers as displaying seemingly irrelevant learning (see book 9 above). His work reaches magnificent extremes of rhetoric and the grotesque (e.g. his description of Caesar enjoying his breakfast among the corpses after Pharsalus, and of the wild beasts devouring the dead). But it is carried through with great vigour and brilliance; the sensational scenes appal and engross the reader; they are interspersed with passages of considerable power and pathos, such as that describing Pompey's farewell to Italy. The author's gift for incisive epigram is evident, and some lines have achieved fame: 'the conquering cause pleased the gods, the losing cause pleased Cato' (*victrix causa deis placuit sed victa Catoni*); of Caesar, 'believing that nothing had been done if anything remained still to do' (*nil actum credens cum quid superesset agendum*); and of friendship, 'nobody ever chooses to be the faithful friend of those already unfortunate' (*nulla fides unquam miseros elegit amicos*). Lucan's feelings for his subject were sincere: he detested Caesar and all he stood for, while admitting his greatness; he makes Pompey a tragic figure and evokes sympathy for him and his cause. The verse sometimes lacks flexibility, but despite the bleakness of its vision the rhetoric is impressive.

**Phei'dias** (active *c.*465–*c.*425 BC) Athenian sculptor, the most famous artist of the ancient world. He was a friend of *Pericles, who gave him a leading role in his great building programme in Athens; most notably he was in charge, according to Plutarch, of the sculptural decoration of the *Parthenon. A good deal of this sculpture survives (much of it in the British Museum), but Pheidias' cult statue of Athena, of gold and ivory ('chryselephantine') over a wooden core, does not; the Greek traveller *Pausanias (1.24.5) gives a description of it, from which several (much smaller) Roman copies have been identified. Another huge cult statue, considered Pheidias' masterpiece, was made for the temple of Zeus at *Olympia, and is known only from its representation on coins and gems. Pheidias' style was serene and majestic; it is said that when asked what model he was going to use for the likeness of Zeus, he replied that he would model it on Homer's lines in the *Iliad*, 'Cronion [Zeus] spoke, and nodded his dark brow, and the ambrosial locks waved from the king's immortal head; and he made great Olympus quake' (1.528). In 432 enemies of Pericles, trying to attack him through his friends, accused Pheidias of embezzling gold intended for the statue of Athena, but he was able to prove his innocence. He was then charged with impiety and put in prison, where Plutarch says he died. It would seem that he was alive in the 430s when his workshop at Olympia was in use, and excavation has revealed tools and even a cup bearing his name.

**Pheidi'ppidēs** The Athenian runner who, according to Herodotus (6.105–6), was sent to request help from Sparta before the battle of Marathon in 490 BC (*see* PERSIAN WARS), arriving in Sparta the next day. He would have covered in that time a distance of 200km (125 miles) or more. On his way back he is said to have met the god *Pan, who was later honoured with a state cult. He is associated with the modern Marathon race (introduced at the first modern Olympic Games at Athens in 1896), perhaps because later legend has confused his name with Philippides, who according to *Lucian was the messenger who brought the news of Marathon to Athens. Philippides, having run from Athens to Marathon (a distance of about

40km or 25 miles) in order to join in the battle against the Persians, then ran back to Athens and, having announced the victory ('Greetings, we win!'), dropped dead. Plutarch (*On the Glory of Athens*) gives the runner's name as Thersippus or Eucles. The distance of 26 miles 385 yards (42.195km) was first used at the 1908 Olympic Games in London, measured between the starting-point at Windsor Castle and the finish at White City Stadium, and was later adopted as standard in 1921.

**Pheidon** (perhaps first half of the seventh century BC, possibly nearly a century earlier) King of *Argos, a Heraclid descended from *Temenus. According to Aristotle, he exceeded his hereditary powers and made himself tyrant. He was clearly an important figure, but his dates and activities are obscure. He was remembered for three achievements: his recovery of the 'lot of Temenus', i.e. his unification of the Argolid; his standardization of weights and measures; and his seizure of the management of the Olympian games from Elis. Evidence suggests that he was a very successful military leader, perhaps responsible for Argos succeeding Chalcis (in Euboea) as the greatest military power in Greece. He may have been responsible for the Argive victory over Sparta at Hysiae.

**Phere'cratēs** Athenian comic poet active between 440 and 430 BC. Only some titles and fragments of his plays survive.

**Pherecy'dēs 1.** (of Syros, an island in the Cyclades) Philosopher of the mid-sixth century BC who was reputedly the teacher of *Pythagoras (because he believed in the immortality of the soul) and was said by some to be the first writer of Greek prose (*see* ANAXIMANDER).

**2.** (of Leros and Athens) A *logographer (1) of the early fifth century BC, sometimes confused with (1) above.

**Philē'bus** Dialogue by *Plato in which an attempt is made to analyse the concept of pleasure so as to estimate its value in people's lives. It emerges that pleasure is closely related to wisdom and knowledge.

**Philē'mōn** One of the chief writers of Greek New Comedy; *see* COMEDY [Greek 6].

**Philē'mōn and Baucis** An old man and his wife, in a story told by Ovid, who entertained Zeus and Hermes in disguise as hospitably as their poverty would allow, after the gods had been repulsed by the rich. Because of this Philemon and Baucis were saved from a deluge which overwhelmed the land where they lived, and their dwelling was transformed into a temple of which they were made the first priest and priestess. They were also granted their request to die at the same time, and were then turned into trees whose boughs intertwined.

**Philē'tās** (perhaps more correctly, Philītas, of Cos; b. *c.*340 BC) Greek poet and grammarian of the *Hellenistic age, tutor of the (subsequent) king of Egypt Ptolemy II Philadelphus. His other distinguished pupils were said to include the scholar *Zenodotus and the poet Theocritus. He was a writer of love-poems, and particularly famed for his literary scholarship and 'learned' poetry. He is mentioned by Ovid and Propertius as their model. Only fragments of his work survive.

**philhellenism** *See* HELLENISM.

**Philip (Philippos) 1. Philip II** (383/2–336 BC) King of *Macedon 359–336 BC. Philip unified Macedon and made it the strongest power in Greece, laying the foundations for the achievements of his son *Alexander the Great. As a boy he had seen his two elder brothers—who reigned for a few years each as Alexander II and Perdiccas III—struggle in vain against rebellious vassal princes and outside interference. Philip came to power after Perdiccas was killed in battle against invading Illyrians. Perhaps initially he was regent for his nephew Amyntas, but he seized the throne for himself and proved a brilliant ruler with a talent for compromise and deviousness. He suppressed opposition, strengthened the economy, and forged a professional army with national spirit. Philip was himself a formidable warrior (he lost his right eye in battle and was wounded many other times), but he was also a skilful politician, and he expanded his territories by diplomacy as well as conquest. The interests of Athens were gravely threatened, especially when Philip's new fleet began to harass the city's trade, and *Demosthenes ((2) 2) in his speech known as the *First Philippic* (351) called upon the Athenians to prepare to fight. However, a precarious peace was kept until various acts of hostility in 341 developed into open war in 340. Athens and Thebes joined forces, despite their inveterate hostility, but Philip crushed their joint army at Chaeronea (338).

He was now master of Greece and made plans for waging a Greek war against Persia, with himself as general. Preparations were made for the invasion, and his commander Parmenio was sent to secure a footing in Asia Minor; but while walking in procession during the celebration of his daughter's marriage to the king of Epirus Philip was murdered by an assassin, Pausanias. Apparently he was pursuing a private grievance, although it has been alleged that it was the result of a plot by Olympias, Philip's wife, who had been deposed in favour of a young bride Cleopatra, and that his son Alexander was aware of it. Excavations at Aegae (Vergina) in Macedonia have uncovered the tombs (most believe) of Philip and his family, with magnificent grave goods and wall-paintings. Philip's own body has been tentatively identified.

**2. Philip V** (238–179 BC) King of *Macedon.

**Phi'lippi** City in Macedonia east of the river Strymon on the border with Thrace, refounded under this name by Philip II of Macedon in 356 BC. It was the scene of two engagements three weeks apart but remembered as one, the defeat on 23 October of the republican forces of (Marcus Junius) Brutus and (Gaius) Cassius by those of Mark Antony and Octavian, and of the death of the two former.

**Phili'ppics** Four political speeches by *Demosthenes (see (2) 2) attacking Philip II, king of Macedon. The title was jokingly adopted by *Cicero ((1) 6) for the speeches that he delivered against Mark Antony.

**Phili'ppides** *See* PHEIDIPPIDES.

**Philī'tas** *See* PHILETAS.

**Philo** *See* PHILON.

**Philo'cratēs, Peace of** Truce between Greece and Philip II of Macedon, 346 BC; *see* DEMOSTHENES (2) 2 and AESCHINES.

**Philoctē'tēs** In Greek myth, son of Poeas. The latter had been persuaded to light the pyre on which *Heracles was burnt alive, by the gift of his bow and arrows. These descended to Philoctetes, who led seven ships from Methone and other towns of Pylos in the expedition to Troy. On their way to Troy the Greeks sacrificed in Tenedos, and there Philoctetes was bitten in the foot by a serpent. The stench from his festering wound and his terrible cries and curses caused the Greeks, persuaded by Odysseus, to abandon him on the solitary coast of the island of Lemnos, where he supported himself by the bow and arrows which never missed their mark. Ten years later the Trojan seer Helenus, captured by Odysseus, revealed that Troy would never fall unless Philoctetes could be persuaded to come and fight with his bow and arrows. Accordingly Odysseus and Neoptolemus (or Diomedes) went to Lemnos and brought him back. *Machaon healed his wound and Philoctetes, by shooting Paris, helped to conquer Troy. According to the *Odyssey* Philoctetes returned home safely. He is mentioned in the *Iliad* and is the subject of a play by Sophocles.

**Philoctē'tēs** Greek tragedy by *Sophocles, produced in 409 BC.

*Philoctetes is living wretchedly on Lemnos, suffering from his wound, supporting himself by shooting birds with his beloved bow of Heracles. Odysseus and Neoptolemus arrive to carry him off to the siege of Troy. Odysseus reveals his plan to Neoptolemus: the latter is to pretend that he has quarrelled with the leaders of the Greek army and is on his way home; he is to heap abuse on Odysseus, and to try to get possession of the bow. Neoptolemus is at first unwilling to join in this deceit, but eventually agrees. He meets Philoctetes and tells his story. Philoctetes makes a pitiful appeal to be taken to Greece, and Neoptolemus agrees. But Philoctetes is seized with a paroxysm of pain, after which he falls asleep. Before sleeping, however, he entrusts his bow to Neoptolemus. When he wakes up, Neoptolemus, stung with remorse, confesses the plot. He is on the point of returning the bow when Odysseus appears and takes it. He and Neoptolemus depart with it to the ships; Philoctetes is left lamenting his loss, while the chorus of sailors try to persuade him to join them. They are about to leave him when Neoptolemus returns, determined to give back the bow but pursued by Odysseus. Philoctetes, having regained the bow, tries to shoot Odysseus but is prevented by Neoptolemus who again tries to persuade Philoctetes to accompany him to Troy. He fails, and reluctantly decides to abide by his promise and take Philoctetes home to Greece. At this point Heracles suddenly appears; he reveals Zeus' plan for Philoctetes, that he is to go to Troy with Neoptolemus; Philoctetes yields to the voice of one whom he cannot disobey.

**Philodē'mus** (of Gadara in Syria) Poet and Epicurean philosopher who came to Rome c.75 BC. His friendship with *Piso Caesoninus, perhaps the owner of the Villa of the Papyri at *Herculaneum, brought about his association with Virgil and Horace (who names him in the *Satires*). Many of his erotic epigrams are to be found in the *Greek *Anthology*. He also wrote on Greek philosophy, his many works being now gradually recovered from the charred papyrus rolls of the villa at Herculaneum. A remarkable aspect of his thought, from a modern perspective, is on *aesthetics, and partially surviving works *On Rhetoric* and *On Music* are also interesting.

**Philola'us** (of Croton, fifth century BC, contemporary with Socrates) Pythagorean philosopher, perhaps the first to write a book about Pythagoreanism. Apart from some fragments his work is lost but enough survives to indicate that it is likely to have been Aristotle's source for his account of that philosophy. Philolaus may have been the first to include the earth as one of the heavenly bodies circling a central fire, and with a counter-earth to make their number up to ten, the Pythagorean perfect number (*see* ASTRONOMY and PYTHAGORAS). *See also* ANATOMY AND PHYSIOLOGY.

**Philomē'la and Procnē** In Greek myth, daughters of Pandīon, a legendary king of Athens. Procne was married to Tereus, king of Thrace. The latter fell in love with Philomela, and after raping her cut out her tongue and hid her in a lonely fortress so that she could not reveal what had happened. But Philomela managed to depict her sufferings on a tapestry which she sent to Procne by a servant. Procne then went to her sister disguised as a *Bacchant during the festival of Dionysus, and smuggled her into the palace similarly disguised. Seeking revenge Procne stabbed her son Itys to death, to deprive Tereus of an heir, and served up his flesh to her husband. When, after the meal, Philomela brought in the boy's head so that Tereus understood what had happened, he drew his sword to kill the sisters, but was changed into a hoopoe; Philomela was changed into a swallow (since, having no tongue, she could merely chatter like one) and Procne into a nightingale (or, according to Latin authors, Philomela into a nightingale and Procne into a swallow).

**Phĭlon** (Lat. Philo) **1. Phi'lon of Lari'ssa** (159–84 BC) The last undisputed head of the *Academy at Athens, from 109 BC. In 88 BC he left for Rome where he probably remained until his death. Cicero became his most devoted pupil. Like Carneades Philon was a moderate Sceptic.

**2. Philo Jūdae'us** ('Philo the Jew', c.30 BC–c. AD 45) A member of a prosperous Jewish family in Alexandria, who took part in an embassy sent to Rome in AD 39–40 to seek exemption for Jews from the obligation to worship the emperor (at that time Caligula). Except for this event nothing is known of his life. He was, with *Josephus, the most important Hellenistic Jew of his age and a prolific author of philosophical and exegetical writings, a large part of which survives. His importance lies in his assimilation of Platonism, Christianity, and Judaism. Philo believed that God was virtually unknowable and therefore a mediator is needed, *logos*, the Word, equivalent to Plato's Forms, to knowledge of which a devotee might aspire (*see* PLATO 4). He also developed allegorical interpretations of Judaic scripture which enabled him to find a great deal of Greek Platonic philosophy in the Old Testament. His works were a strong influence in mediating between Platonism, including *Neoplatonism, and later Greek Christian thought. A considerable portion of them were preserved in the library of Caesarea by Origen and later by Eusebius.

**3. Philon of Byzantium** (third century BC) Greek engineer and mathematician. He wrote a wide-ranging treatise *Mechanics* which survives in part, some of it by way of Arabic. It describes not only mechanical devices but also areas of civil and military engineering. In mathematics he is best known for his method of duplicating the cube (i.e. finding the cube root of 2).

**Philopoe'men** (of Megalopolis in Arcadia, c.253–182 BC) The bold and vigorous general of the *Achaean confederacy, in which post he reorganized its army and repeatedly defeated the Spartans. It is recorded that after one of his victories Philopoemen was present at the Nemean games when Pylades, the most famous singer of his day, was singing part of the *Persians* of *Timotheus (1). At the words, 'who gives to Greece the glorious crown of freedom', the people rose and gave an ovation to the general. Philopoemen and his supporters refused to accept any Roman interference in Achaean internal affairs, thereby dividing Achaean opinion on this issue. In 183 BC, when he was about 70, he took part in an expedition against Messene, which had revolted from the confederacy. He was captured by the Messenians, thrown into prison, and forced to drink poison. His ashes were brought back to Megalopolis, the urn being carried by the young *Polybius.

**philosopher-kings** *See* REPUBLIC.

**philosophy** [Gk. *philosophia*, 'love of knowledge or wisdom'].

**Greek.** For the Greeks, 'philosophy', the pursuit of knowledge by rational enquiry, was an elastic term; it began with scientific speculation on nature and the origins of the world—*cosmology—but it also included speculation as to the conduct of political and social life, and this last was one of the main concerns of philosophers in the fifth and fourth centuries BC. Later post-Aristotelian Greek philosophy dealt with moral and religious questions, the concept of virtue and the individual's relations with the divine; it had by then become not merely a mental activity but a way of life, to be followed in accordance with philosophical beliefs.

Greek philosophy had its origins in the sixth century BC among the Ionian Greeks of Asia Minor (*see* PRESOCRATICS). It was then mainly occupied with speculation about the origins of the universe, and associated with the name of *Thales of Miletus, whose chief successors (also sixth-century Milesians) were *Anaximander and *Anaximenes. These sought the material principle of the universe in some single uncreated and imperishable substance which underwent various modifications to produce the multitude of phenomena in the world: Thales thought that it was water, Anaximander something indeterminate, without specific qualities, and Anaximenes air. *Heracleitus of Ephesus, writing in about 500 BC, stood apart from this Ionian school and rejected the notion of a permanent substance underlying the variations of matter (though he thought the essential stuff of the universe to be pure fire). He saw all things as in a state of flux, and matter itself constantly changing.

*Pythagoras (last quarter of the sixth century BC), was the first to call himself a philosopher. Originally an Ionian Greek from

Samos, he migrated to Croton, an Achaean colony on the toe of Italy, and founded there another school of philosophy which in some ways resembled a mystical sect, having secret doctrines not to be revealed to the uninitiated. The Pythagoreans saw in numbers and their relationships the basis of the universe. Also during the sixth century the Ionian polymath and philosopher *Xenophanes, relying on logic, seems to have constructed a rational theology thus paving the way for future scepticism about the gods.

A third school was that of Elea (also in Magna Graecia), founded by *Parmenides (early fifth century BC) and continued by *Zeno (1). The Eleatics distinguished between what they saw as the One—the true stuff of the universe, single, eternal, and unchangeable—and the unreal phenomena of change, diversity, and motion which are what the senses perceive. *Empedocles of Acragas in Sicily, *Anaxagoras, originally from Clazomenae in Ionia but who lived in Athens, and Leucippus (perhaps Ionian also), all working in the fifth century BC, evolved fresh hypotheses about the physical basis of the universe, assuming not one single basic stuff but plural constituents. (See also Democritus below.)

Empedocles was the first to propound the theory of the four elements, fire, air, earth, and water, out of which everything is composed in varying proportions. Anaxagoras believed in an original mixture containing 'seeds' of every substance; more significantly, however, he introduced the important concept of an Intelligence (*Nous*) as a principle of force and order distinct from matter. Leucippus was said to be the originator of the school of atomist philosophy, which rested on the doctrine that the universe is composed of a vast number of atoms, mechanically combined. This doctrine was developed by Democritus, and then fully expounded by *Epicurus; the most eloquent account of it to survive is that of *Lucretius in Roman times.

Classical Greek philosophy culminated in *Socrates and the *sophists, in the second half of the fifth century BC, and *Plato and *Aristotle, in the fourth. The conquests of Alexander the Great, however, towards the end of the fourth century, swept away the context of their ethical and political teaching, the independent *city-states whose continued existence they had not doubted. However, the new order promoted progress in mathematics and astronomy

centred on Alexandria and the Hellenistic kingdoms. The later philosophies, those in particular of the Stoics (see STOICISM) and Epicureans, show interest not only in the theoretical problems of the nature of reality and the scope of knowledge but also in the practical problems of everyday behaviour. They have been called philosophies of resignation; they seek a road to peace and happiness in the state of mind of the individual, by making him independent of external circumstances. See also ACADEMY; SCEPTICS; CYNICS; MEGARIAN SCHOOL; PERIPATETIC SCHOOL; ARISTIPPUS; THEOPHRASTUS; NEOPLATONISM; SCIENCE, ATTITUDES TO.

**Roman.** Rome came into close contact with Greek civilization, including philosophy, after the conquest of Magna Graecia in the third century BC and the occupation of Sicily, Greece, and part of Asia Minor in the second. At first Rome regarded Greek philosophy with some suspicion, and fears of its possibly subversive effects led to the temporary banishment of Greek philosophers in 173 and again in 161 BC. In 155 *Carneades, Diogenes of Babylon, and Critolaus, the heads respectively of the Academic, Stoic, and Peripatetic schools of philosophy in Athens, were sent on an embassy to Rome (to appeal against a large fine imposed by the Romans on Athens), and, giving lectures there, made a great impression. A little later *Scipio Aemilianus received into his household the Stoic philosopher *Panaetius of Rhodes; and in the early part of the first century BC a successor of the latter, *Poseidonius, became the friend and teacher of Varro in Rome and of Pompey and Cicero in Rhodes. The Romans were not much interested in theories as to the constitution of the universe, nor in elucidating the processes of thought and of acquiring knowledge; and they produced no great original speculative philosophers or metaphysicians. Lucretius alone, in his poem *De rerum natura* ('On nature'), expounded with enthusiasm the atomic theory put forward first by Leucippus and Democritus.

The attention of the Romans was chiefly concentrated on ethical principles, and here they were mainly divided between Epicureans and Stoics, the latter prevailing. Stoic notions of duty and fate appealed to Roman severity. Cicero, who did much to make Greek philosophical thought known to his countrymen, was himself a follower of the New Academy (the Platonic school), with leanings towards the Stoics; he was in fact an eclectic, that is, he did not accept wholly the teaching of any one particular school, but picked out from their various doctrines those which commended themselves to him. *Seneca (2) was the principal Roman Stoic author, and his writings had considerable influence on Christian ethics. The most famous of the later Roman Stoics were Marcus *Aurelius (who wrote his *Meditations* in Greek) and *Epictetus (who also wrote in Greek). The satirist *Persius, under the influence of his teacher Cornutus, and the poet *Lucan were followers of the same school. Under the influence of Seneca and his successors, the general tendency of Stoics was to become more practical and human. The tranquillity which the earlier Greek Stoics thought was the exclusive attainment of the sage who lived in detachment from the world was now seen to be attainable by men living fully in the world, through the exercise of fortitude and self-control. *See also* BOETHIUS.

**Philo'stratus** Name borne by four writers, members of a family belonging to Lemnos, who lived in the second and third centuries AD. The most important works (in Greek) which have come down under this name are: (i) (by Flavius Philostratus) *Lives of the Sophists*, that is, of the *sophists and rhetoricians from Protagoras in the fifth century BC to the author's own times, the foundation of our knowledge of the *Second Sophistic (the term is his invention); (ii) (written for *Julia Domna) a Life of *Apollonius of Tyana, the wandering Pythagorean mystic and miracle-worker of the first century AD (which furnished material for anti-Christians who wanted a pagan narrative to set against the Gospel life of Jesus); (iii) *Eikones* ('Images'), two sets of descriptions in prose of pictures which the author purports to have seen (the first set far fuller than the second; *see* ECPHRASIS); (iv) *Heröicus*, a dialogue in which the ghosts of heroes of the Trojan War appear; and (v) a collection of *Letters*, sophistical exercises for the most part, noteworthy as containing in Epistle 33 the source of Ben Jonson's lyric 'Drink to me only with thine eyes'.

**Phily'ra** In Greek myth, daughter of *Oceanus and Tethys, loved by *Cronus. When Rhea (his wife) found them both together, Cronus changed himself and Philyra into horses. Philyra's child was the Centaur *Chiron; she was so horrified to see the baby's shape that

she prayed to the gods to change her shape also, and she was turned into a lime tree (Gk. *philyra*).

**Phīneus** In Greek myth, a Thracian king, plagued by the *Harpies who stole or defiled all his food. When the *Argonauts arrived at his land he agreed to prophesy to them their future adventures in return for deliverance from the Harpies. The sons of *Boreas (Calais and Zetes) drove them away, turning back at the islands afterwards known as Strophades ('islands of turning'). Phineus' original offence is variously described. The best known version says that he married Cleopatra, daughter of Boreas, and had sons, but at her death remarried; their stepmother so slandered his sons that Phineus blinded them (or let their stepmother do so). Thereupon Zeus gave him the choice of death or blindness; he chose the latter, and Helios (Sun), who sees all, angry at Phineus' choice, sent the Harpies.

**Phle'gethon (Pyriphlegethon)** One of the rivers of the Underworld; *see* HADES.

**Phōcae'a** Most northerly of the Ionian Greek settlements on the coast of Asia Minor, founded by emigrants from Phocis. Because of its two excellent harbours it soon became famous as a maritime city; according to Herodotus the Phocaeans were the first Greeks to sail far west, visiting Tartessus in southern Spain. In about 600 BC it founded the colony of Massalia (Marseilles), giving the Greeks access to southern Gaul. When Ionia was conquered by the Persian king Cyrus in 540 BC, most of the citizens preferred emigration to submission and finally settled at Elea (Velia) in Lucania, south Italy; Phocaea never recovered its former prosperity.

**Phō'cion** ('the Good', 402–318 BC) Athenian general and statesman during the time of Philip II of Macedon and his son Alexander the Great. He commanded universal respect and was elected *strategos* forty-five times. In politics he was an advocate of peace with Macedon, being convinced that Athens was no longer a match for her in military strength. After Athens' defeat at Chaeronea in 338 he assisted Demades in preserving peace with Philip and Alexander, and sought to prevent Athens from joining in the *Lamian War. When democratic rule was (briefly) restored at Athens in 318, Phocion was put to death on a charge of treason. Plutarch's *Life of Phocion* portrays him as a patriot, with a stern and stoical sense of duty.

**Phōcis** Small country of central Greece, to the west of Boeotia, important in Greek history as containing Delphi, of which she occasionally lost control, becoming involved in the Sacred Wars (1). Her bid for independence in the Third Sacred War ended in her subjugation by Philip II of Macedon (346 BC).

**Phocus** *See* TELAMON.

**Phōcy'lidēs** (of Miletus, mid-sixth century BC) Apparently a Greek poet or sage who wrote gnomic hexameters (*see* GNOME) in which he embodied moral observations and precepts; a few of these survive. In each maxim he introduced his own name.

**Phoebē (Phoibe)** ('the bright one') In Greek myth, according to Hesiod, a *Titan, daughter of Uranus (Heaven) and Gaia (Earth); she became the wife of Coeus and mother of *Leto, and is thus grandmother of Apollo and Artemis. In later mythology her name was frequently used for Selene (Moon).

**Phoebus Apo'llo** *See* APOLLO.

**Phoeni'ssae (Phoinissai)** ('Phoenician women') **1.** Greek tragedy (which has not survived) by *Phrynichus (1).

**2.** Greek tragedy by *Euripides, produced in 409 BC. The play derives its name from the chorus of Phoenician maidens dedicated by the citizens of Tyre to the temple of Apollo at Delphi, who happen to be at Thebes on their way to Delphi and witness the events while having no connection with them. Aeschylus' *Seven against Thebes* tells part of the same narrative. *Phoenissae* is the longest Greek tragedy in existence and covers the greatest stretch of story.

The drama takes up the legend of *Oedipus at the start of the quarrel between his two sons: Polyneices has been refused by his brother Eteocles his share of their alternating rule of Thebes, and has come with Adrastus, king of Argos, and the five other leaders of the Argive army, to enforce his rights. Jocasta, wife of Oedipus, endeavours to reconcile their two sons, but her efforts fail and the attack on Thebes becomes inevitable. The seer *Teiresias predicts the victory of Eteocles and Thebes if a son of Creon (brother of Jocasta and friend of Eteocles) is sacrificed. Accordingly Menoeceus, Creon's younger son, gives his

life heroically for his city, in spite of his father's resistance. The Argives are driven back in the first onset, and it is arranged that the quarrel shall be settled by a single combat between the brothers. In this each kills the other, and Jocasta in despair takes her own life with one of their swords; their sister Antigone brings the news to Oedipus. Creon takes over the government and proclaims that Polyneices' body will lie unburied and that the blind Oedipus will be expelled; moreover, Antigone will marry Creon's son Haemon. Antigone refuses, and accompanies her father into exile, announcing that she will return and secretly bury her brother.

**3.** Roman tragedy by *Seneca (2), which survives in an imperfect condition, having only two acts and no choral odes. It appears to combine material from *Oedipus at Colonus* by Sophocles (the blind Oedipus wandering under the guidance of Antigone), with a situation derived from other sources (Antigone at Thebes with her mother Jocasta, who tries in vain to reconcile her two sons). It has been suggested that the surviving portions are fragments of two distinct plays.

**Phoenix 1.** In Greek myth, son of Amyntor, a king in Thessaly. His mother persuaded him to seduce his father's concubine, out of jealousy. When his father found out he cursed him with childlessness; Phoenix left home and went to Phthia, where he was kindly received by Peleus and put in charge of the young *Achilles (Peleus' son). In the Trojan War he was one of the ambassadors sent to bring Agamemnon's offer of reconciliation to Achilles, whom he had accompanied to Troy, and illustrates Achilles' situation with a speech on his own experience.

**2.** The *eponymous ancestor of the Phoenicians, son of Agenor, king of Tyre, and brother of *Cadmus and Europa (or father of Europa).

**Phoenix** Latin poem in elegiacs, 170 lines long, on this mythical Arabian bird, whose resurrection to life from death appealed to Christians and to pagan believers in mystery religions. The poem is usually ascribed to the Christian writer Lactantius (*c.*AD 245–*c.*325). The phoenix is described by Herodotus (2.73), Tacitus (*Annals* 6.28), and others with varying details. In general it was thought to resemble an eagle but with red (*phoinix*) and gold plumage; every 500 years it makes a nest and dies; from the nest arises a new phoenix which carries its parent's body to Heliopolis in Egypt for funeral in the temple of Helios (Sun). The version that has become popular in modern times has the new phoenix arising from the funeral pyre which the old phoenix has made for itself.

**Phōlus** *Centaur by whom Heracles was entertained when in pursuit of the Erymanthian Boar (see HERACLES, LABOURS OF 3). Pholus died after the fight between Heracles and the Centaurs; while inspecting one of Heracles' arrows he dropped it on his foot and was killed by the poison.

**Phorcys** Greek sea-god, son of Nereus or of Pontus (Sea) and Gaia. By his sister Ceto he was father of the *Graeae, the *Gorgons, and *Scylla.

**phorminx** See MUSIC [Greek 3].

**Pho'rmio** Roman comedy by *Terence, based on a Greek play of the third century BC, 'The Claimant', by Apollodorus of Carystus, a writer of Greek New Comedy (see COMEDY [Greek 6]). It was produced at the Roman games in 161 BC.

Antipho, a young Athenian, while his father Demipho is out of the country, has fallen in love with a girl whom he found weeping for her recently dead mother, whose funeral she must arrange, being now alone in the world. Phormio, a resourceful *parasite, taking advantage of the law that orphan girls must be married to their next-of-kin (within the permitted degree), has pretended, in collusion with Antipho, that the latter is the girl's nearest relative and obtained a court order that he is to marry her, and the marriage has taken place. Meanwhile Antipho's cousin Phaedria is desperately in love with a slave-girl, a lute-player, but lacks the money to buy her from the pimp who owns her. His father Chremes, Demipho's brother, has been away in Lemnos. Both fathers return at this juncture. Demipho is furious at his son's marriage and determined to put an end to it. Phormio offers the father, for a sum of money, to take the bride away and marry her himself. Having obtained the money he hands it over to Phaedria who now purchases his lute-player. Meanwhile it has been discovered through a nurse that the girl Antipho has married is in fact the daughter of Chremes, who has bigamously kept a wife on Lemnos; daughter, wife, and nurse had come to Athens to look for him, and there the wife had died. Chremes wishes above all else to keep from his legitimate wife

in Athens any knowledge of his liaison. To avoid trouble the two fathers decide to recognize Antipho's marriage, but their attempt to recover the money paid to Phormio leads to the exposure of Chremes to his wife. She is mollified, however, and all ends happily. The play is aptly named: Phormio dominates it, and no other character in Roman comedy quite reaches his commanding position.

**Pho'rmion** (fourth century BC) Slave and subsequently chief assistant of the Athenian banker *Pasion, and lessee of the bank. He was awarded Athenian citizenship and later married Pasion's widow. Pasion's son *Apollodorus (1) unsuccessfully prosecuted him for embezzling money from the bank. After the lease of Pasion's bank expired Phormion may have become an independent banker.

**phratries** [Gk. *phratriai*, 'brotherhoods'] In many Greek cities, groups of related families or clans (see GENOS). Before the reforms of *Cleisthenes (2) at Athens political power was based on family groups. The four original *tribes were subdivided into phratries, membership of which probably qualified a man for Athenian citizenship and for having a political voice. After Cleisthenes citizenship depended upon membership of a *deme and the phratries lost their political significance in Athens. They continued to exist but with only social and religious functions. They celebrated the festival of Apaturia, with the attendant cult of Zeus Phratrios and Athena Phratria especially. This festival was common to all Ionians (who included the Athenians), and was the time when fathers had their young sons registered in their phratries.

**Phrixus** See ATHAMAS.

**Phrȳnē** Famous *hetaira* of the fourth century BC from Thespiae in Boeotia, whose outstanding beauty gave rise to some notable works of art, including the painting of Aphrodite Anadyomene by *Apelles and *Praxiteles' Aphrodite of Cnidus. There was a gilded statue of her at Delphi dedicated by herself (according to *Pausanias (2)) or by her admirers (according to other authorities). One of these was the orator *Hypereides.

**Phrȳ'nichus 1.** An Athenian tragedian, coupled with *Thespis by some ancient authorities as both being the originators of tragedy. Phrynichus first won a competition for tragedy between 511 and 508 BC and was said to have been the first to introduce female characters into tragedy. Of his plays only scanty fragments survive. He produced, probably in 492, a play dealing with the capture of *Miletus by the Persians in 494 during the Ionian Revolt (see PERSIAN WARS), and was fined by the Athenians because, Herodotus said, he had reminded them too vividly of 'troubles which touched them closely'. His *Phoenissae* ('Phoenician women'), celebrating the Greek victories over the Persians in 480–79, with the chorus composed of the wives of the enemy's Phoenician sailors, was also famous. This may have been produced in 476, a year in which he was victorious and Themistocles was his *choregos*. Aristophanes seems to have admired his lyrical passages particularly, while mocking his dramas' deficiency in action.

2. One of the extreme oligarchs at Athens at the time of the revolution of the *Four Hundred in 411 BC, towards the end of the Peloponnesian War. After his return from Sparta, where he had gone to negotiate peace, he was assassinated in the agora.

**phylae** [Gk. *phylai*, '*tribes'] The divisions of the citizen body of a Greek state in early times.

**Physics** (Lat. *Physica*; Gk. '*Physike akroāsis*, 'Lecture on nature') Treatise by *Aristotle on physics, or nature, in eight books, with the appearance of a collection of essays. It is written against a background of *Parmenides and Plato. Parmenides believed that 'what exists' is one and unchangeable and therefore that 'coming-into-being' and change are impossible. Plato believed that the ordinary world of the senses could not be the object of true knowledge; only the Forms were truly knowable (see PLATO 4). For Aristotle the perceptible world is the true reality which science must investigate, and change is its most notable feature. Most of the *Physics* is concerned with change in its different aspects, change of substance, of quality, of quantity, and of place. In examining change he makes important distinctions between form and matter, and actuality and potentiality. Aristotle formulates the four causes which have to be established to account for the existence of something, namely the material, formal, efficient, and final causes. The treatise investigates the nature of time and space (in which change takes place) and a number of particular problems which we would nowadays think of as belonging to biology or psychology or philosophy rather than to physics

**physiology** *See* ANATOMY AND PHYSIOLOGY.

**Pīcu'mnus and Pīlu'mnus** In ancient Roman religion, two brothers, perhaps agricultural deities, the beneficent gods of matrimony and the protectors of women in childbirth. Pilumnus was thought to be the inventor of the pestle (*pilum*) for grinding corn; Virgil makes him the ancestor of *Turnus.

**Pīcus** ('woodpecker') Italian god of agriculture, sometimes described as a son of *Saturn and as the first king of Italy, possessed of prophetic powers and usually taking the form of Mars' sacred bird, the woodpecker. This bird was of great importance in *augury; omens were drawn from the sight of it and from its note. It was said that it helped to feed Romulus and Remus. There was a story that Picus was turned into a woodpecker by Circe ('hawk'), whose love he had spurned. Virgil makes him the father of *Faunus and grandfather of Latinus.

**Pillars of Hercules** *See* HERACLES, LABOURS OF 10.

**Pīlu'mnus** *See* PICUMNUS.

**Pi'nakĕs** *See* CALLIMACHUS.

**Pindar (Pindaros)** (518–after 446 BC) Greek lyric poet, born near Thebes in Boeotia, famous for his Epinician ('victory') Odes written in honour of the victors at the four great panhellenic games. These odes are accordingly grouped as Olympian, Pythian, Nemean, and Isthmian, commonly abbreviated to *O.*, *P.*, *N.*, and *I.*

Very little is known about Pindar's life. Legend relates that he received instruction in composition from the Boeotian poet *Corinna, and that he went to Athens for his musical education (see LASUS). His devotion to the god Apollo was rewarded by special privileges at *Delphi. His attitude to the great historical events of his time was panhellenic rather than narrowly bound by local loyalties; thus he saw the Persian invasions as a threat to Greece as a whole and her deliverance as a blessing. His personal feelings about the consequences to Thebes of her pro-Persian policy cannot be known, but he laments the sorrow and loss that war brought her; his expressed admiration for Athens was unaffected by the mutual animosity of the two cities. It is said that he was fined by his countrymen for his praises of Athens, but that the Athenians paid him the amount of the fine twice over. Some of his greatest odes were for the Sicilian tyrants, particularly Hieron I of *Syracuse. He attained great fame in his lifetime, and was soon quoted as an authority (e.g. by Herodotus and Plato). In the destruction of Thebes in 335 (a punishment for her revolt against Macedonian rule) Alexander the Great ordered Pindar's house to be spared; its ruins were still visible when *Pausanias (2) visited Thebes c.AD 150.

Pindar's numerous poems, which included all the chief forms of choral *lyric, were grouped by the Alexandrian scholars into seventeen books according to their types. Of these only the four books of Epinician Odes survive, virtually entire, in manuscript. The rest are known mostly from quotations, although discoveries of papyri in the late nineteenth and the twentieth centuries have greatly augmented our knowledge.

Pindar wrote in the literary Dorian dialect but used epic forms as well, particularly for mythical narratives. Close analysis reveals that the odes follow a conventional pattern of praise; but the poet's skill succeeds in intertwining rather disparate elements into an artistic whole, and the reader's attention is distracted from the technical aspects of the composition by the rapid and varied flow of the poetry. The essentially repetitious nature of the subject matter is not particularly obvious even when the forty-four odes are read in sequence, as their author can hardly have supposed they would be; the reader marvels rather at the variety. Pindar has complete control over his medium, and his technique is distinguished by constant variation, complexity, and vitality. Some of his sentences are long and periodic, others are arrestingly short. Sometimes (especially in the later odes) the language seems almost stark, stripped of ornament, and the word order simple and prosaic; in other odes the language is rich and magnificent, the word order intricate. Myths are narrated economically, allusively, and vividly. The poet is skilful at building up climaxes within the ode. Transitions from one topic to another are sometimes made abruptly for rhetorical effect, sometimes unobtrusively. Metaphors and metonomies (e.g. the variety of words used to express 'victory') abound.

The Epinician Odes are written from an essentially religious standpoint; it is this background that imparts grandeur to Pindar's themes and language. Men are nothing by themselves: success is god-given; but men attain an almost divine happiness at the moment of success. The poet himself has a skill that is god-given and cannot be taught; he is 'the mouthpiece of the Muses'. Zeus and Apollo are the gods most often invoked. The gods favour those who have struggled hard for their victory, but the victors are those whose breeding makes them worthy of it; Pindar admires aristocratic qualities, the beauty and strength fostered in the *palaestra, wealth and standing, courage and preparedness, the aristocratic institution of guest-friendship, traditional worship of the gods, devotion to family and homeland; and he warns against the unjust use of power and the envy from lesser men which success brings in its train. The qualities which he admires he sees exhibited in the heroes of old, and especially Heracles, the hero most often cited in the odes. Pindar treats myth with freedom and with sensitivity to its appropriateness, always in a way that comports with the dignity of the occasion.

Horace, in the opening stanzas of *Odes* 4.2, praised Pindar's rushing eloquence, bold originality in metres and diction, and admirable use of myth, and believed that his own odes could never reach such heights. Quintilian shared the general view that Pindar was by far the greatest of the Greek lyric poets. In modern times poets have tried to imitate his free-flowing, vigorous style with varying degrees of success. Of English odes, those of the seventeenth-century poet John Dryden, *Song for St Cecilia's Day* and *Alexander's Feast*, and of the eighteenth-century poet Thomas Gray, *Progress of Poesy* and *The Bard*, capture something of the true feeling.

**Pīrae'us (Peiraieus, Peirāeus)** Chief port of Athens, on a promontory 8km (5 miles) southwest of the ancient city. It was fortified by *Themistocles from the time of his archonship (493/2 BC, a little before the first Persian invasion) in order that the growing Athenian fleet might have a safer anchorage than that provided by the open roadstead of *Phalerum. For the Long Walls connecting Piraeus (and Phalerum) with Athens *see* LONG WALLS. The city was laid out on a grid plan by *Hippodamus in the mid-fifth century. As the base for the fleet, Piraeus was the centre of democratic resistance to the *Thirty Tyrants (*see* OLD OLIGARCH). The fortifications were demolished by the Spartan Lysander in 404 BC, at the end of the Peloponnesian War, but replaced by the Athenian admiral Conon in 393. The Roman general Sulla laid siege to Piraeus and subsequently destroyed it in 87–86 BC.

**Pīrē'nē** *See* PEIRENE.

**Pīri'thŏus (Peirithŏŏs)** King of the Lapiths, friend of *Theseus; *see* CENTAURS.

**Pīsi'stratus** *See* PEISISTRATUS.

**Pīso 1. Lucius Calpurnius Piso Caesonī'nus** Roman consul in 58 BC; his daughter Calpurnia married Julius Caesar. He refused to support Cicero against *Clodius, and was rewarded by the latter with the governorship of the province of Macedonia. His administration there (57–55) was attacked by Cicero in two speeches, *De provinciis consularibus* and *In Pisonem* (*see* CICERO (1) 4). After Caesar's assassination in 44 BC he tried to prevent civil war, but died within a short time. He was an Epicurean and a friend and disciple of the Greek Epicurean philosopher *Philodemus, whom he very probably made a resident of his own magnificent villa at *Herculaneum. The 'Villa of the Papyri' excavated there which contained charred rolls of Philodemus' writings may be Piso's.

**2. Lucius Calpurnius Piso** ('the pontifex') Son of (1) above, and Roman consul in 15 BC. According to an ancient note he and his two sons were the Pisos to whom Horace's *Ars poetica* is dedicated. He was well known as a philhellene and the patron of the poet Antipater of Thessalonika.

**3. Gaius Calpurnius Piso** (d. AD 65) The figurehead of the great conspiracy against the emperor Nero. Exiled during the reign of Caligula (AD 37–41), suffect *consul under his successor Claudius, Piso was a rich and popular figure at Rome, and a great orator. The conspiracy to assassinate Nero and to put Piso on the throne was betrayed and he committed suicide.

**Pi'ttacus** (of Mytilene in Lesbos, mid-seventh century–*c.*570 BC) Statesman, included among the *Seven Sages. He commanded the Mytilenaeans in a war against Athens for the possession of Sigeum at the mouth of the Hellespont, and appears by name in the poetry of his younger contemporary *Alcaeus. The latter savagely attacks him as a former comrade-in-arms in overthrowing tyranny at Mytilene, who has now broken with his old friends and sided with tyranny. The political struggles of the city remain unclear, but the citizens elected Pittacus *aisymnetes* ('dictator') for ten years to restore order. He did not alter the constitution, but reformed the laws; his best-remembered reform doubled the penalty for offences committed when drunk. After his period of office Pittacus laid down the dictatorship and retired to live quietly. Many sayings were attributed to him. His answer to the question 'What is best?' was 'To do the present thing well'. One of his sayings, 'It is hard to be good', was the starting point of a poem by Simonides discussed in Plato's *Protagoras*.

**plague at Athens** *See* PELOPONNESIAN WAR.

**Planu'dēs** *See* ANTHOLOGY.

**Platae'a** City in Boeotia on the border with Attica. Plataea, alone of the Boeotian cities, became allied to Athens when threatened by her Boeotian rival Thebes in the late sixth century BC. At Marathon in 490 the Plataeans were the Athenians' only allies in the battle (*see* PERSIAN WARS). Both cities were sacked by the Persians in 480, but in the following year Plataea was the scene of a great Greek victory over the invaders when some 600 Plataeans fought alongside the other Greeks. Plataea was again sacked (427) in the Peloponnesian War, and yet again in 372 by the Thebans. Alexander the Great restored the city as a symbol of Greek bravery in resisting the Persians, and in Roman times Plutarch describes the Persian War memorial festival, the Eleutheria, as still celebrated.

**Plato (Plătōn)** (b. early-to-mid-420s, d. 347 BC) One of the greatest of Greek philosophers and prose-writers, and founder of philosophical idealism.

1. Plato was born into a rich and noble family. His stepfather Pyrilampes was a democrat and friend of Pericles; his mother's cousin *Critias and his maternal uncle *Charmides took part in the oligarchic revolution of 404 BC (*see* THIRTY TYRANTS). What little we think we know about the events of his life is largely based on thirteen 'Letters' supposedly written by Plato himself but unlikely to be genuine. It is usually accepted that the Seventh Letter, if not by Plato himself, is more or less accurate in its biographical information. At some point in his

youth he met *Socrates whose life and manner of death, at which Plato by his own account was not present, became a formative influence. (A story relates that just before his own death Plato offered up thanks to his *daimon that he had been born a man and not an irrational animal, that he was born a Greek and not in some other country, and that he had been born in the time of Socrates.) He subsequently decided against a political career (and marriage), and devoted the rest of his life to philosophy. His earliest writing was said to have been poetry, but probably none of the surviving epigrams attributed to him is genuine. After Socrates' execution in 399 BC we are told he spent several years in travel, visiting Egypt and Magna Graecia where he met the Pythagoreans and in particular *Archytas of Tarentum. His stay in Sicily where he supposedly met (and soon fell out with) Dionysius I, tyrant of Syracuse, and the latter's young nephew Dion, is the subject of much anecdote in the Letters.

It was upon his return to Athens that he founded the *Academy, primarily a school for philosophy, traditionally in 387 BC. Here Plato and his pupils, who later included Aristotle, engaged in dialectic, epistemology, ethics, logic, metaphysics, political theory, perhaps natural science, perhaps rhetorical and literary theory—all studies that seemed relevant for the education of future leading citizens. Of prime importance was mathematics: 'No one may enter who is ignorant of geometry' (*ageometrētos mēdeis eisito*) was allegedly written on the door. Plato, although not himself a mathematician, was very interested in mathematical procedures and encouraged his pupils to study the subject, insisting in *Timaeus* for example on the importance of mathematics for understanding nature.

2. *Philosophical writings*. Plato published some thirty philosophical dialogues (the authenticity of some dialogues surviving under his name is disputed) and the *Apology (not a dialogue but a supposed reproduction of Socrates' defence at his trial), written over his lifetime, and they all survive. Aristotle makes reference to doctrines not found in the dialogues, the mysterious 'unwritten doctrines' (Gk. *agrapta dogmata*); hence it may be that only Plato's lectures would have given the authentic statement of his views. The dialogues, fictional in form, vary from what could almost be staged as a play to what becomes virtually a mono-

logue. Most participants are known to be historical. Socrates is usually a central character; Plato himself never appears. Thus Plato gives no personal support to any of the arguments, but throughout his work he remained consistent in his view that knowledge could not be conveyed directly from one person to another or through books (*see PHAEDRUS*), but could only be achieved by individual effort through *dialectic. The dialogues are incentives to further thought, not expositions of doctrine. They are very varied in form; some reach no conclusion and are clearly left open; others are hard to interpret. Plato's legacy can therefore be seen not so much as the promulgation of positive doctrines as recognition of the value of a certain amount of scepticism and of a continuing need for argument (*see* ACADEMY [Old Academy]). There also appear conflicts of thought between dialogues, and Socrates' well-known 'irony' lends itself to conflicting interpretation. The precise chronological order of the dialogues is not known, but the evidence of style and the development of ideas suggest a rough division into three periods. (Scholars often disagree about the assigning of particular dialogues to one group or another.) The early period is that of the 'Socratic' dialogues, those in which Socrates is the principal figure, examining and demolishing the views put forward by his interlocutors. Included are the *Apology*, *Charmides*, *Crito*, *Euthyphro*, *Hippias Minor*, *Ion*, *Laches*, *Lysis*, and *Protagoras*. The second period includes *Gorgias*, *Meno*, *Menexenus*, *Euthydemus*, *Phaedo*, Phaedrus, *Republic*, *Symposium*, and *Theaetetus*. In these Socrates is still the foremost figure, and he is now represented as propounding many positive views of his own at some length. The third group, the work of Plato's later years, includes *Cratylus*, *Parmenides*, Critias (*see* TIMAEUS), *Philebus*, *Sophist*, *Statesman*, and Timaeus. The *Laws, Plato's longest and last work, appears to be unrevised and was probably published as it stood after his death.

Many of Plato's dialogues charm the reader as little dramas enacted in an interesting setting by highly individualized characters, none more so than the omnipresent and enigmatic Socrates.

3. It is difficult to know in the early dialogues how far Plato is reproducing Socrates' views and to what extent he has moved beyond

them, but in the later dialogues it is reasonable to think that Plato is propounding his own doctrines. His primary concern is with moral education. Plato believes that on the one hand it is possible to be a good man without properly knowing what it means to be a good man or what goodness is. This is to have right opinion or true belief (*orthe doxa*); as one might think correctly that a road leads to Larissa (Plato's example in *Meno*) without having been along it and reached Larissa oneself. But on the other hand only to have right opinion is to be in a precarious state: meeting a new idea about goodness might throw one into confusion so that one could not judge its value. True knowledge is needed, which is different from right opinion in that with it one is able to define or give an account of what one knows. The early dialogues portray Socrates seeking definitions of particular virtues (*see* ARETE), courage in *Laches*, temperance in *Charmides*, piety in *Euthyphro*, or virtue in general in *Meno*, but without reaching positive conclusions, and sometimes being unable to proceed further (*see* APORIA). Virtue is a matter of knowledge. *Rhetoric therefore, which is simply a matter of persuasion and not in Plato's view concerned with knowledge, should not be the basis of education (see 6 below). Both Socrates and Plato were attracted by the notion that knowledge of virtue is similar in kind to knowledge of how to practise a craft, such as cobbling shoes. It followed for Socrates and Plato (though not for many others) that wrongdoing is the result of ignorance; if people truly knew the good they were bound to do it. In any case knowledge of what goodness is would enable people both to be good themselves and to lead others through dialectic to knowledge of goodness. Only philosophical enquiry, that is, the practice of dialectic, can lead to true knowledge, and it must be preceded by the study of mathematics and of abstract and logical thinking in general, as well as of the science of government. A man having such knowledge would constitute the ideal ruler. Only a select few may be capable of gaining this kind of true knowledge; the rest must be content with having the right opinions.

4. Plato is interested in investigating the qualities not only of the virtuous man but of the virtuous ruler, notably in the *Republic*. Here the rulers are the 'guardians', who have expert knowledge about how to run a *city-state with the help of their auxiliaries and govern the citizens in their own best interests, while the citizens defer to the rulers as a patient defers to a doctor. The city is analogous to the human *soul, where Plato's notional three parts work together in harmony. For Plato all objects of knowledge, including what we think of as abstractions such as 'beauty', were real entities, but like the objects of mathematical knowledge, such as the ideal triangle or circle, these abstractions did not exist in our world of the senses. Plato postulated another world, the world of the Forms or Ideas of things (*see* PLATONISM). He leaves the relationship between the world of Forms and the world of the senses somewhat vague; but he believes that the things we see now in this world remind us of the Forms that they in some way 'partake of', and that we can attain knowledge of the world of Forms only by thought (as is true of the objects of mathematical knowledge). True knowledge can only be of these Forms, because they are eternal and unvarying whereas the objects of our world of the senses are forever changing and decaying. (Aristotle's criticism of this doctrine was that Forms only had reality in so far as they were embodied in particular objects.)

5. Plato believed in a dualism of mortal body and immortal soul which is endlessly reborn into different bodies. The soul before its incarnation at birth is acquainted with the world of Forms; knowledge of the Forms in this life is achieved through the soul's recollection of what it has previously known, a recollection which is brought about by the practice of philosophy (i.e. dialectic). Soul is thus the intellect as well as the principle of life and the individual personality. Life should be devoted to the cultivation of the soul and the suppression of the body (which may hinder the soul's activities). Beyond all other Forms is that of the Good ('the cause of whatever is right and good' (*Republic* 7), knowledge of which it is the soul's ambition to attain. Love of what is good and beautiful in this world can lead by stages, through dialectic, to the soul's contemplation of the Form of the Good in another world, for which it yearns.

6. Plato has become notorious for his hostile attitude to rhetoric, art, and literature, despite being reputedly a poet himself, an admirer of

Homer, and an outstanding prose stylist. His attitude was based on the failure of artists to have knowledge themselves or convey it in any rational way, or to be a moral influence for good. See REPUBLIC [book 10]; PHAEDRUS; AESTHETICS, POETICS.

7. In the disciplines and methods of philosophy, and the rigour of their application, Plato's immediate heir was Aristotle, but ultimately his intellectual heirs are all those who have tried to think systematically about morals and politics, science and mathematics. Plato has exerted an enormous influence on subsequent philosophic and religious thought by his theory of Forms, his sense of an unseen and eternal world behind the changing unrealities of the world of the senses, his conception ( in the late *Timaeus*) of God as Demiurge, the maker of the world, and his connection of morality with religion. In Judaism his influence is felt in the system of Philo the Jew (see PHILON (2)). Among the Romans his philosophy appealed to Cicero in particular, as it did to all who revolted against materialism. In the third century AD Plotinus and others provided systematic exegesis of the dialogues as well as reinterpretations, which together made *Neoplatonism the dominant pagan philosophy of that time. Christian thought was infused with Platonic notions from the time of (the Greek) Clement of Alexandria and Origen (second century AD), and Latin Christianity too was influenced indirectly by Platonic teaching from a variety of sources including *Boethius and, from the ninth century, translations of pseudo-Dionysius the Areopagite (see DIONYSIUS (4)). At the beginning of the Renaissance, reaction by humanists against scholasticism took the form of disparagement of Aristotle and enthusiasm for Plato. Latin translations of his works were made in the fifteenth century by the Italian humanist Marsilio Ficino (1433–99). Knowledge of Plato came to England in the sixteenth century and Platonism was embraced enthusiastically by the seventeenth-century Cambridge Platonists, so-called, who were in this as in much else opposed to the thought of their age. Although nowadays a Platonist philosophy is not usually thought to be tenable, Plato remains a source of philosophical inspiration.

See also SCEPTICS; STOICISM; SOPHIST; MIME.

**Platonism** The term Platonism implies the existence of a systematic philosophical doctrine. *Plato, however, does not express his meaning directly by straightforward exposition. His thoughts emerge only through the medium of literary dialogues, fictional conversations on philosophical topics between Socrates and other individuals, usually well-known historical characters of the generation preceding Plato, composed over a period of some fifty years. Moreover, Plato himself never appears as a participant, the authorial voice is never heard, and though Socrates may seem to be his mouthpiece this is not always the case.

Plato's central doctrine is that of the existence of Forms or Ideas, eternal realities that can only be apprehended by the mind and that exist in a transcendental world beyond the world of the senses in which we live. They resemble mathematical objects, the triangle or the sphere for example, in that they are known only through intellect. Platonists believe that the world in which they exist is the real world, and our world only a reflection of it. The Forms seem also to have been thought of on occasion as ideal standards to which we may aspire, e.g. the Form of justice, and most particularly the Form of the Good. Awareness of this invisible, eternal, and ideal world sometimes has poetic or religious overtones. It can also by contrast lead to close analysis of the realities of this world of the senses.

The first of later philosophers who wished to extract a system from Plato's dialogues were the Neoplatonists (see NEOPLATONISM), notably *Plotinus (third century AD) and *Proclus (fifth century AD). Their concern was first with whether there was or could be any intermediary between the world of the Forms and our world of the senses (such as the *soul, which in Plato's thought can know both worlds) and secondly whether there was any reality beyond the Forms. Plato himself sometimes wrote as if the Form of the Good was in some undefined way just such an ultimate reality. This last idea led to the Neoplatonic concept of the One. Knowledge of or union with this ultimate being, some felt, could be achieved not by the mind or soul but only by the kind of love, *eros*, first described by Plato in the *Symposium*. This idea of spiritual love became for many the essential part of Platonism.

It is notable that the political concerns of Plato, as expressed in the *Republic* for example, took virtually no part in shaping the tradition of thought commonly described as Platonic. See also ACADEMY and MIDDLE PLATONISM.

**Plautus, Titus Ma'ccius (Maccus)** (c.250–184 BC) Roman writer of comedies. He was born at Sarsina in Umbria, reputedly in humble circumstances. Twenty of the 130 plays that were attributed to him have survived, all included in the twenty-one named by *Varro as authentic. Of the twenty-first, the *Vidularia* ('wallet'), only 100 or so lines exist in a *palimpsest. The plays are all adaptations from Greek New Comedy (*see* COMEDY [Greek 6]) of the fourth and third centuries BC, now lost (but *see* DIS EXAPATON); and they reproduce Greek life and, with humorous exaggeration, Greek character, as presented by the Greek originals. They were known among the Romans as *fabulae *palliatae*. They contain no satire on public affairs. Plautus' success in winning the approval of his unsophisticated audience lay in the freedom and liveliness with which he handled the Greek originals. In practice he completely re-created these works, simplifying or abridging the plot and making its progress clear, and at the same time introducing other elements, some incongruous and anachronistic, aimed at appealing to his contemporary Roman audience: short stock scenes where characters exchange threats or insults; stock motifs such as that of the 'running slave' entering to deliver a message ostensibly in a hurry but with a great deal of byplay; the slave in the role of popular entertainer, daringly outspoken and insolent in what the Romans may have felt was the Greek fashion, sometimes contrasted with a loyal slave expressing sentiments towards his masters likely to win the approval of slave-owners in the audience. Above all there was a great deal of exuberant word-play: coarse jokes, alliteration, puns, and boisterous humour. The effect was a never-land blend of Greece and Rome. As well as this, instead of having plays consisting almost entirely of spoken dialogue (*diverbium*), Plautus greatly increased (to about two-thirds of the play) the element of song and recitative (*cantica*), so that the plays resembled musical comedy. The spoken part was written chiefly in iambic senarii, but the scansion was far less regular than in later authors, and was based in great part not on quantity but on stress accent, probably in accordance with colloquial pronunciation. The sung portion was written in a number of lyric metres.

The plays show variety of manner: sentimental comedy in *Captivi*, domestic in *Tri-nummus*, romantic in *Rudens*, burlesque in *Amphitruo*, and farcical in *Miles gloriosus*. Most plots centre on the tricks of a resourceful slave to forward the love affair of his young master who is being thwarted by a rival, a pimp, or a stern father. The girl in question is usually a slave-prostitute who is eventually discovered to be freeborn and so able to marry her Athenian lover. Often the heroine was kidnapped in childhood and her recognition forms the climax of the play. Among the stock characters may be included a boastful soldier, a *parasite, and a cook. (For descriptions of the plays see the entries under their titles.) The best-known are: *Amphitruo*, *Aulularia*, *Bacchides*, *Captivi*, *Menaechmi*, *Mostellaria*, *Miles gloriosus*, *Pseudolus*, *Rudens*, *Trinummus*. Less popular are: *Asinaria*, *Casina*, *Cistellaria*, *Curculio*, *Epidicus*, *Mercator*, *Persa*, *Poenulus*, *Stichus*, *Truculentus*. (For *Vidularia* see above.)

These plays are almost the only evidence we have for the *Latin language at that period. They were greatly admired in the late republic and under the early emperors, but dropped out of favour later because of the difficulty of the language. Plautus was rediscovered and widely translated in the Renaissance, and his influence is traceable in much sixteenth-century English comedy. Henry VIII had two of the comedies performed to entertain the French ambassador in 1526. Shakespeare used the plot of the *Menaechmi* in *The Comedy of Errors* (1594), and Molière's Harpagon in *L'Avare* (1668) is taken from Euclio in *Aulularia*.

**plebei'ans** [Lat. *plebs*, sing., 'the common people'] Name given to the body of Roman citizens other than the privileged *patricians. In the early republic the plebeians were excluded from religious *collegia*, magistracies, and perhaps from the senate, and from intermarriage with patricians by a law of the *Twelve Tables. The 'conflict of the *orders' in the fifth and fourth centuries BC was an eventually successful struggle to have these civil disabilities abolished. *See also* TRIBUNES OF THE PLEBS and SECESSION.

**plebiscite** *See* SECESSION.

**Plei'ādēs** (Eng. Pleiades or Pleiads) In Greek myth, the seven daughters of the Titan *Atlas and of Pleione. Their names were Maia (the mother of Hermes by Zeus), Tāygete, Electra, Alcyone, Asterope, Celaeno, and Merope. They were pursued by *Orion and he and they were turned into constellations (as were their sisters the *Hyades). The Pleiades star cluster has special significance for marking the seasons, in particular the time for sowing and planting. In Hesiod, the first time they rise so as to be visible in the night sky just before sunrise marks harvest-time (early to mid-May), and their setting just before sunrise (at the beginning of November) marks the time for ploughing and sowing, though the expanse of the cluster makes it impossible to determine an exact date. (Hesiod further particularizes with even less exact dating, by snails climbing up and cranes migrating.)

The name Pleiad was given to a group of eight or more Greek writers of tragedy who lived in Alexandria in the reign of Ptolemy II Philadelphus (285–246 BC). None of their tragedies survives. The name was later taken over by various groups of artists, most famously by a group of seven sixteenth-century French poets. See also LYCOPHRON.

**Pleisthenes** An obscure hero in the family tree of *Agamemnon. He sometimes appears to be the son of Atreus and the father of Agamemnon and Menelaus, who after Pleisthenes' death were brought up by Atreus.

**Pliny 1. Pliny the Elder** (Gaius Plinius Secundus, AD 23/4–79) Roman writer on natural history. He was born at Comum (Como) in north Italy (Cisalpine Gaul) of an equestrian family and probably educated at Rome. He was the uncle of *Pliny the Younger and the author of the Naturalis Historia ('Natural History') in thirty-seven books. From the age of about 23 to 35 he spent his life in military service, and was at one time the comrade-in-arms of the future emperor Titus. He returned to Italy in 57 or 58 and perhaps spent a period as an advocate. After the accession of the emperor Vespasian in AD 69 he held a succession of procuratorships in Gaul, Africa, and Spain and became a counsellor (amicus, 'friend') of Vespasian and then of Titus who succeeded in 79, and was appointed commander of the fleet at Misenum (near Naples). It was from there that he sailed on 24 August 79 to observe the eruption of Vesuvius from the neighbourhood of Stabiae (south of Pompeii). His nephew Pliny the Younger describes in a letter to Tacitus (6.16) how his uncle had his attention drawn to the column of smoke rising above the nearer mountains and set off in a light vessel to investigate; how he dictated his observations under a hail of stones, and the next day went out on the shore despite the darkness and explosions, with a pillow around his head for protection against falling debris, but was suffocated by the fumes.

Pliny was a man of extraordinary industry and thirst for knowledge. He slept little, had books constantly read to him, and took an immense quantity of notes. He wrote works which are now lost on cavalry tactics, oratory, grammar, and history but his greatest surviving achievement is the Natural History, dedicated to Titus in 77 and published posthumously. Pliny tells us in the preface that it consists of 20,000 important facts obtained from 100 authors, but the real total of both is much higher. Book 1 consists of a table of contents and list of authorities; book 2 deals with the physics of the universe, and its constituent parts; books 3–6 are on the geography and ethnology of Europe, Asia, and Africa; book 7 on human physiology; books 8–11 on zoology (land animals, sea animals, birds, insects); books 12–19 on botany; books 20–7 on the medicinal properties of plants; books 28–32 on medicines derived from animals; books 33–7 on metals and stones, including the use of minerals in medicine, art, and architecture, with a digression on the history of art, the source of many good anecdotes and much valuable information about Greek artists. In spite of many errors and the tedium of dry catalogues, the work is remarkable for the vast labour and the boundless curiosity of the author that it represents; it contains much that is interesting and entertaining, and much unique information about the art, science, and civilization of the author's day. Pliny is an enthusiastic admirer of nature, and a vigorous critic of his times. In the preface to the Natural History he observes that 'a [fully realized] life entails staying awake' (vita vigilia est); he ends the work with heartfelt and lyrical praise of Italy.

**2. Pliny the Younger** (AD 61/62–c.112) Roman administrator known through his letters. He was called Gaius Plinius Caecilius Secundus after being adopted by his maternal uncle Pliny the Elder ((1) above). He was born at Comum (Como) in north Italy, and studied at Rome under *Quintilian, whose influence may be detected in the simplicity and restraint of his pupil's prose. Another of his teachers was the Stoic philosopher *Musonius. He was three times married, his first two wives dying young; his letters show that his third marriage, to Calpurnia, was a very happy one. He began a career at the bar at the age of 18 and was proud of his oratory. Having passed through the *cursus honorum*, he succeeded by his discretion in avoiding Domitian's persecution of the Stoic opposition, in spite of his sympathy with its views. Under Trajan (AD 98–117) he became one of the officials in charge of the state treasury; he was *consul suffectus* in 100 (*see* CONSULS), then a curator of the river Tiber at Rome. He became augur in 103 (succeeding *Frontinus) and finally in about 110 governor of the disorderly province of *Bithynia–Pontus along the south coast of the Black Sea, where he apparently died in office. His career was similar to that of his friend the historian Tacitus.

Pliny derived great wealth from his estates in Italy and was munificent: he founded a library at Comum and made many large gifts and charitable bequests. His only surviving speech is a revised edition of the *Panegyricus* which he delivered to Trajan on entering on his consulship in AD 100; it is an expression of the relief felt under the new reign after the oppression of Domitian, and throws light on Trajan's reforms.

Pliny's fame rests on his ten books of letters, nine of which were published before he went out to Bithynia. In general the letters are not dated, and Pliny professes to have arranged them haphazardly. Book 10 was published posthumously; it begins with fourteen short official letters to Trajan, and is followed by correspondence relating to Bithynia. The first three books deal with the events of 97–102, ending with a letter on the death of the poet Martial in 103/4. Books 4–7 refer to the events of 103–7; in the last letter of book 7 Pliny hopes he will be included in the *Histories* of Tacitus. Books 8–9 cover the years 108–9, and show Pliny enjoying a leisurely time on the estate of his Tuscan villa at Tifernum (Città di Castello). His appointment to Bithynia ended this period of cultivated leisure.

Pliny's letters resemble short essays on a wide variety of subjects: public affairs, descriptions of his villas or of scenery, or of how he spends his day (sometimes in hunting, but he takes his writing materials too), literary or rhetorical points, ghost stories, the purchase of a statue or an estate, a murder. He writes of his new marriage, his grief at his wife's miscarriage, and his hopes for further children (not to be fulfilled). Several of the letters are addressed to his friends Tacitus and Suetonius, among them the famous letter to Tacitus (6.16) describing the eruption of Vesuvius and his uncle's death. Others include eulogies of the poets *Silius Italicus and Martial (3.7 and 21), an account of the heroism of *Arria, wife of Paetus (3.16), and a bibliography of the works of the Elder Pliny (3.5). Their style is adapted to the subject: they are more studied and artificial than those of Cicero to *Atticus and include some rather bad specimens, but they have natural charm, and depict the life of a wealthy Roman during a happy period of the empire, helping to correct the unfavourable impression left by the bitter satire of Juvenal and the sombre pessimism which Tacitus retained even when writing under Trajan.

The correspondence with Trajan in the tenth book illustrates the administration of an imperial province. It displays Pliny as an honest but timid governor, referring to Rome such small matters as the absence of a fire-brigade and water-buckets at Nicomedia. The emperor's replies are precise and clear and show him encouraging an extraordinary degree of centralization. The most famous of these letters are Pliny's submission of the question how the Christians should be treated, and the emperor's answer (*see* CHRISTIANITY IN THE ROMAN WORLD).

Pliny prided himself not only on his oratory but on his poetry, and published two volumes of verse. His pleasure in his literary fame appears when he tells (9.23) how a Roman *eques*, sitting next to Tacitus at the Circus and conversing with him, asked him who he was, and being answered, 'You know me from your reading', enquired, 'Are you Tacitus or Pliny?'

**Plōtī'nus** (AD *c.*205–*c.*270) Greatest Greek philosopher of late antiquity, the chief exponent of *Neoplatonism, probably born at Lycopolis in Egypt. He settled in Rome in 244, after having accompanied the unsuccessful expedition of the emperor Gordian to Mesopotamia in order to learn something of eastern thought. In the event religious ideas from the East seem to have had little influence on his thinking. He was admired for his extreme spirituality, mysticism, and asceticism. 'He seemed ashamed of being in a body', says his biographer and disciple *Porphyry. Plotinus wrote philosophical essays arising out of discussions and intended for circulation among his pupils. These were collected by Porphyry and arranged in six books of nine essays each, called *Enneads* ('The nines'), published between 300 and 305. Ennead 1 deals with ethics and aesthetics; Enneads 2 and 3 with physics and cosmology; Ennead 4 with psychology; Enneads 5 and 6 with metaphysics, logic, and epistemology. These form a more coherent body of philosophical teaching than anything surviving from an earlier period. Because of his weak sight Plotinus never read through what he had written; the writings read like oral discourse and are brief, elliptical, and allusive, with abrupt transitions, and are therefore very difficult to understand.

Plotinus' philosophy may be summarized as follows. The universe is to be explained as a hierarchy of realities (or hypostases), a great chain of being, in which the higher reality is the cause of and gives existence to whatever is immediately below it; this process Plotinus calls emanation, an 'overflowing' from a higher to a lower level. In this process there is a gradual diminution, so that every existent is slightly inferior to its cause. At the very summit is the One (Gk. *Hĕn*), supreme goodness, which can to a large extent be identified with Plato's Form of the Good (*see* PLATO 5) or the 'One' of the *Eleatic philosophers. It is the foundation of existence and the source of all values. After the One are three divine and descending grades of reality, World Mind, World Soul, and Nature. The first, Mind (Gk. *Nous*), derives its form from contemplating its source. It is a fragmented image of the One, and corresponds to intuitive thought. The Platonic Forms (*see* PLATO 4) are to be found in Mind. *Soul (Gk. *Psȳchē*), which derives from Mind, can only contemplate its objects in succession, moving from one to another, and so it creates time and space. It generates the next reality, Nature (*Physis*), the principle of life and growth. Beyond Nature, at the lowest level of reality, exist material things (matter). Human beings are microcosms, containing within themselves parts of Matter, Nature, Soul, and Mind. What a human being becomes depends on the level to which he or she directs consciousness. By intellectual discipline a person may hope to rise to the level of Mind. It is even possible to rise beyond that, to achieve complete inward unity (Gk. *henōsis*) and be identified with the supreme unity of the One (this ecstatic experience Plotinus says came four times to him). In ethics Plotinus enjoined purification by self-discipline, with a view to ascent, impelled by love and enthusiasm, towards the One. His writings are based on personal experience and are a classic of mysticism. He makes no explicit reference to Christianity, and does not think of unification with the One as being attainable by divine grace. Plotinus also makes an important contribution to aesthetics: whereas Plato had argued that art imitates natural objects, Plotinus propounds the view that art and nature alike impose a form on matter in accordance with an inward vision of archetypal Forms or Ideas.

**Plŭtarch (Ploutarchos)** (AD *c.*46–after 120) Greek biographer, historian, and moral philosopher.

1. Plutarch was born at *Chaeronea in Boeotia, of a wealthy and cultivated family, and spent most of his life there. He studied philosophy at Athens and visited Egypt and Italy, lecturing and teaching at Rome, and acquiring a wide circle of influential friends. But the last thirty years of his life were centred on Chaeronea and *Delphi; he was a priest of Delphi, and served both places with devotion for many years. Neither Pliny the Younger nor Tacitus (his contemporaries) mentions him. Plutarch is one of the most attractive and readable of ancient prose authors, writing with charm, geniality, and tact. An ancient catalogue of his works exists, ascribed to Lamprias. His surviving writings (half his complete works) consist of (i) a series of fifty biographies known as *Parallel Lives* (Gk. *Bioi paralleloi*) in which he relates the life of some eminent Greek (statesman or soldier) followed by the life of some similar Roman offering some points of resemblance, and then adds a short comparison of the two; and (ii) seventy-eight miscellaneous works now known as the *Moralia* (Gk. *Ethika*).

2. *Parallel Lives*. These consist of twenty-three pairs of lives, nineteen of them with comparisons attached, and also four single lives. They include lives of Solon, Themistocles, Aristeides, Pericles, Alcibiades, Nicias, Demosthenes, Philopoemen, Timoleon, Dion, Alexander, Pyrrhus, Marius, Sulla, Pompey, Mark Antony, Brutus, Julius Caesar, and Cicero. Of the Roman emperors, only the lives of Galba and Otho survive. Plutarch's object is

to bring out the moral character in each case, rather than to relate the political events of his time; hence his full treatment of the subject's education and natural disposition, and his relation of anecdotes calculated to reveal the nature of the man, 'a light occasion, a word, or some sport' which 'makes men's natural dispositions more plain than the famous battles won, in which ten thousand men may be killed'. Although Plutarch distorts the truth in order to exemplify virtue or vice, in general he is as reliable as his sources, and sometimes very valuable. He shows no bias or unfairness in his treatment of Greeks and Romans, no flattery of the now dominant power of Rome or vanity in the past glories of his own nation. He believed in the compatibility of Rome the ruler and Greece the educator.

The *Lives* contain, besides interesting anecdotes, many memorable historical passages: the catastrophe in the Peloponnesian War of the Athenian expedition to Syracuse (*Nicias*), Pompey's defeat by Caesar and subsequent murder, the death of the younger Cato, and the suicide of Otho. There are also great battle-pieces: the victory of the Roman general Marius over the German Cimbri, the victory of the Corinthian general Timoleon over the Carthaginians at the river Crimisus, the siege of Syracuse (when Archimedes was there) by the Roman Marcellus; and striking descriptions of a quite different kind, of the happy state of Italy under Numa, of Sicily pacified by Timoleon, and of Cleopatra sailing in her barge up the Cilician river Cydnus to visit Antony at Tarsus, 'Venus come to revel with Bacchus for the happiness of Asia'. The most famous translation of the *Lives* into English was that of Sir Thomas North (1579), made not from Greek but from the French version of Jacques Amyot (1559). It was Shakespeare's major source for *Julius Caesar*, *Antony and Cleopatra*, and *Coriolanus*, and a minor source for *A Midsummer Night's Dream* and *Timon of Athens*.

3. *Moralia*. These treatises are usually referred to by their Latin titles and their subjects are varied. There is one group of rhetorical works and another on moral philosophy (treated in a popular style) on themes such as 'On busybodies' (*De curiositate*), 'On garrulity' (*De garrulitate*), 'On the restraint of anger' (*De cohibenda ira*), 'How to distinguish a flatterer from a friend' (*Quomodo adulator ab amico*

*internoscatur*). Plutarach's warm and sympathetic personality is apparent in his 'Advice to married couples' (*Coniugalia praecepta*) and 'Consolation to my wife' (*Consolatio ad uxorem*) on the death of their infant daughter. There is a religious group, in which Plutarch appears as the interpreter and defender of the old beliefs. It includes the treatise 'On superstition' (*De superstitione*), in which he regards superstition as the opposite extreme to atheism, and piety as the mean between the two. Plutarch was a (not altogether orthodox) Platonist and was opposed to some of the doctrines of the Stoics, and still more to the Epicurean school and its encouragement of withdrawal from the duties of social life: see his treatises on 'The Unnoticed Life' (*An recte dictum sit latenter esse vivendum*), 'Advice on public life' (*Praecepta gerendae reipublicae*), and 'Not even a pleasant life is possible on Epicurean principles' (*Non posse suaviter vivi secundum Epicurum*). There is an interesting treatise 'On the delays of divine justice' (*De sera numinis vindicta*) in which he explains the puzzle of the apparent prosperity of the wicked, and another 'On the E at Delphi' (*De E apud Delphos*), i.e. on the letter E inscribed in the temple of Apollo there (for which he offers a Pythagorean explanation, that it is the Greek for 'Thou Art', identifying the one eternal principle of the universe); also interesting is 'On the cessation of oracles' (*De defectu oraculorum*), which contains a discussion of demons (*see* DAIMON), beings intermediate between gods and men as in Plato's *Symposium*, and refers to the legend of the genii of the British Isles.

Plutarch used the *dialogue form extensively and often to great effect. The nine books of 'Table talk' (*Quaestiones convivales*) are dinner-party conversations of wise men (rhetoricians, physicians, etc., some of them historical characters) on a multitude of subjects. The treatise 'On Socrates' sign' (*De genio Socratis*) combines many elements: exciting narrative (the liberation of Thebes), philosophical conversation, and an elaborate myth, in the manner of Plato, on the fate of the soul after death. A different kind of treatise is that 'On the face in the moon' (*De facie quae in orbe lunae apparet*), a speculation on the cosmos. Several important antiquarian works have also survived: the 'Greek questions' and 'Roman questions' (*Quaestiones Graecae, Romanae*) are a mine of information about religious antiquities. Plutarch wrote some literary criticism, including a comparison of Aristophanes and Menander, and an essay 'On the malignity of Herodotus' (*De malignitate Herodoti; see* HERODOTUS), in which Plutarch's complaint seems to be that Herodotus did not conceal the pro-Persian sympathies of the Boeotians (*see* PERSIAN WARS). It is noteworthy that Plutarch, in spite of his familiarity with Roman society, history, archaeology, and religion, almost completely ignores Roman literature (his knowledge of Latin appears to have been limited). In his *Life of Lucullus* he gives a Greek version of a passage from Horace, but never mentions Virgil or Ovid.

4. Among the *Moralia* have survived several slightly later works not written by Plutarch but of great importance: 'On the education of children' (*De liberis educandis*) was very influential in the Renaissance; 'On fate' (*De fato*) is valuable as a work of Middle Platonist philosophy; 'The lives of the ten orators' (*Vitae decem oratorum*) is an important source for ancient knowledge of the Attic orators from Antiphon to Deinarchus; 'The doctrines of the philosophers' (*De placitis philosophorum*) is another important source book; and 'On music' (*De musica*) is one of the principal sources of modern knowledge about the history of Greek music and lyric poetry.

5. Plutarch's *Moralia* were widely read in medieval times and studied by many later authors. They were translated into French by Amyot in 1572, and into English by Philemon Holland in 1603. These and the *Lives*, perhaps more than the work of any other ancient writer, transmitted to Europe knowledge of the moral and historical traditions of the classical world, and influenced immeasurably its ways of thought.

**Pluto** (the Latin form, commonly used in English, of Ploutōn) In Greek myth, a name given to *Hades, god of the Underworld, meaning 'The wealth-giver' (Gk. *ploutos*, 'wealth'), because wealth comes from the earth (*cf.* PLUTUS). It is also the name of a Titan, mother of *Tantalus.

**Plūtus (Ploutos)** ('Wealth') In Greek myth, the son of *Demeter and *Iasion, and so 'wealth' in the sense of an abundance of crops. He became a figure of popular rather than literary mythology, and was worshipped with Demeter at Eleusis. There was a tradition

that Zeus blinded him in order to make him indiscriminate in the distribution of riches. See the Greek comedy **Plutus* by Aristophanes.

**Plūtus (Ploutos)** ('Wealth') Greek comedy by *Aristophanes produced in 388 BC; at what festival and with what success is not known. It is the last of Aristophanes' extant plays. An earlier play of the same name, now lost, had been produced by him in 408. The lyrics to be sung by the chorus are very scanty in this play, but provision appears to have been made at various places for choral interludes which had no particular connection with the plot (for the diminishing role of the chorus in the latest plays of Aristophanes *see* COMEDY [Greek 5]).

Chremylus is so indignant at seeing bad men grow rich while honest men like himself remain poor that, accompanied by his slave Carion, he has been to consult the Delphic oracle as to whether he should bring up his son to be good or bad if the boy is to succeed in life. The god advises Chremylus to accost the first person he meets on leaving the shrine and induce him to enter his house. This is a blind old man; pestered by Chremylus and Carion he reveals that he is Plutus, god of wealth, whom Zeus has blinded out of ill-will to men so that, being unable to distinguish good men from bad, he will reward them without regard to their virtue. Chremylus decides that the sight of Plutus must be restored so that he may associate only with honest men. Plutus is terrified of the vengeance of Zeus but is persuaded that he himself is more powerful than that god: by not providing men with the money to buy them he can put a stop to Zeus' sacrifices. He therefore consents to be taken to the temple of Asclepius to be cured. The goddess of Poverty intervenes and tries to deter Chremylus, pointing out the disastrous effects of what he proposes to do, for it is Poverty, the source of all virtue and effort, that has made Greece what she is. But Chremylus remains unconvinced, and he and Carion go off to the temple with Plutus. Carion returns to tell Chremylus' wife of the successful cure, with much entertaining detail; presently Plutus returns and enriches Chremylus' house. Then comes a series of visitors: an honest man who has long been poor and is now prosperous; an informer, indignant at being impoverished; an old woman who has lost her young lover now he no longer needs her money; the god Hermes who is desperately hungry since no one bothers to sacrifice to the gods, and is looking for a job; and finally the priest of Zeus who is also hungry because he cannot get his share of the sacrifices. Chremylus seems to identify Plutus and Zeus, and suggests that they install Plutus in the treasure-room of Athena on the Acropolis. A procession for that purpose ensues.

**Pnyx** Small hill at Athens, about 400m (440 yds.) south-west of the Agora, where from the time of *Cleisthenes (2) (end of the sixth century BC) the assembly of the Athenian citizens, the *ecclesia, used to meet. In Roman times (i.e. after 146 BC) the Pnyx lost its importance and the assembly met in the theatre of Dionysus.

**Podalei'rius** See MACHAON.

**Poe'nulus** ('Little Carthaginian') Roman comedy by *Plautus.

The two daughters of Hanno, a Carthaginian, who were stolen from him in their childhood, have been bought by a pimp and taken to Sicyon (in Greece). In the same place is living Agorastocles, son of Hanno's cousin (and the 'little Carthaginian' of the title); he likewise was stolen in infancy and has been adopted by a wealthy citizen of Sicyon. He has fallen in love with the elder of the sisters, not knowing of their kinship to him. He and his slave devise a plot for ruining the pimp in order to free the girl. Meanwhile Hanno, who has been searching every country for his daughters, arrives at Sicyon; he discovers them and his relation Agorastocles, recovers the girls, and bestows the elder on her lover. The play exploits the exoticism of the Carthaginian element. Much is made of Punic 'bad faith' and ability in languages (see BILINGUALISM), and there are even exchanges in the Carthaginian language. See TEXTS, TRANSMISSION OF ANCIENT 4.

**Poetics (Peri poiētikes)** (Lat. *Poetica*) Short treatise by *Aristotle on poetry, usually treated as primarily a work of aesthetic theory. Like his *Rhetoric, however, the *Poetics* has a practical aim: how to create a tragedy. (*See also* AESTHETICS.) Aristotle believed that art is essentially representational and that the basis of the pleasure derived from all forms of art, not only poetry but also music, dancing, painting, and sculpture, is imitation or representation of human life. The artist, by pointing out similarities, gives us the pleasure of understanding things better.

Aristotle divides poetry according to whether it imitates people above or below the average state of humanity (tragedy represents good characters, comedy bad) and according to whether it is narrative (epic) or dramatic. He traces the special origins and development of *tragedy and *comedy. An analysis of tragedy follows: its constituent elements are plot, the imitation of character, verbal expression, the imitation of intellect, spectacle, and songwriting; the plot (the pre-eminent part of tragedy) should represent a single action of a certain magnitude; the poet's aim is to produce pleasure in the spectator by eliciting from the representation the emotions of pity (for others) and fear (for oneself). Plato had attacked tragedy for stimulating the emotions a good man tries to suppress; Aristotle seems to suggest that the *catharsis* (purging) of these emotions may incidentally be beneficial. He discusses the construction of the plot, including the complex (as opposed to the simple) plot which contains 'reversal of fortune' (*peripeteia*) and recognition (*anagnorisis*). This part includes the notable observation that poetry is more like philosophy and more worthwhile than history, because it tells general truths while history tells particular facts, 'what Alcibiades did and what happened to him'. There follow sections on characterization, poetic imagination, and diction. As well as dealing with aesthetic matters Aristotle was analysing, within the conventions of his day, the constituents of a successful play

Aristotle then discusses epic poetry, the rules to which it should conform, and its metre. Finally he deals with criticisms of Homer and how they may be met, and ends with a comparison of tragedy and epic.

The *Poetics* became the most influential book on poetry ever written. It has moreover the peculiarity that the genuine views of Aristotle contributed no more to its influence than the misinterpretation of these views arising from the author's compressed and elliptical style. The dramatic unities of time, place, and action, for example, which were so rigidly adhered to by the French classical dramatists, find their origin in Aristotle's observations on the practice of his day (he insisted only on the necessity for unity of action) but took their absolute nature from the elaborations of Italian Renaissance scholars and in particular from the widely read *Poetics* (1561) of Julius Caesar Scaliger.

**po'lemarch (*polemarchos*)** At Athens, one of the nine *archons appointed annually, originally the commander-in-chief of the army. After 487 BC, when the archons were first appointed partly by lot, the chief command was transferred to the *strategoi* and the polemarch's powers were limited to certain judicial and ceremonial functions.

**police** In the ancient world police forces to maintain order and to enforce the law did not exist. At Athens there were minor officials, *astynomoi*, whose responsibility it was to keep streets clean and supervise the markets, etc. There was also a corps of 300 Scythian archers who kept order in the assembly and lawcourts, but there was no body with powers to investigate, arrest, or prosecute. These activities were left to private citizens who with neighbours and kin practised a kind of self-help. At Rome the *aediles had functions similar to those of the Athenian *astynomoi*. There were also officials who supervised the city gaols and carried out executions, with the help of slaves (*see* PRISON). It was recognized at Rome particularly that in a political crisis it was occasionally necessary to call on the help of armed citizens (*see* e.g. GRACCHI (2)). The Roman emperors instituted something resembling a police force in the *vigiles* and urban cohorts (*see* PRAEFECTUS URBI and PRAEFECTUS VIGILUM). Despite this, law-enforcement remained the responsibility of citizens acting with other like-minded individuals.

**polis** ('city') *See* ACROPOLIS and CITY-STATE.

***Politics (Politica)*** Treatise in eight books by *Aristotle. In its present form it is made up of various parts composed at different times from different perspectives.

Aristotle discusses the science of politics from the point of view of the *city-state (Gk. *polis*), which he assumes to be that most conducive to the fullest life of a citizen. The human excellences (*see* NICOMACHEAN ETHICS) cannot be practised by a solitary individual. Humans are social animals like bees, wasps, ants, and cranes: partnership in these things makes a household and a state, Aristotle believes. He thinks the city-state was developed naturally by the grouping of families in villages, and of villages in a city, in order to secure for the citizens a good and self-sufficing life. Since the essential purpose of the city is to pursue this moral, not material, end, it is necessary that the power

should rest, not with the wealthy or with the whole body of free citizens, but with the good. For Aristotle the city-state must be small: 'it must have the largest population consistent with self-sufficiency, but small enough for no-one to go unnoticed' (Plato in the *Laws* assumed a state of 5,040 citizen-farmers with households of families and slaves). Aristotle discusses citizenship, the classification of actual constitutions, and the various types of these, their failings and remedies. Though he recognizes the advantages of *democracy, producing good policies from the combined knowledge of a diverse population, he finds the highest type in the monarchy of the perfect ruler if such is available, and failing this in an *aristocracy of men of virtue and enlightenment. But this, too, is difficult, and so in practice he regards a limited democracy as the constitution best suited 'for a complete and self-sufficient life'. Another ideal is liberty, the prerogative of citizens. One form of liberty is to live as one pleases, and women do not possess liberty in a real sense. He regards slavery as a natural institution (*see* LAW, NATURAL), so far as it is based on the inferiority of the nature of the slave rather than on right of conquest. But the master must not abuse his authority, and slaves must have the hope of emancipation. However, Aristotle describes many ways in which the state should control the lives of its citizens, and envisages the good life being promoted by a very authoritarian regime.

***Poli'ticus*** *See* STATESMAN.

**Po'llio (Gaius Asi'nius Pollio)** (76 BC–AD 4) Roman historian, literary patron, statesman, and supporter of the emperor Augustus. In his youth he was an associate of the poet Catullus, and a supporter first of Julius Caesar in the civil war against Pompey and later of Mark Antony. He was consul in 40 BC, when he helped to bring about the treaty of *Brundisium between Antony and Octavian. In 39 he obtained a triumph for his victory over an Illyrian tribe, and used the booty to build the first public library in Rome (*see* LIBRARIES). He refused to fight against Antony at Actium, but became a supporter of the Augustan settlement, after which he withdrew from politics. It was he who first recognized the genius of Virgil, and came to his assistance when Virgil's farm near Mantua was confiscated after the battle of Philippi in 42. The poet celebrated him in his fourth and eighth *Eclogues*. His history of the civil wars, from 60 BC to the battle of Philippi in 42 BC (and perhaps continued to the end of the 30s), has unfortunately not survived but was used by Appian and Plutarch; it receives high praise from Horace in *Odes* 2.1. Pollio also wrote tragedies and erotic poems, and won a reputation as an orator. A sharp critic, he ventured to correct Cicero, Caesar, and Sallust, and to criticize Livy for his provincialism (which he calls *patavinitas*). He is said by the Elder Seneca to have introduced the practice of reciting his own works to an audience.

**pollution** The Greeks, in common with many races at all times, believed that people were defiled or polluted by close contact with impurity—bloodshed, birth, death, some sexual activity (incest for example), murder except in war, or sacrilege. The effect of pollution might be similar to the consequences of divine anger: to be in danger. A polluted city, for example (such as Thebes as described at the opening of Sophocles' *Oedipus Rex*), might be struck by sterility and plague; the source of the pollution had to be found and expelled, and purity restored by religious acts of purification. Impurity was abhorrent to the gods, and a polluted person was excluded from temples and all religious occasions. Like *Oedipus, the unwitting perpetrator of parricide and incest, he was contagious and might infect others with his pollution, and therefore his company was shunned.

Pollution could result from contact with something itself unclean, a corpse for example. (At Athens, trials for murder always took place in the open air.) Birth and death were the two commonest natural pollutions, both shunned by the gods (*see* TELEPHUS). Households in which either occurred had to be purified.

The most notable cause of pollution was murder, requiring ritual purification of varying degrees of elaboration to get rid of the victim's blood, thought of as clinging to the murderer's hands. Blood shed in battle could be simply washed away, and similarly the blood of a villain could be easily removed by a straightforward ritual. At the other extreme, the *Alcmaeonidae in the fifth century BC were still dogged by accusations of pollution (or vicarious liability) arising from a murder committed in the seventh (*see* CYLON and DRACO). Epilepsy and madness were commonly regarded as if

they were the result of pollution, and were treated by rites of purification (but *see* HIPPO-CRATES (1)). Occasionally, as if to mark a new beginning, scapegoats carrying a community's impurities were expelled from a city. After the final expulsion of the Persian invaders from Athens in 479 BC (*see* PERSIAN WARS), all the fires in the city 'polluted' by the Persian presence were extinguished and rekindled from the hearth of Apollo's shrine at Delphi (Rome too was purified after the expulsions of the Tarquins and the Gauls).

**Pollux** *See* DIOSCURI.

**Pollux, Julius** (second century AD) Greek scholar and rhetorician of Naucratis in Egypt, and teacher of the Roman emperor *Commodus. He was a lexicographer and the author of an *Onomasticon*, a list of Attic Greek words and technical terms, a much-abridged and interpolated version of which is extant, descended from an epitome possessed by the Byzantine scholar Arethas *c.*AD 900. The arrangement of terms is not alphabetical but according to subject. In its explanation of terms it supplies incidentally a great deal of information on a very wide range of topics in antiquity, perhaps most valuably on music, the ancient theatre, and the Athenian constitution. Its collection of thirty-three terms of abuse for a tax-collector is notable.

**Poly'bius** (*c.*200–after 118 BC) Greek historian of Rome's rise to power, born at Megalopolis in Arcadia, the son of Lycortas, who was a prominent member of the *Achaean confederacy and friend of its general *Philopoemen. Polybius was given the honour of carrying the ashes of Philopoemen to burial in 182. In 181 he was chosen, with his father, to serve on an embassy to Egypt, but this was cancelled when the king there died suddenly. Nothing more is known of his life until 169, when he was made *hipparchos* (cavalry commander) of the confederacy. In 168, in a political purge following the Roman conquest of Macedonia, Polybius was among a thousand prominent Achaeans deported to Rome for examination and kept there for sixteen years without accusation or trial. He was fortunate to become tutor to the sons of Aemilius *Paullus (who had commanded the Roman army at Pydna), the younger of whom became by adoption Publius Cornelius *Scipio Aemilianus. Polybius' enduring friendship with the latter, and his consequent connections with two of the leading philhellenic families in Rome, allowed him on several occasions to intercede between Greece and Rome. The Achaean exiles were permitted to return to Greece in 150, and Polybius went with them, but in 147–146 he accompanied Scipio to the siege of Carthage and witnessed the destruction of that city. When war suddenly broke out between Rome and the Achaean confederacy, leading to a Greek defeat and the sacking of Corinth by Mummius in 146, Polybius acted as intermediary and was entrusted with organizing many details of the new administration. In this difficult task he earned the approval of the Romans and the gratitude of the Greek cities. Little is known of the last twenty years of his life, which must have been largely occupied with his literary work, of which only the *History* survives (in part), written in Greek. According to one source he died as a result of a fall from his horse at the age of 82.

Polybius declares the original aim of his *History* in the introduction: '[to relate] by what means and under what system of government the Romans succeeded in less than fifty-three years [from 220 BC, the start of the Second Punic War, to 168 BC, the end of the Third Macedonian War] in bringing under their rule almost the whole inhabited world'. Subsequently he extended his scheme to cover the preliminary period from the beginning of the First Punic War (264) to the destruction of Carthage and Corinth in 146 (see above). In this extended form the history consisted of forty books, of which only the first five survive complete. Of the rest we have only excerpts and quotations, some quite substantial. Book 6 includes a sketch of the Roman constitution in Polybius' day and a comparison of this with the constitutions of Athens, Thebes, Crete, Sparta, and finally Carthage.

Polybius attributed the greatness of Rome to the perfection of the Roman constitution, an even blend of monarchical, aristocratic, and democratic elements as he saw it, which was to be very influential on later thought. His history was addressed primarily to Greeks but also to the upper-class Romans of his own day who were familiar with the Greek language. His chief aim was to be useful, and he concentrates on political actions in the widest sense. He describes his work as *pragmatike historia*, a factual history and explanation of events in war and politics, with careful avoidance of the emotional and sensational as portrayed in so-called 'tragic history'. His history was breaking new ground (only *Theopompus and *Ephorus had anticipated him) in being a universal history which offered wide scope for exemplifying the various truths that Polybius wanted to communicate, and in particular the significant role that fortune played in the rise of Rome (*see* TYCHE). In using this term Polybius sometimes comes close to suggesting that Rome enjoyed divine favour, but he never attributes events to divine agency, indicating rather that Rome deserved her success because of her own merits: as Terence observed, 'fortune favours the brave'.

Polybius is unusually revealing about the qualities needed by one who would write 'pragmatical history': he must know the countries he is writing about, have personal experience of political life, which includes warfare, and (only thirdly) should have studied documents and the memoirs of others (*see* BOOKS, GREEK AND ROMAN 3). A historian should be first of all a man of action (as the author was). Polybius envisages history as being for the most part about events which can be recalled by those still alive, and regards the interrogation of eyewitnesses as supremely important; most of his own history fell within living memory or within the lifetime of the previous generation. Above all a historian must have a passion for the truth. Polybius systematically seeks the causes of events ('nothing whether probable or improbable can happen without a cause'), tracing the evolution of nations and their decline. He does not shrink from exposing the reasons for the decadence of Greece. His narrative is clear and simple and somewhat monotonous, without rhetorical artifice, written in the *koine* or 'common dialect' of Greek which prevailed from 300 BC, and without the elegance of the Greek prose writers of the classical period. *Dionysius of Halicarnassus included Polybius' history among the works no one ever managed to finish. Polybius himself is severely critical of the methods of other historians.

**Po'lybus** In Greek myth, the childless king of Corinth, who with his wife Merope adopted the infant *Oedipus to rear as their own child.

**Poly'cratēs** Tyrant of Samos from *c*.535 BC. He made the island a strong naval power and dominated the eastern Aegean. In *c*.522 he was lured to the mainland of Asia Minor by the Persian satrap Oroetes, who pretended to be plotting against the Persian king Darius, and was crucified there. Polycrates was a noted art-lover and had many beautiful buildings erected, of which Herodotus praises particularly the temple of Hera, the harbour mole, and the aqueduct for the city. He maintained a sumptuous court where the poets Anacreon and Ibycus enjoyed his patronage. Herodotus relates that Amasis II, king of Egypt, alarmed by the constant good fortune of Polycrates, sent him a letter advising him to throw away something that he valued highly so as to avert the jealousy of the gods. Polycrates accordingly threw into the sea a beautiful seal-ring, his most prized possession, but a few days later the ring was returned to him in the belly of a fish which a fisherman had presented to him. Amasis, concluding that Polycrates was marked down for destruction, renounced his friendship.

**Polydeu'cēs** (Lat. Pollux) Brother of Castor; *see* DIOSCURI.

**Polydō'rus 1.** In Greek myth, the youngest son of *Priam, king of Troy, and his wife Hecuba. According to Euripides' *Hecuba, he was murdered by Polymestor, king of the Thracian Chersonese. In Virgil's narrative (*Aeneid* 3.22), Aeneas, landing in Thrace pulls up some cornel bushes and finds the roots dripping with blood. He hears groans and a voice from the mound telling him that the murdered Polydorus is buried there. Aeneas performs funeral rites and they 'lay his soul to rest in the grave'.

**2.** In Greek myth, one of the *Epigoni.

**Polygnō'tus** (of Thasos, active 475–447 BC, later a citizen of Athens) A famous Greek painter. He may be dated by his friendship with *Cimon for whom he painted Elpinice, Cimon's sister, in the Stoa Poikile ('Painted colonnade'). *Pausanias (2) describes his celebrated murals in the Cnidian Lesche (public room) at *Delphi, of the 'Capture of Troy' (*Iliupersis*) and the 'Descent of Odysseus to the Underworld' (*Nekyia*), each containing about seventy figures. He represented people as serious and dignified in character, but showed advance on earlier art by the life and expression of the faces; for this he is praised by Aristotle and Lucian.

**Polynei'cēs** *See* OEDIPUS.

**Polyphē'mus** In Greek myth, a Cyclops (*see* CYCLOPES), son of *Poseidon. He is represented in Homer's *Odyssey* 9 as one of a race of savage, one-eyed giants, rearing sheep and goats on an island identified in later literature with Sicily. Odysseus with twelve of his men enters Polyphemus' cave. The latter, having returned with his flocks and closed the mouth of the cave with a huge rock, discovers the intruders and kills and eats two of them raw, morning and evening. The next evening Odysseus, who has been kept imprisoned in the cave, makes Polyphemus drunk with wine and destroys his eye with a pointed stake. He has told the Cyclops that his name is No-man (Outis), and when the other Cyclopes come on hearing his cry Polyphemus replies to their enquiries that No-man is killing him; they therefore go away. Next morning Odysseus lashes the rams together in threes, and under each three conceals one of his comrades. When the blinded Polyphemus releases his flocks, they thus escape, Odysseus hiding himself under the shaggy belly of the largest ram. He thereafter taunts Polyphemus, who hurls rocks at Odysseus' departing ship and nearly destroys it. Poseidon, answering his son's prayer for vengeance, tries to prevent Odysseus' fated homecoming in every possible way. Polyphemus appears in Euripides' play *Cyclops.

In the sixth and eleventh Idylls of the Hellenistic poet *Theocritus the boorish Polyphemus is represented as falling in love with the nymph Galatea and being repulsed by her. According to Ovid he crushed Galatea's young lover Acis with a rock; this is the version adopted by John Gay in his libretto to Handel's opera *Acis and Galatea* (*c*.1718).

**Poly'xena (Polyxene)** A daughter of *Priam, king of Troy, and his wife Hecuba. *See* ACHILLES.

**Pōmō'na** Roman goddess of fruit (*pōma*), the wife of Vertumnus. For the story of his wooing of her under various shapes *see* VERTUMNUS.

**Pompe'ii** Port situated on the Bay of Naples and a regional centre in southern Campania, some 240km (150 miles) south of Rome. It was an ancient city: the remains of two Greek temples have been dated to the sixth century BC, the period when Greek settlers were consolidating their cities in *Magna Graecia, and Pompeii probably had links with Etruscan culture. The native population was originally Oscan-speaking but adopted the

*Latin language after the *Social War (2). (Even in Pompeii's latest years someone scratched his name on a wall using Oscan letters.) The city developed through trade and a vigorous and varied agriculture, and flourished economically. It was a popular resort; Cicero who, Plutarch tells us, served in Sulla's army during the siege of Pompeii, later had a villa there, like many other wealthy Romans. Widespread damage caused by an earthquake in AD 62 and by subsequent tremors was still being repaired when the cataclysmic eruption of the volcano on Mount Vesuvius, about 8km (5 miles) to the north-west, occurred in AD 79 (traditionally on 24–25 August). The eruption was described by the Younger *Pliny in his Letters 6.16 and 20. Days before it there were tremors which caused many inhabitants to flee, before the last procrastinators were overwhelmed by a rain of pumice and a surge of seething lava and gases. It has been estimated that about 2,000 died in the city, which was buried in pumice and ash to a depth of several metres (more than ten feet). It seems that a great many returned to rescue their possessions when the eruption was over, but after 79 the city was never reoccupied as hitherto. The site was rediscovered in 1748 and systematic excavation began in 1861. Now about one-quarter of it still remains to be explored. *See also* HERCULANEUM.

**Pompe'ius 1. Gnaeus Pompeius Magnus**
*See* POMPEY.

**2. Sextus Pompeius** (*c.*67–36 BC) Younger son of Pompey the Great, who spent his life in fighting for his father's cause, on the republican side, against the Caesarians. He was defeated in 36, captured, and put to death by one of Antony's officers whom he had once spared.

**Pompey (Gnaeus Pompeius Magnus)** ('the Great', 106–48 BC) Roman general and statesman, famous as the associate and later the opponent of Julius Caesar. Magnus was his official cognomen, granted after 81 BC in imitation of Alexander. He fought so successfully for *Sulla in his civil war against *Marius that he was allowed a triumph by Sulla in 81 or 80, although he was technically ineligible by being still an *eques* and not having held a high magistracy. In 77 he was sent to Spain to suppress the revolt of *Sertorius, and after returning to Italy in 71 he cooperated with *Crassus in putting an end to the slave revolt led by *Sparta-

cus. Again he was granted a triumph, and he and Crassus were elected consuls for 70, even though Pompey was technically too young (*see* CURSUS HONORUM). In 67 Pompey was appointed to expel pirates from the Mediterranean, which he successfully accomplished in three months, and in the following year was given command against *Mithridates VI, king of Pontus, Rome's great enemy in the east. This campaign was Pompey's finest achievement; he utterly defeated Mithridates, made provinces of *Bithynia, *Pontus, and Syria (capturing Jerusalem after a siege), and established an eastern frontier for Rome that lasted—with few changes—for 500 years. In 62 he returned to Italy and in 61 celebrated the most spectacular triumph that Rome had yet seen. However, the ingratitude of the Senate led Pompey to form an alliance in 59 with Caesar and Crassus (called in modern times 'the first triumvirate') and they became in effect rulers of Rome. In 54 the death of Julia (Caesar's daughter who had married Pompey in 59) broke the strongest bond between Caesar and Pompey, and in 53 Crassus was killed in Parthia; the triumvirate was ended and Pompey's popularity waned. He was appointed sole consul in 52 after Clodius' murder (*see* CAESAR (2)). In 49 civil war began between him and Caesar. Pompey commanded the republican forces in Italy, and in 49 transported them to Greece, where Caesar arrived in 48. That year Pompey was defeated in pitched battle at Pharsalus and fled to Egypt, where he was assassinated (for the events of the Civil War *see* CAESAR (2)). There is a Life of Pompey by Plutarch.

**Pompō'nius Mēla** (of Tingentera in Spain, near Gibraltar) Author of the earliest surviving Latin work on *geography, *De chorographia* ('On places'), in three books, composed at the time of Claudius' invasion of Britain in AD 43. The work is intended for general readers and is based on earlier accounts; it was used by Pliny the Elder. After a summary description of the earth and the three continents Europe, Asia, and Africa, he describes in greater detail the countries around the Mediterranean, starting from Mauretania and working round to Spain; then passing to Gaul, Germany, Scythia, the islands (including the British Isles), India, and the Persian Gulf. He occasionally preserves information not found elsewhere, as, for example, on the Druids. He enlivens his account by descriptions of national characteristics and customs, scenery, and natural phenomena, and by references to birthplaces, battle-fields, and historical and legendary associations. He offers explanations of the tides (the action of the moon is one of them) and of the midnight sun, but he writes of the earth as if it were a disc.

**Pons Subli'cius** ('bridge on wooden piles') The oldest bridge, and for several centuries the only bridge, at Rome, famously defended by *Horatius Cocles against the Etruscans. In consequence of the difficulty on that occasion of breaking it down it was rebuilt exclusively of wood, in such a way as to be easily taken apart, by the *pontifices, from which fact the latter were said by Varro to derive their name; any repairs to it were accompanied by religious rites. It was swept away in a flood in AD 69.

*Pontic Epistles* See EPISTULAE EX PONTO.

**po'ntifex ma'ximus** ('chief pontiff') At Rome, the head of the college of pontiffs (*pontifices), elected by a (limited) popular vote from the mid-third century BC. He exercised disciplinary function not only over the pontiffs but over the *Vestal Virgins, whom he appointed, together with the *flamens and *rex sacrorum. He came to be very influential, publishing the decisions (decreta, without the binding force of laws) of the college of pontiffs. He had his official headquarters in the *Regia, and an 'official residence' (Domus Publica). The position was one of great dignity and importance, exercising control over the whole state religion; latterly it was held by Julius Caesar and by all the emperors down to Gratian (who dropped the title after AD 381).

**pontiff, pontifex** See PONTIFICES.

**ponti'fices** (pontiffs, apparently meaning 'bridge-builders'; see PONS SUBLICIUS) At Rome, the most important college of *priests. They had general oversight in matters of state religion involving religious law and procedure, but only in an advisory capacity: their rulings, of which they kept records, had to be put into effect by magistrates. They seem originally to have numbered three, but were successively increased in number until finally (under Julius Caesar) they reached sixteen. Originally they were all *patricians, but after 300 BC half the number was chosen from the *plebeians.

**Pontus 1.** In Greek myth, Sea; according to Hesiod, son of Gaia (Earth) and father of *Nereus and *Phorcys.

**2.** [Gk. *pontos*, 'sea'] In particular, in Greek and Latin, the Black Sea, and by extension the territory to the south of it. The name was especially applied to the region of Asia Minor south of the Black Sea, between Paphlagonia and Colchis, extending southward to Cappadocia. This was the centre of the empire of *Mithridates VI. In 63 BC at the end of the Mithridatic wars Pontus was broken up and reorganized by Pompey, and in AD 64 Nero incorporated the eastern portion in the province of Galatia.

**Poppae'a Sabi'na** Mistress of the emperor *Nero from AD 58, during her second marriage to Otho (friend of Nero and emperor himself briefly in 69). At her instigation, it was said, Nero murdered his mother Agrippina in 59 and in 62 divorced, banished, and executed his first wife Octavia. Nero now married Poppaea, and she bore a daughter Claudia, who died at four months in 63. Poppaea is said to have died (in 65), when she was pregnant again, after Nero kicked her in a fit of temper.

**popular** (as in e.g. 'popular leaders') See POPULARES.

**popula'res** ('on the side of the people') The name adopted at Rome from the time of the *Gracchi (i.e. about 133 BC) by those Roman political leaders who, working through the people (populus) rather than the senate, challenged the political predominance of the oligarchic republican government. Some were motivated by concern for the people; others by the belief that they could promote their own career in this way. Their political opponents called themselves *optimates, 'the best men'.

**populus** ('people') At Rome, the citizen-body. The 'Roman people', populus Romanus, meant the body of those eligible to be soldiers, to participate in public religious rites, and to attend meetings of the popular assembly, together with their families. It seems originally to have denoted the citizens as a military body (in contrast to *Quirites), hence the title magister populi, 'master of the infantry' (see DICTATOR). During the struggles of the *orders between patricians and plebeians populus continued to denote the whole community and not 'people' in the sense of 'plebeians'; however, at a later period populus designated the classes supporting the *populares* in their opposition to the senate. In the phrase, 'The senate and people of Rome', *senatus populusque Romanus*, *populus* denotes the people as the sovereign body.

**Porch, the** Name for the Stoic school of philosophy (*see* STOICISM), derived from the alternative translation of *stoa (usually 'colonnade').

**Po'rcia** (in Shakespeare's *Julius Caesar*, Portia) Daughter of *Cato (2) the Younger and wife of, first, Calpurnius *Bibulus (consul with Julius Caesar in 59 BC) and secondly Marcus *Brutus. Like her second husband and her father she was an ardent supporter of the republican cause, and is said to have inflicted a wound on herself in order to show that she was worthy to share in the secret of the plot against Caesar's life. After Brutus sailed for the East she became ill and in the early summer of 43 committed suicide, it is said by inhaling fumes from a brazier.

**Po'rphyry** (Porphyrios) (AD 234–*c*.305), Neoplatonist philosopher originally from Tyre. He is known by the Greek version of his original Phoenician name Malchus, 'king'. He studied philosophy at Athens and was converted to Neoplatonism by Plotinus with whom he studied at Rome in 263–8. He was particularly hostile to Christianity. His work *Against the Christians* was burnt in the fifth century, and is now known only through quotations. He was the author of numerous philosophical works including a history of philosophy down to Plato, from which a life of Pythagoras survives. His most important work was the editing of the lectures of *Plotinus under the title *Enneads*, and the composition of Plotinus' biography. His 'Introduction' (*Īsagōge*) and short commentary to the 'Categories' of Aristotle survive. The former was later translated into Latin by *Boethius and became very influential in the medieval schools. His treatise on vegetarianism entitled *On Abstinence from Animal Food* forbids the eating of meat for ascetic reasons (the philosopher should free himself from desires and appetites), rejects animal sacrifice (everything material is unclean and not to be offered to the supreme God, 'the One', whom we can approach through reason only), and claims rationality for animals (*see* ANIMALS, ATTITUDES TO). He also wrote on the limits to what could

be achieved by the pagan religious magic known as theurgy.

**Po'rsen(n)a, Lars** King of Clusium, one of the twelve cities of Etruria, at the end of the sixth century BC, who besieged Rome in order to restore the exiled Tarquinius Superbus to the throne (*see* TARQUIN). Porsena was so impressed by the feats of *Horatius Cocles, Mucius *Scaevola, and *Cloelia that he made peace with Rome. There are many contradictory versions of this essentially romantic story.

**portents** *See* DIVINATION.

**Portland vase** Celebrated Roman vase of dark blue glass, about 25cm (10 in.) high, with a cameo-style relief showing historical and/or mythological scenes, including perhaps the wedding of *Peleus and Thetis. It probably dates from the early first century AD and may have been made in Rome by Alexandrian craftsmen. In the seventeenth century it was in the Barberini Palace in Rome; in the following century it was bought by Sir William Hamilton who sold it to the dowager Duchess of Portland in 1784. Two years later her son the third duke lent it to Josiah Wedgwood to copy its cameo style in his jasper ware. In 1810 the Portland family deposited the vase on loan to the British Museum, where in 1845 a drunken visitor deliberately smashed it into more than 200 pieces; it was repaired and eventually bought by the Museum in 1945, since when it has undergone restoration and conservation.

**Portū'nus** Roman god worshipped as protector of harbours. Virgil in *Aeneid* 5.241 makes Portunus give one of the galleys in the boatrace a shove 'into port'. He was represented with a key in his hand. His festival, the Portunalia, was on 17 August. He had a special *flamen, the *flamen portunalis*.

**Posei'don** In Greek myth, the god of earthquakes and of the sea, violent natural forces, and associated with horses. He was the brother of Zeus and Hades and son of *Cronus and Rhea; his wife was Amphitrite, by whom he had a son, *Triton. The derivation of his name is uncertain; the first two syllables seem to contain the Greek for 'lord' or 'husband' and so it has been explained as 'lord of earth' (i.e. husband of Earth). He is an ancient and important god, appearing in the *Linear B tablets at Mycenae and Pylos. As god of the sea his cult was widespread throughout

Greece, as is attested by the city names Potidaea in Chalcidice and Poseidonia in south Italy. He was worshipped on all occasions connected with the sea and navigation. The *Isthmian games were held in his honour near his sanctuary on the Isthmus of Corinth; no doubt Corinth's strategic position, commanding the seas to east and west, made the cult of Poseidon particularly appropriate. His usual representation is with a trident (a fish-spear, or perhaps suggesting lightning). As the god of earthquakes his common epithet is 'earth-shaker' (Enosichthon, Ennosigaios), and perhaps he is to be thought of as the embodiment of elemental forces. Bulls were sacrificed to him. The Greeks also thought of him as the tamer of horses: the cult of Poseidon Hippios ('of horses') was widespread and has been seen as connected with the introduction into Greece from Anatolia of horses and (war) chariots early in the second millennium BC. In mythology he is sometimes represented as the father of the first horse or of magical horses (*see* PEGASUS and ARION (2)); he is also made the father of the monsters *Chrysaor and *Antaeus. He does not have a large mythology, but important myths connect him with Attica. One relates his contest with Athena for ownership of Attica in which he struck a spring of salt water from the Acropolis; Athena with her offer of the olive was adjudged the victor by the Athenians, or by *Cecrops. Another myth makes *Theseus his son, and he was worshipped at Athens as Poseidon Erechtheus. In the Trojan War he was the enemy of the Trojans because he was cheated by *Laomedon, king of Troy, when he and Apollo built the city walls, but he persistently sought the destruction of the Greek hero Odysseus (the outstanding seafarer) because the latter had blinded his son, the Cyclops *Polyphemus. The Romans identified Poseidon with the water-god *Neptune.

**Poseidō'nius (Poseidonios)** (of Apamea in Syria, *c.*135–*c.*50 BC) Stoic philosopher (*see* STOICISM) and a notable polymath with a very wide range of learning some part of which he transmitted to the Roman world. Unfortunately very little of his writing has survived, which makes what little we have difficult to interpret. For several years he studied philosophy at Athens under the Stoic *Panaetius before becoming head of the Stoic School of philosophy at Rhodes. At the end of 87 BC he went from there as envoy to Rome to appease Marius, whom he

disliked intensely. In 78 Cicero, among others who later achieved distinction, was his pupil in Rhodes and often paid tribute to him in his own writings. (He thought Poseidonius would prove a worthy memorializer of his famous consulship but was tactfully rebuffed. 'I have dumbfounded the whole Greek community', was Cicero's self-satisfied comment.)

Poseidonius wrote a history in fifty-two books which was a continuation of the history of Polybius, from 146 BC to the dictatorship of Sulla (81 BC). Very few fragments survive, but Sallust, Caesar, Tacitus, and Plutarch all made use of it in different ways. It embraced the whole Mediterranean world including peoples north of Gaul. He had great influence on the development of Stoic philosophy: he saw the Roman empire as embodying the Stoic view of the kinship of all humanity, since it was intended to cover all the peoples of the world. Poseidonius made considerable modifications to the Stoic doctrines of his day. He did not, for example, think that virtue was sufficient for happiness; it needed to be accompanied by external, bodily good. His Stoicism seems to have admitted influences from other schools of thought, and his best-attested innovation was to reject Chrysippus' view that the passions were misjudgements on the part of reason and to accept Plato's view that they arose from the non-rational part of the soul.

Poseidonius was also an eminent geographer, ethnographer, and astronomer, and wrote on tides and volcanoes. Nothing of these works has survived. His influence on later philosophers seems to have been considerable but remains unclear. In different ways Cicero, Lucretius, Virgil, Manilius, Seneca the Younger, the Elder Pliny, and Strabo, as well as the historians mentioned above, were all indebted to him. He was a most important figure, and the loss of his works a particular misfortune.

**Posterior Analytics** (i.e. *Analytics* Part 2) Logical treatise by *Aristotle investigating the nature of scientific axioms (i.e. self-evident truths). He argues that since science aims for generalized explanations, in order to understand particular cases we must understand how these fit the general pattern. If we are to have true understanding of a science then its subject matter must be systematized. If a science is to be systematized we must be confident that its axioms and theorems are true statements of fact, i.e. propositions. 'We think we know a thing when we think we know the cause of a thing being what it is and why, and when we also know that it is not possible for it to be other than it is.' This is the condition set upon knowledge. The scientist who has knowledge will be able to show how the axioms of his science lead to the theorems which express the facts. *See also* PRIOR ANALYTICS.

**Potidae'a** Corinthian colony founded *c.*600 BC (*see* PERIANDER) on the western prong of Chalcidice in north-east Greece for the purpose of trade with Macedonia. It joined the (Athenian) *Delian League, but the fact that Corinth supplied its annual chief magistrate meant that it was inevitably involved in any hostility between Athens and Corinth. It revolted from Athens in 432 BC after an increase of its tribute but was retaken in 430 after a siege (*see* PELOPONNESIAN WAR). Athenian *cleruchs held it until 404 when it passed to the Chalcidians. It was recovered by Athens in 363, but in 356 fell into the hands of *Philip II of Macedon. Perhaps destroyed in the Olynthian War (348), it was refounded *c.*316 by *Cassander under the name of Cassandreia.

**praefe'ctus** At Rome, 'officer in charge' of a military unit or branch of administration, etc., and in particular of the administration of justice in provincial towns; he was appointed by a higher authority. Under the empire *praefecti* were officers of equestrian rank.

**praefe'ctus anno'nae** ('prefect of the corn-supply') At Rome under the empire, an officer of *equestrian rank in charge of food supplies generally, and particularly of the supply of corn, the regulation of its price, and distributions to the poor.

**praefe'ctus praetō'rio** ('prefect of *praetorians') At Rome under the empire, an officer of equestrian rank who commanded the emperor's praetorian guard. First appointed by Augustus in 2 BC, they were usually two in number, occasionally one or three. Their position sometimes gave them great influence over the emperor (*see* SEJANUS). A few were well-known jurists, but for the most part they were soldiers.

**praefe'ctus urbi** ('prefect of the city') At Rome, originally the temporary deputy of an absent king or consul. Under the empire, Augustus gave this title to a magistrate of senatorial rank, usually a senior ex-consul, who was re-sponsible for maintaining order within the city boundaries. He presided in his own court of justice which by the third century AD had taken over the courts of the regular magistrates.

**praefe'ctus vi'gilum** ('prefect of the fire-brigade') At Rome under the empire, an officer of *equestrian rank in command of the cohorts of *vigiles* (originally slaves, later freedmen) forming the fire-brigade, instituted by Augustus. They occasionally had policing duties as well.

**Praene'stine fī'bula** Brooch found at Praeneste apparently dating from the second half of the seventh century BC, inscribed with a very early specimen of Latin. Its authenticity is very doubtful.

**praenō'men** *See* NAMES [Roman].

**praete'xta, fa'bula** In Roman literature, a serious drama which derived its subject from Roman history. (The *toga praetexta* was the bordered toga worn by magistrates, who were the characters in the plays; *see also* TOGATA.) The invention of the *fabula praetexta* is sometimes attributed to *Naevius. Only one complete *praetexta* survives, the tragedy *Octavia*; there are fragments of or references to others.

**praetor** ('one who goes first [in battle]' At Rome, originally the title of the two *eponymous magistrates who replaced the king as heads of state (*see* ROME 2). In 367 BC a third magistrate was introduced, a patrician praetor as a colleague to the original two, who were now or soon to be called *consuls. He had *imperium, but to a lesser degree than the first two. In the absence from Rome of the consuls the praetor was in charge of the legislature. Rome's closer contact with foreign states led to the appointment *c.*242 BC of a second praetor; the first was now designated *urbanus*, the 'city praetor', and the second was *praetor peregrinus*, the 'praetor for foreigners', who was probably a military commander but may have administered justice where foreigners were involved (*see* LAW, ROMAN). In 227 BC the number of praetors was increased to four for the government of the provinces of Sicily and Sardinia, and to six in 197 BC to include Spain. Sulla increased their number to eight and Julius Caesar to sixteen. Under the empire the office was still an important step in the *cursus honorum*.

**praetorians (praetorian guard)** The household troops of the Roman emperors, formed as a permanent corps by Augustus in 27 BC with nine cohorts, each thought to be 500 or possibly 1,000 strong. They received three times legionary pay and served for sixteen years. Augustus initially kept them under his direct control, not until 2 BC appointing two commanders, the *praefecti praetorio*. Their concentration by *Sejanus in AD 23 into one large barracks on the north side of Rome initiated their political importance and at certain moments the praetorian guard played an important part in the history of the empire; they were responsible, for example, for the accession of Claudius (41) and the murder of Elagabalus (222). Constantine I disbanded the guard in 312 after he defeated Maxentius.

**Pratĭ'nas** Greek poet of the early fifth century BC from Phlius (in Arcadia), reputed to have been the first to compose *satyr plays. He also wrote tragedies, *dithyrambs, and *hyporchemata*.

**Praxi'telēs** One of the most famous Greek sculptors, born at Athens and active 375–330 BC. One surviving marble statue used to be thought his original work, but it is probably a Hellenistic copy; it was discovered in 1877 in the Heraeum at Olympia (where *Pausanias (2) had seen it) and represents the god Hermes with the infant god Dionysus on his arm. His most famous work was the Aphrodite of Cnidus, a statue of the goddess naked supposedly modelled by his *hetaira Phryne, and now known through copies. The Cnidians, who possessed the statue, seem to have been fond of art; they refused the king of Bithynia's offer to pay their public debt in exchange for it. Praxiteles exemplified the tendency of the Greek sculptors of the fourth century to move away from the severe dignity of the fifth century to an art more concerned with human feeling. His iconic representation of the female nude—oval face with centrally parted hair, small breasts, and wide hips—persisted for several centuries.

**prayer** Together with *sacrifice and *divination, one of the three ways of approaching a god in the ancient world. Prayer could be formal or informal, private or public, but was almost always spoken aloud, the petitioner standing with outstretched arms as addressing the god. The earliest example of prayer we have is that of the priest Chryses to Apollo in *Iliad* 1. It has all the usual constituents: invocation of the god by name including relevant cult names, his or her dwelling, functions and qualities; a reminder to the god of why his or her help is particularly appropriate; and some form of eulogy. There follows the petition itself. It appears from literature that private prayers were equally formulaic. At Rome elaborate care would be taken to employ all forms with scrupulous accuracy.

**prefect** *See* PRAEFECTUS.

**Presocratics (Presocratic philosophers)** A modern classification describing early Greek thinkers who flourished not later than the lifetime of *Socrates (469–399 BC) and who had views on nature and on the origins of the universe. Their way of thinking gradually brought into existence the concepts of science and philosophy as fields of study separate from each other and from all other subjects. They were also interested in questions of epistemology—what is it possible to know?—and ethics—how should we behave?—questions which were of the greatest interest to Socrates, who thereby brought about a significant shift in the focus of Greek philosophy. Their works survive only in fragments, mostly in quotations made by later philosophers and early Christian writers. *See* PHILOSOPHY and entries on the following (in roughly chronological order): THALES; ANAXIMANDER; ANAXIMENES; HERACLEITUS; PYTHAGORAS; XENOPHANES; PARMENIDES; ZENO (1); MELISSUS; ANAXAGORAS; EMPEDOCLES; DEMOCRITUS.

**Prīam (Prĭamos)** In Greek myth, son of *Laomedon, king of Troy at the time of the *Trojan War and husband of *Hecuba. He was the father of fifty sons and many daughters, some by Hecuba, the rest by other wives or concubines. His children include Hector, Paris, Polydorus, Cassandra, and Creusa. In Homer's *Iliad* he is already an old man, and a pathetic figure, lamenting the death of many sons and the sufferings of his people, but loyal and kindly to *Helen, the cause of these misfortunes. After Hector's death he goes to the Greek camp secretly, aided by the god Hermes, to ransom his son's body with rich treasures for Achilles. The *Iliupersis* told how, at the fall of Troy, he took refuge in the palace at the altar of Zeus Herkeios and was there killed by *Neoptolemus. The best-known version is that of Virgil in *Aeneid* 2. His name became almost proverbial for a man who had known the extremes of good and bad fortune.

**priamel** [Ger., 'preamble'] A literary figure, a so-called focusing device. Several items are listed and rejected (these are sometimes called 'foils') until the final item is reached which outclasses all the rest. The classic example is the beginning of Sappho's poem 16:

> Some say a host of horsemen, others of infantry, and others of ships, is the most beautiful thing on the dark earth: but I say it is what you love.

**Priāpē'a (Priapeia)** Collection of eighty Latin poems addressed to or supposedly spoken by the god *Priapus, written in the time of the emperor Augustus and collected in the first century AD. Two other poems of this kind are attributed to Tibullus, and three others are found in the *Catalepton* (*see* APPENDIX VIRGILI-ANA). The poems are mainly written in hendecasyllables or elegiacs; they are lively, sometimes witty, and, as befits their subject, of varying degrees of obscenity. Typically he threatens to penetrate any intruder into the garden of which he is the protector.

**Priā'pus** God of fertility, originally worshipped at Lampsacus on the Hellespont, where asses—thought of as symbolizing lust—were sacrificed to him; he was said to be the son of Dionysus and of either Aphrodite or a local nymph. His cult spread to Greece during the Hellenistic age (after *c.*300 BC) and thence to Italy, but he seems never to have been taken very seriously. In Italy he was adopted as a god of gardens, where statues of him were often placed, showing him as a small misshapen creature with an enormous phallus, scaring off thieves and birds, a combined scarecrow and guardian. It was customary to compose short humorous poems or epigrams purportedly (or in fact) to be inscribed on his statues (*see* PRIAPEA).

**priests** In general priests in Greece and Rome performed specific religious duties when required but otherwise engaged in their day-to-day secular activities. They were usually selected on the basis of birth and wealth. There was no priestly group separate from the rest of the community, nor did priests monopolize religious activities, which might be administered by magistrates or male heads of households. They were not regarded as consultants on matters relating to the gods unless they were priests of an oracle who spoke on behalf of the gods. Individuals were more likely to have recourse to experts on divination or ritual. In Greece there were female as well as male priests (females for goddesses, but *see* PYTHIA), often having a role in sacrifices, a few required to be virgin or beyond the age of expected sexual activity.

At Rome priests were male except for the *Vestal Virgins. By tradition *Numa inaugurated three great priesthoods, formed into 'colleges' (Lat. *collegia*). These were the *pontifices, augures* (*see* AUGURY), and *duoviri* ('two men [for performimg rituals]'), the last increased to ten, *decemviri*, in 367 BC and to fifteen, *quindecimviri*, by 51 BC. A fourth college, the *fetiales*, was probably of equal importance. The lesser priesthoods, such as the *Salii and the Luperci formed what were known as 'associations', *sodalitates*. The *arval brethren seem to have been a special category.

**primordial deities** Ancient cosmogonies and genealogies of the gods began with one or two intangible existents such as *Chaos (as in Hesiod's *Theogony*): Nyx (night), Aer (mist or air), Erebus (darkness), and *Tartarus are recorded. Cicero mentions a Stoic genealogy which began with Darkness and Night. The cosmogony in Aristophanes' *Birds* begins with a concentration of gloom: Chaos, Night, Darkness, and Tartarus. Mythical entities of this kind, without origin themselves, are often referred to as primordial deities.

**princeps** ('chief', 'leader') Title taken by the emperor *Augustus (*see* 3), and adopted by his successors to indicate his constitutional position. In the late republic the word had been used in the plural, *principes*, to signify 'the chief men in the state', and the singular had been applied to important individuals like Pompey and Julius Caesar. It was not an official title, and was chosen to indicate the civil nature of Augustus' primacy, not carrying connotations of dictatorship or monarchy. *See* PRINCEPS SENATUS for the use of the term before the first century BC.

**princeps senā'tūs** ('the leader of the senate') At Rome, the senator placed by the *censors at the head of the list of members of the senate and ranked as the senior member. When decisions had to be taken by the senate he was the first to be asked his opinion. It was an office of great dignity and was held by a *patrician, customarily by the senior ex-censor. Sulla abolished the office in 81 BC, not wanting any one senator to have such influence; Augustus revived it and held it, as did his successors, for life.

**Principate** ('The Leadership') At Rome, the term often used in preference to 'empire' to describe the rule of the Roman emperors after 31 BC from *Augustus until (usually) the accession of *Diocletian in AD 284. The word designates the period during which the forms at least of republican government were maintained under the *princeps*. In the words of the English historian Edward Gibbon, it was 'an absolute monarchy disguised by the forms of a commonwealth'. With the accession of Diocletian the senate lost all independent authority and no longer was any attempt made to disguise the monarchical nature of the empire. The period from 284 onwards is often known as the Later Roman Empire. *See* LATE ANTIQUITY.

**Prior Analytics** (i.e. *Analytics* Part 1) The fundamental work on formal logic by *Aristotle, on the conditions necessary for a valid deductive inference. Simple statements, called propositions, affirm something—'every man is mortal', or deny something—'no man is mortal'. Aristotle invented, or discovered, a type of argument where two propositions, the premisses, lead to a third, namely a conclusion which is a valid deductive inference. Each premiss must contain two terms; one of these, called the 'middle term', is common to both but absent from the conclusion, which contains the remaining two terms. Thus, for example, 'if Socrates is a man [premiss 1], and if every man is mortal [premiss 2], Socrates is mortal [conclusion]'. Here 'man' is the middle term absent from the conclusion. Such an argument is known as a syllogism (Gk. *syllogismos*), defined by Aristotle as 'an argument in which, certain things being assumed [the premisses], something different from the things assumed follows necessarily from their being so'.

Aristotle thought that by such means it could be demonstrated that the theorems of science followed from its axioms, i.e. from self-evident truths (as they appeared to Aristotle and his contemporaries) like the common example, that 'if equals are subtracted from equals, the remainders are equal'. He used letters of the alphabet, and was the first to do so, in order to be able to generalize his arguments along the lines of, 'if A is B and B is C then A is also C'. Although his work in this area no longer provides a complete logic, it seemed to most scholars from the Middle Ages to the early twentieth century that it did, and that it was the great

instrument of reason. A few dissenters mocked it as a piece of pedantry which makes no contribution to real knowledge. *See also* POSTERIOR ANALYTICS.

**Pri'scian (Priscianus Caesariensis)** Native of Caesarea in Mauretania and a grammarian at Constantinople under the emperor in the East, Anastasius (ruled AD 491–518). He wrote in Latin a still-surviving *Institutiones grammaticae* ('Grammar') in eighteen books, with the original purpose of teaching Latin to Greek-speakers (Latin was still the official language of the Roman empire in the Greek-speaking East). The work is rich in quotations from the classical Latin authors and also from earlier republican writers, and founded largely on the (Greek) grammatical works of *Apollonius Dyscolus. It became famous in the Middle Ages (with the shorter grammar of Donatus): more than a thousand manuscripts of it are still in existence.

**prison** Imprisonment in a public prison for a period of time as a judicial penalty was sometimes envisaged at Athens (e.g. by Socrates in the *Apology*). According to *Lysias, Andocides was incarcerated for nearly a year. In general, imprisonment only occurred if there was default in payment of a fine (to prevent defaulters escaping). However, imprisonment as a long-term punishment was very rare for freemen in Greece and Rome; there were no resources to cover the expense or the administration. Public prisons administered by the *Eleven in Athens were only for short periods of imprisonment, such as when accused persons were awaiting trial or convicted criminals awaiting execution (*see* CRITO). Rome had a grim and ancient state prison, with a dungeon called the Tullianum (from its founder Servius Tullius) where executions commonly took place, near the Scalae Gemoniae (Gemonian Steps) down which the bodies were thrown into the Forum for public viewing. Here prisoners also awaited trial. *See also* CLAUDIUS (1).

**proa'gōn** At Athens, a day or two before the dramatic competition at the Great *Dionysia, the ceremonial appearance of *choregoi*, poets, actors, and choruses in the Odeum, when the names and subjects of the plays were announced. Actors and choruses appeared without costumes or masks. It was at the *proagon* of 406 BC after the death of Euripides that the audience was greatly moved by the appearance of Sophocles in mourning, with his actors and chorus not wearing the usual garlands.

**Pro A'rchia pōē'ta** Speech by *Cicero (1) delivered in 62 BC, successfully defending the claim of the Greek poet Archias to Roman citizenship.

Archias, a literary figure and known to Cicero, was attached to the household of the general L. Licinius *Lucullus. His claim to Roman citizenship was based on his citizenship of Heraclea in Lucania. Archias' claim had been doubted through lack of documentary evidence of his enrolment. Cicero meets this by producing witnesses of it. He also appeals to the sentiment of the jury by an eloquent and subsequently famous panegyric of literature: 'These studies sharpen youth and give pleasure to old age; they enhance prosperity and provide a refuge and relief in adversity; they enrich private life and do not interfere with public life; at night, on journeys, and in our country retreats, they keep us company' (*Haec studia adulescentiam acuunt, senectutem oblectant, secundas res ornant, adversis perfugium ac solacium praebent, delectant domi, non impediunt foris, pernoctant nobiscum, peregrinantur, rusticantur*).

**probou'loi** ('commissioners') In Greece, in particular at Athens in 413 BC after the failure of the *Sicilian Expedition, men appointed to oversee matters of state, on the assumption, one presumes, that the *ecclesia* and *boule* could not be entrusted unaided with the conduct of the war at such a crisis. They comprised ten men over the age of 40 (and in 413 included the poet Sophocles and the father of *Theramenes).

**Prŏbus, Marcus Vale'rius** (late first century AD) The outstanding Latin grammarian and scholar of his age, from Berytus in Phoenicia, who gathered together a large number of manuscripts and worked particularly on the texts of the Latin republican authors including Plautus, Terence, Sallust, and Virgil. He used critical signs in the manner of the Alexandrian scholar *Aristarchus (*see also* TEXTS, TRANSMISSION OF ANCIENT 1). Some of his notes survive in the scholia to Terence and Virgil, and there are references to Plautus and Sallust; later grammarians quote him, but it is difficult to establish exactly the scope of his work.

**Proclus** (AD 412–85) Neoplatonist philosopher (*see* NEOPLATONISM). He was born in Lycia but spent most of his life at Athens, succeeding to the headship of the *Academy. He was a prolific writer and a scholar of vast learning, so much so that it has been doubted whether all the works that have come down under his name can be genuinely his. Writing as a Neoplatonist (and influenced by the superstitions of his time), he gives in his *Elements of Theology* a concise summary of Neoplatonist metaphysics in some respects differing from Plotinus; he wrote commentaries on Plato's *Timaeus* and *Republic* and an essay on Parmenides as well as commentaries on the works of earlier mathematicians including Euclid. His literary works include a book of hymns, scholia (*see* SCHOLIUM) on Hesiod's *Works and Days*, and a *Chrestomathia* ('Summary of useful knowledge'), a handbook of literature, of which only an epitome exists. It has been thought that this last work, important for preserving summaries of six poems of the *Epic Cycle dealing with the Trojan War, may be the work of an earlier Proclus. His philosophy strongly influenced medieval and Renaissance thought.

**Procnē** *See* PHILOMELA.

**proconsul** At Rome, a *consul whose powers had been prolonged for a further year following his year of office. After 146 BC, when Rome had an increased number of provinces to govern, such prolongation of office (*prorogatio*) became the usual procedure to allow magistrates a further year as governors of provinces.

**Procō'pius** (of Caesarea in Palestine, *c.* AD 500–after 562) Byzantine Greek historian and secretary to Belisarius (the famous general of the Roman emperor *Justinian) whom he accompanied on his early campaigns in Africa and Italy. He returned to Constantinople (then the capital of the Roman empire) in 542. (He is not the Procopius who was made prefect of the city in 562.) His principal work, *History of the Wars of Justinian*, in eight books, covering the years 527–53, is a clear and reliable account of the events of his own times and is our main source for the first two-thirds of Justinian's reign. His chief praise is reserved for Belisarius; Justinian and his empress Theodora are treated with much less enthusiasm. In his work *On Justinian's Buildings*, on the buildings and works of art in Constantinople and the empire, a valuable source of information about the art and architecture of the time, he describes how God himself inspired Justinian to solve problems in the construction of the cathedral of Hagia Sophia when the engineers were baffled. Procopius is also the author of a remarkable supplement to his *History*, a *Secret History* (*Anecdota*), covering the same period but making a virulent attack on the whole policy of Justinian as an adherent of the aristocratic opposition. On the basis, apparently, of court gossip he also makes scurrilous comments on the dubious morals of the empress Theodora. It cannot have been published in the author's lifetime, and was perhaps not known until the tenth century; Photius appears not to have known it, but it is referred to in the *\*Suda*.

**Procris** *See* CEPHALUS.

**Procru'stēs (Damastes)** Legendary brigand said to be the son of Poseidon, who lived beside the road between Athens and Eleusis. He ensnared strangers with hospitality, then seized them and fastened them to a bed which he then made them fit, cutting short their limbs if they were too long for it, or racking them if they were too short. *Theseus applied the same treatment to Procrustes and cut off his head.

**procura'tor** At Rome under the empire, in general, an employee of the emperor in civil administration. In particular, procurators might oversee the revenues in the imperial provinces, and also, independently of the governors, in the senatorial provinces. They could also govern some of the minor provinces.

**Pro'dicus** (of Ceos, fifth century BC) *Sophist and contemporary of Socrates. He was a teacher of rhetoric and by serving on diplomatic missions built up connections with wealthy men whose sons he taught. He was particularly interested in precise semantic distinctions between words of similar meaning. Socrates sometimes professes himself indebted to Prodicus' work, perhaps not always ironically. In late antiquity he was regarded as an atheist (*see* ATHEISM) but his contemporaries do not mention him as such. His writings do not survive, except for a paraphrase by Xenophon of his fable of the Choice of *Heracles between Pleasure and Virtue.

**Proetus** In Greek myth, first king of Tiryns, son of Abas and Aglāia and twin brother of Acrisius (father of *Danaë). The two brothers had a lifelong feud; when Abas left them his kingdom jointly they fought each other for its possession. Acrisius drove Proetus out, but was himself ousted in turn. *See* BELLEROPHON; DIONYSUS; MELAMPUS.

**Pro legĕ Manī'lia** ('In support of the Manilian law'; also known as *De imperio Cn. Pompeii*, 'On the command of Pompey') Speech by Cicero in 66 (*see* CICERO (1) 1) delivered before the people when Cicero was praetor, in support of the proposal of the tribune Manilius to extend Pompey's command in Asia to Bithynia, Pontus, and Armenia so as to enable him to take over the command in the war against *Mithridates. This was Cicero's first speech on purely public affairs, and was delivered in order to promote the interests of the equestrian order (who, being the businessmen of Rome, were suffering severe financial losses because of the disturbed condition of the rich province of Asia Minor). Although this command was against the wishes of the senate the proposal was carried.

**prōleta'rii** At Rome, the citizens placed in the lowest property-class who were too poor to contribute anything to the state except their children (*prōles*). Until the reforms of *Marius they were exempted from compulsory military service except in an emergency. They remained politically disadvantaged throughout the republic.

**prologue** (Gk. *prologos*) In Greek tragedy or comedy, the expository opening scene before the entry of the chorus into the orchestra. *See* TRAGEDY 3.

**Promē'theus** ('Forethinker') In Greek myth, a *Titan, son of Iapetus and Themis (or Clymene, daughter of Oceanus). He was associated with the origin of fire and with Hephaestus; both of them were worshipped at Athens by potters. For some he appears as the champion of humankind against the hostility of the gods. There was also a tradition that he himself created men out of clay (from Panopea, near Chaeronea in Boeotia). When Zeus, having no love for men, deprived them of fire, Prometheus stole a spark from heaven (or from the forge of Hephaestus) and brought it to them in a stalk of fennel (*narthex*). He also taught them all kinds of arts and sciences, thus improving their brutish lives. In the apportionment of sacrificed animals between men and the gods, he induced Zeus by a trick to choose the less desirable portion (bones covered with fat), the meat being left for men. (This story is obviously meant to account for the fact that it was usually the inedible parts of a sacrifice which were allotted to the gods.) To avenge himself Zeus caused Hephaestus to create the first woman, Pandora, fashioned out of clay. Athena breathed life into her, and the other gods endowed her with every charm (whence her name, 'all gifts'), but Hermes taught her flattery and guile. This woman was sent not to Prometheus, who was too cunning to accept such a dangerous gift, but to his brother Epimetheus ('He who thinks afterwards'), who gladly received her, although warned by his brother not to take any gifts from Zeus. She brought with her a jar containing all kinds of evils and diseases from which men had hitherto been free; this she opened, and they all flew out, leaving only Hope inside, under the lid, as a consolation for men. Pandora's jar seems to have become a 'box' in post-classical times by a confusion with the box which *Psyche was forbidden to open in the story in *Apuleius' *Golden Ass*.

Prometheus also knew the secret concerning the marriage of Thetis (*see* PELEUS and *PROMETHEUS BOUND*), but refused to reveal it to Zeus, who wished to marry Thetis himself. To punish him Zeus had him chained to a lonely rock usually said to be in the Caucasus, where an eagle daily fed on his liver which grew again each succeeding night (being a Titan, Prometheus was immortal). This torture continued for long ages until Prometheus was released either by Heracles shooting the eagle with his bow, or by his submitting and revealing the secret about Thetis. He was the father of *Deucalion by a wife variously named.

### Promē'theus Bound (P. desmōtes) (Lat.

*P. vinctus*) Greek tragedy attributed to *Aeschylus, though perhaps completed or even written by another after the former's death in 456 BC. No one in antiquity doubted that it was by Aeschylus, but in several respects the style is markedly different from that of his six other surviving plays. It is the only one of his plays for which there is no didascalic information (*see* DIDASCALIA) about production, date, and trilogy. It is possible that it was the second play of a connected trilogy, followed by *Prometheus lyomenos* ('P. Unbound'), of which a few fragments survive. A play entitled 'Prometheus the Fire-kindler' seems to have been a *satyr play of 472 and unconnected with *Prometheus Bound*. It remains uncertain whether a connected trilogy existed.

*Prometheus the Titan, who in the past has aided Zeus to set up his rule over Cronus and the other Titans, has incurred Zeus' anger by becoming the champion of mortals and giving them fire and the arts. In the opening scene of the play, the god Hephaestus, at the order of Zeus, together with Kratos (Power) and Bia (Force), reluctantly nails Prometheus (possibly represented by a huge dummy figure behind which the actor spoke) to a high rock in the Caucasus, to suffer torment for as long as Zeus pleases. The chorus of Oceanides, the daughters of the Titan *Oceanus, come to grieve with him and comfort him. Oceanus himself also comes, offering to intercede with Zeus if Prometheus will moderate his attitude. Prometheus scornfully rejects his offers, and then enumerates to the chorus all his benefactions to humankind. Another victim of Zeus' tyranny arrives, *Io, a mortal whom Zeus has loved and whom Hera, out of jealousy, has made partly cow-like in form. She is doomed to long wanderings pursued by a gadfly and haunted by the myriad-eyed *Argus. Prometheus tells her about her sufferings, about her descendant Heracles who will eventually release Prometheus, and about the fatal marriage which Zeus will one day make unless Prometheus warns him. After Io departs Hermes enters, sent by Zeus to demand from Prometheus the revelation of his secret; although Hermes predicts increased torments for him Prometheus haughtily refuses and is plunged into the abyss with the Oceanides, who decide to share his fate.

If a reconciliation between Prometheus and Zeus took place in a following play, it is impossible to say how the author devised it. From the fragments of *P. lyomenos*, it seems that the play opened with Prometheus restored to the light after thirty thousand years, and that the chorus was composed of Titans.

As a suffering god, the creator of mankind, and also as the champion of the oppressed and an independent thinker, Prometheus has had a wide appeal to people of various religions and political beliefs. The English poet Shelley (1792–1822) in his 'Prometheus Unbound' could not accept Prometheus' apparent defeat at the end of the play: in his poem Prometheus is released and it is Jupiter (i.e. Zeus) who is vanquished.

**Prope'rtius, Sextus** (*c*.50 BC–after 16 and before 2 BC) Roman elegiac poet. He was born at Asisium (Assisi) in Umbria, his estate diminished when he was young by the confiscations of Octavian in 41–40 BC (after the defeat of the republicans at Philippi), was educated at Rome for the practice of law, but turned to poetry instead. He left four books of elegies, of which the first, published probably in 29 or 28 BC, shows Propertius as a member of a small and intimate group of poets who included Ovid (*Tristia* 4.10.45). The book's great success admitted him to the wider circle around *Maecenas, but he seems to have admired the older poets (e.g. Virgil, in 2.34) rather than known them well. Horace, whom he does not mention, refers to him as aping Callimachus and Mimnermus (*Epistles* 2.2.90). It is as a love-poet that he is best known. His first book of poems, known in antiquity as the *Cynthia monobiblos* ('Cynthia, in one book'), consists almost entirely of elegant and witty love-poems to his mistress 'Cynthia' so-called, a Greek pseudonym for, reputedly, a certain Hostia (cf. 'Lycoris' of the poet *Gallus and 'Delia' of *Tibullus).

Book 2 is improbably long and may be a conflation of two books; no poem in it is later than 25 BC. The text is particularly disordered in the manuscripts, which in many cases give no indication of where individual poems begin and end. In style this book is similar to book 1 though now are included some poems on imperial themes pleasing to the new regime (*see* ROME 5); there is no indication, however, that Propertius was ever financially dependent on Maecenas' patronage as Virgil and Horace were. This book does not quite have the lyrical freshness of its predecessor. Book 3, published soon after 23 BC, shows a wider range of subject matter and includes an important poem to Maecenas, but also shows a greater degree of generalization and abstraction. Although the influence of the Hellenistic Greek poets was perceptible in the earlier books, it is with this book that Propertius first makes his claim to be the Roman Callimachus, writing small-scale poems in a refined style, and no longer confines himself to love-poetry. Only about a third of the poems in this book are concerned with love, and the final poem is a farewell to Cynthia and perhaps to his career as a love-poet. Book

4 appeared after a longish interval, not before 16 BC, perhaps constructed around two commissioned and honorific poems, 6 and 11. Some of the poems are antiquarian in subject, in the manner of Callimachus' *Aitia*; the rest are miscellaneous, and include two of his most brilliantly original on Cynthia (7 and 8). Poem 11, an epicedium (a song sung in mourning over a corpse) for the nobly born Cornelia (daughter of Scribonia, the first wife of Octavian), is written as if spoken by the subject herself, and is a touching expression of the virtues of a Roman matron.

Propertius has an intense visual imagination which colours everything he writes: the setting of a poem must first be grasped and its implications understood if the reader is to make sense of the poet's abrupt changes of mood and his train of thought. Corruptions of the original text add to the difficulties of interpretation. No other Roman poet shows such strong personal characteristics, the recurrent melancholy, the passionate but objective, occasionally obsessive, self-observation, as he records his ecstasy, torment, and humiliation. His passion appears in a great variety of moods, inspired by Cynthia's beauty, or her venality, or her dangerous illness, and by the vicissitudes of his relations with her. The self-absorption, the striking imagery, the bold and difficult language, the political independence, mark a new spirit in Latin literature.

**Propo'ntis** (now the Sea of Marmara) An intermediate sea between the Aegean and the Black Sea. Its principal cities were Byzantium and Chalcedon at the mouth of the Bosporus.

**propraetor** At Rome, a praetor whose powers have been prolonged for a further year. *See* PROCONSUL.

**Propylae'a** At Athens, the great roofed gateway and entrance to the *Acropolis, on the western side, built of Pentelic marble (*see* ATTICA), designed by Mnesicles, and erected as part of Pericles' building programme between 437 and 432 BC, after the completion of the Parthenon. Much of it is still intact.

**Pro Ro'scio Ameri'no** ('For Roscius of Ameria') Speech by *Cicero ((1) 1) in 80 BC in defence of Sextus Roscius (not the actor *Roscius, also defended by Cicero) on a charge of murdering his father. This, Cicero's first speech in a criminal case, gives the origin of the expression *cui bono* ('who profits?'). He quotes it as being the frequent saying of an illustrious judge, L. Cassius Longinus, in trials of this kind, and proceeds to show that the accusers of Roscius had themselves profited.

**proscriptions** At Rome, a *proscriptio* was a published list of Roman citizens who were declared to be outlaws and whose property was confiscated and auctioned by the state. Those proscribed could be killed by soldiers with impunity; rewards and punishments were used to encourage their friends and families to betray them. This procedure was employed by Sulla in 82–81 BC (it is now thought that a little over 500 people were named) and by the triumvirs Antony, Lepidus, and Octavian during the Civil War in 43–42 BC; it was a means both of getting rid of enemies and of acquiring funds and land. Caesar did not employ proscription.

### prose, development of

**Greek.** Prose as a means of literary expression was developed in Greece as in other countries long after poetry. In early times when writing was in its infancy and literary compositions survived by being committed to memory, those written in metrical form were easier to memorize (in Greece, writing was reintroduced at the end of the eighth century BC; *see* ALPHABET). The earliest writers of Greek prose appear to have been the chroniclers (*see* LOGOGRAPHERS (1)) and philosophers (*see* PHILOSOPHY) of Ionia in the sixth century BC; *see* ANAXIMANDER (d. mid-sixth century BC) and PHERECYDES (1) (fl. mid-sixth century BC). From this time onward the development of prose was rapid. Heracleitus in about 500 BC was already writing prose of subtlety and style. By the middle of the fifth century BC a technical prose had been developed which was adequate to express all that was needed for a scientific or philosophical treatise. Democritus (*c.*460–*c.*357 BC), to judge from his fragments, was a competent prose writer, and the earliest works in the Hippocratic Corpus (*see* HIPPOCRATES) show at least the capacity for accurate and concise statement.

The first fully developed prose work that has survived in its entirety is the History of Herodotus (*c.*490–*c.*425 BC).

**Latin.** Latin prose was developed, in its characteristic features, out of public speech, though it originated partly in the *Annales* of the pontiffs (their records of traditional ritual and events of religious importance; *see* ANNALS) which were the origin of written history at Rome. Roman law, published and often learnt by heart, was also a formative influence. Latin prose, unlike Latin poetry, owed little to Greek influences, for it already possessed, before the advent of these, the essential qualities of clarity, precision, and conciseness. In a community like Rome where politics played so great a part, these qualities were naturally esteemed in oratory. *Cato the Elder was not only a noted speaker; his *Origines* was the first history of its kind in Latin.

*Cf.* ORAL POETRY.

**Pro'serpine** (Lat. Proserpina) *See* PERSEPHONE and DIS.

**proskynesis** The Persian custom of prostrating oneself before the king, which implied submission but not worship. Alexander the Great's attempt to make his entourage adopt this custom was unsuccessful.

**proso'dion** In Greek *lyric poetry, a procession song.

**pro'sody** The study of versification; in Greek and Latin in particular, the study of the rules which govern the quantity (i.e. length) of syllables in verse. Syllables are classified according to the length of time they took to pronounce and are called long, short, or anceps ('ambivalent', i.e. either long or short). A syllable is long or short 'by nature' according as it contains either a long vowel or diphthong, or a short vowel. The general rules of Greek and Latin prosody (to which there are exceptions) are the following.

### Greek

(i) By nature the vowels η and ω are long, ε and o short; α, ι, and υ are sometimes long by nature, sometimes short. Diphthongs are long (i.e. αι, αυ, ει, ευ, ηυ, οι, ου, υι, ᾳ, ῃ, ῳ), except that οι and αι, which appear to have been of shorter duration, are sometimes scanned short.

(ii) A syllable long by nature is sometimes shortened if it comes immediately before another vowel. This happens most often at the end of a word (i.e. before another word beginning with a vowel). The shortening is known as *correption (and see (iii) below).

(iii) A syllable that is short by nature is lengthened in pronunciation, and so becomes long 'by position', if the vowel is immediately followed by two (or more) consonants or by a so-called double consonant, ζ (=sd), ξ (=ks), or ψ (=ps), whether or not the consonants are in the same word. There is an exception to this general rule: in Attic poetry (which includes tragedy and comedy), a naturally short syllable usually remains short if it is followed by one of several combinations of two consonants, the first a so-called 'mute' (for this purpose one of π, β, φ, τ, δ, θ, κ, γ, χ), and the second a 'liquid' (λ, ρ, μ, ν). This phenomenon is known as Attic correption.

**Latin**

(i) The vowels a, e, i, o, u (and y) are sometimes long by nature, sometimes short. Diphthongs (ae, au, ei, ou, oe) are long. A vowel which immediately precedes another vowel in the same word but is not part of a diphthong is generally short.

(ii) Correption of a final long syllable (see (ii) above) is rare.

(iii) A syllable that is short by nature is lengthened in pronunciation, and so becomes long 'by position', if the vowel is immediately followed by two (or more) consonants, or by a double consonant, x (= ks) or z (= Greek ζ). (When the 'semi-consonants' i and u are equivalent to English j or v they are counted as consonants; h is discounted; qu is counted as a single consonant.)

(iv) An exception to (iii) is that short syllables remain short before certain combinations of so-called 'mute' and 'liquid' consonants (compare Greek prosody, (iii) above), i.e. b, c, d, f, g, p, t followed by l or r. This licence does not occur when the two consonants belong to different words or to different parts of a compound verb (e.g. ābrumpere).

**prostitution** See HETAIRAI and LOVE AND SEXUALITY.

**Pro Sulla** ('For Sulla') Speech by *Cicero ((1) 3) in defence of P. Cornelius Sulla (elected consul for 65 but convicted of bribery and so disqualified; he was a relation of the famous Sulla, in whose *proscriptions he amassed great wealth). Sulla was acquitted and rewarded Cicero well.

**protagonist** See TRAGEDY 2.

**Prōta'goras** (of Abdera in Thrace, b. c.485 BC) One of the earliest, most famous, and most successful of the *sophists. He professed to teach to young men who could afford his fees *arete, 'virtue' (i.e. human excellence), meaning worldly success achieved through good management of public and private affairs with emphasis on skill in public speaking. In his wide travels he made several visits to Athens where he associated with Pericles, who invited him to draw up a code of laws for the new colony of *Thurii in 443. The story that Protagoras was expelled from Athens for *atheism is improbable since Plato reports that he was universally admired. His two famous books (which have not survived) were *On Truth* and *On the Gods*. In the former he expressed scepticism about the possibility of objectivity and absolute truth. His doctrine is usually summed up as 'Man [Gk. *anthropos*] is the measure of all things', meaning that all appearances and beliefs are true either for the individual who has them or for the human species as a whole, a relativism criticized at length by Plato in the *Theaetetus*. In his book *On the Gods* he adopted an agnostic attitude about their existence and nature (*see* AGNOSTICISM for his aphorism). He appears as the opponent of Socrates in Plato's dialogue *Protagoras*, where he is treated with respect.

**Protagoras** Dialogue by *Plato in which the interlocutors are, besides Socrates, the sophists *Protagoras, *Hippias, and *Prodicus. It is a dialogue on the nature of 'virtue' or 'human excellence', on knowledge, and on politics. Socrates raises the question of whether virtue can be taught. (It is uncertain to what extent Plato intended Socrates' arguments to be taken seriously at the time of composition.) Protagoras tells a story to show how humans developed social institutions in order to survive and that *aidos, shame (or conscience), and justice are needed to preserve these institutions. He argues that virtue (in his sense), leaving aside the question of its nature, is something that can be taught just as well as any other subject, but in this case citizens teach their children and each other. He also argues that the different virtues are distinct parts of a total virtue or excellence, and objects to Socrates' arguments against this position. A poem of Simonides is analysed (first by Protagoras, then by Socrates), on the sophistic theme of 'the good man'. (This dialogue remains its only source; *see* PITTACUS.) When the original discussion resumes Socrates turns to refuting Protagoras and puts forward the peculiarly un-Socratic thesis that pleasure is the good. The dialogue ends with the two main participants maintaining positions opposite to those they started with.

The dialogue contains a noteworthy declaration by Protagoras that under a rational system criminals are punished to deter them from doing wrong again, not as retribution for past misdeeds.

**Prōtesilā'us** In Greek myth, Thessalian prince, son of *Iphiclus. Soon after his marriage he left to take part in the Greek expedition against Troy. When the Greek fleet reached the Trojan coast he was the first to leap ashore, and was subsequently the first to be killed (some said in conscious fulfilment of an oracle that the first to tread on Trojan soil would be the first to die). His wife Laodamia was plunged into such grief at his death that the gods allowed her husband to return to her for three hours, but when he left her again she killed herself.

**Prōteus** In Homer's *Odyssey* (4.351), a minor sea-god, who herds seals, knows all things, and has the power of assuming different shapes in order to escape answering questions; he will answer if held until he resumes his true shape. In Herodotus and in Euripides' tragedy *Helen* he is a virtuous king of Egypt who keeps *Helen safe throughout the Trojan War.

**proto-geometric** Name given to one of the five periods of the Greek era (based on the differences in pottery styles), denoting the early part of the Greek *Iron age, very roughly 1050-875 BC. *Cf.* GEOMETRIC; ORIENTALIZING; ARCHAIC; CLASSIC.

**province, Roman** A territory outside Italy subject to Rome, governed by a resident Roman magistrate (*see* PROCONSUL) and obliged to pay tribute (*see* REPETUNDAE). For *Provincia* ('the Province') *see* GAUL.

**provoca'tio** *See* APPEAL.

**pro'xenos** In a Greek state, a local citizen chosen by another state to look after the interests of citizens from that state in return for favours, a sort of consul (in the modern sense). Pindar at Thebes was *proxenos* of the Athenians staying in that city; Demosthenes at Athens was *proxenos* of the Thebans.

**Pro'xenus** Boeotian friend of Xenophon, at whose invitation he took part in the expedition of Cyrus related in the *Anabasis*.

**prytanē'um** In the chief city of a Greek state, the symbolic 'home' of the whole state, containing the hearth (*see* HESTIA) where a fire was kept continually burning and from which fire was taken to a new colony. Here also were the offices of the local magistrates; it was the place where ambassadors were entertained and distinguished citizens were rewarded by the provision of meals at the state's expense. The prytaneum at Athens was in the agora. *See* PRYTANY.

**pry'tany** (*prytaneia*, 'presidency'), **prytaneīs** ('presidents') At Athens, after the political reforms of *Cleisthenes (2) in 508 BC, each of the newly constituted ten tribes chose by lot every year fifty of its members to serve on the *boule* ('council'). Each group of fifty served as the executive committee of the *boule* for one-tenth of the year, when they were known as *prytaneis*, and the period as a prytany. One *prytanis* was chosen daily by lot to act as chairman of the *boule* and *ecclesia* and to put questions to the vote.

**Pseudo-Callisthenes** Greek author of the *Alexander Romance*, a *novel falsely ascribed to the historian *Callisthenes. The author, of whom nothing is known, lived in Alexandria in the third century AD (probably). His novel survives in many copies in many languages, apparently derived from a variety of fictions and histories about Alexander. It has been continuously read and revised in many countries—Armenia, Persia, Arabia, India, Indonesia, Bulgaria—and Latin versions have circulated in the West for many centuries. In 781 AD Alcuin of York sent the emperor Charlemagne a copy of *Alexander and Dindymus*. In the chivalric Middle Ages Alexander was a household name. Chaucer in the *Monk's Tale* sums it up:

> The storie of Alisaundre is so commune
> That every wight that hath discrecioun
> Hath herd somewhat or al of his fortune.

**Pseu'dolus** Roman comedy by *Plautus produced in 191 BC at the Megalesian games celebrating the dedication of the temple of Cybele at Rome. The title is taken from the name of a character in the play.

A Macedonian captain has bought a girl, Phoenicium, from a pimp for 20 minae, paying 15 down. The girl is to be delivered to his messenger when he sends the 5 minae still owing and a certain token. Calidorus, a young Athenian, is in love with her. The play centres on the trick by which his father's slave, Pseudolus, having intercepted the captain's letter and token, cheats the pimp and carries off Phoenicium for Calidorus. (The part of the pimp Ballio was chosen by *Roscius, the great comic actor of Cicero's day.)

**psyche** See SOUL.

**Psȳchē** ('Soul') The name of the heroine in a tale, told in books 4–6 of the *Golden Ass* of *Apuleius, the narrator being an old woman who is trying to amuse a girl captured by robbers. Psyche was so beautiful that Venus became jealous of her and sent Cupid to make her fall in love with some unsightly creature; however, Cupid himself became her lover. He placed her in a palace but only visited her in the dark, and forbade her to attempt to see him. Her sisters, out of jealousy, told her he was a monster who would devour her. One night she took a lamp and looked at Cupid while he slept, but a drop of hot oil woke him. Thereupon the god left her, angry at her disobedience. Psyche, solitary and remorseful, sought her lover all over the earth, and various superhuman tasks were required of her by Venus. The first was to sort out before nightfall an enormous heap of various kinds of grain. But the ants took pity on Psyche and arriving in hordes did the task for her. By one means or another all the tasks were completed except the last, which was to descend to the Underworld and fetch a casket of beauty from Persephone. Curiosity overcame Psyche and she opened the casket, which contained not beauty but a deadly sleep, to which she succumbed. Jupiter, at Cupid's entreaty, at last consented to their marriage, and Psyche was brought to heaven. This fairytale has often been interpreted as an allegory of the soul's journey through life and its final union with the divine after suffering and death.

**Pto'lemies (Ptolemaioi)** Macedonian Greek dynasty which ruled *Egypt from the death of Alexander the Great in 323 BC until the Roman conquest in 30 BC, the so-called Ptolemaic period; all the kings were called Ptolemy. The first of the dynasty was Ptolemy I Soter, 'Saviour', (b. 367, ruled 323–283 BC) one of Alexander's generals, who received Egypt in the division of Alexander's empire after his death (see DIADOCHI). He moved the Egyptian capital from Memphis to *Alexandria. He himself wrote a notable history of Alexander the Great (now

lost) based on his own recollections and using much official material. It was used by the historian *Arrian. His third wife was *Berenice I, mother of the dynastic line. Other notable members were his son Ptolemy II Philadelphus, b. 308, who ruled 285–246 BC, for the first two years joint ruler with his father, and in whose reign the artistic and cultural life of Alexandria developed; and Ptolemy III Euergetes, b. 284, who ruled 246–221 BC and won for a time a large part of Seleucid Asia. The famous *Cleopatra VII was the sister and wife of Ptolemy XIII (b. 63, ruled 51–47 BC) and ruled with him. The last to bear the name were another brother of Cleopatra, Ptolemy XIV (b. c.59, ruled 47–44 BC jointly with Cleopatra, and murdered on her orders), and Cleopatra's son by Julius Caesar, as she claimed, Ptolemy XV Caesar (b. 47, ruled nominally 44–30 BC, jointly with Cleopatra), better known as *Caesarion.

The Ptolemies were immensely enriched by their exploitation of Egypt, and they raised their capital Alexandria to great wealth and magnificence. By their patronage of art and literature, and especially by the establishment of the *Museum or literary academy of Alexandria, and the *Alexandrian Library, the first Ptolemies made the city a centre of Hellenistic culture. Greek settlements were planted in many parts of Egypt, most extensively in the reclaimed land of the Faiyum. To these Greek settlers we owe numerous papyri, discovered in the nineteenth and twentieth centuries in places where physical conditions have been suitable for their preservation, and on these many fragments of Greek literary works have been discovered (see PAPYROLOGY and OXYRHYNCHUS).

**Pto'lemy (Claudius Ptolemaeus)** Greek astronomer, mathematician, and geographer who produced what was for 1,300 years the definitive work in these areas. He was born at Ptolemais Hermiou in Upper Egypt and worked at Alexandria between AD 146 and c.170. His great work on astronomy is the *Mathematike syntaxis* ('Treatise on mathematics'), translated later into Arabic and generally known as the *Almagest*, a compound of the Arabic for 'the' and the Greek adjective *megiste*, 'greatest [*syntaxis*, treatise]'. The work is in thirteen books. It is not a mere compilation of the astronomical knowledge of his age: Ptolemy was an original mathematician who established Greek *astronomy on a mathematical basis. His use of *o* as zero in a place-value number system is often mentioned. Aided by selected observations he developed theories and compiled tables for computing the positions of the sun, moon, the (five known) planets, and the fixed stars around a stationary earth, an orderly system which his predecessors had almost universally believed in (for the exception *see* ARISTARCHUS). This theory (with modifications) was accepted throughout the West including the Byzantine world and Islam until the time of Copernicus and Kepler in the sixteenth century. Ptolemy himself constructed the first viable theory of the five planets, and his fixed-star table is based on his own fresh observations. The *Almagest* soon became a standard work and remained so until the end of the Middle Ages, not only in the Greek but also in the Arab world, passing thence into medieval Europe (*see* TEXTS, TRANSMISSION OF ANCIENT 7). It is an important source for knowledge of earlier works which were lost following Ptolemy's supremacy.

Ptolemy wrote a number of other scientific treatises, including an important one on optics surviving only in a Latin translation from the Arabic, and one on the mathematics of musical harmony in four books. This is concerned with the ratios of musical intervals (with some valuable information on attunements (*see* MUSIC [Greek 5]) used by contemporary musicians) and extends into the harmonies of the soul and the heavens. Some of his ideas on ratios survived into medieval and Renaissance times through *Boethius. Regarded as authoritative for as long as the *Almagest* was his 'Outline of Geography' (*Geōgraphike hyphegesis*) in seven books describing his division of the world map into 26 smaller maps. The first book has a discussion of maps, and instructions on drawing a world map with two different projections; the following six books are devoted to lists of some 8,000 places located by latitude and longitude, which Ptolemy was the first to employ systematically. There also survives an eighth book containing the famous maps attributed to him. These, descending from a later Byzantine archetype, were probably not part of his original work but later reconstructions. Among numerous errors which the work contained, particularly in areas outside the Roman empire, was the notion that Asia stretched much further to the east than it does. It was this that misled Columbus into thinking that he had reached Asia when he was in fact in the Caribbean. Another error led to the inclusion of a land-mass linking Africa to China (and making the Indian Ocean an inland sea). Ptolemy also wrote on *astrology, in four books in which he attempts to find a scientific basis for the various astrological practices of his time, and this work too exerted great influence. Chaucer's Wife of Bath in his *Canterbury Tales* quotes a proverb from Ptolemy, calling him 'the wise astrologe'.

**publicā'ni** ('publicans', i.e. tax-collectors) In Rome, the collection of public revenue was sold by contract to the highest bidder, who then recouped with as much profit to himself as possible. (Salaried administrators employed by the state, known as *apparitores*, were very few.) Other public works were sold in the same way and to the same people, who were usually of the *equestrian order, since men of senatorial rank were not permitted to engage in trade of this sort. Under the empire this method of collecting taxes was gradually superseded by direct collection by the government through quaestors and procurators.

**Publi'lius Sȳrus** (first century BC) Writer of Latin *mimes who was brought to Rome as a slave, possibly from Antioch, and manumitted. He is known by a collection of moral maxims made for school use which purport to have been selected from his plays. One of his maxims, *iudex damnatur cum nocens absolvitur* ('When the guilty man is let off the judge stands condemned') was adopted by the *Edinburgh Review* (1802) to express its stern attitude in literary criticism.

**punctuation** Neither Greeks nor Romans left spaces between words to aid word recognition, except for using dots on inscriptions (in Greece on some archaic examples, and in Rome commonly). Nevertheless the occasional difficulty of reading continuous writing was recognized: discussion of word-division in Homer began at an early period. Punctuation marks—most commonly the equivalent of the full-stop or comma, but also apostrophes and accents—were present sporadically in Greek papyri from at least the fourth century BC (*see* PAPYROLOGY). Texts were written in narrow columns, as in a modern newspaper, and this was probably an aid to reading, especially to reading aloud, which was the common practice. Aristotle in the *Rhetoric* observes that punctuating Heracleitus is hard work because of the difficulty of telling whether an adverb goes with what precedes or what follows. *See also* BOOKS, GREEK AND ROMAN 2.

**Pūnica** *See* SILIUS ITALICUS.

**Punic Wars** Three wars (264–241 BC; 218–201 BC; and 149–146 BC) in which Rome fought *Carthage for dominance in the western Mediterranean with final success. The name comes from the Latin word *Poeni* ('Carthaginians', adj. *Punicus*, 'Carthaginian'). Rome, having by 270 BC won control of the Italian peninsula, responded to an appeal for help from the *Mamertines *c.*265. At this time the Carthaginians were a rival power who now ruled not only the north and west of Sicily but also the greater part of North Africa, Sardinia, Corsica, and the cities on the coast of southern Spain. The Romans felt that trade and security would be threatened if Carthage encroached further.

The First Punic War was centred on Sicily, where Carthage and Hieron II joined forces. The Romans won sea-battles at Mylae (260) and Cape Ecnomus (256), overcoming superior Carthaginian seamanship by the innovative use of grappling-irons. Mastery of the sea allowed them to land unopposed in Africa, but after early successes there, they were defeated, and *Regulus, who had commanded the force, was captured. However, another Roman sea victory off the Aegates Insulae (242) caused the Carthaginians to sue for peace. They evacuated Sicily (except for the dominion of Hieron II), which then became the first Roman province, and paid a large indemnity.

When the First Punic War ended, Carthage turned to Spain to recoup wealth and manpower, and between 237 and 219 *Hamilcar Barca, *Hasdrubal, and *Hannibal gradually conquered that country. In 219 Hannibal's attack on Saguntum (Rome's Spanish ally and a threat to Carthage's grip on Spain) deliberately precipitated the Second Punic War. This was one of the great struggles of the ancient world, fought in several theatres. Hannibal anticipated the dispatch of Roman expeditions to Spain and Africa and struck first by invading north Italy. There he defeated one great army after another, that of P. Scipio at the river Ticinus in 218, that of Scipio and Tib. Sempronius Longus at the river Trebia in the same year (both rivers tributaries of the Po), and that of

C. *Flaminius at Lake Trasimene in 217, when Flaminius was himself killed. Hannibal then moved to the south to detach the allies from Rome. At this crisis Rome appointed a dictator, Quintus *Fabius (2), who acquired the *cognomen* Cunctator, 'Delayer', from following the invader and harassing him, while refusing a general engagement. In 216 the new consuls C. Terentius Varro and L. Aemilius Paullus were authorized to risk a decisive battle to protect the territory of Rome's allies, with the result that at Cannae Rome suffered the bloodiest of all her defeats, losing perhaps 50,000 men, half of them Roman. Hannibal remained in Italy for fifteen years and was undefeated in battle, but Fabius continued to wear down his strength and the tide began to turn against Carthage. M. Claudius Marcellus captured Syracuse in 211, despite the weapons of war devised by *Archimedes, and thus weakened the power of Carthage in Sicily; Hasdrubal, who had gone to aid Hannibal in Italy, was defeated and killed at the river Metaurus (in Umbria, 207); and Scipio Africanus drove the Carthaginians from Spain (206). The scene of war was now transferred to Africa and Hannibal and the Punic army were recalled from Italy. They were beaten by Scipio in a pitched battle at Zama (202) and Carthage accepted harsh peace-terms. It was the end of her position as a great Mediterranean power.

Carthage retained, however, her commercial importance; she continued to compete successfully with Rome in trade, and her rapid recovery was a source of uneasiness there. She had undertaken to wage no wars in Africa without the consent of Rome, but in 151, when she had paid off the war indemnity, the depredations of *Masinissa, the ruler of the adjoining Numidian kingdom and the friend of Rome, goaded her into retaliation (150). In 149 Rome used this pretext to initiate the Third Punic War. The Elder *Cato, from motives of revenge and fear, urged Carthage's destruction, and an army landed in Africa. The Carthaginians surrendered, handed over hostages and arms, and then heard the terms that they must abandon their city. Unexpectedly they refused to comply and withstood a siege until 146, when *Scipio (2) captured the city and demolished it. With Carthage destroyed her territory was made into the Roman province of Africa.

**purification** In Greece purifications were carried out before important occasions such as marriages or meetings of the *ecclesia* or by individuals before approaching temples, often by doing no more than washing in sea-water or water from a sacred spring. Specific *pollution was removed not so much by actions as by the passage of time. Athens had 'purifiers' who could advise individuals on particular problems. The major pollutant was blood, and blood-guilt required a period of exile before the shedder could be readmitted to the community. The subject impinged upon medicine: certain diseases (epilepsy and madness in particular) were often seen as the province of seers who professed cures (*see* HIPPOCRATES (1), *On the Sacred Disease*). Special sorts of purification were adopted by the adherents of the otherworldly movements of Greek thought, Orphism (*see* ORPHEUS) and Pythagoreanism, which included fasting, in an attempt to escape the polluting effect of the body itself. Apollo at Delphi was frequently consulted on matters of pollution and purification (*see* DELPHIC ORACLE), but the god chiefly responsible was Zeus Katharsios, 'of purification'.

**purple** In Rome the wearing of purple garments was a mark of high rank. Roman emperors wore robes dyed with Tyrian purple (from Tyre in Phoenicia, made from the Mediterranean whelk, *murex*). The emperor Commodus was the first to be described as 'born in the purple' because he was born to the reigning emperor Marcus Aurelius. There was a story that Byzantine empresses were supposed to give birth in a room whose walls were lined with the purple stone porphyry. *See also* TOGA.

**Pydna** (In Macedonia on the Thermaic Gulf) The scene of the battle in 168 BC in which the Romans under L. Aemilius *Paullus decisively defeated Perseus, king of *Macedonia, and ended the Third Macedonian War. Here the Macedonian cavalry phalanx fought its last battle.

**Pygmā'lion 1.** Legendary king of Tyre, brother of Elissa (*Dido), whose husband Sychaeus he killed in the hope of obtaining his fortune.

**2.** Legendary king of Cyprus, who fell in love with a beautiful statue (according to Ovid, made by the king himself). He prayed to Aphrodite to give him a wife resembling the statue; and she did more than this, for she gave the statue life, and Pygmalion married the woman so created. Their child was Paphos, the mother of *Cinyras.

**Pȳ'ladēs 1.** In Greek myth, the constant friend of *Orestes. He was the son of Strophius, king of Phocis, and his wife Anaxibia, sister of Orestes' father Agamemnon. He accompanied Orestes to the land of the Tauri (*see* IPHIGENEIA), and later to Mycenae when Orestes took vengeance on Clytemnestra and Aegisthus (*see* ELECTRA, Sophocles' tragedy). He later killed Neoptolemus at Delphi and married Electra.

**2.** An actor at Rome; *see* PANTOMIME.

**Pȳlos** In classical Greece, the name of several sites which all claimed to be the kingdom of the Homeric hero *Nestor, described by Homer as 'sandy', which suggests it was near the sea. The most important prehistoric site actually called Pylos in the *Linear B tablets found there is some 9km north-east of Navarino Bay and seems to have become a centre of power in Messenia in Mycenaean times. As with other Mycenaean sites the palace was burned *c.*1200 BC but seems not to have been entirely abandoned until the eighth century BC. The adjoining bay of Pylos, and the island of Sphacteria which almost closes the mouth of the bay, were the scene of an important defeat of the Spartans by the light-armed Athenians in 425 BC, thought by other Greeks to be 'the greatest surprise of all the events of this war', according to Thucydides. The Spartans' concern to recover their prisoners was one motive for their accepting the Peace of Nicias in 421 BC (*see* PELOPONNESIAN WAR). The Athenians held Sphacteria with a garrison until 409 BC.

**Py'ramus and Thisbē** Hero and heroine of a love story almost unknown in classical literature except through Ovid's *Metamorphoses*. The two lovers, who were next-door neighbours in Babylon, were forbidden by their parents to marry, but they spoke to each other through a chink in the party-wall. Finally they arranged to meet at the tomb of Nisus outside the city walls, under a white mulberry tree. Thisbe arrived first, but being frightened by a lion coming from its kill, fled into a cave, dropping her cloak which the lion mauled. On his arrival Pyramus found the tattered and blood-stained cloak and the animal's prints and, concluding that Thisbe was dead, stabbed himself with his sword. Thisbe emerging from the cave, distraught at the sight of the dying Pyramus, fell upon his sword. Their blood flowed to the roots of the mulberry tree, which thereafter bore dark red fruit. Their parents buried their ashes in a single urn. The story is acted by Bottom and his fellow tradesmen to entertain the wedding-party in Shakespeare's *A Midsummmer Night's Dream*.

**pyrrhic dance (*pyrrhichē*)** Spartan mimic war-dance, perhaps a form of the *hyporchema*, said to have originated with the Dorians in Crete. It was danced at the Spartan festival of the Gymnopaediae and also at the Athenian festival of the *Panathenaea. The origin of the name is uncertain.

**Pyrrhic victory** See Pyrrhus (1).

**Pyrrhon** See Sceptics.

**Pyrrhus 1.** (319–272 BC) The last great military adventurer of his time, king of Epirus in Greece from 307, second cousin of Alexander the Great. Pyrrhus was ousted from his throne in 302, but with the help of Ptolemy I of Egypt was restored in 297. He hoped to revive Alexander's empire and was at one time (286), after a successful war against *Demetrius Poliorcetes, the most powerful ruler in the European part of it, having secured Thessaly and a portion of Macedonia. But he was soon driven back to Epirus (283) by Lysimachus (one of the *Diadochi, Alexander's 'successors'). He then turned to the West and accepted the invitation of the Greek city of Tarentum in Italy to lead the Italian Greeks of *Magna Graecia against Rome. He won battles in 280 and 279 with a large army and twenty elephants but was unable to establish himself in Italy. The expression 'Pyrrhic victory' to describe a victory gained at too great a cost alludes to an exclamation attributed to him after the battle of Asculum in 279 where he routed the Romans but lost the flower of his army: 'One more victory like that and we are lost.' Pyrrhus then transferred his forces to Sicily, and by 277 had almost succeeded in expelling the Carthaginians from that island. He broke off the war there (perhaps by then a lost cause) and returned to Italy. After more losses in 275 against the Romans at Malventum ('Ill-met', thereafter named by them Beneventum, 'Well-met'), he withdrew to Epirus. Once again in 274 he at-

tempted to conquer Macedonia, with some success, but went on to attack Sparta in 272. He was killed in the same year in an attempt to seize Argos, by a tile thrown from the roof of a house. A brilliant tactician, Pyrrhus was quick to take advantage of an opportunity but made no lasting gains. He wrote an *Art of War* which was still read in the time of Cicero. Hannibal said that of all generals Pyrrhus was the first, Scipio the second, and himself the third. *See also* Fabricius.

**2.** Alternative name of the Greek hero *Neoptolemus.

**Pȳtha'goras** *Presocratic Greek philosopher, mystic, and by tradition mathematician of the sixth century BC, an influential figure in the intellectual life of Greece and reputed by later commentators to be the originator of a long-lasting 'Pythagorean' tendency in some philosophies. Partly perhaps because he wrote nothing himself he is impenetrably mysterious and seems to have been an object of legend even in his own lifetime. The traditions concerning his life are contradictory and confused. He was born in the late seventh or early sixth century BC on the Ionian island of Samos but *c.*580 BC he moved to Croton in *Magna Graecia, where he attracted a group of followers, both men and women, who lived according to his ascetic rule of life. He was also active in the politics of the region. The Pythagorean tradition continued to develop after his death (*c.*500 BC) until at any rate 450 BC, when the communities became unpopular and members were killed or exiled. (Pythagoras himself had felt it prudent to retire to Metapontum in south Italy. Cicero as a cultural tourist went to see the place there where he died, and the chair he sat in.) It is difficult to isolate Pythagoras' original teaching, particularly since there seems to have been no record made of it before the fourth century BC. Assessing the relationship between Pythagoras' original work and the interpretations of *Aristoxenus, *Archytas, *Eudoxus, and *Philolaus (whose works exist only in fragments) as well as of Plato is hazardous, and many philosophical and mathematical theories have been attributed to him which were in fact made later. His intellectual interest reputedly centred on *mathematics, *music, and *astronomy, and was underpinned by religious and ethical mysticism. He was clearly interested in number (and therefore ratios and harmonics) and in the nature of the *soul and its transmigration (also known as metempsychosis), the belief that at death a soul leaves a body to be born later into another body, an idea foreign to Greek tradition and of uncertain origin. The testimony of contemporary philosophers was not kind. Heracleitus thought he practised 'false craft' and that like other philosophers 'much learning ... did not teach him under-standing'. *Xenophanes, a slightly younger contemporary, ridiculed in a poem his belief in metempsychosis. (Xenophanes said that Pythagoras pitied a puppy being whipped 'be-cause it is the soul of a friend. I recognized it when I heard it crying out.') Pythagoras' actual views on the nature of the soul, however, re-main obscure. That Plato was greatly influ-enced by him is indicated by Plato's myths concerning the nature of the soul and judge-ment after death, by his belief in the superiority of soul to body, and by his sympathy for a mathematical view of reality. Aristotle reports that for Pythagoreans all things are or imitate numbers. Also characteristic of early Pythagor-eanism, apparently, was the learning of myste-rious questions and answers called *acusmata* (Gk. *akousmata*, 'things heard', i.e. oral in-structions) apparently embodying precepts and rules of a moral or religious nature. Some sound like taboo-prohibitions, others like tra-ditional wisdom. Pythagoras taught that the soul is immortal, a fallen divinity imprisoned in the body as in a tomb. Since the soul is rational and responsible for its actions, the choices it makes determine the kind of body into which it is reincarnated, human or animal (perhaps even plant). By keeping itself pure from the pollutions of the body the soul of an adherent might eventually win release from it and attain blessedness (*see also* ORPHEUS for Orphic beliefs, with which Pythagoras obvious-ly had much in common). This was an austere regimen the details of which are not clear but which perhaps entailed silence, self-examina-tion, and abstention from eating flesh (not vegetarianism, but prohibition on specific parts of the body) and beans (no reason is known for this latter prohibition).

Pythagoras was credited, perhaps wrongly, with the discovery that the relation between the chief musical intervals produced on a vi-brating string can be expressed as ratios be-tween the first four whole numbers: octave, 2:1; fifth, 3:2; fourth, 4:3. From this evolved the idea that the explanation of the universe is to be sought in numbers and their relations, of which the objects of sense are representations. According to Aristotle, even abstracts like 'opinion' or 'opportunity' or 'injustice' were numbers in the Pythagorean system, and had their place in the cosmos. Since the first four integers can express musical harmonies and since they can be represented as an equilateral triangular array of ten points in rows of one, two, three, and four, it was thought that this pattern, known as the *tetractys* ('foursome'), was of mystical significance. It was thought to embrace the whole nature of number: one could be identified with a point, two with a line, three with a surface, and four with a solid. Pythagoras was also credited with the theorem that still goes under his name, namely that the square on the hypotenuse of a right-angled triangle is equal to the sum of the squares on the other two sides; on discovering it he is said to have made the important sacri-fice of a *hecatomb. The Pythagoreans be-lieved that the earth is a sphere; later adherents (*see* PHILOLAUS) had an astronomical system in which the heavenly bodies (the sphere of the fixed stars, the five planets then known, the sun, moon, earth, and counter-earth, the last included to bring the number of bodies up to ten) revolve around a central fire. *See also* HARMONY OF THE SPHERES.

Plato's science and metaphysics are infused with Pythagorean ideas. Writing between a century and a century-and-a-half after Pythag-oras' death, he was influenced by aspects of contemporary Pythagoreanism, perhaps through his friendship with Archytas, the Pythagorean mathematician. Pythagorean doctrines were later revived at Rome under the early empire, and became confused with Orphic beliefs, to which they had affinities.

**Pythagoreans** *See* PYTHAGORAS.

**Py'theas** (second half of the fourth century BC) Greek explorer from Massalia (Marseille), who, according to Strabo, Diodorus Siculus, and the Elder Pliny, made a courageous voyage up the west coast of Europe to Britain, which he circumnavigated, visiting Cornwall and St Michael's Mount, and reported an island *Thule.

**Py'thia** Priestess of Apollo at *Delphi.

**Py'thian games** The most important Greek games after those at *Olympia, held at the Pythian festival in honour of Apollo Pythius at Delphi. From 582 BC they were held every four years in the third year of each Olympiad.

**Py'thias** *See* DAMON.

**Pȳthon** *See* DELPHI.

# Q

**Quadriga'rius, Claudius** *See* HISTORIOGRA-PHY [Roman].

**quadri'vium** *See* SEVEN LIBERAL ARTS.

**quaestors** ('investigators') *Magistrates at Rome; in the early republic there were two who prosecuted some capital cases. After 447 BC the quaestors became properly constituted magistrates elected annually by the people (*see* DECEMVIRI); in 421 their number was increased to four, two of whom administered the state treasury, *aerarium*, and were called in consequence *quaestores aerarii* or *urbani* ('of the city'). Four more were instituted in 267 and others added later as the number of Roman provinces increased and financial officers were required. Sulla made the office compulsory in the *cursus honorum*, entailing automatic entry to the senate for the holders, and declared that 30 was the minimum age for holding it.

**quindecimviri sacris faciundis** ('the fifteen [priests] for performing rituals', as opposed to *augury) At Rome, one of the four important colleges of priests. Their main function was to guard and consult the Sibylline books (*see* SIBYL) and perform the appropriate religious ceremonies in response to portents. Since this led to the gradual import of Greek cult and rituals, overseeing these 'Greek rites' also became one of their duties.

**quintessence** As the name indicates (Lat. *quintus*, 'fifth'), a pure fifth *element, from which heavenly bodies were believed by some to be composed, a different stuff from the four elements which make up the world. Medieval alchemists tried to distil it. The idea derives ultimately from Aristotle's *Physics*.

**Quinti'lian (Marcus Fabius Quintiliānus)** (b. *c.*AD 35 at Calagurris in Spain; the date of his death is not known, but his *Institutio oratoria* was published about AD 95) A famous teacher of *rhetoric at Rome. He may have received all his education at Rome; at some

period he returned to Spain, whence he was brought back by the emperor Galba in 68. He was the first rhetorician to receive an official salary from the state treasury (under the emperor Vespasian), and he acquired great wealth; the Younger Pliny was among his pupils. He also practised advocacy in the courts. The emperor Domitian made him consul and tutor to his two great-nephews and heirs. He retired, probably in 88, in order to write. Before he retired he married, but his wife died before her nineteenth birthday, and his two sons later, at the ages of 5 and 9; the introduction to the sixth book of his *Institutio* makes clear his grief. His earlier work *De causis corruptae eloquentiae* ('On the causes of the decline of eloquence') is lost.

The *Institutio oratoria* ('Education of an orator'), in twelve books, is Quintilian's most famous work. It covers the training of an orator from babyhood to the grown man. *Book 1* deals with the early education of the future orator; the influence of nurses, parents, slaves; the superiority of school education over education at home; the importance of a thorough study of language as a foundation; and the need for Greek and various other subjects. The subject matter should not be dictated by commercial consideration.

*Book 2*, which begins with the boy's entry to the school of rhetoric, is on the general method and aim of training in rhetoric, on the qualifications of a good teacher and the proper treatment of pupils, and on the need in an orator for moral character as well as wide knowledge.

*Books 3–7* pass on to technicalities: the three kinds of oratory (judicial, deliberative, *epideictic), the parts of a speech (exordium, narrative, etc.), and the arrangement of matters to be dealt with. These are principally related to speeches in the courts, and are illuminating when read in conjunction with the speeches of Cicero.

*Books 8–11* deal with style and delivery. Of these book 10 contains the famous discussion of those authors, Greek and Latin, who are to be studied as 'particularly suitable to those proposing to become orators', and Quintilian's judgements on them, made solely from a rhetorical viewpoint. Of the Greeks he places Homer first for his many qualities and in particular his oratorical skills. Pindar is by far the greatest of the lyric poets, especially for his flood of eloquence; Aristophanes, Eupolis, and Cratinus are the greatest of the writers of Old Comedy, Menander of New. Sophocles and Euripides are the most accomplished of the tragedians, for Aeschylus, in spite of his dignity, is often uncouth. In history he sets far above the others Thucydides ('compressed and concise and always pressing on') and Herodotus ('delightful, clear, and discursive'). He discusses Demosthenes and his lesser rivals. He praises Plato's acuteness, and his 'divine and Homeric' gift of eloquence, Xenophon's unaffected style, and Aristotle's knowledge and penetration. Of the Romans he places Virgil first, as most nearly approaching Homer. The style of Lucretius he thinks difficult. Ennius he compares with those ancient sacred groves whose mighty oaks are admired less for their beauty than for their sanctity. Ovid is too much an admirer of his own genius. Satire, for the Roman Quintilian, is 'all our own'; he places Horace as a satirist before Lucilius, and mentions Persius favourably. In Latin Horace is 'virtually the only lyric poet worth reading' (Catullus is mentioned only for the invective of his iambics). Quintilian thinks the (now lost) *Thyestes* of Varius the equal of any Greek tragedy, and commends the (also lost) *Medea* of Ovid, but makes no high claim for Roman tragedy. Comedy is Rome's weakest point. In history he regards Sallust as equal to Thucydides, Livy to Herodotus. Cicero is a match for any Greek orator: Quintilian compares his style with that of Demosthenes, and though scrupulously fair to the merits of both cannot conceal the pleasure he feels at Cicero's overall brilliance. Caesar might have been his rival had he devoted himself to the subject; as it is he equals Cicero in force, acumen, and vigour. Book 11 discusses the manner of delivery.

*Book 12* sums up Quintilian's view of the ideal orator, not a speaker merely, but a man of highest character, properly trained in morals as well as in taste; Quintilian quotes the words of Cato the Elder: *vir bonus dicendi perītus*, 'a good man who knows how to speak'.

The poet Martial called Quintilian 'the supreme guide of wayward youth'.

**Quintus Smyrnae'us (Quintus of Smyrna)** (third or fourth century AD). Author of an extant epic poem in Greek in fourteen books known by its Latin title, the *Posthomerica* (Gk. *Hoi meth' Homēron logoi*), which filled the gap in events between Homer's *Iliad* and *Odyssey* originally covered by the poems of the *Epic Cycle. The work is mainly of antiquarian interest; its sources probably date from the Hellenistic age.

**Quirī'nal** Most northerly of the *seven hills of Rome, traditionally occupied by Sabines, and one of the four regions (*see* REGIONES) of republican Rome. On it were many famous temples and houses, including at various periods the temple of *Quirinus (293 BC), the ancient citadel (*capitolium vetus*), the temple of Venus Erycina (181 BC), and later the houses of the poet Martial and of Cicero's friend Atticus.

**Quirī'nus** In Roman religion, originally the local deity; he was also a war god of the Sabine community settled on the Quirinal hill before the foundation of Rome. When this community came to be incorporated into Rome, Quirinus was included among the state gods of the city with Jupiter and Mars. Though he became less important, he remained a deity of the people. His festival, the Quirinalia, was celebrated on 17 February. As an early god he had his own *flamen, the *flamen Quirinalis*, but little is known of Quirinus himself and nothing of his ritual. He was thought to be the apotheosis of *Romulus by the Romans of the late republic. In 16 BC Augustus rebuilt the temple of Quirinus, showing the power of Roman myth in the religion of that time.

**Quirī'tes** Name given to the earliest inhabitants of Rome, Latin and Sabine, which survived later in official phraseology to be applied to the Roman people in their civil capacity. It was superseded by the name *Romani* (Romans) or *populus Romanus* (Roman people). The term was not applicable to Romans when serving in the army: Caesar is said to have quelled a mutiny of his soldiers by addressing them as 'Quirites'. The origin of the name is uncertain. The Romans generally believed that it originally signified the inhabitants of the Sabine town of Cures.

# R

**Rape of the Sabines** *See* ROMULUS.

**reading** *See* BOOKS, GREEK AND ROMAN; *see also* LITERACY and PUNCTUATION.

**reception studies** Studies of how texts, works of art, historical events, almost anything from the past, have been 'received' in the past and up to the present day by the generality or by a variety of interested people. The aim is to find if texts, for example, have been accepted at their apparent face-value or reinterpreted, re-written, expurgated, shaped to fit contemporary ideas and situations or an imaginary past, or used symbolically to convey a message. Based on the truism that history belongs to two time-frames, the time at which it is written and the time at which it is read, study of the reception of a text at one particular period often illuminates the thought of that period itself in fresh and unexpected ways. This is a relatively new (twentieth-century) field of study which has been found stimulating and rewarding, opening up new ways of looking at whatever is under consideration and widening investigation into what constitutes meaning.

**Rē'gia** At Rome, the royal palace said to have been built by King *Numa at the foot of the Palatine on the eastern edge of the Forum. The earliest foundations have been dated to the late seventh and sixth centuries BC. It adjoined the precinct of Vesta. In republican times the Regia was the official headquarters of the *pontifex maximus*. The building was several times burnt and restored. In 36 BC it was rebuilt of marble and on its walls were inscribed the *fasti consulares* and *fasti triumphales* (records of consuls and of triumphs at Rome).

**Rēgi'llus, Lake** The site of a Roman victory in the early days of the republic, *c*.496 BC, over the Latins, who were attempting to re-establish the *Tarquins at Rome. For the intervention of the gods Castor and Pollux *see* DIOSCURI.

**rēgio'nēs** ('regions', sing. *regio*) At Rome, the four wards into which the city was divided during the republic; these were the Suburana, which included the Caelian hill, the Esquilina (the *Esquiline hill), the Collina, including the *Quirinal and Viminal hills, and the Palatina (the *Palatine hill). The emperor Augustus divided the city into fourteen new *regiones*.

**Re'gulus, Marcus Atī'lius** Roman consul in 265 and 256 BC. In the latter year as a commander in the First *Punic War he defeated the Carthaginian navy at Cape Ecnomus, but in the following year—leading the Roman expedition to Africa—he was captured. It is said that he was sent on an embassy to Rome to negotiate an exchange of prisoners, the Carthaginians making him swear to return if the negotiations failed. He advised the Romans to continue the war, then kept his word and returned to Carthage, where he was tortured to death. (Carthaginians had a reputation for cruelty as well as for human sacrifice.) The story was well known in the first century BC. As related by Horace in *Odes* 3.5 the issue was one of ransom, which recalled the refusal by Rome to pay ransom to the Carthaginians for their soldiers captured at *Cannae in 216. It has been suggested that the story was invented to excuse his widow's cruel treatment of two Carthaginian prisoners in Rome, in revenge for Regulus' death. Polybius seems not to have heard of the story.

**reincarnation** *See* PYTHAGORAS and *REPUBLIC* [book 10].

**religion**
**Greek.** The classical Greeks had a religion in the sense that they worshipped in communally recognized ways a pantheon of gods and goddesses and a number of somewhat disparate heroes, and generally excluded from their worship the gods of other nationalities (but see below). These Greeks would have agreed with the historian Herodotus that it was the poets Hesiod and Homer who composed the theogonies and gave the gods their names, but it is clear that these developments took place long before their time. The names of many of the

major Greek gods are found in Mycenaean *Linear B tablets, and some elements of cult practice may also date from Mycenaean times. Influence from the Near East is visible from the eighth century BC with the building of large temples containing images of the gods worshipped there, and it may be the case that some elements of animal sacrifice also derive from the East. Certainly many of the Greek myths had Eastern origins. Religion and society were closely entwined in Greece; the whole city joined in the major festivals (*see* e.g. PA-NATHENAEA) and smaller groups—local communities, kinship groups such as phratries, or groups of coevals—came together for celebration and the worship of particular deities (*see* CITY-STATE). These civic connections gradually began to lose their importance during the Hellenistic age.

The gods in Homer are the twelve Olympians (*see* GODS), who constitute a divine family of which the individual members are strongly characterized; they are essentially human in their behaviour and motivated by human desires, but differ from men in their power and in their immortality. Hesiod in the *Theogony* related them to one another in a genealogy and systematized all the many other deities of Greek polytheism. Zeus and the Olympian gods are described as the third generation to hold power; the earlier gods (Titans and primordial deities) were of little religious significance except perhaps for *Gaia (Earth). Zeus was supremely powerful, but his authority did not go unchallenged (in myth at any rate). The Greeks had many other deities apart from the twelve Olympians and there were many other aspects of the divine which Homer excluded but which were of significance in Greek religious life. *Demeter and *Dionysus for example, with their emphases on fertility and on ecstasy, were important in cult in ways scarcely hinted at by Homer (*see also* MYSTERIES and *BACCHAE*). The Greeks also had the idea that the gods were teachers of the arts: Ceres, for example, brought agriculture to humans.

In popular belief gods were to be found in every locality; every spring and river had its god or *nymph, the object of purely local cult and myth; hero-cult and the cult of the dead generally were important (*see* HEROES), as were the cults of phratries and demes. There was no separate priesthood; *priests were not always a necessary part of religious proceedings, and a man might perform his own sacrifices. There

was no firmly asserted connection between religion and an after-life (except for the mystery religions). But certainly divine attitudes shown in Homer's *Odyssey* and Hesiod's *Works and Days* provided a basis for morality.

Greek and Roman religion was tolerant and without dogma. The Greeks did not have a word for 'religion'; *eusebeia*, 'piety', is the word that comes nearest to the idea. Piety lay in the performance of traditional rituals and in the observance of the traditional modes of behaviour expressed in the Delphic maxims (*see* DELPHI). *Cult had little to do with men's ideas about the divine. Socrates seems to have been a scrupulous observer of traditional rites, but accusations of impiety were still made against him. State gods were important for the safety of a city, which had its own tutelary deity for its own needs, Poseidon at Corinth, Hera at Argos, Athena at Athens. As a city expanded and admitted foreigners so it admitted foreign gods also, as Athens took in the Thracian *Bendis and, influenced by special circumstances, *Pan and *Asclepius. Greeks in foreign countries naturally paid homage to the local gods, many of whom were regarded as the familiar Greek deities under different names.

*See* references for AFTER-LIFE; *see also* ATHEISM; CYBELE; DAIMON; DIVINATION; FESTIVALS; GODS; HERMS; MONOTHEISM; MYTHOLOGY; ORACLES; POLLUTION; PRAYER; RULER CULT; SACRIFICE; TYCHE.

**Roman.** Roman religion is essentially a fusion of early Latin beliefs and of Greek religion, from which in very early times the Romans derived many of their myths and ideas about their own gods. They believed that their religion had its origin in the foundation of the city itself by Romulus in 753 BC. The sacred boundary, *pomerium*, had divine approval and the earliest temple, where Romulus dedicated the spoils of his victories, was to Jupiter Feretrius (*see* JUPITER). However other religious traditions were thought to exist already, brought by *Evander from Arcadia (*see* HERCULES). When Aeneas arrived in Italy (and was given a tour of the future site of Rome by Evander) he brought with him his 'household gods', the *penates*, and the *Palladium from Troy, which eventually found a home in the temple of *Vesta.

More religious institutions and priesthoods were established by the second king, *Numa, and subsequent kings created important foundations: the *fetial priests, the temple of *Jupiter, *Juno, and *Minerva on the Capitoline hill, the temple of *Diana on the Aventine. By the end of the sixth century BC, Romans believed, the basic framework of their religious life was in place. It mattered to the Romans even more than to the Greeks that public worship on behalf of the state should be properly performed.

See CHRISTIANITY IN THE ROMAN WORLD; *see also* references as above, and AUGURY; BACCHANALIA; DEIFICATION; *FASTI*; FERIAE; FERIAE LATINAE; GODS [Roman]; SALII; VARRO [res divinae].

**Reme'dia amo'ris** ('Cures of love') Latin poem in elegiacs by *Ovid, of some 800 lines. It professes to give instructions for overcoming unhappy love, for women as well as men, by hunting, travel, agricultural occupations, and avoidance of wine and love-poetry; but the poet's real intent is to amuse the reader, who nowadays takes pleasure in the glimpses of Roman life that the poem gives.

**Rēmus** *See* ROMULUS.

**repetu'ndae** (Lat., in full *res repetundae*, 'property to be recovered') The legal charge of extortion. When Roman provincial magistrates returned to Rome, any accusations made by provincials about extortion were brought before a special court. Radical reform of the judicial process to be followed began with C. Sempronius Gracchus (*see* GRACCHI) and developed into a procedure of much complexity, with emphasis on clear accountability. The penalty was originally simple restitution, but later double repayment. From being a civil offence it became a criminal matter, with ramified political consequences.

**Republic (Politeia)** Dialogue in ten books by *Plato, written *c.*375 BC in the early years of his *Academy (founded to educate future politicians), arguably the greatest philosophical work from antiquity. The traditional English title, derived from the Latin translation, *Res publica*, of the Greek title, is perhaps misleading. The Greek is closer in meaning to 'society' or 'the state'. An ancient (but perhaps not Platonic) title is 'On justice'. The subject is the nature of justice, and the consequences of justice and injustice for the individual and the state. For Plato, justice in any individual is conditional upon the harmonious working of the three parts of that individual's soul. These parts (described in book 4) comprise reason (which exercises control), spirit or courage, and desire or appetite which most needs con-

trol (*see also* PHAEDRUS). Justice will exist in the state when there is similar harmony between the three functionally separate classes of citizens which Plato proposes to establish (see below).

Book 1 has the conversational form of an early Socratic dialogue (*see* PLATO 2), but the rest of the work is a more or less continuous exposition by *Socrates of what may be supposed to be Plato's own views on society at the time of writing. The interlocutors are Socrates, an old man Cephalus (father of the orator *Lysias) and his son Polemarchus, Thrasymachus a sophist, and Plato's brothers Glaucon and Adeimantus. The discussion takes place in the Piraeus at the house of Cephalus, who soon withdraws from the conversation.

The dialogue starts with the question 'What is justice?' The definition offered in the past by the poet Simonides, that justice means giving a person his due, as in the traditional maxim that one should help one's friends and harm one's enemies, is shown to be inadequate. Can reason suggest another answer? Thrasymachus rejects conventional morality and maintains that human behaviour is, and should be, guided by self-interest. Socrates' argument reduces Thrasymachus to silence, but Glaucon and Adeimantus remain unsatisfied and restate his case for him. Glaucon argues that justice is a matter of human convention based on expediency: we would all be unjust to our own advantage if we could. As illustration he tells the story of *Gyges' magic ring of invisibility. Adeimantus argues that justice is pursued only for reputation and reward: Socrates must show that justice is preferable to injustice for its own sake and not for the rewards it brings. Socrates suggests that justice will best be seen in the macrocosm of a perfect *city-state, and thence can be found by analogy in individuals. Accordingly Socrates proceeds to construct the ideal state, so that in its construction one might see also the growth of justice, or injustice. This state is seen to consist of three classes, rulers (known as 'guardians'), in whose education Plato is particularly interested (books 2 and 3), auxiliaries or soldiers, and workers, all classified according to aptitude, upbringing, and education; children can be moved between the classes, but eventually all will be suited to one role only. In the first class resides the wisdom of the state; the guardians alone, by virtue of their aptitude and education, will have expert knowledge of justice and the Good (*see* PLATO 4 and 5), and will rule in the interests of the majority, whose understanding will be limited. The second class will have spirit or courage, and the third will have appetite. Individuals have the qualities of the three classes present in their souls (book 4) but in varying proportions; justice consists in the harmony of all three elements under the control of reason, and the just man is ruled by reason. Socrates explains his proposal that the guardian class should live communally (book 5): it is for the sake of eugenics, and to prevent the guardians from being distracted from their work. Women as well as men are capable of joining this ruling class (an idea that sets him apart from most of his contemporaries).

The *Republic* answers the question of the *Protagoras*, how virtue is passed from one generation to another. It can only happen in a just city, through the unquestioned authority of guardians educated in philosophy, 'philosopher-kings' (who may be women, Socrates reminds the company). They alone have knowledge; others have at best only true belief (book 5). But true philosophers are very few in number (book 6). Socrates expounds their education, which leads ultimately to knowledge of the Good. He explains the nature of this knowledge by using as analogies the sun, a divided line, and most famously an allegory of a cave (book 7). The human condition is, in Plato's view, that of prisoners in a subterranean cave who are chained so as to see only shadows of objects projected on to the rock face in front of them. These shadows are thrown by the light of a fire behind them, which they cannot see. In consequence they take the shadows for the only realities. Those who manage to struggle out of the cave into the everyday world are the guardians, and they will finally see the sun which makes everything visible and symbolizes the Form of Good itself (*see* PLATO 5). To this end their education (book 7) is to continue beyond the age of 20: for the next ten years they will study mathematics and harmonics, then for five years dialectic. From 35 they will gain practical experience and at 50 the best will have attained the vision of the Good, and will thereafter devote their lives to government. In books 8 and 9 Socrates resumes the subject of the various types of political organization, aristocracy, timocracy (as at Sparta), oligarchy, democracy, and tyranny, with their human representatives, ending with

the tyrant/dictator who has every vice, 'making him only less of a calamity to those around him than he is to himself'. Even the just city degenerates in the end, because no earthly institution can avoid decay. All this finally shows that justice in the well-ordered soul produces happiness and benefits its possessors, while injustice produces misery and harm. Rewards are merely a secondary consideration. Contrary to Thrasymachus' view that injustice pays when it goes unpunished, life for the just will be more pleasurable as well as noble. (Plato has in mind the example of Socrates, who was completely happy through 'living well'.)

The final book (10) reads somewhat like an appendix. It starts with some of Plato's most important observations on the relation of art to truth. He attacks poetry and then art in general for being remote from reality, which for Plato is found only in the Forms. (*See* PLATO 4–6; PLATONISM; AESTHETICS; and MIMESIS.) A further objection is that poetic drama, by encouraging an audience to indulge in emotion, has a psychologically damaging effect. (Plato's devaluing of the emotions was to have a powerful effect on *Stoicism.) Plato then turns abruptly to giving a proof of the immortality of the *soul, which will undergo reincarnation according to the soul's own choice, and ends with the myth of Er, who returned to life twelve days after his death and described the fate of souls after death and the cycles of rebirth.

**republic, Roman** *See* ROMAN REPUBLIC.

**Res Gestae** Inscription in Latin (with Greek translation) found in 1555 at Ancyra (modern Ankara, hence the alternative name Monumentum Ancyranum), engraved on the walls of the temple of Rome and Augustus. It contains the text of one of the four documents written by the emperor Augustus and read in the senate after his death, a 'record of his enterprises', *index rerum a se gestarum*, which, in accordance with his wish, was then engraved on bronze tablets and placed outside his mausoleum. The text is not preserved on manuscript, nor has the original inscription survived, but copies were set up in the provinces, of which this is one. Fragments of two other copies have been found at Apollonia and at Antioch, both in Pisidia.

**res publica (respublica)** *See* ROMAN REPUBLIC.

**Return of the Heracleidae** *See* HERACLEI-
DAE.

**Revenues (Poroi)** ('Ways and means', Lat.
*De vectigalibus*) One of the minor works of
*Xenophon, written not before 355 BC and
probably his last work. The ascription to him
has been doubted.

Xenophon discusses various means of increasing the revenue of Athens, so that she is
not constrained to oppress other cities. Harm-
less measures include encouraging the resident aliens (metics), who were engaged in
manufacturing and trade generally; among ingenious suggestions for investment is that accommodation could be rented to visitors and
slaves hired out to operators of the Laurium
silver-mines (a transaction from which the author expected a return of 33 per cent on the
capital expended).

**rex sacrō'rum** ('king for the sacred rites') At
Rome after the expulsion of the kings (510 BC;
*see* TARQUIN (2)), a priest whose duty it was to
perform some of the king's religious functions.
He was a patrician, married by *confarreatio*,
appointed for life, and unlike the *pontifex
maximus* (to whom he was superior in rank
and precedence though inferior in religious
authority) disqualified from playing any part
in political life: he did not even sit in the senate. He and his wife (*regīna*, 'queen', who also
had some religious duties) held a sacrifice on
the Kalends and occasionally appeared in the
Comitium and sacrificed there.

**Rhadama'nthys** (Lat. Rhadamanthus) In
myth, son of Zeus and *Europa; he did not
die but went to *Elysium, where he became a
ruler; in some accounts he was made judge of
the dead in the Underworld, with *Minos and
*Aeacus. In Virgil he presides over *Tartarus
and punishes the wicked.

**Rhampsinī'tus, Rameses III** Pharaoh of
Egypt, of whom the Greek historian Herodotus
(2.121) tells the following folk-tale. He had a
treasury built, in the wall of which the builder
secretly left a movable stone. After his death
the builder's sons, by means of this, were able
to creep in and steal the treasure. The king,
finding the seals of the door unbroken but the
treasure diminished, set a man-trap, in which
one of the brothers was caught. He immediately called to his brother and bade him cut off his

head and take it away to avoid detection, which
was done. (*Cf.* TROPHONIUS.)

**rhapsode, rhapsodist** [Gk. *rhapsōdos*,
'one who stitches songs together', perhaps by
the formulaic technique; *see* ORAL POETRY] In
Greece, a professional reciter of poetry, usually
of Homer (i.e. epic), but also of other poems.
Rhapsodes were a familiar sight at public festivals and games, where they competed for
prizes (at least down to the third century AD)
by reciting from memory. Plato's dialogue *Ion*
is a satire on their pretensions.

**Rhēa** In Greek myth, one of the *Titans,
daughter of Uranus and Gaia, wife (and sister)
of *Cronus, mother of Zeus and other Olympian gods. The Romans identified her with *Ops.

**Rhēa Si'lvia** *See* ILIA.

**Rhēsus** One of the 'selected' tragedies of
*Euripides, but only doubtfully attributed to
him in modern times; if it is his work, it
would appear to be earlier than any other of
his extant plays.

*Rhesus* is a dramatization of the tenth book
of Homer's *Iliad*; the action takes place at
night. The Greeks have been driven back to
their ships, and Hector sends the Trojan
Dolon by night to spy out their intentions.
Rhesus, king of Thrace, arrives at Troy with
his army to support the Trojans. Hector reproaches him for his delay; Rhesus replies
proudly and confidently, and then retires to
rest. Odysseus and Diomedes enter the Trojan
camp; they have killed Dolon after learning the
password from him. Directed by the goddess
Athena they fall upon the sleeping Thracians,
kill Rhesus, and lead away his magnificent
horses. His charioteer relates his death by an
unknown hand and accuses Hector of his murder. Hector is exculpated by the Muse Terpsichore, mother of Rhesus, who descends from
heaven to carry off her son's body. The bones
of Rhesus are connected with the foundation of
Amphipolis.

**rhētor** (Gk. and Lat. *rhetor*) At Athens originally, a public speaker in the *ecclesia, a politician; later at Athens, and at Rome, a teacher of
public speaking, a rhetorician.

**rhetoric** The theoretical art of public
speaking so as to persuade; it is *oratory reduced to a system which can be taught.
The earliest teachers, *rhetors, were Corax

and Teisias, who were active in Sicily in the middle of the fifth century BC when the rule of tyrants gave place to democracy; the law-suits which followed this change of constitution are said to have given Corax the idea of systematizing and writing down the rules for speaking in a law-court. According to Aristotle, *Empedocles too played some part in this development. *Gorgias of Leontini (in Sicily) brought this new style of public speaking to Athens in 427 BC, adopting in particular a poetic style, although it is clear from the earlier plays of Euripides that oratory was already a developed art in the city. Gorgias' influence has been detected in the speeches of Thucydides and *Isocrates. The teaching of rhetoric was part of the stock-in-trade of many *sophists, some of whom specialized in particular aspects of the subject, such as semantics or figures of speech. The sophists and rhetors laid emphasis on the techniques necessary for winning over an audience. The teaching of this kind of rhetoric aroused the hostility of Socrates and especially of Plato, who thought that persuasive speech should be based on knowledge of the truth, and thus introduced the idea of an opposition between rhetoric which aimed to persuade and philosophy which aimed to grasp the truth (*see* GORGIAS). The theoretical study of rhetoric was further developed by Aristotle (*see* ARISTOTLE 4 (vii)), who was probably the first to divide oratory into three kinds, forensic (or judicial), deliberative (or political), and *epideictic (the oratory of 'display', as in a funeral oration or a speech in praise of a person), each with its own particular style.

At Rome during the first century BC (as a consequence of the spread of Greek culture among an aristocracy active in politics) the study of rhetoric became an important part of *education and it exercised an increasing influence on Roman literature during the empire. The elements of rhetoric were treated under the five aspects in which an orator should be competent: invention, arrangement, style, memory, delivery. 'Invention' was the discovery (*inventio*) of the relevant material; 'arrangement' entailed putting the materials together in a structured way; 'style' concerned finding the appropriate register of speech for the occasion, grand, middle, or plain (sometimes known as low or simple). 'Memory' gave guidance on how to memorize speeches, and 'delivery' on the techniques of public speaking.

The following deal with rhetoric: Aristotle, *Rhetoric*; Cicero, *Brutus*, *De inventione*, *De optimo genere oratorum*, *De oratore*; *Demetrius (3); *Dionysius of Halicarnassus, *On the Arrangement of Words*; *Hermogenes; *Longinus on the Sublime*; *Quintilian, *Institutio oratoria*; Tacitus, *Dialogus de oratoribus*; and the *Rhetorica ad Herennium*.

**Rhetoric** Treatise in three books by Aristotle. This and the *Poetics* are the only examples we have of Aristotle's 'study of productive activity' in the arts. Because it is the business of the rhetorician to instruct the orator in the production of a convincing proof, *Rhetoric* is an enquiry into how to compose a good speech. Plato had distrusted *rhetoric on the grounds that it was not based on knowledge. The sophists and Isocrates, however, established the study of rhetoric as the foundation for the higher *education of young men likely to be political aspirants. Aristotle claims that rhetoric is not a mere 'producer of persuasion' (Plato's disparaging phrase) but is worthy to be classed as an art or skill (*techne*), a technique for discovering the persuasive aspects of a case, which in Aristotle's treatment frequently resembles dialectic.

After an introduction on the nature of rhetoric in general Aristotle discusses the three different kinds—forensic, deliberative, and epideictic (for which *see* RHETORIC). Plato in *Phaedrus* had suggested that a rhetoric that was truly a *techne* would be based on knowledge of the 'soul' of the audience. Aristotle takes up the hint by stating the need first to take account of the emotions and prejudices of the audience (with perhaps a certain amount of self-contradiction in the matter of what constitutes proof). He proceeds to the role of argument and those aspects common to all species of proof—the use to be made of possibility, the citing of similar cases, comparisons, maxims, and so on. Finally he deals with composition, points of style, and use of metaphor. In the matter of composition, since the two main functions of a speech are to state the case and prove it, the speech should be structured accordingly. It therefore must cover the narrative of events, proof, prejudice, and refutation. An effective peroration should round it all off: 'I have spoken, you have heard, you have the facts, judge.' The basic virtues of style are clarity and appropriateness: nouns and verbs make for clarity, ancillary words convey appropriateness.

Like the *Poetics* (in the case of tragedy), the *Rhetoric* achieves something additional to its main purpose: it is the first aesthetic evaluation of prose style. With its wealth of apt and enlightening examples it is one of Aristotle's most engaging works, and the most influential of all treatises on the subject.

**Rhēto'rica ad Here'nnium** ('To Herennius, on public speaking') Latin treatise on oratory in four books, written probably between c.86 and 82 BC and addressed to an unidentified C. Herennius by an unknown author; some attribute it to a certain Cornificius, on slight evidence in Quintilian. It is ascribed in the manuscripts to Cicero, and it seems connected in some way with the source of Cicero's early *De inventione*. *Rhetoric is treated under its five aspects; the section on style (book 4) is the oldest surviving treatment in Latin and rich in examples (most from Latin). Despite being modelled on Greek writers, the work is highly critical of Greek rhetoricians and the writer has taken pains to give it a Roman flavour. Its date makes it interesting as a relatively early example of Latin prose.

**rhētra** *See* LYCURGUS and TYRTAEUS.

**Rhodō'pē (Rhodō'pis)** ('Rosie') Nickname of Doricha, a Greek courtesan, said to have been a Thracian and a fellow-slave of Aesop, and to have been taken to Naucratis in Egypt. In a fragmentary poem the Greek poet Sappho mocks her brother Charaxos after he apparently bought Rhodope her freedom.

**Rōbī'gus** (female equivalent Robigo) In Roman religion, the god of 'blight' who averted red mildew or rust from crops. He was propitiated and the pest averted by the annual sacrifice of a rust-coloured dog at the festival of the Robigalia on 25 April, when the stalks were well up and the ears at risk.

**Roman age of Greek literature** Term used to describe Greek literature written from the time when Rome subjugated Greece and the Mediterranean world, i.e. from the second half of the second century BC, to AD 529, when the emperor Justinian closed the schools of philosophy at Athens and ended the long history of that city as a focus of Greek intellectual life and culture. *See also* SECOND SOPHISTIC.

**romance** *See* NOVEL.

**Roman empire** Term applied to (i) the government of Rome under Augustus, the first Roman emperor, and his successors (*see* PRINCIPATE), and (ii) the lands governed by the Romans at any time from about the third century BC, when her power began to expand beyond the Italian peninsula. For the division of the empire into two halves, *see* BYZANTINE AGE and FALL OF ROME.

**Roman republic** Term meaning either (i) the period in Roman history between the abolition of monarchy in 510 BC (*see* KINGS OF ROME) and the accession of Augustus, the first emperor, in 27 BC, or (ii) more loosely, the Roman government of this period, often expressed simply as 'Rome', the seat of Roman authority. The Latin words *res publica* mean 'affairs of state', 'the state' itself, or 'the constitution' of the state. The Roman constitution was that of a republic in the modern sense of the word, in that the supreme power rested with the people; arbitrary rule by an individual (monarchy or tyranny) or by a small group (oligarchy) was renounced, and the right to take part in political life was given to all adult (male) citizens. Although it was thus nominally a democracy in that all laws had to be approved by an assembly of citizens, the republic was in fact organized as an aristocracy or broad-based oligarchy, governed in practice by a fairly small group of about fifty noble families (*see* NOBILES) who regularly held all the *magistracies (but *see* NOVUS HOMO). Magistracies had to be held in a fixed order (*see* CURSUS HONORUM) before a candidate could hold the highest office of all, the consulship. The two consuls, who had equal authority, were in charge of the state for their year of office, their powers limited by the laws and by each other's potential veto and that of the ten *tribunes.

Citizens exercised their political rights in assemblies, *comitia*, and were divided into *tribes or centuries according to the nature of the *assembly. These, however, were far from democratic. The citizens voted only on proposals by the magistrates and could not amend them. The *comitia* themselves discriminated against various classes of voters, and no attempt at reform ever succeeded. Under the empire the election of magistrates and the judicial and legislative functions of the *comitia* lapsed, though they continued in formal existence until the third century AD. In elections and all other matters put to the assemblies, decision was reached by the votes of a majority of these groups; an individual's vote merely helped determine that of his group. The groups of the rich and powerful voted first; those to which the poorest people were allotted voted last. Since the result was declared as soon as a simple majority was reached, the last groups rarely voted at all (see PROLETARII). Voting took place only at Rome, with the consequence that those living in rural areas were usually unable to vote. The assemblies were not deliberative; they could only approve or reject policy decided elsewhere. The sole deliberating body was the senate, which decided upon all policy, relating to both home and foreign affairs. A citizen was not free to address an assembly without the consent of the magistrates and tribunes, who alone had the right to summon a public meeting and to debate. The members of the assembly could only express an unofficial opinion, by shouting, for example.

This organization was reflected in the towns (*municipia*) throughout Italy; their citizens were also (in the later republic) citizens of Rome but the towns retained local autonomy, with their own senate and senators (known as *decuriones*).

See also DICTATOR; ROME; ORDERS, CONFLICT OF.

**Roman revolution, the** See GRACCHI (1) and ROME 4.

**Rome (Rōma)** Ancient Rome stood on the left bank of the river Tiber, about 22km (14 miles) from the sea, in the territory of *Latium near its northern boundary, south of Etruria. The site was already inhabited in the second half of the second millennium BC. Rome's history is divided into three main periods: a largely obscure early period ending when the last king was expelled and a republic set up in 510/509 BC; the republic, lasting from then until 27 BC, when Augustus became the first emperor; and the empire, which ended in the West when the last emperor, Romulus Augustulus, was deposed in AD 476. See also PRINCIPATE.

**1. Early history.** For our information about the foundation and early history of Rome we rely mainly on historians who were writing more than 500 years after the event (see HISTORIOGRAPHY [Roman]), and who were using accounts, now lost themselves, written not before the end of the fourth century BC. By that time it

was not easy to distinguish between fact and legend. Moreover, a desire that Rome should share in some way in Greek achievements had led the Romans to connect their history with that of Greece. By tradition the city was founded by *Romulus in 753 BC (a date fixed by Varro; the first settlement on the site was in fact much earlier). Romulus was given an invented ancestry that made him a grandson of King Numitor of *Alba Longa and a descendant of Aeneas (see also LAVINIUM). The Latin element (see LATINI) was also important: *Latinus' daughter Lavinia became the wife of Aeneas. Reputedly under the kingship of Servius Tullius, but more likely in the fourth century BC, the city was enclosed within a wall (the Servian wall, so called) and now comprised the *seven hills of Rome. The four regions were also created at this time (see REGIONES). Under the kings Rome was a great hill-top fortress, with the Capitoline hill (see CAPITOLIUM) equivalent to the Acropolis at Athens, and with the Aventine hill as a religious centre. According to tradition the city was ruled after Romulus by a succession of six kings (see KINGS OF ROME), some at least of whom have a historical basis. Other kings, such as *Titus Tatius, are recorded who are not in the canonical list.

There appear to have been many wars during the early regal period as a result of which Roman territory was enlarged. Rome destroyed Alba, according to legend, when Tullus Hostilius was king (see HORATII AND CURIATII), and under Ancus Marcius founded a colony at Ostia near the mouth of the Tiber. *Etruscan influence became strong at Rome under *Tarquin (1), said to be an adventurer, half Greek and half Etruscan, who came to try his fortune at Rome and won the throne, and under his two successors (see KINGS OF ROME). It may be that the Etruscans, a powerful commercial and industrial people, conquered Rome; or they may simply have accepted Tarquin as their king.

The Tarquins were expelled in 510 BC, and with their departure the probable domination by Etruscans was ended; despite the efforts at restoration by Lars *Porsen(n)a, monarchy was abolished at Rome. The struggle is reflected in the famous legend of the rape of *Lucretia.

**2. The early republic, 509–290 BC.** The constitution which followed in 509 BC was an aristocratic republic. The king was replaced by two magistrates elected annually (*praetors, later called *consuls). In times of national crisis, their powers might be temporarily superseded by the appointment of a *dictator, but the *senate was now the real governing force in the state. The history of the republic during the next 250 years consists in the main of two struggles: an internal class struggle between the privileged *patricians and the *plebeians who had few rights, during which the republican constitution was hammered out (*see* ORDERS, CONFLICT OF); and an external struggle with the surrounding peoples, at first mainly defensive but subsequently aggressive, at the end of which Rome emerged supreme as the head of a confederacy embracing all Italy. The conflict of the orders saw the plebeians gradually admitted to various offices of state and ended in 287 with the Hortensian Law (passed by the dictator Quintus Hortensius), which made the decrees of the *concilium plebiss* ('assembly of the people') binding on all Romans, not only the plebeians. The outcome of the struggle was the formation of a mixed patrician and plebeian oligarchy of *nobiles*, who monopolized office as exclusively as the patricians alone had done hitherto.

In its external relations, in this early period of the republic, Rome had to face assaults from every side (the legends of Lars *Porsen(n)a, *Horatius Cocles, *Cloelia, and Mucius *Scaevola all refer to Rome's struggles with Etruria). At the beginning of the fifth century BC Rome was faced with a revolt of the Latins (*see* REGILLUS, LAKE), but military alliance enabled Romans and Latins to resist invasions by neighbouring Sabines, Aequi, and Volsci. In the second half of the fifth century Rome passed from defence to aggression, capturing the Etruscan town of Veii in 396 BC, but in about 385 BC Rome itself was sacked by the Gauls, except for the Capitol (according to the usual legend), which was bravely held by a small force under M. Manlius Capitolinus (*see* MANLIUS for the story of the geese saving the Capitol). Thereafter the city was rebuilt and refortified, and Rome entered on a long and arduous period of expansion. A crucial event was the great Latin war of 341–338 (*see* LATIN LEAGUE): Rome's victory and the subsequent settlement were decisive for her expansion. For seventy years she was at odds with the Samnites, a warlike mountain-people of the Abruzzi, east of Rome, before finally subduing them in 295.

**3. The republic, 290–133 BC.** During the third century BC Rome was drawn into southern Italy, where the Greek cities of Magna Graecia were being hard pressed by Lucanian tribes, and by 270 had subjugated the whole region. By successful wars against the Umbrians, Picentes, and Sallentini in 270–266 she became supreme in the whole peninsula south of the river Rubicon, forcing all its peoples to become allies. *Tarentum, which had summoned *Pyrrhus in 280, submitted finally in 272. Peace was at last substituted for war as the normal condition of life in Italy. Rome did not force her civilization on others, but gradually local languages, cults, and customs gave way to a common culture based on the *Latin language and Roman *law. When Ptolemaic Egypt entered into a treaty of friendship (*amicitia*) with Rome in 273 it signalized the fact that Rome was now a Mediterranean power. This was the era to which Romans looked back nostalgically as to an ideal time, the formative period of the Roman character when life was simple and austere, and morality uncorrupted.

As a Mediterranean power Rome came into contact with Carthaginian interests in Sicily. The conflict with Carthage and Rome's eventual triumph (*see* PUNIC WARS) gave her control of the western Mediterranean, and Sicily and Sardinia became her first provinces. Rome wished for no further conquests, but she desired security and that meant crushing any rival power. The alliance of Philip V of Macedon with Carthage provoked the Macedonian wars (*see* FLAMININUS), and Macedonia was annexed as a province in 146. A long series of Spanish campaigns, terminated in 133 by the capture of Numantia, resulted in the subjugation of the greater part of Spain. In the same year Attalus of Pergamum bequeathed his dominions to Rome (*see* ATTALIDS). These were formed into the Roman province of Asia. In the West the southern part of Gaul was made a province, known simply as Provincia, later Gallia Narbonensis, in 121 (*see* GAUL 2). There was thus an enormous expansion of Roman territory in the second century BC. At the same time economic and social life in Rome and Italy underwent profound changes. In many parts peasant husbandry had given place to capitalist farming of huge estates (*see* LATIFUNDIA). Industry and commerce had expanded generally and, although the aristocracy did not take part in these enterprises, the *equites* (*see* EQUESTRIAN ORDER) were considerably enriched. The patrician-plebeian elite dominated the senate. Slavery increased, both on the land and in households. Rome quite suddenly acquired immense wealth from booty and tribute, there was a great increase in luxury of all kinds, and great public building works were undertaken. In all spheres, art and architecture, literature and religion, Greek culture became pervasive; the earliest Roman historians actually wrote in Greek (see HISTORIOGRAPHY [Roman]).

### 4. The republic and the civil wars, 133–27 BC.

The last century of the Roman republic was a period of acute social and political struggle, starting with the election of Ti. Gracchus as tribune in 133 BC initiating what has become known as 'the Roman revolution'(see GRACCHI). There was discontent in the provinces, whose governors were often unscrupulous and ambitious, seeking to enrich themselves and to acquire power. Army commanders were also personally ambitious, and the army increasingly looked to them rather than to the senate to provide bounties and distributions of land, thus introducing a dangerous element into political life. The senate itself had become more oligarchic and less democratic in its attitudes, showing exclusivity towards the Italian allies, denying them citizenship and many of the spoils of war which they had helped to win. The first attempt to deal with some of these problems was made by the Gracchi, who tried to reform agrarian laws in favour of the poorer citizens. Their eventual failure was followed by a conservative reaction, and by a war with *Jugurtha (112–105), a (second) slave revolt in Sicily (104–101), and an invasion of Italy by the Germanic Cimbri and Teutones. These conflicts were conducted so ineffectually by the senate that the people and *equites* acting together had Metellus (see METELLI (2)) superseded and the command given to *Marius. The latter's eventual dispute with *Sulla for the command against Mithridates of Pontus led to Sulla's march on Rome in 88 at the head of his legions, and ushered in a period of civil war and bloodshed. Meanwhile a war had broken out in 91 between Rome and her Italian allies (Socii), known as the *Social War (91–87 BC). It was settled by Rome conceding full citizenship to the allies. Sulla was established as dictator in 81 and sought to re-establish the power of the senate over the tribunate and over army commanders, but these measures did not long survive his retirement in 79.

The second stage of Rome's civil wars is associated with the names of *Pompey, Julius *Caesar, *Crassus, and *Cicero. In this struggle all thoughts about the good of the republic gave way to the ambitions of individuals who sought power for themselves alone. Their fortune was built on their conquests as military commanders and they enjoyed what amounted to private control over loyal and effective troops, who realized that their own profit depended upon the success of their leaders. In 60 was formed the compact between Caesar, Pompey, and Crassus known (in modern times only) as 'the first triumvirate', by which they secured for themselves a commanding position in the state. Pompey had popular support, Crassus money, and Caesar calculated cunning. This compact endured, while Caesar was conquering Gaul and Britain, until Crassus was killed and the Romans defeated by the Parthians at Carrhae in 53, after which the senate was powerless, order almost entirely broke down (see CLODIUS), and rivalry between Caesar and Pompey developed into war. Pompey was utterly defeated by Caesar at Pharsalus (in Thessaly) and was murdered in Egypt in 48. Whether or not Caesar intended to end the republic, his dictatorship introduced the principle of personal autocracy into the constitution (see DICTATOR). His programme of legislation was idealistic but he showed himself to have monarchical, anti-republican tendencies and his reforms were cut short by his assassination at the hands of senatorial conspirators in 44. Instead of the restoration of the republic which the conspirators had hoped for, a third round of civil war followed. Mark *Antony, Caesar's colleague in the consulship of 44 and at first the natural leader of the Caesarian party, found his position threatened by Octavian, Caesar's heir. Antony's defeat at the battle of Actium in 31 and his suicide at Alexandria in 30 left Octavian sole master of Rome and all her territories, and in 27—as Augustus—he became the first emperor.

### 5. The *Principate or early empire, 27 BC–AD 192.

One reason for the collapse of the republic was the lack of a large bureaucracy capable of managing the very complicated empire Rome now governed; another was the rise of military dictators. Using the framework of the old republic Augustus created a new system which was to some extent a compromise: he retained sole control of the military forces and foreign policy as well as general supervision over the machinery of government, but he left a share in administration to the senators and, especially, to the *equites*. Augustus himself adopted the outward appearance and mode of life of a republican magistrate, but his real position far exceeded that of a magistrate and he was in effect raised to a monarchical position. He made a great effort to restore by legislation the traditional religion and morality of the Roman people and to restrain luxury. The effect of his laws for this purpose was at best only temporary. As regards foreign policy, ambitious plans in the East were abandoned, and the efforts of the empire concentrated on the Romanization of Gaul and the acquisition of a strong frontier in the West. During the subsequent 300 years the centre of gravity of the empire was to shift to the East, the constitution of Augustus was to be radically modified, and in the end the West was to be overrun by barbarians. But none of this was to happen until Augustus' aims of Romanizing western Europe had been achieved in a form that would to some extent survive these upheavals.

Augustus died in AD 14. The next four emperors—Tiberius, Caligula, Claudius, and Nero—were related by blood or adoption and are known as the Julio-Claudian emperors, AD 14–68. Events of this period included the conquest of Britain in 43 (under Claudius) and the burning of Rome in 64 (under Nero). The fire gave Nero the opportunity to begin rebuilding Rome on an imposing scale, and he drew up regulations for broad, orderly streets in place of the twisting alleys of the old city. His own great monument, the *Golden House, was destroyed after his death, but this made available to his successors a large area for building, on which were erected some of Rome's greatest landmarks over the next half-century, above all the *Colosseum.

When Nero committed suicide in 68, the last of Augustus' line, there was no constitutional provision for the succession, and civil war broke out, resulting in the 'year of the four emperors', 69. Galba, Otho, and Vitellius were successively and very briefly made emperor by provincial armies until stability was restored under the wise and efficient rule of Vespasian (69–79) and his sons, Titus and Domitian (although Domitian's final years were despotic). Vespasian restored by prudent economy the finances which had been utterly wrecked by the civil war and the prodigality of Nero, strengthened the existing frontiers, and admitted more provincials into the senate so that it became more representative of the empire. Vespasian's son Domitian was succeeded by Nerva, who ruled briefly (96–8) and then by Trajan (98–117). Under Trajan, Hadrian (117–38), and the *Antonines (138–92) the Roman empire reached its greatest extent, stretching from Scotland to North Africa and from Spain to the Persian Gulf, and its peak of peace and prosperity. In a famous passage in his *Decline and Fall of the Roman Empire* Edward Gibbon memorably evoked this age: 'If a man were called to fix the period in the history of the world, during which the condition of the human race was most happy and prosperous, he would, without hesitation, name that which elapsed from the death of Domitian [96] to the accession of Commodus [180].'

**6. Decline and fall, AD 192–476.** As Gibbon's words suggest, it is with Commodus (180–92) that the decline of the empire is usually said to begin. After his murder there was civil war, but Septimius Severus (193–211) established a new dynasty, which ruled until 235. His son Caracalla (211–17) extended Roman citizenship to all freemen throughout the empire. When the last of the dynasty, his cousin Alexander Severus (222–35), was murdered, military anarchy followed, with emperors succeeding one another rapidly and increasingly bad government in the provinces. The frontiers were under pressure from invaders—particularly the Goths in the north—who would eventually overrun the empire (*see* FALL OF ROME). Diocletian (284–305) divided the empire into four administrative units, two eastern and two western, ruled by joint emperors. Constantine (306–37) restored the unity of the empire and moved his capital from Rome to Constantinople, founded on the Greek city of Byzantium, making it his imperial residence in the East. Theodosius I (379–95) was the last ruler of a unified Roman state, the division between east and west becoming permanent at his death. In 402 the capital of the western empire was moved from Rome to Ravenna, and Rome was sacked by Visigoths in 410 and Vandals in 455. The last Roman emperor in the west, Romulus Augustulus, was deposed in 476 by Odoacer, who became the first barbarian king of Italy.

For a period of almost a thousand years after this, Rome declined, and—even though it was the seat of the papacy—became of only marginal or intermittent importance in European affairs. Its history from the fifth to the fourteenth century is one of extraordinary strife and chaos, and it was sacked by the Arabs in 846 and the Normans in 1084. The population, which at the height of the Roman empire probably reached a million, had dropped by the fourteenth century to about 20,000. Large areas within the ancient walls were densely wooded and inhabited by wild beasts, and sometimes only the tops of ancient buildings projected above piles of debris. It was Pope Martin V (reigned 1417–31) who began the restoration of Rome to a great city.

**Ro'mulus** The legendary founder of Rome, his name meaning simply 'Roman'. He and his twin brother Remus (in most Greek authors, Rhomos) were grandchildren of Numitor, king of *Alba Longa, who had been deposed by his younger brother Amulius. To ensure that Numitor's only child, Rhea Silvia, did not marry and produce an heir, Amulius made her a Vestal Virgin, but the god Mars fathered twins upon her. Amulius imprisoned the mother and threw the children into the Tiber. They were washed ashore and suckled by a she-wolf (*see* RUMINA) until discovered by the royal herdsman Faustulus, who with his wife Acca Larentia brought them up. Being eventually recognized they overthrew Amulius and restored Numitor to his kingdom. They then decided to found a new settlement where they had been washed ashore. An omen in the form of a flight of birds settled the kingship in favour of Romulus. He proceeded to build the city named after him on the Palatine Hill; the traditional date for his foundation is 753 BC. Remus showed his contempt for it by jumping over the beginnings of the city wall, and was thereupon killed by Romulus or his lieutenant Celer. Romulus expanded his new city by offering asylum to all fugitives, including slaves and criminals. To secure wives for his people he invited the neighbouring *Sabines to witness the newly established games, the Consualia, during which the Romans carried off the Sabine women ('the Rape of the Sabines', of which there are many ancient versions). War followed, but eventually the two peoples settled down together. It was said that Romulus ruled for forty years until 715 and then disappeared from the earth, enveloped in a cloud during a thunderstorm. Soon after, he made known his divinity as the god *Quirinus to an individual, Proculus Julius. The antiquity of the story is much debated, as is its meaning. It was well known by the beginning of the third century BC, and is retold by, for example, Livy and Plutarch. An alternative story was that Romulus was murdered and 'disappeared' by being cut into tiny pieces and hidden in the senators' togas.

**Ro'mulus Augu'stulus** Last emperor of Rome, AD 475–6; *see* FALL OF ROME.

**Ro'scius Gallus, Quintus** (d. 62 BC) The most famous comic actor of his day at Rome, who also played tragic roles. A member of the equestrian order, he amassed great wealth and was on intimate terms with Catullus and Sulla. Cicero defended him in a private suit (*see* CICERO (1) 1). Though handsome he had a squint, and to conceal it is reported to have introduced into Rome the wearing of masks when acting, wigs having been worn previously. The name of Roscius is occasionally used in English literature to denote a great actor.

**Rosetta Stone** Slab of black basalt from Egypt, now in the British Museum, on which is inscribed an Egyptian decree of 197 BC honouring the king Ptolemy V Epiphanes. The inscription is given in three versions, Greek and two forms of Egyptian: hieroglyphics ('priestly picture-writing') and demotic, the simplified form of hieroglyphic in common use. The discovery of the stone in 1799 made possible the eventual decipherment of hieroglyphics by the French scholar Jean-François Champollion (1790–1832), by first picking out repeated names spelt phonetically rather than pictorially.

**Royal Road** Highway in Persia, described by Herodotus as running from the capital Susa to Sardis (about 2,500km or 1,550 miles) and part of a network linking the royal residences from the Indus to Sardis. Its system of fast couriers greatly impressed the Greeks. (*See also* EUCLID.)

**Ru'bicon** Small Italian river, reddish in colour (hence the name, from *rubicundus*, 'ruddy'), flowing into the Adriatic and marking the boundary in republican times between Italy and the province of Cisalpine Gaul. Julius Caesar, by crossing the river into Italy in 49 BC without disbanding his army as the senate had ordered, effectively declared war on Pompey and the senate. Suetonius gives Caesar the words, *iacta alea est*, 'the die is cast'. 'Crossing the Rubicon' is proverbial for taking an irrevocable decision.

**Rudens** ('The rope') Romantic comedy by *Plautus adapted from a Greek comedy by Diphilus (*see* COMEDY [Greek 6]). This is one of Plautus' best plays, with a well-integrated plot, interesting characterization, and lively dialogue.

The prologue is spoken by the star Arcturus. The scene is the rocky coast of Cyrene near a temple of Venus and the country house of an elderly Athenian, Daemones, whose daughter Palaestra was stolen from him in her childhood. She has fallen into the hands of a young pimp, Labrax of Cyrene; a young Athenian, Plesidippus, has fallen in love with her, and made part-payment for her purchase. But Labrax has thought to improve his fortunes by secretly carrying the girl off to Sicily. Thereupon Arcturus has raised a storm and wrecked the ship near the scene of the play. Palaestra and another girl reach land in a boat and are kindly tended by the priestess of Venus. Labrax is also washed ashore; he discovers the girls and tries to carry them off from the temple. They are defended by Daemones and presently rescued by Plesidippus, who marches Labrax off to justice. A box belonging to Labrax is pulled from the sea in the net of a fisherman, who quarrels over it with a slave of Plesidippus while hauling on the rope (*rudens*) of the net; the quarrel leads to the discovery in the box not only of the gold of Labrax but also of trinkets belonging to Palaestra, which show her to be the lost daughter of Daemones. There is joyful recognition, followed by the betrothal of Palaestra to Plesidippus.

**Rufus, Quintus Cu'rtius** *See* CURTIUS.

**ruler cult** Ruler cult first appears clearly during the reign of *Alexander the Great, inspired by his belief in his own divinity after being addressed by the priest of Ammon at Siwa in 331 BC as 'son of Amon-Ra' (the Egyptian equivalent of Zeus, according to Herodotus). Some cities gave him divine cult, and some of his successor-kings (*Diadochi) became recipients similarly. The cult of the Ptolemies at Alexandria began in 285 BC. Though cults of kings gradually became accepted, the propriety of the practice for human beings was often debated. It seems to have been a tangible demonstration of the accepted power of the king. Roman ruler cult started with Julius Caesar immediately before his assassination, when he was accorded certain rights appropriate only to a god. When the comet appeared at the games held in his honour in the summer of 44 BC, after his death, it was taken as evidence of his apotheosis. He was formally deified on the first day of 42 BC. *See* DEIFICATION and LYSANDER.

**Rumī'na** In Roman religion, goddess who protected mothers suckling their children. She had a sanctuary at the foot of the Palatine hill, where the *ficus Ruminalis* stood, the fig-tree under which *Romulus and Remus were supposed to have been suckled by the wolf.

**Sabā'zios** Phrygian god introduced to Athens in the fifth century BC. Aristophanes refers to him, and wrote a comedy (now lost) in which, Cicero tells us, Sabazios and other foreign gods were brought to trial and expelled from the state. His worship, which apparently included wine drinking and women uttering cries, had connections with that of the Magna Mater ('Great Mother'; *see* CYBELE), and private *mysteries were celebrated in his honour. During the Roman empire his worship was widespread and he was often identified with Zeus or Jupiter. Christians associated him with snake-handling.

**Sabe'lli** Collective name given by the Romans to the tribes of central *Italy who spoke the Oscan-type Italic languages. They include Samnites and Apulians. The Sabelli moved outwards from their original *Sabine homeland, imposing their language upon the populations they settled among; these migrations continued into the fourth century BC.

**Sabines** (Lat. Sabini) An Italian people living north-east of Rome in early times. By tradition they were the ancestors of all the Sabellian peoples (*see* SABELLI), and figure largely in the legends of early Rome, in which they are famous for their bravery, high morality, and strong religious feelings. Many stories indicate a Sabine element in the early development of Rome (*see* ROMULUS), probably arising rather from amalgamation than from conquest. However, Livy records Roman wars against the Sabines, ending in 449 BC (book 3) with a resounding Roman victory. In 290 BC M'. Curius Dentatus conquered them, and they were absorbed into the Roman state, receiving full citizenship in 268. For the Rape of the Sabines *see* ROMULUS. *See also* TITUS TATIUS.

**Sacred Band** (Gk. *hieros lochos*) At *Thebes, an elite corps of 300 hoplites chosen from noble families and professionally trained, formed in 378 BC by the general Gorgidas after the liberation of Thebes from Spartan occupation. The special character of the Sacred Band derived from its being composed of 150 pairs of lovers, each member bound to the other by strong emotional ties of love and loyalty. The corps had a notable leader in *Pelopidas. It was partly responsible for the Theban victories over Sparta at Leuctra in 371 and Mantinea in 362, but it was too small to carry a battle by itself, as was shown at the battle of *Chaeronea in 338 when Athens and Thebes were defeated by Philip II of Macedon. The Band did not share in the general flight but fought to the death. It was never re-formed.

**Sacred Way** At Rome, *see* VIA SACRA; at Athens, the road to Eleusis, leaving the Ceramicus district by the Sacred Gate (*see* MYSTERIES).

**sacrifice** [from Lat. *sacrificium*, 'making sacred']

1. The etymology shows that sacrifice was viewed as a transfer of ownership, a gift to the gods, or, as the occasion required, to heroes or the dead, who were also the recipients of offerings. Sacrifice could be offered for almost any event, and could be a public or a private affair. Except in the case of Underworld deities it was always made upon an altar.

2. *Bloodless offerings.* Fruit, vegetables, and special cakes and bread were offered in many Greek cults, especially to the gods of the Underworld; they were either laid on the altar or burnt. Cheese, honey, wine, and oil were also common offerings; *see* LIBATIONS.

3. *Blood offerings.* The slaughter and consumption of a domestic animal as offering to a god was the most popular form of ancient sacrifice. The most splendid sacrifice was that of a bull, but more usual was that of a sheep, goat, or pig (*see also* HECATOMB). Poultry were also commonly sacrificed, other birds and fish rarely (but *see* VULCAN). The animal was carefully chosen to be without blemish, and often had to be of a colour considered appropriate, e.g. light-coloured for celestial deities,

black for the gods of the Underworld and the dead (cf. the red dog sacrificed to *Robigus at Rome). In a public sacrifice of importance an animal, perhaps an ox, its horns gilded and entwined with ribbons, was escorted to the altar by a procession, preceded by a virgin carrying a basket with the sacrificial knife concealed in grains of barley or cakes. Someone also carried a vessel of water and perhaps incense.

When all stood around the altar, water was poured over the hands of the participants as well as sprinkled on the animal, causing it to jerk its head 'in consent'. An ox was given water to drink, so that he bowed his head and thus appeared a willing victim. The participants took handfuls of barley, and after a prayer to the god, threw them on the altar and on the animal. The official performing the sacrifice took the knife from the basket, cut some hairs from the victim, and threw them on the altar fire. Small animals were held over the altar and their throats cut; an ox was struck with an axe to stun it and its neck artery opened to the accompaniment of shrill cries from the women. The blood was caught in a bowl and poured over the altar. The animal was then skinned and cut up, and the entrails roasted on skewers at the fire. The important participants, perhaps the priests, ate the entrails first. The bones and fat were then burnt on the fire for the gods (*see* PROMETHEUS), together with other offerings such as cakes, and wine poured over so that the flames blazed. After this the rest of the meat was boiled to make a communal feast for those taking part. It was often prescribed for a particular sacrifice that all the meat must be consumed within the sanctuary; the priest was often permitted to keep the skin.

4. Although the principles and function of sacrificial ritual were largely the same in Greece and Rome, Roman sacrifice differed in small details from the Greek, described above, and could incorporate elements of three rituals, Greek, Roman, and Etruscan. At a Roman sacrifice the back of the victim was sprinkled with salted flour, *mola salsa* (hence the Latin *immolare*, 'to sacrifice'). When the dead victim was on its back the front was opened up and the vital organs (*exta*: peritoneum, heart, liver, gall-bladder, and lungs) inspected; if any presented an unusual appearance a fresh sacrifice had to be made. The *exta* were for the gods, the rest was for human consumption. In the Etruscan ritual the *exta* were examined for the purposes of *divination. Sacrifice was performed by the men in authority most suited to the occasion: priests, magistrates, or at Rome the *paterfamilias. Women could not celebrate a public sacrifice. In Roman sacrifices the sacrificer kept his head covered with his toga throughout; in Greece the head was kept uncovered. In both Greece and Rome the sacrifice was accompanied by music (usually on the *aulos, sometimes on the lyre).

There were also blood offerings which were not the prelude to a meal and in which the victim was completely burned; these were known (in Greek) as holocausts. They took place at purifications, at burial of the dead, to the gods of the Underworld and heroes, and before battles or at other times of crisis.

At some sacrifices animals were offered which were not considered human food, dogs to Hecate and Eileithyia, horses to Poseidon and Helios, and (at Rome) asses to Priapus, for example. A pregnant sow was offered to Demeter and Dionysus (to promote fertility).

5. Finds at some Mycenaean sites may indicate human sacrifice, and traces remain in stories. It was reported that at the sacrifice before the battle of Salamis in 480 BC captured Persians were substituted for animals. There were several myths of the sacrifice of—usually willing—maidens before battle, to which class the slaying of *Iphigeneia at Aulis belongs. There was a story that the Romans buried alive two Greeks and two Gauls in the Forum Boarium after the defeat at Cannae in 216 BC, and again in 113 BC when a Gallic invasion threatened. However, human sacrifice soon became abhorrent to the Romans, witness the measures they took against the Druids (*see* BRITAIN 1).

Modern interpreters sometimes see sacrifice as arising either among hunters who thereby atone for the crime of killing, or as a way of legitimizing the eating of meat by ritualizing what precedes it, i.e. the killing of animals.

*See also* ARCADIA and GYMNOSOPHISTS.

**saga** *See* MYTHOLOGY.

**Sa'lamis** 1. Island separated by a narrow channel from the south-west coast of Attica, near Piraeus. In Greek myth it was the home of Telamon, father of *Ajax (1). It originally belonged to Aegina, was occupied by Megara c.600 BC but was soon after conquered by Athens as a result of a stirring appeal by *Solon, thereafter sharing her fortunes. It was the scene in

September 480 BC of the great naval defeat of Persia by the Greeks (*see* PERSIAN WARS), and it was the birthplace of Euripides.

2. In Greek times the principal city of Cyprus, on the east coast, said to have been founded by Telamon's son *Teucer.

**Sa'lii** The Salian priests at Rome (also in many towns of central Italy), so called from the Latin *salire*, 'to dance'. Reputedly founded by Numa, they were an ancient college of twelve, later twenty-four, priests of Mars, of *patrician birth and having both parents living. They wore the distinctive armour of the archaic Italian foot-soldier, with sword, bronze breastplate, short military cloak (the *trabea*), and the conical felt cap, the *apex*. In their right hands they carried a spear or staff, and on their left arms the sacred figure-of-eight shields, *ancilia*. During March and October, the start and end of the campaigning season, the Salii went in procession through the city, halting at certain places and performing elaborate ritual dances, beating the shields with their staves and singing the *carmen saliare* ('Salian song') in the Saturnian metre, a song so ancient that according to Quintilian in the first century AD it had become almost unintelligible, even to the priests themselves. Sacrifices were made to obtain the gods' favour. A few fragments of the song survive. *Cf.* ARVAL BRETHREN.

**Sallust (Gaius Sallustius Crispus)** (86–35 BC) Roman historian, born at Amiternum in the Sabine country, perhaps of a local aristocratic family. He was tribune of the plebs in 52 BC, when he acted against Cicero (*see* CICERO (1) 4) and *Milo. It is said that the hostility he showed to Milo after the murder of Clodius in that year was the result of his being horsewhipped by Milo when caught in the act of adultery with the latter's wife. He was expelled from the senate in 50 BC, perhaps for playing a part in fomenting the riots of 52. He then joined Julius Caesar, commanding a legion in 49. Elected praetor in 47 he became governor of the province of eastern Numidia (Africa Nova) in 46, where he enriched himself considerably at the provincials' expense and was (unsuccessfully) charged with extortion upon his return to Rome. In this respect at least his life was at odds with the moral tenor of his writings. He withdrew from public life, became the owner of fine gardens, *horti Sallustiani*, and devoted the rest of his life to writing: two monographs

of near-contemporary history which survive, the *Bellum Catilinae* ('The War against *Catiline'), written *c.*41–40 BC concerning the events of 63–2 BC, and the *Bellum Iugurthinum* ('The Jugurthine War'), written 41–40 BC on events in Numidia 111–104 BC; *see* JUGURTHA. Of the *Historiae* ('Histories'), covering the period 78–67 BC (the years following Sulla's death in retirement in 78), we have only fragments. Despite his monographs being on subjects not of the first importance, Sallust is greatly admired for the incisive if occasionally over-compressed style in which, in a manner reminiscent of parts of Thucydides, whom he himself admired, he depicts the decay of public morals and growing lawlessness of Rome. His work shows an advance on his annalistic predecessors (*see* HISTORIOGRAPHY [Roman]) both in narrative powers and in its more scientific method: he aims to explain the causes of political events and the motives for men's actions. In the *Bellum Catilinae* his main source must have been Cicero, as well as his own recollection of events, but his heroes were Caesar and Cato the Younger (*see* CATO (2)) whose traditional attitudes he admires; their impressive speeches in the final debate of the senate to decide the fate of the conspirators are reported at length. For the slightly later *Bellum Iugurthinum*, a subject chosen partly 'because it represented the first challenge to the arrogance of the nobility' (*see* MARIUS), Sallust used a variety of sources including the autobiography of Sulla, and the *History* of Sisenna. He had gathered information while in Africa and had had what he refers to as 'Punic books' translated. In selecting Catiline and Jugurtha as subjects he was influenced, as he says himself, by the striking and potentially dangerous nature of their actions. His monographs also have as a theme the struggle of the *populares*, at successive stages, against the entrenched nobles.

Sallust's narrative is enlivened by speeches, letters, digressions, and character studies. Although his political thought is not profound it reflects an essentially Roman moralistic outlook, with emphasis on traditional *virtus* ('virtue'), and a pessimistic attitude towards contemporary corruption. He has also provided posterity with the starting-point of the late republic, dating Rome's moral collapse from the return of Sulla's booty-laden troops from the East and their bloody seizure of Rome in 82 BC. The ancient critics noted the characteristics of Sallust's style: the use of archaisms, brevity to the point of obscurity, innovative vocabulary, Graecisms, epigrams, rapidity. In these respects he influenced the style of later historical writers, and in particular Tacitus.

**Sa'lmacis** *See* HERMAPHRODITUS.

**Salmō'neus** In Greek myth, son of *Aeolus (2) and father of *Tyro, and consequently the ancestor of Pelias and Jason (*see* ARGONAUTS). He is placed by Virgil in the lowest depths of *Tartarus because of his impious arrogance in claiming to be the equal or even the superior of Zeus, driving about in a chariot of bronze to imitate thunder and throwing firebrands to imitate lightning. Zeus destroyed him and his city (Salmone in Elis) with a thunderbolt.

**Sā'mia** ('The girl from Samos') Greek comedy by *Menander, produced probably between 317 and 307 BC; four-fifths of it were recovered in the twentieth century from a papyrus.

While two neighbours, Demeas and Niceratus, are abroad, the latter's daughter Plangon gives birth to a baby by Demeas' son Moschion. A marriage is arranged, and Demeas' mistress Chrÿsis, who has suffered a miscarriage, agrees to keep the baby and pass it off as her own by Demeas. The neighbours return; Demeas overhears an old woman speak of the baby as Moschion's and concludes that since Moschion wants to marry Plangon he was unwillingly seduced by Chrysis. Demeas drives Chrysis and the baby out of the house whereupon they are taken in by Niceratus; both fathers are bewildered by conflicting evidence as to the identity of the baby's parents. Moschion, in despair, prepares to go abroad as a soldier, but eventually all is sorted out and the marriage takes place. (The happy resolution of the plot is lost.)

**Sappho** Greek lyric poet, born in the late seventh century BC at Eresus in *Lesbos, a contemporary of the Lesbian poet Alcaeus. Biographies written centuries later give us (unreliable) information about her life. Her father was Scamandronymus, her mother Clēis. While still young she went into exile in Sicily, presumably because of political troubles in Lesbos. (A statue of her erected in Sicily in the fourth century BC was stolen by the notorious Roman governor *Verres.) She returned to spend the rest of her life at Mytilene. She had three brothers, one of whom, Charaxos, a merchant, became expensively entangled with an Egyptian courtesan named *Rhodope. Sappho married Cercylas and had a daughter Cleis. A famous story related that she fell in love with a certain Phaon who rejected her and in consequence she threw herself off the cliff on Leucas (an island off the west coast of Greece). The date of her death is unknown.

Sappho's poetry, which was almost entirely monody (*see* LYRIC POETRY), was divided into nine books according to metre; book 1 consisted of poems in the sapphic metre, book 2 of poems in dactylic pentameters, and so on. The ninth book contained those epithalamia (*see* MARRIAGE SONGS) which did not fit into the other books for metrical and other reasons. Her dialect was the Lesbian vernacular, a branch of Aeolic Greek. Of her poems only the address to Aphrodite is probably complete; some passages have been preserved in quotations, but for the most part the poems are known from papyrus fragments discovered in the twentieth century. In the most recent (2004, from a mummy-cartonnage in Cologne) she regrets her old age but recalls the fate of *Tithonus. Her subject matter seems to be almost entirely confined to her personal world of family and female friends.

Sappho appears as a leading personality among a circle of women or girls who seem to have comprised her audience. Whether she was in some formal sense their teacher or mentor remains unclear. Her frequent references to partings and absence suggest that they shared their lives only briefly, perhaps before marriage. She was on intimate terms with them and wrote with great simplicity but passionate intensity about her love (and occasionally her hate) for individuals. Her two most famous poems are, first, the address to Aphrodite mentioned above in which she summons the goddess in a style reminiscent of a cult-song and asks to be delivered from unrequited love for a girl; and secondly a declaration of love for a girl, the mere sight of whom moves Sappho intensely while a young man sitting beside her seems godlike in his indifference (Catullus translated this in his poem 51). But she was not described as a lover of women until post-classical times, and there are no explicit references to physical relations in the surviving fragments. However, the poet *Anacreon a generation later seems to be indicating maliciously that the name of the island connotes female homosexuality. The epithalamia are different in tone from these two poems, in some ways more formal and less personal, and contain elements from Lesbian folk-song; but they too have a deceptive simplicity. Sappho created a form of subjective personal lyric never equalled in the ancient world in its immediacy and intensity.

**Sardinia** Taken over by Carthage *c*.500 BC, Sardinia became a Roman province with Corsica in 227 BC after the First Punic War and became an important granary.

**Sarpē'don** In Homer's *Iliad*, son of Zeus and Laodamia, leader (with *Glaucus, his friend and comrade in battle) of the Lycians, and the best warrior among the allies of the Trojans. His death by the spear of Patroclus (*Iliad* 16) is movingly recounted. His father Zeus had wanted to avert his death, but allowed it after being rebuked by Hera. He ordered Apollo to carry Sarpedon's body off the battlefield, and Sleep and Death bore it to Lycia for burial. According to another version Sarpedon was the son of Zeus and Europa, and brother of *Minos and *Rhadamanthys.

**satire** [Lat. *satura*, feminine form of the adjective *satur*, 'full'. Beyond this the origin of the word 'satire' is obscure, but like a stuffed sausage—one possible meaning—satire displays 'variety', 'mixture'] Quintilian claimed satire as 'entirely our own', i.e. a Roman creation: *satura quidem tota nostra est*. From a modern perspective the first satirists were the Greek poets *Archilochus and *Hipponax who wrote malicious *iambic poetry against their enemies, and the writers of Attic Old Comedy (*see* COMEDY [Greek 3]), notably Aristophanes, who attacked the personalities of the day, e.g. Cleon. (Horace at the beginning of his Satire 1.4 cites the authors of Old Comedy as forerunners.) Their influence is visible in the Cynic-Stoic *diatribes of *Bion the Borysthenite and *Menippus. However, it was a Roman achievement to develop satire as a separate literary genre characterized by variety of subject matter and occasionally of form (dialogue, fable, anecdote, precept, verse of various metres, combination of verse and prose). Livy describes as *saturae* early dramatic performances originally put on to placate the gods at a time of plague, combining song, music, and mimetic dancing. (Perhaps he was thinking of Greek *satyr plays.) The mixed literary form of 'satire' was a literary commentary from

a personal viewpoint. The author figures prominently, being good-humoured, biting, or moralizing, discoursing on current topics, social life, literature, and the faults of individuals, in a variety of assumed roles. Roman sources say *Ennius (239–169 BC) was the first to write satires in verse (among much else) but apparently without including invective. *Lucilius (*c*.180–*c*.102 BC) was the first to confine himself entirely to this genre, and it was he who gave it its outspoken character as well as establishing the hexameter as the appropriate metre for it. All later Roman satirists regarded him as their founding father and a symbol of republican liberty. He was followed by M. Terentius *Varro (116–27 BC), who took as a model the satires of Menippus in which prose and verse in a variety of metres were rather oddly intermingled, but who wrote in a less bitter, mildly didactic vein.

The *Satires* (1) of Horace, written in the 30s BC, show the strong influence of Lucilius but are inoffensive in tone, containing no dangerous invective against powerful individuals or serious vices, and the autobiographical stance aims to charm. *Persius (AD 34–62) also felt Lucilius' influence, but his satires, characterized by earnest Stoic moralizing, contain no direct attacks on individuals, and often seem puzzlingly disjointed. He entrusts his secrets only to a hole in the ground or a darkened study. His editor Cornutus toned down a line of verse which the emperor Nero might have resented.

The genre took a different direction in two brilliant Menippean satires which appeared in the reign of the emperor Nero (AD 54–68), Seneca's *Apocolocyntosis, a caricature of the deification of the late emperor Claudius, and the *Satyricon* of *Petronius. Roman satire reached its peak in the *Satires* (2) of Juvenal (published in the first part of the second century AD), whose bitter denunciations of the vice and folly of his own times (safely attached to names of people of the previous generation) embrace most men and all women. *Lucian's satirical prose dialogues are numerous and include some of his most characteristic work, giving him the opportunity to show his wit and inventiveness as well as his hatred of cant, hypocrisy, and fanaticism. In the *Icaromenippus* Menippus, equipped with wings like Icarus and disgusted with the disputes of philosophers, flies to heaven to find out the truth and hears the gods decide to destroy all philosophers as useless drones. He returns to earth to announce with glee to the philosophers their impending doom. In the *Menippus* he visits the Underworld to consult *Teiresias as to the best life to lead, and is told merely to do, with smiling face, the task that lies to hand. In *Nigrinus* and *De merce conductis* Lucian makes sharp observations on Roman culture from his own viewpoint as a Syrian Greek.

In the fourth century AD the emperor Julian wrote (in Greek but in the Roman tradition) the *Caesars*, a character-assessment of his predecessors. The form of Menippean satire, but not the tone or purpose, was followed by Martianus Capella in the *Marriage of Mercury and Philology* and by *Boethius in the *Consolation of Philosophy*.

**Satires** 1. By the Roman poet *Horace, two books of poetic 'conversations' (Lat. *Sermōnes*, also called by Horace *Saturae/Satirae*; *see* SAT-IRE) written in hexameters. The first book contains ten satires, the second eight. They were written in the 30s BC (the first refers to an event of 38 or 37, the second to the events of 30, and so they date from the last years of the Civil War and the first years of a precarious peace). Horace, who was writing the *Epodes* contemporaneously, presents in the first book of *Satires* his views on a variety of topics, moral and literary criticism from a purely personal perspective including simple autobiography. In the second book all the satires except one are written in dialogue form. Painful invective against individuals is almost entirely absent. In this respect Horace differs markedly from his model *Lucilius, as he does also in the deliberately casual and easy style of his language and metre, the hexameters conveying an impression of writing carefully in colloquial but urbane Latin. His criticism of vice is meant to improve himself as well as others, and is done lightly—'to speak the truth with laughter'.

The satires in both books are arranged according to theme. Among them the following are of particular interest to modern readers: 1.5, 'A Journey to Brundisium' (corresponding to Lucilius' 'Journey to Sicily') describes his travels of 38 or 37 in the suite of *Maecenas with the poet Virgil and the tragedian Varius Rufus; 1.6 is interesting for its autobiographical details, an account of Horace's father and of his own introduction to Maecenas; 1.9, *ibam forte via Sacra* ('I was going by chance along the Sacred Way'), is an entertaining description of

an encounter with a bore and the author's efforts to get rid of him; 1.8 is the least personal, a story of witches put to flight in the midst of their incantations by the sudden cracking of a wooden statue of *Priapus. In the second book, the adoption of dramatic form gives life and humorous variety to the illustrations of Roman life: 2.5 is a parody of epic in which Odysseus, in a continuation of the Underworld episode in *Odyssey* 11, consults *Teiresias as to the recovery of his lost fortune and receives advice in the Roman art (or vice) of legacy-hunting; 2.6 is the famous satire on town and country life illustrated by the fable of the town mouse and the country mouse.

2. By the Roman poet *Juvenal, sixteen satires, written in hexameters and published, it seems, in five books during the 110s and 120s AD. They are highly rhetorical, and it has been suggested that they are not so much a reflection of the realities of life at Rome as artfully constructed works in which the narrator assumes poses—the indignant moralist, the angry ranter, the detached, ironic, and cynical observer.

Satire 1 is a programmatic poem in which Juvenal—or the narrator Juvenal purports to be—explains that his subject matter is not taken from outworn mythology but is concerned with 'all the activities of people', *quidquid agunt homines*. The vices of the age provide the stimulus: 'indignation prompts my verse', *facit indignatio versum*. But it is safe to write only of the dead; at the present time 'honesty is praised but left out in the cold', *probitas laudatur et alget*. Satire 2 is an attack on hypocritical homosexual men who give the appearance of being stern moralists but are immoral in their private lives: 'no one becomes vicious all at once', *nemo repente fuit turpissimus*. Satire 3 is a picture of life at Rome and is perhaps Juvenal's best-known satire, imitated by Samuel Johnson in his *London* (1738). Juvenal approves of his honest friend Umbricius for fleeing to the country from the vices and perils of the city, which include 'poets reciting in the month of August'. Umbricius cannot stand the invasion of Greeks and pillories the versatile 'Greek in search of a meal', *Graeculus esuriens*. The honest and poor Roman has no chance in Rome: 'luckless poverty has no misery harder to endure than this, that it exposes men to ridicule', *nil habet infelix paupertas durius in se / quam quod ridiculos homines facit*. Poverty stands in the way of merit: 'it is not easy for men to rise when straitened circumstances at home stand in the way of merit', *haut facile emergunt quorum virtutibus opstat / res angusta domi*. The city is described: the tall houses with pigeons nesting on the roofs, ready to fall about the ears of the inhabitants; the frequent fires, the impossibility of sleep because of the noise of wagons in the narrow, winding streets and the abuse of drovers, the danger of being crushed by a heavy load or hit by rubbish thrown down from open windows. Then the city at night: a great man passing in his scarlet cloak, with torches and a retinue of clients and slaves, the affray with a bully 'if affray it can be called, when you do all the beating and I get all the blows', *si rixa est, ubi tu pulsas, ego vapulo tantum*. When one is finally behind locked doors at home, there is still the danger of being murdered by a burglar.

Satire 4 depicts the courtiers humiliated by the emperor Domitian, who asks their advice on how to dispose of a mullet too large for any dish. Similarly satire 5 is about the humiliation of poor *clients at the tables of their rich patrons. Book 2 consists entirely of satire 6, the longest and most virulent of Juvenal's satires, a denunciation of women. The poet professes astonishment that a friend should contemplate marriage when there is so much rope to be had, and then depicts, at great length, the vices of women, their insatiable and reckless sexual appetite, their extravagance, tyranny, and quarrelsomeness in the home. If you chance on a good woman, who is a 'rare bird on earth, as common as a black swan', *rara avis in terris nigroque simillima cygno*, she will be haughty. It is useless to set a guard on one's wife, for 'who will guard the guards themselves?', *quis custodiet ipsos custodes*?

In a calmer vein, book 3 consists of satires 7–9. Satire 7 is on the unprofitability of the literary professions (unless you are a poet like Horace with a Sabine farm) and especially that of teacher (*Quintilian has been lucky). Moreover, the teacher has to endure much monotonous repetition, 'cabbage served up again and again', *crambe repetita*. Satire 8 attacks pride of ancestry. 'Virtue is the only true nobility', *nobilitas sola est atque unica virtus*. It is the greatest sin to prefer life to honour 'and to lose for the sake of living all that makes life worth having', *et propter vitam vivendi perdere causas*. Satire 9 is the complaint of a man who remains poor despite having obligingly fathered children for his homosexual employer on the latter's wife as well as giving him sexual

favours. In Satire 10 (the model for Samuel Johnson's poem *The Vanity of Human Wishes*, 1749) Juvenal writes on the folly of human prayers; wealth exposes a man to dangers, whereas 'the empty-handed traveller will cheerfully sing when confronted by a robber', *cantabit vacuus coram latrone viator*; power (consider *Sejanus), long life, and beauty are all sources of trouble. Better leave your fate to the gods, or pray for at most 'a healthy mind in a healthy body', *mens sana in corpore sano*, and for courage and endurance. The only things the public cares for are 'bread and circuses', *panem et circenses*. Satire 11 contrasts extravagance and simplicity of living in an Horatian-style invitation to dinner; in Satire 12 Juvenal celebrates a true friend's escape from shipwreck, and attacks the false friendship of legacy-hunters.

Satire 13, the opening poem of book 5, is a condemnation of anger in the form of a plea to a friend not to seek vengeance against one who has defrauded him; the guilty man will be punished by his own conscience: 'it is always the little, weak, and petty mind that delights in vengeance', *quippe minuti / semper infirmi est animi exiguique voluptas / ultio*. The poet refers approvingly to the *Delphic oracle's condemnation of a man who had merely thought of committing an offence: 'for he who secretly meditates a crime has all the guilt of having done the deed', *nam scelus intra se tacitum qui cogitat ullum, / facti crimen habet*. Satire 14 is about the influence of parental example in education. The parents' faults will be copied by the children: 'if you have any shameful deed in mind, the greatest reverence is owed to the young', *maxime debetur puero reverentia, siquid turpe paras*. In Satire 15, after describing a conflict in Egypt, resulting in an act of cannibalism, Juvenal praises tenderness of heart as the quality which distinguishes humans from beasts. Satire 16, on the abusive privileges of the military, is unfinished.

Juvenal's 'savage indignation' had a lasting influence on later satire, especially on Johnson's imitations of 3 and 10, themselves a strong influence on later writers.

**satrap** Title given to a Persian provincial governor, in effect a vassal king with very wide powers; the territory he governed was known as a satrapy. *Darius divided the Persian empire into twenty satrapies which remained the basis for later territorial administration.

**Saturn** (Lat. Sāturnus) Ancient Italian god whose original function remains obscure though his name suggests to some that he may originally have been a god of 'sowing', *sătus*. This supposition is perhaps supported by the date of his festival (the \*Saturnalia) which occurs in the calendar of \*Numa on 17 December, between the Consualia for the god of the granary and the Opalia for the god of plenty. Sacrifices to him were made according to the Greek rite, with head uncovered (*see* SACRIFICE); the Romans themselves thought that he had been introduced from Greece, and identified him at an early stage with the Greek god \*Cronus, who ruled during the \*Golden age. His temple stood at the foot of the Capitoline hill and served as the treasury (*aerarium*) of the Roman people; there too were kept the Tables of the law (*see* TWELVE TABLES) and the records of decrees of the senate. He was regarded as the husband of \*Ops and father of \*Picus.

**Saturnā'lia** In Roman religion, a festival celebrated for seven days in Cicero's time but from 17 to 19 December under Augustus. It was the most cheerful of the year, 'the best of days' according to Catullus, a time of enjoyment, goodwill, and licence, of present-giving and lighting candles, the prototype of some aspects of modern Christmas festivities. The holiday began with a sacrifice at the temple of \*Saturn followed by a public feast open to everyone, but thereafter was a household festival. Slaves were freed from their duties and might even be waited on by their masters. Each household chose a mock king to preside over the festivities. Not everyone enjoyed it: the Younger Pliny built himself a soundproof room to which he retired throughout the holiday. By about the fourth century AD many of these customs were transferred to New Year's Day, and hence were added to the traditional Christmas celebrations.

**Saturna'lia** Dialogue by \*Macrobius.

**Saturnī'nus, Lucius Appule'ius** Roman politician. As tribune of the plebs in 103 and 100 BC he cooperated with the consul \*Marius to enable the latter to get land-allotments for his landless veterans, and he was able to pass other popular measures against optimate opposition, often by violence, and with the help of the praetor \*Glaucia. His personal influence and his ability to act independently of Marius grew considerably. When in 99 he stood again

for the tribunate and Glaucia for the consulship, a rival of Glaucia was assassinated. At this Marius dissociated himself from both of them with the backing of the senate. The latter passed the \**senatus consultum ultimum*—the first time it was used against a tribune in office – and Saturninus and Glaucia were both murdered by a mob.

**Saty'ricōn (*Satyrica*)** *See* PETRONIUS ARBITER.

**satyr plays** At Athens during the classical period it seems that at the City \*Dionysia each trilogy (consisting of three tragedies) was generally followed by a fourth play in a lighter vein, usually a semi-comic satyr play written by the same author, in which the chorus was always composed of \*satyrs, led by \*Silenus represented as father-figure, wearing horses' tails and ears. Aristotle at one point in the *Poetics* expresses the belief that tragedy originated from this type of performance; others however thought that satyr plays were a later development. Euripides' \**Cyclops* is the only complete specimen still surviving, but substantial fragments of the *Dictyulci* ('Net-fishers') of Aeschylus and the *Ichneutae* ('Trackers') of Sophocles have been found in recent times on papyrus (*see* PAPYROLOGY). The subject matter of satyr plays had to suit the satyric character, and was usually a burlesque of some mythical episode sometimes connected with the preceding trilogy, with a certain amount of coarse language and gesturing. \*Pratinas of Phlius, writing at the beginning of the fifth century in Athens, was said to be the first to write satyr plays, and also to have written thirty-two himself.

Occasionally the fourth play of a tetralogy might not be specifically a satyr play (*see* ALCESTIS). Satyric drama, detached from tragedy after the mid-fourth century BC, continued to be written even in Roman times; rules for its composition are given by Horace in the \**Ars poetica*.

**satyrs (*satyroi*)** In Greek mythology, male attendants of the god \*Dionysus, boisterous creatures of the woods and hills. They are generally represented as naked and of mainly human form but with some bestial aspect, e.g. a horse's tail or the legs of a goat (but they are not usually represented as goats until the fourth century BC). Lustful and fond of wine, they were called the sons of Hermes. The Romans identified them with the Fauni (*see* Faunus). The chorus in Attic *satyr plays was dressed to represent satyrs. *See also* Silenus.

**Scaean Gate** ('the gate on the left', presumably) In the Trojan War, the main gate of Troy, leading to the fighting; an oak tree said to belong to Zeus grew nearby. Here Hector met Andromache in the *Iliad*, and here Achilles will break into the city and be killed.

**Scae'vola 1. Gaius Mu'cius Scaevola** Legendary Roman who, when Lars *Porsen(n)a, king of Clusium, was besieging Rome at the end of the sixth century BC, made his way to the enemy camp, attempted but failed to kill Porsena, and mistakenly killed his secretary. He was taken prisoner, and to show his indifference to the prospect of torture, thrust his right hand into the fire. The king was so impressed that he released Mucius, who thus acquired the *cognomen* Scaevola, 'left-handed'.

**2. Publius Mucius Scaevola** See ANNALS.

**3. Quintus Mucius Scaevola** (*c.*170–87 BC) Known as 'the augur', consul in 117 BC, son-in-law of *Laelius and father-in-law of L. Licinius Crassus the orator. He was a distinguished jurist and taught (among others) his son-in-law and Cicero, who greatly admired him. He is one of the interlocutors in Cicero's *De oratore*, *De amicitia*, and *De republica*

**4. Quintus Mucius Scaevola** (*c.*140–82 BC; often referred to as Quintus Mucius) *Pontifex maximus* in 115, consul with L. Licinius Crassus the orator in 95 BC. He was himself an orator and lawyer of distinction, noted, according to Cicero, for the concise accuracy of his language. He published the first systematic treatise (in eighteen books) on civil law, which was still being consulted in the second century AD. He helped to modernize the procedures of civil law and make it morally more acceptable, using the model of a conscientious head of a household (*diligens paterfamilias*) as a pattern of correct behaviour. Cicero in his youth received instruction in the law from him after the death of his relative and namesake, the augur (see (3) above). In his consulship he and Crassus passed the Licinio-Mucian law, instituting proceedings against aliens who had been illegally enrolled as citizens. This brought about the expulsion of many Italians from Rome and was in consequence a contributory cause of the *Social War (2). Cicero remarked on the fact that

such an unfortunate measure was due to such excellent men. Scaevola was assassinated by the Marian party (*see* Marius) in the temple of Vesta.

**scansion** Metrical analysis of poetry into long and short (or stressed and unstressed) syllables, and metra or feet.

**Sceptics** [Gk. *skeptikos*, 'inquirer'—with the implication that the inquirer reaches no conclusion] Philosophers who suspend judgement on everything and teach no doctrine. The term is thought to have been introduced in the first century BC. Before then philosophers of this type would have been known as Pyrrhonists, after Pyrrhon of Elis (*c.*365–*c.*270 BC), the founder of Scepticism. In fact sceptical attitudes were expressed by philosophers, notably the *sophists, long before that. Pyrrhon travelled to India in the train of Alexander the Great and there, tradition relates, met the *gymnosophists and 'magi' who were thought to have influenced his later philosophical views. He returned and lived the rest of his life quietly at Elis. He left no writings, and only fragments survive of the writings of his pupils. Pyrrhon inferred from the deceptions inherent in sense-perceptions and the contradictions in the teachings of 'dogmatic' philosophers that knowledge of the true nature of things is unattainable. Hence the proper attitude is suspension of judgement (*epochē*), and refraining from asserting anything; one should 'say about all things that they no more are than they are not'. The result will be mental quietude (Gk. *ataraxia*).

Our knowledge of Pyrrhon depends on the testimony of his most influential pupil *Timon (2) of Phlius and our chief source of information on the Sceptics in general is the lengthy account by *Sextus Empiricus (late second century AD). It remains unclear what the relationship was between Pyrrhon's Scepticism and that of the *Academy at Athens, introduced by Arcesilaus (head of the Academy *c.*265 BC) and developed a century later by *Carneades. It seems probable that Arcesilaus was influenced by Pyrrhon. The former's criticism of Stoic epistemology led to protracted argument between Academics and Stoics until the first century BC (*see* Academica). After Sextus, Scepticism as a philosophy seems to have petered out.

**Sche'ria (Scheriē)** Name of the island of the Phaeacians (*see* ODYSSEY [book 5]), on the coast of which Odysseus was cast ashore. Some have identified it with Corcyra (modern Corfu).

**scholasticism** *See* TEXTS, TRANSMISSION OF ANCIENT 7.

**schō'lium** (Lat.; Gk. *scholion*) Name given in antiquity to a short explanatory note written to elucidate a difficulty in a text. The plural, scholia, is often used to describe the commentaries on classical texts written in the margins of manuscripts by ancient scholars, and copied along with the text from manuscript to manuscript. In this form they are a compilation, greatly abbreviated and sometimes garbled, made from earlier, fuller commentaries or excerpted from monographs of various dates. Thus they sometimes contain valuable information about antiquity from reliable sources which has not otherwise come down to us. The scholia to Homer, Hesiod, Pindar, Aristophanes, and the tragedians are particularly useful, and although the manuscripts in which they are found are of the later *Byzantine age, the notes sometimes go back to the great scholars of the *Hellenistic age, Zenodotus, Aristophanes (of Byzantium), and Aristarchus. There are also valuable scholia on Latin authors such as Horace.

**science, attitudes to** In the ancient world the development of science was almost entirely a Greek phenomenon. The progress the Romans made in engineering and invention was mostly founded on Greek discoveries. *Lucretius' great poem *On nature* could be regarded as the Romans' most notable foray into scientific speculation, although it is in fact a work of philosophy rather than physics. From origins in Ionia in the late seventh century BC Greek science combined observation of the universe and of life on earth with speculation about the nature and origin of both (*see* PHILOSOPHY). In its early stages it could as well be described under the headings of philosophy or *cosmology, but there is a clear line leading from the early investigators to *Aristotle, who was the first to insist upon the primacy of observation over speculation as well as upon the necessity for an investigator to state causes and give rational explanations.

Most branches of modern science, particularly physics and chemistry, were beyond the reach of the ancient Greeks who lacked not only the concepts necessary for progress such as mass, force, gravity, velocity, temperature, and so on, but above all the technology. However, throughout antiquity the relations between *mathematics and the physical world were closely studied, notably by the Pythagoreans (*see* PYTHAGORAS) and by Plato. For Plato the mathematical perfection of ultimate reality (*see* PLATONISM) can never be wholly present in the physical objects of this world. But the idea that the world order could in some way be described mathematically was pervasive among intellectuals. In the branches of mathematics closest to physics knowledge developed rapidly. Among Aristotle's works (though almost certainly not by Aristotle) is a treatise on mechanics, describing the theory and practice of balances, pulleys, and levers. (*See also* ARCHIMEDES.) Similar progress was made in mathematical and physical *geography (regarded by *Strabo as a branch of scientific enquiry), *astronomy, and optics. This last subject the Greeks advanced considerably, although their work was based on the false belief that vision is achieved by rays emanating from the eye towards the objects seen (the theory adopted by *Euclid in his *Optics* and later by *Ptolemy in his). Though the Greeks did not set up experiments as modern scientists would, Ptolemy reports at length on his investigations into refraction, describing the apparatus used and recording the results. Aristotle too occasionally refers to tests he has made. Pythagoras is said, improbably, to have discovered the intervals of the musical scale after hearing in a blacksmith's forge the sounds produced by hammers on an anvil.

In the life sciences also the Greeks made remarkable progress. *Celsus declares that it was *Hippocrates in the fifth century BC 'who first separated medicine from philosophy'. (*See also* ANATOMY AND PHYSIOLOGY.) The gradual increase in knowledge about drugs and surgery to some extent displaced speculative theory, although in ancient medicine theory, like magic, never entirely disappears.

*See also* POSTERIOR ANALYTICS; ANIMALS, ARISTOTLE ON; BOTANY; DIOSCORIDES; TECHNOLOGY.

**Sci'pio 1. Publius Corne'lius Scipio Africā'nus Maior** ('the Elder', 236–183 BC) Rome's greatest general in the Second *Punic War. He was the son of P. Cornelius Scipio, who was defeated by Hannibal at Ticinus in 218 BC. He is said to have saved his father's life in that battle and to have rallied the survivors of *Cannae in 216. In 210 when only about 25 his exceptional military ability brought about his appointment by the people to the command in Spain, the first *privatus*, 'private citizen', to be granted the *imperium* of a proconsul. By 206 he had driven the Carthaginians out of Spain. He was elected consul for 205, and, managing to get the better of senatorial opposition, especially that of *Fabius (2) who thought Hannibal should be defeated in Italy, crossed over to Africa with his army. He finally defeated Hannibal at the battle of Zama in 202, which earned him the *cognomen* Africanus and a triumph.

In 199 he was elected censor and became *princeps senatus*, 'leader of the senate'; in 194 he was consul for a second time. In 190, although nominally merely the legate of his brother Lucius in the command against Antiochus of Syria, he led the first Roman army into Asia. When the brothers returned to Rome, political attacks, directed by *Cato (1) the Censor, were launched against them both, accusing them of misconduct in public affairs. A series of trials resulted, and although at the last the charges were not pressed home (Scipio is said at one point to have reminded the people that the day of the trial was the anniversary of Zama) the influence of the Scipios was broken, and Africanus retired to his estate at Liternum in Campania, where he died. The Younger Seneca in Epistle 86 vividly evokes the simplicity of his life there. Like many members of his family he was an ardent philhellene; that and his military brilliance and magnetic personality prompted comparisons with Alexander the Great. He married Aemilia, sister of L. Aemilius *Paullus; one of his daughters was *Cornelia, mother of the Gracchi.

**2. Publius Cornelius Scipio Aemiliā'nus** (known as Africanus Minor; *c.*185–129 BC) Roman general and statesman. He was by birth the second son of L. Aemilius *Paullus, the conqueror of Macedonia, but was adopted by P. Scipio, the son of Scipio Africanus Major (see (1) above). He fought under his real father at the battle of Pydna in 168 BC to end the Third Macedonian War, and destroyed Carthage in 146 to end the Third *Punic War. Watching Carthage burn he wept as he remembered Homer and the fate of Troy. Finally he brought the long and costly war in Spain against the Numantines to a successful conclusion in 133. During these campaigns he won major military

decorations. At his return to Rome in 132 he took the lead amongst those opposed to the radical reforms of the *Gracchi, but died suddenly in 129 at the height of the political unrest. It was suspected that he had been murdered, perhaps by his wife Sempronia, sister of the Gracchi. He was a great orator, the leading figure in the philhellenic circle at Rome, and a patron of Greek and Latin literature and learning; his friends included Polybius, Panaetius, Lucilius, Terence, Laelius, and, improbably, *Cato (1) the Elder. His combination of intellectual and active virtues, of high culture with the Roman virtues of outstanding military and political success, moved Cicero to unbounded admiration of him as the ideal statesman. Cicero made him the central character in *De republica and *De senectute. His *De amicitia dwells on the friendship of Scipio and Laelius.

**3. Publius Cornelius Scipio Nasi'ca Sera'pio** Consul in 138 BC, a man of strongly conservative and aristocratic views. In 133 he vigorously opposed his cousin Ti. Gracchus when he was seeking re-election as tribune (*see* GRACCHI (1)), and was leader of the group of senators and clients who attacked and killed him. In later times the murder sharply divided the *optimates who approved and the *populares who condemned it.

**Scipio's Dream** See SOMNIUM SCIPIONIS.

**Scīron** In Greek legend, a brigand who preyed on travellers along the cliff road from Athens to Megara. He made them wash his feet, and as they did so he kicked them over the cliff, where, according to some, they were eaten by a giant tortoise. *Theseus on his way to Athens threw Sciron over the edge, and his bones were turned into the cliffs which bear his name. Other stories relate to Sciros, a connected heroic figure.

**sco'lia** (sing. *scolion*) [from *skolios*, 'crooked'] Short drinking-songs, especially Attic, sung by guests at a Greek *symposium or drinking-party, in succession but in random order, 'crookedly'. They were accompanied by the lyre. *Athenaeus (book 15) preserves a collection of anonymous Attic scolia of the late sixth and early fifth centuries BC. They either comment on some historical incident (such as the assassination attempt of *Harmodius and Aristogeiton) or contain some personal sentiment or comment on life. The singer held a bay- or myrtle-branch while he sang, and when he had finished passed the branch to another. Tradition makes *Terpander the originator of the scolion.

**Scōpads, Scōpas** *See* CRANNON and SIMONIDES.

**Scrībo'nia** Wife of Octavian (later the emperor Augustus). She was married at least three times; by one of her first two husbands she became the mother of that Cornelia whose premature death occasioned an elegy of consolation from Propertius (4.11). Octavian married her for political reasons in 40 BC, but divorced her in 39 after the birth of their daughter *Julia (4). She accompanied Julia into exile in 2 BC and remained with her until the latter's death in AD 14. She herself was still alive in 16.

**scripts** *See* CURSIVE SCRIPT; UNCIALS; TEXTS, TRANSMISSION OF ANCIENT 3 and 5.

**Scȳlax** (of Caryanda in Caria) Explorer sent c.515 BC by the Persian king Darius (521–486 BC) on a voyage of investigation from the Indus round the coast of Arabia. The book Scylax wrote afterwards (*Periplus*, 'Voyage') is apparently quoted by *Hecataeus as well as by Aristotle and Strabo. The surviving *Periplus* attributed to him, describing a clockwise circumnavigation of the Mediterranean and Black Sea which ended along the north coast of Africa, dates from the fourth century BC and may be a compilation of various accounts.

**Scylla 1.** In Greek myth, daughter of *Phorcys and *Hecate. She was sometimes described as originally human but turned into a monster by a rival in love. She is represented as having six heads, each with a triple row of teeth, and twelve feet; she lived in a cave (traditionally situated in the Straits of Messina between Sicily and Italy) with the whirlpool of *Charybdis opposite. Her diet was fish but she devoured sailors if a ship came near. Homer describes the passage of Odysseus' ship past the cave in *Odyssey* 12. To be 'between Scylla and Charybdis' is to be in a situation where the two possible courses of action are equally dangerous.

**2.** Daughter of *Nisus (1), king of Megara.

The Latin poets Virgil, Ovid, and Propertius sometimes confuse the two Scyllas.

**Seasons (Hōrai)** (Eng. 'Hours') In Greek myth, daughters of Zeus and *Themis, attendants on the gods. Homer and Hesiod know three seasons (spring, summer, winter), which Hesiod in the *Theogony* names symbolically as *Eunomia (Good order), Dike (Justice), and Eirene (Peace); without these, the implication is, society cannot flourish. The first two are more often invoked since they are thought of as the goddesses of life and growth, and they are often associated with Aphrodite and the Graces. They also figure at the birth, upbringing, and marriage of gods and heroes. Autumn first appears in the Greek poet Alcman, and after Aristotle and Theophrastus four is the canonical number.

**secession** In Roman history, term used to describe the withdrawal on three known occasions of the Roman *plebs* (*see* PLEBEIANS) from the city to a hill outside the boundary, an extreme form of civil disobedience (especially since it entailed refusal of military service). The traditional date of the first secession was 494 BC at a time of economic hardship, when the plebs set up a political system for themselves (*see* TRIBUNES OF THE PLEBS) and the cult of *Ceres, *Liber, and Libera. This secession was brought to an end by Menenius, a plebeian who had been consul in 503; he told the Greek parable of the body and the limbs (see Livy 2.32.8) to illustrate the mutual dependence of all parts of the citizen-body. A second secession supposedly of 449 BC resulted in the overthrow of the *decemvirs, who had been appointed with consular authority in 451 after plebeian agitation for the laws to be published. The third and last secession was c.287 BC when the patricians conceded that plebiscites (resolutions passed by the plebeian assembly, *concilium plebis*) automatically had the same force as law. *See* ROME 2.

**Second Athenian League** *See* ATHENS 4.

**Second Sophistic** The term applied to the period, roughly AD 60–230, in the Greek-speaking parts of the Roman empire when *declamation became a leading literary activity and its highly-skilled practitioners famous. The name was coined by *Philostratus (1) in his *Lives of the Sophists* (second to third century AD), claiming a link with the Greek *sophists of the first sophistic age, the late fifth and fourth centuries BC. 'Sophists' was the title given to these latter-day practitioners, who at this time were professional *rhetors or orators who gave public displays of their art for entertainment. On the whole these sophists distinguished themselves from philosophers. They replicated the virtuoso performances of the fifth-century sophists as well as carefully imitating the language and style of the best Attic writers, Lysias, Xenophon, Plato, and Demosthenes. These performances met with immense popular success in Athens and the great cities of western Asia Minor—Pergamum, Smyrna, and Ephesus. Their main speech was usually a *suasoria* (*see* SENECA (1)). The audiences were educated and sophisticated and often selected the theme themselves, which the rhetor would meditate on for a few minutes before delivering his declamation extempore. Others preferred to speak on a prepared subject. Although a practice which concentrated so much on form at the expense of content could be seen as stultifying, study of the Attic models infused the rhetoric with something of the philosophy of the originals and helped create for some a new *Platonism, for others a philosophical Hellenism which amalgamated the central beliefs from different Greek philosophical systems. *See* ARISTEIDES (2); DIO CHRYSOSTOM; FAVORINUS; FRONTO; HERODES ATTICUS; LUCIAN; PLUTARCH.

The unsettled conditions of the mid-third century scarcely affected the popularity of declamation and it flourished anew in the late third and fourth centuries, a peaceful and prosperous period in the eastern part of the still undivided empire. *See* HIMERIUS; LIBANIUS; THEMISTIUS; and *cf.* ROMAN AGE OF GREEK LITERATURE.

**Secular Games** During the republic the Romans celebrated the end of one period of a hundred years and the beginning of another with theatrical events and sacrifices in the Campus Martius. A hundred-year period was called the *saeculum*, defined as the longest span of human life. The first attested celebration took place in 249 BC at the hardest point of the First Punic War, and the second in the 140s BC. No games were held in the 40s BC, but Augustus, having had the Sibylline books consulted (*see* SIBYL), discovered a prophecy sanctioning games in 17 BC, and fixed the *saeculum* at 110 years. Secular Games were duly held in that year (exceptionally well-attested), to mark not only the end of an era but the birth of a new age. The celebration combined tradition and innovation. Horace composed the *Carmen Saeculare*, 'Secular Hymn', for the occasion. Claudius next celebrated games in AD 47 but on a new cycle, based on the eight-hundredth

anniversary of the foundation of Rome (753 BC). Games were also held for the next two centenaries, in 148 and 248, but were not counted officially since they were not on the Augustan cycle. That cycle was continued by Domitian, who celebrated games in 88 (six years early) and by Septimius Severus in 204. But no games were held in 314: Constantine and the empire were by then converting to Christianity and the Secular Games were ended.

**seer** *See* DIVINATION.

**seisachthei'a** *See* SOLON.

**Sējā'nus, Lucius Ae'lius** (d. AD 31) Roman politician. Of *equestrian status, he was appointed prefect of *praetorians by the emperor Tiberius in AD 14 and exercised a steadily increasing influence over him. When the latter's son Drusus died suddenly in 23 (murder was later suspected), Sejanus' influence was unequalled. He even hoped to make a dynastic marriage with Drusus' widow, Livilla (*see* LIVIA (2)), in 25 but his background was too humble for the emperor to agree. When at his persuasion Tiberius withdrew to Capri in 27 Sejanus became all the more powerful. Tiberius, however, allegedly warned by his sister-in-law *Antonia (2), denounced him in a letter to the senate (the poet Juvenal's 'long-winded and lengthy letter', *verbosa et grandis epistula*) and Sejanus was brought before the senate, condemned of plotting against the throne, and executed. It is said that after his execution his body was torn to pieces by the people whose hatred he had incurred, and thrown into the Tiber. The execution of many others, including Livilla and his own children, followed.

**Selē'nē** In Greek myth, the moon-goddess (Roman Luna), according to Hesiod the daughter of the *Titans Hyperion and Theia and sister of Helios and Eos (Sun and Dawn); but some writers give different genealogies. She has little cult and few myths (but *see* ENDYMION). She is sometimes identified with the goddess Artemis, perhaps because both had been identified with *Hecate.

**Seleu'cids** Dynasty which eventually obtained Syria and much of Asia as its share in the empire of Alexander the Great (*see* DIADOCHI). The founder of the dynasty was Seleucus I (*c.*358–281 BC), an officer of Alexander, who, after the latter's death, received the governorship of Babylonia (321). After a shaky beginning, by the end of the fourth century he had extended his rule eastwards over all Alexander's provinces as far as India. In 281 Seleucus acquired northern and central Asia Minor by defeating and killing Lysimachus (another of Alexander's generals) at the battle of Corupedium. Now entertaining the hope of winning *Macedonia, the possession of which was still undecided, he invaded Europe, but was assassinated by Ptolemy Ceraunus, a son of Ptolemy I of Egypt, who wanted Macedonia himself. His most remarkable successor was Antiochus III (the Great, c.242–187). The latter's expansionist policy in the West (he invaded Europe in 196 to recover Thrace), led him into conflict with Rome, and after losing three battles against the Romans he was forced to evacuate all Asia Minor west of Mount Taurus. Thereafter, despite its Mediterranean seaboard, the Seleucid empire ceased to be a Mediterranean power. It broke up through dynastic wars into a multitude of free cities and small kingdoms, and territory was lost to the Parthians in the east. Finally, in 64 BC Syria was annexed to Rome by Pompey. The importance of the Seleucids lies in their Hellenization of Asia, particularly in founding scores of cities, more or less Greek in character; Seleucus I founded *Antioch on the Orontes as his Syrian capital and Seleuceia on the Tigris as the capital of his empire.

**sella curū′lis** See CURULE MAGISTRACIES.

**Se′melē** See DIONYSUS.

**Semnai** See FURIES.

**Sēmō′nidēs** (mid-seventh century BC) Greek iambic poet originally of Samos but always connected with Amorgos (an island of the Sporades in the Aegean Sea), where he joined in its colonization. Of his poetry, written in the Ionic dialect, very few fragments survive. The longest piece, almost complete, describes with satirical humour various types of women as having the qualities of the animals from which, according to him, they derive. A piece of elegiac verse on the shortness of life is now known to be a conflation of two passages by *Simonides.

**senate (senātus)** The legislative council of Rome, in origin the council of advisors to the king which survived the abolition of the

monarchy in 510 BC. The number of members first attested is 300, increased by Sulla to 600, by Julius Caesar to 900, and reduced by Augustus again to 600. It may at first have been a purely *patrician body and it became in practice an assembly of ex-magistrates. However, it was traditionally addressed as *patres (et) conscripti*, 'patricians (and) enrolled members', which suggests that the membership was mixed. Senators received no payment. Although a property qualification was not stipulated until the time of Augustus, senators were usually rich men from important families, and membership of the senate tended to be hereditary (see OPTIMATES; NOBILES; NOVUS HOMO). From the fourth century BC members were chosen by the censors according to fixed criteria; expulsion from the senate for serious misconduct was rare, so membership was effectively for life. Owing to its functions and permanence the senate was the real head of the state. It prepared legislative proposals to be brought before the people, and its resolutions, called *decreta* or, more commonly, *senatus consulta*, had some measure of effective if not legal authority (they could be vetoed by the tribunes). It administered the finances, assigned magistrates to provinces, and dealt with foreign relations. It also supervised the practice of the state religion. Since it was a body of ex-magistrates, serious clashes were avoided between the *imperium of the magistrates and the authority of the senate, and in general it exercised strong control over holders of office, tending to use them as its tools. The collapse of the republic came about in the first century BC when the authority of the senate was powerless against military leaders backed by their armies (see ROME 4). Under the empire, although the senate lost its sovereign power, it was not without important functions, and *Augustus (see 3) endeavoured to share with it the administration of the state. But in fact, partly owing to its own inefficiency, its power gradually diminished (see PRINCIPATE).

The senate met for business either in the Curia (senate house), which stood in the Forum, or within a mile of the city in a consecrated place. The first sitting of the year was in the temple of Jupiter Capitolinus. When a decision had to be reached each senator was asked his opinion according to his rank (see CURSUS HONORUM), censors followed by consuls, praetors, aediles, etc., patricians taking precedence over plebeians in each category. The senator heading the list was known as the *princeps senatus*, 'leader of the senate'.

## senā'tūs consu'ltum u'ltimum ('the final resolution of the senate') Resolution issued to the magistrates in a grave emergency, authorizing the consuls to use force for the protection of the state and suspending the right of appeal to the people. It was first used in 121 BC against C. Gracchus (*see* GRACCHI (2)), and, among other occasions, against *Saturninus in 100 and *Catiline in 63. It was last employed (against Salvidienus Rufus) in 40 BC. When the decree led to deaths the *populares* always contested its use, for example in connection with C. Rabirius, who in 63 BC was defended by Cicero (see CICERO (1) 2) for what he did in 100 BC when under Marius' command.

## Se'neca, Lucius Annae'us 1. 'The Elder' or the 'Rhetorician', born at Corduba (Cordoba) in Spain *c*.50 BC of Italian stock and educated at Rome. He died between AD 37 and 41, before the exile of his son and namesake (see (2) below). His history of Rome from the start of the civil wars to his own day is lost. He devoted himself to the study of rhetoric, and in his old age assembled for his sons a collection of *Controversiae* ('Debates') and *Suasoriae* ('Speeches of advice'). These were model exercises on rhetorical themes used in the schools of *rhetoric: the former covered the oratory of the law-courts and took the form of speeches for and against litigants in criminal or civil cases; the latter were exercises in deliberative (political) oratory on such themes as whether the 300 Spartans at Thermopylae should fight the Persians or run away. All the examples, dating from the time of Cicero to Seneca's old age, are extracts from rhetoricians whom Seneca had heard during his long life, a testimony to his astonishing memory (which he himself tells us was unrivalled) and an invaluable source for literary history. Of particular interest are the prefaces to the *Controversiae* where he discusses various orators, their analyses (*divisiones*) and lines of approach (*colores*) to the debates that follow, with many digressions and anecdotes. Only five of the original ten books of *Controversiae* and one book of *Suasoriae* are extant.

**2.** 'The Younger' or 'the Philosopher' (*c*.4 BC–AD 65).

1. He was the second son of Seneca the Elder ((1) above), and like him was born at Corduba. He was brought as a child to Rome and educated there in rhetoric and philosophy. Embarking on a senatorial career he became an advocate, quaestor, and senator, and achieved a considerable reputation as an orator and writer. Under Claudius, Seneca occupied a position at court. In 41 he was banished to Corsica for alleged adultery with Julia (Livilla), the youngest daughter of Germanicus and Agrippina the Elder, and niece of Claudius. Julia's sister, also called Agrippina (the Younger), mother of *Nero, had him recalled in 49 and he was made tutor to the young Nero. In 51 Burrus, who was to become Seneca's friend and colleague, was made the sole prefect of *praetorians. On the accession of Nero in 54 Seneca became the emperor's political adviser, and for the next five years Rome and the empire enjoyed good government, largely under the direction of Seneca and Burrus. But after Nero had his mother murdered in 59 and Seneca wrote Nero's letter to the senate saying that she had committed suicide, Seneca's influence was reduced and he asked permission to retire. He left Rome after the death of Burrus in 62 and devoted the next three years to philosophy and his friends. In 65 he was implicated in the unsuccessful conspiracy of Piso against Nero's life and forced to commit suicide. His courageous death, reminiscent of Socrates', is described by Tacitus (*Annals* 15.64).

The inconsistencies between Seneca's moral principles, his political life, his wealth, and the behaviour of his pupil emperor have provoked accusations of hypocrisy. However, he faced serious dilemmas; he was a humane and tolerant man, for many years a successful politician and an influence for good, and a writer of considerable and varied talent.

2. Seneca wrote voluminously. Besides the works that survive we have titles or fragments of treatises on geography, natural history, and ethics, among many others. His extant prose works comprise, first, the following ten ethical treatises given the name *Dialogi* ('Dialogues'):

*De providentia* ('On providence'), addressed to his friend Lucilius (the Younger), in which he discusses the question why good men meet with misfortune when there exists a providence. The answer is that misfortune serves a useful purpose: it is a school of virtue. *Stoicism provides the remedy of suicide when misfortune becomes intolerable.

*De constantia sapientis* ('On the constancy of the wise man'), addressed to Annaeus Serenus, *praefectus vigilum* under Nero, on the theme that a wise man can suffer neither wrong nor insult.

*De ira* ('On anger', in three books), addressed to his brother Novatus (later Gallio, by adoption). It deals with the nature of anger and means of restraining it.

*De consolatione ad Marciam* ('Consolation to Marcia'), an attempt to console the daughter of Cremutius Cordus (a historian, victim of *Sejanus) for the death of her sons.

*De vita beata* ('On the happy life'), addressed to his brother and surviving incomplete. It opts for the Stoic doctrine that happiness lies in living virtuously in accordance with nature, but accepts that other things such as health and riches have their value.

*De otio* ('On leisure'), addressed to Annaeus Serenus, advocating that leisure should be spent in contemplation.

*De tranquillitate animi* ('On tranquillity of the soul'), addressed to Annaeus Serenus, on pursuing peace of mind.

*De brevitate vitae* ('On the shortness of life'), addressed to an official, Paulinus. On the value of time and the wise use of it, it is considered one of Seneca's best essays.

*De consolatione ad Polybium* ('Consolation to Polybius'), addressed to a freedman of the emperor Claudius (this Polybius appears to have translated Homer into Latin prose and Virgil into Greek). It is an unattractive piece written *c*.43 in an attempt to obtain recall from exile.

*De consolatione ad Helviam matrem.* ('Consolation to Helvia'), written to his mother to console her for his own exile in 41. It shows fortitude and dignity.

Outside this collection of dialogues there are further moral essays, *De clementia* ('On clemency') and *De beneficiis* ('On acts of kindness'), and the *Epistulae morales*, a collection of 124 letters addressed to his friend Lucilius, divided into twenty books. *De clementia* (AD 55–6) is in three books, of which the first and part of the second survive, on the need for clemency in a ruler. Written in the second year of the emperor Nero's reign, its theme was suggested by his exclamation when unwillingly signing a death warrant, 'Would that I had never learnt to write!' The praise of Nero that it contains must be judged in relation to the comparative

mildness of his rule in its early years. The *Epistulae* are also in effect moral essays (the fiction of a genuine correspondence is only sporadically aimed at), and are written in the tradition of the philosophical letter (*see* LETTERS [Latin]) or the *diatribe. The nature of the subject matter—on happiness, the supreme good, riches, the terrors of death, and so forth—and the charm and informality of style, have made them the most popular of Seneca's works. They are persuasive, not dogmatic, in tone, and furnish interesting personal details about the author himself, as well as being illuminating about contemporary life. They were approved and made use of by early Christian writers. Seneca was thought in the Middle Ages to have been a Christian, and was believed by St Jerome and others to have corresponded with the apostle Paul. His treatises were studied by Petrarch (1304–74) and known to Chaucer (*c*.1343–1400).

3. Of a different order are the seven books of Seneca's *Naturales quaestiones*, dedicated to Lucilius and written during Seneca's retirement towards the end of his life. This work is an examination of natural phenomena, not from a scientific but from a Stoic standpoint. It is not a systematic work but a collection of facts about nature. The phenomena are grouped according to their connection with one or other of the four *elements, earth, air, fire, and water, with moral observations scattered throughout. The purpose of the work seems to be to find in nature a foundation for Stoic ethic. Though of little scientific value the work was used in the Middle Ages as a textbook of natural science.

The *Apocolocyntosis* is a clever and original piece of satirical burlesque on the death of the emperor Claudius, written in the form of a Menippean satire in a medley of prose and verse (*see* MENIPPUS).

Most of Seneca's prose work is philosophical, and an important source for the history of Stoicism. His own brand of that philosophy was undogmatic and tempered by experience and common sense, and is often used as the basis for moral exhortation rather than expounded as a system of thought in its own right. The style is lively and rhetorical; it catches the attention immediately, but its unremitting brilliance, lacking depth of thought, is tiring: 'sand without lime' (i.e. cement that crumbles) is how the emperor Caligula described it.

4. Seneca's most important poetical works are the nine tragedies attributed to him and derived from Greek tragedy in general rather than from individual plays: *Hercules furens, Medea, Troades* (*\*Trojan Women*), *Phaedra, Agamemnon, Oedipus, Phoenissae* and the very Sophoclean *Hercules Oetaeus* (neither perhaps by Seneca), and *Thyestes* (a gruesome story with no surviving Greek source). A tenth tragedy, *Octavia*, is obviously not by him. (See individual entries for each of these.) The plays are modelled on Greek tragedy, that is, with five dramatic episodes (written in iambic senarii;) separated by choral odes (in lyric metres, most often anapaestic). The central character, who is neither a hero nor a villain, is often called upon to take vengeance in reaction to a terrible event. We hear a great deal about violence: Seneca loves to dwell on the horrific and macabre elements of the plot. The plays are exaggerations of the Euripidean style, showing psychological insight into passions running out of control, but markedly rhetorical and short in dramatic action. It is likely that they were intended for private recitation rather than acting. But the *stichomythia is often more effective than that of the Greek original, and the ending of Seneca's *Medea* is more dramatic than that of Euripides. There are fine passages of description, much moralizing, and some striking epigrams. The plays also convey the Euripidean sense of the individual as victim. They exerted a great influence in the Italian Renaissance and in Tudor and Jacobean times in England; stock characters in the romantic plays of Shakespeare, such as the ghost, the nurse, and the barbarous villain, were transmitted from the Greek through the medium of Seneca.

The *Anthologia Latina* (*see* ANTHOLOGY [Latin]) includes a number of short poems by Seneca, some containing references to his own life and family.

**Se'ptuagint** (in abbreviation LXX) Greek version of the Hebrew or Aramaic scriptures which became the Old Testament of the Greek-speaking Christians. The name is derived from a story, now known to be false, contained in an Alexandrian Greek work of the mid-second century BC, the *Letter of Aristeas*. The story goes that Ptolemy II Philadelphus (king of Egypt 283–246 BC) wanted for the royal library a translation of the Jewish Law (the Torah, i.e. the Pentateuch, the five books of Moses:

Genesis, Exodus, Leviticus, Numbers, and Deuteronomy). The translators were seventy-two (or seventy, Lat. *septuaginta*) learned Jews, kept in seclusion on the island of Pharos off Alexandria until their task was finished. This story was elaborated to include the other Old Testament books. The translation must in fact have been made by Egyptian Jews working independently of one another and living at different periods in the Hellenistic age. The Septuagint differs from the present Old Testament both in the order of the books and in the inclusion of those books which are usually known as the Apocrypha. There are also textual differences. The Greek-speaking Christian Fathers down to the late fourth century AD regarded the Septuagint as the standard form of the Old Testament and seldom referred to the Hebrew. Origen, however, was very interested in its relation to the Hebrew and to other Greek versions. *See also* LONGINUS ON THE SUBLIME.

**Serā'pis** (Lat.; Gk. Sarapis) A new god, a combination of the Egyptian god Osiris and the sacred embalmed bull Apis, the object of popular cult in Egypt under the early Ptolemies. Serapis was identified with several Greek gods in his several roles. As a divine healer, he was identified with *Asclepius: *Demetrius of Phalerum (a close adviser of Ptolemy I) was cured of his blindness, reputedly by the god, in Alexandria, and in consequence wrote a *paean to him. It is thought that Ptolemy may have prompted Serapis' cult to unite his Greek and Egyptian subjects in the worship of a god whom both could appreciate. The first three Ptolemies had a hand in building the Serapeum, a vast temple to Serapis, at Alexandria; his cult spread widely in the Greco-Roman world.

**Sermō'nes** *See* SATIRES (1).

**Sertō'rius, Quintus** (*c.*126–73 BC) Distinguished Roman soldier, supporter of *Marius, who joined Cinna in his march on Rome in 87 BC but opposed Marius' indiscriminate slaughter. He became praetor and was given Spain as his province in 83–2. In 80 BC he accepted an invitation by the Lusitanians (in western Spain) and Roman exiles hostile to Sulla to lead them in a revolt against Rome. He was successful against many Roman commanders (including *Pompey) and at one time held most of Roman Spain. Gradually losing ground to Metellus and Pompey, and his popularity having waned, he was murdered in 73 or 72 by his lieutenant Perperna, who was subsequently executed by Pompey.

**Se'rvius (Marius Servius Honoratus)** Latin grammarian and commentator of the fourth century AD, whose greatest work was a commentary on Virgil based on the earlier work of *Donatus (1). Since the commentary was intended for school use it concentrates on grammatical, rhetorical, and stylistic points, but some notes on the subject matter are included which contain very valuable information. The commentary is found in the manuscripts in a shorter (the original Servian) and a longer version, the latter known as *Servius auctus* ('augmented Servius') or *Servius Danielis* (named after its discoverer, Pierce Daniel, and published in 1600). This incorporates earlier material from Donatus not included by Servius. Servius was a participant in *Macrobius' *Saturnalia*.

**Se'rvius Tu'llius** Semi-legendary king of Rome, sixth in succession from Romulus; according to tradition he reigned from 578 to 535 BC. He was the successor of Tarquinius Priscus (*see* TARQUIN (1)), in whose house he was brought up as a slave. There were several legends about his birth, some including miraculous elements. He is credited with the enfranchisement of freedmen and his rule is said to have been mild. A number of public works and constitutional reforms, and the institution of the cult of Diana on the Aventine, were attributed to him. (But no sixth-century traces of the 'Servian' wall have been found; *see* ROME 1). Servius was murdered by the order of Lucius Tarquinius (*see* TARQUIN (2)), son of Priscus, at the instigation of his own daughter, Tullia, who was Lucius' wife. Lucius succeeded him and was known as Tarquinius Superbus.

**seste'rtius** (pl. sestertii) (Eng. sesterces) In Roman currency, a small silver coin worth 2½ asses. Despite its comparatively low value the Romans reckoned even very large sums of money in sesterces. *See* MONEY AND COINS.

**Seven against Thebes, The** (*Hepta epi Thebas*) (Lat. *Septem contra Thebas*) Tragedy by *Aeschylus, produced in 467 BC, the third play in a trilogy dealing with related events, the first two plays being *Laius* and *Oedipus*. The *satyr play which followed it was also related in subject matter, being entitled *Sphinx*. All these plays except the *Seven* are lost.

*Oedipus' curse on his sons results in their quarrelling over the throne of Thebes. Polyneices has come, aided by the Argive army, to claim the kingdom, unjustly retained by his brother Eteocles. The scene is the city of Thebes, and the chorus is composed of Theban women. A messenger announces the disposition of the Argive army and describes the seven champions preparing to lead the attack, one at each of the seven gates of Thebes. Their names (as usually given) are: Adrastus, his sons-in-law Polyneices and Tȳdeus, Capaneus, Hippomedon, Parthenopaeus, and *Amphiaraus. Eteocles appoints a Theban opponent to withstand each one, finding himself left to oppose Polyneices; Eteocles rushes out to face his brother in spite of the dissuasions of the chorus. Their deaths at each other's hands are announced, and their bodies are borne in, mourned by the chorus. In a scene probably added by an imitator their sisters Ismene and Antigone join in the lamentation. A herald announces the decree that the body of Polyneices, who has waged war on his own city, will lie unburied. Antigone at once declares that she will defy the edict: she will bury him herself. The ending was probably remodelled after Sophocles' *Antigone*.

For the Argive background *see* ADRASTUS. In other versions of the story two alternative champions were sometimes included, Eteocles, son of Iphis, instead of Adrastus, and Mecisteus, Adrastus' brother, instead of Polyneices. The story was told in the *Thebaïs*, a poem of the *Epic Cycle. *See also* ANTIMACHUS and THEBAÏD.

**seven hills of Rome** The Palatine, Aventine, Capitoline, Caelian, Esquiline, Viminal, and Quirinal hills. (In Latin, the first five are *montes*, 'peaks', 'mountains', the last two *colles*, 'hills', but the distinction bears no apparent relation to their heights.)

**seven kings of Rome** *See* KINGS OF ROME.

**seven liberal arts** A loose classification of the subjects comprising the educational curriculum in the West during the Middle Ages, from the late fifth century AD onwards. The name 'liberal arts' seems to originate with Aristotle, who in the *Politics* talks of *eleutherai epistemai*, 'branches of knowledge worthy of free men', the basic knowledge needed for a properly educated citizen. They were divided into the trivium ('where three ways meet'), namely grammar (i.e. literature), rhetoric, and dialectic (logic), and the more advanced quadrivium ('where four ways meet'), namely arithmetic, geometry, music, and astronomy. These are the four sciences mentioned by Protagoras, in Plato's dialogue of that name, as taught by the sophist Hippias. For the original nine *see* VARRO [*Disciplinae*]; *see also* EDUCATION 3, 4, and 6.

**Seven Sages** Name given by Greek tradition to seven men of practical wisdom—statesmen, law-givers, and philosophers—of the seventh and sixth centuries BC. The list of sages is variously given in the authorities, but generally includes some or all of the following: *Solon of Athens, *Thales of Miletus, *Pittacus of Mitylene, Cleobulus of Rhodes, *Chilon of Sparta, Bias of Priene, and *Periander of Corinth. Many pieces of proverbial wisdom were attributed to them, such as those inscribed at *Delphi, 'Know yourself' and 'Nothing in excess'.

**Seven Wonders of the ancient world** Listed in Hellenistic times, these were the Pyramids of Egypt, the Hanging Gardens of Babylon, the Mausoleum at Halicarnassus (*see* MAUSOLUS), the Temple of Artemis at Ephesus, the statue of Zeus at *Olympia (by *Pheidias), the *Colossus of Rhodes, and the Pharos of *Alexandria.

**Sextus Empi'ricus** (fl. *c.* AD 200) Greek physician obviously of the empiricist school (*see* MEDICINE), whose writings are the chief source of information on the *Sceptics. In his 'Outlines of Pyrrhonism' (*Pyrrhōneioi hypotypōseis*, abbreviated to *PH*) in three books, he states the case for the Sceptics and attacks dogmatic philosophies. In his other work 'Against the professors' (*Pros tous mathematikous*, Lat. *Adversus mathematicos*, abbreviated to *M*) he criticizes the teachers of the various branches of education in succession.

**sexuality** *See* LOVE AND SEXUALITY.

**shaft graves** *See* MYCENAE.

**shame** *See* AIDOS and HUBRIS.

**Shield of Heracles** (*Aspis Herakleous*) Greek narrative poem in 480 hexameters attributed to *Hesiod but written too late (probably in the early sixth century BC) to be by him. The first 56 lines tell the story of Alcmena, mother of Heracles, and come from the *Catalogue of Women* or *Eoeae*, also erroneously attributed to Hesiod. The poem goes on to relate briefly the killing by Heracles of Cycnus, son of Ares. For the encounter Heracles has put on armour given him by Hephaestus, including a shield, the disproportionately long description of which (in imitation of Homer's description of the shield of Achilles in the *Iliad*) gives the poem its title.

**ships** *See* PENTECONTER and TRIREME.

**Sibyl (Sibylla)** General name given by the Greeks and Romans to various women prophets in the Greek and Roman world, who sometimes had individual names as well. The most ancient Sibyl known in legend was Herophile, who prophesied to Hecuba, queen of Troy, before the Trojan War. She was also known as the Erythraean Sibyl from her birthplace Erythrae (perhaps the city of that name on the coast of Asia Minor opposite Chios). Many Sibyls prophesied in an ecstatic state, and were believed to be possessed by a god, usually Apollo, who spoke through them (cf. the Pythia at *Delphi). Their utterances were written down, and cities made official collections of what were believed to be their prophecies; at Athens similar collections of oracles were kept on the Acropolis (*see* ONOMACRITUS and ORACLES).

The most famous Sibyl in antiquity was that of Cumae in Campania (sometimes identified with the Erythraean), whom Virgil represents as being visited by Aeneas (in *Aeneid* 6) and speaking under the inspiration of Apollo. The cave in which she is supposed to have lived still exists. Her prophecies were said to have been inscribed on palm-leaves. According to legend she offered nine volumes of oracles to the last king of Rome, Tarquinius Superbus (*see* TARQUIN (2)), at a high price. When he refused to buy she burned three volumes and offered the remainder at the same price. When he again refused she burned three more, and finally sold the last three to him at the original price. The king is said to have entrusted these Sibylline books (*libri Sibyllini*) to the care of a priestly college (*see* QUINDECIMVIRI).

However acquired, books of oracles in Greek verse certainly existed in Rome at an early date, and were consulted not only for guidance about the future but in order to find out how a threatened calamity, such as earthquake and plague, might be averted. Instituting new cults and rituals was often recommended. The books were kept in a chest in a stone vault under the temple of the Capitoline Jupiter. When they were destroyed in the temple fire of 83 BC, envoys were sent to various places to make a fresh collection of similar oracular sayings, which was subsequently placed by Augustus in the temple of Apollo on the Palatine hill. The last known consultation was in AD 363. The collection was still in existence in the temple when the latter was destroyed early in the fifth century. Fourteen miscellaneous books of oracles, of Judaeo-Hellenistic and Christian origin, still survive from late antiquity. Because of Christian interpolations in the Sibylline oracles, the Sibyls came to be thought of as on an equality with Old Testament prophets, and frequently figure with them in Christian literature and art.

A famous story told of the Cumaean Sibyl relates that the god Apollo once offered her anything she wished if she would take him as her lover. She asked to live as many years as there were grains of sand in a pile of sweepings, and these numbered a thousand, but she failed to ask for continued youth (*cf.* TITHONUS). Trimalchio, a character in *Petronius' Satyricon*, had seen her with his own eyes, he said, hanging from the ceiling of her cave in a bottle, and when children asked her what she wanted, she used to reply, 'I want to die.' In the days of the Greek traveller *Pausanias (second century AD) a jar was shown at Cumae said to contain her bones.

**Sicilian Expedition** (415–413 BC) An episode in the *Peloponnesian War when Athens made an ill-fated invasion of Sicily. Athens responded to an appeal for help from Segesta, who was at war with Selinus, her neighbour on the island, but the real reasons for the expedition were to curb the growing power of Syracuse (Sicily's main city), to gain a foothold on Sicily, and to obtain complete control of the sea. The expedition was the greatest naval and military force ever mounted by a Greek city, but it failed disastrously. It was commanded by the incompatible *Alcibiades, *Lamachus, and *Nicias. Alcibiades was soon recalled on a charge of sacrilege, but he escaped and went over to Sparta; Lamachus was killed in a skirmish. Nicias, who was left in sole command until joined by the general *Demosthenes (1), had opposed the invasion from the beginning and proved an indecisive general. He besieged Syracuse in 414 but was crushingly defeated on land and at sea. (After an eclipse of the moon,

considered a bad omen, he delayed a retreat for twenty-seven days.) Athens lost more than 30,000 men and 200 ships—blows from which she never recovered.

**Sicily** (Gk. Sikelia, Lat. Sicilia) The largest island of the Mediterranean, separated from Italy by the Straits of Messina. The Thrinacia mentioned in Homer's *Odyssey* (from Greek *thrīnax*, 'trident') is perhaps to be identified with it. Trinacria was a Latin poetical name for the island. Its strategic position, fine climate, and fertile soil made it a meeting-place for settlers from east and west, and from Italy and Africa, and gave it great importance in the history of the Mediterranean world. Ancient writers speak of there being three native peoples there, Elymi in the west, Sicani in the west-central, and Siceli in the east. Thucydides says that the Sicanians and Sicels were Iberian and Italian respectively; the Elymi he describes as fleeing from the sack of Troy.

From about the eighth century BC it was colonized variously by Greeks, Phoenicians, and Carthaginians, and its history was often one of bloody conflict (for the Athenian invasion of 415–413 BC *see* SICILIAN EXPEDITION). During the first part of the fifth century BC the courts of the Sicilian tyrants were places of culture and great wealth, as may be seen from odes written for them by *Pindar in celebration of their victories at the Panhellenic games, as well as from the surviving ruins. The main city was *Syracuse, and in the fourth century it came to control all Sicily except for the Carthaginian territories in the far west. After Rome's victory over Carthage in the First *Punic War (264–241 BC) almost the whole island came under Roman rule, which was often harsh and corrupt (*see* VERRES). After the Romans captured Syracuse in 211 (*see* MARCELLUS (1)) Sicily became a Roman province.

Sicily produced many Greeks famous in literary history, among them the poet Stesichorus, the sophist Gorgias, the scientists Empedocles and Archimedes, the historian Timaeus, the pastoral poet Theocritus, and Herodas the writer of mimes.

*Sicyō'nius* ('The Sicyonian') Greek comedy by *Menander, of which some 470 more or less fragmentary lines from the second half have been recovered from a papyrus used by Egyptian mummifiers when making a papier-mâché mummy case (*see* PAPYROLOGY). The play concerns Stratophanes (the Sicyonian of the title), a successful captain of mercenaries who on returning to Athens after service in Caria has taken a house at Eleusis, and his discovery of his real father and of the identity and Athenian citizenship of a girl whom he has purchased as a slave in Caria and now wishes to marry.

**Sige'um** Athens' first possession overseas, in the Troas, acquired in the late seventh century BC by Periander then lost to Mytilene and reconquered by Peisistratus. It became a loyal member of the *Delian League.

**Sīlē'nus (Seilenos)** In Greek myth, Silenus represented the spirit of wild life in a creature half-man, half-animal in form (*cf.* SATYRS; classical authors seem to use the names indistinguishably). Silenus is shown on Attic vases of the early sixth century BC having horse-ears and sometimes horse-legs and a tail. Sometimes a collection of sileni are found. In general, whereas satyrs are young, sileni are thought of as old men, and being old are thought to be wise. A famous story relates how *Midas made Silenus drunk in order to learn his secrets. In Virgil's Eclogue 6, Silenus is caught by two shepherds and sings them songs of ancient myths. He is sometimes represented as *Dionysus' tutor, or depicted in the train of Dionysus, making music or getting drunk. (See also the *Cyclops* of Euripides.) *Socrates was often compared with Silenus, and their likenesses are remarkably similar. The comparison was meant to include not only physical appearance but a common incongruity between outward appearance and inner wisdom.

**Sī'lius Ita'licus (Tiberius Catius Ascōnius Silius Italicus)** (*c*.AD 26–*c*.102) Latin poet. He was the author of the longest surviving Latin poem, *Punica*, an epic comprising over 12,000 lines in seventeen books of hexameters on the Second *Punic War (218–201 BC). His life is chiefly known to us from a letter of the Younger Pliny (3.7), and from references in Martial's epigrams. He was probably born at Patavium (Padua) and having won fame as an advocate was consul in 68, the last year of the emperor Nero's reign. Later, *c*.77, he won praise as proconsul for his administration of Asia. Thereafter he lived in retirement on his estates near Naples. He was a wealthy man, bought country houses (including a villa once belonging to Cicero, whom he revered), and was a collector of books and works of art. He had a profound admiration for Virgil, whose tomb near Naples, on one of his properties, he restored. Finding that he was suffering from an incurable disease he starved himself to death at the age of 75. *Punica* begins with *Hannibal's oath, his appointment to the command, and, except for digressions on the captured Roman general *Regulus and on Anna, sister of the Carthaginian queen Dido, it proceeds in order through the principal episodes of the war, the crossing of the Alps, the battles of the Ticinus, the Trebia, Lake Trasimene, and Cannae, the capture of Syracuse, the battle of the Metaurus, Scipio in Spain and Africa, and the final battle of Zama.

Silius was highly praised as Virgil's poetic heir by Martial, but the Younger Pliny's remark that his epic was written with more diligence than inspiration (*maiore cura quam ingenio*) has been found more apt. It was probably published, not fully revised, at his death. The subject matter came from Livy, the form from study of Virgil and Lucan (*see PHARSALIA*). The theme is the fulfilment of Dido's curse that there should be eternal enmity between her people and Aeneas' descendants. Following Virgil's practice (and in contrast with Lucan) Silius retained the intervention of the gods in the conflict, traditional in epic since Homer. However, to mythicize the real world of Hannibal and Scipio so as to mingle gods and men without incongruity was impossibly difficult; it is, for example, bizarre to find the Carthaginian general Hannibal saved from death by the goddess Juno, just as the legendary Turnus is saved in the *Aeneid*. Also incongruous are the traditional epic ingredients of catalogues (of Hannibal's allies), funeral games, description of a hero's shield (Hannibal's), Nereids (sea-nymphs) disturbed by a vast fleet (Carthaginian), and altercations of antagonists on the battlefield. The greatness of the theme—Rome's heroic rise, with divine sanction, from defeat to victory—is lost through lack of proportion. The realistic descriptions of slaughter (perhaps due to Lucan's influence) exceed those of Homer. By the end it is clear that Rome's victory over Carthage holds the seeds of her own decline. There are some memorable phrases: 'rarely do the altars of the fortunate smoke [with sacrifices]', *rarae fumant felicibus arae*, and 'adversity is the test of men', *explorant adversa viros*.

**silloi** *See* TIMON (2) and XENOPHANES.

**Silvae** The title given by the poet *Statius to his collection of (mostly) short poems published in five books. The Latin word *silva* in its sense of 'raw material' was extended in a literary sense to the raw material of a literary work; *Quintilian explains it as a quickly produced first draft of a poem. It was used in the plural, *silvae*, of collections of occasional poems.

**Silva'nus** ('of the wood') In Roman religion, the god of the countryside beyond the boundaries of the cultivated fields. He thus resembled the Greek *satyrs or *Silenus, and was sometimes identified with them, but more often with the gods *Faunus or *Pan. His cult was regarded as very ancient, and it was important to propitiate him before violating his territory, e.g. cutting down trees.

**Silver age** Term sometimes applied to the post-Augustan period of Latin literature; *see* LATIN LITERATURE, PERIODS OF (iii).

**Sīmo'nidēs** (of Ceos, a small Ionian Greek island off the coast of Attica) Greek lyric and elegiac poet and famous writer of sepulchral *epigrams. Most sources date his birth to 556 BC and report him as living to be 90. He was uncle of the poet Bacchylides. As a professional poet he travelled widely in the Greek world. He was the guest of *Hipparchus at Athens during the Peisistratid tyranny, and subsequently went to Thessaly, where he was the guest of the Scopads and later wrote a dirge lamenting their deaths (see below). After the Persian Wars he became the ally of *Themistocles, on whose behalf he attacked in his poetry the Rhodian poet Timocreon. His *Battle of Plataea* (in or after 479) was finished at the court of Hieron in Syracuse, with whom he stayed until his death. His tomb was to be seen at Acragas.

Very many stories circulated about him, some concerning his fondness for money, which became proverbial (he is said to have been the first Greek poet to write eulogies for pay). The most famous story concerns his visit to the Scopads of Thessaly where at a banquet he sang a lyric glorifying his patron, but including a lengthy digression in praise of Castor and Polydeuces (*see* DIOSCURI). Scopas said that he would pay the poet only half the fee, and he might apply for the rest to the two heroes to whom he had devoted an equal share of the praise. A little later a message came to say that two young men were asking for Simonides at

the door of the hall. Simonides rose to speak to them but found no one there; while he was outside, the roof of the hall collapsed, killing all the other guests. Although the dead were crushed out of recognition Simonides, who had devised a system of mnemonics, was able to remember where each guest sat and so identify each body.

Despite his great reputation in antiquity, most of Simonides' poetry is lost. Comparatively little survives in quotation, and papyrus finds have been very fragmentary. He excelled in many varieties of choral lyric: hymns, dithyramb, partheneia, paeans, scolia, encomia (including the poem to Scopas from which a long passage survives in Plato's *Protagoras*, quoted there as the basis for discussion), *epinicians (he and perhaps *Ibycus were the first to write poems of this genre), and elegies. These last include some historical pieces on the battles of Artemisium and Plataea. He was most famed for *dirges and for epigrams to be inscribed on dedications and tombstones, particularly for those referring to the dead of the Persian Wars, although it is difficult to be sure which ones were genuinely written by him. Best-known (but perhaps not genuine) is that on the Spartan dead at Thermopylae:

> Tell them in Lacedaemon, passer-by,
> That here obedient to their words we lie.

Simonides acquired the reputation of a sage, and many perhaps traditional sayings were attributed to him. The dictum that 'painting is silent poetry and poetry a painting that speaks', adapted by Horace as 'poetry resembles painting' (*ut pictura poesis*), was taken by G. E. Lessing as the starting-point of his *Laokoon* (1766).

**Sīnon** *See* TROJAN HORSE.

**Sīrens (Seirēnes)** In Greek myth, female creatures who had the power of drawing men to destruction by their song. In Homer's *Odyssey* there are two of them who live on an island near *Scylla and *Charybdis (in the Straits of Messina). Odysseus, when his ship was about to pass their island, in order to escape them filled the ears of his men with wax but left his own unblocked and had himself lashed to the mast so that he could hear their singing and yet survive. The song they tempted him with offered omniscience: 'we know of all things that come to pass on the fruitful earth.' According to later legend the Sirens drowned themselves from vexation at his escape. The body of one of them, Parthenope, was washed ashore in the bay of Naples, which originally bore her name. The *Argonauts, on their return voyage, passed near the Sirens; Orpheus, by playing on his lyre more beautifully than the Sirens sang, saved the other Argonauts from listening to their song (except for one man, who sprang overboard but was rescued by Aphrodite). In Homer the Sirens are not described, but in art they are represented as half-women and half-birds; in time they came increasingly to be shown as beautiful women, and also as creators of music; in the myth of Er at the end of Plato's *Republic* they make the music of the spheres (*see* HARMONY OF THE SPHERES); thus in Hellenistic art and literature they came to symbolize music. 'What song the Sirens sang' is said by Suetonius to be one of the impossible questions with which the emperor Tiberius teased the scholars at his court.

**Sīro (Siron)** *See* VIRGIL.

**Si'syphus** In Greek myth, son of Aeolus and Enarete, founder of the city of Corinth (called Ephyre in the *Iliad*), reputedly the most cunning of men. For that reason in some post-Homeric accounts he became the father of Odysseus and was sometimes associated with the master-thief *Autolycus. (When Autolycus stole his cattle Sisyphus was able to recognize his own, having marked their hoofs 'Autolycus stole these'. His revenge was to seduce Autolycus' daughter Anticlea, so that it was suspected that he rather than her husband Laertes was Odysseus' father.) Having observed the seduction of the nymph Aegina by Zeus he revealed the truth to her father, the river-god Asopus, in return for a spring of fresh water on the citadel. Zeus punished Sisyphus by sending Death for him, but Sisyphus chained Death up in a dungeon, so that mortals ceased to die; the gods in alarm sent Ares to release Death, who came after Sisyphus once again. Sisyphus instructed his wife Merope to leave his body unburied and make no offerings, with the result that the Underworld gods Hades and Persephone allowed the supposedly indignant Sisyphus to return from the Underworld to earth to punish his wife and make her bury the body. Once in the world again Sisyphus resumed his life and lived to a great age. However, when he eventually died the gods of the Underworld devised for him a famous punishment: to roll up to the top of a hill a rock which always rolled down again just as it was about to reach the summit. Sisyphus was the father of four sons, one of whom was Glaucus, father of *Bellerophon.

## slavery

**Greek.** The entire manner of Greek life was dependent on the presence of large numbers of slaves. At a rough estimate perhaps a third of the population of Attica in the classical period, numbering say a quarter of a million in all, comprised slaves. On the whole Greeks did not enslave fellow-Greeks but '*barbarians', a situation which gave rise to Aristotle's notorious identification of some people as 'natural' slaves. Despite that, slavery in the ancient world was never based on race alone. The popular idea of slavery has its origin in the so-called 'chattel' slave, an alien acquired through war (often between foreigners) and slave-traders, who was regarded merely as a piece of property (a 'living tool' in Aristotle's phrase) to be used and abused as the owners wished, with no legal or civic rights whatsoever (but *see also* HELOTS). A slave's evidence was admissible in a law-court only if obtained under torture. Athens was a society based on such slaves, but despite lack of rights there was a gradation of their status. The highest class had occupations that could be performed by free men, as in the case of *Pasion and *Phormion. The employment of slaves such as these rather than free men as managers of banks may seem surprising, but all Greeks, or at least all Athenians, thought it demeaning to be employed by a master, which they considered tantamount to slavery. Slaves were employed as *police or as clerks in the state bureaucracy, and in extreme emergencies they were conscripted into the army or navy. Those who fought the Spartans at *Arginusae in 406 BC were rewarded with their freedom, but many Athenian slaves ran away when the Spartans established a base at *Decelea in 413 BC. Thucydides said that more than 20,000 made their way there, most of them skilled workmen. On the other hand, when the Greeks were in control of Chios in 411 BC many slaves, who were punished particularly severely in Chios, deserted to the Athenians. At Athens it was possible for a slave to take refuge either at the temple of *Hephaestus or at the altar of the Eumenides on the Areopagus, and beg someone to buy him from his master.

Another category comprised the skilled slaves owned and trained by craftsmen to carry on a craft for their masters and live independently (known as 'living apart'), retaining a percentage of the profits. The orator *Lysias and his brother Polemarchus, from a rich *metic family, owned a shield factory employing nearly 120 slaves, the largest industrial establishment we know of in ancient Greece. There were also large numbers of household slaves, managed by the housewife; they often had a hard life, especially those men required to do agricultural work, but worst off were slaves employed in the mines, such as the silver mines at Laurium, until released by an early death. The general Nicias is said to have hired out a thousand slaves as miners for a return of one obol a day each. A small class of slaves were those enslaved for debt; but the Athenian statesman *Solon at the beginning of the sixth century BC abolished debt-bondage for citizens altogether. In some states whole communities of slaves existed as population groups, notably the helots at *Sparta. A person whose parents were slaves was himself a slave from birth.

A master could free his slave by making a simple declaration before witnesses. Slaves 'living apart' would hope to buy their freedom. Freed slaves became metics, not citizens as at Rome.

**Roman.** As in Greece, Roman society could function as it did only through slave-ownership. Romans had complete control over the lives of their slaves, including (unlike Athens) that of life and death. The proportion of slaves to free citizens, as far as one can tell, seems to have been the same in Rome as in Greece, i.e. one to two, but the scale of ownership was much larger at Rome, the wealthy possessing hundreds of slaves. Slaves were chiefly procured as a result of war, and Rome's wars of the second and first centuries BC produced large numbers of prisoners. We hear of Aemilius *Paullus selling 150,000 slaves after his victory in 168 BC at Pydna. Pirates, particularly the Cilicians, swamped the famous slave market at Delos with their victims. Children born to slave mothers were themselves slaves.

As at Athens slaves were used on a large scale in the mines. The scale of their use in Italian agriculture in the second and first centuries BC is still debated (see LATIFUNDIA), but it seems to have been relatively high and still so under the empire. In manufacturing, slaves and free men often worked side by side. Roman slaves were quite often freed ('manumitted') by their masters using a simple form of words, or could buy their freedom with their savings (*peculium*). They could then be registered as citizens. They continued to belong to the family of their former master (*patronus*) and both parties were bound by mutual obligations. Home-bred farm slaves seem to have been regarded with sentimental sympathy by town-bred Romans. A freedman often adopted the name and forename (*praenomen*) of his liberator, adding his own as *cognomen* (see NAMES [Roman]).

Running away was common for individual slaves: Cicero was very upset when his slave Dionysius ran off with many of his books. Slave revolts were only likely to occur when there were large concentrations of slaves sharing a nationality or language. Two occurred in Sicily (c.139–132 and 104–100 BC) and were suppressed at great cost. A third was in Italy 73–71 BC, led by *Spartacus. The slaves involved were aiming to seize a territory and live in freedom, not, as far as one knows, to destroy the institution of slavery. In Greece and Rome slavery was taken for granted as a fact of life, and was not opposed even by philosophers who believed in a common humanity (Cynics and Stoics) or by early Christians, who were all in their different ways uninterested in the material conditions of life. See LAW, NATURAL and POLITICS.

**Sleep** (Gk. Hypnos, Lat. Somnus) In Greek myth, the brother of Death (Thanatos), son of Night (*Nyx). Homer, in the episode of Hera seducing Zeus with the aid of Sleep (*Iliad* 14.225), describes his home as a cave on the island of Lemnos; Ovid places it in the dark mists of the far North.

**soccus** The low-heeled, loose-fitting shoe worn by Roman actors of comedy, of Greek origin. The word is often used to symbolize comedy; the poet John Milton speaks of 'Jonson's learned sock'. Cf. COTHURNUS.

**Social War 1.** In Greek history, name given to the war (357–355 BC) between Athens on the one hand and Chios, Cos, and Rhodes (with the support of Byzantium and Mausolus of Caria) on the other, all of which had revolted from Athens' Second League. At the end of the war the independence of the principal members of the league was recognized. *See* ATHENS 4.

**2.** In Roman history, also known as the Marsic or Italic War, an uprising against Rome (91–87 BC, the main fighting being in 90–89) by its Italian allies (*socii*), most of whom were fighting to win Roman citizenship. From a military point of view the fighting was inconclusive, but the Romans conceded the main issue: full citizenship was granted to all Italians south of the Po. *See* SCAEVOLA 4.

**socii** ('allies', of Rome) Although Rome had allies outside Italy, the term commonly denoted her Italian allies, *socii Italici*, those people, Italian, Greek, and Etruscan, living in some 150 communities, who were allied to Rome by formal treaties. The term excluded the Latins, who had a special relationship with Rome and special privileges; *see* LATIN RIGHTS. The allies differed from the Romans and Latins in language, laws, and customs. All were obliged to provide military aid when required and to surrender to Rome control of foreign affairs. Their feelings of injustice led to the outbreak of war in 91 BC (*see* SOCIAL WAR (2)).

**So'cratēs** (469–399 BC) Greek philosopher, a public figure at Athens, and a central figure in the intellectual debates there in the middle-to-late fifth century BC. His influence was enormous though he himself wrote nothing. He was born in the Attic deme of Alopeke near Athens. His father was Sophroniscus, a sculptor or stonemason, and his mother Phaenarete, a midwife. He himself was a stonemason. Rather late in life he married the reputedly shrewish Xanthippe, by whom he had three sons, who were still young at the time of his death. He fought in the Peloponnesian War and as a hoplite soldier he was distinguished by his courage and physical resilience. Although he generally avoided public affairs, when he did take part his behaviour accorded with his principles. He was foreman of the *prytaneis* of the assembly on the day when the generals were tried for abandoning the dead after *Arginusae, and alone voted against the illegal proposal to try them en masse. Under the *Thirty Tyrants he risked his own life by refusing to assist in the arrest of an innocent man condemned to death by the Thirty. His manner of life won him many enemies, and in 399 he was brought to trial by Anytus (a democratic politician), Meletus, and Lycon on the charge of not believing in the

same gods as the Athenians but introducing new gods, and of corrupting the youth of the city. The death penalty was asked for.

Two versions of Socrates' speech in his own defence exist: in the *Apology* (Gk. *apologia*, 'defence') by Plato and, it is thought in a less authentic form, in that by Xenophon, but neither makes exactly clear the precise significance of the charges. These were connected, however, with Socrates' well-known association with many of the Thirty Tyrants who overthrew the democracy, notably *Alcibiades and *Critias. Clearly he had failed to teach them virtue. The attack on him was not merely because of the political views of his protégés: the amnesty of 403 BC prohibited prosecution for most political offences committed before that date. It seems also to have been felt that he had undermined the traditional morality and religion of the city, the practice of which had in former times, it was believed, made Athens great; of his associates, Alcibiades was suspected of sacrilege and Critias was an atheist. It is unlikely that Socrates' accusers wished or expected the death penalty to be inflicted; it would have been possible for him to follow the usual course of going into voluntary exile before the verdict, or of proposing banishment as an alternative to the death penalty, when it would probably have been accepted. However, his unconditional belief that he had done no harm to the city led to his obviously unacceptable counter-proposal that he should be dined for life at public expense (a privilege afforded to great benefactors of the state) or alternatively that his friends should pay a fine on his behalf; a greater number of the jury (we are told by a later writer) voted for the death penalty than had condemned him in the first place, perhaps not surprisingly. Execution was postponed, Xenophon says for a month, during the absence of the state ship on a sacred embassy (*see* DELOS); during this period Socrates was in prison and visited by his friends, their conversations purportedly recorded in Plato's dialogues *Crito and *Phaedo. The latter dialogue describes Socrates' acceptance of the cup of hemlock (by which the death penalty was carried out at Athens).

Socrates himself wrote no books, and we are dependent mainly upon the widely diverging descriptions of Aristophanes, Xenophon, and above all Plato (*see* PLATO 3) for our knowledge of his beliefs and also for our understanding of his uncompromising adherence to the philosophic life. This had such a profound effect upon his contemporaries and, through Plato, on subsequent philosophy, that all earlier Greek philosophers are referred to collectively as *Presocratic. Xenophon conveys his unqualified respect for the man, but the reader feels he was unable to understand his philosophical concerns. Aristophanes' malicious and satirical portrayal in the *Clouds reflected the anti-intellectual prejudices of his audience, depicting Socrates as no different from the other intellectuals of the day, the *sophists, in 'making the weaker argument stronger'. (In Plato's *Apology* Socrates refers to the influence of 'the comic poets' as a factor in his unpopularity; Plato in the *Symposium is at pains to show that a friendly relationship existed between Socrates and Aristophanes in real life.) Plato's picture of Socrates is also in some measure his own creation, but it is possible to identify from it some features which his contemporaries must have known were genuinely those of Socrates: his concern with the difference between true knowledge and opinion or belief which may merely happen to be correct; his search for definitions (What is courage? What is justice?) without which true knowledge in his view is unattainable, in the belief that there are such things as courage and virtue; the method he employed to reach these definitions, by question and answer (*see* ELENCHUS); the question of whether 'goodness' (*arete, 'virtue', 'excellence') can be taught, as the sophists said it could; the feeling that goodness is connected with knowledge of the good, and that once one has that knowledge one cannot deliberately act badly ('no one errs deliberately'); the belief that the good man cannot be harmed (an outlook developed by some later philosophers into extreme asceticism). And all this intellectual examination was aimed, as Socrates insisted, at the practical end of achieving happiness in this life, as Socrates did, by right living: 'the unexamined life is not worth living.'

There is no doubt that this kind of questioning made Socrates highly unpopular with his fellow-citizens, if not with the young who enjoyed seeing their elders ridiculed. He compared himself with the gadfly, stinging people out of their complacency. (Alcibiades compared him with a stingray, inducing a state of numb helplessness.) Unlike the people he questioned, he himself professed complete ignorance, asking his questions purely for information. When his friend Chaerephon visited the Delphic oracle to enquire if any man was

wiser than Socrates, and returned with the answer that there was none, Socrates concluded that his wisdom consisted of knowing his own ignorance, as others did not know theirs. Some thought his assumption of ignorance was merely a pose and described it as an example of 'Socratic irony'. In a famous passage of Plato's *Theaetetus* Socrates is represented as comparing himself with a midwife; he is not a teacher and cannot himself give birth to wisdom, but he can help others to discover and bring to birth the truth within themselves.

Both Plato and Xenophon refer to a less rational aspect of Socrates, his *daimonion* or 'divine sign', which he often called simply 'the customary sign'. Plato has Socrates describe it in the *Apology* (where Socrates supposes it to be the reason behind his indictment for introducing new gods into the city) as a kind of inner voice which since childhood has turned him back from action but never urged him towards it; it was this divine sign that prevented him from taking part in politics. He believed that the sign was sent by the gods, of whom he was unquestioningly respectful and whose worship he observed. He differed from his sophist contemporaries in many respects: for example, he did not teach, in the sense that he did not impart formal knowledge, nor did he ever take fees from the young men who associated with him; far from being sceptical or a moral relativist, he believed that there was such a thing as virtue, that it was knowable, and that the good life had little to do with material success. But the effect on others of his questioning unexamined assumptions had its destructive and demoralizing aspect.

With his broad, flat, turned-up nose, prominent bulging eyes, thick lips, and a paunch, Socrates was famous for his ugliness. Yet his appearance in no way detracted from his magnetic personality. Alicibiades in Plato's *Symposium* contrasted his outward appearance with his inner worth. (*See* SILENUS.)

Much of Socrates' later influence was due not so much to his doctrines as to the integrity and consistency of his life and death, and to the memory he left behind of an inspired talker and an outstanding intellect. The scantiness of and uncertainty about his positive doctrines led to schools of the most diverse opinions being founded by his disciples, among others Plato, *Antisthenes the Cynic, and Aristippus, a predecessor of Epicurus (*see* CYRENAIC SCHOOL). *See also* SCEPTICS; STOICISM; *MEMORABILIA*.

**Sōlī'nus, Julius** Latin author, probably soon after AD 200, of *Collectanea rerum memorabilium* ('Collection of memorable things'), substantially an epitome of the Elder Pliny's *Natural History* and the geography of Pomponius Mela. The title *Polyhistor* ('Very learned') is sometimes given to him. It was he who introduced the name 'Mediterranean Sea' and told us about the absence of snakes in Ireland.

**Sō'lon (Sōlōn)** (*c.*640–after 561 BC) Athenian statesman, celebrated for his humane reform of the city's laws; he was also a poet, and wrote elegiac and iambic poetry to publicize and justify his political policies. For later Greek historians his poetry was the main source of information on the economic and social crisis that he attempted to deal with.

Solon was elected *archon for 594/3 at a time when Athens was on the brink of revolution, largely owing to an agrarian system in which the rich landowners grew richer and the poor were reduced in some cases to *slavery and altogether to despair. Selling a debtor as a chattel slave if his possessions failed to cover the debt was an accepted practice, and many Athenians had found themselves unable to meet their obligations and had either been sold over the border of Attica as slaves or had fled into exile to avoid that fate. Solon's two relief measures were first of all the cancellation of all debts for which land or freedom was the security (a reform known as the *seisachtheia*, 'shaking-off of burdens'), and secondly the prohibition of all future borrowing on the security of the person himself. Perhaps this should be seen rather as the liberation of the *hektemoroi* ('sixth parters') who had to give a sixth of their produce to an overlord, on pain of enslavement. Other economic reforms were credited to him (perhaps not reliably): notably the prohibition of the export of any crops except the olive (thus keeping for home consumption the surplus grain of the rich landowners who had been selling it outside Attica), and the granting of citizenship to immigrant craftsmen, to strengthen home industry. He also introduced a more humane legal code, repealing all the laws of *Draco except those that applied to homicide. He created a category of public law-suits in which any citizen could prosecute an offender, a reform of the old system in which only an injured party could prosecute, and also instituted an appeals procedure. His great reform of the constitution was to grade eligibility to political office in terms of wealth, not birth, and thus to break the hereditary monopoly of power. He famously divided the citizen body into four property classes, in order of wealth: the *pentakosiomedimnoi*, men whose land yielded at least 500 *medimnoi*, 'bushels', of corn or equivalent per annum; the *hippeis*, 'horsemen', 300–500; the *zeugitae*, 'yoke-men', i.e. those who had served in the army as hoplites and enjoyed full citizen rights but were not admitted to the highest magistracies, 200–300; and the *thetes*, 'hired labourers', men who did not own land yielding 200 *medimnoi*, could not afford hoplite armour, and were not admitted to magistracies.

It was said by later writers that after his reforms Solon spent ten years in overseas travel, visiting Egypt and Cyprus among other places (but on chronological evidence almost certainly not meeting *Croesus of Lydia, despite the legends). He returned to find Athens distracted by regional strife and lived long enough to see *Peisistratus voted a bodyguard, the first step towards his tyranny. Solon used verse to express his ideas and explain the motives, indeed the moral philosophy, that lay behind his reforms. His poetic eulogy of 'good order', *Eunomia*, has as much to do with the idea of justice as with its practical application. In a famous reply to the poet Mimnermus, who had said that he wanted to die when he reached 60, Solon declared that the poet should rather say 80. This should probably be taken with another famous line by Solon to the effect that even as he grows old he still continues to learn, *geraskō d'aiei polla didaskomenos*. For democracy *see* CLEISTHENES (2).

**So'mnium Scipiō'nis** ('Dream of Scipio') Surviving portion of the otherwise lost sixth book of Cicero's *De republica*, preserved in the commentary of *Macrobius. It takes the form of a narrative placed in the mouth of *Scipio (2). He relates a visit to the court of *Masinissa, a Numidian ally of Rome in the Second Punic War (218–201 BC), during which there was much talk of the first great Scipio (1), the hero of that war, awarded the *cognomen* Africanus. When the younger Scipio retired to bed, the ghost of the elder appeared to him in a dream, foretold his future, and exhorted him to virtue, patriotism, and disregard of human fame; for those who have served their country well there will be the reward of a heavenly habitation in the after-life (*see* POSEIDONIUS for the Stoic aspect of this idea). The 'Dream' is largely modelled on the myth of Er in the tenth book of Plato's *Republic*.

**sophist (*sophistes*)** Originally, in Greek, a man who had a particular skill and therefore a claim to wisdom. In the fifth century BC it came to be specially, though not exclusively, applied to itinerant teachers of higher education who went from city to city giving popular lectures and specialized private instruction for a fee. The subjects they taught were wide-ranging, such as history, geography, anthropology, mathematics, Ionian science, and linguistics, and in their role as teachers they popularized some aspects of philosophy. However, their overriding purpose was to train rich young men to be successful in public life; in their own words they 'taught excellence (*arete*)'. To this end all of them to some extent included in their curriculum the teaching of rhetoric, the art of public speaking. Some, notably *Gorgias, concentrated on this subject exclusively and gave public performances to advertise their rhetorical skill. The ability to argue persuasively was essential for political advancement, and politics was the career above all other in the ancient world that offered power, fame, and fortune. Persuasion was a powerful goddess to whom the Athenians made annual sacrifice. The poet Pindar speaks of 'the lash of Persuasion'. The sophists satisfied a need among the ambitious for a kind of advanced education not obtainable elsewhere, attuned to the times, inclusive of new knowledge, practical and sophisticated (*see* ISOCRATES). It is not surprising that sophists enjoyed great popularity among those they catered for, and they amassed large fortunes. Their emphasis upon worldly success as well as their advocacy of the idea, which much impressed the Athenians, that the ability to plead a case and win depends on a skill that can be taught rather than on having a just cause (cf. the *Clouds* of Aristophanes), were factors in promoting the scepticism and moral relativism that were associated with their name. Famous sophists were Gorgias of Leontini, *Protagoras of Abdera, *Prodicus of Ceos, *Hippias of Elis, and *Thrasymachus of Chalcedon (*see also* ANTIPHON). Most Athenians of the day would have included *Socrates, not aware of the fundamental differences in his outlook, but seeing that he too was an intellectual who questioned people's unexamined beliefs about the gods, the laws, and traditional values.

The dangerous effect of the sophists was possibly evident in the late fifth-century phenomenon of able, cynical, and recklessly self-seeking politicians, but, on the other side, the intellectual stimulus they provided is manifested in the arguments and educational theories of Plato. Apart from fragments their writings are lost and we rely on Plato, a hostile witness, for much of our knowledge of them. *See also* SOPHIST and NOMOS–PHYSIS ANTITHESIS.

**Sophist, The (*Sophistes*)** Dialogue by *Plato, a sequel to *Theaetetus*. The same characters Theodorus, Theaetetus, and Socrates (here a silent listener) are joined by an unnamed visitor, a philosopher from Elea. Plato once more applies himself to problems raised by the *Eleatics. The visitor distinguishes three types of person often confused: sophist, statesman/politician, and philosopher, and the dialogue starts with the definition of a *sophist. The question then arises whether what the sophist produces is false, and whether there can be a 'false' or 'unreal' thing, since the Eleatics believe that 'what is not', and therefore falsehood, cannot exist (*see* PARMENIDES). The dialogue finds a solution in the doctrine that all things partake of 'difference'; in making a denial we are not making an antithesis between something and nothing, but an opposition between something and something else different from it: 'what is not' is in fact 'what is different'. Plato is thus able to demonstrate the existence of falsehood and error. As in the *Statesman* Plato develops the technique of 'collection and division' in order to reach a definition, a method he first outlined in *Phaedrus*.

**Sophistic, Second** *See* SECOND SOPHISTIC.

**Sophistici elenchi** ('Refutations in the manner of the sophists') Treatise on logic by *Aristotle, an appendix to the *Topica*, consisting of a catalogue of fallacious arguments. It remained throughout the Middle Ages and later an authoritative handbook of bad arguments which a student could learn to recognize and counter, and is the source of most of the names still used for logical fallacies. In his conclusion, having summarized the methods of earlier *sophists, Aristotle points out, modestly, the originality of his own contribution to logic: 'Regarding reasoning we had nothing earlier to refer to, but we had to work things out over a long period by trial and error.'

### Sophists, Against the *See* ISOCRATES.

**So'phoclēs** (*c.*496–406/5 BC) One of the great Athenian tragedians, born at Colōnus near Athens, the son of Sophilus, a wealthy manufacturer of armour. The anonymous ancient biography of the poet gives a great deal of information about him, no doubt much of it unreliable. His beauty and his skill in music and dancing early attracted attention; as a boy he led the chorus which sang the *paean in honour of the Greek victory over the Persian invaders at Salamis in 480 BC. His first victory in the tragic competitions was at the Great *Dionysia in 468 BC, at his first attempt it is said, when he defeated Aeschylus. His early life coincided with the expansion of the Athenian empire, and though he took no active part in politics as far as is known, he was twice elected *strategos* ('general') with Pericles, probably in 441/40. After the failure of the *Sicilian Expedition in 413 he is said to have been one of the ten *probouloi* ('advisers') appointed to deal with the crisis. Amiable and popular, he was a good citizen who lived and died in Athens; he is said to have refused invitations to visit the courts of kings (unlike Aeschylus and Euripides). Aristophanes in the *Frogs*, writing a year after Sophocles' death, described him as 'relaxed' or 'good-tempered', 'among the living, and among the dead'. Only a few months before his own death Sophocles presented his chorus and actors at the *proagon* in mourning garb for the death of Euripides. He left two sons: by Nicostrate, Iophon the tragedian; and by Theoris of Sicyon, Agathon, father of the younger Sophocles, also a tragedian.

Sophocles was credited with more than 120 plays, of which seven were later judged to be spurious, and with winning at least twenty dramatic competitions with his tetralogies, eighteen at the City Dionysia; with the rest he came second, never third. Seven tragedies are extant; the suggested dates are possible but (except for *Philoctetes* and *Oedipus Coloneus*) by no means certain: *Antigone* 441; *Trachiniae* and *Ajax* probably earlier; *Oedipus Tyrannus* soon after 430; *Electra* between 418 and 410; *Philoctetes* 409; *Oedipus Coloneus* probably written 406/5, produced posthumously in 401 by his grandson Sophocles. (For the plots of these plays see their individual titles.) A large fragment of his *satyr play *Ichneutae* ('Trackers') has been recovered from a papyrus found in modern times. Its plot concerned the theft of Apollo's cattle by Hermes soon after the latter's birth. As well as writing tragedies he was the author of a prose treatise, 'On the Chorus'.

According to Aristotle in the *Poetics*, Sophocles was an innovator in tragedy: he added a third to the previously accepted two actors, introduced 'scene painting', and increased the chorus from twelve to fifteen; he also abandoned the Aeschylean practice of writing trilogies on related events (*see* TRAGEDY 2), instead giving each play a self-contained plot. Since the masked actors in Greek tragedy might play more than one part, the introduction of the third actor enabled Sophocles to make plot, dialogue, and the relationship of characters much more complex. His characters were admired by Aristotle for being 'like ourselves only nobler'; nevertheless his characters are not wholly idealized but remain manifestly human. His heroes and heroines, who stand out in conspicuous isolation, must decide upon a course of action, and by their actions, which often have tragic consequences, they show their heroic stature. More than those of the other tragedians, Sophocles' heroes and heroines give the impression that it is their innate characters that initiate the action, and that they could not have behaved otherwise. When, as in *Ajax*, *Antigone*, and *Trachiniae*, the main character dies well before the end of the play and the plot takes a turn in another direction, some slackening of the tension is inevitably felt; but even so, the concluding part still seems to follow necessarily from what has preceded. In the other plays the unity is complete; in particular, the tight-knit plot of *Oedipus Tyrannus* (which for Aristotle represented Greek tragedy at its greatest) is handled with great dexterity and at a rapid pace.

Sophocles rarely introduces into the self-contained world of the play ideas which relate to contemporary affairs, a factor which makes dating the plays on internal evidence difficult. He was a master of dialogue, both in speeches and in *stichomythia. One feature for which he became famous is dramatic irony, of the kind where the speaker's words have additional significance for the audience, already familiar with the outlines of a story drawn from a well-known body of myth (*see* TRAGEDY 1). The language of Sophocles is dignified, avoiding both the grandiose and the over-naturalistic, and often dense, in aid of brevity but not at the expense of clarity. Some of the lyric odes move the audience away from the action to contemplate a more general truth. According to Plutarch, Sophocles distinguished three periods in his own style: the first, when he imitated the 'high-flown' style of Aeschylus; the second, when his style was 'harsh and artificial'; and the third, when it was 'most suitable for expressing characters and best for drama'. His extant plays seem to the modern audience to belong to the third period.

The plays show a conventional but deeply felt piety: that the gods enforce their justice upon human life, and the wise act as best they can in accordance with divine will. In this connection Matthew Arnold's judgement of Sophocles (in his sonnet, 'To a Friend') as one 'who saw life steadily and saw it whole' is often quoted. The poet Shelley had a volume of Sophocles in his pocket when he was drowned in 1822.

**Sophoni'sba** *See* MASINISSA.

**Sō'phron** *See* MIME.

**Sora'nus** Greek physician at Rome in the early first century AD. Most of his writings are lost or very fragmentary but his *Gynaecology* survives and gives valuable information on obstetrics, midwifery and the role of the midwife, and care of the infant at that period. *See* GYNAECOLOGY.

**sortēs** *See* ORACLES and VIRGIL.

**sortition** Election by lot, a method of appointing *magistrates in Greek democracies, best known from its use at Athens. This method of appointment, combined with the prohibition of, or severe restriction on, re-election, allowed considerable rotation in office and reinforced the sovereignty of the citizen assembly. The *strategoi and some financial officers, however, who were required to have some technical skill, were appointed by vote.

**So'sii** Famous booksellers at Rome, referred to by Horace in the *Epistles*.

**Sō'tadēs** (of Maroneia in Thrace, third century BC) Greek iambic poet, said to have been put to death for writing lampoons against the marriage in 276/5 of Ptolemy II Philadelphus and his sister Arsinoe II (a marriage of a kind traditional in pharaonic Egypt but scandalous to Greeks). He invented a flexible form of

metre named after him (sotadean), which was used for several centuries after his time for coarse satires and mythological burlesques. Only a dozen or so lines and a few titles of his works remain.

**soul** (Gk. *psyche*; the Greek and English words do not correspond exactly) In Homer *psyche* is the spirit, in the sense of 'life' or perhaps 'breath', which leaves a person's body at death and goes to the sunless Underworld as an insubstantial image of the living person, lacking strength, wits, and voice. Achilles in *Odyssey* 11 vividly expresses the belief that everyone however wretched his situation prefers life to death. The Underworld was for virtually all souls, regardless of the virtues or vices of their past lives, and there was no judgement (for exceptions to this belief *see* HADES). The Homeric view never quite lost its hold on the Greek imagination. Tragedy frequently reflects it, representing the souls of the dead being greeted by their relations upon arrival in the Underworld. A dead person seen in a dream, as Hecuba sees Polydorus in Euripides' tragedy *Hecuba*, is the *psyche* of that person sent up from the Underworld by the powers below for a short time.

By the end of the sixth century BC the philosophical notion that after death the departing soul might be reincarnated in another body, human or animal, is developed in the worldview of *Pythagoras and *Empedocles. The origin of this notion is unclear, but it is one that will be adopted later by Plato, who will argue for the immortality of the soul. In the first half of the fifth century BC the poet Pindar in his dirges expresses the view that for some souls at least (the most distinguished) there will be a happy after-life, and in the second Olympian ode a condition for this after-life is initiation into a mystery cult (*see* MYSTERIES). At the end of the century, in Aristophanes' comedy *Frogs*, the happy dead are those who have been initiated into such a cult (and sinners lie in the mud). At the same time a belief in judgement after death deciding the fate of the soul was widespread, as the old man Cephalus shows in the first book of Plato's *Republic*. Even without the benefit of initiation the chorus of Euripides' *Alcestis* (438 BC) tentatively hope that Alcestis, having sacrificed her life for her husband, may enjoy some advantage in the Underworld, 'if even there, there is something more for the virtuous': the soul is being thought of as the seat of individual personality.

By the fifth century, in philosophy in general 'soul' implies consciousness and intellect as well as personality, and the term 'soul', meaning 'mind', comes to be contrasted with 'body', as in English 'mind and body'. For Socrates, who regarded the soul as the centre of morality, 'care of the soul' became of the greatest importance. He seems not to have had a view on whether it survived death, but believed that whether it did or not the good man had nothing to fear. For Plato, souls pre-existed birth and survived death; life begins when the immortal soul enters the body. The concept of intellect as an aspect of soul allows him to treat knowledge as the soul's recollection of what it knew before death. Moreover, soul seen as personality makes it meaningful to envisage posthumous rewards and punishments for the soul as well as reincarnation. For Plato the soul is made up of three parts: reason, which in a just person rules the other two parts, a 'spirited' (combative and competitive) part, and a part consisting of hedonistic desires, 'appetite'; *see* PHAEDRUS. In his latest dialogues Plato treats the world itself as a living thing made up of body and soul (as in *Timaeus*) and even suggests that human souls are fragments of a cosmic soul. For a Stoic view of the soul *see* POSEIDONIUS. In philosophy generally, soul is the source of 'self-caused' movement without which, for most philosophers (though not for *Epicurus and his school), the cosmos could not come into existence. The atomist *Democritus believed that although the soul, in his view composed of very fine, round atoms, is the cause of life, it is as material as the body and so perishes with it, the view later adopted most forcefully by Epicurus. For the most part Aristotle takes a biological viewpoint: soul is the form that makes a natural organic body what it is, i.e. gives it its species-form, and it does not survive the death of the body.

## Sparta

1. The capital of *Lacedaemon (or Laconia), a territory in the south-east of the Peloponnese founded by Dorians (*see* DORIAN INVASION and HERACLEIDAE). The city was situated on high ground on the west bank of the river Eurotas, and consisted of little more than a group of villages, without fine buildings, as Thucydides

comments (1.10), and unfortified until the end of the fourth century BC.

By 700 BC all *Messenia, the territory of the eastern coastal strip of Laconia, had been incorporated into the Spartan state, and the population there was either reduced to a condition of limited independence in which they were known as *perioikoi*, 'dwellers round about', or had become serfs, known as *helots, bound to the land which they cultivated for their Spartan masters. The creation of this class was the first stage in a way of life that was to distinguish Sparta from every other Greek state. The helot system relieved the Spartan citizens (Gk. *Spartiatai*) of tending the land themselves and allowed the men to spend an abnormally large amount of time training as soldiers.

2. After the age of 7 the Spartan boy was devoted to a military regime which produced the finest army in Greece and, gradually, a proverbially famous austerity of life. He was taken from home and enrolled in a group of his contemporaries under the leadership of an older boy, and with this group he lived for the next fourteen years, educated for toughness, endurance, and military discipline. Spartan girls also underwent physical training. Music and dancing were part of the curriculum because they had military uses, but only the essentials of reading and writing were taught. Other details are obscure. At the end of his education the Spartan joined the *eirĕnĕs* or young men who had completed their twentieth year, and remained with them living in barracks until he was 30, when he became a full citizen with the right to vote in the assembly. The Spartan political system, associated with the name of *Lycurgus (2) (see 3 below), was a rigid oligarchy in which considerable power was given to the kings, magistrates (*ephors), and council of elders (*gerousia). There were two royal houses (Agiads and Eurypontids), and two kings ruled concurrently. They were the religious representatives of the state and leaders of the army in war, but the ephors had greater power and could even sentence the kings to be fined or imprisoned.

3. In foreign relations, Sparta at first followed a policy of conquest and expansion, establishing her predominance in the Peloponnese, and defeating and weakening her principal rival Argos. During the seventh century there was a serious Messenian revolt, the Second Messenian War (*see* MESSENIA), and Sparta was defeated by Argos at Hysiae in 669 BC. Towards

the middle of the sixth century she abandoned her expansionist policy and set about consolidating her position. She formed a league of the Peloponnesian states (including Corinth and Megara but neither Argos nor Achaea) under her own leadership, which met at Sparta, and was now the strongest power in Greece. At some point she underwent a thorough reorganization of her institutions and way of life, perhaps as a consequence of extending control over Messenia. The date is uncertain, but later it was attributed to a single lawgiver, Lycurgus (2) (*see also* TYRTAEUS). This reform covered three areas. There was a core of several thousand 'Spartans', citizen hoplites debarred from every activity that detracted from their full-time military training; a constitution based on the ephors, the two kings, and the gerousia, with a limited right of veto for the *apella; and a rigorous upbringing (*agoge) for future citizen hoplites. The result was the famous constitutional settlement known as *eunomia, 'good order' i.e. law and order.

Sparta's narrow and inward-looking policy was made evident when in 499 she refused assistance to the Ionian Greeks in their revolt against Persia (*see* PERSIAN WARS). But when Xerxes prepared for war against Greece itself, Sparta combined with Athens in measures of defiance and showed the bravery of her soldiers at the battles of Thermopylae and Plataea. This co-operation ceased after the final defeat of the Persians at Mycale in 479, and Sparta no longer took the lead in Greek affairs. This was partly as a result of the rise in importance of Athens (*see* DELIAN LEAGUE); also, Sparta suffered a devastating earthquake in 464 and a war (464–460) caused by a revolt of the helots. Jealousy and fear of Athenian expansion twice brought about war between Athens and Sparta: in 460–446 (*see* PELOPONNESIAN WAR, FIRST); and in 431–404 (the *Peloponnesian War).

4. The defeat of Athens in 404 left Sparta supreme in Greece, but her falling citizen population (the reasons for which have been much debated), rigid institutions, and the individualist ambitions of her leaders (*see* LYSANDER and AGESILAUS) did not fit her for an imperial role. She entered on a period of arrogant aggrandisement which aroused the hostility of her neighbours and led to a crushing victory for *Thebes (1) over Sparta at Leuctra in 371. Thereafter Thebes took the role of the aggressor. Sparta was repeatedly invaded by the Theban commander *Epaminondas, who dealt her a fatal blow by freeing Messenia (370/69) and refounding it as an independent state after 300 years of servitude to Sparta. The formation of a league of Arcadian cities after Leuctra also weakened Sparta's influence; this too was the work of Thebes. Sparta was not actually captured by Philip II of *Macedon when he invaded the Peloponnese after the battle of Chaeronea in 338, but her territory and power were further diminished, and her important role in Greek history now came to an end. The city became prosperous under the Romans, who admired classical Sparta, but was sacked by Alaric and the Goths in AD 396.

5. Sparta differed from other Greek states not only in her peculiar constitution and in the supreme importance she attached to military efficiency, but in certain other respects: she did not use coined money until the third century BC, the currency taking the form of iron 'spits', *obeloi*; and women enjoyed a position in some respects approaching equality with men, with greater independence and authority than at Athens, and were expected to interest themselves in the welfare of their country. The warlike attitude of the Spartan state meant that it offered virtually no encouragement to the arts, but in the seventh century BC, before militarism because a way of life, Sparta was famous for choral *lyric poetry (*see* ALCMAN; TERPANDER; THALETAS). At the same period Tyrtaeus wrote war-songs. Thereafter, however, the art of poetry seems to have died. The Spartan reputation for terseness has given 'laconic' (from Laconia) to the English language—when Philip of Macedon wrote to them, 'If I invade Laconia I shall turn you out', they wrote back: 'If.'

**Spa'rtacus** Thracian slave-gladiator who in 73 BC escaped from a school of gladiators at Capua with seventy companions and led a revolt, joined by large numbers of other slaves and desperate men. Spartacus' army is said to have numbered 90,000 men, and within the year he had defeated two Roman armies and devastated southern Italy. In 72 he defeated another three armies, and reached Cisalpine Gaul, but his followers refused the chance to escape over the Alps and marched south again to plunder Italy; he was finally defeated and killed in 71 by M. Licinius *Crassus, who subsequently crucified any rebels he captured.

Spartacus' body was never identified. Pompey returned from Spain in time to annihilate the remaining rebels, thereby taking credit for ending the war. Spartacus quickly became a legend, not only for his daring successes but for personal qualities of bravery, strength, and humanity. His name has often been invoked by revolutionaries, but he was fighting for personal liberty rather than trying to bring down Rome. (*See* SLAVERY.)

**Sparti (Spartoi)** *See* CADMUS.

**Speusi'ppus** (*c*.407–339 BC) Plato's nephew and his successor as head of the *Academy from 347 to 339 BC. Of his voluminous writings only fragments survive, together with accounts of his work by later writers. He worked on definition, and wrote ten books on the observable resemblances between different sorts of plants and animals as well as writing on distinctions between words. He also wrote on Pythagorean mathematics but rejected the idea that the elements of number are the elements of everything else, a claim which Aristotle ascribes to Plato as well as to Pythagoras. In ethics Speusippus maintained that pleasure is neither good nor bad in itself.

**Sphacteria** *See* PYLOS.

**spheres, harmony of the** (music of the spheres) *See* HARMONY OF THE SPHERES.

**sphinx** [from *sphingein*, 'to bind fast'] In Greek myth, a monster usually depicted with a human head, male or female, on the body of a lion; bearded male sphinxes are sometimes found in early Greek art, and wings are commonly added. Hesiod made the sphinx the daughter of *Chimaera (or, in the view of some, Echidna) and *Orthrus. In the story of *Oedipus and the Sphinx, the riddle she posed was 'What is it that walks on four legs in the morning, on two at noon, and on three in the evening?' The answer was 'A human', who as an infant crawls on all fours and in old age walks with a stick. Her representation in art can be traced back to Egypt and Mesopotamia in the third millennium BC.

**spo'lia opī'ma** ('spoils of honour') The arms taken by a Roman general, in full command of his army, from the body of the enemy leader he has killed in single combat. They were reckoned by the Romans to have been won three times: by Romulus from Acron, king of the Caeninenses, in the hostilities that followed the Rape of the Sabines; by Aulus Cornelius Cossus, according to Livy in 437 BC, when he killed Lars Tolumnius the Etruscan king; and by M. Claudius Marcellus who killed the Gaul Viridomarus in 222 BC. *Crassus (2) claimed the spoils in 29 BC but was disallowed by Octavian. The spoils were dedicated to Jupiter Feretrius; lesser spoils, *spolia secunda* and *tertia*, were dedicated to Mars and Janus Quirinus.

**SPQR** In Roman documents, inscriptions, etc., abbreviation for *senatus populusque Romanus*, 'the senate and people of Rome'; *see* POPULUS.

**stade, sta'dium (*stădion*)** Greek unit of length (*see* MEASURES), the 'stade', 600 (Greek) feet long (however long the foot), and so in the range 175–200 metres or somewhat less than an English furlong. It was originally the length of a single draught of the plough. Because the most famous running-track, that of *Olympia, was a stade long, the word came to denote any running-track, 'stadium'. A stadium was generally a piece of level ground a little over 200m long and up to about 40m wide, with a starting line at each end. In the middle of each line was a turning-post round which runners had to make a turn for any race longer than a single length. Since level ground of such a size was not easy to find in mountainous Greece, one end of the stadium was often left curving naturally into the hillside. In this way the stadium came to have what is now considered its characteristic U-shape. The best-preserved ancient stadia may be seen at Olympia, Delphi, Athens, and Epidaurus. The stadium at Athens was rebuilt by *Herodes Atticus in marble, with seats to hold 50,000 spectators.

**Stagei'ra (Stageiros)** Greek town near the east coast of Chalcidice, famous as the birthplace of Aristotle, who in consequence is sometimes referred to as 'the Stagīrite'. It was destroyed by Philip II of Macedon in 349 BC, but rebuilt by him in response to a plea by Aristotle, whom he appointed as tutor to his son Alexander.

**Stasī'nus** Of Cyprus, sometimes named as the author of the *Cypria* (*see* EPIC CYCLE).

**stasis** [Gk., 'a standing'] Word used in Greek to describe a group of citizens taking a political stance, thus becoming a party or faction, and by extension applied to political activity leading to civil war and foreign intervention. Thucydides famously analysed *stasis* at Corcyra in book 3 of his history.

**Statei'ra** *See* ALEXANDER (1) 6.

**stater** A Lydian coin which circulated widely in the ancient world, generally having the weight and monetary value of two to four drachmas (*see* MONEY AND COINS and WEIGHTS).

**Statesman (Politicus)** Dialogue by *Plato, a continuation of the *Sophist*. The company is the same but the young Socrates replaces Theaetetus as respondent. The inquiry is primarily into the method for arriving at a definition, 'learning to divide according to kinds', a reference to the method of 'collection and division' first encountered in *Phaedrus*. The nature of statesmanship is nonetheless an important part of the enquiry. The dialogue includes a long cosmic myth and an interesting analogy drawn from weaving in wool, one also used by Lysistrata in Aristophanes' comedy of that name (567–87).

**Stā'tius 1. Caeci'lius Statius** *See* CAECILIUS.
    **2. Publius Papi'nius Statius** (*c.* AD 45–*c.*96) Roman poet, born at Naples, the son of a man who was himself a poet and then a *grammaticus* or schoolmaster and teacher of literature. In Rome Statius recited his poems to large audiences and won a contest held by the emperor Domitian. His (extant) epic in twelve books, the *Thebaïd*, was published in 90 or 91 after twelve years' toil; it is the only complete Roman epic which can be said to have been published as the author wished. The plot is that of the quarrel between Oedipus' sons Eteocles and Polyneices. Soon afterwards Statius began to issue the *Silvae*. The first four books appeared between AD 91 and 95; the fifth was probably put together after Statius' death in 96. The survival of these poems depended on a manuscript discovered in 1417. Most are written in hexameters, but six are in lyric metres, alcaics, sapphics, and hendecasyllables. Statius wrote them for his patrons, who included the emperor Domitian, on a variety of subjects suggested by incidents in the patrons' lives as well as in the poet's own; his poem on the death of a friend's parrot is well known (2.4). He has been accused of sycophancy, and it is true that he wrote what his patrons wanted to hear. But some of the poems are sincere and moving: an invocation to Sleep (5.4), an affectionate address to his wife Claudia (3.5), and an epithalamium on the marriage of his friend Assuntius Stella (1.2). In (probably) 90 he failed to win the Capitoline poetry competition and was deeply disappointed. About this time he retired to Naples, where he began the composition of another epic, the *Achilleïd*, broken off in book 2 by his death, apparently before the murder of Domitian in September 96.

Statius married Claudia, a widow with one daughter, and was greatly attached to her. He had no children of his own; his sorrow at the death of an adopted son is expressed in the last poem of the *Silvae*. He associated with prominent men, including Domitian himself, whom he flattered obsequiously. His lost works include the libretto for a *pantomime *Agave*, on the story of Pentheus, and an epic *De bello Germanico* ('On the German war') on Domitian's campaigns. The *Thebaïd* is a very self-conscious work. The *Silvae*, being simpler, more spontaneous, and less polished, have for many readers a greater appeal, but the epic attracts readers for its greater range and its exploration of violence and madness, drama and pathos.

Statius was much admired in the Middle Ages; regarded by Dante as a Christian, he appears in Cantos 21 and 22 of the *Purgatorio* where his spirit meets that of Virgil, appropriately enough in view of Statius' reverence for the earlier poet. Statius is represented as explaining how he was led to Christianity by certain passages in Virgil.

**Stentor** Greek at the siege of Troy who could shout as loudly as fifty men (*Iliad* 5).

**Stēsi'chorus** ('Choir-setter') Greek lyric poet writing in the first half of the sixth century BC whose real name according to some was Teisias. He was said to have been born at Matauros (Metaurum) in the toe of Italy and to have lived at Himera in Sicily. He wrote narrative *lyric poetry (of what type is not certain) collected in 26 books. It was classified by the ancients as choral lyric because of the metre, the poetic Doric dialect, and the triadic structure (*see* TRIAD; Stesichorus was even said to be the inventor of this particular form). It has seemed to some modern critics that the great length of his poems precludes their being sung and danced by a chorus, and that it is more likely that the poet performed them himself, to the accompaniment of a lyre, in the manner of a Homeric bard (*see* HOMER 4). Certainly the poems were long: evidence suggests that the *Geryonēis* was at least 1,300 lines long (by comparison, not many of Pindar's choral odes are much over 100 lines long), and the *Oresteia* and perhaps *Helen* occupied two books. Only fragments survive, and most of these have been recovered from papyrus in the twentieth century.

Existing titles indicate that the subjects were taken from a wide range of epic sources, from the *Epic Cycle as well as Homer. His *Oresteia* differed from the story in Homer in placing the death of Agamemnon at Sparta (not Mycenae or Argos); as Aeschylus did in the *Choephoroe*, Stesichorus included Clytemnestra's dream and gave some part to Orestes' nurse. The *Geryoneis*, which told of Heracles' search for the cattle of Geryon (*see* HERACLES, LABOURS OF 10) is remarkable for an early mention of the silver mines of Tartessus; it also has a memorable description of the cup of the Sun (*see* HELIOS). The *Funeral Games of Pelias* is connected with the legends of the Argonauts, the *Boar-hunters* with the Calydonian boar-hunt, the *Eriphyle* with Theban legend. The *Iliupersis*, 'Sack of Troy', drew on the Epic Cycle and included an account of Epeus, who made the Wooden Horse; some believe that it may have been the source for the stories of Aeneas' wanderings to Italy (*see* TABULAE ILIA-CAE). Stesichorus told the story of Helen of Troy twice, first in the usual version as the cause of the Trojan War, and secondly in the form familiar from Euripides' play *Helen*, according to which Helen's phantom went to Troy while she herself remained behind in Egypt. Legend relates that he was struck with blindness for 'slandering' Helen in the first poem, and that his sight was restored after he recanted and wrote his famous *Palinode*, blaming Homer for the earlier story. His language and style show the strong influence of epic, but have many features of later choral lyric, e.g. the rich use of epithets. The metre he used was a form of dactylo-epitrite. His influence on contemporary art has been detected in the appearance of many of his subjects on the vases of the day, but in poetry he had no successors.

**Stheneboe'a** *See* BELLEROPHON.

**stichomy'thia** ('talking by the line') In Greek drama, dialogue that is conducted by two characters speaking in alternate lines (though strict regularity is not always maintained). Stichomythia can be very effective in a confrontation, but the difficulty of maintain-ing such a form can lead to artificiality of expression, nicely illustrated in A. E. Housman's famous parody, 'Fragment of a Greek Tragedy':

*Chorus*: Might I then hear at what your presence shoots?
*Alcmaeon*: A shepherd's questioned mouth informed me that—
*Chorus*: What? For I know not yet what you will say.
*Alcmaeon*: Nor will you ever if you interrupt.
*Chorus*: Proceed, and I will hold my speechless tongue.

**Stichus** Roman comedy by *Plautus, performed at the Plebeian Games of 200 BC. The title is taken from the name of one of the characters, a slave. The comedy has little plot. The two daughters of Antipho are married to two brothers. These have gone abroad on a trading venture to retrieve their fortunes, and at the opening of the play they have been absent for three years and no news has been received. Antipho urges his daughters to marry again, but they insist on remaining faithful to their husbands. The husbands have prospered and now return, and their home-coming is a matter of celebration. Much comedy is derived from the behaviour of a hungry *parasite and from the portrayal of slaves enjoying themselves. The motif of the 'running slave', rushing on stage with urgent news only to deliver it long-windedly, features in this play.

**sto'a** Greek word for a roofed colonnade or portico (English 'porch') generally of the Doric order (*see* ARCHITECTURE, ORDERS OF) with a wall on one side, erected as a separate building near temples or gymnasia or in market-places as a sheltered place in which to walk and talk or hold meetings. The wall was often decorated with paintings or inscriptions. Thus the Stoa Poikile ('Painted Colonnade') in the agora at Athens, built *c.*460 BC, was adorned with frescos by famous artists, including one by *Polygnotus representing the destruction of Troy. It was in this stoa, much used by the philosopher Zeno (2) and his disciples, that the Stoic school of philosophy derived its name (and was occasionally known as the Porch; *see* STOICISM).

**Stobae'us, Johannes** (John of Stobi, in Macedonia) Compiler in the early fifth century AD of an anthology of excerpts from (pagan) Greek poets and prose-writers, in the first instance for the instruction of his son Septimius. These excerpts were originally arranged in four books whose subjects included philosophy, physics, rhetoric, poetry, ethics, morals, and politics. They were later grouped under the titles *Eklogai* and *Anthologion*. The latter has survived, and preserves quotations from works which have not otherwise come down to modern times.

**stoichē'don** *See* EPIGRAPHY [Greek].

**Stoicism** A philosophy promulgated in Athens *c.*300 BC by Zeno of Citium (in Cyprus), taking its name from the *Stoa Poikile* (*see* STOA) at Athens where he did his teaching. Zeno came to Athens in 313 BC and first attended lectures at the *Academy (the Platonic school) but was converted to Cynicism by *Crates (2) (*see* CYNICS). After studying the works of *Antisthenes, a devoted follower of Socrates (and regarded by some as the founder of Cynicism), he turned to Socratic philosophy, out of which he developed his own 'Stoic' system, divided into three parts, logic (including theory of logic), physics (including metaphysics), and ethics. At his death Athens honoured him with a public funeral, as a man who 'had made his life an example to all, for he followed his own teaching'. The most influential Stoic was the third head of the school, *Chrysippus of Soli (in Cilicia), in the third century BC, who gave definitive form and expression to Stoicism. Although the school seems to have been less strictly organized than either the Academy or the *Lyceum, it nevertheless had a succession of heads to at least AD 260, and probably for some years after. It gradually faded out, however, and was no longer in existence when the emperor Justinian closed the philosophical schools at Athens in AD 529.

Stoics generally accepted the traditional gods. Their main doctrines were the following. Nature (the whole universe, that is) is controlled by Reason, *logos* (identified with Zeus in *Cleanthes' *Hymn* and *Aratus' proem), and shows itself as Fate (also called Necessity or Providence—they are all the same agency); whatever happens is in accordance with divine or cosmic Reason. It is thus the aim of the wise person who knows this truth to accept what happens and to live in harmony with Nature (or Reason); this is virtue and the only good. Whatever happens to us cannot be otherwise; nevertheless human action is free and morally responsible. The wise aim to achieve willing acquiescence. Not to do this is to show moral weakness instead of virtue, and this is the only evil. (Thus the Stoics adopted the Socratic principle that the only thing that is good in itself is the goodness or well-being of the human soul.) Everything else—pain, poverty, death (even a cold in the head, as the poet Horace ironically observes at the end of his first Epistle)—is indifferent. It is beyond the power of anyone to deprive the wise of virtue; and always knowing the only true good, they therefore achieve happiness, which is the aim of the virtuous person. They are also absolutely brave, since they know that pain and death are not evils, and self-controlled, since they know that pleasure is not the good. They repudiate all emotion.

The Stoics were also materialists, who believed that matter breaks down into the four *elements, earth, water, air, and fire, i.e. the dry, the wet, the cold, and the hot, and is capable of changing from the one to the other. Fire, the element most closely related to cosmic Reason, periodically consumes the other, grosser elements, and out of it in time a new universe arises, and so on for ever. Every person possesses a spark of that divine fire. This belief led, importantly, to the Stoic concept of the kinship of all humankind, without distinction between Greek and *barbarian, free and slave, and of the consequent duty of universal benevolence and justice. In spite of this, Stoicism was in the main a doctrine of detachment from and independence of the outer world.

The immediate successor of Zeno was Cleanthes, who had a religious view of the world expressed in his *Hymn to Zeus*. He was followed in 232 BC by Chrysippus (see above), converted to Stoicism by Cleanthes, but by this time Stoicism was breaking up in different directions. Chrysippus recast and systematized the Stoic doctrine so successfully that it was later said that if there had been no Chrysippus there would have been no Stoa. All these philosophers belonged to the **Early Stoa**, down to Antipater (d. 129 BC). The famous names of the subsequent period, the second and first centuries BC, the so-called **Middle Stoa**, are those of *Panaetius and *Poseidonius. The former, who spent much time in Rome, was the first to reject the doctrine of periodic universal conflagrations, and also rejected the belief that only the absolutely wise can be virtuous, teaching that those who merely aspired to virtue were making progress. While at Rome he, like

Polybius, became a friend of P. *Scipio Aemilianus, and his practical version of Stoic ethics, seemingly adapted for the needs of active statesmen and soldiers, had great influence on his associates. His writings were studied by the Younger Cato, Brutus, Cicero, and many others. Poseidonius submitted the doctrines of the early Stoics to an even more thoroughgoing revision.

During the Roman empire the Stoics were almost exclusively concerned with ethical questions. The most important Stoics of the first century AD were *Seneca the Younger, Cornutus, *Musonius Rufus, and, towards the end of the century, *Epictetus. Stoicism provided the philosophical basis for opposition to the one-man rule of the emperors: Paetus Thrasea and his son-in-law Helvidius Priscus, resolute opponents of Nero, were Stoics; the emperors Vespasian and Domitian both banished the philosophers from Italy. But after Epictetus the emperor M. *Aurelius was the most famous Stoic in the second century. During the third century the school gradually died out, but it had an important and long-lasting effect on the life and thought of many, influencing *Neoplatonism and permeating the Christianity of some of the early Fathers of the Church, such as Tertullian. (*See* DAIMON)

**Strābo (Strabōn)** (64 BC–after AD 21) Greek geographer from Amaseia in Pontus, a member of a distinguished local family. He came to Rome in 44 BC to complete his education and subsequently spent, it seems, long periods in the city. He travelled widely, 'from Armenia to Etruria, and from the Black Sea to the borders of Ethiopia', apparently returning to his home about 7 BC where he remained until his death. Despite seeing so much he argues that most people learn more by hearing than by seeing. At some time he became a Stoic (*see* STOICISM); he also developed a profound admiration for the Romans: like *Poseidonius, he regarded them as the creators of an earthly world-state comparable with the heavenly one.

He was the author of *Hypomnemata* ('Historical notes') in 47 books, now lost, which comprised an outline (in four books) of historical events up to the opening of Polybius' history, followed by a complete history (in 43 books) from 146 BC (where Polybius ended) up to at least the death of Julius Caesar. His surviving masterpiece is the *Geographika* ('Geography') in seventeen books. Strabo insists that his geography is intended for political lea-

ders and generals, 'who bring together peoples and cities into a single empire and political administration'. His aim is to impart practical wisdom, and this includes acceptance of the domination of Rome, in which respect he resembles Panaetius, Poseidonius, and Polybius. He describes the physical geography of the chief countries in the Roman world, giving the broad features of their historical and economic development and an account of anything remarkable in the customs of their inhabitants or in their animal and plant life. The first two books serve as a general introduction; after a remarkable preface in which he discusses geography as a branch of scientific inquiry, Strabo deals with the dimensions of the inhabited world and the position of various places with reference to a simple grid. Books 3–17 embrace Spain, the Isles of Scilly, Gaul, Britain (of which he knows little), Italy, Sicily, north and east Europe (he knows nothing of northernmost Europe and Asia), central Europe, north Balkans, Greece, Asia around the Black and Caspian Seas, Asia Minor, India, Persia, Mesopotamia, Palestine, Arabia, Egypt, Ethiopia, and North Africa (Strabo takes Africa to be a triangle north of the equator). His information is not always up-to-date.

Strabo takes *Eratosthenes as a starting-point but frequently finds fault with him. He regards the earth as a sphere, on which the inhabited world is contained within a quadrilateral area bounded on the south by the equator, on the north by the frozen latitudes, and on the east and west by a meridian. His whole work is invaluable in informing us about the state of geographical knowledge in his day, and though he does not stress geographical wonders he does incidentally include 'some of the trivial things that may arouse the curiosity of the studious or practical man': how the Indians capture elephants and long-tailed apes, how the Arabians get fresh water out of the sea, how the Egyptians feed their sacred crocodiles; the Hanging Gardens of Babylon, the whales of the Persian Gulf, the aromatics of the Sabaeans. The work, in an epitomized form, was used as a schoolbook in the Middle Ages.

**strateg'gos** In Greece, a military commander both on land and on sea. At Athens in the fifth century BC *strategoi* were political as well as military leaders. From 500 BC the board of ten annually elected *strategoi* (one from each tribe) formed an important administrative council, responsible for all duties relating to war and the enlistment of soldiers and sailors. Pericles was *strategos* almost continuously from 443 until his death in 429; Cleon, Nicias, and Alcibiades all held this office. In 406 the eight *strategoi* in command at *Arginusae were all dismissed and condemned to death. *See also* POLEMARCH.

**Strife** *See* ERIS.

**strophē** ('turn') In Greek *lyric poetry (and Latin written in imitation) a stanza. It was said to have derived its name from the performance of choral lyric, in which a stanza or strophe was sung as the chorus proceeded in its dance in one direction, followed by a second stanza, the antistrophe, corresponding exactly in metre with the strophe, sung when the chorus turned and reversed its dance in the opposite direction. *See also* TRIAD. 'Astrophic' composition describes extended lyric passages not written in stanza form.

**Stymphā'lian birds** *See* HERACLES, LABOURS OF 5.

**Styx** ('the Abhorrent') In Greek myth, the principal river of the Underworld (*see* HADES) over which the souls of the dead were traditionally said to be ferried by Charon. According to Hesiod, Styx was one of the daughters of Oceanus and Tethys. Styx and her children, Zelos (Glory), Nike (Victory), Kratos (Strength), and Bia (Force), aided Zeus in his quarrel with the *Titans, in consequence of which she was greatly honoured, and an oath by Styx was held inviolable by the gods. According to the Greek historian Herodotus, people swore solemn oaths by a small river of this name in Arcadia which still falls from a tall cliff (the Mavroneri Falls), leaving a black stain on the rocks; its water was reputed to be poisonous. Plutarch and Arrian report that Alexander the Great was poisoned by this water, sent to him in a mule's hoof (which withstood its reputedly corrosive nature).

**Subli'cian bridge** *See* PONS SUBLICIUS.

**Sublime, Longinus on the** *See* LONGINUS ON THE SUBLIME.

**Successors, the** *See* DIADOCHI.

**Suda, The** (*he Souda*) ('The Fortress', formerly referred to as 'Suidas', as if the name of a person) Name of a Greek lexicon or literary encyclopaedia compiled at the end of the tenth century AD and containing many valuable

articles on Greek literature and history. It is based partly on earlier lexica (*see* HESYCHIUS), partly on texts, with scholia (*see* SCHOLIUM), of Homer, Sophocles, Aristophanes, the Palatine *Anthology which the compiler consulted himself, and the Bible, as well as on excerpts made in earlier times from the works of historians, grammarians, and biographers.

**Suetō'nius 1.** Gaius Suetonius Pauli'nus *See* BRITAIN 2.

**2. Gaius Suetonius Tranqui'llus** (b. *c.*AD 70) Roman biographer of equestrian family. Not much is known about his life. He practised in the law-courts at Rome and was well-known as an author by the 90s. He was a friend of the Younger Pliny. He held three important secretaryships at the imperial palace, where he would have had unrestricted access to the imperial archives, but in 121/2 he was dismissed by Hadrian, together with the praetorian prefect, for some indiscretion involving the empress. After this nothing more is heard of him.

Of his writings, which include works on Roman antiquities, natural sciences, and grammar, much is lost. His fame depends on his lively and anecdotal biographies; after Cornelius *Nepos, Suetonius is the first Latin biographer whose work still exists. The surviving writings consist of the 'Lives of the Caesars' (*De vita Caesarum*) and part of his 'On Famous Men' (*De viris illustribus*). The latter now comprises over half of the section on the grammarians and rhetoricians (*De grammaticis et rhetoribus*). In addition, his Lives of Terence, Horace, Lucan, and the version of his Life of Virgil by *Donatus (1) have been transmitted in manuscripts of these authors' own works; perhaps the surviving Lives of Tibullus and Persius are also derived from Suetonius. 'On the grammarians' sets out the syllabus which these teachers would have taught, i.e. broadly the study of literature, and describes its introduction at Rome by *Crates (1), as well as giving some account of twenty of the principal grammarians. 'On the rhetors' outlines the growth at Rome of the study of *rhetoric, which at first was disapproved of by influential Romans (*see* CATO (1)), explains the method of teaching it, and illustrates the themes used in the schools. An account of five of the principal teachers of rhetoric follows. The 'Lives of the poets' contain fact, anecdote, and misinformation inextricably confused; passages about the personal appearance of the poets have their own fascination: for instance, that Horace was short and fat.

The 'Lives of the Caesars' cover Julius Caesar and the eleven subsequent emperors: Augustus, Tiberius, Gaius (Caligula), Claudius, Nero, Galba, Otho, Vitellius, Vespasian, Titus, and Domitian. The first few chapters of Julius Caesar's Life are lost. The biographies follow a consistent pattern: after describing the subject's ancestry and early life Suetonius lists his successes in fulfilling what readers must have expected of his imperial role, and his personal characteristics. Usually the biography concludes with the subject's death, although sometimes it goes on to describe his appearance, as for the poets. The Lives of Caesar and Augustus are much fuller than those of the later emperors, which suggests that Suetonius was particularly interested in the new form of government that emerged as the *Principate. He quotes frequently from earlier writers and from documents such as the letters of Augustus, having probably had access to them during his secretaryships under Trajan and Hadrian. Since he quotes no emperor later than Augustus it has been thought that only his and Caesar's Lives had been written at the time of his dismissal. He writes not as a historian but as a biographer, concerned first to assess his subject's success as an emperor and then to describe and illustrate his personality and individuality. His Lives include many anecdotes, gossipy and salacious, but lively and with interesting detail.

The work became a model for biography in the Middle Ages but was superseded by Plutarch when the latter's Lives were translated into the vernacular languages. See BIOGRAPHY.

**Sū'idas** See SUDA.

**Sulla, Lucius Corne'lius** (c.138–78 BC) Roman general and leader of the *optimates (aristocratic party) in the civil war against the *popularis *Marius. Born of a patrician but not distinguished family, Sulla was chosen by Marius as his quaestor in 107 BC and had outstanding success that year as a soldier in the war against *Jugurtha, whose surrender he obtained. He served again under Marius in campaigns against German tribes. Praetor urbanus in 97, he was assigned Cilicia as his province and stayed there for several years. Sulla fought with distinction in the *Social War (90–88 BC). Largely through the support of the Metelli he

gained the consulship in 88 and was designated by the senate for the command against *Mithridates, who had invaded the Roman province of Asia. But the tribune of 88, P. *Sulpicius Rufus (1), a supporter of Marius, transferred the command to the latter, and Sulla was forced to leave Rome. The six legions which Sulla had assembled at Capua marched with him against the (legitimate) government at Rome and for the first time a consul entered the city at the head of his army. Marius escaped with difficulty (arriving in Africa after many adventures), and Sulla took control of the city by force, killing Sulpicius and shocking even his friends by his violent measures. His vindictive cruelty was long remembered.

After acquiescing in a temporary political settlement he ignored a summons to go on trial and proceeded to the East, where he defeated Mithridates and acquired a vast amount of booty. Marius meanwhile had died (in 86), but his party had regained the upper hand in Rome. Sulla invaded Italy in 83 and was joined by most aristocrats including *Pompey and *Crassus. A ruthless civil war ensued and Sulla finally seized Rome in 82 after a victory at the *Colline Gate. He was elected dictator and granted complete immunity for all acts, past and future, taking the agnomen (see NAMES [Roman]) Felix, 'Fortunate'. He now adopted in his turn Marius' policy of exterminating his enemies, adding the device of *proscription, the posting-up of the names of victims who might be killed without trial and their property confiscated, while the murderers and informers were rewarded for their efforts. These terrible events marked the advent of a new era, the late republic (see SALLUST), a time when individuals with great personal ambition, made powerful by their leadership of large armies, brought about the ruin of Italy and the collapse of republican government.

After having his eastern settlement ratified, Sulla set about a complete constitutional reform at Rome which aimed to improve administrative efficiency, increase the power of the senate, and restrict that of the people and their tribunes. The equites who supported him (see EQUESTRIAN ORDER) were admitted to the senate, which now numbered 600. One of the few parts of his work to survive the reaction in the 70s which followed his death was the full organization of a system of criminal procedure. After completing his reforms he abdicated his power, restored constitutional government, becoming consul in 80, and retired to private life in 79. He died in 78, having devoted his last year to the composition of his memoirs in twenty-two books; these have not survived.

**Sulmo** (Sulmona) Birthplace of the Roman poet Ovid (43 BC), in a valley of the Apennines east of Rome.

**Sulpi'cia 1.** (second half of the first century BC) Roman poet, the author of six short elegies surviving in the manuscripts of *Tibullus, the only surviving complete poems by a woman in classical Rome. She was the daughter of Servius *Sulpicius Rufus, and niece and ward of *Messala. Her poems are love elegies to a young man addressed, according to the current style of Roman love elegy, by the Greek pseudonym Cerinthus. This display of aristocratic female independence in the matter of love is striking (but *cf.* CLODIA and *see* LOVE AND SEXUALITY).

**2.** (d. 94–98 AD) Roman poet who wrote love-poems to her husband Calenus; only a small fragment survives, but sufficient to confirm the poet Martial's view of her work as expressing faithfulness to her husband in a highly sensual style. Martial commemorated her death (10.38), and she is mentioned several times in later literature.

**Sulpi'cius 1. Publius Sulpicius Rufus** An ambitious aristocrat, *tribune of the plebs in 88 BC and a supporter of *Marius. He proposed that the newly enfranchised Italians should be fairly distributed in all the *tribes and not confined to a few; also that the command against Mithridates should be transferred from *Sulla to Marius (in order to get the latter's help for his political aims). These proposals were carried by force, but when Sulla reacted by marching on Rome in 88 Sulpicius had to flee. He was captured and executed, and his laws annulled.

**2. Servius Sulpicius Rufus** (*c.*106–43 BC) Great Roman jurist and orator, contemporary of Cicero, known to us by the latter's praise of him in his *Brutus* and in the *Ninth Philippic* (though he made fun of him in *Pro Murena*), and by his correspondence with Cicero. He was consul in 51 and a half-hearted supporter of Pompey. He wrote to Cicero two celebrated letters, one describing the murder of M. Marcellus in May 45, the other a consolation on the death of Cicero's daughter Tullia. He died on an embassy to Mark Antony.

**Sū'nium (Sounion)** Cape forming the southernmost point of Attica. It is mentioned by Homer as the point off which Apollo killed the pilot who guided Menelaus on his way to Troy. A temple to Poseidon was built on the promontory in the 440s BC; eleven of its Doric columns still stand.

**Suppliants, The (*Hiketidĕs*)** (Lat. *Supplices*, 'Suppliants' or 'Suppliant women')

**1.** Greek tragedy by *Aeschylus, of uncertain date, but produced in a year, possibly 463 BC, in which Sophocles was also a competitor (the latter's first dramatic production was in 468). It was the first play of its trilogy; the others were *Aegyptii* ('Sons of Aegyptus') and *Danaides* ('Daughters of Danaus'); the *satyr play was the *Amymone*. Like the *Persians* and the *Seven against Thebes* the play envisages a *theatre without a *skene* (a stage building serving as a backdrop) but containing a mound representing the Argive sanctuary with cult images. There are only two actors, so the main interactions are between character and chorus.

The suppliants are the fifty daughters of *Danaus who have fled from Egypt to avoid marriage with their cousins, the fifty sons of the usurping king Aegyptus. They have come with their father to Argos, with which they claim connection through their descent from *Io, to ask for protection from their pursuers. The king of Argos hesitates and consults his people. They vote in favour of the suppliants, and the demand of the enemy herald for their surrender, with threats of war, is rejected.

The role of the suppliants themselves is taken by the chorus, which thus becomes virtually the protagonist; it is quite appropriate therefore that choral lyrics occupy more than half the play. The reason for the suppliants' flight from marriage, not made unambiguously clear by Aeschylus, has been much debated, but inconclusively. The trilogy probably ended with the confirmation of marriage as a natural institution, exemplified by Hypermnestra's sparing of her husband.

**2.** Greek tragedy by *Euripides produced probably *c.*422 BC; the goddess Athena's words at the end relate to an Argive alliance, actual or in view at the time of writing.

The Thebans have refused to allow the burial of the bodies of the Argive chieftains (the '*Seven against Thebes') who have unsuccessfully attacked the city, thus violating the sacred custom of the Greeks. The mothers of the chieftains (who form the chorus of suppliants from whom the play is named) have come with Adrastus, king of Argos, surviving leader of the expedition, to Eleusis in Attica and made supplication at the shrine of Demeter to Aethra, mother of Theseus, king of Athens. Theseus rejects the arrogant demand of the Theban herald for their surrender; he yields to the prayer of the suppliants and recovers the bodies for burial by force. Evadne, widow of Capaneus, one of the chieftains, throws herself on his funeral pyre. The goddess Athena appears at the end to tell Argos to swear never to attack Athens, and promises success against Thebes to the sons of the Seven.

**Su'pplicēs** See SUPPLIANTS.

**surgery** See MEDICINE and CELSUS.

**sy'cophant** [Gk. *sykophantes*, 'fig-denouncer'] At Athens, a man who habitually prosecuted others, ostensibly on behalf of the state, on trumped-up charges, for the sake of private gain. For most offences at Athens there was no public prosecutor; that role was left to a public-spirited private individual ('anyone who wished', in Solon's words) but the system was open to abuse. Since there could be a share of the fine for a successful prosecution, or the possibility of blackmail, those who made a habit of such prosecutions earned this abusive name, the origin of which is obscure. Today 'sycophantic' means 'obsequious'. Aristophanes shows how sycophants behaved in his *Acharnians*.

**syllogism** See PRIOR ANALYTICS.

**Symplē'gadĕs** ('Clashing ones') In Greek myth, the 'clashing rocks' at the north end of the Bosporus through which the *Argonauts had to pass to enter the Black Sea, an adventure described by *Apollonius Rhodius. The rocks were believed to crush ships that passed between them. The Planctae ('Wandering ones') were similar rocks mentioned in the *Odyssey*, in an unspecified place.

**sympo'sium** ('drinking-party') A social occasion in Greece when men drank together after a meal. In fifth-century Athens it was an important institution in the life of aristocratic men. It was held in the *andron*, 'men's apartment', and began and ended with libations and prayers. The (male) guests, their heads gar-

landed with flowers, reclined on couches (an Eastern practice introduced into Greece before the sixth century BC), usually two, sometimes three, to a couch (*kline*), propped on their left arm; low tables to hold food and wine cups were placed in front of the couches. Wine was served from a large mixing-bowl (*krater*) where it was blended with water to make it fairly mild, and poured by young slaves of both sexes, often chosen for their good looks. At least as important as the drinking was the entertainment, in early centuries provided by the guests themselves. A branch of bay or myrtle was passed round and the guest receiving it was expected to cap the previous singer's contribution of a song or recitation, or else start afresh (*see* SCOLIA). An *aulos*-player would provide an accompaniment, or the guest himself might play on a lyre. Much of the lyric of Alcaeus, Anacreon, and Archilochus, and some of the short elegiac poems of Theognis, for example, were written for this kind of setting. Towards the end of the fifth century the entertainment began to change to a more regularized kind; sometimes slaves were hired to sing and dance, or other entertainers like acrobats, or, as in Plato's *Symposium*, the guests might entertain themselves with learned conversation, or less learned riddles and games. The evening might end with a noisy procession (*kōmos*) through the streets. Homosexuality derived much of its vitality as an institution from the circumstances of the symposium, where freeborn respectable women were absent and male beauty, charm, and wit were highly regarded. In a comic scene in Aristophanes' *Wasps*, a socially ambitious son tries to teach acceptable symposiastic behaviour to his embarrassingly boorish father. See also SYMPOSIUM (2) and MUSIC [Roman]. Today, a symposium means no more than a discussion-group.

**Sympo'sium** ('The drinking-party'; misleadingly, often 'banquet' in English. See SYMPOSIUM)

**1.** Dialogue by *Plato, written perhaps *c.*384 BC. The events described are supposed to have taken place at a party held in Athens at the house of the tragic poet *Agathon who is celebrating his first victory in the competitions for tragedy at the *Lenaea of 416 BC. The dialogue is narrated by a friend of Socrates, Apollodorus of Phalerum, who was not present (being too young) but had the story from an eyewitness and admirer of Socrates, Aristodemus. For entertainment each of the guests delivers a short speech in honour of love, Phaedrus from a mythical standpoint, Pausanias from that of a sophist, Agathon from that of a poet, and so on; *Aristophanes turns the dialogue towards comedy. Each speech is a clever parody by Plato of the style of the purported speaker. Socrates takes the discussion on to a higher plane. He has learnt from Diotima, the priestess of Mantinea, that love may have a nobler aspect. The need in a human being which is manifested on a lower plane by sexual love can also take an intellectual form, the desire of the soul to create conceptions of wisdom and beauty such as poets and legislators produce. One should proceed by stages, as when climbing a ladder, from the love of a beautiful body to the perception and love of universal divine beauty, which has no physical aspect. *Alcibiades now joins the party, professedly drunk. He confesses the fascination which Socrates exercises on him and his hope of receiving lessons in wisdom from him. He tells of various incidents in the life of Socrates, including his own failure to seduce him. Socrates, he says, is like the statuettes of *Silenus that conceal images of gods inside them, and like *Marsyas the satyr who with his pipe could charm the souls of men. The party is broken up by the arrival of revellers.

The term 'Platonic love' refers to the argument for the superiority of non-sexual love.

2. A narrative by *Xenophon of an imaginary symposium supposed to have taken place on the occasion of the Great *Panathenaea of 421 BC at the house of *Callias, Socrates being among the guests. Those present are all well-known historical characters except for a comedian called Philippus and a Syracusan in charge of the dancers. The narrative gives a vivid picture of the conversation and amusements at an Athenian symposium. The conversation is a mixture of humour and seriousness, and Socrates is presented in a relaxed mood. There are a good many jokes about his personal appearance; he is the central figure, and, amid all the jokes, delivers a serious speech on the superiority of spiritual to carnal love.

**Syphax** *See* MASINISSA.

**Sȳ'racuse** (Gk. Syrakousai, Lat. Syracusae) Chief city of *Sicily, founded as a colony by Corinth in 733 BC. It was a flourishing place by the end of the sixth century, and was raised to the position of first city in Sicily by *Gelon, who became tyrant c.490 BC and won great glory by repelling a Carthaginian invasion in 480. Gelon was succeeded by his brother Hieron I (478–67), who added to the cultural splendour of Syracuse and was made famous by the Epinician odes of Pindar and Bacchylides, and by the fact that Aeschylus and Simonides spent some time at his court. Xenophon wrote an imaginary dialogue between the latter and Hieron.

Soon after Hieron's death a democracy was set up at Syracuse, and internal dissensions were followed by external aggression against other Sicilian cities, a situation which Athens was led to believe she could turn to her own advantage; her hope of controlling some part of the island led to the disastrous *Sicilian Expedition of 415. Its failure was followed by the rise of Dionysius (later Dionysius I), a man of demagogic power, who was sole ruler from 405 to 367. He made himself master of half Sicily and extended his conquests to the mainland of Italy, winning effective control over most of *Magna Graecia. His rule brought prosperity to Syracuse, but was generally considered oppressive. Plato visited his court (*see* PLATO 1) but there is a legend that when Plato was leaving Syracuse, Dionysius contrived to have him sold into slavery, from which Plato's friends rescued him. Dionysius had a taste for literature and bought for himself the writing-tablets of Aeschylus. Thus inspired, he actually won the prize at the *Lenaea in 367 with a tragedy, the *Ransoming of Hector*; his death is said to have been caused by a drinking-bout in celebration of this victory.

Dionysius II succeeded his father, but was expelled by his uncle and brother-in-law Dion, who was himself assassinated in 353. The relations of Plato with these tyrants form the subject of several of his Epistles (*see* PLATO 6). After Dion's death Syracuse became increasingly anarchic and decline began, though Dionysius II recovered his throne in 346. The Syracusans appealed for assistance against him to their mother-city Corinth, who in 344 sent them *Timoleon. He restored peace to Sicily, introducing at Syracuse a moderately oligarchic government on the Corinthian model, but a further period of unrest followed under Agathocles (d. 289), a demagogue, who made himself first tyrant (317) and then king (305). He attacked other Sicilian cities, and fought against the Carthaginians, who occupied the west of the island. The reign of Hieron II (269–216), mild and just, celebrated by Theocritus in Idyll 16, was the last golden age of Syracuse. He had allied himself with Rome against Carthage in the First *Punic War and contributed to her final victory. After his death Syracuse forsook Rome for Carthage, an act which signalled its final downfall. The city was besieged (213–211) and finally sacked by M. Claudius Marcellus; in their defence the Syracusans were substantially aided by *Archimedes, who perished when the city was taken. Under Roman rule Syracuse retained its beauty and to some extent its importance, but it suffered at the hands of the governor *Verres.

**sȳrinx** *See* PAN and MUSIC [Greek 4].

# T

**Ta'bulae Ī'liacae** Some twenty-two stone reliefs, possibly of the early first century AD, from Rome or its vicinity. Most are of marble, most represent scenes from the Trojan War, and some seem to be from the workshop of a certain Theodorus. On one, found by the Via Appia near Bovillae, about 20km (12 miles) south-east of Rome, an inscription states that the central panel represents the (lost) *Iliupersis* ('Sack of Troy') of *Stesichorus, and its details have been believed to be Stesichorean. Among other things the panel shows Aeneas bearing his father Anchises on his shoulders from Troy, accompanied by his son Ascanius, with an inscription saying that he is sailing to '*Hesperia' (i.e. Italy). If Stesichorus did indeed include this episode, then he is the first authority for the legend of Aeneas' migration to Italy. Some scholars doubt the authenticity of the attribution to Stesichorus.

**Ta'citus, Publius Corne'lius** ('Gaius' rather than Publius in some sources; b. AD 56 or 57, d. after 117) Roman historian. He was probably a native of Narbonese or Cisalpine Gaul. Comparatively little is known about his life, but he had a normal senatorial career, begun under the emperor Vespasian (AD 69–79); he married *Agricola's daughter in 77, was praetor in 88, *consul suffectus* in 97 (*see* CONSULS), and governor of Asia in 112–13. His experience of the tyranny of Domitian's reign (81–96), to which he owed advancement, as he admits, led him to write in the introduction to his *Agricola* and *Histories* of the difficulties of surviving in public life and writing about great deeds in recent times (without naming the emperor). But he won fame during his lifetime: the Younger *Pliny, who was his friend, was proud to be considered his equal in popular estimation.

His *Agricola* was published in 98, early in Trajan's reign. It is essentially a panegyric of his father-in-law, especially of his great achievements in *Britain, on which Tacitus has valuable information; but it is also a defence of the integrity and service of those administrators who, like Agricola and Tacitus himself, as well as Trajan, had managed to survive Domitian's reign. His *Germania* or 'On the Origin and Country of the Germans' was published in the same year. It is an ethnographical work, and the second half contains an account of the various tribes north of the Rhine and the Danube, heavily dependent on earlier writers such as Livy and the Elder Pliny. It describes the Germans as indigenous and racially unmixed; their love of freedom and their vigour and bravery are implicitly compared with the corruption at Rome. His *Dialogus de oratoribus* ('Dialogue on orators') is set in the seventies; three distinguished men of the day discuss the supposed decline of Roman *oratory. The first speaker argues in favour of modern oratory, the second for a return to the old values, and the third attributes the decline to the disappearance of political freedom. Despite its near-Ciceronian style, very different from that of Tacitus' other works, it is now thought to belong to the period 100–5, and the early-seeming style is explained by reference to the requirements of a different literary genre. Tacitus had studied *rhetoric as a young man and he became famous as a speaker. In 97 he delivered a funeral oration over the consul Verginius Rufus (a distinguished general whom his soldiers had wanted to become emperor, and whose consulship Tacitus completed), and in 100 he spoke as advocate for the province of Asia against the ex-governor Marius Priscus; the Younger Pliny notes the eloquence and dignity of the latter speech.

His major works were the *Histories* and the *Annals*. A projected work on the happier reigns of Nerva and Trajan 'which I am saving for my old age' did not materialize. The *Histories*, on which Tacitus was working in 106–7, covered the period AD 69–96, the reigns of the emperors Galba, Otho, Vitellius, Vespasian, Titus, and Domitian, and was written in twelve or perhaps fourteen books. Only the first four and part of the fifth survive, dealing with the events of 69 and 70, but even those two years justify his description of the period as one 'full of catastrophe, fearful in its fighting, torn by mutinies, bloody even in peace'. He gives a vivid picture of the civil wars of 69 (the *'year of the four emperors') and their contenders, ending with the one emperor who 'changed for the better', Vespasian. The *Annals*, on which Tacitus was working *c.*116, originally consisted of eighteen or sixteen books covering AD 14–68, i.e. the reigns of Tiberius, Caligula, Claudius, and Nero. Most of 5 and the whole of 7–10 and the first half of 11 are missing; 16 breaks off in AD 66 before Nero's death. Tacitus' sources overall were the works of other historians, public records, and, where possible, his own experiences.

The *Annals* in particular show Tacitus to have been one of the greatest of historians, with a penetrating insight into character and a sober grasp of the significant issues of the time. He knew that rule by one emperor was to be a permanent institution; and he praised the few individuals who served the state well, but he was deeply pessimistic about Rome's ability to find a good emperor. The impartiality he claimed in writing the histories of the emperors was compromised by his use of innuendo: the suggestion is that the less honourable explanation is likely to be the correct one, and any underlying motive is brought to the reader's attention. He saw it as the historian's function to record virtue and ensure that vice was denounced by posterity (*Annals* 3.65). To this end he created a style as memorable as the events he records, condensed, rapid, and incisive. He avoids trite phraseology and frequently uses metaphor and archaic or poetic words. In his sentence structure he avoids balance, and commonly starts with the main clause, appending what follows in participial constructions, particularly the ablative absolute. This arrangement is particularly effective in undercutting an apparently straightforward statement with a sly insinuation or sardonic comment.

Tacitus' writings barely survived to modern times. The minor works existed in one fifteenth-century manuscript, lost after being copied; *Annals* 1–6 descend from a single manuscript (ninth century), as do *Annals* 11–16 and *Histories* 1–5 (eleventh century in this case).

**talent** A standard weight in the ancient world, representing a man's load; *see* WEIGHTS and MONEY AND COINS.

**Tālōs 1.** In Greek myth, the bronze man of Crete, made by the god Hephaestus and given by him (or Zeus) to King Minos to guard *Europa. He guarded the island by walking round it three times a day; if he saw strangers approaching he threw stones or made himself red-hot and then embraced them when they landed. His one vulnerable spot was a vein of blood which was closed in his foot by a nail. When he tried to drive the *Argonauts away from Crete, *Medea used her magic powers on him; according to one story she removed the nail, causing him to bleed to death.

**2.** The nephew of *Daedalus, sometimes called Perdix.

**Tanaquil** At Rome, wife of Tarquinius Priscus (*see* TARQUIN (1)). Livy represents her as a supportive wife and a dominating political presence. Her name is Etruscan.

**Ta'ntalus** In Greek myth, son of Zeus and the *Titan Pluto ('Wealth'), and king of the region around Mount Sipylus in Lydia. He married Dione, daughter of Atlas, by whom he became the father of Niobe and *Pelops, and thus the ancestor of the Pelopidae. Tantalus offended the gods and was punished in *Tartarus by being 'tantalized': he was set, thirsty and hungry, in a pool of water which always receded when he tried to drink, and under trees whose branches the wind tossed aside when he tried to pick the fruit. Another account of his punishment was that a great stone was suspended over his head, threatening to crush him, so that he was in too much terror to enjoy a banquet before him. His offence is variously described: either he tested the gods by inviting them to dinner and serving his son's flesh to see if they would realize (*see* PELOPS); or he stole nectar and ambrosia from the gods' table, where he had been invited, and gave them to his friends; or he told his friends the gods' secrets.

**Tare'ntum** (Gk. Taras, modern Taranto) Important city and harbour on the 'instep' of south Italy, on the gulf named after it. It was Sparta's only foreign settlement, traditionally founded in 706 BC by the Partheniai, the sons of *helots born to Spartan mothers when their husbands were away fighting the First Messenian War. Originally an aristocracy, Tarentum became a democracy *c*.475 BC, and flourished especially in the fourth century BC during the lifetime of the Pythagorean philosopher and politician *Archytas. The Tarentines quarrelled with the encroaching Romans in 282, relying on help from *Pyrrhus, and thus provoked Rome's Pyrrhic wars. The Romans conquered Tarentum in 272, which became an ally in 270. *Livius Andronicus, probably a Tarentine captive taken to Rome, was an important figure in early Roman literature. Tarentum played an important part in the Second Punic War: in 213 it was captured by Hannibal, and in 209 recaptured by Fabius Cunctator (and thoroughly plundered). Thereafter it suffered a decline in importance if not in wealth. It lay in very fertile country; its honey, olives, scallops, wool, and purple dye were praised by Horace, its pine-woods by Propertius.

**Tarpē'ia** Woman in early Roman history whose legend explained the name of the Tarpeian Rock at a cliff on the Capitoline hill, from which traitors and murderers were thrown. When after the rape of the Sabine women (*see* ROMULUS) the Romans and the Sabines were at war, Tarpeia, the daughter of a Roman officer, undertook to betray the citadel on the Capitol if, she said, the Sabines would give her 'what they had on their left arms', meaning their gold bracelets. But when the Sabines broke in they rewarded her treachery by crushing her under their shields, also worn on the left arm. (In an alternative version Tarpeia was a heroine, her intention being to gain possession of the Sabine shields in order to help the Romans.)

**Tarquin (Tarquinius)** Name of two of the (semi-legendary) kings of Rome.

**1. Tarquinius Priscus, Lucius** Fifth king of Rome (traditionally 616–579 BC), son of *Demaratus of Corinth. Tarquin and his wife *Tanaquil migrated to Rome from Corinth, and he became the indispensable associate of the king *Ancus Marcius. At the latter's death Tarquin was chosen by the *patricians as successor. He was eventually assassinated by the sons of Ancius Marcius, but their attempt to seize the throne was frustrated by Tanaquil, who obtained it for her favourite *Servius Tullius, born as a slave in her household. Tarquin's son, Tarquinius Superbus (see 2 below), succeeded to the throne later. One of his daughters married Servius Tullus, the other M. Brutus by whom she became the mother

of L. Iunius *Brutus (1), who ousted the Tarquins.

**2. Tarquinius Superbus ('the Proud'), Lucius** Seventh and last king of Rome (traditionally 534–510 BC), said to be the son of Tarquinius Priscus (but chronology requires him to be the grandson). For his accession *see* TULLIA (1). He was an active military ruler: he organized the *Latin league into an alliance under Rome, and he made a treaty with the Latin city of Gabii the text of which is said to have survived until Augustan times. He also completed the temple of Jupiter on the Capitol. However his tyrannical rule led to his expulsion by Tarquinius Collatinus and L. Iunius Brutus (*see* LUCRETIA). He subsequently appealed for help to the Etruscan cities of Veii, Tarquinii, and Clusium (where Lars Porsenna ruled) and finally to his son-in-law Manilius, dictator of the Latins. After the Romans defeated the Latins at Lake *Regillus Tarquin fled to Cumae where he died in 495 BC. *See also* SIBYL.

**Ta'rtarus** In Greek myth, a *primordial deity; his father was Aither (Sky), his mother Gaia (Earth), and by his own mother he became the father of Typhoeus. The name also describes the deepest part of the Underworld, 'as far beneath Hades as Heaven is above the earth' (*Iliad*), where the wicked suffer punishment for their misdeeds on earth, especially (in the early poets) those such as *Ixion, *Sisyphus, and *Tantalus who have committed some outrage against the gods. *See* HADES and DEATH, ATTITUDES TO.

**Tatius, Titus** *See* TITUS TATIUS.

**technology** Until recently it was thought that the prevalence of slaves in the ancient world discouraged technological innovation, and that the Greek attitude, later adopted by Roman intellectuals like Cicero, was that philosophical thought and discussion were preferable to the advancement of technology (often qualified as 'banausic' by Plato and Aristotle, from *baunos*, the forge or furnace). But despite the ancient pursuit of intellectual leisure both Greeks and Romans equipped armies, built fortifications and civil edifices including complex systems for supplying and disposing of water for large populations, and provided transport for agricultural and industrial goods. The Romans, far from merely applying the inventions of others, made crucial developments in many areas.

Much Greek technology is now believed to have originated in the Museum at Alexandria in Hellenistic times. A great stimulus was patronage by the ruling Ptolemies; *Philon (3) comments on their *philotechnia* ('love of technical knowledge'), but this may have been chiefly directed towards the tools of war. The book *Mechanical Problems* which has come down to us in the works of Aristotle was probably written at Alexandria between 280 and 260 BC.

Simple machines, known before the archaic age, included the wheel and axle, lever, pulley, winch, wedge, and screw. Gears were probably developed at Alexandria in the early third century BC. Apart from warfare, machines were used mainly in building works, mining, water-lifting, and agriculture; for the most part they were not used in manufacturing. Cranes were first used in Greek building operations in the late sixth century BC, perhaps at first with a rope passed over a simple pulley. The invention of the compound pulley to give mechanical advantage was ascribed, perhaps wrongly, to *Archimedes.

The Hellenistic period saw the introduction of more complicated water-lifting devices than hitherto. The example found in London, built in AD 63, shows that this piece of technology rapidly followed the Roman conquest. The water-lifting screw is attributed to Archimedes, although some would argue for the Near East. These devices made it possible to bring water to places above its natural level. It now seems that the water-mill was invented in the mid-third century BC, after which water power became widely used in the Greco-Roman world for many purposes—rock-crushers in mines, dough-kneaders, pestles for pounding, sawmills, olive- and grape-presses. In the case of mining, although the main innovation during the first millennium BC was the introduction of iron tools, the new sciences of hydrostatics, pneumatics, and mechanics were applied at least empirically to creating deep shafts and long galleries in mines. Glass vessels became everyday objects in the first century BC, when it was discovered that large numbers of them could be produced by glass-blowing instead of their being moulded or formed round a core. *See also* SCIENCE, ATTITUDES TO.

**Tecme'ssa** *See* AJAX.

**Te'gea** Mycenaean occupation site and ancient city in the south-east of Arcadia, mentioned in the *Iliad*. In very early times Tegea fought successfully against Sparta; in the first half of the sixth century the Spartans, reputedly trusting an ambiguous oracle from Delphi, advanced into Tegea to seize the land but were defeated, and Spartan prisoners were made to till the land wearing the chains which they had brought with them for use on the Tegeans. In the mid-sixth century, again on advice from *Delphi, the Spartans were told to find and bring back to Sparta the bones of the hero Orestes (son of Agamemnon). Having brought the bones from Tegea the Spartans were then victorious over the Tegeans who, after agreeing not to harbour Messenians (*see* MESSENIA), were taken into alliance with Sparta.

**Teire'sias** In Greek myth, the blind Theban seer. Several reasons are given for his blindness: one story is that he saw the goddess Athena bathing and she blinded him, but gave him as compensation, since his mother was her friend, the gift of prophecy and a life seven generations long, from the time of *Cadmus (when he was already old) to the *Epigoni. In another version, he saw snakes coupling and killed one of them with a stick, whereupon he changed into a woman; later the same thing happened again and he changed back into a man. Since he was now uniquely qualified to answer, Zeus and Hera consulted him as to whether a man or a woman derived more pleasure from the act of love. When Teiresias replied that women received nine times as much pleasure as men, Hera struck him blind, but Zeus gave him the gift of unerring prophecy. Teiresias plays a part in many myths: in Homer's *Odyssey* Odysseus is sent to the Underworld to consult him about his return to Ithaca; he also figures importantly in Sophocles' *Antigone* and *Oedipus Tyrannus*, in Euripides' *Bacchae* and *Phoenissae*, and in Statius' *Thebaïd*.

**Tei'sias 1.** (of Syracuse, first half of the fifth century BC) Early teacher of *rhetoric and a pupil of *Corax, with whom he is linked as the founder of forensic oratory. He too was interested in arguments from probability and resembled *Gorgias in observing how words could make 'the trivial important and the important trivial'.

**2.** The real name of *Stesichorus.

**Te'lamon** In Greek myth, king of the island of Salamis, son of Aeacus (king of Aegina) and

Endēis, brother of *Peleus, and father of the greater *Ajax and *Teucer. He was one of the Argonauts, and joined in the Calydonian boar-hunt (*see* MELEAGER). He and Peleus killed their half-brother Phocus (whose mother was the Nereid Psamanthe), perhaps at the instigation of Endeis. As a consequence Aeacus exiled them, Telamon going to Salamis. There he married Glauce, daughter of the king, and inherited the throne. After Glauce's death Telamon married Eriboea (or Periboea) and fathered Ajax. He had helped Heracles in an early sack of Troy (*see* LAOMEDON), and Heracles gave him Laomedon's daughter Hesione as concubine. Heracles' prayer that Telamon and Eriboea would have a brave son was shown to have been answered by the appearance of an eagle (Gk. *aietos*) sent by Zeus, after which the baby was named Ajax (Gk. Aias). Hesione also bore Telamon a son, Teucer. Telamon's death is variously narrated. He is usually said to have died at Salamis after banishing Teucer for failing to prevent Ajax' death.

**Telchī'nēs** In Greek myth, magical and malevolent beings associated with Cyprus, Crete, and Rhodes, but also found in mainland Greece, inventors of the craft of metalworking and users of a spiteful magic. They were finally destroyed by a god, usually said to be Zeus, by means of a great flood. The poet *Callimachus applied the name to his literary critics.

**Tele'gonus** According to the *Telegonia* (*see* EPIC CYCLE), the son of *Odysseus by Circe, and the unwitting killer of his father. According to Italian legend Telegonus founded the town of *Tusculum in the Alban hills outside Rome.

**Tele'machus** In Greek myth, the son of Odysseus and Penelope; for his history *see* ODYSSEY. According to the *Telegonia* (*see* EPIC CYCLE), Telemachus married *Circe. Homer in the *Odyssey* (see books 1–4 and 21–23) represents him as at first diffident, lacking his father's energy and resource, but at the end of the story astonishing his mother by taking command of the house and fighting resolutely against the suitors.

**Tē'lephus** In Greek myth, son of Heracles and Auge (daughter of a king of Tegea and priestess of Athena), who gave birth to him secretly in her shrine; because of the pollution the land was struck by plague, and when the king discovered the reason he had the child

exposed and Auge sold overseas. She came into the possession of Teuthras, king of Teuthrania in Mysia, who adopted her. The child was rescued by shepherds, and when he grew up went to Mysia. Here he was about to marry Auge when their relationship was revealed. He became king of Mysia; the Greeks on their way to Troy landed in his kingdom, mistaking it for their destination, and in the fighting that ensued Telephus caught his foot in a vine planted there by Dionysus and was wounded by Achilles. The wound proving incurable, Telephus went to the Greek camp at Aulis to seek Achilles, having been told by the Delphic oracle that the wounder would also heal. 'The wounder' was found to mean the spear, rust from which cured the wound. Euripides wrote a (lost) tragedy on the subject containing a scene, twice parodied by Aristophanes, in which Telephus appears disguised as a beggar, dressed in rags, and saves his own life in melodramatic fashion by seizing Agamemnon's infant son Orestes as hostage. The tetralogy of which it was a part (and which included the still extant *Alcestis*) won second prize in the dramatic competitions of 438 BC.

**Telesi'lla** Argive Greek poet of the fifth century BC, famous for supposedly arming the women of Argos after *Cleomenes (1) of Sparta had defeated the Argive men. Only a few fragments survive of her lyrics, written for choirs of girls. The telesillean metre is named after her.

**Tellus** In Roman religion, the earth-goddess, probably very old, associated with agricultural festivals.

**Te'menus** Among other mythical characters of this name, one of the *Heracleidae, descendants of Heracles. After these had conquered the Peloponnese, Temenus received Argos as his share. He was regarded as the ancestor of the Macedonian royal family.

**templum** At Rome, when taking the auspices, the place and direction from which the sign came were crucially important. A *templum* was an area defined both in the sky and on the ground. The senate house and the Comitium were both considered *templa*. See AUGURY.

**Ten Thousand, the** See ANABASIS.

**Terence (Publius Terentius Āfer)** (d. 159 BC) Roman writer of comedy. The main source for his life is a biography written by Suetonius *c.* AD

100 and preserved in *Donatus' commentary to Terence, but that itself is uncertain about many events. The manuscripts are divided between those who say he died at the age of 24 and those who say 34. He was said to have been born at Carthage ('Afer' means 'African') and to have been a slave at Rome. In composing his plays he was alleged to have been aided by *Scipio Aemilianus, C. *Laelius, and other friends of theirs, allegations to which he himself refers with some pride (at being thought to have such distinguished friends). He is said to have died at sea while returning from a visit to Greece.

Terence wrote six plays all of which survive, with dates (for details see individual titles): *Andria* ('Girl from Andros'), *Hecyra* ('Mother-in-law'), *Heauton timorumenos* ('Self-tormentor'), *Eunuchus* ('Eunuch'), *Phormio*, and *Adelphoe* ('Brothers').

His plays are *fabulae* *palliatae*, and with two exceptions are adapted from *Menander; he follows his Greek originals more closely than *Plautus did, although sometimes combining portions of two plays. He thus represents scenes of the same Greek life as Plautus depicted, but by keeping the settings and conventions of his Greek sources, and excluding specifically Roman elements, he avoids obvious incongruity. Although the characters and subjects (young men's complicated love affairs) are much the same in both playwrights, the spirit is different. In Terence portraiture takes the place of caricature; conversation is much more natural than in Plautus, lacking the boisterous, farcical element of the latter. In all respects Terence is more refined and sophisticated than Plautus, but less robust. He abandoned the expository kind of prologue, and instead inserted necessary background information into the action; he also avoided the somewhat unnatural monologues of his models, rescripting them as dialogues. He introduces a more prosaic note by almost entirely avoiding lyric passages (*cantica*) and opera-like scenes; but only half of his lines are in the spoken metre of iambic senarii; the rest are iambic and trochaic septenarii, which were certainly 'sung' in the form of recitative. In general Terence aims at greater realism, and succeeded in creating a naturalistic style of conversation far closer to everyday life than anything in Plautus, thus contributing to the development of natural-seeming literary Latin.

The plays of Terence did not have popular appeal but were greatly admired by discriminating critics like Cicero and Horace. Several of his lines have become proverbial: *quot homines, tot sententiae* ('as many opinions as there are people'), and *fortīs fortuna adiuvat* ('fortune favours the brave'), both from *Phormio*.

**Tēreus** *See* Philomela.

**Te'rminus** ('boundary-stone') In Roman religion the god who protected stones, the object of an annual ritual (the Terminalia) on 23 February, which included a sacrifice and a feast by the neighbouring landholders. According to Roman myth, the boundary-stone of the god in the temple of Jupiter Optimus Maximus had been there before the temple was built. It was left in position; the temple had an opening in the roof to ensure that the stone remained under the open sky.

**Terpa'nder (Terpandros)** (of Lesbos, early seventh century BC) Greek lyric poet and musician, famous in legend, but of whose life nothing is known for sure. He was said to have won a musical competition during the period 676–673, at the *Carnea in Sparta, where he was believed to have founded a music school, and also won four successive victories for music at the Pythian games. The invention of the seven-stringed lyre (*cithara*) was ascribed to him. He composed *nomes* (settings of epic poetry), preludes or introductions to the singing of epic poetry, and *scolia* (drinking songs); it is very doubtful whether the few surviving fragments ascribed to him are authentic; it seems probable that none of his work was known by the Alexandrian scholars of the Hellenistic age.

**Tethys** According to Hesiod, a *Titan, daughter of Gaia (Earth) and Uranus (Heaven), consort of *Oceanus. Homer in the *Iliad* (14.201) speaks of Tethys and Oceanus as the parents of the gods, but this would appear to derive from a lost theogony which made the primeval waters the origin of the world.

**tetra'logy** In Greek, originally a term used in oratory to describe a group of four speeches (*logoi*) delivered in the same law-suit (two each for the prosecution and defence). For its application to Greek drama *see* TRAGEDY 2.

**Teucer (Teukros) 1.** In Greek myth, legendary king ruling in the neighbourhood of *Troy, son of the river Scamander and a nymph Idaea, who became the ancestor of the Trojan kings through his daughter who married *Dardanus. From him the Trojans are sometimes called Teucri.

**2.** In Greek myth, son of *Telamon and Hesione, and half-brother of *Ajax(1). He was called Teucer (i.e. Trojan) because his mother was a daughter of *Laomedon, king of Troy. He was the greatest archer among the Greeks at the siege of Troy. On his return to Salamis from the siege he was banished by his father for not preventing his brother's death, and went to Cyprus where he founded a town also called Salamis.

## texts, transmission of ancient

1. In Greece the first literature, Homeric epic, was composed and handed down orally (*see* HOMER). According to tradition, it was the Athenian tyrant Peisistratus in the middle of the sixth century BC who first ordered an official text of Homer to be written down, and one may guess that the lyric poetry of Archilochus, Alcaeus, and Sappho circulated in written form also. Certainly from the late seventh century onwards the new prose works, which could not have been as easily memorized as poetry, could hardly have survived by oral transmission and must have been written down. Books were not common until well into the fifth century BC, but soon after the middle of that century some sort of book-trade developed, which made it possible for individuals such as Aristotle in the fourth century BC to collect books and form libraries (for books at this time *see* BOOKS, GREEK AND ROMAN 3)

Aristotle's arrangement of the library at the *Lyceum served as a model for the library at Alexandria set up in the third century BC (*see* ALEXANDRIAN LIBRARY); to the editorial labours of the Alexandrian librarians and scholars, in particular to *Callimachus, *Zenodotus, *Eratosthenes, *Aristophanes of Byzantium, and *Aristarchus, we owe the texts of classical Greek literature that we still possess today, and some of the ancient notes (scholia; *see* SCHOLIUM) which have come down with them. The scholars at Alexandria aimed to collect copies of all the known literature of ancient Greece. Out of this they drew up lists of the best authors in each genre (*see* CANONS), thus facilitating the survival of these works at the expense, it would appear, of the works of lesser authors. The manuscripts which reached Alexandria had been copied with varying degrees of care, and most contained numerous mistakes and deviations from what the authors had written ('corruptions'). The scholars' task was to restore the original texts, as far as was possible, to classify them according to type (in *lyric poetry, for example, there were many different kinds), and also to write commentaries explaining difficult language, literary connections, or forgotten customs. Restoring the original posed problems of convention; spelling in early texts differed according to the version of the Greek alphabet used in the author's own city, and these texts had to be transliterated into the Ionic alphabet which was in general use in Greece after 403 BC (*see* ALPHABET). Some obviously wrong readings found in manuscripts of the Middle Ages go back to errors in transliteration made in the fourth and third centuries BC.

Another problem presented by the manuscripts was that of simple interpretation. Texts were written without word-division and continued to be so written long after the Hellenistic age; it was not until the Middle Ages that there was consistent separation of words. *Accents, a Hellenistic invention which helps word identification as well as being a guide to pronunciation, were likewise not used consistently until the Middle Ages. *Punctuation was rudimentary and used sporadically; in the texts of plays a change of speaker was indicated by a horizontal stroke at the beginning of a line or by a colon, with inevitable inaccuracy. Aristophanes of Byzantium was credited with distinguishing the individual metrical units or cola of poetry, thus aiding recognition of the metre, a discovery which enabled the text to be written in separate lines of verse rather than continuously in the form of prose. The critical signs written in the margins by Alexandrian scholars are in some cases still in use today. Lines thought to be spurious were 'obelized', that is, a horizontal stroke, *obelos*, was placed beside the line in the left-hand margin; the *diplē* > indicated that something in the line was notable; the *asteriskos* ✕ marked a line incorrectly repeated in another place; the sigma and antisigma (⊂ and ⊃) marking two consecutive lines showed that they might be interchanged. Thus there gradually developed the technicalities of scholarship and in particular of *textual criticism as scholars began to suggest alternative readings for what they thought to be errors in the text, fortunately without removing the original readings (*see* DIDYMUS).

2. In the ensuing Roman age, from the second century AD (*see* ROMAN AGE OF GREEK LITERATURE), scholarship declined although there still were scholars engaged in preserving and continuing the tradition of Alexandrian research: in grammar, *Apollonius Dyscolus and *Herodian, in metric *Hephaestion, in the compilation of lexicons Harpocration and *Hesychius. But interest in the old authors was limited, and selections and *anthologies came to be preferred to the complete work of a poet. However, at the same time, in the Greek-speaking eastern part of the Roman empire, there was a revival of interest in classical Attic Greek (*see* SECOND SOPHISTIC). This, combined with the emphasis on rhetoric in education, ensured the survival of the admired prose models, Plato, Xenophon, and Demosthenes, and in verse the popular plays of the tragedians and of Aristophanes. A factor which led to losses at this time, however, was the change in the form of books from the papyrus roll to the parchment codex with leaves as in the modern book (*see* BOOKS, GREEK AND ROMAN 5). It must always have been the case that works were lost simply by the disintegration of papyrus rolls before they had been recopied, but the general change from roll to codex entailed the complete recopying of ancient literature from one form to another during the second to fourth centuries AD. Inevitably, some works did not seem worth the effort. Also, the absence of a roll or two at the time of copying might mean that a work was thereafter transmitted with part missing.

Classical literature was the basis of the whole educational system for Christian and pagan alike, since there were no alternative Christian texts. However, since most Christians had no further interest in reading pagan literature once their education was over, there was less incentive in a Christian society to copy texts apart from those which appeared on the school curriculum, and apparently not enough to ensure their survival through the wars and destructions of the fourth and subsequent centuries. On the other hand there was no appreciable corruption during this time and the quality of surviving texts was hardly impaired.

3. By the end of the sixth century a serious decline in learning and literacy in the eastern empire meant that for three centuries there is little recorded about classical studies. After the eighth century, the darkest period, came peace and a revival in the ninth century associated with the names of Photius and Arethas, who sought out surviving classical books. At the same time there were two important changes in manuscripts, one of material and one of handwriting. First, papyrus became scarce, particularly after the Arab conquest of Egypt (AD 639–42), and was replaced by parchment (made from animal skins) and later by paper (this was not common in the West before about the thirteenth century, but it was used earlier in Byzantium). Secondly, the old-style handwriting, *uncial, was replaced by minuscule, which could be written rapidly in half the space—parchment was expensive, so economical use of it was important. The rewriting of the uncial manuscripts into minuscule began in the ninth century. Although texts in which there was little interest were neglected, the recopying which began then ensured the preservation of the works we still possess: many of the surviving manuscripts of ancient authors descend from only one or two minuscule manuscripts written at that time.

After the losses of the ninth and tenth centuries, the survival of most of what was left of the Greek classics was virtually certain. The literary texts were copied regularly and so too were those of the medical and mathematical writers. Nevertheless, losses still occurred; the libraries of Constantinople must have suffered severely when the city was sacked by the Franks in 1204 during the Fourth Crusade. However, serious though this was it did not for long disrupt the progress of learning. It was followed by a flowering of Greek scholarship from the late thirteenth to the fifteenth centuries, associated particularly with the names of Planudes and Triclinius, when much consolidation of learning took place and resulted in careful editions of the surviving texts. Even before the Turks captured Byzantium in 1453 there had been some emigration of Byzantine scholars to the West and the Italian humanists had been collecting Greek manuscripts from the Byzantine empire. By the time Byzantium fell the survival of Greek literature in the West was assured.

4. Latin literature began in the third century BC and by the middle of the following century a considerable body of texts was in existence, of poetry, plays, and prose. However, although books must have circulated by that time, very little is known about the way in which texts,

presumably written on papyrus rolls as in Greece, were copied and published. The epics of Naevius and Ennius were in a sense a national possession and received some scholarly attention; but dramatic texts, being distributed as acting copies, suffered many alterations and recastings (Plautus' *Poenulus* and Terence's *Andria* each have two different endings preserved in the manuscripts). The influence of *Crates (1), a Pergamene grammarian who visited Rome *c.*168 BC, and scholarship deriving from Alexandria (*see* ALEXANDRIAN LIBRARY and MUSEUM) gave impetus to Roman scholarship. Rome's most famous scholar of the first century BC was *Varro. His research into antiquities, the Latin language, and literary history gave a firm foundation to the work of later textual scholars. Also in the first century BC we have the earliest Roman example of a textbook on rhetoric, the *Rhetorica ad Herennium*. For later examples of literary commentaries *see* DONATUS; PRISCIAN; PROBUS; SERVIUS.

In the second century AD there was again a revival of interest in early Roman writers, and it is to this revival that we owe most of our knowledge of Ennius and Cato the Elder who, though not surviving in manuscript, are quoted and referred to by compilers of excerpts (such as Aulus *Gellius). During the third and fourth centuries many Latin texts were epitomized, continuing and increasing a tendency that had been apparent in the first century AD when Livy was so treated. The last pagan revival came at the end of the fourth century, in the face of the triumph of Christianity during the reign of the emperor Theodosius (378–95). In general, Latin-speaking Christians like their Greek counterparts accepted that the pagan Latin texts were still essential for education and could be used, but with caution. The old Roman educational system prevailed until it came to be replaced much later by that of monastic and episcopal schools. (*See also* MACROBIUS.)

5. The destructions of the fourth and fifth centuries were exceeded by those of the sixth century and by the final collapse of the western Roman empire under waves of invaders (*see* FALL OF ROME). The classically educated world narrowed with the fall of North Africa to the Vandals; Spain, which survived the Frankish invasions of the third century and the Visigothic in the fifth (even transmitting a residuum of Roman culture through Isidore, bishop of Se-

ville), succumbed early in the eighth century to the Arabs; and Gaul under the Franks was not in a position to preserve classical learning. Nevertheless, books continued to be produced in the fourth and fifth centuries, including luxury copies of Virgil. Although the Latin Church was predominantly hostile to pagan literature, pagan Latin texts were still included in the important collections of books being made at the ecclesiastical centres of Rome, Ravenna, and Verona. At the beginning of the sixth century it was still possible to obtain copies of most of the important Latin classical and post-classical authors except for the very early literature which had disappeared in the course of the previous centuries. (For the copying of books in a sixth-century monastic library *see* CASSIODORUS).

In the period from the mid-sixth to the mid-eighth centuries, a dark age in the Latin West as in the Greek East, there was a steep decline of interest in classical literature, texts of which seem scarcely to have been copied at all, while a large number of biblical and patristic works was produced. Many Latin works perished when old parchments had their original text removed by washing and were then reused for religious texts (reused manuscripts are called *palimpsests), less from hostility than from complete lack of interest. The surviving part of Cicero's *De republica* is known only from what has been recovered from underneath the commentary of St Augustine on the Psalms.

But at the same time, from the late sixth century onwards, classical literature was being saved and propagated by Christian missionaries from Ireland. Impelled by a zeal for books and learning, they spread across Europe founding monasteries to which they passed on their own enthusiasm, e.g. at Luxeuil in Burgundy, Bobbio in northern Italy, and St Gall in Switzerland. It was the importation of books into England in great quantity which enabled the biblical scholar and historian Bede (673–735) to acquire his vast learning, though he had never left Northumbria in the north of England. Anglo-Saxons in their turn became missionaries and scholars. A special variety of Latin handwriting, known as 'insular', is associated with the early scholarship of the British Isles.

At the end of the eighth century came a revival of learning in Charlemagne's reconstituted Roman empire of western Europe (and consequently called the Carolingian revival), centred on the monasteries. The scholar monk Alcuin, born in 735 and educated at York, was its chief promoter. He was appointed by Charlemagne to head a school attached to the court at Aachen, where he followed the programme of Cassiodorus in teaching the *seven liberal arts. When he became Abbot of St Martin's at Tours he taught his monks to copy manuscripts, and as a result France was important in the transmission of texts during the ninth and tenth centuries. Caroline minuscule script was developed in France, and from it evolved a minuscule that became the normal script of western Europe. Some of our soundest Latin texts date from this time.

6. By the end of the ninth century the survival of a large number of Latin works was secured by their being part of the educational curriculum or established as works of literature; but there were others which were rarely studied, and some which were represented, as far as can be seen, by only one or two copies. In the late eleventh and early twelfth centuries there was suddenly a renewed interest in the classics, and books on the verge of extinction began to be copied. Because of this we still possess part of Varro's *De lingua Latina* and Frontinus' *De aquis*. During the twelfth century generally a more active intellectual life was being pursued in the cathedral schools. Although education continued to be based on Latin literature it was becoming more secular, but at the same time there was now a leisured class who wanted from literature a reflection of its own life and desires. It is therefore a matter of regret that when for the first time for many centuries love-poetry and satire were in demand for their own sakes, the age was without the poetry of Catullus, Tibullus, and Propertius, which was yet to be rediscovered.

7. The teaching of the seven liberal arts, under the influence of Alcuin, did much to prepare the way in the eleventh century for the application of philosophical method to the study of theology, an educational pattern which became rigid and narrow and was known as scholasticism. To the scholastics, classical literature was no longer important for its form or style or for other literary reasons, but for its material content, information, or moral anecdote. These aspects could be more readily absorbed in excerpts than by reading complete texts. Ovid and Seneca, who can be easily appreciated in selections, became very popular; Virgil, who could not, languished. Most significantly, Aristotle acquired importance, even if only for his works on logic. The result was a revival of interest in Greek. Until the end of the twelfth century Aristotle was known in the West only in the Latin translations of, and commentaries on, a few of his logical works, by *Boethius and others (see ARISTOTLE 5). Plato similarly was known only from a Latin version of the *Timaeus*, made in the fourth century, and from Latin quotations. From the mid-eighth century onwards, translations into Arabic and Syriac of Greek philosophical works in which Islamic thinkers were particularly interested, initiated by a desire for the medical works but including Plato, Aristotle, Theophrastus, Ptolemy, and the mathematical writers, circulated in the Arab world. Towards the end of the twelfth century, Arabic translations and commentaries on these Greek authors by Avicenna (980–1037) and Averroes (1126–98), Aristotle's greatest Islamic disciple, were themselves translated into Latin at Toledo in Spain and diffused rapidly through Europe. But the great step forward came in the thirteenth century when these Latin translations from the Arabic were superseded by others made direct from the original Greek. In England Robert Grosseteste (c.1170–1253) translated Aristotle's *Ethics* and some of the works of pseudo-*Dionysius the Areopagite, and William of Moerbeke (c.1215–86) a number of Greek commentaries on Aristotle, many at the request of Thomas Aquinas (1225–74). Roger Bacon (c.1214–94), a pupil of Grosseteste at Oxford, lamenting the general ignorance of Greek, tried to remedy matters by compiling a Greek grammar.

8. Modern classical scholarship began in north Italy in the fourteenth century, stimulated by the revival of interest in the classics. A wide range of previously unavailable literary and historical texts was now being discovered and studied. A key figure was Petrarch (1304–74), who combined enthusiasm and scholarship (although he never learned Greek). Through his connections with the papacy he gained access to libraries and assembled an impressive library of his own containing both Latin and Greek texts. His belief that the wide range of classical literature was a better basis for education than the narrow syllabus of Aristotelian philosophy proved influential, and Italian

humanists followed his teaching for the next century. There was a revival of Greek teaching, and scholars generally began to possess a modicum of that language. The most important Greek prose works began to circulate in Latin translations. By the end of the fifteenth century many of the techniques of textual and historical criticism had evolved. There were new beginnings in theology also. Lorenzo Valla (*c*.1405–57) anticipated Erasmus (*c*.1466–1536) in arguing that the proper basis for the study of the New Testament was the Greek text and not the Latin Vulgate of Jerome. The invention of printing ensured the survival of the classics, first of the major Latin texts and then, from the 1480s, of the Greek. *See also* PAPYROLOGY.

**textual criticism** Study of surviving copies of a written work with the aim of restoring the author's original text. The manuscripts in which the works of Greek and Latin literature were preserved, before the invention of printing, date from the ninth to the fifteenth centuries AD (*see* TEXTS, TRANSMISSION OF ANCIENT and PAPYROLOGY). They are thus at many removes from the authors' original: in the course of being copied by hand through many centuries, they have been altered ('corrupted') by accidental miscopying and by deliberate rewriting ('interpolation'), and have deteriorated by natural wear and tear. The first stage of textual criticism is to compare the manuscript copies of a text with each other so as to understand their relationships (for example, which manuscripts are copied from others still surviving). This process, known as collation, makes it possible to gain an idea of the state of the text of the nearest common ancestor of them all, known as the archetype. (The archetype, which is very rarely still in existence, is as far back as the manuscript evidence goes, but is itself usually many centuries later than the author's own text.) It is then often possible to group the manuscripts in families. In some cases it is possible to set out these family relationships in a 'family tree' (a *stemma*) descending from the archetype, in which manuscripts are identified by letters of the alphabet. At this stage manuscripts which are found to be direct copies of others still in existence are eliminated as having no independent value. Where a scribe has introduced variant readings from elsewhere or has changed his source, his manu-script is said to be 'contaminated', and may not fit easily into a *stemma*.

The next stage is to examine critically the text of the manuscripts selected as significant (a process sometimes called recension). The editor's task is to identify the authentic readings in those places where the manuscripts differ and to detect places where all of them seem to be in error. These last the editor corrects ('emends') if he can; if he cannot, he isolates the error and indicates that the text is not sound by 'obelizing' the corrupt words, i.e. printing a 'dagger' or obelus before and after them. (The dagger thus † is a modern critical sign: the *obelos* of the Alexandrian scholars was a horizontal line; *see* TEXTS, TRANSMISSION OF ANCIENT 1.) In some places in the texts the manuscripts will offer a variety of readings some or all of which have a claim to be considered as authentic; the editor's task is then to decide between them. Where no given reading is satisfactory the editor may make a suggestion, 'conjecture', of his own or accept another's conjecture. Nowadays the variant readings, together with the plausible emendations or conjectures of previous editors, are printed by the editor at the bottom of each page of text. This part of a modern printed text, usually written in Latin and with considerable use of abbreviations, is known as the *apparatus criticus*, 'critical apparatus', and enables readers to assess for themselves the evidence for and reliability of the text they are reading.

**Thaïs** Famous Athenian *\*hetaira* who accompanied Alexander the Great (*see* ALEXANDER (1) 4). Many examples are recorded of her wit in repartee.

**Thalēs** (of Miletus, fl. *c*.600 BC) By tradition the earliest Greek philosopher-scientist, one of the *\*Seven Sages. He is credited with offering sound advice in many spheres, including politics (to the Ionians, to form a political union to meet the threat from Persia), but he was chiefly famous for his observations of the sky and as a geometer. He left no written work; his fame survived in oral tradition. He is said to have predicted an eclipse of the sun within the year 585 BC which actually took place on the day of the battle of the Halys between the Medes and the Lydians. Though it is highly unlikely for one of his time to have known a system for predicting a solar eclipse at a given latitude he may have known that eclipses were caused by lunar interposition, and have used lunation cycles to arrive at a rough date. Slightly more plausible is the belief that after visiting Egypt he originated geometry by generalizing from Egyptian land-measurement. Aristotle attributed to him the view that all things are modifications of a single eternal (and therefore divine) substance, which Thales held to be water, an idea paralleled in Egyptian and Babylonian myth (and in the opening of Genesis). With this is connected his saying that 'all things are full of gods'. *See* PHILOSOPHY.

**Thalē'tas** Poet from Gortyn in Crete who came to Sparta in the seventh century BC, where, it was said, he founded the *Gymnopaediae in order to rid the Spartans of a plague (by appeasing the god Apollo with his poetry). There he composed *paeans and *hyporchemata for the festivals, using paeonic and cretic metres. Nothing of his work survives.

**Tha'myris (Thamyras)** Legendary Thracian poet and musician. According to Homer, he boasted that he would win a contest even if the Muses opposed him, but they blinded him and made him forget his skill. Later authors attribute various musical inventions to him.

**Thanatos (Death)** *See* HYPNOS.

**Thapsus** City in North Africa, famous as the site of Julius Caesar's victory over the supporters of Pompey in 46 BC.

**Theaetē'tus** Dialogue by *Plato, a sequel to *Parmenides*, named after an Athenian geometer (*c.*414–369 BC) who was the author's friend and pupil. It deals with the nature of knowledge. In the introductory scene Theaetetus is reported to have been taken home, mortally wounded in the Corinthian War between Athens and Corinth (probably in 369) in which he has shown great bravery. A conversation is recalled that took place between him and Socrates shortly before the latter's death in 399, when Theaetetus was only a boy, and since it had been written down (in direct dialogue form), a slave is summoned and reads the manuscript. Various definitions of knowledge are considered, such as 'knowledge is sensible perception', but are all found wanting. Plato makes little or no use here of his doctrine of Forms. The problem is left unresolved and is resumed in the *Sophist*. In the course of the dialogue there occurs Socrates' famous comparison of himself to a midwife, bringing to birth the thoughts of others.

**Thea'genes** Tyrant of *Megara in Greece *c.*640–620 BC, whose son-in-law was *Cylon the would-be tyrant at Athens. He built a famous fountain-house to give Megara a public water-supply; he was later banished.

**Thea'genes and Chariclē'a** Alternative title of the *Aethiopica* of Heliodorus.

**theatre** In both Greece and Rome, plays were performed in the open air in daylight, and the action was generally presumed to take place similarly (but *see* RHESUS).

**Greek.** In Greece theatres were so frequently altered and rebuilt that the early history of the theatre of Dionysus at Athens, where classical drama originated, can only be conjectural (*see* DIONYSUS, THEATRE OF). Theatres are commonly thought to have developed out of the *orchestra*, a flat dancing-place of hard earth where the choruses in Greek drama continued to perform. (There is testimony to an early *orchestra* in the agora at Athens.) Near the theatre of Dionysus was an area of sloping ground convenient for spectators to sit or stand, the *theatron* ('a place for watching', Lat. *auditorium*). Later the area was made semicircular, with seats cut out of the ground. The front rows, perhaps with stone seating, were for priests and officials. At each side of the *orchestra* was a *parodos* or 'way-in', used by the spectators when they entered the theatre and by the chorus and actors on entering and leaving the *orchestra*. In later times a convention grew up that when the scene was Athens, characters purporting to come on the scene from the agora or Piraeus should enter from the audience's right, since these places were situated in fact in that direction; coming from the country they entered from the left. Vase-paintings of the fifth and fourth centuries BC suggest that there was a low wooden stage with steps in the middle down to the *orchestra*, and behind it a stage-building, *skēnē* (originally 'tent' or 'booth') for the use of the actors, which developed into a more substantial wooden structure serving also as a backdrop (English 'scene'). At the opening of Aeschylus' *Agamemnon* the Watchman is positioned on the roof of the *skene*, with dramatic effect. There were large double doors in the middle of the *skene* (and later other doors too) through which the *ekkyklema*, a wheeled platform, could be brought forward with a static display representing events which had taken place indoors, such as Ajax surrounded by dead animals in Sophocles' *Ajax*. A *mēchanē*, 'crane', was erected at the back of one end of the *skene*, which could be used to represent gods flying through the air (in the case of Euripides' *Medea*, Medea herself escaping in the chariot of the Sun). The appearance in this manner of a god who provided a solution in an intractable situation was the origin of the Latin phrase *deus ex machina*, 'a god on a machine', to describe an unexpected outside intervention which resolves a difficulty. Various other stage-properties might be used in the Greek theatre, e.g. statues, altars, or other prominent features of the play, and scenery might be painted on boards. There was, however, no curtain. For the actors and their dress *see* COMEDY [Greek 3] and TRAGEDY 2. For the admission charge *see* THEORIC FUND. *See also* DIONYSIA.

**Roman.** There was no permanent theatre at Rome until 55 BC, when Pompey built one in stone from the spoils of the Mithridatic War with a seating capacity estimated at 10,000. It was erected in the Campus Martius, next to the Curia. Two other stone theatres were subsequently built in Rome, both in the Campus Martius, that of L. Cornelius Balbus dedicated in 13 BC, and that known as the theatre of Marcellus, built by the emperor Augustus and named after his adopted son.

In the time of Plautus, Terence, Ennius, and Pacuvius (late third and the second centuries BC), plays were performed on wooden stages in front of a temporary wooden building having at most three doors opening on to the stage and representing houses opening on to a street. These stages would be erected in the Forum or Circus Maximus, with circles of wooden seats; an attempt to erect a permanent theatre in 155 BC was thwarted by the consul Scipio Nasica, who induced the senate to demolish the building as it constituted a danger to public morality. But in the first century BC even the temporary theatres had linen awnings to keep off the sun.

The *orchestra* was used for seating, reserved for senators, priests, and officials. After 68 BC the *equites* (*see* EQUESTRIAN ORDER) had the right to occupy the first fourteen rows of the auditorium behind the orchestra. Behind the stage was the stage-building. The auditorium was much more enclosed than in a Greek theatre, and could even have the awnings replaced by a roof, as at Pompeii. The uncomfortable nature of the seating is mentioned by Ovid, who refers to the narrow space allotted to each spectator, and to the knees of those behind pressing into the backs of those in front. From the end of the second century BC we hear of a curtain, kept in a slot in the floor of the stage and raised at the end of the play (a convenient way of indicating that the performance was over). Stage scenery was said to have been first introduced in 99 BC. The chorus in the tragedies of Ennius, Pacuvius, and Accius (unlike the chorus of Greek drama) stood on the stage, not in the *orchestra*, and could enter and exit like any other character (whereas with very rare exceptions the Greek chorus did not leave until the end of the play). This was more realistic; the functions of the chorus had changed and there was no longer that important lyrical element in drama for which it had been the mouthpiece.

The players were slaves or freedmen, trained to the profession, and organized in companies under the direction of a manager paid for by the magistrate who gave the *ludi* ('games') at which the plays were performed. The players' pay gradually increased, and although actors (like musicians) were originally despised, the examples of *Roscius and Aesopus showed that popular actors might become rich and socially acceptable. Female parts (except in mimes and late comedy) were played by men. It is said that the type of character was indicated at first by wigs (white for old men, red for slaves, etc.) and later by masks (*see* ROSCIUS), but whether masks were in fact worn in the Roman theatre, and if so, when, is a matter of dispute. Tragic actors wore long flowing robes and high buskins (*see* COTHURNUS); comic actors wore ordinary dress and the *soccus or low-heeled shoe.

**Thē'bāïd** (*Thēbāïs*) Latin epic poem in twelve books of hexameters by *Statius. The author, who spent twelve years on the work, published it in AD 90 or 91.

The subject is the expedition of the *Seven against Thebes in support of the attempt by Polyneices to recover the throne from his brother Eteocles (*see* OEDIPUS). The first three books deal with the preliminaries of the war—the arrival of Polyneices and Tydeus at Argos, the embassy of Tydeus to Thebes and the subsequent attempt by some Thebans to destroy him in an ambush (in book 2 he fights single-handed against fifty Thebans), and the prophecy of Amphiaraus. Books 4, 5, and 6 include the consultation of the seer Teiresias, the Argive march on Thebes, the episode of *Hypsipyle, her account of the massacre at Lemnos, 5.85, and the funeral games for the child Opheltes, including the exciting chariot race, 6.296. With book 7 the fighting begins, after a vain attempt by Jocasta at mediation. The pious Amphiaraus is swallowed up by the earth; the fighting continues through books 8, 9, and 10, with many incidents: the death of Ismene's lover Atys, the episode of Tydeus and Melanippus, the feats of Hippomedon, the self-sacrifice (*devotio*) of Menoeceus, the death of Capaneus by a thunderbolt. Book 11 contains the fatal combat of Eteocles and Polyneices, Creon's refusal of burial to the latter, and Jocasta's suicide. Book 12 completes the story with the meeting between Polyneices' wife Argeia and Antigone, the funeral pyre of the two sons of Oedipus, with its divided flames, the intervention of Theseus, and the death of Creon. At the end, Statius takes leave of his long task, and with a humble reference to Virgil speculates whether his own work will endure.

Statius follows epic tradition in having the gods interfere in men's affairs, writing a catalogue of the forces fighting, describing funeral games, and so on, but he plays with this inheritance and exploits the possibilities of allegory. Many incidents and much of his language are imitated from Virgil, though in some respects his work is more reminiscent of Ovid's *Metamorphoses*, showing great stylistic refinement. The modern reader may find an excess of mythological lore, relieved by the occasional lively narrative, but the deeper themes of civil war and insanity make themselves felt.

**Thēbă'is** See EPIC CYCLE and *THEBAID*.

**Thebes (Thēbai) 1.** The principal city of Boeotia in Greece (in rivalry with Orchomenus) and the most important in Greek history after Athens and Sparta. Its fame in myth and legend was unequalled; Sophocles (in a surviving fragment) described it as 'the only city where mortal women are the mothers of gods' (i.e. of Dionysus and Heracles). For its early legendary history see CADMUS; ANTIOPE; HERACLES; OEDIPUS. According to the usual legend (but see ANTIOPE) the city was founded by the leader of a Phoenician colony, Cadmus, whose daughter Semele gave birth to the god Dionysus. It was probably the centre of a large kingdom in the *Mycenaean age; part of a sub-

stantial palace has been excavated and *Linear B tablets have been found. In myth it was destroyed by the *Epigoni a generation or two before the Trojan War; hence the absence of the name from the catalogue (in *Iliad* 2) of the Greek cities which fought against Troy. After its eclipse in the *Dark age, Thebes recovered by the sixth century BC to take the lead in a loose confederation of Boeotian cities (*see* BOEOTIA), but was never strong enough to unite them into a single state with itself at the head. In the fifth century Thebes was hostile to Athens and supported Persia in the *Persian Wars and Sparta in the *Peloponnesian War. After the Peloponnesian War came a period of rivalry between Thebes and Sparta for supremacy in Greece, and, under the leadership of *Pelopidas and *Epaminondas, Thebes attained its zenith. Not only did the city defeat and humiliate Sparta (in the years following the Spartan defeat at Leuctra in 371), it extended its power in the north, bringing parts of Thessaly under its protection and establishing its authority at the court of Macedon. However, under *Philip II, Macedon swiftly rose to be the strongest state in Greece, posing such a threat that Thebes allied itself with the Athenians. Together they were defeated by Philip at Chaeronea (338); Philip then dissolved the Boeotian confederacy and established a Macedonian garrison in the citadel of Thebes. Shortly after the accession of Philip's son Alexander the Great the Thebans revolted (335) and Alexander destroyed the city. The punishment shocked Greece, and when it was rebuilt by Cassander in 317 many Greek cities helped with contributions. The new Thebes continued to exist throughout Roman times.

*Teiresias and *Amphion in myth, and, historically, the poet Pindar were born at Thebes, and the poet Corinna at Thebes or Tanagra. In the last destruction of the city Pindar's house was spared by Alexander's order.

**2.** Greek name of a city of Upper Egypt, on the site of which Luxor now stands. It became the capital of Egypt at the time of the twelfth dynasty (*c.*2000 BC), supplanting Memphis, the earlier capital, and attained great splendour under the kings of the eighteenth to twentieth dynasties (*c.*1400–1100 BC). Homer calls it 'hundred-gated' and speaks of 200 warriors with horses and chariots issuing from each gate. It is now famous for the remains of its great temples and royal tombs. See also MEMNON.

**Themis** ('Law', 'Right', 'Order') Greek goddess of the generation preceding the Olympian gods, according to Hesiod a *Titan. By Zeus, with whom she is closely associated, she is the mother of the *Seasons (*Horae*), Good Order (*Eunomia*), Justice (*Dike*), Peace (*Eirene*), and, according to some traditions, the *Fates. In Aeschylus' *Prometheus Bound* she is the mother of Prometheus. Later she is herself a personification of justice.

**Themi'stius** (*c.*AD 317–*c.*388) Greek rhetorician from Paphlagonia. He opened a rhetorical school in Constantinople *c.*345, where he was appointed prefect (383–4) by the Christian emperor Theodosius I and tutor to the latter's son, the future emperor Arcadius. He was entrusted with many official missions, and was given the name Euphrades, 'the eloquent'. Thirty-four of his orations survive, many of them panegyrics on the emperors, but including an interesting funeral oration on his father. He wrote paraphrases of Aristotle's works, some of which are extant. A pagan, he advocated toleration of other religious beliefs. A lost address to the pagan emperor Julian prompted a famous reply from the latter describing his proposed restoration of paganism.

**Themi'stoclēs** (*c.*524–459 BC) Athenian politician, son of Neocles. He belonged to the *genos, 'clan', of the Lykomidai but his mother was probably not Athenian. Archon in 493/2, he began developing *Piraeus as Athens' harbour (previously Phalerum). During the 480s he survived the threat of *ostracism, and was instrumental in getting the city to decide to spend the surplus income from the Laurium silver mines on enlarging the navy from 70 to 200 ships, a crucial decision in view of the defeat of the Persian navy at Salamis in 480 (*see* PERSIAN WARS). In that year he commanded the Athenian contingent in the Greek forces ranged against the Persians, and determined their strategy. But in 479, although Themistocles was honoured at Sparta, the Athenian forces were commanded by *Aristeides (1) and *Xanthippus. After the Persian Wars, when the Spartans were hostile to the fortification of any Greek city, let alone Athens, Themistocles won fame for his delaying action during an embassy to Sparta while the Athenians rebuilt their own city walls. However he lost influence to the aristocratic *Cimon, and a tradition also grew up of the democratic Themistocles being op-

posed to the aristocratic Aristeides. At the end of the 470s he was ostracized and retired to Argos, where he stirred up feeling against Sparta. In about 468 Sparta claimed to have evidence that he and *Pausanias (1) were plotting with Persia; he was condemned to death at Athens and his property confiscated. He escaped to Asia by way of Corcyra, Epirus, and Macedonia, and was made governor of Magnesia on the Maeander, where he was much honoured, and died in 459. His remains were brought home, it is said, and buried outside the walls of Piraeus, Athens' harbour, which he had done so much to develop and strengthen. There is a famous sketch of his character by Thucydides (1.138), who admired him for his far-sightedness. *See* BILINGUALISM.

**Theocly'menus 1.** In Greek myth, a seer, descended from *Melampus; *see* ODYSSEY, book 20.
   **2.** *See* HELEN.

**Theo'critus** (first half of the third century BC) Hellenistic Greek poet from Syracuse in Sicily, a near contemporary of Callimachus and the originator of *pastoral or bucolic poetry. He may have lived in south Italy and visited Alexandria during the reign of Ptolemy II Philadelphus. His extant poems, generically known as *Idylls, and mostly in the hexameter metre, include court poems, mythological poems, and epigrams, but his fame stems from the seven or so poems which were primarily bucolic. These were to have a strong influence on Virgil (in the *Eclogues*) and through him on later European literature. Since there is no complete agreement on the criteria that define a bucolic poem, not all readers agree on which of Theocritus' poems are most characteristically bucolic: poems 1, 3, 4, 5, 6, and 11 are always included, 7 and 10 sometimes, and 27 (unlikely to be genuine) occasionally; 8 and 9, known and imitated by Virgil, are not generally considered authentic. Though Theocritus writes in an artificial, literary Doric dialect for a sophisticated literary and urban circle, the poems still convey an impression of timeless pastoral life in the hills of Sicily and south Italy.

The first Idyll contains the lament for *Daphnis, a dirge imitated in the *Adonis* of *Bion and in the *Bion* attributed to *Moschus, and the prototype of later pastoral elegies in English, Milton's *Lycidas*, Shelley's *Adonaïs*, and Matthew Arnold's *Thyrsis*. Another feature which was to have a long literary history is a meticulous description of a single artefact (cf. the Shield of Achilles in *Iliad* 18), in this case a carved wooden cup, its three scenes obliquely emblematic of pastoral themes. Idylls 14 and 15, which are set in towns, recall the mimes of *Herodas; the second of these, entitled *Adonia-zusae* ('Women at the festival of Adonis'), is a conversation between two simple and admiring Syracusan women, now housewives in Alexandria visiting the Adonis festival at the palace there, and closes with a hymn which they hear sung in honour of Adonis and Aphrodite. Idyll 2, *Pharmaceutria* ('Woman preparing a love charm'), cast as a monologue, similarly recalls mime: Simaetha instructs her servant Thestylis how to perform magic so that her lover will either return, or perish. Other Idylls deal with mythological subjects: the love of the one-eyed Cyclops *Polyphemus for the nymph Galatea (11), the abduction of Hylas (13), the fight between Polydeuces and Amycus (24). Two are flattering addresses (in the hope of patronage) to Hieron II, tyrant of Syracuse (17), and Ptolemy II (16), and one is a poetic epistle accompanying the present of a distaff to the wife of a friend (28). The most enigmatic is Idyll 7, entitled *Thalysia* ('Harvest home'), written in the first person by a certain Simichidas, describing a journey he took in his youth on the island of Cos. There he meets a Cretan, Lycidas, described in emphatic terms as a goatherd. They discuss the current state of poetry and engage in a poetic contest, which Simichidas wins. The idyll has been interpreted as Theocritus (Simichidas) claiming validation as a poet (as when the poet Hesiod met the Muses on Mount Helicon: *see* THEOGONY). The end of the poem evokes the feeling of harvest-time in an Aegean island, idyllic in the modern sense (*see* LOCUS AMOENUS). A number of epigrams purportedly written for tombs or statues is also attributed to Theocritus.

**Theodosian Code** A collection of Roman imperial laws published in AD 438 on the authority of Theodosius, emperor of the eastern Roman empire (*see* BYZANTINE AGE). Theodosius, son of Arcadius and grandson of Theodosius I 'the Great', saw the need to revise and harmonize the laws in the two halves of the empire. *Justinian included much of the Theodosian Code in his own Codex.

**Theo'gnis** Of *Megara, Greek elegiac poet, dated in antiquity *c.*550 BC though historical allusions seem to suggest that he lived at least half-a-century earlier. Nearly 1,400 lines of poetry ascribed to him survive in manuscript, mostly in short poems one to six couplets long, divided into two books. However, it is a matter of dispute how much is authentic, since some of the lines are also found in poems ascribed to Tyrtaeus, Mimnermus, and Solon, and some of the poems were clearly written at a much later date and against a different background. The collection seems to be in the nature of an anthology, based on the authentic poems of Theognis but augmented by other poems of similar theme drawn from various sources. It is usually accepted that poems addressed to the boy Cyrnus, with whom Theognis was in love, were authentic. Theognis' poems seem typical of those sung or recited at *symposia; he expects his own to survive in this way far into the future. They express passionate support for the aristocratic belief in the value of good breeding, and deplore the success of new wealth. There are also many poems of moral exhortation and reflection on life which, with the homosexual love-poems, are often expressed with great liveliness. The whole collection is representative of the attitudes found in poetry circulating at symposia from the late seventh to early fifth century BC.

**Theo'gony** (*Theogonia*) Greek poem in about a thousand hexameter lines by *Hesiod, and unique in surviving Greek literature in being a systematic account of the gods of Greece and their genealogy. The poet begins with a famous description of how, while pasturing sheep on Mount Helicon, he was inspired by the Muses to compose this poem. It begins at the beginning of the world, with the coming into being of primordial Chaos ('Chasm', perhaps conceived of as the dark space between Earth and *Tartarus), followed by Gaia (Earth), Tartarus, and Eros (Love). Gaia produced Uranus (Heaven), and these two were the parents of the *Titans, *Cyclopes, and other *giants. Last-born of the Titans was Cronus, who at his mother's instigation castrated Uranus. The Titans Rhea and Cronus were the parents of the Olympian gods, whom Cronus swallowed as soon as they were born, except for Zeus, who was hidden away from him. Zeus later overthrew Cronus and made him restore his other children. This 'succession myth' seems to have come to Greece from the Near East, and has parallels in Akkadian and Hittite texts. One of the Titans, *Prometheus, deceived Zeus in the matter of fair division of sacrificed animals between gods and men, and also stole fire from the gods for men. As his punishment Zeus bound him to a rock where an eagle daily ate his liver, and as a punishment for men Zeus created a woman. War broke out between the older gods, the Titans, and the younger (Olympian) gods, the children of Cronus, led by Zeus. The latter were victorious, and the Titans and *Typhoeus, who helped them, were thrown down to Tartarus by Zeus. The gods then chose Zeus to be their king. He took a series of goddesses to wife, the last of whom was Hera. Their child Hebe married Zeus' mortal son Heracles, who became after death a god himself. The last part of the poem deals with the offspring of goddesses and mortal men, and ends with two post-Hesiodic lines leading into the *Catalogue of Women. Scholars differ as to where the genuinely Hesiodic poem ends.

**Theōn** (of Alexandria, fourth century AD) Greek mathematician and astronomer. His reworkings of *Ptolemy's astronomical tables seem to be the only form in which these were known to Arabic astronomers and through them to medieval Europe. He was the last known member of the Museum at Alexandria, and father of *Hypatia (see also NEOPLATONISM). Others of the same name include a grammarian and commentator on the Hellenistic Greek poets, also from Alexandria, who lived in the first century BC.

**Theophra'stus** (of Eresus in Lesbos, c.370–c.287 BC) Pupil and friend of Aristotle, and his successor (in 322) as head of the *Peripatetic School of philosophy at Athens. He was the teacher of *Deinarchus and of *Demetrius of Phalerum, and was also on friendly terms with *Cassander and Ptolemy I Soter of Egypt. He continued Aristotle's tradition in writing on a great variety of subjects, but of his output only a tiny fraction survives. This includes a Historia plantarum ('Inquiry into plants'), in nine books, and De causis plantarum ('On the aetiology of plants'), in six books (for the content of these works see BOTANY, a subject which he may be said to have created). There also survive a short treatise on metaphysics, and numerous fragments from other philosophical and scientific works, differing from Aristotle in some of the views expressed. In modern times he is best known for a minor work, Charaktērĕs ('Characters'), a collection of thirty descriptive sketches

of various types of character. Each exemplifies some deviation from the proper norm of behaviour, exhibiting some failing such as tactlessness, followed by a list of the things that the tactless person will do. There are touches of humour (e.g. the children of the loquacious man asking their father to talk to them at bedtime 'to put us to sleep'). The 'Characters' delineate in a concise form types similar to those found in the New Comedy of *Menander (who was said to be a pupil of Theophrastus), an aspect of the work which suggests to some that it was connected less with ethics, as studied by Aristotle, and more with the writing of comedy or with forensic rhetoric (in which the orator's ability to characterize was important).

Theophrastus was remembered in late antiquity for the perfection of his Attic Greek: having come to Athens from Lesbos he had to learn the native dialect. According to Cicero he was mortified at being addressed as 'Stranger': no native Athenian could be expected to speak his own dialect so perfectly. Aristotle was reputed to have given him the name 'Theophrastus' because he 'spoke divinely'.

**Theopo'mpus** (of Chios, 378–after 320 BC) Greek historian, pupil of *Isocrates, friend of *Philip II and Alexander the Great of Macedon. He was exiled from Chios for having Spartan sympathies, restored by Alexander, and fled to Egypt at the latter's death in 323. Little remains of his numerous books except for fragments of his two most important works, the Hellenica and Philippica. The former was a continuation of Thucydides, a history of Greece from 411 to the battle of Cnidus in 394; the latter, a vast work in fifty-eight books, used the life of Philip as the connecting thread in what was virtually a world history composed of extensive digressions. It was a late work, published after 324 BC. Numerous fragments survive. He was a great admirer of Philip and declared that Europe had produced no one to match him.

**theo'ric fund** (i.e. spectators' fund) At Athens, a state subsidy for the poorer citizens to enable them to pay for admission to the theatre at the major festivals, introduced, it was said, by Pericles but probably not until very much later.

**Thēra'menēs** (d. 404 BC) Athenian politician, one of those responsible for the setting up of the revolutionary oligarchic council of the *Four Hundred in 411 BC. He was, however, a moderate (although Thucydides' picture of him is hostile) and instrumental in overthrowing the Four Hundred and setting up a broader-based voting assembly of 5,000 citizens. This apparent change of policy gave him an appearance of shiftiness, since it wholly supported neither the extreme oligarchs nor the democrats; his enemy the oligarch *Critias called him 'Cothurnus' (the loose boot, also worn on stage, that fitted either foot). In 410 he was with the fleet in the Hellespont, and in 406 he was one of the two naval commanders (trierarchs) when the Athenians defeated Sparta at *Arginusae. The blame for failure to pick up the dead and wounded was disputed between Theramenes and the generals, the former alleging bad weather as the reason; six of the latter were put to death but Theramenes survived. After Athens' final defeat in the *Peloponnesian War in 404 he was sent to negotiate with the Spartans; the blame for the three months' delay during which Athens starved is often laid at his door. When peace was made he was appointed one of the *Thirty Tyrants, but his moderate position brought him into conflict with the extreme oligarch Critias, who had him put to death. Aristotle regarded him as a politician genuinely seeking a moderate political position.

**Thermo'pylae (Pylae)** ('Hot Gates', from its sulphur springs) Strategic pass linking north with central and southern Greece, between Thessaly and Locris, having in classical times the sea close by on one side (it has now receded) and on the other steep cliffs, the spurs of Mount Oeta. Its weakness was that an invader who knew the way up could walk along the spine of the mountain above it and outflank the defenders. It was the scene of several battles, most notably the heroic defence by a small force of Spartans, who in 480 BC held at bay a large army of invading Persians before being overwhelmed (*see* PERSIAN WARS and LEONIDAS).

**Thēron** Tyrant of *Acragas in Sicily 488–472 BC, who married his daughter Demarete to *Gelon, tyrant of Syracuse. In 483 he seized the city of Himera, and after the latter appealed for Carthaginian help, he and Gelon won a crushing victory there over the Carthaginians in 480. Theron fell out with Hieron, tyrant of Syracuse after Gelon, but war was averted and his niece married Hieron. He repeopled Himera, and made Acragas one of the most beautiful of Greek cities. Pindar wrote his second

and third Olympian odes for him. He claimed descent from *Thersander.

**Thersa'nder** In Greek myth, son of Polyneices (son of Oedipus) and Argeia. He took part in the successful expedition of the *Epigoni against Thebes, and afterwards became king of Thebes. From there he took part in the Greek expedition to Troy, but was killed by *Telephus in Mysia. *Theron claimed descent from him.

**Thersī'tēs** In Homer's *Iliad*, the only low-born character among the Greeks at Troy (though in post-Homeric legend said to be of good family), physically ugly and abusive of the Greek leaders. When he attacked Agamemnon for stealing the girl Briseis from Achilles, and suggested that the army should return to Greece, Odysseus beat him for insolence. For his death *see* AETHIOPIS.

**Thēseus** In Greek myth, the national hero of Athens, and prominent in Athenian tradition from the sixth century BC. He was the son of Aegeus, king of Athens (or the sea-god *Poseidon) and of Aethra, daughter of Pittheus, king of Troezen. Represented as the friend and contemporary of *Heracles (whose exploits he often emulates), he thus belonged to the generation before the Trojan War. When Aegeus left Aethra at Troezen, he told her that when their son reached manhood he was to lift a certain large rock and bring to Athens the sword and sandals which were hidden underneath it. Theseus, the son, in due course lifted the rock easily and with these tokens set out for Athens by the dangerous land route. On the way he destroyed various bandits and monsters including *Procrustes, *Sciron, and Sinis, who used to tie his victims to two pine-trees which he bent to the ground and then released, tearing the victim in two. (It would seem that these adventures have been influenced by the similar stories told of Heracles.) On his arrival at Athens, Medea (*see* ARGONAUTS), who had taken refuge with Aegeus, realizing who he was tried to destroy him by persuading Aegeus to send him against the bull of Marathon. This was, according to some, *Pasiphae's bull brought from Crete by Heracles. On the way to Marathon he was hospitably received by an old woman, Hecale; when after returning from killing the bull he found Hecale dead, he ordered that her memory should be honoured (*see also* CALLIMACHUS). He returned to Athens, where Medea then tried to poison him, but Aegeus recognized his son in time; Medea was obliged to return to Colchis, taking with her Medus, her son by Aegeus.

Theseus now heard of the tribute which *Minos of Crete had imposed on Athens, that seven youths and seven girls had to be sent to be eaten by the Minotaur, and volunteered to be one of the youths. On the way to Crete he demonstrated that Poseidon was his father by diving into the sea and recovering a gold ring Minos had contemptuously thrown in to test him. Minos' daughter *Ariadne with her thread enabled him to find his way out of the Labyrinth after killing the Minotaur. Theseus sailed away with the other Greeks but abandoned Ariadne at Naxos. He had arranged with his father that on returning to Athens his ship would carry a white sail if he was safe, but he forgot to change the black sail, seeing which his father, concluding that Theseus had perished, threw himself from the cliffs to his death. It is possible that his death-leap is commemorated in the name of the Aegean Sea.

Theseus was now king of Athens. He is credited with bringing about the union (synoecism) of the various Attic communities into one state with Athens as the capital city. The event is historical, but its date in Attic history is unknown. With Heracles he joined an expedition against the *Amazons and took the Amazon Antiope (or Hippolyta, the Amazon queen) as his wife. To recover her the Amazons invaded Attica and occupied the Acropolis, but were defeated and withdrew. When Peirithous, king of the Lapiths, raided Marathon he was met by Theseus, and the two became friends. Theseus was present at his wedding-feast and at the subsequent fight between Lapiths and *Centaurs, and later helped Peirithous to enter the Underworld in an attempt to carry off Persephone. Theseus was ultimately rescued by Heracles but Peirithous had to remain below. In gratitude to Heracles he gave him asylum after the latter, in a fit of madness, had killed his own wife and children. Theseus is also said to have carried off *Helen when she was a child, but she was rescued by her brothers Castor and Polydeuces (*see* DIOSCURI). Iphigeneia is said by some poets to be the child of this union. When Creon refused burial to the bodies of the *Seven against Thebes, Theseus supported Adrastus and the sons of the Argive leaders, marched with an army against Creon, and ensured the burial of the dead. Later he

gave refuge to *Oedipus. After the death of his first wife Hippolyta, by whom he became the father of *Hippolytus, he married Phaedra, sister of Ariadne.

Theseus was finally driven from Athens by rebellions following the incursion of the Dioscuri, took refuge in Scyros, and died or was murdered there. He continued to protect his city, however, and was seen in gigantic size fighting for the Greeks at the battle of Marathon (490 BC). In 475 BC after the Persian Wars the Athenian *Cimon, in obedience to an oracle, brought home from Scyros the bones of a huge man which were believed to be those of Theseus, and buried them at Athens.

Theseus was honoured by a festival, the Theseia. Though he was probably purely mythical, the Athenians believed him to have been one of their early kings. There is a Life of him by Plutarch, who brings together the various stories.

**thesis** *See* ARSIS.

**Thesmopho'ria** Three-day festival held in Athens and in almost every part of the Greek world in honour of *Demeter; it was attended only by women and apparently excluded those who were unmarried. Celebrated at Athens during 11–13 Pyanopsion (October/November), before the time of sowing, its ceremonies were a 'mystery', known only to the participants (*see* MYSTERIES). Its purpose was evidently to ensure the fertility of the cereal crops sown at this time of year. Aristophanes' comedy *Thesmophoriazusae* is imagined as taking place during the festival, but reveals no secrets.

**Thesmophoriazū'sae** ('Women celebrating the Thesmophoria') Comedy by Aristophanes produced in 411 BC, probably at the Dionysia.

The women are about to celebrate their private festival, the *Thesmophoria (from which men are excluded). Euripides has learnt that, since his portrayal of legendary wicked women in his tragedies has given all women a bad name, they intend to plot his death. Taking an elderly kinsman with him, he tries to persuade the effeminate tragic poet *Agathon to disguise himself as a woman, attend the rites, and plead the cause of Euripides. Agathon refuses. Thereupon the old man offers to go instead. He is shaved and suitably dressed and goes off to the festival, having made Euripides swear to come to his aid if there is any trouble. The women gather and speeches are made against Euripides; the old man defends him by pointing out how much worse were the charges he might truthfully have made against women. The general indignation he causes is interrupted by the arrival of Cleisthenes (notorious for his effeminacy) with news that a man has got into the festival in disguise. Search is made and the old man is discovered and put under guard. Imitating the hero of Euripides' tragedy *Palamedes* (now lost), the old man writes a message on a votive tablet of the temple and throws it out. He then assumes the character of Helen from Euripides' extant tragedy of that name, and Euripides appears as Menelaus; there is a recognition scene, the only sustained parody by Aristophanes for which we possess the original, but the guard prevents the reunion of the pair. A Scythian policeman now arrives and ties up the old man. Euripides reappears as Perseus and the old man takes on the character of Andromeda, from Euripides' lost tragedy of that name, tied to her rock. But the Scythian stops the attempted rescue. Euripides now comes to terms with the women: he will never again slander them if they release his kinsman. They agree. But the Scythian has to be dealt with. He is lured away by the promise of a dancing-girl, and the old man and Euripides escape.

The old man is nowhere given a name in the text. The single manuscript which is the source of the play calls him Mnesilochus (the name of Euripides' father-in-law) in the scholia (*see* SCHOLIUM), but this may be a guess on the part of a commentator.

**thesmo'thetai** *See* ARCHONS.

**Thespis** From Icaria in Attica, according to one tradition the inventor of Greek tragedy (*see* TRAGEDY 1). He is (unreliably) said to have won the competition when tragedies were first presented at the *Dionysia at Athens between 535 and 533 BC, and to have invented the mask. Aristotle credits him with taking the vital step of transforming a choral performance into drama by inventing an actor who played the part of a character, spoke the prologue, and conversed with the chorus-leader. Four play titles, drawn from mythology, are known, but they may not be genuine. Nothing can be said about the nature of his plays. 'Thespian' now refers to drama in general.

**The'ssaly (Thessalia)** District of north-eastern Greece, consisting of two large fertile plains divided by hills, the whole area almost completely walled in by mountains, including Olympus, Ossa, Pelion, and Pindus. Its chief river was the Peneus, flowing through the Vale of Tempe into the Aegean, and it had limited access to the sea through the Gulf of Pagasae. Its chief cities were Crannon, Larissa, and Pherae. Thessaly was powerful in the seventh century BC, during which time the Thessalians organized themselves into a state with cities ruled by aristocratic families but in a federation under one ruler. From 400 BC Thessaly declined because of inter-city rivalries (the Aleuadae and the Scopadae were rival clans). In the early fourth century it was briefly united under *Jason of Pherae, but late in that century came under Macedonian control. Ostensibly liberated by Rome in 196 (*see* FLAMININUS), it was incorporated into the Roman province of Macedonia in 148 BC.

In mythology Thessaly was the home of the *Centaurs and Lapiths, Chiron, and Achilles; it was from Thessaly that the *Argonauts set out, Pelias and Aeson being rulers of Iolcus. It was regarded as pre-eminently the country of magicians.

**thētēs** In Greece, 'hired labourers' (sing. *thēs*); after *Solon's reforms at the beginning of the sixth century BC they comprised the lowest property class. They were ineligible for holding magistracies and unable to serve as hoplites because they could not afford the armour, but they acquired political importance in wartime as oarsmen in Athens' naval fleet and perhaps as archers.

**Thetis** *See* PELEUS and ACHILLES.

**Thirty Tyrants (the Thirty)** An *oligarchy that governed Athens in 404–403 BC in co-operation with Sparta after Sparta had defeated Athens in the *Peloponnesian War. *Critias led the extreme oligarchs and *Theramenes the moderate. The Thirty abolished the law-courts and began exterminating their democratic opponents and confiscating their property. The franchise was originally limited to 3,000 citizens. When Theramenes tried to extend it further Critias had him executed. About 1,500 citizens and metics are said to have been put to death also, including the brother of the orator *Lysias, who himself barely escaped with his life (see his speech *Against Eratosthenes*). In January 403 a few democrats outside the city led by *Thrasybulus rebelled, and in response the Thirty stationed a Spartan garrison on the

Acropolis, an unpopular move. By May the opposition had grown and Thrasybulus occupied Piraeus. In the fighting Critias was killed. After negotiations full democracy was restored in September. Amnesty was given to all except the Thirty, most of whom were eventually put to death.

**Thirty Years' Peace** The peace agreed between Athens and Sparta and their allies in 446 BC, terminating the state of war which had existed since 460 (see PELOPONNESIAN WAR, FIRST). It was to be for thirty years but in fact lasted barely fifteen: the *Peloponnesian War proper broke out in 431. See also CORONEA (1) and ATHENS 3.

**Thisbē** See PYRAMUS AND THISBE.

**Thracian Chersonese** See CHERSONESE.

**Thra'sea Paetus, Publius Clo'dius** Prominent Roman senator under the emperor Nero, leader of the Stoic and republican opposition. His father-in-law was A. Caecina Paetus, husband of Arria (the elder). He modelled himself on the Younger *Cato, of whom he wrote a Life. Condemned for disloyalty, he committed suicide in AD 66. See also HELVIDIUS PRISCUS.

**Thrasybū'lus 1.** Tyrant of *Miletus in the seventh century BC.
**2.** Athenian naval commander who at Samos in 411 BC led, with *Thrasyllus, the democratic reaction in the Athenian fleet against the oligarchic rule of the *Four Hundred, and recalled Alcibiades. With Thrasyllus he contributed to Athenian naval successes at Cynossema in 411, leading to the recovery of Cyzicus, and in the following years. At *Arginusae he served as trierarch. Banished by the *Thirty Tyrants, he gathered a band of fellow-exiles and in January 403 successfully led them to seize Piraeus and defeat the troops of the Thirty. When, thanks to Sparta, an amnesty was declared he led his men to Athens and the democracy was restored. He was later active in the cause of Athenian imperialism, and was murdered while on campaign in 388.

**Thrasy'llus** Democratic politician and soldier. Elected general for 405, he was one of the Athenian naval commanders executed after the victory of *Arginusae in 406 BC. See also THRASYBULUS.

**Thrasy'machus** (of Chalcedon in Bithynia) Greek *sophist and rhetorician in the last quarter of the fifth century BC, who figures in Plato's *Republic defending the proposition that justice is the interest of the stronger. He played a part in the development of Attic oratorical style, emphasizing the importance of rhythm and of polished sentence structure.

**Thrīna'cia (Thrīnakiē)** In the *Odyssey* (book 12) the island where *Helios kept his cattle.

**Thūcy'dēs (Thoukȳdidēs) 1.** (b. c.500 BC, son of Melesias) Athenian politician. He succeeded *Cimon (a relative by marriage) as leader of the wealthy aristocratic and oligarchical faction, and was the political enemy of Pericles, whose use of tribute money from the *Delian League for building-works in Athens he attacked. He was ostracized in perhaps 443 BC but presumably returned after the statutory ten years. In his old age he was prosecuted in a manner condemned by Aristophanes. He is mentioned by Pindar as a famous trainer of wrestlers. The historian Thucydides (2) was probably of the same family.
**2.** Greek historian, author of the (apparently incomplete) History of the Peloponnesian War between Athens and Sparta, 431–404 BC, in eight books.

1. Thucydides was born probably between 460 and 455 BC; at some time between 430 and 427 he caught the plague (see PELOPONNESIAN WAR) but recovered from it. As *strategos in 424 he was sent to protect the coast of Thrace from the Spartan general *Brasidas but failed to save Athens' valuable colony of Amphipolis from falling into Spartan hands, and was condemned in his absence and exiled. He returned to Athens twenty years later when the war was over, and died probably c.400; there was a tradition that he was assassinated. He seems to have been related to *Cimon and Thucydides (1).

2. He had intended to take his history down to the fall of Athens in 404, but the narrative breaks off in mid-sentence with the events of the winter 411/10. Its continuations by Theopompus and Cratippus are lost, together with the rest of their works. (See OXYRHYNCHUS HISTORIAN). Thucydides says that at the beginning of the Peloponnesian War he realized that it would have a greater importance in the history of Greece than any previous wars (including the Persian Wars) and therefore would be the

more worth writing about. Since he spent most of the war in exile and removed from the immediate action, he might be thought to be in a good position to gain first-hand information from both sides and to have a clearer perspective. His object was to provide an accurate record of what happened and to be instructive, because knowledge of the past is a useful guide to the future. His work was to be a 'possession for all time' (*ktēma es aiei*), not something 'written for display, to make an immediate impression'. Its unity used to be taken for granted but there is now increased awareness of different strata in its composition. A feature of the history is the reporting of speeches, for which he does not claim the same degree of accuracy as for events. With regard to these speeches he says that he kept as closely as possible to the sense of what was actually spoken while setting out the arguments which in his opinion the situation required (the exact meaning of this assertion is still debated). When reporting the first eight years of the war, and the sixteenth to nineteenth years, he includes elaborate speeches. For the intervening ninth to fifteenth years there are virtually no speeches. The reason for this is still a matter of speculation. The speeches serve to reveal the policies or attitudes which lay behind the decisions of the generals and politicians who made them, as Thucydides saw them. Often he presents the speeches of two opponents advocating opposite courses of action. Since all the speeches are reported in Thucydides' own idiosyncratic style, it has been thought that they must be his original compositions, designed to make clear in dramatic form what Thucydides thought to be the fundamental issues, but this is to disbelieve his statement to the contrary. Some critics have also felt that in his search below the surface for underlying causes he resembles the scientists and physicians of his day (*see* e.g. HIPPOCRATES); in his analysis of the causes of the Peloponnesian War he distinguishes between the immediate causes and pretexts—quarrels about the alliances of lesser city states, Corcyra and Potidaea—and the primary cause, Sparta's fear of Athenian expansion. It is possible that this last was added at a later stage of composition, with the benefit of deeper reflection.

3. Of the eight books into which Hellenistic librarians divided the work, book 1 comprises an introduction, giving a brief summary of early Greek history (the so-called 'Archaeology', chapters 1–23) to illustrate the importance of Thucydides' subject by comparison with earlier history and stating his aims in writing the work. There follow a description of events at Corcyra and Potidaea, the political manoeuvrings of 433–432, and a history of the growth of Athenian power during the years 479 to 435 (the Pentekontaetia, 'fifty-year period', is covered in chapters 89–118). Books 2–5.24 describe the main events of the first ten years of war, 431–421, known as the Archidamian War; they include Pericles' Funeral Oration at the end of the first year of war (2.34–46), the plague at Athens (2.47–54), the revolt at Mytilene in 428/7 (3.1–50), the destruction of Plataea in 427 (3.51–68), civil war in Corcyra in 427 (3.69–86), the capture of the Spartan garrison on Sphacteria in 425 (4.1–42), the loss of Amphipolis to Brasidas (4.102–116), and the deaths of Cleon and Brasidas and the Peace of Nicias (5.1–24). The rest of book 5 describes the precarious peace, the Mantinea campaign 418–417 (63–83), and ends with the Melian Dialogue and the destruction of Melos in 415. It functions as a sequel to the Archidamian War and an introduction to the Sicilian Expedition, for which it has a second preface. Books 6 and 7 are devoted to the expedition. Book 8, which is incomplete and contains no speeches, is very full. It covers the beginning of the so-called Decelean War (413–404) and describes the revolt of the Athenian allies and the naval warfare off the coast of Asia Minor, before stopping in 411.

4. Thucydides displayed a passion for accuracy and exactness that no other ancient historian approached and which was probably a product of his own individuality as much as the result of influence from contemporary scientific writers. His aim was to make history intelligible. Moreover, he saw history as explicable entirely in human terms without recourse to the supernatural; omens and oracles were dismissed. He is generally impartial, although in his picture of political leadership it has been felt that his view of Pericles was too favourable and his portrait of a detestable Cleon too prejudiced. His subject is treated with the utmost seriousness and at a high level; there is no room for anecdote or scandal or hearsay, and certainly no room for the romantic. Some critics have thought that the history was modelled on an Attic tragedy; consciously or not Thucydides conveys a sense

of the tragic in human affairs. Apart from Thucydides we have no history of the Peloponnesian War; for the most part we cannot know what he has chosen to omit or test the accuracy of what he includes. His overall attitude is the only justification for our acceptance of his picture of events, both of the facts he gives and his interpretation of them.

His brilliant but difficult style (*see* DIONYSIUS (3)) is well suited to the narration of great events. It has a poetic flavour apparent in, for example, his occasional use of Ionic dialect forms which sound old-fashioned in the context of his normal Attic usage; other poeticisms include making abstract nouns like 'war' or 'hope' sound like personifications, and using an unnatural word-order, for emphasis. Thucydides' sentences, though not usually short, show remarkable compression, the meaning telescoped into a few words (also a poetic trait), his rapidity of thought achieved by a plentiful use of abstract nouns. This impression of concentration is particularly apparent in the speeches; in narrative passages the style, though spare, is relatively simple. *See also* HISTORIOGRAPHY.

**Thulē** Northern land never certainly identified, first noticed by *Pytheas in the fourth century BC on his circumnavigation of Britain and nowadays thought from his route to be Norway or Iceland; it lay six days' sail north of Britain and the sun did not set there at midsummer. *Eratosthenes drew the Arctic circle through it (at 66°); *Ptolemy located it at Shetland (midnight sun notwithstanding); it was probably Shetland that was seen by Agricola's fleet (*see* BRITAIN 2) when they claimed to have seen Thule. From Virgil onwards it was proverbial for remoteness: *ultima Thule* (*Georgics* 1.30) alludes to Britain.

**Thu'rii (Thourioi)** Greek colony founded in 443 BC in south Italy, on the Gulf of Tarentum very near the site of Sybaris (destroyed by the neighbouring city of Croton *c.*510 BC). The descendants of the Sybarites who had been driven out asked the assistance of Sparta and Athens to refound their city there. Under the direction of Pericles Athens agreed. Athenian colonists were sent out under Lampon (a celebrated soothsayer, satirized in the comedy of the day) and a certain Xenocritus in 443 BC, and were joined by others from all parts of the Greek world, reputedly including Herodotus

and Lysias. *Hippodamus may have laid out the city; *Protagoras wrote its law-code.

**Thye'stēs** *See* PELOPS.

**Thye'stēs** Roman tragedy by *Seneca (2), dealing with the gruesome revenge of Atreus against his brother (*see* PELOPS). It was perhaps written in Nero's reign (AD 54–68). No Greek drama on this subject is extant, but the theme had already been used by three Roman writers in tragedies now lost: Ennius in his *Thyestes*, Accius in *Atreus*, and *Varius in his more famous *Thyestes*.

**thyrsus** A wand wreathed in ivy and vine-leaves, with a pine-cone at the top, carried by the worshippers of *Dionysus.

**Tiber (Tiberis, Tibris, Tybris)** The chief river of central Italy, rising in the Apennines and flowing in a generally southerly direction between Etruria on the west, Umbria and the country of the Sabines on the east, and Latium on the south. The silt it carries with it on its journey of 400km (250 miles) accounts for the yellowish tinge of its water. Ancient Rome stood on its left bank about 25km (16 miles) from its mouth at Ostia. *See* TIBERINUS.

**Tiberī'nus** Eponymous hero who gave his name to the river Tiber in Italy. In Roman tradition he is variously described as the son of the god *Janus, or as a descendant of Aeneas and king of *Alba Longa (his father then being Capetus); he was drowned in the river then known as Albula, after which the river was renamed.

**Tibērius (Tiberius Iulius Caesar Augustus)** (b. 42 BC) Roman emperor AD 14–37, elder son of Tiberius Claudius Nero and *Livia. Livia subsequently married the emperor Augustus, who finally and reluctantly accepted his stepson Tiberius as his heir in AD 4, when both his adopted sons (children of his sister Julia) were dead. From 20 BC until AD 12 Tiberius had a wholly successful military career as well as gaining civil powers. In AD 13 his proconsular *imperium* was made equal to that of Augustus, so that when the latter died in 14 Tiberius was already empowered to rule. The economic situation he inherited was poor, with grain shortages at Rome and high taxation and unrest in the provinces. He ruled moderately and parsimoniously; his drastic cutting of luxury expenditure, notably on public shows, strengthened finances but made him unpopular in Rome. Within his own family there was jealousy and continual intrigue. He had been made by Augustus to divorce his wife, Agrippa's daughter Vipsania Agrippina, and marry Augustus' daughter Julia, and many people favoured as heir one or other of Tiberius' stepsons or his nephew *Germanicus whom he had adopted in AD 4. When Germanicus died in 19 and Tiberius' son by Vipsania, Drusus Julius Caesar, in 23, the question of the succession arose again. Tiberius, embittered and increasingly misanthropic, retired to Capri and ruled through *Sejanus. The end of his reign was a time of terror, with spying, prosecutions, vengeance, and suicides. Finally Tiberius was given evidence that Sejanus was plotting against Germanicus' younger son Gaius (the future emperor Caligula), who had become the only likely successor. Sejanus and his followers were executed (31). Tiberius died in 37, to general rejoicing. Stories of his vicious life on Capri are possibly distortions of the truth. Accounts of his reign are given by Tacitus in books 1–6 of the *Annals and by *Velleius Paterculus, and there is a biography in Suetonius' Lives of the Caesars.

**Tibu'llus, A'lbius** (b. between 55 and 48 BC, d. 19 BC) Roman elegiac poet. He was of *equestrian rank, a friend of Horace and Ovid, and belonged to the circle of poets around M. Valerius *Messala Corvinus. Between 31 and 27 BC he set out with Messala to the East but had to return because of illness. He may then have served under him in Gaul. Three books of love-poems have come down to us attached to his name, but only the first two are by Tibullus himself. Book 1 of his poems refers to Messala's triumph in 27 BC and was probably published soon after that event, and after Propertius' first book of elegies. It contains mostly love-elegies, five about his love for Delia (1, 2, 3, 5, and 6) and three for a boy Marathus (4, 8, and 9); Apuleius tells us that Delia was a pseudonym for Plania. The second book contains only six poems, three concerning his love for a girl Nemesis (3, 4, and 6); the opening poem is a dramatization of the country festival, the Ambarvalia, and the poet's song there. The third book comprises poems by other members of Messala's circle, six elegies of one Lygdamus, rather sentimental compositions by a poet who seems to have a connection with Ovid, six short elegies (7–12) by *Sulpicia, Messala's niece, and five poems recording her love for Cerinthus (a pseudonym), possibly by Tibullus himself. Tibullus' favourite themes are romantic love and the pleasures of country life, and sometimes both together, in this way differing from the urban Catullus and Propertius. He avoids using examples from myth. Quintilian calls him tersus atque elegans, 'polished and discriminating'.

**Tibur (Tivoli)** Ancient Latin town (pre-seventh century BC) about 28km (17 miles) north-east of Rome. Many rich Romans had villas there, including Catullus and the emperor Augustus, and perhaps Horace had a town house. The most famous was the great villa of Hadrian (emperor AD 117–38).

**Tigelli'nus, Ofonius** (d. AD 69) The emperor Nero's notorious commander of the praetorian guard (62–8; see PRAETORIANS), who was the cause of many executions at Rome. He was a Sicilian exiled from Rome in 39 for adultery with the emperor Caligula's sisters, but was again at court early in Nero's reign, first as *praefectus vigilum. For his part in discovering the conspiracy of Piso against the emperor in 65 he was lavishly rewarded (see PISO (3)). He abandoned Nero at the end, and after the latter's death was removed from office. He transferred his allegiance to Galba, but when Otho became emperor he was forced to commit suicide.

**Timae'us** (c.350–shortly after 264 BC) Greek historian of Tauromenium in Sicily. He migrated to Athens c.315 and spent the next fifty years there, perhaps returning to Sicily c.265 under Hieron II. His most important work, of which only fragments survive, was a history of Sicily in thirty-eight books from earliest times to 264 BC (before the Romans attacked the Carthaginians there). In fact he covered the whole of the western Mediterranean, including Carthage, and was the first Greek historian to give an account of Roman history up to that date. He seems to have been the first to establish a chronology based on the *Olympiads, synchronizing it with the dating systems of other Greek states, and *Eratosthenes probably took over the system from him. *Polybius, whose history proper starts in 264 BC, praised him for his invention, but also attacked him for neglecting to make first-hand inquiries, 'which is the historian's most important duty'.

**Timae'us** Dialogue by *Plato, usually thought to be a late work, in form a sequel to one of the themes of the *Republic*. Besides Socrates the characters are a certain Timaeus, *Critias, and Hermocrates (the Sicilian general). Socrates asks the others to bring the ideal city to life and show it in action. Critias starts by telling the story of *Atlantis, whose aggressive power had been defeated 9,000 years before Solon by Athens, the ideal city. (This serves as an introduction to the myth of Atlantis as it is narrated in the sequel to *Timaeus*, the unfinished *Critias*.) The main part is a lecture by Timaeus, who appears to be a prominent politician of Locri, interested in Pythagorean philosophy and especially astronomy and cosmology; he expounds the origin and system of the universe. The creator god or Demiurge, being good, created the material universe from the *elements earth, air, fire, and water as a unique copy of the ideal universe which exists only in the realm of (Platonic) Ideas or Forms (*see* PLATONISM). From these elements in various proportions the Demiurge also created the soul of the world, the lower gods, and the stars. The lower gods created men's mortal bodies, though the Demiurge created their immortal souls. Men who lived immoral lives were, 'it is reasonable to suppose', reincarnated first as women, and then if unreformed as animals. Plato refers to the theory that a woman's womb, if it remains unfertilized beyond the normal time, 'wanders around the body, blocking the channels of breath and causing diseases of all kinds'. The origin of sensations and diseases is then traced; the threefold division of the soul into reason, emotion, and appetite, and the fate of the individual after death are briefly indicated.

Cicero translated or adapted *Timaeus* but most of his work is lost. The early part (to 53c) was translated into Latin in the early fifth century AD by a certain Chalcidius, and this became the only form in which it was known to the Christian West until the twelfth century. It was enormously influential, especially on *Neoplatonism with its anticipation of the latter's elaborate spiritual hierarchy; the Demiurge was also easily seen by Christians as the Creator God of Genesis. The idea that the Demiurge created the stars and other heavenly bodies with souls gave authority to *astrology, which regarded them as divine.

**time, measurement of** *See* CALENDARS; CLOCKS; ERA, DATING BY.

**Timo'creon** (first half of the fifth century BC) Greek lyric and elegiac poet from Rhodes, who took the Persian side when the Persians occupied that island. Only small fragments of his work survive in quotation. He was a personal enemy of *Themistocles and *Simonides; the latter pilloried him in a couplet purporting to be his epitaph.

**Timō'leon** (d. *c.*336 BC) Corinthian statesman and general who in *c.*365 BC conspired with his friends in killing his brother Timophanes when the latter attempted to make himself tyrant. Nothing more is heard of him until he was sent by the Corinthians in 345 with a small force of his own mercenaries to their daughter-city *Syracuse whose aristocrats had appealed for help against their tyrant Dionysius II. He defeated the enemy forces, restored order, set up a new constitution, and then retired into private life. Dionysius went into exile at Corinth, and Timoleon remained at Syracuse as the adviser of the people until his death. As a result Sicily experienced a resurgence visible in the archaeological record.

**Timon 1.** Semi-legendary Athenian who, supposedly owing to the ingratitude of his friends, became a notorious misanthrope, refusing to meet anyone except, according to Plutarch, *Alcibiades. Aristophanes is the first to refer to him. Shakespeare's *Timon of Athens* is based on his story as told by Plutarch in his *Life of Mark Antony*, and by Lucian in his dialogue *Timon*.

**2.** (of Phlius, *c.*320–*c.*250 BC) *Sceptic philosopher, author of a book of lampoons, of which only fragments survive, entitled *Silloi* (i.e. 'squint-eyed' pieces), in mock-Homeric hexameters, in which he ridiculed all dogmatic philosophers (in contrast with Pyrrhon).

**Timo'theus 1.** (of Miletus, *c.*450–*c.*360 BC) Greek poet, reputedly a friend of Euripides. He is famous for his *nomes and *dithyrambs. Although most of his eighteen books of poems are lost, some 250 lines of the nome *Persae* have been found on a papyrus of the fourth century BC, one of the oldest surviving Greek literary texts. Euripides wrote the prologue. It is an impression of the battle of Salamis, mainly from a Persian viewpoint, and expressive of the Persian distress. The metres are mainly iambo-trochaic and aeolic (probably the music was as important as the words), and the composition is astrophic (*see* STROPHE).

**2.** (d. 354 BC) Athenian politician, son of *Conon (1) and pupil of *Isocrates. He pursued an imperialist policy, promoting the Second Athenian League (*see* ATHENS 4), capturing Samos from the Persians in 365 and extending the dominion of Athens in the Thracian Chersonese and Chalcidice. In consequence of his failure to support his fellow-general Chares in an attack on Chios in 356 he was tried and fined, and died in exile soon after.

**Tīre'sias** *See* TEIRESIAS.

**Tīro, Marcus Tu'llius** (d. 4 BC, reputedly in his hundredth year) Slave, confidential secretary, and friend of Cicero (*see* CICERO (1) 7), who freed him in 53 BC. He was the author of a Life of Cicero (now lost), and editor of some of his speeches and of his letters *Ad familiares* ('To his friends'), which include letters to Tiro himself. He wrote also on grammar, and developed a system of shorthand; a surviving collection of abbreviations is known as *notae Tironianae*.

**Tiryns** Ancient Greek city in the southern part of Argolis, inhabited from the early Bronze age (before 2200 BC), and called by Homer 'mighty-walled Tiryns'. In myth it was the city of Proetus and Acrisius, and has a role in the story of Heracles. The huge 'Cyclopean' walls (*see* CYCLOPES) and palace foundations, built *c.*1400 BC of roughly hewn blocks of stone, are still standing and among the earliest examples of the Mycenaean palace plan. The city may have functioned as a port for *Mycenae, some 15km to the north, rather than independently, being only 1½km from the sea. *Linear B tablets have been found there. Tiryns shared in the destructions at the end of the Mycenaean Bronze age.

**Tī'sias** *See* TEISIAS.

**Tissaphe'rnēs** The Persian satrap of the coastal provinces of Asia Minor with whom Sparta entered into alliance against Athens *c.*413 BC, and with whom *Alcibiades intrigued. When in 401 Cyrus the Younger of Persia challenged the army of the Persian king Artaxerxes, his brother, at the battle of Cunaxa, Tissaphernes with his cavalry played the decisive part in Artaxerxes' victory. Thereafter he murdered Cyrus' Greek generals, and harassed Xenophon and the Ten Thousand who had fought for Cyrus (*see* ANABASIS). He was once more ruler of the Aegean coast when Sparta began war with Persia in 400, and Xenophon relates in his *Hellenica* and *Agesilaus* how Tissaphernes was outwitted and crushingly defeated by the Spartan king *Agesilaus at Sardis in 395. After this failure he was assassinated by order of Artaxerxes.

**Tītans (Tītānĕs)** (of uncertain meaning; perhaps it once meant 'kings') In Greek myth the older gods of the generation before the Olympian gods (*see* GODS [Greek]), children of Uranus (Heaven) and Gaia (Earth). The story of the marriage of Heaven and Earth and the birth of gods from the marriage is very widespread in myth from all parts of the world. According to Hesiod the Titans were twelve in number, six sons and six daughters: Oceanus, Coeus (Koios), Crīus (Krios), Hyperion, Īapetus, Cronus, and Theia, Rhea, Themis, Mnēmosynē, Phoebē, Tethys. The names are a mixture of Greek, non-Greek (e.g. Oceanus, Iapetus, Cronus) and abstractions (Themis, 'Justice', and Mnemosyne, 'Memory'). Some of their children were also regarded as Titans, notably *Prometheus and *Atlas. When Zeus, aided by his mother Rhea, compelled *Cronus to disgorge his other children, battle ensued (the Titanomachy) between the Titans on the one hand and Zeus and his brothers and sisters on the other (Prometheus fighting on the side of Zeus). The battle lasted for ten years, shaking the universe to its foundations, but eventually the *Cyclopes and *Hecatoncheires came to the help of Zeus, and the Titans were overcome and imprisoned in Tartarus, guarded by the Hecatoncheires; Atlas was punished by being made to support the sky on his shoulders. It was sometimes thought that eventually Zeus freed the Titans. In literature the Titanomachy is often confused with the Battle of Gods and *Giants (the Gigantomachy). Apart from Cronus, the Titans were not the object of cult.

**Tithō'nus** In Homer, son of Laomedon, king of Troy, and brother of Priam. According to others he came from further east and was the father of Memnon (killed at Troy). Eos (Dawn) fell in love with him, and by her he was the father of Emathion (killed while trying to prevent Heracles from stealing the Golden Apples of the Hesperides; *see* HERACLES, LABOURS OF 11). Eos obtained immortality for him from Zeus but forgot to ask also for eternal youth, so that Tithonus became an old shrivelled creature little more than a voice; she put him into a room and shut the door. According to the Homeric Hymn to Aphrodite he was turned into a cicada, which renews its skin every year.

**Tĭtus (Tĭtus Flavius Vespasianus)** (AD 39–81) Roman emperor 79–81, elder son of Vespasian, the first Flavian emperor. He assisted his father in suppressing the Jewish Revolt in 67–70 AD (*see* JOSEPHUS). The Arch of Titus commemorating this, erected in the Forum at Rome by his brother Domitian when the latter succeeded as emperor, is still standing, in part restored. During his campaign in Judaea Titus fell in love with *Berenice (4), daughter of the Jewish king Herod Agrippa I. After his return to Rome she followed him in 75 but the Romans disapproved of the connection and Titus had to dismiss her, probably in 79. In that year he succeeded his father smoothly, having shared the throne with him since 71. Titus was universally popular, and his short reign was remembered as a happy one, despite the eruption of Vesuvius at the beginning of his reign in 79 and the plague and fire in Rome the following year, to all of which he responded energetically. His building works included the completion of the Colosseum (begun by Vespasian) and the Baths of Titus. Suetonius is the source of a famous story about him: one evening at dinner, Titus, realizing that he had done no favour to anyone for twenty-four hours, said, 'Friends, I have wasted a day.'

***Tĭtus Andro′nicus*** Roman tragedy by Shakespeare, whose hero has no counterpart in Roman history or literature. Its story is patterned on that of *Philomela in Ovid's *Metamorphoses*, book 6.

**Tĭtus Tā′tius (Tĭtus)** Legendary king of the *Sabines who, after the reconciliation between his people and the Romans which followed the Rape of the Sabines (*see* ROMULUS), ruled jointly with Romulus over the united community. He was assassinated while sacrificing at Lavinium.

**Ti′tyus** In Greek myth, a *Giant, son of Gaia (Earth), who was killed, for assaulting the goddess Leto, by Zeus or by Apollo and Artemis (Leto's children). Odysseus (in the *Odyssey*, book 11) saw him lying in the Underworld covering 9 *plethra* ('acres') of ground, while two vultures tore at his liver.

**tmēsis** ('division') In grammar, the division of a word into two parts with other words interposed; e.g. in Ennius, *saxo cere comminuit brum*, 'he shattered his skull (*cerebrum*) with a rock'; more obvious is Virgil's *talis Hyperboreo septem subjecta trioni*, 'beneath the Hyperborean sky' (*septentrioni*).

**toga** The usual outer garment worn by Roman men from republican times, and originally by women too. It was a heavy woollen garment, roughly semicircular in shape, typically about 5 metres long and 2 wide although its size varied according to the wearer's taste. The straight edge was placed on the left shoulder from behind, with a third of its length falling in front and supported by the left arm; the toga was then drawn across the back (the straight edge uppermost and the curved edge falling down to the right leg), brought under the right arm and thrown over the left shoulder to hang down at the back. It became the distinctive badge of Roman citizenship. The ordinary *toga virilis* ('man's toga') was entirely white; the *toga praetex(ta)ta* ('bordered toga') had a purple hem and was worn by certain priests and magistrates, and by high-born boys before they received the *toga virilis* on reaching manhood. Girls wearing the toga wore the *praetexta* until they married. The toga was an uncomfortable garment and needed frequent cleaning, but it was dignified and was obligatory dress on formal occasions, even in imperial times when more convenient garments had come into use.

**tŏgā′ta, fabula** ('a play in a toga') These *fabulae* were Roman comedies of the second century BC about Italian life and characters, set in some small Italian town. Nothing of them has survived except for a few titles and quotations. *Afranius was the chief author.

**Tŏmis** (Lat. Tŏmis, Tŏmi, modern Constanţa) Colony of *Miletus on the west coast of the Black Sea. The region was brought under Roman rule in the first century BC; it became the Roman province of Moesia in the early first century AD but was also known as Scythia Minor. Tomis is famous as the place of Ovid's banishment. *See* TRISTIA.

***To′pica*** ('Topics', i.e. forms of argument) Work on logic by Aristotle (*see* ARISTOTLE 4(i)) in which he systematizes dialectical argument, distinguishing four main types of proposition or question, each requiring its own type of argument and counter-argument. He gives examples. Its sequel is the *Sophistici Elenchi*, a catalogue of fallacious and paradoxical arguments which students had to learn to recognize and to counter. For Cicero's abstract of the *Topica see* CICERO (1) 5.

**Torquā'tus** *See* MANLIUS TORQUATUS.

**Trachi'niae** ('Women of Trachis') Greek tragedy by *Sophocles. There is no evidence for the date but some see indications that, with *Ajax* and *Antigone*, it is early among his surviving works, written in the years after Aeschylus' *Oresteia* of 458 BC.

Since his murder of Iphitus, son of Eurytus, *Heracles and his family have been exiled from Tiryns to Trachis (in Malis, a little west of Thermopylae). The chorus is composed of Trachinian women. When the play opens, Heracles has been absent for fifteen months. He had told Deianeira, his wife, that at the end of this period the crisis of his life would come, and he would either die or have a happy life thereafter. Deianeira sends Hyllus, their son, in search of his father. As she reflects on her anxieties a messenger announces the arrival of Heracles in Euboea nearby. This is presently confirmed by the report of a herald, who brings with him a train of captive women taken by Heracles when he sacked Oechalia in Euboea, the city of his enemy Eurytus. Deianeira discovers that these include Iole, daughter of Eurytus, and that Heracles has fallen in love with her. Using a love-charm which she had been given by Nessus, the Centaur, when he was dying at the hands of Heracles, she decides to win back her husband's love, and smears the charm on a robe she is sending him. Too late she discovers that it has shrivelled a piece of wool and is a deadly poison. Hyllus returns, describes the agony of Heracles, his flesh consumed by the robe, and denounces his mother as a murderess. Deianeira goes out in silence, and presently her old nurse enters to say that she has killed herself. The dying Heracles is brought in; he tells Hyllus to carry him to Mount Oeta and there burn him on a pyre before the agony returns, and afterwards to marry Iole. Hyllus reluctantly consents, bitterly reproaching the gods for their pitiless treatment of his father.

**tragedy** Tragic drama, the invention of the Greeks from Gk. *tragōidia*, 'goat song'. There is no satisfactory explanation of this name. It may have arisen because, it has been suggested, the chorus in tragedy originally wore goat-skins, or

in connection with a goat-sacrifice, or even because there was a competition with a goat as prize.

The Monk in Chaucer's *Canterbury Tales* defines the essence of tragedy as he knew it, and as it is in most surviving Greek tragedies:

Tragedie is to seyn a certeyn storie,
As olde bookes maken us memorie,
Of hym that stood in greet prosperitee,
And is yfallen out of heigh degree
Into myserie, and endeth wrecchedly.

There are some Greek tragedies which do not 'end wretchedly' but have a happy ending for the good characters (e.g. Euripides' *Helen*). Aristotle (in the *Poetics*) considered plays of this type to be an inferior form of tragedy. It has been observed that Seneca, not the Greeks, was the first to write what we now think of as tragedy (see 5 below).

**1. The origin of Greek tragedy.** The only Greek tragedy we possess is Athenian; for that reason it is known as 'Attic' tragedy (from the state of Attica, of which Athens was the chief city). Tragedy was usually regarded as an Attic invention (but not always; see below). It is very difficult to trace its history back beyond the fifth century BC. There were several different accounts of its origin current in antiquity. Aristotle in chapter 4 of the *Poetics* reports that the *Dorians claimed the invention of both tragedy and comedy from the improvisations of those who 'led the *dithyramb', a form of choral lyric sung in honour of the god Dionysus. Certainly choral song remained an important constituent of tragedy, and the dialect of the choruses, a literary Doric, suggests that the choral element originated in a Doric-speaking region.

The tradition which gives tragedy a Dorian and Peloponnesian origin claims that the decisive step towards drama was taken in Corinth by *Arion, possibly of the seventh century BC and also credited with the development of the dithyramb into a recognized literary form. He is said to have brought on stage 'satyrs speaking verse'. Aristotle also says that tragedy acquired dignity by development from the style of *satyr plays. Arion may provide a tenuous link between dithyramb, tragedy, and satyr plays, but it is still not clear whether (and how) Attic dithyramb and tragedy evolved from the same background as satyr plays, or to what extent the choral performances in the Peloponnese became dramatic. Drama requires actors. A tradition followed by Horace in the *Ars poetica* attributed the invention of the actor to *Thespis, who came to Athens from Icaria in Attica and was said to have won the tragedy competition between 535 and 533. According to Aristotle, Thespis added prologue and speech to a choral performance. A modern suggestion is that performance of tragedy was instituted at the City *Dionysia by the new *democracy. Thus Attic tragedy may be thought to have originated no earlier than the mid-sixth century BC. The original meaning of the Greek word for actor, *hypokritēs*, is much debated: it has been taken by some to mean 'answerer' and by others 'interpreter'. In the former case the actor's answers to the questions of the *chorus provided the occasion for their song, and their exchanges (by this account) brought drama into existence.

By 472, the date of the earliest surviving play, Aeschylus' *Persians*, tragedy had acquired the dignity and seriousness of which Aristotle spoke (see above), stemming from its concern with human predicaments and their relation to divine ordinance, as told in myth. It is impossible to know how much the development of tragedy was shaped by Aeschylus, since we know so very little of his predecessors and contemporaries (see 4 below). The plot of a Greek tragedy is nearly always based on an episode from myth (for exceptions *see* PERSIANS; PHRYNICHUS; AGATHON), and the influence of Homer is marked.

**2. Performances of Greek tragedies.** Tragedy was not confined to Attica but acquired its form there, and Attic tragedy is virtually all we know. It formed part of religious celebrations and, until the Hellenistic age, appears to have been confined to the festivals of Dionysus. (For the close connection between the god and the performance of drama *see* DIONYSIA and DIONYSUS, THEATRE OF.) Thus plays were produced on only a few occasions during the year, and for a single performance on each occasion. The most important setting for new tragedies was the City Dionysia in March, but tragedies were also produced at the *Lenaea in January (probably from the 430s), and second productions might be staged at the Rural Dionysia. In the fifth century the only second productions at the City Dionysia (with one exception; see below) were revised versions of plays which had been unsuccessful in their original form, such as Euripides' *Hippolytus*, but it may be that comedies

were more often restaged than tragedies. However, in the case of Aeschylus it was decreed after his death that his plays might be produced at the City Dionysia by anyone who wished.

Tragedy was produced under the auspices of the state, supervised by magistrates, and was a matter for competition. Three tragic poets were selected from all those applying and 'granted a chorus' by the archon, i.e. given permission to compete for the prize of best tragic poet. A main actor ('protagonist') was allocated to each poet by lot, from three chosen and paid for by the state. Apart from that the costs of production were borne by the *choregoi*. Each poet staged three tragedies (the trilogy) followed by a fourth of a different character, often a satyr play, the set of four being known as the tetralogy. (These terms we owe to the Alexandrian scholars.) In Aeschylus, unlike Sophocles, the trilogy dealt with related events. The contests were decided by judges, five in number, chosen by lot from lists of names selected by each tribe; no doubt the judges were influenced on occasion by the audience. The successful poet was rewarded with a crown of ivy; from the mid-fifth century the best actor also received a prize. Actors and chorus were all male, and only Athenian citizens were allowed to take part, although *metics were admitted at the Lenaea at a later date.

Greek tragedy contained two elements, choral song in lyric metres combined with dance, to musical accompaniment, and dramatic spoken exchanges between characters, which were mainly in iambic trimeters. Some parts were a blend of the two. The chorus comprised twelve performers in the plays of Aeschylus, increased to fifteen by Sophocles. It was drawn up in a rectangular form (in contrast with the circular chorus of the dithyramb) and its movements were based on this arrangement. The importance of the chorus varied from play to play (in Aeschylus' *Eumenides* it might be considered corporately as one of the main characters). On the whole its role declined in significance towards the end of the fifth century. The dramatic role of the chorus in general is to play the part of spectators of the action, humble in rank, taking a limited part in but rarely initiating action, sympathizing with one or other of the chief characters, and commenting on or interpreting the dramatic situation. The choral songs were composed in a variety of lyric metres arranged in *strophes and antistrophes, occasionally with epodes added (*see* TRIAD). They were accompanied by the double \**aulos*. Very little is known about the dances performed by the chorus after the early fifth century when, we are told, Phrynichus and Aeschylus invented many dances. The term *emmeleia* ('gracefulness') was often used to denote the grave and dignified dance of tragedy. By the end of the fifth century BC the dance was less important and singing by individual actors became more important. Choruses continued to form a part of tragedies throughout the fifth and for part at least of the fourth century BC, after choruses in comedy had been discontinued; but it is not known precisely how long they survived.

To the single actor of Thespis' invention Aeschylus added a second and Sophocles a third, and three actors seem to have remained the norm. Originally the poet acted in his own plays; this is recorded of Thespis and Aeschylus, and of Sophocles in his earliest plays (not extant). From the time of Sophocles the relative importance of the actors was indicated by the names protagonist ('first actor'), deuteragonist ('second actor'), and tritagonist. To the first was assigned the longest and most difficult part, together with other parts which could be combined with it. All the actors and the chorus wore masks (according to one tradition introduced by Thespis) appropriate to their roles; this feature was perhaps a relic of Dionysiac cult, for some parts of which the worshippers were masked. Only the *aulos*-player was unmasked. No fifth-century masks have survived, but it is clear from vase-paintings that they covered the whole front half of the head including the ears and had wigs attached. They seem to have been made of linen stiffened with plaster and painted. The wearing of masks facilitated the doubling of parts by a single actor, or even the splitting of a single part between two actors. In Euripides' *Bacchae*, for example, Dionysus and the messenger were probably played by the same actor; in Sophocles' *Oedipus Coloneus* the doubling and splitting of parts has become extremely complicated, with Theseus played by perhaps three actors, and Ismene by a silent extra (*kōphon prosōpon*, 'dumb mask') unless, exceptionally, a fourth actor was allowed. Non-speaking extras were used, and known, like their modern equivalents, as 'spear-carriers' (*doryphorēmata*). Aeschylus was said to have given the actors

a more dignified costume; by the end of the fifth century they were wearing heavy, long-sleeved, ornamented robes reaching to the ground; Euripides was notorious for clothing his heroes in rags when the plot suggested it. Actors in classical times either went barefooted or wore tall laced boots (\**cothurni*). Female characters were played by men.

### 3. The parts of Greek tragedy.

(i) The prologue (*prologos*), the part preceding the entrance of the chorus, a monologue or dialogue between actors which sets out the subject of the drama and the situation from which it starts. In the earliest tragedies the play begins with the entrance of the chorus, who set the scene without prologue.

(ii) The *parodos* ('entrance'), the song which the chorus sings as it enters the *orchestra* (*see* THEATRE). Once in, the chorus does not usually leave before the end of the play.

(iii) The episodes (*epeisodia*), scenes in which one or more actors take part, with the chorus. The word *epeisodion* probably meant originally the entrance of an actor to announce something to the chorus. The episodes might also contain lyrical passages, such as lamentations or incidental songs by the chorus, but they were divided from each other by the songs of the chorus known as *stasima* (see below).

(iv) *Stasima*, songs of the chorus 'standing in one place', i.e. in the *orchestra*, in contrast with the *parodos* which was sung during its entrance. In the earlier extant tragedies the *stasima* are usually connected, if only obliquely, with the events of or emotions aroused by the preceding episode. But this connection became more tenuous, until \**Agathon* became reputedly the first to introduce choral lyrics which had nothing to do with the plot (and could fit any tragedy), called by Aristotle *embolima*, 'interpolations'.

(v) The *exodos* or final scene, after the last *stasimon*, and the departure of the chorus.

For Aristotle's analysis of the nature of tragedy and its qualitative elements *see* POETICS.

### 4. Principal Greek tragedians. 
Before Aeschylus and apart from Thespis we have the names of \**Phrynichus*, \**Pratinas*, and Choerilus. A few fragments survive, of doubtful authenticity. After Aeschylus, Sophocles, and Euripides the most famous was Agathon, and after him perhaps \**Ion of Chios* and \**Critias*. There were about a dozen others who won

the fifth-century tragedy competitions from time to time. The descendants of Aeschylus and Sophocles included some able tragedians. A younger Euripides produced posthumous plays by the elder Euripides and was himself a dramatist. By the end of the fourth century BC the three great tragedians had acquired classic status (*see* LYCURGUS (3)), but tragedy was still being written in the third century BC at Athens, Alexandria (on a grand scale), and elsewhere. We know nothing except the (otherwise unknown) names of some of the writers and small fragments of their work; nothing more was thought worthy of preservation

**5. Roman tragedy.** For the origins of Roman drama *see* COMEDY [Roman 1]. A new impulse was given when in 240 BC *Livius Andronicus first staged rough adaptations of a Greek tragedy and a Greek comedy, to be followed by other adaptations from Greek. *Naevius, his contemporary, appears to have been the first to compose, besides tragedies on Greek subjects, *fabulae *praetextae*, dramas whose themes were drawn from Roman history or legend. His successors *Ennius, *Pacuvius, and *Accius also wrote occasional *praetextae* as well as tragedies modelled on Greek originals. Tragedy remained important in Rome's cultural and political life from the third to the first century BC, although there was no outstanding tragedian in the later years of the republic. Under the emperor Augustus, Asinius *Pollio wrote tragedies which have perished, as have also the *Medea* of Ovid and the *Thyestes* of Varius Rufus (performed at the celebrations after *Actium). Both of these were popular plays praised by Quintilian. Plays for public festivals continued to be written in the first century AD. To the age of the emperor Nero belong the highly rhetorical tragedies of *Seneca the Younger, which may have been recited in front of small groups rather than on the popular stage. Like most of his predecessors Seneca borrowed his subjects from Greek sources (already familiar to the philhellenic Neronian court). The ordinary metre of Roman tragedy was the iambic senarius; this was used in dialogue. The sung portions were in simple lyrical metres adapted from the Greek. Greek-style choral odes did not entirely disappear but the amount of singing and dancing was greatly reduced. The 'bystander' who undertook this appeared on stage, not, as in Greek tragedy, in the *orchestra*, and could take a greater part in the action. Tragedy did not continue into late antiquity.

Horace in his *Ars poetica* gives critical advice on the writing of tragedy, perhaps because the Pisones to whom the poem is addressed were interested in the genre. But conditions at Rome were unfavourable to tragedy. Performances were not, as they had been at Athens, part of a religious festival with cultic associations and social significance. There was no homogeneous audience in sympathy with the poet's view of things, religious, national, ethical, and social. Tragedies on Roman themes were perhaps problematical for political reasons; they were certainly few. The extinction of political life under the empire would have made it difficult for the playwright to choose a subject that was not liable to sinister interpretation by a suspicious emperor.

*See also* THEATRE.

**Trajan (Marcus Ulpius Trāiānus)** Roman emperor AD 98–117. He was born in Spain, probably in AD 53, his father being of senatorial rank. He had a highly successful military career which earned him his adoption by the emperor Nerva in 97 when he was governor of Upper Germany. After his accession in the following year he did not go immediately to Rome but preferred to organize the Rhine and Danube frontiers. Later he also conquered a large part of the Parthian empire, having previously subdued Dacia, beyond the Danube, and reached the Persian Gulf in the course of his expedition. He strove to be on good terms with the senate, many of whose members he appointed to oversee his schemes such as the subsistence allowances (*alimenta*) paid to poor children in Italy, and he showed concern for the well-being of the provinces. He devoted vast sums of money to building projects at Rome, notably his Forum (Forum Traiani), where the Column of Trajan, decorated with a spiral frieze illustrating the events of the Dacian Wars, was erected in 113 to commemorate his campaigns. *Pliny the Younger delivered a *panegyric on him, and when governor of Bithynia corresponded with him regularly. His decisions and advice on the problems referred to him, notably on the matter of the Christians (Pliny, *Epistles* 10.96–7) illustrate his firm humanity and good sense. He died in Cilicia on his way home from the Parthian campaign; his ashes were deposited in a golden urn in the base of his column, and his successor

Hadrian erected in the Forum Traiani a temple dedicated to him.

Trajan's reign, which saw the Roman empire at its greatest extent, was remembered as a time of peace and prosperity, and set the standard for a good emperor. His column, which stands 38m (125 ft.) high with an internal spiral staircase leading to the top, is still in a good state of preservation. *See* ANTONINES.

**transmigration of souls** (metempsychosis) *See* PYTHAGORAS; ORPHEUS; *REPUBLIC* [book 10].

**Trasimene, Lake** Site of a battle in 217 BC; *see* PUNIC WARS.

**triad** In a Greek lyric poem, a group of three stanzas, of which the first two, called strophe and antistrophe, are symmetrical, i.e. correspond in metre, but the third, called the epode, has a different though related metrical form. If the poem consists of more than one triad the epodes, at least in Pindar, correspond with one another, as do all the strophes and antistrophes. This form of composition, which broke the monotony of a long series of similar stanzas, was thought to have been introduced by *Stesichorus followed by Simonides and Pindar. It is generally believed that lyric poetry written in triadic form was sung and danced by a chorus, whereas monodic lyric was usually sung by an individual (*see* LYRIC POETRY [Greek]).

**tribes** (Gk. *phylai*, Lat. *tribūs*) Subdivisions of the citizen body.

1. In early times the various Greek peoples were divided into large kinship groups known as tribes, which were further subdivided into *phratriai*, 'brotherhoods'. Thus the Dorian people was divided into three tribes known as the *Hylleis*, *Pamphyloi*, and *Dymānēs* which were found in almost all Dorian cities. Tribes were corporate groups, with hereditary membership and their own priests and officials. In early times they were the basis of state administration for military and governmental purposes. At Athens, *Cleisthenes' (2) reforms of the democracy in the late sixth century BC involved the dismantling of the old tribes and the creation of ten new tribes based on the *demes. A similar change was made at Sparta during the Lycurgan reforms, when administration came to be based on the *obai*, the constituent villages, in preference to the tribes.

2. At Rome the people in the earliest times were supposedly divided into three tribes based on kinship, Titienses (abbreviated to Tities), Ramnenses (Ramnes), and Luceres. According to tradition, the king *Servius Tullius replaced these with four urban tribes based on locality (compare Cleisthenes' similar reform at Athens), in order to include in the citizen body the large number of aliens who had settled at Rome. To these were gradually added 'rustic' tribes for the country regions. By 387 BC there were twenty-one tribes in all; by 241 BC the number had reached thirty-five, which was never exceeded. Every citizen had to belong to a tribe, even under the empire. The tribes were the administrative units for the census, taxation, and the military levy, as well as for political *assemblies of the *plebs*.

**tribunes of the plebs** (of the people) (Lat. *tribūni plēbis*) At Rome, magistrates who were themselves *plebeian and of free birth, first appointed, according to tradition, in 494 BC, the date of the first *secession of the plebs, and numbering ten by 449. Their role was to protect the lives and property of the plebeians, and they could thwart elections, laws, and decrees of the senate. Their power derived from the oath sworn by the plebs to guarantee their inviolability (*sacrosanctitas*). They also possessed the right of veto against any act of a magistrate. They were elected annually by the *concilium plebis* ('assembly of the people') and could summon meetings of the plebeians; *patricians could become tribunes only by getting themselves adopted into a plebeian family (see the case of Clodius under CICERO (1) 3). The tribunate became gradually indistinguishable from the other magistracies, but it never wholly lost its revolutionary flavour. Under the empire the emperor was invested with tribunician power (*tribunicia potestas*) and the real tribunes lost all importance.

**tribū'ni mī'litum** ('military tribunes') At Rome in later republican times, senior army officials of equestrian rank, six to a legion; the tribunes of the first four legions recruited each year were elected by the people, and those for additional legions appointed by the commander. Under Julius Caesar the tribunes declined in importance with the rise of *legati as legion commanders. Under the empire one of the six tribunes in a legion was normally a young man of senatorial rank who held the post for a year in order to gain experience. In the course of the first century AD tribunes so-called held many military positions.

**tribū'ni plēbis** *See* TRIBUNES OF THE PLEBS.

**tribute lists, Athenian** Name given to a series of fragmentary inscriptions on stone of 454 to 409 BC, recovered from the Athenian Acropolis, relating to the finances of the \*Delian League. They record the sum of money paid each year by each allied city in the league as an offering to (the treasurers of) the goddess Athena. These payments constituted one-sixtieth part of the total tribute paid by each city, and began after the treasury of the league was moved from Delos to Athens, probably in 454/3 BC when the tribute lists begin. In 413 tribute was replaced by a 5% duty on all goods transported by sea, but it was probably re-instated in 410/09. Assessment of total tribute was normally revised every four years. In addition to these lists of offerings to Athena there also survive fragmentary assessment lists of other years. Modern historians have elicited a great deal of political and social information from the lists.

**tribu'tum** At Rome, up to 167 BC, a property tax paid by individuals to the state, varying in amount from year to year. (It was briefly reintroduced in the crisis after Caesar's murder in 44 BC.) After 167 BC *tributum* denoted the taxes paid by all inhabitants of the provinces, whether Roman citizens or not, in the form of a land-tax or a poll-tax. Under the empire Romans and Italians paid no direct taxes.

**trierarchy** *See* LITURGY.

**trilogy** *See* TRAGEDY 2.

**Trima'lchio's Banquet** *See* PETRONIUS ARBITER.

**Trīna'cria (Trinacia, Thrinacia)** *See* SICILY.

**Trinu'mmus** ('Three pieces of silver') Roman comedy by \*Plautus adapted from a Greek New Comedy by Philemon (*see* COMEDY [Greek 6]). The play takes its name from a coin paid as a day's wages to a hired impostor, whose part in the plot is relatively unimportant. The exact value of the coin is disputed.

While Charmides, a wealthy Athenian, is out of the country, his dissolute son Lesbonīcus has spent all his father's money and even put the house up for sale. At his departure Char-

mides had entrusted his son and daughter to the care of his friend Callicles, and confided to the latter that a treasure was concealed in the house. Callicles therefore, anxious about the treasure, has bought the house himself. Lesbonicus' friend, Lysiteles, wishing to help the financial situation, offers to marry Lesbonicus' sister without a dowry. Lesbonicus, though approving the match, will not accept an arrangement discreditable to his family, and Callicles thinks the sister should have a dowry out of the treasure. The difficulty is how to arrange this without revealing to Lesbonicus the existence of the treasure. Callicles' solution is to hire 'for three pieces of silver' a \*'sycophant' (i.e. a man prepared to do anything for money), who is to deliver to Lesbonicus a thousand gold pieces and a letter purporting to come from his father, explaining that the money is to be used for a dowry (while in fact being part of the treasure). Charmides himself now arrives unexpectedly and meets the sycophant knocking at the door. Learning his errand he discovers the imposture, and then finds out that the house is no longer his own but belongs to Callicles. He begins to abuse the latter, but when all is revealed warmly thanks him, gives his daughter, with a dowry, to Lysiteles, and pardons the now penitent Lesbonicus.

**Triphiodō'rus** *See* TRYPHIODORUS.

**Tripto'lemus** In the \*Homeric Hymn to Demeter, a prince of Eleusis to whom Demeter imparts her \*mysteries. Athenians believed that he was told to go about the world and teach men the skills of agriculture. His parentage is originally obscure and later variously described. His rise to fame (he received sacrifice at Eleusis) probably resulted from Athenian interest in the mysteries. He was also regarded as a lawgiver. Plato made him, with \*Minos and \*Rhadamanthys, a judge of the dead in the Underworld.

**tri'reme** The warship of the Mediterranean from the late sixth century BC to the fourth century AD, replacing the \*penteconter. Although there are no known remains of an ancient trireme it has proved possible to reconstruct a replica from surviving evidence. It was manned by 170 oarsmen, 85 on each side, each man pulling a single oar. The oarsmen were arranged in three slightly staggered rows of unequal length. For long voyages a square linen sail on a mast amidships and a second sail on a foremast could be hoisted, but masts were removed and left on shore before battle. A bronze ram was fitted on the prow at the water-line. Apart from oarsmen she carried ten marines, four archers, and a crew of sixteen, making a complement of 200. The Romans made extensive use of triremes until the fourth century AD.

**Tri'stia** ('Sorrows'), Latin elegiac poems by *Ovid in five books, written in AD 9–12, following his banishment to *Tomis in AD 8. The metre must have seemed appropriate, since elegiac was commonly thought in ancient times to have been originally the metre of lament (*see* ELEGY). The poems are in the form of open letters to his wife and unnamed persons in Rome, written to ensure that he was not forgotten. He laments his fate and prays for some mitigation of his anticipated future suffering. The poems appear to have been sent individually to Rome and then collected in groups for publication.

  *Book 1* consists of poems composed on the long journey to Tomis and sent back to Rome on Ovid's arrival. They include descriptions of storms and hardships encountered. The real destination of these poems is Augustus, on whom Ovid brings moral pressure to rescind his banishment; he reminds the emperor of his status as a poet and of his achievement. The third poem of the book is the moving account of the poet's last night at Rome.

  *Book 2* is a single poem of over 500 lines, a serious defence of the autonomy of poetry, in the face of which the emperor's attitude to the poet is made to seem beside the point since his posthumous reputation is in the hands of his poets. *Books 3, 4,* and *5* include glimpses of life at Tomis, now a seaside resort but seeming to Ovid to be a precariously held Roman outpost of civilization: he describes the flat, treeless landscape, the rigorous climate, the attacks of various tribes on the town (when even Ovid is constrained to take up arms for its defence), and his loneliness among his Getic hosts. Perhaps this is more a landscape of exile than of actuality. There is some monotony in Ovid's complaints, but these are by no means abject, and the poet often runs the risk of making too clear for safety his view that he was a victim of tyrannical injustice. Poem 3.7 is to Ovid's stepdaughter Perilla—the only named addressee in the *Tristia*—who was herself a poet. She too can

achieve immortality, he says, confident of his own: 'When I am gone my fame will endure . . . I shall be read.' Ovid's famous poetic autobiography 4.10 makes it clear that his first loyalty has always been to poetry, which for him was not a matter of choice but a true vocation: 'all I attempted to write turned out as verse' (4.10.26).

**Trīton** In Greek myth, a merman, son of *Poseidon and Amphitrite, with human head and shoulders and a fish tail from the waist down. The origin of his name (as also of Amphitrite) is unknown and may not be Greek. He is commonly shown blowing on a conch-shell, and Virgil describes how the trumpeter Misenus challenged him to a contest on this instrument and was drowned by him. In some stories there are several Tritons (as in the case of Eros). *Pausanias (2) on his travels saw two specimens of what he was told were Tritons.

**trittys** At Athens, 'a third', i.e. of a *tribe. *Cleisthenes (2) in his constitutional reforms created thirty *trittyĕs*, territorial divisions, each containing one or more demes. Each of his (new) ten tribes was composed of three *trittyes*, one each from the city, interior, and coastal regions, according to the *Athenaion Politeia* (1). *See* DEME.

**triumph** At Rome, the celebratory procession of a Roman general who had won a major victory, from the Campus Martius outside the city walls to the temple of Jupiter on the Capitol, by the triumphal gate through which no one else might pass. The triumph was Etruscan in origin, and was regulated by strict rules of a religious nature. To be granted a triumph (by the senate and people) it was at first necessary for the general to hold a magistracy with *imperium*: even Scipio Africanus after his victories in Spain had been denied a triumph through not holding a regular magistracy. A general so qualified had to win a great victory over a foreign enemy, with at least 5,000 of the enemy killed, and finally to have brought home at least a token army to show that the war was won. Later, holding a regular magistracy ceased to be a prerequisite (*see* POMPEY), but the other requirements meant that a triumph was still a fairly rare event. Under the empire only the emperor could celebrate a triumph; the last to do so was Diocletian in AD 302. Preceded by his lictors the *triumphator*, richly dressed in red, his face painted red, and his head wreathed in laurel, rode on a chariot drawn by four white horses, a slave reputedly murmuring to him words to avert the dangers of outstanding success such as 'remember you are mortal'. The army shouted '*io triumphe*' and sang rude songs (*see* FESCENNINE VERSES). The procession was joined by the magistrates and senators, captives, spoils, and sacrificial animals. At the temple of Jupiter Capitolinus the general made sacrifice and surrendered his laurels to the god.

When a triumph was disallowed an *ovatio* was usually granted. This was a less spectacular form of triumph, the general entering Rome on foot or on horseback rather than in a chariot and wearing a crown of myrtle. The last recorded *ovatio* was in AD 47.

**triumvirate** The unofficial coalition of Julius Caesar, Pompey, and Crassus in 60 BC is often referred to for convenience, but strictly speaking incorrectly, as the first triumvirate (*see* CAESAR). The (second) officially constituted triumvirate in 43 BC was formed by Antony, Lepidus, and Octavian (*see* AUGUSTUS 1).

**Tri'via** *See* DIANA.

**tri'vium** *See* SEVEN LIBERAL ARTS.

**Trō'adĕs** *See* TROJAN WOMEN.

**Troas (the Troad)** The territory around *Troy, forming the north-west extremity of Asia Minor, between the Hellespont and the island of Lesbos, including Mount Ida.

**Trogus, Pompē'ius** Roman historian in the time of Augustus, a native of Narbonese Gaul, whose father had been a lieutenant of Julius Caesar. He wrote a universal history in forty-four books entitled *Historiae Philippicae* ('Philippic histories'), centred as the name indicates on the history of *Macedon, especially under Philip II, and probably based on Greek sources (e.g. the important *Theopompus). We have only the tables of contents and an epitome of it by *Justin, which are nevertheless valuable for the history of Macedon and the Hellenistic kingdoms.

**Trōilus** In Greek myth, a younger son of Priam, king of Troy, and Hecuba, mentioned briefly in Homer's *Iliad* as already dead, and, according to the version starting in the *Cypria*, killed by Achilles in an ambush. For the medieval story of Troilus and Cressida (which has

no classical precedent) *see* PANDARUS. Cressida is *Chryseis in the *Iliad*.

**Trojan Horse** Also known as the Wooden Horse, a device resorted to by the Greeks, after the death of Achilles, to capture Troy. The story is known to Homer and is referred to in the *Odyssey* as well as being part of the cycle of stories about Troy (*see* EPIC CYCLE; ILIAD, LITTLE; ILIUPERSIS), but the *Iliad* ends well before this event. Epēius, a skilful craftsman, constructed a very large wooden horse inside which picked Greek warriors, including Odysseus, who devised the plan, were concealed. Then the Greek army sailed out of sight, leaving behind Sinon, one of their number, who pretended to the Trojans that he was a deserter and that the horse was an offering to Athena; if brought within the city it would render it impregnable. In spite of the warning given to the Trojans by Laocŏon (a priest of Apollo) not to trust 'Greek gifts', the Trojans dragged the horse into the city, convinced that the destruction of Laocoon and his sons by two serpents after he had given his warning was a punishment for impiety. Cassandra too prophesied disaster but was disbelieved. At night the Greeks came out of the horse and the city was taken. In Homer's *Odyssey* (book 4) Menelaus reminds Helen how, when the horse was inside the walls of Troy, she had walked round it calling out the names of the men she suspected might be inside, and Odysseus had prevented anyone from answering. In book 8 Odysseus at the court of Alcinous asks the bard to sing the story of the Wooden Horse. Virgil tells the story of the horse in *Aeneid* 2.

**Trojan War** The subject of the most important and most pervasive of Greek legends; an episode in the war is the subject of Homer's *Iliad*, the war's aftermath that of his *Odyssey*. The ancient city of *Troy stood on the Asian side of the Hellespont; archaeological evidence has revealed that one of the occupation levels, known as Troy VIIa, was destroyed with fire and loss of life *c.*1190 BC, which roughly corresponds with *Erastosthenes' calculation of 1184 for the fall of Troy. Herodotus' date was *c.*1280.

In the Homeric account the war was waged by the *Achaeans (i.e. the Greeks) led by Agamemnon to recover *Helen, the wife of Agamemnon's brother Menelaus and the most beautiful woman in the world, who had been abducted by *Paris, a prince of Troy. Helen's father Tyndareus made all her suitors take an oath to protect the rights of the chosen bridegroom, and this accounts for so many Greek leaders going to Troy. The Achaeans laid siege to the city but at the end of nine years had still failed to take it. Then followed the events recounted in the *Iliad*. After this, according to post-Homeric legend, occurred the arrival of the Amazons under Penthesilea (*see* EPIC CYCLE and ACHILLES) and of the Ethiopians under *Memnon to reinforce the Trojans, the death of Achilles, the summoning of *Neoptolemus and *Philoctetes, the incident of the *Trojan Horse, and the fall of the city.

Medieval legend relating to the Trojan War is mainly based on Latin works which purported to be translations of the narratives of Dares Phrygius and *Dictys Cretensis. In England the most prominent form of the medieval legend was the story which Geoffrey of Monmouth (d. 1155) made popular: that Brutus ('Brut'), great-grandson of Aeneas, collected a remnant of Trojans, settled in Britain, which was uninhabited at the time ('except for a few giants'), and became the progenitor of a line of British kings which included King Arthur; and that he founded 'New Troy', Troynovant, later known as London. (The name was based on that of the British tribe the Trinovantes whose territory was north and east of London.) This legend was taken seriously even beyond medieval times.

**Trojan Women** (*Trōadĕs*) **1.** Greek tragedy by *Euripides. It was produced in 415 BC, shortly after the capture of *Melos by the Athenians, who slaughtered its male inhabitants and enslaved its women and children. One of the most poignant of Euripidean dramas, it presents not so much a narrative as a tragic situation: the condition of the Trojan women when their menfolk have been killed and they are at the mercy of their captors. Grieving and anxious, they await their fate. Talthybius, the Greek herald, announces that they are to be distributed among the victors. The Trojan queen Hecuba is to become the possession of the hated Odysseus; her daughter Cassandra has been allotted to Agamemnon, and it is revealed that her other daughter Polyxena has been slaughtered on the tomb of Achilles. The tragic figure of Cassandra appears; having prophetic power she foretells some of the disasters which will come upon the conquerors. Andromache, Hector's widow, en-

ters with her small son Astyanax; she is to be the prize of Neoptolemus. Talthybius returns to carry off Astyanax whose death has been ordered by the Greeks. The meeting of Menelaus and Helen follows; he is determined to destroy her, and Hecuba encourages his anger. But Helen pleads her cause, and when Helen and Menelaus depart their reconciliation has been foreshadowed. Talthybius appears once more with the broken body of Astyanax, and Hecuba prepares the burial. Finally Troy is set on fire and its towers collapse as the women leave for captivity.

**2.** Roman tragedy by *Seneca (2), based on (1) above and combining with it the sacrifice of Polyxena from Euripides' *Hecuba*. This is one of the most popular of the Senecan tragedies, containing passages of great passion and pathos.

**Trophō'nius and Agamē'dēs** In Greek myth, sons of Ergīnus of Orchomenus (in Boeotia) who lived in the time of Heracles. Trophonius ('Nourisher') is sometimes said to be the son of Apollo. They were architects and builders, and according to the *Homeric Hymn to Apollo laid the first courses for the temple of Apollo at Delphi and the golden treasury for the Boeotian king Hyrieus (or for Augeas, king of Elis). The story told about the last is similar to that told of *Rhampsinitus. The two brothers robbed the treasury by means of a movable stone in the wall; the king set a trap, and when Agamedes was caught Trophonius cut off his head to avoid identification. Trophonius was subsequently swallowed up by the earth at Lebadeia in western Boeotia but lived on under the earth as an *oracle. When the Boeotians were suffering from a drought the oracle at Delphi told them to consult Trophonius' oracle. They did not know how to find it, but one of the envoys, following a swarm of bees into a cave, saw a vision of Trophonius who told him he was now the oracle of the cave.

The oracle was consulted by Croesus, king of Lydia, in the sixth century BC, Epaminondas, and Philip II of Macedon, and was still in existence in Roman times. According to Plutarch it was the only Boeotian oracle that remained active in his day (early second century AD). The method of consulting the oracle, the 'descent', *katabasis*, was highly unusual, as we know from *Pausanias (9.39.4), who consulted it himself. After elaborate preparations, which included drinking from the springs of Forgetfulness and Memory, the enquirer descended into a chasm, at the bottom of which was a small opening. Into this he inserted his legs and was immediately snatched away to another place, 'as if a deep fast river was catching a man in a current and sucking him down'. Here the enquirer learned the future from the god himself and from things he saw or heard, before being returned feet-first the same way. The priests then took him to the Throne of Memory and asked him what he had learnt; this was written down and the tablet dedicated to the god. The enquirer emerged pale and terrified, so that it became proverbial to say of people looking gloomy that they had consulted the oracle of Trophonius.

**Trōs** A grandson of *Dardanus, after whom the Troad and the Trojans were named. His elder son was Ilus, from whom Troy is sometimes known as Ilion (Lat. Ilium). Ilus had two sons, *Laomedon, father of *Priam, the king of Troy in the *Iliad*, and *Tithonus.

**Troy** (modern Hisarlik) Ancient Anatolian city famous in legend; its siege by the Greeks is the subject of Homer's *Iliad* (see TROJAN WAR and TROJAN HORSE). It is situated in north-west Asia Minor some 6km (4 miles) from the Aegean Sea, a little south of the Hellespont. Occupied from the early *Bronze age (c.3000 BC), it later became a remote part of the Hittite empire. In 1820 it was identified as a small citadel mound, composed of the accumulated debris of centuries, and excavated by the German archaeologist Heinrich Schliemann between 1870 and 1890. He and later archaeologists established the principal strata representing successive periods of occupation (called Troy I, Troy II, etc.), dating from the early Bronze age to about 700 BC (Troy VIIIc); Troy IX was Hellenistic and Roman, and became a specially revered site. Throughout the Greek classical period the site remained unoccupied. Troy VIIa, dated by pottery finds to the thirteenth century BC, in the late Bronze age, corresponds most closely with what is generally accepted to be the situation and date of Homer's Troy (see ERATOSTHENES). The site has not yet been fully excavated but seems now to indicate a sizeable city. A destruction date of c.1190 BC is a possibility. Though there is not much evidence for the cause of the destruction there are traces of fire, some human bones, and a few arrowheads, which together suggest war, although the damage could also be due to earthquake.

The citadel was repaired (Troy VIIb$_1$) and re-occupied on a small scale until resettled by Greek colonists c.700 BC. If there is any fact at all behind the story that Greeks aimed at the destruction of Troy in the Trojan War, the latest reasonable date for mainland Mycenaean Greece to be making a concerted attack on the city seems to be 1250 or thereabout, when both sides were at the height of their power, since after that time Greece herself was involved in the general upheavals of the Mediterranean world, sometimes described as the Bronze-age collapse, which began in the second half of the century (see MYCENAE).

***Trucule'ntus*** ('The Boor') Roman comedy by *Plautus.

The play, which has little plot, is mainly concerned with the doings of a covetous prostitute who shamelessly exploits her three lovers, a dissolute young Athenian, a boastful soldier, and a young man from the country (whose sour and aggressive slave gives the play its title). She palms off on the soldier a child she has acquired, by pretending that it is his. The child turns out to be that of the dissolute Athenian and a freeborn girl, whom the penitent seducer agrees to marry. The slave tries to prevent his master wasting his money on the prostitute, but then falls in love himself with her maid.

**Tryphiodō'rus** (fourth century AD) Greek epic poet, a native of Egypt. Only his *Capture of Troy* survives. A short epic of 691 lines, it resembles in style the epic of *Nonnus.

**Tucca, Plō'tius** See AENEID.

**Tu'llia 1.** In Roman legendary history, daughter of King *Servius Tullius and wife of Tarquinius Superbus (see TARQUIN (2)). She incited her husband to overthrow her father, and when the latter had been murdered, drove her chariot over his dead body.

**2.** The much-loved daughter of *Cicero (1) and Terentia, born c.79 BC. She was three times married, to Calpurnius Piso Frugi, of whom Cicero was fond, but who died in 57 during the latter's exile; to Furius Crassipes, who divorced her c.51; and thirdly to the dissolute P. Cornelius Dolabella, who supported alternately Julius Caesar and Brutus in the Civil War. Her death in 45 BC threw her father into despair; see CICERO (1) 4 and SULPICIUS RUFUS.

**Tulliā'num** At Rome, the underground execution cell of the prison, at the foot of the Capitoline hill, where most state prisoners were executed, including Jugurtha, the Catilinarian conspirators, and the Gaul Vercingetorix.

**Tullus Hosti'lius** In Roman legendary history the third king of Rome (673-642 BC). His reign was said to have been occupied by constant warfare (hence his name), which included the capture and destruction of Alba Longa (*see* HORATII AND CURIATII).

**Tully** Name by which Marcus Tullius *Cicero was known to English readers down to the early nineteenth century.

*Tū'riae laudā'tio* See LUCRETIUS (2).

**Turnus** In Virgil's *Aeneid*, Italian hero, son of Daunus and the nymph Venilia, brother of the nymph Juturna. He was the king of Ardea, a city of the Rutulians (of Latium), and suitor of Lavinia, daughter of King *Latinus. The Latins and Rutulians fought the incoming Trojans under Aeneas. Turnus killed Pallas, son of Evander, was twice saved by Juno, but was finally killed by Aeneas (*see* AENEID [books 7–12]).

*Tu'sculan Disputations* (*Tusculānae disputātiōnēs*) ('Discussions at *Tusculum', where Cicero had a villa) Philosophical treatise in five books by Cicero on the conditions for happiness. The work was completed in 44 BC (*see* CICERO (1) 5) and is addressed to Marcus *Brutus. It takes the form of conversations between two characters indicated in later manuscripts as M and A, but perhaps intended to stand for Magister (master) and Discipulus (pupil).

After an introduction defending the adoption of philosophy as a subject for treatment in Latin literature, Cicero himself summarizes the contents of the books: 'they examine the essentials for a happy life. The first book shows that death is nothing to be afraid of, and the second that pain is endurable. The third shows how sorrow can be alleviated, the fourth covers other mental disturbances, and the fifth deals with a proposition which brilliantly illuminates the entire field of philosophy, that moral goodness by itself is sufficient for happiness.' In the case of book 1 he asserts that death is either a change of place for the soul or annihilation; in neither case is it an evil; 'How can what is

necessary for all be an evil for one?' In a famous sentence Cicero says, 'by Hercules, I would rather be wrong with Plato [than right with some other philosophers]': *errare, mehercule, malo cum Platone . . .*

**Tu'sculum** Ancient Italian town in the mountains near Frascati about 24km (15 miles) south-east of Rome. Under the late republic and early empire it was a fashionable resort. Cicero had a villa there (his favourite), as did Lucullus and Maecenas. For the legendary founder *see* TELEGONUS.

**Twelve gods** *See* GODS.

**Twelve Tables** The earliest Roman code of laws drawn up by a special commission of ten men with consular *imperium, decemviri legibus scribundis* ('ten men for writing out the laws'), in 451/50 BC, making the law of custom statutory. This was in response to the demand of the *plebeians, in order to put an end to the monopoly of *patricians and priests in interpreting the law, and was possibly part of the conflict of *orders. No complete text of the code survives, and it is known only from quotations and references. According to tradition envoys were sent to Athens to study Greek laws before the decemvirs started work. The Twelve Tables were primarily concerned with civil actions and included only those criminal cases likely to affect an early peasant community. They were never abolished, but later enactments made them obsolete. As late as Cicero's day, although not for much longer, schoolboys still learned them by heart. *See* LAW, ROMAN.

**Tȳchē** ('Chance', 'Fortune', good or bad) In Greek religious thought the incalculable element in life. In popular belief each person and city had its own *tyche*, much like a *daimon*. Pindar calls Tyche one of the Fates, stronger than her sisters, and the child of Zeus Eleutherios, but she is not mentioned in Homer and never became fully personified or a subject of myth. On the whole she is favourable, but Sophocles has Oedipus dangerously calling himself 'the child of Tyche'. In New Comedy she is capricious and senseless; in the novels a useful expedient for a plot. Belief in this abstraction strengthened after the fifth century BC as worship of the old gods declined, and her cult spread. *Cf.* Latin FORTUNA.

**Tȳ'deus** In Greek myth, son of Oineus, king of Calydon. Exiled for homicide (his victim is variously given), at Argos he married Dēipyle, daughter of Adrastus, while Polyneices married her sister Argeia. He was one of the leaders in the expedition of the *Seven against Thebes where he was wounded by Melanippus. When the latter was killed he tried to suck out his brains, an act which so disgusted the goddess Athena that she withheld the immortality that she was about to grant him. His son was *Diomedes, the Greek hero at Troy, who is always conscious of the need to match his father's exploits.

**Tynda'ridae** ('the Tyndarids') Name sometimes given to Castor and Polydeuces (Pollux; see DIOSCURI), whose mother *Leda was wife of Tyndareus, king of Sparta.

**Typhō'eus (Tȳphos)** According to Hesiod, the last child of *Tartarus and Gaia (Earth), born after Zeus' defeat of the *Titans. He was a monster with a hundred serpent heads, fiery eyes, and a tremendous voice; Zeus at once attacked him with thunderbolts and cast him into Tartarus, setting *Aetna (1) on fire on the way. In Pindar and Aeschylus he is the force under that volcano, and he is the source of hurricanes which cause shipwreck and devastation.

**tyrant (*tyrannos*)** ('king', perhaps a Lydian word) In Greece, name given to an absolute monarch who seized power illegally. There were many such in Greek cities of the seventh and sixth centuries BC, often originally members of a ruling oligarchy who led a popular revolt against oppressive government (see PITTACUS). In such cases they sometimes paved the way for democratic government. Under the later democracies of classical Greece, when the idea of tyranny became repugnant, the word 'tyrant' acquired its pejorative overtone; Plato and Aristotle thought tyranny the worst possible form of constitution, but most of the early tyrants made important contributions to the adornment and general cultural standing of

their cities. A tyranny rarely lasted for more than two generations. Spartans boasted that they were never subject to tyrants. The most famous tyrants of the Greek world included *Cleisthenes (1), *Cypselus, *Hippias and Hipparchus, *Peisistratus, *Periander, *Pheidon, and *Polycrates. Later tyrants were military dictators, Gelon and Hieron of *Syracuse, *Theron of Acragas, and in the late fifth and fourth centuries BC Dionysius I and II of Syracuse.

**Tȳro** In Greek myth, daughter of *Salmoneus, a king of Elis, and brought up by a cruel stepmother. Tyro was loved by the god Poseidon who took the form of the Thessalian river Enipeus and made a great wave curl over them. She bore twin sons, Pelias (see ARGONAUTS) and Neleus (father of *Nestor), whom she abandoned. She was married to her father's brother Cretheus and became by him the mother of Aeson and thus grandmother of *Jason. See also MELAMPUS.

**Tyrrhē'nians** See ETRUSCANS.

**Tyrtae'us** (mid-seventh century BC) Spartan elegiac war poet. The Alexandrian scholars collected his works in five books, but only about 250 lines survive, in quotation and on papyri. There are four sizeable passages in which the rank-and-file soldier is constantly exhorted to advance boldly in line, fight bravely and endure until death. The longest passage begins with a *priamel listing several manly qualities before arriving at the one needed in war—high physical courage. These poems were produced in the crisis of the Second Messenian War (see MESSENIA and SPARTA 3) and are of historical interest although the chronology is hard to establish. In another poem later called *Eunomia ('Good order'), written at a time of civic unrest, he reminds the people of the divine origin underlying the roles of kings, council, and people, quoting the four-line hexameter oracle from Delphi which had defined their roles (see LYCURGUS (2)).

**U**

**Uli'xēs** *See* ODYSSEUS.

**U'lpian Library** At Rome, built by Trajan, emperor AD 98–117, and so called from his own name, Ulpius. *See* LIBRARIES.

**Uly'ssēs** *See* ODYSSEUS.

**U'mbrian** The language of Umbria, a region of central *Italy, north-east of Rome. An *Indo-European Italic dialect closely related to Oscan, it survives in inscriptions from *c.*400–90 BC. It was written in a script derived from the alphabet used in western Greece, through the influence of Etruria. The longest texts are the *tabulae Iguvinae*, from *c.*200–100 BC, describing priestly ritual. *See also* LATIN LANGUAGE.

**uncials** In Greek and Latin handwriting, one of the two forms of majuscules or large letters used in papyri and early manuscripts, the other being capitals. Uncials are a curvilinear form of the latter, being easier to write with a pen on soft material than the angular capitals, which are more readily cut on metal or stone. The name first appears in Jerome's preface to the Old Testament book of Job, and is generally taken to mean 'letters an inch long' (Lat. *uncia,* 'inch'), but the derivation is uncertain. *See* TEXTS, TRANSMISSION OF ANCIENT 3.

**Underworld** *See* DEATH, ATTITUDES TO; MYSTERIES; HADES; ORPHEUS; SOUL; TARTARUS.

**Ūra'nia** Title of the goddess *Aphrodite, describing her as 'heavenly', i.e. spiritual, to distinguish her from Aphrodite Pandemos, 'vulgar' love, as in Plato's *Symposium.*

**Ū'ranus (Heaven)** (Gk. Ouranos) In Greek myth, the personification of the heavens. Uranus and *Gaia (Earth), who herself gave birth to Uranus, are the primordial parents in Greek cosmogony. Uranus fathered numerous children but prevented them from being born. Gaia called upon *Cronus, her son by Uranus, to help, and he castrated his father with a sickle (an act which seems to represent the separation of Heaven and Earth, a frequent motif of myth all over the world). Uranus' children could then be born (*see* TITANS; CYCLOPES; HECATONCHEIRES), after which he himself loses importance and disappears from view. Various divine monsters were born from the drops of his blood which fell on the earth, Erinyes (*see* FURIES), *Giants, and Meliae (tree-nymphs). His genital organs were flung into the sea by Cronus, and from the foam that bubbled around them *Aphrodite was born. He had virtually no cult.

**Valē'rius Flaccus, Gaius** Latin poet of whose life little is known except that dateable references in his only known work, the *Argonautica*, indicate that it was written under the Flavian emperors (i.e. between AD 71 and 96). The *Argonautica*, an epic poem written in hexameters, ends abruptly in the eighth book. Valerius' main source was the similarly entitled Hellenistic Greek epic of *Apollonius Rhodius, but other poets including Varro Atacinus had treated the same subject and Valerius may have consulted their works; the Underworld scene in book 1 is indebted to similar scenes in Homer's *Odyssey* and, especially, to Virgil's *Aeneid*, but Valerius also introduces scenes of his own invention. Book 7, and the possibly incomplete book 8, the episode of Jason and Medea, are usually judged the most interesting part of the poem, where with some subtlety and in a graver, less playful manner than Apollonius, he develops the character of Medea, torn between her passion for Jason and loyalty to her father, and enlists the reader's sympathy for her. He leaves Jason contemplating the betrayal of the bride on whom his success depends. It is possible that the work was completed in eight books, and that the last part of book 8 has been lost.

**Valē'rius Maximus** Latin compiler, in the early first century AD, of an extant collection of anecdotes and examples for the use of orators, in nine books. Very little is known of his life. He followed his patron Sextus Pompeius (consul in AD 14) to Asia in AD 27, and dedicated his work to the emperor Tiberius after the fall of Sejanus in AD 31. His nine books of *Facta et dicta memorabilia* ('Memorable deeds and sayings'), mostly drawn from Livy and Cicero, are arranged roughly as follows: book 1, religion, omens, prophecies; book 2, social customs; books 3–6, virtuous conduct (fortitude, moderation, humanity, etc.); books 7–8, a miscellaneous group including good fortune, military stratagems, famous law-suits, eloquence, and many other items; book 9, evil conduct.

The examples on each topic are divided into 'Roman' and 'foreign'. The work shows little originality and the style is highly rhetorical, but it proved useful and was very popular in the Middle Ages; two epitomes were made of it, perhaps in the fourth and fifth centuries.

**Va'rius Rufus, Lucius** Roman poet of the first century BC, friend of Virgil and Maecenas, to whom he and Virgil introduced Horace. Both Virgil and Horace admired his poetry, and regarded him as a leading epic poet in his day. He was the author of a tragedy on the story of *Thyestes, performed in 29 BC at the games in celebration of Octavian's victory at Actium, which earned him a million sesterces from the victor, and which Quintilian thought the equal of any Greek tragedy. Horace alludes to him as pre-eminent in epic. With *Varus (1), Plotius Tucca, and Virgil he was a member of an Epicurean group referred to by *Philodemus. None of his works has survived. After Virgil's death Varius and Plotius Tucca edited the *Aeneid*, upon instructions from Augustus who refused to allow the work to be destroyed as Virgil had wished.

**Varro, Marcus Tere'ntius** (116–27 BC) Roman man of letters, called 'Reātīnus' because he was born at Reātē in Sabine territory. He was opposed to Julius Caesar in politics and was a Pompeian officer in Spain at the time of the Civil War, but was reconciled to Caesar and was to have been the head of the public library whose creation Caesar was contemplating in 47. In 43 he was proscribed by Mark Antony, but escaped with the loss of some property and his library. He was a poet, satirist, antiquarian, jurist, geographer, grammarian, and scientist, and wrote on education and philosophy also. Quintilian called him 'the most learned of Romans'. He had completed 490 books by the start of his seventy-eighth year. Fifty-five titles are known from probably 75 separate works totalling more than 600 volumes of which only his *De re rustica* ('On farming') survives complete. He died pen in hand.

*De lingua Latina* ('On the Latin language') was a systematic treatise in 25 books on Latin grammar, dealing successively with *etymology, inflexion, and syntax, a pioneer work showing occasional penetration, amid many absurd derivations. Books 5–10, much of which we possess, are dedicated to Cicero; the others have not survived (*see* TEXTS, TRANSMISSION OF ANCIENT 6). It was probably published in 43 BC.

The *Saturae Menippeae* ('Menippean satires'), in 150 books, were satires on the model of *Menippus of which we have some 600 fragments, in a mixture of prose and verse, some of them in dialogue or semi-dramatic form. They were critical sketches of Roman life with a wide range of characters and scenes including some from myth; the language is vigorous, earthy, and inventive. Many of the sketches were directed, with humour and nostalgia for the decencies of the previous century, against what he saw as the greed, luxury, and sophisticated pretensions of his own day, as exemplified by the contemporary Greek schools of philosophy.

His *Hebdomades* ('Sevens'), or *Imagines* ('Portraits'), in fifteen books now lost, was a collection of 700 character sketches in prose of celebrated Greeks and Romans, accompanied by coloured portraits of the subjects, to each of which an epigram was appended. Much of our knowledge about the lives of eminent Romans derives ultimately from Varro.

Among his other more important works were (i) the antiquarian treatise *Antiquitates rerum humanarum et divinarum* ('Human and divine antiquities'), a historical encyclopaedia of which roughly speaking the first part dealt with the history of Rome and the second part with Roman religion (the arrangement of facts followed a simple pattern of people, places, dates, and events); (ii) *De gente populi Romani* ('On the Roman nation'), concerning the prehistory and early chronology of Rome; (iii) *De vita populi Romani* ('On the way of life of the Roman people'), concerning the history and style of Roman society; (iv) *Disciplinae* ('Studies'), on the liberal arts (grammar, dialectic, rhetoric, geometry, arithmetic, astronomy, music, medicine, and architecture), all except the last two forming the medieval *trivium* and *quadrivium*, and subsequently utilized by Martianus Capella (*see* SEVEN LIBERAL ARTS); and (v) a treatise on philosophy, *De philosophia*. Many fragments survive of the *Res divinae* ('On religion'), preserved by St Augustine when he attacked it in the *City of God*. Varro was influenced by the Platonism of Antiochus of Ascalon (*see* ACADEMY), as well as by Stoic and Pythagorean ideas, yet he insisted that an ancient city should adhere to its traditional religion, and accepted that the greatness of Rome had depended in part on its religious observances: at the least, religion, if untrue, was useful.

**Vārus 1.** The *cognomen* of a friend of Horace, given the name Quintilius in some manuscripts. He may be P. Alfenus Varus, a jurist and patron of literature, to whom Catullus may also have written a poem. Virgil mentions a Varus, probably him, in the *Eclogues*.

**2. Quinti'lius Varus** Roman general who in AD 9 was entrusted with the settlement of Germany. He and his three legions were lured by the German chief *Arminius into an ambush and annihilated. Varus committed suicide and Roman expansion in north Germany was ended for ever (but *see* GERMANICUS).

**Vatican** At Rome in classical times, an outlying district on the west bank of the river Tiber on the Vatican hill, north-west of the ancient city, not one of the *seven hills of Rome. The region was known for its unhealthy air, unproductive soil, and bad wine. Its only claim to fame in republican times was that here *Cincinnatus was cultivating his four acres when he was summoned to be dictator. Its only building of note was the Mausoleum of the emperor Hadrian, now the Castello di S. Angelo. Here was the Vatican circus where Caligula set up a great obelisk from Egypt and which was traditionally the site of the martyrdom of the apostle Peter, first bishop of Rome. Excavations in the 1940s directly under the high altar of St Peter's basilica revealed a small second-century shrine arguably marking his burial site.

**vau** *See* ALPHABET.

**vegetarianism** *See* ANIMALS, ATTITUDES TO.

**Veii** (modern Isola Farnese) One of the great Etruscan cities captured by Rome in 396 BC (*see* ROME 2).

**Vellē'ius Pate'rculus, Gaius** (*c*.19 BC– after AD 30) Roman historian who served for several years with the army in Germany, quaestor in AD 7 and praetor in AD 15. The only surviving Roman historian between Livy and Tacitus, he was the author of a summary history of Rome from earliest times to AD 29 in two books, the first of which (down to 146 BC) is almost all lost. His history shows partiality for the imperial house of the Caesars and enthusiasm, reaching adulation, for Tiberius. The work is not profound (he admits that he wrote hurriedly), but his interest is in individuals and the biographical sketches are valuable, e.g. that of Tiberius (which is in strong contrast with the picture given by Tacitus) and on a small scale those of Caesar, Pompey, and Maecenas. The history is notable also for its chapters on the evolution of Latin literature. He discusses the reasons for its decline and suggests that the perfection reached in the Augustan age had driven later writers in despair to seek minor fields. The style of the history is artificial and rhetorical, but some of his epigrams are acute. The text survived in a single manuscript, now lost.

**Vēnus** Roman goddess, who did not belong to Rome's earliest pantheon, but by the sixth century BC *Lavinium's federal sanctuary common to all Latins had an altar to Venus. Her name means 'charm'. In Rome from the third century BC she became identified with and acquired the mythology of the Greek goddess *Aphrodite, the goddess of love. Venus of Eryx in Sicily (Venus Erycina), where Aeneas had founded a temple in honour of his father Anchises, had a temple on the Capitoline hill in Rome dedicated in 217 BC at a dire moment in the Second Punic War, and another outside the Colline Gate. Aeneas was the son of Aphrodite/ Venus; the story of his wanderings and final settlement in Italy was particularly important to the Julian family (of which Julius Caesar and the emperors down to and including Nero were members; *see* JULIA, GENS) because it was claimed that they were descended from Aeneas' son Iulus (Ascanius) and so from Venus. She was also associated with the origin of the Roman people as the consort of *Mars. Julius Caesar, in gratitude to her for his success at the battle of Pharsalus, dedicated a temple to Venus Genetrix, 'universal mother', in 46 BC in the Forum Iulium, and under the empire she became officially a major deity. It is in her aspect of universal mother that *Lucretius extols her at the beginning of *De rerum natura*, and that she is celebrated in the *Pervigilium Veneris* written for the spring festival. 'Venus'

was the name given to the highest throw at dice (*see* ASTRAGALOI).

**Venu'sia (Venosa)** Town on the river Aufidus in Apulia, south Italy, near the border of Lucania, famed as the birthplace of Horace.

**Vēra histo'ria** *See* LUCIAN.

**Vercinge'torix** Nobleman of the Gallic tribe of the Arverni who in 52 BC raised a revolt in Gaul against Rome and was acclaimed king and general. He was eventually defeated by Julius Caesar. *See* COMMENTARIES 1 [book 7]. He surrendered and was brought to Rome for Caesar's triumph in 46 BC before being put to death (*see* TULLIANUM).

**Vergil** *See* VIRGIL.

**Vergina** *See* AEGAE.

**Verginia** *See* VIRGINIA.

**Verrēs, Gaius** Roman propraetor in Sicily 73–71 BC. He plundered the province for his personal enrichment, in a way that was typical of many Roman governors of the time but perhaps more thoroughgoing than most. He must have expected to survive a prosecution in the *repetundae (extortion) courts, with the help of bribery, and powerful allies such as the Metelli and Q. *Hortensius to defend him, but he was defeated by the oratorical and legal genius of Cicero, whose *Verrine Orations* have made Verres' crimes notorious (*see* CICERO (1) 1). He kept much of his plundered treasure and retired to Massalia where he died. It was alleged that his treasure attracted the greed of Mark Antony, and that Verres was therefore proscribed and murdered in 43 (*see* PROSCRIPTIONS).

**verse** As well as having the obvious meaning of poetry in general, 'verse' in the context of Latin and Greek poetry usually means 'metrical line', and only rarely 'stanza'. In Latin, *versus* is said originally to have meant 'furrow'.

**Vertu'mnus** *See* VORTUMNUS.

**Vespae** *See* WASPS.

**Vespā'sian (Titus Flavius Sabinus Vespasianus)** (AD 9–79) Roman emperor 69–79, the first of the *Flavians. He rose in the army and by the time of the invasion of Britain in AD 43 commanded the second legion, subduing the south-west as far as Exeter. In 66 he accompanied Nero to Greece and at the end of the year was entrusted with subduing rebellion in Judaea, a task largely complete by 68 (*see* JOSEPHUS). After the death of Nero in that year, there was a chaotic period in which Galba, Otho, and Vitellius briefly ruled, but Vespasian was declared emperor by the army, and after defeating and killing Vitellius was recognized by the senate—the first emperor not to come from an aristocratic family. He was a sound and just ruler, though firm (*see* HELVIDIUS PRISCUS), remarkable for the simplicity of his life and the economy and efficiency of his administration. Among his public works at Rome were the *Colosseum (completed by his son and heir Titus), the reconstruction of the temple of Jupiter Capitolinus, and a temple to Peace (built after his victory in Judaea), thought by the Elder Pliny to be one of the most beautiful buildings in the world. Tacitus claimed that Vespasian was the first man to improve after becoming emperor. His reign was efficient and peaceful, and though largely uneducated himself he founded chairs of rhetoric and philosophy. His insistence on his son Titus succeeding him may have caused controversy.

**Vesta** In Roman religion, the ancient Roman goddess of the hearth-fire, the etymological and religious equivalent of the Greek goddess *Hestia, believed to have been introduced into Rome by Romulus or Numa from Alba Longa. She had the title 'mater', 'mother', but was thought of as virgin. The state cult expressed and guaranteed Rome's permanence: the sacred fire on the symbolic hearth of the state was kept burning, in a small round temple in the Forum. This fire was rekindled every year on 1 March (the ancient New Year's Day), and was looked after for the rest of the year by the *Vestal Virgins. The round temple of Vesta was thought to have represented the original round house and hearth of the king of Rome in ancient times, and the Vestals his daughters. In the temple was the storehouse, *penus*, of the state (*see* PENATES), where sacred objects were kept, including the *Palladium, and for the most part only the Vestals and the *pontifex maximus* were allowed to enter. There was no statue of the goddess. On 9 June each year for the festival of Vesta, the Vestalia, it was opened to married women, who walked barefoot to it in procession, bringing simple food-offerings. This festival was also regarded as the bakers' holiday; asses were freed from the treadmill

and decked with garlands and little cakes. From 9 to 15 June the temple stood open, a time of ill-omen while the building was cleaned. 15 June was marked in the calendar *Q(uando) St(ercus) D(elatum) F(as)*, which meant that it was a normal working day 'when the dirt has been cleaned away'.

**Vestal Virgins** At Rome, one of the most ancient religious associations, going back to earliest times. Six virgins who were considered to represent the daughters of the early Roman kings had a duty to watch in turn, by day and night, the fire in the temple of *Vesta on the state hearth. Their service was housewifely: they tended the fire, guarded and ritually cleaned the storehouse, and garnered the earliest corn to make the salt cake (*mola salsa*) used to sanctify the victim at sacrifices. They also had custody of a number of sacred objects including the *Palladium and the ashes for the Parilia festival. The Vestals, said to have been instituted by the king Numa, and originally drawn from patrician families, were chosen by the *pontifex maximus* from suitable girls aged between 6 and 10. Their period of service was for thirty years, during which they had to maintain strict sexual purity, but generally the Vestals continued to serve the goddess for the rest of their lives. They lived in a house next to the temple of Vesta known as the Atrium Vestae ('hall of Vesta') and were maintained at public expense with all kinds of privileges. They were under the control of the *pontifex maximus* and could be scourged for offences such as letting the fire out. If anything went wrong in their house, the sanctity and security of Rome was threatened. Their purity was all-important: any Vestal who broke the rule of virginity was entombed alive. A letter of the Younger Pliny (4.11) describes such an event under the emperor Domitian. Vestals were held in high repute, and great importance was attached to their intervention on behalf of those in trouble. They wore a linen dress in the old-fashioned style of a matron. The cult was abolished in AD 394.

**veterinary medicine** *See* MEDICINE.

**Via A'ppia** *See* APPIAN WAY.

**Via Sacra** The Sacred Way, the street connecting the Forum with Velia (a narrow ridge joining the Palatine and Oppian hills). Its name is derived from the sacred buildings, including the shrine of Vesta and the Regia, which it passed. There Horace famously encountered his Bore (*Satires* 1.9).

*Vidula'ria* ('The wallet') Title of a play by *Plautus surviving in a *palimpsest of which only fragments are legible. The plot appears to have resembled that of the *Rudens*.

**vi'gilēs** At Rome, the fire-brigade, instituted as a force of 600 slaves by the emperor Augustus after a fire of 23 BC. After another fire in AD 6 he created a corps of 7,000 freedmen under the command of a *praefectus vigilum* appointed by the emperor. They dealt with fires by demolishing buildings; extinguishing flames was beyond their technology.

**villa** In Italy, a country house with land, comprising either a comfortable dwelling for the owner, with specialized farm buildings nearby, gardens, and agricultural land, or the luxurious property of a wealthy landowner for whom the land was used principally for ornamental purposes. An owner would leave Rome in the autumn heat and go down to his villa at vintage-time. In Britain and other provinces where the villas represent a consciously Roman lifestyle, it has been difficult to work out the agricultural purposes for which the land was used, and for how long. *See* BRITAIN 5.

**Viminal** One of the *seven hills of Rome, between the Esquiline and the Quirinal.

**Vindolanda tablets** Wooden writing tablets discovered at the Roman fort of Vindolanda south of Hadrian's Wall in the north of England. Since the 1970s several hundred have been found, some of the type where wood is coated with wax, to be inscribed with a stylus, but most consisting of thin wooden leaves written on with pen and ink. They date from AD 90 to 120 and are mostly letters, official and unofficial, written by soldiers and their families. There are some other texts—fragments of literature, military reports, accounts. They provide a fascinating glimpse of everyday life on the Wall, as well as being interesting for the light they throw on the business of organizing a newly established frontier (building the Wall began in AD 122; *see* BRITAIN 2), and they give new evidence about the Latin language and palaeography. They are important also because it is unusual for wooden tablets to survive.

**Vipsa'nia Agrippina** *See* AGRIPPINA (1) and (2).

**Vi'rbius** *See* DIANA.

**Virgil (Publius Vergilius Maro)** (70–19 BC) Roman poet, born on 15 October at Andes near Mantua (Mantova) in Cisalpine Gaul. According to ancient sources, which may not be altogether reliable, his father was quite rich but of humble origins, his mother perhaps well-connected. He was educated at Cremona and Mediolanum (Milan), and later studied philosophy and rhetoric at Rome; at some time he was a pupil of the Epicurean philosopher Siro at Naples. His family estate suffered loss, it was said, in the confiscations of land for the army veterans of Antony and Octavian which followed the battle of Philippi in 42 BC, but he was on friendly terms with the commissioners for the redistribution of the confiscated lands (*Gallus, *Varus (1), and *Pollio), and may have been given a property near Naples in recompense. It was around 42 BC when he began the composition of the *Eclogues*. Pollio was the first to recognize Virgil's talents, but with the publication of the *Eclogues* (perhaps finally in 37) Virgil moved from the circle of Pollio to the patronage of *Maecenas (to whom he introduced Horace) and Octavian. At this time he lived chiefly in Campania, at Naples and Nola. Horace records their journey together to *Brundisium in 38 or 37 (*Satires* 1.5). He spent the following seven years in the composition of the *Georgics*, published in 29 BC, and immediately afterwards began on the *Aeneid*, which was to occupy him for the remaining ten years of his life. In his last year he undertook a voyage to the East to visit some of the places he had described; he fell ill at Megara in Greece and returned to Italy, dying at Brundisium. His body was brought to Naples and buried outside the city, where his tomb was soon honoured as a shrine. He is said to have dictated the inscription for it on his deathbed:

*Mantua me genuit, Calabri rapuere, tenet nunc
Parthenope: cecini pascua, rura, duces.*

(Mantua brought me life, Calabria death; now Naples holds me: I sang of pastures and farms and heroes.)

(For the name Parthenope *see* SIRENS.) The *Aeneid* was incomplete at the author's death, and Virgil is said to have made *Varius promise to burn it if he died before his return, but on the orders of Augustus it was published after the literary executors Varius and Tucca had 'lightly corrected' it.

The *Eclogues*, *Georgics*, and *Aeneid* are described under those titles. A number of minor poems attributed to the poet are collected in the *Appendix Virgiliana*.

Virgil is described by *Donatus as tall and dark, with the appearance of a countryman, and a number of portraits survive in the manuscripts. His health was weak, he was shy and led a retired life, rarely appearing in Rome. He never married, and his sexual preference was said to be for boys. Although he became famous during his lifetime, he was diffident of his own poetic powers. His fame was based primarily on his position as the epic poet who revealed the greatness of the Roman empire, but his poetic eminence rests also on the technical perfection of his verse, with its sustained beauty and melodiousness, on the poet's tenderness and melancholy, and on his love of nature. He is the poet not only of the destiny of Rome but of the beauty and fertility of Italy, its morality and its religion.

Virgil is said to have been famous even in his lifetime, and his fame grew after his death into superstitious reverence. In the first century AD his birthday was celebrated and his works and tomb were revered as almost objects of cult by *Silius Italicus. From late antiquity he came to be regarded as a magician and miraculous powers were attributed to him. The *sortes Virgilianae*, 'Virgilian lots', attempts to foretell the future by opening his books and picking a line at random, were widely practised from an early date (reputedly as early as the emperor Hadrian in the second century AD). Memoirs of King Charles I relate that when the king was in the Bodleian Library at Oxford during the Civil War he sought his future by this method and hit upon Dido's curse against Aeneas (*Aeneid* 4.615), *At bello audacis populi vexatus et armis*..., 'harassed by war and the hostility of a bold nation...'. Virgil's works soon became one of the most widely used of schoolbooks and the subject of commentaries and learned discussion by Donatus, *Servius, *Macrobius, and others. Early Christian writers often reveal a conflict in their minds between admiration for his poetry and distrust of his paganism. The number and high quality of the manuscripts surviving from the third to the fifth centuries AD attest the great estimation in which he was then held. His ideas were made acceptable to Christians by *allegory (book 2 of

the *Aeneid* signifying the trauma of birth, book 6 the acquisition of enlightenment, for example), this kind of interpretation persisting in the thirteenth century in Dante (although not in the *Divine Comedy*). The widespread feeling that only mischance prevented Virgil from dying a Christian is expressed in the legend that the apostle Paul wept over his tomb at Naples, described by an anonymous poet at Paris in the twelfth or thirteenth century:

> '*quem te', inquit, 'reddidissem*
> *si te vivum invenissem*
> *poetarum maxime.'*

('What would I have made of you, had I found you alive!' he said, 'greatest of poets.')

Dante regarded Virgil not only as *il nostro maggior poeta* ('our greatest poet'), but as a prophet of Christianity, who guided him to the Gates of Paradise but had himself to be excluded. Several English translations preceded John Dryden's famous version of the whole of Virgil in 1697.

**Virgi'nia (Verginia)** According to Roman tradition, daughter of L. Verginius, a centurion, around 450 BC when the *decemvirs had been appointed at Rome to publish a code of laws (*see* TWELVE TABLES). Appius *Claudius (1), one of the decemvirs, intended to seduce her and in order to get her into his possession had one of his dependants claim her as a slave belonging to his own household; Appius Claudius himself pronounced judgement in the case, in favour of his dependant. Before Virginia could be taken away her father stabbed her to death, declaring that her death was better than her dishonour, and made his escape to the army camp. A rising followed in which the decemvirs were overthrown and more democratic procedures instituted. The story is told by Livy (3.44) and retold by Petrarch and by Chaucer in *The Physician's Tale*.

**virginity** *See* CHASTITY.

**Vite'llius, Aulus** (AD 15–69) Roman emperor, the last of three (following Galba and Otho) who ruled briefly in 69 before order was restored by Vespasian. He was supported by most of the western provinces and Africa, and defeated Otho in April 69 at Bedriacum. Otho committed suicide, and Vitellius entered Rome in July, but did nothing to win over the defeated army and by then the legions in the East had declared for Vespasian. Supporters of the latter defeated Vitellius in Rome and on 20 December he was killed. During his life he had been notorious for gluttony, laziness, and incompetence.

**Vitrū'vius Po'llio** Roman engineer and architect of the first century BC, who saw military service under Julius Caesar. He wrote a Latin treatise in ten books, *De architectura* ('On architecture'), dedicated to Octavian. Compiled partly from his own experience and partly from similar works by earlier architects, mostly Greek, it is the only treatise of its kind to have survived. It includes important quotations from Greek Presocratic philosophers and later mathematicians. Although it was fairly well known in manuscript copies in the Middle Ages, it was not until the Renaissance that it assumed great importance, becoming adopted as the supreme architectural authority (in spite of the frequent obscurity of the text). The first printed edition appeared *c.*1486, the first illustrated edition in 1511. The term 'Vitruvian man' refers to his theory of human proportion, in which the human figure is shown to fit into a square circumscribed by a circle (illustrated by Leonardo da Vinci).

Book 1 of *De architectura* deals with town planning, architecture in general, and the qualifications necessary for an architect; 2, building materials (he distrusts Roman concrete constructions); 3 and 4, temples and the orders of *architecture; 5, theatres (and their acoustics), baths, and other public buildings; 6, domestic architecture; 7, interior decoration, mosaic pavements, decorative plasterwork, and the use of colouring; 8, water supplies; 9 includes geometry, astronomy, mensuration, etc., with interesting remarks about water-clocks (*see* CLEPSYDRA); 10, cranes, water-lifting devices, water-mill, force pump, water organ, siege engines. Vitruvius emphasizes architectural design, but omits the architectural engineering that went into Greek building practice.

**Volsci** People of ancient central Italy, who spoke an Italic dialect resembling Umbrian. By 500 BC they had moved to an area in Latium south-east of Rome; three important Volscian towns were Arpinum (birthplace of Marius and Cicero), Antium, and Tarracina (which the Volsci renamed Anxur). They were a threat to the independence of Rome, which Rome met by making alliances with the Latins. The exploits of *Coriolanus relate to this time. By the end of the fourth century BC the Volscians were subject to Rome and they rapidly became Romanized.

**Vortu'mnus (Vertumnus)** Roman god, supposed to be of Etruscan origin. His name, connected by the Romans with *vertere*, 'to turn', was explained variously, as of the god who changes his shape, or who presides over the 'turn' of the year (autumn), or who once turned back a flood of the Tiber. Nothing is known for certain of his function. Ovid seems to have made up the story that he was the husband of *Pomona, whom he wooed in a succession of various forms, reaper, ploughman, pruner, etc.

**Vulcan (Volcānus)** Ancient Roman god of fire, perhaps a god of the smithy, in classical times identified with the Greek god *Hephaestus. He was associated with the goddess *Maia (2), for reasons that are not apparent. His own name, which is not Latin, resists interpretation. His function seems to have been to avert fires, hence his by-name Mulciber, 'he who quenches'. His festival of 23 May coincided with the Tubilustria, and there was another festival, the Volcanalia, in his honour on 23 August when his offering was of live fish from the Tiber, thrown into a fire. He had an important cult at Ostia, where he seems to have been the chief deity.

**war, just** For the concept, *see* FETIALES.

**Wasps (*Sphēkĕs*)** (Lat. *Vespae*) Comedy by *Aristophanes, produced in 422 BC at the *Lenaea, where it won second prize.

The play is a satire on the system of the jury courts at Athens (*see* JURIES) which at that time provided, through payment for jury service, means of support for poor and elderly men who were Athenian citizens. Philocleon ('love-*Cleon') is consumed by a passion for serving on juries. His son Bdelycleon ('loathe-Cleon') has tried to cure him and has finally imprisoned him in his house. Philocleon's friends, the chorus of old jurymen, dressed as wasps to show their readiness to inflict punishment, come along before dawn to take him with them to the courts, and try to bring about his escape. There is a scuffle, and Bdelycleon eventually persuades the chorus to listen while he urges his father to change his ways. A debate follows between father and son, the father dwelling upon the pleasures and benefits of exercising power irresponsibly, the son demonstrating that the jurors' power is an illusion; they are really manipulated by the politicians, who divert the city's revenues for their own ends. The chorus are converted, but Philocleon is reluctant, and as consolation Bdelycleon arranges for him to play the juror at home, the first to be tried being Labes, the house-dog, who has stolen a cheese. Tricked by his son, Philocleon unintentionally acquits the prisoner, the first that he has ever let off. Bdelycleon now takes in hand his father's social life, polishing his manners for the more refined pleasures of a *symposium. Philocleon takes to this with gusto and returns drunk and in high spirits with a kidnapped slave-girl, and followed by threatening tradespeople whom he has assaulted on the way home. Bdelycleon is dismayed, but the play ends in a riotous dance, *cordax, led by Philocleon.

**weights**
**Greek.** In Greece, units of weight had the same names as units of *money (since these latter denote weights of metal), thus

| 6 obols | = 1 drachma (4.31g) |
|---|---|
| 100 drachmas | = 1 mina (431g, about 15 oz.) |
| 60 minas | = 1 talent (25.86kg, about 57 lbs.) |

**Roman.** The Roman units of weight were based on the pound, *libra* (or *as*), their highest weight, equivalent to 327g (about ¾ lb.). It was subdivided into 12 ounces (*unciae*, 'twelfth parts', each roughly equivalent to the ounce avoirdupois), and the ounce was subdivided down to the *scripulum* ('scruple'), its 24th part.

*See also* MEASURES.

**women** Aspects of women's lives in antiquity are mentioned in the following categories:

Attic comedy: *see* ECCLESIAZUSAE; THESMOPHORIAZUSAE; LYSISTRATA.

Childbirth and health: *see* GYNAECOLOGY; MEDICINE; TIMAEUS.

Daily life: see ARS AMATORIA; BATHS; COSMETICS; DANCING; DEATH, ATTITUDES TO; HERODAS; HEROIDES; LITERACY.

Names: *see* NAMES, PERSONAL.

Notable women: *see* ASPASIA; ARTEMISIA; HORTENSIA; LIVIA; OCTAVIA; PHRYNE; THAIS; SULPICIA.

Political status: *see* AENEID; CATO (1) [Oppian law]; CENSUS; CITIZENSHIP; ECCLESIA; LAW, ROMAN; LAW AT ATHENS; POLITICS; REPUBLIC.

Religion: *see* ADONIS; ARTEMIS; *BACCHAE*; BACCHANTS; BONA DEA; CARMENTIS; CYBELE; DIANA; DIONYSUS; FATES; HECATE; HERA; ISIS; JUNO; KANEPHOROI; SACRIFICE 4; THEOCRITUS [Idylls 2 and 15]; VESTA; VESTAL VIRGINS.

Satirical or hostile attitudes: *see* HESIOD; SATIRES (2); SEMONIDES.

Social relations: *see* AGE GROUPS; CONCUBINAGE; FRIENDSHIP; HETAIRA; LESBIANISM; LOVE AND SEXUALITY; LYRIC POETRY; SAPPHO; SYMPOSIUM; and the comedies of PLAUTUS and TERENCE.

Status: *see* ATHLETICS; *HECYRA*; MARRIAGE LAW; PATERFAMILIAS; SPARTA 5.

Women in Euripides: *see* HECUBA; HELEN; MEDEA; PHOENISSAE; SUPPLIANTS; TROJAN WOMEN.

**Wooden Horse** *See* TROJAN HORSE.

***Works and Days*** (*Erga kai hēmerai*) Greek poem in 828 hexameters by *Hesiod; the 'Works' are the activities of the farming year, the 'Days' (from line 765 onward) are an almanac of days in the month that are favourable or unfavourable for different activities. No reason is given for the category of a particular day except for the implication that Zeus has ordained it so. Lucky or unlucky days are scarcely mentioned again in literature until Hellenistic times.

The chief themes of the poem are justice and the need for hard work. After an invocation to the Muses the poet addresses his brother Perses, urging him to a reconciliation of their quarrel (*see* HESIOD). To explain why men have to work hard and act justly he uses myth: *Prometheus and the story of Pandora, the five ages or generations (Golden, Silver, Bronze, Heroic, and Iron; *see* GOLDEN AGE), and the fable of the hawk and the nightingale, illustrating the unjust use of power; the whole is blended with proverbs, moral maxims, and threats of divine anger. In the remaining two thirds of the poem Hesiod gives Perses instructions on how to work as a farmer, which are mostly an enumeration of the tasks of the various seasons with some practical advice, for example on how to construct a plough. There is a fine descriptive passage on the rigours of winter (504–35), balanced by a picture of the farmer enjoying the languorous heat of summer (582–96). There follows some brief advice on sea-trading, a collection of proverbial maxims about religious and social conduct, and the almanac of lucky and unlucky days. The poem is a work of exhortation and instruction, for which parallels exist, but in Near Eastern literature rather than in Greek. Aratus and Virgil admired its elegance. The poems of *Phocylides and *Theognis are comparable in tone, but much more limited in scope. *Works and Days* is given unity chiefly by the personality of the author. Whether the circumstances of its composition are real or imaginary, the poem represents the life-experience of a cautious and conservative farmer, inured to hardship and adversity, suspicious of pleasure, and no lover of women, but one who by reflection had come to believe that the conditions of life were divinely and justly ordained.

**wrestling school** *See* PALAESTRA.

**writing, writing materials** *See* ALPHABET and BOOKS, GREEK AND ROMAN; *See also* TEXTS, TRANSMISSION OF ANCIENT.

**Xanthi'ppē** Wife of *Socrates.

**Xanthi'ppus** Father of *Pericles. In the *Persian Wars he commanded the Athenian fleet after the battle of Salamis and in 479 BC at the battle of Mycale, where he had a large share in the victory. He had earlier married Agariste, niece of Cleisthenes (2) and a member of the *Alcmaeonidae whose political ally he was. He had been ostracized in 484, but recalled at the time of the invasion by Xerxes. He led some of the Greeks in the attack on Sestus which after siege was captured from the Persians.

**Xanthus** (of Lydia) *See* LOGOGRAPHERS (1).

**Xeno'cratēs** Follower of Plato and head of the *Academy 339–314 BC.

**Xeno'phanēs** (of Colophon, in Ionia) A *Presocratic Greek philosopher who spent most of his long life wandering in Greek lands, chiefly perhaps in Sicily. His own words indicate that he was born c.570, and he is said to have lived on to the time of Hieron (tyrant of Syracuse 478–467 BC). According to tradition he was the teacher of *Parmenides, and thus in some sense connected with the origins of *Eleatic philosophy. He is said to have written a poem in hexameters on the foundation of Colophon and the colonization of Elea (in *Magna Graecia), but the surviving fragments of his writings are from three sources, his satirical *Silloi*, occasional elegiac poems, and a poem *On Nature*. He is important for his contribution in two fields, theology and epistemology. He was well known for his attack on the polytheism and anthropomorphism of the traditional Greek religion, and was concerned by the lack of ethical content in stories about the gods found in Homer and Hesiod (the *Silloi*, 'squint-eyed' poems, i.e. lampoons, satirize these myths). His god is single and eternal, in no way resembling men, effecting things by mind alone. This radical *monotheism was new in Greek thought. From the presence of seashells in the moun-

tains and the impression of a fossil fish and of seaweed in the Syracusan quarries, Xenophanes deduced that the land was once covered with water, and infers that it may be so again. In other fragments he shows the same radical and sceptical approach to accepted opinions, denouncing athletic success in the games as of less value than his own intellectual achievement. Fragments which express his awareness of the limits to the chances of humankind attaining knowledge led to Xenophanes' being identified as an early *Sceptic.

**Xe'nophon 1.** (c.428–c.354 BC) Greek historian and disciple of Socrates. He was an Athenian, son of Gryllus, born into a wealthy family, and had two sons Gryllus and Diodorus. Presumably he served in the cavalry (*see* HIPPEIS) and he was an associate of the aristocratic circle of young men around Socrates. He may have found life difficult in Athens after the oligarchic revolution, having fought against the returning democrats (*see* FOUR HUNDRED and THIRTY TYRANTS), and he left in 401. At the invitation of his Boeotian friend Proxenus he joined the expedition of *Cyrus the Younger which he describes in his *Anabasis*. After having extricated the Ten Thousand from this failed adventure by his own determination and military skill (according to his account), he accepted service in 396 with the Spartan king *Agesilaus, to whom he became strongly attached, against the Persian Pharnabazus. When Agesilaus was recalled by events in Greece Xenophon accompanied him and fought on the Spartan side at the battle of Coronea, against Athens and Boeotia, in 394 (*see AGESILAUS*). Exiled for this or perhaps already banished from Athens, and his property confiscated, he settled on an estate given him by the Spartans at Scillus near Olympia, and was made the Spartan *proxenos* for the entertainment of Spartans visiting Olympia. Here he spent the next twenty years, enjoying the country life and writing his books. In 371 Elis claimed Scillus and Xenophon retired to

Corinth. The decree of his banishment from Athens was revoked, probably *c.*368. When the Athenians were expelled from Corinth in 366 he returned to Athens; his two sons fought in the Athenian contingent on the Theban side at the battle of Mantinea in 362 and the elder, Gryllus, was killed.

Xenophon wrote on numerous subjects suggested by his varied experience (see entries for individual titles), and all known works survive. Socrates' personality made a profound impression on him and he wrote three books of recollections, *Memorabilia, Apology,* and *Symposium.* He may have misunderstood Socrates as profoundly as he admired him. (It is related that Socrates first met Xenophon, then a boy, in the street, and stopping him asked where various articles could be got. Xenophon told him. Socrates then asked, 'Where can you get brave and virtuous men?' and when Xenophon was puzzled told him to come with him.) *Oeconomicus* was inspired by his home life; *Anabasis* and *Cyropaedia* by his experiences in Persia; his treatises *The Cavalry Commander, Horsemanship,* and *Cynegeticus* by his military career and devotion to sport; *Hellenica, Agesilaus, Constitution of the Lacedaemonians, Hieron,* and *Revenues,* by his acquaintance with political affairs in various countries. The *Constitution of the Athenians* (*see* OLD OLIGARCH), preserved among his works, is certainly not by him. As a historian Xenophon sometimes omits matters of importance and is guilty of taking sides. On military and sporting matters he is an expert and an enthusiast and writes engagingly. He was a pious man, possessed of great common sense, an easy, lucid, and agreeable writer. Quintilian speaks warmly of his unaffected charm.

**2.** Of Ephesus; *see* NOVEL.

**Xerxēs** (*c.*519–465 BC) King of Persia from 486 BC, the son and successor of *Darius the Great and Atossa. In 480 he launched a huge invasion of Greece, leading his army over the Hellespont on a bridge of boats; *see* PERSIAN WARS. (The first attempt was a failure because a storm destroyed the boats, and Xerxes had the sea whipped in punishment.) He also had a canal cut across the promontory of Mount Athos to spare his fleet a dangerous piece of navigation. The Persians sacked Athens, but after his crushing defeat at Salamis Xerxes returned home. He was assassinated by a member of his court.

**Xūthus (Xouthos)** In Greek myth, the ancestor of the Ionians and Achaeans. He is presented either as the son of *Hellen and brother of Dorus and Aeolus (*see* DEUCALION), or as the son of Aeolus (*see* ION (1)).

**'year of the four emperors'** The year AD 69, when, following the death of Nero in 68, three emperors (Galba, Otho, and Vitellius) briefly held power before order was restored by Vespasian (ruled 69–79).

**years, reckoning of** *See* CALENDARS.

**youth** *See* AGE GROUPS.

**Za'greus** *See* DIONYSUS ZAGREUS.

**Zaleucus** (mid-seventh century BC) Perhaps the earliest lawgiver of the Greek world, legislating in Italian (Epizephyrian) Locri. He prescribed exact penalties for crimes, usually of an 'eye for an eye' nature, and was notorious for the severity of his legislation.

**Zama, battle of** In Numidia in 202 BC, the final defeat of Hannibal by Scipio Africanus to end the Second *Punic War. Its actual location is uncertain.

**Zēno (Zēnōn) 1.** (of Elea, *c.*490–after 445 BC) Greek philosopher. Little is known of his life except that he was the pupil and friend of *Parmenides and thus belonged to the so-called *Eleatic school of Greek philosophy which believed that the basic matter of the universe is single, indivisible, and unchanging. He seems to have written, in support of this belief and against those who made fun of it, a book of philosophical paradoxes which reduce to absurdity the supposition that plurality and motion exist. (Because of his method he was called by Aristotle the inventor of *dialectic.) Only two of his forty arguments against plurality have survived, and the essence of these can be summarized as follows. If there are many things, they must be both limited and unlimited in number (which is absurd): limited, because they are as many as they are; unlimited, because things are only two in number when they can be distinguished from one another, i.e. when they are separated; but things are only separated where there is something in between; that in turn must be separated by two intervening things from those it originally separated, and so on *ad infinitum*.

Of his four arguments (according to Aristotle) against the possibility of motion, the most famous is the paradox of Achilles and the tortoise. If a tortoise is given a start in a race against Achilles, Achilles will never be able to overtake it because when he arrives at the tortoise's starting point it will have moved ahead to a new position, and when he reaches that position the tortoise will again have moved ahead, and so on indefinitely. On this basis the tortoise must always be ahead, by however small a margin. The simplest and usual explanation of fallacy in the argument is that while it takes Achilles an infinite number of these increments of distance to catch the tortoise, their sum, i.e. the total distance required, is in fact finite. Nevertheless, the argument raises questions about the ideas of infinity and divisibility which are philosophically important, and formal refutation is not a trivial matter. One of Zeno's other arguments against motion similarly divides the distance to be covered by an athlete in the stadium into the geometrical series $\frac{1}{2} + \frac{1}{4} + \frac{1}{8} + \ldots$ and asserts that the distance, having an infinite number of divisions, can never be covered, and therefore motion is impossible. It is an argument of the same nature as that of Achilles and the tortoise.

Zeno appears in the dialogue *Parmenides* of Plato.

**2.** Greek philosopher of Citium in Cyprus (*c.*333–262 BC), and founder of the Stoic school. *See* STOICISM.

**Zēno'dotus** Of Ephesus, scholar at Alexandria, pupil of Philetas of Cos, who became the first head of the *Alexandrian Library *c.*285–*c.*270 BC. He is reputed to have divided Homer's *Iliad* and *Odyssey* into twenty-four books each, and to have worked on the text, perhaps even produced an edition. Lines whose genuineness he doubted he marked with the newly invented sign, the *obelos* (*see* TEXTS, TRANSMISSION OF ANCIENT 1). He seems also to have worked on the lyric poets. Traces of his critical work and views survive in the Homeric scholia (*see* SCHOLIUM).

**Ze'phyrus** In Greek myth, the personification of the west wind, sometimes said to be the husband of Iris, goddess of the rainbow. By the Harpy Podarge he became the father of

Achilles' horses Xanthus and Balius. *See* FLORA and HYACINTHUS.

**Zētēs** *See* CALAIS AND ZETES.

**Zēthus** *See* ANTIOPE.

**zeugitae** In Greece, *Solon's third property class, those who served in the army as hoplites.

**Zeus** In Greek myth and religion, the supreme god, the youngest (according to Homer the eldest) son of *Cronus whom he overthrew and succeeded. His name indicates an *Indo-European origin, being found in the Indic sky-god Dyaus pita, the Roman Jupiter, the German Tuesday, Latin *deus*, 'god', *dies*, 'day', and Greek *eudia*, 'fine weather'. His cult is attested in Bronze-age Greece and *Linear B texts mention several sanctuaries belonging to him. For the Greeks he is the god of weather rather than of the 'bright sky' of day. According to his Homeric epithets he is the cloud-gatherer, the thunderer on high, hurler of thunderbolts. He was born in Crete, according to what is probably the oldest myth, or was born in Arcadia and brought to Crete, where he was hidden in a cave on Mount Dicte or Mount *Ida and fed by the goat *Amalthea. The *Curetes, in order to conceal him, drowned his cries by their noisy ritual. (The Cretans also had a peculiar myth of Zeus dead and buried.) After the overthrow of Cronus, Zeus and his brothers divided the universe by casting lots, Zeus obtaining the heavens, Poseidon the sea, and Hades the underworld. Zeus dwells on the tops of mountains where the storm-clouds gather, on Mount Lycaeus in Arcadia, or Mount Ida near Troy, or on Mount *Olympus, the highest mountain in northern Thessaly. The thunderbolt, which only he commands, signifies his irresistible power, over other gods as well as men, and it enabled him to defeat the *Titans, the *Giants, and *Typhoeus. Thus it is Zeus who must be supplicated to grant victory in war. He is the protector of political freedom, Zeus Eleutherios ('Deliverer'), or Soter ('Saviour'), and festivals were instituted in his honour. After the Greek victory at Plataea in 479 BC (*see* PERSIAN WARS) a sanctuary for Zeus Eleutherios and the festival of the Eleutheria were instituted.

Zeus is the only Greek god to have as children other powerful gods, Apollo, Artemis, Hermes, Dionysus, Athena, and Persephone. By his wife Hera he was the father only of Ares, Hebe, and Eileithyia. The mother of *Athena, Metis (Wisdom), was fated to have a second child more powerful than its father, and so Zeus swallowed her, thereafter combining supreme power and wisdom within himself. His mortal children included Heracles, Helen, Perseus, Epaphos, Minos, and the brothers Amphion and Zethus (*see also* DIOSCURI). Zeus is called 'the father of gods and humankind' and had perhaps been so addressed since Indo-European times, although he is not the father of all the gods and did not create humans (for stories about the creation of humankind *see* DEUCALION and PROMETHEUS). He is the author of the order in the world as it now is. Epithets added to his name indicate his particular roles: he is father in the sense of ruler and protector, defender of the house (Herkeios), of the hearth (Ephestios), of the rights of hospitality (Xenios and Hikesios), of oaths (Horkios), and the guardian of property (Ktesios), his image set up in the storeroom. He is also the protector of law and morals; in that capacity the poet Hesiod invokes him in *Works and Days*, and represents the goddess of justice, Dike, as enthroned beside him. The impartiality of his judgements is represented by Homer in the *Iliad* in the image of Zeus holding golden scales in his hand; as Achilles and Hector fight, the fall of a scale indicates that Hector is doomed. Zeus has the power, if he wishes, to save Hector whom he loves, as he might have saved his own son *Sarpedon, but it is the human 'fate' (*moira*) or 'portion' (*aisa*) to die, and Zeus does not overrule the apportionment (*see* FATE).

Zeus is also called Chthonios, 'of the Earth'. Sometimes the phrase simply stands for Hades or Pluto, the god of the Underworld; the sky god is not meant. More often the phrase signifies Zeus whose all-embracing power extends into the earth as well, from which the growth of crops is expected. Apart, however, from general overseership given by his position of supremacy, Zeus had little to do with the day-to-day concerns of people—war, agriculture, crafts, etc.; but the wide scope of his functions made him unique in his importance to all Greece. His festival at *Olympia asserted his supreme position and the essential unity of all who worshipped him. To participate in his festival was to be a Hellene; the admission of the Macedonians and later of the Romans were events of great political significance. The beginnings of his universality are apparent in Aeschylus ('Zeus, whoever you are ...', *Agamemnon* 160) and Sophocles, who sees Zeus' hand in all human affairs ('Nothing of this is not Zeus', *Trachiniae* 1278), and paved the way for the later philosophical pantheism of the Stoics. He corresponds to, and was identified with, the Roman *Jupiter.

**Zeuxis** Of Heraclea in *Magna Graecia, one of the most famous painters of ancient Greece, working in the late fifth century BC. In Plato's *Protagoras*, set in the Athens of *c*.430 BC, he is young and has recently arrived in Athens. One of his most celebrated paintings was a picture of Helen (of Troy) for the temple of Hera at Croton. He is said to have assembled the five most beautiful maidens of the city and combined the best features of each into one figure of ideal beauty. For another famous anecdote about him *see* PARRHASIUS.

**Zmyrna** Miniature Latin epic poem in hexameters on the myth of Myrrha and *Adonis by the learned poet C. Helvius *Cinna (3). Only three lines survive. It was worked on by its author for nine years, and seems to have typified the influence of 'Alexandrianism' on Roman poetry (*see* ALEXANDRIANISM, LATIN). Catullus predicted immortality for it.

**Zō'ilus** Of Amphipolis, *Cynic philosopher, rhetorician, and critic of the fourth century BC, also perhaps a *sophist, who earned notoriety for the bitterness of his attacks on Isocrates, Plato, and especially Homer, earning himself the name of Homeromastix, 'scourge of Homer', by his nine books of criticism. He found fault with Homer mainly on points of invention (such as the description of the companions of Odysseus 'weeping' when turned into swine), but also on points of grammar. His name became proverbial for a carping critic.

**Zo'simus** (late fifth century AD) Greek historian, author of an extant history, in Greek in six books, of the Roman empire from Augustus to AD 410 (just before the sack of Rome by the *Visigoths under Alaric). Book 1 summarizes the events of the first three centuries of the empire, books 2–4 give a fuller account of the fourth century, and books 5 and 6 cover the years 395–410, for which Zosimus is the most important source. Being a pagan he attributes the decline of the empire to the rejection of the pagan gods.

# CHRONOLOGICAL TABLE

Many of the dates given are approximate, especially before *c*.600 BC. The abbreviation *fl*. (*floruit, floruerunt*: flourished) after writers' names is meant only to give an impression of relative dates.

| EVENTS | | LITERATURE |
|---|---|---|

**BC**

| | | |
|---|---|---|
| 2800–1050 | Greek Bronze age | |
| 2000 | Rise of Assyria | |
| 2000–1700 | Writing on clay tablets in Asia Minor | |
| 1800–1000 | Italian Bronze age | |
| 1700–1200 | Hittites dominate central Anatolia | |
| 1600–1125 | Mycenaean period | |
| 1600 | Babylonia powerful | |
| 1375–1200 | Linear B tablets | |
| 1200–1125 | Destruction of Mycenaean and Hittite cities | |
| 1184 | Destruction of Troy | |
| 1100 | Beginning of Dark age; Dorian Invasion | |
| 1050 | Beginning of Iron age in Greece | |
| 1050–875 | Proto-geometric pottery; migration of mainland Greeks to Asia Minor | |
| 1000 | Beginning of Iron age in Italy | |
| 900 | Synoecism at Athens | |
| 875–750 | Geometric pottery | |
| 814 | Phoenicians found Carthage | |
| 776 | First Olympian (Olympic) games | |
| 753 | Foundation of Rome by Romulus | |
| 753–510 | Rome ruled by kings | |
| 750–720 | Sub-geometric pottery; early Greek writing | |
| 747–657 | Corinth ruled by the Bacchiads | |
| 735–715 | First Messenian War | |
| 734 | Greek colonization of Sicily begins | |
| 733 | Foundation of Syracuse | |
| 720 | Greek colonization of S. Italy begins | |

| EVENTS | | LITERATURE | |
|---|---|---|---|
| **BC** | | | |
| 720–620 | Orientalizing period in pottery | | |
| 700–680 | Colonization of Hellespont and Bosporus | *c.*700 | Homer and Hesiod *fl.* |
| 688 | Gela founded | | |
| 683 | Death of Codrus, last king of Athens; archons elected annually | | |
| 680 | Gyges king of Lydia | 675 | Terpander and Callinus *fl.* |
| 669 | Argos defeats Sparta at Hysiae | | |
| 664 | Psammetichus I begins Saite dynasty of Egypt | | |
| 660 | Foundation of Byzantium | | |
| 657 | Cypselus tyrant at Corinth | | |
| 650–620 | Second Messenian War | 650 | Archilochus and Semonides *fl.* |
| 648 | Eclipse of the sun on 6 April, mentioned by Archilochus | | |
| 632 | Megacles the Alcmaeonid acquires hereditary pollution | 640 | Tyrtaeus *fl.* |
| 627–587 | Periander tyrant of Corinth | | |
| 625–600 | Thrasybulus tyrant of Miletus | 630 | Alcman and Mimnermus *fl.* |
| 621 | Laws of Draco put in writing | | |
| 620–480 | Archaic period | | |
| 612 | Melanchrus becomes tyrant of Mytilene; Assyrian empire overthrown by Medes and Nineveh sacked | | |
| 610 | Black-figure vase-painting begins | 610–575 | Alcaeus and Sappho *fl.* |
| | | 610–545 | Anaximander |
| 600 | Foundation of Massalia | 600 | Thales *fl.* |
| 594 | Reforms of Solon | 594 | Solon's poetry |
| 592 | Alcmaeon wins Athens' first victory in the chariot-race at Olympia | | |
| 587 | Nebuchadnezzar II sacks Jerusalem | | |
| 585 | Eclipse of sun, supposedly predicted by Thales | | |
| 582 | Pythian games established | | |
| 581 | Isthmian games established | | |
| 573 | Nemean games established | 570 | Stesichorus *fl.* |
| 570–525 | Attic black-figure vases at their peak | 570–478 | Xenophanes |
| 566 | First celebration of Great Panathenaea at Athens | | |
| 560–556 | Peisistratus tyrant at Athens | | |
| 560–546 | Croesus last king of Lydia | | |
| 550 | Cyrus I of Persia conquers Media | 556–468 | Simonides |

| EVENTS | | LITERATURE | |
|---|---|---|---|
| **BC** | | | |
| 546 | Cyrus I conquers Lydia; death of Croesus | 550 | Anaximenes and Phocylides *fl.* |
| 546–527 | Peisistratus again tyrant | | |
| 540 | Persians under Cyrus I conquer Ionia | | |
| 534 | City Dionysia started by Peisistratus | 540 | Hipponax, Ibycus, and Theognis *fl.* |
| | | 533 | Thespis wins first tragedy competition at the Dionysia |
| 530 | Death of Cyrus I; red-figure pottery begins | 530 | Anacreon and Pythagoras *fl.* |
| 525 | Cleisthenes archon at Athens | 518 | Pindar born |
| 521 | Darius I king of Persia | | |
| 514 | Hipparchus murdered by Harmodius and Aristogeiton | | |
| 510 | Hippias expelled from Athens; last king expelled from Rome | | |
| 509 | Foundation of Roman republic | | |
| 507 | Reforms of Cleisthenes introduce ostracism | | |
| | | 500 | Hecataeus, Heracleitus, and Phrynichus *fl.* |
| 499 | Ionian Revolt | | |
| 496 | Romans defeat Latins at Lake Regillus | | |
| 494 | Ionian Revolt: battle of Lade; Persians sack Miletus First secession of the plebs at Rome | 492 | Phrynichus' tragedy *Capture of Miletus* |
| 490 | Persians invade Greece and are defeated at Marathon | 490–425 | Herodotus |
| 486 | First comedy produced at the Dionysia Beginning of classical period | 484 | Aeschylus: first victory in tragedy competitions |
| 480 | Persian invasion of Greece: battles of Artemisium, Thermopylae, and Salamis; Carthaginian invasion of Sicily: battle of Himera | 480 | Parmenides *fl.* |
| 479 | Battles of Plataea and Mycale | | |
| 478 | Delian League formed | 470 | Bacchylides *fl.* |
| | | 469 | Socrates born |
| | | 468 | Sophocles: first victory in tragedy competitions |

| EVENTS | | | LITERATURE |
|---|---|---|---|
| **BC** | | | |
| 467 | Battle of Eurymedon; fall of meteorite near Aegospotami | | |
| 464 | Helot revolt | | |
| 462 | Reforms of Ephialtes | 462 | Anaxagoras (500–428) in Athens |
| 461–429 | Ascendancy of Pericles at Athens | | |
| 461–456 | Long Walls built | | |
| 460–446 | First Peloponnesian War | | |
| | | 458 | Aeschylus: *Oresteia* |
| | | 458–380 | Lysias |
| | | 456 | Death of Aeschylus |
| | | 455 | Euripides: first production |
| 450 | Twelve Tables published at Rome; Peace of Callias | 450 | Empedocles and Zeno the Eleatic *fl.* |
| 449 | Second secession of the plebs at Rome | | |
| 447 | Battle of Coronea; Parthenon begun | | |
| 446 | Thirty Years' Peace | | |
| | | 440–390 | Andocides |
| | | 436 | Isocrates born |
| | | 435 | Leucippus *fl.* |
| 431 | Start of Peloponnesian War proper | 431 | Thucydides begins his history |
| 430 | Plague at Athens | 430 | Democritus, Hippocrates, Meton, Protagoras, and Socrates *fl.* |
| 429 | Death of Pericles | | |
| | | 427 | Plato born; Gorgias arrives at Athens |
| 425 | Capture of Sphacteria; Cleon influential at Athens | 425 | Aristophanes: *Acharnians*; Hellanicus *fl.* |
| 424 | Battle of Delium | | |
| 422 | Deaths of Brasidas and Cleon | | |
| 421 | Peace of Nicias | | |
| | | 420 | Hippias and Prodicus *fl.* |
| 419 | Peloponnesian War resumed | | |
| 415–413 | Sicilian Expedition | | |
| 411 | Oligarchic revolution at Athens | 411 | Execution of Antiphon |
| 406 | Battle of Arginusae | 406 | Deaths of Euripides and Sophocles |
| 405 | Sparta finally defeats Athens at Aegospotami | 405 | Aristophanes: *Frogs*. |
| 404 | Capitulation of Athens: the Thirty Tyrants | | |
| 404–371 | Sparta supreme in Greece | | |
| 403 | Restoration of democracy at Athens | | |

| EVENTS | | LITERATURE | |
|---|---|---|---|
| **BC** | | | |
| 401 | Expedition of the Ten Thousand: battle of Cunaxa | | |
| 400–386 | Sparta at war with Persia | 400 | Antisthenes and Eucleides *fl.* |
| 396 | Romans capture Veii | 400–325 | Diogenes |
| | | 399 | Trial and death of Socrates |
| 395–386 | Corinthian War | 392 | Aristophanes: *Ecclesiazusae* |
| | | 390 | Aeschines born; Isocrates, Plato, and Xenophon (428–354) *fl.* |
| 386 | Peace of Antalcidas; Academy founded at Athens | 388 | Aristophanes: *Plutus* |
| 385 | Gauls sack Rome | | |
| | | 386 | Death of Aristophanes |
| | | 384 | Aristotle and Demosthenes born |
| 377 | Second Athenian League | | |
| 371 | Thebans defeat Spartans at Leuctra | | |
| | | 370–287 | Theophrastus |
| 369 | Epaminondas founds Megalopolis in Arcadia | | |
| | | 365–285 | Crates the Cynic |
| | | 365–270 | Pyrrhon |
| 362 | Thebans defeat Spartans at Mantinea: Epaminondas killed | | |
| | | 360 | Aeschines, Aristotle, and Demosthenes *fl.* |
| 359–336 | Philip II king of Macedon | | |
| 357–355 | Social War in Greece | | |
| 356 | Alexander the Great born | | |
| 355–352 | Third Sacred War; Philip destroys Phocis | | |
| | | 347 | Death of Plato |
| 346 | Peace of Philocrates | | |
| 343–341 | First Samnite War in Italy | | |
| 341–338 | Latin War in Italy | 342–292 | Menander |
| | | 340 | Ephorus and Theopompus *fl.* |
| 339 | Timoleon defeats Carthaginians at the Crimisus | | |
| 338 | Philip II defeats Athens and Thebes at Chaeronea | 338 | Death of Isocrates; Lycurgus in control of Athenian finance |
| 336–323 | Alexander the Great king of Macedon | 335 | Aristotle founds Lyceum |
| 334 | Battle of the Granicus | | |
| 333 | Battle of Issus; Egypt surrenders to Alexander | | |
| 331 | Alexandria founded; battle of Gaugamela | | |

# Chronological Table

EVENTS                                          LITERATURE

**BC**

| | | | |
|---|---|---|---|
| 330 | Persepolis destroyed | | |
| 327–304 | Second Samnite War in Italy | | |
| 326 | Battle of Hydaspes | | |
| 323 | Death of Alexander | | |
| 323–322 | Lamian War | | |
| | | 322 | Deaths of Aristotle and Demosthenes |
| 321 | Romans surrender to Samnites at Caudine Forks | | |
| 317–307 | Demetrius of Phalerum governor of Athens | | |
| 311–306 | War of Agathocles of Syracuse against Carthage | | |
| | | 307 | Epicurus founds his school at Athens |
| 301 | Battle of Ipsus | | |
| | | 300 | Zeno of Citium founds Stoic school at Athens |
| 298–290 | Third Samnite War in Italy | | |
| 297–272 | Campaigns of Pyrrhus | | |
| | | 285 | Zenodotus head of the Alexandrian Library; Philetas and Euclid *fl.* |
| 287 | Final secession of the plebs at Rome | | |
| 283 | Accession of Ptolemy II Philadelphus in Egypt | | |
| 273 | Egypt makes treaty of friendship with Rome | 280 | Bion the Borysthenite *fl.* |
| | | 271 | Death of Epicurus |
| 266 | Rome dominant in Italy south of the Rubicon | 270 | Aratus, Aristarchus of Samos, Callimachus, Herodas, and Theocritus *fl.* |
| 266–262 | Chremonidean War; Athens surrenders to Macedon | | |
| 264–241 | First Punic War | | |
| | | 260 | Death of Timaeus |
| | | 250 | Apollonius Rhodius *fl.* |
| | | 240 | Archimedes, Eratosthenes, and Livius Andronicus *fl.* |
| | | 235 | Naevius *fl.* |
| 221–179 | Philip V king of Macedon | | |
| 219 | Hannibal captures Saguntum | | |
| 218–202 | Second Punic War | | |
| 217 | Hannibal defeats Romans at Lake Trasimene | | |

| EVENTS | | LITERATURE | |
|---|---|---|---|
| **BC** | | | |
| 216 | Hannibal defeats Romans at Cannae | | |
| 214–205 | First Macedonian War | | |
| 211 | Sicily becomes Roman province | 212 | Archimedes killed in Syracuse; Fabius Pictor *fl.* |
| 202 | Battle of Zama: subjugation of Carthage by Rome | | |
| 200–197 | Second Macedonian War | 200 | Aristophanes of Byzantium head of Alexandrian Library; Ennius and Plautus *fl.* |
| 179 | Perseus king of Macedon | | |
| | | 180 | Aristarchus of Samothrace head of Alexandrian Library; Pacuvius *fl.* |
| 172–168 | Third Macedonian War | | |
| 168 | Rome defeats Perseus at Pydna | 168 | Polybius taken to Rome |
| | | 166–159 | Terence's plays produced |
| | | 155 | Carneades at Rome |
| 149–146 | Third Punic War | 149 | Cato the Censor: *Origines* |
| 146 | Sack of Corinth; Greece becomes a Roman protectorate, Macedonia a province | | |
| | | 145 | Lucilius *fl.* |
| | | 144 | Panaetius at Rome |
| | | 140 | Accius *fl.* |
| | | 135 | Nicander *fl.* |
| 133, 123 | Tribunates of the Gracchi | | |
| | | 116 | Varro born |
| 112–105 | War against Jugurtha | | |
| 107–100 | Reforms of Marius | | |
| | | 106 | Cicero born |
| 100 | Julius Caesar born | 100 | Meleager *fl.* |
| | | 98 | Lucretius born |
| 90–88 | Social War: Rome concedes full citizenship to the Italian allies | | |
| 89–85 | First Mithridatic War | | |
| | | 87–51 | Poseidonius *fl.* |
| 86 | Sulla sacks Athens | | |
| | | 84 | Catullus born |
| 83–82 | Second Mithridatic War | | |
| 82–80 | Reforms of Sulla | | |
| | | 75 | Philodemus comes to Rome |
| 74–63 | Third Mithridatic War | | |
| 73–71 | Slave revolt under Spartacus | | |
| 70 | Consulate of Crassus and Pompey; trial of Verres | | |
| 66–62 | Pompey in the East | | |
| | | 65 | Horace born |

| EVENTS | | LITERATURE | |
|---|---|---|---|
| **BC** | | | |
| 63 | Consulship of Cicero and Catilinarian conspiracy; Augustus (Octavian) born | | |
| 60 | First triumvirate: Caesar, Pompey, and Crassus | 60 | Cornelius Nepos *fl.*; ' Neoterics' active |
| | | 60–30 | Diodorus Siculus compiles his history |
| | | 59 | Livy born |
| 58–57 | Cicero in exile | 58–52 | Caesar: *Commentaries* on the Gallic War |
| 58–49 | Caesar in Gaul | | |
| | | 57–56 | Catullus visits Asia Minor, probably with Cinna |
| 55–54 | Caesar in Britain | 55 | Death of Lucretius |
| | | 54 | Death of Catullus |
| 53 | Parthians defeat Crassus at Carrhae | | |
| 49 | Caesar crosses the Rubicon | | |
| 48 | Battle of Pharsalus; murder of Pompey | | |
| 47–44 | Caesar dictator | | |
| | | 45 | Sallust begins to write histories |
| 44 | Murder of Caesar | 44 | Strabo arrives at Rome |
| 43 | Second triumvirate: Antony, Lepidus, and Octavian; murder of Cicero | 43 | Ovid born |
| 42 | Battle of Philippi | | |
| | | 37 | Virgil: *Eclogues*; joins circle of Maecenas |
| 31 | Battle of Actium | | |
| 30 | Deaths of Mark Antony and Cleopatra | 30 | Didymus *fl.* |
| | | 29 | Virgil: *Georgics*; Propertius: *Elegies* 1 |
| | | 28–23 | Vitruvius: *de Architectura* |
| 27 | Principate of Augustus begins | 27 | Death of Varro |
| | | 23 | Horace: *Odes* 1–3; Propertius: *Elegies* 3 |
| | | 20 | Ovid: *Amores*, first, lost edition |
| | | 19 | Deaths of Tibullus and Virgil |
| | | 8 | Deaths of Horace and Maecenas |
| 4 | Death of Herod the Great | | |
| | | | Ovid: 'single' *Heroides* |
| | | 1 | (or later) Ovid: *Ars Amatoria* 1 and 2 |

| EVENTS | | LITERATURE | |
|---|---|---|---|
| **AD** | | | |
| | | 2 | (onwards) Ovid: *Metamorphoses* and *Fasti* |
| | | 8 | Ovid exiled |
| 14 | Death of Augustus | 13 | Ovid: *Epistulae ex Ponto* 1–3 |
| 14–37 | Tiberius emperor | 17 | Deaths of Livy and Ovid |
| 31 | Execution of Sejanus | 30 | Manilius, Valerius Maximus, and Velleius Paterculus *fl.* |
| 37 | Caligula emperor | 37 | Death of Seneca the Elder |
| | | 39–40 | Philo the Jew in Rome |
| 41 | Claudius emperor | | |
| 43 | Invasion of Britain | | |
| 54–68 | Nero emperor | | |
| 60 | British revolt under Boudicca | 60 | Persius (34–62), Petronius, Lucan (39–65), and Seneca the Younger (4 BC–AD 65) *fl.* |
| 64 | Fire of Rome | | |
| 65 | Pisonian conspiracy | 65 | Suicides of Lucan, Petronius, and Seneca the Younger |
| 66–70 | Jewish revolt | | |
| 69 | Year of the four emperors: Galba, Otho, Vitellius, and Vespasian | 68 | Silius Italicus, author of *Punica*, consul |
| 70 | Destruction of the Temple at Jerusalem | 70 | Valerius Flaccus begins *Argonautica* |
| | | 74 | Frontinus consul |
| 78–85 | Agricola governor of Britain | | |
| 79–81 | Titus emperor | | |
| 79 | Eruption of Vesuvius: destruction of Herculaneum and Pompeii | 79 | Death of Pliny the Elder |
| 80 | Colosseum inaugurated | | |
| 81–96 | Domitian emperor | 81 | Dio Chrysostom, Josephus, Martial, and Quintilian *fl.* |
| | | 89 | Epictetus banished |
| | | 90–1 | Statius: *Thebaïd* |
| | | 92–3 | Plutarch in Rome |
| 96–8 | Nerva emperor | | |
| | | 97 | Tacitus consul |
| 98–117 | Trajan emperor | 97 | (or later) Frontinus: *On the Waters of Rome* |
| | | 100 | Pliny the Younger consul |
| | | 100–27 | Juvenal: *Satires* written |
| 117–38 | Hadrian emperor | 102 | Silius Italicus: *Punica* probably published |
| | | 119–22 | Suetonius: *Lives* published |
| 135 | Final dispersal of the Jews | | |
| 138–61 | Antoninus Pius emperor | | |
| | | 140 | Ptolemy (mathematician) *fl.* |
| | | 143 | Fronto consul |

| EVENTS | | | LITERATURE |
|---|---|---|---|

**AD**

| | | | |
|---|---|---|---|
| | | 150 | Lucian *fl.* |
| | | 155 | Apuleius *fl.* |
| | | 160 | Appian begins his history; Aristeides, Aulus Gellius, Gaius (lawyer), and Pausanias (traveller) *fl.* |
| 161–80 | Marcus Aurelius emperor; first Germanic invasions into Italy | 161 | Herodian (grammarian) *fl.* |
| | | 169 | Galen settles in Rome |
| | | 170–80 | M. Aurelius: *Meditations* (published after 180) |
| 180–92 | Commodus emperor | | |
| 193–211 | Lucius Septimius Severus emperor | | |
| | | 200 | Alexander of Aphrodisias, Athenaeus, Papinian (lawyer), Ulpian (lawyer), and Sextus Empiricus *fl.* |
| 211 | Death of Severus at York | | |
| 211–17 | Caracalla emperor | | |
| 218–22 | Elagabalus emperor | | |
| | | 220 | Paulus (lawyer) *fl.* |
| 222–35 | Alexander Severus emperor | 223 | Murder of Ulpian |
| | | 224 | Philostratus: *Lives of the Sophists*; coins term 'Second Sophistic' |
| | | 229 | Second consulate of Cassius Dio |
| | | 230 | Herodian (historian) and Origen *fl.* |
| | | 240 | Plotinus *fl.* |
| 247 | Millenary celebrations at Rome | | |
| 267 | Herulians (Germanic tribe) sack Athens | | |
| 272 | Emperor Aurelian captures Palmyra | | |
| | | 280 | Porphyry *fl.* |
| 284–305 | Diocletian emperor | | |
| 293 | Tetrarchy established | | |
| | | 300 | Iamblichus *fl.* |
| 303–5 | Great Persecution of Christians | | |
| 306–37 | Constantine (the Great) emperor | | |
| 312 | Battle of the Milvian bridge: toleration and imperial favour given to Christianity | | |
| 325 | Council of Nicaea | | |
| 330 | Constantinople capital of the Roman empire | 330 | Tryphiodorus *fl.* |
| | | 350 | Ausonius and Donatus *fl.* |

| EVENTS | | LITERATURE | |
|---|---|---|---|
| **AD** | | | |
| 360–3 | Julian the Apostate emperor | 360 | Libanius and Themistius *fl.* |
| | | 370 | Ambrose, Ammianus Marcellinus, and Jerome *fl.* |
| 378–95 | Theodosius (the Great) emperor | 380 | Quintus of Smyrna *fl.*; *Historia Augusta* |
| | | 384 | Symmachus *praefectus urbi* |
| 395 | Division of the empire into East and West | | |
| | | 400 | Claudian *fl.* |
| 410 | Sack of Rome by Alaric the Visigoth | | |
| | | 420 | Martianus Capella and Servius *fl.* |
| | | 430 | Death of Augustine; Macrobius *fl.* |
| 439 | Vandals conquer Roman Africa | | |
| 452 | Attila invades Italy | 450 | Nonnus *fl.* |
| 455 | Vandals plunder Rome | | |
| 476 | Fall of Rome | | |
| 527 | Justinian emperor in the East | 524 | Boethius executed |
| 529 | Philosophical schools at Athens closed | 530 | Tribonian (lawyer) *fl.* |

# MAPS

The place-names on the following maps include the majority of those which appear in the text. Sites of battles are not distinguished from those of cities, nor are distinctions made on grounds of relative importance or of period. Mountains are shown as peaks except in a few cases where the names describe a range. Classical names are given in commonly accepted spellings, with the Latinized form generally preferred (thus: Cnossus, not Knossos). Modern place-names are shown in italic on the maps.

In the Gazetteer, a name in parentheses following an ancient name is a modern equivalent. Only one reference is given for places or features which are named on more than one map.

1. Asia Minor and the Middle East
2. Greece and the Aegean
3. Greece
4. Italy
5. The Western Roman Empire
6. Roman Britain

Map 1 Asia Minor and the Middle East

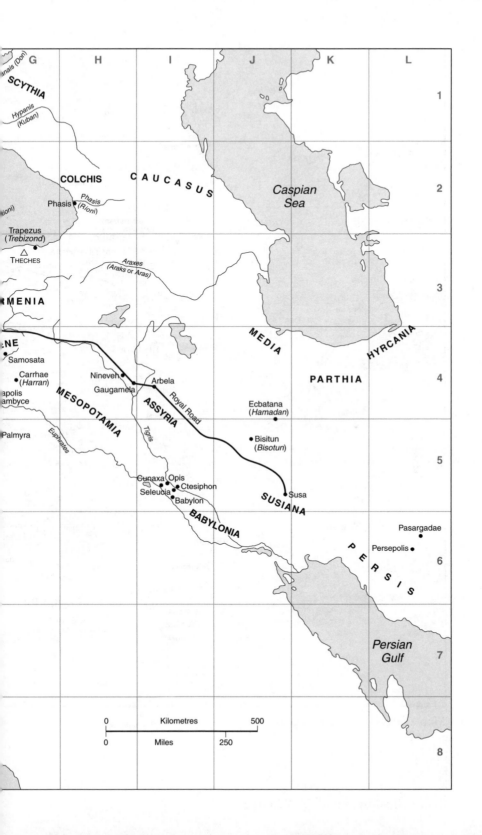

Map 2 Greece and the Aegean

G　　H　　I　　J　　K　　L

**Euxine**
**(Black Sea)**　　1

*C* *E*

• Hadrianopolis
(*Adrianople*)

*Bosporus*

Byzantium or
Constantinople
(*Istanbul*)

• Perinthus　　• Chalcedon

Nicomedia
(*Izmit*)

Maronea •
era •

**Propontis**
**(Sea of Marmara)**　　2

Lysimacheia
Cardia •

**Proconnesus**

Nicaea
(*Iznik*)

• Cios

**B I T H Y N I A**

mothrace

**THRACIAN**
**CHERSONESE**

*Aegospotami* • Parium
Sestus • Lampsacus

• Cyzicus

• Prusa (*Bursa*)

**Imbros**

mnos

Abydos
Cynossema

• • Scepsis

*Granicus*

**M Y S I A**

**P H R Y G I A**　　3

*Hellespont* Sigeum
Troy

**Tenedos**

*Scamander*

Colonae • **TROAS**
(*THE TROAD*)

Assos •

△ IDA

Methymna •

*A* *E* *O* *L* *I* *S*

Antissa •
**Eresus** Pyrrha •
Mitylene

• Pergamum
Atarneus •
• Pitane
• Elaea

**L Y D I A**　　4

**Lesbos**

**Arginusae**

• Cyme
• Phocaea

Magnesia
(*Manisa*)

*Hermus*

Bin
Tepe

**Chios**

Erythrae •
• Clazomenae
• Teos

Sardis •

*Pactolus*

• Smyrna

• Colophon

*Maeander*

• Hierapolis　　5

ndros

Notium
• Ephesus

**Tenos**

**Samos**

MYCALE Magnesia

**Rheneia**

**Icaria**

△ • Priene

**Myconos**
**Delos**

**C A R I A**

ros

• Miletus

**Lade**

6

Naxos

**Leros**

• Caryanda

**Amorgos**

**Cos**

Halicarnassus
(*Bodrum*)

• Cnidus

**L Y C I A**

Ios

• Xanthus

Ialysus • Rhodes

**Telos**

• Camirus

Akroteri **Thera**
(*Santorini*)

• Lindus

7

**Rhodes**

brus (*Maritsa*)

Map 3 Greece

G　　　　H　　　　I　　　　J　　　　K　　　　L

*Cape Artemisium*

Scyros

1

E U B O E A

*Aegean Sea*

2

atea
anopea
Chaeronea
Lebadeia
● Tegyra
Orchomenus
*L. Copais*
ronea
ICON
Thespiae
Leuctra
OPUNTIAN LOCRIS
● Halae
Anthedon ●
Chalcis
*Lefkandi*
Aulis ● Eretria
Delium ● Oropus
Tanagra ● Oenophyta
● Plataea
△ CITHAERON
BOEOTIA
● Haliartus
● Ascra
Thebes
Rhamnus ●
Decelea ●
Eleutherae PARNES △
● Cephissia
Eleusis ● PENTELICUS △
Athens ● Pallene ●
Piraeus ● Marathon
Salamis △ HYMETTUS
Phalerum ● Brauron
Carystus ●

Megara ● Nisaea
inth

A T T I C A

Psyttaleia

3

Tenea

ARGOLIS

Epidaurus ●
auplia

Aegina

LAURIUM △
Sunium

Andros

Ceos

Tenos

4

*Saronic Gulf*

Calaureia

Troezen ●
Hermione ●

Syros

Rheneia

C y c l a d e s

I A
mon)

*Myrtoan Sea*

Seriphos

Paros

5

Melos

6

Cythera

0　　Kilometres　　50

0　　Miles　　25

Cythera

7

Map 4 Italy

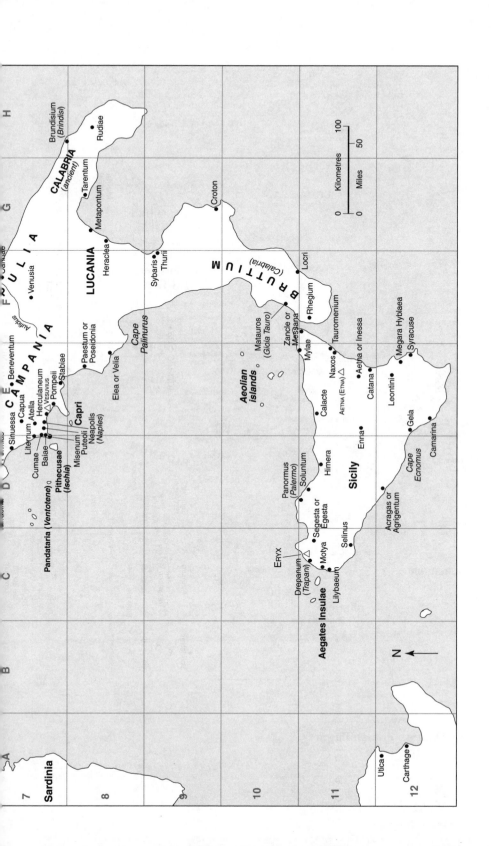

Sardinia

F U L I A

Canusium

Aufidus

Brundisium
*(Brindisi)*

CALABRIA
*(ancient)*

Rudiae

Tarentum

Metapontum

Venusia

LUCANIA

Croton

Heraclea

Thurii

Sybaris

Cape
Palinurus

B R U T T I U M
*(Calabria)*

Locri

C A M P A N I A

Beneventum

Paestum or
Poseidonia

Capua

Atella

Sinuessa

Herculaneum

VESUVIUS

Stabiae

Pompeii

Elea or Velia

Rhegium

Zancle or
Messana

Matauros
*(Gioia Tauro)*

Tauromenium

Mylae

Naxos

Aetna or Inessa

Capri

Liternum

Cumae

Baiae

Misenum

Puteoli

Neapolis
*(Naples)*

Pithecusae
*(Ischia)*

AETNA (ETNA)

Catana

Aeolian
islands

Calacte

Leontini

Megara Hyblaea

Syracuse

Pandataria *(Ventotene)*

Panormus
*(Palermo)*

Soluntum

Himera

Enna

Sicily

Gela

Camarina

Cape
Ecnomus

Segesta or
Egesta

Selinus

Acragas or
Agrigentum

ERYX

Motya

Drepanum
*(Trapani)*

Lilybaeum

Aegates Insulae

N ←

Utica

Carthage

0       50      100    Kilometres
0            50         Miles

7

8

9

10

11

12

A    B    C    D    E    F    G    H

N

| 0 | Kilometres | 500 |
| 0 | Miles | 250 |

Map 5 The Western Roman Empire

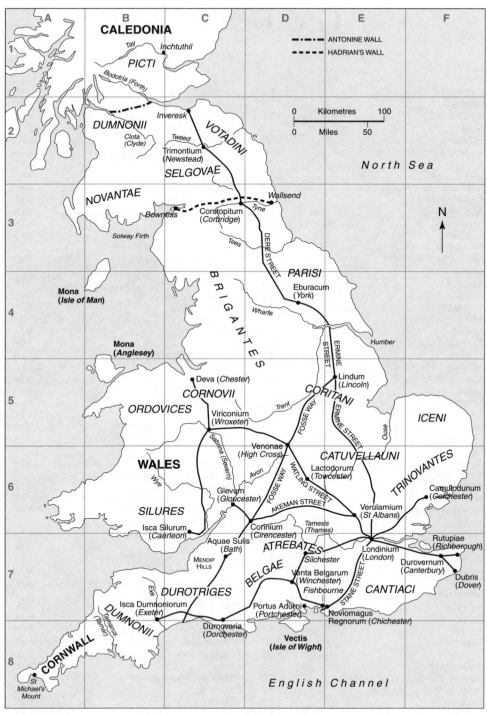

Map 6 Roman Britain

# GAZETTEER